CONTRACTS

CASES, NOTES AND MATERIALS

Canadian Legal Casebook Series

CASTEL: *CONFLICT OF LAWS, Cases, Notes and Materials*

PALMER, PRENTICE AND WELLING: *CASES AND MATERIALS ON COMPANY LAW*

WRIGHT AND LINDEN: *THE LAW OF TORTS, Cases, Notes and Materials*

SCHMEISER: *CRIMINAL LAW, Cases and Comments*

WATSON, BORINS AND WILLIAMS: *CANADIAN CIVIL PROCEDURE, Cases and Materials*

WHYTE AND LEDERMAN: *CANADIAN CONSTITUTIONAL LAW, Cases, Notes and Materials*

CASTEL: *INTERNATIONAL LAW*

FODDEN: *CANADIAN FAMILY LAW, Cases and Materials*

GLASBEEK: *EVIDENCE, Cases and Materials*

SWAN AND REITER: *CONTRACTS, Cases, Notes and Materials*

WALKER AND ASH: *DEBTOR-CREDITOR RELATIONS, Cases and Materials*

CONTRACTS

CASES, NOTES AND MATERIALS

by

JOHN SWAN
Professor of Law
Faculty of Law, University of Toronto

BARRY J. REITER
Professor of Law
Faculty of Law, University of Toronto

BUTTERWORTHS
TORONTO

CANADA: BUTTERWORTH & CO. (CANADA) LTD.
                   TORONTO: 2265 Midland Avenue, Scarborough, M1P 4S1

UNITED KINGDOM: BUTTERWORTH & CO. (PUBLISHERS) LTD.
                   LONDON: 88 Kingsway, WC2B 6AB

AUSTRALIA: BUTTERWORTH PTY. LTD.
                   SYDNEY: 586 Pacific Highway, Chatswood, NSW 2067
                   MELBOURNE: 343 Little Collins Street, 3000
                   BRISBANE: 240 Queen Street, 4000

NEW ZEALAND: BUTTERWORTHS OF NEW ZEALAND LTD.
                   WELLINGTON: 77-85 Customhouse Quay, 1

SOUTH AFRICA: BUTTERWORTH & CO. (SOUTH AFRICA) (PTY.) LTD.
                   DURBAN: 152/154 Gale Street

For further references to copyright see "Acknowledgments" at page viii

Canadian Cataloguing in Publication Data

Swan, John.
    Contracts

(Canadian legal casebook series)

Includes index.
ISBN 0-409-87110-9 bd.   ISBN 0-409-87111-7 pa.

1. Contracts — Canada — Cases. I. Reiter,
Barry J. II. Title. III. Series.

KE850.A7S83   346'.71'02   C78-001376-X

To Meg

PREFACE

These materials have been put together after several years of co-operation between the authors and Professor E. J. Weinrib of this faculty. It is not possible now to attribute sole responsibility to anyone for any of the ideas that we have had. All our ideas have been shaped by conversation among ourselves and with our colleagues, and, of course, by the response we have had from our students. We have adopted ideas and techniques found in a number of American casebooks. The ones we have found particularly useful are: Fuller & Eisenberg, *Basic Contract Law*, 3rd ed., and Macneil, *Contracts, Exchange Transactions and Relations*, 2nd ed. We have taken ideas, the arrangement of cases and suggestions for questions and problems in ways that cannot be expressly and precisely acknowledged. We are grateful for the advice and comments that we have received from those colleagues in other law schools who have used some of our earlier drafts. We have found the earlier drafts of these materials to be useful and effective teaching materials. We hope that others will find these to be so as well.

We would like to thank Kathy O'Rourke and Vaughan Black for help in proof-reading and in preparing the index. Our special thanks, however, go to Alice Ng who, for several years, has endured the boredom of seemingly endless photocopying, the typing of indecipherable manuscript and all the other labour of putting together a casebook. Alice has throughout been cheerful, careful and efficient and she has made our work much less difficult than it might have been.

We are also grateful for the help and encouragement we have received from our publishers, Butterworth & Co. (Canada) Ltd.

ACKNOWLEDGMENTS

A casebook on such a wide subject necessarily contains a great deal of reference to the work of others in the field, in the cases, notes and text, and more especially in the selected reading. The authors and publishers of these articles and textbooks have been most generous in giving permission for the reproduction in this text of work already in print. References, of course, appear where necessary and possible in the text. It is convenient for us to list below, for the assistance of the reader, the publishers and, in several instances, the authors for whose courtesy we are most grateful.

American Law Institute	*Restatement of the Law of Contracts* (1932), § 90, 227.
	Restatement of the Law, Second, Contracts, (1973), Tentative Drafts 1-7, Revised and Edited, §§ 21A, 35, 75, 90, 227.
American Law Institute and National Conference of Commissioners on Uniform State Laws	*Official Text of the Uniform Commercial Code* (1978), §§ 2-207, 2-302, 2-306(2), 2-615, 2-709, 2-716. Reprinted with permission of the Permanent Editorial Board for the Uniform Commercial Code.
Canadian Press	Newspaper article published in Globe & Mail, Toronto, on May 5, 1977.
Columbia Law Review	Fuller, "Consideration and Form", 41 Colum. L. Rev. 799.
	Kessler, "Contracts of Adhesion — Some Thoughts About Freedom of Contract," 43 Colum. L. Rev. 629.
Foundation Press, Inc.	Dawson & Harvey, *Cases and Comment on Contracts* (3rd ed.), pp. 190-193.
	Macneil, *Contracts, Exchange Transactions and Relations* (1st ed.), pp. 3-5; (2nd ed.), pp. 455-477.
Fred B. Rothman & Co.	Fuller, "Law's Precarious Hold on Life", 3 Georgia Law Review 530-545 (1968-69).
Globe & Mail, Toronto	Article on O.L.R.B., published Dec. 8, 1977.
Harvard Journal on Legislation	James McCauley Landis, "Statutes and the Sources of Law", 2 Harvard Journal of Legislation 7.
International Association of Legal Science	*International Encyclopedia of Comparative Law*, Vol. VII, c. 3 (II), pp. 18-34.
Journal of Legal Education	Macneil, "Whither Contracts" (1969), 21 J. of Leg. Ed. 403-417.

Little, Brown & Co.	Karl N. Llewellyn, *The Common Law Tradition: Deciding Appeals* (Boston 1960), pp. 362-371.
Michael Joseph Ltd., Jefferson Smurfit Group	M. Healey, *The Old Munster Circuit* (Dublin, 1939), p. 209.
Northwestern University Press	Havighurst, *The Nature of Private Contract*, pp. 113-118.
Oxford University Press	Jeremy Bentham, *A Comment on the Commentaries*, C. W. Everett (ed.) (1928), p. 194.
Richard A. Posner	Posner, Economic Analysis of Law (2nd ed., 1973), pp. 88-93.
Routledge & Kegan Paul Ltd.	Renner, *The Institutions of Private Law and Their Social Function* (1906), pp. 1-16, pp. 104-122.
Simon & Schuster	Walt Kelley, *Beau Pogo* (1960), pp. 182, 183.
University of Toronto Press	Barry Reiter, "Courts, Consideration and Common Sense," 27 University of Toronto Law Journal 467-71.
West Publishing Company	Fuller & Eisenberg, *Basic Contract* Law (3rd ed., 1972), pp. 89-103, 191-195, 280-282, 1008, 1009.
	Various cases reproduced from the Atlantic, Federal, New York Supreme Court, North Eastern, North Western, Pacific, Southern, and South Western Reporters.
Yale Law Journal Co. & Fred B. Rothman & Co.	Fuller & Perdue, "The Reliance Interest in Contract Damages," 46 Harvard Law Journal pp. 52-68, 84-86.
	K.N. Llewellyn, "On Our Case Law of Contract: Offer and Acceptance," 48 Harvard Law Journal pp. 1, 32.
	Llewellyn, "What Price Contract: An Essay in Perspective," 40 Harvard Law Journal pp. 704, 741-44.
Yale Law School	*Corbin on Contracts* (1960), vol. 3, §§ 573, 574, 582, 597.

SUMMARY OF CONTENTS

CHAPTER 1. Remedies for Breach of Contract 1-1
  A. Introduction 1-1
  B. The Interests Protected 1-19
  C. Specific Performance and Injunctions 1-68
  D. Remoteness of Damage 1-106
  E. The Range of the Interests Protected 1-130
  F. Mitigation 1-139

CHAPTER 2. The Kinds of Promises that the Law Will
          Enforce 2-1
  A. Introduction 2-1
  B. Formal Validity of Contracts 2-44
  C. Consideration 2-49
      (1) The Bargain Theory. Consideration as Exchange 2-49
      (2) Past Consideration 2-58
      (3) Mutual Promises 2-73
      (4) Performance of a Legal Duty as Consideration: Modification
           and Waiver of Contractual Duties 2-98
  D. Third Parties and Consideration 1-122
  E. Reliance as a Basis for the Enforcement of Promises 2-141

CHAPTER 3. Making the Contract 3-1
  A. Introduction 3-1
  B. The Classical Theory of Offer and Acceptance 3-8
      (1) Introduction 3-8
      (2) What is an offer? 3-9
      (3) The Power of Acceptance 3-19
      (4) When do Negotiations Come to an End? The Problem of
           Indefiniteness 3-65
  C. The Battle of the Forms 3-89

CHAPTER 4. Misunderstandings, Misrepresentation and
          Mistakes
  A. Interpretation and Implication 4-1
  B. The Parol Evidence Rule 4-13
  C. Misrepresentation and Warranties 4-29
      The Sale of Goods Act and Third Parties 4-65
  D. Mistakes 4-109
  E. Frustration 4-175
  F. Third Parties and Mistakes 4-209

CHAPTER 5. THE EFFECT OF NON-PERFORMANCE
                BY THE PLAINTIFF 5-1

  A. Excuses for the Defendant's Non-Performance: Herein of Conditions 5-1
      (1) The Effect of Express Conditions 5-1
      (2) The Technique of Implying a Condition 5-16
  B. Excuses for the Plaintiff's Non-Performance 5-30
  C. Restitution in the Event of the Plaintiff's Breach 5-41

CHAPTER 6. THE CONTROL OF CONTRACT POWER 6-1
  A. Introduction 6-1
  B. Standard Form Contracts 6-47
      (1) The "Ticket" Cases 6-47
      (2) Signed Contracts 6-66
         (a) The Problem in the Courts 6-66
            (1) Introduction 6-66
            (2) The Problem Outlined 6-68
            (3) Penalties and Forfeitures 6-117
            (4) A Tentative Solution 6-141
  C. Exemption Clauses and Third Parties 6-189
  D. Unconscionability 6-199
  E. The Legislative Response 6-242

CHAPTER 7. THE STATUTE OF FRAUDS 7-1

CHAPTER 8. ILLEGAL CONTRACTS 8-1

CHAPTER 9. CONTRACTS: POSTSCRIPT AND PRECLUDE 9-1

TABLE OF CONTENTS

Preface vii

Acknowledgments viii

Table of Statutes xxi

Table of Cases xxiii

Introduction xxvii

CHAPTER 1. REMEDIES FOR BREACH OF CONTRACT 1-1

   A. Introduction 1-1

       Fuller and Eisenberg, *Basic Contract Law* 1-1

       Macneil, Cases and Materials on Contracts 1-15

   B. The Interests Protected 1-19

       Peevyhouse v. Garland Coal & Mining Co. 1-19

       Sale of Goods Act 1-27

            Note on Canadian and American Legislation and Law
            Reform 1-28

       Victory Motors Ltd. v. Bayda 1-30

       Fuller and Perdue, "The Reliance Interest in Contract Damages" 1-37

       Posner, Economic Analysis of Law 1-47

       Sunshine Exploration Ltd. v. Dolly Varden 1-51

       Anglia T.V. v. Reed 1-60

       Sullivan v. O'Connor 1-62

   C. Specific Performance and Injunctions 1-68

       Behnke v. Bede Shipping Co. 1-75

       Uniform Commercial Code, § 2-716(1) and § 2-716(3) 1-77

       Sky Petroleum Ltd. v. VIP Petroleum Ltd. 1-77

       Gilbert v. Barron 1-80

       De Rivafinoli v. Corsetti 1-82

       Warner Bros. v. Nelson 1-84

            Note on Labour Relations 1-89
            McGavin Toastmaster Ltd. v. Ainscough 1-90

       Hill v. Parsons 1-92

            Review Problem 1-97

       Wroth v. Tyler 1-97

   D. Remoteness of Damage 1-106

       Hadley v. Baxendale 1-106

       Fuller and Perdue, "The Reliance Interest in Contract Damages" 1-109

            Note on Legal Reasoning 1-110

       Victoria Laundry v. Newman Industries 1-111

       The Heron II. Koufos v. C. Czarnikow Ltd. 1-113

Kerr S.S. Co. v. R.C.A. 1-119

Horne v. Midland Railway 1-123

Freedhof v. Pomalift Industries Ltd 1-128

    Review Problem 1-130

E. The Range of the Interests Protected 1-130

Addis v. Gramophone Co. Ltd. 1-130

Jarvis v. Swans Tours Ltd. 1-133

    Martel v. Duffy-Mott Corp. 1-137

F. Mitigation 1-139

Payzu Ltd. v. Saunders 1-140

White and Carter v. McGregor 1-142

Clark v. Marsiglia 1-148

Finelli v. Dee 1-150

Cockburn v. Trusts & Guarantee Co. 1-151

Review Problem 1-153

CHAPTER 2. THE KINDS OF PROMISES THAT THE LAW WILL
    ENFORCE 2-1

A. Introduction 2-1

Fuller, "Consideration and Form" 2-3

      Matheson v. Smiley 2-23

      Soldiers Memorial Hospital v. Sanford 2-25

      Deglman v. Guarantee Trust & Constantineau 2-27

      Boone v. Coe 2-30

      Boomer v. Muir 2-34

      Review Problem 2-36

      Post v. Jones 2-36

      Chilliback v. Pawliuk 2-38

      Sundell Ltd. v. Emm Yannoulatos 2-41

B. Formal Validity of Contracts 2-44

Dawson and Harvey, "The Seal" 2-46

C. Consideration 2-49

(1) The Bargain Theory. Consideration as Exchange 2-49

Restatement, Second, Contracts § 75 2-49

White v. Bluett 2-50

Thomas v. Thomas 2-51

Hamer v. Sidway 2-52

Note on the Doctrine of Consideration 2-55

(2) Past Consideration 2-58

Mills v. Wyman 2-58

Webb v. McGowin 2-61

Eastwood v. Kenyon 2-63

Roscorla v. Thomas 2-71

Note on Infants' Contracts and the effect of the Statute of Limitations 2-72

(3) Mutual Promises 2-73

G.N.R. v. Witham 2-74

Bernstein v. W.B. Mfg. Co. 2-76

Wood v. Lucy, Lady Duff-Gordon 2-82

U.C.C. § 2.306(2) 2-83

Stewart Macaulay, "The Standardized Contracts of United States Automobile Manufacturers" 2-85

(4) Performance of a Legal Duty as Consideration: Modification and Waiver of Contractual Duties 2-98

Harris v. Watson 2-98

Stilk v. Myrick 2-99

Raggow v. Scougall 2-100

Smith v. Dawson 2-101

Fairgrief v. Ellis 2-103

Gilbert Steel v. University Construction 2-105

Note 2-110

Foakes v. Beer 2-112

The Mercantile Law Amendment Act 2-115

    Bank of Nova Scotia v. MacLellan 2-116
    Rommerill v. Gardener 2-117
    Champlain Ready-Mixed Cement v. Beaupre 2-119

Scotson v. Pegg 2-120

D. Third Parties and Consideration 1-122

Tweddle v. Atkinson 2-122

Note on Third Parties 2-123

Beswick v. Beswick (C.A.) 2-124

Beswick v. Beswick (H.L.) 2-130

Jackson v. Horizon Holidays 2-135

E. Reliance as a Basis for the Enforcement of Promises 2-141

Central London Property v. High Trees 2-142

Imperator Realty v. Tull 2-145

Combe v. Combe 2-148

Restatement, Contracts, § 90 2-152

Fuller and Perdue, "The Reliance Interest in Contract Damages" 2-152

D. & C. Builders v. Rees 2-155

Watson v. Canada Permanent Trust 2-160

Baxter v. Jones 2-163

Sloan v. Union Oil Co. 2-165

Skidmore v. Bradford 2-168

Dalhousie College v. Boutilier Estate 2-170

Re Ross 2-177

Balfour v. Balfour 2-180

Jones v. Padavatton 2-183

    Simpkins v. Pays 2-188

Llewellyn: What Price Contract? An Essay in Perspective 2-191

CHAPTER 3. MAKING THE CONTRACT 3-1

A.   Introduction 3-1

    Hobbs v. Esquimalt and Nanaimo 3-3

    Henkel v. Pape 3-5

    Raffles v. Wichelhaus 3-6

    Restatement Second, Contracts, § 21A 3-8

B.   The Classical Theory of Offer and Acceptance 3-8

    (1)   Introduction 3-8
    (2)   What is an offer? 3-9

    Johnston Bros. v. Rogers Bros. 3-9

    Denton v. G.N.R. 3-11

    Lefkowitz v. Great Minneapolis Surplus Store 3-13

    Pharmaceutical Society v. Boots 3-16

        Combines Investigation Act 3-18
    (3)   The Power of Acceptance 3-19

    Eliason v. Henshaw 3-20

    Williams v. Carwardine 3-22

    Carlill v. Carbolic Smoke Ball 3-23

    Fitch v. Snedaker 3-26

    The Crown v. Clarke 3-28

        "Unkindest Cut" 3-31

    Dickinson v. Dodds 3-32

    Restatement Second, Contracts, § 35 3-37

    Petterson v. Pattberg 3-37

    Errington v. Errington 3-40

    Dawson v. Helicopter Exploration 3-43

        Dennis Reed Ltd. v. Goody 3-45

    Adams v. Lindsell 3-47

    Household Insurance v. Grant 3-49

        Post Office Act 3-56

    Tinn v. Hoffmann 3-56

    Wheeler v. Klaholt 3-62

        Consumer Protection Act 3-64

    K.N. Llewellyn, "Offer and Acceptance" 3-65

    (4)   When do Negotiations Come to an End? The Problem of
        Indefiniteness 3-65
        Problems 3-65

Foley v. Classique Coaches 3-66

Bristol, Cardiff and Swansea Aerated Bread v. Maggs 3-70

Bellamy v. Debenham 3-72

Harvey v. Perry 3-73

Brown v. Gould 3-77

Courteney v. Tolaini 3-84
Labour Relations Act 3-85

Brewer Street Investments v. Barclays 3-86

C. The Battle of the Forms 3-89

Matter of Doughboy Industries Inc. 3-89

Roto-Lith v. Bartlett & Co. 3-93

U.C.C., § 2-207 3-96

Fuller, "Law's Precarious Hold On Life" 3-98

CHAPTER 4. Misunderstandings, Misrepresentation and
Mistakes

A. Interpretation and Implication 4-1

Restatement [First] Contracts, § 227 4-1

Restatement, Second, Contracts, § 227 4-2

Fuller and Eisenberg, *Basic Contract Law* 4-2

Prenn v. Simmonds 4-4

Schuler v. Wickman 4-8

B. The Parol Evidence Rule 4-13

Corbin on Contracts 4-14

Hawrish v. Bank of Montreal 4-16

Zell v. American Seating Co. 4-20

J. Evans & Son v. Andrea Merzario Ltd. 4-26

C. Misrepresentation and Warranties 4-29

Redgrave v. Hurd 4-30

Redican v. Nesbitt 4-35

Misrepresentation Act 4-43

Heilbut, Symons v. Buckleton 4-44

Dick Bentley v. Harold Smith Motors 4-49

Richview Construction v. Raspa 4-51

Shanklin Pier v. Detel 4-57

Andrews v. Hopkinson 4-59

Note on Warranties and The Sale of Goods Act 4-62
The Sale of Goods Act and Third Parties 4-65
McMorran v. Dominion Stores & Crush Int. 4-66
Sigurdson v. Hillcrest Service 4-69

Ranger v. Herbert A. Watts (Quebec), (Ont. H. Ct.) 4-71

Ranger v. Herbert Watts (Quebec), (Ont. C.A.) 4-78

Note on Negligent Misrepresentation 4-79

Esso Petroleum v. Mardon 4-81

Nunes Diamonds v. Dom. Elec. Co. 4-89

Sealand v. McHaffie Ltd. 4-101

    N.W. Mutual Ins. v. J.T. O'Bryan & Co. 4-106

D. Mistakes 4-109

Corbin, Checklist, § 597 4-110

U.S.A. v. Motor Trucks 4-110

Paget v. Marshall 4-113

Norwich Union v. Price 4-116

Bell v. Lever Brothers 4-119

Solle v. Butcher 4-131

Magee v. Pennine Insurance Co. 4-136

Note on Mistake 4-142

    Brooklin Heights Homes v. Major Holdings 4-145

Scott v. Coulson 4-149

Sherwood v. Walker 4-151

    London County Council v. Boot 4-156

Grist v. Bailey 4-157

Hyrsky et al. v. Smith 4-159

Amalgamated Investment v. John Walker & Sons 4-164

    Upton-on-Severn Rural District Council v. Powell 4-169
    Boulton v. Jones 4-171

Review Problems 4-174

E. Frustration 4-175

Paradine v. Jane 4-176

Taylor v. Caldwell 4-177

Krell v. Henry 4-180

Capital Quality Homes v. Colwyn Construction 4-185

Sainsbury Ltd. v. Street 4-193

Appleby v. Myers 4-198

Fibrosa v. Fairbairn 4-200

    The Frustrated Contracts Act 4-207

F. Third Parties and Mistakes 4-209

Prudential Trust Co. v. Cugnet 4-209

Saunders v. Anglia Building Society 4-217

Lewis v. Averay 4-223

A Note on Secured Transactions 4-230

    Ingram v. Little 4-232

CHAPTER 5. THE EFFECT OF NON-PERFORMANCE
BY THE PLAINTIFF 5-1

A. Excuses for the Defendant's Non-Performance: Herein of Conditions 5-1

(1) The Effect of Express Conditions 5-1

Pym v. Campbell 5-2

Turney v. Zhilka 5-3

Beauchamp v. Beauchamp 5-4

Barnett v. Harrison 5-5

Schuler v. Wickman 5-13
(2) The Technique of Implying a Condition 5-16

Kingston v. Preston 5-18

Boone v. Eyre 5-19

Hong Kong Fir v. Kawasaki 5-19

Note on Terminology 5-25

Jacob & Youngs v. Kent 5-26

B. Excuses for the Plaintiff's Non-Performance 5-30

Cort v. The Ambergate Railway Co. 5-31

Hochster v. De La Tour 5-33

Dalrymple v. Scott 5-36

British & Benningtons Ltd. v. North Western Cachar Tea 5-37

C. Restitution in the Event of the Plaintiff's Breach 5-41

Howe v. Smith 5-41

Dies v. British and International Mining 5-42

Sumpter v. Hedges 5-46

Dakin & Co. v. Lee 5-48

Blake v. Shaw 5-50

Hamilton v. Raymond 5-51

Bright v. Ganas 5-53

CHAPTER 6. THE CONTROL OF CONTRACT POWER 6-1

A. Introduction 6-1

Renner, "The Institutions of Private Law and Their Social Function" 6-1

Kessler, "Contracts of Adhesion — Some Thoughts About Freedom of Contract" 6-26

MacNeil, *Cases on Contracts*, "Contracts of Adhesion" 6-34

Harold C. Havighurst, The Nature of Private Contract 6-36

Morrison v. Coast Finance Ltd. 6-43

B. Standard Form Contracts 6-47

(1) The "Ticket" Cases 6-47

Parker v. The South Eastern Railway Co. 6-48

Heffron v. Imperial Parking 6-54

Thornton v. Shoe Lane Parking 6-62

(2) Signed Contracts 6-66
   (a) The Problem in the Courts 6-66
      (1) Introduction 6-66
      (2) The Problem Outlined 6-68

Yeoman Credit v. Apps 6-68

Canadian-Dominion Leasing v. Suburban Superdrug Ltd. 6-72

Federal Discount v. St. Pierre 6-77

Suisse Atlantique v. N.V. Rotterdamsche 6-82

Harbutt's Plasticine v. Wayne Tank 6-97

      Note 6-105

Linton v. C.N.R. 6-106

Toepfer v. Continental Grain 6-114

      (3) Penalties and Forfeitures 6-117

Dunlop v. New Garage 6-118

H.F. Clarke v. Thermidaire 6-120

Stockloser v. Johnson 6-131

Gisvold v. Hill 6-137

      (4) A Tentative Solution 6-141

Llewellyn, The Common Law Tradition 6-141

Gillespie Brothers v. Roy Bowles 6-147

Levison v. Patent Steam Carpet 6-154

Tilden Rent-A-Car v. Clendenning 6-157

McCutcheon v. David MacBrayne 6-167

British Crane Hire v. Ipswich Plant Hire 6-171

Henningsen v. Bloomfield Motors 6-173

Stewart Macaulay, "The Standardized Contracts of United States Automobile Manufacturers" 6-182

C. Exemption Clauses and Third Parties 6-189

Scruttons v. Midland Silicones 6-189

The New Zealand Shipping Co. v. Satterthwaite & Co. 6-193

D. Unconscionability 6-199

Lloyds Bank v. Bundy 6-200

Note on Fiduciary Obligations 6-212

      Regier v. Campbell-Stuart 6-213
      McLeod v. Sweezey 6-214
      Jirna v. Mr. Donut 6-216

McKenzie v. Bank of Montreal 6-218

Sherk v. Horwitz 6-222

Esso Petroleum v. Harper's Garage 6-226

Schroeder v. Macaulay 6-234

E. The Legislative Response 6-242

      The Unconscionable Transactions Relief Act 6-254

Collins v. Forest Hill Investment 6-256

Uniform Commercial Code, § 2-302 6-259

CHAPTER 7. THE STATUTE OF FRAUDS 7-1

CHAPTER 8. ILLEGAL CONTRACTS 8-1

Landis, Statutes and the Sources of Law 8-1

Pearce v. Brooks 8-14

Holman v. Johnson 8-19

Rogers v. Leonard 8-21

The Lord's Day Act 8-32

Kiriri Cotton Co. v. Dewani 8-33

Kingshott v. Brunskill 8-37

Sidmay Ltd. v. Wehttam 8-39

St. John Shipping Corp. v. Joseph Rank Ltd. 8-50

Archbolds Ltd. v. Spanglett Ltd. 8-63

Ashmore v. Dawson 8-68

Davidson & Co. v. McLeery 8-74

CHAPTER 9. CONTRACTS: POSTSCRIPT AND PRECLUDE 9-1

Macneil, I.R., "Whither Contracts" 9-1

TABLE OF STATUTES

1. *Canada*

Bills of Exchange Act. R.S.O. 1970 c. B-5 (as amended)

s. 191 6-254

Combines Investigation Act. R.S.C. 1970 c. C-23 (as amended)

s. 36 6-248

37 3-19

2. *Ontario*

Business Practices Act. R.S.O. 1974, c. 131

s. 2(a) 6-246

(b) 6-250

3 6-250

4 6-250

Consumer Protection Act. R.S.O. 1970 c. 82 (as amended)

s. 36 6-253

39 6-254

42a 4-65, 6-254

44a 6-252

Frustrated Contracts Act. R.S.O. 1970 c. 185

— .... 4-207 — 4-208

Highway Traffic Act. R.S.O. 1970 c. 202 (as amended)

s. 58 6-249

ss. 58b, 58c, 58e 6-248

Insurance Act. R.S.O. 1970 c. 224

s. 211 2-124

Judicature Act. R.S.O. 1970 c. 228 (as amended)

s. 20 1-89

21 1-105

Labour Relations Act. R.S.O. 1970, c. 232

s. 36 1-89

38 1-94

42 2-141

Mercantile Law Amendment Act. R.S.O. 1970 c. 272

s. 16 2-115

Mortgages Act. R.S.O. 1970 c. 279

s. 19 2-140

Motor Vehicle Dealers Act. R.S.O. 1970 c. 475 (as amended)

ss. 1, 3, 4 6-242

ss. 5, 6, 7 6-243

s. 33 6-242

35 6-240

Regulations

s. 7 6-245

16(2) 6-251

20 6-252

Sale of Goods Act. R.S.O. 1970 c. 421

s. 5(1) 7-1, 7-7
    9 3-82
    12(2) 4-63, 5-25
    (3) 4-63
    13-16 4-62
    25 4-230
    29(1) 4-198
    30 5-40
    48 1-27
    49 1-27
    50 1-75

Statute of Frauds. R.S.O. 1970 c. 444

s. 4 .... 7-1, 7-3
    6 7-1
    7 .... 2-73, 7-1
    8 7-1

Unconscionable Transactions Relief Act. R.S.O. 1970 c. 472

— .... 6-254 — 6-256

3. *Nova Scotia*

Public Subscriptions Act. R.S.N.S. 1967 c. 257

— 2-179

4. *English*

Misrepresentation Act, 1967 (15 & 16 Eliz. II. ch. 7)

ss. 1, 2 4-43

5. *American*

Uniform Commercial Code

§ 1-203 6-146
   2-103 6-146
   2-204 3-83
   2-207 3-92
   2-302 6-259
   2-306(2) 2-83
   2-716 1-77

Restatement, Contracts

I.§ 90 2-152
   227 4-1
II.§ 21A 3-8
   35 3-37
   75 .... 2-49, 2-154
   90 2-152
   133 2-139
   142 2-139
   217A 7-9
   227 4-2
   238(2) 404

TABLE OF CASES

[A page number in bold face (black) type indicates that the text of the case or a portion thereof is reproduced. A page number in light face type indicates that the case is merely referred to or mentioned.]

Adams v. Lindsell **3-47**
Addis v. Gramophone Co. Ltd., **1-130**
Amalgamated Investment and Property v. John Walker & Sons, **4-164**
Andrews v. Hopkinson, **4-59**
Anglia T.V. v. Reed, **1-60**
Appleby v. Myers, **4-198**
Archbolds Ltd. v. Spanglett, **8-63**
Ashmore v. Dawson, **8-68**

Balfour v. Balfour, **2-180**
Bank of Nova Scotia v. MacLellan, **2-116**
Barnett v. Harrison, **5-5**
Baxter v. Jones, **2-163**
Beauchamp v. Beauchamp, **5-4**
Behnke v. Bede Shipping Co., **1-75**
Bell v. Lever Brothers, Ltd., **4-119**
Bellamy v. Debenham, 3-72
Dick Bentley v. Harold Smith Motors, **4-49**
Bernstein v. W.B. Mfg. Co., **2-76**
Beswick v. Beswick (C.A.), **2-124**
Beswick v. Beswick (H.L.), **2-130**
Blake v. Shaw, **5-50**
Boomer v. Muir, **2-34**
Boone v. Coe, **2-30**
Boone v. Eyre, **5-19**
Boulton v. Jones, **4-171**
Brewer Street Investments v. Barclays, **3-86**
Bright v. Ganas, **5-53**
Bristol, Cardiff & Swansea Aerated Bread v. Maggs, **3-70**
British & Benningtons Ltd. v. North Western Cachar Tea, **5-37**
British Crane Hire v. Ipswich Plant Hire, **6-171**
Brooklin Heights Homes v. Major Holdings, **4-145**
Brown v. Gould, **3-77**

Canadian-Dominion Leasing Corp. v. Suburban Superdrug, **6-72**
Capital Quality Homes v. Colwyn Construction, **4-185**
Carlill v. Carbolic Smoke Ball, **3-23**
Carson v. Willitts, 1-59
Cehave v. Bremer, 5-26
Central London Property Trust v. High Trees House, **2-142**

Champlain Ready-Mixed Cement v. Beaupré, **2-119**
Chicago Coliseum Club v. Dempsey, 1-123
Chilliback v. Pawliuk, **2-38**
Clark v. Marsiglia, **1-148**
H.F. Clarke v. Thermidaire, **6-120**
Cockburn v. Trusts & Guarantee Co., **1-151**
Collins v. Forest Hill Investment Corp., **6-255**
Combe v. Combe, **2-148**
Coppola v. Kraushaar, 1-122
Cort v. The Ambergate Railway, **5-31**
Cotter v. General Petroleums, 1-58
Courteney v. Tolaini, **3-84**
Cox v. Phillips Industries **1-136**
Crown v. Clarke **3-28**
Currie v. Misa, 2-49

D. & C. Builders v. Rees, **2-155**
Dakin v. Lee, **5-48**
Dalhousie College v. Boutilier Estate, **2-170**
Dalrymple v. Scott, **5-36**
Davidson v. McLeery, **8-74**
Dawson v. Helicopter Exploration, **3-43**
De Rivafinoli v. Corsetti, **1-82**
Deglman v. Guarantee Trust and Constantineau, **2-27**
Dennis Reed Ltd. v. Goody, 3-45
Denton v. G.N.R., **3-11**
Detroit Football v. Dublinski, 1-96
Dickinson v. Dodds, **3-32**
Dies v. British & International Mining & Finance, **5-42**
Dunlop v. Selfridges, 2-49
Dunlop Tyre Company v. New Garage & Motor, **6-118**

Eastwood v. Kenyon, **2-63**
Eliason v. Henshaw, **3-20**
Errington v. Errington, **3-40**
Esso Petroleum v. Harper's Garage, **6-226**
Esso Petroleum v. Mardon, **4-81**
J. Evans & Son v. Andrea Merzario, **4-26**

Fairgrief v. Ellis, **2-103**

Federal Discount Corp. v. St.
    Pierre, **6-77**
Fibrosa v. Fairbairn, **4-200**
Finelli v. Dee, **1-150**
Fitch v. Snedaker, **3-26**
Foakes v. Beer, **2-112**
Foley v. Classique Coaches, **3-66**
Freedhof v. Pomalife Industries, **1-128**
Frost v. Knight, 5-35

G.N.R. v. Witham, **2-74**
Gilbert v. Barron, **1-80**
Gilbert Steel v. University
    Construction, **2-105**
Gillespie Brothers v. Roy Bowles, **6-147**
Gisvold v. Hill, **6-137**
Grist v. Bailey, **4-157**

Hadley v. Baxendale, **1-106**
Hamer v. Sidway, **2-52**
Hamilton v. Raymond, **5-51**
Harbutt's Plasticine v. Wayne Tank
    Co., **6-97**
Harris v. Watson, **2-98**
Harvey v. Facey, 3-11
Harvey v. Perry, **3-73**
Hawkes v. Saunders, 2-67
Hawkins v. McGee, **1-67**
Hawrish v. Bank of Montreal, **4-16**
Heffron v. Imperial Parking, **6-54**
Heilbut, Symonds v. Buckleton, **4-44**
Henkel v. Pape, **3-5**
Henningsen v. Bloomfield
    Motors, **6-173**
Heron II (The); Koufos v.
    Czarnikow, **1-113**
Hill v. Parsons, **1-92**
Hobbs v. Esquimalt & Nanaimo
    Railway, **3-3**
Hochster v. De La Tour, **5-33**
Holman v. Johnson, **8-19**
Hong Kong Fir v. Kawasaki, **5-19**
Horne v. Midland Railway, **1-123**
Household Insurance v. Grant, **3-49**
Howe v. Smith, **5-41**
Hyrsky v. Smith, **4-159**

Imperator Realty v. Tull, **2-145**
Ingram v. Little, **4-232**

Jackson v. Horizon Holidays, **2-135**
Jacob & Youngs v. Kent, **5-26**
Jarvis v. Swans Tours Ltd., **1-133**
Jirna v. Mr. Donut, **6-216**
Johnston Bros. v. Rogers Bros., **3-9**
Jones v. Padavatton, **2-183**

Kerr S.S. v. R.C.A., **1-119**

Kingshott v. Brunskill, **8-37**
Kingston v. Preston, **5-18**
Kiriri Cotton Co. v. Dewani, **8-33**
Krell v. Henry, **4-180**

Lake Ontario Cement v. Golden Eagle
    Oil, 3-70
Lefkowitz v. Great Minneapolis Surplus
    Store, **3-13**
Levison v. Patent Steam Carpet
    Cleaning, **6-154**
Lewis v. Averay, **4-223**
Linton v. C.N.R., **6-106**
Lloyd v. Stanbury, 1-61
Lloyds Bank v. Bundy, **6-200**
London County Council v. Boot, **4-156**

Magee v. Pennine Insurance, **4-136**
Martel v. Duff-Mott Corp., **1-137**
Matheson v. Smiley, **2-23**
Matter of Doughboy Industries
    Inc., **3-89**
Mendelssohn v. Normand Ltd., 6-67
Metropolitan Trust v. Pressure
    Concrete, 1-105
Mills v. Wyman, **2-58**
Moorcock (The), 5-17
Morrison v. Coast Finance Ltd., **6-43**
Munroe Equipment Sales v. Canadian
    Forest Products, 1-127

McCutcheon v. David
    MacBrayne, **6-167**
McGavin Toastmaster Ltd. v.
    Ainscough, 1-90
McKenzie v. Bank of Montreal, **6-218**
McLeod v. Sweezey, **6-214**
McMaster University v. Wilchar Const.
    Ltd., **4-143**
McMorran v. Dominion Stores & Crush
    International, **4-66**

New Zealand Shipping Ltd. v. A.M.
    Satterthwaite, **6-193**
Nicholson v. St. Dennis, 2-31
N.W. Mutual Insurance v. J.T. O'Bryan
    & Co., **4-106**
Norwich Union v. Price, **4-116**
Nunes Diamonds v. Dom. Elec.
    Co., **4-89**

Paget v. Marshall, **4-113**
Paradine v. Jane, **4-176**
Parker v. The South Eastern
    Railway, **6-48**
Payzu v. Saunders, **1-140**
Pearce v. Brooks, **8-14**

Peevyhouse v. Garland Coal & Mining, **1-19**

Petterson v. Pattberg, **3-37**

Pharmaceutical Society v. Boots, **3-16**

Pillans v. Van Mierop, 2-67

Post v. Jones, **2-36**

Prenn v. Simmonds, **4-4**

Prudential Trust v. Cugnet, **4-209**

Pym v. Campbell, **5-2**

Raffles v. Wichelhaus, **3-6**

Raggow v. Scougall, **2-100**

Ranger v. Herbert A. Watts (Ont. High Court), **4-71**

Ranger v. Herbert A. Watts (C.A.), **4-78**

Re Registrar of Used Car Dealers & Rowe Motors, **6-243**

Re Ross, **2-177**

Redgrave v. Hurd, **4-30**

Redican v. Nesbitt, **4-35**

Reference Re Certain Titles to Land in Ontario, **8-79**

Regier v. Campbell-Stuart, **6-213**

Reigate v. Union Manufacturing Co., 5-17

Richview Construction v. Raspa, **4-51**

Rogers v. Leonard, **8-21**

Rommeril v. Gardener, **2-117**

Roscorla v. Thomas, **2-71**

Roto-Lith v. F.P. Bartlett, **3-93**

Sainsbury v. Street, **4-193**

St. John Shipping v. Joseph Rank Ltd., **8-50**

Saunders v. Anglia Building Society, **4-217**

Schroeder v. Macaulay, **6-234**

Schuler A.G. v. Wickman Ltd., **4-8**

Scotson v. Pegg, **2-120**

Scott v. Coulson, **4-149**

Scruttons v. Midland Silicones, **6-189**

Scyrup v. Economy Tractor Parts Ltd., **1-127**

Sealand v. McHaffie Ltd., **4-101**

Shanklin Pier v. Detel, **4-57**

Shaw v. D.P.P., 6-192

Sherk v. Horwitz, **6-222**

Sherwood v. Walker, **4-151**

Shirlaw v. Southern Foundries, 5-17

Sidmay Ltd. v. Wehttam, **8-39**

Sigurdson v. Hillcrest Service Ltd., **4-69**

Simpkins v. Pays, **2-188**

Sir Anthony Shirlyn v. Albany, 2-49

Skidmore v. Bradford, **2-168**

Sky Petroleum v. VIP Petroleum, **1-77**

Sloan v. Union Oil of Canada, **2-165**

Smith v. Dawson, **2-101**

Smith v. Hughes, 4-145

Soldiers Memorial Hospital v. Sanford, **2-25**

Solle v. Butcher, **4-131**

J. Spurling Ltd. v. Bradshaw, 6-54

Steadman v. Steadman, **7-5**

Stilk v. Myrick, **2-99**

Stockloser v. Johnson, **6-131**

Suisse Atlantique v. N.V. Rotterdamsche, 6-82

Sullivan v. O'Connor, **1-62**

Sumpter v. Hedges, **5-46**

Sundell v. Emm Yannoulators, **2-41**

Sunshine Exploration v. Dolly Varden, **1-51**

Taylor v. Caldwell, **4-177**

Thomas v. Thomas, **2-51**

Thornton v. Shoe Lane Parking, **6-62**

Tilden Rent-A-Car v. Clendenning, **6-157**

Tinn v. Hoffmann, **3-56**

Toepfer v. Continental Grain, **6-114**

Trollope & Colls v. N.W. Regional Hospital Board, 5-17

Turney v. Zhilka, **5-3**

Tweddle v. Atkinson, **2-122**

U.S.A. v. Motor Trucks, Ltd., **4-110**

Upton-on-Severn Rural District Council v. Powell, **4-169**

Victoria Laundry v. Newman Industries, **1-111**

Victoria Motors Ltd. v. Bayda, **1-30**

Wallis v. Russell, 4-63

Warner Bros. v. Nelson, **1-84**

Watson v. Canada Permanent Trust Co., **2-160**

Webb v. McGowin, **2-61**

Wennall v. Adney, 2-67

Westlake v. Adams, **2-49**

Wheeler v. Klaholt, **3-62**

White v. Bluett, **2-50**

White & Carter v. McGregor, **1-142**

Williams v. Carwardine, **3-22**

Winnipeg Builders' Exchange Case, 1-88

Wood v. Lucy, Lady Duff-Gordon, **2-82**

Wroth v. Tyler, **1-97**

Yeoman Credit v. Apps, **6-68**

Zell v. American Seating Co., **4-20**

INTRODUCTION

The materials that follow have been prepared for the purpose of exploring the way in which the law of contracts functions now and, to some extent, how it got that way.

We would like to suggest some points which should be kept in mind as you read the cases:

1. Every judgment is a product of the time at which it was delivered and the society in which it is found. In these materials there are cases from Canada, England, the U.S.A., Australia and elsewhere. There are judgments that were written as early as the civil wars in England and, of course, as late as this year. You can never ignore both the place and date of any judgment. It is often the case that a judgment can only be understood when it is realized that it was given by an English judge in, say, 1854, when certain things were happening in the society that existed at that time.

You will find that these facts about a judgment will often be forgotten or ignored. Later judges will often use an earlier case as a precedent without remembering the facts and background out of which it arose. This tendency is productive of much harm. If you have a background in history, economics, political science or English literature you should often be able to fill in the background to the case. If you do this, you will then be able to see how much any judgment can only be seen as a product of a particular period in a particular society. If this is the case, it follows that the judgment may well reflect the prevalent political, economic, moral and social ideas of the time. (By "prevalent", we mean those ideas which are congenial to the judge, his colleagues and the members of the legal profession.)

But, on the other hand, it is equally dangerous to suggest that any judgment is *only* valid for a particular time and place. The law becomes as useless for providing guidance to people who have to rely on it when it is never constant as it does when it is anachronistic. If, therefore, a judge has said that a particular case should be decided in a certain way there may be good reasons for following his lead when another similar case comes up. The balancing of the value represented by the concern for some constancy of the law over time and the need for law to reflect current social values is never likely to be easy or even always satisfactory. It is important to realize that in each case it will be necessary to consider the balance that must be achieved and the values at stake. Part of the key to understanding how this process must go on is to realize that the judge must function in a legal system where he has a special role to fill. The requirements of this role force him to respect, for example, his particular place in the judicial hierarchy, the reasonable expectations that the parties have of the extent of his discretion to decide as he might like, and the existence of legislation which might indicate the direction the legislature thinks he should go. We will see that, just as no case can be properly understood apart from its context, so no judgment can be understood apart from the institutional structure in which the judge is functioning.

2. We have talked about the values that the law exists to serve, and that the business of judging forces the judge to consider a choice between values that often are competing for application in the judgment. For example, the judge may have to consider the question of fairness between the parties to a contract and the need to encourage reliance on promises. In many cases it

may be easy to accommodate both values. In others, however, one can only be achieved at the expense of the other. As you read these materials, it will be necessary for you always to ask whether or not each case makes sense. It may be that a judgment makes no sense given the values that one might expect the court to forward. It may be that a judgment that may be indefensible on the basis that the court has offered, becomes obviously valid when alternative bases for it are considered. But what does it mean to ask if a judgment "makes sense"? Briefly, it can mean anything. It may be an adequate criticism of a case to say that it was unfair — one person may have been treated in a way that offends our sense of fair play. It may be equally valid to suggest that the result is economically expensive and results in a waste of resources. When you are asked whether a case makes sense or not, all that is being expected of you is that you be prepared to find some reason for the decision or some basis for criticism that is not simply to state, "That is the law". *Blind* adherence to rules is never an adequate reason for doing anything in the law. You should not expect that there will be any unanimity in the opinions on any case. The cases in these materials are chosen because they raise difficult problems of balancing competing values. They are chosen because they are interesting from a pedagogic point of view; not because they offer a succinct statement of the law in a non-contentious case.

Since the cases are chosen because they represent difficult or interesting fact situations, it should not be expected that they will only come from Ontario or Canadian courts. Of course, many cases do come from those courts, but a great many come from the U.S., England and elsewhere. The purpose of this course in contracts is not the teaching of the rules of contracts as they are applied in the courts of Ontario (or any other province) but the exploration of possible solutions to a wide range of problems in the area of contracts. Those solutions can, obviously, come from anywhere, and there is no reason to assume that Ontario has unique problems in contracts. The cases therefore can be looked at as simply examples of problems requiring solutions and as attempted solutions to those problems. We will not confine ourselves only to such problems as actual cases disclose, but we will examine hypothetical cases to see what might happen if such cases were ever to come before a court. You should not think that solutions will only be found in the judgment of courts. Problems will be solved through legislation or through recommendations made, for example, by law reform commissions.

3. It was mentioned earlier that the judge has to function in the context of an institutional structure that imposes restrictions on his freedom to do what he wants. In a sense, all law can be seen as the development of restrictions on the power of the person who has to decide questions presented for decision by competing claimants, to decide as he sees fit. Sometimes the person deciding may abdicate responsibility for the decision by relying on divine revelation (*e.g.* by consulting the entrails of sacrificial animals or the ordeal in medieval times) or chance (*e.g.* tossing a coin). But in all legal controversies the decision has to be made in a way that satisfies a number of possibly competing ends. First, it must be assumed that law is a rational enterprise: we have the law because it helps us do things that we could not do without it — we do not have law just because we think that rules are nice things to have. Second, if the law is to be a rational enterprise then it must

operate in a way that permits decisions to be made on an appropriate basis. This means, for example, that there may be a place for the decision based on chance — it is the essence of a lottery, for instance — but that in general decisions have to be rationally defended. Third, the function of any part of the legal process must be carried out in a way that permits such a defence.

Most of the problems that are discussed in these materials are problems which the courts have had to solve. We shall therefore, be focussing our attention principally on the way in which the courts function. The courts function in a process of adjudication. The essence of this process is the way in which the parties participate in the decision. The parties in this process have the right to present proofs of facts that they allege took place, and to address reasoned arguments to the court. The normal trial of any case involves these two aspects. First the evidence on both sides is put in. This involves the calling of witnesses and the examination of correspondence. The second stage is the argument on the law. Counsel for one side may argue that the facts support the application of one rule — counsel for the other side may argue for another rule. The judgment when given by the judge first states the facts as found by him — he may believe one side and not the other — or think that one version is more likely than the other — and then applies the law as he sees it to those facts.

This process of decision making has a number of very important consequences:

1. Before counsel for either side can know what facts to put in, he has to have some idea of the possibly applicable rules of law. If he wants to argue that a particular rule applies he has to make sure that he has the facts to support his argument.
2. The idea of "reasoned argument" presupposes that there are agreed standards of argument that the counsel and judge both know. There can, for example be no reasoned argument if the decision turns on the toss of a coin or the judge's whim.
3. The judge in his role as fact-finder can determine the legal result. If fact "a" is necessary to the application of rule "A", there can be no question of the application of that rule if the judge finds that fact "a" does not exist.
4. The same result will follow if the counsel for the side that wants to argue for the application of rule "A" cannot prove fact "a".
5. Counsel must be prepared to argue his case on the basis of the facts as they are found by the judge, and since on appeal, the appeal court is not normally free either to hear new evidence or to review the findings of fact by the trial judge, the arguments at that level are almost entirely on points of law and there is no point in suggesting how different the result might have been if only the facts were not as they were found to be.

All these points must be borne in mind as you read the cases in these materials. You will have to consider how well counsel got the facts before the judge. (It is one of the features of our legal system that the responsibility for fact gathering rests entirely on the parties.) You will have to consider how well counsel argued the case for his or her client. This will probably be the principal concern of class discussion, but you must not think that, from an entirely practical point of view, this aspect of the process is any more important than any other. You will also have to be able to see whether or not the judge found something to be a "fact" simply to make his job of deciding the case easier. If the fact-finding function is performed by a jury and not by a judge, you will have to consider, first, what question the jury was asked to determine, and, second, how far the jury simply found a fact or made a judgment based on its perception of the propriety of one party's conduct. (See, *e.g., Hadley v. Baxendale, infra.*)

If the process of adjudication is to operate properly, the parties must be able to rely on the judge's acceptance of the rules of law as providing the criteria for his decision. This is the same point that was mentioned earlier in connection with the need for rules to be constant and recognized by the judge as binding. If the law is out of date and in need of reform, it will often be a difficult question how far the judge, consistent with his role in the process, can accommodate the pressures for reform. Will he be undercutting the reasonable reliance of one party on the existing law? Has he got the facts necessary to enable him to make the right decision in the case before him? Does the judge know enough about the likely effects of the adoption of one or other of the rules competing for application? All these are important and difficult questions. The same limitation on the judge operates to restrict both his freedom to find the facts and his recourse to facts not put before him by the parties. A judge who finds facts simply to justify the application of a particular rule is undercutting the process of adjudication. A judge who attempts to find facts other than those presented by counsel is destroying any effective participation from them. Again these issues raise important and difficult questions, since a judge may have an obligation to do more than decide the dispute on the terms that counsel have put forward.

All these questions have to be considered not just at the level of the trial judge but also at the appellate level. Here the issues are slightly changed. The appellate courts may not be free to review the facts as found by the trial judge, but they may be more free to reconsider rules of law that the trial judge could not. The trial judge may properly have regarded himself as bound by a decision of the Ontario Court of Appeal. But that court may be free to reconsider its own previous decision and to do what the trial judge could not do. Similarly, the Supreme Court of Canada, as the ultimate court in Canada, may be more free than the Ontario Court of Appeal to reconsider any area of the law and to decide that the law should be changed or developed in some way. But again there are restrictions on how far even the Supreme Court of Canada can go here. Should the court ignore the fact that parties may have relied on the law being as the lower courts had believed it to be? How far should the Supreme Court of Canada go in changing the law? Should it limit the change to the narrow facts of the case before it, or should it seek to deal with a wider range of cases? What should the appellate court do if it needs more facts before making its decision? These questions raise one of the very basic problems in law reform. This is the question of which of the available bodies to make the reform should do so. Should the court do so or should the legislature do so? Does inactivity by one justify activity by the other? What are the characteristics of each method that would enable us to decide which should make the changes?

4. The present law of contracts is a residual category of the law. Historically, the idea of contract was a "greedy" category and it swallowed up other areas of the law. For example, the ownership of land originally

expressed political and social relationships. Gradually these became less and less important as the freedom of owners of land to sell and use their land became part of their freedom to arrange their affairs through contracts. Recent developments in the law have reversed this trend. A century ago the law of contract governed almost completely the relations of buyer and seller, employer and employee, landlord and tenant, doctor and patient, builder and landowner, etc. Now many of these relations have become subject to legislative control in one form or another. For example, the law of employer and employee is almost entirely outside the scope of contract. The process of collective bargaining is carried out under a statutory scheme; the contents of the employment contract are regulated by statute: The Employment Standards Act, R.S.O. 1970, c. 147; the Canada Labour Code, R.S.C. 1970, c. L-1. The relation of landlord and tenant is now controlled by legislation designed to redress the imbalance of bargaining power between them. In a similar way, the contractual relations of business and consumers are now governed by legislation like The Consumer Protection Act, R.S.O. 1970, c. 82 (as amended) and The Business Practices Act, S.O. 1974, c. 131. More developments of this kind are to be expected in the future.

The significance of this trend for our purposes is that it becomes necessary to study the legislation that has had such a dramatic effect on so much of the traditional law of contracts. We shall have to see what remains of the law of contract and how well it will serve or can be made to serve the functions that society has for it.

The arrangement of the materials reflects our personal approach and we certainly do not believe either that this approach is the only valid one to take or that it is the best that could ever be devised. It represents what we think, at the moment, is a possible arrangement. We think, for example, that it makes sense to begin by investigating the consequences of the breach of a contract, and so we will start this course by examining cases that present problems that, in one sense, arise only at the end of a contractual relationship. We do this for the following reasons:

1. About the only possible way to define a contract is that a contract is a promise which the law will enforce. This definition is not very helpful. To know what promises the law will enforce is only to know the whole law of contracts. However, it does make sense to know what the law will do if it does decide to enforce a promise. This knowledge will make more intelligible the later inquiry into the kinds of promises the law will enforce.

2. The cases on breach are among the simplest cases that can be studied by a beginning law student. This is not to say that any case at the outset of law school is simple, but only to say that it is fairly easy to understand the issues and what is going on in a case like *Peevyhouse v. Garland Coal* — the first case in these materials. The difficulty is, of course, that no case has ever been litigated or a judgment written for a person who knows nothing about the law. The judge and the lawyers involved in any case are functioning in the context of an existing legal system and their respective responsibilities do not permit them to consider the needs of law students. But the issues presented by the case may be readily understandable and anyone may have a valid criticism to make of the result reached by the court and even of the process of getting there.

3. If any single key can be suggested for the understanding of law and of contracts in particular it is that one must always ask in respect of every case, "Who is suing whom, and for what?". As you find out more about the history of the common law, you will discover that the common law has developed by a process which focussed on the remedies available in various situations. The common law has never bothered to define a "contract", instead the law has been concerned with the kind of remedy that will be available in certain circumstances. If we begin our study of the law by focussing on the remedies that the law offers, we will be reflecting the very pragmatic approach of the common law. The lawyer always has to ask himself what he can get for his client: he is not concerned whether or not there is a contract if he cannot obtain any advantage or avoid any harm if there is one.

4. As a practical matter, every lawyer who is asked to consider a contracts dispute will have to decide if the amount in issue makes it worth starting or defending an action. A consideration of the remedies available for breach of contract can give a lawyer an answer to the question, "How much can my client get if we sue?"

Chapter 1

REMEDIES FOR BREACH OF CONTRACT

A. Introduction

The materials that follow discuss some general issues that are raised by the law of contract. The first extract is a discussion of the role of contract in our society. It outlines some of the features of contract that indicate where it works well and where it works badly. The important thing to realize as you read this extract and those that follow is that contracts are intimately involved in the achievement of society's values. As you read every case that follows in these materials you will have to remember that you cannot be indifferent to the way in which the rules that the courts are applying or developing forward or hinder the achievement of these values.

The specific questions that are raised and answered by the first extract are:

1. What specific functions does contract perform in the ordering of human relations generally?

2. It is apparently the case that explicit contractual arrangements are a rarity among primitive peoples. What do such peoples miss by not employing the contractual form in regulating their relations with one another?

3. There are many relationships in modern society that do not lend themselves to regulation by contract. What are those relationships? Why is contract an inept device for putting these in order?

FULLER AND EISENBERG, BASIC CONTRACT LAW
(3rd ed.) pp. 89-103

The Role of Contract in the Ordering Processes of Society Generally

I.

In attempting some answer to questions of this sort we shall begin by listing nine distinct principles of social order. The sequence in which these nine "principles" are listed does not pretend to any logical neatness and certainly does not purport to reflect, item by item, the historical order of their emergence in human affairs. The primary purpose in listing these principles is the practical one of facilitating a comparison of their respective capacities and limitations, with, of course, special reference to the principle of contract.

Nine Principles of Social Ordering

1. The coordination of expectations and actions that arises tacitly out of interaction; illustrated in "customary law" and "standard practice."
2. Contract.
3. Property.

4.   Officially declared law.
5.   Adjudication.
6.   Managerial direction.
7.   Voting.
8.   Mediation.
9.   Deliberate resort to chance; "tossing for it."

The list just offered leaves out many nuances and combinational forms. It does not mention, for example, the principle of kinship or the influence of the "charismatic" leader; these may perhaps be subsumed under other headings, such as legislation, managerial direction and adjudication — all operating, in some measure, within the framework of customary law. Again, money is not listed, but may be regarded as a particularly flexible kind of property. Historically "bread and circuses" have provided an expedient for stilling discontent, but can hardly be regarded as providing an affirmative ordering principle. Finally, any concentration on "order" as an overriding desideratum may obscure the function of conflict in articulating and bringing into the open discords that may then be compromised or reconciled.

The last of the nine listed principles of order — "deliberate resort to chance" — may seem too trivial a device to deserve a place in an analysis devoted to the basic ordering principles by which a society is enabled to function. We should remember, however, that this device is used to select those who must risk their lives in military service as well as those who, as jurors, must decide the fate of others. According to the Scripture land was divided among the tribes of Israel by lot. (It should be observed that the word "allot" contains itself a tacit reminder of this use of chance as an ordering principle.) The significance of the lot in social processes is certainly not underesteemed in the following passage from Proverbs (18:18):

"The lot causeth contentions to cease, and parteth between the mighty."

The practice of deciding important issues by a resort to chance is not only of some importance itself, but it serves also to illustrate how the various principles of order may be interrelated and combined. The use of the lot in particular situations may be prescribed by tradition (that is, by "customary law"), by legislative enactment, or by a contract of the affected parties. It may also appear as an adjunct to managerial direction, as where a military commander might employ it to decide which squad should undertake a particularly dangerous mission. (It will be noted that "managerial direction" as used here carries a very broad connotation. It extends the concept of "management" beyond the usual context of economic activity to include, say, a direction and coordination of efforts to achieve military or therapeutic ends. Managerial direction understood in this sense cannot, for obvious reasons, proceed by laying down the relatively stable rules of duty and entitlement characteristic of a legal system.)

Returning to the social uses made of a deliberate resort to chance, it should be observed that though the lot has been found appropriate to quite diverse situations this does not mean that it offers an all-purpose device ready to solve any kind of problem. Its use to choose the judge who will resolve a particular controversy may be quite acceptable and is not unknown in practice; for the judge himself to decide the case by a throw of the dice represents an absurdity of a magnitude sufficient to insure an enduring place in literary history for Rabelais' Judge Bridlegoose, who not only employed, but extolled the virtues of this expedient.

II.

In discussions of ordering processes a distinction is often taken between order imposed from above and order achieved through reciprocal adjustments on a horizontal plane. On this basis officially declared law and managerial direction would seem to represent a vertical ordering, while contract and customary law would appear as obvious illustrations of a horizontal ordering. There are, however, difficulties with this distinction, difficulties that derive from the inherent complexity of the social processes involved. Thus, if we take officially declared law as the archetypal expression of rules imposed from above, complications appear so soon as we examine the legislative process itself. In a democracy many "horizontal" adjustments of opposing interests take place in the course of drafting and enacting laws. Even the lawmaking of a dictator commonly undergoes some accommodation to demands tacitly expressed in rumbling discontents. These are, of course, trite observations. What is not so evident is that there enters a certain contractual element into any ordering of human relations by declared and published rules. If the lawgiver wants his subjects to accept and act by his rules, he must himself display some minimum respect for those rules in his actions toward his subjects, say, in distributing awards and imposing punishments. This means that the publication of a code of legal rules carries with it a tacit commitment by government to abide by those rules in judging the citizen. If this commitment is grossly disregarded a regime of "officially declared law" will not be achieved, though society may continue after a fashion to function by other principles.

If there is, then, commonly a horizontal element in systems that appear to represent order vertically imposed, the reverse is equally true, that is, the forms of ordering which are thought of as reflecting a horizontal accommodation may in fact be shaped by a downward thrust of control that is all the more powerful for its tacit mode of operation. Thus, a written contract between *A* and *B*, though taking the verbal form of a reciprocal adjustment of their respective interests, may have been in fact wholly drafted by *A* and imposed by him on *B*.

This phenomenon is commonly analysed in terms of an "inequality of bargaining power." But this is a loose way of putting the issue. A noted actor, enjoying a sensational public acclaim, may possess great "bargaining power" in negotiating with a theatrical producer; the actor may be, as we say, almost in a position "to write his own contract." But this bargaining advantage derives from the fact that the actor has attained something (lawfully we are supposing) that his producer wants badly; the actor's bargaining power is as much a function of the producer's needs as it is of the actor's special capacity to satisfy those needs. And the advantage enjoyed by the actor still leaves room for bargaining; at some point his demands may reach a point where the producer will bid him goodbye.

A case to be studied later (*Henningsen v. Bloomfield Motors, Inc., infra* [c. 6]) presents a quite different situation. It appeared in that case that the National Automobile Manufacturers Association employed a standard purchase order to be signed by the buyer of any automobile made by its members; this order stated in effect that the dealer selling the car should not be liable for any physical injuries suffered by the purchaser in driving the car, even though the accident causing the injuries was due to a defect in the car. The court held that the purchaser was not bound by this disclaimer of the dealer's liability. The court observed that though it could be said that there was in such a situation a disparity in bargaining power, the fact was that the purchaser was really "not permitted to bargain at all." By a kind of legislative fiat of the Automobile Manufacturers Association a contract was imposed that excluded any claim for personal injuries.

In the fragmentary analysis just concluded enough has been said to suggest the pervasive nature of the problem of distinguishing between, on the one hand, imposed order and, on the other, order that is, broadly speaking, "contractual" in nature. The complexities and ambiguities presented by this distinction pervade every branch of thought affecting our conception of society and social order. In confronting perplexities of this sort there is a natural tendency for the mind to seek out simplistic formulas that will shape our language, and with it, our thought, in ways offering some reassurance that things are not, after all, utterly chaotic or so complicated as to be inaccessible to analysis.

Perhaps the most famous of these formulas of reassurance is that represented by the theory of an original Social Compact, which reached the height of its influence during the seventeenth and eighteenth centuries. There has always been some obscurity as to whether this notion assigning a contractual origin to all government was intended as a description of historical fact or as the expression of a political ideal. The temper of modern thought is apt to regard this theory as false if presented as an historical fact, though perhaps suggestive if proposed as a model.

What of present-day theory? In our efforts to analyse the forms of social ordering do we see things clearly as they are without distorting fictions and prejudgments? There is serious reason to doubt that our thinking has achieved quite this degree of liberation from the shackles of language and tacit presupposition.

Today, it may be suggested, there runs through legal thinking an assumption that all social ordering is, directly or indirectly, imposed from above. Thus, though contract and property rights serve to organize the relations of citizens to one another, they are thought of as doing this solely because they are recognized and enforced by "law," that is, by state-made rules imposed from above. Probably no one has had more influence on our modern ways of thinking about law than Jeremy Bentham. He declared:

> "Property and law are born and must die together. Before the laws there was no property: take away the laws, all property ceases.... No bargain is void in itself — no bargain is valid of itself: it is the law which in each case gives or refuses validity." (*Works*, 1859, Vol. 1, pp. 309 and 333.)

Certainly it is clear that contracts and property were in some measure functioning social institutions before state-made laws existed or were even conceived of. Today many human relations are effectively organized by contracts that neither party would dream of taking to court; as for property, even wild animals often display some sense of respecting the other fellow's "territory." Yet Bentham's assertion that contract and property rights exist because, and to the extent that, the law of the state enforces and protects them reflects a general predisposition of thought which is today shared by lawyers and laymen alike.

There is in this connection an interesting quirk of linguistic usage as it affects contract. When we speak of "the law of contracts" we mean the law *about* contracts, not the "law" contained *in* a contract; indeed any suggestion that a contract could of itself create "law" would seem bizarre indeed. Yet what shall we say of Article 1134 of the French Civil Code declaring that a contract "serves as law" between the parties? ("*Les conventions légalment formées tiennent lieu de loi à ceux qui les ont faites.*") If the form of expression seems odd it remains perfectly clear that legal rights and duties, enforceable through judicial procedures, may derive from the words of a contract just as they may from the provisions of a statute.

International law is another source of embarrassment to the conception that all law is imposed from above. The "law of nations" is a law deriving primarily from contractual arrangements called "treaties" and the tacit adjustments that give rise to "customary law." Curiously enough this departure from the conception of law as something imposed from above seems to have little influence on the usages associated with ordinary law, that is, state-made law. Here the assumption that all law in the strict sense is imposed from above remains largely intact.

It may be objected at this point that nothing of consequence hinges on the way we *talk* about law or contracts; the question is not what we *say* but what we *do*. That contracts which are unenforceable through court action can nevertheless serve as sources of social order may be interesting as a kind of sociological aside, but it has no significant bearing on the law of contracts; that law is made by legislatures and courts.

But to accept this view is to underestimate the influence of language in shaping our general approach to legal questions. The judge who keeps firmly in mind that the principle of contract can, without his aid, serve as a source of social ordering will approach his task in a spirit different from that of the judge who tends to suppose that the influence of contract in human affairs derives entirely from the state-made law of which he is the official custodian and expositor. The first judge will see himself as one whose task it is to facilitate a form of ordering that could function, in some measure, without his intervention; he will accordingly seek to understand the special role that contract plays in the ordering processes of society and will strive to shape his decisions by the perception thus obtained.

IV.

It will be well at this point to attempt a somewhat systematic analysis of the ways in which the principle of contract is related to the other "principles of social order."

With the first of the listed principles — that of *"customary law"* — the difficulty is not in discerning some relation between it and contract, but in drawing a clear distinction between the two. Customary law may, indeed, be described as the inarticulate older brother of contract. We may describe customary law in general terms as consisting of the reciprocal expectations that arise out of human interaction. It is illustrated when *A* and *B*, as the result of past encounters, begin to shape their conduct toward each other by patterns perceived as emerging from their past interactions. As with language, these patterns will tend to "jell" and to spread from one context to another. Customary law may, indeed, be aptly described as a *language of interaction.*

In many situations it may be difficult to distinguish between contractual obligations and those imposed by customary law. This is particularly true in the area of commercial transactions where repetitive dealings tend to create standardized expectations. Thus, if problems arise which are left without verbal solution in the parties' contract these will commonly be resolved by asking what "standard practice" is with respect to the issues in question. In such a case it is difficult to know whether to say that by entering a particular field of practice the parties became subject to a governing body of customary law or to say that they have by tacit agreement incorporated standard practice into the terms of their contract.

The meaning of a contract may not only be determined by the area of practice within which the contract falls, but by the interactions of the parties themselves after entering their agreement. If the performance of a contract takes place over a period of time, the parties will often evidence by their conduct what courts sometimes call a "practical construction" of their agreement. The interpretation of the contract reflected in the parties' acts may control over the meaning that would ordinarily be attributed to the words of the contract itself. The meaning thus attributed to the contract is, obviously, generated through processes that are essentially those that give rise to customary law.

On a more radical level the courts may imply a contract entirely from the conduct of the parties; though no verbal exchange has taken place the parties may have conducted themselves toward one another in such a way that one can say that a tacit exchange of promises has taken place. Here the analogy between contract and customary law approaches identity; indeed, the only reason for hesitancy about applying the second term derives from a "customary law" of language itself, namely, that it is not a common linguistic practice to speak of "law" as governing a two-party relationship even though a statute, coming from "above," would hardly be denied the designation "law" simply because it happened to regulate the relations of two state officials toward one another.

The prevailing tendency to regard all social order as imposed from above has led to a general neglect of the phenomenon of customary law in modern legal scholarship. Outside the field of international law and that of commercial dealings legal theorists have been uncomfortable about the use of the word "law" to describe the obligatory force of expectations that arise tacitly out of human interaction. The most common escape from this dilemma is to downgrade the significance of customary law and to assert that it has largely lost the significance it once had for human affairs. Another and more radical way out was that taken by Austin (*Lectures on Jurisprudence*, 4th ed., 1879, Vol. 1, p. 105) and followed explicitly or tacitly by many writers since his time. This is to assert that what is called "customary law" becomes truly law only after it has been adopted by a court as a standard of decision and thus received the imprimatur of the state. This linguistic expedient, it should be noted, would deny the designation "law" to a custom so firmly rooted and so plainly just and useful that no one would waste his time taking it to court to be tested for its right to be called "law."

The fact is that the operation of a system of a state-made law is itself permeated with internal customary practices that enable it to function effectively by facilitating a collaboration among its constituent elements. Thus, for example, the drafting and enactment of a statute is a task assigned to the legislature; its interpretation is left to the judiciary. Plainly these two functions must be coordinated by reciprocal expectations displaying some stability. In achieving their goal, the legislative draftsmen have to ask them-

selves, "What will the courts make of our statute? What standards of interpretation will they apply to our literary creation?" If the courts of the state
have generally displayed a decided inclination toward "literalness" in the
interpretation of laws, the legislative draftsmen will take this "standard
practice" into account in phrasing their statute. On the other hand, if the
courts have displayed a tendency toward a broadly purposive interpretation, a quite differently phrased statute, and, perhaps, a much shorter one,
will result from the efforts of the drafting committee. The effective functioning of the total law-making and law-applying process depends, then, upon a
kind of "customary law" that lies behind enacted law and enables it to
achieve its goals effectively. And plainly this "customary law" contains a
strong consensual element, something like a tacit "meeting of minds."

Turning now to the ordering principle of *property*, it is apparent that
there is a close affinity of function between it and contract. Much of what is
normally conceived of as "property" in fact consists essentially of contract
claims, — e.g., bank accounts, insurance policies, bonds, and, for most
practical purposes, corporate stock. On another level, where a man has
"property" that can be assigned to another, he is in a position to commit
himself by contract to make this assignment. Conversely, where a man can
contract to give something to another, this means that he has command
over a value that can in a broad sense be called "property," though, to be
sure, a contract for the rendition of personal services stretches this usage to
the point of metaphor. (*Cf.*, "Outfielder *A* is the property of Baseball Club
X.")

Of *adjudication* it has often been asserted that its historical origins lie in
consensual arrangements; two parties, being in dispute and wishing to
avoid open warfare, agree on a third person to settle their controversy. This,
it is said, is how adjudication got its start as a principle of social ordering.
Certainly there is ample evidence that this voluntarily accepted mode of settlement was often adopted in putting an end to the "blood feud" between
families. Whether, however, it can be asserted that in all societies adjudication had its origin in contract is not clearly established.

Certain it is that adjudicative procedures are often today established by
agreement of the litigating parties. The most familiar example is to be found
in the common practice of submitting commercial and labor disputes to
arbitration, both the selection of the arbitrator and the rules by which he is
to proceed often being determined by an agreement between the parties to
the dispute. Today, with our crowded court dockets, the trial of cases is
often speeded by stipulations of counsel dispensing with the formal proof of
relevant facts and generally simplifying the procedures of trial in the interest of a speedy decision. Even in the criminal law it is notorious that most
convictions are the result of "plea bargaining."

It should also be observed that much of the law of procedure remains
uncodified and derives from a tacit adjustment of expectations of the sort
that create customary law. For example, in the trial of an ordinary law suit
(say, for breach of contract) a private conversation concerning the case
between the judge and one of the litigants out of the presence of the other
would involve a gross violation of the tacit expectations that surround the
whole judicial process. Yet, curiously, though there are long chapters of
complicated rules concerning procedure, an explicit prohibition of this
practice is generally not to be found among them; it is so patently violative

of the judicial proprieties that no one has thought to spell it out and put it down in the books.

Turning now to *managerial direction*, it will be well to begin by setting aside for the moment the managerial functions of government in order to direct our attention to private contracts of employment. In entering such a contract the employee will normally in some measure subject himself to the lawful orders of his employer. Suppose he is directed to perform some task and it turns out that his skills are insufficient to enable him to perform it satisfactorily. Though his services have been engaged for a year he is discharged forthwith or assigned to a different task carrying a lower salary. If the employee sues for damages, the question will be stated formally in terms of an interpretation of his contract. What level of skill did the contract explicitly or implicitly stipulate as being reasonably expected of the employee? Here contract serves as the principle for defining the limits of managerial direction.

In turning to the managerial functions of government we are not concerned with its position as an employer (which would not be radically different from that of a private employer) but chiefly with its function in distributing scarce resources — for example, in allocating television channels, air routes, welfare funds, irrigation waters, etc. In this broad area there is a constant struggle between those who want to keep these functions free from the restraints of fixed legal rules and those who want to "judicialize" and "legalize" them. (Regarding the second term, cf., Webster's *Third New International Dictionary*: "le-gal-ize … 2. to interpret or apply in a legalistic spirit (you persist to legalize the gospel — J. W. Fletcher)."

There is a close affinity between this issue and that we have previously discussed concerning the commitment implied in enacting and publishing rules of law. We suggested that the lawgiver is properly regarded as promising to judge the citizen's actions by rules he has announced in advance as governing those actions. In the case of allocative functions the citizen subject to them tends to read into the actions of government tacit rules of law; he wants to receive what is assigned to him as of right and not as a matter of grace. So it may come about that the disadvantaged applicant will feel that government has cheated on its own rules while the allocative agency will conceive of itself as discharging a function that simply cannot be rule-bound but requires a broad discretion to meet shifting contingencies and changed conditions.

At first glance the ordering principles of *voting* seems to offer no entry for the principle of contract. One cannot hold a meaningful election without at least three voters; a contract ordinarily involves only two parties. Yet there is a kind of consensual arrangement that can be said to involve a two-man voting system. Suppose that at the outset of a law suit the judge proposes to counsel an expedient that will speed the trial by dispensing with some of the usual procedural steps. The judge asks the parties if they will agree to it; if either objects, he will follow the book, if both consent the short cut will be adopted. Though we might hesitate here to speak of a contract or a bargain, there is certainly a consensual arrangement or agreement with significant operative effect. This phenomenon is worthy of mention because we tend to identify contract with the notion of a trade or exchange, and it is well to remember that there are consensual arrangements from which the element of "trade-off" is absent.

That there is a close connection between *mediation* and the ordering principle of contract certainly requires no demonstration here. One of the most common tasks of the mediator is to facilitate the negotiation of complicated contracts, though it should be observed that his services are also sometimes employed in reaching an agreement to rescind a contract.

With respect to the relations between *the lot* and the principle of contract it is obvious that a resort to chance may result from a contract; finding no better way to solve their differences the parties may agree "to toss for it."

The discussion just concluded was primarily concerned with the interrelations between the principle of contract and the various other forms of social ordering. In the course of this exposition it should have become clear that the function of the lawyer is not simply that of telling laymen "what the law is." The lawyer is constantly engaged in fitting into some workable design the relations of men to one another. His task as a social architect can demand creative imagination of a high order.

There is in the books a relatively ancient illustration of the role ingenuity can play in solving problems of interpersonal relations. A father dies leaving all his property to two sons "in equal shares." The estate consists of a miscellany of items: furniture, valuable paintings, a cellar of alcoholic beverages, three horses, shares of stock in an adventurous mining company, etc. How shall the division "in equal shares" be accomplished? The classic solution is as follows: Let the older son divide the property into two parts, let the younger son take his pick. (Would it be better to draw lots to see who should make the division?)

V.

So far we have been chiefly concerned with contract as a principle supplementing and interacting in various ways with other principles of social ordering. It is time now to attempt a general appraisal of contract itself; to examine what it can and cannot do, to inquire for what tasks it is a suited instrument and when its employment may do more harm than good.

Let us begin by supposing the following case. Two neighboring farmers share a dirt road — a private way not maintained by public authority — which provides the only access to their farms. During a heavy rainstorm a large stone rolls down a hillside and completely blocks the road. Neither farmer would be capable of removing the stone without the help of his neighbor. The two farmers meet, discuss their predicament, provide themselves with crowbars and join forces to remove the obstructing boulder.

Now it is hard to imagine that in this situation, before undertaking the removal, either farmer would propose to the other anything like a contractual commitment. It is extremely unlikely that one would say to the other, "I propose a deal. If you will promise to work hard with your crowbar, I will work hard with mine." If any such proposal were advanced the most charitable interpretation its addressee could make of it would be that it was intended as a rather sick joke.

Notwithstanding the seeming triviality of this illustration it will be useful to analyse with some care just why in such a situation the parties would be unlikely to think of expressing their relationship in contractual terms. In the *first* place, the parties have no need of a contract. The self-interest of each combined with the inescapable necessity for their collaboration, provides a motivation for joint action that no contract could augment. *Secondly*, if a contract were seriously insisted on by one of the farmers as a condition precedent to his lending his hand to the effort, it would imply a distrust damaging to the relationship that must obtain between close neighbors. *Thirdly,* if a contract were in fact drawn up and written down it would be largely lacking in any significant prescriptive or directive function. It would be hard to imagine a law suit in which the plaintiff alleged simply that "the defendant didn't try hard enough." If one of the farmers, after signing the agreement, defaulted altogether and failed to make any appearance at the appointed time, one might imagine a successful law suit against him, though in such a case the disapproval of his neighbors would scarcely be any different from what it would have been had he refused from the outset to have anything to do with the job of removal. Once the two farmers had begun the joint task of removing the boulder any outside judgment of the parties' respective performances would be rendered difficult by the intensely collaborative nature of the task; each farmer would have to adjust his efforts in such a way as to reinforce and supplement the efforts of the other. Indeed, it is possible that the best contribution one farmer might make would be to stand off at some distance, where he could obtain an overview of the operation, and direct his perhaps more muscular neighbor how and where to apply his efforts with the crowbar.

Let us assume that the two farmers will be sensible enough to see that they need no contract covering their joint efforts to remove the stone and ask how this particular cooperative endeavour might fit into the larger configuration of their relations over a period of time. It is almost certain that there would be other occasions for joining forces, as, for example, in the routine upkeep of their shared roadway. Again, each might look after the other's property while the other was away on a trip; in the event of an emergency, like getting a crop in on time, a helping hand would be forthcoming from the neighbor. At the end of the year, there might be a rather even balance between these voluntary contributions. If there was a serious imbalance an effort would probably be made by the advantaged party to correct it by some gratuitous offering. At no time would there be likely to enter into their relations any contractual commitment or any explicit exchange of one performance against another, though no doubt tacit expectations would develop that would carry with them a certain sense of obligation.

Early in this essay the statement was made that it is "a commonplace of anthropology that explicit contractual arrangements are a rarity among primitive peoples." The situation just discussed suggests why this should be so. Where the basic physical necessities of life — food, shelter, weapons, some covering for the body — are all produced through the cooperative efforts of the extended family, human beings will generally find themselves in the situation of our two farmers. The members of a small, self-sufficient group are all parts, one of another; all are bound together by a complex network of reciprocal renditions and expectations. In such a human situation any attempt at an explicit verbalized definition of each party's expected performance, and the price to be paid him for it, would certainly not produce order and might produce chaos. The ineptitude of contract as an organizing principle in this type of case becomes especially clear when we take into account the shifting contingencies affecting such a group: storms, droughts, sudden attacks by enemy tribes, and the like. No contractual foresight would be equal to providing in advance what should be done in these emergencies or prescribing how the contribution of each member of the group should be fitted in with that of others, though again, accustomed roles and expectations generated by past actions would serve some directive and coordinative purpose.

In discussing social contexts in which contract is likely to be an inept ordering principle we have so far been considering situations radically removed from the usual commercial relationship in which contract plays its accustomed and often indispensable role. It should be observed, however, that even between business firms intent on maximizing their individual profits a relationship of heavy and complex interdependence can develop that may impair the utility of contract as an instrument for defining their rights and duties toward each other. Supppose, for example, that A is the manufacturer of a piece of electronic equipment; B makes a component part essential to the functioning of the device made by A. The field is one of rapid technological advance; an unanticipated improvement in the design of A's machine may require on short notice a redesign of the component part made by B. Conversely a significant improvement in the component part may require a redesign of the equipment made by A and at the same time greatly enhance its sales appeal. It may be impossible to foresee in advance whether and when such technological improvements will be made. Plainly there is here some difficulty in drafting a contract that will specify delivery dates, design specifications, and prices by standards that will remain constant over a set period of time. Nor would it be easy to specify in advance by what standards changes in the contract should be made when a sudden improvement in design becomes necessary to keep ahead of competition. Here fidelity to explicit contractual commitments must be tempered by a sense of reciprocal dependence and a willingness to meet unexpected developments in a spirit of cooperation.

It is worthy of observation that all contracts, and indeed all rules of law, presuppose some stability in external conditions. This is true even of property rights. Suppose, for example, that X and Y own separate farms on either side of a river; X's thirty acre tract is described in his deed as bounded on the east by the river, while the river marks the west boundary of Y's ten-acre holding. Suddenly, as the result of a seismic disturbance, the river shifts its course, removing ten acres from X's land and adding five to Y's. Who now owns what?

The law of contracts is similarly dependent for its integrity upon some stability of external conditions. Suppose, for example, A agrees to sell Blackacre to B for $10,000, delivery of the deed to take place one year from the time of the signature of the contract. Before the time for performance arrives a drastic monetary inflation has taken place, so that the purchasing power of the dollar is a fraction of what it was when the contract was entered. Does B get Blackacre for ten thousand greatly depreciated dollars? If not, how much should he be required to pay, and, if the inflation continues, as of what date shall the revaluation be made? In situations like this the courts have had to rewrite contracts against a shifting economic situation offering little that could serve as a secure baseline for even-handed justice. (See, e.g., Dawson, "Effects of Inflation on Private Contracts: Germany, 1914-1924", 33 Mich.L.Rev. 171-238 (1935); Dawson and Cooper, "The Effect of Inflation on Private Contracts: United States, 1961-1879", 33 Mich.L.Rev. 7-6-757 (1935).)

A famous historical instance of the wholesale rewriting of contracts occurred as a result of the Great Fire of London in 1666, a fire which consumed in three days more than thirteen thousand buildings. Many of the buildings were occupied by tenants and the practice of the time was to provide in the lease that the tenant was bound to repair any damage suffered by the property during his occupancy. (This may seem a harsh provision, but it should be recalled that this was before the institution of fire insurance, which indeed took its origins in the lessons of the London Fire.) With the wholesale destruction that occurred and with normal business suspended indefinitely, it was essential to make some adjustment in the leases. A special Fire Court was instituted, its judges being drawn from the ordinary common law courts. Proceeding partly by mediation, with a reserved power of imposing a decision if mediative efforts failed, the judges of the Fire Court in effect rewrote hundreds of leases. In some cases, where the lease had only a short time to run, the lessee was excused from the rent in return for a surrender of the premises to the landlord. In other cases, adjustments were made whereby the landlord and tenant would share in varying proportions the cost of rebuilding. Some very "unlegal" considerations were often drawn into account; for example, if during the fire a tenant showed great bravery and selflessness in helping his neighbors fight the fire threatening their homes, this service "beyond the call of duty" was thought to entitle him to special consideration in the apportionment of the loss between him and his landlord. (See Jones (ed.), *The Fire Court*, Vol. I, 1966.)

VI.

So much for the limitations that affect the institution of contract and that may, in special circumstances, impair its efficacy as an ordering principle. It is time now to turn to the opposite side of the coin and to explore the special contribution contract can make to human relations, — benefits it can confer that are not to be derived, or are not to be derived so readily, from other principles of social ordering.

The special virtue of contract lies in its capacity to increase human satisfactions through an exchange, as where A has something B wants, B has something A wants, and where an exchange will increase the satisfactions of both A and B; in Bentham's quaint language "the sum of enjoyment... is augmented by the transaction." Bentham continues,

> "If there be an exchange, there are two alienations, each of which has its separate advantages. This advantage for each of the contracting parties is the difference between the value which they put upon what they give up, and the value of what they acquire. In each transaction of this kind, there are two new masses of enjoyment. In this consists the advantage of commerce." (*Works*, 1859, Vol. 1, p. 331).

Bentham's statement suggests a trade or exchange of commodities. But the reciprocal and separate gains that can result from a carefully negotiated contract are by no means confined to physical objects. This is made clear in the following quotation from Chester Barnard, a famous theorist of business organization:

> "... the rule must be that you give, so far as possible, what is less valuable to you but more valuable to the receiver; and you receive what is more valuable to you and less valuable to the giver. This is common sense, good business sense, good social sense, good technology, and is the enduring basis of amicable and con-

structive relations of any kind. This does *not* mean that you give as little as you can from the receiver's point of view. In terms of money, you give a man dollars for his services which are worth more to you than the dollars. No sane man would admit anything else. If you give services for dollars it must be that the dollars are worth more to you than the services. Unfortunately for simplicity, neither side of the transaction can be confined to or measured completely in dollars, even in commercial enterprises; and in non-commercial enterprises the exchange is extremely intangible.

"What conceals this simple fact of experience so often is that subsequent evaluation may change, though this is then beside the point. I may pay a man $10 today with pleasure, and may find tomorrow that I need $10 very badly, but cannot use the services I paid for. I am then perhaps disposed to think I made a bad exchange. I read the past into the present. This leads to the false view that what exchanges *should* be is as little as possible of what the receiver wants, regardless of its value to me. This philosophy of giving as little as possible and getting as much as possible in the *other man's values* is the root of bad customer relations, bad labor relations, bad credit relations, bad supply relations, bad technology. The possible margins of cooperative success are too limited to survive the destruction of incentives which this philosophy implies." (*The Functions of the Executive*, 1942, pp. 254-255.)

In the statement just quoted Barnard makes two important points: (1) that the elements that enter into the exchange may be "extremely intangible," and (2) that, as with so many human activities, men often forget what kind of game it is they are playing and may cheat themselves in trying to keep the other fellow from getting what he wants.

As illustrating the first point we may mention the negotiation of a collective bargaining agreement between an employer and a labor union. We are apt to suppose that the central issue under discussion would be wage rates, but this is not necessarily so. The issue most ardently pressed by the union may be a demand for a change in seniority provisions, while the company may demand a rephrasing of the clause on management prerogatives. Issues of this sort are not unrelated to monetary costs and benefits, but the relationship may be quite indirect. That the issues are not directly convertible into monetary terms does not mean, however, that the final result of the negotiations will not involve some element of trade-off. The company may accept a rewriting of Article V in return for the union's consent to a rephrasing of Article XII. Both parties may feel that they have gained from this "trade" though each would have been happier if he could have achieved this gain without having to accept language he would be glad to see stricken from the agreement.

It is apparent from what has just been said that the creation of a complex contractual relationship through explicit negotiations requires a certain attitude of mind and spirit on the part of the participants; they must share a common conception of the nature of the game they are playing. Each must seek to understand why the other makes the demands he does, even as he strives to resist or qualify those demands. Each must accept the other's right to work for a solution that will best serve his own interests.

Explicit bargaining involves, then, an uneasy blend of collaboration and resistence. This explains why it does not fit readily into either extreme of the spectrum of human relationships running from intimacy to open hostility. Within the closely-knit family demands for a contractual spelling out of obligations will seem to imply an inappropriate distrust. Between parties openly hostile to one another, the element of cooperation essential for effective bargaining will be absent. Curiously enough, at the two extremes of the spectrum where man cannot bargain with words, they can often half-bargain with deeds; tacit understanding arising out of reciprocally oriented actions will take the place of verbalized commitments. This is true within the closely-knit tribal community; it is also often true of the relations between hostile tribes, where tacit restraints on hostility, or on specific ways of expressing hostility, are common. (It should be observed that today much of the customary law of international relations has the same quality.)

So far we have been emphasizing the influence of "the social context" on the aptness of explicit contract as a principle of social ordering. But personal inclinations and dispositions, the "life style" or *Weltanschauung* of the individual, may also play a role. There are those who love to bargain and take pride in the skill and insight they bring to the enterprise; there are those who find the whole process distasteful.

One strategically located personal inclination of this sort has had a profound influence on human history. Karl Marx expressed in his writings a deep aversion for relations of explicit exchange. This aversion found its most eloquent expression in the youthful "alienation theme." In 1843 Marx wrote of a man as leading a double life; "a life in the *political community* in which he recognizes himself as a *communal being*, and a life in bourgeois society [that is, in a trading society] where he acts as a private person, who regards others as means, reduces himself to the level of a means and becomes the plaything of alien forces." (See Tucker, *Philosophy and Myth in Karl Marx*, 1961, p. 105.)

Explicit defenses of the contractual principle are not common, no doubt because it is generally accepted as an inevitable ingredient in a functioning economy. Perhaps the circumstance that he began his career as a Unitarian minister explains why the famous economist, Philip Wicksteed, felt the need to offer some defense of the principle of exchange as expressed in explicit contractual arrangements:

> "... over the whole range of exchangeable things we can usually act more potently by the indirect method of pursuing or furthering the immediate purposes of others than by the direct method of pursuing our own.... We enter into business relations with others, not because our purposes are selfish, but because those with whom we deal are relatively indifferent to them, but are (like us) keenly interested in purposes of their own, to which we in our turn are relatively indifferent.... There is surely nothing degrading or revolting to our higher sense in this fact of our mutually furthering each other's purposes because we are interested in our own.... The economic nexus [that is, the nexus of exchange] indefinitely expands our freedom of combination and movement; for it enables us to form one set of groups linked by community of purpose, without having to find the "double coincidence" which would otherwise be necessary." (*The Common Sense of Political Economy*, ed. Robbins (1933), pp. 156, 179-180.)

VII.

In closing this account it may be well to return briefly to mediation and its role in assisting contracting parties to reach a satisfactory and viable agreement. Some of the contributions a mediator can make to the negotiations are fairly obvious. The mere presence of a third person may tend to put the parties on their good behavior and generate in them a desire to take positions that will seem fair to an impartial observer. If the mediator is a person with creative imagination, who can draw on a considerable experience in contractual negotiations, he may be able to offer expedients that will resolve differences which on the surface seem intractable to solution.

The mediator's most fundamental and often indispensable function relates, however, to the basic principle that makes possible what have here been called "the gains of reciprocity" — the principle that enables both parties to profit from an agreement because each gives up what he values less in exchange for what he values more. In the negotiation of a complex agreement the fitting together of the diverse evaluations of the parties is often an intricate and subtle task; the outcome of the negotiations, in the absence of a mediator, may depend on accidents in the order in which the issues are discussed and the manner in which they are combined in the proposals made by the one party to the other. Suppose, for example, that early in the negotiations *A* makes a demand of *B* stating that the concession of this demand is vitally important to him. *A*'s demand is made without his knowing how it fits into *B*'s evaluations. It happens, however, that *B* could make the demanded concession with very little cost to himself. Does *B* then say at once, "I'll be glad to give you that; it won't cost me much at all." Looking at the matter from the standpoint of *B*'s interests there are obvious objections to this gratuitous concession of a trading advantage that may become vitally important later at some crucial juncture in the negotiations.

It might be suggested that *B* should grant the demand without delay but explain to *A* that he does so with the understanding that in the later negotiations *A* will offer some reciprocating concession. But this will hardly do. Commonly the various issues under discussion will be interrelated in complex ways; impulsive and premature generosity may impair the whole enterprise of achieving the greatest possible gain for both sides, it being remembered that the "exchange" of Christmas presents is notoriously a poor way of maximizing utilities. The best route to a mutually satisfactory agreement is likely to be that of having each party begin by consulting confidentially with the mediator, making a full disclosure of the internal posture of his interests as perceived by him. The mediator can then manage the negotiations in a way that will realize to the fullest extent the gains of reciprocity.

A more concise statement of some of the basic features of contracts is the following.

MACNEIL, CASES AND MATERIALS ON CONTRACTS
(1st ed.) pp. 1-5.

The concept of exchange is known to everyone who has ever studied economics. Nevertheless, it is perhaps worth repeating here that economic exchange occurs when one person gives to another something of economic value in order to secure something of economic value in return. Every one of us engages in exchanges every day; we cannot spend or earn so much as a dime without doing so.

The subject matter of this book is contracts: transactions and relationships in which economic exchange motivations are significant factors. Since the most universal medium of exchange is money, the law school course in contracts is intimately and directly concerned with money. It would be unfortunate, however, if the countless non-monetary social values involved in these transactions and relationships were to be ignored simply because they are obscured by dollar signs. It would be equally unfortunate to overlook the fact that the ways in which societies deal with money and rights to money themselves reflect numerous social values besides the satisfaction of avarice for money. The fact is that, because our economic structure (and that of other countries, including socialist countries) is based heavily on economic exchange motivations, a great many of our social values are expressed in the ways in which we respond to exchange transactions and relationships.

This book is not intended to supply a basis for making judgments concerning the extent to which American society, or any society, is or should be organized around recognition and implementation of economic exchange motivations or the extent to which other organizational principles do or should apply. It is rather intended to focus on certain significant aspects of exchange transactions and relationships as found in our society, especially the legal aspects. Nevertheless, if you do not relate what you learn from this micro-focus to your political and social philosophy, and vice versa, the book will in considerable part fail in its objective.

Exchange of property and the law. The notion of exchange is postulated on the assumption that the parties to an exchange each have some control of the respective subjects of the exchange. There is thus built into it an idea of "my" (or "our") and "yours" — a notion of property. This idea of property need not necessarily be a legal idea — an exchange can take place even though the property of each party depends entirely upon his ability to keep possession of it by force. Nevertheless, in a regime of law such property rights will in substantial measure be legal property rights. That is to say the legal system will make available to an "owner" sanctions to protect his interests in the property owned. Thus a minimal role of law in a society based on exchange will be legal recognition of property rights.

Since exchange is so commonly associated with systems of private property and capitalism, it is essential to make clear that the property involved in an exchange need not be private property. Exchange of public property can occur just as well as exchange of private property, e.g. between state enterprises in a socialist system. Or the exchange can be of private property on the one hand and public property on the other, e.g. purchases by a government agency from a private seller.

A legal recognition of property rights does not by itself, however, mean that reciprocal transfer of legal property rights through exchange is possible. An exchange can be legally effective only if the law recognizes the two transfers involved. If such recognition is not accorded, the legal property rights remain where they were before the exchange, and in the eyes of the law the exchange is ineffective.

Thus the two minimum requirements for a legally recognized system of exchange are recognition of property rights and recognition of the right to make reciprocal transfers of those rights.

Exchanges relating to the future. If the only exchanges possible were those involving existing property, exchange would encourage and effectuate the specialization of labor upon which every economy is based. With no more than a hope that people would give value for shoes when produced, the village shoemaker might nevertheless go ahead and make them in preference to becoming a less specialized tiller of the land or a hunter or a gatherer. His analysis of the prospective needs and desires of the villagers might, indeed, lead him to think that he had a pretty sure thing — that when the shoes were made villagers would want them badly enough to give value adequate to make production worthwhile. Nor is reliance on hope limited to small villages or to primitive societies. Except to the extent that modern advertising and marketing may be thought to be coercive rather than purely persuasive (an important exception, to be sure) the modern manufacturer-distributor of consumer goods is in much the same position as the village shoemaker.

But if a present exchange can somehow be projected into the future beyond mere hope, its power to effectuate and encourage specialization of labor is vastly increased. Consider again, for example, the village shoemaker. Suppose that he has no leather. If he can exchange shoes to be made in the future in return for leather now he can produce shoes, hopefully at a profit. If he cannot he must either abandon his shoemaking or secure leather by less efficient means, e.g. hunting, a task beyond his special skills. Or suppose that a customer wants and needs shoes already made, but the only thing he has to exchange is a calf which will be born in two months. If the shoemaker can exchange the shoes now for the calf to be delivered in two months, he may think it very worthwhile to do so. Or suppose that a customer comes in and wants shoes to be made to order and is willing to pay with a calf which will be born in two months, about the time the shoes will be finished. If the parties could effectively exchange now the shoes to be made in the future and the calf to be born in the future, the shoemaker could go ahead with the making of the shoes knowing that it will be worth his while to do so.

It is not possible to exchange now things which do not yet exist. Nevertheless *assurance* that the transfer will take place when the things (or services) do exist in the future can be exchanged now. There are two basic, closely related forms which this assurance may take. It may consist of a present transfer of a thing of value as security that the real subject of the exchange will be later transferred, e.g. giving custody now of hostages.... The second form of assurance is a promise, i.e. a communication of an intention to accept responsibility for the transfer's being made at the proper time.

Both of these forms of assurance are illustrated by the modern land financing transaction. A financing institution, e.g. a bank, wants to lend money to the owner of real estate. The owner signs a note promising to repay the amount lent together with interest. The owner's making such a promise has certain consequences in the business-legal world which gives the bank some assurance that it will receive what it wants from the deal: repayment of principal with interest. But normally the bank requires greater assurance. This it gets by requiring owner to transfer to the bank a present interest in his real estate. Owner does this by executing a mortgage which conveys to the lender a security interest in the real estate. If the loan is repaid as promised the lender's security interest terminates and the owner-borrower once again owns the property free and clear. If, however, the loan is not repaid, the lender will take steps, called foreclosure, to realize from the property the debt owed to him. If this happens the owner has forfeited his interest in the property and its proceeds to the extent necessary to pay the debt.

Which of the kinds of assurances — promise or forfeit or both — are used, relied upon or utilized when trouble occurs depend upon the nature of the transaction, and upon such things as business custom and legal rules of various kinds. Neither kind of assurance can be ignored in acquiring a basic understanding of exchanges which are not entirely consummated at a single point of time.

When an immediate exchange of existing property is contemplated the only economic question to be asked by each party is whether what is offered by the other is of greater value to him than the value of what is being asked in return. When, however, the subject of the exchange is an assurance of a future transfer the recipient of the assurance cannot content himself merely with the valuation of the properties (or services) at the time they will be exchanged. He must go further and evaluate the assurance itself. Just how sure is it that the exchange will be completed? To the extent that he is not completely sure the element of risk reduces the value of what he is "assured" that he will receive. Moreover, the value may be so far down that he will not agree to make the deal in the first place even though he would have been overjoyed to have done so if the exchange could have been effected immediately.

It should be plain from the foregoing that the more reliable are the assurances offered in exchanges, the more practical possibility there is of projecting exchanges into the future. No matter how beneficial to both parties the ultimate exchange might be, it may very well never come about if there is not some way they can use the "assurance exchange" first.

The law and exchanges relating to the future. We saw earlier that there are two prerequisites to legal recognition and effectuation of exchanges of existing objects. The first is the existence of legal rights of control over the subjects of the exchange in different identifiable persons or groups of persons. The second is a recognition that such rights can be transferred to some other identifiable person or groups of persons, and specifically that such transfer can be made by exchange.

But what of legal recognition and effectuation of exchanges where one or more of the subjects of exchange is simply an assurance of a future transfer? With respect to the forfeit root the role of law can in considerable measure remain as it is with a present exchange of existing objects. The law need merely recognize that the hostage or other pledge now "belongs" to the transferee until the assured event actually occurs. It is, however, really not quite that simple, because the entire nature of the transaction is such that the transferee himself owes obligations relating to the hostage or pledge, since normally he must return it if the transfer assured thereby is later made. These obligations of the transferee keep the security transaction from being identical with outright present exchanges, and indeed introduce an element of promise-assurance on the part of the holder of the security.

What is the role of the law where there is no transfer of security, where the assurance is a promise? (As shown by the real estate loan described earlier there may, of course, be both security and promise.) A potential role of the law where a subject of the exchange is a promise is obvious: it can add its force to the assurance. It can say that if, in return for A's giving B a cow, B promises to give A twenty bushels of wheat next month, legal mechanisms will be available which will make life unpleasant for B if he does not perform his promise. Or it might be able to do even more and make legal mechanisms available which will in fact accomplish the promised transfer, e.g. court officers will seize the wheat (if there is any) from B. Or it might allow A to go after B's property to recoup losses A has suffered because of the breach of the promise. These mechanisms cannot, of course, make 100% sure that the promise will be fulfilled by the transfer of the wheat, but they may nevertheless add to the assurance. How much they add varies from one situation to another. In any case you should never assume that a promisee's having even ironclad legal rights of enforcement necessarily will result in performance of a promise. Indeed one of the most important recurring questions in contracts is the real life effectiveness of legal contract remedies in a variety of contexts.

B. The Interests Protected

The materials that we have read have made it clear that we cannot be indifferent about contracts. The materials in this section raise the problem of what we do when we have to give some concrete expression to our concern about contracts. The cases all start by accepting the following general proposition: Lord Atkinson in *Sally Wertheim v. Chicoutimi Pulp Co.*, [1911] A.C. 301, at p. 307:

> "And it is the general intention of the law that, in giving damages for breach of contract, the party complaining should, so far as it can be done by money, be placed in the same position as he would have been in if the contract had been performed ... that it is a ruling principle. It is a just principle."

Such a proposition cannot really be described as a rule: Lord Atkinson himself describes it as a "principle". Our problem will be to understand what it means. What does it mean to say that the plaintiff (the party complaining) should be put "in the same position as he would have been in if the contract had been performed"? Specifically, the problem centres on the phrase "same position". In many cases it might be fairly simple to know what the "same position" would be. For example, if a seller agrees to sell goods at a certain price and fails to do so and, as a result, the buyer buys similar goods but at a higher price, payment by the seller to the buyer of the difference between the agreed price and the actual price might be regarded as putting the buyer in the same position as if the contract had been performed. In other cases, however, the problem might be far harder. Exactly this problem is raised in the first case.

PEEVYHOUSE v. GARLAND COAL & MINING CO.

(1963) 382 P. 2d 109. Supreme Court of Oklahoma.

Jackson, Justice: In the trial court, plaintiffs Willie and Lucille Peevyhouse sued the defendant, Garland Coal and Mining Company, for damages for breach of contract. Judgment was for plaintiffs in an amount considerably less than was sued for. Plaintiffs appeal and defendant cross-appeals.

In the briefs on appeal, the parties present their argument and contentions under several propositions; however, they all stem from the basic question of whether the trial court properly instructed the jury on the measure of damages.

Briefly stated, the facts are as follows: plaintiffs owned a farm containing coal deposits, and in November, 1954, leased the premises to defendant for a period of five years for coal mining purposes. A "strip-mining" operation was contemplated in which the coal would be taken from pits on the surface of the ground, instead of from underground mine shafts. In addition to the usual covenants found in a coal mining lease, defendant specifically agreed to perform certain restorative and remedial work at the end of the lease period. It is unnecessary to set out the details of the work to be done, other than to say that it would involve the moving of many thousands of cubic yards of dirt, at a cost estimated by expert witnesses at about $29,000.00. However, plaintiffs sued for only $25,000.00.

During the trial, it was stipulated that all covenants and agreements in the lease contract had been fully carried out by both parties, except the remedial work mentioned above; defendant conceded that this work had not been done.

Plaintiffs introduced expert testimony as to the amount and nature of the work to be done, and its estimated cost. Over plaintiffs' objections, defendant thereafter introduced expert testimony as to the "diminution in value" of plaintiffs' farm resulting from the failure of defendant to render performance as agreed in the contract — that is, the difference between the present value of the farm, and what its value would have been if defendant had done what it agreed to do.

At the conclusion of the trial, the court instructed the jury that it must return a verdict for plaintiffs, and left the amount of damages for jury determination. On the measure of damages, the court instructed the jury that it might consider the cost of performance of the work defendant agreed to do, "together with all of the evidence offered on behalf of either party".

It thus appears that the jury was at liberty to consider the "diminution in value" of plaintiffs' farm as well as the cost of "repair work" in determining the amount of damages.

It returned a verdict for plaintiffs for $5000.00 — only a fraction of the "cost of performance", *but more than the total value of the farm even after the remedial work is done.*

On appeal, the issue is sharply drawn. Plaintiffs contend that the true measure of damages in this case is what it will cost plaintiffs to obtain performance of the work that was not done because of defendant's default. Defendant argues that the measure of damages is the cost of performance "limited, however, to the total difference in the market value before and after the work was performed".

It appears that this precise question has not heretofore been presented to this court. In *Ardizonne v. Archer*, 72 Okl. 70, 178 P. 263, this court held that the measure of damages for breach of a contract to drill an oil well was the reasonable cost of drilling the well, but here a slightly different factual situation exists. The drilling of an oil well will yield valuable geological information, even if no oil or gas is found, and of course if the well is a producer, the value of the premises increases. In the case before us, it is argued by defendant with some force that the performance of the remedial work defendant agreed to do will add at the most only a few hundred dollars to the value of plaintiffs' farm, and that the damages should be limited to that amount because that is all plaintiffs have lost.

Plaintiffs rely on *Groves v. John Wunder Co.*, 205 Minn. 163, 286 N.W. 235, 123 A.L.R. 502. In that case, the Minnesota court, in a substantially similar situation, adopted the "cost of performance" rule as-opposed to the "value" rule. The result was to authorize a jury to give plaintiff damages in the amount of $60,000, where the real estate concerned would have been worth only $12,160, even if the work contracted for had been done.

It may be observed that *Groves v. John Wunder Co., supra,* is the only case which has come to our attention in which the cost of performance rule has been followed under circumstances where the cost of performance greatly exceeded the diminution in value resulting from the breach of contract. Incidentally, it appears that this case was decided by a plurality rather than a majority of the members of the court.

Defendant relies principally upon *Sandy Valley & E. R. Co., v. Hughes,* 175 Ky. 320, 194 S.W. 344; *Bigham v. Wabash-Pittsburg Terminal Ry. Co.,* 223 Pa. 106, 72 A. 318; and *Sweeney v. Lewis Const. Co.,* 66 Wash. 490, 119 P. 1108. These were all cases in which, under similar circumstances, the appellate courts followed the "value" rule instead of the "cost of performance" rule. Plaintiff points out that in the earliest of these cases (*Bigham*) the court cites as authority on the measure of damages an earlier Pennsylvania *tort* case, and that the other two cases follow the first, with no explanation as to why a measure of damages ordinarily followed in cases sounding in tort should be used in contract cases. Nevertheless, it is of some significance that three out of four appellate courts have followed the diminution in value rule under circumstances where, as here, the cost of performance greatly exceeds the diminution in value.

The explanation may be found in the fact that the situations presented are artificial ones. It is highly unlikely that the ordinary property owner would agree to pay $29,000 (or its equivalent) for the construction of "improvements" upon his property that would increase its value only about ($300) three hundred dollars. The result is that we are called upon to apply principles of law theoretically based upon reason and reality to a situation which is basically unreasonable and unrealistic.

In *Groves v. John Wunder Co., supra,* in arriving at its conclusions, the Minnesota court apparently considered the contract involved to be analogous to a building and construction contract, and cited authority for the proposition that the cost of performance or completion of the building as contracted is ordinarily the measure of damages in actions for damages for the breach of such a contract.

In an annotation following the Minnesota case beginning at 123 A.L.R. 515, the annotator places the three cases relied on by defendant (*Sandy Valley, Bigham* and *Sweeney*) under the classification of cases involving "grading and excavation contracts".

We do not think either analogy is strictly applicable to the case now before us. The primary purpose of the lease contract between plaintiffs and defendant was neither "building and construction" nor "grading and excavation". It was merely to accomplish the economical recovery and marketing of coal from the premises, to the profit of all parties. The special provisions of the lease contract pertaining to remedial work were incidental to the main object involved.

Even in the case of contracts that are unquestionably building and construction contracts, the authorities are not in agreement as to the factors to be considered in determining whether the cost of performance rule or the value rule should be applied. The American Law Institute's *Restatement of the Law, Contracts,* Volume 1, Sections 346(1) (a) (i) and (ii) submits the proposition that the cost of performance is the proper measure of damages "if this is possible and does not involve *unreasonable economic waste";* and that the diminution in value caused by the breach is the proper measure "if construction and completion in accordance with the contract would involve *unreasonable economic waste".* (Emphasis supplied.) In an explanatory comment immediately following the text, the *Restatement* makes it clear that the "economic waste" referred to consists of the destruction of a substantially completed building or other structure. Of course no such destruction is involved in the case now before us.

On the other hand, in McCormick, *Damages,* Section 168, it is said with regard to building and construction contracts that "... in cases where the defect is one that can be repaired or cured without *undue expense"* the cost of performance is the proper measure of damages, but where "... the defect in material or construction is one that cannot be remedied without *an expenditure for reconstruction disproportionate to the end to be attained"* (emphasis supplied) the value rule should be followed. The same idea was expressed in *Jacob & Youngs, Inc. v. Kent,* 230 N.Y. 239, 129 N.E. 889, 23 A.L.R. 1429, as follows:

> "The owner is entitled to the money which will permit him to complete, unless the cost of completion is grossly and unfairly out of proportion to the good to be attained. When that is true, the measure is the difference in value."

It thus appears that the prime consideration in the *Restatement* was "economic waste"; and that the prime consideration in McCormick, *Damages,* and in *Jacob & Youngs, Inc. v. Kent, supra,* was the relationship between the expense involved and the "end to be attained" — in other words, the "relative economic benefit".

In view of the unrealistic fact situation in the instant case, and certain Oklahoma statutes to be hereinafter noted, we are of the opinion that the "relative economic benefit" is a proper consideration here. This is in accord with the recent case of *Mann v. Clowser,* 190 Va. 887, 59 S.E.2d 78, where, in applying the cost rule, the Virginia court specifically noted that "... the defects are remediable from a practical standpoint and the costs *are not grossly disproportionate to the results to be obtained"* (Emphasis supplied).

23 O.S.1961 §§ 96 and 97 provide as follows:

> "§ 96.... Notwithstanding the provisions of this chapter, no person can recover a greater amount in damages for the breach of an obligation, than he would have gained by the full performance thereof on both sides...
> "§ 97.... Damages must, in all cases, be reasonable, and where an obligation of any kind appears to create a right to unconscionable and grossly oppressive damages, contrary to substantial justice no more than reasonable damages can be recovered."

Although it is true that the above sections of the statute are applied most often in tort cases, they are by their own terms, and the decisions of this court, also applicable in actions for damages for breach of contract. It would seem that they are peculiarly applicable here where, under the "cost of performance" rule, plaintiffs might recover an amount about nine times the total value of their farm. Such would seem to be "unconscionable and grossly oppressive damages, contrary to substantial justice" within the meaning of the statute. Also, it can hardly be denied that if plaintiffs here are permitted to recover under the "cost of performance" rule, they will receive a greater benefit from the breach than could be gained from full performance, contrary to the provisions of Sec. 96.

An analogy may be drawn between the cited sections, and the provisions of 15 O.S.1961 §§ 214 and 215. These sections tend to render void any provisions of a contract which attempt to fix the amount of stipulated damages to be paid in case of a breach, except where it is impracticable or extremely difficult to determine the actual damages. This results in spite of the agreement of the parties, and the obvious and well known rationale is that insofar as they exceed the actual damages suffered, the stipulated damages amount to a penalty or forfeiture which the law does not favor.

23 O.S.1961 §§ 96 and 97 have the same effect in the case now before us. *In spite of the agreement of the parties*, these sections limit the damages recoverable to a reasonable amount not "contrary to substantial justice"; they prevent plaintiffs from recovering a "greater amount in damages for the breach of an obligation" than they would have "gained by the full performance thereof".

We therefore hold that where, in a coal mining lease, lessee agrees to perform certain remedial work on the premises concerned at the end of the lease period, and thereafter the contract is fully performed by both parties except that the remedial work is not done, the measure of damages in an action by lessor against lessee for damages for breach of contract is ordinarily the reasonable cost of performance of the work; however, where the contract provision breached was merely incidental to the main purpose in view, and where the economic benefit which would result to lessor by full performance of the work is grossly disproportionate to the cost of performance, the damages which lessor may recover are limited to the diminution in value resulting to the premises because of the non-performance.

We believe the above holding is in conformity with the intention of the Legislature as expressed in the statutes mentioned, and in harmony with the better-reasoned cases from the other jurisdictions where analogous fact situations have been considered. It should be noted that the rule as stated does not interfere with the property owner's right to "do what he will with his own" *Chamberlain v. Parker*, 45 N.Y. 569), or his right, if he chooses, to contract for "improvements" which will actually have the effect of reducing his property's value. Where such result is in fact contemplated by the parties, and is a main or principal purpose of those contracting, it would seem that the measure of damages for breach would ordinarily be the cost of performance.

The above holding disposes of all of the arguments raised by the parties on appeal.

Under the most liberal view of the evidence herein, the diminution in value resulting to the premises because of non-performance of the remedial work was $300.00. After a careful search of the record, we have found no evidence of a higher figure, and plaintiffs do not argue in their briefs that a great diminution in value was sustained. It thus appears that the judgment was clearly excessive, and that the amount for which judgment should have been rendered is definitely and satisfactorily shown by the record.

We are asked by each party to modify the judgment in accordance with the respective theories advanced, and it is conceded that we have authority to do so. 12 O.S.1961 § 952; *Busboom v. Smith*, 199 Okl. 688, 191 P.2d 198; *Stumpf v. Stumpf*, 173 Okl. 1, 46 P. 2d 315.

We are of the opinion that the judgment of the trial court for plaintiffs should be, and it is hereby, modified and reduced to the sum of $300.00, and as so modified it is affirmed.

Welch, Davison, Halley, and Johnson, JJ., concur.

Williams, C. J., Blackbird, V. C. J., and Irwin and Berry, JJ., dissent.

Irwin, Justice (dissenting): By the specific provisions in the coal mining lease under consideration, the defendant agreed as follows:

> "... "7b Lessee agrees to make fills in the pits dug on said premises on the property line in such manner that fences can be placed thereon and access had to opposite sides of the pits.
> "c Lessee agrees to smooth off the top of the spoil banks on the above premises.
> "7d Lessee agrees to leave the creek crossing the above premises in such a condition that it will not interfere with the crossings to be made in pits as set out in 7b.
>
> . . .
>
> "7f Lessee further agrees to leave no shale or dirt on the high wall of said pits... "

Following the expiration of the lease, plaintiffs made demand upon defendant that it carry out the provisions of the contract and to perform those covenants contained therein.

Defendant admits that it failed to perform its obligations that it agreed and contracted to perform under the lease contract and there is nothing in the record which indicates that defendant could not perform its obligations. Therefore, in my opinion defendant's breach of the contract was wilful and not in good faith.

Although the contract speaks for itself, there were several negotiations between the plaintiffs and defendant before the contract was executed. Defendant admitted in the trial of the action, that plaintiffs insisted that the above provisions be included in the contract and that they would not agree to the coal mining lease unless the above provisions were included.

In consideration for the lease contract, plaintiffs were to receive a certain amount as royalty for the coal produced and marketed and in addition thereto their land was to be restored as provided in the contract.

Defendant received as consideration for the contract, its proportionate share of the coal produced and marketed and in addition thereto, the *right to use* plaintiffs' land in the furtherance of its mining operations.

The cost for performing the contract in question could have been reasonably approximated when the contract was negotiated and executed and there are no conditions now existing which could not have been reasonably anticipated by the parties. Therefore, defendant had knowledge, when it prevailed upon the plaintiffs to execute the lease, that the cost of performance might be disproportionate to the value or benefits received by plaintiff for the performance.

Defendant has received its benefits under the contract and now urges, in substance, that plaintiffs' measure of damages for its failure to perform should be the economic value of performance to the plaintiffs and not the cost of performance.

If a peculiar set of facts should exist where the above rule should be applied as the proper measure of damages, (and in my judgment those facts do not exist in the instant case) before such rule should be applied, consideration should be given to the benefits received or contracted for by the party who asserts the application of the rule.

Defendant did not have the right to mine plaintiffs' coal or to use plaintiffs' property for its mining operations without the consent of plaintiffs. Defendant had knowledge of the benefits that it would receive under the contract and the approximate cost of performing the contract. With this knowledge, it must be presumed that defendant thought that it would be to its economic advantage to enter into the contract with plaintiffs and that it would reap benefits from the contract, or it would have not entered into the contract.

Therefore, if the value of the performance of a contract should be considered in determining the measure of damages for breach of a contract, the value of the benefits received under the contract by a party who breaches a contract should also be considered. However, in my judgment, to give consideration to either in the instant action, completely rescinds and holds for naught the solemnity of the contract before us and makes an entirely new contract for the parties.

In *Globe v. Bell Oil & Gas Co.*, 97 Okl. 261, 223 P. 371, we held:

> "Even though the contract contains harsh and burdensome terms which the court does not in all respects approve, it is the province of the parties in relation to lawful subject matter to fix their rights and obligations, and the court will give the contract effect according to its expressed provisions, unless it be shown by competent evidence proof that the written agreement as executed is the result of fraud, mistake, or accident."

In *Cities Service Oil Co. v. Geolograph Co. Inc.*, 208 Okl. 179, 254 P.2d 775, we said:

> "While we do not agree that the contract as presently written is an onerous one, we think the short answer is that the folly or wisdom of a contract is not for the court to pass on."

In *Great Western Oil & Gas Company v. Mitchell*, Okl., 326 P.2d 794, we held:

> "The law will not make a better contract for parties than they themselves have seen fit to enter into, or alter it for the benefit of one party and to the detriment of the others; the judicial function of a court of law is to enforce a contract as it is written."

I am mindful of Title 23 O.S.1961 § 96, which provides that no person can recover a greater amount in damages for the breach of an obligation than he could have gained by the full performance thereof on both sides, except in cases not applicable herein. However, in my judgment, the above statutory provision is not applicable here.

In my judgment, we should follow the case of *Groves v. John Wunder Company*, 205 Minn. 163, 286 N.W. 235, 123 A.L.R. 502, which defendant agrees "that the fact situation is apparently similar to the one in the case at bar", and where the Supreme Court of Minnesota held:

> "The owner's or employer's damages for such a breach (i.e. breach hypothesized in 2d syllabus) are to be measured, not in respect to the value of the land to be

improved, but by the reasonable cost of doing that which the contractor promised to do and which he left undone."

The hypothesized breach referred to states that where the contractor's breach of a contract is wilful, that is, in bad faith, he is not entitled to any benefit of the equitable doctrine of substantial performance.

In the instant action defendant has made no attempt to even substantially perform. The contract in question is not immoral, is not tainted with fraud, and was not entered into through mistake or accident and is not contrary to public policy. It is clear and unambiguous and the parties understood the terms thereof, and the approximate cost of fulfilling the obligations could have been approximately ascertained. There are no conditions existing now which could not have been reasonably anticipated when the contract was negotiated and executed. The defendant could have performed the contract if it desired. It has accepted and reaped the benefits of its contract and now urges that plaintiffs' benefits under the contract be denied. If plaintiffs' benefits are denied, such benefits would inure to the direct benefit of the defendant.

Therefore, in my opinion, the plaintiffs were entitled to specific performance of the contract and since defendant has failed to perform, the proper measure of damages should be the cost of performance. Any other measure of damage would be holding for naught the express provisions of the contract; would be taking from the plaintiffs the benefits of the contract and placing those benefits in defendant which has failed to perform its obligations; would be granting benefits to defendant without a resulting obligation; and would be completely rescinding the solemn obligation of the contract for the benefit of the defendant to the detriment of the plaintiffs by making an entirely new contract for the parties.

I therefore respectfully dissent to the opinion promulgated by a majority of my associates.

[The U.S. Supreme Court was asked to review the decision of the Oklahoma Supreme Court but declined to do so: (1963), 375 U.S. 906.]

QUESTIONS AND PROBLEMS

1. What did the majority think that the plaintiffs lost by reason of the defendant's breach of contract?

2. What did the minority think that the plaintiffs lost?

3. To what extent did either the majority or minority accept what Lord Atkinson said was the basis for awarding contract damages? To what extent was the application of Lord Atkinson's principle just?

4. Suppose that in *Peevyhouse v. Garland Coal*, the President of Garland Coal had been asked in cross-examination if his company had planned to breach the contract made with Peevyhouse and had admitted that they had intended to do so. Would this change your view of the case?

5. Mrs. Jones, a lonely old widow living in Oklahoma City, has a pussycat named Fiddler who is her only companion. When Fiddler becomes ill Mrs. Jones takes him to Dr. Vet. Dr. Vet. guarantees to cure the cat. He treats Fiddler with medication and Mrs. Jones pays the bill. But Fiddler gets worse. Mrs. Jones takes him to another veterinarian and learns that cure is possible, but only by surgery costing $500. The value of a healthy Fiddler on the open market is about ten cents. Can Mrs. Jones recover $500 from Dr. Vet? Does your answer depend upon whether she has the operation performed?

6. David promised Joan that he would build a model of Casa Loma in her garden for $20,000. David subsequently changed his mind and refused to do the work. It is

proved that it would now cost $25,000 to complete the model. It is also proved that the value of Joan's property would be reduced by $10,000 if the model were built. Joan now sues David to recover the extra cost of having the model completed by someone else. Can she recover, and if so, how much? If Joan can recover in this case, would this be consistent with the judgments in *Peevyhouse v. Garland Coal?*

7. Suppose that you are asked to negotiate on behalf of a farmer an agreement to allow strip mining on his land. What would you do to avoid the result in *Peevyhouse?*

8. Suppose that the State of Oklahoma had enacted legislation to require the operators of strip mining leases to restore the land at the end of the lease, what effect do you think the court should give to such legislation? Would it make any difference if the statute provided for a penalty of $100. per acre for each acre left unrestored?

9. Owner leased building to tenant. Tenant covenanted to restore at the end of the lease. Tenant made alterations and failed to restore at the end of the lease. Owner sold building for the same amount he would have got had the restoration been made. Owner sues for the cost of restoration. What result?

The problems that we have been discussing come up in all kinds of contracts. In the case of contracts for the sale of goods (goods being defined as chattels generally) the law in regard to damages for breach of such a contract is found in the Sale of Goods Act, R.S.O. 1970, c. 421. This act was passed in England in 1893. It was intended to codify the common law in regard to the sale of goods. The Act has been copied in every Canadian province (except Quebec). It was first passed in Ontario in 1920.

The sections of the Act dealing with the remedies of the seller and buyer in the event of the other's breach are as follows:

48(1) Where the buyer wrongfully neglects or refuses to accept and pay for the goods, the seller may maintain an action against him for damages for non-acceptance.

(2) The measure of damages is the estimated loss directly and naturally resulting in the ordinary course of events from the buyer's breach of contract.

(3) Where there is an available market for the goods in question, the measure of damages is *prima facie* to be ascertained by the difference between the contract price and the market or current price at the time or times when the goods ought to have been accepted, or, if no time was fixed for acceptance, then at the time of the refusal to accept.

49(1) Where the seller wrongfully neglects or refuses to deliver the goods to the buyer, the buyer may maintain an action against the seller for damages for non-delivery.

(2) The measure of damages is the estimated loss directly and naturally resulting in the ordinary course of events from the seller's breach of contract.

(3) Where there is an available market for the goods in question, the measure of damages is *prima facie* to be ascertained by the difference between the contract price and the market or current price of the goods at the time or times when they ought to have been delivered, or, if no time was fixed, then at the time of the refusal to deliver.

QUESTIONS AND PROBLEMS

1. Cathy agreed on August 1st to buy carrots from Ben for 10¢/lb. Ben promised to deliver the carrots on September 1st but did not do so. What is the measure of Cathy's damages in the following circumstances:

(a) on Sept. 1st carrots are selling for 15¢/lb;
(b) On Sept. 1st carrots are selling for 8¢/lb;
(c) On Sept. 1st carrots are selling for 25¢/lb, but, on Sept. 4th, the market collapses and carrots are then selling for 10¢/lb?

2. Do you think that in each case Cathy would be adequately compensated under the Sale of Goods Act?

3. What assumptions are made about the alternative measures that are open to a disappointed buyer or seller under the Act?

NOTE ON CANADIAN AND AMERICAN LEGISLATION AND LAW REFORM

Throughout the course we will look at legislation like the Sale of Goods Act and compare it with equivalent American legislation. This note is designed to explain briefly how that legislation arose, what its principal features are and what other bodies or institutions have a bearing on how the law might develop.

The Sale of Goods Act that was introduced in England in 1893 was part of an attempt to codify large parts of the common law relating to common commercial transactions. In 1882 the Bills of Exchange Act codified the law relating to cheques and other negotiable instruments. The Factors Act of 1889 was part of this development. All of these acts were adopted in Canada. Under the B.N.A. Act, the provinces have exclusive authority in respect of matters covered by the Sale of Goods Act and Factors Act, while the federal parliament has exclusive authority in respect of Bills of Exchange. The law in Canada, therefore, presents a uniform picture. In matters covered by these three Acts the law (apart from the province of Quebec) is very nearly identical across the country. The existence of uniform rules in these areas is a useful feature of Canadian law.

The impetus for reform in the United States arose from two separate, though related pressures. The first pressure arose from a desire to encourage uniformity across the country. The second arose from a desire to reduce the apparent chaos that resulted from the separate rules and courts in nearly 50 jurisdictions. Obviously uniform laws will reduce the impact of multiple jurisdictions each going its own way. The first pressure resulted in 1892 in proposals for the establishment of a body that would promote uniformity where that was desirable. The National Conference on Uniform State Laws was subsequently set up. The first result of this was the publication of the Uniform Negotiable Instruments Law in 1896. This was eventually adopted by all the states. In 1906 a Uniform Sales Law was published. The hope was to produce ultimately a single comprehensive code covering all aspects of commercial law. The drafting of what was to become the Uniform Commercial Code (U.C.C.) began in 1942 under the direction of Karl Llewellyn. A uniform code was produced in 1951. The first state to adopt it was Pennsylvania in 1953. Revisions were made to accommodate the objections of various states (principally New York) and revised drafts were published in 1957, 1958, 1962 and in 1971. The U.C.C. has now been adopted in every state. The Code is organized in nine Articles. Article 1 contains general provisions applicable in each Article. Article 2, with which we shall be most concerned, deals with sales and corresponds to our Sale of Goods Act. There is at the moment a committee in Ontario considering whether or not Ontario should adopt the substance of Article 2 to replace the Sale of Goods Act. Article 9, dealing with security interests in chattels, has been adopted in Ontario as The Personal Property Security Act and is now in force.

Article 8, which deals with the question of the negotiability of shares, has become part of the Ontario and Canadian Business Corporations Acts. The U.C.C. has been supplemented by other uniform acts that have been adopted in various Canadian provinces. The Ontario Business Practices Act and the B.C. Trade Practices Act are largely based on the Uniform Consumer Sales Practices Act in the United States.

The second pressure led to the production in 1932 of the Restatement of Contracts. The Restatement (it was originally intended to cover much of the law) was a project of the American Law Institute which began its existence in 1923. Its purpose was, in part, to alleviate the law's complexity and uncertainty and can be seen, therefore to have been a direct response to the pressure that has been mentioned. The ALI engages in three functions: (1) the preparation of model codes and acts; (2) continuing legal education; and (3) the Restatement. The ALI produced a Model Penal Code in 1962 that is widely referred to. We are most concerned with the provisions of the Restatement of Contracts.

The Restatement is an attempt to reduce the law into the form of propositions of law much like a statute. The Restatement has, of course, no statutory authority, nor is anyone likely to incorporate the provisions into an act. The work of producing a Restatement of any area of the law is under the direction of a "Reporter" who is the principal draftsman of the text. The Reporter for the Restatement of Contracts was Samuel Williston who was assisted by Arthur Corbin (the author of the best text book on the law of contracts: *Corbin on Contracts*). The Restatement was well received by the courts and is regarded as having considerable authority. In 1960 work was begun on a revision of the first Restatement. The process of revision is very time-consuming. The first published draft of the new Restatement comes out in tentative drafts. After these have been discussed, the complete draft is submitted to the Council of the ALI (the Institute's governing body) for final approval. The first Reporter of the Second Restatement of Contracts was Robert Braucher formerly of the Harvard Law School and now a Massachusetts judge. The present Reporter is Allan Farnsworth of Columbia University. So far there have been ten tentative drafts of the new Restatement of Contracts published. The latest one being published in April 1975. No complete draft has yet been published.

Throughout the course we will be looking at extracts from the U.C.C. and the Restatement either as propositions of law which might be applicable in Canada or as different ways of solving problems that we share with the U.S. You must remember that neither the U.C.C. nor the Restatement is of any binding authority in Canada. Neither operate to guide the court to a decision in the way that the Sale of Goods Act does. But this does not mean that they are irrelevant.

There is no Canadian equivalent of the ALI, though some of its functions are carried out in different ways. The Canadian Bar Association (Canadian lawyers' national organization) and the various provincial law societies have extensive programmes for continuing education. Almost every province has a Law Reform Commission, and there is a Canadian Law Reform Commission as well. These Commissions produce recommendations for changes in the law and frequently produce model acts. We will spend some time in this course examining various recommendations of the Ontario Law Reform Commission.

The Canadian equivalent of the U.S. National Conference of Commissioners on Uniform State Laws is the Conference of Commissioners on Uniformity of Legislation in Canada. This body has produced a number of drafts of acts that have been offered to the provinces as uniform acts, many of which have been adopted in several provinces. Very few have had anything like universal acceptance. None of the draft acts of the Commissioners on Uniformity deal with the basic issues in this course. The history of the Canadian Conference and a summary of its work to date are available in the Annual Proceedings of the Conference, published each year. For some reason, the Canadian Conference manages to avoid attracting publicity of any kind inside or outside the legal profession.

The next case provides an example of the application of the Sale of Goods Act.

Would it make any difference to the result if the Act had not been passed?

VICTORY MOTORS LTD. v. BAYDA

[1973] 3 W.W.R. 747. Sask. Dist. Ct.

21st March 1973. **Hughes D.C.J.**: The plaintiff is a dealer in new and used automobiles carrying on business in the City of North Battleford. It brings this action for damages to, in effect, recover a commission of $700 it alleges is owing to it by the defendant. On 12th February 1972 the defendant contracted to purchase from the plaintiff a 1972 Mustang automobile. Following the arrival of the vehicle in North Battleford in mid-March 1972 the defendant declined to take delivery. Once it was clear that the defendant was not going to accept the vehicle it was sold by the plaintiff to another customer. The plaintiff's position is that, notwithstanding its recovery of a commission from the third party on the ultimate sale of the vehicle, it was deprived of its profit, by way of a commission, on its transaction with the defendant due to the defendant's refusal to accept and pay for the vehicle as ordered by him from the plaintiff. At the close of the trial I made a finding which I now formally record that the defendant did wrongfully refuse to accept and pay for the vehicle that he had ordered. The reasons therefor are a matter of record. I reserved judgment on and because of the far more complicated question of damages.

Simply stated, the plaintiff's position is that the ultimate sale to and recovery of a commission from the new purchaser who appeared on the scene is irrelevant insofar as its entitlement to recover from the defendant is concerned. The argument is that the ultimate purchaser would have bought another Mustang vehicle from the plaintiff had the one ordered by the defendant not been available for purchase and hence the plaintiff has, because of the defendant's action, made one profit instead of two, and that accordingly it is entitled to recover its profit, by way of damages, on the transaction contracted for by it with the defendant.

Section 49 of The Sale of Goods Act, R.S.S. 1965, c. 388, spells out a seller's entitlement to damages where a buyer wrongfully neglects or refuses to accept goods that he has ordered. The basis for determining the measure of damages is also spelled out in the section. It reads as follows:

> "49. — (1) Where the buyer wrongfully neglects or refuses to accept and pay for the goods the seller may maintain an action against him for damages for non-acceptance.
>
> "(2) The measure of damages is the estimated loss directly and naturally resulting in the ordinary course of events from the buyer's breach of contract.
>
> "(3) Where there is an available market for the goods in question the measure of damages is *prima facie* to be ascertained by the difference between the contract price and the market or current price at the time or times when the goods ought to have been accepted or if no time was fixed for acceptance then at the time of the refusal to accept."

The initial question for consideration is whether the measure of damages in the instant situation is to be determined under subs. (2) or subs. (3). I am assisted in answering this and subsequent questions by a consideration of English decisions where the identical section in the English Sale of Goods Act, albeit numbered s. 50, was under consideration:

W. L. Thompson Ltd. v. R. Robinson (Gunmakers) Ltd., [1955] Ch. 177, [1955] 1 All E.R. 154. In that case the facts were that on 4th March 1954 the defendants agreed in writing with the plaintiffs, who were motor car suppliers, to purchase from them a Standard Vanguard motor car. On 5th March 1954 the defendants intimated to the plaintiffs that they were not prepared to accept delivery of the motor car. The plaintiffs returned the motor car to their suppliers, who did not seek compensation, and plaintiffs proceeded to claim damages for breach of the agreement against the defendant. The price at which a Standard Vanguard motor car could be sold by the suppliers throughout the country was fixed by the manufacturers and the amount of profit which the plaintiffs would have realized on the sale of the motor car was £61 1s. 9d. The Court held that there was not present "an available market" and accordingly s. 50(3) of the Sale of Goods Act, 1893, c. 71, did not apply. Upjohn J. went on to say, however, at p. 160:

> "But there is this further consideration: even if I accepted the defendants' broad argument that one must now look at the market as being the whole conspectus of trade, organisation and marketing, I have to remember that s. 50(3) provides only a prima facie rule, and, if on investigation of the facts, one finds that it is unjust to apply that rule, in the light of the general principles mentioned above it is not to be applied. In this case, as I said in the earlier part of my judgment, it seems to me plain almost beyond argument that, in fact, the loss to the plaintiffs is £61."

Charter v. Sullivan, [1957] 2 Q.R. 117, [1957] 1 All E.R. 809. In that case the facts were that the plaintiff, a motor car dealer, agreed to sell a Hillman Minx car to the defendant for £773 17s. The retail price of such cars was fixed by the manufacturers. Subsequently the plaintiff received a letter from the defendant refusing to complete the purchase but seven or ten days later the plaintiff sold the car to another purchaser at the same price. He brought an action for damages for breach of contract against the defendant, claiming as damages the loss of profit of £97 15s. which he would have made if he had completed the sale to the defendant in addition to selling a similar car to the second purchaser. Jenkins L.J. stated that it would be difficult for him to hold that there was an "available market" within the meaning of s. 50(3) but that, for the following reason, even if there were, s. 50(2) would be applicable. He said at pp. 811-12:

> "Counsel for the defendant argued that in the present case there was an available market for Hillman Minx de luxe saloon cars within the meaning of s. 50(3) of the Act, and accordingly that the measure of damages ought, in accordance with the prima facie rule laid down by that subsection , to be ascertained by the difference between the contract price and the market or current price at the time of the defendant's refusal to perform his contract. The result of this argument, if accepted, would be that the plaintiff could claim no more than nominal damages, because the market or current price could only be the fixed retail price, which was necessarily likewise the price at which he sold to the defendant and resold to Mr. Wigley.
> "The plaintiff, however, is a motor car dealer whose trade for the present purpose can be described as consisting in the purchase of recurrent supplies of cars of the relevant description from the manufacturers, and selling the cars so obtained, or as many of them as he can, at the fixed retail price. He thus receives, on each sale that he is able to effect, the predetermined profit allowed by the fixed retail price, and it is obviously in his interest to sell as many cars as he can obtain from the manufacturers. The number of sales that he can effect, and consequently the amount of profit which he makes, will be governed, according to the state of trade, either by the number of cars that he is able to obtain from the manufacturers, or by the number of purchasers whom he is able to find. In the former case demand exceeds supply, so that the default of one purchaser involves him in no loss, for he sells the same number of cars as he would have sold if that purchaser

had not defaulted. In the latter case supply exceeds demand, so that the default of one purchaser may be said to have lost him one sale.

"Accordingly, it seems to me that, even if there was within the meaning of s. 50(3) an available market for cars of the description in question, and even if the fixed retail price was the market or current price within the meaning of the same subsection, the prima facie rule which it prescribes should be rejected in favour of the general rule laid down by sub-s.(2); for it does not by any means necessarily follow that, because the plaintiff sold at the fixed retail price to Mr. Wigley the car which the defendant had agreed to buy at the self-same fixed retail price, but refused to take, therefore the plaintiff suffered no 'loss directly and naturally resulting, in the ordinary course of events' from the defendant's breach of contract."

It is the portions of the two foregoing decisions quoted, *supra*, that prompted Fridman in his text, *Sale of Goods*, to comment, I am sure, as follows at p. 296:

"It has also been suggested, in *W. L. Thompson Ltd. v. R. Robinson (Gunmakers) Ltd.* [supra] and *Charter v. Sullivan* [supra], that the market test is inapplicable where its strict application would lead to injustice, because it would produce an inaccurate assessment of the damages suffered by the seller. In such instances, therefore, the court is thrown back on the general principle stated in section 50(2) of the Act, namely, 'the estimated loss directly and naturally resulting in the ordinary course of events, from the buyer's breach of contract.' The court must therefore assess the loss to the seller as best it can, *i.e.*, on the basis of loss of profit."

I believe the reasoning of the two Justices in the foregoing cases to be sound and the summation thereof by the learned author to accurately reflect same. I adopt that reasoning and accordingly turn to a consideration of s. 49(2) as the applicable subsection. I do this without the necessity, for the foregoing reason, of giving direct consideration to the existence or nonexistence, in the instant situation, of "an available market".

The question I must now answer is, what is the "estimated loss directly and naturally resulting in the ordinary course of events from the buyer's breach of contract"? The first case to be considered where the Court addressed itself to that very question is *Re Vic Mill Ltd.*, [1913] 1 Ch. 465. In that case the Vic Company was in voluntary liquidation. Before the winding-up the company had ordered certain machines to be made by a firm of engineers, which, owing to the winding-up, the company was unable to accept. The creditors put in a claim for damages in an amount equal to the profits which they estimated they would have made if the contract had been carried out. Hamilton L.J. said at pp. 473-4:

"It follows that he was entitled to recover the damages directly and naturally resulting in the ordinary course of events from the buyer's breach of contract. If the goods had been broken up, or sold by auction for what they would fetch, as the learned judge surmised, the consequences to the buyers would have been considerably worse than they are. It so happened that after the repudiation of the contract by the Vic Mill another customer of the makers was prepared to place an order with them for frames of that kind and somewhat of those dimensions. They might have taken that order, fulfilled it, made their profit on it, and dealt with the frames left on their hands in any reasonable way that they could. They did in fact at a small cost adapt the frames on their hands, and with them fulfilled the order of this other customer, and so made their profit on his contract. To that extent the buyers in the present case got the benefit of the accident that another customer came forward. That was a reasonable mode of mitigating the damages, but it by no means follows that the damages are confined to the cost, a trivial one, of adapting the machines to the needs of the second customer, and the loss on resale to him, which was only £23, making £28 in all. The fallacy of that is in supposing that the second customer was a substituted customer, that, had all gone well, the makers would not have had both customers, both orders, and both profits. In fact, what they did, acting reasonably, and I think very likely more than reasonably in the interests of the Vic Mill, was to content themselves with earning the profit on the second contract at the cost of adapting the machines, which has been taken at £5; but they are still losers of the profit which they would have made on the Vic Mill contract, because they could, if they had been minded, have performed both the contracts, and have made the profit on both the contracts but for the breach by the Vic Mill Company of their contract."

Buckley L.J., in his judgment, expressed the point as follows [p. 474]:

"As regards No. 1, where the goods were manufactured, the respondents are, I think, entitled to both profits, because they were not bound to give the appellants the benefit of another order that the respondents had received. The respondents were left with these goods on their hands. They altered them and sold them to another buyer, but they could have made, and would otherwise, I suppose, have made, other goods for that buyer, and not employed these goods for that purpose. If they had done so, they would have made both profits."

In *W. L. Thompson Ltd. v. R. Robinson (Gunmakers) Ltd.*, [1955] Ch. 177, [1955] 1 All E.R. 154, it was an admitted fact that in the relevant trading area at the time the contract of sale between the plaintiff and the defendant took place there was no shortage of Vanguard models to meet all immediate demands. It was also common ground that:

"... at this stage, the plaintiffs lost a sale in this sense, that if another purchaser had come into the plaintiffs' premises there was available for another purchaser a Vanguard car for immediate delivery; so that the effect as a fact on the plaintiffs was that they lost their profit on a sale: they sold one Vanguard less than they would otherwise have done. The plaintiffs say that the true measure of damages in those circumstances is no more, no less, than their loss of profit, £61. The defendants say: 'No, the loss is nominal, for you could have sold the car to another customer or you could do what, in fact, you did do, which was to get your suppliers to release you, and you have suffered no damage.' " (Per Upjohn J. at p. 156.)

As a preamble to adopting the reasoning quoted in the judgments of Hamilton L.J. and Buckley L.J. in *Re Vic Mill Ltd.*, supra, Upjohn J. said at p. 157:

"Apart altogether from authority and statute, it would seem to me on the facts to be quite plain that the plaintiffs' loss in this case is the loss of their bargain. They have sold one Vanguard less than they otherwise would. The plaintiffs, as the defendants must have known, are in business as dealers in motor cars and make their profit in buying and selling motor cars, and what they have lost is their profit on the sale of this Vanguard."

And after reviewing the said judgments, Upjohn J. went on to say at p. 158:

"It seems to me that in principle that covers this case. True the motor car in question was not sold to another purchaser, but the plaintiffs did what was reasonable, they got out of their bargain with George Thompson, Ltd., but they sold one less Vanguard, and lost their profit on that transaction."

Judgment was granted to the plaintiff in the amount of £61 1s. 9d.

In *Charter v. Sullivan*, [1957] 2 Q.B. 117, [1957] 1 All E.R. 809, Jenkins L.J., in turning his attention to s. 50(2), said at p. 814:

> "It remains therefore to ascertain the loss (if any) 'naturally resulting, in the ordinary course of events' from the defendant's breach of contract, and the measure of that loss must, in my opinion, be the amount (if any) of the profit he has lost by reason of the defendant's failure to take and pay for the car he agreed to buy. This accords with the view taken by Upjohn, J., in *W. L. Thompson Ltd. v. R. Robinson (Gunmakers) Ltd.*, and also with the principle stated in *Re Vic Mill Ltd.* [supra], which Upjohn, J., followed and applied."

In addressing himself to that consideration Jenkins L.J. gave great weight to the evidence of the plaintiff's sales manager, Mr. Winter, when he said, "Can sell all Hillman Minx we can get." Jenkins L.J. said at pp. 814-15:

> "The matter therefore stands thus. If the defendant had duly performed his bargain, the plaintiff would have made on that transaction a profit of £97 15s. The calculation accordingly starts with a loss of profit through the defendant's default, of £97 15s. That loss was not cancelled or reduced by the sale of the same car to Mr. Wigley, for, if the defendant had duly taken and paid for the car which he agreed to buy, the plaintiff could have sold another car to Mr. Wigley, in which case there would have been two sales and two profits; see *Re Vic Mill Ltd.* and particularly per Hamilton, L.J., at p. 473, and per Buckley, L.J., at p. 474. The matter does not rest there. The plaintiff must further show that the sum representing the profit which he would have made if the defendant had performed his contract has in fact been lost. Here I think he fails, in view of Mr. Winter's evidence to the effect that the plaintiff could sell all the Hillman Minx cars he could get.
> "I have already expressed my opinion as to the meaning of this statement. It comes, I think, to this, that, according to the plaintiff's own sales manager, the state of trade was such that the plaintiff could always find a purchaser for every Hillman Minx car he could get from the manufacturers; and if that is right it inevitably follows that he sold the same number of cars and made the same number of fixed profits as he would have sold and made if the defendant had duly carried out his bargain.
> "Upjohn, J.'s decision in favour of the plaintiff dealers in *W. L. Thompson Ltd. v. R. Robinson (Gunmakers) Ltd.* was essentially based on the admitted fact that the supply of the cars in question exceeded the demand, and his judgment leaves no room for doubt that, if the demand had exceeded the supply, his decision would have been the other way."

The learned Lord Justice then shortly concluded his judgment in favour of the defendant and in so doing made the following observation which very much parallels that which exists in the case now before me. At p. 816 he said:

> "The materials before the court leave a good deal to be desired. The parties were no doubt pre-occupied with the issue of contract or no contract, and the argument in regard to damages based on *Thompson v. Robinson* was perhaps something of an afterthought...".

Sellers L.J. also delivered a judgment in *Charter v. Sullivan*, supra. He reached the same conclusion as Jenkins L.J. and awarded nominal damages of 40s. Relevant portions of his judgment are as follows [p. 817]:

> "If a seller can prove that a profit has been irretrievably lost on a sale of goods by the buyer's default, it would in my opinion be recoverable as damages in accordance with s.50(2). But where there has in fact been a resale of the goods,

the seller has the burden of proving a loss of profit beyond that which on the face of it has been recouped in whole or in part by the resale. In my view the plaintiff has failed to give adequate proof of such a loss in this case. The sales manager for the plaintiff said that he had lost the sale of a car, but he also said that he could sell all the Hillman Minx cars he could get. It was argued that the statement that he could sell all the cars he could get ought not to be taken literally, but should be qualified in some way. Even if that is so, which I see, on the evidence, no reason to concede, it does not establish affirmative evidence that the plaintiff could get all the Hillman Minx cars he could sell.

"If it could be proved that there were in effect unlimited supplies of Hillman Minx cars and a limited number of buyers in the circumstances in which a dealer was trading, then it would appear that the dealer could establish a loss of profit which could not be mitigated."

In his consideration of *W. L. Thompson Ltd. v. R. Robinson (Gunmakers) Ltd.*, supra, Sellers L.J. said at p. 818:

"On those facts the learned judge in my view was right in saying that the plaintiffs had lost a customer and thereby a profit. There was no point in their keeping the car and awaiting a resale, as they could acquire a Vanguard car to meet each purchaser as he presented himself. They could not, in other words, avoid their loss. The reasoning of Hamilton, L.J., and Buckley, L.J., in *Re Vic Mill Ltd.*, [1913] 1 Ch. 465 at 473, 474, quoted by the judge is singularly apt and adaptable to this case. Upjohn, J., [1955] 1 All E.R. 154 at 160, states the possible extreme situations: one, where in the case of rejection 'if any purchaser fell out, there were many waiting to take his place', the other:

" 'But on the assumed facts, circumstances had changed in relation to Vanguard motor cars, and in March, 1954, there was not a demand in the East Riding which could readily absorb all the Vanguard motor cars available for sale.'

"Whether the plaintiff could have proved a similar situation with regard to the Hillman Minx cars in his area I do not know, but I cannot find that it was either admitted or proved. It is for this reason that I would allow this appeal."

It now becomes a matter of my relating the facts in the instant situation to the foregoing English decisions. I have not located a case in this country where the point has received consideration. As I have already intimated, counsels' preoccupation with the question of breach of contract precluded an in-depth consideration of the matter of damages. The president and general manager of the plaintiff company, K. O. Magnuson, gave the following evidence, the "third party" referred to by him being the party who ultimately purchased the vehicle ordered by the defendant:

"Q. Now in connection with this third party, supposing that Mr. Bayda had picked up the car that he had ordered, would you have been able to supply the third party with a car? A. Yes, we would.

"Q. How? A. If not one out of stock we could have special ordered another one.

"Q. You could have ordered another one from the Ford Company? A. Correct."

Meagre as that evidence is, it does indicate to me that, at the relevant time, the existing situation at North Battleford was that the supply of Mustang automobiles, either in the plaintiff's stock or through order from the manufacturer, exceeded the demand for same. That is to say, the plaintiff has given evidence which stands uncontradicted that it had a supply of vehicles at hand and others close at hand, to meet all willing customers presenting themselves at its place of business. The situation in this regard was similar to that found to exist in *Re Vic Mill Ltd.* and *W. L. Thompson*

Ltd. v. R. Robinson (Gunmakers)Ltd., supra, and opposite as to supply and demand existing in *Charter v. Sullivan*, supra. Adopting the consistent reasoning of all three decisions, however, the plaintiff is entitled to judgment against the defendant for the amount of profit lost as a result of the defendant's breach of contract. That amount, once determined, will be "the estimated loss directly and naturally resulting in the ordinary course of events from the buyer's breach of contract": per s. 429(2) of The Sale of Goods Act.

The determination of the amount of profit so lost has required the consideration of a number of factors. The plaintiff suggests that it should be the difference between the purchase price paid by it to the factory of $4,075 and the contractual selling price to the defendant of $4,686.40, or $611.40. I do not see it that way for the following reason: the $4,686.40 was to have come from a cash payment of $2,935.78 (excluding provincial sales tax) and a trade-in allowance on a 1966 Dodge two-door hardtop motor vehicle of $1,750.62. Mr. Magnuson conceded, however, that the trade-in might have sold for as little as $1,500. In that event the plaintiff's profit would be reduced by $250.62 or down to $360.78. That is the amount of the judgment ($360.78) that I award to the plaintiff by way of damages and it will have its costs of the action based upon the amount so recovered. I appreciate that Mr. Magnuson testified that where a trade-in is involved the amount of profit is "debatable because we might have to trade two or three cars to come out but on the other hand we may have sold this car immediately". That rather nebulous statement, however, does not give me a basis for fixing the amount to be recovered at a figure other than as above stated.

QUESTIONS

1. Do you think that the plaintiff was fairly compensated here?

2. Do you think that the distinction between the cases of *Thompson v. Robinson* and *Charter v. Sullivan* is valid? Is it true that a seller would not, in both cases, sell one less vehicle than he would otherwise sell?

3. Do you think that the result would be the same if the contract involved a used car?

4. Do you think that it is relevant that 57% of the judgment of Hughes D.C.J., is a direct quote from text-book writers and other judges?

———————

It is clear that while Lord Atkinson's principle can be simply stated and appears to be clear, there are problems of applying it in concrete cases. To suggest that we are interested in compensating the plaintiff does not always provide a clear answer to each case. What we need are some ways of talking about what compensation is and what it might mean to put the plaintiff in the same position that he would have been in had the contract been performed. The extract that follows is an attempt to provide tools for discussing these issues. The article has had an immense influence on the development of American law, and is one of the most famous articles ever written. As we shall see, Canadian and English courts have yet to adopt any of the analytical methods that are proposed.

FULLER AND PERDUE, "THE RELIANCE INTEREST IN CONTRACT DAMAGES"

(1936), 46 Yale L. Rev., pp. 52-68.

[Footnotes appear at the conclusion of this article.]

The proposition that legal rules can be understood only with reference to the purposes they serve would today scarcely be regarded as an exciting truth. The notion that law exists as a means to an end has been commonplace for at least half a century. There is, however, no justification for assuming, because this attitude has now achieved respectability, and even triteness, that it enjoys a pervasive application in practice. Certainly there are even today few legal treatises of which it may be said that the author has throughout clearly defined the purposes which his definitions and distinctions serve. We are still all too willing to embrace the conceit that it is possible to manipulate legal concepts without the orientation which comes from the simple inquiry: toward what end is this activity directed? Nietzsche's observation, that the most common stupidity consists in forgetting what one is trying to do, retains a discomforting relevance to legal science.

In no field is this more true than in that of damages. In the assessment of damages the law tends to be conceived, not as a purposive ordering of human affairs, but as a kind of juristic mensuration. The language of the decisions sounds in terms not of command but of discovery. We *measure* the *extent* of the injury; we *determine* whether it was *caused* by the defendant's act; we *ascertain* whether the plaintiff has included the *same item* of damage twice in his complaint. One unfamiliar with the unstated premises which language of this sort conceals might almost be led to suppose that Rochester produces some ingenious instrument by which these calculations are accomplished.

It is, as a matter of fact, clear that the things which the law of damages purports to "measure" and "determine" — the "injuries", "items of damage", "causal connections", etc. — are in considerable part its own creations, and that the process of "measuring" and "determining" them is really a part of the process of creating them. This is obvious when courts work on the periphery of existing doctrine, but it is no less true of fundamental and established principles. For example, one frequently finds the "normal" rule of contract damages (which awards to the promisee the value of the expectancy, "the lost profit") treated as a mere corollary of a more fundamental principle, that the purpose of granting damages is to make "compensation" for injury.[1] Yet in this case we "compensate" the plaintiff by giving him something he never had. This seems on the face of things a queer kind of "compensation". We can, to be sure, make the term "compensation" seem appropriate by saying that the defendant's breach "deprived" the plaintiff of the expectancy. But this is in essence only a metaphorical statement of the effect of the legal rule. In actuality the loss which the plaintiff suffers (deprivation of the expectancy) is not a datum of nature but the reflection of a normative order. It appears as a "loss" only by reference to an unstated *ought*. Consequently, when the law gauges damages by the value of the promised performance it is not merely measuring a quantum, but is seeking an end, however vaguely conceived this end may be.

It is for this reason that it is impossible to separate the law of contract damages from the larger body of motives and policies which constitutes the general law of contracts. It is, unfortunately for the simplicity of our subject, impossible to assume that the purposive and policy-directed element of contract law has been exhausted in the rules which define contract and breach. If this were possible the law of contract damages would indeed be simple, and we would have but one measure of recovery for all contracts. Of course this is not the case. What considerations influence the setting up of different measures of recovery for different kinds of contracts? What factors explain the rather numerous exceptions to the normal rule which measures damages by the value of the expectancy? It is clear that these questions cannot be answered without an inquiry into the reasons which underlie (or may underlie) the enforcement of promises generally.

In our own discussion we shall attempt first an analysis of the purposes which may be pursued in awarding contract damages or in "enforcing" contracts generally; then we shall attempt to inquire to what extent, and under what circumstances, these purposes have found expression in the decisions and doctrinal discussions. As the title suggests, the primary emphasis will be on what we call "the reliance interest" as a possible measure of recovery in suits for breach of contract.

The Purposes Pursued in Awarding Contract Damages

It is convenient to distinguish three principal purposes which may be pursued in awarding contract damages. These purposes, and the situations in which they become appropriate, may be stated briefly as follows:

First, the plaintiff has in reliance on the promise of the defendant conferred some value on the defendant. The defendant fails to perform his promise. The court may force the defendant to disgorge the value he received from the plaintiff. The object here may be termed the prevention of gain by the defaulting promisor at the expense of the promisee; more briefly, the prevention of unjust enrichment. The interest protected may be called the *restitution interest*. For our present purposes it is quite immaterial how the suit in such a case be classified, whether as contractual or quasi-contractual, whether as a suit to enforce the contract or as a suit based upon a rescission of the contract. These questions relate to the superstructure of the law, not to the basic policies with which we are concerned.

Secondly, the plaintiff has in reliance on the promise of the defendant changed his position. For example, the buyer under a contract for the sale of land has incurred expense in the investigation of the seller's title, or has neglected the opportunity to enter other contracts. We may award damages to the plaintiff for the purpose of undoing the harm which his reliance on the defendant's promise has caused him. Our object is to put him in as good a position as he was in before the promise was made. The interest protected in this case may be called the *reliance interest*.

Thirdly, without insisting on reliance by the promisee or enrichment of the promisor, we may seek to give the promisee the value of the expectancy which the promise created. We may in a suit for specific performance actually compel the defendant to render the promised performance to the plaintiff, or, in a suit for damages, we may make the defendant pay the money value of this performance. Here our object is to put the plaintiff in as good a position as he would have occupied had the defendant performed his promise. The interest protected in this case we may call the *expectation interest.*

It will be observed that what we have called the *restitution interest* unites two elements: (1) reliance by the promisee, (2) a resultant gain to the promisor. It may for some purposes be necessary to separate these elements. In some cases a defaulting promisor may after his breach be left with an unjust gain which was not taken from the promisee (a third party furnished the consideration), or which was not the result of reliance by the promisee (the promisor violated a promise not to appropriate the promisee's goods). Even in those cases where the promisor's gain results from the promisee's reliance it may happen that damages will be assessed somewhat differently, depending on whether we take the promisor's gain or the promisee's loss as the standard of measurement.[2] Generally, however, in the cases we shall be discussing, gain by the promisor will be accompanied by a corresponding and, so far as its legal measurement is concerned, identical loss to the promisee, so that for our purposes the most workable classification is one which presupposes in the restitution interest a correlation of promisor's gain and promisee's loss. If, as we shall assume, the gain involved in the restitution interest results from and is identical with the plaintiff's loss through reliance, then the restitution interest is merely a special case of the reliance interest; all of the cases coming under the restitution interest will be covered by the reliance interest, and the reliance interest will be broader than the restitution interest only to the extent that it includes cases where the plaintiff has relied on the defendant's promise without enriching the defendant.

It should not be supposed that the distinction here taken between the reliance and expectation interests coincides with that sometimes taken between "losses caused" (damnum emergens) and "gains prevented" (lucrum cessans). In the first place, though reliance ordinarily results in "losses" of an affirmative nature (expenditures of labor and money) it is also true that opportunities for gain may be foregone in reliance on a promise. Hence the reliance interest must be interpreted as at least potentially covering "gains prevented" as well as "losses caused". (Whether "gains prevented" through reliance on a promise are properly compensable in damages is a question not here determined. Obviously, certain scruples concerning "causality" and "foreseeability" are suggested. It is enough for our present purpose to note that there is nothing in the definition of the reliance interest itself which would exclude items of this sort from consideration.)[3] On the other hand, it is not possible to make the expectation interest entirely synonymous with "gains prevented". The disappointment of an expectancy often entails losses of a positive character.[4]

It is obvious that the three "interests" we have distinguished do not present equal claims to judicial intervention. It may be assumed that ordinary standards of justice would regard the need for judicial intervention as decreasing in the order in which we have listed the three interests. The "restitution interest," involving a combination of unjust impoverishment with unjust gain, presents the strongest case for relief. If, following Aristotle, we regard the purpose of justice as the maintenance of an equilibrium of goods among members of society, the restitution interest presents twice as strong a claim to judicial intervention as the reliance interest, since if A not only causes B to lose one unit but appropriates that unit to himself, the resulting discrepancy between A and B is not one unit but two.[5]

On the other hand, the promisee who has actually relied on the promise, even though he may not thereby have enriched the promisor, certainly presents a more pressing case for relief than the promisee who merely demands satisfaction for his disappointment in not getting what was promised him. In passing from compensation for change of position to compensation for loss of expectancy we pass, to use Aristotle's terms again, from the realm of corrective justice to that of distributive justice. The law no longer seeks merely to heal a disturbed status quo, but to bring into being a new situation. It ceases to act defensively or restoratively, and assumes a more active role. With the transition, the justification for legal relief loses its self-evident quality. It is as a matter of fact no easy thing to explain why the normal rule of contract recovery should be that which measures damages by the value of the promised performance. Since this "normal rule" throws its shadow across our whole subject it will be necessary to examine the possible reasons for its existence. It may be said parenthetically that the discussion which follows, though directed primarily to the normal measure of recovery where damages are sought, also has relevance to the more general question, why should a promise which has not been relied on ever be enforced at all, whether by a decree of specific performance or by an award of damages?

It should also be said that our discussion of "reasons" does not claim to coincide in all particulars with the actual workings of the judicial mind, certainly not with those of any single judicial mind. It is unfortunately very difficult to discuss the possible reasons for rules of law without unwittingly conveying the impression that these "reasons" are the things which control the daily operations of the judicial process. This has had the consequence, at a time when men stand in dread of being labelled "unrealistic", that we have almost ceased to talk about reasons altogether. Those who find unpalatable the rationalistic flavor of what follows are invited to view what they read not as law but as an excursus into legal philosophy, and to make whatever discount that distinction may seem to them to dictate.

WHY SHOULD THE LAW EVER PROTECT THE EXPECTATION INTEREST?

Perhaps the most obvious answer to this question is one which we may label "psychological". This answer would run something as follows: The breach of a promise arouses in the promisee a sense of injury. This feeling is not confined to cases where the promisee has relied on the promise. Whether or not he has actually changed his position because of the promise, the promisee has formed an attitude of expectancy such that a breach of the promise causes him to feel that he has been "deprived" of something which was "his". Since this sentiment is a relatively uniform one, the law has no occasion to go back of it. It accepts it as a datum and builds its rule about it.

The difficulty with this explanation is that the law does in fact go back of the sense of injury which the breach of a promise engenders. No legal system attempts to invest with juristic sanction all promises. Some rule or combination of rules effects a sifting out for enforcement of those promises deemed important enough to society to justify the law's concern with them. Whatever the principles which control this sifting out process may be, they are not convertible into terms of the degree of resentment which the breach of a particular kind of promise arouses. Therefore, though it may be assumed that the impulse to assuage disappointment is one shared by those who make and influence the law, this impulse can hardly be regarded as the key which solves the whole problem of the protection accorded by the law to the expectation interest.

A second possible explanation for the rule protecting the expectancy may be found in the much-discussed "will theory" of contract law. This theory views the contracting parties as exercising, so to speak, a legislative power, so that the legal enforcement of a contract becomes merely an implementing by the state of a kind of private law already established by the parties. If A has made, in proper form, a promise to pay B one thousand dollars, we compel A to pay this sum simply because the rule or *lex* set up by the parties calls for this payment...

It is not necessary to discuss here the contribution which the will theory is capable of making to a philosophy of contract law. Certainly some borrowings from the theory are discernable in most attempts to rationalize the bases of contract liability. It is enough to note here that while the will theory undoubtedly has some bearing on the problem of contract damages, it cannot be regarded as dictating in all cases a recovery of the expectancy. If a contract represents a kind of private law, it is a law which usually says nothing at all about what shall be done when it is violated. A contract is in this respect like an imperfect statute which provides no penalties, and which leaves it to the courts to find a way to effectuate its purposes. There would, therefore, be no necessary contradiction between the will theory and a rule which limited damages to the reliance interest. Under such a rule the penalty for violating the norm established by the contract would simply consist in being compelled to compensate the other party for detrimental reliance. Of course there may be cases where the parties have so obviously anticipated that a certain form of judicial relief will be given that we can, without stretching things, say that by implication they have "willed" that this relief should be given. This attitude finds a natural application to promises to pay a definite sum of money. But certainly as to most types of contracts it is vain to expect from the will theory a ready-made solution for the problem of damages.

A third and more promising solution of our difficulty lies in an economic or institutional approach. The essence of a credit economy lies in the fact that it tends to eliminate the distinction between present and future (promised) goods. Expectations of future values become, for purposes of trade, present values. In a society in which credit has become a significant and pervasive institution, it is inevitable that the expectancy created by an enforceable promise should be regarded as a kind of property, and breach of the promise as an injury to that property. In such a society the breach of a promise works an "actual" diminution of the promisee's assets — "actual" in the sense that it would be so appraised according to modes of thought which enter into the very fiber of our economic system. That the promisee had not "used" the property which the promise represents (had not relied on the promise) is as immaterial as the question whether the plaintiff in trespass *quare clausum fregit* was using his property at the time it was encroached upon. The analogy to ordinary forms of property goes further, for even in a suit for trespass the recovery is really for an expectancy, an expectancy of possible future uses. Where the property expectancy is limited (as where the plaintiff has only an estate for years) the recovery is reduced accordingly.[6] Ordinary property differs from a contract right chiefly in the fact that it lies within the power of more persons to work a direct injury to the expectancy it represents. It is generally only the promisor or some one working through or upon him who is able to injure the contract expectancy in a direct enough manner to make expedient legal intervention.

The most obvious objection which can be made to the economic or institutional explanation is that it involves a *petitio principii*. A promise has present value, why? Because the law enforces it. "The expectancy," regarded as a present value, is not the cause of legal intervention but the consequence of it. This objection may be reinforced by a reference to legal history. Promises were enforced long before there was anything corresponding to a general system of "credit", and recovery was from the beginning measured by the value of the promised performance, the "agreed price". It may therefore be argued that the "credit system" when it finally emerged was itself in large part built on the foundations of a juristic development which preceded it.

The view just suggested asserts the primacy of law over economics; it sees law not as the creature but as the creator of social institutions. The shift of emphasis thus implied suggests the possibility of a fourth explanation for the law's protection of the unrelied-on expectancy, which we may call *juristic*. This explanation would seek a justification for the normal rule of recovery in some policy consciously pursued by courts and other lawmakers. It would assume that courts have protected the expectation interest because they have considered it wise to do so, not through a blind acquiescence in habitual ways of thinking and feeling, or through an equally blind deference to the individual will. Approaching the problem from this point of view, we are forced to find not a mere explanation for the rule in the form of some sentimental, volitional, or institutional datum, but articulate reasons for its existence.

What reasons can be advanced? In the first place, even if our interest were confined to protecting promisees against an out-of-pocket loss, it would still be possible to justify the rule granting the value of the expectancy, both as a cure for, and as a prophylaxis against, losses of this sort.

It is a cure for these losses in the sense that it offers the measure of recovery most likely to reimburse the plaintiff for the (often very numerous and very difficult to prove) individual acts and forbearances which make up his total reliance on the contract. It we take into account "gains prevented" by reliance, that is, losses involved in foregoing the opportunity to enter other contracts, the notion that the rule protecting the expectancy is adopted as the most effective means of compensating for detrimental reliance seems not at all far-fetched. Physicians with an extensive practice often charge their patients the full office call fee for broken appointments. Such a charge looks on the face of things like a claim to the promised fee; it seems to be based on the "expectation interest". Yet the physician making the charge will quite justifiably regard it as compensation for the loss of the opportunity to gain a similar fee from a different patient. This foregoing of other opportunities is involved to some extent in entering most contracts, and the impossibility of subjecting this type of reliance to any kind of measurement may justify a categorical rule granting the value of the expectancy as the most effective way of compensating for such losses.

The rule that the plaintiff must after the defendant's breach take steps to mitigate damages tends to corroborate the suspicion that there lies hidden behind the protection of the expectancy a concern to compensate the plaintiff for the loss of the opportunity to enter other contracts. Where after the defendant's breach the opportunity remains open to the plaintiff to sell his services or goods elsewhere, or to fill his needs from another source, he is bound to embrace that opportunity. Viewed in this way the rule of "avoidable harms" is a qualification on the protection accorded the expectancy, since it means that the plaintiff, in those cases where it is applied, is protected only to the extent that he has in reliance on the contract foregone other equally advantageous opportunities for accomplishing the same end.

But, as we have suggested, the rule measuring damages by the expectancy may also be regarded as a prophylaxis against the losses resulting from detrimental reliance. Whatever tends to discourage breach of contract tends to prevent the losses occasioned through reliance. Since the expectation interest furnishes a more easily administered measure of recovery than the reliance interest, it will in practice offer a more effective sanction against contract breach. It is therefore possible to view the rule measuring damages by the expectancy in a quasi-criminal aspect, its purpose being not so much to compensate the promisee as to penalize breach of promise by the promisor. The rule enforcing the unrelied-on promise finds the same justification, on this theory, as an ordinance which fines a man for driving through a stop-light when no other vehicle is in sight.

In seeking justification for the rule granting the value of the expectancy there is no need, however, to restrict ourselves by the assumption, hitherto made, that the rule can only be intended to cure or prevent the losses caused by reliance. A justification can be developed from a less negative point of view. It may be said that there is not only a policy in favor of preventing and undoing the harms resulting from reliance, but also a policy in favor of promoting and facilitating reliance on business agreements. As in the case of the stop-light ordinance we are interested not only in preventing collisions but in speeding traffic. Agreements can accomplish little, either for their makers or for society, unless they are made the basis for action. When business agreements are not only made but are also acted on, the division of labor is facilitated, goods find their way to the places where they are most needed, and economic activity is generally stimulated. These advantages would be threatened by any rule which limited legal protection to the reliance interest. Such a rule would in practice tend to discourage reliance. The difficulties in proving reliance and subjecting it to pecuniary measurement are such that the business man knowing, or sensing, that these obstacles stood in the way of judicial relief would hesitate to rely on a promise in any case where the legal sanction was of significance to him. To encourage reliance we must therefore dispense with its proof. For this reason it has been found wise to make recovery on a promise independent of reliance, both in the sense that in some cases the promise is enforced though not relied on (as in the bilateral business agreement) and in the sense that recovery is not limited to the detriment incurred in reliance.

The juristic explanation in its final form is then twofold. It rests the protection accorded the expectancy on (1) the need for curing and preventing the harms occasioned by reliance, and (2) on the need for facilitating reliance on business agreements. From this spelling out of a possible juristic explanation, it is clear that there is no incompatibility between it and the economic or institutional explanation. They view the same phenomenon from two different aspects. The essence of both of them lies in the word "credit." The economic explanation views credit from its institutional side; the juristic explanation views it from its rational side. The economic view sees credit as an accepted way of living; the juristic view invites us to explore the considerations of utility which underlie this way of living, and the part which conscious human direction has played in bringing it into being.

The way in which these two points of view supplement one another becomes clearer when we examine separately the economic implications of the two aspects of the juristic explanation. If we rest the legal argument for measuring damages by the expectancy on the ground that this procedure offers the most satisfactory means of compensating the plaintiff for the loss of other opportunities to contract, it is clear that the force of the argument will depend entirely upon the existing economic environment. It would be most forceful in a hypothetical society in which all values were available on the market and where all markets were "perfect" in the economic sense. In such a society there would be no difference between the reliance interest and the expectation interest. The plaintiff's loss in foregoing to enter another contract would be identical with the expectation value of the contract he did make. The argument that granting the value of the expectancy merely compensates for that loss, loses force to the extent that actual conditions depart from those of such a hypothetical society. These observations make it clear why the development of open markets for goods tends to carry in its wake the view that a contract claim is a kind of property, a conception which — for all the importance he attached to it — MacLeod seemed to regard as the product of a kind of legal miracle. He who by entering one contract passes by the opportunity to accomplish the same end elsewhere will not be inclined to regard contract breach lightly or as a mere matter of private morality. The consciousness of what is foregone reinforces the notion that the contract creates a "right" and that the contract claim is itself a species of property.

If, on the other hand, we found the juristic explanation on the desire to promote reliance on contracts, it is not difficult again to trace a correspondence between the legal view and the actual conditions of economic life. In general our courts and our economic institutions attribute special significance to the same types of promises. The bilateral business agreement is, generally speaking, the only type of informal contract our courts are willing to enforce without proof that reliance has occurred — simply for the sake of facilitating reliance. This is, by no accident, precisely the kind of contract (the "exchange", "bargain", "trade", "deal") which furnishes the indispensable and pervasive framework for the "unmanaged" portions of our economic activity.

The inference is therefore justified that the ends of the law of contracts and those of our economic system show an essential correspondence. One may explain this either on the ground that the law (mere superstructure and ideology) reflects inertly the conditions of economic life, or on the ground that economic activity has fitted itself into the rational framework of the law. Neither explanation would be true. In fact we are dealing with a situation in which law and society have interacted. The law measures damages by the expectancy *in part* because society views the expectancy as a present value; society views the expectancy as a present value *in part* because the law (for reasons more or less consciously articulated) gives protection to the expectancy....

It is not difficult to demonstrate that the judicial treatment accorded contracts is affected by the relation between the particular contract and what we have called "the credit system." The ideal contract from the standpoint of the credit system is the (bargain) promise to pay money. Here we find a combination of legal qualities which reflects the intimate association of this type of contract with the economic institution of credit: free alienation by the creditor; free substitution of another's performance by the debtor; easy convertibility between present and future claims, the difference being measured by interest; damages measured by a mechanical standard which excludes consideration of the peculiarities of the particular situation; finally, damages measured by the expectancy, with no tendency to substitute a different measure.

If it were not for certain complicating cross currents we might expect to find a uniform increase in the tendency to remit the plaintiff to the reliance interest as we progress away from the credit system. This would come about in two ways, both of which may be illustrated in the contract to adopt. (1) The farther removed a contract is from the credit system the more difficult it is to measure the value of the expectancy. (2) The farther removed a contract is from the credit system, the less is the judicial incentive to grant the expectancy, the less pressing are the basic policies which justify the granting of the expectancy in the ordinary business agreement.

We have referred to complicating factors which prevent a steady increase in the tendency to depart from the rule granting the expectancy as we progress away from the credit system. The chief of these lies in the fact that courts have a natural preference for the rule of recovery which offers the most easily administered standard. This factor has a peculiar relevance to promises coming under § 90 of the Restatement, where the expectancy is generally a definite sum of money. An attempt to trace the influence of this factor will be undertaken in the next section.

THE DIVERGENCE OF MEASURE AND MOTIVE AND THE PROBLEM OF MIXED MOTIVES

We have already intimated the nature of the principal difficulty which is encountered in any analysis of the purposes of contract law. This difficulty consists in the fact that it is impossible to assume that when a court enforces a promise it necessarily pursues only one purpose and protects one "interest", or that the purpose or interest which forms the rationale of the court's action necessarily furnishes the measure of the promisee's recovery. In actuality not only may a court consider itself in a given case as vindicating more than one of the three contract "interests" we have distinguished, but even where it is reasonable to suppose that a single interest furnishes the exclusive *raison d'être* of legal intervention it is still possible that for reasons of convenience and certainty the court may choose a measure of recovery which differs from that suggested by the interest protected.

A difficulty in identifying the "ultimate" motives for enforcing contracts exist even as to the earliest stages of legal history. Without attempting to review here what is known concerning the early history of contract, it may safely be said that in England, in Rome, and perhaps generally in primitive law, a place of favor was accorded what may be called the real contract, the "delivery-promise," or the half-completed exchange. In reliance on a promise by the defendant to pay a named price the plaintiff confers some benefit on the defendant; the defendant fails to pay, and the plaintiff brings suit for the agreed price. This is, in outline form, the real contract. Not only was this the situation where in the absence of formalities courts were most willing to intervene, but it is probable that some such transaction originally furnished an indispensable factual core for most formal contracts.

So long as the law confines its intervention to this situation (or to the extent that it grants certain remedies only in this situation) it would seem that the fundamental purpose of the law is the prevention of unjust enrichment, since enrichment of the promisor at the expense of the promisee is the *sine qua non* of judicial interference. Yet though the prevention of unjust enrichment may seem to supply the underlying rationale of legal intervention in the case of the real contract, the measure of recovery was, as we know, from the very beginning the promised price, the expectancy. Various explanations may be given for this apparent discrepancy between the conditions under which liability was imposed and the terms of the liability itself. Even if it were granted that the sole purpose pursued by the courts was the prevention of unjust enrichment it would be possible to regard the promised price as the most obvious and most simple method of measuring the extent of that enrichment, particularly in an age which veered away from any kind of legal relief which involved estimation. If this is the proper explanation for the measure of damages in real contracts we have in them an illustration of the divergence of measure and motive; or, to speak with less attempt at epigram, a case where though the fundamental motive was prevention of unjust enrichment the court was moved to substitute for the measure which that purpose would normally dictate a simpler and more easily administered measure.

---

1. "In fixing the amount of these damages, the general purpose of the law is, and should be, to give compensation: — that is, to put the plaintiff in as good a position as he would have been in had the defendant kept his contract." 3 WILLISTON, CONTRACTS (1920) §1338.

2. Thus in *Johnston v. Star Bucket Pump Co.*, 274 Mo. 414, 202 S. W. 1143 (1918), a building contractor was allowed to recover in quantum meruit for part performance a sum considerably larger than his out-of-pocket loss. The discrepancy between the reasonable value of his part performance and its actual cost to him arose from the fact that he had made very favorable contracts with subcontractors. In such a case the restitution interest (if we mean by that, compelling the defendant to disgorge) is broader than the reliance interest. It should be pointed out, however, that in a suit for "damages" asking reimbursement for reliance plus the lost profit (RESTATEMENT, CONTRACTS (1932) §333) the saving on the subcontracts, which in the *Johnston* case was reflected in an increased "reasonable value" of the plaintiff's performance, would have been reflected in the lost profit.

In *Cincinnati Siemens Lungren Gas Illuminating Co. v. Western Siemens Lungren Co.*, 152 U. S. 200 (1893), damages for breach of a contract not to compete were restricted to the profit realized by the party guilty of breach. It was assumed, however, that the promisee's loss was at least equal to the defaulter's gain, and the limitation of recovery to the defaulter's profit was imposed partly on the ground that there existed no adequate factual basis for determining the business lost to the promisee. In 6 DEMOGUE, TRAITE DES OBLIGATIONS (1931) §287, the view is expressed that the gain of the defaulter is acceptable as a measure of damages only as a kind of surrogate for the more usual rule measuring damages by the creditor's prospective gain.

3. The German Civil Code limits relief on contract in certain situations to the "negative" (i.e. reliance) interest. The "negative interest" is assumed to cover gains prevented (*entgangener Gewinn*) as well as positive losses. See the annotation to §122 in BUSCH, DAS BÜGERLICHE GESETZBUCH (1929). But apparently the loss of the particular gain must under the circumstances have been foreseeable as a probable consequence of the contract. See §252 and its annotation.

4. For example, in *Eastern Advertising Co. v. Shapiro*, 263 Mass. 228, 161 N. E. 240 (1928), the defendant's failure to take advertising space on certain billboards made it necessary for the plaintiff to expend money in placing "fillers" on the boards.

5. ARISTOTLE, NICOMACHEAN ETHICS, 1132*a*-1132*b*.

6. Commons remarks that MacLeod's view of a debt as an economic commodity was "so strange to the economists that they could not understand it.... Its strangeness to the classical economists consisted in that it contained Futurity as one of its dimensions, as well as the use-value and scarcity value of the older schools. Yet futurity is the essence of the ownership side of a commodity, which they had taken for granted." INSTITUTIONAL ECONOMICS (1934) 394.

[An alternative discussion of the same issues is found in Dobbs, *Remedies*, pp. 786-795.]

The extract that follows presents a slightly different point of view. This extract is part of a larger discussion of the law of contracts from an economic point of view. This is, in turn, part of an economic analysis of law as a whole. This is currently a popular topic for discussion. We shall return to it throughout this work to see how helpful such an analysis can be. Those with an economic background will find this of particular interest. It will be important for anyone who wants to understand the law of contract to be aware of economic ways of looking at problems just as much as ethical or even moral ways.

POSNER, ECONOMIC ANALYSIS OF LAW

(2nd ed. 1973) pp. 88-93.

[Footnotes appear at the conclusion of this article.]

§4.9   FUNDAMENTAL PRINCIPLES OF CONTRACT DAMAGES

When a breach of contract is established, the issue becomes one of the proper remedy.[1] A starting point for analysis is Holmes's view that it is not the policy of the law to compel adherence to contracts but only to require each party to choose between performing in accordance with the contract and compensating the other party for any injury resulting from a failure to perform.[2] This view contains an important economic insight. In many cases it is uneconomical to induce the completion of a contract after it has been breached. I agree to purchase 100,000 widgets custom-ground for use as components in a machine that I manufacture. After I have taken delivery of

10,000, the market for my machine collapses. I promptly notify my supplier that I am terminating the contract, and admit that my termination is a breach of the contract. When notified of the termination he has not yet begun the custom grinding of the other 90,000 widgets, but he informs me that he intends to complete his performance under the contract and bill me accordingly. The custom-ground widgets have no use other than in my machine, and a negligible scrap value. Plainly, to grant the supplier any remedy that induced him to complete the contract after the breach would result in a waste of resources. The law is alert to this danger and, under the doctrine of mitigation of damages, would refuse to permit the supplier to recover any costs he incurred in continuing production after my notice of termination.

Let us change the facts. I need 100,000 custom-ground widgets for my machine but the supplier, after producing 50,000, is forced to suspend production because of a mechanical failure. Other suppliers are in a position to supply the remaining widgets that I need, but I insist that the original supplier complete his performance of the contract. If the law compels completion, the supplier will probably have to make arrangements with other widget producers to complete his contract with me. But it may be more costly for him to procure an alternative supplier than for me to do so directly; indeed, were it cheaper for him than for me, he would do it voluntarily in order to minimize his liability for breach of contract. To compel completion of the contract would again result in a waste of resources and again the law does not compel completion but remits the victim to a simple damages remedy.

The problem exposed in the foregoing example is a quite general one. It results from the fact, remarked earlier, that contract remedies are frequently invoked in cases where there is no presumption that an exchange pursuant to the (defective) contract would in fact increase value (for example, cases of defective communication). Here we clearly do not want a remedy that will induce the party made liable to complete the exchange.

The objective of giving the party to a contract an incentive to fulfill his promise unless the result would be an inefficient use of resources (the production of the unwanted widgets in the first example, the roundabout procurement of a substitute supplier in the second) can usually be achieved by allowing the victim of a breach to recover his expected profit on the transaction. If the supplier in the first example receives his expected profit from completing the 10,000 widgets, he will have no incentive to produce the remaining 90,000. We do not want him to produce them; no one wants them. In the second example, if I receive my expected profit from dealing with the original supplier, I become indifferent to whether he completes his performance.

In these examples the breach was in a sense involuntary. It was committed only to avert a larger loss. The breaching party would have been happier had there been no occasion to commit a breach. But in some cases a party would be tempted to breach the contract simply because his profit from breach would exceed his expected profit from completion of the contract. If his profit from breach would also exceed the expected profit to the other party from completion of the contract, and if damages are limited to loss of expected profit, there will be an incentive to commit a breach. There should be. The opportunity cost of completion to the breaching party is the profit that he would make from a breach, and if it is greater than his profit from completion, then completion will involve a loss to him. If that loss is greater than the gain to the other party from completion, breach would be value-maximizing and should be encouraged. And because the victim of the breach is made whole for his loss, he is indifferent; hence encouraging breaches in these circumstances will not deter people from entering into contracts in the future.

An arithmetical illustration may be helpful here. I sign a contract to deliver 100,000 custom-ground widgets at $.10 apiece to A, for use in his boiler factory. After I have delivered 10,000, B comes to me, explains that he desperately needs 25,000 custom-ground widgets at once since otherwise he will be forced to close his pianola factory at great cost, and offers me $.15 apiece for 25,000 widgets. I sell him the widgets and as a result do not complete timely delivery to A, who sustains $1000 in lost profits from my breach. Having obtained an additional profit of $1250 on the sale to B, I am better off even after reimbursing A for his loss. Society is also better off. Since B was willing to pay me $.15 per widget, it must mean that each widget was worth at least $.15 to him. But it was worth only $.14 to A — the $.10 that he paid plus his expected profit of $.04 ($1000 divided by 25,000). Thus the breach resulted in a transfer of the 25,000 widgets from a less to a more valuable use. To be sure, had I refused to sell to B, he could have gone to A and negotiated an assignment of part of A's contract with me to him. But this would have introduced an additional step and so imposed additional transaction costs.

Thus far the emphasis has been on the economic importance of not awarding damages in excess of the lost expectation. It is equally important, however, not to award less than the expectation loss. Suppose A contracts to sell B for $100,000 a machine that is worth $110,000 to B, i.e., that would yield him a profit of $10,000. Before delivery C comes to A and offers him $109,000 for the machine promised B. A would be tempted to breach were he not liable to B for B's loss of expected profit. Given that measure of damages, C will not be able to induce a breach of A's contract with B unless he offers B more than $110,000, thereby indicating that the machine really is worth more to him than to B. The expectation rule thus assures that the machine ends up where it is most valuable.

In *Groves v. John Wunder Co.*,[3] the defendant, as part of a larger deal, had agreed to level some land owned by the plaintiff, but willfully failed to carry out his agreement. The cost of leveling would have been $60,000 and the value of the land, after leveling, no more than $12,000. The court awarded the plaintiff $60,000, reasoning that he was entitled to get the performance he had contracted for and that it was no business of the defendant whether, or how much, his performance enhanced the market value of the plaintiff's property. However, this was not a case, familiar to us from our discussion of just compensation in the last chapter, where value and market price were different. The land in question was a commercial parcel. If the plaintiff had wanted the performance rather than the $60,000, he would probably have brought an action for specific performance. He did not bring such an action and, even more telling, he did not use the money he won from the defendant to level the land.[4] The measure of damages was incorrect from an economic standpoint because, had it been known to the defendant from the outset, it would have made him indifferent as between breaching his agreement to level the land and performing it, whereas efficiency dictated breach: the $60,000 worth of labor and materials that would have been consumed in leveling the land would have purchased a less than $12,000 increase in value.[5]

The court never alluded to the real economic issue in the case, which was how the contract allocated the risk of a fall in the market for real estate, the Depression of the 1930s having occurred after the contract was signed. Since the plaintiff as owner of the land would have enjoyed the benefit of any general increase in real estate values, the parties probably contemplated that he would also bear the cost of a general decline in those values. The effect of the court's judgment was to give the plaintiff a cushion, for which he had not contracted, against the impact of the Depression on land values.

One superficially attractive alternative to measuring contract damages by loss of expectation (i.e., lost profits) is to measure them by the reliance loss, especially in cases where liability is imposed not to induce performance but to penalize careless behavior. And even in the case where the breach is deliberate, it is arguable that expectation damages may overcompensate the victim of the breach. Suppose I sign a contract to deliver 10,000 widgets in six months, and the day after the contract is signed I default. The buyer's reliance loss — the sum of the costs he has irretrievably incurred as a result of the contract — is, let us say, zero, but his lost profit $1,000. Why should he be allowed to reap a windfall gain by the use of a measure of damages that does not correspond to any actual social cost?

One answer has already been given: the lost-profit measure is necessary to assure that the only breaches made are those that promote efficiency. But there is another answer: that on average, though not in every case, the lost-profit method will give a better approximation than the reliance measure to the actual social costs of contract breach. In long-run competitive equilibrium, the total revenues of the sellers in a market are just equal to their total costs; there are no "profits" in the economic sense. What law and accounting call profits are frequently not profits in that sense at all, but rather reimbursement of the costs of capital, of entrepreneurial effort, and of other inputs. These items of cost are excluded by the reliance measure of damages, which will therefore tend to understate the true social costs of breach.

There are exceptions, however, some sufficiently clear to deserve, and receive, legal recognition. Compare the following cases: (1) A tenant defaults and the landlord promptly rents the property to another tenant at a rental only slightly below that of the defaulting tenant. In a suit against the defaulting tenant for the rental due on the balance of the tenant's lease, should the landlord be required to deduct the rental of the substitute tenant? (2) A manufacturer of widgets receives an order for 1000 widgets from X, but X refuses to accept delivery and the manufacturer resells the widgets to Y at a price only slightly lower than what X had agreed to pay. In a suit against X for the profits that were lost on the sale, should the manufacturer be required to deduct the profits he received on the substitute sale to Y?

The law answers yes in the first case and no in the second, and these answers are correct from an economic standpoint. The good supplied by the landlord is fixed in the short run: he cannot add a room because one more family wants to lease from him. The rental that he receives from the substitute tenant in our first case is a gain *enabled* by the breach of contract by the first tenant.[6] His true loss is, therefore, the difference between the two rentals.[7] But a manufacturer can usually vary his output, at least somewhat, in the short run. X's default did not enable the manufacturer to obtain a profit from selling to Y: if X had not defaulted, the manufacturer could still have supplied Y with 1000 widgets. The profit on the sale to Y is a gain that the manufacturer would have obtained regardless of the default, so his true loss is the entire expected profit from the sale to X.[8]

---

1. For a good discussion of contract remedies from the standpoint of economics see John H. Barton, The Economic Basis of Damages for Breach of Contract, 1 J. Legal Studies 277 (1972).

2. See, e.g., Oliver Wendell Holmes, The Path of the Law, in Collected Legal Papers 167, 175 (1920).

3. 205 Minn. 163, 286 N. W. 235 (1939).

4. See John P. Dawson & William Burnett Harvey, Cases on Contracts and Contract Remedies 12 (2d ed. 1969).

5. Would the defendant in fact have levelled the land had he known what the measure of damages would be? Why not? Does it follow that the economist should be indifferent to the measure of damages in such a case?

6. Must mitigation of damages be required for this damage rule to be efficient?

7. Does this depend on whether all of the other apartments are occupied?

8. A related question is whether overhead expense allocated to a sale should be deducted from damages for breach of contract, on the theory that if the sale falls through, the seller has saved the overhead as well as the direct expense of the sale. As most courts hold, it should not be deducted because it is not in fact saved. Overhead expenses (rent, interest, insurance, etc.) are by definition expenses that do not vary with short-run changes in output. Therefore a reduction in output due to the buyer's breach will not produce a savings in overhead expenses to the seller: his rent, etc., will not be lower just because he did not make the particular sale. The question is incorrectly analyzed in Richard E. Speidel & Kendall O. Clay. Seller's Recovery of Overhead Under UCC Section 2-708(2): Economic Cost Theory and Contract Remedial Policy, 57 Cornell L. Rev. 681 (1972).

QUESTIONS AND PROBLEMS

Re-read *Peevyhouse v. Garland Coal* and *Victory Motors v. Bayda* in the light of the analysis presented by Fuller and Perdue. How would you now analyze those cases?

As you read the cases that follow consider how far the analysis of Fuller and Perdue could help the courts to set out the problems that they face.

SUNSHINE EXPLORATION LTD. v. DOLLY VARDEN MINES LTD. (N.P.L.)

8 D.L.R. (3d) 441, [1970] S.C.R. 2, 70 W.W.R. 418.

[Dolly Varden, the respondent, plaintiff, made a contract with Sunshine, the appellant, defendant, that Sunshine would do certain exploration work on mining property owned by Dolly Varden. The agreement provided for Sunshine to do certain exploratory and developmental work in three stages. If Sunshine completed the first stage it could elect to go on with the second, and, if that was completed, Sunshine would then have a right to participate in the production of the mine. The costs involved in the first two stages (which were at Sunshine's cost) would be recovered from the profits of the mine (should one be developed). To provide security for this deal, Dolly Varden executed a conveyance of a half-interest in the property to Sunshine and Sunshine executed a reconveyance of this to Dolly Varden. This latter agreement was held in escrow, to be delivered to Dolly Varden if Sunshine did not elect to proceed to the second stage or terminated the agreement. Sunshine did some of the work on the first stage and then gave notice that it planned to proceed to the second. Dolly Varden objected that not all the work that should have been done in the first stage was done. The parties then made another agreement under which Sunshine withdrew its notice that it was proceeding to the second stage and, in particular, promised to do work referred to as "Schedule A". Subsequently nothing was done by Sunshine to carry out the work specified in Schedule A.]

Martland J. (delivering the judgment of the court) outlined the facts and continued:

It is admitted, in the argument in this Court, that the agreement came to an end, and that Sunshine was in breach of its contractual obligation to carry out the work prescribed in sch. A which it had agreed to perform.

Dolly Varden commenced action against Sunshine for damages for breach of the agreement. The action was tried between January 30 and February 17, 1967, inclusive. Following the hearing, further documents were filed and argument submitted respecting the consequences of an agreement which took effect on March 9, 1967, between Dolly Varden and Newmont Mining Corporation of Canada Limited (hereinafter referred to as "Newmont").

Briefly, this agreement provided that Dolly Varden would give to Newmont exclusive possession, management and control of the mining properties of Dolly Varden, so as to conduct drilling, exploration and development work thereon. Newmont agreed to conduct a geological survey of the property, in such manner as it decided, and a geophysical survey of such portion of the property as it considered advisable. These surveys were to be completed by December 31, 1967. If this work were completed, as provided, Newmont had the right to terminate the agreement, or to extend its rights for a year, in which event it would be committed to expend not less than $200,000 on or for the benefit of the property. Two further periods of extension, for one year, were similarly provided for, at the option of Newmont, involving expenditure in each year of not less than $300,000. Thereafter Newmont had the right either to terminate the agreement or to equip the property for mining, in which event it would acquire title to the property, for the joint venture. Profits of operation would be divided equally after reimbursement to the parties of their respective expenditures. There was no covenant by Newmont to do the work described in sch. A to the amending agreement with Sunshine.

The learned trial Judge [64 D.L.R. (2d) 283] gave judgment for damages for breach of contract, the award for non-performance of the sch. A work being $314,051 based on evidence as to the cost of performing such work.

Sunshine's appeal from this judgment was dismissed, unanimously, by the Court of Appeal [69 D.L.R. (2d) 209] and a cross-appeal by Dolly Varden seeking an increase in this award was allowed, the damages being increased by $64,976.

The appeal to this Court is based solely on the issue of the measure of damages, it being contended that Dolly Varden had neither proved nor suffered any damage by reason of the non-performance of the sch. A work. It was submitted that it was an error in law to award an amount equivalent to the cost of performance of that work.

The learned trial Judge found, as a fact, that [pp. 316-7]:

> I am of the opinion that the completion of the schedule "A" work was a necessary and economic step in the development of the Torbrit mine.

In the light of this finding and his finding that the officers of Dolly Varden intended the completion of the sch. A work, the learned trial Judge held that the damages should be assessed upon the same basis as was approved by this Court in the case of *Cunningham v. Insinger*, [1924] 2 D.L.R. 433, [1924] S.C.R. 8. In that case a mine owner gave to a mine operator an option to purchase a mine for a cash amount, payable in instalments. When the first instalment fell due, the operator negotiated for an extension of time. This extension was granted by the owner in consideration of the operator agreeing to do certain development work not mentioned in the option, consisting mainly of the driving of certain tunnels. The operator failed to pay, relinquished possession of the mine, and surrendered the option without having done the work. The owner sued for damages in the amount of the cost of this work. This Court decided that he was entitled to recover this amount. Idington, J., dissented. Counsel for the operator, Mr. Lafleur, contended that the owner was only entitled to recover the pecuniary advantage he would have obtained by performance of the contract, which, in this case, would be the equivalent of any increase in the value of the mine arising therefrom.

Duff, J. (as he then was), said, at p. 437:

> It would be inadvisable, I think, to attempt to lay down any general rule for ascertaining the damages to which a mine-owner is entitled for breach of a covenant to perform development work or exploratory work by a person holding an option of purchase. Cases may no doubt arise in which the test suggested by Lafleur's argument would be the only proper test, and difficult and intricate as the inquiry might be, it would be the duty of the Court to enter upon an examination of the effect of doing the work upon the value of the property.
> On the other hand, cases must arise in which the plaintiff's right is plainly to recover at least the cost of doing the work. If it were conclusively made out, for example, that the work to be done formed part and a necessary part of some plan of exploration or development requisite, from the miner's point of view, for developing the property as a working mine, and necessary, from the point of view of businesslike management, so that it might fairly be presumed that in the event of the option lapsing the owner would in the ordinary course have the work completed, then the damages arising in the ordinary course would include the cost of doing the work and would accordingly be recoverable under the rule.

Anglin, J. (as he then was), said, at p. 439:

> Acting on the advice of M. S. Davys, a mining engineer, the plaintiff insisted on the promise by Cunningham to undertake and prosecute this work immediately and continuously as the basis of any extension to be given him. Davys deposes that he and Moore had agreed that the work in question should be done. The plaintiff relied upon Davys, and it is a fair inference not only that he regards the work as essential but that it is work which he will have done. It is probably necessary to reach that conclusion in order to justify the departure made by the trial Judge from the ordinary rule that the measure of damages for breach by a defendant of a contract to perform work on the plaintiff's land is the actual pecuniary

loss sustained by the plaintiff as a result of such breach, *i.e.*, the difference between what would have been the value of the premises had the work contracted for been done and their value with it unperformed. The question is by no means free from difficulty and, as presently advised, it is only because I think the learned trial Judge must have dealt with it on the footing indicated and because his having done so was warranted by the evidence that I accept the measure of damages as determined.

Reference may be had to *Pell v. Shearman* (1855), 10 Exch. 766, 156 E.R. 650; Mayne on Damages, 9th ed., pp. 237-8; Sedgwick on Damages, 9th ed., s. 619; *Wigsell v. School for Indigent Blind* (1882), 8 Q.B.D. 357; *Joyner v. Weeks*, [1891] 2 Q.B. 31. In the last cited case the Court of Appeal (p. 43) treated the breach of a tenant's covenant to yield up premises in good repair as subject to a convenient rule of inveterate practice ordinarily applicable specially to such cases and tantamount to a rule of law that the measure of the lessor's damages should be the cost of making the omitted repairs. A recent decision of an Appellate Divisional Court in Ontario may also be adverted to *O'Brien Ltd. v. Freedman* (1923), 25 O.W.N. 240.

Mignault, J., said, at p. 440:

In my opinion, on the construction of the agreement entered into by the parties, by their letters of October 19, October 26, and November 2, 1918, the carrying on of the development work mentioned in para. 3 of the appellant's letter of October 19, was the consideration of the extension of time granted by the respondent for the payment of the balance of the first instalment under the option contract between the parties. It was in no wise a condition of the original option to be unenforceable in case the option to purchase was not exercised by the appellant. On the contrary, the only possible interest the respondent could have in view when he stipulated for this development work, was in case the appellant relinquished his option. If he purchased the property, and paid for it, it would be a matter of indifference to the respondent what development work had been done. Moreover, the letter stated that the work should begin immediately.

Counsel for Sunshine contends that the learned trial Judge should have applied the decision of this Court in *Cotter v. General Petroleums Ltd. and Superior Oils Ltd.*, [1950] 4 D.L.R. 609, [1951] S.C.R. 154, and should have awarded only nominal damages.

.   .   .

It will be noted, from the passages above cited, that the obligation of the companies to drill a well (as distinct from commencing to drill a well) would arise only if the option had been exercised and they had been granted a sublease. The consideration for the drilling was to be the granting of the sublease and that consideration had not passed to them. In the present case, the consideration for the undertaking of the sch. A work had been received by Sunshine in full. Sunshine had received, under the principal agreement, the transfer to it of a one-half interest in the mining properties. Under the amending agreement, it had received from Dolly Varden the consideration stipulated in that agreement, namely, withdrawal of the notice of default, waiver of the performance of further work under sch. F of the principal agreement, waiver of any prior defaults, and an extension of the term of the first development period. For that consideration Sunshine had given a firm commitment to perform the sch. A work, which it failed and refused to perform.

For these reasons, I do not consider that the reasoning in the *Cotter* case is of assistance to Sunshine in the present appeal.

.   .   .

The submissions made on behalf of Sunshine in this Court have failed to persuade me that, in the circumstances of the case, the Courts below were in error in awarding to Dolly Varden damages equivalent to the expense involved in performing the sch. A work which Sunshine contracted to perform and deliberately failed to carry out. As stated by Lord du Parcq in the passage cited earlier, what has to be decided, in determining damages, is a question of fact, and the *Cunningham* case certainly establishes that there is no rule of law which precludes the application of the method of assessing damages which was adopted by the learned trial Judge in this case, when the Court considers it to be appropriate. For the reasons already stated, I do not think that the *Cotter* case is of any assistance to Sunshine in this appeal.

It was contended, for Sunshine, that Dolly Varden was only entitled to receive, by way of damages, the difference between the value of the premises if the work had been performed, and their value with the work unperformed, and that there was no evidence to establish any damage upon this basis. In the circumstances of this case I do not think that this was a proper test for ascertaining damages.

Counsel for Sunshine, in this connection, relied upon two cases, *Wigsell et al. v. School for Indigent Blind* (1882), 8 Q.B.D. 357, and *James v. Hutton and J. Cook & Sons Ltd.*, [1950] 1 K.B. 9.

In the former case, a grantee of land had covenanted to construct around the land conveyed, on all sides where it abutted on the grantor's land, a 7-ft. brick wall. The wall was not erected and an action was brought for damages. It appeared that the value of the adjoining land was not decreased by the non-erection of the wall to anything like the amount required to construct it.

The Court refused to award damages equivalent to the cost of constructing the wall.

This was a case of a purchaser's covenant, similar to a restrictive covenant, taken by the seller for the protection of his adjoining land, and the measure of damages in such cases is usually the diminution in value of the adjoining land resulting from non-performance. In cases of this kind, the grantor has available the remedy of specific performance, where damages would not adequately protect his rights.

The latter case involved a covenant by a lessee, who, under licence, made an alteration to the front of the store he had leased. The lessee undertook, on request, to restore the building to its original condition on the expiration of the lease. The lessee failed to comply with such a request by the lessor. There was no evidence that the restoration would make the premises suitable for any particular purpose or business or that the premises were adversely affected or made less valuable by reason of the new store front which replaced the old.

The Court held that the lessor was only entitled to recover the damage he had actually suffered, which, in this case, was merely nominal. The Court, however, expressly disclaimed that it was suggested that the plaintiff could not give evidence that he desired to use the premises for a purpose for which the new front was unsuitable.

I do not regard these cases as being analogous to the circumstances of the present case. The covenant of the grantee in the *Wigsell* case was given for the benefit of the adjacent lands retained by the grantor. The extent to which the value of those lands was affected by breach of the covenant was not, in the circumstances of that case, determinable by reference to the cost of construction of the wall. Similarly, in the *James* case, the covenant given by the lessee under the licence granted to him by the lessor, was for the benefit of the reversionary interest of the lessor. In the absence of evidence that breach of the covenant affected the use to which the lands were to be put, or their value, after the expiration of the lease, the lessor was held not entitled to recover the cost of restoration of the store front to its previous condition.

The agreements in the present case related to a joint venture for exploration, development and production of minerals underlying the mining properties. These properties were known to have good prospects. Stage one of the principal agreement provided Sunshine with an opportunity to ascertain whether these properties offered a potential return to it sufficient to warrant a decision to proceed further into stage two. Dolly Varden's interest was in having Sunshine proceed with the various stages into commercial production, but, failing such further progress, it would obtain, pursuant to the provisions of the agreement, full information as to the work done, the results thereof and the cost involved. In a sense, although the agreement provided that it should not be construed as creating a partnership, the parties were partners in a joint venture.

The work described in sch. A to the amending agreement was work which Sunshine had decided would be of advantage, after conducting a study of the Torbrit mine and on the recommendation of its chief geologist. It committed itself to do that work for the consideration given by Dolly Varden, which Sunshine received in full. Sunshine committed itself to perform that work, obviously because it considered the results of it would be of value. Dolly Varden gave the stipulated consideration because, if the results were favourable, it would obtain the further development of its property, and, if Sunshine was not satisfied with the results, it would be the recipient of useful information about its property. Clearly, in this case, both parties considered that the work, contracted to be performed, would be worth the expense of doing it. This is an entirely different situation from the covenants given in the two cases mentioned, which would be of advantage only, if at all, to the grantor and the lessor respectively.

When Sunshine, later, deliberately breached its contract to perform the work, what was the measure of Dolly Varden's damage? If it had paid cash for the work, it would clearly be entitled to a repayment of it, and would also have a claim in damages. The consideration was not in cash, but Sunshine, when it executed the amending agreement, considered it to be of sufficient value to warrant the expenditure necessary to perform the work.

It is pointless, in these circumstances, to suggest that a comparison be made between the value of the mining property with and without the work being done. The result of the sch. A work is unknown, and it is unknown because Sunshine elected to break the contract for its performance. But when Sunshine, by entering the agreement, acknowledged that, in the light of its future potential benefits under the agreement, its own suggested programme of work was worth the cost of performing it, and when Dolly Varden was prepared to give, and did give, valuable consideration for its performance, I consider that it was entirely proper for the learned trial Judge to assess the damage resulting from the breach as being equivalent to the cost of doing the work. In so doing he was seeking to fulfil the underlying principle stated by Lord Atkinson in *Wertheim v. Chicoutimi Pulp Co.*, [1911] A.C. 301 at p. 307, and cited by Cartwright, J., in the *Cotter* case in the passage already quoted [[1950] 4 D.L.R. at p. 627]:

> "And it is the general intention of the law that, in giving damages for breach of contract, the party complaining should, so far as it can be done by money, be placed in the same position as he would have been if the contract had been performed."

Having reached this conclusion, I must go on to consider whether the right to receive damages, determined in this manner, is affected by Dolly Varden having entered into the agreement with Newmont, which did not become effective until after Dolly Varden had asserted its right to damages against Sunshine, and after that action had been tried.

In this Court, counsel for Sunshine did not contend that the benefits accruing to Dolly Varden under that contract should be considered by way of mitigation of damages. His position was that no question of mitigation arises because, he said, Dolly Varden had not established any damages. I have already indicated my reasons for disagreeing with this latter assertion. His submission was that the Newmont agreement was relevant as showing that, from its effective date, Dolly Varden had abandoned any power or intention of doing the sch. A work itself, and, on this basis, this case was not analogous to the *Cunningham* case.

The same submission was made at trial and, in respect of it, the learned trial Judge made the following finding [64 D.L.R. (2d) at p. 318]:

> However I have found that the work was economic and necessary as a part of the over-all scheme of development of Torbrit. I also accept the evidence of the officers of the plaintiff company to the effect that they intend the completion of the schedule "A" work.

> The fact that the new agreement with Newmount does not make specific reference to the work and does not provide for its completion at once does not mean that the plaintiff does not intend to do the work or have it done or exclude the possibility that it will be done, and the work being a necessary step in the development of the mining properties the introduction of a new principal cannot justify a finding, by itself, that the work would not be done.

I am not prepared to disturb this finding. Furthermore, I do not regard the Newmont agreement as having any bearing in this case. The agreement with Sunshine terminated at the end of the first development stage. Sunshine had not given notice of intent to extend that period or to enter the next development stage. It abandoned the agreement. Immediately upon the termination of the agreement, in my opinion, for the reasons already given, Dolly Varden had a valid claim in damages equivalent to the expense of doing the sch. A work, which it asserted by action against Sunshine. On such termination Dolly Varden had the mining property on its hands, and, later, it was able to obtain the agreement with Newmont for its development. Under that contract, the work to be done by Newmont was in its discretion, subject to its commitment, if it entered the second and later stages, to expend stipulated amounts of money "for the benefit of the property." It was not obligated to perform the sch. A work. In view of these circumstances, I do not see how this contract can affect the cause of action of Dolly Varden to recover damages equivalent to the cost of the sch. A work, arising out of Sunshine's failure to do that work, which cause of action arose on the termination of the Sunshine agreement.

I would dismiss this appeal, with costs.

Appeal dismissed

The Supreme Court of Canada referred to another case in the Supreme Court of Canada, *Cotter v. General Petroleums Ltd.*, [1950] 4 D.L.R. 609, [1951] S.C.R. 154. The issue before the Court in that case was the measure of damages to be awarded for breach of a contract to drill an oil well. The respondent, defendant had promised to drill an oil well in return for a sub-lease of half the land leased by the appellant, plaintiff, and a share in any profits from the well. The land was near the new Leduc oil field in Alberta. The defendant refused to drill when it became clear that the chance of finding oil on this land was very small. The plaintiff sued for the cost of drilling (about $50,000). The Supreme Court of Canada refused to award this. Cartwright J. (as he then was) said in regard to the plaintiff's claim at p. 629:

> "In my view, the proper measure of his damages under the circumstances of this case is the difference between the value to him of the consideration for which the respondents agreed to drill the well and the value to him of the consideration which, acting reasonably, he should find it necessary to give to have the well drilled by others. I am unable to find in the record evidence on which the damages can be assessed on this basis. It is well settled that the mere fact that damages are difficult to estimate and cannot be assessed with certainty does not relieve the party in default of the necessity of paying damages and is no ground for awarding only nominal damages, but the onus of proving his damages still rests upon the plaintiff."

Cartwright J. held that there was no evidence from which it could be determined what the plaintiff's damages would be on this test; and, therefore did not award the plaintiff any damages on this basis.

The arrangement that the plaintiff had made with the farmer from whom he had obtained the oil lease provided that Cotter should pay $1,000 to the farmer if he did not drill a well within six months of the grant of the lease. Because the defendant refused to drill as had been agreed, Cotter had to pay $1,000 to the farmer to keep his lease. The Supreme Court of Canada allowed Cotter's claim for the $1,000.

QUESTIONS AND PROBLEMS

1. We may assume that the reason the defendant in *Cotter v. General Petroleums* refused to drill was because there was so small a chance of finding oil that it would not be worth an investment of $50,000. If this is so, then
   (a) Is the measure of damages suggested by Cartwright J. correct? and
   (b) Can one justify the award of the $1,000 in that case?
   (c) Suppose that the defendant were ordered by the court to drill the well, what would you expect the plaintiff to do?
2. The Supreme Court of Canada regarded the fact that in *Sunshine v. Dolly Varden*, Sunshine had received in full the consideration for undertaking the Schedule "A" work as crucial.
   (a) What does this mean? Specifically, does this mean that the plaintiff is suing for a restitution interest?

(b) What interest of Dolly Varden was threatened by Sunshine's breach?

(c) What interest of Dolly Varden was protected by the award?

3. Suppose that the Supreme Court of Canada could have considered ordering Sunshine to do the work that it had promised to do, what would have happened? Consider specifically how Sunshine would (or could) be paid had it performed what it promised to do. If you see problems if Sunshine should be ordered to perform, what does this say about the judgment of the Supreme Court?

4. To what extent are the cases of *Wigsell* and *James v. Hutton* similar to *Peevyhouse v. Garland Coal*? How valid do you find the distinction drawn between those cases and *Sunshine v. Dolly Varden*?

5. Bob was injured when he was thrown to the ground by a policeman during a fracas outside a hotel. Bob consulted Ian, a solicitor, about the possibility of bringing an action for damages against the policeman. Bob instructed Ian to commence an action. Ian negligently let the matter wait until it was too late to sue the policeman. (Such an action had to be commenced within six months under the Public Authorities Protection Act.) Assuming that Ian is in breach of his contractual obligation to Bob, what should the measure of Bob's damages be? See: *Prior v. McNab* (1976), 78 D.L.R. (3d) 319, 16 O.R. (2d) 380, 1 C.C.L.T. 137 (H.C.), Reid J.

The following two cases were not referred to by the Supreme Court of Canada in either *Cotter v. General Petroleums* or *Sunshine v. Dolly Varden*. Should they have been? If they should have been and were not, what does this say about the judgments of the Supreme Court of Canada?

In *Carson v. Willitts* (1930), 65 O.L.R. 456, [1930] 4 D.L.R. 977, Ontario Supreme Court, Appellate Division, the plaintiff sued the defendant for breach of a contract to drill oil wells. The plaintiff offered the defendant a share in the oil wells that were to be drilled. The defendant drilled one well but refused to drill any more. Masten J.A., giving judgment for the Court said at pp. 458-59:

"Then what is the basis on which this Court should now direct the damages to be assessed? In my opinion, what the plaintiff lost by the refusal of the defendant to bore two more wells was a sporting or gambling chance that valuable oil or gas would be found when the two further wells were bored. If the wells had been bored and no oil or gas of value had been found, the effect would be that the plaintiff has lost nothing by the refusal of the defendant to go on boring. On the other hand, if valuable oil or gas had been discovered, by the boring of these two wells, he had lost substantially. It may not be easy to compute what that chance was worth to the plaintiff, but the difficulty in estimating the quantum is no reason for refusing to award any damages.

"In Mayne on Damages, 10th ed., p. 6, it is said:

" 'A distinction must be drawn between cases where absence of evidence makes it impossible to assess damages, and cases where the assessment is difficult because of the nature of the damage proved. In the former case only nominal damages can be recovered. In the latter case, however, the difficulty of assessment is no ground for refusing substantial damages.' "

See also: *Chaplin v. Hicks*, [1911] 2 K.B. 786 (C.A.).

An award of £100 by a jury was upheld by the Court of Appeal where the plaintiff had lost the chance to be one of 50 actresses from whom 12 would be selected for employment. The defendant's argument that only nominal damages were payable since the plaintiff only lost the chance to be chosen at the beauty contest was rejected.

ANGLIA T.V. v. REED

[1971] 3 All E.R. 690. Court of Appeal

Lord Denning M.R.: Anglia Television Ltd were minded in 1968 to make a film of a play for television entitled 'The Man in the Wood'. It portrayed an American married to an English woman. The American has an adventure in an English wood. The film was to last for 90 minutes. Anglia Television made many arrangements in advance. They arranged for a place where the play was to be filmed. They employed a director, a designer and a stage manager, and so forth. They involved themselves in much expense. All this was done before they got the leading man. They required a strong actor capable of holding the play together. He was to be on the scene the whole time. Anglia Television eventually found the man. He was Mr Robert Reed, an American who has a very high reputation as an actor. He was very suitable for this part. By telephone conversation on 30th August 1968 it was agreed by Mr Reed through his agent that he would come to England and be available between 9th September and 11th October 1968 to rehearse and play in this film. He was to get a performance fee of £1,050, living expenses of £100 a week, his first class fares to and from the United States, and so forth. It was all subject to the permit of the Ministry of Labour for him to come here. That was duly given on 2nd September 1968. So the contract was concluded. But unfortunately there was some muddle with the bookings. It appears that Mr Reed's agent had already booked him in America for some other play. So on 3rd September 1968 the agent said that Mr Reed would not come to England to perform in this play. He repudiated his contract. Anglia Television tried hard to find a substitute but could not do so. So on 11th September they accepted his repudiation. They abandoned the proposed film. They gave notice to the people whom they had engaged and so forth.

Anglia Television then sued Mr Reed for damages. He did not dispute his liability, but a question arose as to the damages. Anglia Television do not claim their profit. They cannot say what their profit would have been on this contract if Mr Reed had come here and performed it. So, instead of claim for loss or profits, they claim for the wasted expenditure. They had incurred the director's fees, the designer's fees, the stage manager's and assistant manager's fees, and so on. It comes in all to £2,750. Anglia Television say that all that money was wasted because Mr Reed did not perform his contract.

Mr Reed's advisers take a point of law. They submit that Anglia Television cannot recover for expenditure incurred *before* the contract was concluded with Mr Reed. They can only recover the expenditure *after* the contract was concluded. They say that the expenditure *after* the contract was only £854.65, and that is all that Anglia Television can recover. The master rejected that contention; he held that Anglia Television could recover the whole £2,750; and now Mr Reed appeals to this court.

Counsel for Mr Reed has referred us to the recent unreported case of *Perestrello & Compania Limitada v United Paint Co Ltd (No 2)* [(1969), 113 Sol. Jo. 324] in which Thesiger J quoted the words of Lord Tindal CJ in 1835 in *Hodges v Earl of Litchfield [(1835) 1 Bing. 492 at 498]*:

'The expenses preliminary to the contract ought not to be allowed. The party enters into them for his own benefit at a time when it is uncertain whether there will be any contract or not.'

Thesiger J applied those words, saying: 'In my judgment pre-contract expenditure, though thrown away, is not recoverable...'

I cannot accept the proposition as stated. It seems to me that a plaintiff in such a case as this had an election: he can either claim for his loss of profits; or for his wasted expenditure. But he must elect between them. He cannot claim both. If he has not suffered any loss of profits — or if he cannot prove what his profits would have been — he can claim in the alternative the expenditure which has been thrown away, that is, wasted, by reason of the breach....

If the plaintiff claims the wasted expenditure, he is not limited to the expenditure incurred *after* the contract was concluded. He can claim also the expenditure incurred *before* the contract, provided that it was such as would reasonably be in the contemplation of the parties as likely to be wasted if the contract was broken. Applying that principle here, it is plain that, when Mr Reed entered into this contract, he must have known perfectly well that much expenditure had already been incurred on director's fees and the like. He must have contemplated — or, at any rate, it is reasonably to be imputed to him — that if he broke his contract, all that expenditure would be wasted, whether or not it was incurred before or after the contract. He must pay damages for all the expenditure so wasted and thrown away. This view is supported by the recent decision of Brightman J in *Lloyd v Stanbury* [[1971] 2 All E.R. 267]. There was a contract for the sale of land. In anticipation of the contract — and before it was concluded — the purchaser went to much expense in moving a caravan to the site and in getting his furniture there. The seller afterwards entered into a contract to sell the land to the purchaser, but afterwards broke his contract. The land had not increased in value, so the purchaser could not claim for any loss of profit. But Brightman J held that he could recover the cost of moving the caravan and furniture, because it was 'within the contemplation of the parties when the contract was signed'. That decision is in accord with correct principle, namely, that wasted expenditure can be recovered when it is wasted by reason of the defendant's breach of contract. It is true that, if the defendant had never entered into the contract, he would not be liable, and the expenditure would have been incurred by the plaintiff without redress; but, the defendant having made his contract and broken it, it does not lie in his mouth to say he is not liable, when it was because of his breach that the expenditure has been wasted.

I think the master was quite right and this appeal should be dismissed.

[The other judges agreed with Lord Denning.]

In *Lloyd v. Stanbury*, [1971] 2 All E.R. 267, Chancery Division, (referred to by Lord Denning) the plaintiff had agreed to buy the defendant's farm. As part of the arrangement, the plaintiff had agreed to let the defendant live in the plaintiff's caravan during the period that a house in which the defendant and his family were to live was being built on neighbouring land. The agreement for the purchase of the land was not completed. The plaintiff sued to recover the expenses that he had incurred in moving his caravan from his home to the defendant's land in anticipation of the completion of the sale of the land and the defendant's need for the caravan. Brightman J. had awarded the plaintiff these expenses.

QUESTIONS

1. What interests are being protected by the court (a) in *Anglia T.V. v. Reed*, and (b) in *Lloyd v. Stanbury*?

2. If these interests are not the same, is Lord Denning justified in applying *Lloyd v. Stanbury* as a precedent?

3. Would you think that an argument that the defendant did not cause the plaintiff's loss in *Anglia T.V. v. Reed* is legally relevant? If the plaintiff did not cause the defendant's loss what did?

4. Is it relevant that one reason why the plaintiff's losses are hard to quantify is because the defendant breached the contract?

5. Reed was to be paid £1050 for his work. What do you think would have happened if the losses suffered by Anglia T.V. had been £4,000 £8,000 or £20,000?

6. If we accept that Lord Atkinson's principle states a principle to be followed in determining the amount of damages, then it also implicitly sets a limit on the amount recoverable. To what extent is it correct to say, as Lord Denning does, that the plaintiff has an option: '[H]e can either claim for his loss of profits; or for his wasted expenditure." Specifically, to what extent does Lord Denning ignore what Lord Atkinson says on the basis for awarding contract damages?

The next case raises the problem of damages for breach of contract in a very different context. How well do you think that the analysis presented by the court deals with the peculiar facts of the case?

SULLIVAN v. O'CONNOR

(1973), 296 N.E. 2d 183. Supreme Judicial Court of Massachusetts.

Kaplan, Justice: The plaintiff patient secured a jury verdict of $13,500 against the defendant surgeon for breach of contract in respect to an operation upon the plaintiff's nose. The substituted consolidated bill of exceptions presents questions about the correctness of the judge's instructions on the issue of damages.

The declaration was in two counts. In the first count, the plaintiff alleged that she, as patient, entered into a contract with the defendant, a surgeon, wherein the defendant promised to perform plastic surgery on her nose and thereby to enhance her beauty and improve her appearance; that he performed the surgery but failed to achieve the promised result; rather the result of the surgery was to disfigure and deform her nose, to cause her pain in body and mind, and to subject her to other damage and expense. The second count, based on the same transaction, was in the conventional form for malpractice, charging that the defendant had been guilty of negligence in performing the surgery. Answering, the defendant entered a general denial.

On the plaintiff's demand, the case was tried by jury. At the close of the evidence, the judge put to the jury, as special questions, the issues of liability under the two counts, and instructed them accordingly. The jury returned a verdict for the plaintiff on the contract count, and for the defendant on the negligence count. The judge then instructed the jury on the issue of damages.

As background to the instructions and the parties' exceptions, we mention certain facts as the jury could find them. The plaintiff was a professional entertainer, and this was known to the defendant. The agreement was as alleged in the declaration. More particularly, judging from exhibits, the plaintiff's nose had been straight, but long and prominent; the defendant undertook by two operations to reduce its prominence and somewhat to shorten it, thus making it more pleasing in relation to the plaintiff's other features. Actually the plaintiff was obliged to undergo three operations, and her appearance was worsened. Her nose now had a concave line to about the midpoint, at which it became bulbous; viewed frontally, the nose from bridge to midpoint was flattened and broadened, and the two sides of the tip had lost symmetry. This configuration evidently could not be improved by further surgery. The plaintiff did not demonstrate, however, that her change of appearance had resulted in loss of employment. Payments by the plaintiff covering the defendant's fee and hospital expenses were stipulated at $622.65.

The judge instructed the jury, first, that the plaintiff was entitled to recover her out-of-pocket expenses incident to the operations. Second, she could recover the damages flowing directly, naturally, proximately, and foreseeably from the defendant's breach of promise. These would comprehend damages for any disfigurement of the plaintiff's nose — that is, any change of appearance for the worse — including the effects of the consciousness of such disfigurement on the plaintiff's mind, and in this connection the jury should consider the nature of the plaintiff's profession. Also consequent upon the defendant's breach, and compensable, were the pain and suffering involved in the third operation, but not in the first two. As there was no proof that any loss of earnings by the plaintiff resulted from the breach, that element should not enter into the calculation of damages.

By his exceptions the defendant contends that the judge erred in allowing the jury to take into account anything but the plaintiff's out-of-pocket expenses (presumably at the stipulated amount). The defendant excepted to the judge's refusal of his request for a general charge to that effect, and, more specifically, to the judge's refusal of a charge that the plaintiff could not recover for pain and suffering connected with the third operation or for impairment of the plaintiff's appearance and associated mental distress.

The plaintiff on her part excepted to the judge's refusal of a request to charge that the plaintiff could recover the difference in value between the nose as promised and the nose as it appeared after the operations. However, the plaintiff in her brief expressly waives this exception and others made by her in case this court overrules the defendant's exceptions; thus she would be content to hold the jury's verdict in her favor.

We conclude that the defendant's exceptions should be overruled.

It has been suggested on occasion that agreements between patients and physicians by which the physician undertakes to effect a cure or to bring about a given result should be declared unenforceable on grounds of public policy.... But there are many decisions recognizing and enforcing such contracts, and the law of Massachusetts has treated them as valid, although we have had no decision meeting head on the contention that they should be denied legal sanction.... These causes of action are, however, considered a little suspect, and thus we find courts straining sometimes to read the pleadings as sounding only in tort for negligence, and not in contract for breach of promise, despite sedulous efforts by the pleaders to pursue the latter theory....

It is not hard to see why the courts should be unenthusiastic or skeptical about the contract theory. Considering the uncertainties of medical science and the variations in the physical and psychological conditions of individual patients, doctors can seldom in good faith promise specific results. Therefore it is unlikely that physicians of even average integrity will in fact make such promises. Statements of opinion by the physician with some optimistic coloring are a different thing, and may indeed have therapeutic value. But patients may transform such statements into firm promises in their own minds, especially when they have been disappointed in the event, and testify in that sense to sympathetic juries. If actions for breach of promise can be readily maintained, doctors, so it is said, will be frightened into practising "defensive medicine." On the other hand, if these actions were outlawed, leaving only the possibility of suits for malpractice, there is fear that the public might be exposed to the enticements of charlatans, and confidence in the profession might ultimately be shaken. See Miller, "The Contractual Liability of Physicians and Surgeons", 1953 Wash.L.Q. 413, 416-423. The law has taken the middle of the road position of allowing actions based on alleged contract, but insisting on clear proof. Instructions to the jury may well stress this requirement and point to tests of truth, such as the complexity or difficulty of an operation as bearing on the probability that a given result was promised.

If an action on the basis of contract is allowed, we have next the question of the measure of damages to be applied where liability is found. Some cases have taken the simple view that the promise by the physician is to be treated like an ordinary commercial promise, and accordingly that the successful plaintiff is entitled to a standard measure of recovery for breach of contract — "compensatory" ("expectancy") damages, an amount intended to put the plaintiff in the position he would be in if the contract had been performed, or, presumably, at the plaintiff's election, "restitution" damages, an amount corresponding to any benefit conferred by the plaintiff upon the defendant in the performance of the contract disrupted by the defendant's breach. Thus in *Hawkins v. McGee*, (1929) 84 N.H. 114, 146 A. 641, the defendant doctor was taken to have promised the plaintiff to convert his damaged hand by means of an operation into a good or perfect hand, but the doctor so operated as to damage the hand still further. The court, following the usual expectancy formula, would have asked the jury to estimate and award to the plaintiff the difference between the value of a good or perfect hand, as promised, and the value of the hand after the operation. (The same formula would apply, although the dollar result would be less, if the operation had neither worsened nor improved the condition of the hand.) If the plaintiff had not yet paid the doctor his fee, that amount would be deducted from the recovery. There could be no recovery for the pain and suffering of the operation, since that detriment would have been incurred even if the operation had been successful; one can say that this detriment was not "caused" by the breach. But where the plaintiff by reason of the operation was put to more pain that he would have had to endure, had the doctor performed as promised, he should be compensated for that difference as a proper part of his expectancy recovery. It may be noted that on an alternative count for malpractice the plaintiff in the *Hawkins* case had been nonsuited; but on ordinary principles this could not affect the contract claim, for it is hardly a defence to a breach of contract that the promisor acted innocently and without negligence.

Other cases, including a number in New York, without distinctly repudiating the Hawkins type of analysis, have indicated that a different and generally more lenient measure of damages is to be applied in patient-physician actions based on breach of alleged special agreements to effect a cure, attain a stated result, or employ a given medical method. This measure is expressed in somewhat variant ways, but the substance is that the plaintiff is to recover any expenditures made by him and for other detriment (usually not specifically described in the opinions) following proximately and foreseeably upon the defendant's failure to carry out his promise.... This, be it noted, is not a "restitution" measure, for it is not limited to restoration of the benefit conferred on the defendant (the fee paid) but includes other expenditures, for example, amounts paid for medicine and nurses; so also it would seem according to its logic to take in damages for any worsening of the plaintiff's condition due to the breach. Nor is it an "expectancy" measure, for it does not appear to contemplate recovery of the whole difference in value between the condition as promised and the condition actually resulting from the treatment. Rather the tendency of the formulation is to put the plaintiff back in the position he occupied just before the parties entered upon the agreement, to compensate him for the detriments he suffered in reliance upon the agreement. This kind of intermediate pattern of recovery for breach of contract is discussed in the suggestive article by Fuller and Perdue, "The Reliance Interest in Contract Damages", 46 Yale L.J. 52, 373, where the authors show that, although not attaining the currency of the standard measures, a "reliance" measure has for special reasons been applied by the courts in a variety of settings, including noncommercial settings. See 46 Yale L.J. at 396-401. (Note: Some of the exceptional situations mentioned where reliance may be preferred to expectancy are those in which the latter measure would be hard to apply or would impose too great a burden; performance was interfered with by external circumstances; the contract was indefinite. See 46 Yale L.J. at 373-386; 394-396.)

For breach of the patient-physician agreements under consideration, a recovery limited to restitution seems plainly too meager, if the agreements are to be enforced at all. On the other hand, an expectancy recovery may well be excessive. The factors, already mentioned, which have made the cause of action somewhat suspect, also suggest moderation as to the breadth of the recovery that should be permitted. Where, as in the case at bar and in a number of the reported cases, the doctor has been absolved of negligence by the trier, an expectancy measure may be thought harsh. We should recall here that the fee paid by the patient to the doctor for the alleged promise would usually be quite disproportionate to the putative expectancy recovery. To attempt, moreover, to put a value on the condition that would or might have resulted, had the treatment succeeded as promised, may sometimes put an exceptional strain on the imagination of the fact finder. As a general consideration, Fuller and Perdue argue that the reasons for granting damages for broken promises to the extent of the expectancy are at their strongest when the promises are made in a business context, when they have to do with the production or distribution of goods or the allocation of functions in the market place; they become weaker as the context shifts from a commercial to a noncommercial field. 46 Yale L.J. at 60-63.

There is much to be said, then, for applying a reliance measure to the present facts, and we have only to add that our cases are not unreceptive to the use of that formula in special situations. We have, however, had no previous occasion to apply it to patient-physician cases.

The question of recovery on a reliance basis for pain and suffering or mental distress requires further attention. We find expressions in the decisions that pain and suffering (or the like) are simply not compensable in actions for breach of contract. The defendant seemingly espouses this proposition in the present case. True, if the buyer under a contract for the purchase of a lot of merchandise, in suing for the seller's breach, should claim damages for mental anguish caused by his disappointment in the transaction, he would not succeed; he would be told, perhaps, that the asserted psychological injury was not fairly foreseeable by the defendant as a probable consequence of the breach of such a business contract. See Restatement: Contracts, § 341, and comment a. But there is no general rule barring such items of damage in actions for breach of contract. It is all a question of the subject matter and background of the contract, and when the contract calls for an operation on the person of the plaintiff, psychological as well as physical injury may be expected to figure somewhere in the recovery, depending on the particular circumstances.... Again, it is said in a few of the New York cases, concerned with the classification of actions for statute of limitations purposes, that the absence of allegations demanding recovery for pain and suffering is characteristic of a contract claim by a patient against a physician, that such allegations rather belong in a claim for malpractice.... These remarks seem unduly sweeping. Suffering or distress resulting from the breach going beyond that which was envisaged by the treatment as agreed, should be compensable on the same ground as the worsening of the patient's condition because of the breach. Indeed it can be argued that the very suffering or distress "contracted for" — that which would have been incurred if the treatment achieved the promised result — should also be compensable on the theory underlying the New York cases. For that suffering is "wasted" if the treatment fails. Otherwise stated, compensation for this waste is arguably required in order to complete the restoration of the status quo ante. (Note: Recovery on a reliance basis for breach of the physician's promise tends to equate with the usual recovery for malpractice, since the latter also looks in general to restoration of the condition before the injury. But this is not paradoxical, especially when it is noted that the origins of contract lie in tort. See Farnsworth, "The Past of Promise: An Historical Introduction to Contract," 69 Col. L. Rev. 576, 594-596; ... A few cases have considered possible recovery for breach by a physician of a promise to sterilize a patient, resulting in birth of a child to the patient and spouse. If such an action is held maintainable, the reliance and expectancy measures would, we think, tend to equate, because the promised condition was preservation of the family status quo.... It would, however, be a mistake to think in terms of strict "formulas." For example, a jurisdiction which would apply a reliance measure to the present facts might impose a more severe damage sanction for the wilful use by the physician of a method of operation that he undertook not to employ.)

In the light of the foregoing discussion, all the defendant's exceptions fail; the plaintiff was not confined to the recovery of her out-of-pocket expenditures; she was entitled to recover also for the worsening of her condition, (Note: That condition involves a mental element and appraisal of it properly called for consideration of the fact that the plaintiff was an entertainer....) and for the pain and suffering and mental distress involved in the third operation. These items were compensable on either an expectancy or a reliance view. We might have been required to elect between the two views if the pain and suffering connected with the first two operations contemplated by the agreement, or the whole difference in value between the present and the promised conditions, were being claimed as elements of damage. But the plaintiff waives her possible claim to the former element, and to so much of the latter as represents the difference in value between the promised condition and the condition before the operations.

Plaintiff's exceptions waived.
Defendant's exceptions overruled.

[The result of the case is that the trial judge's direction to the jury on the measure of damages for breach of contract was correct and that the award of $13,500 made by the jury should stand.]

QUESTIONS AND PROBLEMS

1. The judge observes that the justification for the award of expectation damages becomes "weaker as the context shifts from a commercial to a non-commercial field"? Why should this be so? If it is so, what does that say about the role of contracts in the two fields?

2. The evidence in *Sullivan v. O'Connor* was that the plaintiff's appearance would not, or could not be improved by any further operations. Suppose however, that the defendant could introduce evidence that the plaintiff's nose could be improved by another operation performed by the defendant and that the defendant would assume all costs himself and, in addition, compensate the plaintiff for any time lost from her job. This would involve at the most an expenditure of $3,000. What should be the measure of the plaintiff's recovery? Would it make any difference if the operation were to be performed by someone other than the defendant?

NOTE: The leading case before *Sullivan v. O'Connor* was *Hawkins v. McGee* (1929), 146 A. 641 (Supreme Court of New Hampshire). This case is referred to by Kaplan J. In that case, the defendant doctor had promised to cure a bad scar on the plaintiff's hand by grafting skin from the plaintiff's chest onto his hand. As Kaplan J. says, the court there approved a measure of damages based on the expectation interest. The court there had said:

"... the true measure of the plaintiff's damages in the present case is the difference between the value to him of a perfect or a good hand ... and the value of his hand in its present condition ..."

The court ultimately sent the case back for a new trial since it held that the trial judge had not applied the right test to determine the measure of damages.

Part of the evidence of the plaintiff at trial was as follows:
George Hawkins: Direct Examination.... Q. What did he [Dr. McGee] do? A. Remove the scar and instead of removing the scar as I supposed he was going to do, cuts in, in other words, possibly, I imagine, getting a foundation — I say a foundation because as I know the results, he must have been trying to get a foundation, because the scar wasn't taken off as he said he was going to take it off. Q. Whether or not there was more cut off from the palm of your hand than he said was going to be cut? A. There was. Q. What did he do after he cut that out? A. It

must have been — he dressed the hand, and I hadn't seen it, — I wouldn't look at it until two or three days after, possibly three days after, and of course I was anxious to go home, because I had expected to go home in two or three days, and when I inquired whether or not I could go home, then he mentioned skin graft. Q. Up until that time had he mentioned any skin grafting, or had he suggested there was going to be any skin grafting? A. Never.... Q. Were you able to move your hand away from the chest? A. I couldn't move it an inch; it was sewed, and then adhesive tape strapped over to keep it in place. Q. How long did you remain in that condition? A. I should say approximately three weeks; between three and four weeks. Q. Suffer any pain? A. Yes, I did. Every time that — of course, I couldn't move in bed; I couldn't turn around or turn over, because my elbow would interfere with my hand. Q. How long were you sewed up in that condition? A. Between three and four weeks.... Q. What was the condition of your chest after the operation? A. There was a scar there approximately between two and three inches wide, possibly a little wider, and about seven inches long, running across this way, and the wound was deep, — I should say probably three-fourths of an inch deep. It looked as though the flesh was taken in between the ribs. Q. And did that pain you? A. It did pain me, and Dr. McGee had me bend over, and he pulled the skin up and made it meet, and sewed it there so that there was a piece gone and the skin of my stomach and the chest was stretched by being sewed in that position, and that is the way I remained for probably two weeks, until it started to heal, then I gradually straightened up. Q. Was it hard for you to straighten up? A. It was. Q. Can you feel any effects from that now? A. Not often, but at times if I straighten up, I get a pain.... Q. Now is this hand embarrassing to you at some times? A. It is. Q. In what way? A. Oh, if I was introduced to somebody I had never known before, and go to shake hands with him, — and especially a woman, they want to know what is in my hand. Q. Is it embarrassing? A. It is embarrassing. The fellows have a good time making jokes about it. Q. Is that embarrassing to you? A. Of course it is. Q. Ever have any trouble like that before the operation? A. Never.

The parties ultimately settled for $1,400 without going to a new trial. Dr. McGee sought to recover that sum from his malpractice insurer, but the insurer refused to pay on the ground that Dr. McGee was not insured when he was made liable on a "special contract". Ironically Dr. McGee had earlier argued that the verdict of the jury should have been set aside on the ground that the jury had discussed insurance coverage and that he had thereby been prejudiced.

C. Specific Performance and Injunctions

In the cases that we have looked at the plaintiff claimed damages for the defendant's breach of contract. The assumption that we made was that the plaintiff's loss could be quantified and expressed in money. We saw that often this process of quantification was very crude and involved some dubious assumptions about the value that a party attached to the other party's performance. We also saw in our earlier discussion that much more satisfactory results might have been achieved if the court had asserted a power to order the defendant to perform his part of the bargain. At that time it was said that that remedy was not available. To explain why that is so, it is necessary to know some legal history.

The law that we have inherited from England contains two major streams. The first is what is known as the common law. The term "common law" has several meanings but it is used here to refer to the law applied by the common law courts in England. These courts owe their origin to the administrative reforms of Henry II (1154-1189). The word "common" signifies that the law applied in the common law courts was common to the whole of England. Much of the early history of the common law courts involved the struggle of the central administration (represented by the king) against the decentralizing pressure of the barons (the feudal lords). Suffice it to say here that the king won and, as a consequence, his courts, the courts applying a law common to all parts of the kingdom, the common law courts were established as the principal judicial authority.

For a variety of reasons, the remedies that the common law courts could offer to litigants were limited. The limitation that most concerns us here is that the common law courts would only give a remedy expressed in money. The form of the judgment of a common law in favour of a plaintiff was not, as one might have expected, an order that the plaintiff pay a sum of money to the defendant, rather it was an order directed to the sheriff, commanding him to seize the goods of the defendant and sell them to obtain the wherewithal to pay the plaintiff. This is still the method of enforcement in the Ontario courts now.

The writ authorizing the sheriff to seize the defendant's goods, for example, is reproduced overleaf.

In many cases the plaintiff would be quite happy to get his money from the sheriff after the defendant's goods had been sold. (As a practical matter, of course, the defendant may well pay before the sheriff is ever called in.) However, in other situations the failure to get the thing that had been promised would seriously disappoint the plaintiff. The principal example of this would be breach of a promise to sell land. The damages that would be obtained in an action in the common law courts would be the difference between the contract price and the market price of the land. This would often be inadequate compensation for a disappointed buyer since the value of the land to him might be far more than the market or contract price. In one sense each piece of land is unique and cannot be replaced as one can replace promised carrots or a car by going into the market to buy others.

The second stream developed in the following way. Litigants who were disappointed by the remedies available in the common law courts would petition the king, as the final source of justice, to obtain relief that the common law courts would not grant. In the case of the disappointed buyer of land the remedy sought would be an order that the defendant, seller, convey the land to the plaintiff. The remedy sought came to be known as an order of specific performance. Medieval kings were busy men and the king had no time to examine each petition that came to him, and so he passed these petitions on to his Chancellor. The medieval Chancellor was one of the great officers of state. He was usually a cleric — a bishop — and in addition to his duties as a member of the king's council, he carried a heavy administrative burden. The volume of petitions coming before the Chancellor was already large by the end of the twelfth century. When a petition came to the Chancellor (after a while petitions came directly to him) he would call the defendant before him by subpoena to answer, on oath, the allegation that had been made by the plaintiff. This procedure was very different from that of the common law courts where, by means of a writ, the defendant was called upon to answer, not under oath, since parties could not be witnesses, but at trial before a jury which was governed by formalistic and rigid rules.

[This is the front of the writ.]

Writ of fieri facias

REGISTRAR'S
FILE NO. _672/75_

In the Supreme Court of Ontario

Between

Sue Lightly

AND

Owen Mutch

PLAINTIFF(S)

DEFENDANT(S)

Elizabeth the Second, by the Grace of God of the United Kingdom, Canada and Her other Realms and Territories QUEEN, Head of the Commonwealth, Defender of the Faith.

To the Sheriff of the Judicial District of York   Greeting.

We Command You that of the goods and chattels and lands and tenements in your bailiwick of

Owen Mutch

you cause to be made the sum of .... $ 11,547.36

and also interest thereon from .... May 1st _____ 1977, { *day of the judgment or order, or day on which the money is directed to be paid, or day from which interest is directed by the order to run, as the case may be*

which sum of money and interest were by a judgment in this action bearing the date of .... May 1st _____ 1977,

adjudged to be paid by the said _____ Owen Mutch

to _____ Sue Lightly _____ ,

and also the further sum of .... $ 2,126.70 _____ ,

for the taxed costs of the said _____ Plaintiff

mentioned in the said judgment, together with interest at the rate of 5% per annum thereon from .. September 1st _____ 1977, *(the date of the certificate of taxation)*

And We Further Command You that so much thereof as you shall have made from the said goods and chattels and lands and tenements be paid out according to law and if required so to do, make appear to our Justices of the Supreme Court of Ontario in what manner you shall have executed this our writ.

In Witness Whereof this writ is signed for the Supreme Court of Ontario by _____ Andrew Drover _____ Registrar

of the said Court at Toronto , this 1st day of September , 19 77

Andrew Drover
Registrar S.C.O.

[The back looks like this:]

THE FOLLOWING ENDORSEMENT MUST BE COMPLETED BY THE OFFICER AT THE OFFICE WHEREIN THIS WRIT WAS ISSUED OR RENEWED (*as the case may be*).

The ___Plaintiff___ is entitled to receive for this and other writs and renewals of the same, the following sums:

Signature of Officer

For	$
This writ	6.00
1st ren'l	
2nd ren'l	
3rd ren'l	

WHEN APPLICABLE, THE FOLLOWING ENDORSEMENT MUST BE COMPLETED BY THE SHERIFF WITH WHOM THIS WRIT IS FILED OR, IF IT IS NOT FILED WITH A SHERIFF, BY THE REGISTRAR AT THE OFFICE WHEREIN THE WRIT WAS ISSUED.

RENEWAL OF WRIT

This writ has been renewed for a further period of six years from the date indicated hereunder:

Signature of Officer

Date	

S. C. O.

Sue Lightly

vs.

Owen Mutch

Writ of Fieri Facias

This writ was issued by:

Messrs. Argue & Fibbs

of the ___City___ of ___Toronto___

in the ___J.D.___ of ___York___

solicitor(s) for the said

___Plaintiff___

who reside(s) at

393 Bay St. Toronto, Ont.

THE FOLLOWING ENDORSEMENT MUST BE COMPLETED BY THE PERSON FILING THIS WRIT AT OR BEFORE THE TIME OF FILING.

MR. SHERIFF:

Levy the sum of ___$ 11,547.36___

with interest at 5% per annum from ___May 1___ 19 77,

and the sum of ___$ 2126.70___ for costs,

with interest at 5% per annum from ___Sept. 1___ 19 77

and for this writ ___$ 6.00___

together with your own fees, poundage and incidental expenses.

___William Argue___
signature of person filing writ

___393 Bay St. Toronto, Ont.___
address

*when such person is in the employ of a solicitor, the name and address of the solicitor shall be inserted here.

The Chancellor's power could not supplant the power and jurisdiction of the common law courts, but he could remedy the deficiencies in the common law rules as he saw them. Again, for our purposes, we are only concerned here with the remedy of specific performance, though this was one of the less important contributions of the Chancellors to the overall development of English law. Gradually it became established that the Chancellor's remedy would only be available to a litigant if the common law remedy was inadequate. The first few cases in this section discuss this issue.

As has been mentioned, the method of enforcement of a common law judgment was by an order directed to the sheriff commanding him to seize and sell the defendant's goods in satisfaction of the judgment. The method of enforcement by the Chancellor was more direct. A defendant who, for example, disobeyed an order of the Chancellor that he convey land to the plaintiff was guilty of contempt of court. The penalty for this was imprisonment. A recalcitrant defendant would then stay in prison until he obeyed. It may be expected that stay in a medieval prison did much to induce compliance with the Chancellor's orders. This power still remains in the modern successors to the Chancellor's power. As a practical matter, in cases where the plaintiff sought a conveyance from the defendant, the threat of imprisonment was often unnecessary, since a conveyance could be executed on behalf of the defendant by an officer of the Chancellor's court. However, as the cases show, the power of the Chancellor extended to those cases where the defendant could be ordered not to do something that would be in breach of his contract. This power is sometimes referred to as the power to issue an injunction. Then, as now, breach of an injunction renders a person liable to punishment which may include imprisonment. The method of enforcement made the Chancellor's remedies very popular with plaintiffs and some care had to be taken not to prejudice defendants unfairly. Cases like *Warner Bros. v. Nelson* (*infra*) discuss this issue.

The writs and rules applicable in the case where equitable remedies were sought included not only the power to imprison, but also the power to seize the property of the recalcitrant defendant. The Ontario Rules of Practice, for example, provide:

Rule 569.
A judgment requiring any person to do an act, other than the payment of money, or to abstain from doing anything, may be enforced by attachment or by committal.

Rule 572.
If an attachment cannot be executed against the person refusing or neglecting to obey the judgment by reason of his being out of the jurisdiction of the court or of his having absconded or that with due diligence he cannot be found or if in any other case the court thinks proper to dispense with a writ of attachment, an order may be granted for a writ of sequestration against the estate and effects of the disobedient person, and it is not necessary for that purpose to issue an attachment.

If we suppose that the defendant in the case of *Gilbert v. Barron* (*infra*) was refractory then the following writs and orders would be available:

Writ of attachment for contempt
In the Supreme Court of Ontario
Between

James Gilbert, Robert MacDonald

PLAINTIFF(S)

and

John Barron

DEFENDANT(S)

Elizabeth the Second, by the Grace of God of the United Kingdom, Canada and Her other Realms and Territories, **Queen**, Head of Commonwealth, Defender of the Faith.

To the Sheriff of the Judicial District of York **Greeting**.

We Command You to attach John Barron notwithstanding any right of place he is in, so as to have him before our Justices in our Supreme Court of Ontario, immediately after the receipt hereof, then and there to answer to us, as well touching a contempt which he it is alleged hath committed against us, as also such other matters as shall be then and there laid to his charge, and further to perform and abide such order as our said Court shall make in this behalf, and hereof fail not, by reason of any liberty, and bring this writ with you.

In Witness Whereof this writ is signed for the Supreme Court of Ontario by Andrew Drover Registrar of the said Court at Toronto this 10th day of October, 1977.

Andrew Drover
(Signature of officer)

This writ brought the defendant before the court so that he could answer the allegation that he was in contempt of court. If the court found that he was in contempt then the court, after reciting the facts and concluding that the defendant had been guilty of contempt would order:

"1. **This Court Doth Order** that the said **John Barron** do stand committed to the common gaol of the Judicial District of York for his contempt for the term of one month, and that a writ of attachment for the arrest of the said **John Barron** be forthwith issued."

The writ of attachment would then order the Sheriff to arrest and keep the defendant in gaol.

If the defendant's goods were being seized or perhaps more properly quarantined, the following writ would be used:

Writ of sequestration
In the Supreme Court of Ontario
Between

James Gilbert, Robert MacDonald

PLAINTIFF(S)

and

John Barron

DEFENDANT(S)

Elizabeth the Second, by the Grace of God, of the United Kingdom, Canada and Her other Realms and Territories, **Queen,** Head of Commonwealth, Defender of the Faith.

To the Sheriff of the Judicial District of York **Greeting**.

Whereas by a judgment in this action dated 16th Jan. 1958, it was ordered that the said John Barron should not pledge certain shares in Amerwood (Eastern) Canada Ltd. Know ye, therefore, that we have given, and by these presents do give to you full power and authority to enter upon all the lands, tenements and real estate whatsoever of the said John Barron and to collect, receive and sequester in your hands, not only all the rents and profits of his said lands, tenements and real estate, but also all his goods, chattels and personal estates whatsoever.

We therefore command you that you do, at certain proper and convenient days and hours, go to and enter upon all the lands, tenements and real estates of the said John Barron and that you do collect, take and get into your hands not only the rents and profits of his said real estate, but also all his goods, chattels, and personal estate, and detain and keep the same under sequestration in your hands until the said John Barron shall redeem said shares in Amerwood (Eastern) Canada Ltd., and clear his contempt, and our said Court make other order to the contrary.

In Witness Whereof this writ is signed for the Supreme Court of Ontario by Andrew Drover Registrar of the said Court at Toronto this 1st day of May, 1958
(signature of officer)

　　　The original scope of the remedy of specific performance was a remedy for breach of a contract to convey land. This was extended to include contracts for the sale of chattels where the common law remedy would be inadequate. Such cases would involve the promise to sell a unique chattel, *e.g.*, a piece of sculpture or, as in *Behnke v. Bede (infra)*, a special ship.

　　　It was thought to be unfair that a buyer could, through the remedy of specific performance, force the seller to do what he had promised. In a concern that the remedies of each party be symmetrical, the rule developed that, in a contract where the buyer could get specific performance, the seller could too. Since what the seller wanted was the price, his judgment would be for money but the measure of the seller's recovery would be the agreed price of the land. The seller would then get his expectation interest protected, without having to show what he had lost by the buyer's breach. This would, of course, normally be the difference between the market price and contract price of the land. Apart from any concern for symmetry, the seller's remedy for the price may have been a response to the same concerns that originally led to the remedy of specific performance in favour of the buyer. It may be doubted now whether anything other than the concern of symmetry, or "mutuality" as it is referred to, justifies the seller's remedy for the price.

　　　The Chancellor's jurisdiction had always been predicated on the king's right and duty to do justice to his subjects. This appeal to justice gave to the Chancellor's jurisdiction the general name of "Equity". We can refer therefore to the Chancellor's jurisdiction as the jurisdiction of the Court of Equity or the Court of Chancery (the terms are synonymous). The remedies available before the Chancellor were known as equitable remedies as distinguished from the legal remedies of the common law courts.

　　　Since the Chancellor's jurisdiction was supplementary only, it followed that he could not give any remedy which was available in the common law courts, for example, damages. A seller's action for the price would have been brought in the common law courts. If therefore a plaintiff was denied any relief by the Chancellor, he might be able to go to the common law courts to get whatever relief they offered. This separate existence of the two bodies of law persisted until the nineteenth century.

　　　Since the plaintiff before the Chancellor was seeking justice it followed that he too had to be prepared to do justice. This led to the development of limitations on the right of a plaintiff to get an equitable remedy when he had behaved in some way improperly. Some of these limitations are mentioned in the cases that follow. As a further result of the origin of the equitable remedies, these remedies were always discretionary. This means that no plaintiff could ever demand, as of right, that the defendant be compelled to perform a contract specifically, no matter how meritorious the claim and upright the conduct of the plaintiff. Again, this will be seen in the cases that follow. By way of contrast, at common law, a plaintiff could not be denied his remedy if he could show breach of contract and damages. Even if the latter could not be shown he was entitled to judgment for nominal damages.

It is now seven hundred years since the power of the Chancellor was established. During that time his jurisdiction became formalized and reduced to rules. A regular court developed to supplement the work of the individual Chancellor. As was inevitable, friction developed between the jurisdiction of the Chancellor and the common law courts: no one likes to be told that he is being unjust. This dispute was resolved by James I who provided that in any dispute between the rules of the common law and equity, equity should prevail. The Court of Chancery existed as a separate court in England until the Judicature Act of 1873 and in Ontario until the Judicature Act of 1881. Since those dates, any court is able to give either equitable or legal remedies. However, it must be remembered that the historical origin of the separate systems still determines what remedies we call equitable and what we call legal and that the distinctions are still vitally important. Even now, the only way to define Equity or equitable rules is that they refer to that body of rules administered by the courts, which, were it not for the operation of the Judicature Act, would be administered only by those courts which would be known as Courts of Equity.

Further readings: Maitland, *Equity* (1909); Holdsworth, *History of English Law*, Vol. 1, 395-476; Vol. 5, 215-338; Plucknett, *Concise History of the Common Law*, 176-198.

The next case is a simple illustration of the rules of equity. The provision in the English Sale of Goods Act is identical to s. 50 of the Ontario Act which is:

> 50. In an action for breach of contract to deliver specific or ascertained goods, the court may, if it thinks fit, direct that the contract be performed specifically, without giving the defendant the option of retaining the goods on payment of damages, and may impose such terms and conditions as to damages, payment of the price, and otherwise, as to the court seems just.

This section is simply a codification of the law as it was before the act was passed.

BEHNKE v. BEDE SHIPPING CO.

[1927] 1 K.B. 649 K.B.D.

Jan. 18. **Wright J**. read the following judgment.

This is an action tried before me on January 12, 1927, without pleadings under an order of the vacation judge dated January 5 last. The plaintiff, a German shipowner, claims against the defendants, the owners of the British steamship *City*, a declaration that he purchased the *City* by contract from the defendants, and an order for specific performance of that contract, and an injunction; and, in the alternative, damages. The defendants deny the contract, and in the alternative say that it is not enforceable by reason of s. 4 of the Sale of Goods Act, 1893; and in any event say that it is not a case in which specific performance ought to be decreed....

It remains to consider what is the proper remedy. The plaintiff claims a decree of specific performance. This claim is strongly contested on behalf of the defendants. It is curious how little guidance there is on the question whether specific performance should be granted of a contract for the sale of a ship. Sect. 52 of the Sale of Goods Act gives the Court a discretion, if it think fit, in any action for breach of contract to deliver specific or ascertained goods, to direct that the contract shall be performed specifically. I think a ship is a specific chattel within the Act. In Fry on Specific Performance, 6th ed., p. 37, note 4, it is said a ship is probably within the general principle and reference is made to *Claringbould* v. *Curtis*, which, however, is the case of a barge and contains no discussion of principle. *Hart* v. *Herwig* seems to imply that a man who has contracted to purchase a ship is prima facie entitled to have it — that is, by an order for specific performance.

In the present case there is evidence that the *City* was of peculiar and practically unique value to the plaintiff. She was a cheap vessel, being old, having been built in 1892, but her engines and boilers were practically new and such as to satisfy the German regulations, and hence the plaintiff could, as a German shipowner, have her at once put on the German register.

A very experienced ship valuer has said that he knew of only one other comparable ship, but that may now have been sold. The plaintiff wants the ship for immediate use, and I do not think damages would be an adequate compensation. I think he is entitled to the ship and a decree of specific performance in order that justice may be done. What is the position between the defendants and the other buyers, whose contract was later in time than that of the plaintiff, is irrelevant in this action.

I have not overlooked the argument of Mr. Miller, based on the clauses in the contract which provide that before completion and payment of the balance of the purchase price the buyer was to have the option of inspecting the vessel afloat and of requiring the sellers to place her in dry dock for inspection, and of requiring the sellers to repair certain damage if any were found. Mr. Miller contended that as the Court will not decree specific performance of a contract to do work or perform services, these clauses constitute a bar to a decree here. But I think this contention is not sound. The defendants are neither dry dockowners nor ship repairers. All they could be required to do would be to give the appropriate orders to a dry dockowner or ship repairer if necessary. But the plaintiff may not require inspection or dry-docking (which, if no damage be found, will be at his own expense), and no damage requiring repairs may be discovered. Thinking, as I do, that justice can only be satisfied by an order for specific performance, I do not find in the clauses referred to, the only ones relied on by Mr. Miller, any ground why I should not make the decree. There will be judgment, therefore, for the plaintiff, with a declaration that he purchased the *City* from the defendants — I do not make the declaration exactly in the terms stated — and a decree that the contract shall be specifically performed, and that an injunction be granted as prayed, and costs.

Judgment for plaintiff.
Decree for specific performance.

The equivalent provisions of the U.C.C. are as follows:

Uniform Commercial Code
§2-716(1) Specific performance may be decreed when the goods are unique or in other proper circumstances.

The Official Comment to this section states:
"In view of this Article's emphasis on the commercial feasibility of replacement, a new concept of what are 'unique' goods is introduced under this section. Specific performance is no longer limited to goods which are already specific or ascertained at the time of contracting. The test of uniqueness under this section must be made in terms of the total situation which characterizes the contract. Output and requirements contracts involving a particular or peculiarly available source or market present today the typical commercial specific performance situation, as contrasted with contracts for the sale of heirlooms or priceless works of art which were usually involved in the older cases. However, uniqueness is not the sole basis of the remedy under this section for the relief may also be granted 'in other proper circumstances' and inability to cover is strong evidence of 'other proper circumstances'."

§2-716(3) provides that the buyer may claim the goods from the seller if he is unable or likely to be unable to effect cover, *i.e.*, obtain what he needs elsewhere.

The intended scope of the U.C.C. provisions is wider than that of s. 50. However, the courts have managed to reach a very similar position to that of the U.C.C. under the Sale of Goods Act. The following case significantly broadened the scope of s. 50.

SKY PETROLEUM LTD. v. VIP PETROLEUM LTD.

[1974] 1 W.L.R. 576 Chancery Division.

Goulding J. This is a motion for an injunction brought by the plaintiff company, Sky Petroleum Ltd., as buyer under a contract dated March 11, 1970, made between the defendant company, VIP Petroleum Ltd., as seller of the one part and the plaintiffs of the other part. That contract was to operate for a period of ten years, subject to certain qualifications, and thereafter on an annual basis unless terminated by either party giving to the other not less than three months' written notice to that effect. It was a contract at fixed prices, subject to certain provisions which I need not now mention. Further, the contract obliged the plaintiffs — and this is an important point — to take their entire requirement of motor gasoline and diesel fuel under the contract, with certain stipulated minimum yearly quantities. After the making of the agreement, it is common knowledge that the terms of trade in the market for petroleum and its different products changed very considerably, and I have little doubt that the contract is now disadvantageous to the defendants. After a long correspondence, the defendants, by telegrams dated November 15 and 16, 1973, have purported to terminate the contract under a clause therein providing for termination by the defendants if the plaintiffs fail to conform with any of the terms of the bargain. What is alleged is that the plaintiffs have exceeded the credit provisions of the contract and have persistently been, and now are, indebted to the defendants in larger amounts than were provided for. So far as that dispute relates, as for the purposes of this motion it must, to the date of the purported termination of the contract, it is impossible for me to decide it on the affidavit evidence. It involves not only a question of construction of the contract, but also certain disputes on subsequent arrangements between the parties and on figures in account. I cannot decide it on motion, and the less I say about it the better.

What I have to decide is whether any injunction should be granted to protect the plaintiffs in the meantime. There is trade evidence that the plaintiffs have no great prospect of finding any alternative source of supply for the filling stations which constitute their business. The defendants have indicated their willingness to continue to supply the plaintiffs, but only at prices which, according to the plaintiffs' evidence, would not be serious prices from a commercial point of view. There is, in my judgment, so far as I can make out on the evidence before me, a serious danger that unless the court interferes at this stage the plaintiffs will be forced out of business. In those circumstances, unless there is some specific reason which debars me from doing so, I should be disposed to grant an injunction to restore the former position under the contract until the rights and wrongs of the parties can be fully tried out.

It is submitted for the defendants that I ought not to do so for a number of reasons. It is said that, on the facts, the defendants were entitled to terminate and the plaintiffs were in the wrong. That, of course, is the very question in the action, and I have already expressed my inability to resolve it even provisionally on the evidence now before me. Then it is said that there are questions between the parties as to arrangements subsequent to the making of the contract, in particular regarding the price to be paid, and that they give rise to uncertainties which would make it difficult to enforce any order made by way of interlocutory relief. I do not think I ought to be deterred by that consideration, though I can see it has some force. In fact, during September and October, to go no further back, the defendants have gone on supplying and the plaintiffs have gone on paying. There has been nothing apparently impracticable in the contract, although the defendants say, of course, that the plaintiffs have not been paying large enough sums quickly enough.

Now I come to the most serious hurdle in the way of the plaintiffs which is the well known doctrine that the court refuses specific performance of a contract to sell and purchase chattels not specific or ascertained. That is a well-established and salutary rule, and I am entirely unconvinced by Mr. Christie, for the plaintiffs, when he tells me that an injunction in the form sought by him would not be specific enforcement at all. The matter is one of substance and not of form, and it is, in my judgment, quite plain that I am, for the time being, specifically enforcing the contract if I grant an injunction. However, the ratio behind the rule is, as I believe, that under the ordinary contract for the sale of non-specific goods, damages are a sufficient remedy. That, to my mind, is lacking in the circumstances of the present case. The evidence suggests, and indeed it is common knowledge that the petroleum market is in an unusual state in which a would-be buyer cannot go out into the market and contract with another seller, possibly at some sacrifice as to price. Here, the defendants appear for practical purposes to be the plaintiffs' sole means of keeping their business going, and I am prepared so far to depart from the general rule as to try to preserve the position under the contract until a later date. I therefore propose to grant an injunction.

Dealing first with its duration, it will restrain the defendants (in terms I will come to in a moment) until judgment in the action or further order, but not in any event beyond June 30, 1974, without further order of the court. I say that because of a provision in the contract which requires further steps to be taken in relation to the price of supply after that date. The terms which I suggest must, with certain qualifications, follow the notice of motion. If counsel are able to arrive at something more convenient and easier to enforce, they may mention the matter to me at an early date and the wording can be reconsidered, but for the moment I will order that the defendants by themselves, or their servants or agents, in the usual form be restrained from withholding supplies of "motor gasoline and DERV" from the plaintiffs in accordance with the terms of the contract dated March 11, 1970, and such other arrangements, if any, as were agreed between the parties before the issue of the writ in this action. There will be a proviso that the plaintiffs are not to require delivery of more than a specified number of gallons in any one month, and that number is to be ascertained by taking the arithmetical mean of the three months of supply, August, September and October. That will, I hope, prevent any abuse of the injunction by the plaintiffs.

I would be sympathetic to any application by the defendants for the provision of security in some particular sum and form. I do not know whether the plaintiffs can make any specific offer in that respect, or whether the best thing is that all the details should be considered by counsel.

Order accordingly.

QUESTIONS AND PROBLEMS

Consider the application of both s. 50 and the U.C.C. in the following cases:

1. A was constructing an office tower for B. C promised to supply specially made elevator doors to A for the building. C refuses to deliver. It is shown that the doors can be readily obtained elsewhere but only after several weeks delay.

2. Would your answer to Q.1 be the same if the delay would make A liable to pay B heavy damages?

3. Marty promises to sell Rob an antique wash basin for $1,000. Marty subsequently gets an offer from Patricia of $2,000 for the wash basin and refuses to sell to Rob.

4. Would your answer to Q.3 be the same if Rob had been approached by Patricia, who had heard that he had agreed to buy the wash basin from Marty? Rob had at that time said that she could have it from him for $2,500. Patricia said that this was too much to pay and so no deal had been made.

5. If Rob can get specific performance from Marty in this case, what do you think should happen if Marty delivered the wash basin to Patricia who paid Marty the full price of $2,000?

It is generally assumed that in contracts for the sale of land specific performance is always available to the purchaser. There is no reason to think that the general finding that common law damages must be inadequate is inapplicable here. There are cases where courts have refused specific performance on this ground, *i.e.* that damages would be adequate. (*Prittie v. Laughton* (1902), 1 O.W.R. 185 (Ont. Div. C.).)

As we have seen, the requirement of mutuality has led courts to allow a vendor to sue the purchaser for the price. Again, the assumption that this is inevitable can be challenged. (*Centrex Homes Corp. v. Boag* (1974), 320 A. 2d 194 (New Jersey).)

The remedy of specific performance is only one of a number of equitable remedies that may be available to a plaintiff. The following case shows how the remedy of specific performance can be supplemented by (a) an accounting and (b) an injunction. (An accounting is an order that a person disclose the benefits that he has obtained in some particular way and that he pay these benefits to the person entitled to them.)

GILBERT v. BARRON

(1958), 13 D.L.R. (2d) 262. Ont. H.C.

Wilson J.: — This is an action to recover from the defendant Barron, shares in Amerwood (Eastern) Canada Ltd., to which the plaintiffs allege they are entitled under an oral contract with him.

.   .   .

The action has been strongly fought and I make the following findings of fact. The company, Amerwood (Eastern) Canada Ltd., is incorporated as a public company under the Ontario *Companies Act* by letters patent of this Province dated October 26, 1948. Under agreement with an American company it manufactures and sells a plywood product known as Amerwood, and since 1954 it also manufactures and distributes another product known as Cellotex. The dispute in this action arises out of a struggle for control of the ownership of the shares of the Ontario company, hereinafter called Amerwood.

The plaintiff MacDonald, a successful salesman who resides in the City of Toronto, is responsible for the organization of Amerwood. He sold much treasury stock at Owen Sound, where the company, when organized, carried on its manufacturing operations. As was natural, he became one of the principal shareholders. The other two principal shareholders were one Parkes and the plaintiff Gilbert, an investment broker of many years' standing, who resides in Toronto. Gilbert became a shareholder in 1948, and at the annual meeting in February 1950 he was elected a director. In June 1954 he was elected president, an office he held until he was succeeded by Barron in 1956 in the circumstances hereinafter related. Shortly after his election as a director in 1948, he and Parkes, who was the general manager of the company from its inception until his resignation and retirement on account of ill-health on January 2, 1954, and MacDonald, who was a director and vice-president from the organization of the company until the annual meeting in 1957, entered into an agreement with the object of holding and preserving among the three of them stock control of the company. The terms of this agreement were that if any one of the three should purchase shares in the company, he would offer one-third to each of the other two at cost price.

The agreement did not necessarily require the other two shareholders to take up the offer but at least they had this right to purchase. This agreement was acted upon when Parkes' son sold his shares to his father. Gilbert and MacDonald agreed that they should be sold to Parkes Sr. because the quantity of shares made no real difference as to the balance of control.

Early in 1953 Parkes became ill, and subsequent to his resignation in January 1954, he died. In January 1954, before his resignation, he sold most of his shares to the defendant Barron, with the approval of Gilbert and MacDonald, after Barron agreed to the same arrangement with respect to the acquisition of future shares as had existed among Parkes, Gilbert and MacDonald. This agreement was made before Barron acquired his shares. The exact date of the agreement is not of great importance. I am satisfied it was made before Barron acquired Parkes' shares. Moreover, as appears later, the agreement was acted upon, and, later again, acknowledged on a Sunday in February 1955 at a meeting, at which Barron, MacDonald and Gilbert were present in Barron's office at Port Credit. I find that Barron acted upon the agreement when he purchased in December 1954 the shares which were known as the 500 Russell shares. This number did not lend itself to an even division, and after negotiation among the three they were divided 150 shares to each of Gilbert, MacDonald and Barron and 50 shares to a member of the staff, Miss Dorothy Gilbank.

By February 1956, without the knowledge of his two fellow shareholders Gilbert and MacDonald, Barron had decided to secure control of the company. He purchased options to buy enough shares to give him voting control of the company and at the annual meeting he had enough proxies and shares in his name to give him voting control of it. After the meeting he took up the options thus acquiring stock control.

Gilbert and MacDonald learned of this control just before the annual meeting and in due course made demands upon Barron for their shares in accordance with the agreement among them. These demands were not replied to, and on February 8, 1957, this action was commenced. In the interval between this annual meeting and the commencement of the action the plaintiffs were acting upon legal advice.

The evidence has been quite lengthy and very conflicting. After paying close attention to all of it, I have no difficulty in deciding which witnesses, although not always clear or consistent, should be believed. They were MacDonald, Gilbert and Miss Gilbank. If Mrs. Parkes' evidence is to be taken into account, and in my opinion it is not, I find she was a credible witness. Barron was a most unreliable witness.

. . .

The plaintiffs are entitled to specific performance of the agreement in respect of all shares claimed by them. He must tender one-third — that is to say, 816 common and 816 preferred — to each of the plaintiffs who will, upon such tender, pay for them in accordance with the agreement.

. . .

The plaintiffs ask in addition to the relief already referred to for an accounting, of all benefits received as a result of holding the said shares. They are entitled to such relief as against Barron, however, to the extent of the dividends paid by the company and the plaintiffs will have judgment against Barron for the dividends paid by Amerwood on the shares which they are entitled to receive from him, payment to be made when they pay for the shares.

The plaintiffs also ask an injunction restraining the defendants from voting the shares to which they are entitled, and from selling, pledging or transferring them. They will have judgment for this relief (directly and indirectly) in respect of Barron. He has apparently placed the shares in the name of Port Credit Lumber Co., of which he has voting share control. However, it is quite apparent that Barron was only using this company as well as his co-defendants as his agent to break the agreement with the plaintiffs. In any event, Barron has not pleaded that it is impossible for him to comply with the contract.

The plaintiffs also ask damages. To this they are entitled as against Barron. No evidence was adduced to prove the amount of damages suffered. I should think there would be some at least loss of salary as directors, but I am unable to conclude there was more. I think the sum of $200 to each of the plaintiffs as nominal damages would suffice. These are the directors' fees they appear to have lost. In other circumstances, even though the task seems an impossible one from the practical point of view, the damages could be assessed at a much higher figure.

In addition to the costs already dealt with, the plaintiffs will have their costs of the action against the defendant Barron which includes the costs they have incurred against the other defendants.

Judgment for plaintiffs.

At common law the basis for any claim for relief was the breach of a contract. In equity, however, the basis for any remedy was not the breach of contract but the making of the contract. A plaintiff was therefore entitled to come to court to seek an order of specific performance even before breach had occurred. This is already a further advantage of the equitable remedy over the common law remedy, since a plaintiff who had to wait until breach may sometimes find that his defendant is insolvent or has disappeared. The Court of Chancery however would make a party who sought a decree of specific performance too soon and where it was not justified, pay the costs of the action. This operated as an effective deterrent to precipitate recourse to the Chancellor.

The equitable remedies are available in any kind of contract. One class of contracts where their application causes special problems is employment contracts. Here, as we shall see, the remedy of specific performance as the enforcement of a positive obligation may not be available, but, instead, the remedy of an injunction — the enforcement of a negative obligation — may be more usually given. The following cases explore some of these issues.

DE RIVAFINOLI v. CORSETTI

(1833), 4 Paige 264. Court of Chancery of New York.

[This case came before the chancellor on an order for the complainant to show cause why a ne exeat granted against the defendant should not be discharged, or the amount for which the defendant was held to bail reduced. The bill, which was filed in September, 1833, stated that the defendant, in the March preceding, had agreed with the complainant, as manager of the Italian theatre in the city of New-York, to sing, gesticulate and recite, in the capacity of *primo basso*, in all the operas, serious, semi-serious and comic, farces, oratorios, concerts, cantatas and benefits, which should be ordered by the complainant, or his authorized agents, in any city of the United States, where the complainant should think proper; and that he should be present at the times which should be appointed for rehearsals, and contribute to the interest and good conduct of the enterprise, submitting himself to the regulations made by the complainant, and to the fines in such regulations established, for the term of eight months, commencing on the first of November, 1833. For which singing, gesticulating, reciting, etc. the complainant agreed to pay him $1192, in sixteen half monthly payments; each payment to be made in advance, at the commencement of the half month for which the same was to be paid; and to allow the defendant one benefit, he bearing half the expense thereof. And that the defendant also agreed not to make use of his talents in any other theatre, or public hall, without the permission of the complainant, or his agents. For the performance of which agreement each party bound himself to the other, under the penalty of a fine of one third of the salary of the defendant; which fine was to be paid by the party in default, without objection, or exception. The bill further alleged that the complainant had entered into a contract with the trustees of the Italian opera house, in New-York, under heavy penalties, to commence the performance of Italian operas, with a first rate company, on the first of November, 1833; and that he had engaged the defendant as one of such company, and had gone to Europe to procure others to make up a troupe, complete in all its departments. That the defendant was a skilful musician, and was well qualified to sing, perform and exhibit Italian operas, in the capacity in which he had been engaged by the complainant; who had made all his arrangements, and his selections of other performers, in this country and in Europe, on the faith of the defendant's performing his engagement. That the services of the defendant were necessary, in the capacity in which he was engaged, to make up the troupe, or company, and his place could not be supplied without great expense and delay. And also that the complainant would be exposed to great damage, loss and inconvenience, and be liable to fail in his contract to obtain a first rate company by the first of November, if the defendant did not perform his engagement. The bill further charged that the defendant, since the making of the agreement, and in violation thereof, had entered into a contract with another person to go to the Havanna as an opera singer, and to be there on the same day on which, by his agreement with the complainant, his services were to commence at New-York; and that he was about to leave this state for Cuba, in fraud and violation of the rights of the complainant. The bill therefore prayed for a specific performance of the contract with the complainant; that the defendant might be decreed to sing, gesticulate and recite, in the capacity of *primo basso*, according to his said agreement; that he might be restrained from leaving the state; and for general relief. The bill also prayed for a ne exeat; which was granted by an injunction master. And the defendant being unable to find bail, was committed to prison....]

The Chancellor [Walworth]. The material facts alleged in the complainant's bill are not denied; and for the purpose of this application, they must be taken to be true. There is an affidavit, annexed to the bill, that the defendant has declared his intention of going to the Havanna; and the defendant has not denied such intention; although he swears he has not made any engagement to go there. Upon the merits of the case, I suppose it must be conceded that the complainant is entitled to a specific performance of this contract; as the law appears to have been long since settled that a bird that can sing and will not sing must be made to sing. *(Old adage.)* In this case it is charged in the bill, not only that the defendant can sing, but also that he has expressly agreed to sing, and to accompany that singing with such appropriate gestures as may be necessary and proper to give an interest to his performance. And from the facts disclosed, I think it is very evident also that he does not intend to gratify the citizens of New-York, who may resort to the Italian opera, either by his singing, or by his gesticulations. Although the authority before cited shows the law to be in favor of the complainant, so far at least as to entitle him to a decree for the singing, I am not aware that any officer of this court has that perfect knowledge of the Italian language, or possesses that exquisite sensibility in the auricular nerve which is necessary to understand, and to enjoy with a proper zest, the peculiar beauties of the Italian opera, so fascinating to the fashionable world. There might be some difficulty, therefore, even if the defendant was compelled to sing under the direction and in the presence of a master in chancery, in ascertaining whether he performed his engagement according to its spirit and intent. It would also be very difficult for the master to determine what effect coercion might produce upon the defendant's singing, especially in livelier airs; although the fear of imprisonment would unquestionably deepen his seriousness in the graver parts of the drama. But one thing at least is certain; his songs will be neither comic, or even semi-serious, while he remains confined in that dismal cage, the debtor's prison of New-York.

[The judge went on to hold that the defendant could not be kept in prison at the date of judgment, leaving it open to decide what to do if he should later refuse to sing.]

NOTE. The writ of "*ne exeat*" referred to in the judgment was an equitable remedy in the nature of bail at common law. The writ is directed to the Sheriff, commanding him to commit the party to prison until he gives security not to leave the jurisdiction without the permission of the court. Such a proceeding would now be brought under the Fraudulent Debtors Arrest Act, R.S.O. 1970, c. 183.

WARNER BROS. v. NELSON

[1937] 1 K.B. 209.

Branson J. The facts of this case are few and simple. The plaintiffs are a firm of film producers in the United States of America. In 1931 the defendant, then not well known as a film actress, entered into a contract with the plaintiffs. Before the expiration of that contract the present contract was entered into between the parties. Under it the defendant received a considerably enhanced salary, the other conditions being substantially the same. This contract was for fifty-two weeks and contains options to the plaintiffs to extend it for further periods of fifty-two weeks at ever-increasing amounts of salary to the defendant. No question of construction arises upon the contract, and it is not necessary to refer to it in any great detail;

but in view of some of the contentions raised it is desirable to call attention quite generally to some of the provisions contained in it. It is a stringent contract, under which the defendant agrees "to render her exclusive services as a motion picture and/or legitimate stage actress" to the plaintiffs, and agrees to perform solely and exclusively for them. She also agrees, by way of negative stipulation, that "she will not, during such time" — that is to say, during the term of the contract — "render any services for or in any other phonographic, stage or motion picture production or productions or business of any other person ... or engage in any other occupation without the written consent of the producer being first had and obtained."

With regard to the term of the contract there is a further clause, clause 23, under which, if the defendant fails, refuses or neglects to perform her services under the contract, the plaintiffs "have the right to extend the term of this agreement and all of its provisions for a period equivalent to the period during which such failure, refusal or neglect shall be continued."

In June of this year the defendant, for no discoverable reason except that she wanted more money, declined to be further bound by the agreement, left the United States and, in September, entered into an agreement in this country with a third person. This was a breach of contract on her part, and the plaintiffs on September 9 commenced this action claiming a declaration that the contract was valid and binding, an injunction to restrain the defendant from acting in breach of it, and damages. The defence alleged that the plaintiffs had committed breaches of the contract which entitled the defendant to treat it as at an end; but at the trial this contention was abandoned and the defendant admitted that the plaintiffs had not broken the contract and that she had; but it was contended on her behalf that no injunction could as a matter of law be granted in the circumstances of the case.

. . .

I turn then to the consideration of the law applicable to this case on the basis that the contract is a valid and enforceable one. It is conceded that our Courts will not enforce a positive covenant of personal service; and specific performance of the positive covenants by the defendant to serve the plaintiffs is not asked in the present case. The practice of the Court of Chancery in relation to the enforcement of negative covenants is stated on the highest authority by Lord Cairns in the House of Lords in *Doherty v. Allman*, 3 App. Cas. 709, 719. His Lordship says: "My Lords, if there had been a negative covenant, I apprehend, according to well-settled practice, a Court of Equity would have had no discretion to exercise. If parties, for valuable consideration, with their eyes open, contract that a particular thing shall not be done, all that a Court of Equity has to do is to say, by way of injunction, that which the parties have already said by way of covenant, that the thing shall not be done; and in such case the injunction does nothing more than give the sanction of the process of the Court to that which already is the contract between the parties. It is not then a question of the balance of convenience or inconvenience, or of the amount of damage or of injury — it is the specific performance, by the Court, of that negative bargain which the parties have made, with their eyes open, between themselves."

That was not a case of a contract of personal service; but the same principle had already been applied to such a contract by Lord St. Leonards in *Lumley v. Wagner* (1852), 1 De G. M. & G. 604, 619; 42 E.R. 687. The Lord

Chancellor used the following language: "Wherever this Court has not proper jurisdiction to enforce specific performance, it operates to bind men's consciences, as far as they can be bound, to a true and literal performance of their agreements; and it will not suffer them to depart from their contracts at their pleasure, leaving the party with whom they have contracted to the mere chance of any damages which a jury may give. The exercise of this jurisdiction has, I believe, had a wholesome tendency towards the maintenance of that good faith which exists in this country to a much greater degree perhaps than in any other; and although the jurisdiction is not to be extended, yet a Judge would desert his duty who did not act up to what his predecessors have handed down as the rule for his guidance in the administration of such an equity." This passage was cited as a correct statement of the law in the opinion of a strong Board of the Privy Council in the case of *Lord Strathcona Steamship Co. v. Dominion Coal Co.*, [1926] A.C. 108, 125, and I not only approve it, if I may respectfully say so, but am bound by it.

The defendant, having broken her positive undertakings in the contract without any cause or excuse which she was prepared to support in the witness-box, contends that she cannot be enjoined from breaking the negative covenants also. The mere fact that a covenant which the Court would not enforce, if expressed in positive form, is expressed in the negative instead, will not induce the Court to enforce it.

. . .

The conclusion to be drawn from the authorities is that, where a contract of personal service contains negative covenants the enforcement of which will not amount either to a decree of specific performance of the positive covenants of the contract or to the giving of a decree under which the defendant must either remain idle or perform those positive covenants, the Court will enforce those negative covenants; but this is subject to a further consideration. An injunction is a discretionary remedy, and the Court in granting it may limit it to what the Court considers reasonable in all the circumstances of the case.... The case before me is, therefore, one in which it would be proper to grant an injunction unless to do so would in the circumstances be tantamount to ordering the defendant to perform her contract or remain idle or unless damages would be the more appropriate remedy.

With regard to the first of these considerations, it would, of course, be impossible to grant an injunction covering all the negative covenants in the contract. That would, indeed, force the defendant to perform her contract or remain idle; but this objection is removed by the restricted form in which the injunction is sought. It is confined to forbidding the defendant, without the consent of the plaintiffs, to render any services for or in any motion picture or stage production for any one other than the plaintiffs.

It was also urged that the difference between what the defendant can earn as a film artiste and what she might expect to earn by any other form of activity is so great that she will in effect be driven to perform her contract. That is not the criterion adopted in any of the decided cases. The defendant is stated to be a person of intelligence, capacity and means, and no evidence was adduced to show that, if enjoined from doing the specified acts otherwise than for the plaintiffs, she will not be able to employ herself both usefully and remuneratively in other spheres of activity, though not as remuneratively as in her special line. She will not be driven, although she may be tempted, to perform the contract, and the fact that she may be so tempted is no objection to the grant of an injunction. This appears from the judgment of Lord St. Leonards in *Lumley v. Wagner*, where he used the following language: "It was objected that the operation of the injunction in the present case was mischievous, excluding the defendant J. Wagner from performing at any other theatre while this Court had no power to compel her to perform at Her Majesty's Theatre. It is true, that I have not the means of compelling her to sing, but she has no cause of complaint, if I compel her to abstain from the commission of an act which she has bound herself not to do, and thus possibly cause her to fulfil her engagement. The jurisdiction which I now exercise is wholly within the power of the Court, and being of opinion that it is a proper case for interfering, I shall leave nothing unsatisfied by the judgment I pronounce. The effect too of the injunction, in restraining J. Wagner from singing elsewhere may, in the event" — that is a different matter — "of an action being brought against her by the plaintiff, prevent any such amount of vindictive damages being given against her as a jury might probably be inclined to give if she had carried her talents and exercised them at the rival theatre: the injunction may also, as I have said, tend to the fulfilment of her engagement; though, in continuing the injunction, I disclaim doing indirectly what I cannot do directly."

With regard to the question whether damages is not the more appropriate remedy, I have the uncontradicted evidence of the plaintiffs as to the difficulty of estimating the damages which they may suffer from the breach by the defendant of her contract. I think it is not inappropriate to refer to the fact that, in the contract between the parties, in clause 22, there is a formal admission by the defendant that her services, being "of a special, unique, extraordinary and intellectual character" gives them a particular value "the loss of which cannot be reasonably or adequately compensated in damages" and that a breach may "cost the producer great and irreparable injury and damage," and the artiste expressly agrees that the producer shall be entitled to the remedy of injunction. Of course, parties cannot contract themselves out of the law; but it assists, at all events, on the question of evidence as to the applicability of an injunction in the present case, to find the parties formally recognizing that in cases of this kind injunction is a more appropriate remedy than damages.

Furthermore, in the case of *Grimston v. Cuningham*, which was also a case in which a theatrical manager was attempting to enforce against an actor a negative stipulation against going elsewhere, Wills J. granted an injunction, and used the following language: "This is an agreement of a kind which is pre-eminently subject to the interference of the Court by injunction, for in cases of this nature it very often happens that the injury suffered in consequence of the breach of the agreement would be out of all proportion to any pecuniary damages which could be proved or assessed by a jury. This circumstance affords a strong reason in favour of exercising the discretion of the Court by granting an injunction."

I think that that applies to the present case also, and that an injunction should be granted in regard to the specified services.

Then comes the question as to the period for which the injunction should operate. The period of the contract, now that the plaintiffs have undertaken not as from October 16, 1936, to exercise the rights of suspension conferred upon them by clause 23 thereof, will, if they exercise their options to prolong it, extend to about May, 1942... the Court should make the period such as to give reasonable protection and no more to the plaintiffs against the ill effects to them of the defendant's breach of contract. The evidence as to that was perhaps necessarily somewhat vague. The main difficulty that the plaintiffs apprehend is that the defendant might appear in other films whilst the films already made by them and not yet shown are in the market for sale or hire and thus depreciate their value. I think that if the injunction is in force during the continuance of the contract or for three years from now, whichever period is the shorter, that will substantially meet the case.

The other matter is as to the area within which the injunction is to operate. The contract is not an English contract and the parties are not British subjects. In my opinion all that properly concerns this Court is to prevent the defendant from committing the prohibited acts within the jurisdiction of this Court, and the injunction will be limited accordingly.

QUESTIONS

1. What do you think that this decision would do to the effect of the contracts that Warner Bros. had with all their stars? [Bette Davis in fact went back to work for Warner Bros. where she was warmly welcomed.]

2. Suppose that Warner Bros. could not have got an injunction, what would the measure of their damages be?

NOTE: The problem of ordering that a contract be specifically performed has also come up in the context of collective agreements, *i.e.* agreements made between an employer and a union. In the *Winnipeg Builders' Exchange Case* (*I.B.E.W. v. Winnipeg Builders' Exchange*) (1967), 65 D.L.R. (2d) 242, the Supreme Court of Canada unanimously upheld decisions of the Manitoba Court of Appeal and Queen's Bench which had granted an interim injunction to restrain a strike. The strike was in breach of a collective agreement. The judges were aware of the historic reluctance of courts to order the specific enforcement of contracts of personal service. Monnin J.A. in the Manitoba Court of Appeal said, (1966), 57 D.L.R. (2d) 141 at 157:

"The complexity of labour-management relations in a highly industrialized civilization were presumably not even thought of [when the law was being developed]."

In giving the judgment of the S.C.C., Cartwright C.J.C., said, (p. 250):

"[U]nder the terms of the collective agreements existing in the case at bar it was expressly provided that there should be no strike during the life of the agreements.

"In my view the purposes of the Labour Relations Act would be in large measure defeated if the court were to say that it is powerless to restrain the continuation of a strike engaged in in direct violation of the terms of a collective agreement binding on the striking employees and in breach of the express provisions of the Act. The ratio of such decisions as *Lumley v. Wagner*,... does not, in my opinion require us so to hold. There is a real difference between saying to one individual that he must go on working for another individual and saying to a group bound by a collective agreement that they must not take concerted action to break this contract and to disobey the statute law of the Province."

The injunction granted by the trial judge read:

"1. THIS COURT DOTH ORDER that the defendants and each of them, their officers, servants, agents and members and any person acting under their instructions or any other person having notice of this order be and are hereby strictly enjoined and restrained until the trial or other final disposition of this action, from declaring, authorizing, counselling, aiding or engaging in or conspiring with others either direct (sic) or indirectly to bring about or continue an unlawful strike with respect to the employment of employees with the plaintiff Poole Construction Limited or its sub-contractors in combination or in concert or in accordance with a common understanding.

"2. AND THIS COURT DOTH ORDER that the defendants and each of them, their officers, servants, agents and members and any person acting under their instruction or any other person having notice of this order be and are hereby strictly enjoined and restrained under the trial or other final disposition of this action from

"(i) watching, besetting or picketing or attempting to watch, beset or picket at or in the vicinity of The Royal Bank Building premises at the Southeast corner of Fort Street and Portage Avenue, in the City of Winnipeg, in Manitoba;

"(ii) interfering with the servants, agents, employees or suppliers of the plaintiff Poole Construction Limited or its subcontractors or any other persons seeking peaceful entrance to or exit from said premises by the use of forces, threats, intimidations, coercion or other manner or means;

"(iii) ordering, aiding, abetting, counselling or encouraging in any manner whatsoever either directly or indirectly, any person to commit the acts aforesaid or any of them."

How easily do you think that this could be enforced?

The Labour Relations Act of Ontario provides:

36(1) Every collective agreement shall provide that there will be no strikes or lock outs so long as the agreement continues to operate.

(2) If a collective agreement does not contain such a provision as is mentioned in subsection 1, it shall be deemed to contain the following provision:

'There shall be no strikes or lockouts so long as this agreement continues to operate.'

The right to obtain an injunction in a labour dispute is subject to the Judicature Act, s. 20:

20 — (1) In this section, "labour dispute" means a dispute or difference concerning terms, tenure or conditions of employment or concerning the association or representation of persons in negotiating, fixing, maintaining, changing or seeking to arrange terms or conditions of employment, regardless of whether the disputants stand in the proximate relation of employer and employee.

(2) Subject to subsection 7, no injunction to restrain a person from any act in connection with a labour dispute shall be granted ex parte.

(3) In every application for an injunction to restrain a person from any act in connection with a labour dispute, the court must be satisfied that reasonable efforts to obtain police assistance, protection and action to prevent or remove any alleged danger of damage to property, injury to persons, obstruction of or interference with lawful entry upon or exit from the premises in question, or breach of the peace have been unsuccessful.

(4) Subject to subsection 7, evidence in support of an application for an injunction to restrain a person from any act in connection with a labour dispute shall be provided by way of affidavits confined to statements of facts within the knowledge of the deponent, but any party may by notice to the party filing such affidavit, together with the proper conduct money, require the attendance of the deponent to be cross-examined at the hearing of the motion.

(5) An interim injunction to restrain a person from any act in connection with a

labour dispute may be granted for a period of not longer than four days and, subject to subsection 7, only after two days notice of the application therefor has been given to the person or persons named in the application.

(6) At least two days notice of an application for an interim injunction to restrain a person from any act in connection with a labour dispute shall be given to the persons affected thereby and not named in the application,

(a) where such persons are members of a labour organization, by personal service upon an officer or agent of the labour organization; and

(b) where such persons are not members of a labour organization, by posting the notice in a conspicuous place at the location of the activity sought to be restrained where it can be read by any person affected,

and service and posting under this subsection shall be deemed to be sufficient notice to all such persons.

(7) Where notice as required by subsections 5 and 6 is not given, the court may grant an interim injunction where,

(a) the case is otherwise a proper one for the granting of an interim injunction; and

(b) notice as required by subsections 5 and 6 could not be given because the delay necessary to do so would result in irreparable damage or injury, a breach of the peace or an interruption in an essential public service; and

(c) reasonable notification, by telephone or otherwise, has been given to the persons to be affected or, where any of such persons are members of a labour organization, to an officer of that labour organization or to the person authorized under section 77 of The Labour Relations Act, to accept service of process under that Act on behalf of that labour organization or trade union, or where it is shown that such notice could not have been given; and

(d) proof of all material facts for the purposes of clauses a, b and c is established by viva voce evidence.

(8) The misrepresentation of any fact or the withholding of any qualifying relevant matter, directly or indirectly provided by or on behalf of the applicant for an injunction under this section, constitutes a contempt of court.

(9) Any judgment or order in an application under this section may be appealed to the Court of Appeal.

There are also cases where substantial damages for breach of contract have been awarded against a union that has supported an unlawful strike. In *Canadian General Electric Co. Ltd. v. United Electrical Workers* (1952), 3 L.A.C. 1090, an arbitration board set up under a collective agreement (chaired by Professor Bora Laskin) awarded the company over $9,000 for breach of the collective agreement.

The courts' general approach to collective agreements is stated by Laskin C.J.C. in *McGavin Toastmaster Ltd. v. Ainscough* (1975), 54 D.L.R. (3d) 1, in the Supreme Court of Canada. In this case the employees engaged in an illegal strike in an attempt to prevent the employer from phasing out certain operations. The employer then closed the plant. The employees sought to obtain severance pay under the collective agreement. The employer argued that, under the general law of contracts, the breach of contract by the employees in striking illegally, entitled it to discharge the employees without any severance pay. In rejecting this argument and upholding the right of the employees to severance pay, Laskin C.J.C. said (p. 6):

"The reality is, and has been for many years now throughout Canada, that individual relationships as between employer and employee have meaning only at the hiring stage and even then there are qualifications which arise by reason of union security clauses in collective agreements. The common law as it applies to individual employment contracts is no longer relevant to employer-employee relations governed by a collective agreement which, as the one involved here, deals with discharge, termination of employment, severance pay and a host of other matters that have been negotiated between union and company as the principal parties thereto. To quote again from the reasons of Judson, J., in the *Paquet* case, at pp. 353-4, (1959), 18 D.L.R. (2d):

" 'If the relation between employee and union were that of mandator and mandatary, the result would be that a collective agreement would be the equivalent of a bundle of individual contracts between employer and employee negotiated by the union as agent for the employees. This seems to me to be a complete misapprehension of the nature of the juridical relation involved in the collective agreement. The union contracts not as agent or mandatary but as an independent contracting party and the contract it makes with the employer binds the employer to regulate his master and servant relations according to the agreed terms.'

"The collective agreement in the present case makes the foregoing abundantly clear. Wages and hours of work are, of course, dealt with, and persons who come into the employ do so on the terms of the collective agreement as to wages and hours. They also come under the terms of the collective agreement as to promotion, lay-offs, rehiring and preference of transfers to shifts, all of which are regulated in this case by art. XVI of the collective agreement, headed "Seniority". Article V deals with the hiring procedure, and gives the union the prior right to supply staff subject to certain exceptions. Discharge is dealt with both in art. IV and in art. VII. Central to all the benefits and obligations that rest upon the union, the employees and the company under the collective agreement are the grievance and arbitration provisions, about which nothing more need be said here. Standing at the forefront of the substantive terms of the collective agreement is art. I under which the union is recognized by the company as 'the sole collective bargaining agency for all employees coming under the jurisdiction of this agreement'. There is in this collective agreement ample support for the observations of Judson, J., in the *Paquet* case.

"In my view, therefore, questions such as repudiation and fundamental breach must be addressed to the collective agreement if they are to have any subject-matter at all. When so addressed, I find them inapplicable in the face of the legislation which, in British Columbia and elsewhere in Canada, governs labour-management relations, provides for certification of unions for compulsory collective bargaining, for the negotiation, duration and renewal of collective agreements. The Mediation Services Act, which was in force at the material time in this case, provided in s. 8 for a minimum one-year term for collective agreements unless the responsible Minister gave consent to earlier termination, and provided also for the making of collective agreements for longer terms, subject to certain termination options before the full term had run. Neither this Act nor the companion *Labour Relations Act*, R.S.B.C. 1960, c. 205 [since repealed by 1973 (2nd Sess.), c. 122, s. 151], could operate according to their terms if common law concepts like repudiation and fundamental breach could be invoked in relation to collective agreements which have not expired and where the duty to bargain collectively subsists."

The next case is an example of the courts' response to perceived unfairness and the availability of equitable remedies.

HILL v. PARSONS

[1971] 3 All E.R. 1345. Court of Appeal, England. Lord Denning M.R.,
Sachs and Stamp L.JJ.

[The facts are taken from the judgment of **Lord Denning M.R.**]

Mr John William Hill is a chartered engineer, now aged 63. He has been
employed by C.A. Parsons & Co. Ltd. ('the company') for the last 35 years,
and is due to retire in two years' time, when he becomes 65. His salary is
£3,000 a year and is soon to be raised. He is a member of their pension
scheme. It is important for him to serve until the end of his time, because
his pension depends on his average salary for his last three years.

Before 1968 Mr Hill and other professional engineers were not members
of a trade union. But employees of the company of lesser standing, such as
draughtsmen and technicians, belonged to one or other of two trade unions.
Most belonged to DATA (the Draughtsmen's and Allied Technicians'
Association); others belonged to a rival union called ASTMS (the Association of Scientific Technical and Managerial Staffs). DATA then engaged in
a vigorous campaign to increase its membership and to gain exclusive negotiating rights. This led to many disputes. The members of DATA 'worked to
rule' on more than one occasion. Mr Hill and other members of the professional staff were disturbed by these inter-union disputes. They joined a
union of professional engineers called UKAPE (United Kingdom Association of Professional Engineers). This union has no political objectives and
does not seek to use disruptive means of strife.

In March 1970 DATA determined to make all the employees join their
union. They called their members out on strike and threatened to 'black'
the company's products. This placed the company in a critical economic
position. Eventually, on 15th May 1970, the company capitulated to the
demands of DATA. They agreed to make all their employees join DATA.
They signed an agreement with DATA which covered all persons below the
heads of departments and assistant heads. It covered, therefore, professional engineers like Mr Hill. (There was to be a list in an appendix of the
jobs covered, but this appendix has never been issued.) This agreement contained these clauses:

> "1. D.A.T.A. shall have sole negotiating rights for all Technical Staff covered by
> this Agreement.
> "2. Membership of D.A.T.A. will be a condition of service for all new recruits to
> Technical Staff...
> "3. The Company will express to all non-union members of the Technical Staff
> its strong wish and desire that they should forthwith join D.A.T.A. After a period
> of 12 months from the signing of this Agreement it will be a condition of service
> for such staff to be members of D.A.T.A...."

After the 12 months expired, the company sought to comply with the stipulations which DATA had forced on them. On 19th May 1971 the company
wrote to 38 of the professional staff a circular letter. It was in this form:

19th May, 1971.

> "Dear Mr. Hill,
> "In accordance with the Agreement which the Company made with [DATA] on
> the 15th May, 1970, *we hereby give one month's notice of a change in your condi-
> tions of employment.*

"*If you are not already a [DATA]* member, and prior to the 15th May, 1970 were not a member of another trade union affiliated to the T.U.C., *it will be a condition of employment that you are required to become a member of [DATA].*

"If you have not already done so you are requested to comply with this condition.

"If you wish to have further sight of the Company's Agreement with [DATA] you may do so..."

Mr Hill did not agree to the change. He did not become a member of DATA. Nor did the other 37. In consequence, on 30th July 1971, the company gave each one one month's notice to terminate his employment. The letter signed by the managing director was as follows:

"In a letter to you dated 19th May, 1971, the Company gave one month's notice of a change in your conditions of employment, that is, that you must become a member of [DATA]...

"As far as I am able to ascertain, you have not to date complied with this condition and *are therefore in breach of your contract of employment.*

"In view of this, *I regret to have to advise you that your employment with this Company will terminate at 5.15 p.m. on Tuesday, 31st August, 1971,* unless prior to this date you have taken steps to comply with the condition in your contract of employment regarding DATA membership.

"The Company is bound to honour its Agreement of 15th May, 1970, in this matter, and wishes it to be understood that *the sole reason for issuing this notice of termination of employment is the fact that you are in breach of your conditions of employment.*"

Faced with this notice to terminate his employment, Mr Hill, on 13th August 1971, brought this action against the company. It is a test action to test the position of the 38. He asked for an interim injunction to restrain the company from implementing the notice dated 30th July 1971, purporting to determine his employment. He went before the vacation judge on 25th August, but the judge refused the injunction. The judge said:

"To my mind there is no doubt whatever that the Company will be committing a wrongful act against the plaintiff if it terminates his employment on the 31st of August as it threatens to do. However, in my judgement, this Court has no power to restrain that wrong."

After some discussion, he added, 'if I had power to grant an injunction I would have done so but I felt constrained by the law.' Mr Hill told the judge that he desired to appeal. The company very sensibly agreed that, pending the appeal, they would not implement the notice. So the 38 are still at work.

Some further backgroud facts are relevant. The relations between the British Government and the unions during the early 1970's centred on the Industrial Relations Act, 1971. This act was passed by a Conservative Government on 5th August, 1971. It was an attempt to control the unions which, up to then, had operated with very few restrictions. The act did two things in regard to the problem raised in the case. First, the act provided for the registration of trade unions. This was to be voluntary, but a registered union was to have considerable benefits that an unregistered one would not have. Registration was opposed by the union movement generally. However, a union like UKAPE was the kind of union that would register, while DATA was one that would not. An unregistered union could not insist on a "union" or "closed" shop agreement. This meant that once the

I.R.A. came into effect, the plaintiff could not be dismissed for refusing to join DATA. However, the part of the I.R.A. dealing with this (Part II) did not come into effect on the passing of the act (and was not in effect on the date of judgment 10th November 1971) but was expected to be soon in effect. Second, if after Part II of the I.R.A. came into effect, the plaintiff were dismissed for failing to join DATA, an Industrial Tribunal (set up under the act) could either award him reinstatement or up to two years' salary (up to about £4,000).

(The Canadian law of labour relations is very different from the British. Generally speaking, the kind of dispute that led to Mr. Hill's problems cannot come up in Canada in quite the same way. In Canada, an employer is only compelled to bargain with a certified union and the determination of what union shall be certified is made by the Labour Relations Board. The Labour Relations Act contains provisions for dealing with "union" and "closed shops". The position in Ontario is set out in the following provision of the Labour Relations Act (R.S.O. 1970, c. 232):

> 38(1). Notwithstanding anything in this Act, but subject to subsection 4, the parties to a collective agreement may include in it provisions,
> (*a*) for requiring, as a condition of employment, membership in the trade union that is a party to or is bound by the agreement or granting a preference of employment to members of the trade union, or requiring the payment of dues or contributions to the trade union;
> (*b*) for permitting an employee who represents the trade union that is a party to or is bound by the agreement to attend to the business of the trade union during working hours without deduction of the time so occupied in the computation of the time worked for the employer and without deduction of wages in respect of the time so occupied;
> (*c*) for permitting the trade union that is a party to or is bound by the agreement to use the employer's premises for the purposes of the trade union without payment therefor.

The remainder of the section qualifies this in certain cases.)

When the Labour Party defeated the Conservative Government of Edward Heath in 1974, the first piece of legislation passed after the election was the repeal of the Industrial Relations Act.]

The court first held that the plaintiff had been wrongfully dismissed. It was assumed that he was entitled to at least six months' notice. Damages at common law would therefore be based on what he would have earned during that period. It was also assumed that a person in the position of the plaintiff would have no prospect of getting another job, and that he would normally have had the expectation of keeping his job until retirement (earning not only salary but increased pension rights). *Sachs L.J.* said, "It follows that, as in so many cases, the damages recoverable under the common law rule are in practice by no means adequate to compensate this particular plaintiff for the loss he would really suffer..."]

Sachs L.J. continued:

It thus becomes relevant first to consider whether an order in the instant case would contravene the main grounds on which it would be refused in the vast majority of master and servant cases. Foremost amongst the grounds given in Fry on Specific Performance is that it is wrong to enforce a contract which needs personal confidence as between the parties when such confidence may not exist. Here such confidence does exist. Another ground is that common law damages normally provide an adequate remedy. Here they do not. It is well recognised that such cases can in practice arise as regards contracts of employment — hence the new 'compensation' provisions in the Industrial Relations Act 1971, which undoubtedly envisage that account should be taken of factors such as the employees 'legitimate expectations for the future in his employment' (see the Report of the Donovan Commission). For an instance of recognition that such damages can be inadequate see the judgment of Jenkins LJ in the *Vine* case. A further ground is often the difficulty of reinstatment when the plaintiff's post has been filled. That difficulty does not exist here. Next one comes to the other previously mentioned factors introduced by the provisions of the Industrial Relations Act 1971 to which Brightman J was not referred — and which in this particular case produce such an unusual situation.

Looking at the aggregate of the matters just recited it appears to me that this is indeed an exceptional case and that relief should be granted unless there is some good counter argument. For the defendants it was suggested that an order of the court if made as claimed would endanger industrial peace as between the defendant company and its employees. I decline to assume that either DATA as an entity or its individual members would in the highly unusual circumstances act in some way that would be unreasonable and incidentally detrimental to their long-term interests — far less that they would seek to interfere with an order of the court.

Finally it was urged that any order made would run contrary to the policy or trend of previous practice. At the risk of reiterating views expressed in my judgments on other subject-matters, it seems appropriate to repeat that in matters of practice and discretion it is essential for the courts to take account of any important change in that climate of general opinion which is so hard to define but yet so plainly manifests itself from generation to generation. In that behalf account must, inter alia, be taken of the trend of the views of the legislature expressed on behalf of the community in its enactments and also of the trend of judicial decisions. Over the last two decades there has been a marked trend towards shielding the employee, where practicable, from undue hardships he may suffer at the hands of those who may have power over his livelihood — employers and trade unions. So far has this now progressed and such is the security granted to an employee under the Industrial Relations Act 1971 that some have suggested tht he may now be said to acquire something akin to a property in his employment. It surely is then for the courts to review and where appropriate to modify, if that becomes necessary, their rules of practice in relation to the exercise of a discretion such as we have today to consider so that its practice conforms to the realities of the day.

It follows that in my judgment there exists no good reason against regarding the instant case as being one in which an order should be made as proposed by Lord Denning MR; so I too would allow the appeal and make that order.

[Lord Denning M.R. wrote a judgment to the same effect as Sachs L.J. and Stamp L.J. dissented.]

In *Detroit Football Co. v. Dublinski* (1956), 4 D.L.R. (2d) 688, Ontario High Court, McRuer C.J.H.C. commented on the question whether or not an injunction should be granted to restrain the defendant football player from playing for the Toronto Argonauts in breach of his contract to play for Detroit. After referring to the judgment in *Warner Bros. v. Nelson*, McRuer C.J.H.C. said:

> "This is a decision of a single Judge and I not think it applies to this case. If it purports to hold that a Court of equity will enforce a negative covenant attached to a contract of employment by granting an injunction where the injunction will protect no interest by enforcing the negative covenant apart from the interest flowing from the positive covenant, I decline to follow it. But a careful examination of the argument in that case shows that what the plaintiff wished to be protected against was the exploitation of the defendant's services by a company competing with it that had a world market... All through the cases runs the thread of the principle that a Court of equity will only protect a plaintiff for a period against likely damage by reason of the breach of a negative covenant, express or implied..."

The judge went on to hold the defendant's playing for Toronto would do the plaintiff no more harm than if he had remained idle since the teams played in different leagues and before different audiences. The plaintiff club appealed. The Ontario Court of Appeal did not discuss the question of the injunction, but awarded the plaintiff damages for the following calculation:

To paid in acquiring the substitute.................	$10,000.00	
To paid salary of substitute............................	11,200.00	
By credit — Salary of defendant		$7,750.00
By credit — Salary of one traded player		6,500.00
	21,200.00	$14,250.00
	14,250.00	
Net cost to plaintiff..	$6,950.00	

Roach J.A. pointed out that this might be inadequate compensation since it did not take into account the investment made by the plaintiff in training the defendant. (1957), 7 D.L.R. (2d) 9.

QUESTION

What would have happened in *Warner Bros. v. Nelson* if Warner Bros. did not release any movies in England?

In *Baxter Motors v. American Motors*, [1973] 6 W.W.R. 501 (B.C.S.C.), the plaintiff, a franchise dealer for the defendant, sought an interim injunction to force the defendant to keep on supplying cars to the plaintiff. The defendant argued that the plaintiff had breached the franchise agreement between the parties. The court concluded that termination of the agreement by the defendant would cause the plaintiff "irreparable harm", and granted the injunction. The court admitted that the plaintiff would not be enjoined from breaching its contract with the defendant should the parties be reversed.

REVIEW PROBLEM

Canner carries on the business of canning tomatoes. The season for tomatoes lasts about six weeks and during this time enough tomatoes must be harvested and delivered to Canner to keep the plant operating at capacity. To ensure adequate supplies of tomatoes, Canner makes agreements with local farmers under which the farmer agrees to sell his entire crop of tomatoes to Canner at a fixed price. It is never clear at the time that these agreements are made whether the fixed price for the tomatoes will be higher or lower than the market price at the date of delivery. At the time when the fixed price is less than the market price, Farmer refuses to sell to Canner and instead sells to Wholesaler for the market price. Canner sues for specific performance and an injunction. What result?

The next case raises a difficult problem of the relationship between the remedy of specific performance and damages. As you read the case keep in mind the general damages issues that have already been discussed.

WROTH v. TYLER

[1973] 1 All E.R. 897. Chancery Division. Megarry J.

[The plaintiffs sought specific performance of an agreement to sell a bungalow, or damages for breach of contract.

Mr. Tyler owned a bungalow. In May of 1971, he entered into a written agreement to sell the house to Mr. and Mrs. Wroth for £6000 plus £50 for some extras, vacant possession of the property to be given October 31st, 1971. A deposit of £605 was paid to Mr. Tyler's real estate agent. However Mrs. Tyler did not want the house to be sold. Apparently, she did not like the area in which Mr. Tyler intended to buy a new home. Although the house was registered in Mr. Tyler's name alone, Mrs. Tyler was entitled to, and did register a "notice of right to occupy the house", under the Matrimonial Homes Act, 1967. Such a notice, while registered, would prevent any purchaser from Mr. Tyler from evicting Mrs. Tyler from the house. The Act permits Mr. Tyler to apply to a Court to have the notice removed from the land register, and on such an application, the Court may, in its discretion, order removal on such terms as it sees fit (for instance, that a cash settlement will be paid to Mrs. Tyler from the proceeds of the sale). [The Ontario equivalent is the Family Law Reform Act, 1978.] Mrs. Tyler did not disclose to Mr. Tyler or the Wroths that she had registered the notice, and its existence only came to light some three weeks later while investigation of Mr. Tyler's title was being undertaken. Mr. Tyler had already agreed to buy another house in Norfolk when he received a letter from his lawyers telling him about the notice Mrs. Tyler had registered. What transpired thereafter is adequately discussed in the judgment of Megarry J.]

Megarry J.:...He found this letter on his return that evening. Its contents came as a complete surprise to him.

That evening there was a row about the notice between the defendant and his wife, after which he decided to withdraw from both transactions. The next day, Saturday, 19th June, he telephoned the Norfolk vendors to say that he would not be buying the Norfolk property, and he wrote to his solicitors asking them to cancel the Norfolk purchase and also the sale of his bungalow. That day he and his wife hardly spoke to each other. The next day, Sunday, there was a worse row between the defendant and his wife about the cost to the defendant of breaking his contracts. It ended with the defendant slapping his wife, who thereupon sent for the police and called for a doctor. In addition to these two rows, the defendant made some further attempts to persuade his wife to withdraw her notice, though he could not recall the details beyond saying that he did it when she seemed to be in an amiable mood; but she was adamant.

As a result of the defendant's withdrawal, the plaintiffs were taken by an estate agent to visit the defendant on the following Saturday, 26th June; and while they were there the defendant's wife and daughter came in from shopping. The burden of the discussion was whether the defendant and his wife would be willing to buy some other property in the Ashford area and carry through the sale of the bungalow to the plaintiffs. The defendant, his wife and daughter all agreed to look at other properties in the district, and the agent offered his services in driving them to see suitable properties. The plaintiffs came away from the discussion with the impression that all would be well after all.

The same day, and probably after that meeting, the defendant's wife wrote a letter to the defendant's solicitors. It reads as follows:

> "Dear Sir, I understand from my husband that we will probably have to pay about £800 due to withdrawal of the sale of the above address. This is nonsense, and as his solicitor it is up to you to see that he doesn't pay anything. Many of my friends have withdrawn sale of their houses, and not had to pay any compensation. I know I started all this business, but will you please make sure that my husband doesn't lose any money over it. I would also be grateful if you would refrain from telling my husband that I have written to you."

The defendant's wife was critical of the defendant's solicitors; but as the letter shows, she expected them to achieve the impossible, and she must have had a complete lack of understanding of the great difference between withdrawing from a transaction before any contract is made, and withdrawing after contract....

By his defence the defendant admits that at the date for completion and at the date of the defence he was unable to give vacant possession of the bungalow, and that he was thereby in breach of his agreement; and he states his willingness to submit to an enquiry as to damages for the breach. By an amendment made on 13th November, shortly before the hearing began, the defendant contends that if (which is denied) the plaintiffs are otherwise entitled to judgment for specific performance, they have disentitled themselves to it by delay. The plaintiffs' primary claim is to specific performance, with damages as an alternative.

The issues before me may be summarised as follows. (1) Delay apart, are the plaintiffs entitled to specific performance of the contract with vacant possession? If they are, a form of order is sought and will require the defendant to make an application to the court for an order against his wife terminating her rights of occupation under the Matrimonial Homes Act 1967, in accordance with s 1(2). (2) Delay apart, are the plaintiffs, as an alternative, entitled to specific performance of the contract subject to the rights of occupation of the defendant's wife, with damages or an abatement of the purchase price in respect thereof? If they are, they will be able to make the application to the court under the 1967 Act, by virtue of ss 1(2) and 2(3). (3)

If, apart from delay, the plaintiffs would be entitled to an order for specific performance under either of these two heads, is their right to it barred by delay? (4) If the plaintiffs have no right to specific performance, then it is common ground that they are entitled to damages. There is, however, an acute conflict as to the measure of damages. The primary contention of the defendant is that damages are limited by the rule in *Bain v Fothergill* (1874), L.R. 7 H.L. 158, so that the defendant need only release the deposit to the plaintiffs and pay their costs of investigating title, and is not liable to them for more than nominal damages for loss of their bargain. Is this contention sound? (5) If *Bain v Fothergill* does not apply, then the defendant accepts that damages for loss of the bargain are payable; but there is a dispute as to the computation of those damages. The defendant says that the damages must be assessed as at the date of the breach, in accordance with the normal rule; the plaintiffs say that this is a case where damages must be assessed as at the date of assessment, that is, today, if I assess the damages. The valuers on each side have not given evidence, but very sensibly they have agreed a graph which shows the figures at successive dates, and counsel put this in as an agreed document. I can ignore £50 of the contract price, for that was for the various fittings and chattels; and on that footing the contract price was £6,000. It is agreed that at the date fixed for completion the bungalow was worth £7,500; and it is agreed that at the time of the hearing before me it was worth £11,500. Damages assessed as at the date of the breach would be £1,500, but as at the date of the hearing would be £5,500. At which figure should damages for the loss of the bargain be assessed? The defendant says that the former figure applies, in accordance with the general rule, but the plaintiffs say that the latter figure applies, for unless it does, they will be unable to acquire an equivalent house at today's prices....

With that out of the way, I turn to the main question of specific performance. It seems to me that where a third party has some rights over the property to be sold, there are at least three categories of cases. First, there are those cases where the vendor is entitled as of right to put an end to the rights of the third party, or compel his concurrence or co-operation in the sale. Second, and at the other extreme, there are cases where the vendor has no right to put an end to the third party's rights, or compel his concurrence or co-operation in the sale, and can do no more than to try to persuade him to release his rights or to concur in the sale. An example of the first category would be the vendor's right, as mortgagor, to pay off a mortgage, or his right, as a mortgagee, to obtain possession from the mortgagor. An example of the second category would be when the third party is entitled to an easement over the land.

In between those two categories there is a third category, namely, where the vendor cannot as of right secure the requisite discharge or concurrence, but if it is refused he can go to the court, which has power, on a proper case being shown, to secure the release or concurrence. Examples would be a restrictive covenant which may be modified or discharged under the Law of Property Act 1925, s 84 (as amended), or the requisite consent of a landlord to an assignment of a lease where there is a contractual or statutory requirement that the landlord's consent is not to be unreasonably withheld. The powers of the court under s 1(2) of the 1967 Act seem to me to bring the present case within this third and intermediate category.

In the end, I do not think that there was much disagreement between counsel as to the first two categories; the real issue was whether the third category was to be aligned with the first or with the second. Counsel for the defendant did not contend that a decree of specific performance would be refused in every case in which the defendant was required to take proceedings to enforce some right; the burden of his contention was that only in clear cases would specific performance be decreed. Relying on the similarity between injunctions and specific performance, at one stage he cited Halsbury's Laws of England for the proposition that the court would never grant a mandatory injunction (and so would never decree specific performance) if in effect the order would require the defendant to take legal proceedings against a third party. However, I do not think that the authorities carry so general a proposition, at any rate in relation to specific performance; and in the end I think counsel for the defendant accepted this, or at any rate did not violently dissent from it.

On the other hand, I do not think counsel for the plaintiffs contended that specific performance would be decreed if there were no means of compelling the concurrence of some requisite third party. It is true that there are some very old cases in which specific performance was decreed against a husband when his wife's consent was requisite, and if he failed to procure it he was committed to prison in order to induce her consent out of compassion for her husband. It does not appear what happened to the husband if his wife lacked compassion or, worse, was actuated by malevolence. The modern doctrine seems to me to be stated in Fry:

> "As the consent of a third party is, or may be, a thing impossible to procure, a defendant who has entered into a contract to the performance of which such consent is necessary, will not, in case such consent cannot be procured, be decreed to obtain it, and thus perform an impossibility."

.   .   .

These circumstances seem to me to make the case one in which the court should be slow to decree specific performance if any reasonable alternative exists. I shall accordingly turn in due course to the question of damages to see whether they would provide the plaintiffs with an adequate remedy.

Before I consider damages, I must deal with the third main point, that of laches, which is a defence to specific performance, although not, of course, to damages. In the end, counsel for the defendant relied only on the delay between 17th August 1971 and the issue of the writ on 25th January 1972. On 17th August the plaintiffs' solicitors wrote to the defendant's solicitors saying that they were taking counsel's advice and would write further when they obtained it. Not until 30th November 1971 did the plaintiffs' solicitors write to the defendant's solicitors to say that proceedings for specific performance or damages (or both) would be instituted shortly, and that the delay had been occasioned by the plaintiffs' unsuccessful application for legal aid. The period in question was thus some 3½ months or 5½ months, according to whether the terminus ad quem was the letter before action, or the writ.... However, as counsel for the plaintiffs pointed out, in this case the date fixed for completion was 31st October 1971, and it must, he said, at least be open to the plaintiffs to refrain from suing for specific performance until the defendant had broken the contract. Time therefore ought to run not from 17th August but from 31st October, with a consequent reduction of some 2½ months in each of the periods. In any case, the authorities cited were cases of the sale of interests in a colliery, and so sales of highly speculative interests, approaching a trade, to which special considerations applied. It seems plain to me that there has been no unexplained delay of an order which, in the circumstances of this case, would justify holding the remedy of specific performance barred by laches or acquiescence.

I turn to damages. The fourth main point is whether the damages are limited to those recoverable under the rule in *Bain v Fothergill*. The rule is conveniently stated in Williams's Contract of Sale of Land:

> "Where the breach of contract is occasioned by the vendor's inability, without his own fault, to show a good title, the purchaser is entitled to recover as damages his deposit, if any, with interest, and his expenses incurred in connection with the agreement, but not more than nominal damages for the loss of his bargain."

What is said for the defendant is, quite simply, that the statutory charge in favour of the defendant's wife is a defect in title within the rule, just as much as any other charge would be, whether legal or equitable, and so the rule applies.

In *Bain v Fothergill* itself, a distinction was drawn between matters of conveyancing and matters of title. Lord Hatherly said:

> "Whenever it is a matter of conveyancing, and not a matter of title, it is the duty of the vendor to do everything that he is enabled to do by force of his own interest, and also by force of the interest of others whom he can compel to concur in the conveyance."

The right to vacant possession may be regarded as a matter of conveyancing rather than of title, in that vacant possession is required to be delivered only on completion, and a title may be in perfect order even though the vendor is out of possession. By contrast, in *Bain v Fothergill* the vendor had a mere equitable title to the lease of the mining royalty that he had contracted to sell, and he unexpectedly failed to obtain the lessor's consent to the assignment that would have enabled him to convey what he had contracted to sell. That was plainly a matter of title, and the rule applied.

. . .

Let me consider the consequences of holding that the rule applies, in days when a new verb of doubtful etymology has been attracting considerable attention, namely, the verb 'to gazump'.

["Gazump" is an English word conceived during the period of rampant inflation referred to in the judgment. It refers to the practice of many vendors of agreeing in principle to sell to purchaser A, the formal contract to be drawn up shortly, then agreeing to sell to B who made a higher offer in the interim before the formal contract had been entered into. The disappointed purchaser A, had been "gazumped"!!]

The most helpful approach seems to me to take the matter by stages. First, if the mere existence of the wife's charge, before registration, creates a defect in title within the rule, then Parliament has at a blow imposed a defect in title on many millions of homes vested in one or other of the parties to a marriage. On 1st January 1968 millions of perfectly good titles became defective. I should be slow indeed to impute to Parliament any intention to produce this result. This is all the more striking in the case of registered land, where the operation of the rule in *Bain v Fothergill* might be expected to be minimal; for the main purpose of the Land Registration Acts is to simplify titles and conveyancing. Furthermore, if the mere existence of an unregistered charge under the 1967 Act constitutes a defect in title, it is a singularly impotent defect, for on completion of a sale it will be void against the purchaser for want of registration. If instead the vendor refused to complete, plainly he would be refusing to take a step which would remove the defect from his title. As at the date of the contract in this case, I therefore cannot see how the rule in *Bain v Fothergill* could have applied. In other words, looking at matters immediately after the contract had been made, the case could not, in my judgment, be said to fall within either the spirit or the letter of the rule in *Bain v Fothergill.*

When in this case the wife's rights were registered the day after the contract had been made, a different situation arose; for then her rights could no longer be destroyed by completing the sale. On the footing that the wife's rights thereupon became capable of attracting the rule in *Bain v Fothergill*, does the rule apply to cases where, at the date of the contract, the necessary conditions for the application of the rule did not exist, but those conditions first came into being after the contract had been made? It has not been suggested that there is any authority bearing directly on this point. The action is an action for damages for breach of contract, and I should be slow to hold that some supervening event could bring within the rule a case initially outside it. Furthermore, the basis of the rule is that of the contract having been made against a background of the uncertainty of titles to land in England; see, for example, *Bain v Fothergill*, per Lord Hatherley. In *Engell v Fitch* Kelly CB said that the rule was —

> "founded entirely on the difficulty that a vendor often finds in making a title to real estate, not from any default on his part, but from his ignorance of the strict legal state of his title."

As I have indicated, a rule laid down for defects in title which lay concealed in title deeds which were often, in the phrase attributed to Lord Westbury, 'difficult to read, disgusting to touch, and impossible to understand', seems singularly inapposite to the effect of a modern statute on registered land, with its aseptic certainty and clarity of title.

Furthermore, the rule is anomalous, and ... where the court encounters an anomalous rule, it is in general better to confine the anomaly within its established sphere than to extend the anomaly to analogous cases. Here, the wife's rights are the creature of statute, imposed generally, and in no way dependent on the vicissitudes of a particular title to property. The charge itself is sui generis. The wife has personal rights of occupation which she cannot deal with, thus differing greatly from other charges, such as legal or equitable charges for money. If her rights are rights of property at all, they are at least highly idiosyncratic. They do not seem to me to fall within the spirit or intendment of the rule in *Bain v Fothergill*; and so I hold.

That brings me to the fifth main point. If *Bain v Fothergill* does not apply, what is the measure of damages? It was common ground that the normal rule is that the general damages to which a purchaser is entitled for breach of a contract for the sale of land are basically measured by the difference between the contract price and the market price of the land at the date of the breach, normally the date fixed for completion. On the facts of this case, the damages under this rule would be of the order of £1,500. The real issue was whether that rule applies to this case, or whether some other rule applies.

Now the principle that has long been accepted is that stated by Parke B in *Robinson v Harman* (1848), 154 E.R. 363, in which, incidentally, the rule in *Flureau v Thornhill* (1776), 96 E.R. 635, was considered. Parke B said:

> "The rule of the common law is, that where a party sustains a loss by reason of a breach of contract, he is, so far as money can do it, to be placed in the same situation, with respect to damages, as if the contract had been performed."

In the present case, if the contract had been performed, the plaintiffs would at the date fixed for completion have had the house, then worth £7,500, in return for the contractual price of £6,000. If in lieu of the house they had been paid £1,500 damages at that date, they could, with the addition of the £6,000 that they commanded, have forthwith bought an equivalent house. I am satisfied on the evidence that the plaintiffs had no financial resources of any substance beyond the £6,000 that they could have put together for the purchase of the defendant's bungalow, and that the defendant knew this when the contract was made. The plaintiffs were therefore, to the defendant's knowledge, unable at the time of the breach to raise a further £1,500 in order to purchase an equivalent house forthwith, and so, as events have turned out, mitigate their loss. Today, to purchase an equivalent house they need £5,500 in addition to their £6,000. How, then, it may be asked, would the award today of £1,500 damages place them in the same situation as if the contract had been performed? The result that would have been produced by paying £1,500 damages at the date of the breach can today be produced only by paying £5,500 damages, with in each case the return of the deposit. On facts such as these, the general rule of assessing damages as at the date of the breach seems to defeat the general principle, rather than carry it out. In the ordinary case of a buyer of goods which the seller fails to deliver, the buyer can at once spend his money in purchasing equivalent goods from another, as was pointed out in *Gainsford v Carroll*, and so the rule works well enough; but that is a very different case. It therefore seems to me that on the facts of this case there are strong reasons for applying the principle rather than the rule. The question is whether it is proper to do so.

In my judgment, therefore, if under Lord Cairns' Act damages are awarded in substitution for specific performance, the court has jurisdiction to award such damages as will put the plaintiffs into as good a position as if the contract had been performed, even if to do so means awarding damages assessed by reference to a period subsequent to the date of the breach. This seems to me to be consonant with the nature of specific performance, which is a continuing remedy, designed to secure, inter alia, that the purchaser receives in fact what is his in equity as soon as the contract is made, subject to the vendor's right to the money, and so on. On the other hand, a decree may be sought before any breach of contract has occurred, and so before any action lies for common law damages; and on the other hand the right to a decree may continue long after the breach has occurred. On the facts of this case, the damages that may be awarded are not limited to the £1,500 that is appropriate to the date of the breach, but extend to the £5,500 that is appropriate at the present day, when they are being awarded in substitution for specific performance. I should add that no contention has been advanced (in my judgment, quite rightly) that the case does not fall within Lord Cairns' Act. The sale of a house is a case par excellence in which the court 'has jurisdiction to entertain an application... for the specific performance' of a contract, and the plaintiffs have done nothing to disentitle themselves to a decree. The undesirability of granting the decree if any suitable alternative exists springs from the position of the defendant and his wife.

·   ·   ·

The conclusion that I have reached, therefore, is that as matters stand I ought to award damages to the plaintiffs of the order of £5,500, in substitution for decreeing specific performance, with all the doubts and difficulties and probably undesirable consequences that a decree in either form would produce. An award of damages on this scale, I accept, will bear hardly on the defendant. Although he is able in one way or another to raise £1,500 without selling his bungalow, £5,500 is another matter; in all probability he could not raise that sum without selling the bungalow with vacant possession, and he has no power to do this. If, however, he becomes bankrupt, then his trustee in bankruptcy can sell the bungalow free from the wife's rights, even though they are registered: see the 1967 Act, s 2(5). With the money so raised, the trustee in bankruptcy will then be able to pay the plaintiffs their damages, one hopes in full; or it may be possible for the plaintiffs to take the bungalow in satisfaction of their claim. This is a dismal prospect for the defendant, but if the plaintiffs obtain neither a decree of specific performance nor £5,500 by way of damages, theirs also is a dismal prospect. Having made a binding contract to purchase for £6,000 a bungalow now worth £11,500, they would recover neither the bungalow nor damages that would enable them to purchase anything like its equivalent. It is the plaintiffs who are wholly blameless. Nothing whatever can be said against them, or has been, save as to the contention that delay barred them from a decree of specific performance; and that I have rejected. Nor do I think that there was any delay on their part that could affect the measure of damages.

The ultimate truth as between the defendant and his wife I do not know. As the evidence stands, his wife did nothing whatever to warn the plaintiffs that she was not willing to leave the bungalow, but conducted herself so as to lead them to believe that she concurred in the sale. So far as the defendent was concerned, his wife was very cool about the move, and it may well be that the move was one which a strong-willed husband was in effect imposing on a reluctant yet secretive wife. Nevertheless, the consequences of disputes between husband and wife, whether open or concealed, ought not to be visited on innocent purchasers.

In these circumstances, I think that what I ought to do is to make no order today, but, subject to what counsel may have to say, to adjourn the case until the first day of next term. In ordinary circumstances, I would adjourn the case for only a week, but unfortunately the impending vacation makes this impossible. During the adjournment I hope that the defendant and his wife will take advice, separately or together. When I resume the hearing, it may be that the defendant's wife will not have changed her mind about her charge. In that case, I shall award the plaintiffs damages against the defendant of the order of £5,500, even though the probable consequence will be the bankruptcy of the defendant and the sale of the bungalow with vacant possession by his trustee in bankruptcy, free from the wife's rights. On the other hand, the defendant's wife may by then have changed her mind, and rather than force her husband into bankruptcy without avoiding having to vacate the bungalow, she may have taken effective steps to enable the defendant to convey the bungalow to the plaintiffs free from her rights.

In that case I shall decree specific performance of the contract. In this way the plaintiffs will obtain either the bungalow that they bought or else an amount of damages which will enable them to purchase its equivalent. I may add that of course I give each side liberty to apply in the meantime; and I should say that I shall be available until 4.00 pm today. As I have indicated, I feel much sympathy for the defendant as well as for the plaintiffs at being embroiled in this way. Yet as between the two sides both the law and the merits seem to me to point to the plaintiffs as being the parties who should be as little hurt as possible; and they have already suffered considerably, not least in relation to their temporary accommodation pending these proceedings. Counsel will no doubt assist me with any submissions that they may have on this proposed adjournment, which was not mooted during the argument.

[11th January. The defendant's wife refusing to remove her notice, his Lordship ordered that the defendant pay damages to the plaintiffs to be quantified as at the date of judgment, i e 11th January. Counsel having agreed that as no increase in prices had taken place since the date of hearing, damages were assessed at £5,500.]

NOTE: The provision in Ontario that corresponds to that in Lord Cairns' Act referred to by Megarry J. is s. 21 of The Judicature Act which provides:

21. Where the court has jurisdiction to entertain an application for an injunction against a breach of a covenant, contract or agreement, or against the commission or continuance of a wrongful act, or for the specific performance of a covenant, contract or agreement, the court may award damages to the party injured either in addition to or in substitution for the injunction or specific performance, and the damages may be ascertained in such manner as the court directs, or the court may grant such other relief as is considered just.

Canadian courts have considered *Wroth v. Tyler*. In *Metropolitan Trust Co. of Canada et al. v. Pressure Concrete Services Ltd. et al.* (1973), 37 D.L.R. (3d) 649; aff'd. (1976) 60 D.L.R. (3d) 431 (C.A.), the Courts discretionarily declined to decree specific performance of an agreement of purchase and sale of land at the suit of the purchaser. Neither in the reasons for judgment of the trial judge, Holland J., nor in those delivered by the Court of Appeal (Schroeder, Arnup and MacKinnon JJ.A.) was any mention made of the financial status of the purchaser at the time of the vendor's breach of contract. Nonetheless, each Court purported to follow *Wroth et al. v. Tyler*, *supra*, and awarded damages to be calculated as the difference between the value of the property at the date of judgment and the contract price, where the value had increased between breach and judgment.

An interesting discussion of the application of the rule in *Bain v. Fothergill* and of *Wroth v. Tyler* damages may be found in *A. V. G. Management Science Ltd. v. Barwell Developments Ltd.* (1976), 69 D.L.R. (3d) 741 (B.C.S.C, Mackenzie J.)

QUESTIONS

1. How important was it in *Wroth et al. v. Tyler*, *supra*, that the purchasers were, to the knowledge of the vendors, unable to take steps to find alternative accommo-

dation when it became clear that the defendants would not perform. How relevant should such consideration be?

2. What would you do as solicitor for either party in a case like *Wroth v. Tyler* to further your client's interest before litigation starts?

3. Should *Wroth v. Tyler* be applied in a commercial case?

D. Remoteness of Damage

If Napoleon had been unable to get to a crucial location at the battle of Waterloo because his horse had been improperly shod and lost the battle as a consequence, would Napoleon, at common law, have been able to sue the blacksmith for the monetary equivalent of the kingdom?

We might analyse this case in the same terms that we have used so far. There was a breach of contract — we may assume that a blacksmith promises to shoe a horse carefully — and damages flowing from this breach, and then we might conclude that Napoleon would have a good claim aginst the blacksmith. (We can ignore the probable impecuniosity of the blacksmith). We might, however, be bothered by this. There are, of course, causal questions — (though again we could assume those away) but even so we might feel that somehow the blacksmith should not be stuck with this kind of liability. The law has responded to this concern by limiting the damages that someone in Napoleon's position could recover in such circumstances. The cases and extracts that follow explore the reasons for and methods of limiting the damages recoverable by a person who has been harmed by a breach of contract.

The next case is one of the most famous cases ever decided. It was one of the first to articulate the concern for the scope of recovery for breach of contract. As you read the case consider how far (and how well) it responds to the problem of Napoleon and the blacksmith.

HADLEY v. BAXENDALE

(1854), 9 Exch. 341, 156 E.R. 145

[At the trial before Crompton J., at the last Gloucester Assizes, it appeared that the plaintiffs carried on an extensive business as millers at Gloucester; and that, on the 11th of May, their mill was stopped by a breakage of the crank shaft by which the mill was worked. The steam engine was manufactured by Messrs. Joyce & Co., the engineers, at Greenwich, and it became necessary to send the shaft as a pattern for a new one to Greenwich. The fracture was discovered on the 12th, and on the 13th the plaintiffs sent one of their servants to the office of the defendants, who are the well-known carriers trading under the name of Pickford & Co., for the purpose of having the shaft carried to Greenwich. The plaintiffs' servant told the clerk that the mill was stopped, and that the shaft must be sent immediately; and in answer to the inquiry when the shaft would be taken, the answer was, that if it was sent up by twelve o'clock any day, it would be delivered at Greenwich on the following day. On the following day the shaft was taken by the defendants, before noon, for the purpose of being conveyed to Greenwich, and the sum of £2, 4s. was paid for its carriage for the whole distance; at the same time the defendants' clerk was told that a special entry, if required, should be made to hasten its delivery. The delivery of the shaft at Greenwich was delayed by some neglect; and the consequence was, that the plaintiffs did not receive the new shaft for several days after they would otherwise have done, and the working of their mill was thereby delayed, and they thereby lost the profits they would otherwise have received.

On the part of the defendants, it was objected that these damages were too remote, and that the defendants were not liable with respect to them. The learned Judge left the case generally to the jury, who found a verdict with 25l. damages beyond the amount paid into Court.

Whateley, in last Michaelmas Term, obtained a rule *nisi* for a new trial, on ground of misdirection.

Cur. adv. vult.]

The judgment of the Court was now delivered by

Alderson B.:- We think that there ought to be a new trial in this case; but, in so doing, we deem it to be expedient and necessary to state explicitly the rule which the Judge, at the next trial, ought, in our opinion, to direct the jury to be governed by when they estimate the damages.

It is, indeed, of the last importance that we should do this; for, if the jury are left without any definite rule to guide them, it will, in such cases as these, manifestly lead to the greatest injustice. The Courts have done this on several occasions; and, in *Blake v. Midland Railway Company* (18 Q.B. 93), the Court granted a new trial on this very ground, that the rule had not been definitely laid down to the jury by the learned Judge at Nisi Prius.

"There are certain established rules", this Court says, in *Alder v. Keighley* (15 M. & W. 117), "according to which the jury ought to find". And the Court, in that case, adds: "and here there is a clear rule, that the amount which would have been received if the contract had been kept, is the measure of damages if the contract is broken."

Now we think the proper rule in such a case as the present is this: — Where two parties have made a contract which one of them has broken, the damages which the other party ought to receive in respect of such breach of contract should be such as may fairly and reasonably be considered either arising naturally, i.e., according to the usual course of things, from such breach of contract itself, or such as may reasonably be supposed to have been in the contemplation of both parties, at the time they made the contract, as the probable result of the breach of it. Now, if the special circumstances under which the contract was actually made were communicated by the plaintiffs to the defendants, and thus known to both parties, the damages resulting from the breach of such a contract, which they would reasonably contemplate, would be the amount of injury which would ordinarily follow from a breach of contract under these special circumstances so known and communicated. But, on the other hand, if these special circumstances were wholly unknown to the party breaking the contract, he, at the most, could only be supposed to have had in his contemplation the amount of injury which would arise generally, and in the great multitude of cases not affected by any special circumstances, from such a breach of contract. For, had the special circumstances been known, the parties might have specially provided for the breach of contract by special terms as to the damages in that case; and of this advantage it would be very unjust to deprive them. Now the above principles are those by which we think the jury ought to be guided in estimating the damages arising out of any breach of contract.... It is said, that other cases such as breaches of contract in the non-payment of money, or in the not making a good title to land, are to be treated as exceptions from this, and as governed by a conventional rule. But as, in such cases, both parties must be supposed to be cognisant of that well-known rule, these cases may, we think, be more properly classed under the rule above enunciated as to cases under known special circumstances, because there both parties may reasonably be presumed to contemplate the estimation of the amount of damages according to the conventional rule. Now, in the present case, if we are to apply the principles above laid down, we find that the only circumstances here communicated by the plaintiffs to the defendants at the time the contract was made, were, that the article to be carried was the broken shaft of a mill, and that the plaintiffs were the millers of that mill. But how do these circumstances shew reasonably that the profits of the mill must be stopped by an unreasonable delay in the delivery of the broken shaft by the carrier to the third person? Suppose the plaintiffs had another shaft in their possession put up or putting up at the time, and that they only wished to send back the broken shaft to the engineer who made it; it is clear that this would be quite consistent with the above circumstances, and yet the unreasonable delay in the delivery would have no effect upon the intermediate profits of the mill. Or, again, suppose that, at the time of the delivery to the carrier, the machinery of the mill had been in other respects defective, then, also, the same results would follow. Here it is true that the shaft was actually sent back to serve as a model for a new one, and that the want of a new one was the only cause of the stoppage of the mill, and that the loss of profits really arose from not sending down the new shaft in proper time, and that this arose from the delay in delivering the broken one to serve as a model. But it is obvious that, in the great multitude of cases of millers sending off broken shafts to third persons by a carrier under ordinary circumstances, such consequences would not, in all probability, have occurred; and these special circumstances were here never communicated by the plaintiffs to the defendants. It follows, therefore, that the loss of profits here cannot reasonably be considered such a consequence of the breach of contract as could have been fairly and reasonably contemplated by both the parties when they made this contract. For such loss would neither have flowed naturally from the breach of this contract in the great multitude of such cases occuring under ordinary circumstances, nor were the special circumstances, which, perhaps, would have made it a reasonable and natural consequence of such breach of contract, communicated to or known by the defendants. The Judge ought, therefore, to have told the jury, that, upon the facts then before them, they ought not to take the loss of profits into consideration at all in estimating the damages. There must therefore be a new trial in this case.

Rule absolute.

NOTE: The apparent discrepancy between the statement of fact in the first paragraph of the extract above and the statement of Alderson B. that the defendants had not had notice that the mill was stopped is explicable by reference to the law governing masters and servants (or principals and agents) where notice to the servant would not necessarily be notice to the master. In other words, the defendant, the master, was never legally informed of the stoppage of the plaintiff's mill so that he would have knowledge that it was stopped. The jury, of course, would have known of this fact for they all lived in Gloucester and the stoppage of Hadley's mill had been discussed in the local papers.

See: Danzig: "*Hadley v. Baxendale*: A Study in the Industrialization of the Law" (1975), J. of Legal Studies 249.

The proposition of law stated in *Hadley v. Baxendale* has frequently come before the courts where efforts have been made to explain just what the rule means and how it might be applied in various situations.

FULLER & PERDUE, "THE RELIANCE INTEREST IN CONTRACT DAMAGES"

(1936) 46 Yale L.J. 52, pp. 84-86.

THE RELIANCE INTEREST AND HADLEY V. BAXENDALE

Before we discuss the relation between the reliance interest and *Hadley v. Baxendale* it will be necessary to state briefly what seems to us to be involved in that famous case, considering it not so much as an event in legal history but as the accepted symbol for a set of problems. The case may be said to stand for two propositions: (1) that it is not always wise to make the defaulting promisor pay for all the damage which follows as a consequence of his breach, and (2) that specifically the proper test for determining whether particular items of damage should be compensable is to inquire whether they should have been foreseen by the promisor at the time of the contract. The first aspect of the case is much more important than the second. In its first aspect the case bears an integral relation to the very bases of contract liability. It declares in effect that just as it is wise to refuse enforcement altogether to some promises (considerationless, unaccepted, "social" promises, etc.) so it is wise not to go too far in enforcing those promises which are deemed worthy of legal sanction. The answer to the question of *Hadley v. Baxendale* (where shall we stop?) must inevitably be as complex as the answer to the question (where shall we begin?) which is implicit in the law of mutual assent, consideration, and the rules governing the formation of contracts generally.

In its second aspect *Hadley v. Baxendale* may be regarded as giving a grossly simplified answer to the question which its first aspect presents. To the question, how far shall we go in charging to the defaulting promisor the consequences of his breach, it answers with what purports to be a single test, that of foreseeability. The simplicity and comprehensiveness of this test are largely a matter of illusion. In the first place, it is openly branded as inappropriate in certain situations where the line is drawn much more closely in favor of the defaulting promisor than the test of foreseeability as normally understood would draw it. There are, therefore, exceptions to the test, to say nothing of authorities which reject it altogether as too burdensome to the defaulter. In the second place, it is clear that the test of foreseeability is less a definite test itself than a cover for a developing set of tests. As in the case of all "reasonable man" standards there is an element of circularity about the test of foreseeability. "For what items of damage should the court hold the defaulting promisor? Those which he should as a reasonable man have foreseen. But what should he have foreseen as a reasonable man? Those items of damage for which the court feels he ought to pay."

The test of foreseeability is therefore subject to manipulation by the simple device of defining the characteristics of the hypothetical man who is doing the foreseeing. By a gradual process of judicial inclusion and exclusion this "man" acquires a complex personality; we begin to know just what "he" can "foresee" in this and that situation, and we end, not with one test but with a whole set of tests. This has obviously happened in the law of negligence, and it is happening, although less obviously, to the reasonable man postulated by *Hadley v. Baxendale.*

Even if the reasonable man who does the foreseeing is a juristic construct, endowed precisely with those qualities which the court feels he ought to have for the purpose at hand, it does not seem that there is a complete *petitio principii* in the test of foreseeability. When we import into a question of liability the "reasonable man" standard we do at least two things. In the first place we increase the chance that the case will ultimately be determined by the jury. Though the court may define the reasonable man, it cannot be sure that its definition will be regarded by the jury, and any test which speaks of the reasonable man decreases the court's chance of removing the case from the jury. In the second place, whether the case is ultimately decided by the judge or the jury, stating the problem in terms of the reasonable man creates a bias in favor of exempting *normal* or *average* conduct from legal penalties. The reasonable man is not necessarily the average man, but he tends to be, and the notion of what is normal and average puts a bridle on the judicial power of defining reasonableness. But the restraint is far from complete. It becomes illusory in those situations where the concepts "normal" and "average" are without definite content; where the "average man" is as much a juristic construct as the "reasonable man". The restraint is often thrown off even in those fields where, because rather definite lay ways of thought and action are discoverable in them, the notion of the "normal" and "average" has some objective reality. The courts have not hesitated to invest the reasonable man with capacities either greater or less than those of the average man. For an example of this judicial autonomy within the reign of fact one need look no further than the case which originated the test of foreseeability, *Hadley v. Baxendale* itself.

NOTE ON LEGAL REASONING

In courts of law it sometimes happens that opposing counsel are agreed as to the facts and are not trying to settle a question of further fact, are not trying to settle whether the man who admittedly had quarrelled with the deceased did or did not murder him, but are concerned with whether Mr. A. who admittedly handed his long-trusted clerk signed blank cheques did or did not exercise reasonable care, whether a ledger is or is not a document, whether a certain body was or was not a public authority.

In such cases we notice that the process of argument is not a chain of demonstrative reasoning. It is a presenting and representing of those features of the case which severally cooperate in favour of the conclusion, in favour of saying what the reasoner wishes said, in favour of calling the situation by the name by which he wishes to call it. The reasons are like the legs of a chair, not the links of a chain. Consequently although the discussion is a priori and the steps are not a matter of experience, the procedure resembles scientific argument in that the reasoning is not vertically extensive but horizontally extensive — it is a matter of the cumulative effect of several independent premises, not of the repeated transformation of one or two. And because the premises are severally inconclusive the process of deciding the issue becomes a matter of weighing the cumulative effect of one group of severally inconclusive items against the cumulative effect of another group of severally inconclusive items, and thus lends itself to description in terms of conflicting 'probabilities'. This encourages the feeling that the issue is one of fact — that it is a matter of guessing from the premises at a further fact at what is to come. But this is a muddle. The dispute does not cease to be a priori because it is a matter of the cumulative effect of severally inconclusive premises. The logic of the dispute is not that of a chain of deductive reasoning as in a mathematic calculation. But nor is it a matter of collecting from several inconclusive items of information an expectation as to something further, as when a doctor from a patient's symptoms guesses at what is wrong, or a detective from many clues guesses the criminal. It has its own sort of logic and its own sort of end — the solution of the question at issue is a decision, a ruling by the judge. But it is not an arbitrary decision though the rational connections are neither quite like those in vertical deductions or like those in inductions in which from many signs we guess at what is to come; and though the decision manifests itself in the application of a name it is no more merely the application of a name than is the pinning on of a medal merely the pinning on of a bit of metal. Whether a lion with stripes is a tiger or a lion is, if you like, merely a matter of the application of a name. Whether Mr. So-and-So of whose conduct we have so complete a record did or did not exercise reasonable care is not merely a matter of the application of a name or, if we choose to say it is, then we must remember that with this name a game is lost and won and a game with very heavy stakes. With the judges' choice of a name for the facts goes an attitude, and the declaration, the ruling, is an exclamation evincing that attitude. But it is an exclamation which not only has a purpose but also has a logic, a logic surprisingly like that of "futile", "deplorable", "graceful", "grand", "divine".

From: "Gods", by John Wisdom in *Logic & Language* Ed. Flew, 1964, p. 202-204.

VICTORIA LAUNDRY v. NEWMAN INDUSTRIES

[1949] 1 All E.R. 997 (C.A.).

[The plaintiffs carried on business as launderers and dyers. In April 1946 they agreed to purchase from the defendant, an engineering company, a large boiler. The plaintiffs had made it clear to the defendants that they required the boiler "in the shortest possible space of time". The defendants promised to deliver it on June 5, 1946. However, on June 1, the boiler was damaged by the contractors who were dismantling it in preparation for shipping. The boiler was not repaired for 20 weeks. The plaintiffs sought to recover from the defendants their loss of profits during this delay. They proved that they had available extremely lucrative dyeing contracts as well as the normal business of launderers and dyers. The trial judge gave judgment for the plaintiffs for the costs incurred in going to pick up the boiler on June 1 but disallowed any claim for profits. The plaintiffs appealed.]

The judgment of the court was given by **Asquith L.J.**: —... What propositions applicable to the present case emerge from the authorities as a whole, including those analysed above? We think they include the following: (1) It is well settled that the governing purpose of damages is to put the party whose rights have been violated in the same position, so far as money can do so, as if his rights had been observed: *Wertheim v. Chicoutimi Pulp Co.*, (1911) A.C. 301. This purpose, if relentlessly pursued, would provide him with a complete indemnity for all loss *de facto* resulting from a particular breach, however improbable, however unpredictable. This, in contract at least, is recognised as too harsh a rule. Hence, (2): In cases of breach of contract the aggrieved party is only entitled to recover such part of the loss actually resulting as was at the time of the contract reasonably foreseeable as liable to result from the breach. (3) What was at that time reasonably foreseeable depends on the knowledge then possessed by the parties, or, at all events, by the party who later commits the breach. (4) For this purpose, knowledge "possessed" is of two kinds — one imputed, the other actual. Everyone, as a reasonable person, is taken to know the "ordinary course of things" and consequently what loss is liable to result from a breach of that ordinary course. Time is the subject-matter of the "first rule" in *Hadley v. Baxendale*, but to this knowledge, which a contract-breaker is assumed to possess whether he actually possesses it or not, there may have to be added in a particular case knowledge which he actually possesses of special circumstances outside the "ordinary course of things" of such a kind that a breach in those special circumstances would be liable to cause more loss. Such a case attracts the operation of the "second rule" so as to make additional loss also recoverable. (5) In order to make the contract-breaker liable under either rule it is not necessary that he should actually have asked himself what loss is liable to result from a breach. As has often been pointed out, parties at the time of contracting contemplate, not the breach of the contract, but its performance. It suffices that, if he had considered the question, he would as a reasonable man have concluded that the loss in question was liable to result: ...

(6) Nor, finally, to make a particular loss recoverable, need it be proved that on a given state of knowledge the defendant could, as a reasonable man, foresee that a breach must necessarily result in that loss. It is enough if he could foresee it was likely so to result. It is enough, to borrow from the language of LORD DU PARCQ in the same case, if the loss (or some factor without which it would not have occurred) is a "serious possibility" or a "real danger." For short, we have used the word "liable" to result. Possibly the colloquialism "on the cards" indicates the shade of meaning with some approach to accuracy.

If these, indeed, are the principles applicable, what is the effect of their application to the facts of the present case? We have, at the beginning of this judgment, summarised the main relevant facts. The defendants were an engineering company supplying a boiler to a laundry. We reject the submission for the defendants that an engineering company knows no more than the plain man about boilers or the purposes to which they are commonly put by different classes of purchasers, including laundries. The defendant company were not, it is true, manufacturers of this boiler or dealers in boilers, but they gave a highly technical and comprehensive description of this boiler to the plaintiffs by letter of Jan. 19, 1946, and offered both to dismantle the boiler at Harpenden and to re-erect it on the plaintiffs' premises. Of the uses or purposes to which boilers are put, they would clearly know more than the uninstructed layman. Again, they knew they were supplying the boiler to a company carrying on the business of laundrymen and dyers, for use in that business. The obvious use of a boiler, in such a business, is surely to boil water for the purpose of washing or dyeing. A laundry might conceivably buy a boiler for some other purpose, for instance, to work radiators or warm bath water for the comfort of its employees or directors, or to use for research, or to exhibit in a museum. All these purposes are possible, but the first is the obvious purpose which, in the case of a laundry, leaps to the average eye. If the purpose then be to wash or dye, why does the company want to wash or dye, unless for purposes of business advantage.

[Asquith L.J. went on to hold that the defendants would be liable for loss of profits as might reasonably have been expected to be earned in the normal course of their laundry business. But in regard to the particularly lucrative dyeing contracts he said: (p. 1005) "We agree [with the trial judge] that in order that the plaintiffs should recover specifically and as such the profits expected on these contracts, the defendants would have had to know, at the time of their agreement with the plaintiffs, of the prospect and terms of such contracts. We also agree that they did not, in fact, know these things. It does not, however, follow that the plaintiffs are precluded from recovering some general (and perhaps conjectural) sum for loss of business in respect of dyeing contracts to be reasonably expected any more than in respect of laundering contracts to be reasonably expected."

The appeal was therefore allowed and a reference ordered for the purposes of determining the lost profits.]

THE HERON II. KOUFOS v. C. CZARNIKOW LTD.

[1969] 1 A.C. 350 (H.L.). Lords Reid, Morris, Hodson, Pearce and Upjohn.

Lord Reid: — My Lords, by charterparty of October 15, 1960, the respondents chartered the appellant's vessel, *Heron II*, to proceed to Constanza, there to load a cargo of 3,000 tons of sugar; and to carry it to Basrah, or, in the charterer's option, to Jeddah. The vessel left Constanza on November 1, 1960. The option was not exercised and the vessel arrived at Basrah on December 2, 1960. The umpire has found that "a reasonably accurate prediction of the length of the voyage was twenty days." But the vessel had in breach of contract made deviations which caused a delay of nine days.

It was the intention of the respondents to sell the sugar "promptly after arrival at Basrah and after inspection by merchants." The appellant did not know this, but he was aware of the fact that there was a market for sugar at Basrah. The sugar was in fact sold at Basrah in lots between December 12 and 22, 1960, but shortly before that time the market price had fallen, partly by reason of the arrival of another cargo of sugar. It was found by the umpire that if there had not been this delay of nine days the sugar would have fetched £32 10s. 0d. per ton. The actual price realised was only £31 2s. 9d. per ton. The respondents claim that they are entitled to recover the difference as damage for breach of contract. The appellant admits that he is liable to pay interest for nine days on the value of the sugar and certain minor expenses but denies that fall in market value can be taken into account in assessing damages in this case.

McNair J. . . . decided this question in favour of the appellant. He said:

> "In those circumstances, it seems to me almost impossible to say that the shipowner must have known that the delay in prosecuting the voyage would probably result, or be likely to result, in this kind of loss."

The Court of Appeal by a majority (Diplock and Salmon L.JJ., Sellers L.J. dissenting) reversed the decision of the trial judge. The majority held . . . applying the rule (or rules) in *Hadley v. Baxendale* as explained in *Victoria*

Laundry (Windsor) Ltd. v. Newman Industries Ltd. . . . that the loss due to fall in market price was not too remote to be recoverable as damages.

It may be well first to set out the knowledge and intention of the parties at the time of making the contract so far as relevant or argued to be relevant. The charterers intended to sell the sugar in the market at Basrah on arrival of the vessel. They could have changed their mind and exercised their option to have the sugar delivered at Jeddah but they did not do so. There is no finding that they had in mind any particular date as the likely date of arrival at Basrah or that they had any knowledge or expectation that in late November or December there would be a rising or a falling market. The shipowner was given no information about these matters by the charterers. He did not know what the charterers intended to do with the sugar. But he knew there was a market in sugar at Basrah, and it appears to me that, if he had thought about the matter, he must have realised that at least it was not unlikely that the sugar would be sold in the market at market price on arrival. And he must be held to have known that in any ordinary market prices are apt to fluctuate from day to day: but he had no reason to suppose it more probable that during the relevant period such fluctuation would be downwards rather than upwards — it was an even chance that the fluctuation would be downwards.

So the question for decision is whether a plaintiff can recover as damages for breach of contract a loss of a kind which the defendant, when he made the contract, ought to have realised was not unlikely to result from a breach of contract causing delay in delivery. I use the words "not unlikely" as denoting a degree of probability considerably less than an even chance but nevertheless not very unusual and easily foreseeable.

For over a century everyone has agreed that remoteness of damage in contract must be determined by applying the rule (or rules) laid down by the court including Lord Wensleydale (then Parke B.), Martin B. and Alderson B. in *Hadley v. Baxendale.* But many different interpretations of that rule have been adopted by judges at different times. So I think that one ought first to see just what was decided in that case, because it would seem wrong to attribute to that rule a meaning which, if it had been adopted in that case, would have resulted in a contrary decision of that case.

In *Hadley v. Baxendale* the owners of a flour mill at Gloucester which was driven by a steam engine delivered to common carriers, Pickford & Co., a broken crankshaft to be sent to engineers in Greenwich. A delay of five days in delivery there was held to be in breach of contract and the question at issue was the proper measure of damages. In fact the shaft was sent as a pattern for a new shaft and until it arrived the mill could not operate. So the owners claimed £300 as loss of profit for the five days by which resumption of work was delayed by this breach of contract. But the carriers did not know that delay would cause loss of this kind.

Alderson B., delivering the judgment of the court, said:

"We find that the only circumstances here communicated by the plaintiffs to the defendants at the time the contract was made, were, that the article to be carried was the broken shaft of a mill, and that the plaintiffs were the millers of that mill. But how do these circumstances show reasonably that the profits of the mill must be stopped by an unreasonable delay in the delivery of the broken shaft by the carrier to the third person? Suppose the plaintiffs had another shaft in their possession put up or putting up at the time, and that they only wished to send back the broken shaft to the engineer who made it; it is clear that this would be quite consistent with the above circumstances, and yet the unreasonable delay in the delivery would have no effect upon the intermediate profits of the mill. Or, again, suppose that at the time of the delivery to the carrier, the machinery of the mill had been in other respects defective, then, also, the same results would follow."

Then, having said that in fact the loss of profit was caused by the delay, he continued:

"But it is obvious that, in the great multitude of cases of millers sending off broken shafts to third persons by a carrier under ordinary circumstances, such consequences would not, in all probability, have occurred."

Alderson B. clearly did not and could not mean that it was not reasonably foreseeable that delay might stop the resumption of work in the mill. He merely said that in the great multitude — which I take to mean the great majority — of cases this would not happen. He was not distinguishing between results which were foreseeable or unforseeable, but between results which were likely because they would happen in the great majority of cases, and results which were unlikely because they would only happen in a small minority of cases. He continued:

"It follows, therefore, that the loss of profits here cannot reasonably be considered such a consequence of the breach of contract as could have been fairly and reasonably contemplated by both the parties when they made this contract."

He clearly meant that a result which will happen in the great majority of cases should fairly and reasonably be regarded as having been in the contemplation of the parties, but that a result which, though foreseeable as a substantial possibility, would only happen in a small minority of cases should not be regarded as having been in their contemplation. He was referring to such a result when he continued:

"For such loss would neither have flowed naturally from the breach of this contract in the great multitude of such cases occurring under ordinary circumstances, nor were the special circumstances, which perhaps, would have made it a reasonable and natural consequence of such breach of contract, communicated to or known by the defendants."

I have dealt with the latter part of the judgment before coming to the well known rule because the court were there applying the rule and the language which was used in the latter part appears to me to throw considerable light on the meaning which they must have attached to the rather vague expression used in the rule itself. The rule is that the damages "should be such as may fairly and reasonably be considered either arising naturally, i.e., according to the usual course of things, from such breach of contract itself, or such as may reasonably be supposed to have been in the contemplation of both parties, at the time they made the contract, as the probable result of the breach of it."

I do not think that it was intended that there were to be two rules or that two different standards or tests were to be applied. The last two passages which I quoted from the end of the judgment applied to the facts before the court which did not include any special circumstances communicated to the defendants; and the line of reasoning there is that because in the great majority of cases loss of profit would not in all probability have occurred, it followed that this could not reasonably be considered as having been fairly and reasonably contemplated by both the parties, for it would not have flowed naturally from the breach in the great majority of cases.

I am satisfied that the court did not intend that every type of damage which was reasonably foreseeable by the parties when the contract was made should either be considered as arising naturally, i.e., in the usual course of things, or be supposed to have been in the contemplation of the parties. Indeed the decision makes it clear that a type of damage which was plainly foreseeable as a real possibility but which would only occur in a small minority of cases cannot be regarded as arising in the usual course of things or be supposed to have been in the contemplation of the parties: the parties are not supposed to contemplate as grounds for the recovery of damage any type of loss or damage which on the knowledge available to the defendant would appear to him as only likely to occur in a small minority of cases.

In cases like *Hadley v. Baxendale* or the present case it is not enough that in fact the plaintiff's loss was directly caused by the defendant's breach of contract. It clearly was so caused in both. The crucial question is whether, on the information available to the defendant when the contract was made, he should, or the reasonable man in his position would, have realised that such loss was sufficiently likely to result from the breach of contract to make it proper to hold that the loss flowed naturally from the breach or that loss of that kind should have been within his contemplation.

The modern rule of tort is quite different and it imposes a much wider liability. The defendant will be liable for any type of damage which is reasonably foreseeable as liable to happen even in the most unusual case, unless the risk is so small that a reasonable man would in the whole circumstances feel justified in neglecting it. And there is good reason for the difference. In contract, if one party wishes to protect himself against a risk which to the other party would appear unusual, he can direct the other party's attention to it before the contract is made, and I need not stop to consider in what circumstances the other party will then be held to have accepted responsibility in that event. But in tort there is no opportunity for the injured party to protect himself in that way, and the tortfeasor cannot reasonably complain if he has to pay for some very unusual but nevertheless foreseeable damage which results from his wrongdoing. I have no doubt that today a tortfeasor would be held liable for a type of damage as unlikely as was the stoppage of Hadley's Mill for lack of a crankshaft: to anyone with the knowledge the carrier had that may have seemed unlikely but the chance of it happening would have been seen to be far from negligible. But it does not at all follow that *Hadley v. Baxendale* would today be differently decided.

But then it has been said that the liability of defendants has been further extended by *Victoria Laundry (Windsor) Ltd. v. Newman Industries Ltd.* I do not think so....

But what is said to create a "landmark" is the statement of principles by Asquith L.J. This does to some extent go beyond the older authorities and in so far as it does so, I do not agree with it. In paragraph (2) it is said that the plaintiff is entitled to recover "such part of the loss actually resulting as was at the time of the contract reasonably foreseeable as liable to result from the breach." To bring in reasonable foreseeability appears to me to be confusing measure of damages in contract with measure of damages in tort.

A great many extremely unlikely results are reasonably foreseeable: it is true that Lord Asquith may have meant foreseeable as a likely result, and if that is all he meant I would not object further than to say that I think that the phrase is liable to be misunderstood. For the same reason I would take exception to the phrase "liable to result" in paragraph (5). Liable is a very vague word but I think that one would usually say that when a person foresees a very improbable result he foresees that it is liable to happen.

I agree with the first half of paragraph (6). For the best part of a century it has not been required that the defendant could have foreseen that a breach of contract must necessarily result in the loss which has occurred. But I cannot agree with the second half of that paragraph. It has never been held to be sufficient in contract that the loss was foreseeable as "a serious possibility" or "a real danger" or as being "on the cards." It is on the cards that one can win £100,000 or more for a stake of a few pence — several people have done that. And anyone who backs a hundred to one chance regards a win as a serious possibility — many people have won on such a chance...

It appears to me that in the ordinary use of language there is wide gulf between saying that some event is not unlikely or quite likely to happen and saying merely that it is a serious possibility, a real danger, or on the cards. Suppose one takes a well-shuffled pack of cards, it is quite likely or not unlikely that the top card will prove to be a diamond: the odds are only 3 to 1 against. But most people would not say that it is quite likely to be the nine of diamonds for the odds are then 51 to 1 against. On the other hand I think that most people would say that there is a serious possibility or a real danger of its being turned up first and of course it is on the cards. If the tests of "real danger" or "serious possibility" are in future to be authoritative then the *Victoria Laundry* case would indeed be a landmark because it would mean that *Hadley v. Baxendale* would be differently decided today. I certainly could not understand any court deciding that, on the information available to the carrier in that case, the stoppage of the mill was neither a serious possibility nor a real danger. If those tests are to prevail in future then let us cease to pay lip service to the rule in *Hadley v. Baxendale*. But in my judgment to adopt these tests would extend liability for breach of contract beyond what is reasonable or desirable. From the limited knowledge which I have of commercial affairs I would not expect such an extension to be welcomed by the business community and from the legal point of view I can find little or nothing to recommend it....

It appears to me that, without relying in any way on the *Victoria Laundry* case, and taking the principle that had already been established, the loss of profit claimed in this case was not too remote to be recoverable as damages.

[All the judges agreed in the result. Short excerpts from the other judgments follow.]

Lord Morris (p. 399): —... I regard the illuminating judgment of the Court of Appeal in *Victoria Laundry (Windsor) Ltd. v. Newman Industries Ltd.* as a most valuable analysis of the rule. It was there pointed out that in order to make a contract-breaker liable under what was called "either rule" in *Hadley v. Baxendale* it is not necessary that he should actually have asked himself what loss is liable to result from a breach but that it suffices that if he had considered the question he would as a reasonable man have concluded that the loss in question was liable to result. Nor need it be proved, in order to recover a particular loss, that upon a given state of knowledge he could, as a reasonable man, foresee that a breach must necessarily result in that loss. Certain illustrative phrases are employed in that case. They are valuable by way of exposition but for my part I doubt whether the phrase "on the cards" has a sufficiently clear meaning or possesses such a comparable shade of meaning as to qualify it to take its place with the various other phrases which line up as expositions of the rule.

Lord Hodson (p. 410): —... The word "probable" in *Hadley v. Baxendale* covers both parts of the rule and it is of vital importance in applying the rule to consider what the court meant by using this word in its context. The common use of this word is no doubt to imply that something is more likely to happen than not. In conversation, if one says to another "If you go out in this weather you will probably catch a cold" this is, I think, equivalent to saying that one believes there is an odds-on chance that the other will catch a cold.   The word "probable" need not, however, bear this narrow meaning....

A close study of the rule was made by the Court of Appeal in the case of the *Victoria Laundry (Windsor) Ltd. v. Newman Industries Ltd.* The judgment of the court, consisting of Tucker, Asquith and Singleton L.JJ., was delivered by Asquith L.J., who... suggested the phrase "liable to result" as appropriate to describe the degree of probability required. This may be a colourless expression but I do not find it possible to improve on it. If the word "likelihood" is used it may convey the impression that the chances are all in favour of the thing happening, an idea which I would reject.

I find guidance in the use of the expression "in the great multitude of cases" which is to be found in more than one place in the judgment in *Hadley v. Baxendale* and indicates that the damages recoverable for breach of contract are such as flow naturally in most cases from the breach, whether under ordinary circumstances or from special circumstances due to the knowledge either in the possession of or communicated to the defendants. This expression throws light on the whole field of damages for breach of contract and points to a different approach from that taken in tort cases.

Lord Pearce (p. 415): —... In my opinion the expression used in the *Victoria Laundry* case were right. I do not however accept the colloquialism "on the cards" as being a useful test because I am not sure just what nuance it has either in my own personal vocabulary or in that of others. I suspect that it owes its attraction, like many other colloquialisms, to the fact that one may utter it without having the trouble of really thinking out with precision what one means oneself or what others will understand by it, a spurious attraction which in general makes colloquialism unsuitable for definition, though it is often useful as shorthand for a collection of definable ideas. It was in this latter convenient sense that the judgment uses the ambiguous words "liable to result". They were not intended as a further or different test from "serious possibility" or "real danger."

Lord Upjohn (p. 424): —... It is clear that on the one hand the test of foreseeability as laid down in the case of tort is not the test for breach of contract; nor on the other hand must the loser establish that the loss was a near certainty or an odds-on probability. I am content to adopt as the test a "real danger" or a "serious possibility." There may be a shade of difference between these two phrases but the assessment of damages is not an exact science and what to one judge or jury will appear a real danger may appear to another judge or jury to be a serious possibility. I do not think that the application of that test would have led to a different result in *Hadley v. Baxendale*. I cannot see why Pickfords in the absence of express mention should have contemplated as a real danger or serious possibility that work at the factory would be brought to a halt while the shaft was away.

QUESTIONS

1. The rule laid down in *Hadley v. Baxendale* was a rule that related to the instruction that a trial judge should give to a jury. Do you think that a jury would be any more able to make the right kind of decision after being charged in accordance with the judgments of the House of Lords than they would have been under *Hadley v. Baxendale* itself or after *Victoria Laundry v. Newman Industries*?

2. If the decision as to the measure of damages is made by a judge rather than by a jury, do you think that he would have a clearer idea of what he should do after the Heron II?

3. Are you any wiser after reading the Heron II than you were before?

4. Do you think that any more precision in the formulation of the rule is possible? If so, how would you go about developing it?

KERR S.S. CO. v. R.C.A.

(1927), 157 N.E. 140. New York Court of Appeals.

Cardozo, C.J.: — On May 15, 1922, the plaintiff, Kerr Steamship Company, Inc., delivered to defendant, the Radio Corporation of America, a telegram consisting of 29 words in cipher to be transmitted to Manila, Philippine Islands. The telegram was written on one of the defendant's blanks, and is prefaced by the printed words:

> "Send the following radiogram via R.C.A., subject to terms on back hereof which are hereby agreed to."

The defendant had no direct circuit for the transmission of radiograms to the Philippine Islands. A radiogram could have been sent to London, where by transfer to other companies it might have reached its destination. This was expensive for the customer. To reduce the expense and follow a more direct route, the defendant forwarded its Philippine messages over the line of the Commercial Cable Company, which transmitted them by cable. When messages were thus forwarded, the practice was to send them upstairs to be copied. One copy was then handed to the cable company and one kept for the defendant's files. That practice was followed in this instance, except that the copy intended for the cable company was mislaid and not delivered. As a consequence the telegram was never sent.

The telegram on its face is an unintelligible cipher. It is written in Scott's code. Translated into English, it remains at best obscure, though some inkling of the transaction may be conveyed to an ingenious mind. Untranslated, it is jargon. The fact is that one Macondray, to whom the telegram was addressed, had cabled the plaintiff for instructions as to the loading of a ship, the Blossom. The instructions were contained in the undelivered message. As a result of the failure to transmit them, the cargo was not laden and the freight was lost. The trial judge directed a verdict for $6,675.29, the freight that would have been earned if the message had been carried. He held that the cipher, though the defendant could not read it, must have been understood as having relation to some transaction of a business nature, and that from this understanding without more there ensued a liability for the damages that would have been recognized as natural if the transaction had been known. The defendant insists that the tolls which the plaintiff was to pay, $26.78, must be the limit of recovery.

The settled doctrine of this court confines the liability of a telegraph company for failure to transmit a message within the limits of the rule in *Hadley v. Baxendale* (9 Exch. 341). Where the terms of the telegram disclose the general nature of the transaction which is the subject of the message, the company is answerable for the natural consequences of its neglect in relation to the transaction thus known or foreseen.... On the other hand, where the terms of the message give no hint of the nature of the transaction, the liability is for nominal damages or for the cost of carriage if the tolls have been prepaid....

We are now asked to hold that the transaction has been revealed within the meaning of the rule if the length and cost of the telegram or the names of the parties would fairly suggest to a reasonable man that business of moment is the subject of the message. This is very nearly to annihilate the rule in the guise of an exception. The defendant upon receiving from a steamship company a long telegram in cipher to be transmitted to Manila would naturally infer that the message had relation to business of some sort. Beyond that it could infer nothing. The message might relate to the loading of a cargo, but equally it might relate to the sale of a vessel or to the employment of an agent or to any one of myriad transactions as divergent as the poles. Notice of the business, if it is to lay the basis for special damages, must be sufficiently informing to be notice of the risk....

At the root of the problem is the distinction between general and special damage as it has been developed in our law. There is need to keep in mind that the distinction is not absolute, but relative. To put it in other words, damage which is general in relation to a contract of one kind may be classified as special in relation to another. If A. and B. contract for the sale of staple goods, the general damage upon a breach is the difference between the market value and the price. But if A. delivers to X. a telegram to B. in cipher with reference to the same sale, or a letter in a sealed envelope, the general damage upon the default of X. is the cost of carriage and no more. As to him the difference between price and value is damage to be ranked as special, and therefore not recoverable unless the message is disclosed. The argument for a larger liability loses sight of this distinction. It misses a sure foothold in that it shifts from general damage in one relation to general damage in another. The bearer of a message who infers from the surrounding circumstances that what he bears had relation to business of some kind is liable, we are told, for any damages that are natural with reference to the character of the business as to which knowledge is imputed. When we ask, however, to what extent the character of the business will be the subject of imputed knowledge, we are told that it is so much of the business only as will make the damage natural.... Thus we travel in a circle, what is natural or general being adapted to so much of a putative business as is constructively known, and what is constructively known being adapted to what is general and natural. One cannot build conclusions upon foundations so unstable. The loss of a cipher message to load a vessel in the Philippines may mean to one the loss of freight, to another an idle factory, to another a frustrated bargain for the sale or leasing of the cargo. We cannot say what ventures are collateral till we know the ventures that are primary. Not till we learn the profits that are direct can we know which ones are secondary. There is a contradictio in adjecto when we speak of the general damages appropriate to an indeterminate transaction.

The key to *Hadley v. Baxendale* is lost if we fail to keep in mind the relativity of causation as a concept of the law.... The argument for the plaintiff mistakenly assumes that the test of what is general damage in a controversy between the sender of a message and the receiver is also the test between the sender and the carrier. To unify the two relations is to abandon *Hadley v. Baxendale* in its application to contracts for the transmission of a message. If knowledge that a message is concerned with business of some kind is by imputation knowledge of those forms of business, and those only, that are typical or normal, there must be search for a definition of the normal and the typical. The quest is obviously futile. Every effect is natural when there is complete knowledge of the cause. Every damage becomes natural when the transaction out of which it arises has been fully comprehended. Imputed knowledge cannot stop with imputed notice of transactions that are standardized by usage. In the complexities of modern life, one does not know where the ordinary ends and the extraordinary begins. Imputed knowledge, if it exists, must rest upon an assumption less timid and uncertain. The assumption cannot be less than this, that whatever a carrier could ascertain by diligent inquiry as to the nature of the undisclosed transaction, this he should be deemed to have ascertained, and charged with damages accordingly. We do not need to consider whether such a rule might wisely have been applied in the beginning, when the law as to carriers of messages was yet in its infancy. Most certainly it is not the rule announced in our decisions. We cannot accept it now without throwing overboard the doctrine that notice is essential. Notice may indeed be adequate though the transaction is indicated in outline only.... The carrier must draw such reasonable inferences in respect of the character of the business as would be drawn by men of affairs from condensed or abbreviated dispatches. Something, however, there must be to give warning that the subject of the message is not merely business in general, but business of a known order....

We are not unmindful of the force of the plaintiff's assault upon the rule in *Hadley v. Baxendale* in its application to the relation between telegraph carrier and customer. The truth seems to be that neither the clerk who receives the message over the counter nor the operator who transmits it nor any other employee gives or is expected to give any thought to the sense of what he is receiving or transmitting. This imparts to the whole doctrine as to the need for notice an air of unreality. The doctrine, however, has prevailed for years, so many that it is tantamount to a rule of property. The companies have regulated their rates upon the basis of its continuance. They have omitted precautions that they might have thought it necessary to adopt if the hazard of the business was to be indefinitely increased. Nor is the doctrine without other foundation in utility and justice. Much may be said in favor of the social policy of a rule whereby the companies have been relieved of liabilities that might otherwise be crushing. The sender can protect himself by insurance in one form or another if the risk of nondelivery or error appears to be too great. The total burden is not heavy since it is distributed among many, and can be proportioned in any instance to the loss likely to ensue. The company, if it takes out insurance for itself, can do no more than guess at the loss to be avoided. To pay for this unknown risk, it will be driven to increase the rates payable by all, though the increase is likely to result in the protection of a few. We are not concerned to balance the considerations of policy that give support to the existing rule against others that weigh against it. Enough for present pruposes that there are weights in either scale. Telegraph companies in interstate and foreign commerce are subject to the power of Congress. 36 Stat. 539, 544. If the rule of damages long recognized by state and federal decision is to give way to another, the change should come through legislation.

The plaintiff makes the point that the action is one in tort for the breach of a duty owing from a public service corporation, and that the rule of *Hadley v. Baxendale* does not protect the carrier unless sued upon the contract. There is much authority the other way.... Though the duty to serve may be antecedent to the contract, yet the contract when made defines and circumscribes the duty.... Possibly the existing rule of damage would have been rejected at the beginning if the carrier's default had been dissociated from the law of contracts and considered as a tort.... As it is, there is little trace of a disposition to make the measure of the liability dependent on the form of action. A different question would be here if the plaintiff were seeking reparation for a wrong unrelated to the contract, as, e.g., for a refusal to accept a message or for an insistance upon the payment of discriminatory rates. The plaintiff alleges in the complaint that the defendant did accept the message and "promised and agreed" to transmit it, and that the plaintiff has "duly performed each and every condition of the agreement" on its part to be performed and is willing to pay the charges. We do not stop to inquire whether such a complaint is turned into one in tort by the later allegation that the defendant was negligent in the performance of its promise. Upon the acceptance of the message the defendant's duty was to deliver it in accordance with the contract, and the damages recoverable for non-performance of the contract are the damages recoverable for nonperformance of the duty.

The judgment of the Appellate Division and that of the Trial Term should be reversed and judgment directed in favor of plaintiff for $26.78, to be offset against costs in all courts, which are awarded to defendant.

Pound, Crane, Andrews, Lehman, Kellogg, and O'Brien, JJ., concur.

Judgment accordingly.

QUESTIONS

1. Is the judgment in this case of more help than the judgments in the English cases?

2. To what extent should changes in the law in this area come by legislation or by judicial decision?

3. (a) Which party can more easily take steps to reduce the risk of loss?

(b) Which party can more efficiently insure against the risk of loss? Should the answers to these questions be relevant?

NOTES

Coppola v. Kraushaar (1905), 92 N.Y.S. 436. The plaintiff ordered two gowns for his betrothed from the defendant, informing the defendant at the time that he was incurring great expense for a wedding feast, and that the gowns must be ready the day before the wedding. The defendant failed to finish the gowns on time, and in consequence, according to the allegations of the complaint, the engagement was broken off by the plaintiff's fiancee, and the expenses "which the plaintiff went to in buying presents, wines, clothes and other expenses" to the extent of $500 were "expended uselessly". The court took the view that while some disappointment on the part of the prospective bride was natural under the circumstances, the defendant had no reason to foresee that she would refuse altogether to go through with the marriage simply because the two dresses were delayed, especially since it was not alleged that either was the bridal gown. The court held, however, that the trial judge acted improperly in dismissing the complaint since the plaintiff was entitled to a return of the $10 paid to the defendant as a part of the purchase price of the gowns, and in any event would be entitled to nominal damages.

Chicago Coliseum Club v. Dempsey (1932), 265 Ill. App. 542. In March, 1926, Jack Dempsey contracted with the Club to fight Harry Wills for the heavyweight championship of the world the following September. In July, Dempsey repudiated the contract, and late in August the Club obtained a decree in Indiana enjoining Dempsey from fighting Gene Tunney. [Dempsey nevertheless fought Tunney in September in Philadelphia, losing the championship.] The Club then sued Dempsey for damages, and the trial court gave judgment for Dempsey.

Reversing, the Appellate Court passed on four types of damages, and held that only the fourth could be recovered: (1) The lost profits were "purely speculative". (2) Expenses incurred before the contract was signed were "not chargeable to the defendant". (3) As for the injunction suit and other efforts to compel Dempsey to perform, after the repudiation by defendant the plaintiff "took such steps at its own financial risk". (4) But certain expenses incurred after the signing of the agreement and before the July breach "are recoverable if in furtherance of the general scheme."

Dawson & Harvey, *Contracts and Contract Remedies*, give some more information on the *Dempsey* case. Dempsey fought Tunney in September 1926 (in violation of the injunction) that fight brought in $1,895. In 1927 Tunney and Dempsey again fought (Dempsey losing again) and the gate receipts were $2,268,000. Would evidence of what these two fights brought in dispose of the argument that the lost profits were "purely speculative"?

To what extent can it be said after a case like this that specific performance is available when common law damages are inadequate? What does "inadequate" mean? Refer back to *Warner Bros. v. Nelson* (supra).

The cases of *Hadley v. Baxendale* and *Koufos v. Czarnikow* involved claims against carriers for delay in shipping goods. Many cases involve railway and telegraph companies where delay in the transmission of goods or a message may involve losses of many thousands of dollars. Generally the courts have been most unwilling to impose liability in these cases. Even when the plaintiff tells the carrier that the goods must be delivered within a specific time, the carrier may not be liable if he had no reason to suspect that the plaintiff might lose an exceptionally profitable deal by a delay.

HORNE v. MIDLAND RAILWAY

(1873), L.R. 8, C.P. 131. Exchequer Chamber.

[The plaintiffs, shoe manufacturers, were under contract to supply a quantity of shoes for the eventual use of the French army. The price was 4s. per pair — an unusually high price. (The Franco-Prussian war was then being fought). The shoes were to be delivered by Feb. 3, 1871, and the plaintiffs sent them to the defendant's station in time for delivery as required by the plaintiff's contract. Notice was given to the defendant that the shoes had to be delivered by Feb. 3, 1871 or they would be thrown on the plaintiff's hands. The defendant's servant was not told that the plaintiffs had an exceptionally profitable contract. The shoes were not delivered until the 4th and were, consequently, refused by the buyer. The plaintiffs sold them at 2s. 9d. per pair — the best price obtainable (and the market price on Feb 3 and 4) — and sued for the difference. The defendants paid enough into court to cover any ordinary losses but the plaintiffs claimed a further £2,600 for the whole loss.

The Court of Common Pleas gave judgment for the defendants and error was brought from that judgment.

The court held, 5:2, that the plaintiffs could not recover more than the ordinary losses. The defendants had not had notice of the exceptional nature of the plaintiffs' contract. Three judges also held that no notice would have been sufficient unless the defendants had contracted to be liable for the greater amount. Blackburn J. said during argument:

> **Blackburn, J.:** It is clear the plaintiff gave notice that it was important that the goods should be delivered on the 3rd, but he gave no notice of the extraordinary nature of the contract. There is a substantial consideration involved; if the carrier has notice of an extraordinary risk he may perhaps charge a higher rate of carriage to cover it. The real meaning of the limitation as to damages is that the defendant shall not be bound to pay more than he received a reasonable consideration for undertaking the risk of at the time of making the contract....

and in his judgment:

> Then if there was no special contract, what was the effect of the notice? In the case of *Hadley v. Baxendale* it was intimated that, apart from all question of a special contract with regard to amount of damages, if there were a special notice of the circumstances the plaintiff might recover the exceptional damages. This doctrine has been adverted to in several subsequent decisions with more or less assent, but they appear to have all been cases in which it was held that the doctrine did not apply because there was no special notice. It does not appear that there has been any case in which it has been affirmatively held that in consequence of such a notice the plaintiff could recover exceptional damages. The counsel for the plaintiffs could not refer to any such case, and I know of none. If it were necessary to decide the point, I should be much disposed to agree with what my Brother Martin has suggested, viz., that in order that the notice may have any effect, it must be given under such circumstances, as that an actual contract arises on the part of the defendant to bear the exceptional loss. Before, however, deciding the point, I should have wished to take time to consider; but it is not necessary to do so, for even assuming that the law is the contrary of that which I incline to think it to be, to my mind it is clear that there was no such notice in the present case as to raise the question. There was, no doubt, a full intimation to the defendants that the time by which the goods were delivered was of consequence, that the reasonable time which the company had to deliver in must not be protracted beyond the 3rd of February, and I think it may fairly be said that there was an intimation to the defendants that the contract under which the plaintiffs had to deliver was a profitable one; but I cannot see, giving the notice its widest construction, that it amounted to a notice that the plaintiffs would suffer such an exceptional loss as they did by non-delivery of the shoes. So that I think it is not necessary to decide whether the dictum in *Hadley v. Baxendale* is well founded, though I do not wish to disguise my present impressions on the subject.]

Kelly, C.B. I am of opinion that the judgment of the Court below must be affirmed. The rules by which this case must be determined are the creatures of authority, and we have not so much to consider in determining it what might be just or unjust, reasonable or unreasonable, under the circumstances of the case, in the absence of previous decisions, as to consider the cases that have been decided on the subject and deduce from them the general principles that must govern our judgment. It must, in the first place, be noticed that this is the case of a railway company, though it does not seem to have occurred to the court below, or to the counsel in arguing the case there, that there was any material difference between the case of a railway company and that of any ordinary person who had contracted for the delivery of goods. It therefore becomes incumbent upon us to consider what is the nature of the ordinary contract between the consignor of goods and the carrier, and what is the obligation imposed upon a railway company in respect of the carriage of goods of an ordinary character such as those in the present case.…

A question of very great importance has been raised in the course of the argument, to which it is proper to refer, though, for reasons I shall presently state, I do not think it will ultimately become necessary to decide it — that is to say, the question what the position of a railway company is when goods are entrusted to it for carriage with an intimation of the consequences of non-delivery, such as it was argued on behalf of the plaintiffs existed in the present case. The goods with which we have to deal are not the subject of any express statutory enactment; the case with respect to them depends on the common law taken in connection with the Acts relating to the defendants' railway company. Now, it is clear, in the first place, that a railway company is bound, in general, to accept goods such as these, and to carry them as directed to the place of delivery, and there deliver them. But now suppose that an intimation is made to the railway company, such, as Mr. Field contended, this amounted to, not merely that if the goods are not delivered by a certain date they will be thrown on the consignor's hands, but in express terms stating that they have entered into such and such a contract and will lose so many pounds if they cannot fulfil it, what is then the position of the company? Are they the less bound to receive the goods? I apprehend not. If, then, they are bound to receive, and do so without more, what is the effect of the notice? Can it be to impose upon them a liability to damages of any amount, however large, in respect of goods which they have no option but to receive? I cannot find any authority for the proposition that the notice without more could have any such effect. It does not appear to me that the railway company has any power, such as was suggested, to decline to receive the goods after such a notice, unless an extraordinary rate of carriage be paid. Of course they may enter into a contract, if they will, to pay any amount of damages for non-performance of their contract in consideration of an increased rate of carriage, if the consignors be willing to pay it; but in the absence of any such contract expressly entered into, there being no power on the part of the company to refuse to accept the goods, or to compel payment of an extraordinary rate of carriage by the consignor, it does not appear to me any contract to be liable to more than the ordinary amount of damages can be implied from mere receipt of the goods after such a notice as before mentioned.

For these reasons, even if the notice given in the present case could be taken as having the effect contended for by Mr. Field, I do not think, in the absence of any expressed or implied contract by the company to be liable to these damages, that there could be any such liability imposed upon them. But however this may be, and even assuming that there might be such a notice as would render the company liable to the exceptional damages claimed by the plaintiffs, I am clearly of opinion that the intimation given to the company in this case does not amount to such a notice. It certainly gave the defendants notice of what might probably be assumed to be the case without express notice, viz., that the plaintiffs being under contract to deliver the shoes, would have them thrown on their hands if not delivered in due time, but it gave the defendants no notice of the exceptional nature of the contract and the unusual loss that would result from a breach of it. That being so, the case comes within the principle clearly to be deduced from all the authorities (not excepting the case of *Hadley v. Baxendale*) itself, whatever view may be taken of the dictum in that case with respect to the effect of notice) viz., that the damages for a breach of contract must be such as may fairly and reasonably be considered as arising naturally, i.e., according to the usual course of things, from such breach of contract itself, or such as may be reasonably supposed to have been in the contemplation of both parties, at the time they made the contract, as the probable result of the breach of it. The effect of the notice here is, that the company must be taken to have contemplated that the plaintiffs were under a contract to deliver the shoes, and would be liable to lose the benefit of such contract, or to an action for breach of it, if they failed to deliver under it. The loss they would in the usual course of things sustain or the damages they would have to pay on such a contract would depend upon the rise or fall of the market price. We are not told when the contract for the sale of the shoes was made, nor what was the market price at that time. It appears to me, therefore, that the only damage we can consider is the difference between the market price at the time when the goods ought to have been delivered and the market price at the time when they were delivered. There is no evidence before us to shew that the market value of the shoes at the time when they were delivered to the defendants or at the time when they ought to have been delivered to the consignees, differed from their value at the time when they were ultimately sold. So far as appears from the case, it seems to me that it must be taken that the market price was the same at all those periods. Under those circumstances, in the absence of any notice to the defendants of the exceptional nature of the contract into which the plaintiffs had entered, I think the plaintiffs are only entitled to nominal damages, unless, perhaps, in respect of expenses, if any, that were incurred, which would be amply covered by the amount paid into court. It appears to me that very serious consequences might result from making a railway company liable upon a mere notice that the consignor is under contract to deliver, such as that in the present case, for an indefinite amount of damages arising out of a contract of a highly exceptional nature, entered into under very special circumstances.

QUESTIONS

1. In the ordinary case where does the obligation to pay damages come from?

2. Why is it necessary to say that there must be a second contract to pay damages?

3. Suppose that there were such a second contract and, for example, in a case like *Victoria Laundry v. Newman Industries,* the defendant promised to pay £20,000 if the boiler was late, should that contract be enforceable?

4. Conversely, suppose that there is a clause specifically excluding liability. For example, in *Kerr S.S. v. R.C.A.,* on the back of the telegram the following appeared:

It is agreed between the sender of the message on the face hereof and this company, that said company shall not be liable for mistakes or delays in transmission or delivery, nor for non-delivery to the next connecting telegraph company or to the addressee, of any unrepeated message, beyond the amount of that portion of the tolls which shall accrue to this company; and that this company shall not be liable for mistakes or delays in the transmission or delivery, or for delay of non-delivery to the next connecting telegraph company, or to the addressee, of any repeated message beyond the usual tolls and extra sum received by this company from the sender for transmitting and repeating such message; and that this company shall not be liable in any case for delays arising from interruption in the working of its system, nor for errors in cipher or obscure messages.

Should the existence of such a clause influence the court?

PROBLEM

Barry was getting married to Valerie on Saturday, September 30. He wanted to arrange for a limousine to take his bride to the church and from there to the reception. On August 30, he arranged with Autorentals for a Cadillac limousine to be at Valerie's house at 2:00 p.m. on the appropriate day. He did not mention the purpose for which the car was needed. After hearing from his friend, Derek, that Autorentals was unreliable, Barry phoned the company, asked to speak to the manager, Tom, and told him that the car was needed for his wedding and that he would be put to considerable inconvenience, embarrassment and expense if the car was not delivered on time. Tom assured him that he need not worry. The car did not show up on the 30th. Barry could only rent another at short notice for an exorbitant amount and, because of the mix-up, Valerie's father told Barry that he would not be offered the job that he had been promised in Valerie's father's firm. Barry sues Autorentals. What result?

Would it matter if, after Barry had told Tom precisely what would happen if the car was not delivered on time, Tom had deliberately breached the contract because a friend of his wanted to borrow the only car available?

The difficulties of applying the "rules" of *Hadley v. Baxendale* can be seen from a comparison of two cases in the Manitoba Court of Appeal. In *Monroe Equipment Sales Ltd. v. Canadian Forest Products* (1961), 29 D.L.R. (2d) 730, the plaintiff sued the defendant for rental payments due on a second-hand bulldozer. The defendant counterclaimed for damages caused by the fact that the bulldozer had broken down shortly after the contract was made. The defendant claimed damages based on the fact that 3,500 cords of pulpwood were not taken out of the bush. Miller C.J.M. said:

> "In my opinion it is unreasonable to expect that such a burden of responsibility for damages as now claimed by the defendant should be assumed from the rental of a second-hand unit. Surely no reasonable person could contemplate, under the circumstances of the renting of this machine, that the lessor of one second-hand tractor was underwriting and virtually insuring the removal of all this pulpwood from the bush...."

Schultz and Guy JJ.A. agreed with Miller C.J.M. Tritschler and Freedman JJ.A. dissented. Freedman J.A. said that the plaintiff had enough knowledge of the defendant's methods of operation to bring the case within the second rule in *Hadley v. Baxendale.*

In *Scyrup v. Economy Tractor Parts Ltd.* (1963), 40 D.L.R. (2d) 1026, a majority of the same court held the defendant liable for lost profits caused by the break-down of second-hand hydraulic equipment bought by the plaintiff by the defendant. Miller C.J.M. and Guy J.A. applied *Monroe Equipment* and would have decided in favour of the defendant. The majority, however, this time consisting of Freedman, Schultz and Monnin JJ.A., held that the defendant was liable. (Monnin J.A. had been the trial judge in *Monroe Equipment* and had been reversed by the Court of Appeal. Schultz J.A. did not give reasons in either case.) Freedman J.A. said:

> "The *Victoria Laundry v. Newman* case, in considering the *Hadley v. Baxendale* rules, made it clear that damages for breach of contract should be measured by what was reasonably foreseeable as liable to result from the breach. That in turn would depend on the knowledge possessed by the parties or, at all events, by the party who later commits the breach. Knowledge could be either imputed or actual. Imputed knowledge is sufficient to bring into play the first rule; actual knowledge is required for the second.
>
> "Reasonable foreseeability is the test under both rules. Indeed it is not always easy to make a rigid division between the two rules, and one writer comments that "the modern restatement of the rule as a totality is a salutary trend": *vide Mayne & McGregor on Damages*, 12th ed., p. 127.
>
> "It seems to me that whether we say there is one rule or two, or one rule with two branches, the test of reasonable foreseeability in either case operates here in favour of the plaintiff. For if imputed knowledge under the first rule is sufficient, it is not unrealistic to ascribe to the defendant an awareness that his breach of contract in selling this defective equipment to the plaintiff would in the ordinary course of events result in damages in the form of loss of profits as here sustained. If, on the other hand, actual knowledge of special circumstances attaching to the contract is required, the evidence on the record shows that the defendant had such knowledge."

FREEDHOF v. POMALIFT INDUSTRIES LTD.

[1971] 2 O.R. 773. C.A.; Kelly, Evans and Brooke, JJ.A.

[The defendant had agreed to install a ski-lift at the ski-resort owned by plaintiff. The agreement was made in October 1963 and delivery was promised in 60 days. The initial delivery of the lift was two months late and after that things went from bad to worse. The parties attempted to get the lift to operate for two and a half years before abandoning the attempt. The plaintiff had had to mortgage his property to the Industrial Development Bank (now the Federal Business Development Bank) to obtain the money needed to acquire the equipment he had agreed to buy. The plaintiff could not repay the loan and the bank sold the mortgaged land to one Boyt for $28,000 (a surplus of $600 was paid into court). Two years later, Boyt sold the land for $48,000. The plaintiff sued the defendant for damages for breach of contract.

The trial judge, Stewart J., gave judgment for the plaintiff and awarded damages as follows:

1. Amount paid to Pomalift	$5,240.00
2. Loss on operations	17,245.00
3. Loss on Land & Chattels	25,000.00
	$47,485.00

The second head covered extra expenses incurred in getting his land ready for the ski-lift and lost profits during the time that the parties were trying to get the lift in operation. The third head covered the loss suffered by reason of the sale of the land to Boyt which Stewart J. assessed at $25,000 (the difference between the principal amount of the mortgage outstanding at the date of sale and $48,000). The plaintiff's claim for loss of future profits was dismissed. On this, Stewart, J. said:

> "The last item of damages claimed, namely, his future profits, I have not assessed as I am not satisfied that they have been proved with the degree of accuracy which would enable me to come to any reasonable conclusion. In fact, while I have no doubt that such profits would have accrued to the plaintiff, they have not been established. If, however, it is to be held that once a head of damage has been proved a Judge should assess such damages at large, although its detailed assessment (being almost impossible to prove) cannot be made, I would assess them at $24,000. However, as I say, I regard this as being nebulous and vague and, therefore, confine the damages for which the plaintiff shall have judgment to the heads above totalling $47,485. The plaintiff shall also have his costs of this action."]

In the Court of Appeal, the judgment of the court was given, orally, by Kelly J.A. Kelly J.A. first held that the plaintiff could not recover the price paid to the defendant. (The amount was held to represent the value of the equipment left on the land when the contract was abandoned.) The court affirmed the basis for the award under the second head. In regard to the third head of damage awarded by the trial judge, Kelly J.A. said:

Kelly J.A.:-... We do not believe that this item is recoverable as damages for breach of this contract. First, even if the plaintiff suffered such a loss, it is not one so directly related to the defendants' failure to perform the contract with respect to the Pomalift, as to entitle the plaintiff to be compensated for it by the defendants. In our view, where the subject-matter of a contract of sale and purchase is the actual material which the buyer intends to resell at a profit, it would be reasonably within the contemplation of the seller that his failure to perform the contract would bring a loss to the buyer; such loss would meet the test of foreseeability or as has been otherwise stated it would be one that the seller would be aware was not unlikely to occur. Where, as in this contract, what was intended was delivery for use in 1963 of a revenue-generating piece of equipment, it would be reasonable for the defendants to have anticipated that if they failed to deliver a working unit the plaintiff would look to them to be reimbursed for the loss of revenue attributed to the non-working of the lift, at least up to the time when by due diligence the plaintiff could have secured some alternative equipment. But in the first example, if the buyer, by reason of the loss of revenue for which he was entitled to be compensated in damages by the seller, became unable to make payments for other equipment which he had bought on a conditional sales basis and such equipment was repossessed from him because he was unable to meet these payments, he would not be entitled to damages for the loss of that other equipment which was repossessed from him. In the instant case, even if the plaintiff be entitled to be compensated for damages in the amount of loss of revenue, the loss of property through the sale by the Industrial Development Bank because of the plaintiff's failure to keep the mortgage in good standing, does not entitle him to damages measured by the loss he alleges that he suffered in the sale of the property. It does not meet the test of foreseeability.

Even if it be assumed that the loss of property was compensable by damages, the plaintiff cannot recover any pecuniary sum unless and until he has proven, by admissible evidence, that the recovery on the sale of the property was less than the value of the property, a fact which can by no stretch of imagination be proven by the mere fact of the sale of it by Boyt in the year 1968 at a figure of some $48,000. There is no evidence in any way to establish a similarity between the value of the property in 1966 and the sale price in 1968; to accept the difference in those two amounts as the measure of the plaintiff's loss would be to assume that the Industrial Development Bank failed in its obligation to sell the property to the best advantage. On this account, we are of the opinion that the plaintiff has not only failed to prove that he has suffered a compensable loss but has failed to give any evidence of any cogency as to what that loss would have been had he been entitled to recover it.

Since we do not consider that the assessment of damages made by the learned trial Judge proceeded upon the principles properly applicable to the facts of this case, and since we do not consider that it would be appropriate for this Court from the findings of the learned trial Judge and the meagre and unsatisfactory evidence adduced at the trial itself to make an assessment, there should be a reference to the Master to assess the damages upon the footing of the entitlement of the plaintiff as we have stated it, namely, the expenditures directly related to the receipt and installation of the Pomalift and the loss of profit calculated as we have expressed it.

QUESTIONS

1. To what extent was the plaintiff worse off because the trial judge awarded him an amount so clearly based on the wrong factors?
2. What did the plaintiff lose by reason of the breach of contract by the defendant? How adequately was he compensated?
3. Was the amount awarded by the trial judge a fair estimate of the losses suffered by the plaintiff?

REVIEW PROBLEM

Anne agreed to buy Charles' house for $100,000. Her offer was accepted by Charles on October 1, and the deal was to close on January 15th. On October 10, Charles, who had wanted to move, agreed to buy Trudy's house for $120,000. This deal was also to close on January 15. On November 15 Charles arranged mortgage financing with Kevin. Kevin agreed to advance $80,000 to Charles on a first mortgage on his new house. Trudy agreed to buy Tom's house for $150,000. Each purchaser agreed to buy for cash. Each vendor agreed to discharge any existing mortgages. On January 15 Anne refused to complete the purchase from Charles. Charles could not now pay Trudy and had now no need for Kevin's mortgage. Trudy could not now purchase Tom's house.

Who is liable to whom for what?

E. The Range of the Interests Protected

ADDIS v. GRAMOPHONE CO. LTD.

[1909] A.C. 488, House of Lords; Lord Loreburn, L.C., Lords James, Atkinson, Collins, Gorell and Shaw.

[All the judges agreed in the result. Only the judgment of Lord Atkinson is reproduced.

The plaintiff was employed by the defendant as the manager of their business in Calcutta. He was paid £15/week salary and a commission on sales. He could be dismissed by 6 months' notice. The plaintiff was dismissed with notice but without being allowed to work out his notice. The jury awarded the plaintiff damages for wrongful dismissal including a sum of £600 above what he would have earned during the six months. The Court of Appeal dismissed the claim in respect of the £600 and ordered an accounting in respect of what he would have earned. The plaintiff appealed.]

Lord Atkinson:- The rights of the plaintiff, disembarrassed of the confusing methods by which they were sought to be enforced, are, in my opinion, clear. He had been illegally dismissed from his employment. He could have been legally dismissed by the six months' notice, which he, in fact, received, but the defendants did not wait for the expiry of that period. The damages plaintiff sustained by this illegal dismissal were (1.) the wages for the period of six months during which his formal notice would have been current; (2.) the profits or commission which would, in all reasonable probability, have been earned by him during the six months had he continued in the employment; and possibly (3.) damages in respect of the time which might reasonably elapse before he could obtain other employment. He has been awarded a sum possibly of some hundreds of pounds, not in respect of any of these heads of damage, but in respect of the harsh and humiliating way in which he was dismissed, including, presumably, the pain he experienced by reason, it is alleged, of the imputation upon him conveyed by the manner of his dismissal. This is the only circumstance which makes the case of general importance, and this is the only point I think it necessary to deal with.

I have been unable to find any case decided in this country in which any countenance is given to the notion that a dismissed employee can recover in the shape of exemplary damages for illegal dismissal, in effect damages for defamation, for it amounts to that,

. . .

I have always understood that damages for breach of contract were in the nature of compensation, not punishment, and that the general rule of law applicable to such cases was that in effect stated by Cockburn C.J. in *Engel v. Fitch* (1868), L.R. 3 Q.B. 314, 330, in these words: "By the law of England as a general rule a vendor who from whatever cause fails to perform his contract is bound, as was said by Lord Wensleydale in the case referred to, to place the purchaser, so far as money will do it, in the position he would have been in if the contract had been performed. If a man sells a cargo of goods not yet come to hand, but which he believes to have been consigned to him from abroad, and the goods fail to arrive, it will be no answer to the intended purchaser to say that a third party who had engaged to consign the goods to the seller has deceived or disappointed him. The purchaser will be entitled to the difference between the contract price and the market price."

. . .

There are three well-known exceptions to the general rule applicable to the measure of damages for breach of contract, namely, actions against a banker for refusing to pay a customer's cheque when he has in his hands funds of the customer's to meet it, actions for breach of promise of marriage, and actions like that in *Flureau v. Thornhill* (1776), 2 W. Bl. 1078; 96

E.R. 635, where the vendor of real estate, without any fault on his part, fails to make title. I know of none other.

The peculiar nature of the first two of these exceptions justified their existence. Ancient practice upholds the last, though it has often been adversely criticized, as in *Bain v. Fothergill* (1874), L.R. 7 H.L. 158. If there be a tendency to create a fourth exception it ought, in my view, to be checked rather than stimulated; inasmuch as to apply in their entirety the principles on which damages are measured in tort to cases of damages for breaches of contract would lead to confusion and uncertainty in commercial affairs, while to apply them only in part and in particular cases would create anomalies, lead occasionally to injustice, and make the law a still more "lawless science" than it is said to be.

For instance, in actions of tort motive, if it may be taken into account to aggregate damages, as it undoubtedly may be, may also be taken into account to mitigate them, as may also the conduct of the plaintiff himself who seeks redress. Is this rule to be applied to actions of breach of contract? There are few breaches of contract more common than those which arise where men omit or refuse to repay what they have borrowed, or to pay for what they have bought. Is the creditor or vendor who sues for one of such breaches to have the sum he recovers lessened if he should be shewn to be harsh, grasping, or pitiless, or even insulting, in enforcing his demand, or lessened because the debtor has struggles to pay, has failed because of misfortune, and has been suave, gracious, and apologetic in his refusal? On the other hand, is that sum to be increased if it should be shewn that the debtor could have paid readily without any embarrassment, but refused with expression of contempt and contumely, from a malicious desire to injure his creditor?

Few parties to contracts have more often to complain of ingratitude and baseness than sureties. Are they, because of this, to be entitled to recover from the principal, often a trusted friend, who has deceived and betrayed them, more than they paid on that principal's behalf? If circumstances of aggravation are rightly to be taken into account in actions of contract at all, why should they not be taken into account in the case of the surety, and the rules and principles applicable to cases of tort applied to the full extent?

In many other cases of breach of contract there may be circumstances of malice, fraud, defamation, or violence, which would sustain an action of tort as an alternative remedy to an action for breach of contract. If one should select the former mode of redress, he may, no doubt, recover exemplary damages, or what is sometimes styled vindictive damages; but if he should choose to seek redress in the form of an action for breach of contract, he lets in all the consequences of that form of action... One of these consequences is, I think, this: that he is to be paid adequate compensation in money for the loss of that which he would have received had his contract been kept, and no more.

I can conceive nothing more objectionable and embarrassing in litigation than trying in effect an action of libel or slander as a matter of aggravation in an action for illegal dismissal, the defendant being permitted, as he must in justice be permitted, to traverse the defamatory sense, rely on privilege, or raise every point which he could raise in an independent action brought for the alleged libel or slander itself.

In my opinion, exemplary damages ought not to be, and are not according to any true principle of law, recoverable in such an action as the present, and the sums awarded to the plaintiff should therefore be decreased by the amount at which they have been estimated, and credit for that item should not be allowed in his account.

JARVIS v. SWANS TOURS LTD.

[1973] 1 All E.R. 71, C.A.; Lord Denning M.R., Edmund Davies and Stephenson L.JJ.

Lord Denning M.R.:-The plaintiff, Mr. Jarvis, is a solicitor employed by a local authority at Barking. In 1969 he was minded to go for Christmas to Switzerland. He was looking forward to a ski-ing holiday. It is his one fortnight's holiday in the year. He prefers it in the winter rather than in the summer.

Mr. Jarvis read a brochure issued by Swans Tours Ltd. He was much attracted by the description of Morlialp, Giswil, Central Switzerland. I will not read the whole of it, but just pick out some of the principal attractions:

> "HOUSE PARTY CENTRE with special resident host... MORLIALP is a most wonderful little resort on a sunny plateau... Up there you will find yourself in the midst of beautiful alpine scenery, which in winter becomes a wonderland of sun, snow and ice, with a wide variety of fine ski-runs, a skating-rink and an exhilarating toboggan run... Why did we choose the Hotel Krone... mainly and most of all, because of the 'GEMUTLICHKEIT" and friendly welcome you will receive from Herr and Frau Weibel... The Hotel Krone has its own Alphütte Bar which will be open several evenings a week... No doubt you will be in for a great time, when you book this houseparty holiday... Mr. Weibel, the charming owner, speaks English."

On the same page, in a special yellow box, it was said:

> "SWANS HOUSEPARTY IN MORLIALP. *All these Houseparty arrangements are included in the price of your holiday.* Welcome party on arrival. Afternoon tea and cake for 7 days. Swiss Dinner by candlelight. Fondue-party. Yodler evening. Chali farewell party in the 'Alphutte Bar'. Service of representative."

Alongside on the same page there was a special note about ski-packs: 'Hire of Skis, Sticks and Boots... 12 days £11.10.'

In August 1969, on the faith of that brochure, Mr. Jarvis booked a 15 day holiday, with ski-pack. The total charge was £63.45, including Christmas supplement. He was to fly from Gatwick to Zurich on 20th December 1969 and return on 3rd January 1970.

The plaintiff went on the holiday, but he was very disappointed. He was a man of about 35 and he expected to be one of a houseparty of some 30 or so people. Instead, he found there were only 13 during the first week. In the second week there was no houseparty at all. He was the only person there. Mr Weibel could not speak English. So there was Mr Jarvis, in the second week, in this hotel with no houseparty at all, and no one could speak English, except himself. He was very disappointed, too, with the ski-ing. It was some distance away at Giswil. There were no ordinary length skis. There were only mini-skis, about 3 ft long. So he did not get his ski-ing as he wanted to. In the second week he did get some longer skis for a couple of days, but then, because of the boots, his feet got rubbed and he could not continue even with the long skis. So his ski-ing holiday, from his point of view, was pretty well ruined.

There were many other matters, too. They appear trivial when they are set down in writing, but I have no doubt they loomed large in Mr Jarvis's mind, when coupled with the other disappointments. He did not have the nice Swiss cakes which he was hoping for. The only cakes for tea were potato crisps and little dry nutcakes. The yodler evening consisted of one man from the locality who came in his working clothes for a little while, and sang four or five songs very quickly. The 'Alphütte Bar' was an unoccupied annexe which was only open one evening. There was a representative, Mrs Storr, there during the first week, but she was not there during the second week. The matter was summed up by the learned judge:

> "... during the first week he got a holiday in Switzerland which was to some extent inferior... and, as to the second week he got a holiday which was very largely inferior [to what he was led to expect]"

What is the legal position? I think that the statements in the brochure were representations or warranties. The breaches of them give Mr Jarvis a right to damages. It is not necessary to decide whether they were representations or warranties; because, since the Misrepresentation Act 1967, there is a remedy in damages for misrepresentation as well as for breach of warranty.

The one question in the case is: what is the amount of damages? The judge seems to have taken the difference in value between what he paid for and what he got. He said that he intended to give 'the difference between the two values and no other damages' under any other head. He thought that Mr Jarvis had got half of what he paid for. So the judge gave him half the amount which he had paid, namely, £31.72. Mr Jarvis appeals to this court. He says that the damages ought to have been much more.

There is one point I must mention first. Counsel together made a very good note of the judge's judgment. They agreed it. It is very clear and intelligible. It shows plainly enough the ground of the judge's decision; but, by an oversight, it was not submitted to the judge, as it should have been... In some circumstances we should send it back to the judge for his comments. But I do not think we need do so here. The judge received the notice of appeal and made notes for our consideration. I do not think he would have wished to add to them. We will, therefore, decide the case on the material before us.

What is the right way of assessing damages? It has often been said that on a breach of contract damages cannot be given for mental distress. Thus in *Hamlin v Great Northern Railway Co* (1856), 1 H. & N. 408, 411, Pollock CB said that damages cannot be given 'for the disappointment of mind occasioned by the breach of contract'. And in *Hobbs v London & South Western Railway Co.* (1875), L.R. 10 Q.B. 111, 122, Mellor J said that—

> "... for the mere inconvenience, such as annoyance and loss of temper, or vexation, or for being disappointed in a particular thing which you have set your mind upon, without real physical inconvenience resulting, you cannot recover damages."

The courts in those days only allowed the plaintiff to recover damages if he suffered physical inconvenience, such as, having to walk five miles home, as in *Hobbs's* case; or to live in an overcrowded house: see *Bailey v Bullock*, [1950] 2 All E.R. 1167.

I think that those limitations are out of date. In a proper case damages for mental distress can be recovered in contract, just as damages for shock can be recovered in tort. One such case is a contract for a holiday, or any other contract to provide entertainment and enjoyment. If the contracting party breaks his contract, damages can be given for the disappointment, the distress, the upset and frustration caused by the breach. I know that it is difficult to assess in terms of money, but it is no more difficult than the assessment which the courts have to make every day in personal injury cases for loss of amenities. Take the present case. Mr Jarvis has only a fortnight's holiday in the year. He books it far ahead, and looks forward to it all that time. He ought to be compensated for the loss of it.

A good illustration was given by Edmund Davies LJ in the course of the argument. He put the case of a man who has taken a ticket for Glyndbourne. It is the only night on which he can get there. He hires a car to take him. The car does not turn up. His damages are not limited to the mere cost of the ticket. He is entitled to general damages for the disappointment he has suffered and the loss of the entertainment which he should have had. Here, Mr Jarvis's fortnight's winter holiday has been a grave disappointment. It is true that he was conveyed to Switzerland and back and had meals and bed in the hotel. But that is not what he went for. He went to enjoy himself with all the facilities which the defendants said he would have. He is entitled to damages for the lack of those facilities, and for the loss of enjoyment.

A similar case occurred in 1951. It was *Stedman v Swan's Tours* (1951), 95 Sol. Jo. 727. A holiday-maker was awarded damages because he did not get the bedroom and the accommodation which he was promised. The country court judge awarded him £13.15s. This court increased it to £50.

I think the judge was in error in taking the sum paid for the holiday, £63.45, and halving it. The right measure of damages is to compensate him for the loss of entertainment and enjoyment which he was promised, and which he did not get. Looking at the matter quite broadly, I think the damages in this case should be the sum of £125. I would allow the appeal accordingly.

[Edmund Davies and Stephenson L.JJ. agreed with Lord Denning.]

[The court refused to allow the plaintiff's claim for 2 weeks' salary (amounting to £93.27). Is it only coincidence that £93.27 and £31.27 (half the cost of the holiday) comes to £124.99?]

QUESTIONS AND PROBLEMS

1. What interests are being protected in *Jarvis v. Swan's Tours*?

2. Is *Jarvis v. Swan's Tours* in conflict with *Addis v. Gramophone*? Do both courts have the same view of the purpose of awarding damages?

3. Suppose that Mrs. Jarvis had accompanied Mr. Jarvis on his holiday and that she, too, had been disappointed. What would the damages be then?

Jarvis v. Swan's Tours has been followed in a number of cases in Canada. See, *e.g.*, *Keks v. Esquire Pleasure*, [1974] 3 W.W.R. 406. (Lost enjoyment on a holiday.) and *Elder v. Koppe* (1974), 53 D.R.L. (3d) 705 (N.S.S.C.). (Inconvenience and disappointment due to breach by defendant of agreement to rent mobile home for vacation.)

In *Tippett v. Int'l Typographical Union* (1976), 71 D.L.R. (3d) 146, damages for loss of reputation and mental distress were awarded against a union when the plaintiff had been wrongfully expelled.

In *Newell v. C.P. Air* (1976), 74 D.L.R. (3d) 574, damages for mental distress were awarded to the plaintiffs whose dogs had been suffocated while being carried in the baggage compartment of an airplane. The court held that such damages were recoverable under *Hadley v. Baxendale*.

Courts had refused to award damages for mental distress in cases involving the negligence of solicitors, (*e.g. Kolan v. Solicitor* (1969), 7 D.L.R. (3d) 481; aff'd, 11 D.L.R. (3d) 672) on the ground that such damages were too remote. However, in *Heywood v. Wellers*, [1976] Q.B. 446 the English Court of Appeal awarded the plaintiff £150 for mental distress caused when the defendant solicitors negligently failed to prevent her from being molested.

The rule in *Addis v. Gramophone* that damages for loss of employment cannot include any element of mental suffering has recently been departed from. In *Cox v. Philips Industries Ltd.,* [1976] 1 W.L.R. 638; [1976] 3 All E.R. 161, the plaintiff had been wrongfully dismissed. He had been promised a position of greater responsibility after receiving an offer from a competitor, but, later, found that his prospects with his employer were very unpromising. He was subsequently relegated to a position of little authority and with a very vague job description. The plaintiff appeared in person and claimed £20,000 damages. The judge mentioned that he had considered *Jarvis v. Swan's Tours Ltd*, and went on to say:

> "In my judgment this is a case where it was in the contemplation of the parties in all the circumstances that, if that promise of a position of better responsibility without reasonable notice was breached, then the effect of that breach would be to expose the plaintiff to the degree of vexation, frustration and distress which he in fact underwent.
>
> "I have had very helpful submissions from Mr. Eady on this matter suggesting that damages for this kind of loss are really only appropriate when you lose a relative and the funeral procession does not turn up at the right time, or you acquire a wife and the photographer does not turn up at the right time, or you do not have a holiday you are promised. But I can see no reason in principle why, if a situation arises which within the contemplation of the parties would have given rise to vexation, distress and general disappointment and frustration, the person who is injured by a contractual breach should not be compensated in damages for that breach. Doing the best I can, because money can never really make up for mental distress and vexation — this is a common problem of course in personal injury cases — I think the right sum to award the plaintiff under that head is the sum of £500.

QUESTION

To what extent does the freedom to award damages for mental distress and lost enjoyment undercut the argument that specific performance is a necessary remedy to prevent the promisee suffering losses for which the common law can offer no adequate compensation?

MARTEL v. DUFFY-MOTT CORP.

(1969), 166 N.W. 2d 541. Court of Appeals; Michigan. Levin, P.J., Burns and McGregor JJ.

Levin, Presiding Judge:-The plaintiffs appeal a directed verdict granted at the conclusion of their proofs. The complaint charged the defendant, Duffy-Mott Corporation, with both negligence and breach of implied warranty of merchantability. On appeal the plaintiffs rely solely on the statutory implied warranty that to be merchantable goods must be fit for the ordinary purposes for which they are used.

Edwina Martel served her sons, Brian, 8, and Gary, 10, Mott's applesauce as part of their meal. Brian mixed his applesauce with the rest of his food and consumed a sizeable portion of the mixture. Gary ate the applesauce separately and after a spoonful or 2 reported to his mother that the applesauce tasted funny. She tasted and smelled the applesauce — at the trial she and Gary testified that it both tasted and smelled bad — and immediately telephoned the poison control center at Children's Hospital which, on the basis of her description of the applesauce, instructed her to take the children and remaining applesauce to the nearest hospital. When she arrived the applesauce was examined by hospital personnel who decided to and did pump the children's stomachs. Mrs. Martel was advised to watch the children carefully that night for certain symptoms. These symptoms did not appear and no other ill effects were suffered.

There was testimony the children were apprehensive on the way to the hospital although neither Mrs. Martel nor her sons knew of the imminent stomach pumping until after they reached the hospital. Mrs. Martel conceded the children may have gagged because of excitement or fright and not necessarily because of a deleterious substance in the applesauce. On the way to the hospital the boys said they were having a hard time breathing and asked to open the windows. Later they were chilled and asked that the windows be closed.

The boys testified that stomach pumping involves having a tube put through one's nose and swallowing it; the pumping then commences and is a very unpleasant experience. There was also testimony that prior to this incident, applesauce was one of the favorites of the boys and was served 3 or 4 times a week, but since the incident they have refused to eat applesauce at all and even shy away from apples. When asked about their apprehensions, one of the boys stated, "I don't seem to trust it anymore" and the other said, "I don't want to get my stomach pumped again."

The trial judge ruled that the plaintiffs had failed to establish a prima facie case:

> "The court must first find that there was sufficient testimony upon which reasonable minds might differ, that there is some testimony from which individuals might legitimately infer that the applesauce contained a *deleterious* matter; secondly, because of the deleterious matter the minors no longer like applesauce. This, in effect, as the court sees it, is basing an inference upon an inference, which is not sufficient to go to a jury." (Emphasis supplied.)

We reverse and remand for a new trial.

When Michigan adopted the uniform commercial code it enacted the following implied warranty of merchantability for transactions in goods:

"Goods to be merchantable must be at least such as ... are fit for the ordinary purposes for which such goods are used."

In this case there was testimony, by persons well experienced in eating applesauce, that the applesauce tasted and smelled bad. From such direct testimony the jury would have been justified in concluding that the applesauce did in fact taste and smell bad and was inedible. We also note that the hospital personnel, on the basis of their examination of the applesauce, decided to pump the boys' stomachs. If the applesauce was inedible, it was not fit for the ordinary purposes for which it is used.

If the jury were to find that the applesauce was inedible, it could also properly conclude the applesauce so found to be inedible caused the boys to gag and to have their stomachs pumped, whether the precise cause of the gagging was excitement, fright or microbes and irrespective of whether the hospital attendants' decision to pump was well-advised or a mistake in judgment. We are not prepared to say that what is alleged to have occurred was not a proximate consequence of the experiences described. Whether the defendant's breach was a material element and a substantial factor in bringing about the alleged injuries is a question for the trier of fact. It is, of course, open to the defendant to suggest an alternative theory of causation.

Concern has been expressed that if recovery is allowed solely on the basis of a plaintiff's testimony that a manufacturer's food tasted bad or smelled bad, the "floodgates" will have been opened to countless spurious claims. When that occurs, if it does, they can be closed. In the meantime, there is no good reason why in the food area we should so limit the implied warranty that food is merchantable even if inedible as long as not deleterious, when as to every other commodity we apply the "fit for the ordinary purpose for which used" test without a showing that the lack of fitness represents a peril of physical harm.

Nor does any reason appear why biological or laboratory proof should be required as part of plaintiff's case. Accused persons have been convicted and sentenced to serve long terms on one eyewitness's view identification testimony even though the witness's view may have been fleeting, the witness was excited at the time of the incident, or there were other doubt engendering circumstances. A witness may make a mistake in identifying a person because of bad eyesight, ineptitude or preconceived notions — he may lie. In a case such as this one, a witness may mistakenly identify a food substance because he has an uneducated palate, or at the time is subject to some systematical disturbance — he too may lie.

It is the business of juries to determine the credibility of witnesses, to sift out the conflicting claims and to decide the disputed issues. If they go too far afield, it is the trial judge's and our responsibility to correct error. We should not deny recovery of just claims because of fear we cannot recognize and exclude the malingerer.

We have also concluded that, if upon the new trial we have ordered, the jury finds the applesauce unfit for consumption, this is a "proper case" ... for allowing of "consequential damages," including "injury to person or property."

It is a close question whether the plaintiffs should be permitted to recover as part of their consequential damages for past and future loss of enjoyment of applesauce. Applesauce is but one of a large variety of desserts, most of which other desserts can, no doubt, we take judicial notice, fill the gastronomical void created when plaintiffs lost their taste for applesauce. Plaintiffs do not claim permanent injury or loss of taste or appetite in general, or loss of ability to consume or enjoy a basic nutriment or variety of food substances. We could well draw a line — no recovery for loss of enjoyment of applesauce and put a label on it: the claimed damages are "remote", "uncertain", "conjectural", etc. But we decline to do so.

More and more of the food sold to the public comes in cans, frozen, prepared, and even precooked ready to eat. Whole meals can be bought all prepared, ready or almost ready to go on the table. We do not think it a sensible use of the time of the profession or of the bench to construct a body of law as to which foods are of such importance that loss of enjoyment is compensable and those which, as a matter of law, are not of that rank. We think it sounder to permit a plaintiff who can convince a jury that the food product he consumed was inedible and in consequence he no longer enjoys eating it, to recover damages, including damages for loss of enjoyment, if he can additionally convince the jury that a true loss was suffered and that it should add a dollar amount therefor. In some cases loss of enjoyment may be real and substantial, an injury not to be made light of.

We see no need to create rules of law in a narrow area that the good sense of the average jury can handle with greater dispatch and probably sounder results. If a recovery seems disproportionate, the corrective remedies for excessive verdicts are available.

Reversed. Remanded for a new trial. Costs to Appellants.

F. Mitigation

If the purpose of awarding damages for breach of contract be compensation or the protection of the various interests that were violated by the breach, should the law be concerned with the way in which an injured party can respond to the breach so as to reduce the amount of his loss? For example, if the seller breaches a contract for the sale of goods by refusing to deliver, can the buyer allow his losses to mount up by refusing to take any steps to find an alternative source of supply? (If the buyer could do this, there would, of course, be some limit to his recovery under the rule in *Hadley v. Baxendale*.) Generally speaking, the law takes the view that a buyer must take such steps as are reasonable to reduce his loss. The Sale of Goods Act, for example, in s. 49(3) (*supra*), provides that the amount that the buyer can recover by way of damages is the difference between the contract price and market price at the time the goods ought to have been delivered. The assumption here is that the buyer can get his goods from someone else and so the only loss that he will suffer will be due to the fact that he has to pay more in this case. (If the goods have decreased in price, it is much more likely that the buyer will breach than that the seller will do so. If the seller does, then the buyer will have suffered no loss.) The cases in this section are concerned with the obligation of the innocent party to mitigate the loss which is caused by the defendant's breach of contract.

PAYZU LTD. v. SAUNDERS

[1919] 2 K.B. 581. K.B.C. & C.A.

Action tried by **McCardie J.** without a jury.

By a contract in writing dated November 9, 1917, the defendant, who was a dealer in silk, agreed to sell to the plaintiffs 200 pieces of crêpe de chine at 4s. 6d. a yard and 200 pieces at 5s. 11d. a yard, "delivery as required January to September, 1918; conditions, 2½ per cent. 1 month," which meant that payment for goods delivered up to the twentieth day of any month should be made on the twentieth day of the following month, subject to 2½ per cent. discount. At the request of the plaintiffs the defendant delivered, in November, 1917, a certain quantity of the goods under the contract, the price of which amounted to £76, less 2½ per cent. discount. On December 21 the plaintiffs drew a cheque in favour of the defendant in payment of these goods, but the cheque was never received by the defendant. Early in January, 1918, the defendant telephoned to the plaintiffs asking why she had not received a cheque. The plaintiffs then drew another cheque, but owing to a delay in obtaining the signature of one of the plaintiffs' directors, this cheque was not sent to the defendant until January 16. On that day the plaintiffs gave an order by telephone for further deliveries under the contract. The defendant in the belief, which was in fact erroneous, that the plaintiffs' financial position was such that they could not have met the cheque which they alleged had been drawn in December, wrote to the plaintiffs on January 16 refusing to make any further deliveries under the contract unless the plaintiffs paid cash with each order. The plaintiffs refused to do this, and after some further correspondence brought this action claiming damages for breach of contract. The damages claimed were the difference between the market prices in the middle of February, 1918, and the contract prices of the two classes of goods, the difference alleged being respectively 1s.3d. and 1s. 4d. a yard.

. . . .

Now a serious question of law arises on the question of damages. I find as a fact that the defendant was ready and willing to supply the goods to the plaintiffs at the times and prices specified in the contract, provided the plaintiffs paid cash on delivery. Mr. Matthews argued with characteristic vigour and ability that the plaintiffs were entitled to ignore that offer on the ground that a person who has repudiated a contract cannot place the other party to the contract under an obligation to diminish his loss by accepting a new offer made by the party in default.

The question is one of juristic importance. What is the rule of law as to the duty to mitigate damages? I will first refer to the judgment of Cockburn C.J. in *Frost v. Knight* (1872), L.R. 7 Ex. 111, 115, where he said: "In assessing the damages for breach of performance, a jury will of course take into account whatever the plaintiff has done, or has had the means of doing, and, as a prudent man, ought in reason to have done, whereby his loss has been, or would have been, diminished"

The question, therefore, is what a prudent person ought reasonably to do in order to mitigate his loss arising from a breach of contract. I feel no inclination to allow in a mercantile dispute an unhappy indulgence in far-fetched resentment or an undue sensitiveness to slights or unfortunately worded letters. Business often gives rise to certain asperities. But I agree that the plaintiffs in deciding whether to accept the defendant's offer were fully entitled to consider the terms in which the offer was made, its bona fides or otherwise, its relation to their own business methods and financial position, and all the circumstances of the case; and it must be remembered that an acceptance of the offer would not preclude an action for damages for the actual loss sustained. Many illustrations might be given of the extraordinary results which would follow if the plaintiffs were entitled to reject the defendant's offer and incur a substantial measure of loss which would have been avoided by their acceptance of the offer. The plaintiffs were in fact in a position to pay cash for the goods, but instead of accepting the defendant's offer, which was made perfectly bona fide, the plaintiffs permitted themselves to sustain a large measure of loss which as prudent and reasonable people they ought to have avoided. But the fact that the plaintiffs have claimed damages on an erroneous principle does not preclude me from awarding to them such damages as they have in fact suffered, calculated upon the correct basis.... They have suffered serious and substantial business inconvenience, and I conceive that I am entitled to award them damages for that. The authorities are conveniently collected in Arnold on Damages at p. 13. Moreover, even if the plaintiffs had accepted the defendant's offer, they would nevertheless have lost the very useful period of credit which the contract gave them. Taking into consideration all the circumstances of the case I have come to the conclusion that the right sum to award as damages is £50. I give judgment for the plaintiffs for that amount, and in view of the important points involved I give costs on the High Court scale.

Judgment for plaintiffs.

[The plaintiffs appealed on the question of damages.]

Bankes L.J. At the trial of this case the defendant, the present respondent, raised two points: first, that she had committed no breach of the contract of sale, and secondly that, if there was a breach, yet she had offered and was always ready and willing to supply the pieces of silk, the subject of the contract, at the contract price for cash; that it was unreasonable on the part of the appellants not to accept that offer, and that therefore they cannot claim damages beyond what they would have lost by paying cash with each order instead of having a month's credit and a discount of 2½ per cent. We must take it that this was the offer made by the respondent. The case was fought and the learned judge has given judgment upon that footing. It is true that the correspondence suggests that the respondent was at one time claiming an increased price. But in this Court it must be taken that the offer was to supply the contract goods at the contract price except that payment was to be by cash instead of being on credit.

In these circumstances the only question is whether the appellants can establish that as matter of law they were not bound to consider any offer made by the respondent because of the attitude she had taken up.

. . . .

It is plain that the question what is reasonable for a person to do in mitigation of his damages cannot be a question of law but must be one of fact in the circumstances of each particular case. There may be cases where as matter of fact it would be unreasonable to expect a plaintiff to consider any offer made in view of the treatment he has received from the defendant. If he had been rendering personal services and had been dismissed after being accused in presence of others of being a thief, and if after that his employer had offered to take him back into his service, most persons would think he was justified in refusing the offer, and that it would be unreasonable to ask him in this way to mitigate the damages in an action of wrongful dismissal. But that is not to state a principle of law, but a conclusion of fact to be arrived at on a consideration of all the circumstances of the case. Mr. Matthews complained that the respondent had treated his clients so badly that it would be unreasonable to expect them to listen to any proposition she might make. I do not agree. In my view each party was ready to accuse the other of conduct unworthy of a high commercial reputation, and there was nothing to justify the appellants in refusing to consider the respondent's offer. I think the learned judge came to a proper conclusion on the facts, and that the appeal must be dismissed.

[Scrutton L.J. and Fry J. agreed with the reasoning of Bankes L.J.]

WHITE AND CARTER (COUNCILS) LTD. v. McGREGOR

[1962] A.C. 413. House of Lords; Lords Reid, Morton, Tucker, Keith and Hodson.

Lord Reid. My Lords, the pursuers supply to local authorities litter bins which are placed in the streets. They are allowed to attach to these receptacles plates carrying advertisements, and they make their profit from payments made to them by the advertisers. The defender carried on a garage in Clydebank and in 1954 he made an agreement with the pursuers under which they displayed advertisements of his business on a number of these bins. In June, 1957, his sales manager made a further contract with the pursuers for the display of these advertisements for a further period of three years. The sales manager had been given no specific authority to make this contract and when the defender heard of it later on the same day he at once wrote to the pursuers to cancel the contract. The pursuers refused to accept this cancellation. They prepared the necessary plates for attachment to the bins and exhibited them on the bins from November 2, 1957, onwards.

The defender refused to pay any sums due under the contract and the pursuers raised the present action in the Sheriff Court craving payment of £196 4s. the full sum due under the contract for the period of three years. After sundry procedure the Sheriff-Substitute on March 15, 1960, dismissed the action. He held that the sales manager's action in renewing the contract was within his apparent or ostensible authority and that is not now disputed. The ground on which he dismissed the action was that in the circumstances an action for implement of the contract was inappropriate. He relied on the decision in *Langford & Co. Ltd. v. Dutch*, 1952 S.C. 15 and cannot be criticised for having done so.

The pursuers appealed to the Court of Session and on November 2, 1960, the Second Division refused the appeal. The present appeal is taken against their interlocutor of that date. That interlocutor sets out detailed findings of fact and, as this case began in the Sheriff Court, we cannot look beyond those findings. The pursuers must show that on those findings they are entitled to the remedy which they seek.

The case for the defender (now the respondent) is that, as he repudiated the contract before anything had been done under it, the appellants were not entitled to go on and carry out the contract and sue for the contract price: he maintains that in the circumstances the appellants' only remedy was damages, and that, as they do not sue for damages, this action was rightly dismissed.

The contract was for the display of advertisements for a period of 156 weeks from the date when the display began. This date was not specified but admittedly the display began on November 2, 1957, which seems to have been the date when the former contract came to an end. The payment stipulated was 2s. per week per plate together with 5s. per annum per plate both payable annually in advance, the first payment being due seven days after the first display. The reason why the appellants sued for the whole sum due for the three years is to be found in clause 8 of the conditions:

> In the event of an instalment or part thereof being due for payment, and remaining unpaid for a period of four weeks or in the event of the advertiser being in any way in breach of this contract then the whole amount due for the 156 weeks or such part of the said 156 weeks as the advertiser shall not yet have paid shall immediately become due and payable.

A question was debated whether this clause provides a penalty or liquidated damages, but on the view which I take of the case it need not be pursued. The clause merely provides for acceleration of payment of the stipulated price if the advertiser fails to pay an instalment timeously. As the respondent maintained that he was not bound by the contract he did not pay the first instalment within the time allowed. Accordingly, if the appellants were entitled to carry out their part of the contract notwithstanding the respondent's repudiation, it was hardly disputed that this clause entitled them to sue immediately for the whole price and not merely the first instalment.

The general rule cannot be in doubt. It was settled in Scotland at least as early as 1848 and it has been authoritatively stated time and again in both Scotland and England. If one party to a contract repudiates it in the sense of making it clear to the other party that he refuses or will refuse to carry out his part of the contract, the other party, the innocent party, has an option. He may accept that repudiation and sue for damages for breach of contract, whether or not the time for performance has come; or he may if he chooses disregard or refuse to accept it and then the contract remains in full effect. . . .

I need not refer to the numerous authorities. They are not disputed by the respondent but he points out that in all of them the party who refused to accept the repudiation had no active duties under the contract. The innocent party's option is generally said to be to *wait* until the date of performance and then to claim damages estimated as at that date. There is no case in which it is said that he may, in face of the repudiation, go on and incur useless expense in performing the contract and then claim the contract price. The option, it is argued, is merely as to the date as at which damages are to be assessed.

Developing this argument, the respondent points out that in most cases the innocent party cannot complete the contract himself without the other party doing, allowing or accepting something, and that it is purely fortuitous that the appellants can do so in this case. In most cases by refusing co-operation the party in breach can compel the innocent party to restrict his claim to damages. Then it was said that, even where the innocent party can complete the contract without such co-operation, it is against the public interest that he should be allowed to do so. An example was developed in argument. A company might engage an expert to go abroad and prepare an elaborate report and then repudiate the contract before anything was done. To allow such an expert then to waste thousands of pounds in preparing the report cannot be right if a much smaller sum of damages would give him full compensation for his loss. It would merely enable the expert to extort a settlement giving him far more than reasonable compensation.

The respondent founds on the decision of the First Division in *Langford & Co. Ltd. v. Dutch.* There an advertising contractor agreed to exhibit a film for a year. Four days after this agreement was made the advertiser repudiated it but, as in the present case, the contractor refused to accept the repudiation and proceeded to exhibit the film and sue for the contract price. The Sheriff-Substitute dismissed the action as irrelevant and his decision was affirmed on appeal. In the course of a short opinion Lord President Cooper said:

> "It appears to me that, apart from wholly exceptional circumstances of which there is no trace in the averments on this record, the law of Scotland does not afford to a person in the position of the pursuers the remedy which is here sought. The pursuers could not force the defender to accept a year's advertisement which she did not want, though they could of course claim damages for her breach of contract. On the averments the only reasonable and proper course, which the pursuers should have adopted, would have been to treat the defender as having repudiated the contract and as being on that account liable in damages, the measure of which we are, of course, not in a position to discuss".

The Lord President cited no authority and I am in doubt as to what principle he had in mind. In the earlier part of the passage which I have quoted he speaks of forcing the defender to accept the advertisement. Of course, if it had been necessary for the defender to do or accept anything before the contract could be completed by the pursuers, the pursuers could not and the court would not have compelled the defender to act, the contract would not have been completed and the pursuers' only remedy would have been damages. But the peculiarity in that case, as in the present case, was that the pursuers could completely fulfil the contract without any co-operation of the defender. The Lord President cannot have meant that because of non-acceptance the contract had not been completely carried out, because that in itself would have been a complete answer to an action for the contract price. He went on to say that the only reasonable and proper course which the pursuers should have adopted would have been to treat the defender as having repudiated the contract, which must, I think, mean to have accepted the repudiation. It is this reference to "the only reasonable and proper course" which I find difficult to explain. It might be, but it never has been, the law that a person is only entitled to enforce his contractual rights in a reasonable way, and that a court will not support an attempt to enforce them in an unreasonable way. One reason why that is not the law is, no doubt, because it was thought that it would create too much uncertainty to require the court to decide whether it is reasonable or equitable to allow a party to enforce his full rights under a contract. The Lord President cannot have meant that....

Langford & Co. Ltd. v. Dutch is indistinguishable from the present case. Quite properly the Second Division followed it in this case as a binding authority and did not develop Lord Cooper's reasoning: they were not asked to send this case to a larger court. We must now decide whether that case was rightly decided. In my judgment it was not. It could only be supported on one or other of two grounds. It might be said that, because in most cases the circumstances are such that an innocent party is unable to complete the contract and earn the contract price without the assent or cooperation of the other party, therefore in cases where he can do so he should not be allowed to do so. I can see no justification for that.

The other ground would be that there is some general equitable principle or element of public policy which requires this limitation of the contractual rights of the innocent party. It may well be that, if it can be shown that a person has no legitimate interest, financial or otherwise, in performing the contract rather than claiming damages, he ought not to be allowed to saddle the other party with an additional burden with no benefit to himself. If a party has no interest to enforce a stipulation, he cannot in general enforce it: so it might be said that, if a party has no interest to insist on a particular remedy, he ought not to be allowed to insist on it. And, just as a party is not allowed to enforce a penalty, so he ought not to be allowed to penalise the other party by taking one course when another is equally advantageous to him. If I may revert to the example which I gave of a company engaging an expert to prepare an elaborate report and then repudiating before anything was done, it might be that the company could show that the expert had no substantial or legitimate interest in carrying out the work rather than accepting damages: I would think that the de minimis principle would apply in determining whether his interest was substantial, and that he might have a legitimate interest other than an immediate financial interest. But if the expert had no such interest then that might be regarded as a proper case for the exercise of the general equitable jurisdiction of the court. But that is not this case. Here the respondent did not set out to prove that the appellants had no legitimate interest in completing the contract and claiming the contract price rather than claiming damages; there is nothing in the findings of fact to support such a case, and it seems improbable that any such case could have been proved. It is, in my judgment, impossible to say that the appellants should be deprived of their right to claim the contract price merely because the benefit to them, as against claiming damages and re-letting their advertising space, might be small in comparison with the loss to the respondent: that is the most that could be said in favour of the respondent. Parliament has on many occasions relieved parties from certain kinds of improvident or oppressive contracts, but the common law can only do that in very limited circumstances. Accordingly, I am unable to avoid the conclusion that this appeal must be allowed and the case remitted so that decree can be pronounced as craved in the initial writ.

Lord Keith: (dissenting)…. I would refer first to contracts for the sale of goods which were touched on in the course of the debate, for the reason that one of the remedies provided to the seller by the Sale of Goods Act, 1893, is an action for the price. This, however, applies only in two cases. One is where the property in the goods has passed to the buyer. But property cannot pass without the intention of the buyer as well as that of the seller and, except in some such cases as fraud or lack of consensus in idem or breach of contract by the seller, no question of repudiation can arise. The contract is completed and finished apart from delivery and nothing remains but payment of the price. The only other case is where parties have contracted for payment on a day certain, irrespective of delivery or the passing of property. This is a clear case of a contractual debt unconditioned by any question of performance by the other party. A much closer parallel with the present case is a contract to sell future, or unascertained goods. In this case there can be no appropriation of, and therefore passing of, property in the goods without the assent of both buyer and seller. If therefore the buyer repudiates the contract before appropriation, or refuses his assent to appropriation, there can be no passing of property. The seller is then confined to an action of damages for breach of contract. This, of course, is a rule of statute. But the Act is largely declaratory of English law, though not of Scots law. So the rule can only be treated as an analogy, but it is an analogy which seems to me to make a hole in the principle contended for by the appellants.

Repudiation of a contract is nothing but a breach of contract. Except where it is accepted as an anticipatory breach and as a ground for a claim of damages, a repudiation can never be said to be accepted by the other party except in the sense that he acquiesces in it and does not propose to take any action. Otherwise he founds on it as a cause of action....

The contract was to come into operation on November 2, 1957, when the previous contract expired. But it involved, in the absence of other advertising matter supplied by the defender, the display by the appellants of at least the name, business and address of the advertiser. I should hesitate to say that any contractor was entitled to display these particulars of the defender against his wish, even if the withholding of his assent be in breach of contract.

Some play was made by counsel for the appellants with an expression used by Asquith L.J. in *Howard v. Pickford Tool Co. Ltd.*, [1951] 1 K.B. 417, 421 "an unaccepted repudiation is a thing writ in water." A graphic phrase, or expression, has its uses even in a law report and can give force to a legal principle, but it must be related to the circumstances in which it is used. Howard was a managing director with a six years contract of service. He thought that the company with which he was serving had shown by the conduct of its chairman that it no longer intended to be bound by its agreement. He brought an action which, as amended, sought a declaration that the company by so acting had repudiated the contract and excused the plaintiff from further performance of his obligations under it. Evershed M.R. said:

> "It is quite plain... that if the conduct of one party to a contract amounts to a repudiation, and the other party does not accept it as such but goes on performing his part of the contract and affirms the contract, the alleged act of repudiation is wholly nugatory and ineffective in law."

Asquith L.J. said:

> "An unaccepted repudiation is a thing writ in water and of no value to anybody: it confers no legal rights of any sort or kind."

The declaration was held to be academic and the claim struck out. These observations must be read in the light of the facts to which they relate. They were directed to an alleged repudiation unaccepted by the man who said there was a repudiation before any cause of action had arisen. At best the case was no more than one of an intended repudiation, for performance was going on. The servant was still serving and the employer was continuing to employ him. What the court was saying was that the plaintiff had at that time no cause of action. But in the case of repudiation of a contract when performance is tendered, or due to be given by the other party, the repudiation cannot be said to be writ in water. It gives rise immediately to a cause of action. This does not involve acceptance of the repudiation. There has been a breach of contract which the complaining party denies the other had any right to commit. I know of no authority for saying that the offended party can go quietly on as if the contract still continued to be fully operative between both parties. He is put to his remedy at the date of the breach. It has been said that when an anticipatory repudiation is not treated as a cause of action the contract remains alive. It does until the contract would become operative, when the repudiation, if still maintained, then becomes a cause of action and all pleas and defences then existing are available to the respective parties.

The party complaining of the breach also has a duty to minimise the damage he has suffered, which is a further reason for saying that after the date of breach he cannot continue to carry on his part of an executory contract. A breach of a contract of employment will serve to illustrate the nature of this duty. A person is engaged to serve for a certain period, say three months, to commence at a future date. When that date arrives the prospective employer wrongfully refuses to honour the engagement. The servant is not entitled to see out the three months and then sue the recalcitrant employer for three months' wages. He must take steps by seeking other employment to minimise his loss. It is true, of course, that a servant cannot invoke a contract to force himself on an unwilling master, any more than a master can enforce the service of an unwilling servant. But if the appellants' contention is sound, it is difficult to see why, by parity of reasoning, it should not apply to a person who keeps himself free to perform the duties of his contract of service during the whole period of the contract and is prevented from doing so by the refusal of the other contracting party. Yet in *Hochster v. De La Tour* (1853), 2 El. & Bl. 678; 118 E.R. 922, from which the whole law about anticipatory repudiation stems, Lord Campbell plainly indicated that if the courier in that case, instead of accepting as he did the repudiation of his engagement as a cause of action, before it was due to commence, had waited till the lapse of the three months of the engagement he could not have sued as for a debt. The jury, he said, would be entitled to look at all that might "increase" or "mitigate the loss of the plaintiff down to the day of trial." There is no difference in this matter between the law of England and the law of Scotland ...

This brings me to the case of *Langford & Co. Ltd. v. Dutch.* I took part in the judgment in that case, though the only opinion delivered in the case was given by the Lord President (Lord Cooper), with whom I and the other judges of the Division concurred. The judgment was not a reserved judgment and the case was not, I think, so fully argued as the case now before your Lordships. It is, if rightly decided, determinative of the present appeal and is, so far as I am aware, the only other case in which the question raised on this appeal has ever been considered. The circumstances were practically indistinguishable from those in the present case and the pursuers were suing, as here, for recovery of a debt under their contract. The Lord President said that the only reasonable and practical course, which the pursuers should have adopted, would have been to treat the defenders as having repudiated the contract and as being on that account liable in damages.

. . .

I have reconsidered the decision in *Langford & Co. Ltd. v. Dutch* in the light of the further argument on this appeal. I have come to the conclusion that it was rightly decided and that the Second Division in the present case was bound to follow it.

I find the argument advanced for the appellants a somewhat startling one. If it is right it would seem that a man who has contracted to go to Hongkong at his own expense and make a report, in return for remuneration of £10,000, and who, before the date fixed for the start of the journey and perhaps before he has incurred any expense, is informed by the other contracting party that he has cancelled or repudiates the contract, is entitled to set off for Hongkong and produce his report in order to claim in debt the stipulated sum. Such a result is not, in my opinion, in accordance with principle or authority, and cuts across the rule that where one party is in breach of contract the other must take steps to minimise the loss sustained by the breach.

[Lord Hodson and Lord Tucker agreed with Lord Reid in allowing the appeal. Lord Morton dissented in a separate opinion on much the same grounds as Lord Keith.]

QUESTIONS

1. What interests did the House of Lords protect in *White v. McGregor*?
2. Was this the only way that this could have been done?
3. Does the majority opinion acknowledge any of the concerns of the majority in *Peevyhouse v. Garland Coal*?
4. What is the effect of the judgment in *White v. McGregor* on the future conduct of White's advertising business? Is this something the courts ought to encourage?
5. Can you think of any case where the kind of conduct of the plaintiff in *White v. McGregor* would be appropriate?

CLARK v. MARSIGLIA

(1845), 43 Am. Dec. 670.

Error from the New York common pleas. Marsiglia sued Clark in the court below in assumpsit, for work, labor and materials, in cleaning, repairing and improving sundry paintings belonging to the defendant. The defendant pleaded non assumpsit.

The plaintiff proved that a number of paintings were delivered to him by the defendant to clean and repair, at certain prices for each. They were delivered upon two occasions. As to the first parcel, for the repairing of which the price was seventy-five dollars, no defence was offered. In respect to the other, for which the plaintiff charged one hundred and fifty-six dollars, the defendant gave evidence tending to show that after the plaintiff had commenced work upon them, he desired him not to go on, as he had concluded not to have the work done. The plaintiff, notwithstanding, finished the cleaning and repairing of the pictures, and claimed to recover for doing the whole, and for the materials furnished, insisting that the defendant had no right to countermand the order which he had given. The defendant's counsel requested the court to charge that he had the right to countermand his instructions for the work, and that the plaintiff could not recover for any work done after such countermand.

The court declined to charge as requested, but, on the contrary, instructed the jury that inasmuch as the plaintiff had commenced the work before the order was revoked, he had a right to finish it, and to recover the whole value of his labor and for the materials furnished. The jury found their verdict accordingly, and the defendant's counsel excepted. Judgment was rendered upon the verdict.

Mr. C. P. Kirkland, for the plaintiff in error, after stating the point, was stopped by the court.

Mr. A. Taber, for defendant in error. By the contract between these parties, the plaintiff acquired the possession of these pictures, and a right to use his materials and labor upon them, and a lien upon them for payment. He could not be devested of these rights except by his own consent. This case differs from those where a party is in a situation in which he may violate a contract by refusing to perform a stipulation which is indispensable to enable the other party to go on. In such cases the contract is necessarily broken up, and the court can do no more than to compel the payment of such damages as are appropriate to the breach. Here the defendant had not the physical right to violate his contract, and not having the legal or moral right to do it, it cannot be done.

Per Curiam. The question does not arise as to the right of the defendant below to take away these pictures, upon which the plaintiff had performed some labor, without payment for what he had done, and his damages for the violation of the contract, and upon that point we express no opinion. The plaintiff was allowed to recover as though there had been no countermand of the order; and in this the court erred. The defendant, by requiring the plaintiff to stop work upon the paintings, violated his contract, and thereby incurred a liability to pay such damages as the plaintiff should sustain. Such damages would include a recompense for the labor done and materials used, and such further sum in damages as might, upon legal principles, be assessed for the breach of the contract; but the plaintiff had no right, by obstinately persisting in the work, to make the penalty upon the defendant greater than it would otherwise have been.

To hold that one who employs another to do a piece of work is bound to suffer it to be done at all events, would sometimes lead to great injustice. A man may hire another to labor for a year, and within the year his situation may be such as to render the work entirely useless to him. The party employed cannot persist in working, though he is entitled to the damages consequent upon his disappointment. So if one hires another to build a house, and subsequent events put it out of his power to pay for it, it is commendable in him to stop the work, and pay for what has been done and the damages sustained by the contractor. He may be under a necessity to change his residence; but upon the rule contended for, he would be obliged to have a house which he did not need and could not use. In all such cases the just claims of the party employed are satisfied when he is fully recompensed for his part performance and indemnified for his loss in respect to the part left unexecuted; and to persist in accumulating a larger demand is not consistent with good faith towards the employer. The judgment must be reversed, and a venire de novo awarded.

Judgment reversed.

FINELLI v. DEE
(1968), 67 D.L.R. (2d) 393. Ont. C.A.

Laskin, J.A. (orally): — This case arises out of a written contract between the plaintiffs and the male defendant, for the paving of the driveway at the defendants' home. The contract was made on June 18, 1966, and while a price was fixed and other terms included, it did not fix any particular time for the commencement or completion of the work. It appears from the evidence that the parties agreed that the work would not begin immediately because the defendant was then in no position to pay for it, but that it would be performed sometime in October or about that time, in 1966.

There is evidence, which was accepted by the trial Judge, that the defendant telephoned the office of the plaintiffs, after the contract was made and before any performance was contemplated, cancelling the contract, and that the plaintiffs' sales manager at the office who received the telephone call, agreed that it would be cancelled. On or about November 1, 1966, when the defendants were away from home, the plaintiffs carried out the contract and the defendants were confronted with the completed work on their return to their premises in the evening. The plaintiffs sued for the price of the work done under the contract but their claim was rejected by the trial Judge.

On appeal, a question was raised whether the cancellation of the contract amounted to rescission or simply represented a repudiation by the defendant. Of course, if there was rescission (and I should say that, notwithstanding the contrary argument of the plaintiffs' counsel, rescission could be effected by oral agreement even though the contract in question was in writing), then there would be no basis on which an action to enforce the provision as to price could be founded. If, on the other hand, the cancellation amounted to repudiation, a question arises as to the applicability of the principles canvassed by the House of Lords in *White & Carter (Councils), Ltd. v. McGregor,* [1961] 3 All E.R. 1178. It was the view of the majority of that Court that a repudiation by one party to a contract does not preclude the innocent party from carrying out the contract and suing for the price, at least where this can be done without the assent or cooperation of the party in breach. I am not, of course, bound by this judgment, but, respecting as I do the considered opinion of the majority, I must say that I am attracted by the reasons of the two dissenting members of the Court. Repudiation is not something that calls for acceptance when there is no question of rescission, but merely excuses the innocent party from performance and leaves him free to sue for damages. But, even accepting the majority view in the *McGregor* case, I should point out that it was a case in which the innocent party could carry out the contract notwithstanding the repudiation, without the assent or co-operation of the party in breach. This is not the situation here.

In the first place, it was necessary for the plaintiffs to enter upon the defendants' land in order to perform; and without wishing to embark on any issue as to trespass, the plaintiffs, in my view, were obliged to give previous intimation to the defendant that they were prepared to do the work called for by the contract and proposed to do it on a certain day. This, of course, was not done.

It follows that whether the cancellation amounts to rescission or merely to repudiation by the defendant, the plaintiffs are not entitled to recover the contract price. Accordingly, I would dismiss the appeal with costs and with a counsel fee of $25 to the defendants.

Appeal dismissed.

QUESTIONS

1. Suppose that the firm of White and Carter (Councils) Ltd. comes to Toronto and sets itself up in the same line of business here, using the same standard forms for its contracts. A customer is planning to breach her contract in exactly the same way as McGregor did. She comes to you for advice. What do you say?

2. After the customer has breached, the firm comes to you for advice, what do you say?

COCKBURN v. TRUSTS & GUARANTEE CO.

(1917), 37 D.L.R. 701. S.C.C.

[The plaintiff, Cockburn, was employed as general sales manager of Dominion Linen. He had a contract for five years from 1st January 1911 at a salary of $5,000 per year. Payment of Cockburn's salary was guaranteed by Kloepfer. Dominion Linen went into liquidation in December 1913, and Cockburn was dismissed. Kloepfer died and defendant is his administrator. Cockburn bought goods from his former employer, Dominion Linen, and sold them for a $11,000 profit. It was not disputed that Cockburn was entitled to recover something the issue, however, was how much.

The trial judge awarded the plaintiff substantial damages. The Appellate Division of the Supreme Court of Ontario reversed this judgment and awarded the plaintiff no damages. The plaintiff appealed to the Supreme Court of Canada.]

Anglin J.: —... The fundamental basis of the assessment of damages for breach of contract — compensation for pecuniary loss naturally flowing from the breach — and its qualification — that the plaintiff cannot recover any part of the damages due to his own failure to take all reasonable steps to mitigate his loss — are too well settled to admit of controversy. The application of this qualified rule, however, sometimes presents difficulty. The qualification does not impose on the plaintiff claiming damages for the breach "an obligation to take any steps which a reasonable and prudent man would not ordinarily take in the course of his business:" nevertheless,

> when in the course of his business he has taken action arising out of the transaction, which action has diminished his loss, the effect in actual diminution of the loss he has suffered may be taken into account even though there was no duty on him to act.

The action of the appellant in acquiring and disposing at a profit of a considerable part of the manufactured stock of his former employers arose out of his relations with them. It involved the employment by him of time, labour and ability which he had engaged to give to them. For his loss of an opportunity to use these in earning a salary from those employers he is now asking that the respondent shall be compelled to pay by way of damages. It would seem to be manifestly unfair that, if the appellant is thus to be remunerated on a contractual basis by way of damages, he should not be held accountable in mitigation for money made by using for his own purposes the time, labour and ability so to be paid for. The $11,000 profit which he made, although the making of it required some assumption of risk and responsibility and also an expenditure clearly beyond anything involved in his engagement by his former employers, and likewise beyond anything which it was his duty to them, or to the respondent, to undertake, is within the rule of accountability stated by Lord Haldane. The action which produced it arose out of his former employment in the sense in which the Lord Chancellor uses the phrase "arising out of the transaction," as is shewn by his illustration from *Staniforth v. Lyall*, 7 Bing. 169. Again to quote his Lordship (p. 691): "The transaction was... one in which the person whose contract was broken took a reasonable and prudent course quite naturally arising out of the circumstances in which he was placed by the breach."

By devoting his time, energy and skill for 2 years to the service of his former employers the appellant would have earned $10,000. A breakdown in his health, or other unforeseen contingencies might have prevented his doing so. Excused from that service, he was enabled by a happy combination of making use of the time, labour and ability thus set free and taking advantage of the opportunity afforded by his employers' misfortune within 66 days to make a clear profit of $11,000 — and he still had at his disposal, in which to add to his earnings, if so inclined, or to amuse himself if he preferred doing so, the remaining year and 299 days. Were he to be now awarded not the $10,000 claimed in his action but the $4,000 allowed him by the trial judge, he would, as a result of his employers' disaster, be better off by at least $5,000 than he would have been had he put in his 2 years of service — "a somewhat grotesque result," as Lord Atkinson put it in *Erie County Natural Gas and Fuel Co. v. Carroll*, [1911] A.C. 105, 115. Making due allowance for extra time and trouble expended and all other elements proper to be considered involved in the efforts which resulted in the plaintiff's securing the profit of $11,000, and taking into account the year and 299 days left at his disposal after that was accomplished, it seems reasonably clear that he did not sustain any actual damage as a result of losing his position. He was probably, on the whole, better off.

Upon the facts, when "allowed to speak for themselves," not only is the conclusion reached by the Appellate Division in conformity with legal principles and the authorities but any other would shock the common sense of justice.

[Davis J. concurred with Anglin J. Duff J. and Fitzpatrick C.J.C. gave reasons for reaching the same result. Idington J. agreed, but with reservations.]

PROBLEMS

1. Francis is hired by the Gourmet Restaurant as maitre d' for one year at $600 per month. Three months later a French maitre d' is hired to replace Francis. Francis is offered a job as a waiter at $350 per month for the remaining nine months. Francis refuses this offer and goes on unemployment insurance at $100 per month for the remaining period.

Francis sues the Gourmet Restaurant and claims as damages his salary for nine months. The defendant admits the wrongful discharge but argues that the amount defendant offered Francis as a waiter and the U.I.C. benefits should be taken into account in awarding damages. What result?

Unemployment Insurance Act, S.C. 1971, C. 48.

51. Where a claimant receives benefit in respect of a period and pursuant to a labour arbitration award, court judgment or otherwise an employer or a person other than the employer of that claimant subsequently becomes liable to pay remuneration to that claimant in respect of the same period and pays such remuneration, that claimant shall pay to the Receiver General as repayment of an overpayment of benefit an amount equal to the benefits that would not have been paid if the remuneration had been paid or payable at the time the benefits were paid.

52. (1) Where pursuant to a labour arbitration award, court judgment or otherwise an employer or a person other than an employer becomes liable to pay remuneration to a claimant in respect of a period and has reason to believe that benefit has been paid to the claimant in respect of that period, that employer or other person shall ascertain whether an amount would be repayable under section 51 if such remuneration were paid to the claimant and if so shall deduct such amount from the remuneration payable by him to the claimant and remit that amount to the Receiver General as repayment of an overpayment of benefit.

(2) Where a claimant receives benefit in respect of a period and pursuant to a labour arbitration award, court judgment or otherwise the liability of an employer of that claimant to pay him remuneration in respect of the same period is or was reduced by the amount of such benefit or by a portion thereof, the employer shall remit such amount or portion thereof to the Receiver General as repayment of an overpayment of benefit.

2. George owns a house that he has had listed for sale. Charles makes an offer to purchase it for $80,000 on October 1, and this is accepted by George on the same day. The deal is to close on December 15. Two weeks later, the price of housing starts to rise dramatically. By November 1, George's house is worth $90,000 and by December 1, $100,000. George decides that he does not want to sell. On December 15, George formally refuses to complete, but tenders Charles a certified cheque for $25,000 saying, "My house is now worth $105,000. Here, take this and go and buy yourself another one as good as mine". Charles refuses the cheque.

Draft the arguments that each side might make in the event of litigation. (Assume that the house was worth $105,000 on December 15. Ignore any out of pocket expenses that Charles may have incurred. Assume also that the price of the house stabilized at $125,000.)

REVIEW PROBLEM

Frank is an expert in tying fancy knots in string though he works as a used-car salesman. He feels that if he could only get some attention from the world for his hobby he could make his fortune. His hobby is finally noticed by Susan, a C.B.C. producer. She offers him a 15-minute show on TV during which time he can demonstrate his skill. Frank eagerly accepts the offer. One week before the show is to be taped Susan calls to say that the show has been cancelled. She refuses to give any reasons. Frank is absolutely crushed by this, and foresees a lifetime spent selling broken-down used cars.

Frank has started an action against the C.B.C. claiming specific performance of the contract and damages for breach in the alternative. You have been asked to draft the arguments that each side might use in the case.

In addition to the above facts you may assume the following. Two weeks before the show, Frank took three days off from work to practise. This cost him $200 in lost wages and commission. He also bought a $300 suit for the occasion. Frank would have appeared on a weekly programme devoted to the exhibition of novel or unusual artistic skill that has a fairly large audience.

CHAPTER 2

THE KINDS OF PROMISES THAT THE LAW WILL ENFORCE

A. Introduction

One of the most difficult problems that the courts have to face in contracts is the determination of what promises are going to be enforced. It is clear that many promises are not going to be enforced: the promise to meet a friend for lunch, a promise not to forget a friend's birthday. On the other hand, it is equally clear that we assume that many promises will be enforced: the promise to sell a house, to employ someone, to level land. What is it that distinguishes one kind of promise from the other? The first set of promises are made in a social context and the promisor would certainly be surprised to be sued for breach. The second set are commercial and the promisor would hardly have been surprised to be sued. This distinction appears to be important. But why should we enforce even commercial contracts? An answer might be offered along the following lines:

The promise made in a commercial context is enforced because it is believed that without such enforcement business relations would be something quite different from what they are and what we believe they should be. This promise is enforced because the agreement that is the contract represents an exchange transaction that is the basis of most commercial activity. The reasons for the enforcement of contracts like that in *Wroth v. Tyler* are much the same. It may be true that Mr. Tyler (and certainly Mrs. Tyler) are not in the business of selling (or buying) houses, but the kind of contract that they made with the Wroths is a contract very similar to that made by a commercial enterprise. Certainly, from the point of view of the Wroths the contract was as important as any made by a business. The court clearly regarded the contract in this way. We can summarize these points by suggesting that the commercial contract (and those that are similar) present claims for enforcement for the following reasons:

1. Much of modern business activity is dependent on contracts and on their enforcement.

2. Since enforcement of such contracts is the rule, people of all kinds come to rely on contracts in planning their affairs, and in any single case, the existence of such reliance may be a reason for the enforcement of that contract. (Of course, the enforcement of any individual contract increases the feeling that contracts in general will be enforced and so we go round again.)

3. No one is going to be surprised (and certainly not unfairly surprised) by the enforcement of such contracts.

4. The expectations of both parties to the contract are probably fairly obvious and the courts are usually able to enforce them with a clear idea of what was the basis for the contract and what will happen if the contract is enforced or enforced in a particular way. (When this kind of background knowledge is forgotten or ignored we have problems like

those in *Sunshine v. Dolly Varden, supra.* On the other hand if the courts have a particular view of only the commercial aspects of a contract, we get the kinds of problems that came up in *Peevyhouse v. Garland Coal, supra.*)

These points are obviously closely interrelated and, as has been mentioned, there are reinforcing effects.

None of these reasons apply in the case of the social promise. Such problems do not involve any exchange relationship in an economic sense. Yet even here we have to be careful. The promise to meet for lunch may be a promise to attend an important business meeting. A promise to remember a birthday may involve a promise to give a present and this may not be the kind of promise that the law should have to worry about. A promise, however to give $1,000,000 to a hospital or university may involve issues quite important enough to be the concern of the law.

Since the pressures towards enforcement are obviously so different in each case, the determination of the question whether a particular promise will be enforced or not might be expected to focus on the issues that have just been discussed. To some extent this is so. You will see that it will be important to notice that the transaction is a commercial one or a gift-type one, or one where there was obviously reliance on a promise made by one party. It will also be of very great importance to notice the historical evolution of the law. The reasons that are regarded as justifying enforcement in one case and not in another depend almost as much on the social context of the promise that is in issue as on whether the promise is made in a commercial context or not. It has been said that the development of the law and legal ideas has been characterized by the expansion of the scope of the legally relevant. (See, for example, Fuller, "Americal Legal Realism", (1934) 82 U. Pa. L.R. 429, 434.) The range of promises and the circumstances of their making now accorded some legal effect is wider than was the case one hundred years ago. This kind of historical development cannot be ignored.

Unfortunately, as you may by now expect, the approach actually taken by the courts will cover a very wide range of issues. On one hand the courts will be very concerned with the kind of promise that was made and the way in which it was made. But, on the other hand, these concerns will sometimes be subordinated to doctrinal purity, and the reason for a result will be found not in any analysis of the reasons why a particular promise will or will not be enforced, but in whether or not it satisfies certain formal and technical rules that have been laid down. This refers to the mysterious term "consideration", the meaning of which we shall explore at length.

The focus of this chapter will, therefore, be on one of the issues which we bypassed in the first chapter. As the title to this chapter indicates, we will be concerned to know how the law answers the question, "What promises are going to be enforced as contracts and what ones are we going to leave unaffected by any legal remedies?"

Consider the following promises.

Do you think that all these promises present the same claims for recognition by the law? What reasons can you give for recognition or against it in each case?

1. "This agreement, made this 5th day of August, 1885, between the

undersigned, husband and wife, in the interest of peace, and for the best interests of each other and of their family, is signed in good faith by each party, with the promise, each to the other, and to their children, that they will each honestly promise to help each other to observe and keep the same, which is as follows, *to wit*: All past subjects and causes of dispute, disagreement, and complaint, of whatever character or kind, shall be absolutely ignored and buried, and no allusion thereto, by word or talk, to each other, or any one else, shall ever be made. Each party agrees to refrain from scolding, fault-finding, and anger, in so far as relates to the future, and to use every means within their power to promote peace and harmony. That each shall behave respectfully, and fairly treat the other. That Mrs. Miller shall keep her home and family in a comfortable and reasonably good condition, and Mr. Miller shall provide for the necessary expenses of the family, and shall, in addition thereto, pay Mrs. Miller, for her individual use, two hundred dollars per year, payable, $16.67 per month, in advance, so long as Mrs. Miller shall faithfully observe the terms and conditions of this agreement. They agree to live together as husband and wife, and observe faithfully the marriage relations, and each to live virtuously with the other."

2. Father says to son, "I have just made a very successful deal. When I get paid, I shall buy a car for you."

3. Uncle says to niece, "I am so pleased that you have been admitted to law school, I would like to make things a bit easier for you so I shall give you $50 per month until you graduate."

4. David asks Daphne for a date and promises her dinner at the Westbury and the latest show at the Royal Alex. She says that she would just love to come and that she will be ready at 6:30 p.m.

5. Car Dealer promises to sell Customer a new Ford. Customer promises to pay $5,000.

6. Steel Co. promises to buy 1,000,000 tons of coal per year from Coal Co. for a period of 10 years. Coal Co. promises to deliver the coal.

The long extract that follows is one that sets out the framework for analysis that we will be following in this chapter. It will repay study not only now but at several times throughout our study of the cases in this chapter and even throughout the course. As you read each case consider how well the judge perceived the issues regarded as important by Fuller, and how well Fuller's analysis would solve the problem raised by the cases.

FULLER, "CONSIDERATION AND FORM"

(1941), 41 Columbia Law Review, 799.

§ 1. *Introduction.* — What is attempted in this article is an inquiry into the rationale of legal formalities, and an examination of the common-law doctrine of consideration in terms of its underlying policies. That such an investigation will reveal a significant relationship between consideration and form is a proposition not here suggested for the first time; indeed the question has been raised (and sometimes answered affirmatively) whether consideration cannot in the end be reduced entirely to terms of form.

That consideration may have both a "formal" and a "substantive" aspect is apparent when we reflect on the reasons which have been advanced why promises without consideration are not enforced. It has been said that consideration is "for the sake of evidence" and is intended to remove the hazards of mistaken or perjured testimony which would attend the enforcement of promises for which nothing is given in exchange. Again, it is said that enforcement is denied gratuitous promises because such promises are often made impulsively and without proper deliberation. In both these cases the objection relates, not to the content and effect of the promise, but to the manner in which it is made. Objections of this sort, which touch the form rather than the content of the agreement, will be removed if the making of the promise is attended by some formality or ceremony, as by being under seal. On the other hand, it has been said that the enforcement of gratuitous promises is not an object of sufficient importance to our social and economic order to justify the expenditure of the time and energy necessary to accomplish it. Here the objection is one of "substance" since it touches the significance of the promise made and not merely the circumstances surrounding the making of it.

The task proposed in this article is that of disentangling the "formal" and "substantive" elements in the doctrine of consideration. Since the policies underlying the doctrine are generally left unexamined in the decisions and doctrinal discussions, it will be necessary to postpone taking up the common-law requirement itself until we have examined in general terms the formal and substantive bases of contract liability.

I. THE FUNCTIONS PERFORMED BY LEGAL FORMALITIES

§ 2. *The Evidentiary Function.* — The most obvious function of a legal formality is, to use Austin's words, that of providing "evidence of the existence and purport of the contract, in case of controversy." The need for evidentiary security may be satisfied in a variety of ways: by requiring a writing, or attestation, or the certification of a notary. It may even be satisfied, to some extent, by such a device as the Roman *stipulatio*, which compelled an oral spelling out of the promise in a manner sufficiently ceremonious to impress its terms on participants and possible bystanders.

§ 3. *The Cautionary Function.* — A formality may also perform a cautionary or deterrent function by acting as a check against inconsiderate action. The seal in its original form fulfilled this purpose remarkably well. The affixing and impressing of a wax wafer — symbol in the popular mind of legalism and weightiness — was an excellent device for inducing the circumspective frame of mind appropriate in one pledging his future. To a less extent any requirement of a writing, of course, serves the same purpose, as do requirements of attestation, notarization, etc.

§ 4. *The Channeling Function.* — Though most discussions of the purposes served by formalities go no further than the analysis just presented, this analysis stops short of recognizing one of the most important functions of form. That a legal formality may perform a function not yet described can be shown by the seal. The seal not only insures a satisfactory memorial of the promise and induces deliberation in the making of it. It serves also to mark or signalize the enforceable promise; it furnishes a simple and external test of enforceability. This function of form Ihering described as "the facilitation of judicial diagnosis," and he employed the analogy of coinage in explaining it.

> Form is for a legal transaction what the stamp is for a coin. Just as the stamp of the coin relieves us from the necessity of testing the metallic content and weight

— in short, the value of the coin (a test which we could not avoid if uncoined metal were offered to us in payment), in the same way legal formalities relieve the judge of an inquiry *whether* a legal transaction was intended, and — in case different forms are fixed for different legal transactions — *which* was intended. (II² GEIST DES RÖMISCHEN RECHTS (8th ed. 1923) 494. *Cf.*, "In all legal systems the effort is to find definite marks which shall at once include the promises which ought to be enforceable, exclude those which ought not to be, and signalize those which will be." Llewellyn, *What Price Contract?* (1931) 40 YALE L.J. 704, 738.)

In this passage it is apparent that Ihering has placed an undue emphasis on the utility of form for the judge, to the neglect of its significance for those transacting business out of court. If we look at the matter purely from the standpoint of the convenience of the judge, there is nothing to distinguish the forms used in legal transactions from the "formal" element which to some degree permeates all legal thinking. Even in the field of criminal law "judicial diagnosis" is "facilitated" by formal definitions, presumptions, and artificial constructions of fact. The thing which characterizes the law of contracts and conveyances is that in this field forms are deliberately used, and are intended to be so used, by the parties whose acts are to be judged by the law. To the business man who wishes to make his own or another's promise binding, the seal was at common law available as a device for the accomplishment of his objective. In this aspect form offers a legal framework into which the party may fit his actions, or, to change the figure, it offers channels for the legally effective expression of intention. It is with this aspect of form in mind that I have described the third function of legal formalities as "the channeling function."

In seeking to understand this channeling function of form, perhaps the most useful analogy is that of language, which illustrates both the advantages and dangers of form in the aspect we are now considering. One who wishes to communicate his thoughts to others must force the raw material of meaning into defined and recognizable channels; he must reduce the fleeting entities of wordless thought to the patterns of conventional speech. One planning to enter a legal transaction faces a similar problem. His mind first conceives an economic or sentimental objective, or, more usually, a set of overlapping objectives. He must then, with or without the aid of a lawyer, cast about for the legal transaction (written memorandum, sealed contract, lease, conveyance of the fee, etc.) which will most nearly accomplish these objectives. Just as the use of language contains dangers for the uninitiated, so legal forms are safe only in the hands of those who are familiar with their effects. Ihering explains that the extreme formalism of Roman law was supportable in practice only because of the constant availability of legal advice, *gratis.*

The ideal of language would be the word whose significance remained constant and unaffected by the context in which it was used. Actually there are few words, even in scientific language, which are not capable of taking on a nuance of meaning because of the context in which they occur. So in the law, the ideal type of formal transaction would be the transaction described on the Continent as "abstract," that is, the transaction which is abstracted from the causes which gave rise to it and which has the same legal effect no matter what the context of motives and lay practices in which it occurs. The seal in its original form represented an approach to this ideal, for it will be recalled that extra-formal factors, including even fraud and mistake, were originally without effect on the sealed promise. Most of the formal transactions familiar to modern law, however, fall short of the "abstract" transaction; the channels they cut are not sharply and simply defined. The Statute of Frauds, for example, has only a kind of negative canalizing effect in the sense that it indicates a way by which one may be sure of *not* being bound. On the positive side, the outlines of the channel are blurred because too many factors, including consideration, remain unassimilated into the form.

As a final and very obvious point of comparison between the forms of law and those of language, we may observe that in both fields the actual course of history is determined by a continuous process of compromise between those who wish to preserve the existing patterns and those who wish to rearrange them. Those who are responsible for what Ihering called "the legal alphabet" — our judges, legislators, and textwriters — exercise a certain control over the usages of business, but there are times when they, like the lexicographer, must acquiesce in the innovations of the layman. The mere fact that the forms of law and language are set by a balance of opposing tensions does not, of course, insure the soundness of the developments which actually occur. If language sometimes loses valuable distinctions by being too tolerant, the law has lost valuable institutions, like the seal, by being too liberal in interpreting them. On the other hand, in law, as in language, forms have at times been allowed to crystallize to the point where needed innovation has been impeded.

§ 5. *Interrelations of the Three Functions.* — Though I have stated the three functions of legal form separately, it is obvious that there is an intimate connection between them. Generally speaking, whatever tends to accomplish one of these purposes will also tend to accomplish the other two. He who is compelled to do something which will furnish a satisfactory memorial of his intention will be induced to deliberate. Conversely, devices which induce deliberation will usually have an evidentiary value. Devices which insure evidence or prevent inconsiderateness will normally advance the desideratum of channeling, in two different ways. In the first place, he who is compelled to formulate his intention carefully will tend to fit it into legal and business categories. In this way the party is induced to canalize his own intention. In the second place, wherever the requirement of a formality is backed by the sanction of the invalidity of the informal transaction (and this is the means by which requirements of form are normally made effective), a degree of channeling results automatically. Whatever may be its legislative motive, the formality in such a case tends to effect a categorization of transactions into legal and non-legal.

Just as channeling may result unintentionally from formalities directed toward other ends, so these other ends tend to be satisfied by any device which accomplishes a channeling of expression. There is an evidentiary value in the clarity and definiteness of contour which such a device accomplishes. Anything which effects a neat division between the legal and the non-legal, or between different kinds of legal transactions, will tend also to make apparent to the party the consequences of his action and will suggest deliberation where deliberation is needed. Indeed, we may go further and say that some minimum satisfaction of the desideratum of channeling is necessary before measures designed to prevent inconsiderateness can be effective. This may be illustrated in the holographic will. The necessity of reducing the testator's intention to his own handwriting would seem superficially to offer, not only evidentiary safeguards, but excellent protection against inconsiderateness as well. Where the holographic will fails, however, is as a device for separating the legal wheat from the legally irrelevant chaff. The courts are frequently faced with the difficulty of determining whether a particular document — it may be an informal family letter which happens to be entirely in the handwriting of the sender — reveals the requisite "testamentary intention." This difficulty can only be eliminated by a formality which performs adequately the channeling function, by some external mark which will signalize the testament and distinguish it from non-testamentary expressions of intention. It is obvious that by a kind of reflex action the deficiency of the holographic will from the standpoint of channeling operates to impair its efficacy as a device for inducing deliberation.

Despite the close interrelationship of the three functions of form, it is necessary to keep the distinctions between them in mind since the disposition of borderline cases of compliance may turn on our assumptions as to the end primarily sought by a particular formality. Much of the discussion about the parol evidence rule, for example, hinges on the question whether its primary objective is channeling or evidentiary. Furthermore, one or more of the ends described may enter in a subsidiary way into the application of requirements primarily directed to another end. Thus there is reason to think that a good deal of the law concerning the suretyship section of the Statute of Frauds is explainable on the ground that courts have, with varying degrees of explicitness, supposed that this section served a cautionary and channeling purpose in addition to the evidentiary purpose assumed to be primarily involved in the Statute as a whole.

§ 6. *When are Formalities Needed? The Effect of an Informal Satisfaction of the Desiderata Underlying the Use of Formalities.* — The analysis of the functions of legal form which has just been presented is useful in answering a question which will assume importance in the later portion of this discussion when a detailed treatment of consideration is undertaken. That question is: In what situations does good legislative policy demand the use of a legal formality? One part of the answer to the question is clear at the outset. Forms must be reserved for relatively important transactions. We must preserve a proportion between means and end; it will scarcely do to require a sealed and witnessed document for the effective sale of a loaf of bread.

But assuming that the transaction in question is of sufficient importance to support the use of a form if a form is needed, how is the existence of this need to be determined? A general answer would run somewhat as follows: *The need for investing a particular transaction with some legal formality will depend upon the extent to which the guaranties that the formality would afford are rendered superfluous by forces native to the situation out of which the transaction arises* — including in these "forces" the habits and conceptions of the transacting parties.

Whether there is any need, for example, to set up a formality designed to induce deliberation will depend upon the degree to which the factual situation, innocent of any legal remolding, tends to bring about the desired circumspective frame of mind. An example from the law of gifts will make this point clear. To accomplish an effective gift of a chattel without resort to the use of documents, delivery of the chattel is ordinarily required and mere donative words are ineffective. It is thought, among other things, that mere

words do not sufficiently impress on the donor the significance and seriousness of his act. In an Oregon case, however, the donor declared his intention to give a sum of money to the donee and at the same time disclosed to
the donee the secret hiding place where he had placed the money. Though
the whole donative act consisted merely of words, the court held the gift to
be effective. The words which gave access to the money which the donor
had so carefully concealed would presumably be accompanied by the same
sense of present deprivation which the act of handing over the money
would have produced. The situation contained its own guaranty against
inconsiderateness.

So far as the channeling function of a formality is concerned it has no
place where men's activities are already divided into definite, clear-cut business categories. Where life has already organized itself effectively, there is
no need for the law to intervene. It is for this reason that important transactions on the stock and produce markets can safely be carried on in the most
"informal" manner. At the other extreme we may cite the negotiations
between a house-to-house book salesman and the housewife. Here the situation may be such that the housewife is not certain whether she is being presented with a set of books as a gift, whether she is being asked to trade her
letter of recommendation for the books, whether the books are being
offered to her on approval, or whether — what is, alas, the fact — a simple
sale of the books is being proposed. The ambiguity of the situation is, of
course, carefully cultivated and exploited by the canvasser. Some
"channeling" here would be highly desirable, though whether a legal form is
the most practicable means of bringing it about is, of course, another question.

What has been said in this section demonstrates, I believe, that the problem of "form," when reduced to its underlying policies, extends not merely
to "formal" transactions in the usual sense, but to the whole law of contracts and conveyances. Demogue has suggested that even the requirement,
imposed in certain cases, that the intention of the parties be express, rather
than implied or tacit, is in essence a requirement of form. If our object is to
avoid giving sanction to inconsiderate engagements, surely the case for legal
redress is stronger against the man who has spelled out his promise than it is
against the man who has merely drifted into a situation where he appears to
hold out an assurance for the future.

II. THE SUBSTANTIVE BASES OF CONTRACT LIABILITY

§ 7. *Private Autonomy.* — Among the basic conceptions of contract law
the most pervasive and indispensable is the principle of private autonomy.
This principle simply means that the law views private individuals as possessing a power to effect, within certain limits, changes in their legal relations. The man who conveys property to another is exercising this power; so
is the man who enters a contract. When a court enforces a promise it is
merely arming with legal sanction a rule or *lex* previously established by the
party himself. This power of the individual to effect changes in his legal
relations with others is comparable to the power of a legislature. It is, in
fact, only a kind of political prejudice which causes us to use the word
"law" in one case and not in the other, a prejudice which did not deter the
Romans from applying the word *lex* to the norms established by private
agreement.

What has just been stated is not presented as an original insight; the conception described is at least as old as the Twelve Tables. But there is need to reaffirm it, because the issue involved has been obfuscated through the introduction into the discussion of what is called "the will theory of contract." The obfuscation has come partly from the proponents of that theory, but mostly from those who have undertaken to refute it and who, in the process of refutation, have succeeded in throwing the baby out with the bath.[10]

The principle of private autonomy may be translated into terms of the will theory by saying that this principle merely means that the will of the parties sets their legal relations. When the principle is stated in this way certain consequences may seem to follow from it: (1) that the law must concern itself solely with the actual inner intention of the promisor; (2) that the minds of the parties must "meet" at one instant of time before a contract can result; (3) that the law has no power to fill gaps in an agreement and is helpless to deal with contingencies unforseen by the parties; and even (4) that the promisor must be free to change his mind at any time, since it is his will which sets the rule. Since these consequences of the will theory are regarded as unacceptable, the theory is assumed to be refuted by the fact that it entails them.

If we recognize that the will theory is only a figurative way of expressing the principle of private autonomy, we see to what extent this "refutation" of the will theory really obscures the issues involved. In our country a law-making power is vested in the legislature. This fact is frequently expressed by saying that the will of the legislature is the law. Yet from this hackneyed metaphor we do not feel compelled to draw a set of conclusions paralleling those listed above as deriving from the will theory of contract. Specifically, we do not seek the "actual, inner" intention of individual legislators; we do not insist, except in a very formal way, on proof that a majority of the legislators were actually of one mind at one instant of time; we do not hesitate to fill gaps in defective statutes; and, finally, we do not permit a majority of those who voted for a particular law to nullify it by a later informal declaration that they have changed their minds.

The principle of private autonomy, properly understood, is in no way inconsistent with an "objective" interpretation of contracts. Indeed, we may go farther and say that the so-called objective theory of interpretation in its more extreme applications becomes understandable only in terms of the principle of private autonomy. It has been suggested that in some cases the courts might properly give an interpretation to a written contract inconsistent with the actual understanding of either party. What justification can there be for such a view? We answer, it rests upon the need for promoting the security of transactions. Yet security of transactions presupposes "transactions," in other words, acts of private parties which have a law-making and right-altering function. When we get outside the field of acts having this kind of function as their *raison d'être*, for example, in the field of tort law, any such uncompromisingly "objective" method of interpreting an act would be incomprehensible.

A legitimate criticism of the principle of private autonomy may be that it is phrased too narrowly, and excludes by implication private heteronomy. If we look at the matter realistically, we see that men not only make private laws for themselves, but also for their fellows. I do not refer here simply to the frequent existence of a gross inequality of bargaining power between contracting parties, nor to the phenomenon of the standardized contract established by one party for a series of routine transactions. Even without excursion into the social reality behind juristic conceptions, a principle of private heteronomy is visible in legal theory itself, as, for example, where it is laid down as a rule of law that the servant is bound to obey the reasonable commands of his master. Here the employer, within the framework of the agreement and subject to judicial veto, is making a part of "the law" of the relation between himself and his employee.

§ 8. *What Matters Shall be Left to Private Autonomy?* — From the fact that a principle of private autonomy is recognized it does not follow that this principle should be given an unlimited application. Lawmaking by individuals must be kept within its proper sphere, just as, under our constitutional system, law-making by legislatures is kept within its field of competence by the courts. What is the proper sphere of the rule of private autonomy?

In modern society the most familiar field of regulation by private autonomy is that having to do with the exchange of goods and services. Paradoxically, it is when contract is performing this most important and pervasive of its functions that we are least apt to conceive of it as a kind of private legislation. If *A* and *B* sign articles of partnership we have little difficulty in seeing the analogy between their act and that of a legislature. But if *A* contracts to buy a ton of coal from *B* for eight dollars, it seems absurd to conceive of this act as species of private lawmaking. This is only because we have come to view the distribution of goods through private contract as a part of the order of nature, and we forget that it is only one of several possible ways of accomplishing the same general objective. Coal does not have to be bought and sold; it can be distributed by the decrees of a dictator, or of an elected rationing board. When we allow it to be bought and sold by private agreement, we are, within certain limits, allowing individuals to set their own legal relations with regard to coal. ("Bargain is then the social and legal machinery appropriate to arranging affairs in any specialized economy which relies on exchange rather than tradition (the manor) or authority (the army, the U.S.S.R.) for apportionment of productive energy and of product." Llewellyn, *What Price Contract?* (1931) 40 YALE L.J. 704, 717.)

The principle of private autonomy is not, however, confined to contracts of exchange, and historically it perhaps found its first applications outside the relationship of barter or trade. As modern instances of the exercise of private autonomy outside the field of exchange we may cite gratuitous promises under seal, articles of partnership, and collective labor agreements. In all these cases there may be an element of exchange in the background, just as the whole of society is permeated by a principle of reciprocity. But the fact remains that these transactions do not have as their immediate objective the accomplishment of an exchange of values.

When the principle of private autonomy is extended beyond exchange, where does it stop? The answer to this question is by no means simple, even if it be attempted in terms of some particular system of positive law. I shall not attempt to give such an answer here. One question must, however, be faced. When the principle of private autonomy is extended beyond exchange, can it legitimately be referred to as a "substantive basis of contract liability"? When we say that the contracting parties set the law of their relationship are we not giving a juristic construction of their act rather than a substantive reason for judicial intervention to enforce their agreement? It must be admitted that in one aspect the principle of private autonomy is a theory of enforcement rather than a reason for enforcement. But in another aspect the principle always implies at least one broad substantive reason for enforcement, which is identical with that underlying government generally. Though occasional philosophers may seem to dispute the proposition, most of us are willing to concede that some kind of regulation of men's relations among themselves is necessary. It is this general desideratum which underlies the principle of private autonomy. Whenever we can reinforce this general need for regulation by a showing that in the particular case private agreement is the best or the only available method of regulation, then in such a case "the principle of private autonomy" may properly be referred to as a "substantive" basis of contract liability.

§ 9. *Reliance.* — A second substantive basis of contract liability lies in a recognition that the breach of a promise may work an injury to one who has changed his position in reliance on the expectation that the promise would be fulfilled. Reliance as a basis of contract liability must not be identified with reliance as a measure of the promisee's recovery. Where the object of the court is to reimburse detrimental reliance, it may measure the loss occasioned through reliance either *directly* (by looking to see what the promisee actually expended in reliance on the promise), or *contractually* (by looking to the value of the promised performance out of which the promisee presumably expected to recoup his losses through reliance). If the court's sole object is to reimburse the losses resulting from reliance, it may be expected to prefer the direct measure where that measure may be applied conveniently. But there are various reasons, too complicated for discussion here, why a court may find that measure unworkable and hence prefer the contractual measure, even though its sole object remains that of reimbursing reliance. (See Fuller and Perdue, *The Reliance Interest in Contract Damages* (1936-1937) 46 YALE L.J. 52, 66-67 and *passim.*).

What is the relation between reliance and the principle of private autonomy? Occasionally reliance may appear as a distinct basis of liability, excluding the necessity for any resort to the notion of private autonomy. An illustration may be found in some of the cases coming under Section 90 of the Restatement of Contracts. In these cases we are not "upholding transactions" but healing losses caused through broken faith. In another class of cases the principle of reimbursing reliance comes into conflict with the principle of private autonomy. These are the cases where a promisee has seriously and, according to ordinary standards of conduct, justifiably relied on a promise which the promisor expressly stipulated should impose no legal liability on him. In still other cases, reliance appears not as an independent or competing basis of liability but as a ground supplementing and reinforcing the principle of private autonomy. For example, while it remains executory, a particular agreement may be regarded as too vague to be enforced; until it has been acted on, such an agreement may be treated as a defective exercise of the power of private autonomy. After reliance, however, the court may be willing to incur the hazards involved in enforcing an indefinite agreement where this is necessary to prevent serious loss to the relying party. The same effect of reliance as reinforcing the principle of private autonomy may be seen in much of the law of waiver. Finally, in some branches of contract law reliance and principle of private autonomy appear not as reinforcing one another so as to justify judicial intervention where neither alone would be sufficient, but as alternative and independently sufficient bases for imposing liability in the same case. This is perhaps the situation in those cases where the likelihood that reliance will occur influences the court to impose liability on the promisor. On the one hand, we may say that the likelihood of reliance demonstrates that the parties themselves viewed their transaction as an exercise of private autonomy, that they considered that it set their rights and were prepared to act accordingly. On this view, the law simply acquiesces in the parties' conception that their transaction determined their legal relations. On the other hand, we may say that the likelihood that reliance will occur is a sufficient reason for dispensing with proof that it occurred in fact, since where reliance takes negative and intangible forms it may be difficult to prove. On this theory enforcement of the promise is viewed either as protecting an actual reliance which has probably occurred, or as a kind of prophylactic measure against losses through reliance which will be difficult to prove if they occur.

§ 10. *Unjust Enrichment.* — In return for *B*'s promise to give him a bicycle, *A* pays *B* five dollars; *B* breaks his promise. We may regard this as a case where the injustice resulting from breach of a promise relied on by the promisee is aggravated. The injustice is aggravated because not only has *A* lost five dollars but *B* has gained five dollars unjustly. If, following Aristotle, we conceive of justice as being concerned with maintaining a proper proportion of goods among members of society, we may reduce the relations involved to mathematical terms. Suppose *A* and *B* have each initially ten units of goods. The relation between them is then one of equivalence, 10:10. *A* loses five of his units in reliance on a promise by *B* which *B* breaks. The resulting relation is 5:10. If, however, *A* paid these five units over to *B*, the resulting relation would be 5:15. This comparison shows why unjust enrichment resulting from breach of contract presents a more urgent case for judicial intervention than does mere loss through reliance not resulting in unjust enrichment.

Since unjust enrichment is simply an aggravated case of loss through reliance, all of what was said in the last section is applicable here. When the problem is the quantum of recovery, unjust enrichment may be measured either *directly*, (by the value of what the promisor received), or *contractually*, (by the value of the promised equivalent). So too, the prevention of unjust enrichment may sometimes appear openly as a distinct ground of liability (as in suits for restitution for breach of an oral promise "unenforceable" under the Statute of Frauds), and at other times may appear as a basis of liability supplementing and reinforcing the principle of private autonomy (as where the notion of waiver is applied "to prevent forfeiture," and in cases where the inference of a tacit promise of compensation is explained by the court's desire to prevent unjust enrichment).

§ 11. *Substantive Deterrents to Legal Intervention to Enforce Promises.* — I have spoken of "the substantive bases of contract liability." It should be noted that the enforcement of promises entails certain costs which constitute substantive objections to the imposition of contract liability. The first of these costs is the obvious one involved in the social effort expended in the legal procedure necessary to enforcement. Enforcement involves, however, another less tangible and more important cost. There is a real need for a field of human intercourse freed from legal restraints, for a field where men may without liability withdraw assurances they have once given. Every time a new type of promise is made enforceable, we reduce the area of this field. The need for a domain of "free-remaining" relations is not merely spiritual. Business deals can often emerge only from a converging series of negotiations, in which each step contains enough assurance to make worthwhile a further exchange of views and yet remains flexible enough to permit a radical readjustment to new situations. To surround with rigid legal sanctions even the first exploratory expressions of intention would not only introduce an unpleasant atmosphere into business negotiations, but would actually hamper commerce. The needs of commerce in this respect are suggested by the fact that in Germany, where the code makes offers binding without consideration, it has become routine to stipulate for a power of revocation.

§ 12. *The Relation of Form to the Substantive Bases of Contract Liability.* — Form has an obvious relationship to the principle of private autonomy. Where men make laws for themselves it is desirable that they should do so under conditions guaranteeing the desiderata described in our analysis of the functions of form. Furthermore, the greater the assurance that these desiderata are satisfied, the larger the scope we may be willing to ascribe to private autonomy. A constitution might permit a legislature to pass laws relating to certain specified subjects in an informal manner, but prescribe a more formal procedure for "extraordinary" enactments, by requiring, for example, successive readings of the bill before it was put to a vote. So, in the law of contracts, we may trust men in the situation of exchange to set their rights with relative informality. Where they go outside the field of exchange, we may require a seal, or appearance before a notary, for the validity of their promises.

When we inquire into the relevance of form to liability founded on reliance or unjust enrichment, it becomes necessary to discriminate between the three functions of form. As to the desiderata implied in the evidentiary and cautionary functions it is clear that they do not lose their significance simply because the basis of liability has shifted. Even in the law of torts we are concerned with the adequacy of the proof of what occurred in fact, and (sometimes, at least) with the degree of deliberation with which the defendant acted. It is true that in the law of torts these considerations are not usually effectuated in the same way that they are in contract law. This is due to the fact that the channeling function of form becomes, in this field, largely irrelevant, for this function is intimately connected with the principle of private autonomy and loses its significance in fields where that principle has no application. To the extent, then, that the basis of promissory liability shifts from the principle of private autonomy to the reimbursement of reliance or the prevention of unjust enrichment, to that extent does the relevance of the channeling function of form decrease. This function loses its relevance altogether at that indefinite point at which it ceases to be appropriate to refer to the acts upon which liability is predicated as a "transaction."

III. The Policies, "Formal" and "Substantive," Underlying the Common-Law Requirement of Consideration

§ 13. *Reasons for Refusing to Enforce the Gratuitous and Unrelied-on Promise.* — *A* promises to give *B* $100; *B* has in no way changed his position in reliance on this promise, and he has neither given nor promised anything in return for it. In such a situation enforcement of the promise is denied both in the common law and in the civil law. We give as our reason, "lack of consideration"; the civilians point to a failure to comply with statutory formalities. In neither case, of course, does the reason assigned explain the policies which justify excluding this promise from enforcement. An explanation in terms of underlying policies can, however, be worked out on the basis of the analysis just completed.

Looking at the case from the standpoint of the substantive bases of contractual liability we observe, first of all, that there is here neither reliance nor unjust enrichment. Furthermore, gratuities such as this one do not present an especially pressing case for the application of the principle of private autonomy, particularly if we bear in mind the substantive deterrents to judicial intervention. While an exchange of goods is a transaction which conduces to the production of wealth and the division of labor, a gift is, in Bufnoir's words, a "sterile transmission." If on "substantive" grounds the balance already inclines away from judicial intervention, the case against enforcement becomes stronger when we draw into account the desiderata underlying the use of formalities. That there is in the instant case a lack of evidentiary and cautionary safeguards is obvious. As to the channeling function of form, we may observe that the promise is made in a field where intention is not naturally canalized. There is nothing here to effect a neat division between tentative and exploratory expressions of intention, on the one hand, and legally effective transactions, on the other. In contrast to the situation of the immediate gift of a chattel (where title will pass by the manual tradition), there is here no "natural formality" on which the courts might seize as a test of enforceability.

§ 14. *The Contractual Archetype — The Half-Completed Exchange.* — *A* delivers a horse to *B* in return for *B*'s promise to pay him ten dollars; *B* defaults on his promise, and *A* sues for the agreed price. In this case are united all of the factors we have previously analyzed as tending in the direction of enforcement of a promise. On the substantive side, there is reliance by *A* and unjust enrichment of *B*. The transaction involves an exchange of economic values, and falls therefore in a field appropriately left to private autonomy in an economy where no other provision is made for the circulation of goods and the division of labor, or where (as perhaps in primitive society) an expanding economy makes the existing provision for those ends seem inadequate. On the side of form, the delivery and acceptance of the horse involve a kind of natural formality, which satisfies the evidentiary, cautionary, and channeling purposes of legal formalities.

Describing this situation as "the contractual archetype," (*Cf.* Fuller and Perdue, *The Reliance Interest in Contract Damages* (1936) 46 Yale L.J. 52, 67 and references there cited.) we may take it as our point of departure, dealing with other cases in terms of the degree of their deviation from it. Naturally, all kinds of nuances are here possible, and some minor departures from the pattern were the occasion for dispute in the early history of the action of debt. We are concerned here, however, chiefly with two major deviations from the archetype: the situation of the executory exchange, and the situation of reliance without exchange.

§ 15. *The Wholly Executory Exchange. — B* promises to build a house for *A*, and *A*, in return, promises to pay *B* $5,000 on the completion of the house. *B* defaults on his promise, and *A*, without having had occasion to pay anything on the contract, sues *B* for damages. Judicial intervention in this kind of case apparently began in England toward the end of the sixteenth century. This development we describe by saying that after *Strangborough v. Warner* and related cases the bilateral contract as such became for the first time enforceable. It is now generally assumed that so far as consideration is concerned the executory bilateral contract is on a complete parity with the situation where the plaintiff has already paid the price of the defendant's promised performance. Yet if we examine the executory bilateral contract in terms of the policies underlying consideration, it will become apparent that this assumption is unjustified, and that Lord Holt in reality overshot the mark in his assertion that "where the doing a thing will be a good consideration, a promise to do that thing will be so too."

Where a bilateral contract remains wholly executory the arguments for judicial intervention have been considerably diminished in comparison with the situation of the half-completed exchange. There is here no unjust enrichment. Reliance may or may not exist, but in any event will not be so tangible and direct as where it consists in the rendition of the price of the defendant's performance. On the side of form, we have lost the natural formality involved in the turning over of property or the rendition and acceptance of services. There remains simply the fact that the transaction is an exchange and not a gift. This fact alone does offer some guaranty so far as the cautionary and channeling functions of form are concerned, though, except as the Statute of Frauds interposes to supply the deficiency, evidentiary safeguards are largely lacking. This lessening of the factors arguing for enforcement not only helps to explain why liability in this situation was late in developing, but also explains why even today the executory bilateral contract cannot be put on complete parity with the situation of the half-completed exchange.

In the situation of the half-completed exchange, the element of exchange is only one factor tending toward enforcement. Since that element is there reinforced by reliance, unjust enrichment, and the natural formality involved in the surrender and acceptance of a tangible benefit, it is unnecessary to analyze the concept of exchange closely, and it may properly be left vague. In the executory bilateral contract, on the other hand, the element of exchange stands largely alone (I say "largely alone" because there is always the possibility that the court will be influenced by actual reliance on the bargain or by the probability that reliance has taken place or will occur.) as a basis of liability and its definition becomes crucial. Various definitions are possible. We may define exchange vaguely as a transaction from which each participant derives a benefit, or, more restrictively, as a transaction in which the motives of the parties are primarily economic rather than sentimental. Following Adam Smith, we may say that it is a transaction which, directly or indirectly, conduces to the division of labor. Or we may take Demogue's notion that the most important characteristic of exchange is that it is a situation in which the interests of the transacting parties are opposed, so that the social utility of the contract is guaranteed in some degree by the fact that it emerges as a compromise of those conflicting interests. The problem of choosing among these varying conceptions may seem remote and unimportant, yet it underlies some of the most familiar problems of contract law. For example, suppose a nephew promises his uncle that he will not smoke until he is twenty-one, and the uncle promises him $5,000 as a reward if he will keep his promise. Where the nephew sues after having earned the reward by following the prescribed line of conduct recovery has been permitted. But would such an agreement be enforced as an executory bilateral contract? Could the uncle, for example, sue the nephew for smoking a cigarette? In answering this question it is at once apparent that we are faced with the necessity of defining the particular kind of exchange which is essential to the enforcement of a bilateral contract. A similar problem underlies many of the cases involving "illusory promises."

Like consideration, exchange is a complex concept. To the problem of the executory exchange we may, within a narrower compass, apply the same general approach that we have applied to the problem of consideration as a whole. Here our "archetype" is the business trade of economic values in the form of goods, services, or money. To the degree that a particular case deviates from this archetype, the incentives to judicial intervention decrease, until a point is reached where relief will be denied altogether unless the attenuated element of exchange is reinforced, either on the formal side by some formal or informal satisfaction of the desiderata underlying the use of legal formalities, or on the substantive side by a showing of reliance or unjust enrichment, or of some special need for a regulation of the relations involved by private autonomy.

§ 16. *Transactions Ancillary to Exchanges.* — There are various transactions which, though they are not themselves immediately directed toward accomplishing an exchange, are necessary preliminary steps toward exchanges, or are ancillary to exchanges in process of realization. Among these we may mention offers, promises of unpaid sureties, and what Llewellyn has described as "going-transaction adjustments" such as are involved in unilateral concessions or promises of extra compensation granted during performance of a bilateral contract.

Because of their connection with exchanges, these transactions, in varying degrees, participate in the underlying grounds, both "formal" and "substantive," which justify the enforcement of exchanges. Thus, for example, if it were thought that exchanges could in practice only be arranged through the device of preliminary offers and that offers could be effective only if made irrevocable, then the substantive grounds for enforcing bilateral contracts of exchange would extend to offers. Again, a promise of extra compensation to a man already under contract to build a house at a fixed price participates to some extent in the "formal" guaranties which justify the enforcement of exchanges. From the standpoint of the "channeling" function, for example, such a promise receives a certain canalization from being related to an existing business deal. There is not here to the same degree as in purely gratuitous promises a shadowy no-man's land in which it is impossible to distinguish between the binding promise and tentative or exploratory expressions of intention.

How far legal sanction ought to be extended to these transactions bordering on and surrounding exchanges is a legislative question which cannot be discussed here, though it may be observed that it is precisely in this field that the greatest difference between the common law and the civil law exists. Probably our own law is in need of some reform. The written promise of a surety who guarantees the performance of one party to an exchange, for example, probably ought to be made enforceable without consideration. As to offers, the problem is more difficult, and probably some distinction between kinds of offers is in order.

§ 17. *Unbargained-for Reliance.* — An uncle promises to give his nephew one thousand dollars; in reliance on this promise the nephew incurs an indebtedness he would not otherwise have incurred. In this case we have a change of position which is not bargained for as the price of the uncle's promise. Where the element of exchange is removed from a case, the appeal to judicial intervention decreases both in terms of form and of substance. The appeal is diminished substantively because we are no longer in the field which is in modern society the most obviously appropriate field for the rule of private autonomy. From the formal standpoint, when we lose exchange, we lose the formal guaranties which go with the situation of exchange. (See §§ 14 and 15, *supra.*)

Section 90 of the Contracts Restatement provides in effect that a promise which has given rise to unbargained-for reliance may or may not be enforced, depending on the circumstances of the case. The section makes explicit only two criteria bearing on the question whether relief should be granted, namely, the seriousness of the promisee's reliance and its foreseeability by the promisor. On the basis of the analysis presented in this article, the following additional inquiries would be relevant: (1) Was the promise prompted wholly by generosity, or did it emerge out of a context of tacit exchange? (See §§ 15 and 16, *supra.*) (2) Were the desiderata underlying the use of formalities satisfied in any degree by the circumstances under which the promise was made? (See § 6, *supra.*) As bearing on the second question, we may ask whether the promise was express or implied, and whether after the promise was made the promisee declared to the promisor his intention of acting on it.

§ 18. *Nominal Consideration.* — It has been held that a promise to make a gift may be made binding through the payment of a "nominal" consideration, such as a dollar or a cent. The proper ground for upholding these decisions would seem to be that the desiderata underlying the use of formalities are here satisfied by the fact that the parties have taken the trouble to cast their transaction in the form of an exchange. The promise supported by nominal consideration then becomes enforceable for reasons similar to those which justify the enforcement of the promise under seal. (See § 12, *supra.*) From the standpoint of such an analysis any such distinction as is taken in *Schnell v. Nell* (1861), 17 Ind. 29, and Section 76 (c) of the Contracts Restatement is wholly out of place.

§ 19. *Release of Claims.* — There is in our law a noticeable, though not consistently expressed tendency to treat the surrender of rights differently from the creation of rights. The same tendency may be observed in foreign systems. In general it may be said that it is easier to give up a right than to create one. Words like "renunciation," "surrender," "extinction," and "waiver" are associated in the lawyer's mind with laxness, with a letting down of the bars. What is the explanation for this tendency? This is a question which has not, so far as I am aware, been answered at all. I believe that the analysis presented in § 6, *supra,* may give at least a part of the answer.

If when a creditor releases his debtor the desiderata underlying the use of formalities are satisfied by the circumstances surrounding the informal transaction, then we have an explanation for the observed relaxing of "formal" requirements in this situation. An analogy from the law of gifts will again be helpful. Ordinarily the effective gift of a chattel requires either some document of transfer or a delivery of the chattel itself. It has been held, however, that where the chattel is already in the possession of the donee, mere words of donation are sufficient. This is partly because in such a situation donative words are accompanied by a sense of present deprivation which is absent where the chattel remains in the donor's hands. The cautionary function of form is thus satisfied in this situation without the imposition of form. So, I believe, if we look at the problem now under discussion from the standpoint of the cautionary function of form it will be apparent that there is a difference between releasing a claim and creating a claim by a promise. The release of a claim, even if made orally, carries with it normally a sense of deprivation which is lacking in the case of a promise. Where words have this effect, where they tend to produce a psychological wrench on the speaker, they satisfy the desideratum of inducing deliberation as well as a writing or a seal. On the side of "substance," it may be observed that releases are normally transactions ancillary to a relationship of exchange. (See § 16, *supra.*)

What has just been said is not presented as an adequate analysis of the whole problem of waiver and renunciation. Such an analysis could be made, I believe, in terms of the factors outlined in this article, but it would have to take into account the nuances and complexities to which these factors are subject in this field. Among the counter-currents which pull in a direction opposite from the tendency just discussed are the rule of *Foakes v. Beer* (1884), 9 App. Cas. 605, and the peculiar background surrounding the surrender of personal-injury claims.

§ 20. *Moral Obligation as Consideration.* — Courts have frequently enforced promises on the simple ground that the promisor was only promising to do what he ought to have done anyway. These cases have either been condemned as wanton departures from legal principle, or reluctantly accepted as involving the kind of compromise logic must inevitably make at times with sentiment. I believe that these decisions are capable of rational defense. When we say the defendant was morally obligated to do the thing he promised, we in effect assert the existence of a substantive ground for enforcing the promise. In a broad sense, a similar line of reasoning justifies the special status accorded by the law to contracts of exchange. Men *ought* to exchange goods and services; therefore when they enter contracts to that end, we enforce those contracts. On the side of form, concern for formal guaranties justifiably diminishes where the promise is backed by a moral obligation to do the thing promised. What does it matter that the promisor may have acted without great deliberation, since he is only promising to do what he should have done without a promise? For the same reason, can we not justifiably overlook some degree of evidentiary insecurity?

In refutation of the notion of "moral consideration" it is sometimes said that a moral obligation plus a mere promise to perform that obligation can no more create legal liability than zero plus zero can have any other sum than zero. But a mathematical analogy at least equally appropriate is the proposition that one-half plus one-half equals one. The court's conviction that the promisor ought to do the thing, plus the promisor's own admission of his obligation, may tilt the scales in favor of enforcement where neither standing alone would be sufficient. If it be argued that moral consideration threatens certainty, the solution would seem to lie, not in rejecting the doctrine, but in taming it by continuing the process of judicial exclusion and inclusion already begun in the cases involving infants' contracts, barred debts, and discharged bankrupts.

§ 21. *Performance of Legal Duty as Consideration.* — The analysis presented in this article is not sufficient for a comprehension of the factors underlying all the situations where courts have talked about "consideration." For example, cases where courts have said that illegal agreements are void for lack of consideration (since the law must close its eyes to an illegal consideration) obviously involve policies going beyond those analysed in this paper. It is for a similar reason that I have not drawn into the discussion cases laying down the rule that the performance of a legal duty cannot be consideration. These cases involve factors extrinsic to the problems under discussion here. Among those factors are the effects of improper coercion, and the need for preserving the morale of professions, like that of policeman, jockey, and sailor, which involve activities impinging directly on the interests of others. These cases touch the present discussion only in the sense that there is some relation between coercion and the desiderata underlying the use of formalities; whatever tends to guarantee deliberateness in the making of a promise tends in some degree to protect against the milder forms of coercion.

§ 22. *The Future of Form.* — Despite an alleged modern tendency toward "informality," there is little reason to believe that the problem of form will disappear in the future. The desiderata underlying the use of formalities will retain their relevance as long as men make promises to one another. Doubt may legitimately be raised, however, whether there will be any place in the future for what may be called the "blanket formality," the formality which, like the seal, suffices to make any kind of promise, not immoral or illegal, enforceable. It is not that there is no need for such a device. The question is whether with our present-day routinized and institutionalized ways of doing business a "blanket formality" can achieve the desiderata which form is intended to achieve. The net effect of a reform like the Uniform Written Obligations Act, for example, will probably be to add a line or two to unread printed forms and increased embarrassment to the task of judges seeking a way to let a man off from an oppressive bargain without seeming to repudiate the prevailing philosophy of free contract. Under modern conditions perhaps the only devices which would be really effective in achieving the formal desiderata would be that of a nominal consideration actually handed over, or a requirement that the promise be entirely in the handwriting of the promisor. As the holographic will shows, even the second of these devices would be inadequate from the standpoint of the "channeling" function.

§ 23. *The Future of Consideration.* — The future of consideration is tied up to a considerable extent with the future of the principle of private autonomy. If the development of our society continues along the lines it is now following, we may expect, I believe, that private contract as an instrument of exchange will decrease in importance. On the other hand, with an increasing interdependence among the members of society we may expect to see reliance (unbargained-for, or half-bargained-for) become increasingly important as a basis of liability. We may also see an expansion of the principle of private (or semi-private) autonomy to fields outside that of exchange. We get some hint of this second development in the expanding importance of the collective labor agreement. It appears also in the increasing use by business of revocable dealer and distributor agencies, and standing offers, devices which have their *raison d'être* in furnishing a kind of frame-work or private constitution for future dealings. These changes in business practice will inevitably bring with them in time modifications of the doctrine of consideration. For example, the relationship involved in dealer and jobber agencies is one which calls increasingly for some kind of judicial regulation to prevent hardship and oppression. If the assumption that this relationship is "contractual" coupled with existing definitions of consideration operates to exclude judicial intervention, then legal doctrine should be modified so as to permit bringing this relationship within the control of the law.

It has sometimes been proposed that the doctrine of consideration be "abolished." Such a step would, I believe, be unwise, and in a broad sense even impossible. The *problems* which the doctrine of consideration attempts to solve cannot be abolished. There can be little question that some of these problems do not receive a proper solution in the complex of legal doctrine now grouped under the rubric "consideration." It is equally clear that an original attack on these problems would arrive at some conclusions substantially equivalent to those which result from the doctrine of consideration as now formulated. What needs abolition is not the doctrine of consideration but a conception of legal method which assumes that the doctrine can be understood and applied without reference to the ends it serves. When we have come again to define consideration in terms of its underlying policies the problem of adapting it to new conditions will largely solve itself.

Fuller makes it clear that there is more than one basis for the enforcement of promises. He specifically mentions enforcement to prevent unjust enrichment and enforcement on the basis of reliance. These can in one sense be seen as offering a reason for enforcement that is different from the basis usually put forward in the ordinary commercial contract. Much of our time in examining the problems raised by the cases in this chapter will focus on the problems associated with the enforcement of promises on the basis of reliance. Enforcement of a promise to prevent unjust enrichment is, as Fuller suggests, easy to justify and the following cases show how such promises are handled by the courts. To understand the cases one has to know some legal history.

The early common law (before the sixteenth century) recognized contractual obligations in only two situations. The first was the case where the defendant had agreed to pay for services that had been rendered and the price was fixed by the parties. The price could be in either money or goods. If the price was in money, the plaintiff could bring an action of debt. (Strictly speaking debt was available where the plaintiff sought payment in money or in any fungible commodity.) If the price was an agreed, identified thing, then the plaintiff had an action of detinue. The second situation was where the defendant had promised in a sealed document to do something. For breach of a promise made under seal, an action of covenant would lie.

These contractual remedies were deficient in a number of ways. First, the action of covenant was cumbersome since it required a formal document, and, in the Middle Ages, people who could read and write were in the minority in the population. Second, the action of debt could only be brought in respect of an agreement where the plaintiff had performed his part of the bargain. It was not available in cases where neither side had performed. Thus if William promised to sell Robert a horse for £10 and delivered the horse to Robert, he could sue in debt for the £10. But if William refused to deliver the horse, or if Robert refused to accept it, neither could sue the other. The action of debt therefore gave no remedy for the wholly executory contract. The action of covenant provided a remedy for the executory contract, but, as has been said, that was a cumbersome one.

Third, both the action of debt and covenant suffered from procedural difficulties that gravely impaired their usefulness. The principal problem from the plaintiff's point of view was that the defendant in an action of debt could "wage his law". This term refers to the mode of proof of the defendant's allegation that he did not owe what the plaintiff claimed. The defendant who waged his law procured twelve men who would swear, not that the defendant did not owe the money or that he had paid, but that the defendant's oath was good. At a time when oaths may have meant more than they do now, such a device may have offered some realistic check on the freedom of the unconscientious defendant to escape his obligations. But, from the plaintiff's point of view, this was not a very effective guarantee of enforceability. Lawyers for plaintiffs therefore sought to find a way to limit the defendant's right to wage his law.

The way out of the plaintiff's difficulties was found through the importation into contract of tort remedies. The first case where we can see the mixture of tort and contract remedies was a case decided by the King's Bench in 1348. A ferryman on the River Humber accepted the plaintiff's mare for carriage. He overloaded his boat so that it capsized and the mare was drowned. The plaintiff sued in trespass. At this time the defendant could not be made liable in covenant for, not surprisingly, he had made no promise under seal to carry the horse safely. He could not be sued in debt for he was not being sued for anything that was due as payment for services rendered. The court in the Humber Ferryman's case held the defendant liable for the loss of the horse. It is easy to see that imposing liability in a case of this kind could have important consequences. The blacksmith who carelessly shod a horse so that it was lamed could be sued on the same basis as the ferryman; the surgeon who carelessly treated a patient could also be sued. These cases were important to the development of the law of contracts because they gave a remedy that avoided both the dangers of debt and the inadequacies of covenant. From the point of view of torts the cases were significant because they gave a remedy where there was no deliberate infliction of harm or anything approaching criminal conduct.

From 1348 the law developed so that anyone who undertook to do something and did it improperly could be sued. The key word in the writ that brought the case before the court was the word *assumpsit*; the defendant *undertook* to do something. In the beginning of this development, assumpsit (as the writ became known) was only available where the defendant had done something badly, not where he had refused to do what he had promised. But by the fifteenth century even this limitation was no longer significant. With the rise of assumpsit the way was open for the development of a modern law of contracts. A plaintiff who sued in assumpsit could get his case before a jury (this was one of the consequences of the tortious origin of the writ) — the defendant could not wager his law. The writ of assumpsit gave a remedy for breach of the informal executory contract.

Assumpsit could not be a complete replacement for the old actions, since where debt would lie a plaintiff could not bring assumpsit. This rule was avoided by permitting assumpsit where the defendant who was indebted promised to pay, where, in other words, the defendant, being indebted, undertook to pay. This lead to the development of a general remedy for the recovery of money known as *indebitatus assumpsit.* It may be imagined that defendants were not too happy about this development. But, behind the obvious arguments that might be made by the parties, there was also a dispute between the various courts that made up the common law courts. The Court of Common Pleas had had exclusive jurisdiction over all civil matters, including actions of debt and covenant. The Court of King's Bench had originally had jurisdiction over all criminal matters — these were often referred to as pleas of the Crown. The writ of trespass — the basic tort remedy — and the progenitor of the action of assumpsit, was in the jurisdiction of the Court of King's Bench. The judges of this court saw the action of assumpsit as a way of increasing their business, and since judges and officials were paid from court fees, their income.

The action of *indebitatus assumpsit* as a substitute for debt was not allowed unless the debtor had made an express promise to pay. This promise had to be separate from and later than the original promise. In 1602 all the judges of England considered *Slade's Case,* 4 Co. Rep. 91a. Here the jury had found that there was no express promise to pay, the jury had said that "there was no other promise or assumption but only the [original] bargain". The judges held, over the objections of the defendant's counsel that his client was being deprived of his right to wage his law, that, where there was no actual separate and subsequent promise, one could be implied. The allegation that "the defendant being indebted undertook" became a non-traversable allegation that left only the verbal reminder of the action's origin.

With *Slade's Case* the law had reached the point where the possibility of the development of the modern law of contract was opened. The new general action of assumpsit with its fictitious and non-traversable allegation of an undertaking permitted the courts to give a remedy in the case of the simple informal contract where there was no agreed price. For example, if one man did work for another and there was no fixed price for the work — perhaps neither knew how long it would take or how difficult it might turn out to be — the one who did the work could not bring an action of debt for there was no agreed price, nor could he bring an action of covenant since there was no formal document. In this case the law could, after *Slade's Case*, imply a promise to pay what the work was worth and, the issue now being put to a jury, this issue could be determined in a way that was fair and satisfactory.

It is important to remember that the problem of recovery in the example just given must have been resolved in other ways. We are examining the development of contract remedies in the common law courts. These courts were not the only courts in the country. Throughout the period we have been examining the common law courts only had jurisdiction where the amount in issue was greater than 40s. During the Middle Ages this was a sufficiently high limit that only a comparatively small percentage of contract actions would go to the common law courts. There are very few records of how the other, inferior, courts operated, but there the tailor, carpenter, blacksmith, shopkeeper and surgeon must have had adequate remedies. As inflation broadened the effective jurisdiction of the common law courts, the pressure on them to provide adequate remedies for the simple informal contract must have had an impact. Had the common law courts not responded by providing adequate remedies, we may be sure that potential plaintiffs would have gone elsewhere for relief.

The use of the implied promise in the case of one who seeks payment for work done for another gave a remedy in the case where the implication of the promise clearly arose from the facts. The carpenter or tailor expected to be paid and the customer expected to pay. A more drastic use of the power to imply promises was exercised in the following case. Suppose that John owed Thomas £100. By mistake, John pays Thomas £110. Thomas had no right to the extra £10 but is enriched by it. But Thomas has committed no fraud or other tort in accepting the money, nor can it be said that, from these facts, a promise to pay can be implied. Yet John's claim for the return of the £10 is strong. Here again the use was made of an implied assumpsit as a device to give John a remedy. Now the implication arises, not because one party expected to pay and the other to be paid, but because it would be unjust for Thomas to be allowed to keep the extra £10. By permitting John to allege in his pleadings that Thomas "being indebted, promised to pay", the case was formally brought within the scope of *indebitatus assumpsit*. The real focus of the case was not whether Thomas had or had not made any such promise, but whether or not it was unjust for Thomas to keep the money. This is, of course, precisely the issue that needed to be decided. We may say that the promise to pay the carpenter or tailor was a promise implied *in fact* while the promise of Thomas to pay John was implied in *law*.

The use of indebitatus assumpsit in the case of the overpayment is what is now known as the remedy of *quasi-contract*: there is no real contract but the law treats the case as if there were one. Quasi-contract is then the remedy that is generally available in cases where one party alleges that the other has money that he should not, in justice, be allowed to keep.

Additional readings: Milsom, *Historical Foundations of the Common Law;* Simpson, *A History of the Common Law of Contract;* Fifoot, *History and Sources of the Common Law;* Dawson, *The Oracles of the Law.*

A simple case when the courts can imply a promise to pay is the following.

MATHESON v. SMILEY
[1932] 2 D.L.R. 787. Man. C.A.

The judgment of the Court was delivered by

Robson, J.A.: — Appeal by defendant from a judgment of Clement, Co.Ct.J., in the County Court of Brandon.

Plaintiff is a surgeon and brought this action to recover $150 from defendant as executrix of the last will and testament of John J. Smiley, deceased. The claim alleges that the professional services were rendered "by the plaintiff to the said deceased at the defendant's request."

Particulars are: — "1930. August 24. To services as surgeon at an operation upon the deceased in Brandon General Hospital, $150." The defence is in short a denial of request, an allegation that the service could be foreseen to be of no avail and that in any case the charge was exorbitant.

There was no allegation by plaintiff of any status to sue, or as I read the claim, of any request by Smiley, now deceased, upon which to base a contract creating an obligation against the estate. The parties contested the case on the evidence without formal objection and as the issues appear clearly from the evidence there is no reason why this Court should not deal with the appeal in the same way.

The fact is that Smiley was found lying on the floor in an upstairs room in his home in Brandon having received in his body evidently by his own hand the discharge from a shotgun. He was no doubt in a very serious condition. The defendant was not there but two friends named Wright and Cousins were downstairs and on being alarmed and making the discovery one of them immediately sent for Dr. A. T. Condell. Dr. Condell, considering it to be a case for a surgeon, brought in the plaintiff who has specialized in that branch. Smiley was taken to the hospital. Plaintiff did what he could to reduce the effects of the injury but Smiley succumbed.

It is almost needless to say that all that was done by the two friends and Dr. Condell and plaintiff was done in good judgment in the emergency. Plaintiff's present claim is for his remuneration for his professional service on the occasion. I think it may safely be said that it is really the thought that the fee charged is too large that actuates the defendant in contesting the claim. Be that as it may, the defendant is entitled to raise the questions she has raised here....

Smiley was conscious and did say something to plaintiff but it is clear that he was in such an extreme condition that no words of his then should be construed as a request for the plaintiff's services or as an acquiescence in their being rendered on a contractual footing. Smiley was in no shape for that. But that does not seem to me to end the matter. I think it is not within reason that even in such circumstances as are revealed here a person in such a plight should simply be allowed to die without an effort being made by those in contact with him and without resort to all reasonable means to secure his recovery that may be at hand to them. And surely the person to pay should be the person for whose benefit the service is rendered. I hardly think it an answer to say in any case there was no hope. In such circumstances no one gives up while a spark remains....

I think the friends of the deceased present, Wright and Cousins, only acted within their duty in calling in Dr. Condell and that his calling the plaintiff was merely a natural sequence in the nature of the case....

I look upon the surgeon's service here as a necessary for Smiley even though the effort was unavailing. I therefore think a right to recover from defendant's estate exists in favour of the plaintiff.

This leaves the question of reasonableness of the plaintiff's charge still to be considered.

The plaintiff described the removal of the patient to the hospital, the cleaning, the anaesthetic and the examination. He said there was evidence "that a wound — that a gun was pointing upwards and outwards. The skin was torn, the muscles of the chest were torn. The pleura was torn, that there was evidence that the wound went in and out of the chest, that is, we will call it a scoop wound. It kind of scooped the tissues and the lower part of the lung was torn." The plaintiff narrated in detail his procedure towards the repair of this lacerated condition. He stated that the patient died, as he thought, from shock.

As to reasonableness of the fee charged, the plaintiff being questioned on the subject said: — "Well, I think for an operation of that kind it was a very, very reasonable fee." The learned trial Judge thought the fee charged proper, saying: — "In an emergency such as this one the services of a surgeon are not to be measured by the length of time required to perform the operation but by the skill and services rendered."

. . .

[The trial judge], sitting as a Judge of fact, concluded that $150 was not unreasonable. It seems to me that he had evidence on which he could come to that conclusion.

For these reasons I think the appeal should be dismissed, with costs.

SOLDIERS MEMORIAL HOSPITAL v. SANFORD
[1934] 2 D.L.R. 334 (N.S.S.C.).

Doull, J.: — The defendant interfered in a fight between his father and some preventive officers in the County of Annapolis in the year 1928 and got badly used up in consequence. He was bruised about the head and was shot in the groin. In the end the officers were the victors and the defendant was being taken to gaol when some one suggested that the hospital was a more suitable place for him than the gaol, and he was taken to the hospital at Middleton, owned and operated by the plaintiff.

There is some doubt as to whether he was conscious or unconscious at the time he entered the hospital. In the evidence he was asked: "Q. Were you conscious when you were injured? A. Yes to a certain extent. Q. Did you know that you were being taken to the Soldiers Memorial Hospital? A. Yes, sir."

On the other hand, his own counsel indicates that he was unconscious: "Q. And by the time you got to the Middleton Hospital you were unconscious? A. Yes."

Conscious or unconscious, in the view I take of the matter, the plaintiff can only recover on the ground of a contract, express or implied. There is no express contract proven although the defendant does not expressly deny that he may have promised to pay.

The plaintiff must therefore succeed if at all by virtue of an implied contract.

Contracts to pay in favour of physicians and surgeons are implied as against the patient in cases where in an emergency the services become necessary and it is unreasonable or impossible to wait to make a bargain...

There are, however, limits to this doctrine; thus if a family physician is provided, another who happens to be called by one of the children would not be able to collect from the head of the family who already had provided for necessary attendance. Nor if there were any other means of attendance at hand, would the emergency be held to exist.

The liability depends in these cases on a contract implied by the law for one who is not capable for the time being of contracting for himself and implies for the benefit of the attending physician a promise to pay.

If the police had found the defendant on the road and had taken him to the hospital to save his life, I would have had no hesitation about the matter: I would have held that a contract was implied which would fix upon the defendant the same liability that is fixed on a patient in favour of a doctor in a similar case.

The doubt about the matter arises from the fact that the defendant was in the custody of the preventive officers or of some officers of the law. They were controlling his actions and were taking him either to gaol or to hospital not only without his consent but doubtless in active opposition to his wishes.

The sole question for decision is whether the law will imply a contract as against an injured man in a case where he has no freedom of physical action and is in the custody of the law. The cases cited throw no light upon that proposition. It does not help us to find that some other party is liable; for several may be liable. The only question is whether the injured prisoner is liable.

Probably we may decide this best if we try to ascertain the basis of the liability of persons who are treated in an emergency. The doctor knows very well that the bystander who calls him does not intend to make himself liable, he knows that he has not time to make a bargain with the man, or even to ask him if he wishes his services, therefore the law implies a contract in favour of the doctor as against the man.

The liability implied in these cases has a twofold significance. It fixes with liability the man who cannot act for himself and it protects from liability the good samaritan who calls the physician, or the hospital ambulance, but does not wish to be liable for the expense involved. The hospital knows very well that the bystander is only the voluntary messenger of the injured man and that it can not charge such messenger unless he definitely assumes liability.

Do the same principles apply when a man bound with handcuffs and under arrest is brought in? The police officers are not the ordinary bystander; they are in charge of the man, themselves charged with the duty of keeping him safely until he is delivered in due course of law. Under these circumstances is the hospital justified in assuming that when the police officer calls up and makes arrangement for taking care of a wounded prisoner that he is acting as a voluntary agent and that the liability is implied as being the prisoner's?

I think that the circumstances of this case where the prisoner was taken handcuffed and in custody and where he continued as a prisoner during his term in the hospital and thereafter are sufficient to rebut the presumption which arises in the case of a stranger picking a man up on the road and that the implication is that the officers were looking after the defendant in the course of their duty to safely keep and deliver him or bring him before a Magistrate in accordance with law.

The appeal therefore in my opinion fails and should be dismissed with costs.

[Graham and Carroll JJ. agreed with Doull J.; Ross J. dissented on the ground that the case was covered by *Matheson v. Smiley* and that the attitude of the person in extremity could not be considered.]

QUESTIONS

Would it matter to the result in *Matheson v. Smiley*, if the deceased immediately before he committed suicide had said in writing:
a) "I specifically direct that neither I nor my estate will assume any liability to pay for any medical services rendered to me in any attempt to prevent my dying from the injuries that I am about to inflict on myself", or;
b) The same as in (a) except that Dr. Matheson was specifically mentioned as one doctor the deceased would never consent to pay?
Assume that in both cases Dr. Matheson knew of these statements.

The next cases offer the same basis for enforcement but in very different circumstances. The problems of the Statute of Frauds will be discussed later in Chapter 7. For the moment it is sufficient that the effect of the Statute of Frauds is to render the express promise to pay unenforceable.

DEGLMAN v. GUARANTEE TRUST CO. OF CANADA AND CONSTANTINEAU

[1954] 3 D.L.R. 785. S.C.C.; Rinfret C.J.C., Taschereau, Rand, Estey, Locke, Cartwright and Fauteux JJ.

RINFRET C.J.C. and TASCHEREAU J. concur with RAND J.

Rand J.: — In this appeal the narrow question is raised as to the nature of part performance which will enable the Court to order specific performance of a contract relating to lands unenforceable at law by reason of s. 4 of the *Statute of Frauds,* R.S.O. 1950, c. 371. The respondent Constantineau claims the benefit of such a contract and the appellant represents the next-of-kin other than the respondent of the deceased, Laura Brunet, who resist it.

The respondent was the nephew of the deceased. Both lived in Ottawa. When he was about 20 years of age, and while attending a technical school, for 6 months of the school year 1934-35 he lived with his aunt at No. 550 Besserer St. Both that and the house on the adjoining lot, No. 548, were owned by the aunt and it was during this time that she is claimed to have agreed that if the nephew would be good to her and do such services for her as she might from time to time request during her lifetime she would make adequate provision for him in her will, and in particular that she would leave to him the premises at No. 548. While staying with her the nephew did the chores around both houses which, except for an apartment used by his aunt, were occupied by tenants. When the term ended he returned to the home of his mother on another street. In the autumn of that year he worked on the national highway in the northern part of Ontario. In the spring of 1936 he took a job on a railway at a point outside of Ottawa and at the end of that year, returning to Ottawa, he obtained a position with the city police force. In 1941 he married. At no time did he live at the house No. 548 or, apart from the 6 months, at the house No. 550.

The performance consisted of taking his aunt about in her own or his automobile on trips to Montreal and elsewhere, and on pleasure drives, of doing odd jobs about the two houses, and of various accommodations such as errands and minor services for her personal needs. These circumstances,

Spence J. at trial and the Court of Appeal [[1953] O.W.N. 665], finding a contract, have held to be sufficient grounds for disregarding the prohibition of the statute.

.   .   .

[Rand J. held that the promise was within the statute and was therefore unenforceable.]

There remains the question of recovery for the services rendered on the basis of a *quantum meruit.* On the findings of both Courts below the services were not given gratuitously but on the footing of a contractual relation: they were to be paid for. The statute in such a case does not touch the principle of restitution against what would otherwise be an unjust enrichment of the defendant at the expense of the plaintiff. This is exemplified in the simple case of part or full payment in money as the price under an oral contract; it would be inequitable to allow the promisor to keep both the land and the money and the other party to the bargain is entitled to recover what he has paid. Similarly is it in the case of services given.

This matter is elaborated exhaustively in the Restatement of the Law of Contract issued by the American Law Institute and Professor Williston's monumental work on Contracts, 1936, vol. 2, s. 536 deals with the same topic. On the principles there laid down the respondent is entitled to recover for his services and outlays what the deceased would have had to pay for them on a purely business basis to any other person in the position of the respondent. The evidence covers generally and perhaps in the only way possible the particulars, but enough is shown to enable the Court to make a fair determination of the amount called for; and since it would be to the benefit of the other beneficiaries to bring an end to this litigation, I think we should not hesitate to do that by fixing the amount to be allowed. This I place at the sum of $3,000.

The appeal will therefore be allowed and the judgment modified by declaring the respondent entitled to recover against the respondent administrator the sum of $3,000; all costs will be paid out of the estate, those of the administrator as between solicitor and client.

ESTEY AND LOCKE JJ. concur with CARTWRIGHT J.

Cartwright J.: — The facts out of which this appeal arises are stated in the reasons of my brother Rand.

The appeal was argued on the assumption, that there was an oral contract made between the respondent and the late Laura Constantineau Brunet under the terms of which the former was to perform certain services in consideration whereof the latter was to devise No. 548 Besserer St. to him, that the contract was fully performed by the respondent and that there was no defence to his claim to have the contract specifically performed other than the fact that there was no memorandum in writing thereof as required by the *Statute of Frauds*, which was duly pleaded.

It is clear that none of the numerous acts done by the respondent in performance of the contract were in their own nature unequivocally referable to No. 548 Besserer St., or to any dealing with that land. On the other hand there are concurrent findings of fact, which were not questioned before us, that the acts done by the respondent were in their nature referable to some contract existing between the parties. On this view of the facts the learned trial Judge and the Court of Appeal were of opinion that the acts done by the respondent in performance of the agreement were sufficient to take it out of the operation of the *Statute of Frauds* and that it ought to be specifically enforced....

I have already expressed the view that the acts relied upon by the respondent in the case at bar are not unequivocally and in their own nature referable to any dealing with the land in question and on this point the appellant is entitled to succeed.

It remains to consider the respondent's alternative claim to recover for the value of the services which he performed for the deceased and the possible application to such a claim of the *Limitations Act*, R.S.O. 1950, c. 207.

I agree with the conclusion of my brother Rand that the respondent is entitled to recover the value of these services from the respondent administrator. This right appears to me to be based, not on the contract, but on an obligation imposed by law.

In *Fibrosa Spolka Akcyjna v. Fairbairn Lawson Combe Barbour Ltd.*, [1943] A.C. 32 at p. 61, Lord Wright said: "It is clear that any civilized system of law is bound to provide remedies for cases of what has been called unjust enrichment or unjust benefit, that is to prevent a man from retaining the money of or some benefit derived from another which it is against conscience that he should keep. Such remedies in English law are generically different from remedies in contract or in tort, and are now recognized to fall within a third category of the common law which has been called quasi-contract or restitution."

And at p. 62: "Lord Mansfield does not say that the law implies a promise. The law implies a debt or obligation which is a different thing. In fact, he denies that there is a contract; the obligation is as efficacious as if it were upon a contract. The obligation is a creation of the law, just as much as an obligation in tort. The obligation belongs to a third class, distinct from either contract or tort, though it resembles contract rather than tort."

Lord Wright's judgment appears to me to be in agreement with the view stated in Williston on Contracts referred by my brother Rand.

.   .   .

In the case at bar all the acts for which the respondent asks to be paid under his alternative claim were clearly done in performance of the existing but unenforceable contract with the deceased that she would devise 548 Besserer St. to him, and to infer from them a fresh contract to pay the value of the services in money would be... to draw an inference contrary to the fact.

In my opinion when the *Statute of Frauds* was pleaded the express contract was thereby rendered unenforceable, but the deceased having received the benefits of the full performance of the contract by the respondent, the law imposed upon her, and so on her estate, the obligation to pay the fair value of the services rendered to her.

If this is, as I think, the right view of the nature of the obligation upon which the respondent's claim rests it follows that the *Limitations Act* can have no application... In my opinion the obligation which the law imposes upon the respondent administrator did not arise until the deceased died intestate. It may well be that throughout her life it was her intention to make a will in fulfilment of the existing although unenforceable contract and until her death the respondent had no reason to doubt that she would do so. The statutory period of limitation does not commence to run until the plaintiff's cause of action has accrued; and on the facts of the case at bar the cause of action upon which the respondent is entitled to succeed did not accrue until the death of the deceased intestate.

For the above reasons I would dispose of the appeal as proposed by my brother Rand.

FAUTEUX J. concurs with CARTWRIGHT J.

QUESTION

Suppose that the value of the house were less than the amount awarded by the court; would that matter?

BOONE v. COE

(1913), 154 S.W. 900. Court of Appeal of Kentucky.

[The defendant orally agreed to lease property in Texas to the plaintiffs. In reliance on this promise, the plaintiffs moved from Kentucky to Texas (taking 55 days to get there). When the plaintiffs arrived in Texas, the defendant refused to lease them any land. The plaintiffs returned to Kentucky (in 4 days) and sued defendant for breach of his oral promise.]

Clay, C.: The statute of frauds (section 470, subsecs. 6 and 7, Kentucky Statutes) provides as follows: "No action shall be brought to charge any person: 6. Upon any contract for the sale of real estate, or any lease thereof, for longer term than one year; nor 7. Upon any agreement which is not to be performed within one year from the making thereof, unless the promise, contract, agreement, representation, assurance, or ratification, or some memorandum or note thereof, be in writing, and signed by the party to be charged therewith, or by his authorized agent; but the consideration need not be expressed in the writing; it may be proved when necessary, or disproved by parol or other evidence." A parol lease of land for one year to commence at a future date, is within the statute.

The question sharply presented is: May plaintiffs recover for expenses incurred and time lost on the faith of a contract that is unenforceable under the statute of frauds?... Indeed, it is the general rule that damages cannot be recovered for violation of a contract within the statute of frauds....

To this general rule there are certain well-recognized exceptions, and in a number of other cases, it has been held that, where services have been rendered during the life of another, on the promise that the person rendering the service should receive at the death of the person served a legacy, and the contract so made is within the statute of frauds, a reasonable compensation may be recovered for the services actually rendered. It has also been held that the vendee of land under a parol contract is entitled to recover any portion of the purchase money he may have paid, and is also entitled to compensation for improvements.

And under a contract for personal services within the statute an action may be maintained on a quantum meruit. The doctrine of these cases proceeds upon the theory that the defendant has actually received some benefits from the acts of part performance; and the law therefore implies a promise to pay. In 29 Am. & Eng. Ency. 836, the rule is thus stated: "Although part performance by one of the parties to a contract within the statute of frauds will not, at law, entitle such party to recover upon the contract itself, he may nevertheless recover for money paid by him, or property delivered, or services rendered in accordance with and upon the faith of the contract. The law will raise an implied promise on the part of the other party to pay for what has been done in the way of part performance. But this right of recovery is not absolute. The plaintiff is entitled to compensation only under such circumstances as would warrant a recovery in case there was no express contract; and hence it must appear that the defendant has actually received, or will receive, some benefit from the acts of part performance. It is immaterial that the plaintiff may have suffered a loss because he is unable to enforce his contract." ...

In the case under consideration the plaintiffs merely sustained a loss. Defendant received no benefit. Had he received a benefit, the law would imply an obligation to pay therefor. Having received no benefit, no obligation to pay is implied. The statute says that the contract of defendant made with plaintiffs is unenforceable. Defendant therefore had the legal right to decline to carry it out. To require him to pay plaintiffs for losses and expenses incurred on the faith of the contract, without any benefit accruing to him, would, in effect, uphold a contract upon which the statute expressly declares no action shall be brought. The statute was enacted for the purpose of preventing frauds and perjuries. That it is a valuable statute is shown by the fact that similar statutes are in force in practically all, if not all, of the states of the Union. Being a valuable statute, the purpose of the lawmakers in its enactment should not be defeated by permitting recoveries in cases to which its provisions were intended to apply.

The situation in *Boone v. Coe* is that the plaintiffs have suffered losses but the defendant has received no benefit. If we regard both parties starting with $10.00, after the case the plaintiffs have $9.00 and defendant still has only $10.00. Had the plaintiffs been successful, then the relative positions of the parties would simply have been reversed. The common law has, until quite recently, had no power to apportion losses. It might be thought fair that the plaintiff could recover one half of his losses so that both parties would end up with $9.50, but the courts could not do this. The plaintiff either got all or nothing.

Note: The Statute of Frauds is discussed below, Chapter 7.

QUESTIONS

1. What do you think the court means by saying that the Statute of Frauds is a "valuable statute"?

2. Why do you think that the statute was meant to prevent any claim by the plaintiff in *Boone v. Coe* but not in *Deglman*?

3. What is the statute for?

In *Nicholson v. St. Denis* (1975) 8 O.R. (2d) 315, the Ontario Court of Appeal (Gale C.J.O., Arnup and MacKinnon JJ.A.) reversed the decision of a county court judge who had awarded to the plaintiff the cost of installing aluminum siding on a house. The plaintiff had installed the siding at the request of one Labelle, the purchaser under an agreement of purchase and sale. The defendant was the vendor under this agreement who had retaken possession on the purchaser's default. The trial judge relied on the following statement:

"It is clear that any civilized system of law is bound to provide remedies for cases of what has been called unjust enrichment or unjust benefit, that is to prevent a man from retaining the money of or some benefit derived from another which it is against conscience that he should keep." [(*Fibrosa v. Fairbain Lawson*, [1943] A.C. 32 at 61, House of Lords.)]

MacKinnon J.A., giving the judgment of the court said:

If this were a true statement of the doctrine then the unruly horse of public policy would be joined in the stable by a steed of even more unpredictable propensities. The law of unjust enrichment, which could more accurately be termed the doctrine of restitution, has developed to give a remedy where it would be unjust, under the circumstances, to allow a defendant to retain a benefit conferred on him by the plaintiff at the plaintiff's expense. That does not mean that restitution will follow every enrichment of one person and loss by another. Certain rules have evolved over the years to guide a Court in its determination as to whether the doctrine applies in any particular circumstance.

It is difficult to rationalize all of the authorities on restitution and it would serve no useful purpose to make that attempt. It can be said, however, that in almost all of the cases the facts established that there was a special relationship between the parties, frequently contractual at the outset, which relationship would have made it unjust for the defendant to retain the benefit conferred on him by the plaintiff — a benefit, be it said, that was not conferred "officiously". This relationship in turn is usually, but not always, marked by two characteristics, firstly, knowledge of the benefit on the part of the defendant, and secondly, either an express or implied request by the defendant for the benefit, or acquiescence in its performance.

He went on to hold that there was no relationship between the parties here as would justify the conclusion reached by the trial judge.

One particular aspect of this problem has been covered by statute:

Conveyancing and Law of Property Act, R.S.O. 1970, c. 85.
38(1). Where a person makes lasting improvements on land under the belief that it is his own, he or his assigns are entitled to a lien upon it to the extent of the amount by which its value is enhanced by the improvements, or are entitled or may be required to retain the land if the court is of opinion or requires that this should be done, according as may under all circumstances of the case be most just, making compensation for the land, if retained, as the court directs.

But, of course, this was of no help to the plaintiff in *Nicholson v. St. Denis*.

On the facts of *Nicholson v. St. Dennis*, the plaintiff would have had a right to assert a mechanic's lien against the property under the *Mechanics Lien Act*, R.S.O. 1970, c. 267. This would allow the plaintiff to register his claim in the Land Registry office as a claim against the property. Had this been done before the defendant had retaken possession of the house, it would have been enforceable against the defendant. Do you think that this influenced the court in refusing the plaintiff a remedy?

Of course, the plaintiff could have sued Labelle for his price.

The remedy based on unjust enrichment that we have been discussing is also available in some cases of breach of contract. As we have seen the normal measure of damages for breach is based on the plaintiff's claim to be put in the position that he would have been in had the contract been performed. In some cases the plaintiff may seek to be put into the position that he would have been in if the contract had never been made. Damages measured in such a way would usually be either reliance or restitution damages.

The case we are concerned about here is the claim to protect the restitution interest. A typical case would be the following:

> Alan agrees to buy Jennifer's house for $80,000. He pays a deposit with the offer of $2,000. Jennifer accepts the offer and takes the deposit. She subsequently refuses to complete the sale.

Alan, as we know, could sue to protect his expectation interest by suing either for damages for breach of contract, i.e. his lost profit, or for specific performance. He may not choose to do either; he may, for example, believe that the house is now worth only $75,000. In this case, Alan will want to get back the $2,000 that he has paid. To do so he has to sue on the basis of quasi contract. Jennifer has not expressly promised to return it, but, since she breached the contract, she would be enriched by keeping the deposit. It is clear that this enrichment would be unjust. *Bowes v. Vaux* (1918), 43 O.L.R. 521, Ontario High Court, is authority for the proposition that Alan can sue to recover his deposit.

An example of the problem that can be caused by a lawyer not keeping clearly in mind the distinction between a claim based on the expectation interest and one based on the restitution interest is provided by the case of *Horsler v. Zorro*, [1975] Ch. 302. It was there held that where a vendor of land refuses to complete the sale, the purchaser may either sue for damages for breach or specific performance or he may regard the contract as at an end and sue to recover what he has paid. Once the purchaser has elected to regard the contract as at an end, that election is final and cannot be retracted and the measure of his recovery is the deposit that he has paid and any reliance losses incurred in checking the vendor's title. When a purchaser elects to regard the contract as at an end he is said to have elected to "rescind" the contract. A claim for rescission entitles the purchaser to claim his restitution and some of his reliance losses but not to claim his expectation losses. In other words, a plaintiff has the choice of asking to be put in the position that he would have been in had the contract been performed, or in the position he would have been in had the contract never been made. He cannot ask for both.

Consider the following problem:

Alan agreed to buy a cow and one ton of hay from Derek. The price was $100 which Alan paid. Derek gave Alan the cow but refused to deliver the hay. It cost Alan $10 to go to fetch the cow (and would cost the same to return it) and during the cow's stay with Alan it cost $5 to feed.

Which of the following remedies are open to Alan?

(a) Return the cow, recover the $100 paid and the cost of
    (i)   picking up the cow,
    (ii) returning the cow,
    (iii) the cost of feed for the cow.

(b) Return the cow, recover the $100 paid, the cost of feed and the profit that he would have made had the contract been performed.

(c) Keep the cow, recover the value of the undelivered hay, plus any expenses incurred in preparing to pick up the hay.

The next case raises some further problems of the interrelationship of contractual and quasi-contractual claims.

BOOMER v. MUIR

(1933), 24 P. 2d 570. District Court of Appeal, California.

[Boomer undertook to do sub-contract work for the defendant (who was in partnership with Storrie). The defendant was under contract to build a dam. Boomer was to be paid for his work according to an agreed schedule of unit prices for the work done. Friction developed between the parties. A supplemental agreement was entered into under which Boomer agreed to do a specific amount of work and the defendant agreed to pay 10% more. Eventually Boomer abandoned the work alleging that the defendant had failed to supply the materials that Boomer needed and that the defendant had promised to supply under the contract. The work was substantially complete and Boomer had poured the third slab of concrete on the dam. Boomer sued Storrie and Muir and Storrie's sureties (who would have to pay any damages that Boomer obtained).]

Dooling J.: — It is well settled in California that a contractor who is prevented from performing his contract by the failure of the other party to furnish materials has a choice of three remedies: He may treat the contract as rescinded and recover upon a quantum meruit so far as he has performed; he may keep the contract alive, offering complete performance, and sue for damages for delay and expense incurred; or he may treat the repudiation as putting an end to the contract for purposes of performance and sue for the profits he would have realized. Storrie & Co. and Storrie's sureties admit this rule, but claim that the evidence will not support a finding that Boomer was prevented from performance by Storrie & Co.'s failure to furnish materials.

The court instructed the jury: "If you find from the evidence in this case, that Boomer did not intend to use any materials that might have been furnished after he had completed the pouring of the third slab in December, 1927, and Storrie & Company were aware that if such materials were furnished they would not be used, then there was no obligation upon Storrie & Company's part to furnish such materials at that time, or until they were advised by Boomer that such materials would be needed."

Under this instruction the jury must have found that Boomer intended to proceed if materials were furnished. We are satisfied that under the evidence this was a question of fact for the determination of the jury, and that their implied finding on this point is not without substantial support in the evidence.

It is also argued that Boomer was not prepared to proceed further under winter conditions which then existed, and that sufficient materials were actually reasonably available to proceed had Boomer desired. On both these questions we have examined the record and are satisfied that as to both there was a substantial conflict in the evidence.

The jury was fairly instructed on the question of prevention of performance, no complaint is made of such instructions on this appeal, and the case is the familiar one of a conflict in the evidence on this point as to which the jury's verdict is conclusive on appeal.

It is further urged that, "assuming that prevention of performance was shown, the contractor may not, where the contract has been fully liquidated up to a given stage, re-open the part of the contract which has been fully executed on both sides and seek to have his past work revalued." In this connection it is pointed out that, at the time Boomer left the job in December, 1927, the monthly estimates provided for in the contract had been made up to November 25, 1927, and Boomer had been paid in full for all work covered by these estimates, with the exception of the retained percentage of 10 per cent for three months after May, 1927, in which months Boomer had not placed 40,000 cubic yards of material in the dam as provided in the supplemental agreement. It is conceded that the general rule, and the one followed in California, is that, where a contract has been rescinded for prevention of performance, the plaintiff may recover the reasonable value of what he has done or supplied under the contract, even though such recovery may exceed the contract price. It is insisted, however, that this general rule does not apply in cases where specific payment is provided in the contract for specific portions of the work, and such portions have been fully performed and payment for which has been fully ascertained and liquidated prior to the breach by the adverse party. It being settled as the general rule that upon prevention of performance the injured plaintiff may treat the contract as rescinded and recover upon a quantum meruit without regard to the contract price, why should he be limited to the contract price in case payments for portions of the entire contract have been made or liquidated? Those payments were received in full only on condition that the entire contract be performed. But, if the contract is rescinded, the prices fixed by the contract are also rescinded.

To hold that payments under the contract may limit recovery where the contract is afterwards rescinded through the defendant's fault seems to us to involve a confusion of thought. A rescinded contract ceases to exist for all purposes. How then can it be looked to for one purpose, the purpose of fixing the amount of recovery? "A contract is extinguished by its rescission". Civ. Code, § 1688. "Generally speaking, the effect of rescission is to extinguish the contract. The contract is annihilated so effectually that in contemplation of law it has never had any existence, even for the purpose of being broken."

Storrie & Co. and Storrie's sureties say that to permit such recovery in this case is to allow Boomer to recover over $250,000, when if he had completed the contract, he would have received no more than $20,000.

Even if it were true, then, that Boomer would only have received an additional $20,000 for the completion of his contract, we are of the opinion that that does not prevent him from recovering the reasonable value of his services upon its rescission for Storrie & Co.'s breach. But Boomer points out that he had large claims for damages against Storrie & Co. for continued delays and increased expense of operation due to their misconduct. Upon the rescission of the contract, it ceased to exist for all purposes, including the purpose of relying upon its terms for the purpose of recovering damages for any breach. If Boomer had valid claims for damages arising under the contract by reason of the fact that his cost of operation had been wrongfully increased, it would seem inequitable to limit him to the recovery of the contract price upon a rescission for Storrie & Co.'s failure of performance.

QUESTIONS

1. Why should Boomer be able to claim more than the contract price for his services?

2. If Boomer can claim more than the contract price here, is there any reason to worry about the value of the promised house in *Deglman v. Guarantee Trust?*

REVIEW PROBLEM

Winston, a wealthy investor, has a fervent belief in astrology. He asks Eleanor to learn astrology so that she can assist him in his investments. In return, Winston promises to give Eleanor his cottage on his death. Eleanor attends courses and reads books and gives Winston astrological advice for several years. Winston dies without fulfilling his promise. Eleanor cannot sue on the promise because of the Statute of Frauds. The Statute by s. 4 provides:

> No action shall be brought... upon any contract (for) sale of land... unless the agreement upon which the action is brought, or some memorandum or note thereof is in writing and signed by the party to be charged therewith...

What remedy does Eleanor have?

Just as the existence of a claim based on unjust enrichment can offer good reasons for enforcing a contract when there may be no express promise that can be enforced, so there are cases where, even though there is an express promise, there are good reasons for refusing enforcement. The next two cases illustrate some of these reasons. These are only two cases out of very many. They are put in the materials at this point for four reasons:

1. The courts can refuse to enforce promises because they think that, in spite of appearances, the contract is in some way objectionable.
2. These objectionable features can be talked about and made the basis of the courts' refusal to enforce.
3. There is no justification for a court, faced with an objectionable contract, to refuse to talk about the objectionable features of the contract.
4. If there are no objectionable features is a court justified in refusing to enforce a contract that would (on the grounds indicated in the introductory note and by Fuller) be enforceable?

POST v. JONES

(1856), 60 U.S. (19 How.) 150. U.S. Supreme Court.

Mr. Justice Grier delivered the opinion of the court.

... The Richmond, after a ramble of three years on the Pacific, in pursuit of whales, had passed through the sea of Anadin, and was near Behring's Straits, in the Arctic ocean, on the 2d of August, 1849. She had nearly completed her cargo, and was about to return; but, during a thick fog, she was run upon rocks, within half a mile of the shore, and in a situation from which it was impossible to extricate her. The master and crew escaped in their boats to the shore, holding communication with the vessel, without much difficulty or danger. They could probably have transported the cargo to the beach, but this would have been unprofitable labor, as its condition would not have been improved. Though saved from the ocean, it would not have been safe. The coast was barren; the few inhabitants, savages and thieves. This ocean is navigable for only about two months in the year; during the remainder of the year it is sealed up with ice. The winter was expected to commence within fifteen or twenty days, at farthest. The nearest port of safety and general commercial intercourse was at the Sandwich

Islands, five thousand miles distant. Their only hope of escape from this inhospitable region was by means of other whaling vessels, which were known to be cruising at no great distance, and who had been in company with the Richmond, and had pursued the same course.

On the 5th of August the fog cleared off, and the ship Elizabeth Frith was seen at a short distance. The officers of the Richmond immediately went on board, and the master informed the master of the Frith of the disaster which had befallen the Richmond. He requested him to take his crew on board, and said, "You need not whale any more; there is plenty of oil there, which you may take, and get away as soon as possible." On the following day they took on board the Frith about 300 barrels oil from the Richmond. On the 6th, the Panama and the Junior came near; they had not quite completed their cargoes; as there was more oil in the Richmond than they could all take, it was proposed that they also should complete their cargoes in the same way. Captain Tinkham, of the Junior, proposed to take part of the crew of the Richmond, and said he would take part of the oil, "provided it was put up and sold at auction." In pursuance of this suggestion, advertisements were posted on each of the three vessels, signed *by* or *for* the master of the Richmond. On the following day the forms of an auction sale were enacted; the master of the Frith bidding one dollar per barrel for as much as he needed, and the others seventy-five cents. The ship and tackle were sold for five dollars; no money was paid, and no account kept or bill of sale made out. Each vessel took enough to complete her cargo of oil and bone. The transfer was effected in a couple of days, with some trouble and labor, but little or no risk or danger, and the vessels immediately proceeded on their voyage, stopping as usual at the Sandwich Islands.

Now, it is evident, from this statement of the facts, that, although the Richmond was stranded near the shore upon which her crew and even her cargo might have been saved from the dangers of the sea, they were really in no better situation as to ultimate safety than if foundered or disabled in the midst of the Pacific ocean. The crew were glad to escape with their lives. The ship and cargo, though not actually derelict, must necessarily have been abandoned. The contrivance of an auction sale, under such circumstances, where the master of the Richmond was hopeless, helpless, and passive — where there was no market, no money, no competition — where one party had absolute power, and the other no choice but submission — where the vendor must take what is offered or get nothing — is a transaction which has no characteristic of a valid contract. It has been contended by the claimants that it would be a great hardship to treat this sale as a nullity, and thus compel them to assume the character of salvors, because they were not bound to save this property, especially at so great a distance from any port of safety, and in a place where they could have completed their cargo in a short time from their own catchings, and where salvage would be no compensation for the loss of this opportunity. The force of these arguments is fully appreciated, but we think they are not fully sustained by the facts of the case. Whales may have been plenty around their vessels on the 6th and 7th of August, but, judging of the future from the past, the anticipation of filling up their cargo in the few days of the season in which it would be safe to remain, was very uncertain, and barely probable. The whales were retreating towards the north pole, where they could not be pursued, and, though seen in numbers on one day, they would disappear on the next; and, even when seen in greatest numbers, their capture was uncertain. By this transaction, the vessels were enabled to proceed at once on their home voyage; and the certainty of a liberal salvage allowance for the property rescued will be ample compensation for the possible chance of greater profits, by refusing their assistance in saving their neighbor's property.

It has been contended, also, that the sale was justifiable and valid, because it was better for the interests of all concerned to accept what was offered, than suffer a total loss. But this argument proves too much, as it would justify every sale to a salvor. Courts of admiralty will enforce contracts made for salvage service and salvage compensation, where the salvor has not taken advantage of his power to make an unreasonable bargain; but they will not tolerate the doctrine that a salvor can take the advantage of his situation, and avail himself of the calamities of others to drive a bargain; nor will they permit the performance of a public duty to be turned into a traffic of profit....

The case is therefore remitted to the Circuit Court, to have the amount due to each party adjusted, according to the principles stated.

CHILLIBACK v. PAWLIUK

(1956), 1 D.L.R. (2d) 611. Alberta Supreme Court.

Egbert J.: — The plaintiff, who was a gratuitous passenger in the defendant's car, sues for damages arising out of injuries sustained in an accident allegedly caused by the gross negligence of the defendant.

The defence is twofold — that the defendant was not grossly negligent, and secondly, that if he did become liable to compensate the plaintiff, the latter subsequently released the defendant by signing a written release under seal.

At the conclusion of the trial I found on the evidence that the accident, and the plaintiff's consequent injuries had been caused by the gross negligence of the defendant. Counsel for the defendant then asked for leave to file a written argument on the second line of defence, relating to the alleged release. This leave was granted and both counsel have now filed written arguments on this point.

The accident occurred on June 10, 1953. This action was commenced on June 8, 1954. In the interval, on October 30, 1953, the plaintiff signed the alleged release.

The parties were on friendly terms before the accident and remained on similar terms after the accident, until at least some time after the execution of the alleged release at the end of October, 1953, although after the accident they did not see one another so frequently, since the plaintiff, because of his injuries, was unable to continue his work in Big Valley, where the defendant was also located, and where the parties frequently saw one another.

On October 30, 1953, the plaintiff went into the beer parlour of an hotel in Edmonton. According to his evidence he had some six glasses of beer with a friend who cannot now be located, when another friend, Mercer, came along. Each of the three men had another four or six beers. At this point, when the plaintiff had been in the beer parlour about three hours, the defendant entered, found the group, and said to the plaintiff, "I have a paper here I'd like you to sign, because I'd like to get my driver's licence back" (or very similar words). The plaintiff had once had his own driver's licence taken away for "impaired driving", and knew what the defendant was talking about. The plaintiff then signed a paper which the defendant handed to him. He received no money or other consideration for signing, and says that he signed to help the defendant get his licence back. He had consulted Mr. Dubensky, a solicitor in Edmonton, before this about the possibility of taking action against the defendant, but says that he did not know this paper had anything to do with the lawsuit. He admits that the defendant used no force, or threat or promise to induce him to sign the paper. He denies that he was drunk when he signed the document. The defendant made any insertions or alterations in the document that appear in hand-writing. (These consist of the insertion of the date, and the insertion of the word "nil" in two places.) The plaintiff signed the document and Mercer signed it as witness to the plaintiff's signature. The document itself is contained on one sheet of paper, and reads as follows:

"Release and Discharge

"In consideration of the payment or settlement of the sum of ($)
Nil   Dollars, the receipt whereof is hereby acknowledged), I Fred Chilliback do hereby release and forever discharge William Pawliuk from all and any
actions, cause of actions, claims and demands for, upon or by reason of any
damage, loss or injury which heretofore have been or which hereafter may be
sustained by   in   in consequence of   the   accident of June 10th, 1953 It being further agreed and understood that the payment of the said ($)   nil   Dollars is not to be construed as
an admission on the part of the said William Pawliuk of any liability whatever in
consequence of said accident. I further state that I have carefully read the foregoing release, and know the contents thereof, and I sign the same of my own free
will.

In witness whereof, I have hereunto set my hand and seal this   30   day
of   October   1953.

Signed, Sealed and Delivered)
                  in the presence of)
(Name) 'J. F. Mercer'   )   (Signature) 'F. Chilliback'
(Address) 10860 — 73 St.   )   (Seal)
)   To bear the signature of
)   Fred Chilliback
                Witness"   )

In the space in the right lower corner marked "Seal" is affixed a red wafer seal.

It appears to be common ground that this document was prepared by the Motor Vehicles Branch of the Highways Department, but it is not common ground that that Branch affixed the seal before the document was sent out, or, in fact, that the seal had actually been placed on the document before the plaintiff signed it. The evidence of both parties and of the witness Mercer, appears to be silent on this point. In the absence of evidence, and in the light of a statement made to me by counsel for the defendant, I think I must assume that the seal had been affixed to the document by the Motor Vehicles Branch, and was affixed to it at the time the plaintiff signed it, despite the suggestion of counsel for the plaintiff that it was affixed at some later time.

The defendant states in his evidence that the plaintiff read over the release before he signed it, and had no difficulty in understanding it, and himself suggested that the defendant write in the word "nothing" in the space relating to the consideration. This is not denied by the plaintiff. The defendant admits that he gave the plaintiff no consideration for the release.

The defence resolves itself into the sole question of whether the complete lack of consideration is offset by the presence of the red seal opposite the plaintiff's signature. I am left with no doubt that if there had been no seal the release would have been inoperative because of the absence of consideration. Does the presence of the small, red wafer seal make it operative?

I have no doubt on the evidence, or possibly I should say on the lack of evidence touching the matter of the seal, that both the plaintiff and the defendant were, at the time of the execution of the release, entirely oblivious to its existence, and to the effect of its presence. Indeed, counsel for the defendant states in his argument "neither the plaintiff nor the defendant were at all concerned, nor probably even cognizant of the fact that a seal was on the document or required to be on the document". With this statement I entirely agree. There is no evidence that the plaintiff said any word or did any act which in any way amounted to an adoption by him of the seal as *his* seal. So far as the plaintiff was concerned, he was *signing* a document submitted to him by the defendant — that was the transaction and the whole transaction insofar as he understood it. Nevertheless the document he signed did have affixed to it, opposite the space for his signature, the seal now in question, and the defendant now produces a release purporting to be signed and sealed by the plaintiff.

As is stated in most textbooks and in many ancient authorities, a seal was said to "import" consideration, so that a document under seal might be enforced even though no consideration appeared on the face of the instrument. In other words, the seal itself constituted *prima facie* proof that consideration had passed: O'Brien, Cyclopedia of Conveyancing, 8th ed., pp. 21 *et seq.* But how can it be said that a seal "imports" consideration when the document itself expressly states that there is no consideration? In this case we not only have an express negation of consideration in the instrument, but all the available evidence proves conclusively that no consideration passed from the defendant to the plaintiff, and that the plaintiff himself recorded that fact in the instrument.

In my view, the evidence discloses that the parties did not intend that this document should be executed as a sealed document.

.   .   .

... (W)hen a person signs his name to an instrument already sealed, he is presumed to have adopted the seal affixed — this is one of the equivalents above referred to accepted by the law. But it is only a presumption which is raised, and this presumption may be rebutted by evidence by which a contrary intention is proved or from which it may be inferred. In this case, as I have said, the evidence is, in my view, clear that both parties were quite oblivious to the presence of the seal, and that there was no intention on the part of either of them that the document should be sealed...

I think I am justified in holding that the mere presence of the *testimonium* clause is not sufficient if the evidence otherwise leads to a conclusion that the intention to execute the document under seal did not exist.

I accordingly hold, in the first place, that the release is not an instrument under seal, and therefore since no consideration passed to the plaintiff, it is not enforceable by the defendant.

In the second place, I hold that even if the document is under seal, it is, under the circumstances, not enforceable for want of consideration. As I have said, the document itself, as well as the surrounding evidence, negatives consideration, so that the mere presence of a seal cannot "import" consideration, or raise an irrebuttable presumption of a consideration which did not, in fact, exist. The Court, in the exercise of its equitable jurisdiction may look at the true bargain between the parties, and refuse to enforce an otherwise unenforceable agreement, merely because it is under seal...

[The judge awarded the plaintiff $10,000 general damages.]

SUNDELL LTD. v. EMM YANNOULATOS LTD.

(1955), 56 S.R. (N.S.W.) 323. Supreme Court of N.S.W. (in banco); Roper C.J. in Eq., Hardie J. and Manning A.J.

[The defendant agreed to sell iron to the plaintiff for £109.15.0 per ton. The plaintiff established a letter of credit in favour of the defendant. Later the defendant informed the plaintiff that a price increase of £27 per ton was inevitable and requested an increase in the letter of credit. The defendant made it clear that unless the plaintiff paid the amount of the increase, the iron would not be delivered. The plaintiff ultimately agreed to pay £140 per ton. After the iron had been shipped and paid for, the plaintiff sued to recover the amount of the increased price that it had had to pay. The trial judge gave judgment for the plaintiff, the defendant appealed. The following is the judgment of the court.]

... It asserted that the original contract had never been varied or determined, that the additional price had been paid under protest, and that such payment was not voluntary in the sense that it was made in circumstances which have been variously described as under "duress" or "compulsion."

There is no doubt that the respondent urgently required the iron to carry out its commitments and that the arrangement made in April, 1951 was made by it under a threat that if it failed to do as it was required to do no iron at all would be delivered. It was by virtue of this threat that the letter of credit was increased and the funds thus provided which enabled the appellant to obtain payment.

The submissions made on behalf of the appellant in this appeal may be summarized as follows:—

1. That the original contract was varied or superseded by a new contract made orally on 17th April, 1951, and confirmed by the parties by their conduct thereafter and that the respondent was thereby obliged to pay the increased price.

2. That a payment cannot be said to have been made under "practical compulsion" within the meaning of the principle laid down in the cases cited, where a threat is made by the payee to withhold from the payer a contractual right as distinct from a right of possession of property, a statutory right or some proprietary right.

3. That in any case the payment in question in this case was not made in circumstances which amount to "practical compulsion."

The question as to what was the contractual relation between the parties at the relevant time is not free from difficulty.

Mr. *Evans* for the appellant argued that at a time when the appellant did not have the goods, it was made clear that it did not intend to perform the contract because it could get the goods from France only at a greatly increased price; that this amounted to a repudiation of the original contract that the respondent was then entitled to elect whether to treat the contract as at an end or to treat it as continuing; that the respondent was most desirous of getting delivery of the goods; that a new contract was that entered into which determined the rights and liabilities of the parties under the original contract and that this new contract bound the appellant to supply the same goods but at an increased price; and that the consideration which the appellant gave for the respondent's promise to pay the increased price was that it would do certain things in France which would result in the goods coming forward. It was said that this gave the respondent something more than it previously had. Originally it was left merely with an action for damages. Under the new agreement it would almost certainly get the goods.

We are satisfied that Mr. Sundell's promise made on 17th April, 1951, that he would increase the amount of the letter of credit and extend the period of its currency, amounted to no more than a promise to provide sufficient funds to enable payment to be made for the goods to the French manufacturer and that any increased price would be payable by his company only if it was ascertained later that the appellant was entitled to payment of such increase.

His letter of 18th April, 1951, certainly indicates that such was his belief as to the arrangements. Mr. Hazleton, during the discussions with Mr. Sundell, maintained quite positively that as he was merely an importer — as distinct from a manufacturer — this circumstance gave his company the right to require payment of any increase which the manufacturer could lawfully compel it to pay.

In our view, the whole of the circumstances indicate that Mr. Sundell did no more than agree to pay any increase to which this or any other circumstance would entitle the appellant as against the respondent.

But even if such a promise was made as is alleged, we are of opinion that it was not binding because there was no consideration for it. The only consideration which was suggested in argument as being given in exchange for the alleged promise was that the appellant would do what was necessary to ensure that the goods were delivered. But we are satisfied that the appellant was bound so to do under the original contract. In our view every promise allegedly given to the plaintiff by the defendant under the so-called second agreement was identical with a promise given under the original agreement.

One person cannot by any promise or performance which does not go beyond the limits of his pre-existing legal duty to another person provide a new consideration for a promise by that other person in his favour. In contemplation of law it is no detriment to a party merely to perform, and no promise of a detriment merely to promise to perform what is already his legal duty to the other party to the alleged contract.

Accordingly we are of opinion that the original contract at all relevant times remained in force and that it was not varied or superseded by what was alleged to have been a new contract.

The second question is within a comparatively narrow compass. We do not think we are doing an injustice to Mr. *Evans'* comprehensive and able submissions by summarizing them as follows: That the cases relating to the circumstances in which a payment will be said to be made "under compulsion" are limited and should not be extended, and that these cases include instances where the payee has been under a statutory duty; where he has been in possession of the payer's goods; where he has held the legal title to land of which the payer was the equitable owner; and other cases where the "compulsion" was exercised in relation to the property of the payer. But, so the argument went, the principle has never been applied to a case where a compulsive threat has been made to refrain from performing merely a contractual duty as distinct from a threat to refrain from performing a statutory duty or a threat to interfere with a proprietary right of the payer. And it was said that to treat a threat to refrain from performing a contractual duty as a sufficient "compulsion," would be to break new ground, and to extend the principle in this way would be contrary to the rule laid down by Lord *Sumner* in *Sinclair v. Brougham*, [1914] A.C. 398, 453, and adopted by *Knox* C.J., in *Smith v. William Charlick Ltd.* (1924), 34 C.L.R. 38, at 51.

In the first place we are of opinion that the statements in the cases on which the appellant seeks to rely do not justify his contention. The authorities were reviewed by *Long Innes* J. in *Nixon v. Furphy* (1925), 25 S.R. (N.S.W.), 151, 160, and his Honour said:

> " 'Compulsion' in relation to a payment of which refund is sought... includes every species of duress or conduct analogous to duress, actual or threatened, exerted by or on behalf of the payee and applied to the person or the property *or any right* of the person who pays or, in some cases, of a person related to or in affinity with him."

If we are correct in the views we have expressed above it remains only to consider the third question which, as stated above, is a question of fact. In this regard we are content to say that we agree with the conclusion arrived at by *Kinsella* J. for the reasons stated by him.

In our opinion the appeal should be dismissed with costs.

In *Stoltze v. Fuller*, [1939] S.C.R. 235, the Supreme Court of Canada held that the respondent, plaintiff, was entitled to set aside an agreement on the ground of duress. The plaintiff had been employed by the defendant as the manager of the Reliance Lumber Co. in Saskatoon. The defendant owned the company. The plaintiff owned shares in the company worth $30,000. He was induced to transfer these shares to the defendant in return for the discharge of a bank loan of $3,000. The plaintiff alleged, and the jury believed, that he had been induced to transfer the shares because of his fear for his reputation caused by the defendant's making completely unfounded allegations of dishonourable conduct and threatening to publish them.

QUESTION

Do you think that the disparity between the value of the shares and the price paid for them would be an important factor in deciding whether or not relief should be given on the ground of duress?

Another class of problems in this area arises in cases where one party lacks the capacity to contract. For example, the contract of a minor (a person under the age of 18 or 19 (depending on the province)) may be avoided by the minor. (At common law the contract was voidable. The Infants Relief Act in England and in B.C. used the words "absolutely void".) This appears to mean that the minor can always escape liability on his contracts. In practice, this cannot be so, for otherwise no one would lend money to a minor to buy food or clothing. The contract of minors for necessaries are, therefore, enforceable at common law. (A contract that was for the benefit of a minor could always be enforced by him. (The English and B.C. legislation caused problems since it appeared to prevent this.))

There is abundant case law on all these problems. It is not necessary to refer to it here, as the reduction of the age of majority from 21 to 18 or 19 (in B.C., N.B., N.S., N.W.T and Yukon), substantially reduced the incidence of cases in this area.

The special problem of the ratification of a contract made by a person as a minor after that person has reached his majority is dealt with later. Chapter 2 C(ii).

The protection afforded minors is justified on the ground that young people cannot look after themselves and so the law must protect them. The same reason justifies the protection of people who are mentally incapable of looking after themselves. We will examine in Chapter 6 the problems of people who are in a *relatively* weaker position than the other contracting party. Here it is sufficient to know that one cannot make a contract with a person of unsound mind.

There are some general problems in this area when the courts have to worry about the possibility of unjust enrichment of the person being protected, and about the possibility of the minor or mental incompetent being sued in tort and not in contract. Again, we will not spend time in these issues here.

B. Formal Validity of Contracts

Every legal system must provide a method whereby promises are binding just because the document satisfies certain formal requirements. At common law the seal provided this consequence.

There are still a great many cases on seals. These usually involve banks and particularly contracts of guarantee. A promise made by a guarantor is frequently made without any consideration — *i.e.,* is gratuitous — and in the absence of a seal would be unenforceable by the bank. Banks' action on promises of guarantee may depend on the seal being effective to make the contract enforceable.

GUARANTEE

TO THE BANK OF NOVA SCOTIA

IN CONSIDERATION OF THE BANK OF NOVA SCOTIA (herein called the "Bank") agreeing to deal with or to continue to deal with

....

.(herein called the "Customer") the undersigned and each of them, if more than one, hereby jointly and severally guarantees payment to the Bank of all debts and liabilities, present or future, direct or indirect, absolute or contingent, matured or not, at any time owing by the Customer to the Bank or remaining unpaid by the Customer to the Bank, whether arising from dealings between the Bank and the Customer or from other dealings or proceedings by which the Bank may be or become in any manner whatever a creditor of the Customer, and wherever incurred, and whether incurred by the Customer alone or with another or others and whether as principal or surety, including all interest, commissions, legal and other costs, charges and expenses (such debts and liabilities being herein called the "guaranteed liabilities"), the liability of the undersigned hereunder being limited to the sum of

[Insert Limit, if any.] .... dollars with interest from the date of demand for payment at the rate set out in paragraph 5 hereof.

AS WITNESS the hand and seal of the Guarantor at _____, this   day of   , 19   .

SIGNED SEALED AND DELIVERED
        in the presence of   SIGNATURE AND SEAL

....

....

....

....

....

N.B.-Signature of this Guarantee involves personal liability.
The following extract, gives a short account of the principal features of the seal.

IN WITNESS whereof I have hereunto set my hand and seal.

SIGNED, SEALED AND DELIVERED
in the presence of:

_____ { Affix Seal }
                    (Purchaser)

_____ { Affix Seal }
                    (Purchaser)

That part of the document which starts, "In witness,..." is the "testimonium". The attestation clause states that the document is "signed, sealed and delivered". In practice none of these are necessary. Signing is not strictly necessary (though nowadays it is probably invariably present) since the use of the seal antedated the widespread practice of signing documents. At common law the seal originally had to be wax and imprinted — according to Coke. Now a red wafer or printed blob or circle (usually with the letters "l.s" in the middle) suffices. Delivery of a sealed instrument is not necessary: the document can bind even though it never left the obligor's possession. The promise must, however, be in writing.

There are several other consequences of a promise being made under seal, for example, an action on a sealed instrument can be brought at any time within 20 years after making as opposed to the usual six-year limitation period.

DAWSON and HARVEY
3rd. ed. pp. 190-193

AUTHENTICATION THROUGH SEAL OR WRITING

1. The Seal

By the late Middle Ages the English common law had developed a highly serviceable, all-purpose formality, the seal. It was used to authenticate transfers of ownership, especially transfers of interests in land by way of "deed", and also to make promises enforceable. For breach of a promise under seal the action of covenant, leading to a judgment for damages, became a standard common law remedy. Indeed, until about 1500 it was almost the only remedy available for breach of promise. There was, it is true, the still more ancient action of debt... but its utility was limited: it could be used only to recover a sum of money already due and fixed in amount. It was not until relatively late — the sixteenth century — that common law courts developed a generalized damage remedy for breach of contract, which acquired the title of special assumpsit. It gave damages for breach of a variety of informal promises that did not fit the pattern of the half-completed exchange for which debt could be used. Until then, and indeed for a long time thereafter, especially in transactions that had been carefully planned because the interests at stake were important, the contract under seal was the prototype for consensual transactions and carried the main workload.

By the tests suggested in the passage just quoted, describing the functions that legal formalities can perform, the seal in its heyday deserved a high rating. The requirements were strict. In the early seventeenth century, according to the testimony of a well-known judge-reporter, Sir Edward Coke, it was necessary for a valid seal that heated wax, impressed with a mark, be actually affixed to the document that was to be authenticated. As to the mark itself there was some leeway: persons of importance would no doubt use their own family seals embellished with mottos but the impression could be made with a signet ring, a finger or, according to one early report, the bite of a foretooth. Heating the seal and placing an imprint on the document would be quite likely to arrest the participants' attention. Signature or a mark by the person making the transfer or promise would also be required. And there was one more step, delivery — a physical surrender of the document to the grantee or promisee or someone authorized to act on his behalf. A ceremony with all these elements was surely calculated (deliberately calculated, it seems, by those who conceived it) to produce persuasive evidence, to make a sharp impression on the participants and provide visible signs of authenticity.

If the prescribed formalities were followed, nothing more was needed to make a promise under seal enforceable. The requirement of consideration, which we will soon encounter, was invented as a control over informal (unsealed) promises long after promises under seal had come to be regularly enforced. Some modern decisions have mentioned a "presumption" of consideration that the seal produces but in states where the seal still has its common law effects the presumption is conclusive or, in other words, consideration is not needed. One of the questions to keep in mind is whether persons who are fully capable and not under the influence of drugs or alcohol should have power to bind themselves by promise merely because they seriously intend to do so. One way to confer this power is to provide a ceremonial — a stereotyped formality — such as the signing, sealing and delivery of a written document. In more than half our states this is no longer possible.

In its classical development, during the fifteenth and sixteenth centuries, common law doctrine made the sealed promise not only enforceable but almost invulnerable to attack. The individual whose signature and seal appeared on a document could no doubt show that both were placed there through forgery and without his knowledge. If he did in fact sign and seal he could show that the nature and legal effect of the document had been misrepresented to him ("fraud in the factum"). But he could not show in a common law action any other kind of fraud or mistake (e.g., that the diseased horse for which he had promised under seal to pay had been fraudulently described as healthy). Nor could he show that he had not received the performance promised him in return, or that he had already fully performed his own obligation without securing a cancellation or release under seal, or that the agreement evidenced by the sealed document had been superseded by a subsequent informal agreement of the parties.

These attitudes of common law courts were quite a bit less than half the story since the Chancellor took very different attitudes that he usually made prevail. Indeed, relief against misuse or abuse of sealed instruments had become, by the sixteenth century at least, a major activity of the Chancery. Fraud or mistake in the making of sealed contracts, payment without securing cancellation or release, and subsequent modification by informal agreement became standard grounds for intervention by the Chancellors. The correctives they introduced served to bring the sealed instrument back within the framework of a rational scheme of contract law. Some of these correctives were so obviously needed that they were gradually absorbed within the common law system. It has been true for a long time, for example, that payment can be pleaded directly as a defense by the obligor when sued at law on a sealed instrument. In many states this is also true of fraud or mistakes in the formation of the transaction, though in others a legacy remains in the form of a distinction making defenses of fraud, mistake, or breach by the opposite party "equitable" issues that must be decided, when issues of fact are disputed, by a judge rather than a jury. There were other problems that took longer to solve, such as the invulnerability of sealed promises to modification or revision by mutual agreement (the older law required an instrument of "equal dignity") and the limitation of the right to sue to the parties to the covenant (thus barring beneficiaries and undisclosed principals). Difficulties of this kind were not inherent or inevitable features of formalized legal transactions. They reflected the technicality and rigidity that the common law system showed in many other areas as well. In states that preserve the seal these problems have been dealt with, sometimes by courts without help from express legislation.

In order to preserve a legal formality a price must be paid. The history of the seal makes it plain that the opinion-makers in Anglo-American law did not consider the advantages gained to be worth the price. That history can be summarized briefly: gradual erosion of the requirements of form gradually drained off the solemnity and thereby destroyed the usefulness of the seal. The erosion occurred in several ways. Dilution of the requirement of delivery can illustrate the mental processes at work. It is clear and has been clear for a long time that the mere physical surrender of a document is meaningless of itself — the purpose may be merely to permit another person to inspect it. The essential factor is the intent of the transferor to endow the document, by that act, with legal consequences. So a delivery to some third person or various kinds of "symbolic" delivery should do just as well and restrictions or qualifications desired by the transferor (e.g., postponing all legal effect until some future event should occur) should be enforced. Then if it was intent, not acts, that counted, why insist on the ancient formalities; was it really necessary to heat up wax and stick it on a piece of paper? Why not use another piece of paper on which a mark of some kind had been made and stick it on with adhesive? Or why was it not enough for the signer merely to recite in the document that he considered it to be under seal? As printed forms came into wider circulation it became common practice simply to print after the space provided for signature the word "seal" or the letters "L.S.". Even signers who remembered some Latin would have no particular reason to know that L.S. is short-hand for the Latin phrase *locus sigilli*, meaning "place of the seal". These various dilutions of the ancient formality were clearly inspired by impatience with what seemed to be purely external trivia as compared with the overriding purpose of enforcing the signers' intent. Accepting these various substitutes could seem fully justified by the result, *enlarging* the power of promisors to bind themselves by promise if they used the right words or did the right acts. The irony was that the words and acts used for the purpose lost meaning, especially as they became standard features of widely used printed forms, so that the impulse grew stronger to cut off this path to promissory obligation and destroy the power altogether.

The attitudes that have inspired much modern legislation were well expressed by the New York Law Revision Commission in 1940 in recommending a statute that deprived the seal of all legal effect (Report, pp. 359-360):

> "The seal has degenerated into a L.S. or other scrawl which, in modern practice, is frequently a printed L.S. upon a printed form. To the average man it conveys no meaning, and frequently the parties to instruments upon which it appears have no idea of its legal effects. Moreover, under the present law, the character of an instrument which bears the magic letters, but which contains no recital of sealing, is left uncertain as to whether it is sealed, depending upon parol evidence of intent to be later adduced (Transbel Investment Co. v. Venetos, 279 N.Y. 207, 18 N.E.2d 129 (1938)). It would seem, therefore, that if a method of making promises binding without consideration is desirable, some method should be devised which more clearly than the seal brings to the attention of the promisor what he is doing, and which fixes the character of the instrument as of the time of its execution....
>
> "Concerning the broader question whether, and to what extent, a person should be able to bind himself by a promise without consideration, the Commission doubts the wisdom of any device that is applicable to all kinds of promises under all circumstances. Certainly the seal is not the best device, assuming some such device is desirable."

NOTE: Chilliback v. Pawliuk (supra, Sec. A) makes it clear that the mere existence of a seal does not remove the general problems of the enforceability of agreements.

C. Consideration

(1) THE BARGAIN THEORY. CONSIDERATION AS EXCHANGE

The following statements are often quoted as the classic statements of the doctrine of consideration:

Currie v. Misa (1875), L.R. 10 Ex. 153, 162; affirmed, 1 App. Cas. 554. Lush J:
> ... A valuable consideration, in the sense of the law, may consist either in some right, interest, profit, or benefit accruing to the one party, or some forbearance, detriment, loss, or responsibility, given, suffered, or undertaken by the other.

Dunlop v. Selfridges, [1915] A.C. 847, 855. Lord Dunedin:
> ... I am content to adopt from a work of Sir Frederick Pollock, to which I have often been under obligation, the following words as to consideration: "An act or forbearance of one party, or the promise thereof is the price for which the promise of the other is bought, and the promise thus given for value is enforceable. (Pollock on Contracts, 8th ed., p. 175.)

Hobbes, *Leviathan*, 1651, Ch. 15.
> ... The value of all things contracted for, is measured by the Appetite of the Contractors: and therefore the just value, is that which they be contented to give.

Sir Anthony Shirlyn v. Albany, Q.B., (1587), 1 Cro. Eliz. 67.
> ... for when a thing is to be done by the plaintiff be it never so small, this is a sufficient consideration to ground an action.

Westlake v. Adams (1858), 5 C.B. (N.S.) 248, 265; 141 E.R. 99, 106. Byles J:
> ... It is an elementary principle, that the law will not enter into an inquiry as to the adequacy of the consideration; so that much less consideration than here existed might have sufficed.
>
> Lastly, it must be remembered that the defendant in this case has received a full performance of the terms of the indenture at the hands of the plaintiff. The jury have, I think, made an end of the question; for, they have found (as they well might) that the defendant received what he bargained for, and all that he bargained for.

Do you think that they are useful in deciding what promises should be enforced?

The requirement of consideration in the Restatement II (Tentative Draft # 2, 1965) is the following:

§ 75. Requirement of Exchange; Types of Exchange.
(1) To constitute consideration, a performance or a return promise must be bargained for.
(2) A performance or return promise is bargained for if it is sought by the promisor in exchange for his promise and is given by the promisee in exchange for that promise.
(3) The performance may consist of
(a) an act other than a promise, or
(b) a forbearance, or
(c) the creation, modification or destruction of a legal relation.
(4) The performance or return promise may be given to the promisor or to some other person. It may be given by the promisee or by some other person.

Do you think that this is helpful?

The following cases illustrate some of the problems of determining what promises will be enforced.

WHITE v. BLUETT

(1853), 23 L.J. Ex. (N.S.) 36.

The declaration contained a count upon a promissory note made by the defendant payable to the testator, and a count for money lent.

. . .

And the defendant further saith, that the said J. Bluett was the father of the defendant, and that afterwards, and after the accruing of the causes of action to which this plea is pleaded, and before this suit, and in the lifetime of the said J. Bluett, the defendant complained to his said father that he, the defendant, had not received at his hands so much money or so many advantages as the other children of the said J. Bluett, and certain controversies arose between the defendant and his said father concerning the premises, and the said J. Bluett afterwards admitted and declared to the defendant that his, the defendant's, said complaints were well founded, and therefore, afterwards, &c. it was agreed by and between the said J. Bluett and the defendant, that the defendant should for ever cease to make such complaints, and that in consideration thereof, and in order to do justice to the defendant, and also out of his, the said J. Bluett's, natural love and affection towards the defendant, he, the said J. Bluett, would discharge the defendant of and from all liability in respect of the causes of action to which this plea is pleaded, and would accept the said agreement on his, the defendant's, part in full satisfaction and discharge of the said last-mentioned causes of action; and the defendant further saith, that afterwards, and in the lifetime of the said J. Bluett, and before this suit, he, the said J. Bluett, did accept of and from the defendant the said agreement as aforesaid, in full satisfaction and discharge of such mentioned causes of action.

. . .

Pollock, C.B. — The plea is clearly bad. By the argument a principle is pressed to an absurdity, as a bubble is blown until it bursts. Looking at the words merely there is some foundation for the argument, and, following the words only, the conclusion may be arrived at. It is said, the son had a right to an equal distribution of his father's property, and did complain to his father because he had not an equal share, and said to him, I will cease to complain if you will not sue upon this note. Whereupon the father said, if you will promise me not to complain I will give up the note. If such a plea as this could be supported, the following would be a binding promise: A man might complain that another person used the public highway more than he ought to do, and that other might say, do not complain, and I will give you five pounds. It is ridiculous to suppose that such promises could be binding. So, if the holder of a bill of exchange were suing the acceptor, and the acceptor were to complain that the holder had treated him hardly, or that the bill ought never to have been circulated, and the holder were to say, Now, if you will not make any more complaints, I will not sue you. Such a promise would be like that now set up. In reality, there was no consideration whatever. The son had no right to complain, for the father might make what distribution of his property he liked; and the son's abstaining from doing what he had no right to do can be no consideration.

THOMAS v. THOMAS
(1842) 2 Q.B. 851; 144 E.R. 330.

... At the trial, before Coltman J., at the Glamorganshire Lent Assizes, 1841, it appeared that John Thomas, the deceased husband of the plaintiff, at the time of his death, in 1837, was possessed of a row of seven dwelling houses in Merthyr Tidvil, in one of which, being the dwelling house in question, he was himself residing; and that by his will he appointed his brother Samuel Thomas (since deceased) and the defendant executors thereof, to take possession of all his houses, &c., subject to certain payments in the will mentioned, among which were certain charges in money for the benefit of the plaintiff. In the evening before the day of his death, he expressed orally a wish to make some further provision for his wife; and on the following morning he declared orally, in the presence of two witnesses, that it was his will that his wife should have either the house in which he lived and all that it contained, or an additional sum of 100l. instead thereof.

This declaration being shortly afterwards brought to the knowledge of Samuel Thomas and the defendant, the executors and residuary legatees, they consented to carry the intention of the testator so expressed into effect; and, after the lapse of a few days, they and the plaintiff executed the agreement declared upon; which, after stating the parties, and briefly reciting the will, proceeded as follows.

"And, whereas the said testator, shortly before his death, declared, in the presence of several witnesses, that he was desirous his said wife should have and enjoy during her life, or so long as she should continue his widow, all and singular the dwelling house," &c., "or £100, out of his personal estate," in addition to the respective legacies and bequests given her in and by his said will; "but such declaration and desire was not reduced to writing in the lifetime of the said John Thomas and read over to him; but the said Samuel Thomas and Benjamin Thomas are fully convinced and satisfied that such was the desire of the said testator, and are willing and desirous that such intention should be carried into full effect: now these presents witness, and it is hereby agreed and declared by and between the parties, that, in consideration of such desire and of the premises," the executors would convey the dwelling house, &c. to the plaintiff and her assigns during her life, or for so long a time as she should continue a widow and unmarried: "provided nevertheless, and it is hereby further agreed and declared, that the said Eleanor Thomas, or her assigns, shall and will, at all times during which she shall have possession of the said dwelling house, &c., pay to the said Samuel Thomas and Benjamin Thomas, their executors, &c., the sum of 1l. yearly towards the ground rent payable in respect of the said dwelling house and other premises thereto adjoining, and shall and will keep the said dwelling house and premises in good and tenantable repair:" with other provisions not affecting the questions in this case.

The plaintiff was left in possession of the dwelling house and premises for some time: but the defendant, after the death of his co-executor, refused to execute a conveyance tendered to him for execution pursuant to the agreement, and shortly before the trial, brought an ejectment, under which he turned the plaintiff out of possession....

Ultimately a verdict was found for the plaintiff on all the issues; and, in Easter term last, a rule nisi was obtained pursuant to the leave reserved.

...

Lord Denman C.J. There is nothing in this case but a great deal of ingenuity, and a little wilful blindness to the actual terms of the instrument itself. There is nothing whatever to shew that the ground rent was payable to a superior landlord; and the stipulation for the payment of it is not a mere proviso, but an express agreement. (His Lordship here read the proviso.) This is in terms on express agreement, and shews a sufficient legal consideration quite independent of the moral feeling which disposed the executors to enter into such a contract. Mr. Williams's definition of consideration is too large: the word causa in the passage referred to means one which confers what the law considers a benefit on the party. Then the obligation to repair is one which might impose charges heavier than the value of the life estate.

Patteson J. It would be giving to causa too large a construction if we were to adopt the view urged for the defendant: it would be confounding consideration with motive. Motive is not the same thing with consideration. Consideration means something which is of some value in the eye of the law, moving from the plaintiff: it may be some benefit to the plaintiff, or some detriment to the defendant; but at all events it must be moving from the plaintiff. Now that which is suggested as the consideration here, a pious respect for the wishes of the testator, does not in any way move from the plaintiff; it moves from the testator; therefore, legally speaking, it forms no part of the consideration. Then it is said that, if that be so, there is no consideration at all, it is a mere voluntary gift; but when we look at the agreement we find that this is not a mere proviso that the donee shall take the gift with the burthens; but it is an express agreement to pay what seems to be a fresh apportionment of a ground rent, and which is made payable not to a superior landlord but to the executors. So that this rent is clearly not something incident to the assignment of the house; for in that case, instead of being payable to the executors, it would have been payable to the landlord. Then as to the repairs: these houses may very possibly be held under a lease containing covenants to repair; but we know nothing about it: for any thing that appears, the liability to repair is first created by this instrument. The proviso certainly struck me at first as Mr. Williams put it, that the rent and repairs were merely attached to the gift by the donors; and, had the instrument been executed by the donors only, there might have been some ground for that construction; but the fact is not so. Then it is suggested that this would be held to be a mere voluntary conveyance as against a subsequent purchaser for value: possibly that might be so: but suppose it would: the plaintiff contracts to take it, and does take it, whatever it is, for better for worse: perhaps a bona fide purchase for a valuable consideration might override it; but that cannot be helped.
Rule discharged
   [Coleridge J.'s judgment was to the same effect.]

HAMER v. SIDWAY

(1891), 27 N.E. 256. Court of Appeals of New York.

... The plaintiff presented a claim to the executor of William E. Story, Sr., for $5,000 and interest from the 6th day of February, 1875. She acquired it through several mesne assignments from William E. Story, 2d. The claim being rejected by the executor, this action was brought. It appears that William E. Story, Sr., was the uncle of William E. Story, 2d; that at the celebration of the golden wedding of Samuel Story and wife, father and mother of William E. Story, Sr., on the 20th day of March, 1869, in the presence of the family and invited guests, he promised his nephew that if he would refrain from drinking, using tobacco, swearing, and playing cards or billiards for money until he became 21 years of age, he would pay him the sum of $5,000. The nephew assented thereto, and fully performed the conditions inducing the promise. When the nephew arrived at the age of 21 years, and on the 31st day of January, 1875, he wrote to his uncle informing him that he had performed his part of the agreement, and had thereby become entitled to the sum of $5,000. The uncle received the letter, and a few days later, and on the 6th day of February, he wrote and mailed to his nephew the following letter: "Buffalo, Feb. 6, 1875. W. E. Story, Jr. — Dear Nephew: Your letter of the 31st ult. came to hand all right, saying that you had lived up to the promise made to me several years ago. I have no doubt but you have, for which you shall have five thousand dollars, as I promised you. I had the money in the bank the day you was twenty-one years old that I intend for you, and you shall have the money certain. Now, Willie, I do not intend to interfere with this money in any way till I think you are capable of taking care of it, and the sooner that time comes the better it will please me. I would hate very much to have you start out in some adventure that you thought all right and lose this money in one year. The first five thousand dollars that I got together cost me a heap of hard work. You would hardly believe me when I tell you that to obtain this I shoved a jack-plane many a day, butchered three or four years, then came to this city, and, after three months' perseverance, I obtained a situation in a grocery store. I opened this store early, closed late, slept in the fourth story of the building in a room 30 by 40 feet, and not a human being in the building but myself. All this I done to live as cheap as I could to save something. I don't want you to take up with this kind of fare. I was here in the cholera season of '49 and '52, and the deaths averaged 80 to 125 daily, and plenty of small-pox. I wanted to go home, but Mr. Fisk, the gentleman I was working for, told me, if I left them, after it got healthy he probably would not want me. I stayed. All the money I have saved I know just how I got it. It did not come to me in any mysterious way, and the reason I speak of this is that money got in this way stops longer with a fellow that gets it with hard knocks than it does when he finds it. Willie, you are twenty-one, and you have many a thing to learn yet. This money you have earned much easier than I did, besides acquiring good habits at the same time, and you are quite welcome to the money. Hope you will make good use of it. I was ten long years getting this together after I was your age. Now, hoping this will be satisfactory, I stop. One thing more. Twenty-one years ago I bought you 15 sheep. These sheep were put out to double every four years. I kept track of them the first eight years. I have not heard much about them since. Your father and grandfather promised me that they would look after them till you were of age. Have they done so? I hope they have. By this time you have between five and six hundred sheep, worth a nice little income this spring. Willie, I have said much more than I expected to. Hope you can make out what I have written. To-day is the seventeenth day that I have not been out of my room, and have had the doctor as many days. Am a little better to day. Think I will get out next week. You need not mention to father, as he always worries about small matters. Truly yours; W. E. STORY. P.S. You can consider this money on interest." The nephew received the letter, and thereafter consented that the money should remain with his uncle in accordance with the terms and conditions of the letter. The uncle died on the 29th day of January, 1887, without having paid over to his nephew any portion of the said $5,000 and interest....

Parker, J., (*after stating the facts as above.*) The question which provoked the most discussion by counsel on this appeal, and which lies at the foundation of plaintiff's asserted right of recovery, is whether by virtue of a contract defendant's testator, William E. Story, became indebted to his nephew, William E. Story, 2d, on his twenty-first birthday in the sum of $5,000. The trial court found as a fact that "on the 20th day of March, 1869,... William E. Story agreed to and with William E. Story, 2d, that if he would refrain from drinking liquor, using tobacco, swearing, and playing cards or billiards for money until should become twenty-one years of age, then he, the said William E. Story, would at that time pay him, the said William E. Story, 2d, the sum of $5,000 for such refraining, to which the said William E. Story, 2d, agreed," and that he "in all things fully performed his part of said agreement." The defendant contends that the contract was without consideration to support it, and therefore invalid. He asserts that the promisee, by refraining from the use of liquor and tobacco, was not harmed, but benefited; that that which he did was best for him to do, independently of his uncle's promise, — and insists that it follows that, unless the promisor was benefited, the contract was without consideration, — a contention which, if well founded, would seem to leave open for controversy in many cases whether that which the promisee did or omitted to do was in fact of such benefit to him as to leave no consideration to support the enforcement of the promisor's agreement. Such a rule could not be tolerated, and is without foundation in the law. The exchequer chamber in 1875 defined "consideration" as follows: "A valuable consideration, in the sense of the law, may consist either in some right, interest, profit, or benefit accruing to the one party, or some forbearance, detriment, loss, or responsibility given, suffered, or undertaken by the other." Courts "will not ask whether the thing which forms the consideration does in fact benefit the promisee or a third party, or is of any substantial value to any one. It is enough that something is promised, done, forborne, or suffered by the party to whom the promise is made as consideration for the promise made to him." Anson, Cont. 63. "In general a waiver of any legal right at the request of another party is a sufficient consideration for a promise." Pars. Cont. *444. "Any damage, or suspension, or forbearance of a right will be sufficient to sustain a promise." 2 Kent, Comm. (12th Ed.) *465. Pollock in his work on Contracts, (page 166), after citing the definition given by the exchequer chamber, already quoted, says: "The second branch of this judicial description is really the most important one. 'Consideration' means not so much that one party is profiting as that the other abandons some legal right in the present, or limits his legal freedom of action in the future, as an inducement for the promise of the first." Now, applying this rule to the facts before us, the promisee used tobacco, occasionally drank liquor, and he had a legal right to do so. That right he abandoned for a period of years upon the strength of the promise of the testator that for such forbearance he would give him $5,000. We need not speculate on the effort which may have been required to give up the use of those stimulants. It is sufficient that he restricted his lawful freedom of action within certain prescribed limits upon the faith of his uncle's agreement, and now, having fully performed the conditions imposed, it is of no moment whether such performance actually proved a benefit to the promisor, and the court will not inquire into it; but, were it a proper subject of inquiry, we see nothing in this record that would permit a determination that the uncle was not benefited in a legal sense...

All concur.

QUESTIONS

1. Consider in each of these cases whether the promises involve gifts or exchanges? Can they all be put in one or other category?

2. Are the results consistent with the expected consequences of your classification?

3. Do you think that it was important in *Hamer v. Sidway* that the promise was made at the golden wedding anniversary party?

4. What is meant by the phrase, "the son had no right to complain..." in *White v. Bluett*?

PROBLEMS

1. Margaret is discovered by her sister, Maureen, reading Playgirl magazine. Both know that this magazine is regarded as grossly obscene by their father. Margaret promises to pay Maureen $100 if Maureen does not tell her father. Can Maureen recover from Margaret?

2. Harvey is a very nervous law student, especially when writing exams. When about to write the final exam in Contracts, he announces to all the students in the examination room that if there is no coughing, shuffling of feet, etc. in the examination he will pay them each $10. Is he liable if the other students comply with his request?

3. What would be the result if he asked them to stop smoking and there was a sign stating that smoking was prohibited?

The doctrine of consideration is the principal method the common law has for determining what contracts should be enforced. But it is capable of hiding many other factors which might reasonably be expected to enter into the court's judgment whether or not any particular contract should be enforced. We must disentangle many of the issues that the use of the doctrine of consideration leaves untouched and unarticulated. For example, some of the cases and problems we have discussed have raised the issue of inequality of bargaining power between the parties. Others have led us to consider why one enforces promises made as part of an exchange transaction and not gift promises.

In Milner, *Cases and Materials on Contracts*, the following story from *Huckleberry Finn* is re-told. This extract is taken from Pound, "Law in Books and Law in Action" (1910) 44 American L.R. 12.

"When Tom Sawyer and Huck Finn had determined to rescue Jim by digging under the cabin where he was confined, it seemed to the uninformed lay mind of Huck Finn that some old picks the boys had found were the proper implements to use. But Tom knew better. From reading he knew what was the right course in such cases, and he called for case-knives. 'It don't make no difference', said Tom, 'how foolish it is, it's the right way — and it's the regular way. And there ain't no other way that ever I heard of, and I've read all the books that gives any information about these things. They always dig out with a case-knife.' So, in deference to the books and the proprieties, the boys set to work with case-knives. But after they had dug till nearly midnight and they were tired and their hands were blistered, and they had made little progress, a light came to Tom's legal mind. He dropped his knife and, turning to Huck, said firmly, 'Gimme a case-knife.' Let Huck tell the rest:

" 'He had his own by him, but I handed him mine. He flung it down and says, "Gimme a case-knife."

" 'I didn't know just what to do — but then I thought, I scratched around amongst the old tools and got a pickaxe and give it to him, and he took it and went to work and never said a word.

" 'He was always just that particular. Full of principle.'

"Tom had made over again one of the earlier discoveries of the law. When tradition prescribed case-knives for tasks for which pickaxes were better adapted, it seemed better to our forefathers, after a little vain struggle with case-knives, to adhere to principle — but use the pickaxes. They granted that law ought not to change. Changes in law were full of danger. But, on the other hand, it was highly inconvenient to use case-knives. And so the law has always managed to get a pickaxe in its hands, though it steadfastly demanded a case-knife, and to wield it in the virtuous belief that it was using the approved instrument."

The doctrine of consideration is a "case-knife". It is used by the courts as a test which performs a multitude of functions.

The first point which must be borne in mind is that the law has developed historically. We have not so far, made much of the fact that one case may have been decided in 1854, e.g. *Hadley v. Baxendale* and another in 1967, *e.g., The Heron II*. But the changes in society, in economic relations, in political, economic and social ideas between 1854 and 1967 have been dramatic. There is little basis for a belief that what was a sensible result in 1854 will be sensible in 1967, or 1978. To understand the doctrine of consideration we have to keep in mind its historical development.

It has been argued that the doctrine of consideration is a purely nineteenth century development. Thus Professor Gilmore of the Yale Law School has suggested that Holmes and Langdell (the father of the so-called "case method") together invented the doctrine. (*The Death of Contract*, Columbus, Ohio, 1974). The development of consideration, on this view is part of a theory that Gilmore describes as follows: (pp. 14, 15)

The theory seems to have been dedicated to the proposition that, ideally, no one should be liable to anyone for anything. Since the ideal was not attainable, the compromise solution was to restrict liability within the narrowest possible limits. Within those limits, however, liability was to be absolute: as Holmes put it, "The only universal consequence of a legally binding promise is, that the law makes the promisor pay damages if the promised event does not come to pass." Liability, although absolute — at least in theory — was nevertheless, to be severely limited. The equitable remedy of specific performance was to be avoided so far as possible — no doubt we would all be better off if Lord Coke's views had prevailed in the seventeenth century and the equitable remedy had never developed at all. Money damages for breach of contract were to be "compensatory," never punitive; the contract-breaker's motivation, Holmes explained, makes no legal difference whatever and indeed every man has a right "to break his contract if he chooses" — that is, a right to elect to pay damages instead of performing his contractual obligation. Therefore the wicked contract-breaker should pay no more in damages than the innocent and the pure in heart. The "compensatory" damages, which were theoretically recoverable, turned out to be a good deal less than enough to compensate the victim for the losses which in fact he might have suffered. Damages in contract, it was pointed out, were one thing and damages in tort another; the contract-breaker was not to be held responsible, as the tortfeasor was, for all consequences of his actions. Another aspect of the theory was that the courts should operate as detached umpires or referees, doing no more than to see that the rules of the game were observed and refusing to intervene affirmatively to see that justice or anything of that sort was done. Courts do not, it was said, make contracts for the parties. The parties themselves must see that the last i is properly dotted, the last t properly crossed; the courts will not do it for them. And if A, without the protection of a binding contract, improvidently relies, to his detriment, on B's promises and assurances, that may be unfortunate for A but is no fit matter for legal concern. Contract liability, furthermore, was to be sharply differentiated from tort liability and there was to be no softening or blurring of the harsh limitations of contract theory by the recognition of an intermediate no-man's-land between contract and tort; the idea which later flourished as "quasi-contract" was no part of the Holmesian theory.

A key part of this view of contracts was the notion of consideration. Consideration in Holmes' view was not simply either benefit or detriment. It was only consideration if the parties dealt with it as consideration. The function that the doctrine of consideration had was therefore to make sure that very few obligations would be imposed by contract. This view of consideration does, as we shall see, bear some resemblance to what the courts have done with it. It can be used to provide a theoretical basis for a great many rules that are very hard to justify.

The Death of Contract is well worth reading and there are enough ideas to stimulate a lot of discussion about contract theory. However a word of warning is necessary. The nineteenth century did have a fantastic impact on the law that we have today. To a truly amazing extent ideas that were first formulated then have proved to be extremely durable. Sometimes these ideas were useful and lead to better solutions to problems that might bother us. More often, the ideas were harmful and we shall see that much of the modern developments in the law are simply efforts to avoid rules that we should never have had in the first place. It is far harder than Gilmore suggests, however, to pin the blame for what happened on people like Holmes and Langdell. The actual appearance of the legal theories taken over by Holmes and Langdell did not take place at the end of the century when they were writing. There are cases as early as 1809 where the view that we can characterize as nineteenth century can be found. There are cases as late as 1869 where eighteenth century ideas are very much alive. It is also a mistake to think (though Gilmore does not make this mistake) that only in contracts do we find the "nineteenth century" phenomenon. The courts are doing odd things in many areas of the law. We shall, of course, be principally concerned with the contractual manifestations of this phenomenon.

The significance of Gilmore's theory is that it bears on the following issues:

1. To what extent are the rules that we have the product of a particular view of contracts that may be no longer valid?
2. To what extent has the development of the law been influenced by,
   (a)   the views of particular writers, and
   (b)   the fact that certain cases and not others became "leading cases"?
   (c)   the subdivision of the law into discrete categories with little or no attempt at synthesis. (Such subdivision occurs in works like Cana-

dian Abridgments, Halsbury's Laws of England and even in text-books. Cases on contracts, mortgages, insurance and real estate transactions are put in different volumes.)

3. We cannot begin to understand the development of the law unless we realize that it must, at each stage of its development, share the prevalent philosophies, social and economic views of those who participate in its development.

As you read the cases that follow keep these issues in mind.

[For comments on Gilmore's book, see:

Milhollin: (1974), 24 Catholic University Law Review, 29.

Gordon: Book Review, [1974] Wisconsin Law Review, 1216.

Speidel: Book Review (1975), 27 Stanford Law Review, 1161.

Gordley: Book Review (1975), 89 Harv. L.R. 452.

Horwitz: Book Review (1975), 42 U. of Chic. L.R. 787.]

An alternative view of the development of the law of contracts in the nineteenth century is offered in: Horwitz, *The Transformation of American Law, 1780-1860.* 1977, especially chapter 6.

The sections that follow raise specific problems of the doctrine of consideration. To what extent are the problems real or simply the result of theoretical or conceptual views of the doctrine?

(2) PAST CONSIDERATION

The first group of problem cases are cases where the promise being sued upon is unenforceable because the consideration is said to be past. The first case, *Mills v. Wyman,* is typical of this class. There the defendant had promised to pay the plaintiff for looking after the defendant's son before the son died. The plaintiff had not looked after the defendant's son at the defendant's request and what the plaintiff did occurred before the promise to pay was made. The consideration for the defendant's promise was therefore "past".

The questions that we have to answer in this case include the following:

1. Are there any good reasons for being worried about the enforcement of this kind of promise?

2. What interest of the plaintiff would be protected by enforcement?

3. What distinguishes the cases in this section from those like *Deglman v. Guaranty Trust, Matheson v. Smiley, etc.?*

4. What is the court afraid of when it refuses to recognize a moral obligation as the basis for enforcement?

5. What ways are there around the problems caused by the fact that consideration is past?

MILLS v. WYMAN

(1825), 3 Pick. (Mass.) 207. Supreme Judicial Court of Massachusetts.

[This was an action of assumpsit brought to recover a compensation for the board, nursing, etc., of Levi Wyman, son of the defendant, from the 5th to the 20th of February, 1821. The plaintiff then lived at Hartford, in Connecticut; the defendant, at Shrewsbury, in this county. Levi Wyman, at the time when the services were rendered, was about 25 years of age, and had long ceased to be a member of his father's family. He was on his return from a voyage at sea, and being suddenly taken sick at Hartford, and being poor and in distress, was relieved by the plaintiff in the manner and to the extent above stated. On February 24, after all the expenses had been incurred, the defendant wrote a letter to the plaintiff, promising to pay him such expenses. There was no consideration for this promise, except what grew out of the relation which subsisted between Levi Wyman and the defendant. Howe J., before whom the cause was tried in the court of common pleas, thinking this not sufficient to support the action, directed a nonsuit. To this direction the plaintiff filed exceptions.]

The opinion of the Court was read, as drawn up by

Parker C.J.: General rules of law established for the protection and security of honest and fair-minded men, who may inconsiderately make promises without any equivalent, will sometimes screen men of a different character from engagements which they are bound in *foro conscienticoe* to perform. This is a defect inherent in all human systems of legislation. The rule that a mere verbal promise, without any consideration, cannot be enforced by action, is universal in its application, and cannot be departed from to suit particular cases in which a refusal to perform such a promise may be disgraceful.

The promise declared on in this case appears to have been made without any legal consideration. The kindness and services towards the sick son of the defendant were not bestowed at his request. The son was in no respect under the care of the defendant. He was twenty-five years old, and had long left his father's family. On his return from a foreign country, he fell sick among strangers, and the plaintiff acted the part of the good Samaritan, giving him shelter and comfort until he died. The defendant, his father, on being informed of this event, influenced by a transient feeling of gratitude, promises in writing to pay the plaintiff for the expenses he had incurred. But he has determined to break this promise, and is willing to have his case appear on record as a strong example of particular injustice sometimes necessarily resulting from the operation of general rules.

It is said a moral obligation is a sufficient consideration to support an express promise; and some authorities lay down the rule thus broadly; but upon examination of the cases we are satisfied that the universality of the rule cannot be supported, and that there must have been some pre-existing obligation, which has become inoperative by positive law, to form a basis for an effective promise. The cases of debts barred by the statute of limitations, of debts incurred by infants, of debts of bankrupts, are generally put for illustration of the rule. Express promises founded on such pre-existing equitable obligations may be enforced; there is a good consideration for them; they merely remove an impediment created by law to the recovery of debts honestly due, but which public policy protects the debtors from being compelled to pay. In all these cases there was originally a *quid pro quo*; and according to the principles of natural justice the party receiving ought to pay; but the legislature has said he shall not be coerced; then comes the promise to pay the debt that is barred, the promise of the man to pay the debt of the infant, of the discharged bankrupt to restore to his creditor what by the law he had lost. In all these cases there is a moral obligation founded upon an antecedent valuable consideration. These promises therefore have a sound legal basis. They are not promises to pay something for nothing; not naked pacts; but the voluntary revival or creation of obligation which before existed in natural law, but which had been dispensed with, not for the benefit of the party obliged solely, but principally for the public convenience. If moral obligation, in its fullest sense, is a good substratum for an express promise, it is not easy to perceive why it is not equally good to support an implied promise. What a man ought to do, generally he ought to be made to do, whether he promise or refuse. But the law of society has left most of such obligations to the *interior* forum, as the tribunal of conscience has been aptly called. Is there not a moral obligation upon every son who has become affluent by means of the education and advantages bestowed upon him by his father, to relieve that father from pecuniary embarrassment, to promote his comfort and happiness, and even to share with him his riches, if thereby he will be made happy? And yet such a son may, with impunity, leave such a father in any degree of penury above that which will expose the community in which he dwells, to the danger of being obliged to preserve him from absolute want. Is not a wealthy father under strong moral obligation to advance the interest of an obedient, well disposed son, to furnish him with the means of acquiring and maintaining a becoming rank in life, to rescue him from the horrors of debt incurred by misfortune? Yet the law will uphold him in any degree of parsimony, short of that which would reduce his son to the necessity of seeking public charity.

Without doubt there are great interests of society which justify withholding the coercive arm of the law from these duties of imperfect obligation, as they are called; imperfect, not because they are less binding upon the conscience than those which are called perfect, but because the wisdom of the social law does not impose sanctions upon them.

A deliberate promise, in writing, made freely and without any mistake, one which may lead the party to whom it is made into contracts and expenses, cannot be broken without a violation of moral duty. But if there was nothing paid or promised for it, the law, perhaps wisely, leaves the execution of it to the conscience of him who makes it. It is only when the party making the promise gains something, or he to whom it is made loses something, that the law given the promise validity. And in the case of the promise of the adult to pay the debt of the infant, of the debtor discharged by the statute of limitations or bankruptcy, the principle is preserved by looking back to the origin of the transaction, where an equivalent is to be found. An exact equivalent is not required by the law; for there being a consideration, the parties are left to estimate its value: though here the courts of equity will step in to relieve from gross inadequacy between the consideration and the promise.

These principles are deduced from the general current of decided cases upon the subject, as well as from the known maxims of the common law. The general position, that moral obligation is a sufficient consideration for an express promise, is to be limited in its application, to cases where at some time or other a good or valuable consideration has existed.

A legal obligation is always a sufficient consideration to support either an express or an implied promise; such as an infant's debt for necessaries, or a father's promise to pay for the support and education of his minor children. But when the child shall have attained to manhood, and shall have become his own agent in the world's business, the debts he incurs, whatever may be their nature, create no obligation upon the father; and it seems to follow, that his promise founded upon such a debt has no legally binding force.

The cases of instruments under seal and certain mercantile contracts, in which considerations need not be proved, do not contradict the principles above suggested. The first import a consideration in themselves, and the second belong to a branch of the mercantile law, which has found it necessary to disregard the point of consideration in respect to instruments negotiable in their nature and essential to the interests of commerce.

Instead of citing a multiplicity of cases to support the positions I have taken, I will only refer to a very able review of all the cases in the note in 3 Bos. & Pul. 249. [This is the note to *Wennall v. Adney* set out, *infra*, after *Eastman v. Kenyon*.] The opinions of the judges had been variant for a long course of years upon this subject, but there seems to be no case in which it was nakedly decided, that a promise to pay the debt of a son of full age, not living with his father, though the debt were incurred by sickness which ended in the death of the son, without a previous request by the father proved or presumed, could be enforced by action.

It has been attempted to show a legal obligation on the part of the defendant by virtue of our statute, which compels lineal kindred in the ascending or descending line to support such of their poor relations as are likely to become chargeable to the town where they have their settlement. But it is a sufficient answer to this position, that such legal obligation does not exist except in the very cases provided for in the statute, and never until the party charged has been adjudged to be of sufficient ability thereto. We do not know from the report any of the facts which are necessary to create such an obligation. Whether the deceased had a legal settlement in this commonwealth at the time of his death, whether he was likely to become chargeable had he lived, whether the defendant was of sufficient ability, are essential facts to be adjudicated by the court to which is given jurisdiction on this subject. The legal liability does not arise until these facts have all been ascertained by judgment, after hearing the party intended to be charged.

For the foregoing reasons we are all of opinion that the nonsuit directed by the Court of Common Pleas was right, and that judgment be entered thereon for costs for the defendant.

WEBB v. McGOWIN

(1935), 168 So. 196. Court of Appeals of Alabama.

Bricken, Presiding Judge. This action is in assumpsit. The complaint as originally filed was amended. The demurrers to the complaint as amended were sustained, and because of this adverse ruling by the court the plaintiff took a non-suit, and the assignment of errors on this appeal are predicated upon said action or ruling of the court.

A fair statement of the case presenting the questions for decision is set out in apppellant's brief, which we adopt.

"On the 3d day of August, 1925, appellant while in the employ of the W. T. Smith Lumber Company, a corporation, and acting within the scope of his employment, was engaged in clearing the upper floor of mill No. 2 of the company. While so engaged he was in the act of dropping a pine block from the upper floor of the mill to the ground below; this being the usual and ordinary way of clearing the floor, and it being the duty of the plaintiff in the course of his employment to so drop it. The block weighed about 75 pounds.

"As appellant was in the act of dropping the block to the ground below, he was on the edge of the upper floor of the mill. As he started to turn the block loose so that it would drop to the ground, he saw J. Greeley McGowin, testator of the defendants, on the ground below and directly under where the block would have fallen had appellant turned it loose. Had he turned it loose it would have struck McGowin with such force as to have caused him serious bodily harm or death. Appellant could have remained safely on the upper floor of the mill by turning the block loose and allowing it to drop, but had he done this the block would have fallen on McGowin and caused him serious injuries or death. The only safe and reasonable way to prevent this was for appellant to hold to the block and divert its direction in falling from the place where McGowin was standing and the only safe way to divert it so as to prevent its coming into contact with McGowin was for appellant to fall with it to the ground below. Appellant did this, and by holding to the block and falling with it to the ground below, he diverted the course of its fall in such way that McGowin was not injured. In thus preventing the injuries to McGowin appellant himself received serious bodily injuries, resulting in his right leg being broken, the heel of his right foot torn off and his right arm broken. He was badly crippled for life and rendered unable to do physical or mental labor.

"On September 1, 1925, in consideration of appellant having prevented him from sustaining death or serious bodily harm and in consideration of the injuries appellant had received, McGowin agreed with him to care for and maintain him for the remainder of appellant's life at the rate of $15 every two weeks from the time he sustained his injuries to and during the remainder of appellant's life; it being agreed that McGowin would pay this sum to appellant for his maintenance. Under the agreement McGowin paid or caused to be paid to appellant the sum so agreed on up until McGowin's death on January 1, 1934. After his death the payments were continued to and including January 27, 1934, at which time they were discontinued. Thereupon plaintiff brought suit to recover the unpaid installments accruing up to the time of the bringing of the suit."

The action was for the unpaid installments accruing after January 27, 1934, to the time of the suit.

The principal grounds of demurrer to the original and amended complaint are: (1) It states no cause of action; (2) its averments show the contract was without consideration; (3) it fails to allege that McGowin had, at or before the services were rendered, agreed to pay appellant for them; (4) the contract declared on is void under the statute of frauds.

1. The averments of the complaint show that appellant saved McGowin from death or grievous bodily harm. This was a material benefit to him of infinitely more value than any financial aid he could have received. Receiving this benefit, McGowin became morally bound to compensate appellant for the services rendered. Recognizing his moral obligation, he expressly agreed to pay appellant as alleged in the complaint and complied with this agreement up to the time of his death; a period of more than 8 years.

Had McGowin been accidentally poisoned and a physician, without his knowledge or request, had administered an antidote, thus saving his life, a subsequent promise by McGowin to pay the physician would have been valid. Likewise, McGowin's agreement as disclosed by the complaint to compensate appellant for saving him from death or grievous bodily injury is valid and enforceable.

Where the promisee cares for, improves, and preserves the property of the promisor, though done without his request, it is sufficient consideration for the promisor's subsequent agreement to pay for the service because of the material benefit received. . . .

It follows that if, as alleged in the complaint, appellant saved J. Greely

McGowin from death or grievous bodily harm, and McGowin subsequently agreed to pay him for the service rendered, it became a valid and enforceable contract.

2. It is well settled that a moral obligation is a sufficient consideration to support a subsequent promise to pay where the promisor has received a material benefit, although there was no original duty or liability resting on the promisor....

3. Some authorities hold that, for a moral obligation to support a subsequent promise to pay, there must have existed a prior legal or equitable obligation, which for some reason had become unenforceable, but for which the promisor was still morally bound. This rule, however, is subject to qualification in those cases where the promisor, having received a material benefit from the promisee, is morally bound to compensate him for the services rendered and in consideration of this obligation promises to pay. In such cases the subsequent promise to pay is an affirmance or ratification of the services rendered carrying with it the presumption that a previous request for the service was made....

Under the decisions above cited, McGowin's express promise to pay appellant for the services rendered was an affirmance or ratification of what appellant had done raising the presumption that the services had been rendered at McGowin's request.

4. The averments of the complaint show that in saving McGowin from death or grievous bodily harm, appellant was crippled for life. This was part of the consideration of the contract declared on. McGowin was benefited. Appellant was injured. Benefit to the promisor or injury to the promisee is a sufficient legal consideration for the promisor's agreement to pay.

QUESTION

Would it matter in a case like *Webb v. McGowen* that there was or was not a scheme of compensation available to the plaintiff similar to that in Ontario under the Workmen's Compensation Act? (This act provides for compensation to employees who are injured in the course and scope of their employment.)

EASTWOOD v. KENYON

(1840), 11 A. & E. 438, 113 E.R. 482. Q.B.

[The plaintiff was the executor of the will of John Sutcliffe, John Sutcliffe died leaving an infant daughter, Sarah, who married the defendant. The plaintiff, acting as Sarah's guardian and agent, spent £140 of his own money in looking after Sarah's estate. The plaintiff had to borrow this money from one Blackburn to whom he gave a promisory note. When Sarah became of full age she assented to the loan, asked the plaintiff to let one Stansfield manage her affairs, and promised to pay the amount of the loan from Blackburn. Sarah also paid one year's interest on the loan. When Sarah married the defendant, he promised to pay Blackburn and discharge the loan. The plaintiff sued when the defendant did not pay.

At trial, there was a verdict for the plaintiff, subject, however, to a motion to enter a verdict for the defendant on the ground that the promise was unenforceable under the Statute of Frauds. A rule nisi was obtained according to the leave reserved, and also for arresting judgment on the ground that the declaration showed no consideration for the promise alleged.]

Lord Denman delivered the judgment of the court. (That portion of the judgment dealing with the Statute of Frauds is omitted. The court held that the promise was outside the Statute and, therefore, enforceable.)

Lord Denman: —... "The second point arose in arrest of judgment, namely, whether the declaration showed a sufficient consideration for the promise.

. . .

Upon motion in arrest of judgment, this promise must be taken to have been proved, and to have been an express promise, as indeed it must of necessity have been, for no such implied promise in law was ever heard of. It was then argued for the plaintiff that the declaration disclosed a sufficient moral consideration to support the promise.

Most of the older cases on this subject are collected in a learned note to the case of *Wennall v. Adney* (1802) (3 B. & P. 249), and the conclusion there arrived at seems to be correct in general, "that an express promise can only revive a precedent good consideration, which might have been enforced at law through the medium of an implied promise, had it not been suspended by some positive rule of law; but can give no original cause of action, if the obligation, on which it is founded, never could have been enforced at law, though not barred by any legal maxim or statute provision". Instances are given of voidable contracts, as those of infants ratified by an express promise after age, and distinguished from void contracts, as of married women, not capable of ratification by them when widows; *Loyd v. Lee* (1718) (1 Stra. 94); debts of bankrupts revived by subsequent promise after certificate; and similar cases. Since that time some cases have occurred upon this subject which require to be more particularly examined. *Barnes v. Hedley* (1809) (2 Taunt. 184), decided that a promise to repay a sum of money, with legal interest, which sum had originally been lent on usurious terms, but, in taking the account of which, all usurious items had been by agreement struck out, was binding. *Lee v. Muggeridge* (1813) (5 Taunt. 36), upheld an assumpsit by a widow that her executors should pay a bond given by her while a feme covert to secure money then advanced to a third person at her request. On the latter occasion the language of Mansfield C.J. and of the whole Court of Common Pleas, is very large, and hardly susceptible of any limitation. It is conformable to the expression used by the Judges of this Court in *Cooper v. Marten* (1803) (4 East, 76), where a stepfather was permitted to recover from the son of his wife, after he had attained his full age, upon a declaration for necessaries furnished to him while an infant, for which, after his full age, he promised to pay. It is remarkable that in none of these there was any allusion made to the learned note in 3 Bosanquet and Puller above referred to, and which has been very generally thought to contain a correct statement of the law. The case of *Barnes v. Hedley* is fully consistent with the doctrine in that note laid down. *Cooper v. Martin* also, when fully examined, will be found not to be inconsistent with it. This last case appears to have occupied the attention of the Court much more in respect of the supposed statutable liability of a stepfather, which was denied by the Court, and in respect of what a Court of Equity would hold as to a stepfather's liability, and rather to have assumed the point before us. It should, however, be observed that Lord Ellenborough in giving his judgment says, "The plaintiff having done an act beneficial for the defendant in his infancy, it is a good consideration for the defendant's promise after he came of age. In such a case the law will imply a request; and the fact of the promise has been found by the jury;" and undoubtedly the action would have lain against the defendant whilst an infant, inasmuch as it was for necessaries furnished at his request in regard to which the law raises an implied promise. The case of *Lee v. Muggeridge* must however be allowed to be decidedly at variance with the doctrine in the note alluded to, and is a decision of great authority. It should however be observed that in that case there was an actual request of the defendant during coverture, though not one binding in law; but the ground of decision there taken was also equally applicable to *Littlefield v. Shee* (1831) (2 B. & Ad. 811), tried by Gaselee J. at N.P., when that learned Judge held, notwithstanding, that "the defendant having been a married woman when the goods were supplied, her husband was originally liable, and there was no consideration for the promises declared upon". After time taken for deliberation this Court refused even a rule to shew cause why the nonsuit should not be set aside. *Lee v. Muggeridge* was cited on the motion, and was sought to be distinguished by Lord Tenterden, because there the circumstances raising the consideration were set out truly upon the record, but in *Littlefield v. Shee* the declaration stated the consideration to be that the plaintiff had supplied the defendant with goods at her request, which the plaintiff failed in proving, inasmuch as it appeared that the goods were in point of law supplied to the defendant's husband, and not to her. But Lord Tenterden added, that the doctrine that a moral obligation is a sufficient consideration for a subsequent promise is one which should be received with some limitation. This sentence, in truth, amounts to a dissent from the authority of *Lee v. Muggeridge*, where the doctrine is wholly unqualified.

The eminent counsel who argued for the plaintiff in *Lee v. Muggeridge* spoke of Lord Mansfield as having considered the rule of nudum pactum as too narrow, and maintained that all promises deliberately made ought to be held binding. I do not find this language ascribed to him by any reporter, and do not know whether we are to receive it as a traditional report, or as a deduction from what he does appear to have laid down. If the latter, the note to *Wennall v. Adney,* shews the deduction to be erroneous. If the former, Lord Tenterden and this Court declared that they could not adopt it in *Littlefield v. Shee*. Indeed the doctrine would annihilate the necessity for any consideration at all, inasmuch as the mere fact of giving a promise creates a moral obligation to perform it.

The enforcement of such promises by law, however plausibly reconciled by the desire to effect all conscientious engagements, might be attended with mischievous consequences to society; one of which would be the frequent preference of voluntary undertakings to claims for just debts. Suits would thereby be multiplied, and voluntary undertakings would also be multiplied, to the prejudice of real creditors. The temptations of executors would be much increased by the prevalance of such a doctrine, and the faithful discharge of their duty be rendered more difficult.

Taking then the promise of the defendant, as stated on this record, to have an express promise, we find that the consideration for it was past and executed long before, and yet it is not said to have been at the request of the defendant, nor even of his wife while sole (though if it had, the case of *Mitchinson v. Hewson* (1797) (7 T.R. 348), shews that it would not have been sufficient), and the declaration really discloses nothing but a benefit voluntarily conferred by the plaintiff and received by the defendant, with an express promise by the defendant to pay money.

If the subsequent assent of the defendant could have amounted to a *ratihabitio*, the declaration should have stated the money to have been expended at his request, and the ratification should have been relied on as matter of evidence, but this was obviously impossible, because the defendant was in no way connected with the property or with the plaintiff, when the money was expended. If the ratification of the wife while sole were relied on, then a debt from her would have been shewn, and the defendant could not have been charged in his own right without some further consideration, as of forbearance after marriage, or something of that sort; and then another point would have arisen upon the Statute of Frauds which did not arise as it was, but which might in that case have been available under the plea of non assumpsit.

In holding this declaration bad because it states no consideration but a past benefit not conferred at the request of the defendant, we conceive that we are justified by the old common law of England.

Lampleigh v. Brathwait (1615) (Hob. 105), is selected by Mr. Smith (1 Smith's Leading Cases, 67), as the leading case on this subject, which was there fully discussed, though not necessary to the decision. Hobart C.J. lays it down that "a mere voluntary courtesy will not have a consideration to uphold an assumpsit. But if that courtesy were moved by a suit or request of the party that gives the assumpsit, it will bind; for the promise, though it follows, yet it is not naked, but couples itself with the suit before, and the merits of the party procured by that suit; which is the difference"; a difference brought fully out by *Hunt v. Bate* (1568) (Dyer, 272 (a)), there cited from Dyer, where a promise to indemnify the plaintiff against the consequences of having bailed the defendant's servant, which the plaintiff had done without request of the defendant, was held to be made without consideration; but a promise to pay £20 to plaintiff, who had married defendant's cousin, but at defendant's special instance, was held binding.

The distinction is noted, and was acted upon, in *Townsend v. Hunt* (1635) (Cro. Car. 408), and indeed in numerous old books; while the principle of moral obligation does not make its appearance till the days of Lord Mansfield, and then under circumstances not inconsistent with this ancient doctrine when properly explained.

Upon the whole, we are of opinion that the rule must be made absolute to arrest the judgment.

Rule to enter verdict for defendant, discharged.

Rule to arrest judgment, absolute.

[In 1840 Sarah's husband would have been entitled at common law to all of his wife's property and so would have received the ultimate benefit of the expenditure made by the plaintiff. Could you use this in any way to strengthen the plaintiff's claim?]

———————

A. Dicey in Lectures on the Relation between "Law and Public Opinion in England during the Nineteenth century" described Lord Denman as very much a Benthamite liberal. Why would Lord Denman think that in 1840 the law should be found in "the old common law of England" and not in the approach of Lord Mansfield in the Eighteenth century? *Eastwood v. Kenyon* is usually taken as putting an end to the liberalizing ideas of Lord Mansfield. Lord Mansfield, for example, said in *Hawkes v. Saunders* (1782) 1 Cowp, 289; 98 E.R. 1091:

> "When a man is under a moral obligation, which no Court of Law or Equity can enforce, and promises, the honesty and rectitude of the thing is consideration... [T]he ties of conscience upon an upright mind are a sufficient consideration."

He therefore held that a promise by an executrix to pay a legacy "in consideration of assets" was enforceable. And in the great case of *Pillans v. Van Mierop* (1765), 3 Burr 1663; 97 E.R. 1035, he had said in a commercial context:

> "I take it, that the ancient notion about the want of consideration was for the sake of evidence only; for when it is reduced into writing, as in covenants, specialties, bonds, etc., there was no objection to the want of consideration... In commercial cases among merchants, the want of consideration is not an objection."

If it be true that Lord Denman could be regarded as a Benthamite liberal, what does the decision in *Eastwood v. Kenyon* say about Benthamite liberals?

As a young man Bentham had written:

> "Hail noble Mansfield! Chief among the just,
> The bad man's terror and the good man's trust."

but later, after his ideas about law had developed, he said:

> "Should there be a judge who, enlightened by genius, stimulated by honest zeal to the work of reformation, sick of the caprice, the delays, the prejudices, the ignorance, the malice, the fickleness, the suspicious ingratitude of popular assemblies, should seek with his sole hand to expunge the effusions of traditionary imbecility, and write down in their room the dictates of pure and native justice, let him but reflect that partial amendment is bought at the expense of universal certainty; the partial good thus purchased is universal evil; and that amendment from the judgment seat is confusion."

Does this help explain why Lord Denman did as he did? Would the horror that Bentham foresaw have occurred if the decision in *Eastwood v. Kenyon* had gone the other way? Is Bentham's view of the proper role of the judge defensible? How important is certainty in the law?

It is dangerous to believe either that Benthamite ideas provided the sole reason for the judgment of Lord Denman or that the theory of Gilmore, (*supra*) is the only view of the origin of the so-called traditional ideas of the doctrine of consideration. It is probable that Benthamite ideas had a significant influence on people like Lord Denman and that the views of Langdell and Holmes had a powerful effect on the formulation of the doctrine.

Lord Denman refers to the case of *Wennall v. Adney* ((1802) 3 B. & P. 249; 127 E.R. 137) and to a note by the editors of that series of reports. (This note is also referred to by the judge in *Mills v. Wyman*.) The note is as follows:

> "An idea has prevailed of late years that an express promise, founded simply on an antecedent moral obligation, is sufficient to support an assumpsit. It may be worth consideration, however, whether this proposition be not rather inaccurate, and whether that inaccuracy had not in a great measure arisen from some expres-

sions of Lord Mansfield and Mr. Justice Buller, which, if construed with the qualifications fairly belonging to them, do not warrant the conclusion, which appears to have been rather hastily drawn from thence. In *Atkins v. Hill* (1775) 1 Cowp. 288, which was assumpsit against an executor on a promise by him to pay a legacy in consideration of assets, Lord Mansfield said, "It is the case of a promise made upon a good and valuable consideration which in all cases is a sufficient ground to support an action. It is so in cases of obligations which would otherwise only bind a man's conscience, and which without such promise he could not be compelled to pay". And in *Hawkes v. Sanders* (1782), 1 Cowp. 290, which was a similar case with *Atkins v. Hill*, Lord Mansfield said that the rule laid down at the bar, "that to make a consideration to support an assumpsit there must be either an immediate benefit to the party promising or a loss to the person to whom the promise was made", was too narrow; and observed, "that a legal or equitable duty is a sufficient consideration for an actual promise; that where a man is under a moral obligation, which no Court of law or equity can enforce, and promises, the honesty and rectitude of the thing is a consideration". His Lordship then instanced the several cases of a promise to pay a debt barred by the statute of limitations, a promise by a bankrupt after his certificate to pay an antecedent debt, and a promise by a person of full age to pay a debt contracted during his infancy. The opinion of Mr. Justice Buller in the last case was to the same effect, and the same law was again laid down by Lord Mansfield in *Trueman v. Fenton* (1777), 1 Cowp. 544. Of the two former cases it may be observed, that the particular point decided in them has been overruled by the subsequent case of *Deeks v. Strutt* (1794), 5 T.R. 690. And it may further be observed, that however general the expressions used by Lord Mansfield may at first sight appear, yet the instances adduced by him as illustrative of the rule of law, do not carry that rule beyond what the older authorities seem to recognize as its proper limits; for in each instance the party bound by the promise had received a benefit previous to the promise. Indeed it seems that in such instances alone as those selected by Lord Mansfield will an express promise have any operation, and there it only becomes necessary, because though the consideration was originally beneficial to the party promising, yet, inasmuch as he was not of a capacity to bind himself when he received the benefit, or is protected from liability by some statute provision, or some stubborn rule of law, the law will not as in ordinary cases imply an assumpsit against him. The same observation is applicable to *Trueman v. Fenton*, that being an action against a bankrupt on a promise made by him subsequent to his certificate respecting a debt due before the certificate. There is however rather a loose note of a case of *Scott v. Nelson*, Westminster sittings (1764), 4 Geo. 3, cor. Lord Mansfield (see Esp. N.P. 945), in which his Lordship is said to have held a father bound by his promise to pay for the previous maintenance of a bastard child. And there is also an Anonymous case (1683), 2 Show. 184, where Lord Ch. J. Pemberton ruled that "for meat and drink for a bastard child an indebitatus assumpsit will lie." Although the latter case does not expressly say that there was a previous request by the Defendant, yet that seems to have been the fact, for Lord Hale's opinion is cited to shew 'that where there is common charity and a charge", the action will lie; which seems to imply that if a charge be imposed upon one person by the charitable conduct of another, the latter shall pay; and though he adds "and undoubtedly a special promise would reach it", that expression does not necessarily import a promise subsequent to the charge being sustained, but may be supposed to mean that where a party is induced to undertake a charge by the engagement of another to pay, the latter will certainly be liable even though he should not be so where the charge was only induced by his conduct without such engagement. The case of *Watson v. Turner* (1767), Bull N.P. 147, has sometimes been cited in support of what has been supposed to be the general principle laid down by Lord Mansfield, because in that case overseers were held bound by a mere subsequent promise to pay an apothecary's bill for care taken of a pauper; but it may be observed, that "this was adjudged not to be nudum pactum, for the overseers are bound to provide for the poor"; which obligation being a legal obligation distinguishes the case. Indeed in a late case of *Atkins v. Banwell (1802), 2 East, 505,* that distinction does not seem to have been sufficiently adverted to, for *Watson v. Turner* was cited to shew that a mere moral obligation is sufficient to raise an implied assumpsit, and though the Court denied that proposition, yet Lord Ellenborough observed that the promise given in the case of *Watson v. Turner* made all the difference between the two cases, without alluding to another distinction which might have been taken, viz. that though the parish officers were bound by law in *Watson v. Turner,* the Defendants in the principal case were not so bound, because the pauper had been relieved by the Plaintiff's as overseers of another parish, though belonging to the parish of which the Defendants were overseers. In the older cases no mention is made of moral obligation; but it seems to have been much doubted whether mere natural affection was a sufficient consideration to support an assumpsit, though coupled with a subsequent express promise. Indeed Lord Mansfield appears to have used the term moral obligation not as expressive of any vague and undefined claim arising from nearness of relationship, but of those imperative duties which would be enforceable by law, were it not for some positive rule, which, with a view to general benefit, exempts the party in that particular instance from legal liability. On such duties, so exempted, an express promise operates to revive the liability and take away the exemption, because if it were not for the exemption they would be enforced at law through the medium of an implied promise. In several of the cases it is laid down, that to support an assumpsit the party promising must derive a benefit, or the party performing sustain an inconvenience occasioned by the plaintiff; per Coke and all the Justices, *Hatch and Caples case,* Godb. 203, per Reeve J. Mar. 203, per Coke Ch.J. and Dodderidge J. 3 Bulst. 162, and per Coke Ch. J. Roll. Rep. 61, pl. 4. And in *Lampleigh v. Braithwaite* (1615), Hob. 105, it was resolved "that a mere voluntary curtesy will not have a consideration to uphold an assumpsit. But if that curtesy were moved by a suit or request of the party that gives the assumpsit, it will bind; for the promise, though it follows, is not naked, and couples itself with the suit before, and the merits of the party procured by that suit". And in *Bret v. J.S. and his Wife* (1600), Cro. Eliz. 755, where the first husband of the wife sent his son to table with the Plaintiff for three years at £8 per ann. and died within the year, and the wife during her widowhood, in consideration that the son should continue the residue of the time, promised to pay the Plaintiff £6 13s. 4d. for the time past, and £8 for every year after, and upon which promise the Plaintiff brought his action; the Court held that natural affection was not of itself a sufficient ground for an assumpsit; for although it was sufficient to raise an use, yet it was not sufficient to ground an action without an express quid pro quo; but that as the promise was not only in consideration of affection but that the son should afterwards continue at the Plaintiff's table, it was sufficient to support a promise. In *Harford v. Gardner* (1588), 2 Leo. 30, it was said by the Court that love and friendship are not considerations to found actions upon, and in *Best v. Jolly,* 1 Sid. 38, where a father was held liable for his own and his son's debt, because he had promised to pay them if the Plaintiff would forbear to sue for them, yet the Court said, "he was not liable for his son's debt", but having induced forbearance, which is a damage to the Plaintiff, he was held liable, "though as to the son's debt it was no benefit to the Defendant". So in *Besfisch v. Coggil* (1624) Palm. 559, it was debated whether the Defendant was liable upon an express promise to repay the Plaintiff money laid out by him in Spain for the Defendant's son, and the charges of his funeral, Hyde Ch. J. and Whitelock being of opinion that the action could not be maintained; Jones and Dodderidge è contrà that it could. The former of which it should seem was the better opinion; for in *Butcher v. Andrews* (1698) Carth. 446, on assumpsit for money lent by the Plaintiff to the Defendant's son at his instance and request, and verdict for the Plaintiff, the judgment was arrested, Holt Ch. J. saying, "if it had been an indebitatis for so much money paid by the Plaintiff at the request of the Defendant unto his son, it might have been good, for then it would be the father's debt, and not the son's; but when the money is lent to the son, it is his proper debt, and not the father's." But in *Church v. Church*, B.R. 1656, cit. Sir. T. Ray. 260, where defendant promised to repay the Plaintiff the charges of his son's funeral, the latter was held entitled to recover, though no request was laid in the declaration. Of which case it may be observed, that possibly after verdict the Court presumed a request proved; for in *Hayes v. Warren* (1732), 2 Str. 933, though the Court would not presume a request after judgment by default, yet they said they would have presumed it after verdict. However, in *Style v. Smith*, cited, by Popham J. 2 Leon. 111, it was determined that if a physician in the absence of a father give his son medicine, and the father in consideration thereof promise to pay him an action will lie for the money. But the case of *Style v. Smith*, if closely examined, will not perhaps be found so discordant with the principle laid down in *Bret v. J.S. and his Wife* as may be supposed. From the expression "in the absence of a father", used in that case, it may be inferred that the son lived with the father, and that the medicine was administered to the son in the house of the father, while the latter was absent, from whence it results that the physicians' debt, though not founded on any immediate benefit to the father, or on his request, was most probably founded on his credit; which credit, it (sic) fairly inferred from circumstances by the physician, might operate to charge the father in the same way as his request would operate, the physician having sustained a loss in consequences of that credit. Indeed if any of the cases could be sustained on the principle that a father is, by the mere force of moral obligation, bound to pay what has been advanced for his son, because he has subsequently promised to pay it; by the same rule the son should be liable for the debt of the father upon a similar promise; for the same moral obligation exists in both cases. Yet in *Barber v. Fox*, 2 Saund. 136, the Court arrested the judgment in an action of assumpsit on a promise made by the Defendant, to avoid being sued on a bond of his father, it not being alleged that the Defendant's father had bound himself and his heirs; for they refused to intend even after verdict that the bond was in the usual form, and consequently held the promise of the Defendant nudum pactum, he not appearing to have been liable to be sued upon the bond. And this last case was confirmed in *Hunt v. Swain* (1665) 1 Lev. 165. Sir T. Ray. 127. 1 Sid. 248. See note 2 to *Barber v. Fox*, by Mr. Serjt. Williams. Indeed it is clear from *Lloyd v. Lee* (1718) 1 Str. 94, and *Cockshott v. Bennett* (1788), 2 T. R. 763, and if a contract between two persons be void, and not merely voidable, no subsequent express promise will operate to charge the party promising, even though he has derived the benefit of the contract. Yet according to the commonly received notion respecting moral obligations and the force attributed to a subsequent express promise, such a person ought to pay. An express promise, therefore, as it should seem, can only revive a precedent good consideration, which might have been enforced at law through the medium of an implied promise, had it not been suspended by some positive rule of law, but can give no original right of action if the obligation on which it is founded never could have been enforced at law, though not barred by any legal maxim or statute provision. In addition to the cases already collected upon this subject, it may be observed, that in *Mitchinson v. Hewson* (1797) 7 T.R. 348, the Court of King's Bench, upon the authority of *Drue v. Thorn* (1644), All. 72, held a husband not liable to be sued alone for the debt of his wife, contracted before marriage, though the objection was only taken in arrest of judgment, and consequently a promise by him to pay the debt appeared upon the record. From whence this principle may be extracted, that an obligation to pay in one right, even though it be a legal obligation, and coupled with an express promise, will not support an assumpsit to pay in another right."

QUESTIONS

1. Does the note reproduced above provide satisfactory reasons for deciding *Mills v. Wyman* or *Eastwood v. Kenyon* in the way those courts did?

2. What view did the reporters have of judicial decision-making?

3. Are the reporters faithful to that view?

4. Do you share that view?

5. Does Lord Mansfield have the same view of the law and of contracts generally as the reporters or Lord Denman?

What this note makes clear is that the doctrine of consideration, in the form in which Lord Denman understood it, was developed as early as 1802. The development of the so-called nineteenth century approach to law is a very complex event.

See also: Horwitz, *The Transformation of American Law*, 1780-1860.

The next case raises very different issues from those in the preceding cases. Are the reasons for refusing enforcement in this case the same as in the others? To what extent is Lord Denman justified in referring to the Note to *Wennell v. Adney* or to *Eastwood v. Kenyon*?

ROSCORLA v. THOMAS

(1842), 3 Q.B. 234, 114 E.R. 496.

Before Lord Denman C.J., Patteson, Williams, and Wightman JJ.

Lord Denman C.J., delivered this judgment of the Court.

This was an action of assumpsit for breach of warranty of the soundness of a horse. The first count of the declaration, upon which alone the question arises, stated that, in consideration that the plaintiff, at the request of the defendant, had bought of the defendant a horse for the sum of £30., the defendant promised that it was sound and free from vice. And it was objected, in arrest of judgment, that the precedent executed consideration was insufficient to support the subsequent promise. And we are of opinion that the objection must prevail.

It may be taken as a general rule, subject to exceptions not applicable to this case, that the promise must be coextensive with the consideration. In the present case, the only promise that would result from the consideration, as stated, and be coextensive with it, would be to deliver the horse upon request. The precedent sale, without a warranty, though at the request of the defendant, imposes no other duty or obligation upon him. It is clear, therefore, that the consideration stated would not raise an implied promise by the defendant that the horse was sound or free from vice.

But the promise in the present case must be taken to be, as in fact it was, express: and the question is, whether that fact will warrant the extension of the promise beyond that which would be implied by law; and whether the consideration, though insufficient to raise as implied promise, will nevertheless support an express one. And we think that it will not.

The cases in which it has been held that, under certain circumstances, a consideration insufficient to raise an implied promise will nevertheless support an express one, will be found collected and reviewed in the note to *Wennall v. Adney* and in the case of *Eastwood v. Kenyon*. They are cases of voidable contracts subsequently ratified, of debts barred by operation of law, subsequently revived, and of equitable and moral obligations, which, but for some rule of law, would of themselves have been sufficient to raise an implied promise. All these cases are distinguishable from, and indeed inapplicable to, the present, which appears to us to fall within the general rule, that a consideration past and executed will support no other promise than such as would be implied by law.

The rule for arresting the judgment upon the first count must therefore be made absolute.

Rule absolute.

[We must assume that in *Roscorla v. Thomas* the statements that were made about the horse were made *after* the sale, *i.e.*, after the plaintiff had agreed to pay £30 and the defendant had agreed to sell the particular animal.]

PROBLEMS

1. Bruce and Colin are neighbouring owners on a lake where both have boats. At a time when only Bruce is at the lake, a storm occurs and threatens to damage Colin's boat. Bruce spends considerable time and effort in making sure that no damage is caused to Colin's boat. He also uses one of his new fenders to prevent damage to the hull. The fender, which cost $50, is badly damaged by the storm. When Colin hears what Bruce has done he says he will pay him $100 and will reimburse him for the fender. What can Bruce recover?

2. Winston had a badly run-down house that he lent to his daughter Mary to live in. Mary had a friend, Tom, a painter. Mary asked Tom to paint a mural on one of the walls and agreed to pay him $200. Tom painted a very beautiful mural that has increased the value of the house by $2,000. When Winston saw the mural, he promised to pay Tom the $200 that Mary promised to pay. Would Tom be successful if he were to sue Winston?

3. Alan and Don are neighbours. When Don was going away on his summer vacation he asked Alan to look after his house, mow his lawn and weed his garden. Alan agreed to do so. Both expected that Don would return the kindness when Alan went on his holiday. However, Alan could not get away that year. In the fall, Don said to Alan, "Since I could not return the favour you did me, I'll pay you $500 for the work that you did. Is that O.K. with you?" Alan said that was fine.

Don and Alan have now fallen out, and Alan wants to sue Don for the amount he promised to pay. How can you put his case to avoid the problems of *Eastwood v. Kenyon*?

NOTE ON INFANTS' CONTRACTS AND THE EFFECT OF THE STATUTE OF LIMITATIONS

Certain kinds of contracts raise the problem of past consideration in a special way. The contracts of an infant are, at common law, void. (An infant, now called a "minor", is any person under 18 years of age: Age of Majority and Accountability Act, 1971. At common law an infant was any person less than 21 years old. A person became 21 at 12.01 a.m. on the day *before* his or her 21st birthday.) However, if a person on reaching the age of majority affirmed a contract that he or she had entered into as an infant, the person was liable on that contract even though the consideration was past. Thus in *Eastwood v. Kenyon*, had Sarah been sued she would have been liable. Since she was married, she could only be sued through her husband and, in any case, she had no assets. The new promise to pay made after the person has come of full age is a promise for which the consideration is past. But, in this case, this is not fatal to an action on the promise. Note that the promise to pay in such circumstances must be in writing: Statute of Frauds, R.S.O. 1970, c. 444, s. 7:

> No action shall be maintained whereby to charge a person upon a promise made after full age to pay a debt contracted during infancy or upon a ratification after full age of a promise or simple contract made during infancy, unless the promise or ratification is made by a writing signed by the party to be charged therewith or by his agent duly authorized to make the promise or ratification.

Under The Statute of Limitations (now The Limitations Act, R.S.O. 1970, c. 246, s. 45) an action upon a simple contract must be commenced within six years after the cause of action arose. An action brought more than six years afterwards is said to be statute-barred. However, it is well established that the time from which the statute runs can be reopened by an acknowledgement by the debtor that the amount is due. Thus if A owes money to B for goods purchased and the cause of action arose on October 1, 1970, B cannot maintain an action on this debt if the writ is not issued before October 1, 1976. However, if A acknowledged the debt in May 1973, then the period runs from that date and the action will be barred only in May 1979. It might be thought that the action in the latter case would be on a promise made in May 1973 for which the consideration was past. However the courts, as a practical matter, have never been bothered by this. It is clear law that an acknowledgment of the debt takes it out of the statute and an action can be brought even thought six years may have passed from the original cause of action. This is rationalized by saying that the action is still on the original contract, and that the only effect of the later acknowledgment is to take the case out of the statute. A comprehensive discussion of this area of the law is found in the judgment of the House of Lords in *Spencer v. Hemmerde*, [1922] 2 A.C. 507. Note that an acknowledgment that operates to extend the time for bringing an action must be in writing: Limitations Act, s. 51.

(3) MUTUAL PROMISES

As you know from some of the extracts dealing with the history of the law of contract, the wholly executory contract was not recognized in English law until the end of the sixteenth century. The courts have never had much difficulty with the enforcement of this kind of contract where it is clear that A promises to do something for B in return for B's promise to pay (or do something) for A. Many of the difficulties arose with academics who tried to fit mutual promises into the classic bargain framework of consideration. For example, if the bargain theory of consideration requires a detriment to the promisee, how can there be any detriment in the simple case where A promises to buy B's car for $1,000 and B promises to sell? A has incurred no detriment in return for B's promise unless his promise is enforceable, but to assume that A's promise is enforceable is arguing in a circle, since A's promise is no more enforceable than B's. Sir Frederick Pollock was moved to say, "What logical justification is there for holding mutual promises good consideration for each other? None it is submitted."((1912) 28 L.Q.R. 101). Two years later he called this "one of the secret paradoxes of the common law" ((1914) 30 L.Q.R.).

We can ignore the kind of difficulty that faced people like Pollock. The courts will enforce mutual promises — the wholly executory contract. However there still remain several problems which are related to the logical problem of enforcement. It is clear that the following promises are enforceable:

A promise on July 1 to work for B for one year starting January 1. B promises to pay A $20,000 for the year's work. If A refuses to start work on January 1, B can sue A for damages for breach. If B refuses to allow A to work, A can sue B.

But what about the following promises?

A promises to give B $1,000 on the condition that B will promise to accept it. B. promises to do so. Can B sue A for the $1,000? The transaction is in form an exchange of promises, but, in substance, it is a gift. Is this the kind of contract you would expect the court to enforce? Are there any more reasons to support this promise than the ordinary gift promise? There will inevitably be problems in the transformation of an unenforceable gift promise into an "exchange" promise by such a device as this. Probably the courts will not enforce what is essentially a gift promise simply because the form has been changed.

Suppose that in *Hamer v. Sidway*, the uncle had repudiated his promise one month after he made it. If we could assume that the nephew had promised to do what the uncle asked, would the contract be enforceable as an executory contract?

These problems illustrate one difficulty which we have to consider in enforcing mutual promises. One promise may turn out on examination to be a promise which obligates the promisor to do nothing. It is usually said in supporting the enforceability of mutual promises that if doing something would be good consideration then a promise to do it would be good consideration (see: Holt C.J. in *Thorp v. Thorp* (1702), 12 Mod. 455; 87 E.R. 1448). If then the return promise is a promise to do nothing, the original promise may not be enforceable.

A second problem has to do with the requirement that both parties must be bound or neither is bound. This is sometimes referred to as the requirement of mutuality. This requirement is not absolute for many kinds of promises are enforceable on one side only: the person defrauded by another may sue on the contract while the other may not, an infant (minor) may sue on a contract while the other may not.

These issues are raised in the material which follows.

G.N.R. v. WITHAM

(1873), L.R. 9 C.P. 16. Common Pleas.

The cause was tried before Brett, J., at the sittings at Westminster after the last term. The facts were as follows: — In October, 1871, the plaintiffs advertised for tenders for the supply of goods (amongst other things iron) to be delivered at their station at Doncaster, according to a certain specification. The defendant sent in a tender, as follows: —

> "I, the undersigned, hereby undertake to supply the Great Northern Railway Company, for twelve months from the 1st of November, 1871, to 31st of October, 1872, with such quantities of each or any of the several articles named in the attached specification as the company's store-keeper may order from time to time, at the price set opposite each article respectively, and agree to abide by the conditions stated on the other side. (Signed) "Samuel Witham."

The company's officer wrote in reply, as follows: —

"Mr. S. Witham.

"Sir, — I am instructed to inform you that my directors have accepted your tender, dated, &c., to supply this company at Doncaster station any quantity they may order during the period ending 31st of October, 1872, of the descriptions of iron mentioned on the inclosed list, at the prices specified therein. The terms of the contract must be strictly adhered to. Requesting an acknowledgment of the receipt of this letter, (Signed) "S. Fitch, Assistant Secretary."

To this the defendant replied, — "I beg to own receipt of your favor of 20th instant, accepting my tender for bars, for which I am obliged. Your specifications shall receive my best attention. S. Witham."

Several orders for iron were given by the company, which were from time to time duly executed by the defendant; but ultimately the defendant refused to supply any more, whereupon this action was brought.

A verdict having been found for the plaintiffs,

Nov. 5. *Digby Seymour, Q.C.,* moved to enter a nonsuit, on the ground that the contract was void for want of mutuality. He contended that, as the company did not bind themselves to take any iron whatever from the defendant, his promise to supply them with iron was a promise without consideration.

Keating, J. In this case Mr. Digby Seymour moved to enter a nonsuit. The circumstances were these: — The Great Northern Railway Company advertised for tenders for the supply of stores. The defendant made a tender in these words, — "I hereby undertake to supply the Great Northern Railway Company, for twelve months, from &c. to &c., with such quantities of each or any of the several articles named in the attached specifications as the company's store-keeper may order from time to time, at the price set opposite each article respectively," &c. Some orders were given by the company, which were duly executed. But the order now in question was not executed; the defendant seeking to excuse himself from the performance of his agreement, because it was unilateral, the company not being bound to give the order. The ground upon which it was put by Mr. Seymour was, that there was no consideration for the defendant's promise to supply the goods; in other words, that, inasmuch as there was no obligation on the company to give an order, there was no consideration moving from the company, and therefore no obligation on the defendant to supply the goods.... If before the order was given the defendant had given notice to the company that he would not perform the agreement, it might be that he would have been justified in so doing. But here the company had given the order, and had consequently done something which amounted to a consideration for the defendant's promise. I see no ground for doubting that the verdict for the plaintiffs ought to stand.

Brett, J. The company advertised for tenders for the supply of stores, such as they might think fit to order, for one year. The defendant made a tender offering to supply them for that period at certain fixed prices; and the company accepted his tender. If there were no other objection, the contract between the parties would be found in the tender and the letter accepting it. This action is brought for the defendant's refusal to deliver goods ordered by the company; and the objection to the plaintiffs' right to recover is, that the contract is unilateral. I do not, however, understand what objection that is to a contract. Many contracts are obnoxious to the same complaint. If I say to another, "If you will go to York, I will give you £100.," that is in a certain sense a unilateral contract. He has not promised to go to York. But, if he goes, it cannot be doubted that he will be entitled to receive the £100. His going to York at my request is a sufficient consideration for my promise. So, if one says to another, "If you will give me an order for iron, or other goods, I will supply it at a given price;" if the order is given, there is a complete contract which the seller is bound to perform. There is in such a case ample consideration for the promise. So, here, the company having given the defendant an order at his request, his acceptance of the order would bind them. If any authority could have been found to sustain Mr. Seymour's contention, I should have considered that a rule ought to be granted. But none has been cited. This is matter of every day's practice; and I think it would be wrong to countenance the notion that a man who tenders for the supply of goods in this way is not bound to deliver them when an order is given. I agree that this judgment does not decide the question whether the defendant might have absolved himself from the further performance of the contract by giving notice.

[This case is an example of a very common type of contract. What are the motivations on both sides that might induce them to enter into such an arrangement?]

QUESTIONS

1. What did the G.N.R. promise to do?
2. What did Witham promise to do?
3. Would it make any difference if G.N.R. had promised to buy from Witham all the supplies covered by the contract that they might need during the year, or if G.N.R. had promised not to buy from X, a competitor of Witham, or from anyone else?
4. What if Witham had promised to sell any iron he might produce to G.N.R.?
5. How would you re-draft the letters so that the contract might more closely reflect the parties' expectations?
6. Both Keating J. and Brett J. use the word 'unilateral" to describe the contract. Do they both mean the same thing? In the "walk to York case" mentioned by Brett J. can any action be brought by either party while the contract remains executory?

PROBLEM

The University of Toronto requires a large amount of paper for producing casebooks in the Faculty of Law. The amount needed cannot be known in advance, but the best estimate put the minimum amount at 500 cartons and the maximum at 1,500 cartons. The price of paper has been steadily rising, (but may fall) and the supply has been erratic. The University has been approached by a salesman for Paper Supply Co. who says that his company is prepared to supply paper to the University for a fixed price for one year. This price is slightly higher than the current market price. The University thinks that this is a good deal.

List the concerns that both parties have in this deal.

Draft the clauses that each part would like to see in the contract.

BERNSTEIN v. W.B. MFG. CO.

(1921), 131 N.E. 200 Supreme Judicial Court of Massachusetts.

Pierce, J. This is an action to recover damages for the alleged breach of a contract, which the plaintiff claims resulted from an order that the defendant admits it placed with the plaintiff for the delivery of certain goods.

The order so given called for the sale and delivery of one hundred and seventy-four dozen boys' wash suits, and five sets of samples thereof at $16.50 a dozen. The admitted facts and evidence show that the plaintiff delivered to the defendant on August 20, 1918, the five sets of samples called for by the order, and that it was paid therefor by the defendant in September, 1918. The evidence also shows that the plaintiff on December 15, 1918, shipped to the defendant seventy-two dozen wash suits; that they were delivered in the shipping room of the defendant; that the defendant "opened them up" and immediately notified the plaintiff that it would not accept the goods. A memorandum of the order was made by the representative of the plaintiff on a printed order blank of the plaintiff. It was not signed by the defendant, and it contained the following printed clause:

"This order is given and accepted subject to a limit of credit and determination at any time by us."

At the close of the evidence the defendant excepted to the refusal of the judge to direct a verdict for the defendant.

Because of the clause above quoted the defendant contends that the agreement was invalid in its inception for want of mutuality of obligation; and rests its defense upon the accepted legal maxim that in a bilateral agreement both of the mutual promises must be binding or neither will be, for if one of the promises is for any reason invalid the other has no consideration and so they both fall. Bernstein v. W.B. Manufacturing Co., 235 Mass. 425, 427, 126 N.E. 796. The plaintiff admits the legal force of the rule invoked by the defendant, and replies thereto that the clause does not have the effect of reserving to the plaintiff the right to determine the contract (which otherwise resulted from the placing and acceptance of the order) but is obviously only referable to a determination of "a limit of credit." Giving to the clause a fair construction, we think the right of "determination" was intended to embrace the "order" as well as "a limit of credit."

The plaintiff next contends that the delivery and acceptance of the five sample suits were such partial performance by the plaintiff as afforded a sufficient consideration for the defendant's promises, even though there was no obligation to support the contract at its inception. We do not think the agreement which was void in its inception for want of mutuality became an agreement which was supported by a sufficient consideration upon the delivery and acceptance of part of the goods called for in the order of the defendant, because the plaintiff was not thereby precluded from exercising his reserved option. He was not bound to fill the balance of the order unless he chose to do so, and the defendant gained thereby no additional contractual right against the plaintiff. . . .

It becomes unnecessary to consider the defense of the statute of frauds. It results that the motion to direct a verdict for the defendant should have been granted, that the exceptions must be sustained, and that judgment be now entered for the defendant.

FULLER and EISENBERG

3rd ed. pp. 191-195.

PREVIOUS APPEAL IN BERNSTEIN v. W. B. MFG. CO.

On a previous appeal of this case (235 Mass. 425, 126 N.E. 796) the court interpreted another clause of the order which read as follows: "All orders accepted to be delivered to the best of our [the seller's] ability, but will under no circumstances hold ourselves liable for failure to deliver any portion of orders taken, sometimes caused by circumstances over which we have no control." The trial court held that this excuse clause was so broadly phrased as to make the plaintiff's undertaking illusory and directed a verdict for the defendant. The Supreme Judicial Court held this ruling to be in error and ordered a new trial. It interpreted the excuse clause to mean that the seller was bound to deliver unless he was prevented from doing so by causes beyond his control. (Arguing the case on the second appeal for the seller, what use would you make of this previous decision, and the clause that it interpreted?)

AN ARGUMENT AGAINST THE HOLDING IN BERNSTEIN v. W. B. MFG. CO.

An argument against the decision rendered on the second appeal may be advanced along the following lines.

If possible, the language of the sales order should be so construed that it will make business sense in the context in which it was used. An order for wash suits accepted by the seller, but subject to cancelation by him at any time, is not a transaction that, in normal times at least, would have any readily perceivable business or economic purpose. It is true that the cancelation of orders is not viewed by business ethics in the same manner as it is by the law of contracts, at least as that law is usually formulated. Where the seller has a valid reason for canceling the order, and he is apparently treating his customers alike, the buyer may acquiesce in the cancelation, though advised by his lawyers that he has legal grounds for objecting. (Naturally, he is more likely to adopt this attitude when goods are scarce and he anticipates having to look to the seller for his next season's supply.) On the other hand, even in an atmosphere of business relations dominated more by good faith and fair treatment than by rigid lines of obligation, an order, accepted by the seller, that carries with it no commitment at all by the seller, is a kind of nonesuch, lacking any definable function.

Accordingly, the clause involved in the *Berstein* Case should not be construed to give an unrestricted power of cancelation to the seller if there is any other interpretation that can reasonably be put on it. In deciding whether there is such an interpretation, the following facts should be noted. One of the principal problems confronting the manufacturer of clothing is the credit of his buyers. He often deals with a large number of them and their credit may change very rapidly, operating, as they do, in a hazardous field where economic casualties are high. The legal rules protecting the seller in case the buyer's credit business becomes impaired are, from the seller's point of view, unsatisfactory, UCC § 2-702 provides that the seller may refuse delivery except for cash if he discovers the buyer to be insolvent. In effect, this gives the seller the power to convert the transaction from a sale on credit to a sale for cash, *if* the buyer is "insolvent," as, for example, where the seller is in a position to prove in court that the buyer had "ceased to pay his debts in the ordinary course of business or cannot pay his debts as they become due." UCC § 1-201 (23). Knowing that the buyer's affairs are not in good shape, and that he has ceased to be a good risk, is, of course, something quite different from being able to prove in court that his condition corresponds to the formal definition of insolvency given in the UCC. For this reason, the right to convert the credit sale into a sale for cash where the buyer becomes "insolvent" is a procedure too hazardous to be satisfactory to the seller. (NOTE: The UCC provisions referred to above are substantially similar to Uniform Sales Act §§ 54, 76, which were in force at the time of the *Bernstein* Case. UCC § 2-609 would be relevant today, but there was no such provision in the Sales Act.)

In a field closely allied in business practice to that involved in the *Bernstein* Case, that is, in the sale of cotton grey goods (unfinished cloth as it comes from the loom) the trade associations affected (representing both buyers and sellers) have worked out a standard form that gives the seller the unrestricted right, in his own judgment, "to limit any credit extended" the buyer or "to require payment before delivery." This form has been employed by some of the textile mills selling finished goods direct to jobbers and retailers, so that it is used by them in their sales orders in essentially the same business context as that involved in the *Bernstein* Case.

With these facts in mind, it may be argued that the seller of wash suits in the *Bernstein* Case was attempting to obtain for himself by his sales order form the same protection given the seller of grey goods under the Worth Street Rules. The disputed clause meant that the order was "subject to a limit of credit" (that is, the total *amount* of credit to be extended at any time, say $1000 or $5000, could be limited by the seller) "and [this credit was in turn subject to] determination" by the seller (that is, the seller could cancel the credit term altogether and require payment before delivery). This gives the clause in the *Bernstein* Case the same meaning as the clause in the standard form of the Worth Street Rules. On this interpretation, the expression "determination" is used in apposition to the term "limit" and both qualify "credit"; in short, credit could either be limited or canceled (that is, "determined") by the seller. This interpretation gives the clause a purpose that is entirely understandable in the business context in which the parties were dealing.

The line of reasoning just advanced is in no sense conclusive. Against it one may argue that it takes liberties with the grammatical construction of the disputed clause, and that, in any event, ambiguities in the language of a contract should be construed against the interest of the party who used the language, in this case, the seller. (Note, on the facts of this case, it was to the seller's interest to show that he had bound himself; the holding that he had not resulted in his losing his suit against the buyer.)

It should be observed that the argument in the preceding paragraphs to show that the holding in the *Bernstein* Case was wrong requires going much beyond "the four corners of the instrument" and necessitates drawing freely on the entire business background of the transaction involved. It is apparent from the decision that no consideration was given to this background by the court, and an examination of the briefs reveals no reference to it by counsel.

PROVING THE BUSINESS BACKGROUND OF A CONTRACT

The basic problem faced by a court attempting to ascribe a proper meaning to the language of a contract is: What were these parties trying to accomplish? This is obviously a question that cannot be answered satisfactorily unless one is familiar with the general business and economic environments in which the parties were operating. To attempt to answer the question without a knowledge of that environment is like trying to understand the movements of players in a game without knowing the object of the game itself or what its rules are.

Where a contract containing ambiguous language is executed in the context of a particular field of business practice one cannot safely proceed to the task of interpretation unless one is in a position to answer questions like the following: What are the hazards that are most important in this field? Against which of these hazards are the parties most likely to erect legal safeguards? What kinds of transactions will serve an understandable economic purpose in this field, and what will not? What are the practices in related fields, and is there any tendency for the practices in this field to develop in the same direction?

The lawyer who attempts to get before the court facts that will answer these questions will find that he is seriously handicapped by our traditions of forensic procedure and by the existing rules of evidence. In the same manner, the judge who seeks to broaden his understanding of the general business background of the case will find himself limited by those traditions and rules. See Note, Social and Economic Facts — Appraisal of Suggested Techniques for Presenting Them to the Courts, 61 Harv.L.Rev. 692 (1948).

Under the formal limitations of our law of procedure, the judge can generally take account of facts of the sort set forth in the last note in two ways only: 1) by subsuming the facts under the heading of "judicial notice"; 2) by receiving in court the testimony of qualified expert witnesses.

The doctrine of judicial notice is an exception to the general rule that only facts proved in court can be considered in arriving at the decision. In general, the rule is stated to be that the the court may act on facts that are so much a matter of "general knowledge" that no proof of them is necessary. Wigmore on Evidence, 3d ed., §§ 2565-2570. Thus, a court might well take judicial notice of the existence of an economic depression, and might construe a contract in the light of the economic conditions generally prevailing at the time it was written. On the other hand, facts of the detailed sort outlined in the last note would generally fall outside the scope of judicial notice.

If, therefore, an attorney were to attempt to get those facts before the court the technically proper way to accomplish this would be by putting expert witnesses on the stand, who would testify to the business practices relevant to the interpretation of the contract. There are, however, serious practical difficulties in this procedure. It is often difficult to secure anyone who will testify as an expert. Those really qualified (for example, the executive secretary of a trade association) are often in a position where they are reluctant to do anything that would seem to suggest "taking sides" in a controversy. They are likely to avoid appearing if they can; if they do appear, their testimony is likely to be colorless and non-committal. Furthermore, the law surrounding the reception of expert testimony is such as to open the

way for time-consuming wrangles in court. The witness must first be qualified, that is, it must be demonstrated that he has a sufficient background
and training to be properly considered an expert. When he begins his testimony, the manner in which questions may be put to him is severely restricted. Wigmore on Evidence, 3d ed., §§ 555-563. Finally, when the facts to be
proved are like those discussed in the last note, the immediate relevance of
any particular fact is difficult to demonstrate, though the cumulative effect
of a whole series of related facts may be persuasive. If the witness is asked
to state whether the word "determination" has acquired a definite and recognized meaning in the trade, there is little difficulty. But if he is asked to
convey to the court the general background of the transaction, the marketing problems of the sellers of wash suits, and the practices in related fields,
there will almost certainly be vociferous objection from the other side, and
the attorney who wishes to introduce this testimony will be hard put to it to
show what he is driving at. For statutory efforts to clarify the procedure, see
UCC §§ 1-205, 2-302(2).

In actual practice, the plight of the advocate may not be as bad as the
account just presented would imply. This is a field in which the trial judge
has a wide discretion. It would be a rare case in which the admission of
facts of the sort suggested would be reversible error. Accordingly, if the trial
judge really wants to inform himself of the whole background of the case,
he can usually do this by allowing the testimony to range over a somewhat
wider area than that which can be logically defended under the rules of evidence as they are formally laid down. A common occurrence in trials is for
one attorney to object to the introduction of certain testimony, and for the
judge to permit its introduction provisionally with the understanding that it
will be disregarded if it turns out not to be relevant or to violate some rule
of exclusion. This procedure permits the offered proof to approach its goal
indirectly and relieves the attorney from the necessity of demonstrating at
each turn just what he is attempting to prove.

Furthermore, in cases involving a considerable technical background, it
is not uncommon for attorneys to include in their argument to the court a
good deal of factual material that is not actually supported by testimony
formally presented in court. This is, strictly, an irregular procedure, and in
cases of this sort there is often some banter (which may or may not be good-
natured) about attorneys "testifying." If the judge is eager to broaden his
own understanding of the case he is likely to allow a considerable leeway in
this respect, so that much more is conveyed to him than is possible under
the formal conceptions of proper procedure.

The insight thus obtained by the trial judge may, of course, be lost on the
appeal and the appellate court may judge the case in abstraction from its
practical background. Here again, however, the situation is not always in
reality as bad as it seems in theory. Attorneys often insert in their briefs
assertions of fact (supported wherever possible by printed sources) that will
assist the court in securing an insight into the general business environment
of the case. Sometimes, opposing counsel will object that these assertions
"go beyond the record", but objections of this sort consume valuable time
during the oral argument and may impress the court adversely if the court
itself is really eager to see the case in its whole setting. On the oral argument, again, a good deal of factual material is likely to be woven into the
legal argument, especially where the background of the case is of a technical nature.

The fact that our system works better in practice than one might suppose from a study of its formal elements does not mean that it works well. Indeed, the limitations on the judicial procedure for obtaining "background facts" is one of the causes for the enormous growth of administrative tribunals in recent years. Our present judicial practice, with all its covert tolerances, is a far cry from that followed by Mansfield when he undertook toward the end of the eighteenth century to bring English law into closer conformity with business practice. In the trial of commercial cases he arranged to have the jurymen drawn from a special panel carefully selected from among the merchants. During the trial he would often interrogate the jurors on matters of commercial usage, and take their responses into account in drafting his final instructions on the law. For the further advancement of his knowledge of commercial usage, it is said that he often entertained his jurymen at dinner (See 4 Campbell, Lives of the Chief Justices, 1899, p. 119, n. 2.)

WOOD v. LUCY, LADY DUFF-GORDON

(1917), 118 N.E. 214. New York Court of Appeals.

Cardozo, J. The defendant styles herself "a creator of fashions". Her favor helps a sale. Manufacturers of dresses, milinery, and like articles are glad to pay for a certificate of her approval. The things which she designs, fabrics, parasols, and what not, have a new value in the public mind when issued in her name. She employed the plaintiff to help her to turn this vogue into money. He was to have the exclusive right, subject always to her approval, to place her indorsements on the designs of others. He was also to have the exclusive right to place her own designs on sale, or to license others to market them. In return she was to have one-half of "all profits and revenues" derived from any contracts he might make. The exclusive right was to last at least one year from April 1, 1915, and thereafter from year to year unless terminated by notice of 90 days. The plaintiff says that he kept the contract on his part, and that the defendant broke it. She placed her indorsement on fabrics, dresses, and millinery without his knowledge, and withheld the profits. He sues her for the damages, and the case comes here on demurrer.

The agreement of employment is signed by both parties. It has a wealth of recitals. The defendant insists, however, that it lacks the elements of a contract. She says that the plaintiff does not bind himself to anything. It is true that he does not promise in so many words that he will use reasonable efforts to place the defendant's indorsements and market her designs. We think, however, that such a promise is fairly to be implied. The law has outgrown its primitive stage of formalism when the precise word was the sovereign talisman, and every slip was fatal. It takes a broader view to-day. A promise may be lacking, and yet the whole writing may be "instinct with an obligation", imperfectly expressed. ... If that is so, there is a contract.

The implication of a promise here finds support in many circumstances. The defendant gave an exclusive privilege. She was to have no right for at least a year to place her own indorsements or market her own designs except through the agency of the plaintiff. The acceptance of the exclusive agency was an assumption of its duties. ... Many other terms of the agreement point the same way. We are told at the outset by way of recital that:

"The said Otis F. Wood possesses a business organization adapted to the placing of such indorsements as the said Lucy, Lady Duff-Gordon, has approved."

The implication is that the plaintiff's business organization will be used for the purpose for which it is adapted. But the terms of the defendant's compensation are even more significant. His sole compensation for the grant of an exclusive agency is to be one-half of all the profits resulting from the plaintiff's efforts. Unless he gave his efforts, she could never get anything. Without an implied promise, the transaction cannot have such business "efficacy, as both parties must have intended that at all events it should have". Bowen, L.J., in the *Moorcock* (1889), 14 P.D. 64, 68. But the contract does not stop there. The plaintiff goes on to promise that he will account monthly for all moneys received by him, and that he will take out all such patents and copyrights and trade-marks as may in his judgment be necessary to protect the rights and articles affected by the agreement. It is true, of course, as the Appellate Division has said, that if he was under no duty to try to market designs or to place certificates of indorsement, his promise to account for profits or take out copyrights would be valueless. But in determining the intention of the parties the promise has a value. It helps to enforce the conclusion that the plaintiff had some duties. His promise to pay the defendant one-half of the profits and revenues resulting from the exclusive agency and to render accounts monthly was a promise to use reasonable efforts to bring profits and revenues into existence. For this conclusion the authorities are ample....

The judgment of the Appellate Division should be reversed, and the order of the Special Term affirmed, with costs in the Appellate Division and in this court.

Cuddeback, McLaughlin, and Andrews JJ., concur. Hiscock C.J., and Chase and Crane JJ., dissent.

Order reversed, etc.

QUESTION

Suppose that Wood had an exactly similar contract with another prominent woman, and that he gave Lucy only 10% of the business that he did through both women. Could she sue him? If so, what damages could she get?

U.C.C. § 2.306(2) and Comment.
§ 2 — 306. Output, Requirements and Exclusive Dealings

(2) A lawful agreement by either the seller or the buyer for exclusive dealing in the kind of goods concerned imposes unless otherwise agreed an obligation by the seller to use best efforts to supply the goods and by the buyer to use best efforts to promote their sale.

Official Comment

5. Subsection (2), on exclusive dealing, makes explicit the commercial rule embodied in this Act under which the parties to such contracts are held to have impliedly, even when not expressly, bound themselves to use reasonable diligence as well as good faith in their performance of the contract. Under such contracts the exclusive agent is required, although no express commitment has been made, to use reasonable effort and due diligence in the expansion of the market or the promotion of the product, as the case may be. The principal is expected under such a contract to refrain from supplying any other dealer or agent within the exclusive territory. An exclusive dealing agreement brings into play all the

good faith aspects of the output and requirement problems of subsection (1). It also raises questions of insecurity and right to adequate assurance under this Article.

The following are examples of problems that can come up.

1. An agreement between a printer and the Province of Quebec under which the printer agreed to print any documents the Province might ask him to print, was held to give no protection when the contract was cancelled (six months after it was made) by a newly elected government. The Province had not promised to give any work to the printer: *R. v. Demers*, [1900] A.C. 103. P.C.

2. An agreement giving the buyer the right to cancel the order at any time before shipment was held to be enforceable by the buyer since he would be bound if shipment were made before cancellation: *Gurfein v. Werbelovsky* (1922), 118 A. 32.

3. An agreement gave the licensee the right to manufacture and distribute "Orange Crush" in a certain territory. The licensor agreed to supply the concentrate and to advertise the product. The licence was perpetual, but the licensee could cancel the contract at any time. The licensor cancelled and licensee sought to prevent licensor doing so. The court held that there was no consideration and that the action failed: *Miami Coco-Cola Bottling Co. v. Orange Crush Co.* (1924), 296 F. 693.

QUESTIONS

a) Suppose that the concentrate supplied by the licensor was contaminated, could licensee sue for damages?

b) Suppose that the licensor breached the promise to advertise, could licensee sue, and, if so, for how much?

c) What interests are protected and what are not?

d) Would it make any difference that licensee had to give notice before it could cancel? Would one day's notice be enough? one month? one year?

See *Linder v. Mid Continent Petroleum Corp.* (1952), 252 S.W. 2d 631.

PROBLEM

Gargantua Ltd. gave Valerie Small an exclusive franchise to sell home freezers in Smithville, Ontario, a village of 400 people. The agreement gave Gargantua the power "to cancel this agreement at any time upon written notice, for any reason within the absolute discretion of the company." Valerie went to work selling freezers and in the first three months after making the agreement she had saturated Smithville. Sales then fell rapidly. Four months after the agreement was made Valerie received notice that the agreement was cancelled. Valerie was convinced that she could have continued to make some money for herself and for Gargantua had she been able to keep the dealership.

Has Valerie got any claim against Gargantua?

Would it matter whether Valerie had conducted her business out of her home or had rented store space for one year and erected (at her expense) a large sign advertising Gargantua freezers?

If the U.C.C. applied in Ontario would that make any difference to her claim?

The following extract shows how the law of contract functions in practice in a very significant business area. To what extent is the dichotomy between the law in practice and the law in the books justifiable? What is the *law*?

STEWART MACAULAY. "THE STANDARDIZED CONTRACTS OF UNITED STATES AUTOMOBILE MANUFACTURERS".

7 International Encyclopedia of Comparative Law. Chapter 3, Part 2.

[Most footnotes have been omitted.]

INTRODUCTION

21. The automobile industry in the United States is large, very complex and has great economic power. The major manufacturers are run as bureaucratic structures designed to operate efficiently at all levels. Those people and organizations that deal with the manufacturers have patterned their conduct to accommodate this model of economic efficiency. However, new models of automobiles must be designed several years before they are offered to the public and the demand for new automobiles fluctuates significantly. Bureaucratic operation in the service of economic efficiency, time-span and fluctuating demand are all critical factors which are reflected in many different kinds of exchange transactions found in this industry. In this paper we will consider some of the exchange relationships between the manufacturers, and their suppliers, their dealers and their customers in order to generalize about contract as it is found in this kind of large scale industry. This discussion will be limited to practices within the United States and the consequences of those practices under its legal system. We lack data for a full comparative analysis. Nonetheless what is said here is likely to have relevance in other nations. The automobile manufacturers are important transnational corporations and their practices are models for other large corporations. While the precise legal techniques used will differ, it is likely that the goal of risk avoidance and minimization will be pursued in all nations in which such organizations operate.

A. CONTRACTS TO BUILD AND SELL CARS

i. *The Manufacturers and Their Suppliers*

a. Description of the Relationship

22. Although the manufacturers can and do make in their own plants some of almost all of the parts which go into an assembled automobile, they also buy many of these parts from suppliers. There are a number of reasons why they purchase from outside suppliers. First, the manufacturer gets a product without investing additional capital in buildings, machines and a trained work force. Second, the manufacturer gets a yardstick which can be used to measure the efficiency of its own division making the same item. If a division making grease seals can produce them at 2 cents each, but an outside supplier can make them for 1½ cents each, the manufacturer knows he must reexamine the efficiency of his internal operation. Third, the manufacturer increases the chance that he may benefit from technological innovation. The supplier's designers and engineers may be able to suggest a different design or an improved manufacturing process. On the other side, most businesses, but not all, that can produce parts for automobiles want to sell their output to the automobile manufacturers because of the possibilities for extremely high volume production which, in an efficiently managed firm, can be highly profitable.

There are three additional factors influencing the course a manufacturer-supplier relationship takes: First, the mass production techniques of

American automobile manufacturing require that the assembly line not be stopped. When, for example, a particular Ford sedan arrives at a certain point on the assembly line four hubcaps must be there ready to be installed. It would be extremely costly to the manufacturer if the line had to be stopped because the supplier's machines that stamp out hubcaps broke down, because a suppliers' inventory was not great enough to meet the demand or because the parts were lost in shipment. However, demand for automobiles and even for particular types of automobiles fluctuates. To a great extent, this second factor offsets the first. The easiest way to avoid stopping assembly lines would be to produce large quantities of parts far in advance of need. Yet this approach increases costs because of the possibility of waste and the loss of the use of funds thus devoted to inventories. If, for example, the demand for station wagons declines during the year, exhaust pipes that fit only station wagons that will never be produced are mere scrap metal. Third, component parts can be defective, the defect can cause injury to property or person, and in United States law the injured party in such cases has increasingly been gaining rights against manufacturers. Not surprisingly, one finds that manufacturers wish to hold suppliers responsible for such claims, and the suppliers must defend themselves against the costly results of seemingly minor defects in the parts they make.

b. The Blanket Order System
aa. The System Described

23. The *manufacturers* have accommodated all of these economic and legal factors in an imaginative piece of transaction architecture which is usually called a "blanket order." [Many divisions of the General Motors Corporation use what are called requirements contracts rather than blanket orders. However, because of the way the General Motors' requirements contracts are written and administered, the two systems are essentially the same in operation. The General Motors' standard agreement form for production requirements calls for it to "purchase... approximately the percentage shown on the attached exhibit (of) the Buyer's requirements..." Legally, the key word would be "approximately" since it might be interpreted to undercut any commitment to buy.] Coupled with the suppliers' great desire to do business with the automobile manufacturers, the blanket order system almost always insures that parts will arrive at the assembly plants at the right time, that the suppliers will take the risk of scrapped parts caused by fluctuations in demand, and that the suppliers will be responsible for claims caused by defects. Moreoever, the system gives the manufacturers great leverage to ward off price increases caused by the suppliers' increased costs.

This is how it works: Some time before the beginning of the model year, the manufacturer will issue a blanket order to a supplier of, for example, tail pipes designed specifically for one of the manufacturer's station wagons. The blanket order states a number of "agreements". One of the most important is the price per unit. This price is computed on the basis of an estimated number of units to be ordered, and it will not be increased if fewer are actually ordered. Thus, the manufacturer has made the supplier run the risk that he will not even recover his cost of producing the items actually shipped to the manufacturer in the event that the manufacturer uses substantially fewer than the estimated number. And the blanket order does not oblige the manufacturer to take and pay for *any* of the parts described in it. The obligation comes only when the manufacturer sends the supplier documents called "releases." The idea seems to be that the blanket order creates a force which is held back until released little by little.

Each month, sometimes more often, the manufacturer sends the supplier a release, ordering him to manufacture and ship a specified number of the parts each week. On the release form, the manufacturer also will estimate the number of parts he will require for the next two or three months, but this estimate, to quote one manufacturer's form, "is for planning purposes only and does not constitute a commitment." Typically, manufacturers do not send releases calling for more parts than they will need in a month since their monthly estimates of sales are fairly accurate. However, sometimes they do order too few or too many parts. If there is an increase in public demand for a particular model, the blanket order allows the manufacturer to send another release form calling for increased deliveries. Such sudden increases may be a great strain on the supplier if he does not have unused capacity for production. Moreover, a supplier must always guard against a break-down of his machinery, which temporarily destroys his ability to meet the manufacturer's demands. As a result, the supplier usually makes more than the number of parts ordered by the manufacturer so that the supplier will have an inventory to cover anticipated future demands. He builds his inventory at his own risk since the blanket order clearly provides that "Seller shall not fabricate any articles covered by this order, or procure materials required therefor, or ship any articles to Purchaser, except to the extent authorized by ... written releases ... Purchaser will make no payments for finished work, work in process or raw material fabricated or produced by Seller in excess of Purchaser's written releases."

If a manufacturer his "released" too many parts in light of a sudden decrease in demand, the blanket order gives it the right to cancel the amount ordered in whole or in part. It then is obligated to pay the contract price for each part finished and "the cost to Seller (excluding profit or losses) of work in process and raw material, based on any audit Purchaser may conduct and generally accepted accounting principles ... "

bb. Blanket Orders and American Contract Law
(1) Legal Enforceability

24. American contract law would likely support the manufacturer's plan for the transaction so that, when the law is combined with the market situation, the manufacturer's interests would be favored. Under that law there must be an exchange of promises or of performances to create a legally enforceable contract. In a blanket order the manufacturer makes no promise until it sends a "release" and so until then there has been no exchange and contract rights have not been created. In effect, at the manufacturer's request, the supplier makes an offer – a promise to supply certain goods if they are ordered – which the manufacturer accepts every time it sends a release. The continuing offer and the many acceptances create a series of contracts. It is possible that two developing doctrines in the Common Law of the United States might be applied in the future to offer remedies despite the absence of a contract. Reliance by the manufacturer on the supplier's promise to fill all orders might receive legal protection, in the unlikely event it were needed, by the growing "firm offer" doctrine. Reliance by the supplier on any assurances (most likely implied ones) of the manufacturer that it would order a reasonable quantity might be protected by the development of rules requiring fairness in negotiations.

25. One can only speculate about the legal situation in light of general principles of contract law and the Uniform Commercial Code, since litigation testing these conclusions is unlikely. The large automobile manufacturers try to avoid placing total reliance on any one supplier, and other suppliers usually can increase production so that a manufacturer's assembly line is not stopped for lack of an item. Thus manufacturers tend to avoid injury rather than litigate for compensation. On the other hand, no automobile parts supplier is likely to bring a case against a manufacturer; the loss on any one order is very unlikely to be large enough to justify jeopardizing future business. Of course, the trustee of a bankrupt supplier would be free of this constraint. However, in light of the uncertainty of the supplier's legal position, many trustees would think it unwise to risk the cost of legal action against a manufacturer.

26. What are the consequences of the legal situation? If we assume that the developing reliance and fairness doctrines would not apply, the parties get legal rights only after the manufacturer has issued a release and only as to the goods ordered in that release. This means that there can be a great deal of reliance by the supplier which is unprotected by contract rights. On the other hand, legally the supplier would be free to refuse to continue the relationship by revoking his outstanding offer to supply the parts as ordered by the release forms. As we have said previously, few suppliers who were not going out of business could afford to exercise such a right; very few situations short of bankruptcy would justify losing the good will of General Motors, Ford, Chrysler or American Motors. Most importantly for the manufacturer, it does get legal rights once a release is issued. As a result, it manages to avoid any question that the supplier will bear liability for injuries caused by defective parts which it ships. Once the parts are ordered by a release there is a contract which the manufacturer has written, and the disclaimers and limitations of remedy so typically found in documents drafted by sellers are thus avoided. As between Chrysler and its suppliers, the responsibility for compliance with federal safety and air pollution regulations is also clearly placed on the supplier.

(2) Remedies

27. The standard blanket order documents drastically limit the remedies to which a supplier would otherwise be entitled under American contract law once a legally binding contract is created by the issuance of a release. Typically, the manufacturer reserves a right to cancel the goods ordered by its release, either in whole or in part. Under American contract law such a cancellation would be a breach if not authorized by the agreement, and, absent a contract provision to the contrary, the seller would be entitled to recover what he had spent in performance before the buyer's notice of cancellation plus the profit he would have made had he been allowed to complete his performance. Most blanket order cancellation clauses, however, exclude a right to profit except as to those parts which have been completed before cancellation. Thus even when a contract is formed by a release, the supplier's rights in most situations will be minimal. The manufacturer gains a practical commitment from the supplier to meet the demands of its assembly line. It retains maximum flexibility by making no commitment to buy any parts until a release is given and making only a very limited payment if it wishes to cancel after one is sent.

c. The Absence of a Reform Movement

28. There are no statutes attempting to regulate this relationship, and no movement seeking such legislation has been discovered. Insofar as statutes in the United States are the result of pluralistic struggle and compromise, one essential element of pluralism seems lacking. It would be hard to form a group of suppliers to seek legislation. Supplying the manufacturers is very profitable for a firm that can accept all of the risks allocated to it by the blanket order system. Such successful firms would hesitate to jeopardize their standing with the manufacturers by supporting an organization taking a stand antagonistic to the manufacturers' interests. Without the most successful firms, such a group would lack political power. Firms that do not wish to assume the risks of the blanket order system can easily seek other customers since their facilities are not limited to producing original-equipment automobile parts. "Exit" is a relatively cheap remedy for dissatisfaction in this case. The facilities devoted to producing original-equipment parts can be converted readily to producing parts for repairing automobiles – the so-called "after market" – or to supplying related industries such as truck or industrial engine manufacturers which, generally, do not have the bargaining power to use the blanket order system. "Voice" – using private or legal power to change the allocation of risks – would entail high costs and the chances of success would not be great in light of the many resources of the manufacturers.

Moreover, insofar as statutes flow from the efforts of those with access to the communications media attempting to enhance their status and power by acting as champions of the deserving underprivileged, this seems an unpromising area. The auto parts suppliers typically are not small businessmen but only smaller organizations than the giant auto manufacturers. The image of the suppliers is that of junior partners who are well-paid for taking large but acceptable risks: it would be hard for an ambitious United States Senator to champion them as the exploited victims of the corporate system.

Finally, insofar as one explains United States legislation as an instrument of the powerful to further their interests, no statutory action is needed in this area. The Common Law of contracts serves to legitimate and support the manufacturers' procedures by minimizing or denying rights to the suppliers.

29. In summary, the manufacturers have tailored a relationship whereby they get most of the advantages of producing parts in a division of their own firms while preserving most of the advantages of dealing with an outside organization. The suppliers are offered a chance to make high profits in exchange for assuming great risks. Most suppliers are eager for the chance to play the blanket order game. The public may get better automobiles at a lower price as a result of the system, but one cannot be sure. There are important parallels to the contract system used by the United States government to procure military equipment such as tanks and aircraft. Since experience may change the need for a weapon or call for a modification in its design, the government retains great power to change or terminate its orders to private industry while paying less than the damages specified in general contract law (see *infra* ch. 4). It is thought that the risks in dealing with the United States government are reflected in higher prices paid to the weapons industry on government contracts. The automobile manufacturers may also pay for the flexibility in the blanket order system. However, unlike the United States government, the manufacturers make some of their own

needs of each type of part. They can turn to their own division if prices are too high, and they can negotiate about prices with suppliers in the light of detailed knowledge about what it costs to make the item. Moreover, unlike the government's, the manufacturers' decisions and negotiations are not directly subject to political process.

ii. *The Manufacturers and Their Dealers*
a. Description of the Relationship

30. The automobile manufacturers sell most of their cars through networks of "franchised" dealers. The dealers are independent businessmen. The franchise system offers, or at one time offered, a number of advantages to manufacturers as compared to operation of their own stores at the retail level. Instead of having its capital tied up in show-rooms and garages, the manufacturer can pass this burden on to a dealer. Moreover, a dealer who has invested his own money in the business has incentives which would not work as forcefully on an employee managing a factory-owned sales branch. The dealer will want to maximize his own return by his sales success. Selling cars is also a trading business since most potential customers have an older machine to trade in on a new one. A dealer will have more incentive to keep a trade-in allowance at a reasonable level than would an employee. As to the public interest, independent dealerships offer advantages of decentralization in decisionmaking. The dealer should be able to treat the customer as an individual rather than merely apply rules developed by a home office for governing branch office operations. These are the reasons usually offered to explain the franchise system. Today, however, the manufacturers may not need the contributions of capital from their dealers, and they may have adequate incentives and controls as bureaucratic techniques have developed. Nonetheless, the manufacturers would face significant political opposition if they attempted to end the franchise system suddenly and openly. American society has been concerned about the size and power of the automobile industry for a number of years, and such a display of power and the resulting injury to small businessmen would likely prompt some governmental response.

The franchise contracts impose certain controls which are designed, primarily, to serve the *manufacturers'* goals. A dealer might want to sell fewer units at a high profit on each one; the manufacturer wants to sell more units and wants dealers to take a smaller profit on each to maximize volume. It is easier to coordinate a network of dealers across the Unites States if there is a certain amount of standardization. A manufacturer wants its trade name used so as to exploit its advertising, but some actions of a dealer can injure that trade name. For example, customers may identify poor service with the manufacturer when the local dealers' performance is poor. All in all, the manufacturer wants to gain the advantages of having a network of independent businessmen handling problems at the retail level while still enjoying the advantages of the control it would have if it ran its own retailing entirely.

The dealer sees the franchise as a way to run a very profitable business, trading on the good name of the manufacturer. And most dealers are among the most successful retailers in their communities. But dealers tend to want independence from factory control; they want freedom to run "their" business as they see fit. From a standpoint of bargaining power, the relationship is one of dependance of the dealers on the manufacturer. A dealer's building, organization and skills cannot readily be shifted into another type of business, and there are few alternative franchises available. Rarely, will a manufacturer ever need the services of a specific dealer.

b. The Original Dealer Franchise: A Contract at Will

31. Sometime in the mid-1950's, the manufacturers changed the relationships they had with their dealers because of the impact of the legal system. Before this time, the relationship with the dealers was very similar to the one they have with the parts suppliers. The franchise document typically was relatively short; it required, in effect, that the dealer keep the company satisfied with his sales, service, facilities, and personality; carefully said that the manufacturer was not promising to fill any of the dealer's orders for cars or parts and that the dealer was not an agent for the company; and allowed either party to terminate the relationship at will. The dealer had no contract rights that could be enforced in court, third parties would have had trouble holding the company responsible for the dealer's actions, and the company could press for greater sales by being hard to satisfy and using its right to terminate at will as a sanction. Upon cancellation a dealer lost any going-business value and found himself with a sales and service building which could not easily be put to any other use. And manufacturers did threaten to cancel franchises and in fact did so. Moreover, dealers were coerced to purchase hard-to-sell types of cars and accessories from the manufacturers. During the depression of the 1930's, manufacturers pushed dealers relentlessly for more sales, sales which were extremely difficult to make. During the early 1950's, General Motors and Ford competed for dominance in the market, and both used great pressure on their dealers to outsell the competition.

c. Reform Through the Legal System
aa. The Law of Contracts

32. Increasingly during this period, cancelled automobile dealers turned to the legal system to try to offset the manufacturers' power under the franchise system. Some sued for breach of contract, attempting to convince courts to construe the franchises as imposing a duty of good faith on the manufacturers. Most of these suits were unsuccessful as the courts stressed that the dealers had assumed the risks of the franchise system voluntarily when they entered into such one-sided relationships. The standard of free contract served to justify the use of the manufacturers' economic power.

bb. The State Legislation

33. In 1937, an automobile dealers' trade association successfully lobbied for legislation in Wisconsin which was to become the model for legislation in 20 other states. The most successful of these statutes required manufacturers and their representatives who contracted dealers to obtain state licenses. Licenses could be revoked if a manufacturer or his representative: (1) induced or coerced a dealer to accept delivery of cars or other things that he did not order, or attempted to do this; (2) induced or coerced a dealer to enter any agreement with the manufacturer or "to do any other act unfair to said dealer" by threatening to cancel the dealer's franchise, or attempting to do this; (3) "(u)nfairly, without due regard to the equities of said dealer and without just provocation..." cancelled the franchise of a dealer. As a result of these statutes, in many states informal mediation procedures have evolved. Dealers with complaints meet representatives of the manufacturers

in informal hearings before the agencies which administer these statutes
and bargain out their differences. Typically, it is unnecessary to hold formal
hearings for license revocation or to go to court for enforcement of private
rights granted by the statutes, steps which are expensive for both parties
and used only as a last resort for recouping losses or for vengeance when all
else fails. The statutes create and maintain bargaining power for the dealers
to offset, to some degree, the manufacturers' natural advantages.

While many of these state statutes were highly effective, some were not.
In a few cases, state supreme courts declared them unconstitutional. In
other states, the statutes assigned enforcement responsibilities to agencies
which had neither the desire nor the resources to enforce them. Finally, the
automobile manufacturers successfully lobbied to prevent passage of such
statutes in many states. All of this prompted an appeal to the federal government.

cc. The Federal Legislation
(1) The Impact of Hearings

34. The National Association of Automobile Dealers sought help before
the Federal Congress in 1954. Full dress hearings were held before two Senate Committees and received wide press and television coverage. As a result
of, and in defense against these hearings, the manufacturers rewrote their
franchise agreements. Most significantly, they set up standards of performance. In order to justify cancellation, a dealer would have to fail to meet
one of these standards; no longer did the manufacturers reserve the power
to cancel at will. For example, now a Ford dealer's sales performance is
measured by first comparing the dealer's sales to (1) the total registration of
all cars in his locality, (2) the sales objectives established by Ford for his
locality, and (3) the sales of Chevrolet, Plymouth and American Motors in
his locality. Secondly, the dealer's sales are compared to (1) those of three
other Ford dealers of comparable size in the nearest comparable areas, and
(2) the average of all Ford dealers in his zone, district, region, and nationally. In making these comparisons Ford will also consider (1) the history of
the dealer's sales performance, (2) the availability of cars to the dealer, and
(3) "special local conditions that might affect the dealer's sales
performance." While this is a more limited right to cancel than the old
requirement that a dealer sell "to the satisfaction" of Ford, the factory still
retains broad discretion to increase the sales objectives for an area as it con-
ducts new surveys, to select the areas for comparison purposes, and to judge
both whether cars were available and whether there were local conditions
which adversely affected sales. In addition to rewriting the franchise documents, the manufacturers created internal review systems to which dealers
could appeal if they were unhappy with the administration of the relationship. General Motors has an umpire, who acts as a judge within their private legal system.

(2) The "Dealers Day in Court" Act

35. In addition to these manufacturer-initiated changes, the hearings
before Congress in the mid-1950's produced legislation. The federal
"Dealers Day in Court" Act giving dealers the right to sue manufacturers
who failed to act in "good faith" was passed. "Good faith" was defined as:
"the duty of each party to any franchise... to act in a fair and equitable
manner toward each other so as to guarantee the one party freedom from

coercion, intimidation, or threat of coercion or intimidation from the other party: *Provided,* that recommendation, endorsement, exposition, persuasion, urging or argument shall not be deemed to constitute a lack of good faith."

The *proviso* was drafted by the Ford Motor Company and accepted by a House of Representatives Committee. Many dealers have sought relief under the Act, but only a handful have won judgments which have not been reversed by the appellate courts. The *proviso* and the Committee Report on the statute have been used to construe the statute so that it does not apply to any conduct likely to occur within the manufacturer-dealer relationship. Although it is possible that judicial construction may open a new avenue leading to change, so far the statute cannot be shown to have been an important influence on transactions between manufacturers and their dealers.

dd. New Problems: New Attempts at Reform

36. In the mid-1960's, a new problem became significant. Manufacturers, particularly the Chrysler Corporation, turned to creating very large dealerships located in the fastest growing areas in large cities. The factories either put up buildings and ran the dealerships themselves or financed a man to begin such a dealership. The older established dealers were angered – and often financially hurt – by the new competition. They turned to suits under the Dealers Day in Court Act, to lobbying for more state statutes to license manufacturers and to a new round of hearings before the United States Senate. This battle continues.

B. CONCLUSIONS

i. *The Balance of Power and Risk*

a. The Manufacturers' Power

48. One can see some common elements in all of these relationships between manufacturers and others. Generally, the automobile manufacturer has great power and the market does not prevent him from writing a contract to serve his own interests, whether the other party is a supplier, dealer or new car buyer. For example, the manufacturer offers both suppliers and dealers the chance to earn unusually great returns on their investments which for most suppliers and dealers makes the power of the manufacturers easy to accept. Buyers of automobiles have relatively few manufacturers to choose from, and there is little competitive advantage in assuming a liability for injuries caused by defects in cars since a manufacturer could not advertise that he had assumed such a responsibility without, at the same time, drawing to the attention of potential buyers the fact that cars are sometimes defective and hurt people. Also buyers often are concerned with the appearance of a car and its price far more than with its safety and reliability – qualities which they just take for granted. Even in the rare instances where the other party – a supplier, for example, writes the contract, the automobile manufacturer's economic power serves to deter any attempt to use rights formally reserved. For example, Ford and Reynolds Aluminum Corporation had a contract drafted by Reynolds whereby it received a legal right to supply up to 30 per cent of the dollar volume of Ford's annual purchases of aluminum products. A Reynolds executive responded to a question from a Congressional Committee by saying:

"I don't think I agree with you that the contract requires Ford to buy 30 per cent from us ... Maybe that is the final legal commitment but we are not in position to require Ford to do much of anything at the time we try to sell it."

A Ford executive stressed that Ford viewed the contract, despite its express terms, as merely giving Reynolds "an opportunity to quote" prices.

b. Dependent Relationships

49. What kinds of relationships do manufacturers create when they exercise their power? They create contracts of adhesion with all the characteristics of standardization to serve the ends of coordinating large scale enterprise. These contracts can be viewed profitably as a type of private legislation – the Ford dealer franchise document even looks like a statute; it has a preamble, an elaborate organization with cross references and definitions, and a detailed index. Much first class legal and business talent has been applied to planning and drafting these "contracts." These men have produced elaborate systems for dealing with complicated situations in uniform ways. Transaction plans have been mass produced so that lower status personnel have relatively few important decisions to make. Moreover, economic power and standardization have been used to ward off risks by transferring them to others. If demand for automobiles falls, suppliers must assume some of the loss. If the factory wants to replace a dealer, he takes the risk of a loss of going business value. If there is an accident, the consumer takes the risk of injury. Of course, as a matter of administering these relationships the manufacturers can grant favors to suppliers, dealers or buyers, but these are favors and not legal rights except in the instances where legal regulation has interfered.

50. These standardized contracts are carefully worded to avoid contractual liability in most instances. No major commitments are made under blanket orders which could justify a suit for breach of contract. Originally, a dealer franchise was terminable at will. Now it can only be terminated for failure to comply with a complex standard which, however, gives the manufacturer the power to make a series of judgments as to the adequacy of a dealer's sales. While the courts might find that these judgments must be made in good faith, it is unlikely that this would be a serious limitation on the manufacturer's power to behave so as to maximize its economic interests. To a great extent, in these areas freedom of contract is the freedom to have no contract – as far as having a legally enforceable agreement is concerned. The new car warranty granted to buyers, on the other hand, is designed as a legally enforceable contract, but the main reason it is designed to be legally enforceable is to disclaim a liability which would be imposed if no contract were made concerning it. It, too, is an attempt to avoid legal control over private power.

ii. *Evaluation: Benefits at What Price?*
a. The Balance of Gains and Costs

51. Undoubtedly, this kind of rationalized planning has advantages. It is not an insignificant part of a system which has produced great wealth for executives of automobile manufacturers, stockholders in these companies, automobile dealers, parts suppliers, and even, to some extent, for workers employed by this industry and its satellites. The high demand for automobiles produces opportunities for profit and jobs in many related industries and has a major impact on the total American economy. The system may have produced less expensive automobiles than could be made by any other, since one can assume that if the manufacturers had had to assume all of the risks they avoid by these contracts, they would have passed on these costs to buyers in the form of higher prices for new cars.

52. However, these benefits have not come without important economic and social costs. Perhaps the most significant cost is the contribution that this rationalization has made to a system of private transportation based on replacing private machines before the end of their useful lives. One can point to the waste of scarce resources and the misallocation of public funds that this society has used for super-highways and car storage at the price of the decline of the mass transportation system and the neglect of the needs of those who cannot and do not wish to drive their own automobiles.

There are also costs even if one assumes that the United States' system of transportation based largely on the private automobile is, on balance, a good thing. The planning structures which have been described here maximize economic rationality at the cost of other values, most of which we can categorize as personal concerns. Parts suppliers and automobile dealers must operate under great emotional pressure, constantly facing economic tests that are hard to pass. The blanket order and the dealer franchise are designed to minimize the pull of considerations such as sympathy and forgiveness of mistakes. These mechanisms call for people to devote major portions of their lives to a kind of competitive "sport" – can Jones Corporation make a grease seal more cheaply than Ford's own division can? Can the Ford dealer in a particular city overtake the Chevrolet dealer and sell more cars? Moreover, in order for rationalized economic plans to work, parts suppliers, dealers and automobile buyers must surrender important amounts of control of their own destinies and enter relationships of dependency on large and relatively impersonal organizations. For example, an executive for a major supplier to the automobile industry has described to me the frustration of trying to talk about changes in the blanket order system or in its administration with a representative of the manufacturer. The representative with whom the executive could talk have no authority to make changes in procedures. The executive tried to get an appointment with officials who had this power, but these men refused to see him. Automobile dealers make similar complaints. They must use advertising designed by the manufacturer, install the manufacturer's bookkeeping and accounting system, and rely on the manufacturer to offer and make available to the dealers the kinds of cars that they can sell without having any voice themselves in these matters. This dependency and control stands in sharp contrast with the usual invocation of the advantages of being an "independent businessman" in the American "free enterprise" system. The new car buyer similarly cannot negotiate with those who have power to bind the manufacturer; the buyer must deal with a dealer who lacks this authority. The buyer usually gets an automobile of a certain degree of reliability and safety. However, a buyer's ability to purchase cars produced by competitors is only one of many influences on that degree of reliability and saftey since most cars offered to the public are about equally safe and reliable. Also, there are few channels of information about the matter so that most buyers will lack knowledge. Manufacturers do warrant their cars against certain defects for a given period of time, but automobile buyers have complained that often they have real difficulty in getting a dealer even to make the warranted repairs. In order to control dealers who might too liberally make repairs for good-will purposes at the manufacturer's expense, the manufacturers have set up great economic disincentives that discourage dealers from performing warranty repairs except in clear cases. If a dealer refuses a claimed warranty repair, there is little a buyer can do. If the buyer writes to the manufacturer, he will be referred back to the dealer. Such a letter and reference will serve to insure that the dealer is applying the manufacturer's standards for repairs which should be made under the warranty. However, the buyer is subject to the manufacturer's interpretation of its warranty, an interpretation not necessarily consonant with the buyer's expectations based on the manufacturer's advertising. Private lawsuits are too expensive to offer a remedy in any but a few cases. Few buyers have the resources or courage to follow the successful tactics adopted by one man who was very dissatisfied with his new Chevrolet and the dealer's and manufacturer's attempts to fix it. This buyer continually telephoned the home of the man who was then the head of the Chevrolet Division of General Motors and asked for action. Finally, in exchange for an agreement not to harass the Chevrolet executive, General Motors gave its dissatisfied customer a new car.

53. One could point to a mitigating factor, perhaps. One could argue that in each instance an individual made a choice to enter the relationship with the automobile manufacturer. To some extent this is true. The parts supplier is, perhaps, the most free. Exit is a real option for him. There are alternative uses for the supplier's enterprise, most suppliers know the implications of the system, and blanket orders are written anew each year in most cases. If a supplier is willing to sacrifice the chance for a high return offered by the automobile industry, he can turn to other kinds of business. Dealers, too, are probably aware of the implications of the franchise system, but they are locked in with few alternatives. There are few, if any, other uses for their skills, capital investment and going business value. Buyers of new cars neither know the system nor have realistic alternatives. Essentially the same disclaimer is used by all four American manufacturers of automobiles; practically, one cannot bargain for a different contract to buy a new car if one wanted to do so since a consumer must negotiate with a dealer who lacks authority to increase the obligations assumed by the manufacturer; and the disclaimer is, as a practical matter, effectively hidden from the consumer – at the time of the sale, it is not easy to find the disclaimer clause and if one does notice it, its wording would carry meaning only to a lawyer.

Of course, if a manufacturer were to acquire a reputation for producing unreliable or unsafe cars, consumers could deal with its competitors. Whatever the problems with the legal response to disclaimers and poor service, the possibility of this kind of exit could minimize the number of unsafe or unreliable cars produced. Undoubtedly, this is an important sanction influencing manufacturers to build safer and more reliable automobiles or to use public relations techniques to avoid a bad reputation. It has been suggested, however, that dissatisfied customers may tend to cancel each other out thereby lessening the impact of this sanction – unhappy buyers of Fords purchase new Chevrolets only to be replaced as Ford customers by unhappy buyers of Chevrolets. Insofar as cost pressures mean that all automobiles selling for a comparable price will be of about equal quality, exit will produce no signal to the managements of manufacturers that there is real dissatisfaction.

b. Legal Ideology and Reality

54. The law of any country tends to support its prevailing economic structures. The United States is no exception. However, bureaucratic

rationality is a principle which often clashes with older individualistic values also found in Western culture and in its law. Recently, the accommodations between these competing values made in the late nineteenth and early twentieth centuries have been giving way. English and American contract law have long been based on an ideology of free choice or manifested free choice. Yet economic rationality has been furthered by standardization that disregards individual differences. Large organizations have controlled risks and set patterns with form contracts that minimize the element of even manifested choice. On one hand, these documents originally were drafted to give the party dealing with the organization few or no rights. Until recently, courts were willing to accept this, and they reconciled such economic planning with their individualistic doctrines by speaking of assuming the risk of what might be written in a standard form contract if one did not read and understand it. Where it was obvious that the individual in no way had led the large organization's representatives to understand that he was assuming a particular risk assigned to him by the organization's forms, courts responded by talking of the duty to read and what the individual ought to have known. On the other hand, where the documents purported to create legally enforceable obligations, the courts were willing to enforce them although the individual had very little opportunity to discover particular provisions or to understand them. For example, disclaimers are often buried in small type on the backs of forms. Before 1960, most buyers of new cars could discover the disclaimer of liability for injuries caused by defects in the car only after they took delivery of the automobile and long after they signed the contract to buy it. Courts did not give serious consideration to the question of whether the disclaimer ever had made its way into the contract between the parties. In a real sense, courts were willing to distort the legitimating ideals of contract law – that is, choice or manifest choice – in the service of economic development through facilitating large scale private corporate economic power. To be sure, liability for what one "should have" known can be made to appear consistent with manifested choice, but the appearance is a matter of form rather than substance in light of the announced purposes of the manifest choice doctrine. Perhaps, such a cover for facilitating rational bureaucratic operations of private corporations was once socially useful; perhaps, in certain industries, such a policy could be defended openly today.

55. But recently there has been a trend toward recognition of the fictitious quality of the individual choice assumed in the application of contract doctrine and toward substitution of rules imposed by government for those imposed by one party and adhered to by the other. The *Henningsen* decision that overturned the manufacturers' uniform disclaimer is but one manifestation of this. Moreover, government has begun to move in other, perhaps more effective, ways. Publicity techniques of a congressional committee may be the most effective control of a powerful industry such as automobiles. The operations of the automobile industry are now of great concern to a number of United States Senators, and this concern is publicized in the news media. Charges of unsafe cars, unfair treatment of dealers and customers and atmospheric pollution by the internal combustion engine get attention in the newspapers and on television. Restrictive legislation is introduced. Some is passed. Even that which does not pass is a threat to the industry. Perhaps at one time automobile manufacturing was an

infant industry in the United States to be fostered by all means available, including the legal. Today, many would have it face an accounting measured by values other than economic efficiency – most goods for least cost – and bureaucratic rationality. In fact, the success of this view in the past 10 to 20 years has prompted some to worry about the costs of imposing these new standards. Concern for suppliers, dealers and purchasers of new cars could increase the price of new automobiles and decrease job opportunities in making, selling and repairing the vehicles insofar as increased cost causes decreased demand. To the extent that this is the case, the middle class part supplier, the automobile dealer and the customer of more costly cars will be benefited at the expense of workers who will lose jobs and the less well off who no longer will be able to afford a car in a society where a car is often both a symbol of success and an economic necessity.

(Completed in April 1973)

[Professor Macaulay also discussed the relationship between the automobile manufacturers and the purchasers of new cars. This part has been omitted for this extract, though as you can see he discussed it extensively in his conclusion. The problems of the automobile manufacturers and their customers is discussed in Chapter 6 of these materials. (See, *Henningsen v. Bloomfield Motors* (*infra*).)]

(4) *PERFORMANCE OF A LEGAL DUTY AS CONSIDERATION: MODIFICATION AND WAIVER OF CONTRACTUAL DUTIES*

The next few cases raise one of the most important current problems of the law of consideration. Here, perhaps more clearly than in any other aspect of the doctrine of consideration we can see the influence of unarticulated premises and conceptualism. We must again be prepared to ask what reasons might there be for refusing to enforce any particular promise?

HARRIS v. WATSON

(1791), Peake 102; 170 E.R. 94. At Nisi Prius.

In this case the declaration stated, that the plaintiff being a seaman on board the ship "Alexander," of which the defendant was master and commander, and which was bound on a voyage to Lisbon: whilst the ship was on her voyage, the defendant, in consideration that the plaintiff would perform some extra work, in navigating the ship, promised to pay him five guineas over and above his common wages. There were other counts for work and labour, &c.

The plaintiff proved that the ship being in danger, the defendant, to induce the seamen to exert themselves, made the promise stated in the first count.

Lord Kenyon. — If this action was to be supported, it would materially affect the navigation of this kingdom. It has been long since determined, that when the freight is lost, the wages are also lost. This rule was founded on a principle of policy, for if sailors were in all events to have their wages, and in times of danger entitled to insist on an extra charge on such a promise as this, they would in many cases suffer a ship to sink, unless the captain would pay any extravagant demand they might think proper to make.

The plaintiff was nonsuited.

STILK v. MYRICK

(1809), 2 Camp. 317; 170 E.R. 1168. At Nisi Prius.

This was an action for seaman's wages, on a voyage from London to the Baltic and back.

By the ship's articles, executed before the commencement of the voyage, the plaintiff was to be paid at the rate of £5 a month; and the principal question in the cause was, whether he was entitled to a higher rate of wages? — In the course of the voyage two of the seamen deserted; and the captain having in vain attempted to supply their places at Cronstadt, there entered into an agreement with the rest of the crew, that they should have the wages of the two who had deserted equally divided among them, if he could not procure two other hands at Gottenburgh. This was found impossible; and the ship was worked back to London by the plaintiff and eight more of the original crew, with whom the agreement had been made at Cronstadt.

Garrow for the defendant insisted, that this agreement was contrary to public policy, and utterly void. In West India voyages, crews are often thinned greatly by death and desertion; and if a promise of advanced wages were valid, exorbitant claims would be set up on all such occasions. This ground was strongly taken by Lord Kenyon in *Harris v. Watson*, Peak. Cas. 72, where that learned Judge held, that no action would lie at the suit of a sailor on a promise of a captain to pay him extra wages, in consideration of his doing more than the ordinary share of duty in navigating the ship; and his Lordship said, that if such a promise could be enforced, sailors would in many cases suffer a ship to sink unless the captain would accede to any extravagant demand they might think proper to make.

The Attorney-General, *contra*, distinguished this case from *Harris v. Watson*, as the agreement here was made on shore, when there was no danger or pressing emergency, and when the captain could not be supposed to be under any constraint or apprehension. The mariners were not to be permitted on any sudden danger to force concessions from the captain; — but why should they be deprived of the compensation he voluntarily offers them in perfect security for their extra labour during the remainder of the voyage?

Lord Ellenborough. — I think *Harris v. Watson* was rightly decided; but I doubt whether the ground of public policy, upon which Lord Kenyon is stated to have proceeded, be the true principle on which the decision is to be supported. Here, I say, the agreement is void for want of consideration. There was no consideration for the ulterior pay promised to the mariners who remained with the ship. Before they sailed from London they had undertaken to do all that they could under all the emergencies of the voyage. They had sold all their services till the voyage should be completed. If they had been at liberty to quit the vessel at Cronstadt, the case would have been quite different; or if the captain had capriciously discharged the two men who were wanting, the others might not have been compellable to take the whole duty upon themselves, and their agreeing to do so might have been a sufficient consideration for the promise of an advance of wages. But the desertion of a part of the crew is to be considered an emergency of the voyage as much as their death; and those who remain are bound by the terms of their original contract to exert themselves to the utmost to bring the ship in safety to her destined port. Therefore, without looking to the policy of this agreement, I think it is void for want of consideration, and that the plaintiff can only recover at the rate of £5 a month.

Verdict accordingly.

[The plaintiff's counsel included one Espinasse. Espinasse also published a report of this case, (6 Esp. 129; 170 E.R. 851). In that report Lord Ellenborough made no mention of the problem of consideration and was quite content to follow *Harris v. Watson*. Espinasse, however, is not held in very high regard as a reporter (one judge is reported to have said that he did not want to "hear from Espinasse or any other ass"!) and we assume that Campbell (whose entire report is given above) was reasonably accurate. On the other hand, the arguments of counsel are based entirely on the applicability of the public policy decision in *Harris v. Watson*. We cannot know now just what Lord Ellenborough said, and it does not really matter for the case has been treated as a "leading case" and is now authority for the proposition that a new promise by a person who is already bound to perform for the defendant is unenforceable. See: Gilmore, *The Death of Contract*, chap. 1.]

RAGGOW v. SCOUGALL

(1915), 31 T.L.R. 564. Divisional Court.

This was an appeal by the defendants, Messrs. Scougall and Co., who were a firm of mantle-makers, from a decision of Judge Rentoul in the City of London Court, by which the plaintiff, a mantle designer, recovered judgment for £58.

Mr. Frampton appeared for the appellants; and Mr. Tyfield for the respondent.

In August, 1913, the plaintiff by an agreement in writing agreed to become the defendants' designer for two years at a certain salary. It was provided that if the business should be discontinued during the period the agreement should cease to be of any effect. When the war broke out many customers cancelled orders which they had given to the firm, and the defendants had to consider whether they should close the business altogether. They called their employees together, and most of them agreed to a reduction of wages during the war if the defendants would continue the business. The plaintiff entered into a new agreement in writing, in which he, like other employees of the firm, agreed to accept a smaller salary for the duration of the war, provided that when the war was over the terms of the old agreement should be revived. He went on with his work and accepted the new salary until February last, when the defendants received a solicitor's letter claiming payment in full at the rate fixed in the old agreement; and as they refused to pay the excess this action was brought.

In the Court below judgment was given for the plaintiff on the ground that no consideration had been shown for the new agreement to accept a reduced payment.

Mr. Frampton now submitted that the new agreement had annulled the old one, and had entirely replaced it.

Mr. Tyfield submitted that the new agreement was merely a variation of the old in one particular, the amount of salary, and that in all other respects the old one remained in force; there was, therefore, no consideration for the promise to accept a less sum and the new agreement was void within *Foakes v. Beer* (9 App. Cas., 605).

Mr. Justice Darling said that the appeal must be allowed. It was clear from the provision in the new agreement that the terms of the old one should be revived when the war came to an end, and that until the war ended the old agreement was dead. The parties had in fact torn up the old agreement and made a new one by mutual consent. They could have done it by recitals setting out the existence and rescission of the old agreement, but they had adopted a shorter course. The new agreement was an agreement contemplating employment on certain terms while the war lasted, and on certain other terms, which could be ascertained by reference to the older document, after the war had ended. The point, therefore, as to want of consideration failed and the appeal succeeded. He was the more glad to be able to arrive at this conclusion on the law, for it was evident that the plaintiff was trying to do a very dishonest thing.

Mr. Justice Coleridge agreed.

QUESTIONS

1. Why does the court accept the argument that the parties made a new agreement here and not in *Stilk v. Myrick*?

2. Why is this plaintiff *dishonest*? Compare this case with *Foakes v. Beer* (1884) 9 App. Cas. 605 (Reproduced, *infra*). The House of Lords did not call Mrs. Beer *dishonest*, yet how does that case differ from *Raggow v. Scougall*?

3. If there was rescission in this case why was there not rescission in *Stilk v. Myrick*?

4. Would any of the parties in either *Stilk v. Myrick* or *Raggow v. Scougall* have regarded themselves at any time as being completely discharged from further performance? If not, how then can there be rescission in either case? Is rescission as much of a "case-knife" as consideration?

SMITH v. DAWSON

(1923), 53 O.L.R. 615. Ontario Supreme Court, Appellate Division.

[The plaintiffs agreed to build a house for the defendant for $6,464. When the house was nearly finished, a fire took place in it, doing considerable damage. The defendant had insured the building, and received $2,150 from the insurers. (She also insured her furniture for $1,000.) The plaintiffs took out no insurance. After the fire, the defendant asked the plaintiff to go on and complete the work and gave them to understand that she would pay over the $2,150 to them. The County Court Judge gave judgment for the plaintiffs for $1,666. The defendant appealed.]

Riddell J.: — ... The situation then seems quite clear — the plaintiffs, learning that the defendant had received some insurance money on the house, objected to go on without having some kind of assurance that they were to get the insurance money — the defendant demurred, as she had lost considerably by the destruction of her furniture, but finally said, "All right, go ahead and do the work." If this constituted a contract at all, it was that she would give them the insurance money which she had received, if they would go ahead and do the work they were already under a legal obligation to do.

In some of the United States a doctrine has been laid down that (at least in building contracts) the contractor has the option either to complete his contract or to abandon it and pay damages. These Courts have accordingly held that the abandonment by the contractor of his option to abandon is sufficient consideration for a promise to pay an extra amount.

The Courts of Illinois, Indiana, and Massachusetts seem to have adopted this rule: 9 Corpus Juris, p. 720, "Building and Construction Contracts," sec. 53; 13 Corpus Juris, p. 354.

But such a course is to allow a contractor to take advantage of his own wrong, and other American Courts reprobate it: 9 Corpus Juris, p. 720; 13 Corpus Juris, p. 354, sec. 210, and cases cited in notes.

This is not and never was law in Ontario, as it is not and never was law in England.

It has long been text-book law that "not the promise or the actual performance of something which the promisee is legally bound to perform" is a consideration for a promise: Halsbury's Laws of England, vol. 7, p. 385, para. 798; "the performance of an existing contract by one of the parties is no consideration for a new promise by the other party:" Leake on Contracts, 7th ed., p. 455, and cases cited.

I am of opinion that the promise (if there was one) to pay for the work to be done was not binding for want of consideration, and would allow the appeal with costs here and below.

If there be any difficulty in moulding the judgment, one of us may be spoken to.

Middleton J.: — Unless the legal situation is clearly kept in mind, the case seems to present some aspect of hardship.

The plaintiffs undertook to build the house for the contract price and to hand it over complete to the defendant. In the absence of any provision to the contrary in the contract, the destruction of the building by fire would not afford any excuse for non-performance of the contract.

When the work was going on, the material and labour which went into the building became the defendant's property subject to any lien in the plaintiffs' favour; so she had an insurable interest in the property, and she effected an insurance for her own protection.

The builders had an insurable interest, not only because of their lien, but also because the destruction of the property by fire would injure them, as under the building contract they would be bound to replace. They did not insure, preferring to carry the risk themselves. There was no obligation on the part of the owner to insure for the benefit of the contractors, and the contractors have no equitable or other claim upon the money received by the owner as the result of her prudence and expenditure.

As I understand the evidence, there was no more than a demand by the owner upon the contractor to complete his contract. If there was more, it did not amount to a new contract, as there was no consideration.

In its essence the defence is an attempt to shift the loss resulting from the fire — legally a loss falling upon the contractors — to the shoulders of the owner, who, fortunately for her, is not liable.

It may also be regarded as an attempt, by one who had an insurable interest but did not insure, to appropriate insurance money belonging to another, who also had an insurable interest and did insure.

The appeal should be allowed.

[Latchford and Logie JJ. agreed in the result.]

QUESTION

To what extent are the reasons to refuse enforcement in this case the same as those in cases like *Stilk v. Myrick*?

This case is very close to the line of enforceability. The following case indicates how close it is. Does this (or should this) influence how one should approach a case like *Smith v. Dawson*?

FAIRGRIEF v. ELLIS
(1935), 49 B.C.R. 413. B.C.S.C.

McDonald, J.: Defendant is a retired gentleman, 72 years of age, owning and residing upon a small parcel of land on Lulu Island, worth approximately $2,500. For some years his relations with his wife have been strained; she refused to live with him in British Columbia and maintained her residence in California.

Plaintiffs are sisters, cultured maiden ladies about 50 years of age, who until the year 1933 lived in Winnipeg where they had been employed in clerical work though in recent times they were for considerable periods out of employment. They had been close friends of the defendant over a period of some 25 years and their relations may be judged from the fact that they called him "Dad." In the spring of 1933 the plaintiff Cornelia Fairgrief came to British Columbia on an excursion and visited with the defendant for some three days. Following that occasion some letters passed between the defendant and the plaintiff Anne Fairgrief wherein the plaintiff Anne Fairgrief was invited to visit the defendant. This invitation she declined. In August of that year defendant's son, who had for some months been residing with him, departed for the United States whereupon defendant wrote the plaintiff Anne Fairgrief stating that he was alone and that he required a housekeeper and that he wished the plaintiffs to come and keep house for him, final arrangements to be made after their arrival. Plaintiffs thereupon came to the defendant's home and took up their residence with him upon a verbal agreement that if they would become his housekeepers and take charge of his home during his lifetime the home would become theirs upon his death.

Pursuant to the above agreement plaintiffs entered upon their duties, took full charge of the home, performed all the household duties and did a good deal of work outside including painting, cleaning up the ground and other works of a more or less permanent nature. In addition to being his housekeepers they were his congenial companions and the three lived comfortably and happily until August, 1934, when the defendant's wife (much to his surprise for he had expected nothing of the sort) suddenly arrived in Vancouver. Defendant requested the plaintiffs to remain and be kind to his wife while she should reside with them, he feeling quite assured that her stay would not be a lengthy one. At the end of about a month defendant told the plaintiffs that he was grieved to be obliged to tell them that his wife insisted that they should depart the premises as she intended to remain and take charge. Defendant, knowing of his obligation to the plaintiffs, promised them if they would give up their rights under the agreement already entered into, and would depart from his home he would on or about the 1st of October, 1934, pay them $1,000. That offer was accepted and plaintiffs removed themselves from the premises. The plaintiffs now bring action to recover that sum of $1,000. I have no doubt at all that the defendant's repudiation of his agreement resulted from the interference of his wife. Having persistently refused to live with him and assist him in making a happy and comfortable home, she was determined that the plaintiffs should not be allowed to render that assistance which she herself declined to render. Incidentally it may be said that her further actions justify to some extent this assumption for she again left her husband on November 2nd, 1934, and has not returned to him. Although there is a conflict of evidence I find the facts to be as above stated.

On the above facts, can the plaintiffs succeed?

. . .

[McDonald J. held that the first agreement was caught by the Statute of Frauds.]

(H)owever, I cannot understand why the plaintiffs cannot succeed on their claim for $1,000. When the agreement was made in September to pay the plaintiffs $1,000 the defendant thought that he was under an obligation to the plaintiffs and in order to be released from that obligation and so that the plaintiffs might agree to peacefully vacate his premises, he made the second agreement. Even although he was not in law bound to perform the first agreement nevertheless I think there was good consideration to support the promise to pay $1,000.

. . .

I agree with plaintiffs' counsel that this case comes more nearly within the principle of the decision in *Haigh v. Brooks* (1839), 10 A. & E. 309. There the plaintiff in consideration of the defendant's promise sued on gave up to the defendant a guarantee which was in fact unenforceable by reason of section 4 of the Statute of Frauds. The Court held that nevertheless the promise sued upon could be enforced. There the defendant, just as the defendant here, even although he might have been mistaken as to his legal rights, in consideration of his promise, obtained that which he desired and he must be held to his bargain. There will be judgment for the plaintiffs for $1,000. Inasmuch however as the plaintiffs were obliged to amend their statement of claim, in order to comply with the evidence, I think there is "good cause" for depriving the plaintiffs of their costs.

Judgment for plaintiffs.

[An interesting example of the same argument is found in the case of *Waugh v. Slavik* (1975), 62 D.L.R. (3d) 577 (B.C.S.C.).]

QUESTIONS

1. What reasons for enforcement exist in *Fairgrief v. Ellis* that do not exist in *Smith v. Dawson*? Or, conversely, what reasons are there in *Smith v. Dawson* that would justify a decision to refuse enforcement, and that are not present in *Fairgrief v. Ellis*?

2. Would it matter if the plaintiffs in *Smith v. Dawson* had reasonably thought that they had no obligation to build?

3. Would it matter if the plaintiffs in *Fairgrief v. Ellis* had known that the first promise made by the defendant was unenforceable at the time of the second promise?

4. Middleton J. in *Smith v. Dawson* says that "the defence is an attempt to shift the loss resulting from the fire — legally a loss falling upon the contractors — to the shoulders of the owner, who fortunately for her, is not liable."

(a) Is there anything wrong with shifting the loss?

(b) Why should the result be 'fortunate'?

(c) The purpose of fire insurance is to compensate the insured for the loss caused by fire. Has this insured suffered any loss through this fire since she had her house rebuilt at no cost to her? How could she defend an action brought by the insurers to recover what they had paid her? If she has no defence, does this make the judgment more or less sensible?

5. How would you, as counsel for the plaintiff in *Smith v. Dawson* have handled the case to avoid the result that happened?

The next case is an example of a very common situation. To what extent is it important that such arrangements are commonly made in business?

GILBERT STEEL LTD. v. UNIVERSITY CONSTRUCTION LTD.

(1976), 12 O.R. (2d) 19. Ontario Court of Appeal; Gale C.J.O., Howland and Wilson JJ.A.

The judgment of the court was given by **Wilson, J.A.:** — This is an appeal from the Order of Mr. Justice Pennell [(1973) 36 D.L.R. (3d) 496] dismissing the plaintiff's action for damages for breach of an oral agreement for the supply of fabricated steel bars to be incorporated into apartment buildings being constructed by the defendant. The case raises some fundamental principles of contract law.

The circumstances giving rise to the action are as follows. On September 4, 1968 the plaintiff entered into a written contract to deliver to the defendant fabricated steel for apartment buildings to be erected at three separate sites referred to in the contract as the "Flavin, Tectate and University projects". The price fixed by that contract was $153 per ton for "Hard grade" and $159 per ton for "Grade 60,000". Deliveries for the Flavin and Tectate projects were completed in August, 1969, and October, 1969, respectively, and paid for at the agreed-upon prices.

Two apartment buildings calling for the supply of 3,000 tons of fabricated steel were to be erected at the University site. However, prior to the defendant's notifying the plaintiff of its intention to commence construction on the first of these two buildings, the owners of the steel mill announced an increase in the price of unfabricated steel. They also gave warning of a further increase to come. The plaintiff approached the defendant about a new contract for the University project and a written contract dated October 22, 1969, was entered into for the supply of fabricated steel for the first building. The new price was $156 per ton for "Hard grade" and $165 per ton for "Grade 60,000". In fact this increase in price did not reflect the full amount of the initial increase announced by the mill owners.

On March 1, 1970, while the building under construction was still far from completion, the mill owners announced the second increase in price and a further discussion took place between John Gilbert and his brother Harry representing the plaintiff and Mendel Tenenbaum and Hersz Tenenbaum representing the defendant with respect to the price to be paid for the steel required to complete the first building. It is this discussion which the plaintiff alleges resulted in a binding oral agreement that the defendant would pay $166 per ton for "Hard grade" and $178 per ton for "Grade 60,000". Although the plaintiff submitted to the defendant a written contract embodying these revised prices following their meeting, the contract was not executed. It contained, in addition to the increased prices, two new clauses which the trial Judge found had not been the subject of any discussion with the defendant but were unilaterally imported into the written document by the plaintiff. The trial Judge also found, however, that the defendant agreed at the meeting to pay the increased price.

From March 12, 1970, until the completion of the first building the defendant accepted deliveries of the steel against invoices which reflected the revised prices but, in making payments on account, it remitted cheques in rounded amounts which at the date of the issuance of the writ resulted in a balance owing to the plaintiff in accordance with the invoices.

Having found on the evidence that the defendant had orally agreed to pay the increased prices, the legal issue confronting Mr. Justice Pennell was whether that agreement was legally binding upon the defendant or whether it failed for want of consideration. Counsel for the defendant submitted at the trial that past consideration is no consideration and that the plaintiff was already obliged before the alleged oral agreement was entered into to deliver the steel at the original prices agreed to in the written contract of October 22, 1969. Where then was the *quid pro quo* for the defendant's promise to pay more?

Counsel for the plaintiff sought to supply this omission from the evidence of Hersz Tenenbaum who, during the course of discussions which took place in September, 1970, with a view to a contract for the supply of steel for the second building at the University site, asked whether the plaintiff would give him "a good price" on steel for this building. Plaintiff's counsel argued that the promise of a good price on the second building was the consideration the defendant received for agreeing to pay the increased price on the first. The trial Judge rejected this submission and found the oral agreement unenforceable for want of consideration. In the course of his reasons for judgment the trial Judge adverted briefly to an alternate submission made by the plaintiff's counsel. He said:

> "I should, in conclusion, mention a further point which was argued with ingenuity by Mr. Morphy. His contention was that the consideration for the oral agreement was the mutual abandonment of right under the prior agreement in writing. I must say, with respect, that this argument is not without its attraction for me."

On the appeal Mr. Morphy picked up and elaborated upon this submission which had intrigued the trial Judge. In launching his main attack on the trial Judge's finding that the oral agreement was unenforceable for want of consideration, he submitted that the facts of this case evidenced not a purported oral variation of a written contract which failed for want of consideration but an implied rescission of the written contract and the creation of a whole new contract, albeit oral, which was subsequently reneged on by the defendant. The consideration for this new oral agreement, submitted by Mr. Morphy, was the mutual agreement to abandon the previous written contract and to assume the obligations under the new oral one. Mr. Morphy submitted to the Court for its consideration two lines of authority, the first line illustrated by the leading case of *Stilk v. Myrick* (1809), 2 Camp. 317, in which the subsequent agreement was held to be merely a variation of the earlier agreement and accordingly failed for want of consideration and the other line illustrated by *Morris v. Baron & Co.*, [1918] A.C. 1, in which the subsequent agreement was held to have rescinded the former one and was therefore supported by the mutual agreement to abandon the old obligations and substitute the new. Mr. Morphy invited us to find that the oral agreement to pay the increased price for steel fell into the second category. There was, he acknowledged, no express rescission of the written contract but price is such a fundamental term of a contract for the supply of goods that the substitution of a new price must connote a new contract and impliedly rescind the old.

It is impossible to accept Mr. Morphy's submission in face of the evidence adduced at the trial. It is clear that the sole reason for the discussions between the parties in March, 1970, concerning the supply of steel to complete the first building at the University site was the increase in the price of steel by the mill owners. No changes other than the change in price were discussed. The trial Judge found that the other two changes sought to be introduced into the written document submitted by the plaintiff to the defendant for signature following the discussions had not even been mentioned at the meeting. Moreover, although repeated references were made at trial by the Gilbert brothers to the fact that the parties had made a "new contract" in March, 1970, it seems fairly clear from the evidence when read as a whole that the "new contract" referred to was the agreement to pay the increased price for the steel, *i.e.*, the agreement which effected the variation of the written contract and not a new contract in the sense of a contract replacing *in toto* the original contract of October 22, 1969.

I am not persuaded that either of the parties intended by their discussions in March, 1970, to rescind their original contract and replace it with a new one. Indeed, it is significant that no such plea was made in the statement of claim which confined itself to an allegation that "it was orally agreed in March 1970 that the prices as set forth in the said contract [*i.e.*, of October 22, 1969] would be varied...". Accordingly, consideration for the oral agreement is not to be found in a mutual agreement to abandon the earlier written contract and assume the obligations under the new oral one.

Nor can I find consideration in the vague references in the evidence to the possibility that the plaintiff would give the defendant "a good price" on the steel for the second building if it went along with the increased prices on the first. The plaintiff, in my opinion, fell far short of making any commitment in this regard.

Counsel for the appellant put before us as an alternate source of consideration for the agreement to pay the increased price the increased credit afforded by the plaintiff to the defendant as a result of the increased price. The argument went something like this. Whereas previously the defendant had credit outstanding for 60 days in the amount owed on the original prices, after the oral agreement was made he had credit outstanding for 60 days in the amount owed on the higher prices. Therefore, there was consideration flowing from the promisee and the law does not enquire into its sufficiency. Reliance was placed by counsel on the decision of Chief Justice Meredith in *Kilbuck Coal Co. v. Turner & Robinson* (1915), 7 O.W.N. 673. This case, however, is clearly distinguishable from the case at bar, as Mr. Justice Pennell pointed out in his reasons, on the basis of the *force majeure* clause which had relieved the plaintiff of its obligations under the original contract. In undertaking to supply coal despite the strike the plaintiff was unquestionably providing consideration of real substance in that case. I cannot accept counsel's contention, ingenious as it is, that the increased credit inherent in the increased price constituted consideration flowing from the promisee for the promisor's agreement to pay the increased price.

The final submission put forward by counsel for the appellant was that the defendant, by his conduct in not repudiating the invoices reflecting the increase in price when and as they were received, had in effect acquiesced in such increase and should not subsequently be permitted to repudiate it. There would appear to be two answers to this submission. The first is summed up in the maxim that estoppel can never be used as a sword but only as a shield. A plaintiff cannot found his claim in estoppel. Secondarily, however, it should perhaps be pointed out that in order to found an estoppel the plaintiff must show, not only that the conduct of the defendant was clearly referable to the defendant's having given up its right to insist on the original prices, but also that the plaintiff relied on the defendant's conduct to its detriment. I do not think the plaintiff can discharge either of these burdens on the facts of this case.

In summary, I concur in the findings of the trial Judge that the oral agreement made by the parties in March, 1970 was an agreement to vary the written contract of October 22, 1969 and that it must fail for want of consideration.

. . .

The judgment of Pennell, J., should be varied to provide that the plaintiff shall have judgment for interest at the rate of 5% on the payments which were overdue for more than 60 days under the contract dated October 22, 1969. Subject to this variation the appeal should be dismissed with costs.

The respondent cross-appealed on the subject of costs. The trial judge made no order as to costs although the defendant was successful in the action. Mr. Starkman submits that, in failing to award costs to his successful client, Mr. Justice Pennell did not exercise his discretion with respect to costs judicially. A review of Mr. Justice Pennell's reasons for judgment indicates that he was motivated to withhold costs by his assessment of the conduct of the defendant which led up to this litigation and, since he was in a better position than this Court to make such an assessment, I see no reason to interfere with his disposition as to the costs at trial.

The cross-appeal should accordingly be dismissed. There will be no order as to costs of the cross-appeal.

Appeal and cross-appeal dismissed

QUESTIONS AND PROBLEMS

1. What advice did the defendant's solicitor give to his client?

2. If you had been solicitor for the plaintiff what advice would you have given plaintiff?

3. What are the dangers in enforcing this kind of contract?

4. What do you think Wilson J.A. means when she says that, "the case raises some fundamental principles of contract law"? What is a *fundamental* principle? In particular, what fundamental principle is relevant here? Draft a statement of the principle applied by Wilson J.A.

5. If the court in *Raggow v. Scougall* was prepared to hold that the parties had entered into a new agreement, why not do the same in any of these cases? *Raggow v. Scougall* was cited to the Court of Appeal in the argument in *Gilbert Steel v. University Construction*.

6. Suppose that the seamen in *Stilk v. Myrick* had each given the captain a peppercorn or a canary, would the result have been the same?

7. Gargantua Construction Ltd. is under a contract to build a convention centre. The completion date is November 1. It is known that if the centre is not completed by that time Gargantua will be liable in heavy damages. Gargantua subcontracted excavation work to Deepole Ltd. and the plumbing work to Sinks Ltd. A few weeks after excavation began the president of Deepole came to the representative of Gargantua and said that quite unforeseen difficulties had been encountered in excavation, that the contract price would have to be doubled and that Deepole faced almost certain bankruptcy if the price were not increased. The representative of Gargantua said, "You have us over a barrel; but since we would have to pay anyone the higher price now, we will pay." Two weeks before completion, the president of Sinks Ltd. told Gargantua, "If you want this building ready on time, you must pay us double the agreed price." The representative of Gargantua said, "You have us over a barrel, we have no choice, we will pay."

How would the court treat the claims of Deepole and Sinks?

A more complete account of the facts in this case is contained in the following passage:

In 1968, Gilbert Steel was the largest supplier of fabricated reinforcing steel in Metropolitan Toronto, purchasing steel bars from steel mills and fabricating the bars in accordance with engineers' specifications for particular projects. University Construction was an apartment construction company. On September 4, 1968, Gilbert Steel and University Construction signed a written agreement under which Gilbert Steel agreed to deliver fabricated steel for use in apartment buildings, to be built by University Construction at three separate sites. Two grades of steel were required, and University Construction undertook to pay $153 per ton for "Hard Grade" and $159 per ton for "Grade 60,000" steel.

At the first two building sites, deliveries were made and paid for as agreed. However, before Gilbert Steel was notified (early in October, 1969), of University Construction's intent to proceed with the first of two buildings at the third site (the "University site"), steel mill owners announced an increase in the price of unfabricated steel, the increase to take effect in two stages. The price to Gilbert Steel would increase on August 1, 1969 by $8.50 per ton for "Hard Grade" and $11.50 per ton for "Grade 60,000"; and a second increase of a then unspecified amount would become effective as of March 1, 1970.

Gilbert Steel was obliged by the September 4, 1968, agreement to supply a sufficient quantity of steel for the erection of both buildings at the "University site". However, in the changed circumstances, Gilbert Steel "suggested a new contract for the University Project", and on October 22, 1969, the parties signed a new written contract under which Gilbert Steel would supply fabricated steel for one building only at the University project at a price of $156 per ton for "Hard Grade" and $165 per ton for "Grade 60,000". Although the certainty of a further price increase by the millers was foreseen by both parties no escalation clause was included in the new contract.

Construction began in November, 1969, and many deliveries of steel were made. Each delivery was immediately billed to University Construction by invoices describing the steel delivered, the unit price, and the total invoice price. The prices charged were those established by the new agreement of October 22, 1969. University Construction accepted all steel delivered without protest, and until March 11, 1970, regularly paid the amount billed by each invoice by a cheque which "squared precisely on every occasion with the amounts shown as debits in the invoices."

On March 1, 1970, while the first building at the "University site" was still "far from completion" the steel millers announced the anticipated second price increase. Intent on not wholly absorbing the increase themselves, John and Harry Gilbert, officers of Gilbert Steel, met with Mendel and Hersz Tenenbaum, officers of University Construction, with a view to procuring another new contract. The Gilberts asked the Tenenbaums to consider a new contract, since construction had not progressed as expected. Hersz Tenenbaum had "agreed to accommodate" the Gilberts but "in consequence of the accommodation [University] should be given favourable consideration by the contract to be arranged for the second building at the University project."

Harry Gilbert then prepared a "contract" dated March 1, 1970, and mailed it to University Construction. The contract was a duplicate of the October 22, 1969, contract except that the price of the steel to be supplied was increased. University did not sign or return this "new contract", but it did accept deliveries of steel invoiced at the new March 1, 1970, agreement rates "regularly from [Gilbert Steel] without any protest and without any claim to abate the price which was invoiced against them". However, Hersz Tenenbaum adopted a new method of payment after this date. He no longer paid by cheques corresponding to the invoice amounts, but cast the cheques in rounded figures that tended to over-payment at first, but by the end of construction resulted in a net balance of $22,615.56 owing by University Construction to Gilbert Steel.

As construction of the first building at the University site neared completion, the comptroller of Gilbert Steel pressed for payment in full of the account. In a conversation on September 24, 1970, Hersz Tenenbaum told the comptroller that he expected a mortgage draw by October 10, 1970, and that he would pay the account in full at that time. About the same time, Hersz Tenenbaum met with the Gilberts to discuss a contract for the supply of steel for the second building at the University Project. Tenenbaum "reminded ... [the Gilberts] ... that he had twice agreed to new contracts." He asked them whether they could give him a good price. The Gilberts made an offer, and Tenenbaum said that he would consider it. The meeting was conducted and concluded in an atmosphere of good will. Tenenbaum did not complain about the price increase of March, 1970. He later decided not to accept the Gilberts' offer for the second project and indicated for the first time that University Construction would not pay its past due account as increased by the March agreement. Gilbert Steel sues for this balance.

NOTE

The decision in *Gilbert Steel* suggests that the "doctrine of consideration" represents the time-tested all-embracing opinion of the common law about which promises are, and which are not enforceable. It is as if the common law had consciously attempted to find a compendious means of identifying that state of affairs which, if it existed, would justify enforcing any promise, and if it did not, would alone, justify a refusal to enforce. It is as though a theory of enforceability had been carefully built around "consideration" so that the enforcement or not of any promise should follow logically from the major premise and the major premise alone.

Almost nothing could be farther from the truth. The courts never set out to create a theory which would decisively answer the question whether any promise was or was not enforceable. They were concerned with the much less esoteric and much more practical problem of deciding whether or not it seemed desirable to enforce the particular promise alleged to have been made in the case before them. No simple and uniform doctrine by which enforceability can be deductively determined ever was evolved. The "doctrine" meant very different things at different times in its history. Although it has come to be most associated with a meaning given it extrajudicially during the nineteenth century (and ostensibly accepted by the courts then), "the very changes which the doctrine of consideration has undergone are warning that there is nothing in it more peculiarly fundamental than in many other legal doctrines and that a theory which has changed so much in the past may very well change once again." As a cornerstone for the law of contract, the doctrine has been widely criticized and it is foolhardy to attempt to defend it as an exercise in logic. It can be understood only in the light of its history and of the society which produced it. The doctrine is a most convincing demonstration of the truth of Holmes' oft-quoted assertion that, "The life of the law has not been logic, it has been experience". These dogmatic comments must be justified.

We have already seen how the common law courts developed a general theory of contractual obligation in the process leading up to *Slade's Case* in 1602. This decision did far more than settle a disputed pleading point, for it was quickly recognized as providing a basis for the general enforcement of promises, a basis which could replace the pockets of law which had been developing around debt, covenant and other contract-like actions. The writs in general assumpsit usually set out the facts said to have made the defendant indebted, and then alleged that "in consideration of" those facts, defendant had promised to pay plaintiff and had defaulted. During the sixteenth century, it became customary to refer to the recited facts as "the considerations" for the later promise, but no technical meaning attached to these words. Once the later promise was to be conclusively presumed (*i.e.* after *Slade's Case*), attention shifted from the making of that promise, to the earlier "considerations", which were no longer merely sufficient reasons to enforce a subsequent promise, but were now, sufficient alone, to establish liability. What sort of "considerations" would justify imposing liability in assumpsit? Certainly, where debt or assumpsit had lain before, indebitatus assumpsit would lie now. But it is clear that immediately after *Slade's Case*, the courts began to experiment and to find new fact situations, new considerations, which would justify liability in assumpsit.

The benefit to the defendant, quid pro quo, restitution sentiment of the action of debt gave some shape to the new assumpsit action. So too did the notion of detrimental reliance of the plaintiff, upon which older assumpsit actions had been founded. From the Chancery came the notion that all promises deliberately made ought to be enforced, particularly where the promises involved an exchange of rough equivalents. There was some influence from the general theories of obligations of the civilians, and from the mercantile law, itself much influenced by continental thinking. The pressure which any one or any combination of these factors would exert in a given case would vary with the facts, with the judges, and with the proximity of the case to the influence of one of the older "pockets of law" which had built up around a particular type of fact situation. However, a trend towards the enforcement of a greater number of promises was visible shortly after *Slade's Case* freed juries to consider whether or not assumpsit was made out; and the passage of the Statute of Frauds some 75 years later was undoubtedly hastened by the alarming ease with which a defendant, incompetent as a witness, could be charged and found liable on a promise. The courts often referred to a presence or absence of "consideration" (or "considerations") sufficient to support an assumpsit; but they were using the terms in no technical, no unitary and no orthodox sense. For some two hundred years, a finding that there was consideration (or that there were sufficient considerations) in any case, meant no more than the legal conclusion that on the facts assumpsit would lie. There was no concept of what could count as sufficient consideration beyond the examples of cases in which assumpsit had been held to lie before, although there was no suggestion that the old cases constituted a complete catalogue of the range of assumpsit. Indeed, the old cases were referred to constantly in new efforts to broaden the scope of assumpsit. It was clear that in some cases the notion of the rectitude of performing promises gave much of the push towards actionability in assumpsit. In cases involving businessmen dealing amongst themselves, notions of enforceability derived from the law merchant might be seen to be paramount and to justify allowing assumpsit. Cases which concerned family arrangements revealed wholly different conceptions about what sort of considerations would justify liability in assumpsit. There was simply no unitary conception of contract or of consideration. During the seventeenth and eighteenth century the results of the operation of the "doctrine of consideration" as it was being developed by the courts, strongly resembled the results which might be expected had a functional approach been overtly employed, and Wilmot J. was not exercising a fanciful imagination when he said, in 1765, in *Pillans v. Van Mierop*, that, "[C]onsideration has been melting down into common sense, of late".

But one would have needed an exceptionally vivid imagination to make the same observation just one hundred years later. For the nineteenth century produced a sharp break with contractual (assumpsit) developments of the past, even of the (then) very recent past. The break was engineered with a double-edge sword: within one century (and in theory at least) wide-ranging notions of what sorts of considerations would suffice to found an assumpsit were gobbled up first by the bargain theory generally, then by the oversimplification of detriment-to-the-promisee *or* benefit-to-the promisor, and finally by the intensive over-simplification of detriment to the promisee only. At the same time a unitary approach to promise enforcement was winning formal acceptance: the narrowing view of what constituted consideration was to be applied equally to all promises, and functional differences between contract-modifying and contract-initiating promises; between promises to pay for benefits received and wholly gratuitous promises; between contracts in a family setting and commercial transactions; and between contracts which might be specifically enforced and those which would not, were ignored. [Reiter, "Courts, Consideration and Common Sense" (1978), 27 U.T.L.J. 439.]

The next case represents possibly the high-water mark of the view of consideration that is identified with the nineteenth century.

FOAKES v. BEER

(1884), 9 App. Cas. 605. House of Lords.

[Mrs. Beer got a judgment for £2990.19.0 against Dr. Foakes. The parties entered into an agreement under which Dr. Foakes paid £500 on signing and paid the balance in instalments over about five years. Mrs. Beer promised not to claim any interest. Mrs. Beer sued for the interest due. The jury found that the principal had been paid as agreed. The Court of Appeal reversed and gave judgment for the interest. The defendant appealed.]

W.H. Holl, Q.C., for the appellant: — Apart from the doctrine of *Cumber v. Wane* (1718), 1 Str. 426 there is no reason in sense or law why the agreement should not be valid, and the creditor prevented from enforcing his judgment if the agreement be performed. It may often be much more advantageous to the creditor to obtain immediate payment of part of his debt than to wait to enforce payment, or perhaps by pressing his debtor to force him into bankruptcy with the result of only a small dividend. Moreover if a composition is accepted friends, who would not otherwise do so, may be willing to come forward to assist the debtor. And if the creditor thinks that the acceptance of part is for his benefit who is to say it is not? The doctrine of *Cumber v. Wane* has been continually assailed, as in *Couldery v. Bartrum* (1881), 19 Ch. D. 394, 399 by Jessel M.R. In the note to *Cumber v. Wane* (1 Smith L.C. 4th ed. p. 253, 8th ed. p. 367) which was written by J.W. Smith and never disapproved by any of the editors, including Willes and Keating JJ., it is said "that its doctrine is founded upon vicious reasoning and false views of the office of a Court of law, which should rather strive to give effect to the engagements which persons have thought proper to enter into, than cast about for subtle reasons to defeat them upon the ground of being unreasonable. Carried to its full extent the doctrine of *Cumber v. Wane* embraces the exploded notion that in order to render valid a contract not under seal, the adequacy as well as the existence of the consideration must be established. Accordingly in modern times it has been, as appears by the preceding part of the note, subjected to modification in several instances." *Cumber v. Wane* was decided on a ground now admitted to be erroneous, viz. that the satisfaction must be found by the Court to be reasonable. The Court cannot inquire into the adequacy of the consideration. *Reynolds v. Pinhowe* (1595) Cro. Eliz. 429, which was not cited in *Cumber v. Wane*, decided that the saving of trouble was a sufficient consideration; "for it is a benefit unto him to have his debt without suit or charge." ... *Pinnel's Case* (1602) 5 Co. Rep. 117a, was decided on a point of pleading: the dictum that payment of a smaller sum was no satisfaction of a larger, was extra-judicial, and overlooked all considerations of mercantile convenience, such as mentioned in *Reynolds v. Pinhowe*; and it is also noticeable that it was a case of a bond debt sought to be set aside by a parol agreement. It is every day practice for tradesmen to take less in satisfaction of a larger sum, and give discount, where there is neither custom nor right to take credit.... It has often been held that a sheet of paper or a stick of sealing wax is a sufficient consideration. The result of the cases is that if *Cumber v. Wane* be right, payment of a less sum than the debt due, by a bill, promissory note or cheque is a good discharge; but payment of such less sum by sovereigns or Bank of England notes is not. Here the agreement is not to take less than the debt, but to give time for payment of the whole without interest. Mankind have never acted on the doctrine of *Cumber v. Wane*, but the contrary; nay few are aware of it. By overruling it the House will only declare the universal practice to be good law as well as good sense.

Earl of Selborne L.C.: — Whatever may be the ultimate decision of this appeal the House is much indebted to Mr. Holl for his exceedingly able argument.

[Winch followed on the same side, and contended that on the true construction of the agreement no provision was made for interest.]

Bompas, Q.C. (Gaskell with him) for the respondent: — The agreement was not intended to and does not deprive the respondent of her right to interest. But if it does it is void for want of consideration. There is a strong current of authority that what the law implies as a duty is no consideration. Therefore where a debt is due part payment is no reason for giving up the residue. The doctrine is too well settled to be now over-thrown: ... Where law and practice are so well established this House will not now depart from them: ...

Holl, Q.C., in reply: — The cases about seamen's wages have always been based on questions of public policy: see *Harris v. Watson*...

[The House took time for consideration.]

Earl of Selborne L.C.: —... The question, therefore, is nakedly raised by this appeal, whether your Lordships are now prepared, not only to overrule, as contrary to law, the doctrine stated by Sir Edward Coke to have been laid down by all the judges of the Common Pleas in *Pinnel's Case* in 1602, and repeated in his note to Littleton, sect. 344, but to treat a prospective agreement, not under seal, for satisfaction of a debt, by a series of payments on account to a total amount less than the whole debt, as binding in law, provided those payments are regularly made; the case not being one of a composition with a common debtor, agreed to, inter se, by several creditors. I prefer so to state the question instead of treating it (as it was put at the Bar) as depending on the authority of the case of *Cumber v. Wane*, decided in 1718. It may well be that distinctions, which in later cases have been held sufficient to exclude the application of that doctrine, existed and were improperly disregarded in *Cumber v. Wane*; and yet that the doctrine itself may be law, rightly recognised in *Cumber v. Wane*, and not really contradicted by any later authorities. And this appears to me to be the true state of the case. The doctrine itself, as laid down by Sir Edward Coke, may have been criticised, as questionable in principle, by some persons whose opinions are entitled to respect, but it has never been judicially overruled; on the contrary I think it has always, since the sixteenth century, been accepted as law. If so, I cannot think that your Lordships would do right, if you were now to reverse as erroneous, a judgment of the Court of Appeal, proceeding upon a doctrine which has been accepted as part of the law of England for 280 years.

The doctrine, as stated in *Pinnel's Case*, is "that payment of a lesser sum on the day" (it would of course be the same after the day), "in satisfaction of a greater, cannot be any satisfaction for the whole, because it appears to the Judges, that by no possibility a lesser sum can be a satisfaction to the plaintiff for a greater sum". As stated in Coke Littleton, 212(b), it is, "where the condition is for payment of £20, the obligor or feoffer cannot at the time appointed pay a lesser sum in satisfaction of the whole, because it is apparent that a lesser sum of money cannot be a satisfaction of a greater"; adding (what is beyond controversy), that an acquittance under seal, in full satisfaction of the whole, would (under like circumstances) be valid and binding.

The distinction between the effect of a deed under seal, and that of an agreement by parol, or by writing not under seal, may seem arbitrary, but it is established in our law; nor is it really unreasonable or practically inconvenient that the law should require particular solemnities to give to a gratuitous contract the force of a binding obligation. If the question be (as, in the actual state of the law, I think it is), whether consideration is, or is not, given in a case of this kind, by the debtor who pays down part of the debt presently due from him, for a promise by the creditor to relinquish, after certain further payments on account, the residue of the debt, I cannot say that I think consideration is given, in the sense in which I have always understood that word as used in our law. It might be (and indeed I think it would be) an improvement in our law, if a release or acquittance of the whole debt, on payment of any sum which the creditor might be content to receive by way of accord and satisfaction (though less the whole), were held to be, generally, binding though not under seal; nor should I be unwilling to see equal force given to a prospective agreement, like the present, in writing though not under seal; but I think it impossible, without refinements which practically alter the sense of the word, to treat such a release or acquittance as supported by any new consideration proceeding from the debtor. All the authorities subsequent to *Cumber v. Wane*, which were relied upon by the appellant at your Lordships' Bar have proceeded upon the distinction, that, by giving negotiable paper or otherwise, there had been some new consideration for a new agreement, distinct from mere money payments in or towards discharge of the original liability. I think it unnecessary to go through those cases, or to examine the particular grounds on which each of them was decided. There are no such facts in the case now before your Lordships. What is called "any benefit, or even any legal possibility of benefit", in Mr. Smith's notes to *Cumber v. Wane*, is not (as I conceive) that sort of benefit which a creditor may derive from getting payment of part of the money due to him from a debtor who might otherwise keep him at arm's length, or possibly become insolvent, but is some independent benefit, actual or contingent, of a kind which might in law be a good and valuable consideration for any other sort of agreement not under seal.

My conclusion is, that the order appealed from should be affirmed, and the appeal dismissed, with costs, and I so move your Lordships.

Lord Blackburn (after making a thorough review of the cases, concluded): ... What principally weighs with me in thinking that Lord Coke made a mistake of fact is my conviction that all men of business, whether merchants or tradesmen, do every day recognise and act on the ground that prompt payment of a part of their demand may be more beneficial to them than it would be to insist on their rights and enforce payment of the whole. Even where the debtor is perfectly solvent, and sure to pay at last, this often is so. Where the credit of the debtor is doubtful it must be more so. I had persuaded myself that there was no such long-continued action on this dictum as to render it improper in this House to reconsider the question. I had written my reasons for so thinking; but as they were not satisfactory to the other noble and learned Lords who heard the case, I do not now repeat them nor persist in them.

I assent to the judgment proposed, though it is not that which I had originally thought proper."

[Lords Fitzgerald and Watson gave judgment to the same effect.]

THE MERCANTILE LAW AMENDMENT ACT

R.S.O. 1970, c. 272, s. 16.

16. Part performance of an obligation either before or after a breach thereof when expressly accepted by the creditor in satisfaction or rendered in pursuance of an agreement for that purpose, though without any new consideration, shall be held to extinguish the obligation.

This Act was originally passed in 1885 — a pointed legislative comment on *Foakes v. Beer*!

Would this Act, if applicable to the case of *Foakes v. Beer*, have produced a different result?

What would have happened under the Act if Mrs. Beer had sued for the whole sum unpaid, with interest, two years after the agreement was made?

The following case shows how far a court will go in an attempt to get around the problems caused by *Foakes v. Beer*.

BANK OF NOVA SCOTIA v. MACLELLAN

(1977), 78 DLR (3d) 1. N.S.S.C. Appeal Division; MacKeigan C.J.N.S., Coffin and Macdonald JJ.A.

The judgment of the Court was delivered by
MacKeigan, C.J.N.S.: — This appeal from a decision of the Honourable Mr. Justice Hart turns on the following point of law:

Is an agreement made by the appellant bank to accept from the respondent $610.13, one-quarter of the amount then owing by her on a promissory note signed by her and her husband, in "settlement" of her debt, enforceable against the bank, after having been repudiated by the bank before she paid the sum agreed upon?

The respondent and her then husband, Brian Hoey, from whom she was divorced in September, 1973, signed a promissory note on December 21, 1972, for $5,940. By April, 1975, Mr. Hoey had left the Halifax area and the bank was pressing the respondent to pay the then balance of $2,440.55. Mr. Donald Oliver, the respondent's solicitor at the time, proposed the settlement to a Mr. Dudka, an official of the bank. The learned trial Judge held:

> Although I am satisfied that the plaintiff bank did not in fact accept the offer made on behalf of the defendant by Mr. Oliver I find that Mr. Dudka was a person with the ostensible authority to communicate the bank's decision on the matter to the defendant. I find that Mr. Dudka did indicate to Mr. Oliver that the bank had accepted his client's offer of settlement and that the bank is estopped from denying its acceptance.

The settlement was rejected by the bank before any of the $610.13 agreed upon had been paid by the respondent. The bank claims that the settlement agreement was unsupported by any fresh or additional consideration. It cannot be disputed that such consideration is necessary to complete an accord and satisfaction of a debt such as this. The principle is described in Cheshire and Fifoot, *Law of Contract*, 9th ed. (1976), p. 541:

> The agreement, if supported by the necessary consideration, is called accord and satisfaction. This has been judicially defined as follows:
> "Accord and satisfaction is the purchase of a release from an obligation, whether arising under contract or tort, by means of any valuable consideration, not being the actual performance of the obligation itself. The accord is the agreement by which the obligation is discharged. The satisfaction is the consideration which makes the agreement operative." [*British Russian Gazette Ltd. v. Associated Newspapers, Ltd.*, [1932] 2 K.B. 616 at pp. 643-4]

If such consideration is found we need not be concerned with the possible application of more esoteric principles, such as promissory estoppel, as in *Central London Property Trust Ltd. v. High Trees House Ltd.*, [1947] K.B. 130 (Denning, J., as he then was).

Mr. Justice Hart found that some consideration was given by the respondent, saying:

> When I look at the dealings between Mr. Oliver and the various officials of the bank as a whole I am satisfied that there was some consideration for the compromise agreement of settlement. In Mr. Drapeau's original letter in which he indi-

cated that the bank was prepared to discuss settlement, he made it clear that such a settlement would envisage their continued contact with the defendant from time to time in an attempt to locate her ex-husband for the purpose of recovering the balance due under the note. Mr. Oliver's letter of April 25, 1975, provided information on this subject, and it is apparent that the parties were assuming that the defendant undertook this obligation as well as the payment of 25% of the debt in exchange for a release of liability. When the bank official communicated the acceptance of the settlement to Mr. Oliver it was on the understanding that Linda MacLellan's co-operation would be forthcoming, and, in my opinion, this amounted to the exchange of a promise for a promise, which is sufficient consideration for the agreement to accept 25% of the debt in satisfaction of the whole.

The appellant contends that the trial Judge erred in drawing these inferences from the evidence. I cannot say, however, that he was wrong in so doing. The respondent can be said to have at least faintly promised to help find her ex-husband. This promise, though slight and of little real value, is enough to meet the legal test of consideration.

It follows that we should dismiss the appeal with costs, and affirm the judgment of the learned trial Judge allowing the appellant $610.13 plus costs to the date on which that sum was paid into Court.

Appeal dismissed.

QUESTION

Would it matter whether there was or was not Nova Scotia legislation equivalent to s. 16 of the Mercantile Law Amendment Act?

ROMMERIL v. GARDENER

(1962), 35 D.L.R. (2d) 717. B.C.C.A.

The judgment of the Court was delivered by

Davey, J.A.: — By an oral judgment that was not recorded, the learned County Court Judge found that the defendant (respondent) agreed to pay and the plaintiff (appellant) to accept $599.19 in full of his claim for commissions amounting to $1,187.23. There is ample evidence to support that finding.

From the learned Judge's notes of the evidence of the respondent and her husband it would appear that the respondent either told the appellant that she would pay the amount by Easter, 1960, or agreed that it was to be paid by that date. Appellant's evidence is no help on this point because he denied the agreement. The learned County Court Judge must have thought that the agreement to accept the $599.19 in full was not terminated by the failure to pay that amount by Easter. We are quite unable to say from the fragmentary notes of the evidence that the learned Judge was wrong in not regarding the promise to pay by Easter as a condition of the settlement.

The appellant wrote in October of that year demanding payment of $1,187.23. The respondent then sent him a cheque for $599.19, which he retained but did not cash; thereupon he commenced action for $1,187.23. Two days before trial the respondent paid appellant $599.19, which he accepted on account and proceeded to trial. The learned County Court Judge held, so counsel tell us, that the payment was as good as if made at Easter and dismissed the action. Appellant appeals.

Unless respondent can bring the payment of $599.19 within the terms of

s. 2(33) of the *Laws Declaratory Act*, R.S.B.C. 1960, c. 213, it is obvious that the payment of the lesser amount without new consideration will not satisfy the greater sum of $1,187.23 otherwise due.

The clause, which is substantially the same as enactments in Ontario, Saskatchewan and Alberta, and similar to one in Manitoba, reads as follows:

> (33) Part performance of an obligation either before or after a breach thereof, when expressly accepted by the creditor in satisfaction or rendered in pursuance of an agreement for that purpose, though without any new consideration, shall be held to extinguish the obligation.

The first branch of the subsection may be dismissed at once for both counsel agree that the $599.19 was not accepted by the appellant in satisfaction of the greater amount. If the payment of $599.19 extinguished the obligation it must be because it was rendered in pursuance of the agreement that it be paid and accepted in full of the obligation.

To that appellant's counsel makes two submissions:

First: He says that the agreement mentioned in the clause means a contract under seal or supported by consideration, and that there was no consideration for the parol agreement in question.

Secondly: He contends that the appellant in October, 1960, had before payment demanded the whole amount of $1,187.23, and consequently effectively terminated any agreement to take the lesser amount in full.

In support of his first submission counsel relies upon the judgment of Gregory, J., in *Bell v. Quagliotti et al.* (1918), 25 B.C.R. 460 in which he held that the agreement mentioned in the clause means a binding agreement, supported by consideration when not under seal, *i.e.*, a contract, . . .

The weight of subsequent authority seems to be against the view expressed by Gregory, J., in *Bell v. Quagliotti, supra.* As a matter of pure construction, I should think that for the purposes of the clause the agreement need not by itself be a binding contract, and consequently need not be supported by consideration. The words "though without any new consideration", while relating grammatically to the verbs "accepted" and "rendered", in my opinion point significantly to the purpose of the clause. Moreover a part performance rendered pursuant to a binding contract based upon a new consideration to accept that part performance in full would by that very fact constitute an accord and satisfaction at common law. When the clause says rendered without any new consideration, it must mean that there need not be consideration for the agreement upon which the part performance is rendered.

Appellant cannot succeed on that branch of his argument.

Turning to the second ground of appeal, the respondent admits that about October, 1960, the appellant demanded payment of the full sum of $1,187.23, in response to which she sent him the cheque for $599.19, which was never cashed. But the letter making that demand is not before us, and so far as the notes of evidence go there was no secondary evidence of its contents, consequently we do not know the tenor of the demand. It is unlikely that it was a demand terminating the unperformed agreement because of default, because the appellant denied at the trial that there was such an agreement. I suppose that under some circumstances a bare demand of the greater sum might terminate an unperformed agreement made without consideration to take a lesser sum in full satisfaction of the indebtedness, but it is by no means evident to me at the moment that such a bare demand would by itself necessarily terminate an agreement that the creditor denied. Without the letter I am unable to come to any conclusion upon this ground of appeal. This makes it unnecessary to consider whether under cl. (33) such a creditor can terminate at will a voluntary agreement before it has been partly performed....

I would dismiss the appeal.

CHAMPLAIN READY-MIXED CEMENT v. BEAUPRE
[1971] 3 O.R. 568. C.A.

APPEAL from a judgment of a Division Court dismissing a claim alleged to have been discharged by satisfaction.

Jessup, J.A. (orally): — This is an appeal from a judgment rendered in the Sixth Division Court of the County of Simcoe dismissing the plaintiff's action with costs.

The facts can be stated quite briefly. The defendant was indebted to the plaintiff in the amount of $930.85 for concrete supplied by the plaintiff to the defendant. In February of 1970 the defendant wrote to the plaintiff advising that he was in financial difficulties and stating that he proposed a settlement with his creditors on the basis of 50 cents on the dollar. Subsequently, there was a discussion by telephone with a representative of the plaintiff in which the representative of the plaintiff said he would look into the situation with other creditors of the defendant. Having done so, the representative of the plaintiff had another telephone discussion with the defendant in which he advised the defendant that the proposal was not acceptable.

Shortly afterwards the defendant sent to the plaintiff a cheque for $500 on the reverse of which he had typed the following endorsement "$500.00 has been accepted by Mr. Coldwell as payment in full". When the cheque was received by the plaintiff, Mr. Coldwell for the plaintiff "x'd" out by typewriter the words "in full" and added to the endorsement made by the defendant the words "on account, balance $430.85".

There was evidence given on behalf of the plaintiff that subsequently some two weeks later a bill was sent to the defendant for the balance owing on the account of $430.85. The defendant said that he heard nothing with respect to the balance he owed until he received the Division Court summons. The plaintiff, of course, cashed the cheque after altering the endorsement, as I have mentioned, and the action in the Division Court was for the sum of $400 representing the balance of $430.85 with an abandonment of the $30.85 which was in excess of jurisdiction.

In these circumstances, the rights of the parties are governed by s. 16 of the *Mercantile Law Amendment Act*, R.S.O. 1960, c. 238 [now R.S.O. 1970, c. 272], which provides:

> 16. Part performance of an obligation either before or after a breach thereof when expressly accepted by the creditor in satisfaction or rendered in pursuance of an agreement for that purpose, though without any new consideration, shall be held to extinguish the obligation.

It is quite clear on the facts that the cheque for $500 was not rendered in pursuance to an agreement for part performance within the meaning of s.

16 and the only question, therefore, is whether on the evidence it can be held that there was an express acceptance by the plaintiff of the cheque in partial payment tendered by the defendant.

In the course of his judgment the learned trial Judge said:

> In my view, if a party receives a cheque marked "payment in full", the cheque may be cashed and a claim made for the balance owing, but it is incumbent upon the creditor to forthwith write the debtor and advise him that the cheque is not being accepted as payment in full.

With the greatest respect for the learned trial Judge, I do not find support in the authorities for that statement of law. It is a question of fact in every case, whether or not there has been express acceptance of part performance in satisfaction of an obligation; and while the silence of a creditor may be some evidence which is to be considered with all the other evidence in deciding whether or not there has been express acceptance, in my view it is not a factor which is singly governing the rights of the parties.

In any event, in this case the evidence of the plaintiff was that a revised billing had been sent out at the end of the month and the endorsement on the cheque having been altered, its alteration would have necessarily come to the attention of the defendant when the cheque was returned to him from his bank. A defendant, pleading s. 16 of the *Mercantile Law Amendment Act*, has in my opinion a heavy onus. He must prove an express acceptance of part performance. In my view, on the facts of this case, that onus was not met.

In the result, I think the appeal must be allowed and the judgment below set aside. In its place a judgment will go for the plaintiff for $400 and costs to include a counsel fee of $25. The plaintiff is entitled to its costs of this appeal.

Appeal allowed; judgment for plaintiff.

A variation on the preceding cases is the case where A promises to pay B if B will perform his contract with C. It has been sometimes said that B has given A no consideration for his promise to pay B since B is bound to perform his contract with C. It is an important question whether it is proper to draw any analogy between the three-party case and the two-party case. What reasons might there be for refusing to enforce A's promise to pay B?

SCOTSON v. PEGG

(1861), 6 H. & N. 295; 158 E.R. 121. Exch.

[Vendors of coal sold to the defendant and employed the plaintiff to deliver the coal to defendant. The defendant promised the plaintiff, that, if the coal were delivered to him, he (defendant) would unload it at a certain rate. The defendant did not unload the coal as rapidly as he had promised, and the plaintiff sued for damages for breach of contract. The defendant argued that, the plaintiff being already bound to deliver the coal to the defendant by the contract with the vendors, there was no consideration for his promise.]

Martin, B. I am of opinion that the plea is bad, both on principle and in law. It is bad in law because the ordinary rule is, that any act done whereby the contracting party receives a benefit is a good consideration for a promise by him. Here the benefit is the delivery of the coals to the defendant. It is consistent with the declaration that there may have been some dispute as to the defendant's right to have the coals, or it may be that the plaintiffs detained them for demurrage; in either case there would be good consideration that the plaintiffs, who were in possession of the coals, would allow the defendant to take them out of the ship. Then is it any answer that the plaintiffs had entered into a prior contract with other persons to deliver the coals to their order upon the same terms, and that the defendant was a stranger to that contract? In my opinion it is not. We must deal with this case as if no prior contract had been entered into. Suppose the plaintiffs had no chance of getting their money from the other persons who might perhaps have become bankrupt. The defendant gets a benefit by the delivery of the coals to him, and it is immaterial that the plaintiffs had previously contracted with third parties to deliver to their order.

Wilde, B. I am also of opinion that the plaintiffs are entitled to judgment. The plaintiffs say, that in consideration that they would deliver to the defendant a cargo of coals from their ship, the defendant promised to discharge the cargo in a certain way. The defendant, in answer, says, "You made a previous contract with other persons that they should discharge the cargo in the same way, and therefore there is no consideration for my promise." But why is there no consideration? It is said, because the plaintiffs, in delivering the coals are only performing that which they were already bound to do. But to say that there is no consideration is to say that it is not possible for one man to have an interest in the performance of a contract made by another. But if a person chooses to promise to pay a sum of money in order to induce another to perform that which he has already contracted with a third person to do, I confess I cannot see why such a promise should not be binding. Here the defendant, who was a stranger to the original contract, induced the plaintiffs to part with the cargo, which they might not otherwise have been willing to do, and the delivery of it to the defendant was a benefit to him. I accede to the proposition that if a person contracts with another to do a certain thing, he cannot make the performance of it a consideration for a new promise to the same individual. But there is no authority for the proposition that where there has been a promise to one person to do a certain thing, it is not possible to make a valid promise to another to do the same thing. Therefore, deciding this matter on principle, it is plain to my mind that the delivery of the coals to the defendant was a good consideration for his promise, although the plaintiffs had made a previous contract to deliver them to the order of other persons.

Judgment for the plaintiffs.

PROBLEMS

1. Fred was employed as a jockey to ride the mare "Grace" in the Queen's Plate. The mare's dam, sire and two full brothers were owned by Patricia. Patricia promised Fred that, if he won the race, she would pay him $1,000. "Grace" did win. The value of the horses owned by Patricia has now been greatly increased. Fred sued Patricia for the $1,000. What result?

2. A fire occurs at the home of David and Daphne. David rushes out into the street and tells Brad, a fireman who has just arrived on the scene, that he will give him $1,000 if he saves his wife. Brad plunges into the flames and rescues Daphne. Brad sues David. What result?

3. Mary, a policewoman, is called to Tom's house after a burglary. Tom tells her that he has just lost a valuable heirloom which he very much wants back. He prom-

ises Mary that if she recovers the heirloom and gets the criminals convicted he will pay her $1,000. Through Mary's efforts the property is recovered and the criminals convicted. Can Mary sue Tom?

D. Third Parties and Consideration

In the last few cases the situation was that A promised to pay B, if B would perform his contract with C. The actions that we considered were between A and B. The cases we are now going to examine are those where A and B make a promise that, if performed, will benefit C. The question we will have to consider is whether C can sue either A or B for breach of promise if the benefit that was intended for C does not materialize.

The classical position is found in the next case:

TWEDDLE v. ATKINSON

(1861), 1 B. & S. 393, 121 E.R. 762. Queen's Bench; Wightman, Crompton and Blackburn JJ.

[The plaintiff had married the daughter of William Guy. The plaintiff's father and William Guy had made an agreement that they would each pay £100 and £200 respectively to the plaintiff. Neither father paid and both are now dead. The plaintiff sued the executor of William Guy for the £200 that was promised.]

Wightman J. Some of the old decisions appear to support the proposition that a stranger to the consideration of a contract may maintain an action upon it, if he stands in such a near relationship to the party from whom the consideration proceeds, that he may be considered a party to the consideration. The strongest of those cases is that cited in *Bourne v. Mason* (1669) (1 Ventr. 6), in which it was held that the daughter of a physician might maintain assumpsit upon a promise to her father to give her a sum of money if he performed a certain cure. But there is no modern case in which the proposition has been supported. On the contrary, it is now established that no stranger to the consideration can take advantage of a contract, although made for his benefit.

Crompton J. It is admitted that the plaintiff cannot succeed unless this case is an exception to the modern and well established doctrine of the action of assumpsit. At the time when the cases which have been cited were decided the action of assumpsit was treated as an action of trespass upon the case, and therefore in the nature of a tort; and the law was not settled, as it now is, that natural love and affection is not a sufficient consideration for a promise upon which an action may be maintained; nor was it settled that the promisee cannot bring an action unless the consideration for the promise moved from him. The modern cases have, in effect, overruled the old decisions; they shew that the consideration must move from the party entitled to sue upon the contract. It would be a monstrous proposition to say that a person was a party to the contract for the purpose of suing upon it for his own advantage, and not a party to it for the purpose of being sued. It is said that the father in the present case was agent for the son in making the contract, but that argument ought also to make the son liable upon it. I am prepared to overrule the old decisions, and to hold that, by reason of the principles which now govern the action of assumpsit, the present action is not maintainable.

Blackburn, J. agreed in the result.

Judgment for the defendant.

QUESTIONS

1. What do you think Crompton J. means when he says that it would be a monstrous thing for a person (like the plaintiff) to be able to sue on a contract but not be liable on it? There was no evidence that the plaintiff had promised anything.

2. What is the purpose of the doctrine of consideration here?

3. Does this court have the same conception of its role as the court in *Eastwood v. Kenyon*?

The rule laid down by the court in *Tweddle v. Atkinson* became accepted as one of the axioms of the common law. It was stated either as that a person who was not a party to a contract could not sue on it, or as that no action could be maintained by a person who gave no consideration for the promise sued upon. Lord Haldane L.C. said, for example, in *Dunlop v. Selfridges*, [1915] A.C. 847 (H.L.):

"My lords, in the law of England certain principles are fundamental. One is that only a person who is a party to a contract can sue upon it. Our law knows nothing of a jus quaesitum tertio arising by way of contract".

The history of the cases since 1861, in spite of what Lord Haldane said in 1915, has been one constant attempt to get around the problem posed by the rule that third parties cannot sue. Two common law methods for getting around the rule are to use the rules of agency or assignment.

Thus a contract can be enforced by one person P, when the contract has been made with T by A who is P's agent. This is possible even though T had no knowledge of P's existence or that A was acting for P, and even though A was not authorized to act for P when he made the contract with T, so long as P subsequently ratifies the act done on his behalf by A.

Similarly where D owes money to C, C can assign the benefit of his claim against D to A, who, as assignee, can sue D in his own name. In this situation the assignment of C's claim against D operates much like a transfer of property except that a legal claim rather than property is being transferred.

In addition, the equitable device of the trust was frequently used to avoid the doctrinal problems facing the third party. Thus if A made a promise to B for the benefit of C it was said that B, the promisee, held the promise *in trust* for C. The rules of equity would then allow C either to sue A directly or to force B to sue A on C's behalf. (There are even cases where the courts have held that A is the trustee. These are conceptually quite impossible, since it is hard to see what A holds in trust. Such a case is *Mulholland v. Merriam* (1872), 19 Grant 282, Ontario Court of Chancery. The existence of such cases only underlines the strength of the courts' determination to enforce these contracts.)

The importance of these devices for avoiding the operation of the rule that a third person cannot sue on a promise to which he is not a party or for which he has given no consideration is that it is clear that there is no problem avoiding the application of the rules provided that one is careful. As we saw, such care would have avoided the plaintiffs' problems in *Smith v. Dawson*. The important question that the courts have left with us is not so much what is the rule — that is all too clear — but when will they pick up one of the tools available to them and avoid the application of the rule. Corbin, in an article published in 1930, "Contracts for the Benefit of Third

Persons" (1930), 46 L.O.R. 12, pointed out that the English courts, in spite of what they had said in *Tweddle v. Atkinson* and *Dunlop v. Selfridges* were perfectly happy to enforce third party beneficiary promises. He referred in particular to the use of the trust as a device to get around the rule. It is possible to believe that this so annoyed the English judges that the Privy Council in *Vandepitte v. Preferred Accident Ins. Corp.*, [1933] A.C. 70, a case on appeal from B.C., took the opportunity to show that they were concerned about doctrinal purity and that the rule that third parties could not sue would be strictly enforced. In this case a father had bought insurance from the respondent company against liability from the use of his car. His daughter drove the car and had an accident. She was sued by the person she injured. She had no assets and so the injured person, the appellant, sued the company. The policy provided that the coverage would extend "to any person... legally operating the automobile... with the permission of the assured." It was argued that the father was trustee for his daughter. On this, Lord Wright said, "in the present case... there is no evidence that (the father) had any intention to create a beneficial interest for (his daughter). ..."

One wonders what the father thought he was doing if he was not intending to provide protection for his daughter! (Of course, as might have been expected, the law was altered by legislation. See, e.g., *Insurance Act*, R.S.O. 1970, c. 224 (as amended) ss. 207, 208, s. 211 provides: "Any person insured by but not named in a contract to which section 207 or 208 applies may recover indemnity in the same manner and to the same extent as if named therein as the insured, and for that purpose shall be deemed to be a party to the contract and to have given consideration therefor.") Having thus told the upstart American that the English (!) courts were not going to put up with that kind of analysis, the rules of third party beneficiary contracts were confirmed. The Privy Council never said, of course, why doctrinal purity was important.

The next cases show that the English courts are again seeking to find ways around the rule that third parties cannot sue.

BESWICK v. BESWICK

[1966] 1 Ch. 538 C.A. (England); Lord Denning M.R., Danckwerts and
Salmon L.JJ.

Lord Denning M.R. Old Peter Beswick was a coal merchant in Eccles, Lancashire. He had no business premises. All he had was a lorry, scales and weights. He used to take the lorry to the yard of the National Coal Board, where he bagged coal and took it round to his customers in the neighbourhood. His nephew, John Joseph Beswick, helped him in the business.

In March, 1962, old Peter Beswick and his wife were both over 70. He had had his leg amputated and was not in good health. The nephew was anxious to get hold of the business before the old man died. So they went to a solicitor, Mr. Ashcroft, who drew up an agreement for them. The business was to be transferred to the nephew: old Peter Beswick was to be employed in it as a consultant for the rest of his life at £6 10s. a week. After his death the nephew was to pay to his widow an annuity of £5 per week, which was to come out of the business. The agreement was quite short and I will read it in full:

"1. Peter Beswick to assign to John Joseph Beswick the goodwill, motor lorry, scales, weights and other trade utensils of the business of a coal merchant hitherto carried on by him in consideration of the transferee employing the transferor as consultant to the said business for the remainder of the transferor's life at a weekly salary of £6 10s. 2. For the like consideration the transferee, in the event of the death of the transferor, to pay to the transferor's widow an annu to be charged on the said business at the rate of £5 per week. 3. The transferee not to sell the said business in any way freed from his liability to the transferor, which liability shall cease only on the death of the survivor of them the transferor and his said widow. 4. The agreement between the parties to be deemed for all purposes to have commenced to operate as from March 2, 1962. 5. The transferor to be free to devote only such time to the conduct of the said business as he shall find convenient or shall at his own absolute discretion decide. 6. For the consideration aforesaid the transferee to take over the transferor's liability to the following creditors of the transferor: George and Lydia Turner in the sum of £187, Joseph Beswick in the sum of £250 or such lesser sums as shall be agreed with the said creditors whether by compounding or otherwise."

After the agreement was signed, the nephew took over the business and ran it. The old man seems to have found it difficult at first to adjust to the new situation, but he settled down. The nephew paid him £6 10s. a week. But, as expected, he did not live long. He died on November 3, 1963, leaving his widow, who was 74 years of age and in failing health. The nephew paid her the first £5. But he then stopped paying her and has refused to pay her any more.

On June 30, 1964, the widow took out letters of administration to her husband's estate. On July 15, 1964, she brought an action against the nephew for the promised £5 a week. She sued in the capacity of administratrix of the estate of Peter Beswick, deceased, and in her personal capacity she claimed £175 arrrears and a declaration. By amendment she claimed specific performance and the appointment of a receiver. The action came for hearing before the Vice-Chancellor of the County Palatine of Lancaster, who held that she had no right to enforce the agreement. He dismissed the action.

If the decision of the Vice-Chancellor truly represents the law of England, it would be deplorable. It would mean that the nephew could keep the business to himself, and at the same time repudiate his promise to pay the widow. Nothing could be more unjust. I am sure the Vice-Chancellor would have decided in favour of the widow if he had not felt himself bound by the decision of Wynn-Parry J. in *In re Miller's Agreement*, [1947] Ch. 615. That case is cited in the textbooks as if it were the last word on the subject: see Anson on Contracts, 22nd ed. (1964), p. 381; Cheshire and Fifoot on Contracts, 5th ed. (1960), p. 377. It is very like this case. So we must examine it with some care. In *In re Miller's Agreement* there were three partners. One of them had retired and transferred his interest to the other two. By a deed of covenant made by the three partners, the two continuing partners agreed to pay the retiring partner £5,000 a year during his life, and after his death to pay £1,000 a year to his three daughters during their lives. The two continuing partners also charged their interest in the firm with payment of those sums. The Revenue authorities claimed that estate duty was payable on the annuities payable to the daughters. That depended on whether the daughters had such an interest in property as would be protected in a court of law or equity. Wynn-Parry J. held that they had no such interest. "At common law," he said, "so far as the plaintiffs" (the daughters) "are concerned, the deed is res inter alios acta, and they have no right thereunder." As to section 56 of the Law of Property Act, 1925, "the section," he said, "has not the effect of creating rights, but only of assisting the protection of rights shown to exist." As to the charge: "The central function of a charge is to secure the performance of an obligation, and the charge is essentially ancillary." He concluded: "I cannot find... that the deed confers upon any of the daughters any right to sue... the payments, if and when made, will be no more than voluntary payments...." He held, accordingly, that estate duty was not payable on the daughters' annuities.

I can understand the desire of the judge in that case to save the daughters from death duties, but I cannot subscribe to the way he did it. He was wrong in saying that the daughters had no enforceable interest. We have here the standard pattern of a contract for the benefit of a third person. A man has a business or other assets. He transfers them to another and, instead of taking cash, takes a promise by that other that he will pay an annuity or other sum to his widow or children. Can the transferee take the assets and reject the promise? I think not. In my opinion a contract such as this, for the benefit of widow and children, is binding. The party who makes the promise must honour it, unless he has some good reason why he should not do so. He may, for instance, be able to say that the contract should be rescinded as being induced by fraud or misrepresentation, or that it was varied or rescinded by agreement between the parties, before the widow or children knew about it and adopted it. But unless he has some good reason, he is bound. The executor of the dead man can sue to enforce it on behalf of the widow and children. The widow and children can join with the executor as plaintiffs in the action. If he refuses to sue, they may sue in their own names joining him as a defendant. In this way they have a right which can be enforced. I will prove this by reference to the common law, reinforced by equity, and now by statute.

1. THE COMMON LAW

The common law on this subject was much considered in *Dutton v. Poole* in 1678 (8 T. Raym. 302). It was regarded at the time as a case of great consequence and is reported by no less than five of the old reporters. It was similar in principle to our present case. The facts were these: Sir Edward Poole owned timber trees in a wood in Oaksey Park, Wiltshire. He had several children, including his son and heir, Nevil, and a daughter Grizel. Sir Edward proposed to cut down the trees and sell them so as to raise portions for the younger children. The eldest son did not want him to do this, because he was the heir and would inherit the trees if they were left standing. There was a meeting between the father and mother and the eldest son. The son asked the father not to cut down the trees, and promised him that, if he did not cut them down, he would pay £1,000 to the daughter Grizel. In reliance on the promise, the father did not cut down any of the trees, and died. The eldest son inherited and had the benefit of them. The daughter Grizel (who had married Sir Ralph Dutton) claimed £1,000 from the eldest son. He refused to pay it to her.

The mother was the executrix of the father's estate. She could as executrix have sued to enforce the agreement. But she was the only person present when it was made, and if she brought the action, she would not be a competent witness. So the daughter and her husband themselves sued the eldest son for the £1,000. In that action the mother was a competent witness. She proved the agreement, and the plaintiffs obtained judgment for £1,000. The eldest son appealed to the Court of King's Bench sitting in banc. The case was argued twice. John Holt appeared for the eldest son. He said that the action ought to be brought by the father's executor for the benefit of the daughter; and not by the daughter herself, as she was "not privy to the promise nor consideration." Pollexsen appeared for the daughter. He said that the action was maintainable either by the party to whom the promise was made, or by the daughter. When the case was first argued, two of the four judges were disposed to accept Holt's argument and hold that the daughter could not sue. But at the second argument Scroggs C.J. with his three brethren all held that the daughter could sue, "for the son hath the benefit by having of the wood, and the daughter hath lost her portion by this means." The eldest son appealed to the Court of Exchequer Chamber, but the appeal was dismissed.

Two things appear from that case: First, it was accepted on all hands that the father's executrix could have sued for the benefit of the daughter. Second, that in the special circumstances of that case (when a party could not give evidence), the daughter herself could sue on the contract although she was not a party to it. It was a decision of the Court of Exchequer Chamber and has never been overruled. It was approved by Lord Mansfield himself in 1776 in *Martyn v. Hind*, 2 Cowp. 437, 443, who thought it so plain that "it is matter of surprise how a doubt could have arisen in that case." I know that in the 19th century some judges said that it was wrongly decided, but the criticism is not merited. It would have been shocking if the daughter had been refused a remedy.

The case of *Tweddle v. Atkinson* is readily distinguishable. John Tweddle married Miss Guy. After the marriage the two fathers of the young couple made an agreement between themselves, the two fathers, to pay these sums: The husband's father promised to pay his son £100: the wife's father promised to pay his son-in-law £200: such payments to be made on or before August 21, 1855. Clearly the payments were to be mutual for the benefit of the young couple. Neither of the fathers made the promised payments: and afterwards both fathers died. Then the young husband sued the executor of his wife's father for the £200. The action failed for the very good reason that the husband's father had not done his part. He had not paid his promised £100. The son could not himself be sued for his father's failure to pay the £100: for he was no party to the contract. So he could not be allowed to sue his wife's father for the £200. Crompton J. said:

> "It would be a monstrous proposition to say that a person was a party to the contract for the purpose of suing upon it for his own advantage, and not a party to it for the purpose of being sued."

But if the husband's father had paid his £100 and thus wholly performed his part, then the husband's father in his lifetime, or his executor after his death, could have sued the wife's father or his executor for the £200. As Wightman J. observed:

> "If the father of the plaintiff had paid the £100 which he promised, might not he have sued the father of the plaintiff's wife on his express promise?"

To which the answer would undoubtedly be: "Yes, he could sue and recover the £200," but he would recover it not for his own benefit, or for the benefit of the estate, but for the benefit of the son.

Those two cases give the key at common law to the whole problem of contracts for the benefit of a third person. Although the third person cannot as a rule sue alone in his own name, nevertheless there is no difficulty whatever in the one contracting party suing the other party for breach of the promise. The third person should, therefore, bring the action in the name of the contracting party, just as an assignee used to do. Face to face with the contracting party, the defaulter has no defence. He is sued by one who has provided consideration and to whom he has given his promise to pay the third person. He has broken his promise and must pay damages. The defaulter sometimes seeks to say that the contracting party can only recover nominal damages because it is not he but the third person who has suffered the damage. The common law has never allowed the defaulter to escape by such a shifty means. It holds that the contracting party can recover the money which should have been paid to the third person. He can get judgment for the sum and issue a writ of fi. fa. or other machinery to enforce payment: but when he recovers it, he holds the proceeds for the benefit of the third person. He cannot retain the money himself because it belongs to the third person and not to him: see *In re Schebsman, Ex parte the Official Solicitor, the Trustee. Cargo Superintendents (London) Ltd. v. Schebsman,* [1943] d. 83. It is money had and received to the use of the third person. In *Robertson v. Wait* (1853), 8 Exd 299, 301, Martin B. said: "If a person makes a contract whereby another obtains a benefit, why may not the former sue for it?" And in *Lloyd's v. Harper* (1880), 16 Cl. D. 290, 321 Lush L.J. said:

> "I consider it to be an established rule of law that where a contract is made with A for the benefit of B, A can sue on the contract for the benefit of B and recover all that B could have recovered if the contract had been made with B himself."

Such was the position at common law if the action was brought in the name of the contracting party by himself alone. But nowadays when joinder of parties is freely permissible, it is far better for the contracting party and the third person to join as co-plaintiffs. Judgment will be given for the plaintiffs for the amount: and on payment, it will go at once to the third person who is entitled to it.

2. EQUITY

Sometimes one of the contracting parties makes the contract on trust for the third person, in this sense, that from the very beginning the right to sue is vested in him as trustee for the third person as beneficiary. Such a contract is different from those we are considering. It cannot be rescinded or varied except with the consent of the third person beneficiary.... In such a case it is clearly established that the third person himself can sue in equity to enforce the contract... but even so, he ought as a rule to join the trustee as a party. Here we have a case where there is admittedly no trust of the contractual right. Peter Beswick and his nephew might by agreement before his death have rescinded or varied the agreement, if they so wished. Nevertheless, although there is no trust, I do not think equity is powerless. It has in its hands the potent remedy of ordering a party specifically to perform his contract. If a party makes a promise to pay money to a third person, I see no reason why a court of equity should not order him to perform his promise. The action must be brought, of course, in the name of the other contracting party; but, that being done, there is no bar to a decree for specific performance being made. True it is for the payment of money, but a court of equity often decrees specific performance of a promise to pay money. It can enforce it by the appointment of a receiver, or other appropriate machinery. We have been referred to three cases where this has been done, although there was no trust. The first is *Keenan v. Handley* (1864) 12 W.R. 1021. Ellen Keenan was the mistress of Captain Handley. They lived as Mr. and Mrs. Coverdale and had a baby daughter called Lucy Coverdale. Captain Handley wrote this letter to Miss Keenan: "I will allow you £150 a year, to be continued to you while you live and to your child after your death, should she survive you." She and her daughter sued for specific performance. Kindersley V.-C. granted it. He ordered deeds to be executed for payment of the annuities, including the amounts to the daughter, although she was not a party to the agreement. The next case is *Peel v. Peel* (1869) 17 W.R. 586. William Peel was in financial difficulty. His brother Edmund Peel agreed with his cousin, Sir Robert Peel, that Edmund would pay off William's debts and that Sir Robert would during his life pay William an annuity of £164 a year. Edmund paid off the debts but Sir Robert Peel did not pay the amounts. Edmund Peel and William Peel sued for specific performance. James V.-C. granted it. He ordered Sir Robert to pay William Peel £164 a year, although William was not a party to the agreement. The third case is *Hohler v. Aston*, [1920] 2 Ch. 420 where Mrs. Aston agreed with her nephew, Mr. Hohler, to make provision for her niece and her husband, Mr. and Mrs. Rollo. Mrs. Aston died before doing so. Mr. Hohler and Mr. and Mrs. Rollo sued the executors for specific performance. Sargant J. granted it. He said:

> "Mr. E.T. Hohler was entitled, and is now entitled, to enforce for the benefit of the third parties, Mr. and Mrs. Rollo, a contract made with Mrs. Aston for those third parties. The third parties, of course, cannot themselves enforce a contract made for their benefit, but the person with whom the contract is made is entitled to enforce the contract."

These cases in equity fit in exactly with the common law.

.   .   .

4. CONCLUSION

The general rule undoubtedly is that "no third person can sue, or be sued, on a contract to which he is not a party": but at bottom that is only a rule of procedure. It goes to the form of remedy, not to the underlying right. Where a contract is made for the benefit of a third person who has a legitimate interest to enforce it, it can be enforced by the third person in the name of the contracting party or jointly with him or, if he refuses to join, by adding him as a defendant. In that sense, and it is a very real sense, the third person has a right arising by way of contract. He has an interest which will be protected by law. The observations to the contrary in *In re Miller's Agreement* and *Green v. Russell*, [1959] 2 Q.B. 226, are in my opinion erroneous. It is different when a third person has no legitimate interest, as when he is seeking to enforce the maintenance of prices to the public disadvantage, as in *Dunlop Pneumatic Tyre Co. Ltd. v. Selfridge & Co. Ltd.*: or when he is seeking to rely, not on any right given to him by the contract, but on an exemption clause seeking to exempt himself from his just liability. He cannot set up an exemption clause in a contract to which he was not a party: see *Midland Silicones Ltd. v. Scruttons Ltd.*, [1962] A.C. 446.

The widow here sues in her capacity as executrix of her husband's estate (and therefore as contracting party), and also in her personal capacity (and therefore as a third person). This joint claim is clearly good. She is entitled to an order for specific performance of the agreement, by ordering the defendant to pay the arrears of £175, and the instalments of £5 a week as they fall due. The order for paying the arrears of £175 is equivalent to a judgment for that sum and can be enforced by fi. fa. or other appropriate machinery: see R.S.C. Ord. 42, r. 3. When the money is recovered, it will go to the widow for her own benefit, and not to her husband's estate. I would allow the appeal accordingly.

[Danckwerts and Salmon L.JJ. gave judgments to the same effect.]
[The defendant appealed to the House of Lords.]

BESWICK v. BESWICK

[1968] A.C. 58 (H.L.). Lords Reid, Hodson, Guest, Pearce and Upjohn.

Lord Upjohn [After stating the facts, continued]: As it is necessary to keep clear and distinct the rights of the widow as administratrix of her husband and personally, I think it will be convenient to use letters: letter A represents the deceased and A1 the widow, as personal representative, B the widow in her personal capacity and C the appellant. And in other examples I shall give, these letters will serve the same purpose.

Much is common ground between the parties: (1) B was not a party to the agreement; (2) A did not enter into the agreement as trustee for B in relation to the annuity to be paid to her; (3) A1 stands for all relevant purposes in the shoes of A and is entitled to sue C for breach of his admitted repudiation of the agreement (see paragraph 5 of the defence), but the parties differ fundamentally as to the remedy to which A1 is entitled in such an action.

Counsel for the respondent has not felt able to support the view, expressed by Lord Denning M.R., that apart from section 56 of the Law of Property Act, 1925, B is entitled to sue C at common law. I think that he was right to make this concession, for whatever may have been the state of the law before *Tweddle v. Atkinson* it is difficult to see how your Lordships can go back over 100 years in view of the decisions in this House of *Dunlop Pneumatic Tyre Co. Ltd.* v. *Selfridge & Co. Ltd.* and *Scruttons Ltd.* v. *Midland Silicones Ltd.* [1962] A.C. 496.

Leaving section 56 out of account, there was no real dispute between the parties as to their respective rights (as distinct from remedies) under the agreement. (*a*) B has no rights thereunder. But it was clear from the whole tenor of the agreement that the annuity was to be paid to her for her own beneficial enjoyment, so if C paid it to her she could keep it and did not hold it as a constructive trustee for A1; (*b*) C would completely perform his obligation under the contract by continuing to pay the annuity to B during her life. Neither A nor A1 could compel C to pay it to A or A1, but (*c*) A or A1 and C could, if they pleased, agree to modify, compromise or even discharge further performance of the contract by C, and B would have no right to complain. If authority be wanted for these fundamental propositions, it is to be found in *In re Schebsman*, [1944], Ch. 83, and *In re Stapleton-Bretherton*, [1941] Ch. 482.

My Lords, to return to this case. Admittedly A1 can sue from time to time for damages at common law on failure to pay each instalment of the annuity. But surely on a number of grounds this is a case for specific performance.

First, here is the sale of a business for full consideration wholly executed on A's part who has put C into possession of all the assets. C is repudiating the obligations to be performed by him. To such as case the words of Kay. J. in *Hart v. Hart*, 18 Ch. D. 670, 885, are particularly appropriate:

> "... when an agreement for valuable consideration between two parties has been partially performed, the court ought to do its utmost to carry out that agreement by a decree for specific performance."

The fact that A by the agreement was to render such services as consultant as he might find convenient or at his own absolute discretion should decide may be ignored as de minimis and the contrary was not argued. In any event the fact that there is a small element of personal service in a contract of this nature does not destroy that quality of mutuality (otherwise plainly present) want of which may in general terms properly be a ground for refusing a decree of specific performance...

In the courts below, though not before your Lordships, it was argued that the remedy of specific performance was not available when all that remained was the obligation to make a money payment. Danckwerts L.J. rightly demolished this contention as untenable for the reasons he gives.

But when the money payment is not made once and for all but in the nature of an annuity there is an even greater need for equity to come to the assistance of the common law. Equity is to do true justice to enforce the true contract that the parties have made and to prevent the trouble and expense of a multiplicity of actions. This has been well settled for over a century: *Swift v. Swift* (1841), 3 In. Eq. R. 267. In that case an annuity of £40 p.a. was payable to a lady quarterly and Lord Plunket L.C. enforced specific performance of it. He said:

> "It is said she has a complete remedy at law for the breach of this contract, and that, therefore, this court should not interfere. Now, the remedy at law could only be obtained in one of two ways, either by at once recovering damages for all the breaches that might occur during the joint lives of herself and the defendant, or by bringing four actions in each year, and recovering in each the amount of a quarterly payment of the annuity. Those are the two modes of redress open to the plaintiff at Law. And I am called on to refuse relief here on the ground that such remedies are equally beneficial and effectual for the plaintiff as that which this court could afford. To refuse relief on such a ground would not, in my opinion, be a rational administration of justice. I do not see that there is any authority for refusing relief, and certainly there is no foundation in reason for doing so."

Then, after referring to the case of *Adderley v. Dixon*, (1824), 1 Sim. & St. 607, he continued:

> "Applying this to the present case, leaving the plaintiff to proceed at law and to get damages at once for all the breaches that might occur during the joint lives of her and the defendant, would, in effect, be altering the entire nature of the contract that she entered into: it would be compelling her to accept a certain sum, a sum to be ascertained by the conjecture of a jury as to what was the value of the annuity. This would be most unreasonable and unjust: her contract was for the periodical payment of certain sums during an uncertain period; she was entitled to a certain sum of money, and she agreed to give up that for an annuity for her own and the defendant's lives, and to insist on her now accepting a certain sum of money in the shape of damages for it, would be in effect to make her convert into money, what she, having in money, exchanged for an annuity. As to her resorting four times every year to a Court of Law for each quarterly payment of this annuity, it is a manifest absurdity to call that a beneficial or effectual remedy

for the plaintiff; and resting the case on that ground alone, I think I am warranted by the highest authority in granting the relief sought."

It is in such common sense and practical ways that equity comes to the aid of the common law and it is sufficiently flexible to meet and satisfy the justice of the case in the many different circumstances that arise from time to time.

To sum up this matter: had C repudiated the contract in the lifetime of A the latter would have had a cast iron case for specific performance. Can it make any difference that by the terms of the agreement C is obliged to pay the annuity after A's death to B? Of course not. On the principle I have just stated it is clear that there can be nothing to prevent equity in A's specific performance action making an appropriate decree for specific performance directing payment of the annuity to A but during his life and thereafter to B for her life.

There is abundant authority to support that proposition. The first is *Keenan v. Handley* (1864), 12 W.R. 930; 2 De G.J. & Sm. 283, and on appeal, the facts of which are sufficiently set out in the judgment of Lord Denning M.R. That case seems to me dead in point and I do not accept the argument that the mother, Ellen Keenan, was contracting as trustee for her child; such a relationship cannot be spelt out of Captain Handley's letter. As one of the contracting parties she was suing to enforce her rights under the letter, as later modified by agreement for payment of £100 a year to herself for her life and £50 a year to the child and after Ellen Keenan's death £150 a year to the child for her life. True it is that no point was taken either at first instance or in the Court of Appeal that the infant could not sue but, as *Tweddle v. Atkinson* had only been decided some three years before, that point cannot have been overlooked. I draw the inference that it never occurred to those distinguished equity judges who tried that case that there could be any difficulty in making an order upon C at the instance of A to pay B. That is made clear by the order in that case which is to be found in that great book of authority, Seton on Judgments and Orders (see 7th edition (1912), vol. 3, p. 2212). That was followed by *Peel v. Peel* (1869), 17 W.R. 586, also discussed by Lord Denning M.R. Then came the Irish case of *Drimmie v. Davies*, [1899], I.R. 176, a very familiar type of case where the parties in a firm agreed together to pay annuities to the dependants of a partner when he should die. The executors of a deceased partner brought an action to enforce payment of the annuities and succeeded. Although my noble and learned friend, Lord Pearce, has set out the observations of Holmes L.J. in that case in his speech, it so exactly expresses my own view that I set it out again. Holmes L.J. said:

> "In this case Davies, junior, covenanted for valuable consideration with Davies, senior, that in certain events he would pay certain annuities to the children of the latter. If such annuities had become payable in the life of the covenantee, and they were not paid, what legal obstacle would there be to his suing the covenantor? Indeed, I believe that it is admitted that such an action would lie, but that it would only result in nominal damages. A result more repugnant to justice as well as to legal principle, I can hardly imagine. The defendant would thereby escape from paying what he had undertaken to pay by making an illusory payment never contemplated by either party. Well, if Davies, senior, would have been entitled to sue in his lifetime if the annuities were then payable, his executors would have the same right of action after his death. As I have already said, the question is elementary."

Finally there was the rather unusual case of *Hohler v. Aston*, [1920], 2 Cl. 420, also mentioned by Lord Denning M.R. who quotes the relevant passage from the judgment of Sargant J. (as he then was). This again shows the extent of the power of equity to assist the common law, limited only by canons of common sense and the practical limitations on the power to oversee and administer specific performance decrees. So the power and indeed duty, in proper cases, of the court of equity to make specific performance orders in favour of third parties at the instance of one of the contracting parties is not in doubt.

But when A dies and his rights pass to A1, it is said that the remedy of specific performance is no longer appropriate against C. The argument was first that the estate of A suffered no damage by reason of C's failure to pay B; so A1 is entitled to nominal damages but as she is not otherwise interested in the agreement as such it would be wrong to grant specific performance; for that remedy is available only where damages will be an inadequate remedy. Here nominal damages are adequate. Further, it was argued, to do so would really be to confer upon B a right which she does not have in law or equity to receive the annuity. Then, secondly, it was said that if the remedy of specific performance is granted it might prejudice creditors of A so that the parties ought to be left to their strict rights at law. Thirdly, it is said that there are procedural difficulties in the way of enforcing an order for specific performance in favour of a third party. I will deal with these points, though in reverse order.

As to procedural difficulties, I fear I do not understand the argument. The point if valid applies to an action for specific performance by A just as much as by A1 yet in the authorities I have quoted no such point was ever taken; in *Drimmie v. Davies* indeed the action was by executors. Further, it seems to me that if C fails to obey a four-day order obtained by A1, B could enforce it under the clear and express provisions of R.S.C., Ord. 45, r. 9 (formerly Ord. 42, r. 26). Alternatively A1 could move for and obtain the appointment of a receiver of the business upon which the annuity is charged and the receiver would then be directed by the Court to pay the annuity to B out of the profits of the business. Finally, A1 could issue a writ of fi fa under Ord. 45, r. 1, but as A1 would then be enforcing the contract and not modifying or compromising it the court would obviously in executing its order compel her to carry out the contract in toto and hand the proceeds of execution to B. This point is entirely without substance.

Then as to the second point. Let me assume (contrary to the fact) that A died with substantial assets but also many creditors. The legal position is that prima facie the duty of A1 is to carry our her intestate's contracts and compel C to pay B; but the creditors may be pressing and the agreement may be considered onerous; so it may be her duty to try and compromise the agreement with C and save something for the estate even at the expense of B.... So be it, but how can C conceivably rely upon this circumstance as a defence by him to an action for specific performance by A1? Of course not; he, C, has no interest in the estate; he cannot plead a possible jus tertii which is no concern of his. It is his duty to fulfil his contract by paying C. A1 alone is concerned with the creditors, beneficiaries or next of kin of A and this point therefore can never be a defence by C if A1 in fact chooses to sue for specific performance rather than to attempt a compromise in the interest of the estate. This point seems to me misconceived. In any event, on the facts of this case there is no suggestion that there are any unpaid creditors and B is sole next of kin, so the point is academic.

Then, as to the first point. On this question we were referred to the well-known dictum of Lush L.J. in *Lloyd's v. Harper*:

> "I consider it to be an established rule of law that where a contract is made with A for the benefit of B, A can sue on the contract for the benefit of B and recover all that B could have recovered if the contract had been made with B himself."

While in the circumstances it is not necessary to express any concluded opinion thereon, if the learned Lord Justice was expressing a view on the purely common law remedy of damages, I have some difficulty in going all the way with him. If A sues for damages for breach of contract by reason of the failure to pay B he must prove his loss; that may be great or nominal according to circumstances.

I do not see how A can, in conformity with clearly settled principle in assessing damages for breach of contract, rely at common law on B's loss. I agree with the observations of Windeyer J. in the as yet unreported case of *Coulls v. Bagot's Executor and Trustee Co. Ltd.* (1967), 40 A.L. J. R. 471, in the High Court of Australia. But I note, however, that in *Lloyd's v. Harper* James and Cotton L.JJ. treated A as trustee for B and I doubt whether Lush L.J. thought otherwise.

However, I incline to the view that on the facts of this case damages are nominal for it appears that A died without any assets save and except the agreement which he hoped would keep him and then his widow for their lives. At all events let me assume that damages are nominal. So it is said nominal damages are adequate and the remedy of specific performance ought not to be granted. That is, with all respect, wholly to misunderstand that principle. Equity will grant specific performance when damages are inadequate to meet the justice of the case.

But in any event quantum of damages seldom affects the right to specific performance. If X contracts with Y to buy Blackacre or a rare chattel for a fancy price because the property or chattel has caught his fancy he is entitled to enforce his bargain and it matters not that he could not prove any damage.

In this case the court ought to grant a specific performance order all the more because damages are nominal. C has received all the property; justice demands that he pay the price and this can only be done in the circumstances by equitable relief. It is a fallacy to suppose that B is thereby obtaining additional rights; A1 is entitled to compel C to carry out the terms of the agreement. The observations of Holmes L.J. already quoted are very much in point.

My Lords, in my opinion the Court of Appeal were clearly right to grant a decree of specific performance. That is sufficient to dispose of the appeal but as your Lordships have heard much argument on the true scope and ambit of section 56 of the Law of Property Act, 1925, I propose to express some views thereon, though necessarily obiter.

The discussion of s. 56 of the Law of Property Act, 1925, is omitted. The other judges agreed with Lord Upjohn in separate judgments.

JACKSON v. HORIZON HOLIDAYS

[1975] 1 W.L.R. 1468. Court of Appeal (England); Lord Denning M.R., Orr
and James L.JJ.

Lord Denning, M.R. Mr. Jackson is a young man, in his mid twenties. He
has been very successful in his business. He is married with three small children. In November 1970 there were twin boys of three years of age; and his
wife had just had her third child. He had been working very hard. They
determined to have a holidy in the sun. He decided upon Ceylon. He
inquired of Horizon Holidays Ltd. He made arrangements with their agent,
a Mrs. Bremner, for a holiday at a hotel, the Pegasus Reef Hotel, Hendala
Point, Ceylon. He wrote them a letter which shows that he wanted everything of the highest standard:

> "With reference to our telephone conversation would you please confirm that
> you can arrange for my wife myself and my two twin boys aged three years to
> stay for 28 days from January 23 at the Hotel Pegasus Reef, Hendala Point, Cey-
> lon. Would you also arrange that the children's room has an adjoining door to
> our room; this is essential and is a condition of me booking this holiday. Would
> you please make sure that the balcony is facing the sea and would you also con-
> firm the distance the hotel is from the sea. Would you confirm that the meals are
> four course with a choice of three or four dishes to each course. Could you con-
> firm that there have been arrangements made that an English speaking doctor
> would call on the hotel if needed. Would you please make a clear answer to all
> these questions appreciating that you might have difficulties in answering some
> of these questions and not to send an evasive answer to any of these questions."

He spoke on the telephone to Mrs. Bremner. She led him to believe that
the hotel would come up to his expectations. She wrote on the booking
form:-

> "Remarks Twins' room with connecting door essential. Total charge £1432."

He sent it in and booked the holiday.

In the middle of January it was discovered that the Pegasus Reef Hotel
would not be ready in time. So Horizon Holidays recommended a substitute. This was Brown's Beach Hotel. It was described in the advertisement
as being

> "superbly situated right on the beach, with all facilities for an enjoyable holiday
> including mini-golf, excellent restaurant, cocktail lounge, and gift shop.... The
> bedrooms are well furnished and equipped in modern style. *All rooms have private
> bath, shower, w.c., sea view and air-conditioning.*"

Mr. Jackson had some hesitation about this other hotel. But Horizon
Holidays assured him that it would be up to his expectation. So Mr. Jackson accepted it. But Horizon Holidays reduced the charge. Instead of the
price being the total sum of £1,432 it would, because of the change of hotel,
be £1,200. That included air travel to Ceylon and back and a holiday for
four weeks. So they went there. The courier, Miss Redgrove, met them and
took them to Brown's Beach Hotel. But they were greatly disappointed.
Their room had not got a connecting door with the room for the children at
all. The room for the children was mildewed — black with mildew, at the
bottom. There was fungus growing on the walls. The toilet was stained. The
shower was dirty. There was no bath. They could not let the children sleep
in the room. So for the first three days they had all the family in one room.

The two children were put into one of the single beds and the two adults slept in the other single bed. After the first three days they were moved into what was said to be one of the best suites in the hotel. Even then they had to put the children to sleep in the sitting room and the parents in the bedroom. There was dirty linen on the bed. There was no private bath but only a shower; no mini-golf course; no swimming pool; no beauty salon; no hairdressers' salon. Worst of all was the cooking. There was no choice of dishes. On some occasions, however, curry was served as an alternative to the main dish. They found the food was very distasteful. It appeared to be cooked in coconut oil. There was a pervasive taste because of the manner of cooking. They were so uncomfortable at Brown's Beach Hotel that after a fortnight they moved to the Pegasus Reef Hotel. It appears that by that time it was nearing completion. But a lot of building work was still going on. At any rate, for the second fortnight they were in the Pegasus Reef Hotel, where things were somewhat better than at Brown's Beach Hotel. They stayed out the four weeks, and came home.

Soon after their return, Mr. Jackson wrote a letter setting out all his complaints from the beginning to the end. Then Mr. Jackson brought an action for damages in respect of the loss of his holiday for himself, his wife and the two small children. Horizon Holidays admitted liability. The contest was only on the amount of damages.

In *Jarvis v. Swans Tours Ltd.* [1973] Q.B. 233, it was held by this court that damages for the loss of a holiday may include not only the difference in value between what was promised and what was obtained, but also damages for mental distress, inconvenience, upset, disappointment and frustration caused by the loss of the holiday. The judge directed himself in accordance with the judgments in that case. He eventually awarded a sum of £1,100. Horizon Holidays Ltd. appeal. They say it was far too much.

The judge did not divide up the £1,100. Counsel has made suggestions about it. Mr. Cheyne for Horizon Holidays suggests that the judge gave £100 for diminution in value and £1,000 for the mental distress. But Mr. Davies for Mr. Jackson suggested that the judge gave £600 for the diminution in value and £500 for the mental distress. If I were inclined myself to speculate, I think Mr. Davies' suggestion may well be right. The judge took the cost of the holidays at £1,200. The family only had about half the value of it. Divide if by two and you get £600. Then add £500 for the mental distress.

On this question a point of law arises. The judge said that he could only consider the mental distress to Mr. Jackson himself and that he could not consider the distress to his wife and children. He said:

"The damages are the plaintiff's.... I can consider the effect upon his mind of the wife's discomfort, vexation, and the like, although I cannot award a sum which represents her own vexation."

Mr. Davies, for Mr. Jackson, disputes that proposition. He submits that damages can be given not only for the leader of the party — in this case, Mr. Jackson's own distress, discomfort and vexation — but also for that of the rest of the party.

We have had an intersting discussion as to the legal position when one person makes a contract for the benefit of a party. In this case it was a husband making a contract for the benefit of himself, his wife and children. Other cases readily come to mind. A host makes a contract with a restaurant for a dinner for himself and his friends. The vicar makes a contract for a coach trip for the choir. In all these cases there is only one person who makes the contract. It is the husband, the host, or the vicar, as the case may be. Sometimes he pays the whole price himself. Occasionally he may get a contribution from the others. But in any case it is he who makes the contract. It would be a fiction to say that the contract was made by all the family, or all the guests, or all the choir, and that he was only an agent for them. Take this very case. It would be absurd to say that the twins of three years old were parties to the contract or that the father was making the contract on their behalf as if they were principals. It would equally be a mistake to say that in any of these instances there was a trust. The transaction bears no resemblance to a trust. There was no trust fund and no trust property. No, the real truth is that in each instance, the father, the host or the vicar, was making a contract himself for the benefit of the whole party. In short, a contract by one for the benefit of third persons.

What is the position when such a contract is broken? At present the law says that the only one who can sue is the one who made the contract. None of the rest of the party can sue, even though the contract was made for their benefit. But when that one does sue, what damages can he recover? Is he limited to his own loss? Or can he recover for the others? Suppose the holiday firm puts the family into a hotel which is only half built and the visitors have to sleep on the floor? Or suppose the restaurant is fully booked and the guests have to go away, hungry and angry, having spent so much on fares to get there? Or suppose the coach leaves the choir stranded halfway and they have to hire cars to get home? None of them individually can sue. Only the father, the host or the vicar can sue. He can, of course, recover his own damages. But can he not recover for the others? I think he can. The case comes within the principle stated by Lush L.J. in *Lloyd's v. Harper* (1880) 16 Ch.D. 290, 321:

"I consider it to be an established rule of law that where a contract is made with A, for the benefit of B., A. can sue on the contract for the benefit of B., and recover all that B. could have recovered if the contract had been made with B. himself."

It has been suggested that Lush L.J. was thinking of a contract in which A was trustee for B. But I do not think so. He was a common lawyer speaking of common law. His words were quoted with considerable approval by Lord Pearce in *Beswick v. Beswick* [1968] A.C. 58, 88. I have myself often quoted them. I think they should be accepted as correct, at any rate so long as the law forbids the third persons themselves from suing for damages. It is the only way in which a just result can be achieved. Take the instance I have put. The guests ought to recover from the restaurant their wasted fares. The choir ought to recover the cost of hiring the taxis home. Then is no one to recover from them except the one who made the contract for their benefit? He should be able to recover the expense to which he has been put, and pay it over to them. Once recovered, it will be money had and received to their use. (They might even, if desired, be joined as plaintiffs). If he can recover for the expense, he should also be able to recover for the discomfort, vexation and upset which the whole party have suffered by reason of the breach of contract, recompensing them accordingly out of what he recovers.

Applying the principles to this case, I think that the figure of £1,100 was about right. It would, I think, have been excessive if it had been awarded only for the damage suffered by Mr. Jackson himself. But when extended to his wife and children, I do not think it is excessive. People look forward to a holiday. They expect the promises to be fulfilled. When it fails, they are greatly disappointed and upset. It is difficult to assess in terms of money; but it is the task of the judges to do the best they can. I see no reason to interfere with the total award of £1,100. I would therefore dismiss the appeal.

Orr and James L.JJ. agreed with Lord Denning MR.

Appeal dismissed with costs.
Leave to appeal to House of of Lords refused.

QUESTIONS

1. Would it have been relevant that Mrs. Jackson had, in fact, thoroughly enjoyed her holiday?
2. Does Mr. Jackson have any obligation to pass on the damages he has recovered for Mrs. Jackson to her? If not, then, presumably in any of the examples given by Lord Denning the contracting party can keep the total damages that have been awarded. But Lord Denning seems to say that they have a right to the money. Does this then mean that they can compel the contracting party to sue? If this is so, have the courts got around the third party beneficiary rule?

The case is reported in Vol. 1. W.L.R. this means that the editor did not think it important enough to be included in the Law Reports. Yet if Lord Denning is saying that C can now compel A or B to sue the other, and can get the damages that are recovered, the so-called doctrine of privity of contract has been dealt a severe blow, and the case is revolutionary.

NOTE

Our focus here has been entirely on ways around the third party beneficiary rule established in *Tweddle v. Atkinson*. As we have seen, there are a variety of ways to let C, the third party, sue A, the promisor. So long as C can use (or has to use) devices like agency, assignment and the concept of the trust, then C's claim fits into a generally accepted legal framework. The fact is, of course, that there are often difficulties in constructing a relationship that corresponds to one of these three devices for getting around the third party rule. What we ultimately need is to come to grips with the issue and consider two questions:

1. What reasons might there be that would justify a refusal to allow C to sue A? and
2. If we once let A be sued directly by C as a third party beneficiary, what problems might we have to deal with?

The first question can be answered in a number of ways. First, there are doctrinal problems — the kind that found expression in *Dunlop v. Selfridges* — usually expressed in the language of *Tweddle v. Atkinson* that only a party to a contract or a party to the consideration can sue on it. This may mean that A's promise was made to B, not to C. It may mean that consideration did not move from C. It may also mean that C did not assent to the agreement since the agreement was between A and B. The consideration problem is usually regarded as being the principal objection in English and

Canadian law. The doctrinal problems cannot be much further reasoned about. If we believe that the answer to legal problems can be deduced from some general legal premise, and that this is the right way to resolve problems, then we have an answer to the first question.

The second way of answering the first question focuses not on the doctrine but on the development of satisfactory rules that are a reflection of the way in which this kind of problem has to be resolved. The concern for doctrine forces us to find doctrinally acceptable ways around the doctrinal impasse. The concern for a functional analysis raises the issue of the reasons for granting or refusing enforcement that are hidden (or, more accurately, ignored) by the doctrinal approach. A functional approach sees the existence of doctrinally acceptable devices as irrelevant unless the remedy that C can obtain depends on the device that is used. The focus on the reasons for not allowing C to sue A leads to some interesting questions. Thus if A promises B to confer a benefit on C, whether C has any effective remedy may depend on who B is. If B was, say, C's uncle, who wanted to make a gift to C, on B's death, B's executor may be quite uninterested or even reluctant in bringing any action on C's behalf. It may therefore be necessary to allow C to sue directly in such a case. But to allow C to sue in all cases may not be satisfactory. If Peter Beswick had wanted to vary the arrangement that he had with his nephew, should his wife be able to prevent such a change because she was a third party beneficiary?

The Americans have always been more willing to allow a third party to sue (see: *Lawrence v. Fox* (1859), 20 N.Y. 268. Court of Appeals of New York). They have therefore had to resolve some of these issues. The *Restatement (Second)* contains the following provisions.

§133. *Intended and Incidental Beneficiaries.*
(1) Unless otherwise agreed between promisor and promisee, a beneficiary of a promise is an intended beneficiary if recognition of a right to performance in the beneficiary is appropriate to effectuate the intention of the parties and either (a) the performance of the promise will satisfy an obligation of the promisee to pay money to the beneficiary; or (b) the promise manifests an intention to give the beneficiary the benefit of the promised performance.
(2) An incidental beneficiary is a beneficiary who is not an intended beneficiary
...

An intended beneficiary can sue the promisor directly. The comment to that section discusses examples of intended beneficiaries and incidental beneficiaries. §142 of the *Restatement (Second)* provides that the promisor and promisee "retain the power to discharge or modify the duty" to the beneficiary unless "a term of the promise creating the duty precludes such discharge or modification." This may be further limited when the beneficiary had changed his position in justifiable reliance on the promise, commenced an action on the promise, or manifested his assent to it in a manner invited by the promisor and promisee.

As a matter simply of what is practically necessary, the attitude of the common law to third party cases must be kept in check. There are far too many cases where these promises have to be kept. It is also the fact that, as we have already seen, the legislature has had to step in to remove the risk that the common law (doctrinally pure) rules may be used inappropriately. (An example of such inappropriateness being *Vandepitte v. Preferred Accident (supra)*). The following common situations raise clear problems of third party beneficiary contracts:

1. The joint bank account. B opens a joint account for himself and C at the A bank. B deposits $10,000 in the account and dies. On what basis can C sue A for the money? (See: Willis, "The Nature of a Joint Bank Account" (1936), 14 Can. Bar Rev. 457, and *McEvoy v. Belfast Banking Co.*, [1935] A.C. 24).

2. Fire Insurance on mortgaged premises. B, mortgagor, promises C, mortgagee, to insure the mortgaged premises against fire. B arranges insurance with A Ins. Co. The property is destroyed by fire. On what basis can C sue A for the insurance proceeds?

As a practical matter, neither the A bank nor the A Ins. Co. will refuse to pay. (Preferred Accident Ins. Corp. got no more business in B.C. after refusing to pay the Vandepitte claim.) Can one defend a legal rule that, even in theory, permits the Bank or Insurance Company to refuse to pay the designated beneficiary?

Other equally common situations have been amended by statute. We have seen one example in automobile insurance. Similarly, the beneficiary under a policy of life insurance has a statutory right to sue on the death of the insured: *The Insurance Act*, R.S.O. 1970, c. 224, s. 169. (It is worth noting that The Insurance Act has to add provisions spelling out the power of the insured to deal with the policy when the beneficiary can sue as a third party: ss. 171-174.)

A major potential problem arises in the area of mortgages. Under the standard mortgage, the mortgagor, B, does two things. He promises to pay the mortgage (this is known as the personal covenant) and he transfers his land as security. Should the mortgagor default the mortgagee can recover his money by selling the land. It can happen that the land is insufficient to satisfy the debt. The mortgagee can then sue the mortgagor on his personal covenant to pay. If a mortagor should sell the land he will want the buyer to take over the obligations under the mortgage (assuming that the mortgage is not paid off and a new mortgage arranged.) The seller will want the buyer to do two things: (1) promise to pay the mortgagee and (2) promise to indemnify the seller should the seller subsequently be sued on his personal covenant. The buyer's promise to pay the mortgagee is, at common law, unenforceable because the mortgagee is a third party to the contract of sale. The mortgagee can, of course, sue the seller (the original mortgagor) but he may be unavailable. Again, the situation had to be remedied by statute. There are problems with this legislation, but its purpose is reasonably clear.

The Mortgages Act, R.S.O. 1970, c. 279.

19.(1) In this section, "original mortgagor" means any person who by virtue of privity of contract with the mortgagee is personally liable to the mortgagee to pay the whole or any part of the moneys secured by the mortgage.

(2) Notwithstanding any stipulation to the contrary in a mortgage, where a mortgagor has conveyed and transferred the equity of redemption to a grantee under such circumstances that the grantee is by express convenant or otherwise obligated to indemnify the mortgagor with respect to the mortgage, the mortgagee has the right to recover from the grantee the amount of the mortgage debt in respect of which the grantee is obligated to indemnify the mortgagor; provided that the right of the mortgagee to recover the amount of the mortgage debt under this section from the grantee of the equity of redemption shall as against such grantee terminate on the registration of a grant or transfer of the equity of redemption by such grantee to another person unless prior to such registration an action has been commenced to enforce the right of the mortgagee.

(3) Where a mortgagee has the right to recover the whole or any part of moneys secured by a mortgage from an original mortgagor and also has a right by virtue

of this section to recover from a grantee of the equity of redemption from a mortgagor, if the mortgagee recovers judgment for the amount of the mortgage debt against the original mortgagor, the mortgagee thereupon forever ceases to have a right to recover under this section from a grantee, and if the mortgagee recovers judgment under this section against a grantee he thereupon forever ceases to have a right to recover from the original mortgagor; provided that where there is more than one original mortgagor this section does not affect the right of a mortgagee after the recovery of judgment against one original mortgagor to recover judgment against the other original mortgagor or mortgagors.

Notice again, that once we move to permit an action by a third party beneficiary, some care has to be taken that the right is no wider than necessary, and that the third party is no better off than he would be had the parties to the contract been able to arrange the whole thing between themselves.

In cases where a union has negotiated a collective agreement for the employees of an employer, the employees can be held to be third party beneficiaries. (See: *Young v. Canadian Northern Railway*, [1931] A.C. 83. Note the date of the case!) This too had to be changed by statute.

The Labour Relations Act, R.S.O. 1970, c. 232.
42. A collective agreement is, subject to and for the purposes of this Act, binding upon the employer and upon the trade union that is a party to the agreement whether or not the trade union is certified and upon the employees in the bargaining unit defined in the agreement.

There are, however, problems. For example, if a union will not take (or press) a grievance on behalf of an employee, the employee may have no standing to make any effective complaint, and s. 42 does not help him.

The cases where the rules have been changed by statute show that amending the common law rules is not easy and great care has to be taken. The use of devices like agency, assignment and trust presents equally serious problems. If C is held to be the beneficiary under a trust or a principal for purposes of suing A, then A and B may find themselves unable to change the agreement. The use of the trust device may impose very heavy burden on B, in particular. These devices have a proper and useful function: the use of them outside their proper scope can be dangerous.

It remains to be seen if the courts will continue to cling to a doctrine that has increasingly lost touch with the world where people, for the best of reasons, are determined to make contracts for the benefits of third parties.

E. Reliance as a Basis for the Enforcement of Promises

At the beginning of this chapter, it was suggested that there were many factors which should be taken into account in enforcing promises. This section looks in particular at one factor: reliance. The basic question here will be whether or not the reliance of the promisee on the promise made by the promisor will be enough to justify enforcement. We have already seen that the notion of reliance on a promise is a powerful tool for analysing the correct legal response to a contract problem. In these cases it will be important to consider what, precisely, the acts in reliance were and what the consequences of protecting or denying protection to such reliance might be.

We have seen that when, for example, the basis for enforcement is not the promise but the fact of unjust enrichment, we have to consider carefully the consequences of the change, and how we determine the remedy that the plaintiff should have. The same problems arise when we change the basis from the promise to reliance.

At a more general level the question will be whether the use of reliance (coupled with unjust enrichment in appropriate cases) can become a complete substitute for consideration.

The following questions have to be raised in each case:

1. What was the reliance of the promisee? Reliance can consist of either an act that causes the promisee loss or a failure to take steps to find an alternative method of protection.

2. Is the existence of reliance of one of these kinds a sufficient reason for enforcement?

3. To what extent should the remedy given be measured by the reliance that triggered the enforcement of the promise?

4. To what extent is it relevant that the promise is made in a commercial or non-commercial setting?

CENTRAL LONDON PROPERTY TRUST LTD. v. HIGH TREES HOUSE LTD.

[1947] 1 K.B. 130, King's Bench Division.

ACTION tried by Denning J.

By a lease under seal made on September 24, 1937, the plaintiffs, Central London Property Trust Ltd., granted to the defendants, High Trees House Ltd., a subsidiary of the plaintiff company, a tenancy of a block of flats for the term of ninety-nine years from September 29, 1937, at a ground rent of £2,500 a year. The block of flats was a new one and had not been fully occupied at the beginning of the war owing to the absence of people from London. With war conditions prevailing, it was apparent to those responsible that the rent reserved under the lease could not be paid out of the profits of the flats and, accordingly, discussions took place between the directors of the two companies concerned, which were closely associated, and an arrangement was made between them which was put into writing. On January 3, 1940, the plaintiffs wrote to the defendants in these terms, "we confirm the arrangement made between us by which the ground rent should be reduced as from the commencement of the lease to £1,250 per annum," and on April 2, 1940, a confirmatory resolution to the same effect was passed by the plaintiff company. On March 20, 1941, a receiver was appointed by the debenture holders of the plaintiffs and on his death on February 28, 1944, his place was taken by his partner. The defendants paid the reduced rent from 1941 down to the beginning of 1945 by which time all the flats in the block were fully let, and continued to pay it thereafter. In September, 1945, the then receiver of the plaintiff company looked into the matter of the lease and ascertained that the rent actually reserved by it was £2,500. On September 21, 1945, he wrote to the defendants saying that rent must be paid at the full rate and claiming that arrears amounting to £7,916 were due. Subsequently, he instituted the present friendly proceedings to test the legal position in regard to the rate at which rent was payable. In the action the plaintiffs sought to recover £625, being the amount represented by the difference between rent at the rate of £2,500. and £1,250. per annum for the quarters ending September 29, and December 25, 1945. By their defence the defendants pleaded (1.) that the letter of January 3, 1940, constituted an agreement that the rent reserved should be £1,250. only, and that such agreement related to the whole term of the lease, (2.) they pleaded in the alternative that the plaintiff company were estopped from alleging that the rent exceeded £1,250. per annum and (3.) as a further alternative, that by failing to demand rent in excess of £1,250. before their letter of September 21, 1945 (received by the defendants on September 24), they had waived their rights in respect of any rent, in excess of that at the rate of £1,250., which had accrued up to September 24, 1945....

Denning J. stated the facts and continued: If I were to consider this matter without regard to recent developments in the law, there is no doubt that had the plaintiffs claimed it, they would have been entitled to recover ground rent at the rate of £2,500. a year from the beginning of the term, since the lease under which it was payable was a lease under seal which, according to the old common law, could not be varied by an agreement by parol (whether in writing or not), but only by deed. Equity, however stepped in, and said that if there has been a variation of a deed by a simple contract (which in the case of a lease required to be in writing would have to be evidenced by writing), the courts may give effect to it... That equitable doctrine, however, could hardly apply in the present case because the variation here might be said to have been made without consideration. With regard to estoppel, the representation made in relation to reducing the rent, was not a representation of an existing fact. It was a representation, in effect, as to the future, namely, that payment of the rent would not be enforced at the full rate but only at the reduced rate. Such a representation would not give rise to an estoppel, because, as was said in *Jorden v. Money* (1854) 5 H.L.C. 185, a representation as to the future must be embodied as a contract or be nothing.

But what is the position in view of developments in the law in recent years? The law has not been standing still since *Jorden v. Money*. There has been a series of decisions over the last fifty years which, although they are said to be cases of estoppel are not really such. They are cases in which a promise was made which was intended to create legal relations and which to the knowledge of the person making the promise, was going to be acted on by the person to whom it was made, and which was in fact so acted on. In such cases the courts have said that the promise must be honoured... As I have said they are not cases of estoppel in the strict sense. They are really promises — promises intended to be binding, intended to be acted on, and in fact acted on. *Jorden v. Money* can be distinguished, because there the promisor made it clear that she did not intend to be legally bound, whereas in the cases to which I refer the proper inference was that the promisor did intend to be bound. In each case the court held the promise to be binding on the party making it, even though under the old common law it might be difficult to find any consideration for it. The courts have not gone so far as to give a cause of action in damages for the breach of such a promise, but they have refused to allow the party making it to act inconsistently with it. It is in that sense, and that sense only, that such a promise gives rise to an estoppel. The decisions are a natural result of the fusion of law and equity: for the cases of *Hughes v. Metropolitan Ry. Co.* (1877), 2 App. Cas. 439, *Birmingham and District Land Co. v. London & North Western Ry. Co.* (1888), 40 Ch.O. 268, and *Salisbury (Marquess) v. Gilmore*, [1942] 2 K.B. 38, afford a sufficient basis for saying that a party would not be allowed in equity to go back on such a promise. In my opinion, the time has now come for the validity of such a promise to be recognized. The logical consequence, no doubt is that a promise to accept a smaller sum in discharge of a larger sum, if acted upon, is binding notwithstanding the absence of consideration: and if the fusion of law and equity leads to this result, so much the better. That aspect was not considered in *Foakes v. Beer.* At this time of day however, when law and equity have been joined together for over seventy years, principles must be reconsidered in the light of their combined effect. It is to be noticed that in the Sixth Interim Report of the Law Revision Committee, pars. 35, 40, it is recommended that such a promise as that to which I have referred, should be enforceable in law even though no consideration for it has been given by the promisee. It seems to me that, to the extent I have mentioned, that result has now been achieved by the decisions of the courts.

I am satisfied that a promise such as that to which I have referred is binding and the only question remaining for my consideration is the scope of the promise in the present case. I am satisfied on all the evidence that the promise here was that the ground rent should be reduced to 1,250l. a year as a temporary expedient while the block of flats was not fully, or substantially fully let, owing to the conditions prevailing. That means that the reduction in the rent applied throughout the years down to the end of 1944, but early in 1945 it is plain that the flats were fully let, and, indeed the rents received from them (many of them not being affected by the Rent Restrictions Acts), were increased beyond the figure at which it was originally contemplated that they would be let. At all events the rent from them must have been very considerable. I find that the conditions prevailing at the time when the reduction in rent was made, had completely passed away by the early months of 1945. I am satisfied that the promise was understood by all parties only to apply under the conditions prevailing at the time when it was made, namely, when the flats were only partially let, and that it did not extend any further than that. When the flats became fully let, early in 1945, the reduction ceased to apply.

In those circumstances, under the law as I hold it, it seems to me that rent is payable at the full rate for the quarters ending September 29 and December 25, 1945.

If the case had been one of estoppel, it might be said that in any event the estoppel would cease when the conditions to which the representation applied came to an end, or it also might be said that it would only come to an end on notice. In either case it is only a way of ascertaining what is the scope of the representation. I prefer to apply the principle that a promise intended to be binding, intended to be acted on and in fact acted on, is binding so far as its terms properly apply. Here it was binding as covering the period down to the early part of 1945, and as from that time full rent is payable.

I therefore give judgment for the plaintiff company for the amount claimed.

Judgment for plaintiffs.

IMPERATOR REALTY v. TULL

(1920), 127 N.E. 263. New York Court of Appeal.

[The parties had entered into a written contract for the exchange of land. Under the agreement, the parties undertook to remove any restrictions on the properties arising from, inter alia, violation of municipal by-laws. The piece of land owned by the plaintiff had restrictions against title. The defendant orally agreed that on closing the plaintiff could put up a cash deposit instead of removing the restrictions. When the time came for closing, the defendant defaulted, and gave as his reason the failure of the plaintiff to remove the restrictions. The plaintiff sued. At trial, the jury believed the plaintiff and judgment was given for him. The defendant appealed and the Appellate Division allowed the appeal. The plaintiff appealed.]

Chase, J.: It is claimed by the defendant that the contract with the plaintiff was in writing under seal and could not be changed as claimed by an oral agreement so as to be binding upon either party to it. The contract was also within the provisions of section 259 of the Real Property Law (Consol. Laws, c. 50), and it was therefore necessary that it should be in writing as stated in the statute. . . .

After the execution of a written contract including one within the statute the parties may, of course, reconsider the subject-matter thereof and decide to modify or rescind it. The oral agreement found in this case was made after the execution of the written contract. It is not the right to make a new and independent contract to modify a prior unperformed written contract that we are considering, but the effect, if any, of an oral contract upon a contract under seal or required by the statute to be in writing. We must assume in this case that the oral contract as claimed by the plaintiff, to accept a deposit in cash in place of the payment of outstanding violations, was actually made upon a sufficient consideration. The jury has so found. The oral contract did not purport to be inconsistent with any material part of the written contract, nor to substitute a new oral contract for any material part of the written contract. The plaintiff was simply told in effect to let the violations stand unsatisfied until the due day and then provide for the expense of satisfying the same by a deposit in cash. The extent of the violations was inconsiderable. Both parties were convenienced by waiving the necessity of having them actually cancelled and satisfied before the due day.

In *Thomson v. Poor* (1895), 147 N.Y. 402, 409, 42 N.E. 13, 15, which was an action to recover upon a balance claimed to be due pursuant to a written contract which was within the statute, this court say:

> "We know of no principle of law which will permit a party to a contract, who is entitled to demand the performance by the other party of some act within a specified time and who has consented to the postponement of the performance to a time subsequent to that fixed by the contract, and where the other party has acted upon such consent and in reliance thereon has permitted the contract time to pass without performance, to subsequently recall such consent and treat the non-performance within the original time as a breach of the contract. The original contract is not charged by such waiver, but it stands as an answer to the other party who seeks to recover damages for non-performance induced by an unrecalled consent. The party may, in the absence of a valid and binding agreement to extend the time, revoke his consent so far as it has not been acted upon, but it would be most inequitable to hold that a default, justified by the consent, hap-

pening during its extension, should furnish a ground of action. It makes no difference, as we conceive, what the character of the original contract may be, whether one within or outside the statute of frauds. The rule is well understood that, if there is a forbearance at the request of a party, the latter is precluded from insisting upon non-performance at the time originally fixed by the contract as a ground of actions... Until he gives notice of withdrawal he has no just right to consider the latter in default, although meanwhile the contract time has elapsed. We think the principle of equitable estoppel applies in such case."

The court further say that the principle of estoppel applies equally to sealed and unsealed contracts.

More recently this court in *Arnot v. Union Salt Co.* (1906), 186 N.Y. 501, 79 N.E. 719, held that, where the time of payment under a contract had been extended by parol and the party required to make the payment had acted upon such extension, the party waiving such time of payment cannot consider the debtor in default unless he withdraws the waiver before the time of payment has arrived.

The oral contract in the case before us modified the written contract simply as to the manner of charging the plaintiff with the amount required to satisfy the violations. Such oral contract if carried out in good faith made unnecessary the haste otherwise required to make the slight changes to comply with the notices which constituted the incumbrances or so-called violations.

The defendant by his mutual oral contract with the plaintiff is estopped from now claiming that the plaintiff who relied thereon was in default on the due day of the written contract because of its omission to then have the property free of the violations. He should not be allowed to take advantage of an omission induced by his unrevoked consent. *Thomson v. Poor*, [*supra*]
...

The judgment of the Appellate Division should be reversed, and that of the Trial Term affirmed, with costs in the Appellate Division and in this court.

Cardozo, J. (concurring in result). The statute says that a contract for the sale of real property "is void unless the contract, or some note or memorandum thereof, expressing the consideration, is in writing, subscribed by the ... grantor, or by his lawfully authorized agent." Real Property Law (Consol. Laws, c. 50) § 259 (statute of frauds). In this instance, each party was a grantor, for the sale was an exchange. I think it is the law that, where contracts are subject to the statute, changes are governed by the same requirements of form as original provisions.... Abrogated by word of mouth such a contract may be, but its obligation may not be varied by spoken words of promise while it continues undissolved... I think it is inadequate to say that oral changes are effective if they are slight and ineffective if they are important. Such tests are too vague to supply a scientific basis of distinction. "Every part of the contract in regard to which the parties are stipulating must be taken to be material."... The field is one where the law should hold fast to fundamental conceptions of contract and of duty, and follow them with loyalty to logical conclusions.

The problem, thus approached, gains, I think, a new simplicity. A contract is the sum of its component terms. Any variation of the parts is a variation of the whole. The requirement that there shall be a writing extends to one term as to another. There can therefore be no contractual obligation when the requirement is not followed. This is not equivalent to saying that what is ineffective to create an obligation must be ineffective to discharge one. Duties imposed by law irrespective of contract may regulate the relations of parties after they have entered into a contract. There may be procurement or encouragement of a departure from literal performance which will forbid the assertion that the departure was a wrong. That principle will be found the solvent of many cases of apparent hardship. There may be an election which will preclude a forfeiture. There may be an acceptance of substituted performance, or an accord and satisfaction.... What there may not be, when the subject-matter is the sale of land, is an executory agreement, partly written and partly oral, to which, by force of the agreement and nothing else, the law will attach the attribute of contractual obligation.

The contract, therefore, stood unchanged. The defendant might have retracted his oral promise an hour after making it, and the plaintiff would have been helpless. He might have retracted a week before the closing, and, if a reasonable time remained within which to remove the violations, the plaintiff would still have been helpless. Retraction even at the very hour of the closing might not have been too late if coupled with the offer of an extension which would neutralize the consequences of persuasion and reliance.... The difficulty with the defendant's position is that he did none of these things. He had notified the plaintiff in substance that there was no need of haste in removing the violations, and that title would be accepted on deposit of adequate security for their removal in the future. He never revoked that notice. He gave no warning of a change of mind. He did not even attend the closing. He abandoned the contract, treated it as at an end, held himself absolved from all liability thereunder, because the plaintiff had acted in reliance on a consent which, even in the act of abandonment, he made no effort to recall.

I do not think we are driven by any requirement of the statute of frauds to sustain as lawful and effective this precipitate rescission, this attempt by an ex post facto revocation, after closing day had come and gone, to put the plaintiff in the wrong. "He who prevents a thing from being done may not avail himself of the nonperformance, which he has, himself, occasioned, for the law says to him, in effect: 'This is your own act, and, therefore, you are not damnified. '"... Sometimes the resulting disability has been characterized as an estoppel, sometimes as a waiver.... We need not go into the question of the accuracy of the description.... The truth is that we are facing a principle more nearly ultimate than either waiver or estoppel, one with roots in the yet larger principle that no one shall be permitted to found any claim upon his own inequity or take advantage or his own wrong.... The statute of frauds was not intended to offer an asylum of escape from that fundamental principle of justice. An opposite precedent is found in *Thomson v. Poor.* In deciding that case, we put aside the question whether a contract within the statute of frauds could be changed by spoken words. We held that there was disability, or, as we styled it, estoppel, to take advantage of an omission induced by an unrevoked consent.... A like principle is recognized even in the English courts, which have gone as far as those of any jurisdiction in the strict enforcement of the statute. They hold in effect that, until consent is acted on, either party may change his mind. After it has been acted on, it stands as an excuse for nonperformance.... The defendant by his conduct has brought himself within the ambit of this principle. His words did not create a new bilateral contract. They lacked the written form prescribed by statute. They did create a unilateral contract. Aside from the same defect in form, they did not purport to offer a promise for an act. They did, however, constitute the continuing expression of a state of mind, a readiness, a desire, persisting until revoked. A seller who agrees to change the wall paper of a room ought not to lose his contract if he fails to make the change through reliance on the statement of the buyer that new paper is unnecessary and that the old is satisfactory. The buyer may change his mind again and revert to his agreement. He may not summarily rescind because of the breach which he encouraged. That is what the defendant tried to do. When he stayed away from the closing and acted upon an election to treat the contract as rescinded, he put himself in the wrong.

I concur in the conclusion that the judgment must be reversed.

Hiscock, C.J., concurs with Chase, J.

Cardozo, J., concurs in an opinion in which Pound and Andrews, JJ., also concur.

Collin and Crane, JJ., dissent.

Judgment reversed, *etc.*

QUESTION

How does this case differ from *Boone v. Coe (supra)*?

COMBE. v. COMBE

[1951] 1 A11 E.R. 767. Court of Appeal, England.

Denning, L.J.: In this case a wife who has divorced her husband claims maintenance from him — not in the Divorce Court, but in the King's Bench on an agreement which is said to be embodied in letters. The parties were married in 1915. They separated in 1939. On Feb. 1, 1943, on the wife's petition, a decree nisi of divorce was pronounced. Shortly afterwards letters passed between the solicitors with regard to maintenance. On Feb. 9, 1943 (eight days after the decree *nisi*), the solicitor for the wife wrote to the solicitor for the husband:

"With regard to permanent maintenance, we understand that your client is prepared to make [the wife] an allowance of £100 per year free of income tax."

In answer, on Feb. 19, 1943, the husband's solicitors wrote:

"The respondent has agreed to allow your client £100 per annum free of tax."

On Aug. 11, 1943, the decree was made absolute. On Aug. 26, 1943, the wife's solicitors wrote to the husband's solicitors, saying:

"Referring to your letter of Feb. 19 last, our client would like the £100 per annum agreed to be paid to her by your client to be remitted to us on her behalf quarterly. We shall be glad if you will kindly let us have a cheque for £25 for the first quarterly instalment and make arrangements for a similar remittance to us on Nov. 11, Feb. 11, May 11, and Aug. 11 in the future."

A reply did not come for nearly two months because the husband was away, and then he himself, on Oct. 18, 1943, wrote a letter which was passed on to the wife's solicitors:

"... regarding the sum of £25 claimed on behalf of Mrs. Combe ... I would point out that whilst this is paid quarterly as from Aug. 11, 1943, the sum is not due till Nov. 11, 1943, as I can hardly be expected to pay this allowance in advance."

He never paid anything. The wife pressed him for payment, but she did not follow it up by an application to the divorce court. It is to be observed that she herself has an income of her own of between £700 and £800 a year, whereas her husband has only £650 a year. Eventually, after nearly seven years had passed since the decree absolute, she brought this action in the King's Bench Division on July 28, 1950, claiming £675 being arrears for six years and three quarters at £100 a year. BYRNE, J., held that the first three quarterly instalments of £25 were barred by the Limitation Act, 1939, but he gave judgment for £600 in respect of the instalments which accrued within the six years before the action was brought. He held ... that there was no consideration for the husband's promise to pay his wife £100, but, nevertheless, he held that the promise was enforceable on the principle stated in *Central London Property Trust, Ltd. v. High Trees House, Ltd.*, and *Robertson v. Minister of Pensions*, [1949] 2 All E.R. 767, because it was an unequivocal acceptance of liability, intended to be binding, intended to be acted on, and, in fact, acted on.

Much as I am inclined to favour the principle of the *High Trees* case it is important that it should not be stretched too far lest it should be endangered. It does not create new causes of action where none existed before. It only prevents a party from insisting on his strict legal rights when it would be unjust to allow him to do so, having regard to the dealings which have taken place between the parties. That is the way it was put in the case in the House of Lords which first stated the principle — *Hughes v. Metropolitan Ry. Co.*, (1877), 2 App. Cas. 439 — and in the case in the Court of Appeal which enlarged it — *Birmingham and District Land Co. v. London & North Western Ry. Co.* (1888), 40 Cl. D. 268. It is also implicit in all the modern cases in which the principle has been developed. Sometimes it is a plaintiff who is not allowed to insist on his strict legal rights. Thus, a creditor is not allowed to enforce a debt which he has deliberately agreed to waive if the debtor has carried on business or in some other way changed his position in reliance on the waiver ... *Central London Property Trust, Ltd. v. High Trees House, Ltd.* A landlord who has told his tenant that he can live in his cottage rent free for the rest of his life is not allowed to go back on it if the tenant stays in the house on that footing: *Foster v. Robinson,* [1951] 1 K.B. 149. Sometimes it is a defendant who is not allowed to insist on his strict legal rights. His conduct may be such as to debar him from relying on some condition, denying some allegation, or taking some other point in answer to the claim. Thus, a government department, who had accepted a disease as due to war service, were not allowed afterwards to say it was not, when the soldier, in reliance on the assurance, had abstained from getting further evidence about it: *Robertston v. Minister of Pensions.* A buyer who had waived the contract date for delivery was not allowed afterwards to set up the stipulated time as an answer to the seller: *Charles Rickards, Ltd. v. Oppenheim,* [1950] 1 K.B. 616. A tenant who had encroached on an adjoining building, asserting that it was comprised in the lease, was not allowed afterwards to say that it was not included in the lease: *J. F. Perrott & Co., Ltd. v. Cohen,* [1950] 1 K.B. 705. A tenant who had lived in a house rent free by permission of his landlord, thereby asserting that his original tenancy had ended, was not afterwards allowed to say that his original tenancy continued: *Foster v. Robinson.* In none of these cases was the defendant sued on the promise, assurance, or assertion as a cause of action in itself. He was sued for some other cause, for example, a pension for a breach of contract, or possession, and the promise, assurance, or assertion only played a supplementary role, though, no doubt, an important one. That is, I think, its true function. It may be part of a cause of action, but not a cause of action in itself. The principle, as I understand it, is that where one party has, by his words or conduct, made to the other a promise or assurance which was intended to affect the legal relations between them and to be acted on accordingly, then, once the other party has taken him at his word and acted on it, the one who gave the promise or assurance cannot afterwards be allowed to revert to the previous legal relations as if no such promise or assurance had been made by him, but he must accept their legal relations subject to the qualification which he himself has so introduced, even though it is not supported in point of law by any consideration, but only by his word.

Seeing that the principle never stands alone as giving a cause of action in itself, it can never do away with the necessity of consideration when that is an essential part of the cause of action. The doctrine of consideration is too firmly fixed to be overthrown by a side-wind. Its ill effects have been largely mitigated of late, but it still remains a cardinal necessity of the formation of a contract, although not of its modification or discharge. I fear that it was my failure to make this clear in *Central London Property Trust, Ltd. v. High Trees House, Ltd.*, which misled BYRNE, J., in the present case. He held that the wife could sue on the husband's promise as a separate and independent cause of action by itself, although, as he held, there was no consideration for it. That is not correct. The wife can only enforce the promise if there was consideration for it. That is, therefore, the real question in the case: Was there sufficient consideration to support the promise?

If it were suggested that, in return for the husband's promise, the wife expressly or impliedly promised to forbear from applying to the court for maintenance — that is, a promise in return for a promise — there would clearly be no consideration because the wife's promise would not be binding on her and, therefore, would be worth nothing. Notwithstanding her promise, she could always apply to the divorce court for maintenance — perhaps, only with leave — but nevertheless she could apply. No agreement by her could take away that right... There was, however, clearly no promise by the wife, express or implied, to forbear from applying to the court. All that happened was that she did, in fact, forbear — that is, she did an act, in return for a promise. Is that sufficient consideration? Unilateral promises of this kind have long been enforced so long as the act or forbearance is done on the faith of the promise and at the request of the promisor, express or implied. The act done is then in itself sufficient consideration for the promise, even though it arises ex post facto, as PARKER, J., pointed out in *Wigan v. English and Scottish Law Life Assurance Assocn.* ([1909] 1 Ch. 298). If the findings of BYRNE, J., are accepted, they are sufficient to bring this principle into play. His finding that the husband's promise was intended to be binding, intended to be acted on, and was, in fact, acted on — although expressed to be a finding on the principle of the *High Trees House* case — is equivalent to a finding that there was consideration within this long-settled rule, because it comes to the same thing expressed in different words... My difficulty, however, is to accept the findings of BYRNE, J., that the promise was "intended to be acted on." I cannot find any evidence of any intention by the husband that the wife should forbear from applying to the court for maintenance, or, in other words, any request by the husband, express or implied, that the wife should so forbear. He left her to apply, if she wished to do so. She did not do so, and I am not surprised, because it is very unlikely that the divorce court would have made any order in her favour, since she had a bigger income than her husband. Her forbearance was not intended by him, nor was it done at his request. It was, therefore, no consideration.

It may be that the wife has suffered some detriment because, after forbearing to apply to the court for seven years, she might not now get leave to apply... The court, however, is, nowadays much more ready to give leave than it used to... and I should have thought that, if the wife fell on hard times, she would still get leave. Assuming, however, that she has suffered some detriment by her forbearance, nevertheless, as the forbearance was not at the husband's request, it is no consideration.

. . .

The doctrine of consideration is sometimes said to work injustice, but I see none in this case... I do not think it would be right for this wife, who is better off than her husband, to take no action for six or seven years and then demand from him the whole £600. The truth is that in these maintenance cases the real remedy of the wife is, not by action in the King's Bench Division, but by application in the Divorce Court. I have always understood that no agreement for maintenance, which is made in the course of divorce proceedings prior to decree absolute, is valid unless it is sanctioned by the court — indeed, I said so in *Emanuel v. Emanuel* ([1945] 2 All E.R. 496). I know that such agreements are often made, but their only valid purpose is to serve as a basis for a consent application to the court. The reason why such agreements are invalid, unless approved, is because they are so apt to be collusive. Some wives are tempted to stipulate for extortionate maintenance as the price of giving their husbands their freedom. It is to remove this temptation that the sanction of the court is required. It would be a great pity if this salutary requirement could be evaded by taking action in the King's Bench Division. The Divorce Court can order the husband to pay whatever maintenance is just. Moreover, if justice so requires, it can make the order retrospective to decree absolute. That is the proper remedy of the wife here, and I do not think she has a right to any other. For these reasons I think the appeal should be allowed.

[Asquith and Birkett L. JJ. agreed in allowing the appeal.]

[Asquith L.J. in his judgment said that the doctrine of promissory estoppel could only be used as a shield: it could not be used as a sword.]

QUESTIONS AND PROBLEMS

1. Suppose that the husband had asked his wife to forbear from bringing proceedings for maintenance, would that make it any more sensible to enforce the agreement?

2. Was there any evidence of any reliance by the wife on the husband's promise?

3. *Combe v. Combe* involves a family situation: the others involve commercial relations. Is there any reason for assuming that the same rules should apply to both?

4. Should a wife be allowed to claim as a creditor of the husband's estate if, for instance, he had died insolvent or had gone bankrupt?

5. Uncle promises to give $1,000 to his nephew, Johnny. In reliance on this promise, Johnny buys a car for $500. Uncle refuses to pay the $1,000 that he promised.

Johnny sues Uncle. What result, and how much should Johnny get if he should get anything?

6. Walter had had a life insurance policy with Styx Life Insurance Co. He paid the premiums for 10 years and then stopped. In accordance with the terms of the policy, the company advised Walter that the cash surrender value of the policy was being used to provide insurance until December 1, 1975. The letter went on to say, "This means that you are fully covered until that date for the full amount of the policy, $50,000." Walter did not reply to this letter. Walter died on November 1, 1975. His executor submitted the necessary papers to the company and claimed the face value of the policy. The company rechecked its records and found that there had been an error in the original calculation and that the policy should have lapsed on October 1, 1975. Walter's executor sues the company. What result?

7. The City of Toronto had plans for a new convention centre in the downtown area. Part of the land that would be needed was already owned by the City but plans called for the acquisition of an area of land owned by Trudy's Catering. Trudy's Catering was planning to move to larger premises away from the downtown area but did not feel that the economic situation justified such a move. On the other hand, modification of the existing plant was inadvisable given that the City might expropriate. Discussion took place between the City and Trudy's Catering for sale of the land, but no agreement on price could be reached. Ultimately the city decided to expropriate. At that moment, an extremely attractive property came on the market and Trudy's Catering immediately agreed to purchase it. The City, however, changed its plans and decided not to expropriate. Trudy's Catering would much rather not move, but will now face considerable losses in getting back to its original position. Has Trudy's Catering any remedy against the City?

8. An uncle writes to his nephew: "My friend Green is in town and tells me that you have been talking to him about buying his grocery store. I hope you go ahead with this deal. He has a good location, and I've always wanted to see you in business for yourself. I'm pretty sure that you will want to buy the store when you learn the news I have for you. I have just deposited $50,000 in the Bank of Nova Scotia in your name. You are free to draw on this to finance the deal with Green and set yourself up in business". The nephew received this letter the next day, and immediately entered into a contract with Green to buy the store for $30,000. A few hours after the contract was signed, the uncle was killed in a traffic accident. No money was ever deposited by him in the nephew's name. It appears that he had intended to arrange the transfer of funds shortly after mailing the letter, but had absentmindedly neglected to do so. The uncle's executor refuses to recognize any claim in favor of the nephew.

Consider:

Restatement of Contracts, Washington, 1932. American Law Institute.

§90. A promise which the promisor should reasonably expect to induce action or forbearance of a definite and substantial character on the part of the promisee and which does induce such action or forebearance is binding if injustice can be avoided only by enforcement of the promise.

Second Restatement (Tentative draft, 1964)

90. A promise which the promisor should reasonably expect to induce action or forbearance on the part of the promisee or a third person and which does induce such action or forbearance is binding if injustice can be avoided only by enforcement of the promise. The remedy granted for breach may be limited as justice requires.

How would the application of this section solve any of the above problems?

Fuller and Perdue in their article, "The Reliance Interest in Contract Damages" (1936), 46 Yale L.J. 52, discuss some of the problems of the measure of damages under §90 of the original *Restatement*. The authors suggest that the justification for awarding damages measured by the expectation interest is that this may be the best way of protecting the reliance interest. This, of course, justifies reliance and because there is reliance we must now protect it. They go on to say: (p. 63) (The discussion in the footnote refers to the problem of the action by Johnny against Uncle that has just been raised):

The combined juristic and economic explanation which has just been developed may seem vulnerable to one serious objection. This lies in the fact that the "normal" rule, which measures damages by the expectancy, has been frequently applied to promises of a type having no conceivable relation to "the credit system," the division of labor, or the organization of economic activity. Professor Williston apparently goes so far as to assume that the "normal" rule is the only permissible rule of recovery even in the case of promises made enforceable by §90 of the Contracts Restatement, that is, in the case of promises for which no price has been given or promised and which are enforced only because they have been seriously relied on.[1] Most of the arguments for the rule measuring damages by the expectancy which we developed under our combined economic and juristic explanation have no application to such promises. The suggestion that the expectation interest is adopted as a kind of surrogate for the reliance interest because of the difficulty of proving reliance can scarcely be applicable to a situation where we actually insist on proof of reliance, and indeed, reliance of a "definite and substantial character." The notion that the expectancy is granted as compensation for foregoing the opportunity to enter other similar contracts is also without application in this situation, if for no other reason than because no contract is here "entered" at all. Finally the policy in favor of facilitating reliance can scarcely be extended to all promises indiscriminately. Any such policy must presuppose that reliance in the particular situation will normally have some general utility. Where we are dealing with "exchanges" or "bargains" it is easy to discern this utility since such transactions form the very mechanism by which production is organized in a capitalistic society. There seems no basis for assuming any such general utility in the promises coming under §90, since they are restricted only by a negative definition — they are not bargains.

Is the application of the "normal" rule of damages to non-bargain promises then an unanswerable refutation of the explanation which we have attempted of the rule? We think not. In the first place, it is obviously possible that courts have, through force of habit, given a broader application to the rule than a philosophic inquiry into its possible bases would justify. In the second place, it is by no means clear, from the decisions at any rate, that the rule of recovery in the case of these "non-bargain" promises *is* necessarily that which measures damages by the expectancy.

---

[1]"*Mr. Coudert*: ... Would you say, Mr. Reporter, in your case of Johnny and the uncle, the uncle promising the $1,000 and Johnny buying the car — say he goes out and buys the car for $500 — that uncle would be liable for $1,000 or would he be liable for $500?

"*Mr. Williston*: If Johnny had done what he was expected to do, or is acting within the limits of his uncle's expectation, I think the uncle would be liable for $1,000; but not otherwise.

"*Mr. Coudert*: In other words, substantial justice would require that uncle should be penalized in the sum of $500.

"*Mr. Williston*: Why do you say 'penalized'?

"... *Mr. Coudert*: Because substantial justice there would require, it seems to me, that Johnny get his money for the car, but should he get his car and $500 more? I don't see.

"*Mr. Williston*: Of course, it would be possible to say that for Section 88

[now §90] should be substituted a section in the restatement of quasi-contract that under these circumstances the promisee should be allowed to recover such a sum as would represent the injury he had suffered... "
Quoted from the discussion of what is now §90 of the CONTRACTS RESTATEMENT reported in AMERICAN LAW INSTITUTE, PROCEEDINGS, Vol. IV, Appendix (1926) 98-99.

In a later discussion of the case of uncle and Johnny, Professor Williston was reported as saying in answer to a repetition of the question why Johnny should receive more than $500. "Either the promise is binding or it is not. If the promise is binding it has to be enforced as it is made. As I said to Mr. Coudert, I could leave this whole thing to the subject of quasi contracts so that the promisee under those circumstances shall never recover on the promise but he shall recover such an amount as will fairly compensate him for any injury incurred; but it seems to me you have to take one leg or the other. You have either to say the promise is binding or you have to go on the theory of restoring the status quo." *Id.* at 103-104.

Cf., "A promise of one thousand dollars with which to buy a motor car may thus be binding if it induces the purchase of the car." 1. WILLISTON, CONTRACTS (2d ed. 1936) §140.

On the other hand, Professor Gardner seems to assume that in cases coming under §90 the promisee should be merely "indemnified for loss suffered in reliance" on the promise. He regards the "assumption that a suit for breach of promise must necessarily be a suit to recover the value of the asserted power" as "both analytically and historically incorrect." Gardner, *An Inquiry into the Principles of the Law of Contracts* (1932) 46 HARV. L. REV. 1, 23.

§90 in the Second Restatement has been modified in response to the concern about the measure of recovery where enforcement of the promise is based on reliance. How well do you think that the redraft of §90 deals with the issue?

The following cases are further examples of the courts' response to the problems presented by reliance. There are two questions to be kept in mind as you read them.

1. To what extent is the courts' concern for the protection of reliance overborne by a worry that the whole doctrine of consideration can be circumvented by reliance? For example, simply in terms of the Restatement, to what extent is §75 superseded by §90?. §75 is in the following terms:

§75. Requirement of Exchange; Types of Exchange.
(1) To constitute consideration, a performance or a return promise must be bargained for.
(2) A performance or return promise is bargained for if it is sought by the promisor in exchange for his promise and is given by the promisee in exchange for that promise.
(3) The performance may consist of
    (a) an act other than a promise, or
    (b) a forbearance, or
    (c) the creation, modification or destruction of a legal relation.
(4) The performance or return promise may be given to the promisor or to some other person. It may be given by the promisee or by some other person.

2. How useful is the sword/shield approach that stems from *Combe v.*

Combe? What guidance are the courts giving on the question of the scope of the doctrine of promissory estoppel?

D. & C. BUILDERS v. REES

[1965] 3 All E.R. 837.

Lord Denning, M.R.: D. & C. Builders, Ltd. ("the plaintiffs") are a little company. "D" stands for Mr. Donaldson, a decorator, "C" for Mr. Casey, a plumber. They are jobbing builders. The defendant, Mr. Rees, has a shop where he sells builders' materials.

In the spring of 1964 the defendant employed the plaintiffs to do work at his premises, 218, Brick Lane. The plaintiffs did the work and rendered accounts in May and June, which came to £746 13s. 1d. altogether. The defendant paid £250 on account. In addition the plaintiffs made an allowance of £14 off the bill. So in July, 1964, there was owing to the plaintiffs the sum of £482 13s. 1d. At this stage there was no dispute as to the work done. But the defendant did not pay.

On Aug. 31, 1964, the plaintiffs wrote asking the defendant to pay the remainder of the bill. He did not reply. On Oct. 19, 1964, they wrote again, pointing out that the "outstanding account of £480 is well overdue". Still the defendant did not reply. He did not write or telephone for more than three weeks. Then on Friday, Nov. 13, 1964, the defendant was ill with influenza. His wife telephoned the plaintiffs. She spoke to Mr. Casey. She began to make complaints about the work: and then said: "My husband will offer you £300 in settlement. That is all you'll get. It is to be in satisfaction." Mr. Casey said he would have to discuss it with Mr. Donaldson. The two of them talked it over. Their company was in desperate financial straits. If they did not have the £300, they would be in a state of bankruptcy. So they decided to accept the £300 and see what they could do about the rest afterwards. Thereupon Mr. Donaldson telephoned to the defendant's wife. He said to her: "£300 will not even clear our commitments on the job. We will accept £300 and give you a year to find the balance." She said: "No, we will never have enough money to pay the balance. £300 is better than nothing." He said: "We have no choice but to accept." She said: "Would you like the money by cash or by cheque. If it is cash, you can have it on Monday. If by cheque, you can have it tomorrow (Saturday)." On Saturday, Nov. 14, 1964, Mr. Casey went to collect the money. He took with him a receipt prepared on the company's paper with the simple words: "Received the sum of £300 from Mr. Rees." She gave him a cheque for £300 and asked for a receipt. She insisted that the words "in completion of the account" be added. Mr. Casey did as she asked. He added the words to the receipt. So she had the clean receipt: "Received the sum of £300 from Mr. Rees in completion of the account. Paid, M. Casey." Mr. Casey gave in evidence his reason for giving it: "If I did not have the £300 the company would have gone bankrupt. The only reason we took it was to save the company. She knew the position we were in."

The plaintiffs were so worried about their position that they went to their solicitors. Within a few days, on Nov. 23, 1964, the solicitors wrote complaining that the defendant had "extricated a receipt of some sort or other" from them. They said that they were treating the £300 as a payment on account. On. Nov. 28, 1964, the defendant replied alleging bad workmanship. He also set up the receipt which Mr. Casey gave to his wife, adding: "I assure you she had no gun on her". The plaintiffs brought this action for the balance. The defendant set up a defence of bad workmanship and also that there was a binding settlement. The question of settlement was tried as a preliminary issue. The judge made these findings:

> "I concluded that by the middle of August the sum due to the plaintiffs was ascertained and not then in dispute. I also concluded that there was no consideration to support the agreement of Nov. 13 and 14. It was a case of agreeing to take a lesser sum, when a larger sum was already due to the plaintiffs. It was not a case of agreeing to take a cheque for a smaller account instead of receiving cash for a larger account. The payment by cheque was an incidental arrangement."

The judge decided, therefore, the preliminary issue in favour of the plaintiffs. The defendant appeals to this court. He says that there was here an accord and satisfaction — an *accord* when the plaintiffs agreed, however reluctantly, to accept £300 in settlement of the account — and *satisfaction* when they accepted the cheque for £300 and it was duly honoured...

This case is of some consequence: for it is a daily occurrence that a merchant or tradesman, who is owed a sum of money, is asked to take less. The debtor says he is in difficulties. He offers a lesser sum in settlement, cash down. He says he cannot pay more. The creditor is considerate. He accepts the proffered sum and forgives him the rest of the debt. The question arises: is the settlement binding on the creditor? The answer is that, in point of law, the creditor is not bound by the settlement. He can the next day sue the debtor for the balance, and get judgment. The law as so stated in 1602 by LORD COKE in *Pinnel's Case* — and accepted in 1884 by the HOUSE OF LORDS in *Foakes v. Beer*.

Now, suppose that the debtor, instead of paying the lesser sum in cash, pays it by cheque. He makes out a cheque for the amount. The creditor accepts the cheque and cashes it. Is the position any different? I think not. No sensible distinction can be taken between payment of a lesser sum by cash and payment of it by cheque. The cheque, when given, is conditional payment. When honoured, it is actual payment. It is then just the same as cash. If a creditor is not bound when he receives payment by cash, he should not be bound when he receives payment by cheque. This view is supported by the leading case of *Cumber v. Wane* (1721), 1 Stra. 426, which has suffered many vicissitudes but was, I think rightly decided in point of law.

· · ·

In point of law payment of a lesser sum, whether by cash or by cheque, is no discharge of a greater sum.

This doctrine of the common law has come under heavy fire. It was ridiculed by SIR GEORGE JESSEL, M.R. in *Couldery v. Bartrum* (1881), 19 Cl. D. 394, 399. It was held to be mistaken by LORD BLACKBURN in *Foakes v. Beer*. It was condemned by the Law Revision Committee in their Sixth Interim Report (Comnd. 5449), para. 20 and para. 22. But a remedy has been found. The harshness of the common law has been relieved. Equity has stretched out a merciful hand to help the debtor. The courts have invoked the broad principle stated by LORD CAIRNS, L.C., in *Hughes v. Metropolitan Ry. Co.* (1877), 2 App. Cas. 439, 448

> "... it is the first principle upon which all courts of equity proceed if parties, who have entered into definite and distinct terms involving certain legal rights...

afterwards by their own act, or with their own consent, enter upon a course of negotiation which has the effect of leading one of the parties to suppose that *the strict rights arising under the contract will not be enforced,* or will be kept in suspense, or held in abeyance, that the person who otherwise might have enforced those rights *will not be allowed to enforce them where it would be inequitable, having regard to the dealings which have taken place between the parties.*"

It is worth noticing that the principle may be applied, not only so as to suspend strict legal rights, but also so as to preclude the enforcement of them.

This principle has been applied to cases where a creditor agrees to accept a lesser sum in discharge of a greater. So much so that we can now say that, when a creditor and a debtor enter on a course of negotiation, which leads the debtor to suppose that, on payment of the lesser sum, the creditor will not enforce payment of the balance, and on the faith thereof the debtor pays the lesser sum and the creditor accepts it as satisfaction: then the creditor will not be allowed to enforce payment of the balance when it would be inequitable to do so. This was well illustrated during the last war. Tenants went away to escape the bombs and left their houses unoccupied. The landlords accepted a reduced rent for the time they were empty. It was held that the landlords could not afterwards turn round and sue for the balance: see *Central London Property Trust, Ltd. v. High Trees House, Ltd.* This caused at the time some eyebrows to be raised in high places. But they have been lowered since. The solution was so obviously just that no-one could well gainsay it.

In applying this principle, however, we must note the qualification. The creditor is barred from his legal rights only when it would be *inequitable* for him to insist on them. Where there has been a true accord, under which the creditor voluntarily agrees to accept a lesser sum in satisfaction, and the debtor *acts on* that accord by paying the lesser sum and the creditor accepts it, then it is inequitable for the creditor afterwards to insist on the balance. But he is not bound unless there has been truly an accord between them.

In the present case, on the facts as found by the judge, it seems to me that there was no true accord. The debtor's wife held the creditor to ransom. The creditor was in need of money to meet his own commitments, and she knew it. When the creditor asked for payment of the £480 due to him, she said to him, in effect: "We cannot pay you the £480. But we will pay you £300 if you will accept it in settlement. If you do not accept it on those terms, you will get nothing. £300 is better than nothing." She had no right to say any such thing. She could properly have said: "We cannot pay you more than £300. Please accept it on account." But she had no right to insist on his taking it in settlement. When she said: "We will pay you nothing unless you accept £300 in settlement", she was putting undue pressure on the creditor. She was making a threat to break the contract (by paying nothing) and she was doing it so as to compel the creditor to do what he was unwilling to do (to accept £300 in settlement): and she succeeded. He complied with her demand. That was on recent authority a case of intimidation (see *Rookes v. Barnard,* [1964] A.C. 1129, and *J. T. Stratford & Son, Ltd. v. Lindley,* [1964] A.C. 269). In these circumstances there was no true accord so as to found a defence of accord and satisfaction. There is also no equity in the defendant to warrant any departure from the due course of law. No person can insist on a settlement procured by intimidation.

In my opinion there is no reason in law or equity why the creditor should not enforce the full amount of the debt due to him. I would, therefore, dismiss this appeal.

Danckwerts, L.J.: I agree with the judgment of LORD DENNING, M.R. *Foakes v. Beer*, applying the decision in *Pinnel's Case*, settled definitely the rule of law that payment of a lesser sum than the amount of a debt due cannot be a satisfaction of the debt, unless there is some benefit to the creditor added so that there is an accord and satisfaction.

In *Foakes v. Beer*, the EARL OF SELBORNE, L.C., while approving *Cumber v. Wane* did not overrule the cases which appear to differ from *Cumber v. Wane*, saying:

> "All the authorities subsequent to *Cumber v. Wane*, which were relied upon by the appellant, such as ... *Goddard v. O'Brien* (1882), 9 Q.B.D.37, have proceeded upon the distinction, that, by giving negotiable paper or otherwise, there had been some new consideration for a new agreement, distinct from mere money payments in or towards discharge of the original liability."

LORD SELBORNE was distinguishing those cases from the case before the House.

The giving of a cheque of the debtor, however, for a smaller amount than the sum due is very different from "the gift of a horse, hawk, or robe, etc." mentioned in *Pinnel's Case*. I accept that the cheque of some other person than the debtor, in appropriate circumstances, may be the basis of an accord and satisfaction, but I cannot see how in the year 1965 the debtor's own cheque for a smaller sum can be better than payment of the whole amount of the debt in cash. The cheque is only conditional payment, it may be difficult to cash, or it may be returned by the bank with the letters "R.D." on it, unpaid. I think that *Goddard v. O'Brien* either was wrongly decided or should not be followed in the circumstances of today.

I agree also that, in the circumstances of the present case, there was no true accord. Mr. and Mrs. Rees really behaved very badly. They knew of the plaintiffs' financial difficulties and used their awkward situation to intimidate them. The plaintiffs did not wish to accept the sum of £300 in discharge of the debt of £482, but were desperate to get some money. It would appear also that the defendant and his wife misled the plaintiffs as to their own financial position. Mr. Rees, in his evidence, said: "In June (1964) I could have paid £700 odd. I could have settled the whole bill." There is no evidence that by August, or even by November, their financial situation had deteriorated so that they could not pay the £482. Nor does it appear that their position was altered to their detriment by reason of the receipt given by the plaintiffs. The receipt was given on Nov. 14, 1964. On Nov. 23, 1964, the plaintiffs' solicitors wrote a letter making it clear that the payment of £300 was being treated as a payment on account. I cannot see any ground in this case for treating the payment as a satisfaction on equitable principles.

In my view the county court judge was right in applying the rule in *Foakes v. Beer*, and I would dismiss the appeal.

Winn, L.J.; ... The question to be decided may be stated thus. Did the defendant's agreement to give his own cheque for £300 in full settlement of his existing debt to the plaintiffs of £482 13s. 1d. and the plaintiffs' agreement to accept it in full payment of that debt, followed by delivery and due payment of such a cheque, constitute a valid accord and satisfaction discharging the debt in law?

Apart altogether from any decided cases bearing on the matter, there might be a good deal to be said, as a matter of policy, in favour of holding any creditor bound by his promise to discharge a debtor of his paying some amount less than the debt due: some judges no doubt so thought when they held readily that acceptance by the creditor of something of a different nature from that to which he was entitled was a satisfaction of the liability ... A like approach might at some time in the past have been adopted by the courts to all serious assurances of agreement, but as English law developed, it does not now permit in general of such treatment of mere promises. In the more specific field of discharge of monetary debt there has been some conflict of judicial opinion.

.   .   .

In my judgment it is an essential element of a valid accord and satisfaction that the agreement which constitutes the accord should itself be binding in law, and I do not think that any such agreement can be so binding unless it is either made under seal or supported by consideration. Satisfaction, viz., performance, of an agreement of accord does not provide retroactive validity to the accord, but depends for its effect on the legal validity of the accord as a binding contract at the time when it is made: this I think is apparent when it is remembered that, albeit rarely, existing obligations of debt may be replaced effectively by a contractually binding substitution of a new obligation.

In my judgment this court should now decline to follow the decision in *Goddard v. O'Brien* and should hold that where a debtor's own cheque for a lesser amount than he indisputably owes to his creditor is accepted by the creditor in full satisfaction of the debt, the creditor is to be regarded, in any case where he has not required the payment to be made by cheque rather than in cash, as having received the cheque merely as conditional payment of part of what he was entitled to receive: he is free in law, if not in good commercial conscience, to insist on payment of the balance of the amount due to him from the debtor.

I would dismiss this appeal

Appeal dismissed

QUESTIONS AND PROBLEMS

1. Since *Foakes v. Beer* has been to some extent legislatively overruled by the Mercantile Law Amendment Act, s. 16 (*supra*), what would have happened had *D. & C. Builders Ltd. v. Rees* come up in Ontario?

2. Does *D. & C. Builders Ltd. v. Rees* differ from *Post v. Jones* (*supra*)?

3. Suppose that the defendant had had the forethought to give a peppercorn with the cheque would the result have been the same? Could it have been the same? Does Lord Denning give any clear guidance when he will relieve the debtor and when he will not?

4. If you like the result in *D. & C. Builders v. Rees*, but dislike that in *Foakes v. Beer*, state your reasons precisely.

5. You are a County Court judge in England. A case involving *Foakes v. Beer* has just been argued before you. Would you regard youself as bound by *Foakes v. Beer* after *D. & C. Builders v. Rees*?

WATSON v. CANADA PERMANENT TRUST CO.

(1972), 27 D.L.R. (3d) 735. B.C.S.C.

[As part of a complicated process of financing a moribund company, Arivaca, the plaintiff, in common with the other major shareholders of Arivaca, entered into an agreement with the defendant under which the plaintiff agreed to sell his shares in Arivaca to Pan Arctic. In the meantime the shares were held in a "pool" until various securities commissions have given permission for their release. The agreement set out the price that would be paid for the shares. The refinancing was successful to the point that the shares of Arivaca were being sold at a price higher than the price provided for in the agreement and the plaintiff sought to get out of the agreement. Twenty-five percent of the shares involved were released by the Alberta Securities Commission and the plaintiff received payment at the agreed price, $0.45 per share, for one quarter of his shares. The plaintiff later commenced an action for damages for failure to return the rest of his shares.]

Anderson J. . . . Thus it is clear that unless some consideration passed from Pan Arctic to the plaintiff the offer to sell could be withdrawn by the plaintiff at any time. As there is no consideration shown on the face of the agreement, it remains to ascertain whether consideration not set out in writing, passed to the plaintiff from Pan Arctic at the time of execution of the agreement.

Before dealing with the law in respect of this matter, I should set out my findings of fact relating to the question of consideration:

(a) No money or other property passed from Pan Arctic to the plaintiff.

(b) Pan Arctic did state prior to the execution of the agreement that it would take steps to revive the company which was dormant or "dead".

(c) Pan Arctic would not have taken the steps which it did if it had known that the agreement was merely an offer which could be withdrawn at any time.

(d) The plaintiff believed that Pan Arctic was desirous of obtaining options on all the issued shares in Arivaca which options could not be withdrawn.

(e) The plaintiff assisted Pan Arctic in getting other shareholders to sign option agreements.

(f) Both Pan Arctic and the plaintiff believed that the offer to sell could not be withdrawn.

(g) Pan Arctic did take steps to revive Arivaca and had it not been for the work and expenditures made by Pan Arctic it is clear that Arivaca would have remained "dead".

(h) While Pan Arctic entered into a binding contract with Arivaca on November 6, 1968, the statements made by Pan Arctic to the plaintiff did not constitute a binding contract which could be enforced by the plaintiff.

(i) Pan Arctic was induced by the conduct of the plaintiff in all the circumstances of this case to believe that the plaintiff would not withdraw his offer to sell on the terms outlined in the agreement.

(j) The plaintiff had a *moral* obligation not to withdraw his offer to sell.

(k) The plaintiff had nothing to lose but everything to gain if Pan Arctic was successful in causing Arivaca to make a distribution to the public and build up a public market for the shares of Arivaca.

This would be a simple case to decide if the plaintiff was bound as an honourable person to carry out his bargain. As Lord Mansfield said in *Hawkes v. Saunders* (1782), 1 Cowp. 289 at p. 290, 98 E.R. 1091:

> Where a man is under a moral obligation, which no Court of Law or Equity can inforce, and promises, the honesty and rectitude of the thing is a consideration... the ties of conscience upon an upright mind are a sufficient consideration.

The judgment of Lord Mansfield was repudiated in the case of *Eastwood v. Kenyon* (1840), 11 Ad. & E. 438, 113, E.R. 482, where it was held that a moral obligation did not constitute consideration. "Consideration means something which is of value in the eye of the law, moving from the plaintiff: it may be some benefit to the plaintiff or some detriment to the defendant": see *Thomas v. Thomas* (1842), 2 Q.B. 851 at p. 859, 114 E.R. 330.

In this case, at the time of execution of the option agreement as there was no enforceable promise by Pan Arctic, there was nothing of value "in the eye of the law" moving from Pan Arctic to the plaintiff.

The question then remains as to whether, in all the circumstances the plaintiff was estopped from withdrawing his promise (not to withdraw his offer).

Counsel for the plaintiff relies on *Combe v. Combe*, [1951] 2 K.B. 215, and submits that as the "promise" made by Pan Arctic was unenforceable and of no legal effect that the doctrine of promissory estoppel is not applicable. I find, however, that not only is *Combe v. Combe, supra,* distinguishable but that the judgments in that case support the position taken by counsel for the defendant.

Denning, L.J., who gave the judgment in *Central London Property Trust, Ltd. v. High Trees House, Ltd.,* [1947] K.B. 130, in giving his judgment in *Combe v. Combe, supra,* said in part at p. 220:

> The principle, as I understand it, is that, where one party has, by his words or conduct, made to the other a promise or assurance which was intended to affect the legal relations between them and to be acted on accordingly, then, once the other party has taken him at his word and acted on it, the one who gave the promise or assurance cannot afterwards be allowed to revert to the previous legal relations as if no such promise or assurance had been made by him, but he must accept their legal relations subject to the qualification which he himself has so introduced, even though it is not supported in point of law by any consideration but only by his word.
>
> Seeing that the principle never stands alone as giving a cause of action in itself, it can never do away with the necessity of consideration when that is an essential part of the cause of action. The doctrine of consideration is too firmly fixed to be overthrown by a sidewind.

In the same case Lord Asquith said in part at p. 225.

> The judge has decided that, while the husband's promise was unsupported by any valid consideration, yet the principle in *Central London Property Trust, Ltd. v. High Trees House Ltd.*, [1947] K.B. 130, entitles the wife to succeed. It is unnecessary to express any view as to the correctness of that decision, though I certainly must not be taken to be questioning it; and I would remark, in passing, that it seems to me a complete misconception to suppose that it struck at the roots of the doctrine of consideration. But assuming, without deciding, that it is good law, I do not think, however, that it helps the plaintiff at all. What that case decides is that when a promise is given which (1.) is intended to create legal relations, (2.) is intended to be acted upon by the promisee, and (3.) is in fact so acted upon, the promisor cannot bring an action against the promisee which involves the repudi-

ation of his promise or is inconsistent with it. It does not, as I read it, decide that a promisee can sue on the promise. On the contrary, Denning, J., expressly stated the contrary.

It will be seen that a cause of action cannot be based on promissory estoppel, but if the defendant can bring himself within the principles enunciated by the learned Judges he can prevent the plaintiff from asserting his legal rights (withdrawing his offer and suing for the return of the shares or damages).

In this case the plaintiff knew that the plan outlined by Pan Arctic depended on the obtaining by Pan Arctic of a binding option over all or a large part of the issued "pool" shares. He knew, as a knowledgeable securities salesman, that Pan Arctic would not attempt to "salvage" Arivaca unless it could purchase the issued "pool" shares at a price less than the price to be paid by the public. He knew as a person involved in speculative issues that a "promotor" (Pan Arctic) would not even consider embarking on the "salvage" operation if the options over the issued "pool" shares could be withdrawn at will. With this knowledge he made a promise (unsupported by legal consideration) which any reasonable optionee would believe was not to be withdrawn.

He knew that Pan Arctic intended to act on his promise. Pan Arctic did act on the promise and the plaintiff cannot now repudiate that promise or act inconsistently with it. It should also be noted than Pan Arctic would have suffered great prejudice if the plaintiff were permitted to repudiate his promise. Accordingly, I would hold that the plaintiff could not withdraw his offer to sell and that the option was properly exercised within the time limited by the option.

.   .   .

In the result the action must be dismissed with costs.

If I am wrong and should have found for the plaintiff, I would have fixed damages in the sum of $52,500 (15,000 shares at $3.50 per share) being the highest price obtainable for all the shares in the circumstances during the period June 11, 1969 to June 27, 1969. There was no real market after that time. I did not make any deduction for the fact that 15,000 shares would have been placed on the market because of the balance of probabilities it was not proven that the plaintiff could not have fed his shares into the market in small lots during the 17 day period available to him.

Action dismissed.

[The judgment of *Anderson, J.* was affirmed by the B.C. Court of Appeal (1974), 66 D.L.R. (3d) 85, on different grounds. McFarlane, J.A., who gave the judgment of the court orally, said, "... it is ... unnecessary to consider the subject of estoppel of whatever kind."]

QUESTIONS

1. Is Anderson J. using the doctrine of promissory estoppel as a shield or as a sword?

2. How long and pointed can a shield become before it becomes a sword?

BAXTER v. JONES

(1903), 6 O.L.R. 360. Ontario Court of Appeal.

[The defendant, an insurance agent, had arranged insurance for the plaintiffs in January 1900. The plaintiffs increased their insurance by $500 in January 1901. Under the terms of their existing policies, the other insurers had to be informed of the increase in the amount. The defendant told the plaintiffs that he would give the necessary notices, but he failed to do so. As a result, when a fire occurred, the plaintiffs had inadequate insurance. The plaintiffs sued for the loss they had suffered. The action was brought in negligence. The trial judge found that the defendant had made the agreement to give notice and that it had been breached. He gave judgment for the plaintiffs. The defendant appealed.].

Osler J.A. The question is whether on this evidence, any agreement is made out, for the breach of which the defendant is responsible. The plaintiffs cannot, in my opinion, rely upon anything which took place in January, 1900, when the four policies were effected, because their manager's statement of what the defendant then undertook to do is too vague and indefinite to establish a general engagement by the defendant to give notice of subsequent insurance effected or obtained by him; nor were the policies left in his custody to be looked after. The plaintiffs must, therefore, rely on what took place in January, 1901. The defendant did then undoubtedly at some time promise to give the necessary notices of the new insurance to the companies on the existing policies. Was this as part of the employment he then undertook, or was his employment confined to procuring the new policy, the promise to give notice being an independent or subsequent promise made without consideration, and therefore a gratuitous one which imposed no liability in the event of its non-performance?

If the defendant's employment and promise was entire to do both acts, viz., to procure the new insurance and to give the notices, then, even if it was, as it has been held in the Court below, a gratuitous promise, yet having proceeded upon his employment the defendant would be liable for negligently performing it in such a manner as to cause loss or injury to the plaintiffs. He knew the importance of giving the notices, and the effect of the omission to do so, upon the plaintiffs' other policies. To stop when he had only obtained the insurance was simply to go so far with the business as to cause a direct injury to the plaintiffs if he failed to follow it up by notice to the other insurers, and cannot be regarded otherwise than as actionable negligence.

It would rather appear that nothing was said of giving notice when the defendant was first employed or instructed to procure the insurance, but before the business was complete, and while the plaintiffs might have still withdrawn, they requested the defendant and the latter undertook to give it. Defendant might have refused to assume that duty, and the plaintiffs would then have known that they must look after it themselves, or could have withdrawn their application and sought insurance elsewhere. But the whole business having been ultimately entrusted to and assumed by the defendant before any part of it had been completed, the plaintiffs have a right to complain that the defendant negligently proceeded with it only so far as to be detrimental to them.

I think the learned Judge rightly regarded the transaction as one of mandate, so that if the defendant had not entered upon the execution of the business entrusted to him he would have incurred no liability, *Coggs v. Bernard* (1703), 2 Ld. Raym. 909, 1 Smith's L.C. 11th ed. p. 173, but "it is well established that one who enters upon the performance of a mandate or gratuitous undertaking on behalf of another, is responsible not only for what he does, but for what he leaves unfulfilled, and cannot rely on the want of consideration as an excuse for the omission of any step that is requisite for the protection of any interest intrusted to his care:"

        .   .   .

Maclennan, J.A.: — I think the case depends wholly upon what took place between the parties in January, 1901, when the $500 policy was effected, and is not affected by anything which passed in connection with the previous insurances. . . .

The defendant was an agent of the Millers & Manufacturers Co., and also of the other companies which had risks for the plaintiffs on the same property, and Mr. Baxter says he went to him for this additional insurance just because his other risks were in his office, and, it is not contended that there was any consideration between the plaintiffs and defendant in connection with the business. The only consideration in the matter was the premium which was paid to the company. As between the plaintiffs and defendant, therefore, the whole business was voluntary. It was contended that the procurement of the policy and the promise to notify the companies were one single transaction, and that having undertaken the business and performed it negligently, the defendant was responsible although there was no consideration for the contract: *Coggs v. Bernard,* 1 Sm. L.C. 11th ed. p. 173, and *Elsee v. Gatward* (1800), 5 T.R. 143.

I have had a good deal of doubt and hesitation in this case, and I think the question is a very nice one. It is clear that if the defendant's promise to give notice had been made after the insurance had been completed, he would not have been liable, for want of some consideration. But it was made at latest at the moment of completion, and what was promised had a very material and important bearing upon the principal business. I think the transaction is not to be regarded as an application by the plaintiffs to the defendant, merely as the agent of and representing the Millers & Manufacturers Insurance Company for insurance in that company: but that the plaintiffs applied to the defendant to procure insurance *for them* in some company to be selected and recommended by him, the effect being that he procured this insurance for them at their request, and in connection with it, promised to give the required notices to the other companies. Now he did everything which he undertook to do except to give the notices. The new insurance was perfectly regular and valid in every respect. The company had due notice given to them of all the concurrent insurance, and it was embodied and expressed in the policy. The notices to the other companies were not essential to the completion or to the validity of the new insurance, and so were something distinct. The plaintiffs might have given the notices themselves. Mr. Baxter might have gone to the bank where the existing policies were held as security, and have given the notices immediately after signing the application and paying the premium. If the defendant had been acting solely for the insurance company in effecting the insurance, his promise to give the notices would have stood by itself, and the breach of it would not have been actionable. But because he was procuring the insurance at the request of the plaintiffs, to that extent he was acting for them, which makes it necessary to consider how far, if at all, he was bound to give the notices, although all that he did was as between him and the plaintiffs purely voluntary.

. . .

Now, in this case, unless notice of the new insurance was given to the existing insurers, the new policy was certain to work injury to the plaintiffs by making void the existing policies. This the defendant knew, and as part of his undertaking to procure the new insurance, I think that he undertook and agreed that it should not be done injuriously to the plaintiffs. His omission to give the notices has that effect. It put the plaintiffs at the mercy of the former insurers, when the loss occurred, and compelled them to accept whatever they chose to pay, which was $1000 less than they would, as I think, having read the evidence, have received. Upon the whole I think the judgment is right and should be affirmed.

Moss, C.J.O. and Garrow, J.A. concurred.

QUESTIONS

1. What is the basis of the defendant's liability?
2. What would have happened if the defendant had informed the plaintiff that he would not give the required notice and had given this information,

  (a) one month before the fire; or
  (b) one day before the fire; or
  (c) one minute before the fire?

SLOAN v. UNION OIL CO. OF CANADA
[1955] 4 D.L.R. 664. B.C.S.C.

ACTION by former employee to recover termination allowance.

Wilson J.: — The plaintiff sues for $1,416.44 which he says is due him as "termination allowance" following the termination, on August 31, 1945, by the defendant of his employment by it as credit manager.

The plaintiff had worked for 19 years, first as assistant credit manager and latterly as credit manager for the defendant company when, on August 31, 1945, it sold its assets to British-American Oil Co. Ltd.

The terms of his employment included, in addition to the provision of a salary, certain other considerations referred to by his counsel as fringe benefits. This phrase, in labour terminology, had acquired, through usage, a certain accepted meaning. It connotes things such as vacation pay, termination allowance, insurance protection, pension schemes and medical aid given by an employer to an employee in addition to his wages or salary.

. . .

About mid-August of 1945 the plaintiff, with certain other senior officials, was advised that the defendant expected to sell its business to British American Oil Co. Ltd., which I shall hereafter call B.A. Oil. On August 17, 1945, the sale was consummated by a contract, ex. 5, to take effect August 31, 1945, which contained this reference to the defendant's employees: "Purchaser shall have the right, but without the obligation, to retain any employee of Seller."

The plaintiff did not subscribe to this agreement and knew nothing of its terms.

On August 31st there were two meetings of employees, one at noon and one in the evening. The object of these meetings was undoubtedly to explain to the employees what had happened and to try to induce them to accept, in lieu of their former jobs, which ended that day, new employment with B.A. Oil Co. at the same tasks they had formerly performed for the defendant. This was, of course, very necessary from the standpoint of the B.A. Oil Co.; a wholesale defection of employees would have paralyzed their new business.

. . .

The plaintiff, on September 4, 1945, went to work as credit manager for B.A. Oil. He was told nothing at this time about his terms of employment but he later discovered that while he drew the same pay as before, B.A. Oil did not provide fringe benefits, as had Union Oil, and particularly did not provide a termination allowance. He was informed by one Bennett, his immediate superior, that B.A. Oil would regard unfavourably any employee of theirs who tried to collect termination allowance from the defendant. He got legal advice to the effect that he was entitled to termination allowance from the defendant but advanced no claim for it until after he left the service of B.A. Oil in 1950; in fact his first claim against the defendant was asserted in a letter which briefly preceded the issue of the writ in this action. The writ was issued at the last possible moment to avoid the operation of the *Statute of Limitations,* R.S.B.C. 1948, c. 191. I may say that I attach no importance to the delay in taking action. The plaintiff's explanation that action would imperil his employment by B.A. Oil is acceptable to me and the delay does not, of itself, constitute waiver and has caused no prejudice to the defendant. If there is, as there was here, a statutory bar, the plaintiff is entitled to the full statutory period before his claim becomes unenforceable: see *Archbold v. Scully* (1861), 9 H.L.C. 360 at p. 383, 11 E.R. 769.

I must decide whether or not there was a contract by the defendant to pay the plaintiff a termination allowance if he was discharged without cause.

. . .

The defendant had, in a series of communications from 1941 to 1945, told the plaintiff he would be paid such an allowance. I have no doubt that such statements constitute an offer by the defendant; a promise that it would, if he continued in its employment until such time, short of retirement age, as it should without cause, dismiss him from its service, pay him certain stated sums. The offer is clear. It is equally clear that there was no verbal or written acceptance of the offer; no consideration by way of a promise that he would so continue to serve. Therefore, if a consideration moved from the plaintiff to the defendant, that consideration was not a promise but a performance, the doing of an act. For undoubtedly he did fulfil the terms of the defendant's offer, he did serve them until dismissed, and it is this, and this only, that must be relied on as consideration.

Now he was, of course, already bound to serve them during his period of employment and the consideration for that service was his salary. But he was not bound to continue to serve them until he was dismissed. He could, at any time, have quit his employment. By staying until he was discharged he did something that was not required by his contract of employment and he says that his knowledge of the provision for a termination allowance was one of the factors which induced him to continue his employment.

. . .

I now proceed to deal with some recent English decisions.
Central London Property Trust Ltd. v. High Trees House Ltd., [1947] K.B.
130.

. . .

The promise or assurance here was not used, as in the *High Trees House*
case, *supra*, to resist a claim but to enforce one.

By 1950 Denning J. who had become a Lord Justice of Appeal sat with
other Judges on *Chas. Rickards Ltd. v. Oppenhaim*, [1950] 1 K.B. 616, and
applied the principle he had stated in the *High Trees House* case to another
set of facts, as he did later in *Perrott (J.F.) & Co. v. Cohen*, [1951] 1 K.B. 705.

Combe v. Combe, [1951] 1 All E.R. 767, was tried by the Court of Appeal
in 1951. The Court was Asquith, Denning and Birkett L.JJ. After a decree
nisi of divorce, but before the decree absolute the husband agreed to pay
the wife £100 per annum as permanent maintenance. Six years later the wife
brought an action for arrears due under the agreement. The action failed,
on the basis of lack of consideration. The husband had not stipulated, when
agreeing to pay the wife £100 per year, that she should refrain from asking
the Court for an award of alimony. Nor had the wife agreed that she would
so abstain. If she had done so, her agreement would not have constituted
consideration because it would have been unenforceable. But the Court did
not rest its judgment on this latter point.

The decisive point in the case seems to me to have been not the rejection
of the wife's forbearance as consideration but the finding that there was no
offer by the husband to pay the money for the act of forbearance. I cite
from the judgment of Denning L.J. at pp. 770-1:

> "There was, however, clearly no promise by the wife, express or implied, to for-
> bear from applying to the court. All that happened was that she did, in fact, for-
> bear — that is, she did an act in return for a promise. Is that sufficient
> consideration? Unilateral promises of this kind have long been enforced so long
> as the act or forbearance is done on the faith of the promise and at the request of
> the promisor, express or implied. The act done is then in itself sufficient consider-
> ation for the promise, even though it arises *ex post facto* . . . ."

I think . . . that a majority of the Court would have enforced the promise
to pay £100 per year if it had been coupled with a condition that the wife
abstain from taking proceedings to collect alimony and if the wife had so
abstained. This, of course, apart from the other point that I have mentioned
which might have defeated her claim. The interesting thing here is that
Denning L.J., if I read him correctly, would have enforced the husband's
promise on a basis entirely unrelated to his judgment in the *High Trees
House* case, and on what he calls a long-settled rule that a finding that there
was a promise intended to be binding, intended to be acted upon and in
fact acted upon is equivalent to a finding that there was consideration.

. . .

It appears to me that *Combe v. Combe* brings latter day English law
regarding consideration into a very near relationship with American law on
the same subject. I propose to quote at some length from American authorities which seem to have anticipated the reasoning in *Combe v. Combe*, and
have the added advantage of applying that reasoning to the relation of master and servant. I first cite this general statement from Corbin on Contracts,
vol. 1, p. 221:

> "There are cases in which an employer has promised a 'bonus', some form of

benefit in addition to agreed wages or salary, on condition that the employee or employees remain in service for a stated period. In such cases the offered promise is almost always so made as to make it unnecessary for the employee to give any notice of his assent.

"It is sufficient that he continues in the employment as requested. It is certain that after so continuing in performance, the employer cannot withdraw or repudiate his promise without liability either in damages or for a proportionate part of the bonus promised. A unilateral contract exists."

. . .

It seems to me there are here the essentials of a contract, offer and acceptance, promise and consideration. In the part of ex. 3 (section 1) where provision is made for termination allowance, certain paid holidays are listed and certain rights to vacations with pay are granted. Could it be argued that an employee who had taken the vacation granted would have no right of action against the company for wages for the period covered by the vacation? Surely not. The concession by an employer to an employee of the right to holiday pay or a termination allowance is as much a part of the consideration for his services as is his right to wages. It is part of the contract of employment.

. . .

The plaintiff will have judgment for $1,416.44 and costs.

Judgment for plaintiff.

QUESTIONS

1. Would the application of § 90 help us solve these cases?
2. How much would the plaintiff in *Sloan v. Union Oil* recover under § 90?

The next cases move away from the commercial area. To what extent does the application of any of the solutions that we have so far worked out apply in these cases?

SKIDMORE v. BRADFORD

(1869), L.R. 8 Eq. 134.

[The testator (Jacob Bradford) had arranged to buy a warehouse from Charles Johnson for £5,000. When Jacob came to pay the deposit on the purchase price, he asked Johnson to amend the agreement by writing in his nephew's name, Edward Bradford, as purchaser. At this time Jacob said, "I've bought the warehouse for my nephew." Johnson changed the name on the agreement and Jacob paid Johnson £1,000 as a deposit. Johnson made out the receipt in Edward Bradford's name. Edward subsequently signed the agreement to purchase. Jacob paid a further £500 on the purchase price, but died before paying any more. Johnson required Edward to pay the balance of the purchase price of the warehouse. The court was asked to determine whether Jacob's estate was liable for the balance of the purchase price that Edward had had to pay.]

Sir John Stuart, V.C.: — ... If *Edward Bradford* were a mere volunteer there is no principle on which he would be entitled to come to this Court to have the testator's intended act of bounty completed, and the balance of the purchase-money paid out of the assets. But if on the faith of the testator's representation he has involved himself in any liability, or has incurred any obligation, he cannot be regarded as a volunteer, and if so, the testator's assets are liable to make good the representation on the faith of which the nephew has entered into this contract.

. . .

In this case it is beyond all doubt that the real contracting party was *Jacob Bradford,* the testator, and that in making the purchase his intention was to confer a benefit upon his nephew. The vendor knew all the circumstances of the purchase. It is beyond all doubt that when the contract was prepared the testator desired the contract to be altered so as to have the name of the nephew inserted in the contract, and in consequence of that alteration the nephew came under a legal obligation to pay the purchase-money. The case, therefore, is one in which the purchaser became liable to be sued, and incurred that liability on the faith of the representations of the testator that he would give him the warehouse which was the subject matter of the contract and would provide the purchase-money.

. . .

Upon this principle *Crosbie v. M'Doual* (1806), 13 Ves. 148 was decided by Lord *Erskine*, and *Redington v. Redington* (1794), 3 Ridg. by Lord *Clare*, and that principle is this, "that although upon a mere voluntary promise an action does not lie, yet if one man binds himself to pay and does pay money in consequence of an obligation undertaken by another, the one has money which in equity and conscience ought to be the money of the other; and that is not *nudum pactum*."

I am therefore of opinion that the assets of the testator are liable to make good the obligation which has been incurred by *Edward Bradford*, and he is entitled to have the balance of the purchase-money paid out of the testator's estate.

QUESTIONS

1. What is the extent of the nephew's reliance in this case.?

2. Does the judgment protect this reliance, or does it go far beyond any protection that may be required by the reliance interest involved?

3. If so, what is the basis for the judgment and can it be defended?

PROBLEMS

1. George purchased a cemetery plot for $10. When George's sister Sarah said that she would buy one for herself and her husband, George said, "You need not buy a plot. I will give you and your man burial in my plot". Is there a contract?

2. Sarah replied to George, "If you give me a plot, I will put a tombstone there." Is there a contract?

3. Sarah bought a tombstone and had her own and her husband's names cut on it, and, on the death of her husband, erected it on the plot. George died, and his nephew, his executor (who was also planning to be buried in the same plot) sought to prevent Sarah having anything more to do with the plot and also to have Sarah's husband's body removed. What results?

If one were to conclude that there was a contract in this case when was it made? Was the original offer by George part of any exchange transaction? If not, where is the consideration?

See: *Hubbs v. Black* (1918), 44 O.L.R. 545. Ontario Appellate Division.

4. Father says to son, "I will give you $1,000 for Christmas". Son replies, "I will now go and buy the motorcycle I've always wanted, I can pay for it when I get your

gift." Is there a contract? Would it matter whether the son bought the motorcycle or not?

5. Mary and Eleanor were good friends. Mary inherited a large lake front lot from her father. She invited Eleanor to share the lot and said that she would give her ¼ of the lot. Both women then walked the lot and marked out the part that was to be Eleanor's. Eleanor said that the place was so beautiful that she planned to build a house there, which she did. The friendship has now ended and Eleanor, who never had any deed to the property, would like a conveyance to protect the investment she has made in the house. Can she get one? See: *Loranger v. Haines* (1921), 50 O.L.R. 268 (Appellate Division).

DALHOUSIE COLLEGE v. BOUTILIER ESTATE

[1934] S.C.R. 642. S.C.C.; Duff C.J.C., Rinfret, Cannon, Crocket and Hughes JJ.

The judgment of the court was delivered by
Crocket, J. — This appeal concerns a claim which was filed in the Probate Court for the County of Halifax, Nova Scotia, in the year 1931, by the appellant College against the respondent Estate for $5,000, stated as having been "subscribed to Dalhousie Campaign Fund (1920)", and attested by an affidavit of the College Bursar, in which it was alleged that the stated amount was justly and truly owing to the College Corporation.

The subscription, upon which the claim was founded, was obtained from the deceased on June 4, 1920, in the course of a canvass which was being conducted by a committee, known as the Dalhousie College Campaign Committee, for the raising of a fund to increase the general resources and usefulness of the institution and was in the following terms:

> For the purpose of enabling Dalhousie College to maintain and improve the efficiency of its teaching, to construct new buildings and otherwise to keep pace with the growing need of its constituency and in consideration of the subscription of others, I promise to pay to the Treasurer of Dalhousie College the sum of Five Thousand Dollars, payment as follows:

> Terms of payment as per letter from Mr. Boutilier.
> A. 399.

> Date June 4th, 1920.   Name Arthur Boutilier.
> Make all cheques payable to the Treasurer of Dalhousie College.

So far as the record discloses, the subscription was not accompanied or followed by any letter from the deceased as to the terms of payment. He died on October 29, 1928, without making any payment on account. It appears that some time after he signed the subscription form he met with severe financial reverses which prevented him from honouring his pledge. That he desired and hoped to be able to do so is evidenced by a brief letter addressed by him to the President of the University on April 12, 1926, in reply to a communication from the latter, calling his attention to the subscription and the fact that no payments had been made upon it. The deceased's letter, acknowledging receipt of the President's communication, states:

> In reply I desire to advise you that I have kept my promise to you in mind. As you are probably aware, since making my promise I suffered some rather severe reverses, but I expect before too long to be able to redeem my pledge.

The claim was contested in the Probate Court by the Estate on two grounds, viz.: that in the absence of any letter from the deceased as to terms of payment, the claimant could not recover; and that the claim was barred by the Statute of Limitations. Dr. A. Stanley MacKenzie, who had retired from the Presidency of the University after 20 years' service shortly before the trial, and others gave evidence before the Registrar of Probate. Basing himself apparently upon Dr. MacKenzie's statement that in consideration of the moneys subscribed in the campaign referred to, large sums of money were expended by the College on the objects mentioned in the subscription card, between the years 1920 and 1931, the Registrar decided that there was a good consideration for the deceased's subscription, citing *Sargent v. Nicholson*, a decision of the Appeal Court of Manitoba (1915), 25 D.L.R. 638, and *Y.M.C.A. v. Rankin,* a decision of the Appeal Court of British Columbia (1916), 27 D.L.R. 417, and that no supplementary letter was necessary to complete the agreement. He further held that the deceased's letter of April 12, 1926, constituted a sufficient acknowledgement to take the case out of the Statute of Limitations.

An appeal to the Judge of the County Court sitting as Judge of the Probate Court was dismissed, but on a further appeal to the Supreme Court of Nova Scotia *en banc,* this decision was reversed by the unanimous judgment of Chisholm, C.J., and Mellish, Graham, Carroll and Ross, JJ., on the ground that the subscription was a mere *nudum pactum,* and that nothing was shewn either by the document itself or by the evidence which imposed any binding contractual obligation upon the deceased in connection therewith. This, I take it, to be the gist of the reasons for the judgment of the Appeal Court as delivered by the learned Chief Justice, and embodies the whole problem with which we have now to deal.

There is, of course, no doubt that the deceased's subscription can be sustained as a binding promise only upon one basis, viz.: as a contract, supported by a good and sufficient consideration. The whole controversy between the parties is as to whether such a consideration is to be found, either in the subscription paper itself or in the circumstances as disclosed by the evidence.

So far as the signed subscription itself is concerned, it is contended in behalf of the appellant that it shews upon its face a good and sufficient consideration for the deceased's promise in its statement that it was given in consideration of the subscription of others. As to this, it is first to be observed that the statement of such a consideration in the subscription paper is insufficient to support the promise if, in point of law, the subscriptions of others could not provide a valid consideration therefor. I concur in the opinion of Chisholm, C.J., that the fact that others had signed separate subscription papers for the same common object or were expected so to do does not of itself constitute a legal consideration. Although there have been some cases in the United States in which a contrary opinion has been expressed, these decisions have been rejected as unsound in principle both by the Supreme Court of Massachusetts and the Court of Appeals of the State of New York. See *Cottage Street M.E. Church v. Kendall* (1877), 121 Mass. 528; *Hamilton College v. Stewart* (1848), 1 N.Y. Rep. 581; and *Albany Presbyterian Church v. Cooper* (1889), 112 N.Y. Rep. 517. In the last mentioned case the defendant's intestate subscribed a paper with a number of others, by the terms of which they "in consideration of one dollar" to each of them paid "and of the agreements of each other" severally promised and agreed to and with the plaintiff's trustees to pay to said trustees the sums severally subscribed for the purpose of paying off a mortgage debt on the church edifice on the condition that the sum of $45,000 in the aggregate should be subscribed and paid in for such purpose within one year. The Court of Appeals held that it must reject the consideration recited in the subscription paper, the money consideration, because it had no basis in fact, and the mutual promise between the subscribers, because there was no privity of contract between the plaintiff church and the various subscribers.

A perusal of the reasons for judgment of the Appeal Court of Manitoba, as delivered by Cameron, J.A., in *Sargent v. Nicholson*, already referred to, shews that that court also rejected the contention that it was a sufficient consideration that others were led to subscribe by the subscription of the defendant. In fact Cameron, J.A.'s opinion quotes with approval a passage from the opinion of Gray, C.J., in *Cottage Street M.E. Church v. Kendall*, that such a proposition appeared to the Massachusetts Supreme Court to be "inconsistent with elementary principles." The decision of the Appeal Court of British Columbia in *Y.M.C.A. v. Rankin* fully adopted the opinion of Cameron, J.A., in *Sargent v. Nicholson*, and is certainly no authority for the acceptance of other subscriptions as a binding consideration in such a case as the present one.

The doctrine of mutual promises was also put forward on the argument as a ground upon which the deceased's promise might be held to be binding. It was suggested that the statement in the subscription of the purpose for which it was made, viz.: "of enabling Dalhousie College to maintain and improve the efficiency of its teaching, to construct new buildings and otherwise to keep pace with the growing need of its constituency," constituted an implied request on the part of the deceased to apply the promised subscription to this object and that the acceptance by the College of his promise created a contract between them, the consideration for the promise of the deceased to pay the money being the promise of the College to apply it to the purpose stated.

I cannot think that any such construction can fairly be placed upon the subscription paper and its acceptance by the College. It certainly contains no express request to the College either "to maintain and improve the efficiency of its teaching" or "to construct new buildings and otherwise to keep pace with the growing need of its constituency," but simply states that the promise to pay the $5,000 is made for the purpose of enabling the College to do so, leaving it perfectly free to pursue what had always been its aims in whatever manner its Governors should choose. No statement is made as to the amount intended to be raised for all or any of the purposes stated. No buildings of any kind are described. The construction of new buildings is merely indicated as a means of the College keeping pace with the growing need of its constituency and apparently to be undertaken as and when the Governors should in their unfettered discretion decide the erection of any one or more buildings for any purpose was necessary or desirable.

It seems to me difficult to conceive that, had the deceased actually paid the promised money, he could have safely relied upon the mere acceptance of his own promise, couched in such vague and uncertain terms regarding its purpose, as the foundation of any action against the College Corporation.

So far as I can discover, there is no English or Canadian case in which it has been authoritatively decided that a reciprocal promise on the part of the promisee may be implied from the mere fact of the acceptance by the promisee of such a subscription paper from the hands of the promisor to do the thing for which the subscription is promised. There is no doubt, of course, that an express agreement by the promisee to do certain acts in return for a subscription is a sufficient consideration for the promise of the subscriber. There may, too, be circumstances proved by evidence, outside the subscription paper itself, from which such a reciprocal promise on the part of the promisee may well be implied, but I have not been able to find any English or Canadian case where it has actually been so decided in the absence of proof that the subscriber has himself either expressly requested the promisee to undertake some definite project or personally taken such a part in connection with the projected enterprise that such a request might be inferred therefrom.

It is true that there are expressions in the judgments of the Manitoba Court of Appeal in *Sargent v. Nicholson* and of Wright, J., of the Supreme Court of Ontario, in *Re Loblaw*, [1933] 4 D.L.R. 264, which seem to support the proposition that a request from the promisor to the promisee may be implied from the mere statement in the subscription paper of the object for which the subscription is promised and a reciprocal promise from the promisee to the promisor to carry out that purpose from the mere fact of the acceptance of the subscription, but an examination of both these judgments makes it clear that these expressions of opinion do not touch the real ground upon which either of the decisions proceeds.

There is no doubt either that some American courts have held that by acceptance of the subscription paper itself the promisee impliedly undertakes to carry out the purpose for which the subscription is made and treated this implied promise of the promisee as the consideration for the promise to pay. This view, however, has been rejected, as pointed out in 60 Corpus Juris, 959, on the ground that the promise implied in the acceptance involves no act advantageous to the subscriber or detrimental to the beneficiary, and hence does not involve a case of mutual promises and that the duty of the payee would arise from trusteeship rather than a contractual promise, citing *Albany Presbyterian Church v. Cooper*, above referred to. No suggestion of mutual promises was made in the last named case, notwithstanding that the subscription there involved was expressly stated to be for the single purpose of erecting a designated church building; neither was it made in the leading New York case of *Barnes v. Perine* (1854) 2 Kernan's Rep. (12 NY. Appeals) 18, where the subscription was also stated to be for the erection of a specific church edifice.

As to finding the consideration for the subscription outside the subscription itself, the only evidence relied upon is that of Dr. MacKenzie that increased expenditures were made by the College for the purposes stated between the years 1920 and 1931 on the strength of the subscriptions obtained in the canvass of 1920. It is contended that this fact alone constituted a consideration for the subscription and made it binding. The decisions in *Sargent v. Nicholson*; *Y.M.C.A. v. Rankin*; and the judgment of Wright, J., of the Supreme Court of Ontario, in *Re Loblaw*, adopting the two former decisions, are relied upon to sustain this proposition as well as some earlier Ontario cases: *Hammond v. Small* (1858), 16 U.C. Q.B. 371;

Thomas v. Grace (1865), 15 U.C.C.P. 462; *Anderson v. Kilborn* (1875), 22 Grant. 385; and *Berkeley Street Church v. Stevens* (1875), 37 U.C. Q.B. 9, and several American decisions.

There seems to be no doubt that the first three cases above mentioned unqualifiedly support the proposition relied upon, as regards at least a subscription for a single distinct and definite object, such as the erection of a designated building, whether or not the expenditure would not have been made nor any liability incurred by the promisee *but for the promise* or not. The earlier Ontario cases relied upon, however, do not appear to me to go that far. They all shew that there was either a direct personal interest on the part of the subscriber in the particular project undertaken or some personal participation in the action of the promisee as a result of which the expenditure or liability was incurred.

Regarding the American decisions, upon which *Sargent v. Nicholson* appears to have entirely proceeded — more particularly perhaps on the dictum of Gray, C.J., in *Cottage Street M.E. Church v. Kendall* than any other — it may be pointed out that there are other American cases which shew that there must be something more than the mere expenditure of money or the incurring of liability by the promisee on the faith of the promise. *Hull v. Pearson* (1899), 56 N.Y. Sup. 518, a decision of the Appellate Division of the Supreme Court of New York, in which many of the American cases are reviewed, should perhaps be mentioned in this regard. One W. subscribed a certain sum for the work of the German department of a theological seminary. There was no consideration expressed in the memorandum, and there was no evidence of a request on the part of W. that the work should be continued, or of any expenditures on the part of the theological seminary in reliance on such request. Such department had been continued, but there was no evidence that it would not have been continued as it had been for a series of years but for the subscription. It was held that the subscription was without consideration and could not be enforced. Woodward, J., in the course of his reasons, in which the full court concurred, said:

> It is true that there is evidence that the German department has been continued, but this does not meet the requirement. There is no evidence that it would not have been continued as it had been for a series of years if the subscription of Mr. Wild had not been made.

And further:

> He undoubtedly made the subscription for the purpose of aiding in promoting the work of the German department; but, in the absence of some act or word which clearly indicated that he accompanied his subscription by a request to do something which the corporation would not have done except for his subscription, there is no such request as would justify a constructive consideration in support of this promise.

These latter dicta seem to accord more with the English decisions, which give no countenance to the principle applied in *Sargent v. Nicholson* and *Y.M.C.A. v. Rankin* and in the earlier American cases, as is so pointedly illustrated by the judgments of Pearson, J., in *In Re Hudson* (1885), 33 W.R. 819, and Eve, J., in *In Re Cory* (1912), 29 T.L.R. 18. The head note in *In Re Hudson* states:

> A. verbally promised to give £20,000 to the Jubilee Fund of the Congregational Union, and also filled up and signed a blank form of promise not addressed to

anyone, but headed "Congregational Union of England and Wales Jubilee Fund," whereby he promised to give £20,000, in five equal annual instalments of £4,000 each, for the liquidation of chapel debts. A. paid three instalments of £4,000 to the fund within three years from the date of his promise, and then died, leaving the remaining two instalments unpaid and unprovided for.

The Congregational Union claimed £8,000 from A.'s executors, on the ground that they had been led by A.'s promise to contribute larger sums to churches than they would otherwise have done; that money had been given and promised by other persons in consequence of A.'s promise; that grants from the Jubilee Fund had been promised to cases recommended by A.; and that churches to which promises had been made by the committee, and the committee themselves, had incurred liabilities in consequence of A.'s promise.

His Lordship held there was no consideration for the promise. "There really was," he said, "in this matter, nothing whatever in the shape of a consideration which could form a contract between the parties."

And he added:

I am bound to say that this is an attempt to turn a charity into something very different from a charity. I think it ought to fail, and I think it does fail. I do not know to what extent a contrary decision might open a new form of posthumous charity. Posthumous charity is already bad enough, and it is quite sufficiently protected by law without establishing a new principle which would extend the doctrine in its favour far more than it has been extended or ought to be extended.

In the *Cory* case a gift of 1,000 guineas was promised to a Y.M.C. Association for the purpose of building a memorial hall. The sum required was £150,000, of which £85,000 had been promised or was available. The committee in charge decided not to commit themselves until they saw that their efforts to raise the whole fund were likely to prove successful. The testator, whose estate it was sought to charge, promised the 1,000 guineas and subsequently the committee felt justified in entering into a building contract, which they alleged they were largely induced to enter into by the testator's promise. Eve, J., held there was no contractual obligation between the parties and therefore no legal debt due from the estate.

Chisholm, C.J., in the case at bar, said that without any want of deference to eminent judges who have held otherwise he felt impelled to follow the decisions in the English cases. I am of opinion that he was fully justified in so doing, rather than apply the principle contended for by the appellant in reliance upon the decision in *Sargent v. Nicholson*, based, as the latter case is, upon the decisions of United States courts, which are not only in conflict with the English cases, but with decisions of the Court of Appeals of the State of New York, as I have, I think, shewn, and which have been subjected to very strong criticism by American legal authors, notably by Prof. Williston, as the learned Chief Justice of Nova Scotia has shewn in his exhaustive and, to my mind, very convincing judgment.

To hold otherwise would be to hold that a naked, voluntary promise may be converted into a binding legal contract by the subsequent action of the promisee alone without the consent, express or implied, of the promisor. There is no evidence here which in any way involves the deceased in the carrying out of the work for which the promised subscription was made other than the signing of the subscription paper itself.

I may add that, had I come to the opposite conclusion upon the legal question involved, I should have felt impelled, as Chisholm, C.J., did, to seriously question the accuracy of the statement relied upon by the appellant that "this work was done and the increased expenditures were made on the strength of the subscriptions promised," if that statement was meant to refer to all the increased expenditures listed in the comparative statements produced by Dr. MacKenzie. The statement relied on does not profess to set out verbatim the language of the witness. The record of the evidence is apparently but a brief summary taken down by the Registrar. That the summary is inaccurate was shewn by the admission made on the argument before us that it was not $220,000 which was subscribed in all in 1920, but $2,200,000. The statement produced of expenditures on buildings, grounds and equipment since 1920 shews a grand total for the more than ten years of but $1,491,687 — over $700,000 less than the aggregate of the 1920 campaign subscriptions — and this grand total includes over $400,000 for Shirriff Hall, which it is well known was the object of a special donation contributed by a wealthy lady, now deceased, as a memorial to her father. In the light of this correction it becomes quite as difficult to believe that the College Corporation, in doing "this work" and making "the increased expenditures" did so in reliance upon the deceased's subscription, as if the aggregate of the subscriptions had been but $220,000, as the Registrar took the figures down, and the Nova Scotia Supreme Court supposed, and the total expenditures $1,491,687. This evidence would assuredly seem to shut out all possibility of establishing a claim against the deceased's estate on any such ground as estoppel. The appeal, I think, should be dismissed with costs.

Appeal dismissed with costs.

QUESTIONS

1. Suppose that Boutilier had died with a net estate of $1,000,000, and that under his will all his assets were given to his widow, would your sympathies be with the University or not?

2. But now suppose that the net estate is only $60,000 and again that everything was to go to his widow, is the problem of enforcing the promise the same as in the case where Boutilier had $1,000,000?

The effect of enforcing the promise is that the University would become a creditor of the estate. This would mean that the assets would go first to the creditors and then be available to the family. But if there were not enough for all the creditors, (in other words, the deceased died insolvent) then all creditors would share *pro rata* and the University would get the same proportion as the creditors who had given value. If, on the other hand, the promise to Dalhousie were simply a charitable donation made by will, it would, first be subordinated to the claims of creditors, and second, could be challenged by the family under such statutes as the Succession Law Reform Act, 1977, on the ground that the testator did not leave enough for his wife and children.

The question of the enforceability of promises to charities involves more far-reaching issues than the application of the doctrine of consideration. These issues are not resolved by deciding if there was or was not satisfaction of the technical requirements of the doctrine. The presence of a seal would make the promise binding. Would you sign a United Way pledge card that had a seal, testimonium and attestation clause?

Conversely, the charity may have relied on the promise. Should this elevate its claim to that of a creditor? Should we say that the reliance of a charity on a pledge is never reasonable?

See: C.A. Wright (1935), 13 Can. Bar Rev. 108; Swan (1976) 15 U.W.O. L.Rev. 83.

Compare the following Quebec case with *Dalhousie v. Boutilier*:

RE ROSS

[1931] 4 D.L.R. 689. S.C.C.; Anglin C.J.C., Newcombe, Rinfret, Lamont and Cannon JJ.

[J.K.L. Ross had gone bankrupt. A claim was filed against his estate by McGill University. The claim was based on a promissory note for $100,000 signed by Ross in 1925. The amount, including interest (at 6%) came to $118,862.19. The trustee in bankruptcy refused the claim. The judge of first instance and the Court of King's Bench upheld the claim of the university. The trustee appealed.

The trustee argued that no consideration had been given for the note. The facts that led to the making of the note were as follows: In 1914 Ross pledged $150,000 to McGill for the erection of a gymnasium to be known as the Ross Memorial Gymnasium. The university agreed to contribute a further $100,000 (the amount of a legacy left to the university by Ross' father). This scheme was postponed because of the war. In 1920, during an endowment campaign for the university, Ross arranged to be released from his earlier obligation and promised $200,000 to the endowment campaign. He paid $100,000 of this amount. By 1924 Ross was in financial difficulties. In 1925 the university, in response to a request by Ross for more time to pay, agreed to give him time, but requested that Ross give a promissory note for the $100,000 due under his pledge of 1920. This was the note that was the basis of the claim of the university.]

Newcombe J. outlined the facts and referred to the events of 1920. He said:

... The university was formally released from the obligation of erecting the building, of contributing the $100,000 received from the late Mr. James Ross and of naming it "The Ross Memorial Gymnasium." Mr. J. K. L. Ross, on the other hand, was released from the obligation of contributing the $150,000. There was, as Sir Arthur Currie truly stated, "a mutual release and discharge."

Now, if as the appellant contends, the matter is governed by the common law of England, the mutual release and discharge upon which he relies really satisfies the requirement of valuable consideration. Obviously, when Ross's offer of 1914 was accepted, it became a promise; and it is unnecessary to consider whether or not he had power to revoke that promise; he never did revoke it or manifest any intention to exercise any power of revocation, if any, which he may have had. ...

And, when, in 1920, Mr. Ross arranged with the university authorities the terms of his present subscription, it was one of his stipulations, and a term of the bargain upon which he insisted, that the amount promised for the gymnasium should, with the consent of the university, be diverted from that object and figure in the Endowment Fund. It was upon that footing that he consented to subscribe, and the substitution of the new agreement must be regarded as consideration of value to both parties.

. . .

If therefore, as I think, Mr. Ross's subscription to the Endowment Fund upon the terms agreed involved him in liability for the stipulated payments, the forbearance or extension of time limited for the balance of those payments which he subsequently obtained by the giving of the note was valuable consideration within the meaning of the law. This, I think, is established beyond doubt by the English authorities.

. . .

I would have thought that the question as to whether Mr. Ross's agreement of 1920 to contribute to the Endowment Fund was binding and enforceable would naturally fall to be determined by the law of Quebec, the province in which the parties resided and made the agreement and where it was meant to be performed; but, if that question is governed by the law of Quebec, the appellant's difficulty is greater and becomes even more obvious. It is true that the rules of the common law of England, including the law merchant, apply to bills of exchange and promissory notes, because the parliament of Canada has, by the Bills of Exchange Act, so declared in the exercise of its exclusive legislative authority over that subject; but the Dominion legislation does not and was not intended to affect a subscriber's liability to implement his subscription, and, as I understood the argument, no contention to the contrary was submitted.

I quote arts. 982 and 984 of the Civil Code of Quebec: —

"982. It is essential to an obligation that it should have a cause from which it arises, persons between whom it exists, and an object."
"984. There are four requisites to the validity of a contract:
Parties legally capable of contracting;
Their consent legally given;
Something which forms the object of the contract;
A lawful cause or consideration."

It is essential therefore that an obligation shall have "a cause from which it arises," and that a contract shall have "a lawful cause or consideration;" but it is not meant that a contract which has a lawful cause within the meaning of art. 984 shall be void or defective for lack of that which, under the English authorities, would constitute valuable consideration.

. . .

My interpretation of the authorities, as applicable to the facts of this case, leads me to the view that there were both lawful cause and consideration for Mr. Ross's subscription, within the meaning of the Civil Code of Quebec; and that, as to the note, by the giving of which Mr. Ross, at his urgent request, secured an extension of the time limited for the payment of the balance of his subscription, the consideration was valuable and satisfied the requirements of the common law and of the Bills of Exchange Act.

A considerable part of the appellant's argument was devoted to a contention that a promissory note cannot be the subject of a gift by the maker to the payee; but it is not necessary to determine that question in this case if, as I think, the note was intended not as a gift, but as evidence of the maker's promise, in consideration of the extension of his term of credit, to pay the balance of his subscription in accordance with the tenor of the note.

I would dismiss the appeal with costs.

[The other judges agreed with Newcombe J. without reasons.]

[This problem was the subject of a lengthy annotation in the Dominion Law Reports by Robert Kanigsberg, [1931] 4 D.L.R. 702-712.]

QUESTIONS

1. Is Newcombe J. correct that there would be consideration at common law? Is there an alternative basis for enforcement? Is the conclusion that the agreement should be enforced inevitable?

2. What reasons are there for and against enforcement in this case?

3. What interest of the university is protected by the decision?

Does this decision present all the difficulties that the decision in *Dalhousie v. Boutilier* avoided?

The following act was passed in an apparent attempt to deal with the problems of charitable subscriptions.

PUBLIC SUBSCRIPTIONS ACT

R.S.N.S. 1967, c. 257.

1 Where any subscription list is opened and any subscription is made in aid of the erection of any road, bridge, place of worship, school house, or in aid of any other undertaking of public utility, or which is designated in the subscription list as, or appears therefrom to be, a public undertaking, and such undertaking is commenced, every person who has engaged by written subscription to contribute money, labour or other aid towards the undertaking, shall be held liable to perform such engagement, notwithstanding any apparent want of consideration in the agreement for the same.

2 (1) The following persons may require every person who has so subscribed to perform his engagement, that is to say:

(a) where a public grant is made in aid of such undertaking, the commissioner or other person appointed to expend such grant;

(b) where no public grant is made, the person to whom the performance or superintendence of such undertaking has been entrusted; and

(c) the person who has engaged in, and is then carrying on, such undertaking.

(2) If any subscriber, after a written notice of at least one month, refuses or neglects to perform his engagement, he may be sued by such commissioner or other person in this Section mentioned, or by the person to whom the subscription is payable.

(3) Nothing in this Section shall be construed to bind or make liable the executors or administrators of, or the estate of, any subscriber, unless it expressly appears from the instrument subscribed by him that he intended that his estate should be liable by binding his executors or administrators.

3 All moneys or other aid so subscribed and recovered shall be applied and expended for the purpose for which the same have been so subscribed, and for no other purpose whatever.

QUESTIONS AND PROBLEMS

1. To what extent does the act avoid the problems of the cases?

2. The pledge card for the United Way is as follows:

1977 UNITED WAY OF METROPOLITAN TORONTO

UNIVERSITY/COLLEGE

In consideration of the fact that I would give to all or most of the organizations if they appealed to me separately during the year, I hereby consolidate my giving and make one pledge through the United Way for 1978 needs.

I authorize	I will	
PAYROLL	PAY DIRECT	I enclose
☐ DEDUCTION	MONTHLY ☐	☐ CASH or
of	☐ QUARTERLY ☐	☐ CHEQUE
	or _____	Payable to United
$ ___ per day	(please bill me)	Way of Metro Toronto

MY TOTAL DONA-
TION $.

MY CASH GIFT OR   BALANCE
DOWN PAYMENT $.   DUE $.

a) After reading these cases would you recommend any changes to the wording?
b) How would you change the wording if the Nova Scotia act were in force in Ontario?

The next group of cases are not usually found under the heading of consideration, for they raise an issue that is usually referred to as one of intention. It is said that before a promise can become binding, there must be an intention to create legal relations. The word "intention" is a very dangerous word and whenever it is used it must be treated with caution. Part of the difficulty stems from the fact that the parties never put their intention into any recognizable statement. The conclusion that they had or had not any particular intention is almost always an inference. When courts are free to draw inferences, as they are when the issue is one of intention, the danger is that the conclusion is often result selective. This is a danger not because the result might not be right — the judges are usually sensible enough to know what the right result is — but because we cannot know what the real reason for the decision might have been.

The first case that follows is always regarded as giving the classical statement of the law in this area. The others are variations on this theme.

BALFOUR v. BALFOUR

[1919] 2 K.B. 571. Court of Appeal, England; Warrington, Duke and Atkin
L.JJ.

[The parties were married in 1900. The husband had a job in Ceylon, where they lived. They came to England in 1915. In August 1916 the husband had to return to Ceylon but the wife remained in England. As he was leaving, the husband promised to give his wife £30 per month until she should go out to Ceylon. They never lived together again. In 1918 she obtained an order for alimony on the basis of the husband's desertion.

The wife sued the husband for the amount promised in the agreement made in 1916. The trial judge, Sargant J., held in favour of the wife, the husband appealed.]

Warrington L.J. (after stating the facts). Those being the facts we have to say whether there is a legal contract between the parties, in other words, whether what took place between them was in the domain of a contract or whether it was merely a domestic agreement such as may be made every day between a husband and wife who are living together in friendly intercourse. It may be, and I do not for a moment say that it is not, possible for such a contract as is alleged in the present case to be made between husband and wife. The question is whether such a contract was made. That can only be determined either by proving that it was made in express terms, or that there is a necessary implication from the circumstances of the parties, and the transaction generally, that such a contract was made. It is quite plain that no such contract was made in express terms, and there was no bargain on the part of the wife at all. All that took place was this: The husband and wife met in a friendly way and discussed what would be necessary for her support while she was detained in England, the husband being in Ceylon, and they came to the conclusion that 30*l* a month would be about right, but there is no evidence of any express bargain by the wife that she would in all the circumstances treat that as in satisfaction of the obligation of the husband to maintain her. Can we find a contract from the position of the parties? It seems to me it is quite impossible. If we were to imply such a contract in this case we should be implying on the part of the wife that whatever happened and whatever might be the change of circumstances while the husband was away she should be content with this 30*l* a month, and bind herself by an obligation in law not to require him to pay anything more; and on the other hand we should be implying on the part of the husband a bargain to pay 30*l* a month for some indefinite period whatever might be his circumstances. Then again it seems to me that it would be impossible to make any such implication. The matter really reduces itself to an absurdity when one considers it, because if we were to hold that there was a contract in this case we should have to hold that with regard to all the more or less trivial concerns of life where a wife, at the request of her husband, makes a promise to him, that is a promise which can be enforced in law. All I can say is that there is no such contract here. These two people never intended to make a bargain which could be enforced in law. The husband expressed his intention to make this payment, and he promised to make it, and was bound in honour to continue it so long as he was in a position to do so. The wife on the other hand, so far as I can see, made no bargain at all. That is in my opinion sufficient to dispose of the case.

It is unnecessary to consider whether if the husband failed to make the payments the wife could pledge his credit or whether if he failed to make the payments she could have made some other arrangements. The only question we have to consider is whether the wife has made out a contract which she has set out to do. In my opinion she has not.

I think the judgment of Sargant J. cannot stand, the appeal ought to be allowed and judgment ought to be entered for the defendant.

Atkin L.J. The defence to this action on the alleged contract is that the defendant, the husband, entered into no contract with his wife, and for the determination of that it is necessary to remember that there are agreements between parties which do not result in contracts within the meaning of that term in our law. The ordinary example is where two parties agree to take a walk together, or where there is an offer and an acceptance of hospitality. Nobody would suggest in ordinary circumstances that those agreements result in what we know as a contract, and one of the most usual forms of agreement which does not constitute a contract appears to me to be the arrangements which are made between husband and wife. It is quite common, and it is the natural and inevitable result of the relationship of husband and wife, that the two spouses should make arrangements between themselves — agreements such as are in dispute in this action — agreements for allowances, by which the husband agrees that he will pay to his wife a certain sum of money, per week, or per month, or per year, to cover either her own expenses or the necessary expenses of the household and of the children of the marriage, and in which the wife promises either expressly or impliedly to apply the allowance for the purpose for which it is given. To my mind those agreements, or many of them, do not result in contracts at all, and they do not result in contracts even though there may be what as between other parties would constitute consideration for the agreement. The consideration, as we know, may consist either in some right, interest, profit or benefit accruing to one party, or some forbearance, detriment, loss or responsibility given, suffered or undertaken by the other. That is a well-known definition, and it constantly happens, I think, that such arrangements made between husband and wife are arrangements in which there are mutual promises, or in which there is consideration in form within the definition that I have mentioned. Nevertheless they are not contracts, and they are not contracts because the parties did not intend that they should be attended by legal consequences. To my mind it would be of the worst possible example to hold that agreements such as this resulted in legal obligations which could be enforced in the Courts. It would mean this, that when the husband makes his wife a promise to give her an allowance of 30*s*. or 2*l*. a week, whatever he can afford to give her, for the maintenance of the household and children, and she promises so to apply it, not only could she sue him for his failure in any week to supply the allowance, but he could sue her for non-performance of the obligation, express or implied, which she had undertaken upon her part. All I can say is that the small Courts of this country would have to be multiplied one hundredfold if these arrangements were held to result in legal obligations. They are not sued upon, not because the parties are reluctant to enforce their legal rights when the agreement is broken, but because the parties, in the inception of the arrangement, never intended that they should be sued upon. Agreements such as these are outside the realm of contracts altogether. The common law does not regulate the form of agreements between spouses. Their promises are not sealed with seals and sealing wax. The consideration that really obtains for them is that natural love and affection which counts for so little in these cold Courts. The terms may be repudiated, varied or renewed as performance proceeds or as disagreements develop, and the principles of the common law as to exoneration and discharge and accord and satisfaction are such as find no place in the domestic code. The parties themselves are advocates, judges, Courts, sheriff's officer and reporter. In respect of these promises each house is a domain into which the King's writ does not seek to run, and to which his officers do not seek to be admitted. The only question in this case is whether or not this promise was of such a class or not. For the reasons given by my brethren it appears to me to be plainly established that the promise here was not intended by either party to be attended by legal consequences. I think the onus was upon the plaintiff, and the plaintiff has not established any contract. The parties were living together, the wife intending to return. The suggestion is that the husband bound himself to pay 30*l.* a month under all circumstances, and she bound herself to be satisfied with that sum under all circumstances, and, although she was in ill-health and alone in this country, that out of that sum she undertook to defray the whole of the medical expenses that might fall upon her, whatever might be the development of her illness, and in whatever expenses it might involve her. To my mind neither party contemplated such a result. I think that the parol evidence upon which the case turns does not establish a contract. I think that the letters do not evidence such a contract, or amplify the oral evidence which was given by the wife, which is not in dispute. For these reasons I think the judgment of the Court below was wrong and that this appeal should be allowed.

[Duke L.J. agreed.]

QUESTIONS

1. How much is the wife claiming?
2. Has there been reliance? Could the wife have protected herself without relying on the agreement?
3. Was the wife's reliance reasonable?
4. Would you think that the husband would have been (a) surprised, (b) unfairly surprised by being held liable?
5. Are there better reasons for the decision than are given in the judgments?

JONES v. PADAVATTON

[1969] 2 All E.R. 616. Court of Appeal, England; Danckwerts, Salmon and Fenton Atkinson L.JJ.

[The plaintiff was the mother of the defendant. The parties came from Trinidad. The daughter lived in Washington, D.C. with her son, Tommy. She had a job at the Indian Embassy. The mother was very anxious for her daughter to get called to the English bar. She told her daughter that she would support her while she studied for the bar at the rate of $200 per month. (The daughter thought that the mother meant $U.S., the mother paid in Western Indian dollars. The daughter, however, ultimately accepted the amount that the mother paid.) In 1962 the daughter went to England to study for the bar. In 1964 the arrangement was changed. The mother bought a house for her daughter to live in, and which could also be rented. The daughter was to live off the rental income. The daughter married in 1965. By 1967 the daughter had hardly progressed at all in her studies for the bar. In that year the mother came to England and tried to recover possession of the house. She eventually commenced proceedings to recover possession. The trial judge dismissed the mother's claim for possession, and, on the daughter's counter-claim awarded her the value of repairs to the house made by her. The mother appealed.]

Danckwerts L.J. . . . Before us a great deal of time was spent on discussions as to what were the terms of the arrangements between the parties, and it seemed to me that the further the discussions went, the more obscure and uncertain the terms alleged became. The acceptable duration of the daughter's studies was not finally settled, I think. There was a lack of evidence on the matter, and the members of the court were induced to supply suggestions based on their personal knowledge. At any rate, two questions emerged for argument: (i) Were the arrangements (such as they were) intended to produce legally binding agreements, or were they simply family arrangements depending for their fulfilment on good faith and trust, and not legally enforceable by legal proceedings? (ii) Were the arrangements made so obscure and uncertain that, though intended to be legally binding, a court could not enforce them?

Counsel for the daughter argued strenuously for the view that the parties intended to create legally binding contracts.... Counsel for the mother argued for the contrary view that there were no binding obligations, and that if there were they were too uncertain for the court to enforce. His stand-by was *Balfour v. Balfour.* The principles involved are very well discussed in CHESHIRE AND FIFOOT ON CONTRACT (6th Edn.), at pp. 94-96. Of course, there is no difficulty, if they so intend, in members of families entering into legally binding contracts in regard to family affairs. A competent equity draftsman would, if properly instructed, have no difficulty in drafting such a contract. But there is possibly in family affairs a presumption against such an intention (which, of course, can be rebutted). I would refer to ATKIN, L.J.'s magnificent exposition in regard to such arrangements in *Balfour v. Balfour.*

There is no doubt that this case is a most difficult one, but I have reached a conclusion that the present case is one of those family arrangements which depend on the good faith of the promises which are made and are not intended to be rigid, binding agreements. *Balfour v. Balfour* was a case of husband and wife, but there is no doubt that the same principles apply to dealings between other relations, such as father and son and daughter and mother. This, indeed, seems to me a compelling case. The mother and the daughter seem to have been on very good terms before 1967. The mother was arranging for a career for the daughter which she hoped would lead to success. This involved a visit to England in conditions which could not be wholly foreseen. What was required was an arrangement which was to be financed by the mother and was such as would be adaptable to circumstances, as it in fact was. The operation about the house was, in my view, not a completely fresh arrangement, but an adaptation of the mother's financial assistance to the daughter due to the situation which was found to exist in England. It was not a stiff contractual operation any more than the original arrangement.

In the result, of course, on this view, the daughter cannot resist the mother's rights as the owner of the house to the possession of which the mother is entitled. What the position is as regards the counterclaim is another matter. It may be, at least in honesty, that the daughter should be re-imbursed for the expenditure which she had incurred. In my opinion, therefore, the appeal should be allowed.

Salmon, L.J.: I agree with the conclusion at which DANCKWERTS, L.J., has arrived, but I have reached it by a different route. The first point to be decided is whether or not there was ever a legally binding agreement between the mother and the daughter in relation to the daughter's reading for the Bar in England. The daughter alleges that there was such an agreement, and the mother denies it. She says that there was nothing but a loose family arrangement which had no legal effect. The onus is clearly on the daughter. There is no dispute that the parties entered into some sort of arrangement. It really depends on: (a) whether the parties intended it to be legally binding; and (b) if so, whether it was sufficiently certain to be enforceable.

Did the parties intend the arrangement to be legally binding? This question has to be solved by applying what is sometimes (although perhaps unfortunately) called an objective test. The court has to consider what the parties said and wrote in the light of all the surrounding circumstances, and then decide whether the true inference is that the ordinary man and woman, speaking or writing thus in such circumstances, would have intended to create a legally binding agreement.

Counsel for the mother has said, quite rightly, that as a rule when arrangements are made between close relations, for example, between husband and wife, parent and child or uncle and nephew in relation to an allowance, there is a presumption against an intention of creating any legal relationship. This is not a presumption of law, but of fact. It derives from experience of life and human nature which shows that in such circumstances men and women usually do not intend to create legal rights and obligations, but intend to rely solely on family ties of mutual trust and affection. This has all been explained by ATKIN, L.J., in his celebrated judgment in *Balfour v. Balfour*. There may, however, be circumstances in which this presumption, like all other presumptions of fact, can be rebutted.

. . .

In the present case the learned county court judge, having had the advantage of seeing the mother and the daughter in the witness box, entirely accepted the daughter's version of the facts. He came to the conclusion that on these very special facts the true inference must be that the arrangement between the parties prior to the daughter's leaving Washington were intended by both to have contractual force. On the facts as found by the learned county court judge this was entirely different from the ordinary case of a mother promising her daughter an allowance whilst the daughter read for the Bar, or a father promising his son an allowance at university if the son passed the necessary examinations to gain admission. The daughter here was 34 years of age in 1962. She had left Trinidad and settled in Washington as long ago as 1949. In Washington she had a comfortable flat and was employed as an assistant accountant in the Indian embassy at a salary of $500 a month (over £2,000 a year). This employment carried a pension. She had a son of seven years of age who was an American citizen, and had, of course, already begun his education. There were obviously solid reasons for her staying where she was. For some years prior to 1962, however, the mother, who lived in Trinidad, had been trying hard to persuade her to throw up all that she had achieved in Washington and go to London to read for the Bar. The mother would have been very proud to have a barrister for a daughter. She also thought that her plan was in the interest of her grandson, to whom she was much attached. She envisaged that, after the daughter had been called to the Bar, she would practise in Trinidad and thereafter presumably she (the mother) would be able to see much more of the daughter than formerly. The daughter was naturally loath to leave Washington, and did not regard the mother's suggestion as feasible. The mother, however, eventually persuaded the daughter to do as she wished by promising her that, if she threw up her excellent position in Washington and came to study for the Bar in England, she would pay her daughter an allowance of $200 a month until she had completed her studies.

The mother's attorney in Trinidad wrote to the daughter to confirm this. I cannot think that either intended that if, after the daughter had been in London, say, for six months, the mother dishonoured her promise and left her daughter destitute, the daughter would have no legal redress.

In the very special circumstances of this case, I consider that the true inference must be that neither the mother nor the daughter could have intended that the daughter should have no legal right to receive, and the mother no legal obligation to pay, the allowance of $200 a month.

The point was made by counsel for the mother that the parties cannot have had a contractual intention since it would be unthinkable for the daughter to be able to sue the mother if the mother fell on hard times. I am afraid that I am not impressed by this point. The evidence which the learned county court judge accepted showed that the mother was a woman of some substance, and prior to the agreement had assured the daughter that there would be no difficulty in finding the money. The fact that, if contrary to everyone's expectation the mother had lost her money, the daughter would have been unlikely to sue her throws no light on whether the parties had an intention to contract. The fact that a contracting party is in some circumstances unlikely to extract his pound of flesh does not mean that he has no right to it. Even today sometimes people forbear from mercy to enforce their undoubted legal rights.

The next point made by counsel for the mother was that the arrangements between the mother and the daughter in 1962 were too uncertain to constitute a binding contract. It is true that the mother said $200 a month without stipulating whether she meant West Indian or United States dollars. Obviously she meant West Indian dollars. The daughter says that she thought her mother meant United States dollars. This point does not, however, appear to have given rise to any difficulty. For two years from November 1962 until December 1964 the mother regularly paid her daughter £42, the equivalent of $ (West Indian) 200, a month, and the daughter accepted this sum without demur. Then it is said on the mother's behalf that the daughter's obligations are not sufficiently stated. I think that they are plain, to leave Washington, with all that entailed, come to London and genuinely study for the Bar there. If the daughter threw up her studies for the Bar, maybe the mother could not have recovered damages, but she would have been relieved of any obligation to continue the allowance.

Then again it is said that the duration of the agreement was not specified. No doubt, but I see no difficulty in implying the usual term that it was to last for a reasonble time. The parties cannot have contemplated that the daughter should go on studying for the Bar and draw the allowance until she was seventy, nor on the other hand that the mother could have discontinued the allowance if the daughter did not pass her examinations within, say, 18 months. The promise was to pay the allowance until the daughter's studies were completed, and to my mind there was a clear implication that they were to be completed within a reasonable time. Studies are completed either by the student being called to the Bar or giving up the unequal struggle against the examiners. It may not be easy to decide, especially when there is a paucity of evidence, what is a reasonable time. The daughter, however, was a well-educated intelligent woman capable of earning the equivalent of over £2,000 a year in Washington. It is true that she had a young son to look after, and may well (as the learned judge thought) have been hampered to some extent by the worry of this litigation. But, making all allowance for these factors and any other distraction, I cannot think that a reasonable time could possibly exceed five years from November 1962, the date when she began her studies.

It follows, therefore, that on no view can she now in November 1968 be entitled to anything further under the contract which the learned county court judge, rightly I think, held that she made with the mother in 1962. She has some of Part I of the Bar examination still to pass, and necessarily the final has not yet even been attempted.

During a visit to England in 1964 the mother found that her daughter was living in one room in Acton costing £6 17s. 6d. a week. This rent represented about three-quarters of the daughter's total income. The mother therefore hit on the idea of buying a house in London in which the daughter could live more comfortably and cheaply than in Acton. The rest of the house was to be let off in furnished rooms or flats and after paying the out-goings the daughter was to pay herself the maintenance and remit any balance that there might be to her mother in Trinidad. This scheme, so long as it lasted, provided a convenient method of paying the £42 a month due under the 1962 agreement. Accordingly, the mother acquired no. 181, Highbury Quadrant for £6,000 or so in December 1964. The daughter moved in in the following month, furnished and equipped the house largely by hire-purchase, and tenants began to arrive in February 1965.

The learned county court judge has concluded that in December 1964 the original contract between the mother and the daughter was varied, or a new contract was entered into whereby the daughter acquired the right to stay on in the mother's home indefinitely, whether the mother liked it or not. I am afraid that I cannot accept this conclusion. It was for the daughter to make out such a variation or new contract. In my view she totally failed to do so.

There is no evidence that the mother bargained away her right to dispose of her house, or to evict the daughter (who was a mere licensee) whenever she wished to do so. The evidence shows that all the arrangements in relation to the house were very vague and made without any contractual intent. By this arrangement the mother was trying primarily to help the daughter, and also perhaps to make a reasonable investment for herself. When the mother brought the arrangement to an end (as she was entitled to do at any time) she would, of course, have to go on paying £42 a month as long as the 1962 agreement lasted. There is no evidence to suggest that the mother intended the daughter ever to have more than the equivalent of $ (West Indian) 200 a month after December 1964. Nothing was said as to how much the daughter might pay herself out of the rents for maintenance. Certainly she would have to debit herself with some reasonable figure in respect of her accommodation, no doubt something less than £6 17s. 6d. a week that she had been spending in Acton, but not less, I should think, than about £5 a week. This would leave about £22 a month to be deducted from the rents for maintenance up till November 1967 when in my view the 1962 agreement ran out. In fact for nearly four years, that is, from December 1964 until today, the mother had not received a penny from the daughter in respect of no. 181, Highbury Quadrant nor, in spite of repeated requests, any proper accounts.

I am not at all surprised that the mother's patience became exhausted in

March 1967 when she gave notice determining her daughter's licence to remain in the house. The daughter ignored the notice and has continued in occupation with her husband and son, apparently with the intention of doing so indefinitely. She is still there. She seems to take the view (as does the learned county court judge) that she has a legal claim on the mother to house her and contribute to her support and that of her son and husband, perhaps in perpetuity. In this she is mistaken, and so in my judgment is the learned county court judge. The mother began this action for possession of no. 181, Highbury Quadrant in 1967. For the reasons I have indicated, there is in my view no defence to the action, and I would accordingly allow the appeal.

The learned county court judge has referred the counterclaim. If this reference is pursued, it will involve an account being meticulously taken of all receipts and expenditures from December 1964 until the date on which the daughter yields up possession. This will certainly result in a great waste of time and money, and can only exacerbate ill-feeling between the mother and the daughter. With a little goodwill and good sense on both sides, this could and should be avoided by reaching a reasonable compromise on the figures. I can but express the hope that this may be done, for it would clearly be to the mutual benefit of both parties.

[Fenton Atkinson L.J. gave a judgment to the same effect.]

QUESTIONS

1. Suppose that one year after the daughter had come to England, the mother refused to pay any more, what would have happened,
   (a) under the approach of Danckwerts L.J.;
   (b) under the approach of Salmon L.J.?
2. Which result is preferable?
3. Does this say anything about the utility of the approach found in *Balfour v. Balfour*?

In *Berryere v. Berryere* (1972), 26 D.L.R. (3d) 764 (B.C.S.C.), a mother's claim for payment from her daughter for looking after the daughter's child was dismissed. Ruttan J. held that there had been no intention to create a legally binding relationship. He made reference to both *Balfour v. Balfour* and *Jones v. Padavatton*; and spoke of the presumption against an intention to enter a legally binding contract when the parties are closely related.

What reasons are there for the presumption that Ruttan J. refers to?

SIMPKINS v. PAYS

[1955] 3 All E.R. 10.

Sellers, J.: Happily this is an unusual type of case to come before a court of law, and it arises out of what seems to be a popular occupation of the public — competing in a competition in a Sunday newspaper. In this particular case there was a contest, No. 397, in the "Sunday Empire News" of June 27, 1954, a competition whereby readers were invited to place, in order of merit, eight fashions, or articles of attire. The plaintiff and the defendant, along with the defendant's grand-daughter, sent in a coupon with three forecasts on it. The middle line of the second forecast chanced to be successful, as appeared in the publication of the same newspaper on Sunday, July 4, 1954. This coupon won the prize of £750, being apparently the only coupon containing what was said to be the correct forecast, and this action is brought to recover one-third of that amount, £250.

The plaintiff had been living in the defendant's house from some time in 1950, since some six months after the defendant's husband died. The defendant, who gave evidence here, was a lady of some eighty-three years of age. The plaintiff was much younger. They lived together in harmony, the plaintiff paying a weekly sum for her board and lodging to the defendant. I am satisfied that the plaintiff was greatly interested in betting and in competing, where chance was an element, for some fortuitous prize, and she had been competing for some time in newspaper competitions, including those in the "News of the World" and the "Sunday Empire News", before she went to these premises. When she became a lodger at the defendant's premises she found that the defendant was competing in the "News of the World" competitions, and they seem to have joined forces. At the same time, however, until about the beginning of May, 1954, the plaintiff, apparently unbeknown to the defendant, was filling up alone, week by week, a similar sort of competition in the "Sunday Empire News", which she kept in her room. About the beginning of May, 1954, something happened which brought the two parties to this action to take an interest in the "Sunday Empire News". They do not give the same version as to how that came about, and it does not matter very much, except that it may assist one in trying to see where the truth lies. The plaintiff says that she left a copy of the "Sunday Empire News" in the living room of the house occupied by the defendant and that the defendant took it up, took an interest in it and discussed competing in the competition in the paper. The defendant says that it was the plaintiff who brought the paper down and said: "Why don't you compete in this as well?" It may be that the truth lies somewhere between the two, but on the whole I think that the plaintiff's version is the preferable one, and that, when the defendant did get to know about the paper and they were discussing it, the plaintiff may have said to her: "Well, why don't you compete?"

The result of it was that each week for the next seven or eight weeks the two parties to this action, together with the defendant's grand-daughter, Miss Esme Pays, sent in a coupon with forecasts on it. As far as the "Sunday Empire News" is concerned, I am satisfied that the method of doing this was for the defendant to make her forecast, put it on a piece of paper, for the grand-daughter to make hers and put it on the same piece of paper, and then, when the plaintiff came home, perhaps rather late at night, when the defendant was in bed, the plaintiff would pick this piece of paper up and would fill in the coupon in her own room, putting her own line in first, then putting the grand-daughter's line in second, and the defendant's line in third, and the coupon would be dispatched on the Monday. The evidence is a little uncertain as to who actually paid for the necessary stamps for the postage, or for the twopence-halfpenny stamps which had to be sent for each line forecast. On the final week, the winning week, payment was, I think, made by the plaintiff, but it was not a matter between them of much moment. The amount involved was not very great, and I accept the plaintiff's evidence that the payment was made by each of them more or less alternately, and possibly the defendant paid more frequently. It depended a little on who most frequently had the stamps. There was no hard and fast rule. In regard to the winning coupon, the defendant had asked the plaintiff to get the stamps and deduct the amount from her weekly payment for board and lodging, but, apparently, it was not deducted. The weekly payment was 30s., and, as I understood the defendant, the plaintiff paid 30s. that week. There may have been a little confusion there; I do not think it matters. The entrance money is not a vital matter in this sort of transaction. It might well be done informally, one party paying one time, the other party paying another time. It might be the case that, in fact, all the stamps were bought and paid for by the defendant. The substantial matter was, on what basis were these forecasts being made?

On each of the occasions when the plaintiff made out the coupon during those seven or eight weeks, she put down the forecasts in the way which I have indicated, and entered in the appropriate place on the coupon, "Mrs. Pays, 11, Trevor Street, Wrexham", that is to say, the defendant's name and address, as if the coupon had been the defendant's. There were, in fact, three forecasts on each coupon, and I accept the plaintiff's evidence that, when the matter first came to be considered, what was said, when they were going to do it in that way, was: "We will go shares", or words to that effect. Whether that was said by the plaintiff or by the defendant does not really matter. "Shares" was the word used, and I do not think anything very much more specific was said. I think that that was the basis of the arrangement; and it may well be that the plaintiff was right when she said in her evidence, that the defendant said: "You're lucky, May, and if we win we will go shares".

If my conclusion that there was an arrangement to share any prize money is not correct, the alternative position to that of these three persons competing together as a "syndicate", as counsel for the plaintiff put it, would mean that the plaintiff, despite her propensity for having a gamble, suddenly abandoned all her interest in the competition in the "Sunday Empire News" when the defendant became interested, and handed the competition over to the defendant. I think that that is most improbable, and I accept the plaintiff's evidence that she did not do that. She combined her efforts with the defendant's in the way which I have indicated, and from then onwards she had shares in the result. In a family circle — and this household had some element of a family circle about it although there was no relationship between the plaintiff and the defendant and her grand-daughter — or even among very close friends, the facts might indicate that, if anyone rendered a service to an old lady in filling up her coupon, that person also intended to render a service by making some forecasts, and, in such a case, all that the other person was doing was to help the old lady to make her forecasts, and to give her the benefit of the other person's skill or capacity to guess, whichever it is, so that the venture would be entirely that of the person in whose name the coupon was sent. On the facts of this case, and on the probabilities as I see them, I do not think that that was what happened here, and I prefer the plaintiff's evidence to that given on behalf of the defendant as to how the arrangement came into being, and how it was carried out.

[HIS LORDSHIP reviewed the evidence, and continued:] Although the coupon sent in the defendant's name was successful, the competition was not, in fact, won by the forecast of either the plaintiff or the defendant, because the middle line was composed, not by either of the parties, but by the defendant's grand-daughter. The defendant's case involves that, which-ever forecast won — whether it was the plaintiff's or the defendant's, or the grand-daughter's — the whole prize was to go to the defendant. I think that that is highly improbable.

On the finding of fact that the plaintiff's evidence is right as to what was said about the shares, learned counsel for the defendant not unnaturally said: "Even if that is so, the court cannot enforce this contract unless the arrangement made at the time was one which was intended to give rise to legal consequences". It may well be there are many family associations where some sort of rough and ready statement is made which would not, in a proper estimate of the circumstances, establish a contract which was contemplated to have legal consequences, but I do not so find here. I think that in the present case there was a mutuality in the arrangement between the parties. It was not very formal, but certainly it was, in effect, agreed that every week the forecast should go in in the name of the defendant, and that if there was success, no matter who won, all should share equally. It seems to be the implication from, or the interpretation of, what was said that this was in the nature of a very informal syndicate so that they should all get the benefit of success. It would, also, be wrong, I think, to say from what was arranged that, because the grand-daughter's forecast was the one which was successful of those submitted by the defendant, the plaintiff and the defendant should receive nothing. Although the grand-daughter was not a party before the court and I have not had the benefit of her evidence, on this arrangement she would, in my opinion, be as entitled to a third share as the others, because, although she was not, apparently, present when this bargain was made, both the others knew, at any rate soon after the outset, that she was coming in. It is possible, of course, although the plaintiff is not concerned in this, that the grand-daughter's effort was only to assist the defendant. The grand-daughter may accept that, but it makes no difference to the fact that the plaintiff and the defendant entered into an agreement to share, and, accordingly the plaintiff was entitled to one-third. I so find and give judgment for the amount of £250.

Judgment for the plaintiff.

QUESTIONS

1. What are the pressures towards enforcement in this case?
2. Is there reliance here?

LLEWELLYN: WHAT PRICE CONTRACT? AN ESSAY IN PERSPECTIVE

(1931) 40 Yale L.J. 704, 741-744.

Consideration

But with us the machinery evolved fits both descriptions; the much discussed requirement, and sufficiency, of a consideration. In purpose consideration surely approximates closely the rough description given above of *causa*: any sufficient justification for court-enforcement. In broad effects, that purpose is accomplished. In detail, however, the machinery is embarrassed by a number of rules not too well designed to meet the purpose, yet sufficiently crystallized to make continuous trouble in such cases as involve them.

Neither causes nor processes of the development of the consideration concept are at all clear in detail. We do not know how the Germanic system of awarding what one may speak of as the advantage of proof to the apparently sounder side came to degenerate into the debt-defendant's power as of right to swear himself out of judgment. We do not know whether the fear of stout swearers or the growth of commercial transactions was the more vital factor in developing assumpsit; we know little if anything of the details of the latter pressure on the courts from, say, 1570 to 1620. We do not know in any clarity the process by which the case-misfeasance-tort root and the *quid-pro-quo* root out of debt were built together. What is clear, is the emergence of a current definition in terms of benefit to the promisor or detriment to the promisee as the agreed equivalent and inducing cause of the promise; a definition which purports both to show what is adequate and what is necessary to a successful action in assumpsit or its heirs. The current formulation has the merit of covering most cases, even if it does not cover all. Indeed it is obvious that as soon as the arbitrary but utterly necessary logical jump is made, of making mutual promises serve to support each other, the great bulk of business promises are comfortably cared for.

Four troublesome classes of cases remain. There are business promises such as "firm offers," understood to be good for a fixed time, but revoked before. They are frequent; they are and should be relied on. As to them our consideration doctrine is badly out of joint. Closely related in orthodox doctrine, less so in practice, is the second class: promises which call for acceptance by extended action (such as laying twenty miles of track), revoked while the work is in process. A third and hugely important class is that of either additional or modifying business promises made after an original deal has been agreed upon. Law and logic go astray whenever such dealings are regarded as truly comparable to new agreements. They are not. No business man regards them so. They are going-transaction adjustments, as different from agreement-formation as are corporate organization and corporate management; and the line of legal dealing with them which runs over waiver and estoppel is based on sound intuition. The fourth main trouble-making class has only a doctrinal connection with business; it lies chiefly in the field of family affairs; it includes the promise made and relied on, but which did not bargain for reliance, and in the case of promises to provide it laps over into the third party beneficiary problem. As to all of these classes but the first, a distinct but very uneven tendency is observable in the courts to strain by one dodge or another toward enforcement. That tendency is healthy. It may be expected to increase. It has already had some effects on orthodox doctrine, (*e.g.*, RESTATEMENT OF CONTRACTS (Am. L. Inst. 1927) §§ 45, 90, 135.) and may be expected to have more. Meanwhile the first class mentioned goes largely untouched.

When one attempts to estimate the net value of the consideration requirement the first step is to repeat that it does fit most normal cases in life, that it gives trouble only on the fringes. As a test of what promises *not* to enforce, it must be regarded as somewhat formalistic. The existence of bargain equivalency does indeed commonly evidence positively that the promise was deliberate — considered — meant. Such equivalency gives also fair ground for believing that *some* promise was in fact made; and thereby much reduces the danger from possible perjury, and even from misunderstanding. The giving of a bargain equivalent, be it by promise or by action, is furthermore an excellent objective indication not only of the creation of expectation in the promisee, but of the reasonableness of there being expectation, and of its being related to the promise. (And the size of the equivalent may help to "interpret" the expectation.) Yet it will be observed that the handing over of a signed promise in writing (which is *not* enough for enforcement) would go far in most circumstances to assure the same values; no lawyer, *e.g.,* can fail to be struck by the closeness with which exemptions from the requirement of writing under the statute of frauds are related to the presence of unambiguous consideration which is *substantially equivalent in fact* to the promise claimed. Nor is it apparent why in many cases deliberateness, due assurance that the promise was made and relied on, and properly so, might not all be evidenced by circumstances apart from either writing or consideration. The problem is acute only within the family. Outside, a writing might well be made a condition to "reasonableness" of any reliance; though very possibly, as with the statute of frauds on sales an exception might be needed for pretty transactions. All in all, then, as a test for non-enforcement, our consideration requirement must be regarded as not yet wholly just to our needs.

As a positive test, a test for what promises *to* enforce, the same must be said. For here the requirement of the positive law runs in terms not of *factual* equivalency, but of *formal* equivalency under the bargain as stated. A consideration which in fact is largely, even wholly formal, may be enough; release of injury-claim for a dollar. This is well enough when the promise is one whose enforcement is in itself socially desirable: a charitable subscription, a promise to provide for a child on marriage, an option to buy land. And it is enforcement in such cases which has given foothold for the draftsmen in cases of a — socially — different character. But when the courts in such cases recognize in general language the adequacy of thoroughly formal consideration, they obscure the problem discussed above, as to government by contract; the same problem so clearly seen by the courts in usury and mortgage cases, and by the legislature in regulation of employment: that of discrepancy in bargaining power and semi-duress in fact. Though obscured, that problem recurs. It is therefore not surprising that the last quarter century has seen — in business cases — the incursion into the doctrine of consideration of a further doctrine of so-called "mutuality" whereby particular promises are matched off against each other, and some equivalency in fact (*e.g.,* to buy if the other party has agreed to sell) frequently insisted on, even when formally adequate consideration is present. It is to be expected that this tendency will continue: and it is not unlikely that it will develop, as in the past, peculiarly to relieve the weaker bargainer. The lop-sidedness of bargain-result is thus taken as the mark of lop-sidedness of bargain-making. But the motivation being apparently not wholly conscious, the result has been (as so often during case-law growth) confusion in doctrine and uncertainty in outcome; and — natural enough in a business economy — a relief of smaller business men which finds little counterpart in the case of the laborer.

CHAPTER 3

MAKING THE CONTRACT

A. Introduction

In many of the cases that we have examined so far, it was apparent that the parties had conducted fairly lengthy negotiations before they reached an agreement that could then be enforced. We saw a hint of such negotiations in cases like *Sunshine Exploration v. Dolly Varden Mines supra*, and *Gilbert Steel v. University Construction supra*. In this chapter we shall be focussing on the process of negotiation. Before any contract can be enforced, it has to be decided that there is the kind of contract that the law will enforce — that was the focus of the last chapter — and that the parties have reached enough agreement that there can be said to be a contract. It is clear, for example, that, if a seller wants to sell something for $1,200 and the buyer will only pay $1,000, there is no agreement on the price, and that it would be difficult to enforce any contract in such circumstances.

In this chapter we will examine several cases where the parties engaged in a process of negotiation that eventually appeared to result in an agreement. The question before the court will be whether or not there was such a measure of agreement that there is an enforceable contract. In many situations, however, it is obviously false to suggest that there is any negotiation. If one wants to fly from Toronto to Vancouver there can be no dickering about the price of the ticket or any of the terms of the contract. The ticket is offered on a "take-it-or-leave-it" basis. The same goes for many of the contracts that we as consumers might make with many of the businesses from which we buy anything. For example, there is little or no room for dickering over the terms of one's telephone service, over a car-rental agreement, over one's Chargex agreement, etc. When rules of law that have been developed to handle the contract created through a process of negotiation are projected into these kinds of situations odd things can happen. We shall begin in this chapter to examine a phenomenon that will occupy much of our time in this course — the mass-produced contract.

Many of the cases in this chapter are 50 to 100 years old. There are two reasons for this. One is that the law in this area was settled by decisions of the courts at that time, and the other is that the rules that were settled then were peculiarly durable and, for reasons that are not wholly clear, have a peculiar fascination for lawyers. (In this regard, you might read the extract at the end of Section B3 and the article from which it is taken.)

It should be clear by now that the role of the lawyer is not just that of advising his clients what they can do when something goes wrong. It is much more that of advising his clients how to do things so that problems won't occur, or, if they do, so that they can be handled more easily or with more predictable results. As you read these cases you must always consider how you could have helped the parties to avoid the problems that came up.

The rules of law in this area are stated in fairly simple terms that appear to offer easy, black-letter solutions to most issues. This is an illusion. Behind the rules are some very complex problems of understanding how the rules work in real life and, in particular, how they operate in the context of the judicial process that is provided for the resolution of disputes. There will be many cases where the power of the judge to find facts will have the effect of leaving the so-called rules very imprecise and haphazard in their operation. There will be examples of "definitions" which turn out to be conclusions. Running through many of the cases (especially the older ones) will be ideas about the basis for contractual liability that are a curious blend of doctrinal belief and commercial convenience. The untangling of these elements and the understanding of what is going on are the purposes of this chapter.

The group of cases that follow raise a problem that we shall return to throughout the course. This is the problem of what to do when the parties appear to have reached agreement but, when, on further investigation, it turns out that they were "agreed about different things". What should the court do in such circumstances? There are a number of possibilities:

1. Hold the parties to what appeared to be the agreement?
2. Do this only if doing so protects one of the parties, who, in the circumstances, is entitled to protection?
3. Refuse to enforce the agreement because there was no "real" agreement?

Sometimes, as a solution, it will be suggested that the courts will look at the "objective" meaning of the parties. "Subjective" meanings are then not to be given effect to. It is important to realize that this cannot be the final answer. It is difficult, however, to know when it is the answer and when it is not. Subjective meanings cannot be ignored.

Consider the following case:

A says to B, "I will sell you my cow for $100". B, knowing that A meant to say "horse" and that the word "cow" is a slip of the tongue, says, "I accept".

Is there a contract? If so, is it for the horse or the cow?

The original *Restatement* took the position that there was no contract. The *Restatement (Second)* says that in these circumstances there is a sale of the horse and not of the cow. Is there any difficulty in supporting this conclusion? Is the agreement as enforced based on the subjective or objective meanings of the parties?

Few actual cases raise facts quite as clear as this. The next few cases raise the problem in various ways. The important question in these cases can be worded in one of two ways. One can ask either, (1) is there any good reason why the person who is seeking to escape the consequences of the apparent contract should be able to do so? or, (2) which side should be stuck with the meaning attached to a word or phrase used by the other? These two questions will be picked up later, the first in connection with mistake (one party may have made a mistake) and the second as part of the problem of the interpretation of contracts. Here the questions bear on the problem of the court's response to agreement (apparent or real). The fact that we will return to these questions is simply a further example of the inter-relationship of all contractual problems and solutions.

HOBBS v. ESQUIMALT AND NANAIMO RAILWAY CO.

(1899), 29 S.C.R. 450. Supreme Court of Canada.

APPEAL from a decision of the Supreme Court of British Columbia [6 B.C.R. 228] varying the decree at the trial which declared the plaintiff entitled to a conveyance but not to specific performance:

The action was brought by the appellant to enforce specific performance of an agreement by the railway company to sell to him certain land in British Columbia. The agreement is contained in the following document delivered to appellant in pursuance of his request for an allotment.

"ESQUIMALT & NANAIMO RAILWAY CO. — LAND DEPARTMENT."

VICTORIA, B.C., NOV. 28th, 1889.

"Received of Frank Vicker Hobbs, the sum of one hundred and twenty dollars ($120.00), being a first payment on account of his purchase from the E. & N. Ry. Company of one hundred and sixty (160) acres of land in Bright District, at the Price of three dollars ($3.00) an acre. Commencing at a point about two (2) miles west of Louis Stark's Crown Grant in Cranberry District; thence running west forty chains to Berkeley Creek; thence south 40 chains; thence east 40 chains, thence north 40 chains to place of commencement, the balance of purchase money to be paid in three equal instalments of seventy-five (75) cents an acre, at the expiration of one, two and three years from date, with interest at the rate of 6 per cent per annum."

(Sgd.)   JOHN TRUTCH,

"Land Commissioner."

The question in dispute between the parties is whether or not the railway company, in executing the conveyance to carry out this agreement, is entitled to reserve the minerals in the land therein described.

The company claims that Mr. Trutch had no authority to convey the minerals, and that in its forms of conveyance the word land is always used to mean surface rights only. The trial Judge held that the claim as to want of authority was well founded, but that the company had ratified the agreement. As he was of opinion, however, that the ratification was made under a mistake as to the legal effect of the agreement he refused to decree specific performance but declared in his judgment that the plaintiff was entitled at his option to a conveyance as offered by defendants or to repayment of the purchase money with interest and compensation for improvements. The plaintiff appealed and the decree was varied by a direction that the plaintiff was entitled to a conveyance reserving the minerals without option of repayment. The plaintiff then appealed to this court.

King J. — The facts are stated in the judgment of the late Chief Justice Davie before whom the case was tried.

It is found by him that Mr. Trutch acted beyond the scope of his authority in agreeing to a sale of the land without reservation of the minerals, but that the contract so made was rectified [*sic*] by the company. He, however, was of opinion that, in so ratifying it, the company were under a mistake as to its legal effect, and upon this ground he declined to compel performance but left the plaintiff to his common law remedy for breach of contract.

A first question is as to whether there was, by reason of the alleged mistake, a contract at all.

.   .   .

Here the parties were *ad idem* as to the terms of the contract. It was expressed in perfectly unambiguous language in the offer of the plaintiff and in the acceptance of defendants, and the alleged difference is in a wholly esoteric meaning which one of them gives to the plain words.

. . .

The alleged mistake is given in the evidence of Mr. Dunsmuir, the vice-president of the company. Speaking of the contract entered into by Mr. Trutch, he says:

> It only sold the surface. That is, we term it land in our office. We do not say surface right, we say land, land minus the minerals.

It is evident then that we may put Mr. Trutch aside, and treat the case on this point as if the company, upon an application by plaintiff for purchase of the 160 acres of land, had entered into an agreement to sell the land in the identical words used by Mr. Trutch. In effect they say:

> We agreed to sell the land, but this means land reserving the minerals.

It may well be that in the administration of their varied business a loose but convenient form of speech may have been used in the office, but it is not stated that it was supposed to be a correct one, and it appears incredible that a company, a large part of whose business is that of a land company, could reasonably suppose that in dealings with third persons for the sale of land, the word "land" means land with reservations of minerals. Mr. Trutch does not say that he misconceived the meaning of the word. His impression was that he had verbally notified the plaintiff that the minerals were to be reserved, and if he had done so the plaintiff would be precluded from obtaining the specific performance he seeks; but it has been found that notice was not given. The form of the company conveyances expressly reserving the minerals show that they were aware how to effect such object. The alleged mistake was therefore an unreasonable and careless one, and in view of the fact that the plaintiff went into possession under the contract, I do not think that it can be said to be unconscionable or highly unreasonable to enforce the specific performance of the contract.

Taschereau J. [dissenting]: I would dismiss this appeal. The reasons given in the courts below against the appellant's right to specific performance are, in my opinion, unanswerable. There has been no contract between this company and Hobbs. The company thought they were selling the land without the minerals; Hobbs thought he was buying the land with the minerals. So that the company did not sell what Hobbs thought he was buying, and Hobbs did not buy what the company thought they were selling. Therefore there was no contract between them. Hobbs would not have bought if he had known that the company were selling only surface rights, and the company would not have sold if they had thought that Hobbs intended to buy the land with the minerals. The ratification by the company stands upon no better ground. It was nothing but the ratification of a sale without the minerals. . . .

The rule that any one dealing with another has the right to believe that this other one means what he says, or says what he means, is one that cannot be gainsaid. But it has no application here. Assuming that the agent sold the land with the minerals, he did what he had not the power to do. However, he did not do it.

I would dismiss the appeal with costs.

[Gwynne, Sedgewick and Girouard JJ. agreed with King J. An appeal to the Privy Council was dismissed upon settlement: 31 S.C.R. xxviii].

QUESTIONS

1. Do King J. and Taschereau J. have the same view of the purpose of contracts?
2. Do they agree on the role of the court when asked to enforce an agreement?

HENKEL v. PAPE

(1870), L.R. 6 Exch. 7. Kelly C.B. Bramwell, Pigott and Cleasby BB.

DECLARATION for goods bargained and sold, and for goods sold and delivered.

Pleas, first, except as to 7*l*. never indebted; and, secondly, as to 7*l*. payment into Court. The plaintiffs accepted the money paid into Court, and joined issue on the first plea.

The plaintiffs are gun manufacturers in London and Birmingham, and the defendant is a gun-maker at Newcastle-upon-Tyne. On the 4th of June, 1870, the plaintiffs received from the defendant the following letter:— "Send sample Snider, with sword-bayonet, forward immediately. I can fix an order for fifty, I think, and it may lead to many large orders. Can you do them at 34*s*. nett cash on delivery, so as to secure the order? I shall have to cut very fine, and several will be in for it." In reply the plaintiffs wrote: "We have forwarded you this day sample Snider, with sword-bayonet. We cannot possibly do them for less than 35*s*. nett cash." With this letter the sample was sent. On the 7th of June the plaintiffs received the following telegram purporting to come from the defendant: "Send by mail immediately *the* Snider rifles same as pattern. Must be here in the morning. Ship sails then." The plaintiffs on receipt of this communication sent fifty rifles to the defendant. On the 9th of June they received the following letter from him: "I am surprised that you sent fifty instead of three rifles. The telegram was to send *three*." In fact, the clerk who sent the telegraphic message had by mistake telegraphed the word "the" instead of "three." The defendant had written "three," and not "the," on the message paper. Under these circumstances the plaintiffs insisted on the defendant accepting the fifty rifles sent, but the defendant declined to take more than three. This action was then brought. The defendant paid a sum into court sufficient to cover the price of three rifles and their carriage. He denied his liability as to the residue of the plaintiffs' claim, contending that he could not be made responsible for the mistake of the telegraph clerk.

The cause was tried before Blackburn, J., at the Surrey Summer Assizes, 1870, when a verdict was directed for the defendant, with leave to move to enter a verdict for the plaintiffs for the invoice price of the remaining forty-seven rifles.

H. Thompson Chitty moved accordingly:—The telegraph clerk was the defendant's agent to transmit the message, and the defendant is responsible for the mistake in the transmission. Chitty on Contracts, 6th ed. p. 197. There is no privity between the plaintiffs and the telegraph clerk, nor can they proceed against the Post-office, his employers. ... Their right remedy is against the defendant. Suppose in a letter written by himself he had made the mistake, he would clearly have been liable; and in the transmission of each particular message the telegraph clerk is the agent of the sender. Upon the sender therefore must rest the responsibility of any error committed by the agent in the course of his employment.

Kelly, C.B. We are of opinion that in this case there should be no rule. The question is whether the defendant has entered into a contract to purchase fifty rifles, and there is no doubt he might have bound himself either by letter or a telegraphic message. But the Post-office authorities are only agents to transmit messages in the terms in which the senders deliver them. They have no authority to do more. Now in this case the evidence is that the defendant agreed to take three rifles, and three only, and he authorized the telegraph clerk to send a message to that and to no other effect. That being so, there was no contract between the plaintiffs and defendant for the purchase of fifty rifles. The defendant cannot be made responsible because the telegraph clerk made a mistake in the transmission of the message. There was no contract between the parties such as the plaintiffs rely on. The verdict therefore ought to stand.

[Bramwell, Pigott, and Cleasby BB., concurred.]

NOTE: At the date of *Henkel v. Pape*, the telegraph company would not have been liable to the plaintiff: *Dickson v. Reuter's Telegram Co. Ltd.* (1877), 2 C.P.D. 62 (C.A.) (England).

PROBLEMS AND QUESTIONS

1. Suppose that the things being sold are such that there is a considerable difference in value per item if they are sold in small quantities. Has the defendant any right to keep even the three that he wanted?

2. Pape asks Henkel to quote the price on a rifle for which Pape has a large potential market. Henkel quotes a price that is acceptable to Pape. Pape telegraphs to Henkel, "I offer to pay your price on 5,000 rifles, do you accept?" The telegram when received by Henkel reads 50. Henkel wires his acceptance. Pape sues for failure to deliver 4,950 rifles. What result?

RAFFLES v. WICHELHAUS

(1864), 2 H. & C. 906, 159 E.R. 375. Exchequer Court.

Declaration. For that it was agreed between the plaintiff and the defendants, to wit, at Liverpool, that the plaintiff should sell to the defendants, and the defendants buy of the plaintiff, certain goods, to wit, 125 bales of Surat cotton, guaranteed middling fair merchant's Dhollorah, to arrive ex "Peerless" from Bombay; and that the cotton should be taken from the quay, and that the defendants would pay the plaintiff for the same at a certain rate, to wit, at the rate of 17¼d. per pound, within a certain time then agreed upon after the arrival of the said goods in England. Averments: that the said goods did arrive by the said ship from Bombay in England, to wit, at Liverpool, and the plaintiff was then and there ready, and willing and offered to deliver the said goods to the defendants, &c. Breach; that the defendants refused to accept the said goods or pay the plaintiff for them.

Plea. That the said ship mentioned in the said agreement was meant and intended by the defendants to be the ship called the "Peerless," which sailed from Bombay, to wit, in October; and that the plaintiff was not ready and willing and did not offer to deliver to the defendants any bales of cotton which arrived by the last mentioned ship, but instead thereof was only ready and willing and offered to deliver to the defendants 125 bales of Surat cotton which arrived by another and different ship, which was also called the "Peerless," and which sailed from Bombay, to wit, in December.

Demurrer, and joinder therein.

Milward, in support of the demurrer. The contract was for the sale of a number of bales of cotton of a particular description, which the plaintiff was ready to deliver. It is immaterial by what ship the cotton was to arrive, so that it was a ship called the "Peerless." The words "to arrive ex 'Peerless,'" only mean that if the Vessel is lost on the voyage, the contract is to be at an end. [Pollock, C. B. It would be a question for the jury whether both parties meant the same ship called the "Peerless."] That would be so if the contract was for the sale of a ship called the "Peerless"; but it is for the sale of cotton on board a ship of that name. [Pollock, C. B. The defendant only bought that cotton which was to arrive by a particular ship. It may as well be said, that if there is a contract for the purchase of certain goods in warehouse A., that is satisfied by the delivery of goods of the same description in warehouse B.] In that case there would be goods in both warehouses; here it does not appear that the plaintiff had any goods on board the other "Peerless." [Martin B. It is imposing on the defendant a contract different from that which he entered into. Pollock, C. B. It is like a contract for the purchase of wine coming from a particular estate in France or Spain, where there are two estates of that name.] The defendant has no right to contradict by parol evidence a written contract good upon the face of it. He does not impute misrepresentation or fraud, but only says that he fancied the ship was a different one. Intention is of no avail, unless stated at the time of the contract. [Pollock, C. B. One vessel sailed in October and the other in December.] The time of sailing is no part of the contract.

Mellish (Cohen with him), in support of the plea. There is nothing on the face of the contract to shew that any particular ship called the "Peerless' was meant; but the moment it appears that two ships called the "Peerless" were about to sail from Bombay there is a latent ambiguity, and parol evidence may be given for the purpose of shewing that the defendant meant one "Peerless," and the plaintiff another. That being so, there was no consensus ad idem, and therefore no binding contract. He was then stopped by the Court.

Per Curiam. There must be judgment for the defendants.

QUESTIONS

1. If the court that decided *Raffles v. Wichelhaus* were to consider the question whether there was a sale of the horse or the cow (or neither), how do you think that they would have decided it?

2. Why is the court bothered by the possibility of ambiguity in this case? Is there any evidence that it mattered to anyone which ship the cotton came on?

The case is conventionally put under the rubric of mistake. For example, in Cheshire and Fifoot (9th ed.) p. 227, the case is explained as being one where the court could not determine the sense of the promise since the expressed terms were ambiguous because the parties had each made a mistake about the ship that the other side had meant.

Cheshire and Fifoot refer to this case as a "leading case". Is there not something very odd about a case that has a one line judgment becoming a "leading case". This is even more odd when the judges quite clearly had not the faintest idea of the argument of the counsel for the plaintiff. Notice how the argument was on a demurrer to the defendant's plea that the parties had meant different ships. The plaintiff is quite clearly saying, "So what?", to the defendant's argument.

Suppose that the price had gone up rather than down, which side then would be suing for breach? Would the arguments be the same? Would the result be the same? The case is discussed by Gilmore, *The Death of Contract*, pp. 35-39.

QUESTIONS

1. Could the method used in *Hobbs v. Esquimalt and Nanaimo R. Co.* be used in either *Raffles v. Wichelhaus*, or *Henkel v. Pape*?

2. Can these three cases be reconciled? Surely if Cheshire and Fifoot maintain that there was a mistake in *Raffles v. Wichelhaus* (they do not refer to *Henkel v. Pape*) there was a mistake in *Hobbs v. Esquimalt and Nanaimo R. Co.*

PROBLEM

A and B are merchants who communicate in code. They do this to save money (the messages can be shorter than they would be in plain language) and to keep their business dealings secret. A sends an offer to B in the code which B translates as, "will charter ship, 'Peerless' for two voyages from Bombay to London for $200,000 per voyage", B accepts. In fact the message should have read, one voyage and not two. Is there a contract?

Consider the following cases. Do you think that any of these should result in contracts?

1. Jean bought a horse for $500. She took it for a ride the next day and it threw her twice. She came back to the stable quite disgusted and offered it to anyone for $10. Bob, a good friend, of Jean, knowing what she had paid for it, accepted.

2. Suppose that Jean gave Bob the horse and he took it home with him to his stable. That night the horse was killed in a fire. Could Jean sue Bob for the value of the horse?

3. Would it make any difference if Bob had not been a friend of Jean and had not known what she paid for the horse?

Do you think that any of these problems are satisfactorily resolved by the following provision of *Restatement Second*:

§ 21A. Effect of Misunderstanding.

(1) There is no manifestation of mutual assent to an exchange if the parties attach materially different meanings to their manifestations and

    (a)   neither party knows or has reason to know the meaning attached by the other; or

    (b)   each party knows or each party has reason to know the meaning attached by the other.

(2) The manifestations of the parties are operative in accordance with the meaning attached to them by one of the parties if

    (a)   that party does not know of any different meaning attached by the other, and the other knows the meaning attached by the first party; or

    (b)   that party has no reason to know of any different meaning attached by the other, and the other has reason to know the meaning attached by the first party.

B. The Classical Theory of Offer and Acceptance

(1) Introduction

In the cases that we have just discussed there was at least the appearance of an agreement. The next cases examine the anatomy of agreement more closely. As we have seen, there can be no contract if a seller will only sell something for $1,200 and the buyer will only pay $1,000. The more usual problem is that the parties may have agreed on the majority of the terms of the contract but not on all. The question then is whether there can be a contract. The way in which the common law (and most legal systems) have solved this problem is to require that one side put *all* the terms on which he is prepared to do business in a proposal to the other. This is called the offer. The offeree then has the opportunity to reject the offer or not. If he accepts, then a contract is made.

This structure looks well in theory: it is another matter, however, to impose it on the process of negotiation actually undertaken by the parties. There are a number of related issues that have to be kept in mind:

1. To what extent is the court justified in requiring the parties to fit their negotiations into the process that the rules require?
2. To what extent do the rules reflect real concerns that arise when the process of negotiation does not run smoothly?
3. What are the respective responsibilities of the parties and the court in filling in any blanks that might remain?
4. To what extent is the court's expressed concern for doctrinal consistency a reflection of unarticulated functional concerns?

(2) What is an offer?

JOHNSTON BROS. v. ROGERS BROS.

(1899), 30 O.R. 150. Divisional Court

The judgment of the Court was delivered by

Falconbridge, J.:— The facts and the correspondence are fully set out in the very careful judgment of the learned Judge.

I shall not refer to the second and third grounds of appeal further than to say that they have been fully considered, and, to my mind, satisfactorily disposed of, by the trial Judge.

The real crux of the case is whether there is a contract.

Leaving out the matters of inducement (in both the legal and the ordinary sense) in the letter of the 26th, the contract, if there is one, is contained in the following words:

Letter defendants to plaintiffs.
"26th April, 1898.

We quote you, F. O. B. your station, Hungarian $5.40 and strong Bakers $5.00, car lots only, and subject to sight draft with bill of lading."

Telegram plaintiffs to defendants.
"27th April, 1898.

We will take 2 cars Hungarian at your offer of yesterday."

I should have expected to find American authority as to the phrase "we quote you," which must be in very common use amongst brokers, manufacturers, and dealers in the United States; but we were referred to no decided case, and I have found none where that phrase was used.

In the American and English Encyclopaedia of Law, 2nd ed., vol. 7, p. 138, the law is stated to be: "A quotation of prices is not an offer to sell, in the sense that a complete contract will arise out of the mere acceptance of the rate offered or the giving of an order for merchandize in accordance with the proposed terms. It requires the acceptance by the one naming the price, of the order so made, to complete the transaction. Until thus completed there is no mutuality of obligation."

Of the cases cited in support of this proposition, *Moulton v. Kershaw* (1884), 59 Wis. 316.; 48 Am. Rep. 516, is the nearest to the present one, but in none is the word "quote" used.

The meaning of "quote" is given in modern dictionaries as follows:

Standard — (Com.) To give the current or market price of, as bonds, stocks, commodities, etc.

Imperial, ed. 1884 — In *com.*, to name, as the price of an article; to name the current price of; as, what can you quote sugar at?

Century — (Com.) To name as the price of stocks, produce, etc.; name the current price of.

Webster — (Com.) To name the current price of.

Worcester — To state as the price of merchandize.

See also Black's Law Dictionary, *sub tit.* "Quotation."

There is little or no difference between any of these definitions. Now if we write the equivalent phrase into the letter — "We give you the current or market price, F. O. B. your station, of Hungarian Patent $5.40 . . . — " can it be for a moment contended that it is an offer which needs only acceptance in terms to constitute a contract?

The case of *Harty v. Gooderham* (1871), 31 U. C. R. 18, is principally relied on by the plaintiffs. But that case presents more than one point of distinction. There the first inquiry was from the plaintiff, which, I think, is an element in the case. He writes the defendants to let him "know your lowest prices for 50 O.P. spirits," etc. To which defendants answered, mentioning prices and particulars: "Shall be happy to have an order from you, to which we will give prompt attention," which the Court held to be equivalent to saying "We will sell it at those prices. Will you purchase from us and let us know how much?" And so the contract was held to be complete on the plaintiff's acceptance.

But there is no such offer to sell in the present defendants' letter. *Harvey v. Facey*, [1893] A. C. 552, is strong authority against the plaintiffs.

I have not overlooked the concluding paragraph of the letter, viz., "We would suggest your using the wire to order, as prices are so rapidly advancing that they may be beyond reach before a letter would reach us." The learned Judge considers this to be one of the matters foreign to a mere quotation of prices. I venture, on the contrary, to think that this suggestion is more consistent with, and perhaps consistent only with, a mere quotation of prices, which might vary from day to day or from hour to hour. There could be no question of the prices becoming "beyond reach" in a simple offer to sell at a certain price.

In my opinion, the plaintiffs have failed to establish a contract, and this appeal must be allowed with costs, and the action dismissed with costs.

·   ·   ·

QUESTIONS

1. What do you think that each party intended by the first communication that each made?

2. Suppose that in *Harty v. Gooderham* the plaintiff had ordered 1,000,000 gallons — or about 10 years' purchase of the defendant's distillery — would the defendant have been surprised to find himself in such a bargain? Is this relevant?

3. What is the relevance of the dictionary meanings of "quote"?

4. How would you use this case in any case in which you might be involved today?

In *Harvey v. Facey*, [1893] A.C. 552 (P.C.) the plaintiff sent the defendant the following telegram, "Will you sell us Bumper Hall Pen? Telegraph lowest cash price — answer paid". The defendant replied, "Lowest price for Bumper Hall Pen £900". The plaintiff then telegraphed, "We agree to buy Bumper Hall Pen for the sum of £900 asked by you." The Privy Council, on appeal from the Supreme Court of Jamaica, held that there was no contract. The plaintiff's first telegram asked two questions, and the defendant answered only one.

How could this case be authority for or against either party in *Johnston Bros. v. Rogers Bros.*?

DENTON v. GREAT NORTHERN R. CO.
(1856), 5 E. & B. 860, 119 E.R. 701. Queen's Bench.

[The plaintiff wished to go from London to Hull via Peterborough. He consulted a timetable published by the defendant. Some time before the timetable was published the defendant knew that this journey was not possible at the time that the plaintiff wished to travel. The timetables were published without alteration. The plaintiff sued to recover damages that he had suffered by his late arrival in Hull.]

Lord Campbell C.J. This is a case of some importance, both as regards the public and the railway companies. It seems to me that the representations made by railway companies in their time tables cannot be treated as mere waste paper; and in the present case I think the plaintiff is entitled to recover, on the ground that there was a contract with him, and also on the ground that there was a false representation by the Company.

It seems to me that, if the Company promised to give tickets for a train, running at a particular hour to a particular place, to any one who would come to the station and tender the price of the ticket, it is a good contract with any one who so comes. I take it to be clear that the issuing of the time tables in this way amounts in fact to such a promise; any one who read them would so understand them. Then, is it a good contract in law? The consideration is one which is a prejudice to the person who makes his arrangements with a view to the fulfilment of the contract, and comes to the station on the faith of it. Is it not then within the principle of those cases in which it has been held that an action lies on a contract to pay a reward? There the promise is to the public at large, exactly as it is here; it is in effect the same as if made to each individual conditionally; and, on an individual fulfilling the condition, it is an absolute contract with him, and he may sue. That being so, there is, I think, a contract; and there is no excuse shewn for breaking it. It is immaterial that the defendants are not owners of the line the whole way to Hull. It is admitted to have been often rightly held that, where there is a ticket taken out to go to a station, the contract binds the Company issuing the ticket, though it is not specified how much of the line over which the journey is to be belongs to that Company. Then reliance is placed on the class of cases which decide that an absolute contract must be fulfilled whatever happens, which, it is said, shews that there cannot be a contract here. But from the nature of the contract I think there might be implied exceptions. A carrier by sea excepts the perils of the sea. It may be from the nature of this contract that the perils of the railroad are excepted. I see no inconvenience likely to arise from holding this a contract. It is put, as an example of inconvenience, that a shipowner who has advertised that his ship is bound for Calcutta as a general ship, and that he will take on board goods brought to her, would be liable to an action if when goods were brought on the faith of the advertisement he said he had got a better freight, and was now bound for Jamaica; but I see no reason why he should not be liable. It seems to me, therefore, that this is a contract, and that the plaintiff who has acted on it has his remedy on that ground. But on the other ground there is no doubt. The statement in the time tables was untrue, and was made so as to be what the law calls a fraudulent representation. It was not the original printing that was blameable: but, after notice that the train was withdrawn, the defendants continue, down to the 25th March, to issue these tables. Was not that a representation that there was such a train? And, as they knew it had been discontinued for some time, was it not a false representation? It is all one as if a person, duly authorized by the Company, had, knowing it was not true, said to the plaintiff: "there is a train from Milford Junction to Hull at that hour." The plaintiff believes this, acts upon it, and sustains loss. It is well established law that, where a person makes an untrue statement, knowing it to be untrue, to another who is induced to act upon it, an action lies. The facts bring the present case within that rule.

(Coleridge J. was absent.)

Wightman J. It seems to me that the publication of these time tables amounted to a promise to any one of the public who would come to the station and pay for a ticket, that he shall have one by the train at seven. It is said that this will make the Company liable though there be inevitable accidents. But the provision at the foot of the time tables protects the Company in cases of delay by accident, though the proviso does not apply to the present case where the train is altogether taken off.

But, whether there be a contract or not, the defendants are liable as having induced the plaintiff by a continued knowingly false representation to believe that there was a train at seven to Hull, which he, believing, acted upon to his prejudice. All the essentials for an action for a false representation are here. The representation is untrue; it is known by the persons making it to be untrue; it is calculated to induce the plaintiff to act; and he, believing it, is induce to act accordingly.

Crompton J. I also think that the plaIntiff is entitled to judgment.

I entirely agree in what has been said by my Lord and my brother Wightman, that an action in the nature of an action for deceit lies here. The Company makes a fresh statement at every moment whilst they continue to hold out these time tables as their's. I am besides much inclined to think that they are liable also on the ground that they have committed a breach of their duty as public carriers. A public carrier of goods must carry according to his public profession; I think, however, that there has been no decision that carriers of passengers are under the same obligation; though in Story on Bailments, s. 591, it is said they are. I cannot doubt that the defendants publicly professed to be carriers of passengers by this train; and therefore I am inclined to think an action would lie on that ground. But I am not prepared to say that there is a contract. As I agree that the defendants are liable, there is no occasion to decide this; and it is true that the cases as to the recovery of rewards have an analogy to this case. But there is a difference: where a reward is offered, it is generally offered to procure a service which is entirely performed by the party claiming the reward. I never was able to see any good reason why in such cases he might not sue for work and labour done at the request of the defendant. But in the present case, or in that which might be put of a shopkeeper advertising that he had cheap goods in his shop, I doubt if the labour of coming to the station, or of crossing the threshold of the shop, really is part of the consideration at all. If it be, it is a very small one. I agree, however, that any consideration, however small, will support a promise; and perhaps the difference between me and my Lord and my brother Wightman is rather as to the fact than the law. I doubt whether the promise here in fact was in consideration of coming to the station. If it was, I see difficulty in saying that the shopkeeper does not promise to have his wares for those who will take the trouble to leave the street and come into his shop. But it is quite unnecessary for the decision of this case to come to a determination on that. I am clearly of opinion that the action lies as for a false representation. I think, though less decidedly, that it lies on the ground of their duty as public carriers of passengers to act up to their public profession. But I doubt whether they are answerable on a contract to do all that may be found in the time tables, if there be anything there beyond what would be implied as part of their duty as carriers.

Judgment for plaintiff.

QUESTION

If you had been counsel to the defendant what would you have done after this case? Draft any clauses that you would recommend the company to add to its published timetable.

LEFKOWITZ v. GREAT MINNEAPOLIS SURPLUS STORE

(1957), 86 N.W. 2d 689. Supreme Court of Minnesota.

Murphy, Justice:— This is an appeal from an order of the Municipal Court of Minneapolis denying the motion of the defendant for amended findings of fact, or, in the alternative, for a new trial. The order for judgment awarded the plaintiff the sum of $138.50 as damages for breach of contract.

This case grows out of the alleged refusal of the defendant to sell to the plaintiff a certain fur piece which it had offered for sale in a newspaper advertisement. It appears from the record that on April 6, 1956, the defendant published the following advertisement in a Minneapolis newspaper:

> "Saturday 9 A.M. Sharp
> 3 Brand New
> Fur
> Coats
> Worth to $100.00
> First Come
> First Served
> $1
> Each"

On April 13, the defendant again published an advertisement in the same newspaper as follows:

> "Saturday 9 A.M.
> 2 Brand New Pastel
> Mink 3-Skin Scarfs
> Selling for $89.50

> Out they go
> Saturday. Each....$1.00
> 1 Black Lapin Stole
> Beautiful,
> worth $139.50....$1.00
> First Come
> First served"

The record supports the findings of the court that on each of the Saturdays following the publication of the above-described ads the plaintiff was the first to present himself at the appropriate counter in the defendant's store and on each occasion demanded the coat and the stole so advertised and indicated his readiness to pay the sale price of $1. On both occasions, the defendant refused to sell the merchandise to the plaintiff, stating on the first occasion that by a "house rule" the offer was intended for women only and sales would not be made to men, and on the second visit that plaintiff knew defendant's house rules.

The trial court properly disallowed plaintiff's claim for the value of the fur coats since the value of these articles was speculative and uncertain. The only evidence of value was the advertisement itself to the effect that the coats were "Worth to $100.00," how much less being speculative especially in view of the price for which they were offered for sale. With reference to the offer of the defendant on April 13, 1956, to sell the "1 Black Lapin Stole ... worth $139.50..." the trial court held that the value of this article was established and granted judgment in favour of the plaintiff for that amount less the $1 quoted purchase price.

1. The defendant contends that a newspaper advertisement offering items of merchandise for sale at a named price is a "unilateral offer' which may be withdrawn without notice. He relies upon authorities which hold that, where an advertiser publishes in a newspaper that he has a certain quantity or quality of goods which he wants to dispose of at certain prices and on certain terms, such advertisements are not offers which become contracts as soon as any person to whose notice they may come signifies his acceptance by notifying the other that he will take a certain quantity of them. Such advertisements have been construed as an invitation for an offer of sale on the terms stated, which offer, when received, may be accepted or rejected and which therefore does not become a contract of sale until accepted by the seller; and until a contract has been so made, the seller may modify or revoke such prices or terms.

. . . .

The defendant relies principally on *Craft v. Elder & Johnston Co.* [(1941), 38 N.E. 2d 417]. In that case, the court discussed the legal effect of an advertisement offering for sale, as a one-day special, an electric sewing machine at a named price. The view was expressed that the advertisement was... "not an offer made to any specific person but was made to the public generally. Thereby it would be properly designated as a unilateral offer and not being supported by any consideration could be withdrawn at will and without notice." It is true that such an offer may be withdrawn before acceptance. Since all offers are by their nature unilateral because they are necessarily made by one party or on one side in the negotiation of a contract, the distinction made in that decision between a unilateral offer and a unilateral contract is not clear. On the facts before us we are concerned with whether the advertisement constituted an offer, and, if so, whether the plaintiff's conduct constituted an acceptance.

There are numerous authorities which hold that a particular advertisement in a newspaper or circular letter relating to a sale of articles may be construed by the court as constituting an offer, acceptance of which would complete a contract....

The test of whether a binding obligation may originate in advertisements addressed to the general public is "whether the facts show that some performance was promised in positive terms in return for something requested." 1 Williston, Contracts (Rev. ed.) § 27.

The authorities above cited emphasize that, where the offer is clear, definite, and explicit, and leaves nothing open for negotiation, it constitutes an offer, acceptance of which will complete the contract.

· · ·

Whether in any individual instance a newspaper advertisement is an offer rather than an invitation to make an offer depends on the legal intention of the parties and the surrounding circumstances.

· · ·

We are of the view on the facts before us that the offer by the defendant of the sale of the Lapin fur was clear, definite, and explicit, and left nothing open for negotiation. The plaintiff having successfully managed to be the first one to appear at the seller's place of business to be served, as requested by the advertisement, and having offered the stated purchase price of the article, he was entitled to performance on the part of the defendant. We think the trial court was correct in holding that there was in the conduct of the parties a sufficient mutuality of obligation to constitute a contract of sale.

2. The defendant contends that the offer was modified by a "house rule" to the effect that only women were qualified to receive the bargains advertised. The advertisement contained no such restriction. This objection may be disposed of briefly by stating that, while an advertiser has the right at any time before acceptance, to modify his offer, he does not have the right, after acceptance, to impose new or arbitrary conditions not contained in the published offer....

QUESTION

Are the terms of the offer the same in both cases?

These cases bear a family resemblance to some of the cases discussed in Chapter 2. (*Balfour v. Balfour, etc.*) In this chapter, the question is whether or not the party who initiates the transaction had the intention to bind himself by what he did. The railway and the store may have been surprised by the conclusion that the court reached. What are the differences between the two kinds of cases that would justify the different results reached in, *e.g.*, a case like *Balfour v. Balfour* and the cases here?

The conclusion reached by the courts in these cases is that the defendant made an offer which the plaintiff accepted. It is quite clear that the parties could all have worded the "offers" differently and could have prevented the courts from concluding that they had made an offer. We have already considered what the railway company could have done, and clearly the store could have done something that would not have resulted in a binding contract had it chosen to do so. The investigation of what parties may have intended has the appearance of a factual inquiry (in much the same way as has the inquiry into what is "reasonable") but the question will always be how far such an inquiry can ever be factual.

PHARMACEUTICAL SOCIETY OF GREAT BRITAIN v. BOOTS CASH CHEMISTS (SOUTHERN) LTD.

[1953] 1 Q.B. 401. Court of Appeal.

APPEAL from Lord Goddard C.J.

Special case stated by the parties under R.S.C., Ord. 34, r. 1.

The defendants carried on a business comprising the retail sale of drugs at premises at Edgware, which were entered in the register of premises kept pursuant to section 12 of the Pharmacy and Poisons Act, 1933, and from which they regularly sold drugs by retail. The premises comprised a single room, so adapted that customers might serve themselves, and the business there was described by a printed notice at the entrance as "Boot's Self-"Service." On entry each customer passed a barrier where a wire basket was obtained. Beyond the barrier the principal part of the room, which contained accommodation for 60 customers, contained shelves around the walls and on an island fixture in the centre, on which articles were displayed. One part of the room was described by a printed notice as the "Toilet Dept.," and another part as the "Chemists' Dept." On the shelves in the chemists' department drugs, including proprietary medicines, were severally displayed in individual packages or containers with a conspicuous indication of the retail price of each. The drugs and proprietary medicines covered a wide range, and one section of the shelves in the chemists' department was devoted exclusively to drugs which were included in, or which contained substances included in, Part I of the Poisons List referred to in section 17 (1) of the Pharmacy and Poisons Act, 1933; no such drugs were displayed on any shelves outside the section, to which a shutter was fitted so that at any time all the articles in that section could be securely inclosed and excluded from display. None of the drugs in that section came within Sch. I to the Poisons Rules, 1949 (S.I. 1949, No. 539).

The staff employed by the defendants at the premises comprised a manager, a registered pharmacist, three assistants and two cashiers, and during the time when the premises were open for the sale of drugs the manager, the registered pharmacist, and one or more of the assistants were present in the room. Each customer selected from the shelves the article which he wished to buy and placed it in the wire basket; in order to leave the premises the customer had to pass by one of two exits, at each of which was a cash desk where a cashier was stationed who scrutinized the articles selected by the customer, assessed the value and accepted payment. The chemists' department was under the personal control of the registered pharmacist, who carried out all his duties at the premises subject to the directions of a superintendent appointed by the defendants in accordance with the provisions of section 9 of the Act.

The pharmacist was stationed near the poisons section, where his certificate of registration was conspicuously displayed, and was in view of the cash desks. In every case involving the sale of a drug the pharmacist supervised that part of the transaction which took place at the cash desk and was authorized by the defendants to prevent at the stage of the transaction, if he thought fit, any customer from removing any drug from the premises. No steps were taken by the defendants to inform the customers, before they selected any article which they wished to purchase, of the pharmacist's authorization.

On April 13, 1951, at the defendants' premises, two customers, following the procedure outlined above, respectiVely purchased a bottle containing a medicine known as compound syrup of hypophosphites, containing 0.01% W/V strychnine, and a bottle containing medicine known as famel syrup, containing 0.23% W/V codeine, both of which substances are poisons included in Part I of the Poisons List, but, owing to the small percentages of strychnine and codeine respectively, hypophosphites and famel syrup do not come within Sch. I to the Poisons Rules, 1949.

The question for the opinion of the court was whether the sales instanced on April 13, 1951, were effected by or under the supervision of a registered pharmacist, in accordance with the provisions of section 18 (1) (*a*) (iii) of the Pharmacy and Poisons Act, 1933.

> Pharmacy and Poisons Act, 1933, s. 18:
> (1)... it shall not be lawful — (*a*) for a person to sell any poison included in Part I of the Poisons List, unless — (i) he is an authorized seller of poisons; and (ii) the sale is effected on premises duly registered under Part I of this Act; and (iii) the sale is effected by, or under the supervision of, a registered pharmacist.

The Lord Chief Justice answered the question in the affirmative.
The Pharmaceutical Society appealed.

Somervell L.J.:— This is an appeal from a decision of the Lord Chief Justice on an agreed statement of facts, raising a question under section 18 (1) (*a*) (iii) of the Pharmacy and Poisons Act, 1933. The plaintiffs are the Pharmaceutical Society, incorporated by Royal charter. One of their duties is to take all reasonable steps to enforce the provisions of the Act. The provision in question is contained in section 18. [His Lordship read the section and stated the facts, and continued:] It is not disputed that in a chemist's shop where this self-service system does not prevail a customer may go in and ask a young woman assistant, who will not herself be a registered pharmacist, for one of these articles on the list, and the transaction may be completed and the article paid for, although the registered pharmacist, who will no doubt be on the premises,will not know anything himself of the transaction, unless the assistant serving the customer, or the customer, requires to put a question to him. It is right that I should emphasize, as did the Lord Chief Justice, that these are not dangerous drugs. They are substances which contain very small proportions of poison, and I imagine that many of them are the type of drug which has a warning as to what doses are to be taken. They are drugs which can be obtained, under the law, without a doctor's prescription.

The point taken by the plaintiffs is this: it is said that the purchase is complete if and when a customer going round the shelves takes an article and puts it in the receptacle which he or she is carrying, and that therefore, if that is right, when the customer comes to the pay desk, having completed the tour of the premises, the registered pharmacist, if so minded, has no power to say: "This drug ought not to be sold to this customer." Whether and in what circumstances he would have that power we need not inquire, but one can, of course, see that there is a difference if supervision can only be exercised at a time when the contract is completed.

I agree with the Lord Chief Justice in everything that he said, but I will put the matter shortly in my own words. Whether the view contended for by the plaintiffs is a right view depends on what are the legal implications of this layout — the invitation to the customer. Is a contract to be regarded as being completed when the article is put into the receptacle, or is this to be regarded as a more organized way of doing what is done already in many types of shops — and a bookseller is perhaps the best example — namely, enabling customers to have free access to what is in the shop, to look at the different articles, and then, ultimately, having got the ones which they wish to buy, to come up to the assistant saying "I want this"? The assistant in 999 times out of 1,000 says "That is all right," and the money passes and the transaction is completed. I agree with what the Lord Chief Justice has said, and with the reasons which he has given for his conclusion, that in the case of an ordinary shop, although goods are displayed and it is intended that customers should go and choose what they want, the contract is not completed until, the customer having indicated the articles which he needs, the shopkeeper, or someone on his behalf, accepts that offer. Then the contract is completed. I can see no reason at all, that being clearly the normal position, for drawing any different implication as a result of this layout.

The Lord Chief Justice, I think, expressed one of the most formidable difficulties in the way of the plaintiffs' contention when he pointed out that, if the plaintiffs are right, once an article has been placed in the receptacle the customer himself is bound and would have no right, without paying for the first article, to substitute an article which he saw later of a similar kind and which he perhaps preferred. I can see no reason for implying from this self-service arrangement any implication other than that which the Lord Chief Justice found in it, namely, that it is a convenient method of enabling customers to see what there is and choose, and possibly put back and substitute, articles which they wish to have, and then to go up to the cashier and offer to buy what they have so far chosen. On that conclusion the case fails, because it is admitted that there was supervision in the sense required by the Act and at the appropriate moment of time. For these reasons, in my opinion, the appeal should be dismissed.

This case arose out of a criminal prosecution. The relevance of the case to the general rules of contract has never been doubted. The case has been followed in prosecutions for "offering" certain prohibited goods for sale. The display of a switch-blade knife in a store window is not an offer for sale of the knife: *Fisher v. Bell*, [1960] 3 All E.R. 731: the display on a used-car dealer's lot of cars in violation of a statute was not an "offering for sale". *R. v. Bermuda Holdings Ltd.* (1969), 9 D.L.R. (3d) 595 (B.C.S.C.). Why should it be supposed that the word "offer" must have the same meaning in a case like *Johnston Bros. v. Rogers Bros.* and in prosecutions for unlawfully "offering" something for sale? What purpose does the court's inquiry in a case like *Johnston Bros. v. Rogers Bros.* serve? What is it for? If you displayed a switch-blade knife in a store window would you be surprised if you were convicted of "offering" one for sale? What is the purpose of display in a store window? Conversely, if a conviction were to be sustained in such circumstances, would that be any reason for saying that any display in a window is an offer for *all* purposes?

The result of the cases on the display of goods permitted a seller of goods to display goods that he had no intention of selling. A seller could thus entice people into his store and attempt to sell them other goods. This is known as "bait and switch" selling or advertising. This practice is now covered by the Combines Investigation Act, R.S.C. 1970, c. C-23 (as amended):

37(1) For the purposes of this section, "bargain price" means

   (a)   a price that is represented in an advertisement to be a bargain price, by reference to an ordinary price or otherwise; or

   (b)   a price that a person who reads, hears or sees the advertisement would reasonably understand to be a bargain price by reason of the prices at which the product advertised or like products are ordinarily sold.

(2) No person shall advertise at a bargain price a product that he does not supply in reasonable quantities having regard to the nature of the market in which he carries on business, the nature and size of the business carried on by him and the nature of the advertisement.

(3) Subsection (2) does not apply to a person who establishes that

   (a)   he took reasonable steps to obtain in adequate time a quantity of the product that would have been reasonable having regard to the nature of the advertisement, but was unable to obtain such a quantity by reason of events beyond his control that he could not reasonably have anticipated;

   (b)   he obtained a quantity of the product that was reasonable having regard to the nature of the advertisement, but was unable to meet the demand therefor because that demand surpassed his reasonable expectations; or

   (c)   after he became unable to supply the product in accordance with the advertisement, he undertook to supply the same product or an equivalent product of equal or better quality at the bargain price and within a reasonable time to all persons who requested the product and who were not supplied therewith during the time when the bargain price applied and that he fulfilled the undertaking.

(4) Any person who violates subsection (2) is guilty of an offence and is liable on summary conviction to a fine not exceeding twenty-five thousand dollars, or to imprisonment for one year or to both.

QUESTION

If the common law rule regarding the display of goods were different, would it forward, ignore or frustrate the purpose of s. 37?

(3) The Power of Acceptance

Once one party has made an offer, a power of acceptance is conferred on the other party. The first party, the offeror, has indicated to the other, the offeree, the terms on which he is prepared to deal. The offeree then has the opportunity of accepting or rejecting the terms that have been proposed. In a process of negotiation, the offeree may reject the offer outright or he may propose a modification and he then becomes the offeror and the other party has the power to accept or reject the new offer. Classical contracts theory requires that one party eventually become the offeror and the other, the offeree.

An offer, in the classical theory, must contain all the terms of the agreement and the acceptance, when made, must be a mirror image of the offer. Any variation from the terms of the offer in the acceptance results in a counter-offer, not an acceptance. That this must be so is clear in a case where two parties are dickering over the price of a car or a piece of land. But it is much less clear when the dickering involves a number of terms or where it is not obvious what will constitute acceptance of the offer.

The offeror controls the contract: he can set out all the terms in which he is prepared to do business, he can determine how the acceptance must be made.

ELIASON v. HENSHAW

(1819), 3 Wheaton, 225. U. S. Supreme Court.

Washington, Justice, delivered the opinion of the court. — This is an action, brought by the defendant in error, to recover damages for the non-performance of an agreement, alleged to have been entered into by the plaintiffs in error, for the purchase of a quantity of flour, at a stipulated price. The evidence of this contract, given in the court below, is stated in a bill of exceptions, and is to the following effect:

A letter from the plaintiffs to the defendant, dated the 10th of February 1813, in which they say: "Capt. Conn informs us, that you have a quantity of flour to dispose of. We are in the practice of purchasing flour at all times, in Georgetown, and will be glad to serve you, either in receiving your flour in store, when the markets are dull, and disposing of it, when the markets will answer to advantage, or we will purchase at market price, when delivered; if you are disposed to engage two or three hundred barrels at present, we will give you $9.50 per barrel, deliverable the first water, in Georgetown, or any service we can. If you should want an advance, please write us by mail, and will send you part of the money in advance." In a postcript, they add, "Please write by return of wagon, whether you accept our offer." This letter was sent from the house at which the writer then was, about two miles from Harper's Ferry, to the defendant, at his mill, at Mill Creek, distant about 20 miles from Harper's Ferry, by a wagoner then employed by the defendant to haul flour from his mill to Harper's Ferry, and then about to return home with his wagon. He delivered the letter to the defendant, on the 14th of the same month, to which an answer, dated the succeeding day, was written by the defendant, addressed to the plaintiffs, at Georgetown, and dispatched by a mail which left Mill Creek on the 19th, being the first regular mail from that place to Georgetown. In this letter the writer says, "Your favor of the 10th inst. was handed me by Mr. Chenoweth last evening. I take the earliest apportunity to answer it by post. Your proposal to engage 300 barrels of flour, delivered in Georgetown, by the first water, at $9.50 per barrel, I accept, shall send on the flour, by the first boats that pass down from where my flour is stored on the river; as to any advance, will be unnecessary — payment on delivery is all that is required."

On the 25th of the same month, the plaintiffs addressed to the defendant an answer to the above, dated at Georgetown, in which they acknowledge the receipt of it, and add, "Not having heard from you before, had quite given over the expectation of getting your flour, more particularly, as we requested an answer by return of wagon, the next day, and as we did not get it, had bought all we wanted." The wagoner, by whom the plaintiffs' first letter was sent, informed them, when he received it, that he should not probably return to Harper's Ferry, and he did not, in fact, return in the defendant's employ. The flour was sent down to Georgetown, some time in March, and the delivery of it to the plaintiffs was regularly tendered and refused.

Upon this evidence, the defendants in the court below, the plaintiffs in error, moved that court to instruct the jury, that if they believed the said evidence to be true, as stated, the plaintiff in this action was not entitled to recover the amount of the price of the 300 barrels of flour, at the rate of $9.50 per barrel. The court being divided in opinion, the instruction prayed for was not given. The question is, whether the court below ought to have given the instruction to the jury, as the same was prayed for? If they ought, the judgment, which was in favor of the plaintiff in that court, must be reversed.

It is an undeniable principle of the law of contracts, that an offer of a bargain by one person to another, imposes no obligation upon the former, until it is accepted by the latter, according to the terms in which the offer was made. Any qualification of, or departure from, those terms, invalidates the offer, unless the same be agreed to by the person who made it. Until the terms of the agreement have received the assent of both parties, the negotiation is open, and imposes no obligation upon either.

In this case, the plaintiffs in error offered to purchase from the defendant two or three hundred barrels of flour, to be delivered at Georgetown, by the first water, and to pay for the same $9.50 per barrel. To the letter containing this offer, they required an answer by the return of the wagon, by which the letter was dispatched. This wagon was, at that time, in the service of the defendant, and employed by him in hauling flour from his mill to Harper's Ferry, near to which place the plaintiffs then were. The meaning of the writers was obvious. They could easily calculate, by the usual length of time which was employed by this wagon, in travelling from Harper's Ferry to Mill Creek, and back again with a load of flour, about what time they should receive the desired answer, and therefore, it was entirely unimportant, whether it was sent by that, or another wagon, or in any other manner, provided it was sent to Harper's Ferry, and was not delayed beyond the time which was ordinarily employed by wagons engaged in hauling flour from the defendant's mill to Harper's Ferry. Whatever uncertainty there might have been as to the time when the answer would be received, there was none as to the place to which it was to be sent; this was distinctly indicated by the mode pointed out for the conveyance of the answer. The place, therefore, to which the answer was to be sent, constituted an essential part of the plaintiff's offer.

It appears, however, from the bill of exceptions, that no answer to this letter was at any time sent to the plaintiffs, at Harper's Ferry. Their offer, it is true, was accepted by the terms of a letter addressed Georgetown, and received by the plaintiffs at that place; but an acceptance communicated at a place different from that pointed out by the plaintiffs, and forming a part of their proposal, imposed no obligation binding upon them, unless they had acquiesced in it, which they declined doing. It is no argument, that an answer was received at Georgetown; the plaintiffs in error had a right to dictate the terms upon which they would purchase the flour, and unless they were complied with, they were not bound by them. All their arrangements may have been made with a view to the circumstance of place, and they were the only judges of its importance. There was, therefore, no contract concluded between these parties, and the court ought, therefore, to have given the instruction to the jury, which was asked for.

Judgment reversed, and cause remanded, with directions to award a *venire facias de novo.*

QUESTION

What do you think would have happened if the defendant had met the plaintiff and had said that he would accept?

The next cases raise the problem of the validity of an acceptance in a slightly different situation. The first two cases show that acceptance may be made in a way that does not call for notification to the offeror. The general form of the contract in these cases is similar to the "walk to York case" discussed earlier in *G.N.R. v. Witham.* The next two cases provide a gloss on these problems.

A common example of these kinds of contracts would be the standing offer that the T.T.C. (and other similar bodies) make to pay $100 for information leading to the arrest and conviction of vandals. The offer to pay the reward is an offer in the legal sense. Acceptance of such an offer can only be made by performing the act called for. Acceptance by the offeror is then performance.

WILLIAMS v. CARWARDINE

(1833), 4 B & Ad. 621, 110 E.R. 590, King's Bench.

Assumpsit to recover £20., which the defendant promised to pay to any person who should give such information as might lead to a discovery of the murder of Walter Carwardine. Plea, general issue. At the trial before Parke J., at the last Spring Assizes for the county of Hereford, the following appeared to be the facts of the case:— One Walter Carwardine, the brother of the defendant, was seen on the evening of the 24th of March 1831, at a public-house at Hereford, and was not heard of again till his body was found on the 12th of April in the river Wye, about two miles from the city. An inquest was held on the body on the 13th of April and the following days till the 19th; and it appearing that the plaintiff was at a house with the deceased on the night he was supposed to have been murdered, she was examined before the magistrates, but did not then give any information which led to the apprehension of the real offender. On the 15th of April the defendant caused a handbill to be published, stating that whoever would give such information as should lead to a discovery of the murder of Walter Carwardine should, on conviction, receive a reward of £20.; and any person concerned therein, or privy thereto, (except the party who actually committed the offence) should be entitled to such reward, and every exertion used to procure a pardon; and it then added, that information was to be given, and application for the above reward was to be made to Mr. William Carwardine, Holmer, near Hereford. Two persons were tried for the murder at the Summer Assizes 1831, but acquitted. Soon after this, the plaintiff was severely beaten and bruised by one Williams; and on the 23d of August 1831, believing she had not long to live, and to ease her conscience, she made a voluntary statement, containing information which led to the subsequent conviction of Williams. Upon this evidence it was contended, that as the plaintiff was not induced by the reward promised by the defendant, to give evidence, the law would not imply a contract by the defendant to defendant, to pay her the £20. The learned Judge was of opinion, that the plaintiff, having given the information which led to the conviction of the murderer, had performed the condition on which the £20. was to become payable, and was therefore entitled to recover it; and he directed the jury to find a verdict for the plaintiff, but desired them to find specially whether she was induced to give the information by the offer of the promised reward. The jury found that she was not induced by the offer of the reward, but by other motives.

Curwood now moved for a new trial. There was no promise to pay the plaintiff the sum of £20. That promise could only be enforced in favour of persons who should have been induced to make disclosures by the promise of reward. Here the jury have found that the plaintiff was induced by other motives to give the information. They have, therefore, negatived any contract on the part of the defendant with the plaintiff.

Denman C.J. The plaintiff, by having given information which led to the conviction of the murderer of Walter Carwardine, has brought herself within the terms of the advertisement, and therefore is entitled to recover.

Littledale J. The advertisement amounts to a general promise, to give a sum of money to any person who shall give information which might lead to the discovery of the offender. The plaintiff gave that information.

Parke J. There was a contract with any person who performed the condition mentioned in the advertisement.

Patteson J. I am of the same opinion. We cannot go into the plaintiff's motives. Rule refused.

CARLILL v. CARBOLIC SMOKE BALL CO.

[1893] 1 Q.B. 256, C.A. England; Lindley, Bowen and A.L. Smith L.JJ.

APPEAL from a decision of Hawkins, J.

The defendants, who were the proprietors and vendors of a medical preparation called "The Carbolic Smoke Ball," inserted in the *Pall Mall Gazette* of November 13, 1891, and in other newspapers, the following advertisement:

> "£100. reward will be paid by the Carbolic Smoke Ball Company to any person who contracts the increasing epidemic influenza, colds, or any disease caused by taking cold, after having used the ball three times daily for two weeks according to the printed directions supplied with each ball. £1000. is deposited with the Alliance Bank, Regent Street, shewing our sincerity in the matter.

> "During the last epidemic of influenza many thousand carbolic smoke balls were sold as preventives against this disease, and in no ascertained case was the disease contracted by those using the carbolic smoke ball.

> "One carbolic smoke ball will last a family several months, making it the cheapest remedy in the world at the price, 10*s*., post free. The ball can be refilled at a cost of 5*s*. Address, Carbolic Smoke Ball Company, 27, Princes Street, Hanover Square, London."

The plaintiff, a lady, on the faith of this advertisement, bought one of the balls at a chemist's, and used it as directed, three times a day, from November 20, 1891, to January 17, 1892, when she was attacked by influenza. Hawkins, J., held that she was entitled to recover the £100. The defendants appealed.

Lindley, L.J. [The Lord Justice stated the facts, and proceeded:—] I will begin by referring to two points which were raised in the Court below. I refer to them simply for the purpose of dismissing them. First, it is said no action will lie upon this contract because it is a policy. You have only to look at the advertisement to dismiss that suggestion. Then it was said that it is a bet. Hawkins, J., came to the conclusion that nobody ever dreamt of a bet, and that the transaction had nothing whatever in common with a bet. I so entirely agree with him that I pass over this contention also as not worth serious attention.

Then, what is left? The first observation I will make is that we are not dealing with any inference of fact. We are dealing with an express promise to pay £100. in certain events. Read the advertisement how you will, and twist it about as you will, here is a distinct promise expressed in language which is perfectly unmistakable — "£100. reward will be paid by the Carbolic Smoke Ball Company to any person who contracts the influenza after having used the ball three times daily for two weeks according to the printed directions supplied with each ball."

We must first consider whether this was intended to be a promise at all, or whether it was a mere puff which meant nothing. Was it a mere puff? My answer to that question is No, and I base my answer upon this passage: "£1000. is deposited with the Alliance Bank, shewing our sincerity in the matter." Now, for what was that money deposited or that statement made except to negative the suggestion that this was a mere puff and meant nothing at all? The deposit is called in aid by the advertiser as proof of his sincerity in the matter — that is, the sincerity of his promise to pay this £100. in the event which he has specified. I say this for the purpose of giving point to the observation that we are not inferring a promise; there is the promise, as plain as words can make it.

Then it is contended that it is not binding. In the first place, it is said that it is not made with anybody in particular. Now that point is common to the words of this advertisement and to the words of all other advertisements offering rewards. They are offers to anybody who performs the conditions named in the advertisement, and anybody who does perform the condition accepts the offer. In point of law this advertisement is an offer to pay £100. to anybody who will perform these conditions, and the performance of the conditions is the acceptance of the offer. That rests upon a string of authorities, the earliest of which is *Williams* v. *Carwardine*, which has been followed by many other decisions upon advertisements offering rewards.

But then it is said, "Supposing that the performance of the conditions is an acceptance of the offer, that acceptance ought to have been notified." Unquestionably, as a general proposition, when an offer is made, it is necessary in order to make a binding contract, not only that it should be accepted, but that the acceptance should be notified. But is that so in cases of this kind? I apprehend that they are an exception to that rule, or, if not an exception, they are open to the observation that the notification of the acceptance need not precede the performance. This offer is a continuing offer. It was never revoked, and if notice of acceptance is required ... the person who makes the offer gets the notice of acceptance contemporaneously with his notice of the performance of the condition. If he gets notice of the acceptance before his offer is revoked, that in principle is all you want. I, however, think that the true view, in a case of this kind, is that the person who makes the offer shews by his language and from the nature of the transaction that he does not expect and does not require notice of the acceptance apart from notice of the performance.

We, therefore, find here all the elements which are necessary to form a binding contract enforceable in point of law, subject to two observations. First of all it is said that this advertisement is so vague that you cannot really construe it as a promise — that the vagueness of the language shews that a legal promise was never intended or contemplated. The language is vague and uncertain in some respects, and particularly in this, that the £100.

is to be paid to any person who contracts the increasing epidemic after having used the balls three times daily for two weeks. It is said, When are they to be used? According to the language of the advertisement no time is fixed, and, construing the offer most strongly against the person who has made it, one might infer that any time was meant. I do not think that was meant, and to hold the contrary would be pushing too far the doctrine of taking language most strongly against the person using it. I do not think that business people or reasonable people would understand the words as meaning that if you took a smoke ball and used it three times daily for two weeks you were to be guaranteed against influenza for the rest of your life, and I think it would be pushing the language of the advertisement too far to construe it as meaning that. But if it does not mean that what does it mean? It is for the defendants to shew what it does mean; and it strikes me that there are two, and possibly three, reasonable constructions to be put on this advertisement, any one of which will answer the purpose of the plaintiff. Possibly it may be limited to persons catching the "increasing epidemic" (that is, the then prevailing epidemic), or any colds or diseases caused by taking cold, during the prevalence of the increasing epidemic. That is one suggestion; but it does not commend itself to me. Another suggested meaning is that you are warranted free from catching this epidemic, or colds or other diseases caused by taking cold, whilst you are using this remedy after using it for two weeks. If that is the meaning, the plaintiff is right, for she used the remedy for two weeks and went on using it till she got the epidemic. Another meaning, and the one which I rather prefer, is that the reward is offered to any person who contracts the epidemic or other disease within a reasonable time after having used the smoke ball. Then it is asked, What is a reasonable time? It has been suggested that there is no standard of reasonableness; that it depends upon the reasonable time for a germ to develop! I do not feel pressed by that. It strikes me that a reasonable time may be ascertained in a business sense and in a sense satisfactory to a lawyer, in this way; find out from a chemist what the ingredients are; find out from a skilled physician how long the effect of such ingredients on the system could be reasonably expected to endure so as to protect a person from an epidemic or cold, and in that way you will get a standard to be laid before a jury, or a judge without a jury, by which they might exercise their judgment as to what a reasonable time would be. It strikes me, I confess, that the true construction of this advertisement is that £100. will be paid to anybody who uses this smoke ball three times daily for two weeks according to the printed directions, and who gets the influenza or cold or other diseases caused by taking cold within a reasonable time after so using it; and if that is the true construction, it is enough for the plaintiff.

I come now to the last point which I think requires attention — that is, the consideration. It has been argued that this is nudum pactum — that there is no consideration. We must apply to that argument the usual legal tests. Let us see whether there is no advantage to the defendants. It is said that the use of the ball is no advantage to them, and that what benefits them is the sale; and the case is put that a lot of these balls might be stolen, and that it would be no advantage to the defendants if the thief or other people used them. The answer to that, I think, is as follows. It is quite obvious that in the view of the advertisers a use by the public of their remedy, if they can only get the public to have confidence enough to use it, will react and produce a sale which is directly beneficial to them. Therefore, the advertisers get out of the use an advantage which is enough to constitute a consideration.

But there is another view. Does not the person who acts upon this advertisement and accepts the offer put himself to some inconvenience at the request of the defendants? Is it nothing to use this ball three times daily for two weeks according to the directions at the request of the advertiser? Is that to go for nothing? It appears to me that there is a distinct inconvenience, not to say a detriment, to any person who so uses the smoke ball. I am of opinion, therefore, that there is ample consideration for the promise.

It appears to me, therefore, that the defendants must perform their promise, and, if they have been so unwary as to expose themselves to a great many actions, so much the worse for them.

[Bowen and A.L. Smith L.JJ. agreed.]

FITCH v. SNEDAKER

(1868), 38 N.Y. 248. New York Court of Appeals.

Clerke, J. In consequence of the murder of a woman in the county of Wayne, on the 25th September, 1859, the governor offered a reward, on the 3d of October following, of $500, to any person or persons "who would give such information as should lead to the apprehension and conviction" of the murderers. On the 14th of October, the defendant, as sheriff of the said county, offered a reward of $200, in addition to that offered by the governor, to any person or persons "who will give such information as shall lead to the apprehension and conviction of the person or persons guilty of the murder," etc.

On the trial, Jones, one of the plaintiffs, testified that he gave information of the murder on the 26th of September, the day the woman was found dead. Several questions were asked of this witness, relative to the person to whom he gave this information, and relative to other information which he had given in relation to the murder and the murderer, before the reward was offered, or before he heard of it. The judge at the Circuit sustained the objection and excluded the evidence. This was correct. It is palpably unnecessary to refer to authority to show that any information given by the plaintiffs previous to the offer of the reward could not entitle them to the benefit of it. The defendant, as sheriff, contracted for information to be thereafter given. He did not promise to reward any person for past information gratuitously given. In fact, no part of the plaintiff's conduct was in reference to the reward. Jones expressly says so in his testimony before the county judge. He says: "I told what I knew prior to the 11th October, 1859; all that I told of, I did without reference to any reward, and without expectation of receiving any reward for so telling; I did it for the public good." For this gratuitous service to the State, this patriot now claims the benefit of the reward.

The complaint was properly dismissed. The judgment should be affirmed, with costs.

Woodruff, J. . . . It is entirely clear that in order to entitle any person to the reward offered in this case, he must give such information as shall lead to both apprehension and conviction. That is, both must happen, and happen as a consequence of the information given. No person could claim the reward whose information caused the apprehension, until conviction followed; both are conditions precedent. No one could therefore claim the reward, who gave no information whatever until after the apprehension, although the information he afterward gave was the evidence upon which conviction was had, and, however clear, that had the information been concealed or suppressed there could have been no conviction. This is according to the plain terms of the offer of the reward.

. . .

The question in this case is simple. A murderer having been arrested and imprisoned in consequence of information given by the plaintiff before he is aware that a reward is offered for such apprehension, is he entitled to claim the reward in case conviction follows?

The ruling on the trial excluding all evidence of information given by the plaintiffs before they heard of this award, necessarily answers this question in the negative.

The case of *Williams v. Carwardine*, 4 Barn. & Ald. 621, and same case at the Assizes, 5 Carr. & Payne, 566, holds that a person who gives information according to the terms of an offered reward is entitled to the money, although it distinctly appeared that the informer had suppressed the information for five months, and was led to inform not by the promised reward, but by other motives. The court said the plaintiff had proved performance of the condition upon which the money was payable, and that established her title; that the court would not look into her motives. It does not appear by the reports of this case whether or not the plaintiff had ever seen the notice or handbill posted by the defendant, offering the reward; it does not therefore reach the precise point involved in the present appeal.

I perceive however no reason for applying to an offer of reward for the apprehension of a criminal any other rules than are applicable to any other offer by one accepted or acted upon by another, and so relied upon as constituting a contract.

The form of action in all such cases is *assumpsit*. The defendant is proceeded against as upon his contract to pay, and the first question is, was there a contract between the parties?

To the existence of a contract there must be mutual assent, or in another form, offer and consent to the offer. The *motive* inducing consent may be immaterial but the consent is vital. Without that there is no contract. How then can there be consent or assent to that of which the party has never heard? On the 15th day of October, 1859, the murderer, Fee, had in consequence of information given by the plaintiffs, been apprehended and lodged in jail. But the plaintiffs did not in giving that information, manifest any assent to the defendant's offer, nor act in any sense in reliance thereon; they did not know of its existence. The information was voluntary, and in every sense (material to this case) gratuitous. The offer could only operate upon the plaintiffs after they heard of it. It was *prospective* to those who will in the future give information, etc.

An offer cannot become a contract unless acted upon or assented to.

Such is the elementary rule in defining what is essential to a contract. Chitty Cont. (5th Am. ed.) Perkins' notes, p. 10, 9 and 2, and cases cited. Nothing was here done to procure or lead to Fee's apprehension in view of this reward. Indeed, if we were at liberty to look at the evidence on the first trial, it would appear that Fee was arrested before the defendant offered the reward.

I think the evidence was properly excluded and the nonsuit necessarily followed.

The judgment should be affirmed.

Judgment affirmed.

THE CROWN v. CLARKE

(1927), 40 C.L.R. 227. High Court of Australia; Isaacs A.C.J., Higgins and Starke JJ.

Isaacs A.C.J. This is an appeal from the judgment of the Full Court of Western Australia. Evan Clarke proceeded, by petition of right under the *Crown Suits Act* 1898, to sue the Crown for £1,000 promised by proclamation for such information as should lead to the arrest and conviction of the person or persons who committed the murders of two police officers, Walsh and Pitman. The defence was first a comprehensive denial of the petitioner's allegation that on 10th June 1926 he "gave the said information," and next an affirmative allegation that he made on that date a confession but not with the view of obtaining the reward. The petitioner was thus put to the proof of his case. At the trial the Chief Justice gave judgment for the Crown. In the Full Court, by a majority, the judgment of *McMillan* C.J., the trial Judge, was reversed. In the result, two learned Judges thought the Crown should succeed while two others thought Clarke should succeed ... The difference of opinion arose with respect to the effect or the accuracy, or both, of the case of *Williams v. Carwardine.*

The facts of this case, including inferences, are not, as I understand, in dispute. They amount to this: The information for which Clarke claims the reward was given by him when he was under arrest with Treffene on a charge of murder, and was given by him in circumstances which show that in giving the information he was not acting on or in pursuance of or in reliance upon or in return for the consideration contained in the proclamation, but exclusively in order to clear himself from a false charge of murder. In other words, he was acting with reference to a specific criminal charge against himself, and not with reference to a general request by the community for information against other persons. It is true that without his information and evidence no conviction was probable, but it is also abundantly clear that he was not acting for the sake of justice or from any impulse of conscience or because he was asked to do so, but simply and solely on his own initiative, to secure his own safety from the hand of the law and altogether irrespective of the proclamation. He has, in my opinion, neither a legal nor a moral claim to the reward. The learned Chief Justice held that Clarke never accepted or intended to accept the offer in the proclamation, and, unless the mere giving of the information without such intention amounted in law to an acceptance of the offer or to performance of the condition, there was neither "acceptance" nor "performance," and therefore there was no contract. I do not understand either of the learned Judges who formed the majority to controvert this. But they held that *Williams v. Carwardine* had stood so long that it should be regarded as accurate, and that, so regarded, it entitled the respondent to judgment. As reported in the four places where it is found, it is a difficult case to follow. I cannot help thinking that it is somewhat curtly reported. When the various reports in banc are compared, there are some discrepancies. But two circumstances are important. One is the pregnant question of *Denman* C.J. as to the plaintiff's knowledge of the handbill. The question appears in the reports in *Carrington & Payne* (1883), 5 C. & P. 566, 574, and in *Nevile & Manning* (1833), 1 N. & M. 418, 419, but is omitted from the report in *Barnewall & Adolphus.* The other circumstance is the stress placed on motive. The Lord Chief Justice clearly attached importance to the answer given to his question. He, doubtless, finally drew the inference that, having knowledge of the request in the handbill, the plaintiff at last determined to accede, and did accede, to that request, and so acted in response to it, although moved thereto by the incentive supplied by her stings of conscience. Making allowance for what is in all probability an abridged report of what was actually said, I cannot help thinking, on the whole, that not only *Denman* C.J. but also some at least of the other members of the Court considered that the motive of the informant was not inconsistent with, and did not in that case displace, the prima facie inference arising from the fact of knowledge of the request and the giving of the information it sought. Motive, though not to be confused with intention, is very often strong evidence of that state of mind, both in civil and criminal matters. The evidentiary force of motive in the circumstances of *Williams v. Carwardine* is no criterion of its force in the circumstances of any other case, and it can never usurp the legal place of intention. If the decision in *Williams v. Carwardine* went no further than I have said, it is in line with the acknowledged and settled theories of contract. If it goes so far as is contended for by the respondent, I am of opinion that it is opposed to unimpeachable authority, and I agree with the suggestion of Sir *Frederick Pollock*, in the preface to vol. 38 of the *Revised Reports*, that it should be disregarded. It is unquestionable — putting aside what are called formal contracts or quasi-contracts — that to create a contractual obligation there must be both offer and acceptance. It is the union of these which constitutes the binding tie, the *obligatio.* The present type of case is no exception. It is not true to say that since such an offer calls for information of a certain description, then, provided only information of that description is in fact given, the informant is entitled to the reward. That is not true unless the word "given" is interpreted as "given in exchange for the offer" — in other words, given in performance of the bargain which is contemplated by the offer and of which the offer is intended to form part. Performance in that case is the implied method of acceptance, and it simultaneously effects the double purpose of acceptance and performance. But acceptance is essential to contractual obligation, because without it there is no agreement, and in the absence of agreement, actual or imputed, there can be no contract. Lord *Kinnear* in *Jackson v. Broatch* (1900), 37 S.L.R. 707, 714, said: "It is an excellent definition of a contract that it is an agreement which produces an obligation."

. . . .

The controlling principle, then, is that to establish the *consensus* without which no true contract can exist, acceptance is as essential as offer, even in a case of the present class where the same act is at once sufficient for both acceptance and performance. But acceptance and performance of condition, as shown by the judicial reasoning quoted, involve that the person accepting and performing must act on the offer.

I may here refer to a weighty American authority, that of *Shaw* C.J. in *Loring v. City of Boston* ((1844), 7 Metc. 409.) At p. 411 the learned Chief

Justice said of an action to recover a reward offered for the conviction of an incendiary:-"There is now no question of the correctness of the legal principle on which this action is founded. The offer of a reward for the detection of an offender, the recovery of property, and the like, is an offer or proposal, which anyone, capable of performing the service, may accept at any time before it is revoked, and perform the service; and such offer on one side, and acceptance and performance ... on the other, is a valid contract made on good consideration, which the law will enforce." In the case then before the Court the offer was published more than three years before the information relied on was given, and in the circumstances the Court held the offer had ceased to operate. The important matter, however, is that the Court, in nonsuiting the plaintiff, said: "We are therefore of opinion, that the offer of the City had ceased before the plaintiffs accepted and acted upon it as such, and that consequently no contract existed upon which this action, founded on an alleged express promise, can be maintained." The reasoning quoted seems to me to be as exact and as modern as that in *Carlill's Case* and to be hardly capable of advantageous alteration.

Instances easily suggest themselves where precisely the same act done with reference to an offer would be performance of the condition, but done with reference to a totally distinct object would not be such a performance. An offer of £100 to any person who should swim a hundred yards in the harbour on the first day of the year, would be met by voluntarily performing the feat with reference to the offer, but would not in my opinion be satisfied by a person who was accidentally or maliciously thrown overboard on that date and swam the distance simply to save his life, without any thought of the offer. The offeror might or might not feel morally impelled to give the sum in such a case, but would be under no contractual obligation to do so.

. . .

We have had cited to us the case of *Fitch v. Snedaker*, decided in 1868. As is seen, it was twenty-four years later than the judgment of *Shaw* C.J. It was there held in a case of the present type that, in order to create a contract, there must be both offer and consent to the offer, that motive inducing consent may be immaterial but the consent is vital. *Clerke* J., held that as no part of the plaintiff's conduct was "in reference to" the reward — since it was prior to the offer — he could not succeed. *Woodruff* J. said that the plaintiff did not "act in any sense in reliance" on the offer, and added: "An offer cannot become a contract unless acted upon or assented to." ... In 1875, in *Shuey* v. *United States* [(1875), 92 U.S. 73, 76] *Strong* J., speaking for the Supreme Court of the United States, said that an offer of a reward for the apprehension of a man was revocable "at any time before it was accepted, and before anything had been done in reliance upon it." These last-mentioned cases are entirely consonant with and illustrative of the general principles so clearly stated by *Shaw* C.J. in *Loring* v. *City of Boston*, and by the Court of Appeal in *Carlill's Case*. In *Holmes on the Common Law* the learned author, writing in 1881, says at pp. 293, 294: "The root of the whole matter is the relation of reciprocal conventional inducement, each for the other, between consideration and promise." As to the reward cases, he says, with reference to something being done in ignorance of the offer:— "In such a case the reward cannot be claimed, because the alleged consideration has not been furnished on the faith of the offer. The tendered promise has not induced the furnishing of the consideration." The learned author also applied the term motive when it is the "conventional" motive, and not merely the independent motive of the person doing the act, as equivalent to acting on the faith of the offer. That may or not be accurate; but it is not a necessary part of the problem with which we are concerned.

On the question of fact whether Clarke in making his statement of 10th June acted upon the offer in the proclamation, the learned Chief Justice, who saw and heard him give his testimony, answered that question in the negative. Reading the notes of the trial, which apparently are to some extent abbreviated, and reading also the statement itself, so far from finding anything which would lead me, with all the disadvantages of an appellate Court, to reverse that finding, I quite agree with it. The learned Judges of the Full Court do not appear to have thought differently on that point.

. . . .

The appeal, however, should, in my opinion, for the reasons stated, be allowed, and the judgment of *McMillan* C.J. restored.

[Higgins and Starke JJ. gave judgment to the same effect.]

The Globe and Mail, Thursday, May 5, 1977, p. F5.

UNKINDEST CUT

Washington (CP) — Security men, alerted by a woman's shrieks, easily caught an armed raider in a South Dakota supermarket recently. The woman received a $405 reward for her "vigilance" despite admitting that she hadn't seen the gunman, but was shrieking in horror at the price of her beef.

PROBLEMS

1. Albert had a dog, Ralph, which escaped from his backyard. He phoned a local radio station which broadcast a description of the dog and Albert's offer of $100 to the finder. The dog was found by Stanley and returned to Albert.

What would happen in the following circumstances:

(a) Stanley had no knowledge of the reward.

(b) Stanley heard of the reward when, just before he caught Ralph, he heard a bystander say, "There's a reward for catching that dog."

(c) Stanley had already caught the dog when he heard that there was a reward.

(d) Stanley heard of the reward and then caught the dog but Stanley was employed as a dog-catcher by the city.

(e) Stanley heard of the reward and caught the dog but before he had returned the dog to Albert, Albert revoked his offer of the reward.

2. Margaret finds a Wintario ticket on the street. It turns out to be a winning ticket. Can she recover the value of the prize?

———————

It is treated as axiomatic in English law that an offer once made can be revoked at any time before acceptance. Thus if O makes an offer to A to purchase A's car for $2,000, but, before A can accept, O revokes his offer, the power of acceptance that O's offer conferred on A is terminated and the offer can no longer be accepted. However, the rule is that the revocation must be *communicated* to the offeree, A, before acceptance.

Thus in *Henthorn v. Fraser*, [1892] 2 Ch. 27, O, on July 7, offered to sell property to A. A accepted by mailing a letter at 3:50 p.m. on July 8, and O received the acceptance at 8:30 a.m. on July 9. O, however, at 12:30 p.m. on

July 8 had mailed a letter revoking his offer to A. A received this letter at 8:30 p.m. on July 8. The Court of Appeal held that the revocation was ineffective as it had not reached the offeree before he mailed his acceptance. (As we shall see, the mailing of an acceptance is the time when an acceptance is made, even though it is not received by the offeror until after the revocation has been received by the offeree.)

See also: *Byrne & Co. v. Van Tienhoven & Co.* (1880), 5 C.P.D. 344.

The rule in regard to revocation can be spelled out in the following black-letter proposition:

> "Revocation is possible and effective at any time before acceptance. This is so even though the offeror has declared himself ready to keep the offer open for a given period, and has not bound himself by a separate contract to do so." (Based on Cheshire and Fifoot, 9th ed. p. 50).

Sometimes it has been said that an offer is in "its nature revocable".

Why should this be so? What are the reasons for regarding an offer as revocable?

The following comparative law information may be of interest:

1. *French law.* An offer is revocable, in theory, at least. But the French courts have held that an offer may be irrevocable for a period. It is sometimes said that the offer must be kept alive long enough for the offeree to learn about the offer and examine it.

2. *German law.* The normal rule is that an offer is irrevocable, though the offer may reserve the right to revoke at any time up to acceptance. However, the courts tend to regard an offer with a reservation to revoke as not an offer but as an invitation to deal. If the offeror gives the offeree a stated time to accept the offer, it is irrevocable for that period.

Italian law tends to agree with French law. The law of the Socialist countries of Europe tends to agree with German law.

QUESTIONS

1. If you were negotiating a contract under German law would you reserve the power to revoke or not?

2. In any system of law imposing any restrictions on the revocability of offers, how do you think the courts would treat the presence or absence of reliance on the offer? If the offeree had not, in fact, relied on the offer, is there any reason for holding the offer to be irrevocable? What might evidence of reliance look like in these circumstances?

The leading English case on the revocability of offers is:

DICKINSON v. DODDS

(1876), 2 Ch. D. 463. Court of Appeal, England.

On Wednesday, the 10th of June, 1874, the Defendant *John Dodds* signed and delivered to the Plaintiff, *George Dickinson*, a memorandum, of which the material part was as follows:-

> "I hereby agree to sell to Mr. *George Dickinson* the whole of the dwelling-houses, garden ground, stabling, and outbuildings thereto belonging, situate at *Croft*, belonging to me, for the sum of £800. As witness my hand this tenth day of June, 1874.

£800. (Signed) *John Dodds.*
P.S. — This offer to be left over until Friday, 9 o'clock, A.M. *J.D.* (the twelfth),
12th June, 1874.
(Signed) *J. Dodds.*"

The bill alleged that *Dodds* understood and intended that the Plaintiff should have until Friday 9 A.M. within which to determine whether he would or would not purchase, and that he should absolutely have until that time the refusal of the property at the price of £800, and that the Plaintiff in fact determined to accept the offer on the morning of Thursday, the 11th of June, but did not at once signify his acceptance to *Dodds*, believing that he had the power to accept it until 9 A.M. on the Friday.

In the afternoon of the Thursday the Plaintiff was informed by a Mr. *Berry* that *Dodds* had been offering or agreeing to sell the property to *Thomas Allan*, the other Defendant. Thereupon the Plaintiff, at about half-past seven in the evening, went to the house of Mrs. *Burgess*, the mother-in-law of *Dodds*, where he was then staying, and left with her a formal acceptance in writing of the offer to sell the property. According to the evidence of Mrs. *Burgess* this document never in fact reached *Dodds*, she having forgotten to give it to him.

On the following (Friday) morning, at about seven o'clock, *Berry*, who was acting as agent for *Dickinson*, found *Dodds* at the *Darlington* railway station, and handed to him a duplicate of the acceptance by *Dickinson*, and explained to *Dodds* its purport. He replied that it was too late, as he had sold the property. A few minutes later *Dickinson* himself found *Dodds* entering a railway carriage, and handed him another duplicate of the notice of acceptance, but *Dodds* declined to receive it, saying, "You are too late. I have sold the property."

It appeared that on the day before, Thursday, the 11th of June, *Dodds* had signed a formal contract for the sale of the property to the Defendant *Allan* for £800, and had received from him a deposit of £40.

The bill in this suit prayed that the Defendant *Dodds* might be decreed specifically to perform the contract of the 10th of June, 1874; that he might be restrained from conveying the property to *Allan*; that *Allan* might be restrained from taking any such conveyance; that, if any such conveyance had been or should be made, *Allan* might be declared a trustee of the property for, and might be directed to convey the property to, the Plaintiff; and for damages.

The cause came on for hearing before Vice-Chancellor *Bacon* on the 25th of January, 1876.

Bacon, V.C., after remarking that the case involved no question of unfairness or inequality, and after stating the terms of the document of the 10th of June, 1874, and the statement of the Defendant's case as given in his answer, continued:-

I consider that to be one agreement, and I think the terms of the agreement put an end to any question of *nudum pactum*. I think the inducement for the Plaintiff to enter into the contract was the Defendant's compliance with the Plaintiff's request that there should be some time allowed to him to determine whether he would accept it or not. But whether the letter is read with or without the postscript, it is, in my judgment, as plain and clear a contract for sale as can be expressed in words, one of the terms of that contract being that the Plaintiff shall not be called upon to accept, or to testify his acceptance, until 9 o'clock on the morning of the 12th of June. I see, therefore, no reason why the Court should not enforce the specific perform- ance of the contract, if it finds that all the conditions have been complied with.

. . . .

There will be a decree for specific performance, with a declaration that *Allan* has no interest in the property; and the Plaintiff will be at liberty to deduct his costs of the suit out of his purchase-money.

From this decision both the Defendants appealed, and the appeals were heard on the 31st of March and the 1st of April, 1876.

James, L.J., after referring to the document of the 10th of June, 1874, continued:-

The document, though beginning "I hereby agree to sell," was nothing but an offer, and was only intended to be an offer, for the Plaintiff himself tells us that he required time to consider whether he would enter into an agreement or not. Unless both parties had then agreed there was no con- cluded agreement then made; it was in effect and substance only an offer to sell. The Plaintiff, being minded not to complete the bargain at that time, added this memorandum — "This offer to be left over until Friday, 9 o'clock A.M., 12th June, 1874." That shews it was only an offer. There was no consideration given for the undertaking or promise, to whatever extent it may be considered binding, to keep the property unsold until 9 o'clock on Friday morning; but apparently *Dickinson* was of opinion, and probably *Dodds* was of the same opinion, that he (*Dodds*) was bound by that promise, and could not in any way withdraw from it, or retract it, until 9 o'clock on Friday morning, and this probably explains a good deal of what afterwards took place. But it is clear settled law, on one of the clearest principles of law, that this promise, being a mere *nudum pactum* was not binding, and that at any moment before a complete acceptance by *Dickinson* of the offer, *Dodds* was as free as *Dickinson* himself. Well, that being the state of things, it is said that the only mode in which *Dodds* could assert that freedom was by actually and distinctly saying to *Dickinson*, "Now I withdraw my offer." It appears to me that there is neither principle nor authority for the proposi- tion that there must be an express and actual withdrawal of the offer, or what is called a retractation. It must, to constitute a contract, appear that the two minds were at one, at the same moment of time, that is, that there was an offer continuing up to the time of the acceptance. If there was not such a continuing offer, then the acceptance comes to nothing. Of course it may well be that the one man is bound in some way or other to let the other man know that his mind with regard to the offer has been changed; but in this case, beyond all question, the Plaintiff knew that *Dodds* was no longer minded to sell the property to him as plainly and clearly as if *Dodds* had told him in so many words, "I withdraw the offer." This is evident from the Plaintiff's own statements in the bill.

The Plaintiff says in effect that, having heard and knowing that *Dodds* was no longer minded to sell to him, and that he was selling or had sold to some one else, thinking that he could not in point of law withdraw his offer, meaning to fix him to it, and endeavouring to bind him, "I went to the house where he was lodging, and saw his mother-in-law, and left with her an acceptance of the offer, knowing all the while that he had entirely changed his mind. I got an agent to watch for him at 7 o'clock the next morning, and I went to the train just before 9 o'clock, in order that I might catch him and give him my notice of acceptance just before 9 o'clock, and when that occurred he told my agent, and he told me, you are too late, and he then threw back the paper." It is to my mind quite clear that before there was any attempt at acceptance by the Plaintiff, he was perfectly well aware that *Dodds* had changed his mind, and that he had in fact agreed to sell the property to *Allan*. It is impossible, therefore, to say there was ever that existence of the same mind between the two parties which is essential in point of law to the making of an agreement. I am of opinion, therefore, that the Plaintiff has failed to prove that there was any binding contract between *Dodds* and himself.

Mellish, L.J.:- I am of the same opinion. The first question is, whether this document of the 10th of June, 1874, which was signed by *Dodds*, was an agreement to sell, or only an offer to sell, the property therein mentioned to *Dickinson*; and I am clearly of opinion that it was only an offer, although it is in the first part of it, independently of the postscript, worded as an agreement. I apprehend that, until acceptance, so that both parties are bound, even though an instrument is so worded as to express that both parties agree, it is in point of law only an offer, and, until both parties are bound, neither party is bound. It is not necessary that both parties should be bound within the *Statute of Frauds*, for, if one party makes an offer in writing, and the other accepts it verbally, that will be sufficient to bind the person who has signed the written document. But, if there be no agreement, either verbally or in writing, then, until acceptance, it is in point of law an offer only, although worded as if it were an agreement. But it is hardly necessary to resort to that doctrine in the present case, because the postscript calls it an offer, and says, "This offer to be left over until Friday, 9 o'clock A.M." Well, then, this being only an offer, the law says — and it is a perfectly clear rule of law — that, although it is said that the offer is to be left open until Friday morning at 9 o'clock, that did not bind *Dodds*. He was not in point of law bound to hold the offer over until 9 o'clock on Friday morning. He was not so bound either in law or in equity. Well, that being so, when on the next day he made an agreement with *Allan* to sell the property to him, I am not aware of any ground on which it can be said that that contract with *Allan* was not as good and binding a contract as ever was made. Assuming *Allan* to have known (there is some dispute about it, and *Allan* does not admit that he knew of it, but I will assume that he did) that *Dodds* had made the offer to *Dickinson*, and had given him till Friday morning at 9 o'clock to accept it, still in point of law that could not prevent *Allan* from making a more favourable offer than *Dickinson*, and entering at once into a binding agreement with *Dodds*.

Then *Dickinson* is informed by *Berry* that the property has been sold by *Dodds* to *Allan*. *Berry* does not tell us from whom he heard it, but he says that he did hear it, that he knew it, and that he informed *Dickinson* of it. Now, stopping there, the question which arises is this — If an offer has been made for the sale of property, and before that offer is accepted, the person who has made the offer enters into a binding agreement to sell the property to somebody else, and the person to whom the offer was first made receives notice in some way that the property has been sold to another person, can he after that make a binding contract by the acceptance of the offer? I am of opinion that he cannot. The law may be right or wrong in saying that a person who has given to another a certain time within which to accept an offer is not bound by his promise to give that time; but, if he is not bound by that promise, and may still sell the property to some one else, and if it be the law that, in order to make a contract, the two minds must be in agreement at some one time, that is, at the time of the acceptance, how is it possible that when the person to whom the offer has been made knows that the person who has made the offer has sold the property to someone else, and that, in fact, he has not remained in the same mind to sell it to him, he can be at liberty to accept the offer and thereby make a binding contract? It seems to me that would be simply absurd. If a man makes an offer to sell a particular horse in his stable, and says, "I will give you until the day after to-morrow to accept the offer," and the next day goes and sells the horse to somebody else, and receives the purchase-money from him, can the person to whom the offer was originally made then come and say, "I accept," so as to make a binding contract, and so as to be entitled to recover damages for the non-delivery of the horse? If the rule of law is that a mere offer to sell property, which can be withdrawn at any time, and which is made dependent on the acceptance of the person to whom it is made, is a mere *nudum pactum*, how is it possible that the person to whom the offer has been made can by acceptance make a binding contract after he knows that the person who has made the offer has sold the property to some one else? It is admitted law that, if a man who makes an offer dies, the offer cannot be accepted after he is dead, and parting with the property has very much the same effect as the death of the owner, for it makes the performance of the offer impossible. I am clearly of opinion that, just as when a man who has made an offer dies before it is accepted it is impossible that it can then be accepted, so when once the person to whom the offer was made knows that the property has been sold to some one else, it is too late for him to accept the offer, and on that ground I am clearly of opinion that there was no binding contract for the sale of this property by *Dodds* to *Dickinson*, and even if there had been, it seems to me that the sale of the property to *Allan* was first in point of time. However, it is not necessary to consider, if there had been two binding contracts, which of them would be entitled to priority in equity, because there is no binding contract between *Dodds* and *Dickinson*.

Baggallay, J.A.:- I entirely concur in the judgments which have been pronounced.

QUESTIONS

1. What does this case say about the theory on which the Rules of Offer and Acceptance rests?
2. What did the parties intend? Is this relevant? If so, how?

PROBLEMS

1. A and B are negotiating for the purchase and sale of a quantity of lumber. A tells B that he (A) will buy the lumber for $10,000. B says that he would like to think about it for a few hours. B, one hour later, tells C that he will accept A's offer. C, without any authorization from B, tells A. Is there a contract?
2. Suppose that instead of telling C that he would accept A's offer, B told C that he would not accept A's offer and that when C told this to A, A bought the lumber from D. B then formally accepted one hour later and now sues A for breach. Is there a contract?

Do any of the considerations that we might have in mind in dealing with these problems help us to deal with the problem in *Dickinson v. Dodds?* Would it help here to ask what the parties intended?

The following provision of the *Restatement Second* (Tentative Draft) summarizes the rules in this area as follows:

§ 35. Methods of Termination of the Power of Acceptance.
(1) An offeree's power of acceptance may be terminated by
    (a) rejection or counter-offer by the offeree, or
    (b) lapse of time, or
    (c) revocation by the offeror, or
    (d) death or incapacity of the offeror or offeree.
(2) In addition, an offeree's power of acceptance is terminated by the failure of any condition of acceptance arising under the terms of the offer.

The remaining problems with the cases in this area arise through the application of the "rule" of *Dickinson v. Dodds.* In the ordinary executory contract the revocation of an offer, even when the offeror has promised to let it stand open for acceptance for a time, may not cost the offeree very much. In other words, reliance, if it exists, will usually consist of inaction. Any reliance may be unreasonable, in any event. (Notice now the converse of our usual circular argument.) The case that causes problems arise when, after A has promised B $100 if B will climb the flagpole, A revokes his offer when B is half way up. The following cases raise this problem. The cases show the readiness of the courts to find ways to prevent A revoking, though, as we would expect, doctrine sometimes gets in the way. It is interesting to consider the relationship between the pressure to prevent A revoking to protect B's reliance and the general concern for reliance that we found in the cases in the preceding chapter.

PETTERSON v. PATTBERG

(1928), 161 N.E. 428. New York Court of Appeals.

Kellogg, J. The evidence given upon the trial sanctions the following statement of facts: John Petterson, of whose last will and testament the plaintiff is the executrix, was the owner of a parcel of real estate in Brooklyn, known as 5301 Sixth avenue. The defendant was the owner of a bond executed by Petterson, which was secured by a third mortgage upon the parcel. On April 4, 1924, there remained unpaid upon the principal the sum of $5,450. This amount was payable in installments of $250 on April 25, 1924, and upon a like monthly date every three months thereafter. Thus the bond and mortgage had more than five years to run before the entire sum became due. Under date of the 4th of April, 1924, the defendant wrote Petterson as follows:

> "I hereby agree to accept cash for the mortgage which I hold against premises 5301 6th Ave., Brooklyn, N.Y. It is understood and agreed as a consideration I will allow you $780 providing said mortgage is paid on or before May 31, 1924, and the regular quarterly payment due April 25, 1924, is paid when due."

On April 25, 1924, Petterson paid the defendant the installment of principal due on that date. Subsequently, on a day in the latter part of May, 1924, Petterson presented himself at the defendant's home, and knocked at the door. The defendant demanded the name of his caller. Petterson replied: "It is Mr. Petterson. I have come to pay off the mortgage." The defendant answered that he had sold the mortgage. Petterson stated that he would like to talk with the defendant, so the defendant partly opened the door. Thereupon Petterson exhibited the cash, and said he was ready to pay off the mortgage according to the agreement. The defendant refused to take the money. Prior to this conversation, Petterson had made a contract to sell the land to a third person free and clear of the mortgage to the defendant. Meanwhile, also, the defendant had sold the bond and mortgage to a third party. It therefore became necessary for Petterson to pay to such person the full amount of the bond and mortgage. It is claimed that he thereby sustained a loss of $780, the sum which the defendant agreed to allow upon the bond and mortgage, if payment in full of principal, less that sum, was made on or before May 31, 1924. The plaintiff has had a recovery for the sum thus claimed, with interest.

Clearly the defendant's letter proposed to Petterson the making of a unilateral contract, the gift of a promise in exchange for the performance of an act. The thing conditionally promised by the defendant was the reduction of the mortgage debt. The act requested to be done, in consideration of the offered promise, was payment in full of the reduced principal of the debt prior to the due date thereof. "If an act is requested, that very act, and no other, must be given." Williston on Contracts, § 73. "In case of offers for a consideration, the performance of the consideration is always deemed a condition." Langdell's Summary of the Law of Contracts, § 4. It is elementary that any offer to enter into a unilateral contract may be withdrawn before the act requested to be done has been performed. Williston on Contracts, § 60; Langdell's Summary, § 4.

. . .

An interesting question arises when, as here, the offeree approaches the offeror with the intention of proffering performance and, before actual tender is made, the offer is withdrawn. Of such a case Williston says:

> "The offeror may see the approach of the offeree and know that an acceptance is contemplated. If the offeror can say 'I revoke' before the offeree accepts, however brief the interval of time between the two acts, there is no escape from the conclusion that the offer is terminated." Williston on Contracts, § 60b.

In this instance Petterson, standing at the door of the defendant's house, stated to the defendant that he had come to pay off the mortgage. Before a tender of the necessary moneys had been made, the defendant informed Petterson that he had sold the mortgage. That was a definite notice to Petterson that the defendant could not perform his offered promise, and that a tender to the defendant, who was no longer the creditor, would be ineffective to satisfy the debt. "An offer to sell property may be withdrawn before acceptance without any formal notice to the person to whom the offer is made. It is sufficient if that person has actual knowledge that the person who made the offer has done some act inconsistent with the continuance of the offer, such as selling the property to a third person." Dickinson v. Dodds, headnote... Thus it clearly appears that the defendant's offer was withdrawn before its acceptance had been tendered. It is unnecessary to determine, therefore, what the legal situation might have been had tender been made before withdrawal. It is the individual view of the writer that the same result would follow. This would be so, for the act requested to be performed was the completed act of payment, a thing incapable of performance, unless assented to by the person to be paid. Williston on Contracts, § 60b. Clearly an offering party has the right to name the precise act performance of which would convert his offer into a binding promise. Whatever the act may be until it is performed, the offer must be revocable. However, the supposed case is not before us for decision. We think that in this particular instance the offer of the defendant was withdrawn before it became a binding promise, and therefore that no contract was ever made for the breach of which the plaintiff may claim damages.

The judgment of the Appellate Division and that of the Trial Term should be reversed, and the complaint dismissed, with costs in all courts.

Lehman, J. (dissenting). The defendant's letter to Petterson constituted a promise on his part to accept payment at a discount of the mortgage he held, provided the mortgage is paid on or before May 31, 1924. Doubtless, by the terms of the promise itself, the defendant made payment of the mortgage by the plaintiff, before the stipulated time, a condition precedent to performance by the defendant of his promise to accept payment at a discount. If the condition precedent has not been performed, it is because the defendant made performance impossible by refusing to accept payment, when the plaintiff came with an offer of immediate performance. "It is a principle of fundamental justice that if a promisor is himself the cause of the failure of performance either of an obligation due him or of a condition upon which his own liability depends, he cannot take advantage of the failure." Williston on Contracts, § 677. The question in this case is not whether payment of the mortgage is a condition precedent to the performance of a promise made by the defendant, but, rather, whether, at the time the defendant refused the offer of payment, he had assumed any binding obligation, even though subject to condition.

The promise made by the defendant lacked consideration at the time it was made. Nevertheless, the promise was not made as a gift or mere gratuity to the plaintiff. It was made for the purpose of obtaining from the defendant something which the plaintiff desired. It constituted an offer which was to become binding whenever the plaintiff should give, in return for the defendant's promise, exactly the consideration which the defendant requested.

Here the defendant requested no counter promise from the plaintiff. The consideration requested by the defendant for his promise to accept payment was, I agree, some act to be performed by the plaintiff. Until the act requested was performed, the defendant might undoubtedly revoke his offer. Our problem is to determine from the words of the letter, read in the light of surrounding circumstances, what act the defendant requested as consideration for his promise.

The defendant undoubtedly made his offer as an inducement to the plaintiff to "pay" the mortgage before it was due. Therefore, it is said, that "the act requested to be performed was the completed act of payment, a thing incapable of performance, unless assented to by the person to be paid." In unmistakable terms the defendant agreed to accept payment, yet we are told that the defendant intended, and the plaintiff should have understood, that the act requested by the defendant, as consideration for his promise to accept payment, included performance by the defendant himself of the very promise for which the act was to be consideration. The defendant's promise was to become binding only when fully performed; and part of the consideration to be furnished by the plaintiff for the defendant's promise was to be the performance of that promise by the defendant. So construed, the defendant's promise or offer, though intended to induce action by the plaintiff, is but a snare and delusion. The plaintiff could not reasonably suppose that the defendant was asking him to procure the performance by the defendant of the very act which the defendant promised to do, yet we are told that, even after the plaintiff had done all else which the defendant requested, the defendant's promise was still not binding because the defendant chose not to perform.

I cannot believe that a result so extraordinary could have been intended when the defendant wrote the letter. "The thought behind the phrase proclaims itself misread when the outcome of the reading is injustice or absurdity." See opinion of Cardozo, C.J., in *Surace v. Danna,* 248 N.Y. 18, 161 N.E. 315. If the defendant intended to induce payment by the plaintiff and yet reserve the right to refuse payment when offered he should have used a phrase better calculated to express his meaning than the words: "I agree to accept." A promise to accept payment, by its very terms, must necessarily become binding, if at all, not later than when a present offer to pay is made.

I recognize that in this case only an offer of payment, and not a formal tender of payment, was made before the defendant withdrew his offer to accept payment. Even the plaintiff's part in the act of payment was then not technically complete. Even so, under a fair construction of the words of the letter, I think the plaintiff had done the act which the defendant requested as consideration for his promise. The plaintiff offered to pay, with present intention and ability to make that payment. A formal tender is seldom made in business transactions, except to lay the foundation for subsequent assertion in a court of justice of rights which spring from refusal of the tender. If the defendant acted in good faith in making his offer to accept payment, he could not well have intended to draw a distinction in the act requested of the plaintiff in return, between an offer which, unless refused, would ripen into completed payment, and a formal tender. Certainly the defendant could not have expected or intended that the plaintiff would make a formal tender of payment without first stating that he had come to make payment. We should not read into the language of the defendant's offer a meaning which would prevent enforcement of the defendant's promise after it had been accepted by the plaintiff in the very way which the defendant must have intended it should be accepted, if he acted in good faith.

The judgment should be affirmed.

Cardozo, C.J., and Pound, Crane, and O'Brien, JJ., concur with Kellogg, J.

Lehman, J., dissents in opinion, in which Andrews, J., concurs. Judgments reversed, *etc.*

ERRINGTON v. ERRINGTON

[1952] 1 All E.R. 149. Court of Appeal, England; Sommervell, Denning and Hodson L.JJ.

Denning, L.J.: The facts are reasonably clear. In 1936 the father bought the house for his son and daughter-in-law to live in. The father put down £250 in cash and borrowed £500 from a building society on the security of the house, repayable with interest by instalments of 15s. a week. He took the house in his own name and made himself responsible for the instalments. The father told the daughter-in-law that the £250 was a present for them, but he left them to pay the building society instalments of 15s. a week themselves. He handed the building society book to the daughter-in-law and said to her: "Don't part with this book. The house will be your property when the mortgage is paid." He said that when he retired he would transfer it into their names. She has, in fact, paid the building society instalments regularly from that day to this with the result that much of the mortgage has been repaid, but there is a good deal yet to be paid. The rates on the house came to 10s. a week. The couple found that they could not pay those as well as the building society instalments so the father said he would pay them and he did so.

It is to be noted that the couple never bound themselves to pay the instalments to the building society, and I see no reason why any such obligation should be implied. It is clear law that the court is not to imply a term unless it is necessary, and I do not see that it is necessary here. Ample content is given to the whole arrangement by holding that the father promised that the house should belong to the couple as soon as they had paid off the mortgage. The parties did not discuss what was to happen if the couple failed to pay the instalments to the building society, but I should have thought it clear that, if they did fail to pay the instalments, the father would not be bound to transfer the house to them. The father's promise was a unilateral contract — a promise of the house in return for their act of paying the instalments. It could not be revoked by him once the couple entered on performance of the act, but it would cease to bind him if they left it incomplete and unperformed, which they have not done. If that was the position during the father's lifetime, so it must be after his death. If the daughter-in-law continues to pay all the building society instalments, the couple will be entitled to have the property transferred to them as soon as the mortgage is paid off, but if she does not do so, then the building society will claim the instalments from the father's estate and the estate will have to pay them. I cannot think that in those circumstances the estate would be bound to transfer the house to them, any more than the father himself would have been.

What is the result in law of those facts? The relationship of the parties is open to three possible legal constructions: (i) That the couple were tenants at will paying no rent. That is what the judge thought they were. He said that in the present case ... the defendant "was in exclusive possession, and was, therefore, not a mere licensee, but in the position of a tenant at will." But, in my opinion, it is of the essence of a tenancy at will that it should be determinable by either party on demand, and it is quite clear that the relationship of these parties was not so determinable. The father could not eject the couple as long as they paid the instalments regularly to the building society. It was, therefore, not a tenancy at will. I confess that I am glad to reach this result because it would appear that, if the couple were held to be tenants at will, the father's title would be defeated after the lapse of thirteen years, long before the couple paid off the instalments, which would be quite contrary to the justice of the case. (ii) That the couple were tenants at a rent of 15s. a week, such rent being for convenience paid direct to the building society instead of to the father and the tenancy being either a weekly tenancy or a tenancy for the duration of the mortgage repayments. But I do not think that 15s. can possibly be regarded as rent, for the simple reason that the couple were not bound to pay it. If they did not pay it, the father could not sue for it or distrain for it. He could only refuse to transfer the house to them. If the 15s. was not rent, then it affords no ground for inferring a tenancy. (iii) That the couple were licensees, having a permissive occupation short of a tenancy, but with a contractual right, or, at any rate, an equitable right to remain so long as they paid the instalments, which would grow into a good equitable title to the house itself as soon as the mortgage was paid. This is, I think, the right view of the relationship of the parties.

.   .   .

Applying the foregoing principles to the present case, it seems to me that, although the couple had exclusive possession of the house, there was clearly no relationship of landlord and tenant. They were not tenants at will, but licensees. They had a mere personal privilege to remain there, with no right to assign or sub-let. They were, however, not bare licensees. They were licensees with a contractual right to remain. As such they have no right at law to remain, but only in equity, and equitable rights now prevail. I confess, however, that it has taken the courts some time to reach this position. At common law a licence was always revocable at will, notwithstanding a contract to the contrary... The remedy for a breach of the contract was only in damages. That was the view generally held until a few years ago: see, for instance, what was said in *Booker v. Palmer* ([1942] 2 All E.R. 677); *Thompson v. Park* ([1944] 2 All E.R. 479). The rule has, however, been altered owing to the interposition of equity. Law and equity have been fused for nearly eighty years, and since 1948 it has become clear that, as a result of the fusion, a licensor will not be permitted to eject a licensee in breach of a contract to allow him to remain: see *Winter Garden Theatre (London), Ltd. v. Millennium Productions, Ltd.* ([1946] 1 All E.R. 680), *per* Lord Greene, M.R. ([1947] 2 All E.R. 336), *per* Viscount Simon; nor in breach of a promise on which the licensee has acted, even though he gave no value for it: see *Foster v. Robinson* ([1950] 2 All E.R. 346), where Sir Raymond Evershed, M.R., said that as a result of the oral arrangement to let the man stay, he "was entitled as licensee to occupy the cottage without charge for the rest of his days..." This infusion of equity means that contractual licences now have a force and validity of their own and cannot be revoked in breach of the contract. Neither the licensor nor anyone who claims through him can disregard the contract except a purchaser for value without notice.

.   .   .

In the present case it is clear that the father expressly promised the couple that the property should belong to them as soon as the mortgage was paid, and impliedly promised that, so long as they paid the instalments to the building society, they should be allowed to remain in possession. They were not purchasers because they never bound themselves to pay the instalments, but nevertheless they were in a position analogous to purchasers. They have acted on the promise and neither the father nor his widow, his successor in title, can eject them in disregard of it. The result is that, in my opinion, the appeal should be dismissed and no order for possession should be made. I come to this conclusion on a different ground from that reached by the learned judge, but it is always open to a respondent to support the judgment on any ground. If there is a dispute between the son and the daughter-in-law as to their respective rights in the house, that must be decided under s. 17 of the Married Women's Property Act, 1882. If the father's widow should cease to pay the rates, the actual occupier must pay them, because the father did not bind himself to pay them. He only did so out of paternal affection.

QUESTIONS

1. If the offeror's power to revoke is going to be limited in a case like *Errington v. Errington* it is presumably being done for a good reason. Why was the offeror's power to revoke restricted in *Errington v. Errington*?

2. What interest of the offeree was threatened by the exercise of the power to revoke?

3. What interest of the offeree was protected by the decision?

4. If these interests are not identical what does one do about the decision?

DAWSON v. HELICOPTER EXPLORATION CO. LTD.

[1955] 5 D.L.R. 404. Supreme Court of Canada; Kerwin C.J.C., Rand, Estey, Cartwright and Fauteux JJ.

[The plaintiff appellant had staked a mineral deposit in northern B.C. These claims had lapsed. In 1951, the plaintiff wanted to interest a mining company in these claims. One Springer wrote to the plaintiff after hearing that the plaintiff wanted to get the claims developed. Springer offered the plaintiff a 10% interest in the claims in return for the plaintiff's help. The plaintiff was called up for the U.S. Army (he was an American and the Korean War was on) but expressed to Springer his continued willingness to co-operate in the development of the claims on the terms proposed by Springer. Springer repeated his offer in a subsequent letter of March 5, 1951, and said "if you take us in to the showings and we think that they warrant staking, we will stake all claims and give you a 10% non-assessable interest." The plaintiff replied on April 12, 1951, "If you will inform me... I will immediately take steps for a temporary release in order to be on hand." Springer wrote on June 7, 1951, to say that they would not be going in that year. However, an exploration party sent by the defendant respondent (for whom Springer worked), located the claims and made arrangements to develop them.

The plaintiff commenced an action for his share. The trial judge and the B.C. Court of Appeal dismissed the action. The plaintiff appealed.]

Rand J.:- ... The substantial contention of the respondent is that any offer contained in the correspondence and in particular the letter of March 5th called for an acceptance not by promise but by the performance of an act, the location of the claims by Dawson for the respondent. It is based upon the well-known conception which in its simplest form is illustrated by the case of a reward offered for some act to be done. To put it in other words, no intention was conveyed by Springer when he said "I hereby agree" that Dawson, if agreeable, should have replied "I hereby accept" or words to that effect: the offer called for and awaited only the act to be done and would remain revocable at any time until every element of that act had been completed.

The error in this reasoning is that such an offer contemplates acts to be performed by the person only to whom it is made and in respect of which the offeror remains passive, and that is not so here. What Dawson was to do was to proceed to the area with Springer or persons acting for him by means of the respondent's helicopter and to locate the showings. It was necessarily implied by Springer that he would participate in his own proposal. This involved his promise that he would do so, and that the answer to the proposal would be either a refusal or a promise on the part of Dawson to a like participation. The offer was unconditional but contemplated a performance subject to the condition that a pilot could be obtained by the respondent.

Dawson's answer of April 12th was, as I construe it, similarly an unqualified promissory acceptance, subject as to performance to his being able to obtain the necessary leave. It was the clear implication that Springer, controlling the means of making the trip, should fix the time and should notify Dawson accordingly. As the earlier letters show, Dawson was anxious to conclude some arrangement and if he could not make it with Springer he would seek it in other quarters.

Although in the circumstances, because the terms proposed involve such complementary action on the part of both parties as to put the implication beyond doubt, the precept is not required, this interpretation of the correspondence follows the tendency of Courts to treat offers as calling for bilateral rather than unilateral action when the language can be fairly so construed, in order that the transaction shall have such "business efficacy as both parties must have intended that at all events it should have": Bowen L.J. in *The "Moorcock"* (1889), 14 P.D. 64 at p. 68. In theory and as conceded by Mr. Guild, an offer in the unilateral sense can be revoked up to the last moment before complete performance. At such a consequence many Courts have balked; and it is in part that fact that has led to a promissory construction where that can be reasonably given. What is effectuated is the real intention of both parties to close a business bargain on the strength of which they may, thereafter, plan their courses.

This question is considered in Williston on Contracts, vol. 1, pp. 76-77, in which the author observes:

> "Doubtless wherever possible, as matter of interpretation, a court would and should interpret an offer as contemplating a bilateral rather than a unilateral contract, since in a bilateral contract both parties are protected from a period prior to the beginning of performance on either side — that is from the making of the mutual promises.
>
> "At the opening of the present century the courts were still looking for a clear promise on each side in bilateral contracts. A bargain which lacked such a promise by one of the parties was held to lack mutuality and, therefore, to be unenforceable. Courts are now more ready to recognize fair implications as effective: 'A promise may be lacking, and yet the whole writing may be "instinct with an obligation," imperfectly expressed' which the courts will regard as supplying the necessary reciprocal promise."

The expression "instinct with an obligation" first used by Scott J. in *McCall Co. v. Wright* (1909), 133 App. Div. (N.Y.) 62 is employed by Cardozo J. in *Wood v. Lady Duff-Gordon* (1917), 222 N.Y. 88 at pp. 90-1, in the following passage: "It is true that he does not promise in so many words that he will use reasonable efforts to place the defendant's indorsements and market her designs. We think, however, that such a promise is fairly to be implied. *The law has outgrown its primitive stage of formalism when the precise word was the sovereign talisman, and every slip was fatal.* . . . A promise may be lacking, and yet the whole writing may be 'instinct with an obligation,' imperfectly expressed."

These observations apply obviously and equally to both offer and acceptance.

The question of an anticipatory breach by the letter of June 7th was raised, but that was superseded by the subsequent events. Dawson was bound to remain ready during a reasonable time prior to that mentioned for the trip to endeavour, upon notice from Stringer, to obtain leave of absence. But in promising Dawson that the company would co-operate, Springer impliedly agreed that the company would not, by its own act, prevent the complementary performance by Dawson. In doing what it did, the company not only violated its engagement, but brought to an end the subject-matter of the contract. By that act it dispensed with any further duty of readiness on the part of Dawson whether or not he was aware of what had taken place. Even assuming the technical continuance of the obligations and the necessity of an affirmative step in order to treat an anticipatory breach as a repudiation, the action was not brought until long after the time for performance had passed. Being thus excused, Dawson's obtaining leave, apart from any pertinency to damages, became irrelevant to the cause of action arising from the final breach.

I would, therefore, allow the appeal and remit the cause to the Supreme Court of British Columbia for the assessment of damages. The appellant will have his costs throughout.

[Estey, Cartwright and Fauteux JJ. reached the same conclusion as Rand J. Kerwin C.J.C. dissented.]

There may, of course, be cases where one party may properly want to retain the power to revoke until the other has climbed the flagpole to the top. When an agent participates in a real estate deal, the agent may want to be paid as soon as he has obtained an offer, the vendor may only want to pay when the deal has been signed. Such contracts raise the same problem as in the flagpole case. In *Dennis Reed Ltd. v. Goody*, [1950] 2 K.B. 277 (Court of Appeal, England), the real estate agent, the plaintiff, had attempted to "lower the flagpole" by making the commission payable on the introduction of a person "ready, able and willing to purchase". The deal had ended when the purchaser withdrew his offer. When the agent sued for the commission, Denning L.J. said:

> "... So many cases have now come before the courts on claims by house agents to commission that the document cannot, I think, be interpreted in vacuo. It must be interpreted in the light of the general law on the subject, which I will endeavour to state. When a house owner puts his house into the hands of an estate agent, the ordinary understanding is that the agent is only to receive a commission if he succeeds in effecting a sale; but if not, he is entitled to nothing. That has been well understood for the last 100 years or more.... The agent in practice takes what is a business risk: he takes on himself the expense of preparing particulars and advertising the property in return for the substantial remuneration — reckoned by a percentage of the price — which he will receive if he succeeds in finding a purchaser: see *Luxor (Eastbourne) Ltd. v. Cooper.*
> "No particular words are needed to create the relationship. All the familiar expressions 'please find a purchaser', 'find someone to buy my house', 'sell my

house for me', and so on, mean the same thing: they mean that the agent is employed on the usual terms; but none of them gives any precise guide as to what is the event on which the agent is to be paid. The common understanding of men is, however, that the agent's commission is payable out of the purchase price. The services rendered by the agent may be merely an introduction. He is entitled to commission if his introduction is the efficient cause in bringing about the sale.... But that does not mean that commission is payable at the moment of the introduction: it is only payable on completion of the sale. The house-owner wants to find a man who will actually buy his house and pay for it. He does not want a man who will only make an offer or sign a contract. He wants a purchaser 'able to purchase and able to complete as well'...

"Some confusion has arisen because of the undoubted fact that, once there is a binding contract for sale, the vendor cannot withdraw from it except at the risk of having to pay the agent his commission. This has led some people to suppose that commission is payable as soon as a contract is signed: and I said so myself in *McCallum v. Hicks.*

"But this is not correct. The reason why the vendor is liable in such a case is because, once he repudiates the contract, the purchaser is no longer bound to do any more towards completion: and the vendor cannot rely on the non-completion in order to avoid payment of commission, for it is due to his own fault.... When it is not the vendor, but the purchaser, who withdraws, the case is entirely different; for, even though a binding contract has been made, nevertheless, if the purchaser is unable or unwilling to complete, the agent is not entitled to his commission.... The vendor is not bound to bring an action for specific performance or for damages simply to enable the agent to get commission; but, if he does get his money, he will probably be liable to pay the commission out of it. It only remains to add that, when no binding contract has been made the vendor can himself withdraw at any time without being liable to pay commission: *Luxor (Eastbourne) Ltd. v. Cooper.* A fortiori, if the purchaser withdraws, the vendor is not liable for commission.

"It is against that background that we have to interpret this document. Some estate agents have recently put a special clause in their printed forms, and used special words in their confirming letters. Their object is to get commission if they introduce a person who makes an offer to buy on the named terms, even though it never becomes a binding contract. It often happens that a house owner puts his house into the hands of several agents, and that each of the agents introduces someone who makes an offer. According to the agents, the house owner is liable under this new clause to pay commission, not only on the one offer which he accepts, but also on the other offers which he refuses. This contention has actually succeeded in at least one case that has come before the courts, and the house owner has found himself liable to pay double commission: see *E. P. Nelson & Co. v. Rolfe.* In the present case the agents go further: they say that, once an offer is made by someone whom they introduce, they are entitled to commission even though it is withdrawn by him the next day. They say that, if the person introduced is ready, able and willing at the time of the offer, that is sufficient even if he thereafter becomes unable or unwilling.

"The new clause has been described by judges of this court as 'rather stringent' and 'rather undesirable'. If it has the effect for which the agents contend, these descriptions are not one whit too strong. When an agent gets an offer which the house owner does not accept, it might be quite reasonable for the agent to ask for his out-of-pocket expenses or even for a reasonable reward for his time and labour; but it is not reasonable for him to ask for full commission at the same rate as if he had actually procured a sale. The commission is a substantial remuneration, based not on the time, labour or money expended — which may be little — but on a percentage of the purchase price. Remuneration on such a scale cannot be justified except on the footing that it is to come out of the purchase money; and it should therefore in reason only be payable on completion of the purchase. I know that agents often say that they have earned their commission when they have done their part. But that is a fallacy: an agent does not earn commission as a labourer earns wages. Even though he has done his part, he does not become entitled to his commission until the purchase is completed."

The rules of offer and acceptance have traditionally been most prominent in the case of contracts made by mail. The reason for this is that the time lag between the various stages permits the parties to change their minds, and the rules have, therefore, been most frequently tested. Because the rules were largely developed before the era of instantaneous long-distance communication by telephone and telex, the case-law on contracts made by mail is far larger than its present day importance would justify. But this case law permits us to explore some of the problems of the process of contract formation in very neat situations where the sequence of events is very precisely documented.

The early cases refer to the eighteenth century case of *Cooke v. Oxley* (1790), 3 T.R. 653, 100 E.R. 785. This case illustrates a curious conceptual problem. In this case the offeror had made an offer to sell tobacco. The offeror had allowed the offeree several hours to make up his mind. Within the time allowed, the offeree purported to accept the offer. The court held that there was no contract because the offeror had not been shown to have been still ready to deal on the terms of the offer when the offeree accepted it. The court required a kind of almost metaphysical "meeting of the minds" at the moment of acceptance. Such an attitude would, of course, virtually preclude the making of contracts except by parties dealing in a face to face situation. When it became clear that businessmen would persist in making contracts in ways that the courts found conceptually awkward, the courts had to change. The device that they adopted is shown in the next case.

ADAMS v. LINDSELL

(1818), 1 B. & Ald. 681, 106 E.R. 250. King's Bench.

Action for non-delivery of wool according to agreement. At the trial at the last Lent Assizes for the county of Worcester, before Burrough J. it appeared that the defendants, who were dealers in wool, at St. Ives, in the county of Huntingdon, had, on Tuesday the 2d of September 1817, written the following letter to the plaintiffs, who were woollen manufacturers residing in Bromsgrove, Worcestershire. "We now offer you eight hundred tods of wether fleeces, of a good fair quality of our country wool, at 35s. 6d. per tod, to be delivered at Leicester, and to be paid for by two months' bill in two months, and to be weighed up by your agent within fourteen days, receiving your answer in course of post."

This letter was misdirected by the defendants, to Bromsgrove, Leicestershire, in consequence of which it was not received by the plaintiffs in Worcestershire till 7 p.m. on Friday, September 5th. On that evening the plaintiffs wrote an answer, agreeing to accept the wool on the terms proposed. The course of the post between St. Ives and Bromsgrove is through London, and consequently this answer was not received by the defendants till Tuesday, September 9th. On the Monday September 8th, the defendants not having, as they expected, received an answer on Sunday September 7th, (which in case their letter had not been misdirected, would have been in the usual course of the post,) sold the wool in question to another person.

Under these circumstances, the learned Judge held, that the delay having been occasioned by the neglect of the defendants, the jury must take it, that the answer did come back in due course of post; and that then the defendants were liable for the loss that had been sustained: and the plaintiffs accordingly recovered a verdict.

Jervis having in Easter term obtained a rule nisi for a new trial, on the ground that there was no binding contract between the parties,

Dauncey, Puller, and Richardson, shewed cause. They contended, that at the moment of the acceptance of the offer of the defendants by the plaintiffs, the former became bound. And that was on the Friday evening, when there had been no change of circumstances. They were then stopped by the Court, who called upon

Jervis and Campbell in support of the rule. They relied on *Payne v. Cave* (1789), 3 T.R. 148, and more particularly on *Cooke v. Oxley*. In that case, Oxley, who had proposed to sell goods to Cooke, and given him a certain time at his request, to determine whether he would buy them or not, was held not liable to the performance of the contract, even though Cooke, within the specified time, had determined to buy them, and given Oxley notice to that effect. So here the defendants who have proposed by letter to sell this wool, are not to be held liable, even though it be now admitted that the answer did come back in due course of post. Till the plaintiffs' answer was actually received, there could be no binding contract between the parties; and before then, the defendants had retracted their offer, by selling the wool to other persons. But

The Court said, that if that were so, no contract could ever be completed by the post. For if the defendants were not bound by their offer when accepted by the plaintiffs till the answer was received, then the plaintiffs ought not to be bound till after they had received the notification that the defendants had received their answer and assented to it. And so it might go on ad infinitum. The defendants must be considered in law as making, during every instant of the time their letter was travelling, the same identical offer to the plaintiffs; and then the contract is completed by the acceptance of it by the latter. Then as to the delay in notifying the acceptance, that arises entirely from the mistake of the defendants, and it therefore must be taken as against them, that the plaintiffs' answer was received in course of post.

Rule discharged.

The device of regarding the offer as being remade every instant until acceptance was gradually forgotten by the courts. It became clearly established that a contract could be made by mail. However, as happened in *Adams v. Lindsell*, things could go wrong. In that case the risk of loss that was caused by the delay in the mail, fell on the party who had made the mistake in the address on the offer. Some rule had to be found to determine which party should bear the risk when, through no fault of either party, the mail miscarried. The solution was determined in the next case.

Notice that even now the courts are bothered by conceptual problems. The Post Office has to be regarded as the agent of the offeror so that delivery of the acceptance to the Post Office is delivery to the offeror. Is this decision any more necessary than the device used in *Adams v. Lindsell*? Do you think that the allocation of risk made in this case is sensible? Could this kind of risk allocation help to solve a case like *Henkel v. Pape (supra)*?

HOUSEHOLD INSURANCE v. GRANT

(1879), 4 Ex. D. 216. Court of Appeal (England); Baggallay, Thesiger and Bramwell L.JJ.

Thesiger, L.J. In this case the defendant made an application for shares in the plaintiffs' company under circumstances from which we must imply that he authorized the company, in the event of their allotting to him the shares applied for, to send the notice of allotment by post. The company did allot him the shares, and duly addressed to him and posted a letter containing the notice of allotment, but upon the finding of the jury it must be taken that the letter never reached its destination. In this state of circumstances Lopes, J., has decided that the defendant is liable as a shareholder. He based his decision mainly upon the ground that the point for his consideration was covered by authority binding upon him, and I am of opinion that he did so rightly, and that it is covered by authority equally binding upon this Court.

The leading case upon the subject is *Dunlop v. Higgins* (1848), 1 H.L. Cas. 387.

. . .

In short . . . as a rule, a contract formed by correspondence through the post is complete as soon as the letter accepting an offer is put into the post, and is not put an end to in the event of the letter never being delivered. My view of the effect of *Dunlop v. Higgins* is that taken by James, L.J., in *Harris' Case* (1872), 2 Ch. App. 587, there he speaks of the former case as "a case which is binding upon us, and in which every principle argued before us was discussed at length by the Lord Chancellor in giving judgment," he adds, the Lord Chancellor "arrived at the conclusion that the posting of the letter of acceptance is the completion of the contract; that is to say, the moment one man has made an offer, and the other has done something binding himself to that offer, then the contract is complete and neither party can afterwards escape from it." Mellish, J., also took the same view, he says "in *Dunlop v. Higgins* the question was directly raised whether the law was truly expounded in the case of *Adams v. Lindsell*. The House of Lords approved of the ruling of that case.

. . .

He then referred to the case of *Adams v. Lindsell*, and quoted the observation of Lord Ellenborough, C.J. That case therefore appears to me to be a direct decision that the contract is made from the time when it is accepted by post." Leaving *Harris' Case* for the moment, I turn to *Duncan v. Topham* (1849), 8 C.B. 225, in which Creswell, J., told the jury that if the letter accepting the contract was put into the post office and lost by the negligence of the post office authorities, the contract would nevertheless be complete; and both he and Wilde, C.J., and Maule, J., seem to have understood this ruling to have been in accordance with Lord Cottenham's opinion in *Dunlop v. Higgins*. That opinion therefore appears to me to constitute an authority directly binding upon us. But if *Dunlop v. Higgins* were out of the way, *Harris' Case* would still go far to govern the present. There it was held that the acceptance of the offer at all events binds both parties from the time of the acceptance being posted, and so as to prevent any retraction of the offer being of effect after the acceptance has been posted. Now, whatever in abstract discussion may be said as to the legal notion of its being necessary, in order to the effecting of a valid and binding contract, that the minds of the parties should be brought together at one and the same moment, that notion is practically the foundation of English law upon the subject of the formation of contracts. Unless therefore a contract constituted by correspondence is absolutely concluded at the moment that the continuing offer is accepted by the person to whom the offer is addressed, it is difficult to see how the two minds are ever to be brought together at one and the same moment. This was pointed out by Lord Ellenborough in the case of *Adams v. Lindsell*, which is recognized authority upon this branch of the law. But on the other hand it is a principle of law, as well established as the legal notion to which I have referred, that the minds of the two parties must be brought together by mutual communication. An acceptance, which only remains in the breast of the acceptor without being actually and by legal implication communicated to the offerer, is no binding acceptance. How then are these elements of law to be harmonised in the case of contracts formed by correspondence through the post? I see no better mode than that of treating the post office as the agent of both parties, and it was so considered by Lord Romilly in *Hebb's Case* (1867), L.R. 4 Eq. 9, 12, when in the course of his judgment he said: "*Dunlop v. Higgins* decides that the posting of a letter accepting an offer constitutes a binding contract, but the reason of that is, that the post office is the common agent of both parties." Alderson, B., also in *Stocken v. Collin* (1841), 7 M.W. 515, 516, a case of notice of dishonour, and the case referred to by Lord Cottenham, says: "If the doctrine that the post office is only the agent for the delivery of the notice were correct no one could safely avail himself of that mode of transmission." But if the post office be such common agent, then it seems to me to follow that, as soon as the letter of acceptance is delivered to the post office, the contract is made as complete and final and absolutely binding as if the acceptor had put his letter into the hands of a messenger sent by the offerer himself as his agent to deliver the offer and receive the acceptance. What other principle can be adopted short of holding that the contract is not complete by acceptance until and except from the time that the letter containing the acceptance is delivered to the offerer, a principle which has been distinctly negatived? This difficulty was attempted to be got over in the *British and American Telegraph Co. v. Colson* (1871), L.R. 6 Ex. 108, which was a case directly on all fours with the present, and in which Kelly, C.B., is reported to have said, "It may be that in general, though not in all cases, a contract takes effect from the time of acceptance and not from the subsequent notification of it. As in the case now before the Court, if the letter of allotment had been delivered to the defendant in the due course of the post he would have become a shareholder from the date of the letter.... And hence perhaps the mistake has arisen that the contract is binding upon both parties from the time when the letter is written and put into the post, although never delivered; whereas although it may be binding from the time of acceptance, it is only binding at all when afterwards duly notified." But with deference I would ask how a man can be said to be a shareholder at a time before he was bound to take any shares, or to put the question in the form in which it is put by Mellish, L.J., in *Harris' Case* how there can be any relation back in a case of this kind as there may be in bankruptcy. If, as the Lord Justice said, the contract after the letter has arrived in time is to be treated as having been made from the time the letter is posted, the reason is that the contract was actually made at the time when the letter was posted. The principle indeed laid down in *Harris' Case* as well as in *Dunlop v. Higgins*, can really not be reconciled with the decision in the *British and American Telegraph Co. v. Colson* (1871), L.R. 6 Exch. 108. James, L.J., in the passage I have already quoted affirms the proposition that when once the acceptance is posted neither party can afterwards escape from the contract, and refers, with approval, to *Hebb's Case.* There a distinction was taken by the Master of the Rolls that the company chose to send the letter of allotment to their own agent, who was not authorized by the applicant for shares to receive it on his behalf, and who never delivered it, but he at the same time assumed that if, instead of sending it through an authorized agent they had sent it through the post office, the applicant would have been bound although the letter had never been delivered. Mellish, L.J., really goes as far, and states forcibly the reasons in favour of this view. The mere suggestion thrown out (at the close of his judgment, at p. 597), when stopping short of actually overruling the decision in the *British and American Telegraph Co. v. Colson,* that although a contract is complete when the letter accepting an offer is posted, yet it may be subject to a condition subsequent that, if the letter does not arrive in due course of post, then the parties may act on the assumption that the offer has not been accepted, can hardly, when contrasted with the rest of the judgment, be said to represent his own opinion on the law upon the subject. The contract as he says, is actually made when the letter is posted. The acceptor, in posting the letter, has, to use the language of Lord Blackburn, in *Brogden v. Directors of Metropolitan Ry. Co.* (1877), 2 App. Cas 666, 691, "put it out of his control and done an extraneous act which clenches the matter, and shews beyond all doubt that each side is bound." How then can a casualty in the post, whether resulting in delay, which in commercial transactions is often as bad as no delivery, or in non-delivery, unbind the parties or unmake the contract? To me it appears that in practice a contract complete upon the acceptance of an offer being posted, but liable to be put an end to by an accident in the post, would be more mischievous than a contract only binding upon the parties to it upon the acceptance actually reaching the offerer, and I can see no principle of law from which such an anomalous contract can be deduced.

There is no doubt that the implication of a complete, final, and absolutely binding contract being formed, as soon as the acceptance of an offer is posted, may in some cases lead to inconvenience and hardship. But such there must be at times in every view of the law. It is impossible in transactions which pass between parties at a distance, and have to be carried on through the medium of correspondence, to adjust conflicting rights between innocent parties, so as to make the consequences of mistake on the part of a mutual agent fall equally upon the shoulders of both. At the same time I am not prepared to admit that the implication in question will lead to any great or general inconvenience or hardship. An offerer, if he chooses, may always make the formation of the contract which he proposes dependent upon the actual communication to himself of the acceptance. If he trusts to the post he trusts to a means of communication which, as a rule, does not fail, and if no answer to his offer is received by him, and the matter is of importance to him, he can make inquiries of the person to whom his offer was addressed. On the other hand, if the contract is not finally concluded, except in the event of the acceptance actually reaching the offerer, the door would be opened to the perpetration of much fraud, and, putting aside this consideration, considerable delay in commercial transactions, in which despatch is, as a rule, of the greatest consequence, would be occasioned; for the acceptor would never be entirely safe in acting upon his acceptance until he had received notice that his letter of acceptance had reached its destination.

Upon balance of conveniences and inconveniences it seems to me, applying with slight alterations the language of the Supreme Court of the United States in *Tayloe v. Merchants Fire Insurance Co.* (1850), 9 How 390, more consistent with the acts and declarations of the parties in this case to consider the contract complete and absolutely binding on the transmission of the notice of allotment through the post, as the medium of communication that the parties themselves contemplated, instead of postponing its completion until the notice had been received by the defendant. Upon principle, therefore, as well as authority, I think that the judgment of Lopes, J., was right and should be affirmed, and that this appeal should therefore be dismissed.

[Baggallay LJ. gave a judgment to the same effect as Thesiger, LJ.]

Bramwell, L.J. [dissenting] The question in this case is not whether the post office was a proper medium of communication from the plaintiffs to the defendant. There is no doubt that it is so in all cases where personal service is not required. It is an ordinary mode of communication, and every person who gives any one the right to communicate with him, gives the right to communicate in an ordinary manner and so in this way and to this extent, that if an offer were made by letter in the morning to a person at a place within half an hour's railway journey of the offerer, I should say that an acceptance by post, though it did not reach the offerer till the next morning, would be in time. Nor is the question whether, when the letter reaches an offerer, the latter is bound and the bargain made from the time the letter is posted or despatched, whether by post or otherwise. The question in this case is different. I will presently state what in my judgment it is. Meanwhile I wish to mention some elementary propositions which, if carefully borne in mind, will assist in the determination of this case:

First. Where a proposition to enter into a contract is made and accepted, it is necessary, as a rule, to constitute the contract that there should be a communication of that acceptance to the proposer, per Brian, C.J., and Lord Blackburn: *Brogden v. Metropolitan Ry. Co.*

Secondly. That the present case is one of proposal and acceptance.

Thirdly. That as a consequence of or involved in the first proposition, if the acceptance is written or verbal, i.e., is by letter or message, as a rule, it must reach the proposer or there is no communication, and so no acceptance of the offer.

Fourthly. That if there is a difference where the acceptance is by a letter sent through the post which does not reach the offerer, it must be by virtue of some general rule or some particular agreement of the parties. As, for instance, there might be an agreement that the acceptance of the proposal may be by sending the article offered by the proposer to be bought, or hanging out a flag or sign to be seen by the offerer as he goes by, or leaving a letter at a certain place, or any other agreed mode, and in the same way there might be an agreement that dropping a letter in a post pillar box or other place of reception should suffice.

Fifthly. That as there is no such special agreement in this case, the defendant, if bound, must be bound by some general rule which makes a difference when the post office is employed as the means of communication.

Sixthly. That if there is any such general rule applicable to the communication of the acceptance of offers, it is equally applicable to all communications that may be made by post. Because, as I have said, the question is not whether this communication may be made by post. If, therefore, posting a letter which does not reach is a sufficient communication of acceptance of an offer, it is equally a communication of everything else which may be communicated by post, e.g., notice to quit. It is impossible to hold, if I offer my landlord to sell him some hay and he writes accepting my offer, and in the same letter gives me notice to quit, and posts his letter which, however, does not reach me, that he has communicated to me his acceptance of my offer, but not his notice to quit. Suppose a man has paid his tailor by cheque or banknote, and posts a letter containing a cheque or banknote to his tailor, which never reaches, is the tailor paid? If he is, would he be if he had never been paid before in that way? Suppose a man is in the habit of sending cheques and banknotes to his banker by post, and posts a letter containing cheques and banknotes, which never reaches. Is the banker liable? Would he be if this was the first instance of a remittance of the sort? In the cases I have supposed, the tailor and banker may have recognised this mode of remittance by sending back receipts and putting the money to the credit of the remitter. Are they liable with that? Are they liable without it? The question then is, is posting a letter which is never received a communication to the person addressed, or an equivalent, or something which dispenses with it? It is for those who say it is to make good their contention. I ask why is it? My answer beforehand to any argument that may be urged is, that it is not a communication, and that there is no agreement to take it as an equivalent for or to dispense with a communication. That those who affirm the contrary say the thing which is not. That if Brian, C.J., had had to adjudicate on the case, he would deliver the same judgment as that reported. That because a man, who may send a communication by post or otherwise, sends it by post, he should bind the person addressed, though the communication never reaches him, while he would not so bind him if he had sent it by hand, is impossible. There is no reason in it; it is simply arbitrary. I ask whether any one who thinks so is prepared to follow that opinion to its consequence; suppose the offer is to sell a particular chattel, and the letter accepting it never arrives, is the property in the chattel transferred? Suppose it is to sell an estate or grant a lease, is the bargain completed? The lease might be such as not to require a deed, could a subsequent lessee be ejected by the would-be acceptor of the offer because he had posted a letter? Suppose an article is advertised at so much, and that it would be sent on receipt of a post office order. Is it enough to post the letter? If the word "receipt" is relied on, is it really meant that that makes a difference? If it should be said let the offerer wait, the answer is, may be he may lose his market meanwhile. Besides, his offer may be by advertisement to all mankind. Suppose a reward for information, information posted does not reach, some one else gives it and is paid, is the offerer liable to the first man?

It is said that a contrary rule would be hard on the would-be acceptor, who may have made his arrangements on the footing that the bargain was concluded. But to hold as contended would be equally hard on the offerer, who may have made his arrangements on the footing that his offer was not accepted; his non-receipt of any communication may be attributable to the person to whom it was made being absent. What is he to do but to act on the negative, that no communication has been made to him? Further, the use of the post office is no more authorized by the offerer than the sending an answer by hand, and all these hardships would befall the person posting the letter if he sent it by hand. Doubtless in that case he would be the person to suffer if the letter did not reach its destination. Why should his sending it by post relieve him of the loss and cast it on the other party. It was said, if he sends it by hand it is revocable, but not if he sends it by post, which makes the difference. But it is revocable when sent by post, not that the letter can be got back, but its arrival might be anticipated by a letter by hand or telegram, and there is no case to shew that such anticipation would not prevent the letter from binding. It would be a most alarming thing to say that it would. That a letter honestly but mistakenly written and posted must bind the writer if hours before its arrival he informed the person addressed that it was coming, but was wrong and recalled; suppose a false but honest character given, and the mistake found out after the letter posted, and notice that it was wrong given to the person addressed.

Then, as was asked, is the principle to be applied to telegrams? Further, it seems admitted that if the proposer said, "unless I hear from you by return of post the offer is withdrawn," that the letter accepting it must reach him to bind him. There is indeed a case recently reported in the *Times*, before the Master of the Rolls, where the offer was to be accepted within fourteen days, and it is said to have been held that it was enough to post the letter on the 14th, though it would and did not reach the offerer till the 15th. Of course there may have been something in that case not mentioned in the report. But as it stands it comes to this, that if an offer is to be accepted in June, and there is a month's post between the places, posting the letter on the 30th of June will suffice, though it does not reach till the 31st of July; but that case does not affect this. There the letter reached, here it has not. If it is not admitted that "unless I hear by return the offer is withdrawn" makes the receipt of the letter a condition, it is to say an expression condition goes for nought. If it is admitted, is it not what every letter says? Are there to be fine distinctions, such as, if the words are "unless I hear from you by return of post, &c.," it is necessary the letter should reach him, but "let me know by return of post," it is not; or if in that case it is, yet it is not where there is an offer without those words. Lord Blackburn says that Mellish, L.J., accurately stated that where it is expressly or impliedly stated in the offer, "you may accept the offer by posting a letter," the moment you post this letter the offer is accepted. I agree; and the same thing is true of any other mode of acceptance offered with the offer and acted on — as firing a cannon, sending off a rocket, give your answer to my servant the bearer. Lord Blackburn was not dealing with the question before us; there was no doubt in the case before him that the letter had reached.

.   .   .

I am at a loss to see how the post office is the agent for both parties. What is the agency as to the sender? merely to receive? But suppose it is not an answer, but an original communication. What then? Does the extent of the agency of the post office depend on the contents of the letter? But if the post office is the agent of both parties, then the agent of both parties has failed in his duty, and to both. Suppose the offerer says, "My offer is conditional on your answer reaching me." Whose agent is the post office then? But how does an offerer make the post office his agent, because he gives the offeree an option of using that or any other means of communication.

I am of the opinion that this judgment should be reversed. I am of opinion that there was no bargain between these parties to allot and take shares, that to make such bargain there should have been an acceptance of the defendant's offer and a communication to him of that acceptance. That there was no such communication. That posting a letter does not differ from other attempts at communication in any of its consequences, save that it is irrevocable as between the poster and post office. The difficulty has arisen from a mistake as to what was decided in *Dunlop v. Higgins*, and from supposing that because there is a right to have recourse to the post as a means of communication, that right is attended with some peculiar consequences, and also from supposing that because if the letter reaches it binds from the time of posting, it also binds though it never reaches. Mischief may arise if my opinion prevails. It probably will not, as so much has been said on the matter that principle is lost sight of. I believe equal if not greater, will, if it does not prevail. I believe the latter will be obviated only by the rule being made nugatory by every prudent man saying, "your answer by post is only to bind if it reaches me." But the question is not to be decided on these considerations. What is the law? What is the principle? If Brian, C.J., had had to decide this, a public post being instituted in his time, he would have said the law is the same, now there is a post, as it was before, viz., a communication to affect a man must be a communication, i.e., must reach him.

Judgment affirmed.

PROBLEMS

1. Monica writes to Hilda a letter offering to sell a quantity of scrap iron. Hilda receives the letter and immediately writes accepting Monica's offer. One day later, before the letter is delivered, Hilda phones Monica to say that she does not want to buy the scrap iron. Is there a contract?

2. Would it make any difference if, in reliance on Hilda's refusal of her offer, Monica sold the scrap iron to Duncan?

In *Introduction to the Law of Contract* by J.E. Côté, 1974 (the first Canadian textbook on contracts), the author says: (p. 30)

"It would seem to follow [from the rule that a contract is made when the acceptance is mailed] that once the contract is so formed it cannot be unilaterally rescinded by either party, and so a purported withdrawal of the acceptance would be ineffective, even if it were dispatched by some faster means and arrived before the letter of acceptance did."

In an earlier passage dealing with the problems of communication of the acceptance in general, Côté said: (p. 28)

"Because one of the major purposes of the law of contracts is to create certainty and allow parties to buy and sell risks and guarantees of performance, it is important the parties know whether or not they are bound by a contract."

Do you think that these are adequate to explain the result that Côté would believe follows in the problems?

Are the following provisions of the Post Office Act (R.S.C. 1970, c. P-14) relevant?
41. Subject to the provisions of this Act and the regulations respecting undeliverable mail, mailable matter becomes the property of the person to whom it is addressed when it is deposited in a post office. R.S., c. 212, s. 39.
42. Neither Her Majesty nor the Postmaster General is liable to any person for any claim arising from the loss, delay or mishandling of anything deposited in a post office, except as provided in this Act or the regulations. R.S., c. 212, s. 40.

TINN v. HOFFMANN

(1873), 29 L.T.R. (N.S.) 271. Court of Exchequer.

This was an action brought by the plaintiff against the defendants to recover damages in respect of a breach of contract to deliver 800 tons of iron; and by the consent of the parties, and by order of Martin, B., dated May 30th, 1872, the facts were stated for the opinion of the Court of Exchequer in the following special case:

1. The plaintiff, Mr. Joseph Tinn, is an iron manufacturer, carrying on business at the Ashton Row Rolling Mills, near Bristol; and the defendant, who trades under the name and style of Hoffmann & Co., is an iron merchant, carrying on business at Middlesbro'-on-Tees.

2. In the months of November and December, 1871, the following correspondence passed between the plaintiff and the defendant relating to the proposed purchase and sale of certain iron, the particulars of which fully appear in the letters hereinafter set forth:
The plaintiff to the defendant:

"November 22, 1871.

"Messrs. Hoffmann & Co.:
"Dear Sirs: Please quote your lowest price for 800 tons No. 4 Cleveland, or other equally good brand, delivered at Portishead at the rate of 200 tons per month March, April, May, and June, 1872. Payment by four months' acceptance.
"Yours truly,   J. Tinn."

3. The defendants' reply:
"Royal Exchange Buildings, Middlesbro'-on-Tees,

"November 24, 1871.

"Joseph Tinn, Esq., Bristol:
"Dear Sir: We are obliged by your inquiry of the 22d inst., and by the present beg to offer you 800 tons No. 4 forge Middlesbro' pig iron (brand at our option, Cleveland if possible), at 69s. per ton delivered at Portishead, delivery 200 tons per month, March, April, May, and June, 1872, payment by your four months' acceptance from date of arrival.
"We shall be very glad if this low offer would induce you to favor us with your order, and waiting your reply by return, we remain, dear sir, yours truly,
"A. Hoffmann & Co."

4. The plaintiff to the defendant:

"Bristol, November 27, 1871.

"Messrs. Hoffmann & Co.:
"Dear Sirs: The price you ask is high. If I made the quantity 1200 tons, delivery 200 tons per month for the first six months of next year I suppose you would make the price lower? Your reply per return will oblige
"J. Tinn."

5. The defendant to the plaintiff in reply:
"Royal Exchange Buildings, Middlesbro'-on-Tees,

"November 28, 1871.

"Joseph Tinn, Esq., Bristol:

"Dear Sir: In reply to your favor of yesterday, we beg to state that we are willing to make you an offer of further 400 tons No. 4 forge Middlesbro' pig iron, 200 tons in January, 200 tons in February, at the same price we quoted you by ours of the 24th inst., though the rate of freight at the above-named time will doubtless be considerably higher than that of the following months.

"Our today's market was very firm again, and we feel assured we shall see a further rise ere long.

"Kindly let us have your reply by return of post as to whether you accept our offers of together 1200 tons and oblige yours truly,

"A. Hoffmann & Co."

6. The plaintiff to the defendant:

"Bristol, November 28, 1871.

"Messrs. Hoffman & Co.

"No. 4 Pig iron.

"Dear Sirs: You can enter me 800 tons on the terms and conditions named in your favor of the 24th inst., but I trust you will enter the other 400, making in all 1200 tons, referred to in my last, at 68s. per ton.

"Yours faithfully,   Joseph Tinn."

7. The defendants' reply:

"Royal Exchange Buildings,
Middlesbro'-on-Tees,

"November 29, 1871.

"Joseph Tinn, Esq.

"Dear Sir: We are obliged by your favor of yesterday, in reply to which we are sorry to state that we are not able to book your esteemed order for 1200 tons Nov. 4 forge at a lower price than that offered to you by us of yesterday — viz., 69s., and even that offer we can only leave you on hand for reply by tomorrow before twelve o'clock. Waiting your reply, we remain, dear sir, yours truly,

"A. Hoffmann & Co."

8. On December 1st, 1871, the plaintiff sent a telegram to the defendant, of which the following is a copy:

"From Tinn, Ashton.

"To Hoffman & Co.,
Middlesbro'-on-Tees.

"Book other 400 tons pig iron for me, same terms and conditions as before."

And on the same day the plaintiff sent a letter to the defendant, of which the following is a copy:

"December 1, 1871.

"Messrs. Hoffmann & Co.:

"Dear Sirs: I have your favor of the 29th ult. Please enter the remaining 400 tons No. 4 Forge Pig at 69s ex-ship Portishead, delivery to commence January 1872, payment by four months' acceptance against delivery. Kindly send me sold note for the 800 and 400 tons, and oblige,

yours truly,   J. Tinn."

9. The following correspondence then took place between the plaintiff and the defendants' clerk, duly authorized in that behalf.

The defendants' clerk to the plaintiff:

"Royal Exchange Buildings,
Middlesbro'-on-Tees,

"December 1, 1871.

"Joseph Tinn, Esq., Bristol:

"Dear Sir: We have your telegram on this day, 'Book other 400 tons Pig Iron, same terms and conditions as before,' which we note and shall lay before our Mr. Hoffmann on his return next week.

"Yours truly, for A. Hoffmann & Co.,

C. Jerveland."

10. Memorandum.

"December 2, 1871.

"From A. Hoffmann & Co.,
Middlesbro'-on-Tees.

"To Joseph Tinn, Esq., Bristol:

"The contents of your yesterday's favor is noted and we shall lay same before our principal on his return next week."

11. The defendants to the plaintiff:

"The Queen's Hotel, Manchester,

"December 4, 1871.

"Joseph Tinn, Esq., Bristol:

"Dear Sir: I am in receipt of telegram 'Book other 400 tons, same terms and conditions as before,' and favor of 1st inst. addressed to my firm, in reply to which I very much regret to state that I am not able to book the 1200 tons in question, as your reply to ours of November 28th and 29th did not reach us within the stipulated time; and as I had other offers for the same lot, I disposed of the latter previous to my leaving Middlesbro' and receiving your decision.

"Trusting to be more fortunate in future, I remain, dear sir, yours truly,

A. Hoffmann & Co."

12. The plaintiff to the defendant:

"December 5, 1871.

"Messrs. Hoffmann & Co.:

"Dear Sirs: I regret you cannot enter me the 400 tons No. 4 Forge Pig on the same terms as the 800 tons. Please send me sold note for 800 tons per return.

Yours truly,   J. Tinn."

13. The reply of the defendants:

"Royal Exchange Buildings,
Middlesbro'-on-Tees,

"December 6, 1871.

"Joseph Tinn, Esq., Bristol:

"Dear Sir: Your favor of yesterday to hand, in reply to which we have to state that we cannot send you contract for pig iron, having sold you none.

"The quotation for 1200 tons in our respect of 29th ult. was for your acceptance by 12 o'clock the 30th; and failing to receive such we disposed of the iron, being under other offers, as already intimated to you by our Mr. Hoffmann, and it is now utterly impossible for us to book you the quantity you require, or you may rest assured that we willingly would do so. We are, dear sir, yours truly,

"Pro A. Hoffmann & Co.

C. Jerveland."

14. It is agreed that all the facts and circumstances mentioned in the above correspondence are true, and that the court are to have power to draw all inferences of facts in the same way as a jury might do.

15. The course of post between Bristol and Middlesbrough is one day.

16. The plaintiff contends that he has a binding contract with the defendant whereby the defendants are bound to deliver to him 800 tons of iron. The defendants, on the other hand, contend that there is no such contract, and refuse to deliver any of the said iron.

The questions for the opinion of the Court are, first, whether, upon the facts stated and documents set out in the case, there is any binding contract on the part of the defendants to deliver 800 tons of iron to the plaintiff; secondly, whether, upon the facts and documents set out in the case, there is any binding contract on the part of the defendants to deliver any quantity of iron to the plaintiff, and if yea, what quantity and on what terms and conditions.

[The Court of Exchequer (Bramwell, Channell, and Pigott, BB.) gave judgment for the defendant; Kelly, C.B., dissenting on the ground that there was a contract for 800 tons. The plaintiff brought error to this Court.]

Honyman, J. I am of opinion that the judgment of the Court below was wrong, and that judgment ought to be entered for the plaintiff in respect of 800 tons. The question depends entirely on the construction and effect of the defendants' letter of the 24th and the two letters of November 28th, 1871, one written by the plaintiff and the other by the defendants. The plaintiff had been inquiring at what price the defendants would let him have 800 tons of iron, and by their letter of November 24th they named 69s. per ton as the price for the 800 tons, to be delivered at the rate of 200 tons per month, in the four months of March, April, May, and June, 1872; and that letter concluded thus, "waiting your reply by return." Mr. Kingdon, on the part of the plaintiff, admitted, and I think very properly, that the meaning of that was, we offer you that price, provided you accept it by return. Inasmuch as it was not accepted by return, as it stood, I presume had it stopped there, there would have been no contract. The plaintiff not only did not accept by return, but, on the contrary, he objected to the price, for on November 27th he wrote saying that the price was too high, and asking whether if he increased the quantity to 1200 tons, to be deliverable 200 tons per month — that is to say, in addition to the quantity he had already proposed for, to be delivered in March, April, May, and June, 1872, 400 tons more, to be delivered 200 tons in January and 200 in February, 1872, that would make the price lower. Upon that, on November 28th, the defendants wrote the following letter, on the construction of which I believe the difference of opinion among the members of the Court mainly arises [Reads letter of that date.] What is the meaning of that letter? It amounts to this: On November 24 we offered you 800 tons for delivery at 69s.; we now repeat to you that offer, and in addition to that, we make a further offer of 400 tons more — that is, we renew the offer of November 24th, and we make you a further offer of 400 tons, provided you accept those offers "by return of post." That does not mean exclusively a reply by letter by return of post, but you may reply by telegram or by verbal message, or by any means not later than a letter written and sent by return of post would reach us. If that is so, then comes the plaintiff's letter, written on the same day, November 28th, which crosses the defendants' letter of the same date, in which the plaintiff said, "You can enter me 800 tons on the terms and conditions named in your favor of the 24th inst., but I trust you will enter the other 400, making in all 1200 tons, referred to in my last, at 68s. per ton, ex ship Portishead."

I cannot agree in the opinion said to have been expressed by my Brothers Pigott and Channell in the Court below. As I understand, my Brother Pigott certainly says this is not a clean offer, or a clean acceptance of 800 tons, but that it is 800 tons on the condition or hope or trust that they would lower the price of the other 400 tons. I cannot accede to that view of the case. I assume that it plainly amounts to this, "I will take your 800 tons on the terms and conditions mentioned in the letter of the 24th inst., but I hope you will let me have the other lot at 68s. per ton; if you choose to do that, well and good." I cannot understand how it can be said that that is not an absolute acceptance of the 800 tons, supposing it was competent to the plaintiff to accept that quantity. In the Court below it seems to have been treated as if the offer of November 28th was one offer of 1200 tons. I do not think so. I think it is a repetition of the offer of 800 tons coupled with a further offer of 400 tons, and that it was competent to the plaintiff to accept one and not accept the other. My Brother Bramwell appears to have thought that it was not material to consider whether it was two separate offers of 400 tons and 800 tons, or an offer of 1200 tons, because in either view of the case, the plaintiff could not accept the one and reject the other. If it is to be construed as strictly one offer of 1200 tons, I can understand it, and then of course he could not accept the one and reject the other. But I do not think it is one offer of 1200 tons, nor two offers, one of 400, and the other of 800 tons, but that it is a repetition of the offer of 800 tons, with a further offer of further 400 tons. To say that he could not accept the 400 tons without the 800 tons seems, in my view of the matter, to throw no light on the question whether he might accept the 800 tons without the 400 tons. That being so, it being in my judgment a separate offer of 800 tons, and 400 tons in addition, I should have thought, had the plaintiff's letter of the 28th been written on November 29th, that nobody, but for the opinions which have been expressed here to-day, could have entertained a doubt that it would have been an acceptance. What, then, is the effect when the two letters are written on the same day and crossed each other in the post? Does that make any difference?

On this part of the case, as far as I can gather from the notes that have been given us of the judgments below, my Brother Bramwell is of the same opinion as I am, because I understand him to say that, if he had thought that these were two offers, and that the two offers were capable of being accepted the one without the other, then the fact of the acceptance crossing the offer would have been no bar to the contract. After the plaintiff had written the letter of November 28th mentioning the 800 tons, it could not be said that he would not have been bound by the defendants' letter of the same date, if it had been written on November 29th. I do not see how it can be contended that there would not then have been a valid contract for 800 tons, except with regard to the question of whether it were one offer, or two offers. Of course, if it is one offer, that is one thing; but if it be two offers, then, if the defendants' letter of November 28th had been written on the 29th, after he had received the plaintiff's letter of the 28th, it could not be said that that did not make a good contract for 800 tons. I cannot see why the fact of the letters crossing each other should prevent their making a good contract. If I say I am willing to buy a man's house on certain terms, and he at the same moment says that he is willing to sell it, and these two letters are posted so that they are irrevocable with respect to the writers, why should not that constitute a good contract? The parties are ad idem at one and the same moment. On these grounds it appears to me that the judgment of the Court below was wrong, and ought to be reversed. I speak with some hesitation in this case when I find that the opinion of the majority of my Brothers is against me, and also when the question turns entirely on the construction of a somewhat ambiguously written letter.

Brett, J. The question is, whether upon a true construction of this correspondence, there is a binding contract between the plaintiff and the defendants for the 800 tons of iron at 69s. It is argued on the one side that such a contract is disclosed because it is said that the defendants' letter of November 24th is an offer for the sale of 800 tons of iron, and this letter of November 28th leaves open the time for accepting that offer of November 24th, and makes a new offer with regard to another 400 tons; and that the defendants' offer of November 24th being thus opened by their letter of the 28th, the plaintiff's letter of the 28th is an acceptance of the defendants' offer of the 24th. On the other side it is argued that the defendants' letter of November 28th is not an opening of their offer of the 24th, but that it is an offer with regard to 1200 tons; and that even if it were a separate offer with regard to 800 tons and 400 tons, still that the true view of the matter is not that it reopens the letter of the 24th, but that it makes a new offer with regard to the 800 tons, and another separate offer, with regard to 400 tons; and that, upon such a view, the renewed offer with regard to 800 tons is not accepted, because the letter of the plaintiff of November 28th was not in answer to that offer, but was a letter crossing it.

Now with regard to the construction of the defendant's letter of November 28th, it seems to me that we must consider that the defendant's letter of November 24th is in answer to a request of the plaintiffs of November 22nd for an offer with regard to 800 tons, and is therefore an offer by them with regard to 800 tons. That offer left it open to the plaintiff to accept it within a period which is to be computed by the return of post. I agree that the words, "Your reply by return of post" fix the time for acceptance, and not the manner of accepting. But that time elapsed; there was no acceptance within the limited time. So far from there being an acceptance, it seems to me that the plaintiff's letter of November 27th rejects that offer; it rejects it on the ground the price is higher than the plaintiff is willing to give. That offer is therefore, not accepted within the limited time, but is rejected, and it seems to me is at once dead. The letter of the 27th then asks for an offer with respect to 1200 tons, and the letter of November 28th is a letter written "In reply to your favor of yesterday," that is, In reply to your request for an offer with regard to 1200 tons. "I now make you this offer." That seems to me to show that the letter of November 28th of the defendants is an offer with regard to 1200 tons, and not with regard to 800 tons and 400 tons separately. The way in which the offer with regard to the 1200 tons is made is this: "With regard to the first 800 of them, I make you a new offer upon the same terms as I made in the former offer on the 24th. With regard to the remaining 400 tons, I offer you to deliver them at the same price, but at different periods of delivery."

I think that the defendants' letter of November 28th, being a letter in answer to a request with regard to 1200 tons, is an offer with regard to 1200 tons, and that no such offer was ever accepted; but even if it could be taken that it was a separate offer with regard to 800 tons and 400 tons, I cannot accede to the view that it reopened the offer of November 24th. That offer was dead, and was no longer binding upon the defendants at all, and therefore it seems to me to be a wrong phrase to say that it reopened the offer of November 24th. The only legal way of construing it is to say that it is a new offer with regard to 800 tons. If it were a separate offer, which I should think it was not, it then would be a new offer with regard to 800 tons, and a separate offer with regard to 400 tons, but, even if it were so, I should think that the new offer with regard to the 800 tons had never been accepted, so as to make a binding contract. The new offer would not, in my opinion, be accepted, by the fact of the plaintiff's letter of November 28th crossing it. If the defendants' letter of November 28th is a new offer of the 800 tons, that could not be accepted by the plaintiff until it came to his knowledge, and his letter of November 28th could only be considered as a cross offer. Put it thus: If I write to a person and say, "If you can give me £6000 for my house, I will sell it to you," and on the same day, and before that letter reaches him, he writes to me, saying, "If you will sell me your house for £6000 I will buy it," that would be two offers crossing each other, and cross offers are not an acceptance of each other, therefore there will be no offer of either party accepted by the other. That is the case where the contract is to be made by the letters, and by the letters only. I think it would be different if there were already a contract in fact made in words, and then the parties were to write letters to each other, which crossed in the post, those might make a very good memorandum of the contract already made, unless the Statute of Frauds intervened. But where the contract is to be made by the letters themselves, you cannot make it by cross offers, and say that the contract was made by one party accepting the offer which was made to him. It seems to me, therefore, in both views, that the judgment of the Court below was right.

Judgment of the Court below affirmed.

[In separate opinions, Quain, J. agreed with Honyman, J., and Archibald, Blackburn, Grove, and Keating, JJ., agreed with Brett, J.]

QUESTIONS

1. What concept of offer does the majority have that would lead them to conclude that a contract cannot be made by cross-offers?

2. In what direction would argument based on commercial convenience point?

It is usually said that silence cannot be acceptance. Thus if A offers to sell his shares in B Ltd. to C and says, "If I don't hear from you, I shall take it that the deal is on", there is no contract. The case usually cited in support of this proposition is *Felthouse v. Bindley* (1862), 11 C.B. (N.S.) 869; 142 E.R. 1037 where an offer by a buyer to split the difference in the price between the buyer and seller ended with the words, "If I hear no more about him, I consider the horse mine at £30.15.0." There was held to be no contract even though it was clear that the seller intended the buyer to have the horse at the price offered by the buyer. The case is complicated by the fact that the action was brought by the buyer against an auctioneer who had sold the horse by mistake. The buyer's claim against the auctioneer could only have succeeded if at the date of the sale by the defendant, the horse was owned by the plaintiff.

But even this rule has exceptions.

WHEELER v. KLAHOLT

(1901), 59 N.E. 756. Massachussetts Supreme Judicial Court.

Holmes, C.J. This is an action for the price of one hundred and seventy-four pairs of shoes, and the question raised by the defendants' exceptions is whether there was any evidence, at the trial, of a purchase by the defendants. The plaintiffs contend that the defendants waived their exceptions by presenting and arguing a motion for a new trial upon the ground, among others, of the proposition of law on which their exceptions are based, they not having filed their exceptions until afterwards. The plaintiffs excepted to a ruling that the defendants had not waived their rights. The judge did not require the defendants to waive their exceptions as a condition of entertaining their motion so far as it went on the same ground, and there is nothing to show that his ruling on this preliminary point was not entirely right....

The evidence of the sale was this. The shoes had been sent to the defendants on the understanding that a bargain had been made. It turned out that the parties disagreed, and if any contract had been made it was repudiated by them both. Then, on September 11, 1899, the plaintiffs wrote to the defendants that they had written to their agent, Young, to inform the defendants that the latter might keep the goods "at the price you offer if you send us net spot cash at once. If you cannot send us cash draft by return mail, please return the goods to us immediately via Wabash & Fitchburg Railroad, otherwise they will go through New York City and it would take three or four weeks to get them." On September 15, the defendants enclosed a draft for the price less four per cent., which they said was the proposition made by Young. On September 18 the plaintiffs replied, returning the draft, saying that there was no deduction of four per cent., and adding, "if not satisfactory please return the goods at once by freight via Wabash & Fitchburg Railroad." This letter was received by the defendants on or before September 20, but the plaintiffs heard nothing more until October 25, when they were notified by the railroad company that the goods were in Boston.

It should be added that when the goods were sent to the defendants they were in good condition, new, fresh and well packed, and that when the plaintiffs opened the returned cases their contents were more or less defaced and some pairs of shoes were gone. It fairly might be inferred that the cases had been opened and the contents tumbled about by the defendants, although whether before or after the plaintiff's final offer perhaps would be little more than a guess.

Both parties invoke *Hobbs v. Whip Co.* (1893), 158 Mass. 194, 33 N. E. 495, the defendants for the suggestion on page 197, 158 Mass., and page 495, 33 N. E., that a stranger by sending goods to another cannot impose a duty of notification upon him at the risk of finding himself a purchaser against his own will. We are of opinion that this proposition gives the defendants no help. The parties were not strangers to each other. The goods had not been foisted upon the defendants, but were in their custody presumably by their previous assent, at all events by their assent implied by their later conduct. The relations between the parties were so far similar to those in the case cited, that if the plaintiffs' offer had been simply to let the defendants have the shoes at the price named, with an alternative request to send them back at once, as in their letters, the decision would have applied, and a silent retention of the shoes for an unreasonable time would have been an acceptance of the plaintiffs' terms, or, at least, would have warranted a finding that it was....

The defendants seek to escape the effect of the foregoing principle, if held applicable, on the ground of the terms offered by the plaintiffs. They say that those terms made it impossible to accept the plaintiffs' offer, or to give the plaintiffs any reasonable ground for understanding that their offer was accepted, otherwise than by promptly forwarding the cash. They say that whatever other liabilities they may have incurred they could not have purported to accept an offer to sell for cash on the spot by simply keeping the goods. But this argument appears to us to take one half of the plaintiffs' proposition with excessive nicety, and to ignore the alternative. Probably the offer could have been accepted and the bargain have been made complete before sending on the cash. At all events, we must not forget the alternative, which was the immediate return of the goods.

The evidence warranted a finding that the defendants did not return the goods immediately or within a reasonable time, although subject to a duty in regard to them. The case does not stand as a simple offer to sell for cash received in silence, but as a twofold offer to one who was subject to a duty to return the goods, allowing him either to buy or to return the shoes at once, followed by a failure on his part to do anything. Under such circumstances a jury would be warranted in finding that a neglect of the duty to return imported an acceptance of the alternative offer to sell, although coupled with a failure to show that promptness on which the plaintiffs had a right to insist if they saw fit, but which they also were at liberty to waive.

Exceptions overruled.

The Consumer Protection Act (R.S.O. 1970, c. 82) provides:

46.(1) In this section,
    (a) "credit" means the advancing of money, goods or services to or on behalf of another for repayment at a later time, whether or not there is a cost of borrowing, and includes variable credit;
    (b) "unsolicited goods" means personal property furnished to a person who did not request it and a request shall not be inferred from inaction or the passing of time alone, but does not include,
        (i) personal property that the recipient knows or ought to know is intended for another person, or
        (ii) personal property supplied under a contract in writing to which the recipient is a party that provides for the periodic supply of personal property to the recipient without further solicitation.
(2) No action shall be brought by which to charge any person upon any arrangement for the extension of credit evidenced by a credit card unless the person to whom credit is to be extended requested or accepted the credit arrangement and card in writing, and the obtaining of credit by the person named in the credit card shall be deemed to constitute such written acceptance by him.
(3) No action shall be brought by which to charge any person for payment in respect of unsolicited goods notwithstanding their use, misuse, loss, damage or theft.
(4) Except as provided in this section, the recipient of unsolicited goods or of a credit card that has not been requested or accepted in accordance with subsection 2 has no legal obligation in respect of their use or disposal.
(5) This section applies in respect of credit cards and unsolicited goods received on or after the 3rd day of December, 1970.

The following extract may help to explain why it is that the rules of offer and acceptance have exercised such a strong fascination over the minds of lawyers. It may be necessary that you see the rabbit-hole — perhaps every lawyer must have experienced its attractive warmth, where all questions can be answered and where there is nothing to disturb the serenity and certainty of life as lived by rules. But, having experienced this, you must remember that, as Holmes said, "certainty generally is illusion and repose is not the destiny of man". No lasting answers to any problems are likely to be found in the rabbit-hole, and it is the purpose of this course to drag you from it.

" The rules of Offer and Acceptance have been worked over; they have been written over; they have been shaped and rubbed smooth with pumice, they wear the rich deep polish of a thousand classrooms; they have a grip on the vision and indeed on the affections held by no other rules "of law", real or pseudo. For it was Offer and Acceptance which first led each of us out of laydom into The Law. Puzzled, befogged, adrift in the strange words and technique of cases, with only our sane feeling of what was decent for a compass, we felt the warm sun suddenly, we knew that we were arriving, we knew we too could "think like a lawyer": That was when we learned to down seasickness as A revoked when B was almost up the flag-pole. Within the first October, we had achieved a technical glee in justifying judgment then for A; and succulent memory lingers, of the way our dumber brethren were pilloried as Laymen still. This is therefore no area of "rules" to be disturbed. It is an area where we want no disturbance, and will brook none. It is the Rabbit-Hole down which we fell into the Law, and to him who has gone down it, no queer phenomenon is strange; he has been magicked; the logic of Wonderland we then entered makes mere discrepant decision negligible. And it is not only hard, it is obnoxious, for any of us who have gone through that experience to even conceive of Offer and Acceptance as perhaps in need of re-examination.

K. N. Llewellyn (1938) 48 Yale L.J. 1, 32"

(4) When do negotiation come to an end? The problem of indefiniteness

The cases that have just been discussed have been concerned with whether or not one party made an offer to the other that the other could accept and whether there was an acceptance. Sometimes the problem is even more basic. This is the problem that was mentioned in the introduction to this chapter of deciding if the parties' negotiations have progressed far enough for the courts to be able to say that any kind of enforceable agreement had been reached.

PROBLEMS

Patricia owns a car which she finds too expensive to run. She tells her friend, Valerie, that she is planning to sell her car. The following conversation takes place:

P.: "My old car cost me $100 last month for repairs alone, I shall have to sell it."

V.: "I need a car — even one as expensive to run as yours if I can get it cheap enough."

P.: "Well, I would be happy to sell the car to you if you can pay me a decent amount."

V.: "Great, then it's a deal."

1. Would you think that a contract had been made? If not, why not? The conversation continues:

P.: "Hey, hold on a minute, we have not settled on the price."

V.: "Oh, I know, that that's only a formality. I now know that you will sell it only to me."

P.: "But that still depends on the price."

V.: "I expect to pay no more than any used car dealer will pay you and they have a book telling them what price should be paid for any used car."

P.: "But my car is in a very good condition and you could not buy a used one for the price that they would give me."

V.: "O.K. Then I'll give you the going price for your car and 20% more. Their markup would be about that."

P.: "Fine."

2. Would you now think that a contract had been made? If not, why not? The conversation continues:

V.: "Of course, I cannot pay you all at once. I should be able to pay you about $100 per month. Is that O.K.?"

P.: "Like hell it is. I expected to get cash. The deal is off."

3. Patricia subsequently sells the car to Muriel. Valerie sues for damages for breach of contract. What result?

The next three cases explore the courts' approach to this problem. As you read these cases consider the following questions:

1. Are these cases authority for any propositions of law?

2. If so, what are the propositions?

3. Are the cases consistent?

FOLEY v. CLASSIQUE COACHES, LTD.

[1934] 2 K.B. 1. Court of Appeal (England); Scrutton, Greer and Maughan L.JJ.

APPEAL from a decision of Lord Hewart C.J.

The plaintiff was a retail dealer in petrol and the defendants were the owners of motor coaches who carried on business at premises adjoining those of the plaintiff at 481 Lea Bridge Road, Leyton.

By an agreement in writing dated April 11, 1930, it was agreed that the plaintiff should sell and the defendants should purchase for £1100. the free-hold property which immediately adjoined that retained by the plaintiff. The sale was made subject to certain conditions, among others that the defendants would enter into an agreement with the plaintiff as to the sale of petrol and/or oil, the terms of which had been agreed between them. On the same date the agreement as to the sale of petrol and/or oil was signed. It recited that it was "supplemental to an agreement bearing even date here-with and made between the same parties as are parties thereto and whereby the vendor has agreed to sell and the company to purchase" the property in the already mentioned agreement, and "whereas the vendor and his present wife are the proprietors of a petrol and oil filling station at his said address and the company are proposing to carry on the business of a char-a-banc and garage proprietors on the said adjoining land and it has been agreed that the vendor shall supply to the company and the company will take from the vendor all petrol as shall be required by the company as herein-after mentioned. Now it is hereby agreed as follows: —

> "1. The vendor shall sell to the company and the company shall purchase from the vendor all petrol which shall be required by the company for the running of their said business at a price to be agreed by the parties in writing and from time to time.
>
> "2. The vendor shall deliver the said petrol to the company from the vendor's pumps now or hereafter on his said land.
>
> "3. This agreement shall remain in force during the life of the vendor and his present wife if she survives him."

Clause 4 dealt with the contingency of a strike or lock-out.

> "5. In the event of the company being wound up... the vendor may determine

this agreement at any time after the commencement of such winding-up by giving one week's notice in writing of his intention so to do ... and upon the expiration of such notice this agreement shall cease ... but without prejudice to the right of action of the vendor in respect of any breach of the company's agreements herein contained.

"6. The company shall not purchase any petrol from any other person or corporation so long as the vendor is able to supply them with sufficient petrol to satisfy their daily requirements but nothing herein contained shall prevent the vendor from selling petrol and/or oil to any other person or corporation to be used for any purposes whatever provided that the company and their servants shall be at liberty to purchase such petrol as may be found necessary to complete the particular journey when engaged on journeys over a distance necessitating the re-fuelling of their vehicles.

"7. The vendor shall supply the said petrol of a standard and quality at present supplied by the vendor or of such other standard and quality as the company may reasonably approve.

"8. If any dispute or difference shall arise on the subject matter or construction of this agreement the same shall be submitted to arbitration in the usual way in accordance with the provisions of the Arbitration Act, 1889."

The land, the subject of the first agreement, was duly conveyed to the company, and from April 26, 1930, till October 7, 1933, the defendants bought petrol from the plaintiff in pursuance of the agreement at prices charged by the plaintiff in accounts delivered by him to the defendants each week.

Disputes then arose between the parties as to the price and quality of the petrol, and eventually the defendants' solicitor wrote this letter to the plaintiff dated September 29, 1933 :

"It appears that although you have supplied petrol to my clients as and when they have required it no agreement in writing as to price has ever been made, nor any agreement of any sort thereunder. My clients have from time to time sent you their cheque in payment of statements of account rendered by you. Having considered this alleged agreement and the aforesaid facts, I have advised my clients that this document is of no force or effect, and therefore, acting on their behalf, I hereby give you notice that my clients do not intend to be bound by any of the provisions contained in this alleged agreement. As from October 8, 1933, my clients will be purchasing their petrol supplies elsewhere."

The plaintiff thereupon issued a writ claiming (1.) a declaration that the petrol agreement was valid and binding upon the parties; (2.) an injunction to restrain the defendants from purchasing any petrol required by them for the carrying on of their said business from any persons other than the plaintiff; (3.) an account of all petrol bought by the defendants in breach of the said petrol agreement from any person other than the plaintiff; and (4.) damages for breach of contract.

The defendants pleaded that no price at which petrol should be sold to them by the plaintiff had been agreed; that the provision relating to the supply of petrol did not constitute a binding and/or complete agreement; that clause 6 of the agreement was an unreasonable and unnecessary restraint of the defendants' trade and was contrary to public policy and illegal; and further, or in the alternative, that that provision was applicable when, and only so long as, the parties agreed the price at which petrol was to be supplied.

.   .   .

His Lordship therefore granted an injunction restraining the defendants their agents and servants from any breach of clause 6 and awarded an amount of damages to be ascertained.

The defendants appealed. The appeal was heard on March 15 and 16, 1934....

Scrutton L.J. In this appeal I think that the Lord Chief Justice's decision was right, and I am glad to come to that conclusion, because I do not regard the appellants' contention as an honest one.

The nature of the case is this: the respondent, the plaintiff in the action, had some land, part of which was occupied by petrol pumps. Adjoining that land was some vacant land belonging to him which the appellants wanted to use as the headquarters for their char-à-bancs, and they approached the respondent, who was willing to sell on the terms that the appellants obtained all their petrol from him. It is quite clear that unless the appellants had agreed to this they would never have got the land. There was a discussion whether this term about the petrol and the agreement to purchase the land should be put in one document or in two, but ultimately it was decided to put them in two documents of even date. One relates specifically to the sale and purchase of the land, and that was to go through on condition that the appellants undertook to enter into the petrol agreement, the terms of which had been already agreed. On the same day the second agreement was signed reciting that it was supplemental to the agreement of even date, that is the agreement for the sale of the land. The petrol agreement included a clause that if any dispute or difference should arise on the subject-matter or construction "the same shall be submitted to arbitration in the usual way." It is quite clear that the parties intended to make an agreement, and for the space of three years no doubt entered the mind of the appellants that they had a business agreement, for they acted on it during that time. The petrol supplied by the respondent was non-combine petrol, but he had also combine petrol pumps. The non-combine petrol was supplied to the appellants at a price lower than that paid by the public, and an account was rendered periodically in writing and paid. In the third year some one acting for the appellants thought he could get better petrol elsewhere, and on September 29, 1933, their solicitor, thinking he saw a way out of the agreement, wrote on behalf of the appellants the letter of September 29, 1933, repudiating the agreement. Possibly the solicitor had heard something about the decision of the House of Lords in *May & Butcher v. The King* [reported as a note] but probably had not heard of *Braithwaite v. Foreign Hardwood Co.*, [1905] 2 K.B. 543, in which the Court of Appeal decided that the wrongful repudiation of a contract by one party relieves the other party from the performance of any conditions precedent. If the solicitor had known of that decision he would not have written the letter in the terms he did. Thereafter the respondent brought his action claiming damages for breach of the agreement, a declaration that the agreement is binding, and an injunction to restrain the appellants from purchasing petrol from any other person. The Lord Chief Justice decided that the respondent was entitled to judgment, as there was a binding agreement by which the appellants got the land on condition that they should buy their petrol from the respondent. I observe that the appellants' solicitor in his letter made no suggestion that the land would be returned, and I suppose the appellants would have been extremely annoyed if they had been asked to return it when they repudiated the condition.

A good deal of the case turns upon the effect of two decisions of the House of Lords which are not easy to fit in with each other. The first of these cases is *May & Butcher v. The King*, which related to a claim in respect of a purchase of surplus stores from a Government department. In the Court of Appeal two members of the Court took the view that inasmuch as there was a provision that the price of the stores which were to be offered from time to time was to be agreed there was no binding contract because an agreement to make an agreement does not constitute a contract, and that the language of clause 10 that any dispute as to the construction of the agreement was to be submitted to arbitration was irrelevant, because there was not an agreement, although the parties thought there was. In the second case, *Hillas & Co. v. Arcos* (1932), 38 Com. Cas. 23, there was an agreement between Hillas & Co. and the Russian authorities under which Hillas & Co. were to take in one year 22,000 standards of Russian timber, and in the same agreement they had an option to take in the next year 100,000 standards, with no particulars as to the kind of timber or as to the terms of shipment or any of the other matters one expects to find dealt with on a sale of a large quantity of Russian timber over a period. The Court of Appeal, which included Greer L.J. and myself, both having a very large experience in these timber cases, came to the conclusion that as the House of Lords in *May & Butcher v. The King* considered that where a detail had to be agreed upon there was no agreement until that detail was agreed, we were bound to follow the decision in *May & Butcher v. The King* and hold that there was no effective agreement in respect of the option, because the terms had not been agreed. It was, however, held by the House of Lords in *Hillas & Co. v. Arcos* that we were wrong in so deciding and that we had misunderstood the decision in *May & Butcher v. The King*. The House took this line: it is quite true that there seems to be considerable vagueness about the agreement but the parties contrived to get through it on the contract for 22,000 standards, and so the House thought there was an agreement as to the option which the parties would be able to get through also despite the absence of details. It is true that in the first year the parties got through quite satisfactorily; that was because during that year the great bulk of English buyers were boycotting the Russian sellers. In the second year the position was different. The English buyers had changed their view and were buying large quantities of Russian timber, so that different conditions were then prevailing. In *Hillas & Co. v. Arcos* the House of Lords said that they had not laid down universal principles of construction in *May & Butcher v. The King*, and that each case must be decided on the construction of the particular document, while in *Hillas & Co. v. Arcos* they found that the parties believed they had a contract. In the present case the parties obviously believed they had a contract and they acted for three years as if they had; they had an arbitration clause which relates to the subject-matter of the agreement as to the supply of petrol, and it seems to me that this arbitration clause applies to any failure to agree as to the price. By analogy to the case of a tied house there is to be implied in this contract a term that the petrol shall be supplied at a reasonable price and shall be of reasonable quality. For these reasons I think the Lord Chief Justice was right in holding that there was an effective and enforceable contract, although as to the future no definite price had been agreed with regard to the petrol.

. . .

The appeal therefore fails, and no alteration is required in the form of the injunction that has been granted.

Appeal dismissed.

[The judgments of Greer and Maughan L.JJ. have been omitted.]

QUESTION

Could the solicitor for the defendants in *Foley v. Classique* have improved his clients' case by a differently drafted letter? If so, how?

An example of the same issue in a recent Ontario case is provided by *Lake Ontario Cement Ltd. v. Golden Eagle Oil Ltd.* (1974), 46 D.L.R. (3d) 659 (Ont.), Parker J. The parties had engaged in negotiations for the purchase by the plaintiff of large amounts of fuel oil from the defendant. Telephone calls and letters passed between the parties. No formal contract was ever signed, since the defendant found the deal would be unprofitable. The trial judge found that a concluded contract had been reached even in the absence of a formal contract. The parties eventually settled for $2,700,000 to be paid by the defendant to the plaintiff.

The case is a good example of the problem of deciding when the parties have reached an agreement. The judgment documents the exchange of phone calls and letters but the decision of the judge is found in one paragraph,

> "I accept the evidence of the plaintiff's witnesses. While there is language in the correspondence and in the draft agreements which is consistent with the submissions of either counsel, I find that the intent of the parties was to enter into a firm contract and that they did so. They did not have in mind any specific subject-matter that required clarification."

The conclusion is a finding of fact that is, in effect, unappealable — the large sum agreed on in settlement is the best evidence possible of this.

BRISTOL, CARDIFF AND SWANSEA AERATED BREAD CO. v. MAGGS

(1890), 44 Ch. D. 616. Chancery Division (England).

This was an action by the Plaintiffs, the *Bristol, Cardiff, and Swansea Aërated Bread Company (Limited)*, against the Defendant, a baker and confectioner carrying on business at 15, *Duke Street, Cardiff,* for the specific performance of a contract alleged to be constituted by two letters. The first was written by the Defendant to Colonel *Guthrie*, a director of the Plaintiff company, and was as follows: —

"*Cardiff,* 29th of May, 1899.

"Dear Sir, — I beg to submit to you the following conditions for disposal of my business carried on at 15, *Duke Street, Cardiff.* Lease and goodwill, £450 (lease from the 29th of September, 1888, for fourteen years). All fixtures, fittings,utensils, &c., stock-in-trade connected with the premises to be taken at valuation.

"Yours truly,

"R. Maggs.

"This offer to hold good for ten days."

The letter did not on the face of it shew to whom it was written. Colonel *Guthrie*, writing with the authority of the board of directors of the company, replied as follows: —

"Cardiff, 1st of June, 1889.

"Dear Sir, — On behalf of the *Bristol, Cardiff, and Swansea Aërated Bread Company (Limited)*, I accept your offer for shop and lease, &c., 15, *Duke Street, Cardiff*.

"Yours truly,

"John Guthrie.

"For *B., C., and S. Aërated Bread Company.*

"Mr. *R. Maggs*,

"15, *Duke Street, Cardiff*."

On the 2nd of June, 1889, the Defendant's solicitor sent Colonel *Guthrie* a formal memorandum of agreement for approval, with an accompanying letter. This memorandum was altered by the Plaintiffs' solicitors, mainly by the insertion of a clause preventing the vendor for five years from carrying on a like business within the borough of *Cardiff* or within a distance of five miles from the Townhall. The memorandum so altered was returned on the 4th of June, with a letter of the Plaintiffs' solicitors. On the 5th of June the Defendant's solicitor wrote sending the draft again to the Plaintiffs' solicitors, with a modification of the proposed additional clause. On the 6th of June the Plaintiffs' solicitors wrote that they could not themselves agree to the proposed modification, but that they had asked Colonel *Guthrie* to call about it.

On the 7th the Defendant's solicitor wrote that he regretted the Plaintiffs' solicitors had not agreed to the terms of the draft contract, and continued: "Colonel *Guthrie* has not been near me, and by my client's instructions I beg to inform you that he declines to proceed further in the matter."

On the 8th Colonel *Guthrie* saw the Defendant's solicitor and said he had come to settle the agreement which had been returned to him. The answer was that he was too late; the Defendant had made other arrangements. Colonel *Guthrie* replied he was prepared to sign the agreement leaving out the disputed clause. The solicitor declined; and Colonel *Guthrie* went immediately to the Defendant, who told him that he wished to have the agreement cancelled, because his son was very much against his parting with the shop. The Defendant, it appeared, did not suggest that there was no agreement, but asked Colonel *Guthrie* to use his influence with his co-directors to get the sale cancelled. The memorandum of agreement contained several terms not expressed in the letters; for example, it provided for the book debts and books of account being reserved to the vendor and for the payment of a deposit of £45; it fixed the 24th of June as the day for completion of the purchase and delivery of possession; it provided for delivery of abstract of title and the date from which it was to commence, and for other matters, all of which were more or less of a formal nature.

The action now came on for trial.

1890. March 5. **Kay, J.** (after stating the facts, continued): —

The contested stipulation in the memorandum of agreement as to restricting the vendor from carrying on a like business to that which he had sold was not by any means a matter of form. After some conflict of opinion, it has been decided…, that a man who sells the goodwill of a business may not only set up a similar business next door and say that he is the person who carried on the old business, but that he may also solicit the customers of the old business to continue to deal with him, although by these proceedings he might not only destroy all benefit to the purchaser of the thing which he had bought, but might recover to himself the actual possession of it. Such a fraudulent proceeding, according to the decision, cannot be prevented by any Court of Law or Equity. It follows that the stipulation which the company's solicitors introduced into the draft was one which they were not entitled to insert if the two letters which I have read were a complete contract. In other words, they were trying to obtain an additional and most important concession from the vendor. Now, put aside for a moment the *Statute of Frauds* and decided cases, and suppose this to pass in conversation: *A.* offers to *B.* his business, lease, and goodwill for £450. *B.* says, "I accept." A day or two afterwards *B.* asks *A.* to engage not to carry on a similar business within a distance of five miles. *A.* answers, "I cannot agree to that, but I will if you say three miles." *B.* takes time to consider, saying he will send an agent next day to settle the terms. The agent does not go next day, and *A.* accordingly says to *B.*, "I put an end to the matter." No one could doubt that that would be a continuous negotiation, and that *B.* could not say, "I will disregard all that followed the acceptance of the first offer, and insist on there being a complete contract by that acceptance." Well, then, still leaving out of sight the statute and authorities, suppose all this to take place by letters between *A.* and *B.* instead of conversation; it is obvious the result must be the same. Some of the letters being by the principals and some by the solicitors could not make any difference. …

It was suggested that the ten days during which the offer was to remain open had not expired when it was withdrawn. But this can make no difference. The offer was not a contract, and the term that it should remain open for ten days was therefore not binding. It has often been held that such an offer may, notwithstanding, be withdrawn within the time limited…

I decide this case against the Plaintiffs upon the ground, that although the two letters relied on would, if nothing else had taken place, have been sufficient evidence of a complete agreement, yet the Plaintiffs have themselves shewn that the agreement was not complete by stipulating afterwards for an important additional term, which kept the whole matter of purchase and sale in a state of negotiation only, and that the Defendant was therefore at liberty to put an end to the negotiations, as he did, by withdrawing his offer.

The action must be dismissed with costs.

PROBLEM

What would you do as solicitor for the purchaser to get your client out of the mess that he found himself in?

In *Bellamy v. Debenham* (1890), 45 Ch. D. 481, North J. said:

"… Mr. Justice Kay, in *Bristol, Cardiff, and Swansea Aerated Bread Co. v. Maggs* … by way of illustration [puts] the case of a definite offer to sell a business, lease, and good will, and a definite acceptance, and after that negotiations between the parties as to whether a new term, limiting the area within which the vendor of the business was to carry on a similar business, should be introduced, and said that in such a case he thought that the purchaser could not disregard all that followed the acceptance of the prior offer, and insist on there being a complete contract by that acceptance.... In my opinion, subsequent negotiations, first commenced on new points after a contract complete in itself has been signed, cannot be regarded as constituting a part of the negotiations going on at the time when it was signed... I do not in any way dissent from the view which Mr. Justice Kay took of the case then before him; but those remarks of his, if they meant as much as they might possibly mean, seem to me to go too far, and I should not be prepared to follow them."

PROBLEM

Alexander is anxious to have his wife's picture painted by an eminent portrait painter, Miriam. He contacts Miriam who offers to do the portrait for $5,000. Alexander wants to have the sittings start before his wife's birthday, May 11, but even if this is not possible, he wants to accept Miriam's offer. Miriam's portraits are very popular and there is a great demand for her work.

Which of the following acceptances should he use?

a) "I accept your offer to paint my wife's portrait on the understanding that the sittings will begin before May 11."

b) "I accept your offer to paint my wife's portrait but request that the sittings begin before May 11."

HARVEY v. PERRY

[1953] 1 S.C.R. 233. Supreme Court of Canada; Kerwin, Taschereau, Estey, Locke and Cartwright JJ.

[The parties had been negotiating for the sale of eight oil leases in Alberta. The appellant defendant, Harvey, as vendor, and the respondent plaintiff, Perry, as agent for purchasers, exchanged a number of letters. The material ones are reproduced in the judgment. The trial judge found a contract in the letters of May 2, 8, 15 and August 24 and in Harvey's sending the leases. This judgment was upheld by the Alberta Supreme Court, Appellate Division.

Harvey appealed to the Supreme Court of Canada.

The judgment of the court was given by]

Estey J.: —... The letter of May 2nd is written by respondent in the name of his firm and points out that appellant's terms, as submitted on April 26th (above quoted), are so high "we cannot handle it at all," but then continues:

"However, you might consider the following and if you feel that you could accept these terms, I am sure we could put a deal over for you...."

On May 8th appellant wrote: "I will accept your proposition..."

The respondent, in his letter of May 2nd, submits terms upon which "I am sure we can put a deal over for you". The appellant's reply of May 8th, when read and construed in relation thereto, discloses that the terms are submitted as a basis for respondent's negotiating a deal. In fact respondent's letter of May 15th makes it clear that the terms were so regarded:

"We will proceed immediately to try and consummate a deal for you at the earliest possible moment. There will, in all probability, be a counter proposal or two from our clients, and if such is the case, we will submit them to you at once."

In the correspondence that follows respondent continues to write in the name of the firm, explaining delays but always hopeful of concluding an agreement.

. . .

On August 24th the respondent's solicitors enter into the correspondence and write the letter which the learned trial Judge and their Lordships in the Appellate Division particularly refer to as constituting an acceptance of an offer made by the appellant. The material part of the solicitors' letter of August 24th reads as follows:

> "Re: P. & N.G. Leases Nos. 76411 to 76418 both inclusive in Alberta
>
> "This letter is written at the request of and under the instructions of Mr. A.C. Perry of this city, who advises that he is in a position to take these leases under the terms and conditions contained in his letter to you of the 2nd May last and your letter to his firm dated May 8th, 1950.
>
> "Mr. Perry has asked us to prepare the Assignment and other necessary papers, but in order to do that it will be necessary that we have access to the above leases now in your possession.
>
> "If you will forward these leases to us we hereby give our undertaking to hold them under our control until we are in a position to remit to you the compensation you are entitled to receive."

This, with great respect, is not the language of an acceptance, but rather that of an agent informing his principal that he himself "is in a position to take these leases under the terms and conditions contained in his letter to you of the 2nd May last and your letter to his firm dated May 8th, 1950". That it was not intended to conclude a contract appears from respondent's solicitors' further letter of August 26th, in which they state "some discussion between you will be necessary before adequate instructions can be given to draw such an Agreement". On the same date, August 26th, respondent indicates that he is not accepting an offer and thereby making a contract when he writes to the appellant, in part, as follows: "Mr. Howatt of Howatt and Howatt, my solicitor, is sending through a copy of the proposed agreement. However you and I will get together and complete the terms."

While the letters of May 2nd and 8th were intended as a basis for negotiations, as already stated, it is fair to conclude that a sale upon the terms thereof would have been agreeable to appellant. Even if, however, they be construed to be an offer, the letter of August 24th is not an acceptance because of both its own language and that of the letters of August 26th, which discloses that the respondent was not accepting an offer, as he contemplated "you and I will get together and complete the terms".

The respondent, however, contends that the appellant's conduct in forwarding the leases, as requested in the letter of August 24th, discloses an intention on his part that the letter was an acceptance. It must be observed that these leases were sent in order that an assignment might be prepared as requested by the respondent. That such an assignment could only be and was intended by the respondent to be but a proposed assignment is clear upon a reading of the above quotations from the letter of August 24th and the two of August 26th. There were then, as respondent himself stated, terms to be completed. In these circumstances the sending of the leases goes no further than to indicate a willingness that negotiations might continue, rather than that an agreement had been concluded.

. . .

Moreover, when the whole of the correspondence and conversations are considered it is clear that the parties had not agreed upon the terms of a contract.

However, negotiations continued. The "get together" contemplated by respondent's letter of August 26th (above quoted) took place at Saginaw on September 1st. Respondent says that the parties hereto did there "complete the terms" of the contract and then went to the appellant's solicitor's office where they were detailed to him. It is common ground that these terms were not reduced to writing upon that date and, therefore, at that time there was no compliance with the requirements of the *Statute of Frauds*.

Inasmuch as the learned trial Judge accepted the respondent's evidence "where there is any conflict" between his and that of the appellant, the foregoing, as to what took place at Saginaw, must be accepted, even though the appellant's evidence may be somewhat to the contrary.

The respondent deposes that just before leaving appellant at Saginaw "I then said to Mr. Harvey, we had made a deal and we will rush it through as quickly as we can; and we shook hands on that deal right there and then in front of the hotel: and I went to my hotel room and immediately phoned Mr. Howatt's office". In that telephone conversation he gave instructions relative to the contents of the agreement. As a result, when he arrived at Edmonton and went straight to Mr. Howatt's office, the agreement which was enclosed in the letter of September 2nd to appellant was in the course of preparation. The parties hereto had agreed at Saginaw that the assignment of leases, properly executed, would be deposited in the Royal Bank of Canada, Main Branch, Edmonton, and surrendered to respondent upon payment of $20,000 within a period of 15 days. Notwithstanding that agreement, the proposed agreement, as prepared at Edmonton, signed by the respondent and enclosed with the letter of September 2nd, included no such provision. On the contrary, it provided: "The Assignee shall pay to the Assignor in cash the sum of Twenty Thousand American ($20,000.00) Dollars or its equivalent in Canadian dollars forthwith after the assignments of the said leases have been filed with and accepted by the Department of Mines and Minerals of the Province of Alberta."

The appellant's solicitors replied under date of September 7th...

"The procedure contemplated by your letter is considerably at variance with that discussed with Mr. Perry....

"If Mr. Perry is unwilling to consummate the transaction in the manner above outlined then we assume there is no cause for further negotiations, unless you can suggest a substituted procedure which will afford Mr. Harvey the same protection.

"In the interim, the documents enclosed with your said letter dated the 2nd instant are herewith returned."

On September 9th respondent's solicitor replied, in part: "We have your favour of the 7th instant and the terms are acceptable." He therein submitted a redraft of the consideration in the assignment with respect to which the letter stated: "We trust this will meet with your approval."

The record does not suggest that the insertion of a provision as to the payment of $20,000 so completely different from that agreed upon at Saginaw was an error, but rather that respondent did so in order that he might obtain terms more satisfactory to himself. This view is supported, not only by his conduct throughout, but by his statement, when referring to the 24-month drilling period, "I never give up until the contract is signed".

Notwithstanding the express admission in the letter of September 9th that the provision relative to the payment of the $20,000 ought to have been as stated in appellant's solicitors' letter of September 7th, the respondent, under date of September 13th, forwarded a second agreement executed by himself, in which he retained the provision relative to the $20,000 in identical terms to that enclosed in his letter of September 2nd.

This agreement enclosed in the letter of September 13th contained another important variation.

. . .

Neither the appellant nor his solicitors made any further communication after the letter of September 7th. The respondent's correspondence received thereafter remained unanswered. The position of the parties, therefore, remained as above described until about the middle of September, when appellant went to Edmonton and advised the respondent that he would himself undertake the drilling operations which, of course, concluded the negotations.

. . .

The letter of September 2nd, the proposed agreement enclosed therewith and respondent's solicitors' letter of September 9th, might support a conclusion that the parties had agreed, but, when read, as they must be, with respondent's solicitors' letter of September 13th and the proposed agreement enclosed therewith, it is clear that the respondent had not agreed. The minds of the parties had not met. There was no *consensus ad idem* because the respondent was still negotiating for better terms.

. . .

The position of the respondent is analogous to that of the plaintiff in *Bristol, Cardiff & Swansea Aerated Bread Co. v. Maggs* (1890), 44 Ch. D. 616. There, after an agreement, as evidenced by two letters, had been arrived at, the vendor's (defendant's) solicitors submitted an agreement for approval and the purchaser's (plaintiff's) solicitors inserted a new clause which the vendor refused to agree to. Thereafter the purchaser sought to accept the original offer and to enforce the contract. Kay J. stated at pp. 624-5:

> "Their position, therefore, is, that they were not satisfied with the terms of the two letters, but themselves reopened the matter by negotiating for another most important advantage; and having thus treated the two letters as part of an incomplete bargain, it would be most inequitable to allow them to say, 'Although we thus treated the matter as incomplete and a negotiation only, yet the Defendant had no right to do so, but was bound by a completed contract'. . . .

The correspondence and the conversations, when considered as a whole, do not establish a contract between the parties. The appeal should, therefore, be allowed and the action dismissed.

. . .

The appellant is entitled to his costs throughout, both in respect to the action and the counterclaim.

Appeal allowed.

If A offers goods to B and B contacts A to find out more about the offer one would not expect to find that either B had accepted A's offer or had rejected his offer. Obviously, it may be a fine line between a rejection and, possibly, a counter offer, and a simple query. For example, if B says, "Do you mean that the price is $5/lb. or $5 per piece, if the latter, I could only pay $4?" it is not transparently clear that this is either a query or a counter-offer. You do not need case authority to convince you that each case will depend on the words used and the context of the negotiations. If you do need to be convinced by a case, see *Stevenson v. McLean* (1880), 5 Q.B.D. 346.

BROWN v. GOULD

[1971] 2 All E.R. 1505. Chancery Division (England).

Megarry J. This originating summons raises two questions, only one of which is in issue. Put shortly, the question is whether or not a tenant's option for renewal contained in a lease is void for uncertainty. The time for exercising the option is past, and it is not suggested that the option, if valid, has not been effectually exercised; and although there has been a devolution of the reversion, there is no suggestion that the defendants, who are the present reversioners, are not bound by the option. The plaintiff, who has the good fortune to live at Arabin House, High Beech, Essex (see Megarry's Arabinesque-at-Law (1969) p xi) is the original lessee.

The lease is dated 17th November 1949. The property demised consists of commercial buildings in Loughton, Essex. The term is 21 years from 29th September 1949, at a rent of £500 a year, with certain additional payments. I think I can go straight to the option clause, cl 3(c). This forms part of the covenants made by the landlord with the tenant. It reads as follows:

> "That the Landlord will on the written request of the Tenant made within twelve months before the expiration of the term hereby created and if there shall not at the time of such request be any existing breach or non-observance of any of the covenants on the part of the Tenant hereinbefore contained at the expense of the Tenant grant to him a Lease of such part of the demised premises as shall then be in the actual occupation of the Tenant but not including any portion thereof as shall have been and still be sub let by the Tenant and not then be in his own occupation such new Lease to be for a further term of Twenty one years at a rent to be fixed having regard to the market value of the premises at the time of exercising this option taking into account to the advantage of the Tenant any increased value of such premises attributable to structural improvements made by the Tenant during the currency of this present Lease such new Lease also containing the like covenants and provisions as are herein contained with the exception of the present covenant for renewal the Tenant on the execution of such renewed Lease to execute a Counterpart thereof in the usual way."

It will be observed that the clause provides no machinery for fixing the rent: and in this connection counsel for the defendants referred me by way of contrast to four other portions of the lease. The reddendum provides for the tenant to pay by way of further or additional rent a proportional part 'to be fixed by the Landlord or her Agent' of the insurance premiums paid by the landlord. By cl 2 (d) the tenant covenants to pay 'a fair proportion to be conclusively determined by the Landlord's Surveyors' of the expenses of repairing certain common roofs, drains and so on. By cl 3 (a) the landlord covenants to keep the buildings insured, and in the case of destruction or damage making the premises unfit for use and occupation, to abate the whole or a fair proportion of the rent, with a provision for arbitration in the case of disputes. Finally, cl 4 (c) provides that disputes between landlord and tenant as to how any development charges under the Town and Country Planning Act 1947 shall be borne are to be determined by arbitration on the basis there stated.

The plaintiff has spent some £30,000 in rebuilding the premises and seeks to exercise his option of renewal, which is more advantageous to him at this stage than any rights that he may have under the Landlord and Tenant Act 1954, as amended. The defendants are willing to grant him a new tenancy under that Act, but, as I have indicated, contend that the option for renewal contained in the lease is void for uncertainty. That is the sole question that I have to determine. Stated briefly, the proper approach, I think, is that the court is reluctant to hold void for uncertainty any provision that was intended to have legal effect. In this case it is very properly accepted that the option was intended to have business efficacy.

With that in mind, I approach the attack made on the present clause. Counsel for the defendants concentrated on three phrases in the clause, the words 'a rent to be fixed', the words 'having regard to' the market value of the premises at the time of exercising the option, and the words 'taking into account' to the advantage of the tenant any increased value of the premises attributable to his structural improvements. In addition, he pointed to the absence of any machinery for working out this formula, by contrast with the other provisions in the lease that I have mentioned. Taken together, he said, these considerations showed that the clause provided neither a clear basis for determining the rent nor any means of quantifying that basis, and accordingly the option was void for uncertainty.

At least three types of option may be distinguished. First, the option may be for renewal simply 'at a rent to be agreed'. In that case, no formula for quantifying the rent is laid down, and prima facie the option will, as in *King's Motors (Oxford) Ltd v Lax,* [1969] 3 All E.R. 665, be void as being a mere contract, to make a contract, or, perhaps more properly, as being an agreement to make a contract, or a contract dependent upon the making of an agreement. In *Smith v Morgan,* [1971] 2 All E.R. 1500, Brightman J held that a right of pre-emption in a conveyance 'at a figure to be agreed upon' was not void for uncertainty, but imposed on the person granting it an obligation to offer the land to the grantee at the price at which she was willing to sell it. On this, I would make two comments. First, it illustrates the attitude of the court in striving to avoid holding a provision void for uncertainty. Second, it illustrates one of the differences between an option and a right of pre-emption. Under an option, only one step is normally needed to constitute a contract, namely, the exercise of the option. Under a right of pre-emption, two steps will usually be necessary, the making of the offer in accordance with the right of pre-emption, and the acceptance of that offer. The failure to provide either a price or a formula for ascertaining the price is accordingly far more serious in the case of an option than under a pre-emption: he who exercises such an option may well be virtually signing a blank cheque, whereas he who is entitled to a right of pre-emption can at least refrain from accepting the grantor's offer if the price be too high.

The second type of option is one that is expressed to be exercisable at a price to be determined according to some stated formula, without any effective machinery being in terms provided for the working out of that formula. That is the present case. Thirdly, the option may be one which provides both a formula and the machinery, as, for example, arbitration. In this last case, it may be that the machinery can do something to cure defects in the formula: I do not have to decide that. What is before me is a formula that is assailed for its uncertainty, and the absence of any specified machinery that can do anything to cure that uncertainty. I shall consider the question of machinery first.

On behalf of the plaintiff, counsel submitted that the authorities established two propositions. First, if an option provides some machinery for fixing the price or rent, then the court will not step into the breach and provide some other machinery if the specified machinery breaks down. Second (and this is the proposition that he was concerned to establish), if the option provides no machinery, the court will, if necessary, determine the matter itself. The principal authority on which counsel for the plaintiff relied was *Milnes v Gery* (1807), 14 Ves. 400. That was a case of an agreement for sale according to the valuation of two persons, one to be nominated by each party, or an umpire to be chosen by the two nominees; and the two could not agree either on the price or on an umpire. One party then sued for specific performance, seeking the appointment of a valuer or the ascertainment of the value in such other manner as the court should direct; but Sir William Grant MR dismissed the bill. With the wealth of punctuation characteristic of those days, he said:

> "In this instance the parties have agreed upon a particular mode of ascertaining the price. The agreement, that the price shall be fixed in one specific manner, certainly does not afford an inference, that it is wholly indifferent, in what manner it is to be fixed. The Court, declaring, that the one shall take, and the other shall give, a price, fixed in any other manner, does not execute any agreement of their's; but makes an agreement for them; upon a notion, that it may be as advantageous as that, which they made for themselves. How can a man be forced to transfer to a stranger that confidence, which upon a subject, materially interesting to him, he has reposed in an individual of his own selection? No substantial difference arises from the circumstance, that in this case the decision may ultimately fall to an umpire, not directly nominated by the parties; as through the medium of the original nominees they had an influence upon the choice. No one could be chosen without the concurrence of the persons, in whose judgment they reciprocally confided. The case of an agreement to sell at a fair valuation is essentially different... In that case no particular means of ascertaining the value are pointed out: there is nothing therefore, precluding the Court from adopting any means, adapted to that purpose."

It may indeed be that the distinction is not as clearly bottomed on binding decisions as it might be; but seeking as I do to avoid holding the clause void for uncertainty, I do not have to be compelled to accept the distinction: it suffices if I am enabled. And accept it I do.

The question, then, is whether the language of the clause provides a proper formula, or whether it is too uncertain to be valid. Counsel for the defendants referred me to *Gregory v Mighell* (1811), 18 Ves. 328, where there was an agreement for a lease at a 'fair and just annual rent', to be fixed by arbitration. The tenant had taken possession and spent money on the premises, and Sir William Grant MR decreed specific performance in his favour. He said:

"That is a case in which the failure of the arbitrators to fix the rent can never affect the agreement. It is in part performed; and the Court must find some means of completing its execution; as I have already said, the Plaintiff is not to be considered as a trespasser. Some rent he must pay: the amount must be fixed in some other mode; and it seems to me, that it should be ascertained by the Master, without sending it to another arbitration; which might possibly end in the same way."

Counsel for the defendants, while recognising that the machinery of the Master assessing the rent was there adopted, contended that the case was an entirely different case, not merely because of the part performance but also because the phrase 'fair and just annual rent' provided the certainty that was lacking in the case before me. If in the present case cl 3 (c) had provided for a 'fair and just rent', and no more, he accepted that there would have been no uncertainty; but those words were not there, and even if they had been, the addition of the phrases 'having regard' and 'taking into account' would have taken away that certainty. In their context, these phrases, he said, made the whole basis discretionary. The rent was not to be a rent equal to the market rental value; it merely had to be fixed 'having regard' to the market value. This view, he said, was supported by the words 'to be fixed'.

By way of reinforcement, counsel for the defendants cited *Harvey v Pratt*, [1965] 2 All E.R. 786, as demonstrating that freeholds and leaseholds were regarded quite differently in this respect, in that under an agreement to sell the freehold, stating no date for completion, it will be implied that completion is to take place within a reasonable time, whereas under an agreement to grant a lease, no implication will be made as to when the term is to commence. I do not think that the case supports the proposition that is put forward. The essential distinction seems to me to be that on the sale of the fee, it is an existing estate that is being sold; the date is no part of the estate. On the grant of a lease, on the other hand, a new estate is being brought into being, and unless the date of commencement is known, the estate to be granted lacks one of its essentials.

I readily accept that the words of cl 3 (c) might have been more precise. But that is not the point: the point is whether it is void for uncertainty. If one approaches the formula stated in the clause with reasonable goodwill, as I think I am entitled and, indeed, required to do, does it appear to embody such uncertainty of concept as to make it void? Without saying that there is no room for argument on the details, I would answer No to that question, or, indeed, to any other reasonable way of formulating the question that I can conceive. The question is not, I think, whether the clause is proof against wilful misinterpretation, but whether someone genuinely seeking to discover its meaning is able to do so. To that question I would answer Yes. The rent is to be fixed by whatever method is adopted: in the phrase of Sir William Grant MR, there is nothing to preclude the court 'from adopting any means, adapted to that purpose'. In the process, regard must be had to the market value of the premises when the option is exercised; but then there is to be taken into account, for the benefit of the tenant, any increased value of the premises attributable to any structural improvements that he has made during the lease. Having regard to the market value thus adjusted, a rent is to be fixed for a term of 21 years from the expiration of the lease on all the terms of that lease except the option for renewal. In all probability, if such a formula were to be given to a valuer employed by the landlords and a valuer employed by the tenant, the figures produced by the two valuers would not be identical; valuation is like that. Yet in all probability also, if those valuers gave evidence before the court and were duly cross-examined, the court could reach a conclusion: courts and tribunals have long been hardened to resolving such conflicts. On that footing, I cannot see where the uncertainty lies. In the face of language such as cl 3 (c) employs, it seems to me somewhat wilful to say that although the rent is to be fixed 'having regard' to such matters, nevertheless the fixing of the rent is to be basically a discretionary matter, with the person fixing the rent obliged merely to 'have regard' to certain matters, and then, provided he does not altogether forget these matters or depart from the rational, being fancy-free in the rent that he fixes. This is a clause in a lease; it is far removed from the powers of trustees under a discretionary trust, and so on.

Furthermore, it does not seem to me that counsel for the defendants has been able to demonstrate that this is a case of uncertainty in either of the two main ways in which that can be done. A provision may be void for uncertainty because it is devoid of any meaning. As some critics of certain modern writings might testify, there may be an unintelligible collocation of ordinary English words, or there may be mere gibberish, such as the phrase 'fustum funnidos tantaraboo' cited in the *Fawcett* case. The present case manifestly does not fall under this head. The other main head is where there is a variety of meanings which can fairly be put on the provision, and it is impossible to say which of them was intended. Mere ambiguities may some-times be resolved by the application of legal presumptions, and so on: but where the language used is equally consistent with a wide range of different meanings, it may be impossible to discern the concept which the provision was intended to enshrine. If a case is to be brought under this head, the attack will usually start with the demonstration of a diversity of meanings which are consistent with the language used; and if this is not done, the attack will usually fail. In the present case, there has been no demonstration of this kind which has brought me anywhere near to the point of saying that the clause is void for uncertainty.

In the result, therefore, I reject the only grounds on which it has been contended that cl 3 (c) is invalid. That being so, I answer Question 1 of the summons, asking whether the option is valid and enforceable, by saying Yes. As I have mentioned, it is accepted that the option, if valid, has been duly exercised, and so I make no answer to Question 2.

Order accordingly.

The problem in the cases that we have been examining in this chapter has been to see whether there is an enforceable agreement or not. The prob-lem in the last few cases has been to see if the parties have done enough so that the court can be asked to enforce the contract. It was assumed that if there was no agreement then there could be no contract. The choice between an enforceable agreement or no agreement at all is one that often forces the courts into finding an agreement if they possibly can. This can have two consequences. First, it may catch one party by surprise and, since expectation damages may be available, involve that party in heavy dam-ages. (Such may have happened in the case of *Hillas v. Arcos* which was discussed in *Foley v. Classique Coaches, supra.*) Second, there may well be reliance by one party on part of the agreement as it is being gradually negotiated and agreement reached on each point. This reliance might also arise simply on one party's promise to negotiate. If the choice is between an enforceable agreement or no agreement — between full expectation damages and no remedy — it can happen that reliance losses can go unprotected. This is, of course, part of the problem of consideration and of the cases where A revokes when B is half way up the flagpole. We, therefore, need some basis for finding an intermediate position: a position where there may be some protection for one party but not necessarily the protection that would be afforded were there an enforceable agreement.

At the same time that we may want the courts to recognize some sort of intermediate position, we have to realize that the parties may have carried on their negotiations in such a way that both parties are to be free at any time to withdraw until the final agreement has been reached: "signed, sealed and delivered." This is, for example, the usual case in the typical sale of land in England. In Canada, the acceptance of the offer to purchase creates an enforceable contract. In England, the agreement of sale (even though the offer has been accepted) is often expressed to be "subject to contract." These words are usually taken to mean that there is no enforceable bargain until the formal contract has been drawn up by the parties' solicitors. It may therefore be unfair and unwise to move the date of the enforceable agreement backward where that would catch a party unawares. (As a practical matter, the English rule is very awkward for purchasers who can never know whether they can safely rely on the "agreement" for quite some time after the negotiations have been concluded. The English attitude to the agreement for the sale of land led to the practice of "gazumping" referred to in *Wroth v. Tyler.* This would not be possible here.)

In cases where it is clear that the parties are not negotiating with complete freedom to withdraw at any time there are at least two situations where they may feel in some way bound. The first is where the parties might regard themselves as fully bound unless there is an excuse that would discharge the parties in any executory contract. There may be an agreement that leaves some points to be settled later. When these terms are to be settled by arbitration, for example, the courts have usually held the agreement to be enforceable. Thus the Sale of Goods Act provides:

> "9 — (1) The price in a contract of sale may be fixed by the contract or may be left to be fixed in manner thereby agreed or may be determined by the course of dealing between the parties.
> (2)   Where the price is not determined in accordance with the foregoing provisions, the buyer shall pay a reasonable price, and what constitutes a reasonable price is a question of fact dependent on the circumstances of each particular case."

There are also cases where almost the whole agreement can be determined by arbitration: *Calvan Consolidated v. Manning* (1959), 17 D.L.R. (2d) 1. Such agreements, even though far from complete, are enforceable because, as the courts say, they can be made certain by a process provided for by the parties. There are many problems in knowing when the agreement is complete enough for this. The courts will not themselves perform the job of an arbitrator. (Is there any reason to assume that an arbitrator can do a better job than the courts? To what extent is the process of arbitration different from the process of adjudication?) If the parties have provided no machinery for resolving the issues left unagreed, the bargain may be unenforceable: *May and Butcher v. The King*, [1934] 2 K.B. 17.

The second case is where the parties regard themselves as bound to the extent that agreement is reached. Both regard themselves as bound to negotiate in good faith and as committed to the deal unless any aspect still to be negotiated agreement cannot be reached. Under such an understanding, the parties would not be free to withdraw for any reason. This is the case where the common law has no readily available method to enforce the obligation to negotiate in good faith. Cases where this kind of problem have come before American courts have involved such things as a change in the terms to be offered to one, who in reliance on certain offered terms, undertook preparations for an eventual deal. Thus in *Hoffman v. Red Owl Stores* (1965), 133 N.W. 2d 267, the plaintiff was assured that for $18,000 capital he would be able to open a Red Owl store. The plaintiff took steps to get the experience necessary to run the store and bought land for the store. When the plaintiff began negotiations in earnest he was told that he would need almost twice as much capital. The Wisconsin Supreme Court awarded the plaintiff damages for what the defendant had done. The court relied on § 90 of the Restatement. It remains to be seen how widely this case will be applied and the extent to which any remedy is dependant on § 90.

The U.C.C. has the following provisions:

§ 2-204. Formation in General
(1) A contract for sale of goods may be made in any manner sufficient to show agreement, including conduct by both parties which recognizes the existence of such a contract.
(2) An agreement sufficient to constitute a contract for sale may be found even though the moment of its making is undetermined.
(3) Even though one or more terms are left open a contract for sale does not fail for indefiniteness if the parties have intended to make a contract and there is a reasonably certain basis for giving an appropriate remedy."

The comment to Subsection 3 is as follows:

"Subsection (3) states the principle as to 'open term' underlying later sections of the Article. If the parties intend to enter into a binding agreement, this subsection recognizes that agreement as valid in law, despite missing terms, if there is any reasonably certain basis for granting a remedy. The test is not certainty as to what the parties were to do nor as to the exact amount of damages due the plaintiff. Nor is the fact that one or more terms are left to be agreed upon enough of itself to defeat an otherwise adequate agreement. Rather, commercial standards on the point of 'indefiniteness' are intended to be applied, this Act making provision elsewhere for missing terms needed for performance, open price, remedies and the like.
"The more terms the parties leave open, the less likely it is that they have intended to conclude a binding agreement, but their actions may be frequently conclusive on the matter despite the omissions."

There are, of course, problems of what remedy can be given for the breach of an obligation to bargain in good faith. Would specific performance be an acceptable remedy? To what extent should recovery be limited to the reliance interest? What if the only evidence of reliance is a failure to take steps to find, say, an alternative source of supply?

This problem is discussed by Knapp, "Enforcing the Contract to Bargain" (1969), 44 N.Y.U. L.Rev. 673.

The next two cases show, first, the traditional common law approach and, second, one that acknowledges broader concerns.

COURTENEY v. TOLAINI

[1975] 1 All E.R. 716. Court of Appeal.

[The defendant wanted to build a hotel. He approached the plaintiff who agreed to introduce to the defendant a person who would supply the financing. In return for this service, the defendant agreed to let the plaintiff have the contract to build the hotel. The plaintiff fulfilled his part of the bargain, but the parties could not agree on a price for the construction. The defendant had the hotel built by someone else, though he took advantage of the financing that had been arranged through the efforts of the plaintiff. The court was asked to decide a preliminary question whether there was a contract between the parties or not.]

Lord Denning M.R. [p. 720]: — ... But then this point was raised. Even if there was not a contract actually to build, was not there a contract to negotiate? In this case Mr. Tolaini did instruct his quantity surveyor to negotiate, but the negotiations broke down. It may be suggested that the quantity surveyor was to blame for the failure of the negotiations. But does that give rise to a cause of action? There is very little guidance in the book about a contract to negotiate. It was touched on by Lord Wright in *Hillas & Co. Ltd. v. Arcos Ltd.* (1932), 38 Com. Cas. 23 where he said: "There is then no bargain except to negotiate, and negotiations may be fruitless and end without any contract ensuing." Then he went on:

> "... yet even then, in strict theory, there is a contract (if there is good consideration) to negotiate, though in the event of repudiation by one party the damages may be nominal, unless a jury think that the opportunity to negotiate was of some appreciable value to the injured party."

That tentative opinion by Lord Wright does not seem to me to be well founded. If the law does not recognise a contract to enter into a contract (when there is a fundamental term yet to be agreed) it seems to me it cannot recognise a contract to negotiate. The reason is because it is too uncertain to have any binding force. No court could estimate the damages because no one can tell whether the negotiations would be successful or would fall through; or if successful, what the result would be. It seems to me that a contract to negotiate, like a contract to enter into a contract, is not a contract known to the law. ... I think we must apply the general principle that when there is a fundamental matter left undecided and to be the subject of negotiation, there is no contract. So I would hold that there was not any enforceable agreement in the letters between the plaintiff and the defendants. I would allow the appeal accordingly.

Lord Diplock. I agree and would only add my agreement that the dictum — for it is no more — of Lord Wright in *Hillas & Co. Ltd. v. Arcos Ltd.* to which Lord Denning MR has referred, though an attractive theory, should in my view be regarded as bad law.

Lawton L.J. I agree with both the judgments which have been delivered.

The Ontario Labour Relations Act, R.S.O. 1970, c. 232, provides as follows:

13. Following certification, the trade union shall give the employer written notice of its desire to bargain with a view to making a collective agreement.
14. The parties shall meet within fifteen days from the giving of the notice... and they shall bargain in good faith and make every reasonable effort to make a collective agreement.

A failure to bargain in good faith may make a party liable to criminal penalties under the Act.

QUESTIONS

1. If a failure to bargain in good faith under The Labour Relations Act may be a criminal offence for which a party may be fined, is the position of the common law as stated by Lord Denning defensible?
2. If the Court of Appeal had held that there would be an enforceable contract to bargain in good faith, how would one determine what the damages should be?
3. Would the fact that damages may be hard to determine any reason for refusing to give any?

———————

The problem of the content of the obligation to bargain in good faith is raised in the following account of the application of the provisions of The Labour Relations Act.

The Globe and Mail, December 8, 1977, p. 5.

OLRB can't redress imbalance of bargaining power, head says

The chairman of the Ontario Labor Relations Board, in a decision dealing with a labor dispute at the Ottawa Journal, has stated that it is not the job of the labor board to redress any imbalance of bargaining power between a union and an employer.

In a majority decision submitted to the disputing parties last week, board chairman D.D. Carter dismissed an application by the Ottawa Typographical Union and the Ottawa Newspaper Guild that the board reconsider an earlier decision that confined itself to ordering both parties to bargain in good faith.

The two unions argued that the Journal was continuing a pattern of bargaining in bad faith and that a more specific order should be issued by the board.

The unions, along with three others that have since reached a settlement and returned to work, were locked out by the newspaper in October, 1976, in a dispute that centred on a clash between the Ottawa Typographical Union and the newspaper over automation.

Three unions returned to work under a new agreement last September. Employees within the Guild jurisdiction, most of whom were hired as replacements, have filed an application to have the Guild decertified. Hearings before the labor board on the application have not been completed.

Mr. Carter stated in his decision that remedies proposed by counsel for the two unions are all designed to redress what they regard as an unfavorable bargaining situation.

He wrote that a request for an order directing the employer to table proposals that it made before the lockout and were rejected by the unions would result indirectly in the board imposing at least those terms on the parties. A less drastic remedy of ordering the employer to give preference to Typographical Union members when filling jobs in the Guild bargaining unit would have the same defect (because many of those locked out are no longer available for work).

The board would be dictating specific terms for the collective agreement that should be arrived at by the operation of the collective bargaining process. Mr. Carter also rejected a request that the board postpone the decertification hearings.

He said protection for the union in the circumstances is limited under the labor act. Economic conflict is not allowed to continue interminably where employee-support for a bargaining agent disappears. Extension of the time limit would serve to alter the balance of bargaining power between the parties. The board stated that the unions have not established that events following the original order to bargain in good faith altered the bargaining situation to make the earlier order clearly inappropriate.

The board said when it issued its original order last June that it was apparent that it would not be easy for the two sides to compromise their differences.

The chairman set out the board's role in these terms:

> "The duty to bargain in good faith is administered by this board in such a way as to improve and facilitate the practice and procedure of collective bargaining. This approach recognizes however, that the results of collective bargaining are necessarily dictated by the relative economic strength of the bargaining parties. Although the board should make every effort to restore a bargaining relationship and re-establish the dialogue between the parties to that relationship, it should not go so far as to redress any imbalance of bargaining power that might exist in a particular bargaining situation..."

In the next case the English Court of Appeal gave a remedy even though the parties had reached no agreement. As you read the case consider these questions:

    1. What is the basis for the imposition of liability on the defendants?

    2. What does Denning L.J. mean by "fault"?

    3. Does the use of the word "fault" indicate that there could be a breach of an obligation to bargain in good faith and that there could be an award of damages for such a breach?

    4. To what extent does it matter that the losses were easy to calculate?

    5. What interest of the plaintiff was being protected here?

BREWER STREET INVESTMENTS v. BARCLAYS WOOLLEN CO. LTD.

[1954] 1 Q.B. 428.

Denning L.J. This case raises questions of considerable interest. The landlords seek to recover from the prospective tenants the moneys which they have had to pay to their own contractors for the work done on the alterations before the negotiations for the lease broke down. The question is whether they can do so.

It is not easy to state the legal basis of the landlords' claim. The difficulty arises because, although the prospective tenants agreed to pay the cost of the alterations, nevertheless those alterations were never completed. The work was abandoned before it was finished. Once the negotiations for a lease broke down, both sides realized that the work must be stopped. It was a very sensible thing to do, but it means that the landlords cannot sue for the price as on a completed contract. Nor can they sue the prospective tenants for damages for breach of contract, because the prospective tenants have not been guilty of a breach. Let me give an instance. One item of the work was a lift door to be made, fixed and installed for the lump sum of £48 10s. At the time when the work was abandoned, the lift door had been made in the provinces but it had not been transported to London, let alone fixed or installed. Nevertheless the landlords have had to pay to their contractors the full sum of £48 10s., presumably by way of damages, and they seek to recover it from the prospective tenants. They clearly cannot recover on a quantum meruit as ordinarily understood. The way they put their claim on this item and the others in the statement of claim is money paid on request. The prospective tenants, however, made no request in fact to the landlords to pay the money. Their request, if any, was to pay on completion of the work, and it was not completed. In these circumstances, the proper way to formulate the claim is on a request implied in law, or, as I would prefer to put it in these days, on a claim in restitution.

It is clear on the facts that the parties proceeded on a fundamental assumption — that the lease would be granted — which has turned out to be wrong. The work done has been wasted. The question is: on whom is the loss to fall? The parties themselves did not envisage the situation which has emerged and did not provide for it; and we do not know what they would have provided if they had envisaged it. Only the law can resolve their rights and liabilities in the new situation, either by means of implying terms or, more simply, by asking on whom should the risk fall.

. . .

[The question to ask is:] what was the reason for the negotiations breaking down? If it was the landlords' fault, as, for instance, if they refused to go on with the lease for no reason at all, or because they demanded a higher rent than that which had been already agreed, then they should not be allowed to recover any part of the cost of the alterations. Even if the landlords derived no benefit from the work, they should not be allowed to recover the cost from the prospective tenants, seeing that it was by their fault that the prospective tenants were deprived of it.

On the other hand, if it was the prospective tenants' fault that the negotiations broke down, as for instance, if they sought a lower rent than that which had been agreed upon, then the prospective tenants ought to pay the cost of the alterations up to the time they were stopped. After all, they did promise to pay for the work, and they should not be able to get out of their promise by their own fault, even though the alterations were not completed. It is a very old principle laid down by Sir Edward Coke that a man shall not be allowed to take advantage of a condition brought about by himself.

I do not think, however, that in the present case it can be said that either party was really at fault. Neither party sought to alter the rent or any other point which had been agreed upon. They fell out on a point which had not been agreed at all. From the very beginning the prospective tenants wanted an option to purchase, whereas the landlords were only ready to give them the first refusal. Each of them in the course of the negotiations sought on this point to get more favourable terms — the prospective tenants to get a firm option to purchase, the landlords to give a first refusal of little value — but their moves in the negotiations can hardly be considered a default by one or other.

What, then, is the position when the negotiations go off without the default of either? On whom should the risk fall? In my opinion the prospective tenants ought to pay all the costs thrown away. The work was done to meet their special requirements and was prima facie for their benefit and not for the benefit of the landlords. If and in so far as the work is shown to have been of benefit to the landlords, credit should be given in such sum as may be just. Subject to such credit, the prospective tenants ought to pay the cost of the work, because they in the first place agreed to take responsibility for it; and when the matter goes off without the default of either side, they should pay the costs thrown away. There is no finding here that the work was of any benefit to the landlords, and in the circumstances the prospective tenants should, I think, pay the amount claimed.

[Counsel for the defendant] argued that... it was not right... to ask whose fault it was, or on whom should the risk fall, because each side had an absolute right to withdraw from the negotiations: and could not be said to be at fault in doing so. He referred to *Luxor (Eastbourne) Ld. v. Cooper*, [1941] A.C. 108, and argued that, even if the landlord, for instance, demanded a higher rent and thus caused the negotiations to fall through, he could still recover the cost of the alterations. I do not think that that is right. Estate agents are employed on the footing that they get a large commission if a sale is completed, but nothing if it is not. They take the risk of the deal falling through. The cases on the subject are, therefore, illustrations of the same test; on whom in all the circumstances should the risk fall?

In the present case I think that the risk should fall on the prospective tenants and that they should pay the costs of the alterations. On the question of illegality I have nothing to add to what has been said. I agree that the appeal should be dismissed.

In *William Lacey Ltd. v. Davis*, [1957] 2 All E.R. 712, Q.B.D. (England), a firm of builders was held to be entitled to recover from the defendant the cost of preparing plans and estimates for rebuilding property owned by the defendant. The trial judge (Barry J.) had held that the builders had been led to believe that they would have obtained the contract for the actual work to be done. The work done was held to have gone far beyond that normally done by a builder who submits a tender, and so, when the defendant sold the property without giving the work to the plaintiffs, he was liable for their costs (£250).

QUESTIONS AND PROBLEMS

1. Should the plaintiff in *William Lacey Ltd. v. Davis* be able to recover the costs that would have been incurred in normal tendering?

2. Would the plaintiff (and any other builders concerned) have a cause of action if the defendant advertised for tenders and, after the tenders had been prepared, cancelled the proposed development?

3. How does *Brewer Street v. Barclays* differ from those involving promissory estoppel, *e.g.*, *High Trees* and *Combe v. Combe*?

4. Farmer makes an application for insurance on a form provided by Insurance Co. that states that Farmer will pay all premiums *etc.*, and that the policy will run from the day of the application. One month later, Insurance Co. notifies Farmer that his application is rejected. That day Farmer suffers a loss which would have been covered. Farmer shows that if notified earlier he could have obtained alternative insurance. What arguments could you make on Farmer's behalf in any action that he might bring against Insurance Co.?

C. The Battle of the Forms

Seller, as a prudent businessman, has decided that he needs standard forms for his business. He calls his lawyer and a form is drafted giving Seller certain advantages over Buyer when the form is used. A large supply of these forms is printed and the employee who handles orders for Seller is instructed to send a form with each order. The form is an invoice which states (*inter alia*):

"Goods cannot be returned for credit after delivery."

Buyer, as an equally prudent businessman, has his own stack of appropriately drafted forms which his employees use. Buyer's form, a purchase order, contains the following clause (*inter alia*):

"Buyer may reject goods at any time up to one week after receipt."

Buyer and Seller carry on business for several years without any problems. The typical transaction is that Buyer's employee phones Seller's employee and orders the goods. A purchase order is mailed the same day. When the goods are shipped, about three weeks later, an invoice is included. Eventually one order is defective and Buyer refuses to pay. How can each side use the rules of offer and acceptance and the differences in the forms to support their arguments?

What went on here is what is described as the "Battle of The Forms". It is quite clear that the parties had been doing business for years on the assumption that they had a valid contract. It is equally clear that they never bothered to think about the fact that their forms did not coincide. Had they done so, one side or the other might refuse to do business except on the basis of its own form.

This problem is discussed in the next two cases.

MATTER OF DOUGHBOY INDUSTRIES INC.

(1962), 233 N.Y.S. 2d. 488. Supreme Court of New York, Appellate Division.

Breitel, Justice. This case involves a conflict between a buyer's order form and a seller's acknowledgment form, each memorializing a purchase and sale of goods. The issue arises on whether the parties agreed to arbitrate future disputes. The seller's form had a general arbitration provision. The buyer's form did not. The buyer's form contained a provision that only a signed consent would bind the buyer to any terms thereafter transmitted in any commercial form of the seller. The seller's form, however, provided that silence or a failure to object in writing would be an acceptance of the terms and conditions of its acknowledgement form. The buyer never objected to the seller's acknowledgment, orally or in writing. In short, the buyer and seller accomplished a legal equivalent to the irresistible force colliding with the immovable object.

Special Term denied the buyer's motion to stay arbitration on the ground that there was no substantial issue whether the parties had agreed to arbitrate. For the reasons to be stated, the order should be reversed and the buyer's motion to stay arbitration should be granted. As a matter of law, the parties did not agree in writing to submit future disputes to arbitration (Civil Practice Act, §§ 1448, 1449).

Of interest in the case is that both the seller and buyer are substantial businesses — a "strong" buyer and a "strong" seller. This is not a case of one of the parties being at the bargaining mercy of the other.

The facts are:

During the three months before the sale in question the parties had done business on two occasions. On these prior occasions the buyer used its purchase order form with its insulating conditions, and the seller used its acknowledgment form with its self-actuating conditions. Each ignored the other's printed forms, but proceeded with the commercial business at hand.

The instant transaction began with the buyer, on May 6, 1960, mailing from its office in Wisconsin to the seller in New York City two purchase orders for plastic film. Each purchase order provided that some 20,000 pounds of film were to be delivered in the future on specified dates. In addition, further quantities were ordered on a "hold basis", that is, subject to "increase, decrease, or cancellation" by the buyer. On May 13, 1960 the seller orally accepted both purchase orders without change except to suggest immediate shipment of the first part of the order. The buyer agreed to the request, and that day the seller shipped some 10,000 pounds of film in partial fulfillment of one purchase order. On May 16, 1960, the buyer received the seller's first acknowledgment dated May 13, 1960, and on May 19, 1960 the seller's second acknowledgment dated May 16, 1960. Although the purchase orders called for written acceptances and return of attached acknowledgments by the the seller no one paid any attention to these requirements. Neither party, orally or in writing, objected to the conditions printed on the other's commercial form. Later, the buyer sent change orders with respect to so much of the orders as had been, according to the buyer, on a "hold basis".

The dispute, which has arisen and which the parties wish determined, the seller by arbitration, and the buyer by court litigation, is whether the buyer is bound to accept all the goods ordered on a "hold basis". The arbitration would take place in New York City. The litigation might have to be brought in Wisconsin, the buyer's home state.

The buyer's purchase order form had on its face the usual legends and blanks for the ordering of goods. On the reverse was printed a pageful of terms and conditions. The grand defensive clause reads as follows:

"ALTERATION OF TERMS — None of the terms and conditions contained in this Purchase Order may be added to, modified, superseded or otherwise altered except by a written instrument signed by an authorized representative of Buyer and delivered by Buyer to Seller, and each shipment received by Buyer from Seller shall be deemed to be only upon the terms and conditions contained in this Purchase Order except as they may be added to, modified, superseded or otherwise altered, notwithstanding any terms and conditions that may be contained in any acknowledgment, invoice or other form of Seller and notwithstanding Buyer's act of accepting or paying for any shipment or similar act of Buyer."

The buyer's language is direct; it makes clear that no variant seller's acknowledgment is to be binding. But the seller's acknowledgment form is drafted equally carefully. On its front in red typography one's attention is directed to the terms and conditions on the reverse side; and it advises the buyer that he, the buyer, has full knowledge of the conditions and agrees to them unless within 10 days he objects in writing.

The seller's clause reads:

"IMPORTANT

"Buyer agrees he has full knowledge of conditions printed on the reverse side hereof; and that the same are part of the agreement between buyer and seller and shall be binding if either the goods referred to herein are delivered to and accepted by buyer, or if buyer does not within ten days from date hereof deliver to seller written objection to said conditions or any part thereof."

On the reverse side the obligations of the buyer set forth above are carefully repeated. Among the conditions on the reverse side is the general arbitration clause.

This case involves only the application of the arbitration clause. Arguably, a different principle from that applied here might, under present law, govern other of the terms and conditions in either of the commercial forms. The reason is the special rule that the courts have laid down with respect to arbitration clauses, namely, that the agreement to arbitrate must be direct and the intention made clear, without implication, inveiglement or subtlety
...

It should be evident, as the buyer argues, that a contract for the sale of goods came into existence on May 13, 1960 when the seller made a partial shipment, especially when following upon its oral acceptance of the buyer's purchase order (Restatement, Contracts, § 63; Williston on Sales [rev. ed.] § 5b; Personal Property Law, § 85, subd. 1 [b]). The contract, at such time, was documented only by the buyer's purchase order form. However, that is not dispositive. It is equally evident from the prior transactions between these parties, and general practices in trade, that more documents were to follow. Such documents may help make the contract, or modify it (12 Am.Jur., Contracts, § 405; 10 N.Y.Jur., Contracts, § 403). Whether the subsequent documents were necessary to complete the making of the contract (as would be true if there had been no effective or valid acceptance by partial shipment), or whether they served only to modify or validate the terms of an existing contract (as would be true if there had been a less formal written acceptance, merely an oral acceptance, or an acceptance by partial shipment of goods) is not really too important once the commercial dealings have advanced as far as they had here. By that time, there is no question whether there was a contract, but only what was the contract.

Recognizing, as one should, that the business men in this case acted with complete disdain for the "lawyer's content" of the very commercial forms they were sending and receiving, the question is what obligation ought the law to attach to the arbitration clause. And in determining that question the traditional theory is applicable, namely, that of constructive knowledge and acceptance of contractual terms, based on prior transactions and the duty to read contractual instruments to which one is a party.

But, and this is critical, it is not only the seller's form which should be given effect, but also the buyer's form, for it too was used in the prior transactions, and as to it too, there was a duty to read. Of course, if the two commercial forms are given effect, they cancel one another. (Certainly, the test is not which is the later form, because here the prior form said the buyer would not be bound by the later form unless it consented in writing. It needs little discussion that silence, a weak enough form of acceptance, effective only when misleading and there is a duty to speak, can be negatived as a misleading factor by announcing in advance that it shall have no effect as acceptance [Restatement, Contracts, § 72; Corbin on Contracts, §§ 72-75; 9 N.Y.Jur., Contracts, §§ 34, 45].)

As pointed out earlier, an agreement to arbitrate must be clear and direct, and must not depend upon implication, inveiglement or subtlety.... It follows then that the existence of an agreement to arbitrate should not depend solely upon the conflicting fine print of commercial forms which cross one another but never meet.

. . .

In this case, the supposed condition happened, the acknowledgment made no reference to the purchase order, and, moreover, the prior purchase order disavowed the future application of any subsequent differing acknowledgment. And, the arbitration clause was one of the "specific changes" from the purchase order, which even under the rule in the Wachusett case would not be binding on the other party.

Consequently, as a matter of law there was no agreement to arbitrate in this case, if one applies existing principles.

But the problem of conflicting commercial forms is one with which there has been much concern before this, and a new effort at rational solution has been made. The new solution would yield a similar result. The Uniform Commercial Code (L.1962, ch. 553) takes effect in this State September 27, 1964 (§ 10-105). It reflects the latest legislative conclusions as to what the law ought to be. It provides:

"§ 2-207 Additional Terms in Acceptance or Confirmation

"(1) A definite and seasonable expression of acceptance or a written confirmation which is sent within a reasonable time operates as an acceptance even though it states terms additional to or different from those offered or agreed upon, unless acceptance is expressly made conditional on assent to the additional or different terms.

"(2) The additional terms are to be construed as proposals for addition to the contract. Between merchants such terms become part of the contract unless:

   "(a) the offer expressly limits acceptance to the terms of the offer;
   "(b) they materially alter it; or
   "(c) notification of objection to them has already been given or is given within a reasonable time after notice of them is received.

"(3) Conduct by both parties which recognizes the existence of a contract is sufficient to establish a contract for sale although the writings of the parties do not otherwise establish a contract. In such case the terms of the particular contract consist of those terms on which the writings of the parties agree, together with any supplementary terms incorporated under any other provisions of this Act."

While this new section is not in its entirety in accordance with New York law in effect when the events in suit occurred (see 1 Report of N.Y. Law Rev. Comm. on Uniform Commercial Code [1955] p. 627 et seq.), in its particular application to the problem at hand it is quite useful. The draftsmen's comments to section 2-207 are in precise point (Uniform Commercial Code [U.L.A.] § 2-207, comments 3 and 6). Thus, it is said:

"3. Whether or not additional or different terms will become part of the agreement depends upon the provisions of subsection (2). If they are such as materially to alter the original bargain, they will not be included unless expressly agreed to by the other party. If, however, they are terms which would not so change the bargain they will be incorporated unless notice of objection to them has already been given or is given within a reasonable time....

"6. If no answer is received within a reasonable time after additional terms are proposed, it is both fair and commercially sound to assume that their inclusion has been assented to. Where clauses on confirming forms sent by both parties conflict each party must be assumed to object to a clause of the other conflicting with one on the confirmation sent by himself. As a result the requirement that there be notice of objection which is found in subsection (2) is satisfied and the conflicting terms do not become a part of the contract. The contract then consists of the terms originally expressly agreed to, terms on which the confirmations agree, and terms supplied by this Act, including subsection (2)."

On this exposition, the arbitration clause, whether viewed as a material alteration under subsection (2), or as a term nullified by a conflicting provision in the buyer's form, would fail to survive as a contract term. In the light of the New York cases, at least, there can be little question that an agreement to arbitrate is a material term, one not to be injected by implication, subtlety or inveiglement. And the conclusion is also the same if the limitation contained in the offer (the buyer's purchase order) is given effect, as required by subsection 2(a) of the new section.

Accordingly, the order denying petitioner-appellant buyer's motion to stay arbitration should be reversed, on the law, with costs to petitioner-appellant and the motion should be granted.

Order, entered on April 13, 1962, denying petitioner-appellant buyer's motion to stay arbitration, unanimously reversed, on the law, with $20 costs and disbursements to appellant, and the motion granted. All concur.

ROTO-LITH, LTD. v. F.P. BARTLETT & CO.

(1962), 297 F. 2d 297. U.S. Court of Appeals First Circuit.

Aldrich, Circuit Judge. Plaintiff-appellant Roto-Lith, Ltd., is a New York corporation engaged *inter alia* in manufacturing, or "converting," cellophane bags for packaging vegetables. Defendant-appellee is a Massachusetts corporation which makes emulsion for use as a cellophane adhesive. This is a field of some difficulty, and various emulsions are employed, depending upon the intended purpose of the bags. In May and October 1959 plaintiff purchased emulsion from the defendant. Subsequently bags produced with this emulsion failed to adhere, and this action was instituted in the district court for the District of Massachusetts. At the conclusion of the evidence the court directed a verdict for the defendant. This appeal followed.

Defendant asks us to review the October transaction first because of certain special considerations applicable to the May order. The defense in each instance, however, is primarily the same, namely, defendant contends that the sales contract expressly negatived any warranties. We will deal first with the October order.

On October 23, 1959, plaintiff, in New York, mailed a written order to defendant in Massachusetts for a drum of "N-132-C" emulsion, stating "End use: wet pack spinach bags." Defendant on October 26 prepared simultaneously an acknowledgment and an invoice. The printed forms were exactly the same, except that one was headed "Acknowledgment" and the other "Invoice," and the former contemplated insertion of the proposed, and the latter of the actual, shipment date. Defendant testified that in accordance with its regular practice the acknowledgment was prepared and mailed the same day. The plaintiff's principal liability witness testified that he did not know whether this acknowledgment "was received, or what happened to it." On this state of the evidence there is an unrebutted presumption of receipt.... The goods were shipped to New York on October 27. On the evidence it must be found that the acknowledgment was received at least no later than the goods. The invoice was received presumably a day or two after the goods.

The acknowledgment and the invoice bore in conspicuous type on their face the following legend, "All goods sold without warranties, express or implied, and subject to the terms on reverse side." In somewhat smaller, but still conspicuous, type there were printed on the back certain terms of sale, of which the following are relevant:

> "1. Due to the variable conditions under which these goods may be transported, stored, handled, or used, Seller hereby expressly excludes any and all warranties, guaranties, or representations whatsoever. Buyer assumes risk for results obtained from use of these goods, whether used alone or in combination with other products. Seller's liability hereunder shall be limited to the replacement of any goods that materially differ from the Seller's sample order on the basis of which the order for such goods was made.
>
> "7. This acknowledgment contains all of the terms of this purchase and sale. No one except a duly authorized officer of Seller may execute or modify contracts. Payment may be made only at the offices of the Seller. *If these terms are not acceptable, Buyer must so notify Seller at once.*" (Ital. suppl.)

It is conceded that plaintiff did not protest defendant's attempt so to limit its liability, and in due course paid for the emulsion and used it. It is also conceded that adequate notice was given of breach of warranty, if there were warranties. The only issue which we will consider is whether all warranties were excluded by defendant's acknowledgment.

.   .   .

Section 2-207 provides:

> "(1) A definite and seasonable expression of acceptance or a written confirmation which is sent within a reasonable time operates as an acceptance even though it states terms additional to or different from those offered or agreed upon, unless acceptance is expressly made conditional on assent to the additional or different terms.
>
> "(2) The additional terms are to be construed as proposals for addition to the contract. Between merchants such terms become part of the contract unless:
>
>> "(a)   the offer expressly limits acceptance to the terms of the offer;
>> "(b)   they materially alter it; or
>> "(c)   notification of objection to them has already been given or is given within a reasonable time after notice of them is received."

Plaintiff exaggerates the freedom which this section affords an offeror to ignore a reply from an offeree that does not in terms coincide with the original offer. According to plaintiff defendant's condition that there should be no warranties constituted a proposal which "materially altered" the agreement. As to this we concur. See Uniform Commercial Code comment to this section, Mass.Gen.Laws annotation, supra, paragraph 4. Plaintiff goes on to say that by virtue of the statute the acknowledgment effected a completed agreement without this condition, and that as a further proposal the condition never became part of the agreement because plaintiff did not express assent. We agree that section 2-207 changed the existing law, but not to this extent. Its purpose was to modify the strict principle that a response not precisely in accordance with the offer was a rejection and a counteroffer.... Now, within stated limits, a response that does not in all respects correspond with the offer constitutes an acceptance of the offer, and a counteroffer only as to the differences. If plaintiff's contention is correct that a reply to an offer stating additional conditions unilaterally burdensome upon the offeror is a binding acceptance of the original offer plus simply a proposal for the additional conditions, the statute would lead to an absurdity. Obviously no offeror will subsequently assent to such conditions.

The statute is not too happily drafted. Perhaps it would be wiser in all cases for an offeree to say in so many words, "I will not accept your offer until you assent to the following:..." But businessmen cannot be expected to act by rubric. It would be unrealistic to suppose that when an offeree replies setting out conditions that would be burdensome only to the offeror he intended to make an unconditional acceptance of the original offer, leaving it simply to the offeror's good nature whether he would assume the additional restrictions. To give the statute a practical construction we must hold that a response which states a condition materially altering the obligation solely to the disadvantage of the offeror is an "acceptance... expressly... conditional on assent to the additional... terms."

Plaintiff accepted the goods with knowledge of the conditions specified in the acknowledgment. It became bound.... Whether the contract was made in Massachusetts or New York, there has been no suggestion that either jurisdiction will not give effect to an appropriate disclaimer of warranties.... This disposes of the October order.

With respect to the May order a different situation obtains. Here plaintiff ordered a quantity of "N-136-F," which was defendant's code number for a dry-bag emulsion. The order stated as the end use a wet bag. Accordingly, defendant knew, by its own announced standards, that the emulsion ordered was of necessity unfit for the disclosed purpose. In this bald situation plaintiff urges that the defendant cannot be permitted to specify that it made no implied warranty of fitness.

We do not reach this question. In the court below, when plainly asked to state its opposition to the direction of a verdict, plaintiff did not advance the arguments it now makes, and in no way called the court's attention to any distinction between the May and the October orders. An appellant is not normally permitted to have the benefit of a new theory on appeal. It is true that this is not an absolute prohibition. The court in its discretion may relax the rule in exceptional cases in order to prevent a clear miscarriage of justice. Plaintiff's point, however, is by no means clear cut. Financially the consequences are not large. Plaintiff was represented by competent counsel, and has had an eight-day trial. We do not think the case one for making an exception to the salutary rule that a party is normally entitled to but one "day" in court.

No question remains as to the counterclaim.

Judgment will be entered affirming the judgment of the District Court.

———————

The U.C.C. attempted to resolve this problem by § 2-207:

§ 2-207. Additional Terms in Acceptance or Confirmation
(1) A definite and seasonable expression of acceptance or a written confirmation which is sent within a reasonable time operates as an acceptance even though it states terms additional to or different from those offered or agreed upon, unless acceptance is expressly made conditional on assent to the additional or different terms.
(2) The additional terms are to be construed as proposals for addition to the contract. Between merchants such terms become part of the contract unless:

    (a)   the offer expressly limits acceptance to the terms of the offer;
    (b)   they materially alter it; or
    (c)   notification of objection to them has already been given or is
           given within a reasonable time after notice of them is
           received.

(3) Conduct by both parties which recognizes the existence of a contract is sufficient to establish a contract for sale although the writings of the parties do not otherwise establish a contract. In such case the terms of the particular contract consist of those terms on which the writings of the parties agree, together with any supplementary terms incorporated under any other provisions of this Act.

Official Comment
Prior Uniform Statutory Provision: Sections 1 and 3, Uniform Sales Act.
Changes: Completely rewritten by this and other sections of this Article.
Purposes of Changes:
1. This section is intended to deal with two typical situations. The one is the written confirmation, where an agreement has been reached either orally or by informal correspondence between the parties and is followed by one or both of the parties sending formal memoranda embodying the terms so far as agreed upon and adding terms not discussed. The other situation is offer and acceptance, in which a wire or letter expressed and intended as an acceptance or the closing of an agreement adds further minor suggestions or proposals such as "ship by Tuesday," "rush," "ship draft against bill of lading inspection allowed," or the like. A frequent example of the second situation is the exchange of printed purchase order and acceptance (sometimes called "acknowledgment") forms. Because the forms are oriented to the thinking of the respective drafting parties, the terms contained in them often do not correspond. Often the seller's form contains terms different from or additional to those set forth in the buyer's form. Nevertheless, the parties proceed with the transaction. [Comment 1 was amended in 1966.]
2. Under this Article a proposed deal which in commercial understanding has in fact been closed is recognized as a contract. Therefore, any additional matter contained in the confirmation or in the acceptance falls within subsection (2) and must be regarded as a proposal for an added term unless the acceptance is made conditional on the acceptance of the additional or different terms. [Comment 2 was amended in 1966.]
3. Whether or not additional or different terms will become part of the agreement depends upon the provisions of subsection (2). If they are such as materially to alter the original bargain, they will not be included unless expressly agreed to by the other party. If, however, they are terms which would not so change the bargain they will be incorporated unless notice of objection to them has already been given or is given within a reasonable time.
4. Examples of typical clauses which would normally "materially alter" the con-

tract and so result in surprise or hardship if incorporated without express awareness by the other party are: a clause negating such standard warranties as that
of merchantability or fitness for a particular purpose in circumstances in which
either warranty normally attaches; a clause requiring a guaranty of 90% or 100%
deliveries in a case such as a contract by cannery, where the usage of the trade
allows greater quantity leeways; a clause reserving to the seller the power to
cancel upon the buyer's failure to meet any invoice when due; a clause requiring
that complaints be made in a time materially shorter than customary or reasonable.

5. Examples of clauses which involve no element of unreasonable surprise and
which therefore are to be incorporated in the contract unless notice of objection
is seasonably given are: a clause setting forth and perhaps enlarging slightly
upon the seller's exemption due to supervening causes beyond his control, similar
to those covered by the provision of this Article on merchant's excuse by failure
of presupposed conditions or a clause fixing in advance any reasonable formula
of proration under such circumstances; a clause fixing a reasonable time for
complaints within customary limits, or in the case of a purchase for sub-sale, providing for inspection by the sub-purchaser; a clause providing for interest on
overdue invoices or fixing the seller's standard credit terms where they are within
the range of trade practice and do not limit any credit bargained for; a clause
limiting the right of rejection for defects which fall within the customary trade
tolerances for acceptance "with adjustment" or otherwise limiting remedy in a
reasonable manner (see Sections 2-718 and 2-719).

6. If no answer is received within a reasonable time after additional terms are
proposed, it is both fair and commercially sound to assume that their inclusion
has been assented to. Where clauses on confirming forms sent by both parties
conflict each party must be assumed to object to a clause of the other conflicting
with one on the confirmation sent by himself. As a result the requirement that
there be notice of objection which is found in subsection (2) is satisfied and the
conflicting terms do not become a part of the contract. The contract then consists of the terms originally expressly agreed to, terms on which the confirmations
agree, and terms supplied by this Act, including subsection (2). The written confirmation is also subject to Section 2-201. Under that section a failure to respond
permits enforcement of a prior oral agreement; under this section a failure to
respond permits additional terms to become part of the agreement. [Comment 6
was amended in 1966.]

7. In many cases, as where goods are shipped, accepted and paid for before any
dispute arises, there is no question whether a contract has been made. In such
cases, where the writings of the parties do not establish a contract, it is not necessary to determine which act or document constituted the offer and which the
acceptance. See Section 2-204. The only question is what terms are included in
the contract, and subsection (3) furnishes the governing rule. [Comment 7 was
added in 1966.]

§ 2-207 has not been very successful in its attempt to solve the problem
posed by the Battle of the Forms. The purpose of § 2-207 was to reject the
common law rule that an acceptance has to be the mirror image of the offer.
This was intended to keep any party who wanted out of the deal in. The
problem was that once the parties were kept in the deal, what were the
terms of the agreement? This is a very complex matter. On one hand the law
must be able to nullify the efforts of "fine-print" lawyers. On the other
hand, it must be able to protect the reasonable expectations of the parties in
their reliance on the contract. It must do all this in an even-handed way
realizing that many of the terms are, in fact, not negotiated. There are at
least seven different types of problems with which § 2-207 must deal.

(1) Cases in which the parties send printed forms to one another, and a

crucial term is covered one way in one form and the other way in the other form. (Assume, for example, that buyer's form states that seller warrants the goods to be of a certain kind and seller's form disclaims all warranties.)

(2) Cases in which a crucial term is found in the first form sent (the offer), but no term on that question appears in the second.

(3) Cases in which a crucial term is found in the second form (the acceptance), but there is no consistent or conflicting term in the first.

(4) Cases in which at least one form contains a term that provides that no contract will be formed unless the other party accedes to all of the terms on that form and offers no others.

(5) Cases in which there is a prior oral agreement. (In cases (1) through (4) we have assumed that there may be prior oral negotiations but that no oral agreement was reached before parties sent their forms.)

(6) Cases in which the parties do not use forms but send a variety of messages and letters and conduct intermittent oral negotiations that ultimately produce an agreement.

(7) Cases in which the second form differs so radically from the first that it does not constitute an "acceptance".

Since the deal that the court is asked to enforce under § 2-207 is essentially a non-negotiated one in respect of the terms where there is disagreement, it is important that neither side get any unfair advantage by reason of being the first (or second) party in any exchange of forms. Once the rule that the acceptance must be the mirror image of the offer is abolished there should be no primacy given to either the "offeror" or the "offeree". Yet under § 2-207 this is a difficult task.

For example, the court in *Roto-Lith Ltd. v. Bartlett,* held that a response "which states a condition materially altering the obligation solely to the disadvantage of the offeror is an 'acceptance... expressly... conditional on assent to the additional... terms' " (§ 2-207(1)). This has the effect of making the second document govern in most cases because there will have been no acceptance of the offer and the first party's performance will be acceptance of the second's counter-offer. It is suggested that in *Roto-Lith,* the extent of the difference between the documents was not so great as to come within the proviso to § 2-207(1) and therefore should have come within § 2-207(2). The effect of § 2-207(2) is to restrict the enforceable terms of the agreement to what can be regarded as the common terms in both documents. The drafters of the Code did not like the decision in *Roto-Lith* and made an attempt to get around it by re-drafting comment 7. This was designed to lessen the importance given in *Roto-Lith* to the common law rule that an acceptance which is not the mirror image of the offer is a counter-offer. This would appear to be more sensible than the result in that case.

The fate of § 2-207 is illustrative of what happens when legislation attempts to clear up an area of the common law where traditional rules have almost no bearing on the facts that are presented to the court. It is worth considering this as part of a much wider problem in the law.

FULLER, "LAW'S PRECARIOUS HOLD ON LIFE"

(1968-69) 3 Georgia L.R. 530-545.

INTRODUCTION

In 1916 Roscoe Pound delivered a famous address under the title, *The Limits of Effective Legal Action.* In that address Pound sought to demonstrate to his hearers that the law is not an all-purpose tool, that there are social problems it cannot solve, that the practice of calling out its rough engine in answer to every social alarm can not only damage society, but also may end by destroying the effectiveness of the law itself, even for those tasks for which it is eminently suited.

My theme has a considerable affinity with that pursued by Pound in 1916. Both have to do with cases where the law fails to be effective and with the reasons for its failures. At the same time there are important differences. Pound was concerned with situations where the law overreaches itself, where it attempts clumsily and unsuccessfully to force the shifting currents of life into its own rigid forms. I am concerned, on the other hand, with cases where the law projects itself, as it were, into a vacuum, with situations where the stream of life simply does not offer a sufficient substance to keep afloat even the most modest demands of the law.

To develop a little further the nature of the distinction between our themes, it may be useful to invoke an analogy from family life — though I hasten to add that this analogy is not to be taken too seriously and that it may do some injustice to the subtlety of Pound's analysis. With this apology let me, in any event, cast father in the role of the law and son in the role of the citizen subject to law. Pound was concerned with the legalistic father who approaches every problem of family life with a book of rules in one hand and a rod in the other. These two instruments are his sovereign remedy for every shortcoming of the son, whether it be ingratitude, thoughtlessness toward his mother, or a lack of interest in his studies. My theme has a more contemporary ring. It deals with cases where father and son do not, as we say, communicate. Son is not stifled or oppressed by father's rules, he simply shrugs them off; they do not enter meaningfully into his life at all, either as impediments or as guides to conduct.

In the course of my remarks I shall deal, first, with three illustrations drawn from the contemporary American scene where law fails to take hold on life simply because its forms largely lose their meaning when projected into the areas they are intended to control.

In the second portion of my observations I shall deal at some length with the difficulties encountered in trying to make law — that is, what *we* call "law" — take hold in the life of peoples not accustomed to shaping their conduct by rules written down on paper. We must remember that during most of history, and over most of the world today, law, as something deliberately made and reduced to authoritative written expression, is quite unknown. Most of the inhabitants of this globe have shaped their conduct toward one another, not by numbered paragraphs in printed volumes, but by something we call by the inadequate name of "custom." These peoples find it very difficult, in Walter Bagehot's words, even "to imagine a rule which is obligatory, but not traditional." They find it even more difficult to understand how such a rule can bind them when they have never seen its words with their own eyes and probably could not understand them if they did.

But postponing this broader theme, let me turn now to our own contemporary American experience.

Due Process of Law on Skid-Row

In discussing the law and skid-row I shall draw heavily on a perceptive study published in a recent issue of the *American Sociological Review.* The author of this report set himself the task of finding out what it is like to be an officer of the law on skid-row. The method he followed is known in sociology as that of the "participant observer"; over a period of nearly three months he actually went out with patrolmen on their beats in skid-row and shared with them their responsibilities and frustrations.

It might seem at first glance that enforcing the law on skid-row would be no different from enforcing it anywhere else. Indeed, skid-row might be considered a particularly easy assignment. The normal stimulants to violence — sex and money — are at a minimum, and the alcoholic derelict himself is not likely to be a dangerous adversary.

The conscientious patrolman encounters real difficulties, however, in trying to project the forms of law on a society too chaotic to sustain them. Take, for example, the protection of property rights. How do we protect such rights in an area where no one is ever quite sure what he owns and where it came from?

Let me quote at some length a passage from the study on which I am drawing:

> [A]n officer was called to help in settling a violent dispute in a hotel room. The object of the quarrel was a supposedly stolen pair of trousers. As the story unfolded in the conflicting versions of participants, it was not possible to decide who was the complainant and who was alleged to be the thief, nor did it come to light who occupied the room in which the fracas took place, or whether the trousers were taken from the room or to the room. Though the officer did ask some questions, it seemed, and was confirmed in later conversation, that he was there not to solve the puzzle of the missing trousers but to keep the situation from getting out of hand. In the end, the exhausted participants dispersed, and this was the conclusion of the case. The patrolman maintained that no one could unravel mysteries of this sort because "these people take things from each other so often that no one could tell what 'belongs' to whom." In fact, he suggested, the terms owning, stealing and swindling, in their strict sense, do not really belong on skid-row, and all efforts to distribute guilt and innocence according to some rational formula of justice are doomed to failure.

In his own operational terms, the patrolman on skid-row sees his mission, not as enforcing rules of law, but as keeping the "inhabitants from sinking deeper into the misery they already experience." As for arrests, there are always more people who could properly be arrested than there is space for them in vans or jails. Furthermore, the implications of an arrest are quite different from what they would be elsewhere, for virtually no one on skid-row has a job, or a family, or a reputation that could be impaired by having to spend a night in jail. Something of the spirit of the area is conveyed in the following quotation:

> Sometimes drunk arrests are made mainly because the police van is available. In one case a patrolman summoned the van to pick up an arrested man. As the van was pulling away from the curb the officer stopped the driver because he sighted another drunk stumbling across the street. The second man protested saying that he "wasn't even half drunk yet." The patrolman's response was, "OK, I'll owe you half a drunk."

In the eyes of the police the plainest justification for making an arrest — whatever its ostensible grounds may be — is refusal to answer a question.

This is so even though the question asked has no immediate relationship to anything observed in the conduct of the person being interrogated. To arrest a man simply because he refuses to answer a question, however remote the question may be from anything he is then engaged in, is plainly not a ground of arrest that would appeal very strongly to our Supreme Court. But it may make good sense in terms of the mission of the police as they themselves see it and as perhaps it has to be. To discharge his job on skid-row properly, the patrolman needs, above all else, to know what is going on: who is feuding with whom, who is newly arrived in the neighborhood, why Jim's Bar is unaccountably empty tonight. The policeman is like mother returning from a shopping trip and asking the children, "Where is the cat? What happened to the parcel left by the postman this morning? Why is the light on in the basement?" Mother needs to arrive at some definition of the situation she confronts and this may require a free-ranging and exploratory interrogation. So it is with the policeman seeking to preserve some kind of order in the human wilderness which is his domain.

So much for skid-row. Let me now turn to some problems characteristically arising out of modern business practice in the use of printed forms. This may seem an abrupt transition from the alcoholic incoherence of cheap bars and run-down rooming houses. Let me assure you, however, that a sober business man holding in his hands a stack of ready-made purchase and sales orders can accomplish as much sheer legal chaos as could ever be found on skid-row.

Interpreting the Contractual Intention of Parties Who Make No Serious Attempt to State the Terms of Their Contract

For illustration I shall draw on a decision rendered in 1962 by the Appellate Division in New York. Over a period of months the buyer had bought from the seller various quantities of plastic film. In all cases the only covering documents were the purchase order used by the buyer and the sales order used by the seller. These were printed forms, used indiscriminately for every kind of transaction. Their respective provisions were utterly out of jibe with one another, but no one had ever bothered to straighten out their discrepancies.

Finally, from one of these transactions arose the dispute that gave rise to litigation. The buyer had ordered some 40,000 pounds of film and an additional quantity on what was called a "hold basis," that is, subject to "increase, decrease, or cancellation by the buyer." Just what this "hold basis" order meant was apparently not clarified, either by past practice or by any covering document.

A dispute arose about the "hold basis" order provision and the preliminary question was whether this dispute was subject to arbitration or had to be taken to the regular courts. The seller's form said that any dispute should be arbitrated; the buyer's form said nothing about arbitration, which is the legal equivalent of saying that there should be no arbitration without the consent of both parties. The seller wanted to arbitrate; the buyer wanted to go to court.

The next question then was whether there was any stipulation in either of the forms that could resolve the conflict about arbitration. The seller's form, which stipulated arbitration, stated that it was to be deemed accepted by the buyer, and its terms should bind both parties, unless the buyer registered his dissent in writing within ten days. This he did not do; hence by its own terms the seller's form determined the rights of the parties. The buyer's form, on the other hand, declared very plainly that it should be taken as the authoritative statement of the contract unless the buyer himself, by a writing over his signature, agreed to a change. Since the buyer had not thus agreed to any change, his form claimed to be the only authentic statement of the contract.

The court observed:

> In short, the buyer and seller accomplished a legal equivalent to the irresistible force colliding with the immovable object.

The court might have added that the parties confronted the court itself with a problem that was the legal equivalent of asking a physicist to say what would really happen if an immovable object was hit by an irresistible force. It was, of course, not open to the court to say, as the physicist no doubt would, "Don't be ridiculous."

I shall not attempt here to retrace the ingenious route by which the court finally arrived at its decision. Suffice it to say that the case itself merely brought to somewhat dramatic expression a pervasive problem in the modern law of contracts — a problem that arises out of the fact that the parties often simply do not attempt to reach agreement on the terms of their bargain, but content themselves with dispatching back and forth unrelated printed forms. The experience of skid-row reveals that the law of property may lose much of its meaning where men make no real attempt to keep their belongings separated and reasonably identified. So too the law of contracts must assume that men will strive in some measure at least to spell out the terms of their agreements. Even the so-called objective theory of contractual intention presupposes that direction of effort.

My third illustration from the contemporary American scene carries the subtitle,

Due Care at Sixty Miles an Hour on an Eight-Lane Throughway

I am sure it is not hard to guess that my illustration this time has to do with the legal treatment of automobile accidents.

It has been a kind of platitude of legal history that the general development of the law has been away from what we call strict liability — that is, liability imposed regardless of fault — and toward a principle that holds a man responsible for an injury suffered by another only where he inflicted that injury intentionally or where it came about through some carelessness on his part. Though this principle, which requires fault in the sense of a wrongful intent or negligence, has always been subject to exceptions, it has been held before us as the ideal toward which the law should strive.

But what shall we do with situations where it is plain there was no intent to harm, but where at the same time it is impossible to determine whether or not the harm resulted from carelessness, and if so, from *whose* carelessness? This is, of course, where the automobile comes in. The existing law requires us, before we can impose liability on a driver or his insurance company, to pinpoint the human source of fault that brought about a collision or accident. How remote this principle can be from the conditions of modern highway traffic is dramatically revealed in the following account taken from a recent issue of *Fortune Magazine*. This account related to

> An intricate series of events that took place on a smoggy day... in California, on a stretch of U.S. Highway 101 called Slaughter Alley. It began with the collision

of two passenger cars. A Greyhound bus driver, trying to be helpful, stopped a heavily loaded van to borrow warning flares. The van failed to pull completely off the edge of the road. To avoid hitting the van, an oncoming car swerved in front of a gasoline tanker, causing the tanker to hit the barrier between the lanes. Subsequently, a tractor-trailer rammed another car, knocking it into the tanker, which burst into flames. A second tanker stopped short, was hit by two cars. Then a third tanker hit the second and both exploded and burned. In all, seven people were killed and twenty vehicles destroyed. The claims filed totaled $2,180,000, and involved more than twenty insurance companies. Who was at fault? This is the question, in truth unanswerable, to which the tort-liability system requires an exact answer before the injured can demand reimbursement by the offender's insurance company.

Here, plainly, a rule of law demanding proof of negligence is projected upon a situation where it simply loses its meaning. The law and the facts speak a different language. One of the difficulties of law enforcement on skid-row is that it is often impossible to secure credible witnesses who can testify as to how some brawl or assault came about; the trouble may of course be that all who witnessed the affair had their powers of observation so impaired by alcohol that they could give no coherent account of what happened, even if they wished to do so. In the case of the California highway pileup described in the passage I have quoted, even the most sober witness, with all his reflexes in excellent order, would not be able to report later exactly what happened and just where, in the chain of interrelated human actions, the failure occurred. Events that take place beyond the reach of ordinary human powers of observation and judgment are equally beyond the reach of any legal rule that requires us to decide just who was to blame for what happened.

This completes my survey of three instances, all drawn from current American experience, where law fails to achieve an effective hold on life. It should be noted that in all these cases law fails of its full mission, not because it is repulsed by some counterforce, but because it projects itself upon a social terrain incapable of supporting it. To revert to a figure I have already invoked, in the cases I have reviewed the law speaks a language that simply fails to convey its intended meaning within the environment where it attempts to function.

I come now finally to a problem greatly transcending in importance any I have so far discussed. The subtitle for this concluding portion of my remarks is a lengthy one:

Establishing the Rule of Law Among Peoples Who Are Not Accustomed to Thinking of Law as Something Made or Enacted

What I have in mind here is, of course, the attempt now going on in so many parts of the world to establish "the rule of law" — "Western" or "European" style — among the newly emerging nations, that is, among peoples who have previously lived by customary rules and who have had, therefore, little experience in regulating their behavior by paper rules enacted through legislative procedures.

The subject is a vast one and a truly adequate treatment not only lies beyond my competence, but would be impossible in the space available. I shall, therefore, largely concentrate on attempting to expose for scrutiny some of the provincialisms and unconscious biases that seem to me often to infect our thinking about this problem.

It is not difficult for us to perceive that the notion of a law deliberately enacted by a legislative assembly is a fairly sophisticated thing and that anyone encountering it for the first time would be mystified by it. But are we sure that the incomprehension in this case does not run in both directions? To understand the problems of a transition from customary law to enacted law we have to perceive what is being abandoned as well as what is being embraced. Are we sure we really know what it means to live by the rules of a system we classify as customary law? I think we have the resources for obtaining such an understanding, but it is not clear that we always draw on those resources when we come to deal with cultures that seem remote from our own.

If, in an effort to understand what customary law is and what lends moral force to it, we consult treatises on jurisprudence, we are apt to encounter some such explanation as the following, which I have in fact paraphrased from an article in an encyclopedia: "Customary law expresses the force of habit that prevails so strongly in the early history of the race. One man treads across an area previously unexplored, following a pattern set by accident or some momentary purpose of his own; others then follow the same track until a path is worn." Though what I have just quoted is familiar to the point of being trite, it presents, I believe, a grotesque caricature of what customary law really means in the lives of those who govern themselves by it.

To get a better perspective let us consider at some length a practice that has grown up and become customary in the administration of our own criminal law. In legal theory the criminal law and the law of torts are entirely distinct. If a man takes my watch wrongfully, I have a tort claim against him for the value of what he took from me, and it is up to me to assert that claim. By stealing my watch the taker also commits a crime, and the prosecution of that crime rests, not with me, but with the public authorities. The law of torts serves the purpose of reimbursing the person injured; the law of crimes serves a public purpose, that of punishment, deterrence, prevention and rehabilitation. In theory these two purposes are entirely distinct.

The reality is quite different. In the actual administration of the criminal law, the distinction between tort and crime is — over wide areas of criminal behavior — not only not observed, but is deliberately ignored. In the case of certain types of crime, in certain kinds of cases where it seems appropriate, it is everywhere standard practice for the authorities to withhold any criminal sanction if the offender is willing to make restitution to his victim or otherwise offer amends for the harm he has inflicted. This practice is common in the case of embezzlements, small thefts, bad-check writing, and petty damage to property, such as window breaking. What this means is that if, for example, a man gives a check to a retail store, knowing full well he is overdrawing his account, criminal charges may be withheld if he makes some settlement with the store. In the reaching of such a settlement the police or the prosecutor will play a role, and needless to say, a somewhat persuasive one.

The principle embodied in this practice extends over a wide portion of the human apparatus of law enforcement; it begins with the patrolman on his beat, extends through the prosecutor's office and into the judiciary, at least as far as the trial level. The practice is institutionalized and is conducted according to its own tacitly understood rules. In one large American city — perhaps in others — there is a regular office of the police department called the Restitution Division.

The most remarkable thing about this body of practice is that it may often involve an act by the public authorities which is itself a crime. The crime involved goes by the ugly name of "compounding a felony." A patrolman says to an arrested person, for example, "Bring that watch out of hiding, give it back to the man you took it from, and I'll let you go, with my assurance you won't be called into court." In making this proposal the law's representative becomes himself a criminal. A more cautious and sophisticated officer would, of course, avoid any explicit deal, observing merely that it has been his experience that those who make restitution in cases like this never go to jail, thus leaving it to the offender to decide for himself whether he wants to act as any sensible man would in his situation. Between these extremes there are ambiguous way-stations; a complex game is often played in giving the right complexion to the discussion that leads to the dropping of criminal charges.

Is not the practice I have been describing a form of customary law? We may wince at applying that title to it since, when measured against the law in books, it not uncommonly embraces within itself an element of illegality. But putting any scruples on that score to one side, let us examine the practice dispassionately for whatever insight it may yield into the nature of the thing we call customary law when it appears in primitive society.

Now the first thing to notice is that the practice has little to do with any blind following of tradition; it is not something our ancestors did and we go on doing simply because we are too unimaginative to think of doing things differently. The practice is a purposive thing; it has arisen — in response to similar needs — in many different places at different times. It has its fringes of uncertainty; it requires to be interpreted in the light of its function and purpose. The man who passes a check he knows will overdraw his account is normally eligible for dispensation; the forger plainly is not. The man who draws a check on a bank where he has no account at all may be a borderline case.

We may perhaps best capture the spirit of the practice by quoting from a study sponsored by the American Bar Association. This study reports a case that involved a somewhat novel extension of the practice of forgiving the criminal who squares things with his victim. The case is thus summarized in the study in question:

> A young man was charged with statutory rape when the father of the underage girl, upon discovering that his daughter was pregnant, complained to the prosecuting attorney. The trial judge dismissed the charge when the young man agreed to marry the girl on the grounds that this was "the proper solution to this kind of problem."

While I would not want to recommend generally marriages arranged at the police station, or in the criminal court, the case as reported is suffused with the spirit of primitive law and primitive procedures of dispute settlement. There is the wrong complained of, the face-to-face confrontation of the parties immediately affected, the search for an acceptable solution, and finally a settlement reached in a spirit of forgive, forget and start over. In the minds of those responsible for it, the final settlement was "the proper solution for this kind of problem," and this in spite of the fact that it was completely unauthorized by the written law.

The practice in the administration of criminal law that I have been discussing has counterparts throughout our society. Within the administration of justice itself, there are countless little practices — at every level — that have no sanction in the books and are often subtly or flagrantly inconsistent with what is written there. The same observation holds for our organizational life as a whole — for corporations, governmental agencies, the armed services, universities and churches. Within these organizations it is very seldom that the law in action corresponds exactly with the law in books. Sometimes the internal unwritten laws of these institutions disserve the proper aims of the institutions themselves; they may, indeed, involve outright abuses. At other times, however, it will be found that the practices sanctioned by custom actually serve organizational aims more effectively than formal written rules that were conceived in abstraction from the concrete circumstances of their application.

So it is not a question of our being unfamiliar with customary law, but of our being unable to draw on our own experience when we come to deal with societies different from our own. In part we cannot draw on that experience because we do not know we have it. For it is a characteristic of customary rules of action that they disappear from view precisely when they are most effective, when they appear not as rules at all, but simply as apt responses to an immediate reality, as part of "the way things are." And as for any sense of guilt about an infringement of formal rules, the perceived needs of an immediate situation may speak so loudly that they drown out the voice of enacted law, all of us being, in this respect, like the patrolman on skid-row: busy with the task of keeping our little domain in order, we simply do not hear advice coming from an uncomprehending outside source.

What I have just been saying may seem to suffer from an internal contradiction since I have asserted that certain informal practices provide an example of customary law, and, at the same time, I have spoken of these practices as constituting a direct response to the perceived demands of an immediate situation. This second characterization appears to deny to them any rule-bound quality and accordingly any right to be called "law".

But that there is no real contradiction here may be seen if we consider again the practice of dismissing criminal charges when the offender is willing to make amends to his victim. This is not a practice that manifests itself arbitrarily and sporadically over the whole spectrum of criminal conduct. Only certain kinds of criminal acts are considered appropriate for this kind of settlement. In any such practice there is a built-in drive toward regularity and toward the formulation of tacit rules. This urge toward consistency of treatment derives from two related sources.

First, the conscientious policeman or prosecutor would surely feel some pangs of conscience if he discovered in his actions no discernible tendency to give like treatment to like cases, no impulse toward fairness and equity in the exercise of the power of dispensation placed in his hands. Though his conception of fairness and equity might not equate with that of an outside observer, he nevertheless would be likely to experience at least some discomfort if he found himself departing capriciously from the precedents set by his own practice.

The second source of a drive toward consistency lies in the fact that some degree of administrative regularity is demanded in the interest of organizational efficiency and effective communication among those who administer the practice. Unless the patrolman, the police superintendent, and the prosecuting attorney accept some shared standards for determining the kinds of cases suitable for settlement, no one will be able effectively to coordinate his action with that of others.

The analogy of language may in this connection be illuminating. We should certainly be surprised if a visitor from Outer Space should on his return report to his fellow creatures that the Earthlings have the peculiar habit of sticking by the forms of their language, that they go on using the same ways of declining verbs, employ repetitiously the same variations in word order to distinguish questions from assertions, and generally exhibit great timidity in linguistic experiment, being unwilling apparently to tamper at all with the basic elements of their language. If we were informed of any such reaction to our linguistic habits, we would respond that we are motivated, not by a fear of innovation, but by a desire to maintain communication with our fellows. Without some stability of linguistic forms, communication becomes impossible. If we think of human interaction as a language, not of words, but of conduct, then any mystery in the persistence of relatively stable patterns disappears.

If what I have been saying is correct then we already know much more about customary law than we realize. We also know more than we are perhaps ready to admit about the tendency of customary law to modify and even supplant formal enactment. This should help us to understand at least a part of the struggle involved in attempting to establish the "rule of law" — that is, the rule of enacted law — in the newly emerging nations.

What I have so far been saying may seem to suggest a very simple solution for the legal problems of the new nations: Let them stick by their rules of customary law and forego any venture into the unfamiliar field of enacted law. Unfortunately this solution is excluded by the very forces that drive the newly enfranchised peoples toward nationhood.

Customary law is primarily a law of intimate, face-to-face relations. It is concerned with such things as coming of age, marrying, burying the dead, and sharing in common ventures like fishing and harvesting. When it extends to more distant and impersonal relations, customary law commonly assumes a negative form; it imposes, not rules for effective cooperation, but the minimum restraints essential to guide limited interaction away from open hostility.

The task of the new nation, on the other hand, is to bring under a single system of rules peoples who have previously been divided legally by tribe, dialect, skin-color, caste, occupation and place of residence. Where previously there may have been almost as many legal systems as there were cultural divergencies within the population, the new nation must establish, as rapidly and effectively as it can, a common legal order for all its citizens. This is a tremendous undertaking. The problems it presents are not only unfamiliar to those directly concerned, but they fall largely outside any relevant experience of our own.

Let me mention briefly two problems that commonly come to the fore in the course of this drastic reorientation. I refer to the problems of political corruption and the cult of personality, the tendency to substitute personal rule for the corporate forms contemplated by democracy.

As for political corruption, we must realize that in this field we confront perplexing problems of our own. These problems arise not simply from over-present human frailty, but from the difficulty of drawing manageable lines of distinction that will separate the innocent from the vicious, that will enable us, for example, to permit a man to give financial aid to a political cause without his obtaining a tacit right to preferential treatment from the prospective office holders whose candidacy is furthered by his contribution. The solution for problems of this sort cannot be achieved merely by preaching; it requires the drawing of reasonably clear institutional guidelines that will give intellectual substance to the distinctions we seek to achieve.

Now it is precisely the general absence of such institutional guidelines that chiefly distinguishes the situation of the new nations from our own. Customary law, it should be observed, does not always distinguish clearly the powers of political office from those conferred by property; more generally, it may not distinguish between politics and economics. That a society can function without this distinction — in the form in which we now know it — is sufficiently demonstrated in English history by the feudal system. And many societies governed by customary law, it should be remembered, are essentially feudal in their basic organization.

Let me suggest by means of a somewhat contrived illustration what is missed when no distinction is taken between the prerogatives of office and those of ownership. My illustration is tailored to dimensions that will facilitate a comparison with primitive society. Suppose I live on the outskirts of town and keep a cow. I have no pasture for my cow, so I strike a bargain with a farmer-neighbor by which in return for a fee he will let my cow graze on his pasture. Now I might in such a case be displeased by the amount of the fee demanded by my neighbor, but it would never occur to me to charge him with corruption; he may be a skinflint but he is not a crook. On the other hand, if the city official in charge of snow removal calls on me and says that he will, in exchange for a fee, do an especially thorough and careful job of removing the snow from the street in front of my home, I will feel that I have received an invitation to participate in outrageous corruption.

Now what I want to suggest is that the distinction you and I would take between these two cases may not be apparent to one raised entirely on customary law, which does not always recognize a distinction between office and ownership. We must then realize that in the newly emerging nations there will largely be lacking the institutional boundaries by which we orient our own judgments and decide where tolerance ends. This is something we must keep in mind when we are tempted to pass moral judgment on the acts of those who of necessity live in a social world where the signposts are placed differently from the way they are with us.

As to the tendency for personal rule to supplant constitutionalism, this is a complex problem with, I believe, many unexplored dimensions. One may venture the generalization that when anything like a central political power first emerges in a society based on customary law this power will be devoted, not to making law, but to issuing special orders and decrees. These special orders and decrees may be made to meet some emergency resulting from natural disaster or the outbreak of war. Or, a special decree may be designed to adjust customary law to the peculiar quirks of some unusual situation. These special adjustments effected through an exercise of authority will, in any event, take the form, not of general rules, but of specific commands. Political power, in other words, finds its first use not in making laws, but in issuing orders.

Now it is a fact even with us that special orders or commands are ordinarily issued, not in the name of the collectivity, but in the name of some official. This is so even though in fact the command is the product of collective deliberations. General laws, on the other hand, are normally issued in the name of the state, or of the legislature speaking for the state — in other words in the name of the collectivity. This is true even in the case of a law known to result from the initiative of an individual.

If these observations are correct, then it is understandable that a people for whom the whole idea of enacted law is mysterious, will be likely to find at least as mysterious orders issued in the name of the collectivity. Surrender to the cult of personality may therefore represent, not so much an abandonment of moral principle, as a retreat from a conceptual world that seems unreal into a more familiar intellectual environment.

As offering some support for the line of thought just suggested, let me offer a few lines from Walter Bagehot:

> The best reason why Monarchy is a strong government is, that it is an intelligible government. The mass of mankind understand it, and they hardly anywhere in the world understand any other.... When you put before the mass of mankind the question, "Will you be governed by a king, or will you be governed by a constitution?" the inquiry comes out thus — "Will you be governed in a way you understand, or will you be governed in a way you do not understand?"
> ... [W]e have whole classes unable to comprehend the idea of a constitution — unable to feel the least attachment to impersonal laws.

The words I have just quoted were written about a hundred years ago. They report the conclusions of an astute observer about the common man of his times. This common man, be it remembered, lived in a country that can be said to have offered for the first time in history a truly secure haven for constitutionalism and due process of law. Some reflection on these words may help us to curb our natural American tendency to moralize ourselves out of any capacity to understand what is happening in social environments radically different from our own.

CHAPTER 4

MISUNDERSTANDINGS, MISREPRESENTATION AND MISTAKES

This chapter contains a heterogeneous mixture of cases which cover a wide range of categories in the traditional division of topics in contracts. They are put together here because they have in common the fact that one of the parties to the contract has not got from the deal what he expected. The issue that runs through all the cases is how far the law can protect one party's disappointed expectations. The cases will also have important consequences for the lawyer who is called upon to draft agreements. If it is important for your client to get something from the transaction, how can he best be protected from disappointment?

A. Interpretation and Implication

At some point or another in the courts' handling of contracts it has to be decided just what the parties did agree to do. We cannot begin to understand what their (legally relevant) expectations might be until we know what it was that they thought they were getting from the contract. It will be useful, therefore, to examine how one determines what it is that the parties may have meant by words used in the agreement that they made.

We have seen the courts determining the meaning of words and clauses in contracts in the process of deciding, for example, whether a particular communication was an offer or not. The process of interpretation is basic to any issue of contract. Most of the time this process is largely implicit. Much might be said about the process of interpretation. However, all that will be said here is that the process consumes a large amount of judicial time and requires from lawyers and judges a high degree of philological and grammatical skill. Two cases are offered as examples of how one court sees its function.

Further Readings

Patterson, "The Interpretation and Construction of Contracts" (1964), 64 Col. L.R. 833.

Farnsworth, " 'Meaning' in the Law of Contracts" (1967), 76 Yale L.J. 939.

Restatement [First] Contracts

§ 227: A standard of interpretation is the test applied by the law to words and to other manifestations of intention in order to determine the meaning to be given to them.

Comment: a. [This comment lists six "conceivable standards of interpretation," as follows:]

1. The standard of general usage;

2. A standard of limited usage, which would attach the meaning given to language in a particular locality, or by ... those engaged in a particular occupation ... (the distinction between 1 and 2 is a difference in degree, since generality of usage does not necessarily imply universality);

3. A mutual standard, which would allow only such meanings as conform to an intention common to both or all the parties, and would attach this meaning although it violates the usage of all other persons;

4. An individual standard, which would attach to words or other manifestations

of intention whatever meaning the person employing them intended them to express, or that the person receiving the communication understood from it;

5. A standard of reasonable expectation, which would attach to words or other manifestations of intention the meaning which the party employing them should reasonably have apprehended that they would convey to the other party;

6. A standard of reasonable understanding, which would attach to words or other manifestations of intention the meaning which the person to whom the manifestations are addressed might reasonably give to them."

Restatement, Second, Contracts
§ 227:

(1) Where the parties have attached the same meaning to a promise or agreement or a term thereof, it is interpreted in accordance with that meaning.

(2) Where the parties have attached different meanings to a promise or agreement or a term thereof, it is interpreted in accordance with the meaning attached by one of them if at the time the agreement was made

    (a)   that party did not know of any different meaning attached by the other, and the other knew the meaning attached by the first party; or

    (b)   that party had no reason to know of any different meaning attached by the other, and the other had reason to know the meaning attached by the first party.

(3) Except as stated in this section, neither party is bound by the meaning attached by the other, even though the result may be a failure of mutual assent.

See also §21A (reproduced supra, Chapter 2).

FULLER AND EISENBERG, BASIC CONTRACT LAW

3rd ed. pp. 280 – 282.

IS THE INTERPRETATION OF WRITTEN CONTRACTS A QUESTION OF LAW OR OF FACT?

Until recently, it seemed fairly well settled that the interpretation of written contracts was a question of "law," not "fact" — *i.e.*, was for the lawfinder rather than the factfinder to determine — unless it involved the *credibility* of extrinsic evidence. "Although the code by which the meaning of language is to be tested must frequently be discovered by admitting evidence of facts and circumstances, the actual interpretation of a writing has largely been withdrawn from the jury pursuant to long established precedent and placed in the hands of the judiciary. Upon countless occasions, the courts have declared it to be the responsibility of the judge to interpret and construe written instruments, whatever their nature." 4 Williston § 601 (3d ed. 1961) (footnotes omitted). "It is ... solely a judicial function to interpret a written instrument unless the interpretation turns upon the credibility of extrinsic evidence." Traynor, C.J., in *Parsons v. Bristol Development Co.,* 62 Cal.2d 861, 865, 44 Cal. Rptr. 767, 402 P.2d 839, 842 (1965).

In recent years, however, this approach has come under question. For example, the standard "disputes" clause in contracts with the Federal Government provides that all disputes concerning "questions of fact" arising under the contract shall be decided by the contracting officer subject to appeal to the head of the department or his representative, whose decision shall be final. In *United States v. Moorman,* 338 U.S. 457, 70 S.Ct. 288, 94 L.Ed. 256 (1950), the Supreme Court referred to "the oft-repeated conclusion of the Court of Claims that questions of 'interpretation' are not questions of fact"; without deciding the point, the Court said "there is much to be said for the argument that 'interpretation' here presents a question of fact."

In *Wunderlich v. United States,* 117 Ct.Cl. 92, 212-213 (1950), reversed on another claim, 342 U.S. 98 (1951), the Court of Claims quoted from the *Moorman* case and said, "In view of this observation of the Supreme Court, we have re-examined the doctrine heretofore applied by this court to this problem.

"We are, of course, aware that questions of the interpretation of written documents are not, speaking with analytical accuracy, in most cases questions of law in the sense that a lawyer or judge has the special skill needed to answer them. They may be questions of agriculture, or engineering, or finance, or medicine, or law. In the division of judicial functions between the judge and the lay jury which only by accident would have the requisite skill in a particular case, the judge reserved this function to himself, presumably as being more competent than the jury. And judges and lawyers began to call the questions 'questions of law,' as a short way of saying that they should be decided by the judge. This method of expression, though analytically inaccurate was, so far as we know, quite universal. All the courts, including the Supreme Court of the United States, used it, and applied it with serious consequences ... Where appellate courts have had jurisdiction to review questions of law but not questions of fact, they have held that they could review questions as to the interpretation of contracts. ... Similar statements and decisions were early made by this court with reference to the finality of the decisions of a designated officer in problems arising in government contracts. ... The Government has cited us no authority to the contrary."

In *Meyers v. Selznick Co.,* 373 F.2d 218 (2d Cir. 1966), Judge Friendly forcefully supported an intermediate view: that questions of interpretation are for the jury whenever evidence extrinsic to the written instrument is relevant to its interpretation, even though there is no issue as to the credibility of the evidence, but merely as to its *significance*:

"The books are indeed studded with statements that 'The construction of all *written instruments* belongs to the court.' 9 Wigmore, Evidence § 2556 at 522 (3d ed. 1940); 4 Williston, Contracts § 616 at 649 (3d ed. 1961). If this really were an unvarying rule, there would seem to be no sound reason why it should not also apply to contracts that are partly written and partly oral or wholly oral, except for the possible impracticability in some cases of severing the jury's task in ascertaining what was said from the judge's in interpreting what was meant, see 3 Corbin on Contracts § 554 at 223 (2d ed. 1960) — although such a distinction has been drawn. ... However, the traditional formulation goes considerably beyond the authorities, at least for the federal courts. In a case often cited in support of the orthodox view, *Hamilton v. Liverpool & London and Globe Ins. Co.,* 136 U.S. 242, 255, 10 S.Ct. 945, 950, 34 L.Ed. 419 (1890), Mr. Justice Gray, in holding that in that case the question was solely for the court, was careful to point out that there the answer 'did not depend in any degree ... on oral testimony or extrinsic facts'. ...

"With the courts' growing appreciation of Professor Corbin's lesson that words are seldom so 'plain and clear' as to exclude proof of surrounding circumstances and other extrinsic aids to interpretation, see 3 Corbin on Contracts § 542, the exception bids fair largely to swallow the supposed general rule. About all that is left of the latter, at least where parol evidence has been properly admitted, is that, save for contracts so technical or complex as to lie beyond a jury's comprehension, 'If the meaning after taking the parol evidence, if any, into account is so clear that no reasonable man could reach more than one conclusion as to the meaning of the writing under the circumstances,' 4 Williston, supra, § 616 at 661-62, the court will instruct the jury as to the proper interpretation in the light of its findings with respect to the parol evidence or, where the parol evidence is undisputed, will direct a verdict — just as it would do on any other question where the evidence would warrant only one result.

"Whether determination of meaning be regarded as a question of fact, a question of law, or just itself, reliance on the jury to resolve ambiguities in the light of extrinsic evidence seems quite as it should be, save where the form or subject-matter of a particular contract outruns a jury's competence; indeed, the old formulation may have rested to some extent on the jurors' then illiteracy and inability to understand more than exceedingly simple terms.... Resolution of [issues involving the determination of meaning] may hinge in no small degree on notions of fairness — the very kind of decision laymen are ideally equipped to make." (Footnotes omitted.)

This intermediate view is adopted in Restatement (Second) of Contracts § 238 (2), which provides that "A question of interpretation of an integrated agreement is to be determined by the trier of fact if it depends on the credibility of extrinsic evidence *or on a choice among reasonable inferences to be drawn from extrinsic evidence.* Otherwise a question of interpretation of an integrated agreement is to be determined as a question of law." (Emphasis added.) The rule is rationalized and elaborated in comments d and e:

"Analytically, what meaning is attached to a word or other symbol by one or more people is a question of fact. But general usage as to the meaning of words in the English language is commonly a proper subject for judicial notice without the aid of evidence extrinsic to the writing. Historically, moreover, partly perhaps because of the fact that jurors were often illiterate, questions of interpretation of written documents have been treated as questions of law in the sense that they are decided by the trial judge rather than by the jury. Likewise, since an appellate court is commonly in as good a position to decide such questions as the trial judge, they have been treated as questions of law for purposes of appellate review. Such treatment has the effect of limiting the power of the trier of fact to exercise a dispensing power in the guise of a finding of fact, and thus contributes to the stability and predictability of contractual relations. In cases of standardized contracts such as insurance policies, it also provides a method of assuring that like cases will be decided alike.... Even though an agreement is not integrated, or even though the meaning of an integrated agreement depends on extrinsic evidence, a question of interpretation is not left to the trier of fact where the evidence is so clear that no reasonable man would determine the issue in any way but one. But if the issue depends on evidence outside the writing, and the possible inferences are conflicting, the choice is for the trier of fact."

PRENN v. SIMMONDS

[1971] 3 All E.R. 237. House of Lords; Lords Reid, Donovan, Wilberforce, Pearson and Diplock.
[All the other judges concurred in the judgment of Lord Wilberforce:]

Lord Wilberforce. My Lords, Dr Simmonds's claim in this action is that, under the terms of an agreement under seal dated 6th July 1960, he is entitled to acquire from Mr Prenn, for a consideration of £6,000, a 4 per cent interest in the ordinary capital of a company controlled by Mr Prenn called now Controls & Communications Ltd, but at the relevant date Radio & Television Trust Ltd ('RTT'). This interest was worth at the date of the trial about £200,000. Mr Prenn disputes the claim on the ground that a necessary condition set by the agreement has not been satisfied because less than £300,000 profits available for dividend on the ordinary stock of RTT over the relevant period has been earned. Dr Simmonds maintains that the condition has been fulfilled. The dispute relates not to the figures, which are agreed, but to the definition of profits of RTT available for dividend on its ordinary stock. If this means the separate profits of RTT alone, the amount over the period fell just short of the target, by less than £10,000. If it means the consolidated profits of the group consisting of RTT and subsidiaries, the amount was largely exceeded. The small margin of deficiency, although capable of arousing sympathy for Dr Simmonds, is not an argument for one or other side. A similar situation might arise on either interpretation and is inherent in the nature of 'target' agreements.

The question is thus simply one of construction of the agreement and it should be capable of resolution shortly and cheaply. But Dr Simmonds has claimed in the alternative that, if the agreement did not bear the meaning he contended for, it should be rectified so as to do so. This let in a mass of evidence, oral and documentary, as to the parties' intentions, which would not be admissible on construction, although (as I shall explain) counsel for Dr Simmonds tried to bring some of it in on that issue. It also involved some issues of law. This part of the case overshadowed the rest, so that by far the greater part of the time spent both at first instance and in the Court of Appeal was concerned with it. In this House argument was heard first exclusively on the question of construction and, as your Lordships reached on it a conclusion in favour of Dr Simmonds, no argument on rectification was heard. I now deal with this construction issue.

In order for the agreement of 6th July 1960 to be understood, it must be placed in its context. The time has long passed when agreements, even those under seal, were isolated from the matrix of facts in which they were set and interpreted purely on internal linguistic considerations. There is no need to appeal here to any modern, anti-literal, tendencies, for Lord Blackburn's well-known judgment in *River Wear Comrs v Adamson* (1877), 2 App. Cas. 743, 763, provides ample warrant for a liberal approach. We must, as he said, enquire beyond the language and see what the circumstances were with reference to which the words were used, and the object, appearing from those circumstances, which the person using them had in view. Moreover, at any rate since 1859 (*Macdonald v Longbottom* (1860), 1 E & E 977) it has been clear enough that evidence of mutually known facts may be admitted to identify the meaning of a descriptive term.

Counsel for Dr Simmonds, however, contended for even greater extension of the court's interpretative power. They argued that later authorities have gone further and allow prior negotiations to be looked at in aid of the construction of a written document. In my opinion, they did not make good their contention. A modern authority in this House, which counsel for Dr Simmonds invoked, is *Hvalfangerselskapet Polaris Aktieselskap v Unilever Ltd* (1933), 39 Com. Cas. 1, where it was necessary to interpret the words 'entire production'. There, as here, there was a claim for rectification in the alternative so that a great deal of evidence of matters prior to the contract was called. But the speeches give no support for a contention that negotiations leading up to the contract can be taken into account; at most they support the evidence to establish a trade or technical meeting (not in question here) and, of course, they recognise the admissibility of evidence of surrounding circumstances. But they contain little to encourage, and much to discourage, evidence of negotiation or of the parties' subjective intentions.

I may refer to one other case to dispel the idea that English law is left behind in some island of literal interpretation. In *Utica City National Bank v Gunn* (1918), 118 N.E. 607, the New York Court of Appeals followed precisely the English line. Cardozo J in his judgment refers to 'the genesis and aim of the transaction' citing Stephen's Digest of the Law of Evidence, and Wigmore on Evidence. Surrounding circumstances may, he says, 'stamp upon a contract a popular or looser meaning' than the strict legal meaning, certainly when to follow the latter would make the transaction futile. 'It is easier to give a new shade of meaning to a word than to give no meaning to a whole transaction.' The whole judgment, as one may expect, combines classicism with intelligent realism.

So I think that Dr Simmonds gains little support from authority. On principle, the matter is worth pursuing a little, because the present case illustrates very well the disadvantages and danger of departing from established doctrine and the virtue of the latter. There were prolonged negotiations between solicitors, with exchanges of draft clauses, ultimately emerging in cl 2 of the agreement. The reason for not admitting evidence of these exchanges is not a technical one or even mainly one of convenience (although the attempt to admit it did greatly prolong the case and add to its expense). It is simply that such evidence is unhelpful. By the nature of things, where negotiations are difficult, the parties' positions, with each passing letter, are changing and until the final agreement, although converging, still divergent. It is only the final document which records a consensus. If the previous documents use different expressions, how does construction of those expressions, itself a doubtful process, help on the construction of the contractual words? If the same expressions are used, nothing is gained by looking back; indeed, something may be lost since the relevant surrounding circumstances may be different. And at this stage there is no consensus of the parties to appeal to. It may be said that previous documents may be looked at to explain the aims of the parties. In a limited sense this is true; the commercial, or business object, of the transaction, objectively ascertained, may be a surrounding fact. Cardozo J thought so in the *Utica Bank* case. And if it can be shown that one interpretation completely frustrates that object, to the extent of rendering the contract futile, that may be a strong argument for an alternative interpretation, if that can reasonably be found. But beyond that it may be difficult to go; it may be a matter of degree, or of judgment, how far one interpretation, or another, gives effect to a common intention; the parties, indeed, may be pursuing that intention with differing emphasis, and hoping to achieve it to an extent which may differ, and in different ways. The words used may, and often do, represent a formula which means different things to each side, yet may be accepted because that is the only way to get 'agreement' and in the hope that disputes will not arise. The only course then can be to try to ascertain the 'natural' meaning. Far more, and indeed totally, dangerous is it to admit evidence of one party's objective — even if this is known to the other party. However strongly pursued this may be, the other party may only be willing to give it partial recognition, and in a world of give and take, men often have to be satisfied with less than they want. So, again, it would be a matter of speculation how far the common intention was that the particular objective should be realised. In the present case, Lord Denning MR seems to have taken into account Dr Simmonds's anxiety (as testified by a witness) to protect himself against unilateral decisions by Mr Prenn; and an argument pressed on us was that, if Mr Prenn's interpretation (i e that only the holding company's profits were relevant) was correct, Dr Simmonds would, in this matter on which he felt so anxious, in some respect at least, be completely in Mr Prenn's hands, for Mr Prenn could decide just how much, or how little, of the subsidiaries' profits were to be passed to the holding company. I cannot see how any of this can be admissible because, I repeat, I cannot see how it is helpful. Given the fact of Dr Simmonds's anxiety, the whole question is how far does the agreement meet it; how can we know, except by interpreting the agreement, how far Mr Prenn was willing to meet him or how far Dr Simmonds decided to take what he could get? Even the argument that Mr Prenn's interpretation would put Dr Simmonds in his hands, although apparently attractive, I find to be dangerous; a man in Dr Simmonds's position — a professional man — entering into relations with the source of finance and benefits to come, might decide, in his own interest, that if he could not get all the protection he wanted, the risk of partial protection was one to accept; that Mr Prenn had to be trusted to act fairly. To say that the clause had this result is not to say that it was futile or frustratory: it is to say that a better clause could, with hindsight, in Dr Simmonds's interest have been drawn. But the court cannot construct such a clause out of the material given.

In my opinion, then, evidence of negotiations, or of the parties' intentions, and a fortiori of Dr Simmonds's intentions, ought not to be received, and evidence should be restricted to evidence of the factual background known to the parties at or before the date of the contract, including evidence of the 'genesis' and objectively the 'aim' of the transaction.

As to the circumstances, and the objective of the parties, there is no controversy in the present case. The agreement itself, on its face, almost supplies enough, without the necessity to supplement it by outside evidence. But some expansion, from undisputed facts, makes for clearer understanding and I include a reference to these in what follows.

. . .

To sum up, Mr Prenn's construction does not fit in any way the aim of the agreement, or correspond with commercial good sense, nor is it, even linguistically, acceptable. The converse of each of these propositions applies to Dr Simmonds's interpretation. I would accept it. It follows, in consequence, that the alternative claim for rectification does not arise....

QUESTIONS

1. Does what Lord Wilberforce says here have any bearing on the following problem (which we have already considered):

A says to B, "I will sell you my cow for $100." B, knowing that A meant to say "horse" and that the word "cow" is a slip of the tongue, says, "I accept"?

2. Suppose that in *Hobbs v. E.&N. Railway (supra)* the facts were:

(a) Trutch said to Hobbs, "By land we mean land without the mineral rights."

(b) The price paid by Hobbs was such that any reasonable purchaser would have known that the land that was being sold was either (i) being sold without mineral rights, or (ii) being sold at a price substantially less than would have been the case of land sold with the mineral rights.

Does Lord Wilberforce say anything about the admissibility of evidence of these facts?

3. A rule that says that certain facts are inadmissible is usually based on the

ground that the facts are irrelevant. (Lord Wilberforce does say that evidence of the negotiations is unhelpful). To what extent is it useful to say that the facts are *inadmissible*? If the *Hobbs v. E. & N. Railway* facts are relevant, and if one can get evidence in by alleging, for example, that the agreement as signed does not represent the true agreement (the basis for a claim for rectification) what useful purpose does the decision serve?

4. What, as a practical matter, are the things that a court (and counsel) should have in mind in introducing evidence, having regard to the following issues:

1. The degree to which the court's sympathy can be obtained for one side;
2. The need to explain to the court the business background of a particular transaction; and
3. The possible broadening of the issues of law should an appeal be taken and the consequent need for facts to support arguments that might not be open to a trial judge to accept, but which may be open to the Supreme Court of Canada.

SCHULER A.G. v. WICKMAN LTD.

[1973] 2 All E.R. 39. House of Lords; Lords Reid, Morris, Wilberforce, Simon and Kilbrandon.

[The parties had entered in an agreement under which the respondent had the exclusive right to sell certain products of the appellant. The respondent undertook to try to sell the appellant's products by, among other things, arranging for frequent visits of the respondent's salesmen on certain potential customers. The term in the agreement was referred to as a "condition". The respondent failed on several occasions to have its salesmen call on the potential customers and the appellant maintained that this breach of the agreement, being a breach of a "condition", entitled them to put an end to the arrangement. The respondents resisted this.

The House of Lords, (Lord Wilberforce, dissenting) dismissed the appeal of the appellant from the judgment of the Court of Appeal, upholding the decision of an arbitrator, and held that the breaches that had occurred did not entitle the appellant to terminate the agreement. Extracts are taken from the judgment of Lord Wilberforce and Lord Simon on the correct approach to the interpretation of the written agreement.]

Lord Simon:

Construction by subsequent conduct

The majority of the Court of Appeal came to their conclusion in favour of Wickman by construing the agreement by reference to the subsequent conduct of the parties thereunder. They recognised that it had been stated by four of their Lordships who decided *James Miller and Partners Ltd v Whitworth Street Estates (Manchester) Ltd*, [1970] A.C. 583, that the conduct of the parties under a contract is not available as an aid to construction; but held that this rule only applied when the instrument to be construed is unambiguous, and that *Watcham v Attorney-General of East Africa Protectorate*, [1919] A.C. 533, (which was not cited in the *Whitworth Street Estates* case) was authority entitling the court to have recourse to subsequent conduct of the parties under this contract to resolve the ambiguity that they descried therein. The distribution agreement is not drafted with entire felicity, and therefore presents difficulties in construction. But this is not the same as embodying an ambiguity. Agreeing as I do with the interpretation of my noble and learned friend, Lord Reid, I cannot on final resolution find that there is any ambiguity in the agreement. Nevertheless, the question of the availability of subsequent conduct as an aid to interpretation is an important one which ought not if possible to be left in its present state of uncertainty; and, since it was fully and carefully argued before your Lordships, I do not feel that I would be justified in remaining silent on it.

The *Whitworth Street Estates* case was concerned with a contract (containing an arbitration clause) between an English and a Scots company which was to be performed in Scotland, but was silent whether the contract (and the arbitration thereunder) was to be governed by English or by Scots law. Disputes having arisen, an arbitration took place in Scotland. The issue before the Court of Appeal and your Lordships' House was whether the arbiter could be required to state a case for the opinion of the English High Court, which in turn depended on what was the curial law of the arbitration. If the contract was to be governed by Scots law, that too would be the curial law of the arbitration; but it was argued that even if the law of the contract were English the curial law of the arbitration was Scottish. In the Court of Appeal Lord Denning MR held that the crucial question in determining what was the law governing the contract was to ask: 'what is the *system of law* with which the transaction has the closest and most real connection?' He concluded that that was English law. He went on:

> "I am confirmed in this view by the subsequent conduct of the parties. This is always available to aid the interpretation of a contract and to find out its closest connections. On two occasions the parties seem to have assumed that the transaction was governed by English law."

Davies LJ agreed. Widgery LJ, who also agreed that English was the proper law of the contract, said:

> "To solve a problem such as arises in this case one looks first at the express terms of the contract to see whether that intention is there to be found. If it is not, then in my judgment the next step is to consider the conduct of the parties to see whether that conduct shows that a decision in regard to the proper law of the contract can be inferred from it. If the parties' conduct shows that they have adopted a particular view with regard to the proper law, then it may be inferred that they have agreed that that law shall govern the contract accordingly."

When the *Whitworth Street Estates* case came to your Lordships' House it was argued that the subsequent conduct of the parties could not be looked at to determine what was the proper law of the contract. Four of the five members of the appellate committee dealt expressly with this matter. My noble and learned friend, Lord Reid, said:

> "It has been assumed in the course of this case that it is proper, in determining what was the proper law, to have regard to actings of the parties after their contract had been made. Of course the actings of the parties (including any words which they used) may be sufficient to show that they made a new contract. If they made no agreement originally as to the proper law, such actings may show that they made an agreement about that at a later stage. Or if they did make such an agreement originally such actings may show that they later agreed to alter it. But with regard to actings of the parties between the date of the original contract and the date of Mr Underwood's appointment, I did not understand it to be argued that they were sufficient to establish any new contract, and I think that they clearly were not. As I understood him, counsel sought to use those actings to show that there was an agreement when the original contract was made that the proper law of that contract was to be the law of England. I must say that I had thought it now well settled that it is not legitimate to use as an aid in the con-

struction of the contract anything which the parties said or did after it was made. Otherwise one might have the result that a contract meant one thing the day it was signed, but by reason of subsequent events meant something different a month or a year later."

My noble and learned friend, Lord Hodson, said:

"I should add that I cannot assent to the view which seems to have found favour in the eyes of Lord Denning MR and Widgery LJ that as a matter of construction the contract can be construed not only in its surrounding circumstances but also by reference to the subsequent conduct of the parties."

My noble and learned friend, Viscount Dilhorne, said:

"I do not consider that one can properly have regard to the parties' conduct after the contract has been entered into when considering whether an inference can be drawn as to their intention when they entered into the contract although subsequent conduct by one party may give rise to an estoppel."

My noble and learned friend, Lord Wilberforce, said:

"... once it was seen that the parties had made no express choice of law, the correct course was to ascertain from all relevant contemporary circumstances including, but not limited to, what the parties said or did at the time, what intention ought to be imputed to them on the formation of the contract. Unless it were to be found an estoppel or a subsequent agreement, I do not think that subsequent conduct can be relevant to this question."

It will be noticed that, except perhaps for Widgery LJ's, all these pronouncements (both in the Court of Appeal in favour of there being a rule whereby subsequent conduct is available as an aid to interpretation and contra in your Lordships' House) are perfectly general, none drawing the distinction which was drawn by the majority of the Court of Appeal in the instant case between ambiguous and unambiguous instruments. It must therefore be determined, first, whether or not the *Whitworth Street Estates* case was one where the instrument was ambiguous; secondly, if not, whether the situation there was so closely analogous to an ambiguity that it would be wrong to draw a distinction; thirdly, whether what was said on the matter in the *Whitworth Street Estates* case was part of the ratio decidendi or obiter; and, fourthly, if the latter, whether it should nonetheless be regarded as settling the law. It is convenient to consider together the first and second and the third and fourth points respectively.

The problem posed by the *Whitworth Street Estates* case was that the contract made no express provision on a matter which turned out to be crucial, namely, whether English or Scots law governed the contract and the arbitration. The only way of distinguishing such a situation from an ambiguity would be to say that in a situation such as *Whitworth* the difficulty facing the court was that the contract was silent on a crucial point, whereas in a case such as *Watcham* a patent ambiguity appeared on the face of the instrument, i.e., to regard the former as a case where the court was invited to take account of subsequent conduct to add an absent term, the latter as one where the court was invited to take account of subsequent conduct to determine which of two present but inconsistent terms was to be preferred. But such a distinction would, in my view, merely be to complicate the law and to introduce intolerable refinements. There was, it is true, considerable older authority which suggested that, although extrinsic evidence could be adduced to resolve ambiguity (although never direct evidence of intention in the case of a patent ambiguity), it could not be adduced to influence the interpretation of an unambiguous instrument (see Norton on Deeds). The justification for the adduction of extrinsic evidence to resolve an ambiguity must be that it might be the last resort to save an instrument from being void for uncertainty. This type of practical consideration is characteristically potent in shaping our law; but in this field its practical recommendation is, in my judgment, outweighed by the inconveniences and anomalies involved. In particular, the distinction between the admissibility of direct and circumstantial evidence of intention seems to me to be quite unjustifiable in these days. And the distinctions between patent ambiguities, latent ambiguities and equivocations as regards admissibility of extrinsic evidence are based on outmoded and highly technical and artificial rules and introduce absurd refinements. What was said in *Whitworth* should, therefore, in my judgment, be taken to apply generally to documentary construction, even when an ambiguity can be spelt out.

This brings me to consider how far what was said about this matter in *Whitworth* was part of its ratio decidendi. Lord Reid held the contract to be governed by Scots law; and he therefore did not find it necessary to determine whether, if the proper law of contract were English the arbitration was nevertheless governed by Scots law. In order to arrive at the conclusion that the law of the contract was Scottish, Lord Reid had, in my view, necessarily to determine whether to take into account the subsequent conduct of the parties which had been relied on by the Court of Appeal in holding the law of the contract to be English. In other words, what he said about the availability of subsequent conduct as an aid to interpretation of a contract was part of the ratio decidendi of his judgment. It is true that, on strict analysis, what was said by Lord Hodson, Viscount Dilhorne and Lord Wilberforce cannot be regarded as a vital step towards their conclusions; but, as I have already ventured to demonstrate, the point was directly in issue between the parties in your Lordships' House. I am therefore firmly of opinion that what was said should be regarded as settling the law on this point. I am reinforced in this opinion because, in my view, *Whitworth Street Estates* was a correct decision on the point for reasons additional to those given in the speeches. First, subsequent conduct is of no greater probative value in the interpretation of an instrument than prior negotiations or direct evidence of intention; it might, indeed, be most misleading to let in subsequent conduct without reference to these other matters. But *Prenn v Simmonds* gives convincing reasons why negotiations are not available as an aid to construction; and it does not, and could not consistently, with its reasoning, make any exception in the case of ambiguity. As for direct evidence of intention, there is clear authority that this is not available in the case of a patent ambiguity; and I have already ventured to submit to your Lordships the undesirability of distinguishing between direct and circumstantial evidence and between latent and patent ambiguities in this regard. Secondly, subsequent conduct is equally referable to what the parties meant to say as to the meaning of what they said; and, as the citation from Norton shows, it is only the latter which is relevant. Sir Edward Sugden's frequently quoted and epigrammatic dictum in *Attorney-General v Drummond* (1842), Dr & War 353, 368: '... tell me what you have done under such a deed, and I will tell you what that deed means' really contains a logical flaw: if you tell me what you have done under a deed, I can at best tell you only what you think that deed means. Moreover, Sir Edward Sugden was expressly dealing with 'ancient instruments'. I would add, thirdly, that the practical difficulties involved in admitting subsequent conduct as an aid to interpretation are only marginally, if at all, less than are involved in admitting evidence of prior negotiations.

. . .

Lord Wilberforce. My Lords, with two qualifications, this case is one of interpretation of the written agency or distributorship agreement between the appellants and the respondents dated 1st May 1963, in particular of cl 7 (b) of that agreement.

The first qualification involves the legal question whether this agreement may be construed in the light of certain allegedly relevant subsequent actions by the parties. Consideration of such actions undoubtedly influenced the majority of the Court of Appeal to decide, as they did, in the respondents' favour: and it is suggested, with much force that, but for this, Edmund Davies LJ would have decided the case the other way. In my opinion, subsequent actions ought not to have been taken into account. The general rule is that extrinsic evidence is not admissible for the construction of a written contract; the parties' intentions must be ascertained, on legal principles of construction, from the words they have used. It is one and the same principle which excludes evidence of statements, or actions, during negotiations, at the time of the contract, or subsequent to the contract, any of which to the lay mind might at first sight seem to be proper to receive. As to statements during negotiations this House has affirmed the rule of exclusion in *Prenn v Simmonds*, and as to subsequent actions (unless evidencing a new agreement or as the basis of an estoppel) in *James Miller and Partners Ltd v Whitworth Street Estates (Manchester) Ltd.*

There are of course exceptions. I attempt no exhaustive list of them. In the case of ancient documents, contemporaneous or subsequent action may be adduced in order to explain words whose contemporary meaning may have become obscure. And evidence may be admitted of surrounding circumstances or in order to explain technical expressions or to identify the subject-matter of an agreement: or (an overlapping exception) to resolve a latent ambiguity. But ambiguity in this context is not to be equated with difficulty of construction, even difficulty to a point where judicial opinion as to meaning has differed. This is, I venture to think, elementary law. On this test there is certainly no ambiguity here.

The arguments used in order to induce us to depart from these settled rules and to admit evidence of subsequent conduct generally in aid of construction were fragile. They were based first on the Privy Council judgment in *Watcham v Attorney-General of East Africa Protectorate*, not, it was pointed out, cited in *Whitworth's* case. But there was no negligence by counsel or incuria by their Lordships in omitting to refer to a precedent which I had thought had long been recognised to be nothing but the refuge of the desperate. Whether in its own field, namely, that of interpretation of deeds relating to real property by reference to acts of possession, it retains any credibility in the face of powerful judicial criticism is not before us. But in relation to the interpretation of contracts or written documents generally I must deprecate its future citation in English courts as an authority. It should be unnecessary to add that the well-known words of Lord St Leonards (*Attorney-General v Drummond*) 'tell me what you have done under *such* a deed, and I will tell you what *that deed* means' relate to ancient instruments and it is an abuse of them to cite them in other applications. Secondly, there were other authorities cited, *Hillas & Co Ltd v Arcos Ltd* and *Foley v Classique Coaches Ltd.* But, with respect, these are not in any way relevant to the present discussion, and the judgment of Lawrence J in *Radio Pictures Ltd v Inland Revenue Comrs*, so far as it bears on this point was disapproved in the Court of Appeal and in my opinion was not correct in law.

In my opinion, therefore, the subsequent actings relied on should have been left entirely out of account: in saying this I must not be taken to agree that the particular actings relied on are of any assistance whatever towards one or other construction of the contract. Indeed if one were to pursue the matter, the facts of the present case would be found to illustrate, rather vividly, the dangers inherent in entertaining this class of evidence at all.

. . .

QUESTIONS

1. Suppose that after the sale in *Hobbs v. E. & N. Railway* had been closed, Hobbs had gone into occupation of the land, and, over the course of a year, had regularly allowed teams of geologists employed by the railway to enter his land to prospect for minerals. It is also proved that he had said to an official of the railway, "If I had known that you guys were going to be tramping all over my land looking for your minerals, I would never have bought it."

Does the decision of the House of Lords rule this evidence inadmissible?

2. What pegs are there on which counsel for either side in any subsequent case can get around the rule laid down by the House of Lords?

3. How would you know what is a "latent ambiguity"? In the problem of the horse and the cow, is there any latent ambiguity?

4. What is the purpose of the rule laid down by the House of Lords?

There is no unanimity on the issue of the admissibility of subsequent conduct. The position in Canada is probably contrary to that in *Schuler v. Wickman*. The cases on both sides are collected in Waddams, *The Law of Contracts*, p. 193.

B. The Parol Evidence Rule

The next few cases discuss an issue that needs to be raised at some time in the course. There is no uniquely appropriate place to raise it, but since it bears on the issue of the terms of contract it is raised here.

The extract from Corbin that follows sets out the issues in a very clear form. The cases that follow are examples of how the courts have handled the issues. The issue raised by the parol evidence rule is very similar to that discussed by Lord Wilberforce in *Prenn v. Simmonds*. This is the extent to which it is important that the parties have reduced their agreement to a single expression of the terms on which each party is prepared to deal. The parol evidence rule presents the same problems as the rule of the admissibility of evidence of negotiations. There are many ways around such a rule and so many good reasons why there cannot be a *rule* that it makes little sense to talk of a rule at all.

CORBIN ON CONTRACTS

(1960) Vol. 3, §§ 573, 574.

[Footnotes have been omitted.]

§ 573. The Rule is a Rule of Substantive Contract Law, Not a Rule of Evidence

When two parties have made a contract and have expressed it in a writing to which they have both assented as the complete and accurate integration of that contract, evidence, whether parol or otherwise, of antecedent understandings and negotiations will not be admitted for the purpose of varying or contradicting the writing. This is in substance what is called the "parol evidence rule," a rule that scarcely deserves to be called a rule of evidence of any kind, and a rule that is as truly applicable to written evidence as to parol evidence. The use of such a name for this rule has had unfortunate consequences, principally by distracting the attention from the real issues that are involved. These issues may be any one or more of the following: (1) Have the parties made a contract? (2) Is that contract void or voidable because of illegality, fraud, mistake, or any other reason? (3) Did the parties assent to a particular writing as the complete and accurate "integration" of that contract?

In determining these issues, or any one of them, there is no "parol evidence rule" to be applied. On these issues, no relevant evidence, whether parol or otherwise, is excluded. No written document is sufficient, standing alone, to determine any one of them, however long and detailed it may be, however formal, and however many may be the seals and signatures and assertions. No one of these issues can be determined by mere inspection of the written document.

In determining these issues, however, there is no necessity for being gullible or simple minded. The party presenting the writing will testify to its execution and to its accuracy and completeness. The form and substance of the document may strongly corroborate his testimony; or it may not. There may be disinterested witnesses who corroborate him; or who contradict him. There may be corroboration in other circumstances that are proved; or there may not. When the other party testifies to the contrary on any of these issues, he should always be listened to; but he does not have to be believed. His testimony may be so overwhelmed that it would be credited by no reasonable man; or it may not. Perhaps a verdict should be directed; but perhaps not. This is a question of weight of evidence, not of admissibility.

In hundreds of cases stating and purporting to apply the "parol evidence rule," the reported opinion does not show the basis of the court's finding (or assumption) that the writing presented in court was in fact assented to as the complete and final integration of agreement. Such cases are of little or no service as precedents; and it is futile to cite them in a treatise. In many such cases, it may not be substantially disputed that the writing was executed as a complete integration; and the testimony that is offered may be solely for the purpose of showing that earlier negotiations were different and that the document would not have been executed if those negotiations had been recalled to mind at the time of execution. But such forgetfulness does not prevent the written contract from being enforceable according to its expressed terms, unless there has been such a "mistake" as justifies recission or reformation. The "parol evidence rule" has never been asserted to exclude evidence of mistake; but the question of what constitutes such a mistake is not an easy one to answer.

Again, although the party may definitely assert that the writing was not assented to as a complete statement of agreed terms, the evidence that he offers to prove the assertion may be quite unworthy of belief. This is mainly a question for the trial court. When the appellate court later says that the evidence offered to vary or contradict the writing was not admissible, it may in fact be merely assenting to the trial court's finding after listening to the evidence. Such cases can be of little service as precedents when the report does not show the basis of that finding.

Thirdly, it may be that both the trial court and the appellate court have assumed the completeness and correctness of the writing, merely by reason of the form and content of the document itself; but the opinion of the appellate court is seldom sufficient to show that they made such an assumption without supporting evidence. In such cases, we cannot tell whether or not the decision is correct; and once more the report fails to show a precedent that can be followed.

All the cases may indeed be accepted as precedents for the proposition that if the parties have stated the terms of their contract in the form of a complete written integration, it cannot be varied or contradicted by proof of antecedent negotiations and agreements. This is a mere statement of the obvious. There is no need to support it by a thousand citations. A brief illustration or two may be of service. Where one has contracted in writing to pay money, or to complete a building, or to deliver goods, or to convey land, by a specified date, that contract supersedes and nullifies all antecedent understandings or agreements that this performance is to be rendered by a different date. Parol testimony to prove such an antecedent agreement would be utterly irrelevant and immaterial, as long as it is not part of an attack upon the validity of the subsequently made written contract. Again, if one contracts in writing (or orally) to buy and pay for property on the express condition that no war shall break out between this country and another before the day set for performance, neither oral nor written testimony will be relevant or material that the parties had a previous understanding or agreement to buy and pay for the property even if a war should break out.

It should be clearly observed that a written integration has no greater effect upon antecedent parol understandings and agreements than a parol integration has upon antecedent written agreements. In both cases alike, the later agreement discharges the antecedent ones in so far as it contradicts or is inconsistent with the earlier ones. In both cases alike, the later agreement must be shown to have been in fact made, that its terms were assented to, especially those terms that vary or contradict antecedent expressions and agreements.

§ 574. All Contracts can be Discharged by a Substituted Agreement

Any contract, however made or evidenced, can be discharged or modified by subsequent agreement of the parties. No contract whether oral or written can be varied, contradicted, or discharged by an antecedent agreement. Today may control the effect of what happened yesterday; but what happened yesterday cannot change the effect of what happens today. This, it is believed, is the substance of what has been unfortunately called the "parol evidence rule."

By the early common law, a written contract, sealed and delivered, could be modified or discharged only by a similarly executed instrument. Some traces of this rule may still exist; we are not troubled by them at this point. It is now perfectly clear that informal contracts, whether written or oral, can be modified and discharged by a subsequent agreement, whether written or oral. The subsequent agreement, even though it is in writing, does not discharge the previous oral agreement if it is not agreed that it shall and it is not inconsistent therewith.

The existence and the terms of this modifying or discharging agreement can be proved by the same kinds of evidence that are admissible to prove any other kind of contract; and one denying the making or the terms of such an agreement can support his denial by the usual kinds of testimony, written or oral.

But after these issues have been determined and the court finds, as a fact, the making and the terms of the modifying or discharging agreement, we are no longer interested in the terms of the antecedent contract for purposes of enforcement of them, in so far as those terms have been nullified by the new agreement. They are of yesterday; and their jural effect has been nullified by the events of today. This is the ordinary substantive law of contracts; it is not a rule of evidence and is not stated in the language of evidence, parol or otherwise.

If the foregoing is true of antecedent contracts that were once legally operative and enforceable, it is equally true of preliminary negotiations that were not themselves mutually agreed upon or enforceable at law. The new agreement is not a discharging contract, since there were no legal relations to be discharged; but the legal relations of the parties are now governed by the terms of the new agreement. This is so because it is the agreement of today, whether that which had happened yesterday was itself a contract or was nothing more than inoperative negotiation.

It is obvious that this rule was as applicable in equity as at common law. The Chancellor did not deny to two parties the power to integrate their agreements or to nullify and supplant their agreements and negotiations by subsequent agreements. Oral, or written, evidence of those supplanted agreements, for the purpose of enforcing them, was just as immaterial in equity as at common law. It is true that the Chancellor was somewhat readier to listen to evidence of fraud or mistake, for the purpose of avoiding the new substituted agreement; but by statute, procedural rules, and court unification the rules and practice of nearly all courts have become those of the court of equity.

.   .   .

HAWRISH v. BANK OF MONTREAL

(1969), 2 D.L.R. (3d) 60. Supreme Court of Canada; Abbott, Judson, Ritchie, Hall and Spence JJ.

The judgment of the Court was delivered by

Judson, J.: — This action was brought by the Bank of Montreal against Andrew Hawrish, a solicitor in Saskatoon, on a guarantee which the solicitor had signed for the indebtedness and liability of a newly formed company, Crescent Dairies Limited. This company had been formed for the purpose of buying the assets of Waldheim Dairies Limited, a cheese factory in which Hawrish had an interest.

By January, 1959, the line of credit granted by the bank to the new company was almost exhausted. The bank then asked Hawrish for a guarantee, which he signed on January 30, 1959. The guarantee was on the bank's usual form and stated that it was to be a continuing guarantee and to cover existing as well as future indebtedness of the company up to the amount of $6,000.

The defence was that when he signed the guarantee, Hawrish had an oral assurance from the assistant manager of the branch that the guarantee was to cover only existing indebtedness and that he would be released from his guarantee when the bank obtained a joint guarantee from the directors of the company. The bank did obtain a joint guarantee from the directors on July 22, 1959, for the sum of $10,000. Another joint guarantee for the same amount was signed by the directors on March 22, 1960. Between the dates of these two last-mentioned guarantees there had been some changes in the directorate.

Hawrish was never a director or officer of the new company but at the time when the action was commenced, he was a shareholder and he was interested in the vendor company. At all times the new company was indebted to the vendor company in an amount between $10,000 and $15,000. Hawrish says that he did not read the guarantee before signing. On February 20, 1961, Crescent Dairies Ltd., whose overdraft was at that time $8,000, became insolvent. The bank then brought its action against Hawrish for the full amount of his guarantee — $6,000.

The trial Judge [48 D.L.R. (2d) 374] dismissed the bank's action. He accepted the guarantor's evidence of what was said before the guarantee was signed and held that parol evidence was admissible on the ground that it was a condition of signing the guarantee that the appellant would be released as soon as a joint guarantee was obtained from the directors. He relied upon *Standard Bank v. McCrossan*, 55 D.L.R. 238, 60 S.C.R. 655, [1920] 3 W.W.R. 846. The Court of Appeal [63 D.L.R. (2d) 369, 61 W.W.R. 16] reversed this decision and gave judgment for the bank. In their view the parol evidence was not admissible and the problem was not the same as that in *Standard Bank v. McCrossan*. Hall, J.A., correctly stated the *ratio* of the *Standard Bank* case in the following paragraph of his reasons [p. 373]:

> In my opinion the learned trial Judge erred in holding that the respondent was able to establish such condition by parol evidence. The condition found, if indeed it is one, was not similar to that which existed in *Standard Bank v. McCrossan, supra*, in that it did not operate merely as a suspension or delay of the written agreement. It may be permissible to prove by extraneous evidence an oral agreement which operates as a suspension only.

The relevant provisions of this guarantee may be summarized as follows:
(a) It guarantees the present and future debts and liabilities of the customer (Crescent Dairies Ltd.) up to the sum of $6,000.
(b) It is a continuing guarantee and secures the ultimate balance owing by the customer.
(c) The guarantor may determine at any time his further liability under the guarantee by notice in writing to the bank. The liability of the guarantor continues until determined by such notice.
(d) The guarantor acknowledges that no representations have been made to him on behalf of the bank; that the liability of the guarantor is embraced in the guarantee; that the guarantee has nothing to

do with any other guarantee; and that the guarantor intends the guarantee to be binding whether any other guarantee or security is given to the bank or not.

The argument before us was confined to two submissions of error contained in the reasons of the Court of Appeal:

(a)   that the contemporaneous oral agreement found by the trial Judge neither varied nor contradicted the terms of the written guarantee but simply provided by an independent agreement a manner in which the liability of the appellant would be terminated; and

(b)   that oral evidence proving the making of such agreement, the consideration for which was the signing of the guarantee, was admissible.

I cannot accept these submissions. In my opinion, there was no error in the reasons of the Court of Appeal. This guarantee was to be immediately effective. According to the oral evidence it was to terminate as to all liability, present or future, when the new guarantees were obtained from the directors. But the document itself states that it was to be a continuing guarantee for all present and future liabilities and could only be terminated by notice in writing, and then only as to future liabilities incurred by the customer after the giving of the notice. The oral evidence is also in plain contradiction of the terms of para. (d) of my summary above made. There is nothing in this case to permit the introduction of the principle in *Pym v. Campbell* (1856), 6 El. & Bl. 370, 119 E.R. 903, which holds that the parol evidence rule does not prevent a defendant from showing that a document formally complete and signed as a contract, was in fact only an escrow.

The appellant further submitted that the parol evidence was admissible on the ground that it established an oral agreement which was independent of and collateral to the main contract.

In the last half of the 19th century a group of English decisions, of which *Lindley v. Lacey* (1864), 17 C.B. (N.S.) 578, 144 E.R. 232; *Morgan v. Griffith* (1871), L.R. 6 Ex. 70, and *Erskine v. Adeane* (1873), L.R. 8 Ch. 764, are representative, established that where there was parol evidence of a distinct collateral agreement which did not contradict nor was inconsistent with the written instrument, it was admissible. These were cases between landlord and tenant in which parol evidence of stipulations as to repairs and other incidental matters and as to keeping down game and dealing with game was held to be admissible although the written leases were silent on these points. These were held to be independent agreements which were not required to be in writing and which were not in any way inconsistent with or contradictory of the written agreement.

The principle formulated in these cases was applied in *Byers v. McMillan* (1887), 15 S.C.R. 194. In this case Byers, a woodcutter, agreed in writing with one Andrew to cut and deliver 500 cords of wood from certain lands. The agreement contained no provision for security in the event that Byers was not paid upon making delivery. However, before he signed, it was orally agreed that Byers was to have a lien on the wood for the amount to which he would be entitled for his work and labour. Byers was not paid and eventually sold the wood. The respondents, the McMillans, in whom the contract was vested as a result of various assignments, brought an action of replevin. It was held by a majority of this Court that they could not succeed on the ground that the parol evidence of the oral agreement in respect of the lien was admissible. Strong, J., with whom the other members of the majority agreed, said at pp. 202-3:

> *Erskine v. Adeane*, 8 Ch. App. 764; *Morgan v. Griffith*, L.R. 6 Ex. 70; *Lindley v. Lacey*, 17 C.B. (N.S.) 578, afford illustrations of the rule in question by the terms of which any agreement collateral or supplementary to the written agreement may be established by parol evidence, provided it is one which as an independent agreement could be made without writing, and that it is not in any way inconsistent with or contradictory of the written agreement.
>
>   .   .   .
>
> These cases (particularly *Erskine v. Adeane* which was a judgment of the Court of Appeal) appear to be all stronger decisions than that which the appellant calls upon us to make in the present case, for it is difficult to see how an agreement, that one who in writing had undertaken by his labor to produce a chattel which is to become the property of another shall have a lien on such product for the money to be paid as the reward of his labor, in any way derogates from the contemporaneous or prior writing. By such a stipulation no term or provision of the writing is varied or in the slightest degree infringed upon; both agreements can well stand together; the writing provides for the performance of the contract, and the consideration to be paid for it, and the parol agreement merely adds something respecting security for the payment of the price to these terms.

In *Heilbut, Symons & Co. v. Buckleton*, [1913] A.C. 30 at p. 47, a case having to do with the existence of a warranty in a contract for the sale of shares, there is comment on the existence of the doctrine and a note of caution as to its application:

> It is evident, both on principle and on authority, that there may be a contract the consideration for which is the making of some other contract. "If you will make such and such a contract I will give you one hundred pounds," is in every sense of the word a complete legal contract. It is collateral to the main contract, but each has an independent existence, and they do not differ in respect of their possessing to the full the character and status of a contract. But such collateral contracts must from their very nature be rare. The effect of a collateral contract such as that which I have instanced would be to increase the consideration of the main contract by £100, and the more natural and usual way of carrying this out would be by so modifying the main contract and not by executing a concurrent and collateral contract. Such collateral contracts, the sole effect of which is to vary or add to the terms of the principal contract, are therefore viewed with suspicion by the law. They must be proved strictly. Not only the terms of such contracts but the existence of an animus contrahendi on the part of all the parties to them must be clearly shewn. Any laxity on these points would enable parties to escape from the full performance of the obligations of contracts unquestionably entered into by them and more especially would have the effect of lessening the authority of written contracts by making it possible to vary them by suggesting the existence of verbal collateral agreements relating to the same subject-matter.

Bearing in mind these remarks to the effect that there must be a clear intention to create a binding agreement, I am not convinced that the evidence in this case indicates clearly the existence of such intention. Indeed, I am disposed to agree with what the Court of Appeal said on this point. However, this is not in issue in this appeal. My opinion is that the appellant's argument fails on the ground that the collateral agreement allowing for the discharge of the appellant cannot stand as it clearly contradicts the terms of the guarantee bond which state that it is a continuing guarantee.

The appellant has relied upon *Byers v. McMillan*. But upon my interpretation that the terms of the two contracts conflict, this case is really against him as it is there stated by Strong, J., that a collateral agreement cannot be established where it is inconsistent with or contradicts the written agreement. To the same effect is the unanimous judgment of the High Court of Australia in *Hoyt's Proprietary Ltd. v. Spencer* (1919), 27 C.L.R. 133, which rejected the argument that a collateral contract which contradicted the written agreement could stand with it. Knox, C.J., said at p. 139:

> A distinct collateral agreement, whether oral or in writing, and whether prior to or contemporaneous with the main agreement, is valid and enforceable even though the main agreement be in writing, provided the two may consistently stand together so that the provisions of the main agreement remain in full force and effect notwithstanding the collateral agreement. This proposition is illustrated by the decisions in *Lindley v. Lacey* (17 C.B. (N.S.), 578), *Erskine v. Adeane* (L.R. 8 Ch., 756), *De Lassalle v. Guildford* ([1901] 2 K.B., 215) and other cases.

I would dismiss the appeal with costs.

Appeal dismissed.

ZELL v. AMERICAN SEATING CO.

(1943), 138 F. 2d 641. U.S. Circuit Court of Appeals, 2nd Circuit; L. Hand, Swan and Frank JJ.

The judgment of the court was delivered by Frank J.

Frank, Circuit Judge. On defendant's motion for summary judgment, the trial court, after considering the pleadings and affidavits, entered judgment dismissing the action. From that judgment, plaintiff appeals.

On a motion for summary judgment, where the facts are in dispute, a judgment can properly be entered against the plaintiff only if, on the undisputed facts, he has no valid claim; if, then, any fact asserted by the plaintiff is contradicted by the defendant, the facts as stated by the plaintiff must, on such a motion, be taken as true. Accordingly for the purpose of our decision here, we take the facts as follows:

Plaintiff, by a letter addressed to defendant company dated October 17, 1941, offered to make efforts to procure for defendant contracts for manufacturing products for national defense or war purposes, in consideration of defendant's agreement to pay him $1,000 per month for a three months' period if he were unsuccessful in his efforts, but, if he were successful, to pay him a further sum in an amount not to be less than 3% nor more than 8% of the "purchase price of said contracts". On October 31, 1941, at a meeting in Grand Rapids, Michigan, between plaintiff and defendant's President, the latter, on behalf of his company, orally made an agreement with plaintiff substantially on the terms set forth in plaintiff's letter, one of the terms being that mentioned in plaintiff's letter as to commissions: it was orally agreed that the exact amount within the two percentages was to be later determined by the parties. After this agreement was made, the parties executed, in Grand Rapids, a written instrument dated October 31, 1941, appearing on its face to embody a complete agreement between them; but that writing omitted the provision of their agreement that plaintiff, if successful, was to receive a bonus varying from three to eight per cent; instead, there was inserted in the writing a clause that the $1,000 per month "will be full compensation, but the company may, if it desires, pay you something in the nature of a bonus". However, at the time when they executed this writing, the parties orally agreed that the previous oral agreement was still their actual contract, that the writing was deliberately erroneous with respect to plaintiff's commissions, and that the misstatement in that writing was made solely in order to "avoid any possible stigma which might result" from putting such a provision "in writing", the defendant's President stating that "his fears were based upon the criticism of contingent fee contracts". Nothing in the record discloses whose criticism the defendant feared; but plaintiff, in his brief, says that defendant was apprehensive because adverse comments had been made in Congress of such contingent-fee arrangements in connection with war contracts. The parties subsequently executed further writings extending, for two three-month periods, their "agreement under date of October 31, 1941." Through plaintiff's efforts and expenditures of large sums for travelling expenses, defendant, within this extended period, procured contracts between it and companies supplying aircraft to the government for war purposes, the aggregate purchase price named in said contracts being $5,950,000. The defendant has refused to pay the plaintiff commissions thereon in the agreed amount (i.e., not less than three percent) but has paid him merely $8,950 (at the rate of $1,000 a month) and has offered him, by way of settlement, an additional sum of $9,000 which he has refused to accept as full payment.

Defendant argues that the summary judgment was proper on the ground that, under the parol evidence rule, the court could not properly consider as relevant anything except the writing of October 31, 1941, which appears on its face to set forth a complete and unambiguous agreement between the parties. If defendant on this point is in error, then, if the plaintiff at a trial proves the facts as alleged by him, and no other defenses are successfully interposed, he will be entitled to a sum equal to 3% of $5,950,000.

. . .

It is not surprising that confusion results from a rule called "the parol evidence rule" which is not a rule of evidence, which relates to extrinsic proof whether written or parol, and which has been said to be virtually no rule at all. As Thayer said of it, "Few things are darker than this, or fuller of subtle difficulties." The rule is often loosely and confusingly stated as if, once the evidence establishes that the parties executed a writing containing what appears to be a complete and unambiguous agreement, then no evidence may be received of previous or contemporaneous oral understandings which contradict or vary its terms. But, under the parol evidence rule correctly stated, such a writing does not acquire that dominating position if it has been proved by extrinsic evidence that the parties did not intend it to be an exclusive authoritative memorial of their agreement. If they did intend it to occupy that position, their secret mutual intentions as to the terms of the contract or its meaning are usually irrelevant, so that parties who exchange promises may be bound, at least "at law" as distinguished from "equity", in a way which neither intended, since their so-called "objective" intent governs. When, however, they have previously agreed that their written promises are not to bind them, that agreement controls and no legal obligations flow from the writing. It has been held virtually everywhere, when the question has arisen that (certainly in the absence of any fraudulent or illegal purpose) a purported written agreement, which the parties designed as a mere sham, lacks legal efficacy, and that extrinsic parol or other extrinsic evidence will always be received on that issue. So the highest court of Michigan has several times held. It has gone further: In *Woodard v. Walker*, 192 Mich. 188, 158 N.W. 846, that court specifically enforced against the seller an oral agreement for the sale of land which had been followed by a sham written agreement, for sale of the same land at a higher price, intended to deceive the seller's children who were jealous of the buyer.

We need not here consider cases where third persons have relied on the delusive agreement to their detriment or cases in other jurisdictions (we find none in Michigan) where the mutual purpose of the deception was fraudulent or illegal. For the instant case involves no such elements. As noted above, the pleadings and affidavits are silent as to the matter of whom the parties here intended to mislead, and we cannot infer a fraudulent or illegal purpose. Even the explanation contained in plaintiff's brief discloses no fraud or illegality: No law existed rendering illegal the commission provision of the oral agreement which the parties here omitted from the sham writing; while it may be undesirable that citizens should prepare documents so contrived as to spoil the scent of legislators bent on proposing new legislation, yet such conduct is surely not unlawful and does not deserve judicial castigation as immoral or fraudulent; the courts should not erect standards of morality so far above the customary. *Woodard v. Walker* leaves no doubt that the Michigan courts would hold the parol evidence rule inapplicable to the facts as we have interpreted them.

Candor compels the admission that, were we enthusiastic devotees of that rule, we might so construe the record as to bring this case within the rule's scope; we could dwell on the fact that plaintiff, in his complaint, states that the acceptance of his offer "was partly oral and partly contained" in the October 31 writing, and could then hold that, as that writing unambiguously covers the item of commissions, the plaintiff is trying to use extrinsic evidence to "contradict" the writing. But the plaintiff's affidavit, if accepted as true and liberally construed, makes it plain that the parties deliberately intended the October 31 writing to be a misleading, untrue, statement of their real agreement.

We thus construe the record because we do not share defendant's belief that the rule is so beneficent, so promotive of the administration of justice, and so necessary to business stability, that it should be given the widest possible application. The truth is that the rule does but little to achieve the ends it supposedly serves. Although seldom mentioned in modern decisions, the most important motive for perpetuation of the rule is distrust of juries, fear that they cannot adequately cope with, or will be unfairly prejudiced by, conflicting "parol" testimony. If the rule were frankly recognized as primarily a device to control juries, its shortcomings would become obvious, since it is not true that the execution by the parties of an unambiguous writing, "facially complete", bars extrinsic proof. The courts admit such "parol" testimony (other than the parties' statements of what they meant by the writing) for a variety of purposes: to show "all the operative usages" and "all the surrounding circumstances prior to and contemporaneous with the making" of a writing; to show an agreed oral condition, nowhere referred to in the writing, that the writing was not to be binding until some third person approved; to show that a deed, absolute on its face, is but a mortgage. These and numerous other exceptions have removed most of that insulation of the jury from "oral" testimony which the rule is said to provide.

The rule, then, does relatively little to deserve its much advertised virtue of reducing the dangers of successful fraudulent recoveries and defenses brought about through perjury. The rule is too small a hook to catch such a leviathan. Moreover, if at times it does prevent a person from winning, by lying witnesses, a lawsuit which he should lose, it also, at times, by shutting out the true facts, unjustly aids other persons to win lawsuits they should and would lose, were the suppressed evidence known to the courts. Exclusionary rules, which frequently result in injustice, have always been defended — as was the rule, now fortunately extinct, excluding testimony of the parties to an action — with the danger-of-perjury argument. Perjury, of course, is pernicious and doubtless much of it is used in our courts daily with unfortunate success. The problem of avoiding its efficacious use should be met head on. Were it consistently met in an indirect manner — in accordance with the viewpoint of the adulators of the parol evidence rule — by wiping out substantive rights provable only through oral testimony, we would have wholesale destruction of familiar causes of action such as, for instance, suits for personal injury and for enforcement of wholly oral agreements.

The parol evidence rule is lauded as an important aid in the judicial quest for "objectivity", a quest which aims to avoid that problem the solution of which was judicially said in the latter part of the fifteenth century to be beyond even the powers of Satan — the discovery of the inner thoughts of man. The policy of stern refusal to consider subjective intention, prevalent in the centralized common law courts of that period, later gave way; in the latter part of the 18th and the early part of the 19th century, the recession from that policy went far, and there was much talk of the "meeting of the minds" in the formation of contracts, of giving effect to the actual "will" of the contracting parties. The obstacles to learning that actual intention have, more recently, induced a partial reversion to the older view. Today a court generally restricts its attention to the outward behavior of the parties: the meaning of their acts is not what either party or both parties intended but the meaning which a "reasonable man" puts on those acts; the expression of mutual assent, not the assent itself, is usually the essential element. We now speak of "externality", insisting on judicial consideration of only those manifestations of intention which are public ("open to the scrutiny and knowledge of the community") and not private ("secreted in the heart" of a person). This objective approach is of great value, for a legal system can be more effectively administered if legal rights and obligations ordinarily attach only to overt conduct. Moreover, to call the standard "objective" and candidly to confess that the actual intention is not the guiding factor serves desirably to high-light the fact that much of the "law of contracts" has nothing whatever to do with what the parties contemplated but consists of rules — founded on considerations of public policy — by which the courts impose on the contracting parties obligations of which the parties were often unaware; this "objective" perspective discloses that the voluntary act of entering into a contract creates a jural "relation" or "status" much in the same way as does being married or holding a public office.

But we should not demand too much of this concept of "objectivity"; like all useful concepts it becomes a thought-muddler if its limitations are disregarded. We can largely rid ourselves of concern with the subjective reactions of the parties: when, however, we test their public behavior by inquiring how it appears to the "reasonable man", we must recognize, unless we wish to fool ourselves, that although one area of subjectivity has been conquered, another remains unsubdued. For instance, under the parol evidence rule, the standard of interpretation of a written contract is usually "the meaning that would be attached to" it "by a reasonably intelligent person acquainted with all operative usages and knowing all the circumstances prior to and contemporaneous with, the making" of the contract, "other than oral statements by the parties of what they intended it to mean". We say that "the objective viewpoint of a third person is used". But where do we find that "objective" third person? We ask judges or juries to discover that "objective viewpoint" — through their own subjective processes. Being but human, their beliefs cannot be objectified, in the sense of being standardized. Doubtless, there is some moderate approximation to objectivity, that is, to uniformity of beliefs, among judges — men with substantially similar training — although less than is sometimes supposed. But no one can seriously maintain that such uniformity exists among the multitude of jurymen, men with the greatest conceivable variety of training and background. When juries try cases, objectivity is largely a mirage; most of the objectivity inheres in the words of the "reasonable man" standard which the judges, often futilely, admonish juries to apply to the evidence. Certain aspects of subjectivity common to all men seem to have been successfully eliminated in the field of science through the "relativity theory" — which might better be called the "anti-relativity" or "absolute" theory. But equal success has not attended the anti-relativity or objective theory in the legal field. Perhaps nine-tenths of legal uncertainty is caused by uncertainty as to what courts will find, on conflicting evidence, to be the facts of cases. Early in the history of our legal institutions, litigants strongly objected to a determination of the facts by mere fallible human beings. A man, they felt, ought to be allowed to demonstrate the facts "by supernatural means, by some such process as the ordeal or the judicial combat; God may be for him, though his neighbors be against him." We have accepted the "rational" method of trial based on evidence but the longing persists for some means of counter-acting the fallibility of the triers of the facts. Mechanical devices, like the parol evidence rule, are symptoms of that longing, a longing particularly strong when juries participate in trials. But a mechanical device like the parol evidence rule cannot satisfy that longing, especially because the injustice of applying the rule rigidly has led to its being riddled with exceptions.

   Those exceptions have, too, played havoc with the contention that business stability depends upon that rule, that, as one court put it "the tremendous but closely adjusted machinery of modern business cannot function at all without" the assurance afforded by the rule and that, "if such assurance were removed today from our law, general disaster would result…" We are asked to believe that the rule enables businessmen, advised by their lawyers, to rely with indispensable confidence on written contracts unimpeachable by oral testimony. In fact, seldom can a conscientious lawyer advise his client, about to sign an agreement, that, should the client become involved in litigation relating to that agreement, one of the many exceptions to the rule will not permit the introduction of uncertainty-producing oral testimony. As Corbin says, "That rule has so many exceptions that only with difficulty can it be correctly stated in the form of a rule". One need but thumb the pages of Wigmore, Williston, or the Restatement of Contracts to see how illusory is the certainty that the rule supplies. "Collateral parol agreements contradicting a writing are inadmissible", runs the rule as ordinarily stated; but in the application of that standard there exists, as Williston notes, "no final test which can be applied with unvarying regularity". Wigmore more bluntly says that only vague generalizations are possible, since the application of the rule, "resting as it does on the parties' intent, can properly be made only after a comparison of the kind of transaction, the terms of the document, and the circumstances of the parties... Such is the complexity of circumstances and the variety of documentary phraseology, and so minute the indicia of intent, that one ruling can seldom be controlling authority or even of utility for a subsequent one." The recognized exceptions to the rule demonstrate strikingly that business can endure even when oral testimony competes with written instruments. If business stability has not been ruined by the deed-mortgage exception, or because juries may hear witnesses narrate oral understandings that written contracts were not to be operative except on the performance of extrinsic conditions, it is unlikely that commercial disaster would follow even if legislatures abolished the rule in its entirety.

In sum, a rule so leaky cannot fairly be described as a stout container of legal certainty. John Chipman Gray, a seasoned practical lawyer, expressed grave doubts concerning the reliance of businessmen on legal precedents generally. If they rely on the parol evidence rule in particular, they will often be duped. It has been seriously questioned whether in fact they do so to any considerable extent. We see no good reason why we should strain to interpret the record facts here to bring them within such a rule.

Reversed and remanded.

[Note: Frank J. provided extensive footnotes. These have been omitted.]

QUESTIONS

1. Do you find the judgment of Judson J. or that of Frank J. more useful from any of the following points of view,

    a) a contract draftsman;

    b) a student of law;

    c) a person concerned with the development of a rational system of law; or

    d) a person seeking to codify the law of contracts.

2. The parol evidence rule is stated as follows in Fridman, *The Law of Contract*, 1976, p. 245:

> "The fundamental rule is that if the language of the written contract is clear and unambiguous, then no extrinsic parol evidence may be admitted to alter, vary, or interpret in any way the words used in the writing."

Reference is then made to *Hawrish v. Bank of Montreal*. No reference is made to *Zell v. American Seating* or to Corbin.

    a) Do you think that such a definition is useful?

    b) Why do you think that Fridman would refer to *Hawrish v. Bank of Montreal* and not to Corbin or *Zell v. American Seating*?

J. EVANS & SON (PORTSMOUTH) LTD. v. ANDREA MERZARIO LTD.

[1976] 2 All E.R. 930.

Lord Denning MR. Strangely enough, this is the first case we have had in this court about container traffic. The motor vessel the Ruhr was not purpose built for containers. It was built as a merchant ship but it had been converted so as to carry containers. On 3rd November 1968 the Ruhr was going from Rotterdam to Tilbury. Twenty containers were under the deck. Eight containers were on deck. She met with a slight swell. Two containers fell off and went to the bottom of the water. One of them contained a special injection moulding machine of about £3,000 in value. It was completely lost.

No claim lies against the shipowners. They had issued a bill of lading which said: 'Shipped on deck at shippers' risk.' The claim we have to consider is by the English importers against the forwarding agents. They claim that the containers ought not to have been carried on deck.

The importers were Evans of Portsmouth. They had bought the machines from an Italian manufacturer in Milan. The English importers employed forwarding agents to make all the transport arrangements. The forwarding agents were a company, Andrea Merzario Ltd. They have an associated company in Holland and also their parent company in Italy. These forwarding agents made arrangements under which the goods were carried by rail from Milan to Rotterdam, then by ship for Tilbury, unloaded at Tilbury and carried to the destination in England. The forwarding agents had for some years previously arranged for these machines to be imported, but they had been packed in crates and not in containers. The forwarding agents had always arranged that these machines so packed in crates should be carried under deck; because they were liable to rust if carried on deck. When it was proposed to change over to packing them in containers, the forwarding agents talked to the English importers about it. Their manager, Mr Spano, who was visiting Portsmouth, saw Mr Leonard of the importers. He said that they proposed to use containers in future. Mr Leonard said: 'I have heard about these containers. I am afraid that our machines may get rusty if they are carried on deck. They must not be carried on deck.' Mr Spano assured Mr Leonard: 'If we do use containers, they will not be carried on deck.' The judge accepted that that assurance was given. He said: '... Mr Leonard was assured by Mr Spano that, insofar as the goods were subsequently to be transported in containers, they would be carried under deck in the same way as all goods transported by the defendants.' On getting that assurance, Mr Leonard was content. The forwarding agents gave a quotation for the new charges for carrying in containers. The English importers accepted it. The containers went forward on that basis. Invoices were sent and goods carried on the usual terms and conditions appearing on the form. Nothing was put in writing about being carried under deck.

Unfortunately there was some mistake made somewhere during the forwarding of this consignment from Italy to England. The Dutch company failed to ensure that the containers which contained these machines were loaded under deck at Rotterdam. They allowed them to be shipped on deck and accepted a bill of lading which contained the excepting clause: 'Shipped on deck at shippers' risk.'

So, after these containers fell off the deck into the water, the English importers, through their insurers, claimed damages against the forwarding agents. In reply the forwarding agent said there was no contractual promise that the goods would be carried under deck. Alternatively, if there was, they relied on the printed terms and conditions. The judge held there was no contractual promise that these containers should be carried under deck. He thought that, in order to be binding, the initial conversation ought to be contemporaneous, and that here it was too remote in point of time from the actual transport; furthermore that, viewed objectively, it should not be considered binding. The judge quoted largely from the well-known case of *Heilbut, Symons & Co v Buckleton* in which it was held that a person is not liable in damages for an innocent misrepresentation; and that the courts should be slow to hold that there was a collateral contract. I must say that much of what was said in that case is entirely out of date. We now have the Misrepresentation Act 1967 under which damages can be obtained for innocent misrepresentation of fact. This Act does not apply here because we are concerned with an assurance as to the future. But even in respect of promises as to the future, we have a different approach nowadays to collateral contracts. When a person gives a promise, or an assurance to another, intending that he should act on it by entering into a contract, and he does act on it by entering into the contract, we hold that it is binding: see *Dick Bentley Productions Ltd v Harold Smith (Motors) Ltd.* That case was concerned with a representation of fact, but it applies also to promises as to the future. Following this approach, it seems to me plain that Mr Spano gave an oral promise or assurance that the goods in this new container traffic would be carried under deck. He made the promise in order to induce Mr Leonard to agree to the goods being carried in containers. On the faith of it, Mr Leonard accepted the quotations and gave orders for transport. In those circumstances the promise was binding. There was a breach of that promise and the forwarding agents are liable — unless they can rely on the printed conditions.

It is common ground that the course of dealing was on the standard conditions of the forwarding trade. Those conditions were relied on. Condition 4 which gives the company complete freedom in respect of means, route and procedure in the transportation of goods. Condition 11 which says that the company will not be liable for loss or damage unless it occurs whilst in their actual custody and then only if they are guilty of wilful neglect or default. Condition 13 which says that their liability shall not exceed the value of the goods or a sum at the rate of £50 per ton of 20 cwt. The question is whether the company can rely on those exemptions. I do not think so.

. . .

[In] *Mendelssohn v Normand Ltd*, [1970] 1 Q.B. 177, I said: 'The printed condition is rejected because it is repugnant to the express oral promise or representation.' During the argument Roskill LJ put the case of the Hague Rules. If a carrier made a promise that goods would be shipped under deck and, contrary to that promise, they were carried on deck and there was a loss, the carrier could not rely on the limitation clause. Following these authorities, it seems to me that the forwarding agents cannot rely on the condition. There was a plain breach of the oral promise by the forwarding agents. I would allow the appeal.

Roskill LJ. I agree that this appeal should be allowed for the reasons which Lord Denning MR has given. I venture to add to those reasons out of respect for Kerr J, from whom in a matter of this kind I differ with hesitation. But this case has been put before us rather differently from the way it was put before the learned judge, though, as counsel for the plaintiffs said a moment ago, the point on which he succeeds was in fact first mentioned to the learned judge.

. . .

The matter was apparently argued before the learned judge on behalf of the plaintiffs on the basis that the defendants' promise (if any) was what the lawyers sometimes call a collateral oral warranty. That phrase is normally only applicable where the original promise was external to the main contract, the main contract being a contract in writing, so that usually parol evidence cannot be given to contradict the terms of the written contract. The basic rule is clearly stated in the latest edition of Benjamin on Sale to which I refer but which I will not repeat. But that doctrine, as it seems to me, has little or no application where one is not concerned with a contract in writing (with respect, I cannot accept counsel for the defendants' argument that there was here a contract in writing) but with a contract which, as I think, was partly oral, partly in writing and partly by conduct. In such a case the court does not require to have recourse to lawyers' devices such as collateral oral warranty in order to seek to adduce evidence which would not otherwise be admissible. The court is entitled to look at and should look at all the evidence from start to finish in order to see what the bargain was that was struck between the parties. That is what we have done in this case and what, with great respect, I think the learned judge did not do in the course of his judgment. I unreservedly accept counsel for the defendants' submission that one must not look at one or two isolated answers given in evidence; one should look at the totality of the evidence. When one does that, one finds first, as I have already mentioned, that these parties had been doing business in transporting goods from Milan to England for some time before; secondly, that transportation of goods from Milan to England was always done on trailers which were always under deck; thirdly, that the defendants wanted a change in the practice — they wanted containers used instead of trailers; fourthly, that the plaintiffs were only willing to agree to that change if they were promised by the defendant that those containers would be shipped under deck, and would not have agreed to the change but for that promise. The defendants gave such a promise which to my mind against this background plainly amounted to an enforceable contractual promise. In those circumstances it seems to me that the contract was this: 'If we continue to give you our business, you will ensure that those goods in containers are shipped under deck'; and the defendants agreed that this would be so. Thus there was a breach of that contract by the defendants when this container was shipped on deck; and it seems to me to be plain that the damage which the plaintiffs suffered resulted from that breach. That being the position, I think that counsel for the defendants' first argument fails.

. . .

For those reasons, which I have given at some length out of deference to Kerr J, in addition to those given by Lord Denning MR, I would allow this appeal and enter judgment for the plaintiffs for the sum claimed.

[Geoffrey Lane L.J. wrote a concurring opinion.]

In an effort to convince the court that the written contract is the complete agreement, a draftsman sometimes puts in an "integration clause". Such a clause usually comes at the end of the agreement and looks like this:

> "The above and the terms (and the relevant warranty, if any) on the back hereof shall comprise the entire agreement affecting this purchase and no other agreement, understanding, representation, condition or warranty, either expressed or implied by law or otherwise is a part of this transaction, any such agreement, understanding, representation, condition or warranty being hereby expressly excluded."

It should cause no surprise that such a clause will not always be effective. See *e.g., Ferland v. Keith & Bowerbank* (1958), 15 D.L.R. (2d) 472, Ontario Court of Appeal. The above integration clause was there held to be ineffective in excluding a collateral promise to provide liability insurance on a car that had been purchased from a used car dealer.

QUESTION

What would happen to an integration clause under Corbin's analysis?

C. Misrepresentation and Warranties

We know without having to think much about it that if one person is induced to buy something in reliance on deliberately false statements of the seller about the thing's quality, the buyer can get some form of relief. We know as well that if the seller promises explicitly that a thing has some particular quality, and it does not, the buyer can sue for relief for breach of contract. The problems that concern us arise in those cases where there may have been neither a deliberate and intentional falsehood nor an explicit promise about something's quality. The issues that we have to explore are two:

1. In what circumstances will we give a disappointed party any relief?
2. If we do give any kind of relief, what should it be? What are the choices?

The more narrowly legal questions that arise from these two questions are:

1. What specific facts are likely to influence the court?
(a)   The extent of the knowledge the parties have of the subject matter of the contract;
(b)   How the allocation of the risk between them should be made: the scope of the maxim, *caveat emptor*;
(c)   The ease with which a remedy can be given;
(d)   The consequences of giving relief; and
(e)   The availability of non-contractual bases for relief?
2. What remedy can be given in what circumstances?
(a)   The characteristics of each remedy: its scope and limitations;
(b)   The relief available.

3. To what extent can one plan, so that one's client's affairs can run smoothly?

4. What underlying policy reasons indicate how the problem should be resolved?

5. What role is played by doctrinal concerns?

The first two cases raise the problem of innocent misrepresentation.

REDGRAVE v. HURD

(1881), 20 Ch. D. 1. Court of Appeal (England); Jessel M.R., Baggallay and Lush L.JJ.

In January, 1880, the Plaintiff, a solicitor of *Birmingham,* inserted in the *Law Times* the following advertisement: —

"Law Partnership. — An elderly solicitor of moderate practice, with extensive connections in a very populous town in a midland county, contemplates shortly retiring, and having no successor would first take as partner an efficient lawyer and advocate about forty, who would not object to purchaser advertiser's suburban residence, suitable for a family, value £1600, three-fourths of which might remain on security — no premium for business and introduction. A large field is here open for an efficient man, and great advantages for free education of sons. Address *R. J.,* No. 1919, 10 *Wellington Street, Strand."*

The Defendant applied by letter to the address indicated, and a correspondence ensued, the negotiation proceeding on the footing that the Plaintiff should receive the Defendant as his partner and transfer to him a moiety of his practice and the Plaintiff's leasehold house for £1600. On the 12th of February the Plaintiff and Defendant had two interviews, at the latter of which the Defendant's wife was present. There was a direct conflict of evidence as to what passed at these interviews, the Plaintiff asserting that he stated the business to bring him in about £200 a year, the Defendant and his wife saying that the Plaintiff stated it to bring in from £300 to £400 a year. The parties were examined orally in Court, and Mr. Justice *Fry* held that greater weight was to be attributed to the evidence of the Defendant and his wife than to that of the Plaintiff, and held that the Plaintiff had either represented his business as bringing in about £300 a year, or from £300 to £400 a year.

On the 14th of February the Defendant wrote to the Plaintiff:

"Of course I should duly rely on your promise to do all you could to extend the business among your friends. Still I should be glad to have some idea as to the amount of business done at your office in the past three years and the nature of the nucleus with which we should start. Would you, therefore, be able to give me an hour next Tuesday to go into this matter and settle the terms of partnership?"

On Tuesday, the 17th of February, the parties accordingly had an interview at the Plaintiff's office. The Plaintiff produced to the Defendant three summaries of business done in 1877, 1878, 1879. These summaries shewed gross receipts not quite amounting to £200 in a year. The Defendant asked how the difference was made up, and the Plaintiff shewed him a quantity of letters and papers which he stated to relate to other business which he had done. No books of account were produced, the Plaintiff not having kept any books which shewed the amount of his business, but the Plaintiff shewed the Defendant some letter-books and diaries and a day-book. The

Defendant did not examine any of the books, letters, and papers thus produced, but only looked cursorily at them, and ultimately agreed to purchase the house and take a share in the business for £1600. Mr. Justice *Fry* came to the conclusion that if the letters and papers to which the Plaintiff referred had been examined they would only have shewn business to the amount of £5 or £6 a year. The Defendant wished the written agreement to set out that the £1600 was the consideration for the purchase both of the house and the share in the practice, but the Plaintiff refused to assent to this, and an agreement was drawn up and signed on the 2nd of March, 1880, by which the Defendant agreed to purchase the house for £1600, the practice not being referred to. The Defendant paid a deposit of £100, and on the 17th of April, 1880, was let into possession of the house, and removed thither with his family from *Stroud;* but finding, as he alleged, that the practice was utterly worthless, he gave up possession, and refused to complete the purchase. The Plaintiff, in June, 1880, commenced an action for specific performance of the written agreement to purchase the house.

Jessel, M.R.: — This is an appeal from a decision of Mr. Justice *Fry*, granting specific performance of a contract by the Defendant to buy a house from the Plaintiff, and dismissing with costs a counterclaim by the Defendant asking to rescind the contract, and also asking for damages on the ground of deceit practised by the Plaintiff in respect to the agreement.

As regards the Defendant's counter-claim, we consider that it fails so far as damages are concerned, because he has not pleaded knowledge on the part of the Plaintiff that the allegations made by the Plaintiff were untrue, nor has he pleaded the allegations themselves in sufficient detail to found an action for deceit. It only remains to consider the claim of the Plaintiff for specific performance, and so much of the counter-claim of the Defendant as asks to have the contract rescinded.

Before going into the details of the case I wish to say something about my view of the law applicable to it, because in the text-books, and even in some observations of noble Lords in the House of Lords, there are remarks which I think, according to the course of modern decisions, are not well founded, and do not accurately state the law. As regards the rescission of a contract, there was no doubt a difference between the rules of Courts of Equity and the rules of Courts of Common Law — a difference which of course has now disappeared by the operation of the *Judicature Act*, which makes the rules of equity prevail. According to the decisions of Courts of Equity it was not necessary, in order to set aside a contract obtained by material false representation, to prove that the party who obtained it knew at the time when the representation was made that it was false. It was put in two ways, either of which was sufficient. One way of putting the case was, "A man is not to be allowed to get a benefit from a statement which he now admits to be false. He is not to be allowed to say, for the purpose of civil jurisdiction, that when he made it he did not know it to be false; he ought to have found that out before he made it." The other way of putting it was this: "Even assuming that moral fraud must be shewn in order to set aside a contract, you have it where a man, having obtained a beneficial contract by a statement which he now knows to be false, insists upon keeping that contract. To do so is a moral delinquency: no man ought to seek to take advantage of his own false statements." The rule in equity was settled, and it does not matter on which of the two grounds it was rested. As regards the rule of Common Law there is no doubt it was not quite so wide. There were, indeed, cases in which, even at Common Law, a contract could be rescinded for misrepresentation, although it could not be shewn that the person making it knew the representation to be false. They are variously stated, but I think, according to the later decisions, the statement must have been made recklessly and without care, whether it was true or false, and not with the belief that it was true. But, as I have said, the doctrine in equity was settled beyond controversy, and it is enough to refer to the judgment of Lord *Cairns* in the *Reese River Silver Mining Company v. Smith* (1869), L.R. 4 H.L. 64, in which he lays it down in the way which I have stated.

There is another proposition of law of very great importance which I think it is necessary for me to state, because, with great deference to the very learned Judge from whom this appeal comes, I think it is not quite accurately stated in his judgment. If a man is induced to enter into a contract by a false representation it is not a sufficient answer to him to say, "If you had used due diligence you would have found out that the statement was untrue. You had the means afforded you of discovering its falsity, and did not choose to avail yourself of them." I take it to be a settled doctrine of equity, not only as regards specific performance but also as regards rescission, that this is not an answer unless there is such delay as constitutes a defence under the *Statute of Limitations.* That, of course, is quite a different thing. Under the statute delay deprives a man of his right to rescind on the ground of fraud, and the only question to be considered is from what time the delay is to be reckoned. It had been decided, and the rule was adopted by the statute, that the delay counts from the time when by due diligence the fraud might have been discovered. Nothing can be plainer, I take it, on the authorities in equity than that the effect of false representation is not got rid of on the ground that the person to whom it was made has been guilty of negligence. One of the most familiar instances in modern times is where men issue a prospectus in which they make false statements of the contracts made before the formation of a company, and then say that the contracts themselves may be inspected at the offices of the solicitors. It has always been held that those who accepted those false statements as true were not deprived of their remedy merely because they neglected to go and look at the contracts. Another instance with which we are familiar is where a vendor makes a false statement as to the contents of a lease, as, for instance, that it contains no covenant preventing the carrying on of the trade which the purchaser is known by the vendor to be desirous of carrying on upon the property. Although the lease itself might be produced at the sale, or might have been open to the inspection of the purchaser long previously to the sale, it has been repeatedly held that the vendor cannot be allowed to say, "You were not entitled to give credit to my statement." It is not sufficient, therefore, to say that the purchaser had the opportunity of investigating the real state of the case, but did not avail himself of that opportunity.

Now the facts to my mind are clear, and I am glad to say, with one exception, they are in writing. The Plaintiff *Redgrave* advertised in the *Law Times* for a law partnership. The *Law Times* is not a publication in which people ordinarily advertise for the sale of a house, but is one in which they do advertise for partners in law partnerships. [His Lordship then read the advertisement.] That means this: "There is a moderate practice, I shall not take a premium for it if you will take my house off my hands;" that is, the purchase of the house is the consideration for giving him the partnership in the moderate business. A man issuing such an advertisement cannot be heard to say that he had no business worth mentioning to sell. I agree that his main object was to get rid of the house, and that he had little else to dispose of. It appears on his own evidence that his gross business was £200 a year, what its nett value was I am unable to say, but I should think £100 a year a very high estimate of its nett value. He says by the advertisement that he is elderly and has no successor, which implies that there is a succession to something of some value. He says it is "a moderate practice with extensive connection," which is not a truthful description of a practice such as I have mentioned, a practice which would give £50 a year nett to each of the two partners. We start then with an advertisement containing a misrepresentation, and as far as I can see, of facts within the advertiser's own knowledge, for he does not pretend to say that he did not know that his business had a gross value of only £200 a year; on the contrary, he says in his evidence that he told the Defendant so.

Interviews then took place. The first interview was on the 12th of February. There is a conflict of evidence as to what passed at that interview, and the learned Judge below gave credit to the evidence of *Hurd* and his wife that *Redgrave* stated his practice to be between £300 and £400 a year. Having regard to the advertisement, it is most probable that he did make some such statement, for he had made representations in the advertisement which were inconsistent with its amounting only to £200 a year. But I do not rely on that. The rule of the Court of Appeal is that when there is direct conflicting oral testimony, and the Judge who has seen the witnesses believes one party and disbelieves the other, this Court, not having seen the witnesses, cannot disturb that decision any more than it could disturb the verdict of a jury under similar circumstances. We must, therefore, take it as a fact that *Redgrave* presented to *Hurd* on the 12th of February that his business was worth about £300 a year, or between £300 and £400 a year, it does not matter which.

Another interview took place between the Plaintiff and the Defendant on the 17th of February. Before proceeding to what is said by the learned Judge as to what took place on the 17th of February, I will refer to the observations which he made just before. "Then comes, in the second place, this very material inquiry. Did the Defendant purchase the house and go on with the negotiations upon the footing and upon the faith of that representation so made by the Plaintiff" (that is, the representation made on the 12th of February)? "I have come to the conclusion that he did not. I think that the letter of the 14th of February is worthy of all the weight which has been attributed to it by the Plaintiff's counsel. The Defendant in that letter says this: 'While relying on your effort to extend the business among your connection, I feel I should like to have some idea of the amount of business done at your office during the past three years, and the nature of the nucleus with which we should start.' " Now to my mind that means this: "You have told me you are making between £300 and £400 a year, but I should like to know what is the average of the past three years. What you are making for one year is not sufficient for me." Therefore, the Defendant does not rely exclusively on the statement of the £300 a year because he wants further information, but he does not give up the reliance on the statement. "Accepting your statement that you are making £300 a year, tell me what you made during the last three years." That that is the true meaning of the letter is, I think, shewn by the nature of the documents produced on the 17th of February to the Defendant by the Plaintiff: "The Defendant does, by the Plaintiff's invitation, visit him on the 17th of February, and then and there are produced to the Defendant by the Plaintiff the papers which relate respectively to the years 1877, 1878, and 1879, which have sometimes been called bills of costs, and sometimes called estimates, and they shew, roughly speaking, a gross amount of business done to the extent of about £200 a year. Then the common case of the Plaintiff and the Defendant is that in answer to an inquiry from the Defendant, the Plaintiff said there was other business which was not entered upon those papers." Now that inquiry as I understand it was this, "You were doing £300 a year, you shew in those papers only £200 a year, where is the rest?" And the answer was, "Oh, there is a lot of papers here containing business which will account for the rest." Well, it appears to me, that that being the common case of both parties, it shews that *Hurd*, though still relying on the representation that the business was at least £300 a year, when he found that the papers shewed only a gross £200 a year, wanted to know where the business was that made up the £300 a year, and he is told, "Oh there are a lot of papers there; I have not made out my bills of costs fully, but you will find the business if you look through those papers;" but he did not look through them. The learned Judge continues: "I cannot attribute much weight to that other business, and for this reason, that in my judgment if the Defendant had meant to rely upon this extraneous business, which was not mentioned in the papers, he would have made some inquiry about it." I am sorry to say I differ from every word of that. The Defendant did make an inquiry. All that the Plaintiff had prepared for him were these summaries. He says, "Where is the rest of the business?" "Oh it is in that parcel of papers." How could the Defendant make out bills of costs from the parcel of papers? he could do nothing but rely on the Plaintiff's statement that the parcel of papers did contain the business. Then the learned Judge goes on to say: "According to the conclusion which I come to upon the evidence, the books were there before the Defendant, and although he did not trouble to look into them he had the opportunity of doing so. In my judgment if he had intended to rely upon that parol representation of business beyond that which appeared in the papers, having the materials before him, he would have made some inquiry into it. But he did nothing of the sort." Now in that respect I am sorry to say that the learned Judge was not correct. There were no books which shewed the business done. The Plaintiff did not keep any such books, and had nothing but his diaries, and some letter books; and therefore, it is a mistake to suppose that there were any books before the Defendant which he could look into to ascertain the correctness of the statements made by the Plaintiff; and the whole foundation of the judgment on this part of the case, even if it had been well founded in law, fails in fact, because the Defendant was not guilty of negligence in not doing that which it was impossible to do, no books being in existence which would shew the amount of business done. Then the learned Judge continues: "He did nothing of the sort: I think the true result of the evidence is this, that the Defendant thought that if he could have even such a nucleus of business as these papers disclosed, he could by the energy and skill which he possessed make himself a good business in *Birmingham.*" Then that being so the learned Judge came to the conclusion either that the Defendant did not rely on the statement, or that if he did rely upon it he had shewn such negligence as to deprive him of his title to relief from this Court. As I have already said, the latter proposition is in my opinion not founded in law, and the former part is not founded in fact; I think also it is not founded in law, for when a person makes a material representation to another to induce him to enter into a contract, and the other enters into that contract, it is not sufficient to say that the party to whom the representation is made does not prove that he entered into the contract, relying upon the representation. If it is a material representation calculated to induce him to enter into the contract, it is an inference of law that he was induced by the representation to enter into it, and in order to take away his title to be relieved from the contract on the ground that the representation was untrue, it must be shewn either that he had knowledge of the facts contrary to the representation, or that he stated in terms, or shewed clearly by his conduct, that he did not rely on the representation. If you tell a man, "You may enter into partnership with me, my business is bringing in between £300 and £400 a year," the man who makes that representation must know that it is a material inducement to the other to enter into the partnership and you cannot investigate as to whether it was more or less probable that the inducement would operate on the mind of the party to whom the representation was made. Where you have neither evidence that he knew facts to shew that the statement was untrue, or that he said or did anything to shew that he did not actually rely upon the statement, the inference remains that he did so rely, and the statement being a material statement, its being untrue is a sufficient ground for rescinding the contract. For these reasons I am of opinion that the judgment of the learned Judge must be reversed and the appeal allowed.

As regards the form of the judgment, as the appellant succeeds on the counter-claim, I think it would be safer to make an order both in the action and the counter-claim, rescinding the contract and ordering the deposit to be returned. As I have already said, it is not a case in which damages should be given.

QUESTIONS

1. What interest of the defendant was protected by this decision?
2. What did the defendant claim as damages and what interests did this claim represent?
3. What reasons are there for the difference between the claim of the defendant and what he got?
4. Suppose that the defendant had been able to show that the plaintiff had been fraudulent, what would be the measure of his recovery then?

REDICAN v. NESBITT

[1924] S.C.R. 135. Supreme Court of Canada; Davies C.J.C., Idington, Duff, Anglin and Mignault JJ.

Anglin J. — The defendants entered into a contract to purchase a leasehold property from the plaintiff represented by one Wing, her agent. In due course an assignment of lease executed by the plaintiff and assented to by the landlord (the city of Toronto) was delivered to the defendants' solicitor with the keys of the property, the cheque of one of the defendants for the purchase money being simultaneously handed to the plaintiff's solicitor. The defendants also took an assignment of insurance and paid some arrears of taxes. On inspecting the property two days later — which is said to have been their first opportunity of doing so — they discovered, as they allege, that it had been misrepresented to them by Wing in several particulars, which they claim are of such importance that, had they known the truth in regard to them, they would not have purchased. On learning of these matters they stopped payment of the cheque given for the purchase money having first notified the vendor's husband that that would be done. An action by the vendor was at once begun, the writ bearing the following special indorsement:

> The plaintiff's claim is against the defendants for the sum of $2,969.84 being the amount owing by the defendants to the plaintiff as balance of account owing under an offer to purchase by the defendants from the plaintiff on lots 4 and 5, plan 336 in the city of Toronto.
> The following are the particulars:
> To balance owing under a contract for the sale by the plaintiff to the defendants of lots 4 and 5, plan 336, in the city of Toronto, which said contract has been signed by the defendants (being the amount of a cheque given by the defendants to the plaintiff), $2,969.84.

Under the Ontario practice this indorsement constituted the plaintiff's statement of claim. The words in brackets were added by amendment at the trial.

The action was tried by a jury. The judgment of the trial court, affirmed by the Appellate Division, upheld the plaintiff's claim. The defendants appeal to this court.

That this is not an action on the cheque referred to in the amendment of the special indorsement allowed at the trial, as the plaintiff now seeks to maintain, is made clear by the facts that the claim and the judgment are not against the maker of the cheque alone but are against her and her co-purchaser jointly. The amendment made at the trial should not therefore be regarded as having changed the cause of action as originally stated. It merely added an allegation facilitating proof of the amount of the plaintiff's claim as a sum liquidated. The action remained one for money due and owing upon the contract.

It is, however, equally clear that it is in no sense the equitable action for specific performance. The plaintiff asserted a purely common law claim for payment of a sum of money due under a contract, perfectly valid ... subject to any defence to which such a claim is open. He did not require the aid of a court of equity to be relieved of the leasehold with its burdens; the defendants by taking the conveyance had assumed them. For the recovery of the purchase money the common law remedy was adequate and there was no ground for the plaintiff invoking the interference of a court of equity.... It follows that the defendants will not necessarily succeed by establishing a case which would have disentitled the plaintiff to specific performance in a court of equity. That remedy is so distinctly discretionary that the court may withhold it although a case for rescission has not been made out.

But innocent misrepresentation, such as will support a demand for rescission in equity, though unavailing at common law, will serve as a good equitable defence to a claim for payment under the contract as well as afford ground for a counter-claim for rescission. Rescission is, of course, destructive of the basis of the plaintiff's claim; the right to rescission when established is an effective defence. But whether misrepresentation is set up by way of equitable defence or as the basis of a counter-claim for rescission, the burden on the defendant is the same. If the case made by him would not warrant a decree for rescission it will not avail as a defence to the claim for payment. In preferring this defence a defendant assumes the role of actor and a plea which, if established, would defeat a counter-claim for rescission is equally effective by way of reply to the defence of misrepresentation if set up by the plaintiff. 20 Hals. Laws of Eng., pp. 756, 746, 750.

In the present case the defendants plead misrepresentation as a ground both of defence and of counter-claim. They assert that it was fraudulent and, alternatively, that if innocent it was so material as to afford ground for rescission.

The jury negatived fraud and on this branch of the case, if they are not entitled to have the action dismissed on the other, the defendants ask for a new trial on the ground of misdirection and refusal by the learned trial judge to submit an essential element of it to the jury. I defer dealing with that aspect of the appeal.

The jury found that innocent misrepresentations inducing the contract had been made by the plaintiff's agent, and upon them the defendants maintain they are entitled to rescission. The trial judge rejected this claim on the ground that the contract for sale had been fully executed by the delivery of the deed and the acceptance of the cheque in payment, and that rescission of a contract after execution cannot be had for mere innocent misrepresentation unless it be such as renders the subject of sale different in substance from what was contracted for (*Kennedy v. Panama, etc.* (1867), L.R. 2 Q.B. 580). The suggestion that the property differed so completely in substance from what the defendants intended to acquire that there was a failure of consideration is not borne out by the facts. Neither is there any foundation for a suggestion of mutual mistake as a basis for rescission.... The trial judge regarded the handing over of the cheque as absolute payment and as a completion of the contract by the defendants just as the delivery of the conveyance and possession constituted completion on the part of the plaintiff.

In the Appellate Divisional Court this judgment was sustained, the late Sir W. R. Meredith C.J.O. giving the judgment of the majority of the court, on the ground that the contract became "executed" upon delivery and acceptance of the conveyance, whether the giving and taking of the cheque should or should not be regarded as payment of the purchase money.

Although Mr. Pollock in his treatise on the Law of Contracts (9 ed. p. 593) would seem to imply the existence of some doubt as to the doctrine enunciated in Lord Campbell's dictum in *Wilde v. Gibson* (1848), 1 H.L. Cas. 605, that

where the conveyance has been executed... a Court of Equity will set aside the conveyance only on the ground of fraud,

pointing out that it has not been uniformly followed (see Fry on Specific Performance, 9th ed., p. 312) it is too well established to admit of controversy, assuming that his Lordship meant where the contract had been fully carried out....

But on the question when a contract will, for the purposes of this rule, be deemed to have ceased to be "executory" and to have become "executed" the authorities are not so clear. I have not found any reported case in which it has been determined whether or not after delivery and acceptance of the conveyance and taking of possession a contract of sale remains "executory" until actual payment of the purchase money then due; nor indeed have I found any authority in which the contrary has been categorically determined. In many of the cases it is broadly stated, as it was by Lord Campbell, that after conveyance rescission will not be granted for innocent misrepresentation. But, on examination of the facts in such cases, it is clear either that payment of the purchase money had been made or as in the case of a contract for a lease, ... that all that the plaintiff seeking rescission was required by the contract to do had been done. On the other hand we find in the leading text books such statements as that

complete execution on both sides must be established — that the contract has been completely executed and exhausted on both sides;

17 Hals. Laws of Eng., p. 742 and note (*o*); that the doctrine of the court of equity is that a contract for the sale of land will not be set aside for innocent misrepresentation "after it has been completed by conveyance and payment of the purchase money;" Williams on Vendor and Purchaser (3rd ed.) p. 796; and again

completion of the contract consists, on the part of the vendor in conveying with a good title the land sold and delivering up the actual possession or enjoyment thereof; on the purchaser's part it lies in accepting such title, preparing and tendering the conveyance for the vendor's execution, accepting such conveyance, taking possession and paying the price. Ibid pp. 545, 546.
 After a conveyance has been executed, the court will set aside a transaction only on the ground of actual fraud;

Kerr on Fraud, 5 ed., p. 407. Mr. Dart's statement of the rule, however, is that the principle on which courts of equity rescind contracts for innocent misrepresentation

could not be extended to the taking away after completion the price of the property, which at law had become absolutely the vendor's.... Misrepresentation is no ground for setting aside an executed contract.

Vendors and Purchasers (7 ed.) 808. Mr. Snell (Principles of Equity (18 ed.), p. 436) says

the contract cannot be avoided after conveyance of property has taken place thereunder.

Morrison in his work on Rescission says (p. 143), that

the term "executed contract" is properly applied only when what has been performed is what was agreed to be performed.

 The foundation of the rule that an executed contract will not be rescinded for innocent misrepresentation appears to be somewhat obscure. In *Angel v. Jay*, [1911] 1 K.B. 666, Darling J. states, apparently without disapproval, the contention of counsel that "the foundation of the doctrine" is that

when property has passed the persons concerned cannot be placed in the same position as they were in before the estate became vested.

In numerous cases the vesting of the property has been referred to as a serious obstacle to rescission. In other cases the supersession of the contract for sale by the executed conveyance accepted by the purchaser and the resultant restriction of his rights to those assured by the latter instrument appears to be the ground upon which rescission of the contract after acceptance of conveyance is refused. So far does the court go in maintaining this doctrine that, where under a court sale the purchase money was still in court, the purchaser who had accepted the title and taken his conveyance was refused relief in respect of subsequently discovered incumbrances....

In the case now before us it is probably unnecessary to determine the effect on the right of a purchaser to rescission of his acceptance of a conveyance and taking of possession without making payment. What might have been a formidable obstacle to the granting of rescission to the defendants was suggested by the trial judge, namely, the inability of the court to compel the landlord's assent to a re-assignment of the leasehold to the plaintiff. The effect of the acceptance of the conveyance assented to by the lessor and of the taking of possession of the property by the defendants may have been to give to the lessor rights against them as tenants the relinquishment of which the court could not exact.

Although the execution of the contract does not afford an answer to a claim for rescission in cases of fraudulent misrepresentation, inability to effect *restitutio in integrum,* unless that has become impossible owing to action of the wrong-doer, will ordinarily preclude rescission. Kerr on Fraud (5 ed.) 387-90. *A fortiori* is this the case where innocent misrepresentation only is relied upon. See, however, *Lagunas Nitrate Co. v. Lagunas Syndicate,* [1899] 2 Ch. 392 for an instance of circumstances under which the court will grant relief in a case of fraud which it would withhold if fraud were not established. But

the court has full power to make all just allowances ... the practice has always been for a Court of Equity to give relief by way of rescission whenever by the exercise of its powers it can do what is practically just, though it cannot restore the parties precisely to the state they were in before the contract.

Here, however, neither the impossibility of *restitutio in integrum* nor the intervention of a *jus tertii* has been pleaded by the plaintiff, as it should have been if she meant to rely upon it either by way of reply to the defence or of defence to the counter-claim. Had that issue been raised on the pleadings the defendants might have produced at the trial and tendered for the plaintiff's acceptance a reassignment of the lease duly assented to by the landlord or other satisfactory assurance that such assent would be forthcoming; or, if not, a judgment might have been pronounced in terms similar to those of the decree made in *Lindsay Petroleum Co. v. Hurd* (1874), L.R. 5 P.C. 221....

But I strongly incline to the view that, while the acceptance of the cheque as payment was in this sense conditional that, if it should be dishonoured, the right to sue for the money due under the contract would revive, the transaction was, nevertheless, intended to be closed and the contract completely executed so far as the purchasers were concerned by their taking of the deed and the keys and handing over the cheque. They had obtained the full consideration for which they contracted and, if the vendor saw fit to accept the cheque they tendered in payment in lieu of cash, they should not be heard to say that the contract had not been fully executed. I cannot think that the vendor's right to have the contract treated as executed and completed can be defeated by the fact that she took a cheque as the equivalent of a cash payment, and still less by the accident that the cheque was not presented for payment during two days which intervened between the closing of the sale and the stopping of payment. Bearing in mind the well established custom of solicitors with regard to the closing of sales of real estate, when delivery of conveyance and possession was given and accepted and a cheque (then good) for the purchase money was tendered and taken, what was performed was what the parties intended should be done when they contracted.

Without, therefore, necessarily affirming the position taken in the judgment of the majority of the learned judges of the Appellate Divisional Court, I am of the opinion that, under all the circumstances of this case, the contract for sale was executed and that, according to a well settled rule in equity, rescission for innocent misrepresentation is not an available remedy for the defendants.

I am clearly of the opinion, however, that a new trial must be directed because the issue of fraud was not properly presented to the jury. In substance the learned trial judge charged that, in order to establish fraud, the defendants must show that Wing actually knew his representations were false. He did not tell the jury that the representations would be fraudulent if they were false and were made without belief in their truth, or recklessly, careless whether they were true or false. *Derry v. Peek* (1889), 14 App. Cas. 337. Wing denied having made the statement that the house was lighted by electricity and added that he "did not know how it was lighted." The jury found that he had made the statement. If adequately instructed, or if a properly framed question had been submitted to them, they might have found that it had been fraudulently made. The only questions put on this branch of the case read as follows:

> Did Mrs. Nesbitt's agent, Wing, knowingly make any untrue statements as to the house or its contents for the purpose of deceiving the defendants in any material way and inducing them to make the offer to purchase? And did they make the offer relying upon such statements?

In charging the jury the learned judge said to them

> was there a deliberate lie told by Wing?... You have to decide whether Wing deliberately told an untruth in order to earn a commission.

There was no qualification of this direction. He added,

> what the defendants are entitled to will depend on your answers to the questions as to whether there was deliberate intention to defraud or innocent misrepresentation. The word "innocent" is used in law to convey "not knowingly," and it may be that she should not be relieved from her bargain, but if there was intent, and an untrue statement made, there might be relief.

At the close of the charge to the question of a juror,

> the one question we have to decide is whether the mis-statements that it is claimed were made, were made intentionally or not?

the learned judge replied "Yes."

The Appellate Divisional Court refused the defendants relief on this branch of the case because "no objection was made to the charge" on this ground, and because

> the finding that the misrepresentations were innocent implies that they were not made recklessly careless of whether they were true or false.

Had the jury been properly instructed upon the distinction between innocent and fraudulent misrepresentation their finding that the misrepresentations had been innocent would, no doubt, cover the ground. But how can that be said in view of the explicit instruction given them that "the word 'innocent' is used in law to convey 'not knowingly' " and that only a deliberate and intentional lie would justify a finding that the misrepresentations had been fraudulent?

At the close of the evidence the trial judge handed to counsel the questions he proposed to submit to the jury. Thereupon the following discussion ensued, Mr. Grant representing the defendants:

Mr. Grant: They were made intentionally, my Lord, but whether they were intentionally fraudulent or wrong is another question.

His Lordship: I will leave out those words. I have divided the case first as to whether there was intention to deceive the defendants, and secondly, innocent misrepresentations, which may have the effect of giving the defendant what you want, or may not.

Mr. Grant: I would suggest that you put it: "Were there untrue statements made by Wing, whether intentional or not, which induced the making of the contract?" Then: "Were there any statements made by Wing that were untrue, that he knew to be untrue, or which he made without caring whether they were true or false, to induce the contract?"

I think that would be a better form in which to put the questions, if I may so suggest, my Lord.

His Lordship: No; there must be intention in an action for deceit.

Mr. Grant: No, my Lord; there need not be intention. If he makes the statements recklessly, not caring whether they were true or false, it is as fraudulent as though he knew they were false. Perhaps after your Lordship has charged the jury on that point, we may have something to say.

His Lordship: In the meantime I think I have covered the case.

Mr. Grant: Your Lordship is putting the first question as to whether the statements were fraudulent or not?

His Lordship: Yes.

Mr. Grant: And, secondly, whether they were innocently made, although untrue?

His Lordship: I do not use the word "fraudulently" because the jury does not know the exact meaning of "fraudulently" but they do know the meaning of "intentionally."

The attention of the trial judge was thus pointedly drawn to the feature of fraudulent misrepresentation which his question did not cover. Counsel expressly asked that it should be covered. The learned judge distinctly stated his view that intention to deceive was essential and impliedly that a false statement made with reckless carelessness as to its truth or falsehood would not be fraudulent. He declined to amend the questions as suggested, stating that he had "covered" the case.

Counsel is not obliged to quarrel with the judge or to press an objection *ad nauseam*. Having stated his position and his request for the submission of a proper question having been refused Mr. Grant had, I think, sufficiently discharged his duty and was not called upon to renew the same objection at the close of the charge. The learned judge had definitely expressed his purpose to adhere to an adverse view of the law. *Lex neminem coget ad vana seu inutilia*. The refusal to put to the jury the question whether Wing's statements were made without caring whether they were true or false coupled with the instruction that, although so made, they were innocent and not fraudulent, unless there was an intention to deceive — to tell a deliberate lie — was clearly misdirection and entitles the defendants to a new trial....

While the costs of the abortive trial may properly abide the result, I see no good reason why the appellants should not have their costs in this court and the Appellate Division.

[Davies C.J.C. and Mignault J. agreed with Anglin J. Idington and Duff JJ. wrote judgments to the same effect.]

NOTE

The following passage from Jeremy Bentham (taken from the *Comment on the Commentaries*, Everett, Ed. Oxford 1928, p. 194) who is here castigating Blackstone ("our Author") is appropriate here. (This is not to say that it is not also appropriate elsewhere.) Blackstone, the author of one of the most important works on the common law (*Commentaries on the Laws of England,* 1st ed. 1765) was the first Vinerian Professor of Law in the University of Oxford.

" 'Not', continues our Author, 'that the particular reason of every rule in the law can at this distance of time be always precisely assigned; but it is sufficient that there be nothing in the rule flatly contradictory to reason,' says our Author, 'and then (by a charitable and unnecessary presumption) the law (that is any chance lawyer who is weak enough to talk so) will presume it to be well founded.' Of this more in a few moments. 'And', concludes our Author for the present, 'it hath been an ancient observation in the laws of England, that whenever a standing rule of law, of which the reason perhaps could not be remembered or discerned, hath been *wantonly*† broken in upon by *statutes* or new resolutions, the wisdom of the rule hath in the end appeared from the inconveniencies that have followed the innovation.'

"Thus much to serve for an irrefragable plea for obstinacy: and to confirm that malady which in weak minds and cold bosoms the accumulated influence of interest, and envy and timidity, and ignorance is but too apt to propagate, a malady for which no certain name has yet been found by our pathologists, but which might perhaps be termed, the hydrophobia of innovation.

"The curious circumstance in the passage, and that which justifies this censure is that Statutes are in this respect put upon a footing with resolutions, as if it had the same effect whether a doctrine of Law were overthrown by a new resolution, the will of a Judge or by a Statute, the will of an acknowledged Legislator. 'The doctrine of the law then', continues our Author, 'is this: that precedents and rules must be followed, unless flatly absurd or unjust: for though their reason be not obvious at first view, yet we owe such a deference to — ins. 2, No. 2 — former times as not to suppose that they acted wholly without consideration. To illustrate this doctrine by examples. It has been determined, time out of mind, that a brother of the half blood shall never succeed as heir to the estate of his half brother, but it shall rather escheat to the king, or other superior lord. Now this is a positive law, fixed and established by custom, which custom is evidenced by judicial decisions; and therefore can never be departed from by any modern judge without a breach of his oath, and the law. For herein there is nothing repugnant to natural justice; though the artificial reason of it, drawn from the feudal law, may not be quite obvious to everybody. And therefore, though a modern judge, on account of a supposed hardship upon the half brother, might wish it had been otherwise settled, yet it is not in his power to alter it. But if any court were now to determine, that an elder brother of the half blood might enter upon and seize any lands that were purchased by his younger brother, no subsequent judges would scruple to declare that such prior determination was unjust, was unreasonable, and therefore was *not law*. So that *the Law*, and the *opinion of the judge*, are not always convertible terms, or one and the same thing; since it sometimes may happen that the judge may *mistake* the Law.'

" 'Though the reason'... 'of precedents and rules'... 'be not obvious at first view, yet we owe such a deference to former times as not to suppose they acted wholly without consideration.' So far our Author. For my part, I know not that we owe any such deference to former times. I know not that we owe any deference to former times that we owe not to our own. I know not that we owe them any such deference as to suppose a reason for what they did, when none is visible. Sure I am that it is unnecessary to have recourse to any such defence to justify the adherence to this rule. Whether it never had a reason, or whether having once had a reason, that reason is now ceased makes no difference with respect to the reason we now have for adhering to it. This reason, which may be expressed by one word, stability, our Author had already given us but the page before, tho now as if it never made any impression on him, or so weak an one as to have been obliterated already, abandoned, as it seems, for these false and trivial ones."
† That '*wanton*' proceedings in matter of Law are apt to be productive of 'inconvenience', is what there needed not a Professor from Oxford to have told us. But this word wantonly seems to have been put in for a sort of scapegoat of our Author's. Having said as much as the sentence amounts to without it, he seems to have been afraid of what he had said: and to have put in this word, in order to be able in case of being hard pushed, to reduce the something he before had said into nothing.

It is almost impossible to overestimate the importance of Blackstone's work. Its influence on the common law, particularly in the United States, was great. In England, at least, Blackstone's reputation never recovered from the attacks of Bentham. A good selection of Blackstone's work is found in *The Sovereignty of the Law*, Jones, ed. Toronto, 1973.

QUESTIONS

1. Does Anglin C.J.C. give any satisfactory reason why there should be no remedy for innocent misrepresentation? Would Blackstone expect him to do so?

2. What reasons might there be for regarding the fact of execution alone as relevant? Would it matter whether the representation referred to a matter of title, a condition of the land readily observable by inspection, or a latent defect of any kind?

The law in England has been amended by the Misrepresentation Act, 1967 (15 & 16 Eliz. II. ch. 7):

1. Where a person has entered into a contract after a misrepresentation has been made to him, and —

    (a)   the misrepresentation has become a term of the contract; or

    (b)   the contract has been performed;

or both, then, if otherwise he would be entitled to rescind the contract without alleging fraud, he shall be so entitled, subject to the provisions of this Act, notwithstanding the matters mentioned in paragraphs (a) and (b) of this section.

2. — (1) Where a person has entered into a contract after a misrepresentation has been made to him by another party thereto and as a result thereof he has suffered loss, then, if the person making the misrepresentation would be liable to damages in respect thereof had the misrepresentation been made fraudulently, that person shall be so liable notwithstanding that the misrepresentation was not made fraudulently, unless he proves that he had reasonable ground to believe and did believe up to the time the contract was made that the facts represented were true.

(2) Where a person has entered into a contract after a misrepresentation has been made to him otherwise than fraudulently, and he would be entitled, by reason of the misrepresentation, to rescind the contract, then, if it is claimed, in any pro-

ceedings arising out of the contract, that the contract ought to be or has been rescinded, the court or arbitrator may declare the contract subsisting and award damages in lieu of rescission, if of opinion that it would be equitable to do so, having regard to the nature of the misrepresentation and the loss that would be caused by it if the contract were upheld, as well as to the loss that rescission would cause to the other party.

(3) Damages may be awarded against a person under subsection (2) of this section whether or not he is liable to damages under subsection (1) thereof, but where he is so liable any award under the said subsection (2) shall be taken into account in assessing his liability under the said subsection (1).

The law in Canada has been changed as well by statute but only in regard to consumer transactions. We will look at this legislation later.

QUESTIONS

1. What is the measure of damages contemplated by the Act?
2. Would the passing of the Act have any tendency to *discourage* courts from giving relief for a misrepresentation?

The next group of cases are cases where the courts considered whether there was a warranty. There are two issues in these cases:
1. How can one tell whether something is a warranty or a representation?
2. What is the relationship between the rules regarding warranties and other ways of protecting interests that arise in contractual situations?

The first three cases deal with the first question: the remaining cases with the second.

HEILBUT, SYMONS & CO. v. BUCKLETON

[1913] A.C. 39. House of Lords; Viscount Haldane L.C., Lords Atkinson and Moulton.

Lord Moulton. My Lords, in this action the plaintiff sought relief in damages against the defendants in respect of two contracts whereby the defendants undertook to procure for the plaintiff, and the plaintiff undertook to accept, the allotment of 5000 and 1000 shares in a company called the Filisola Rubber and Produce Estates, Limited. The claim for such relief was mainly based on the allegation that the plaintiff had been induced to enter into these contracts by the false and fraudulent representation of the defendants that the said company was a rubber company. This was the sole ground for relief which was put forward by the plaintiff in the proceedings before action and in the indorsement on the writ; but in the statement of claim an alternative claim for damages was included, based on the breach of an alleged warranty given by the defendants that the company was a rubber company.

At the trial the substantial case which was sought to be made on behalf of the plaintiff had reference solely to the alleged false and fraudulent representation. Evidence was given by the plaintiff and not challenged by the defendants as to a conversation which took place over the telephone between the plaintiff and Mr. Johnston, a representative of the defendants, in which undoubtedly Mr. Johnston stated that the company was a rubber company. The making of the alleged representation was therefore not in issue, and the whole of the evidence on both sides was directed to the issue whether such representation was false, and whether, if so, it was fraudulently made. No evidence was given upon the issue of a warranty having been given by the defendants that the company was a rubber company other than so far as the proof of the conversation above referred to may have amounted to such evidence.

In answer to questions put to them by the judge, the jury found (1.) that the company could not properly be described as a rubber company; (2.) that the defendants did not fraudulently represent, but that (3.) they did warrant that it was a rubber company. Against the second of these findings there is no appeal, so that the only questions before us are as to whether the first and third of these findings can stand.

The alleged warranty rested entirely upon the following evidence. The plaintiff got a friend to ring up on the telephone Mr. Johnston (a representative of the defendants, for whose acts they accept the full responsibility) to tell him that the plaintiff wished to speak to him. The plaintiff's evidence continues thus: "I went to the telephone and I said 'Is that you, Johnston?' He said 'Yes.' I said 'I understand that you are bringing out a rubber company,' and he said 'We are.' "

The material part of the evidence ends here. The further conversation related to the soundness of the company, but no claim for relief is based on what then passed either by way of fraudulent representation or warranty.

The plaintiff then asked if he could have some shares. Mr. Johnston said he thought he could let him have 5000 at a premium of 1s. 3d., which the plaintiff expressed himself ready to take, but no bargain was then concluded. On the next day, however, Mr. Johnston accepted in writing the offer of the plaintiff as to taking 5000 shares. Later on the plaintiff applied to Mr. Johnston for a further 1000 shares and obtained them at a somewhat higher premium. In each case the terms of the contract were reduced to writing by Mr. Johnston, acting for the defendants, and sent to the plaintiff. The contracts were not contracts of sale of the shares of the company (which had not then been issued), but contracts whereby the defendants (who were underwriters of the shares in the forthcoming issue) undertook to procure for the plaintiff the allotment of the shares on his applying for them. There is, of course, no conflict as to the actual terms of these contracts, which appear from the letters. They were acted upon by the plaintiff, who duly applied for and received the allotments of 5000 and 1000 shares of the company, such allotments having been procured by the defendants by the exercise of their rights as underwriters. The plaintiff parted with some of his shares but retained the remainder, and it is in respect of these latter that the damages are claimed in this action.

There is no controversy between the parties as to certain points of fact and of law. It is not contested that the only company referred to was the Filisola Rubber and Produce Estates, Limited, or that the reply of Mr. Johnston to the plaintiff's question over the telephone was a representation by the defendants that the company was a "rubber company," whatever may be the meaning of that phrase; nor is there any controversy as to the legal nature of that which the plaintiff must establish. He must shew a warranty, i.e., a contract collateral to the main contract to take the shares, whereby the defendants in consideration of the plaintiff taking the shares promised that the company itself was a rubber company. The question in issue is whether there was any evidence that such a contract was made between the parties.

It is evident, both on principle and on authority, that there may be a contract the consideration for which is the making of some other contract. "If you will make such and such a contract I will give you one hundred pounds," is in every sense of the word a complete legal contract. It is collateral to the main contract, but each has an independent existence, and they do not differ in respect of their possessing to the full the character and status of a contract. But such collateral contracts must from their very nature be rare. The effect of a collateral contract such as that which I have instanced would be to increase the consideration of the main contract by 100*l.*, and the more natural and usual way of carrying this out would be by so modifying the main contract and not by executing a concurrent and collateral contract. Such collateral contracts, the sole effect of which is to vary or add to the terms of the principal contract, are therefore viewed with suspicion by the law. They must be proved strictly. Not only the terms of such contracts but the existence of an animus contrahendi on the part of all the parties to them must be clearly shewn. Any laxity on these points would enable parties to escape from the full performance of the obligations of contracts unquestionably entered into by them and more especially would have the effect of lessening the authority of written contracts by making it possible to vary them by suggesting the existence of verbal collateral agreements relating to the same subject-matter.

There is in the present case an entire absence of any evidence to support the existence of such a collateral contract. The statement of Mr. Johnston in answer to plaintiff's question was beyond controversy a mere statement of fact, for it was in reply to a question for information and nothing more. No doubt it was a representation as to fact, and indeed it was the actual representation upon which the main case of the plaintiff rested. It was this representation which he alleged to have been false and fraudulent and which he alleged induced him to enter into the contracts and take the shares. There is no suggestion throughout the whole of his evidence that he regarded it as anything but a representation. Neither the plaintiff nor the defendants were asked any question or gave any evidence tending to shew the existence of any animus contrahendi other than as regards the main contracts. The whole case for the existence of a collpteral contract therefore rests on the mere fact that the statement was made as to the character of the company, and if this is to be treated as evidence sufficient to establish the existence of a collateral contract of the kind alleged the same result must follow with regard to any other statement relating to the subject-matter of a contract made by a contracting party prior to its execution. This would negative entirely the firmly established rule that an innocent representation gives no right to damages. It would amount to saying that the making of any representation prior to a contract relating to its subject-matter is sufficient to establish the existence of a collateral contract that the statement is true and therefore to give a right to damages if such should not be the case.

In the history of English law we find many attempts to make persons responsible in damages by reason of innocent misrepresentations, and at times it has seemed as though the attempts would succeed. On the Chancery side of the Court the decisions favouring this view usually took the form of extending the scope of the action for deceit. There was a tendency to recognize the existence of what was sometimes called "legal fraud," i.e., that the making of an incorrect statement of fact without reasonable grounds, or of one which was inconsistent with information which the person had received or had the means of obtaining, entailed the same legal consequences as making it fraudulently. Such a doctrine would make a man liable for forgetfulness or mistake or even for honestly interpreting the facts known to him or drawing conclusions from them in a way which the Court did not think to be legally warranted. The high-water mark of these decisions is to be found in the judgment pronounced by the Court of Appeal in the case of *Peek v. Derry* (1887), 37 Ch. D. 541, when they laid down that where a defendant has made a misstatement of fact and the Court is of opinion that he had no reasonable grounds for believing that it was true he may be made liable in an action of deceit if it has materially tended to induce the plaintiff to do an act by which he has incurred damage. But on appeal to your Lordships' House this decision was unanimously reversed, and it was definitely laid down that, in order to establish a cause of action sounding in damages for misrepresentation, the statement must be fraudulent or, what is equivalent thereto, must be made recklessly, not caring whether it be true or not. The opinions pronounced in your Lordships' House in that case shew that both in substance and in form the decision was, and was intended to be, a reaffirmation of the old common law doctrine that actual fraud was essential to an action for deceit, and it finally settled the law that an innocent misrepresentation gives no right of action sounding in damages.

On the Common Law side of the Court the attempts to make a person liable for an innocent misrepresentation have usually taken the form of attempts to extend the doctrine of warranty beyond its just limits and to find that a warranty existed in cases where there was nothing more than an innocent misrepresentation. The present case is, in my opinion, an instance of this. But in respect of the question of the existence of a warranty the Courts have had the advantage of an admirable enunciation of the true principle of law which was made in very early days by Holt C.J. with respect to the contract of sale. He says: "An affirmation at the time of the sale is a warranty, provided it appear on evidence to be so intended." [See: *Medina v. Stoughton* (1700), 1 Selk. 210.] So far as decisions are concerned, this has, on the whole, been consistently followed in the Courts of Common Law. But from time to time there have been dicta inconsistent with it which have, unfortunately, found their way into text-books and have given rise to confusion and uncertainty in this branch of the law. For example, one often sees quoted the dictum of Bayley, J. in *Cave v. Coleman* (1828), 3 Man. & Ry. 2., where, in respect of a representation made verbally during the sale of a horse, he says that "being made in the course of dealing, and before the bargain was complete, it amounted to a warranty" — a proposition that is far too sweeping and cannot be supported. A still more serious deviation from the correct principle is to be found in a passage in the judgment of the Court of Appeal in *De Lassalle v. Guildford*, [1901] 2 K.B. 215, which was cited to us in the argument in the present case. In discussing the question whether a representation amounts to a warranty or not the judgment says: "In determining whether it was so intended, a decisive test is whether the vendor assumes to assert a fact of which the buyer is ignorant, or merely states an opinion or judgment upon a matter of which the vendor has no special knowledge, and on which the buyer may be expected also to have an opinion and to exercise his judgment."

With all deference to the authority of the Court that decided that case, the proposition which it thus formulates cannot be supported. It is clear that the Court did not intend to depart from the law laid down by Holt C.J. and cited above, for in the same judgment that dictum is referred to and accepted as a correct statement of the law. It is, therefore, evident that the use of the phrase "decisive test" cannot be defended. Otherwise it would be the duty of a judge to direct a jury that if a vendor states a fact of which the buyer is ignorant, they must, as a matter of law, find the existence of a warranty, whether or not the totality of the evidence shews that the parties intended the affirmation to form part of the contract; and this would be inconsistent with the law as laid down by Holt C.J. It may well be that the features thus referred to in the judgment of the Court of Appeal in that case may be criteria of value in guiding a jury in coming to a decision whether or not a warranty was intended; but they cannot be said to furnish decisive tests, because it cannot be said as a matter of law that the presence or absence of those features is conclusive of the intention of the parties. The intention of the parties can only be deduced from the totality of the evidence, and no secondary principles of such a kind can be universally true.

It is, my Lords, of the greatest importance, in my opinion, that this House should maintain in its full integrity the principle that a person is not liable in damages for an innocent misrepresentation, no matter in what way or under what form the attack is made. In the present case the statement was made in answer to an inquiry for information. There is nothing which can by any possibility be taken as evidence of an intention on the part of either or both of the parties that there should be a contractual liability in respect of the accuracy of the statement. It is a representation as to a specific thing and nothing more. The judge, therefore, ought not to have left the question of warranty to the jury, and if, as a matter of prudence, he did so in order to obtain their opinion in case of appeal, he ought then to have entered judgment for the defendants notwithstanding the verdict.

It will, of course, be evident that I have been dealing only with warranty or representation relating to a specific thing. This is wholly distinct from the question which arises when goods are sold by description and their answering to that description becomes a condition of the contract. It is, in my opinion, a failure to recognize that in the present case the parties were referring (as is evident by the written contracts) to one specific thing only that led Farwell L.J. to come to a different conclusion from that to which your Lordships ought, in my opinion, to come in this appeal.

Order of the Court of Appeal reversed and judgment entered for the appellants. The respondent to pay the costs in the Courts below and of the appeal to this House.

[Viscount Haldane and Lord Atkinson gave judgments to the same effect.]

[The contract in this case was made at the height of a "rubber boom" in the stock market, and the shares of "rubber" companies were selling at very high prices. The Filisola Rubber Co. was later found to have far less rubber trees than had been expected and its shares fell dramatically.

Heilbut, Symons & Co. v. Buckleton is the leading case in the law of warranties.]

QUESTIONS

1. What proposition of law could one deduce from it?
2. To what extent does any such proposition bind future courts?
3. Why was the court so concerned to protect the defendant from liability?
4. What would have been the measure of damages had the court found that there had been a warranty?
5. Is the result of the case appropriate?

In regard to similar transactions now you should realize that the operation of the Ontario (and other provincial) Securities Commissions has completely changed the law.

The Ontario Securities Act, R.S.O. 1970, c. 426, s. 65, in part;

65. – (1) A person or company that is a party to a contract as purchaser resulting from the offer of a security in the course of primary distribution to the public... has a right to rescind the contract while still the owner of the security if the prospectus and any amended prospectus then filed with the Commission in compliance with section 55 received by the purchaser, as of the date of receipt, contains an untrue statement of a material fact or omits to state a material fact necessary in order to make any statement contained therein not misleading in the light of the circumstances in which it was made.

The Act requires that, before any primary distribution of shares can be made to the public, a prospectus be filed with the Ontario Securities Commission. There are also criminal penalties provided for making false statements in a prospectus. The Act also allows any purchaser of securities a 48-hour period within which he can change his mind without giving any reasons and even if the prospectus is completely accurate (s. 64(2)).

DICK BENTLEY PRODUCTIONS LTD. v. HAROLD SMITH MOTORS LTD.

[1965] 2 All E.R. 65. Court of Appeal (England); Lord Denning M.R., Danckwerts and Salmon L.JJ.

Lord Denning, M.R.: The second plaintiff, Mr. Charles Walter Bentley, sometimes known as Dick Bentley, brings an action against Harold Smith (Motors), Ltd., for damages for breach of warranty on the sale of a car. Mr. Bentley had been dealing with Mr. Smith (to whom I shall refer in the stead of the defendant company) for a couple of years and told Mr. Smith he was on the look-out for a well vetted Bentley car. In January, 1960, Mr. Smith found one and bought it for £1,500 from a firm in Leicester. He wrote to Mr. Bentley and said: "I have just purchased a Park Ward power operated hood convertible. It is one of the nicest cars we have had in for quite a long time." Mr. Smith had told Mr. Bentley earlier that he was in a position to find out the history of cars. It appears that with a car of this quality the makers do keep a complete biography of it.

Mr. Bentley went to see the car. Mr. Smith told him that a German baron had had this car. He said that it had been fitted at one time with a replacement engine and gearbox, and had done twenty thousand miles only since it had been so fitted. The speedometer on the car showed only twenty thousand miles. Mr. Smith said the price was £1,850, and he would guarantee the car for twelve months, including parts and labour. That was on the morning of Jan. 23, 1960. In the afternoon Mr. Bentley took his wife over to see the car. Mr. Bentley repeated to his wife in Mr. Smith's presence what Mr. Smith had told him in the morning. In particular that Mr. Smith said it had done only twenty thousand miles since it had been refitted with a replacement engine and gearbox. Mr. Bentley took it for a short run. He bought the car for £1,850, gave his cheque and the sale was concluded. The car was a considerable disappointment to him. He took it back to Mr. Smith from time to time. [HIS LORDSHIP referred briefly to some work done on the car and continued:] Eventually he brought this action for breach of warranty. The county court judge found that there was a warranty, that it was broken, and that the damages were more than £400, but as the claim was limited to £400, he gave judgment for the plaintiffs for that amount.

The first point is whether this representation, namely that the car had done twenty thousand miles only since it had been fitted with a replacement engine and gearbox, was an innocent misrepresentation (which does not give rise to damages), or whether it was a warranty. It was said by HOLT, C.J. (1700), 1 Salk. 210, and repeated in *Heilbut, Symons & Co. v. Buckleton*:

> "An affirmation at the time of the sale is a warranty, provided it appear on evidence to be so intended."

But that word "intended" has given rise to difficulties. I endeavoured to explain in *Oscar Chess, Ltd. v. Williams* [1957] 1 All E.R. 325 that the question whether a warranty was intended depends on the conduct of the parties, on their words and behaviour, rather than on their thoughts. If an intelligent bystander would reasonably infer that a warranty was intended, that will suffice. What conduct, then? What words and behaviour, lead to the inference of a warranty?

Looking at the cases once more, as we have done so often, it seems to me that if a representation is made in the course of dealings for a contract for the very purpose of inducing the other party to act on it, and it actually induces him to act on it by entering into the contract, that is prima facie ground for inferring that the representation was intended as a warranty. It is not necessary to speak of it as being collateral. Suffice it that the representation was intended to be acted on and was in fact acted on. But the maker of the representation can rebut this inference if he can show that it really was an innocent misrepresentation, in that he was in fact innocent of fault in making it, and that it would not be reasonable in the circumstances for him to be bound by it. In the *Oscar Chess* case the inference was rebutted. There a man had bought a second-hand car and received with it a logbook, which stated the year of the car, 1948. He afterwards resold the car. When he resold it he simply repeated what was in the log-book and passed it on to the buyer. He honestly believed on reasonable grounds that it was true. He was completely innocent of any fault. There was no warranty by him but only an innocent misrepresentation. Whereas in the present case it is very different. The inference is not rebutted. Here we have a dealer, Mr. Smith, who was in a position to know, or at least to find out, the history of the car. He could get it by writing to the makers. He did not do so. Indeed it was done later. When the history of this car was examined, his statement turned out to be quite wrong. He ought to have known better. There was no reasonable foundation for it.

[HIS LORDSHIP summarised the history of the car, and continued:] The county court judge found that the representations were not dishonest. Mr. Smith was not guilty of fraud. But he made the statement as to twenty thousand miles without any foundation. And the judge was well justified in finding that there was a warranty. He said:

> "I have no hesitation that as a matter of law the statement was a warranty. Mr. Smith stated a fact that should be within his own knowledge. He had jumped to a conclusion and stated it as a fact. A fact that a buyer would act on."

That is ample foundation for the inference of a warranty. So much for this point. I hold that the appeal fails and should be dismissed.

[Danckwerts and Salmon L.JJ. agreed.]

QUESTIONS

1. Does Lord Denning have the same view of the law as Lord Moulton?
2. Would Lord Denning decide *Heilbut, Symons v. Buckleton* in the same way?
3. If you had the chance to cross-examine Johnson, the defendants' representative, in the trial of the action in *Heilbut, Symons*, before a judge now, what questions would you ask him?

RICHVIEW CONSTRUCTION CO. LTD. v. RASPA

(1975), 11 O.R. (2d) 377, Ontario Court of Appeal; Brooke, Arnup and Howland JJ.A.

The judgment of the Court was delivered by

Arnup, J.A.: — This appeal is concerned with the following clause in an agreement of purchase and sale of a vacant lot in a residential subdivision:

> It is understood and agreed that this is a vacant lot and the purchaser as the priviledge to erect a single family dwelling on plans approved by the borough of Etobicoke. Being a fully serviced Lot [*sic*].

The plaintiff is a construction company engaged in "drain and concrete and building construction". Its president is Michael Grella. He controls it. Grella was looking for a building lot, saw a "for sale" sign, and telephoned the agent.

The lot was listed at $24,000. Grella offered $23,000, and $23,500 was finally agreed upon. Before the offer to purchase was executed, Grella asked the agent "if the lot was a fully serviced lot". Grella testified that the agent replied: "Yes, everything is there." In the same conversation the agent referred to the clause already quoted, and said:

> ... look at the second paragraph. You have everything. It is a fully serviced lot. You have everything that is required, sewers, sanitary sewers and everything.

The offer was accepted on September 20, 1971, and the sale was closed on November 4, 1971. The plaintiff did not contact the Borough of Etobicoke before closing to find out if there were lateral connections from the trunk services in the street to the edge of the lot it was buying, nor did it instruct its solicitor to do so. There were no requisitions of any kind submitted on behalf of the plaintiff, and the purchase was closed by a simple deed, containing no reference to services.

In March, 1972, the plaintiff had an architect draw plans for a house to be erected on the lot. In April the plaintiff began to build the house, and could find no lateral connections. Grella went to the borough, who got out the subdivision plan and said there were no lateral services to this lot. The plaintiff then arranged with the borough to install the necessary laterals. They cost $2,860.

The vendor did not give evidence, but her real estate agent apparently thought that a "fully serviced lot" was one where the necessary trunk services were in the street and capable of being connected by laterals to individual lots, at the expense of the lot owner. An engineer called for the defendant testified that the expression "fully serviced lot" was used by him "very seldom", and was "not recognized in his industry". He also testified:

> Q. If you did not know where the services were how would you go about it? A. You would go to the Engineering Department. THE COURT: Q. The Engineering Department? A. Yes, because they have the exact location of every catch basin, every valve, etc.

The plaintiff then sued its vendor for the cost of installing the laterals, plus $500 damages "for breach of contract". The statement of claim included this clause:

> 6. It is the plaintiff's contention that the defendant breached the contract of purchase and sale above referred to by not, on closing, conveying to the plaintiff a fully serviced lot.

Fraud was not alleged, and a motion to amend by alleging fraudulent misrepresentation by the defendant was dismissed at the opening of the trial. That ruling is not appealed against. The defence was that the lot was fully serviced, and that a fully serviced lot does not include lateral connections. By an amendment allowed well before trial, the defendant pleaded the absence of any requisition requiring evidence that the lot was fully serviced or that lateral connections had been installed, and pleaded that the plaintiff was now thereby "barred" from recovering the cost of the laterals. The defendant also counterclaimed for $2,861.50 which the plaintiff had withheld from its payments on the mortgage given back to the vendor.

The trial Judge dealt with the meaning of "fully serviced lot" as follows:

> In my opinion the decision in this case depends to a considerable extent on the proper definition of the term "fully serviced lot" as used in the contract of sale dated September 21, 1971 (ex. 1). Does it mean the existence of trunk sewers and water mains down the centre of the street or does it go further and mean trunks and lateral connections from the trunks to the lot line?
>
> There seems to be a dearth of judicial authority on this point so I must interpret these words as best I can myself. There is no doubt whatever the owner of a vacant lot who builds a house on it is responsible for connecting the sewers and water from the lot line to the house itself. What significance there is to be attached to the word "fully serviced"? I have come to the conclusion that to give the word "fully" its ordinary significance one must come to the conclusion that everything possible has been done to complete the servicing of the lot. There can be no doubt that the provision of the lateral connection from the trunks to the lot line was within the power of the vendor of the land. I am therefore of the opinion that the words "Being a fully serviced Lot" in this contract of sale means that the lot is serviced by sewer and water lateral connection as far as the lot line.

I agree with this conclusion. I would make it clear, however, that we are not writing a definition of "fully serviced lot" for a dictionary, from which it can be extracted for use in interpreting all contracts, in all factual situations. We are deciding what the words mean, in this contract, against the factual background of this case. Generally speaking, a fully serviced lot in an urban municipality is one to the boundary of which the municipal services have been installed, so that the "on site" or household services can be connected up to the municipal system. However, particular fact situations may show that something different was intended by the parties.

The other branch of the case raises questions of law of great difficulty. It having been found that the lot was not a "fully serviced lot", does the plaintiff have a remedy? The purchase has been closed. The deed delivered, and accepted, is silent about services. No question of fraud arises. The plaintiff does not want rescission.

The clause is to be read as if it said, on this point: "It is understood and agreed... that this is a fully serviced lot." How is such a provision to be characterized, in terms of contract law? Different results follow if it is a "mere representation", a "collateral warranty", a "collateral contract", or a "term of the contract". These are terms used in various of the decided cases, and not always — according to the textwriters and commentators — with accuracy and precision.

It is small comfort, at this stage, to recognize that no problem would have arisen if the offer to purchase had read: "The vendor warrants that this is a fully serviced lot, and agrees that this warranty shall survive the closing of the sale", or if the deed had included: "The [vendor] warrants, covenants and agrees that [the lot] is a fully serviced lot."

The trial Judge, while referring to the clause at one stage as a "representation", finally concluded that it was a "warranty collateral to the contract", and was not merged in the deed. He therefore gave judgment for the plaintiff for $2,860 (the claim for $500 damages not being pressed), and dismissed the counterclaim without costs.

In my view, the clause here in question is not a "mere representation". Such a representation, if made innocently (*i.e.*, without fraud) gives no cause of action for damages after closing although it turns out to be untrue. This is shown by the line of cases which includes *Heilbut, Symons & Co. v. Buckleton*, [1913] A.C. 30, especially at p. 51, and *Waxman v. Yeandle et al.*, [1953] O.R. 367, [1953] 2 D.L.R. 475.

To elevate a "mere representation" to the category of a "warranty" it is not enough to show that the statement, originally made orally, has been included in the written contract. Such inclusion simply puts it beyond dispute that the representation was made: *Waxman v. Yeandle*, at p. 375 O.R. p. 478 D.L.R.

What is required to lead a Court to construe a provision as a warranty has been expressed in a number of ways. In *Waxman v. Yeandle*, at p. 376 O.R., p. 479 D.L.R., Roach, J.A., said:

> In order to succeed in this action the plaintiff would have to prove that the defendants contracted with him that the representation was true and that in the event of its turning out to be untrue they would indemnify him against any loss that might thereby be occasioned to him.

At p. 377 O.R., pp. 479-80 D.L.R., he said:

> I am unable to conclude from the language used in the paragraph in question that it was the intention that that paragraph should constitute a warranty. A person can be made liable if he warrants the truth of a representation, but it must be made abundantly clear that the warranty was in fact given.

The statement in that case concerned the number of gallons of beer sold during the previous 12 months in the hotel which was the subject of the sale. One of the considerations that led Roach, J.A., to his conclusion was "the reasonable assumption that the plaintiff in any event would have recourse to the records of the Liquor Control Board" (where the precise information could be obtained): see p. 377 O.R., p. 480 D.L.R.

While this feature of the *Waxman* case exists also in the present case, since the true facts regarding services could have been obtained from the municipality, and in both cases the purchaser did not want rescission, one factual difference is that in *Waxman* the purchaser discovered the misrepresentation before he closed, and purported to close while reserving his right to sue for damages.

In *Heilbut, Symons & Co. v. Buckleton, supra*, it was said, on the basis of cases going back to the 17th century, that it must appear to have been the intention of the representor that he was giving a warranty of the truth of the fact asserted (p. 43). Lord Atkinson was seeking to determine if there was a "collateral contract" (p. 44). Lord Moulton, at p. 47 said:

> He [the plaintiff] must shew a warranty, i.e., *a contract collateral to the main contract* to take the shares, whereby the defendants in consideration of the plaintiff taking the shares *promised* that the company itself was a rubber company. The question in issue is whether there was any evidence that such a contract was made between the parties.

(Emphasis added.) It must be observed that Lord Moulton was influenced in part by the fact that the alleged "collateral contract" was oral, and its effect was to add to the terms of the "principal contract". Such collateral contracts, Lord Moulton said, were "viewed with suspicion by the law".

Lord Moulton criticized [at p. 50], as a "still more serious deviation from the correct principle", a passage in the judgment of the Court of Appeal in *De Lassalle v. Guildford*, [1901] 2 K.B. 215 at p. 221, where, in discussing whether a representation amounted to a warranty or not, the Court of Appeal had said:

> In determining whether it was so intended a decisive test is whether the vendor assumes to assert a fact of which the buyer is ignorant, or merely states an opinion or judgment upon a matter of which the vendor has no special knowledge, and on which the buyer may be expected also to have an opinion and to exercise his judgment.

Lord Moulton said the phrase "decisive test" could not be defended. He agreed that the features referred to by the Court of Appeal "may be criteria of value" in deciding as a question of fact whether or not a warranty was intended, but were not "decisive tests". The intention of the parties could only be deduced from the totality of the evidence.

In the *De Lassalle* case, which involved the lease of a house, the lessee refused to hand over the executed lease until he received an assurance that the drains were in order (a matter which he obviously could not determine for himself, being not yet in possession). The required assurance was given orally. The lease made no reference to drains, which were not in good order. The lessee recovered damages, on appeal, on the basis that the representation constituted a warranty collateral to the lease. At p. 221, A. L. Smith, M.R., said:

> Now what constitutes a warranty in law, or a mere representation? To create a warranty no special form of words is necessary. It must be a collateral undertak-

ing forming part of the contract by agreement of the parties express or implied, and must be given during the course of the dealing which leads to the bargain, and should then enter into the bargain as part of it.

At p. 222 the Master of the Rolls continued:

> The next question is, Was the warranty collateral to the lease so that it might be given in evidence and given effect to? It appears to me in this case clear that the lease did not cover the whole ground, and that it did not contain the whole of the contract between the parties. The lease is entirely silent about the drains, though there is a covenant that the lessee during the term should do the inside repairs, and the lessor the outside repairs, which would, I suppose, include the drains which happened to be inside or outside the house. There is nothing in the lease as to the then condition of the drains — i.e., at the time of the taking of the lease, which was the vital point in hand. Then why is not the warranty collateral to anything which is to be found in the lease? The present contract or warranty by the defendant was entirely independent of what was to happen during the tenancy. It was what induced the tenancy, and it in no way affected the terms of the tenancy during the three years, which was all the lease dealt with. The warranty in no way contradicts the lease, and without the warranty the lease never would have been executed.

De Lassalle v. Guildford was followed by the Manitoba Court of Appeal in *Gilmour v. Trustee Co. of Winnipeg et al.*, [1923] 4 D.L.R. 344, [1923] 3 W.W.R. 177, 33 Man. R. 351 (a warranty as to acreage), which in turn was followed by Kelly, J., in *A.-G. Can. v. Corrie* (1951), 3 W.W.R. (N.S.) 207, 59 Man. R. 94 (warranty that the well water was suitable for human consumption).

Reverting to the definition of "warranty", Stuart, J.A., in *Woolley v. Goldman* (1922), 66 D.L.R. 324, [1922] 1 W.W.R. 618, 17 Alta. L.R. 254 (App. Div. Alta.), said that "to establish a warranty it must be shewn that there was an actual collateral contract entered into by which the defendant has guaranteed or warranted that certain facts exist" (p. 325 D.L.R., p. 619 W.W.R.).

The authors of 9 Hals., 4th ed., *tit.* "Contract", pp. 220-1, paras. 346-7, treat the distinction as being between "representations" and "terms [of the contract]". A representation intended to have contractual force amounts to a "contractual term". The authors express it thus in para. 347:

> Basically, the problem is one of determining the intention of the parties as evidenced by their words and conduct, so that no general principle of interpretation can be universally true. Because, however, the intention of the parties seldom clearly appears, the courts have had regard to any one or more of a number of factors for attributing an intention. These factors should be regarded as valuable, although not decisive, tests.

Of the six factors listed, none is inconsistent with the clause here in question being intended as a warranty, and two definitely point toward warranty. These are the fact that the purchaser would not have made the purchase at all without the assurance given (as Grella here testified), and that the fact stated was one which was or should have been within the vendor's knowledge.

Di Castri in his *Canadian Law of Vendor and Purchaser* (1968), at p. 242, para. 290, uses a combination of terms:

> An oral representation, made at the time of sale, may constitute a *warranty collateral to a contract for the sale of land*, if not inconsistent therewith and if given dur-

ing the course of dealing leading to the contract so as to constitute an *essential term of the contract*.

(Emphasis added.)

The authors of Cheshire and Fifoot, *The Law of Contract*, 8th ed. (1972), prefer to distinguish between what is a representation leading to formation of a contract, on the one hand, and what has become a "term of the contract", on the other. They suggest that "collateral contract" has been adopted in several cases "to avoid the dilemma of 'term' or 'representation' " (p. 114), and assert (at p. 118) that much confusion has resulted over many years by the failure to define either "condition" or "warranty" with precision.

I have no difficulty in concluding, as did the trial Judge, that the clause in question constitutes a warranty and not a "mere representation". While the form of the wording is not conclusive, the use of the words "it is agreed and understood" are contractual in connotation and not those of representation. The subject-matter of the facts dealt with were important to the purchaser. The vendor knew the purchaser — a construction company — was buying the lot to build a house on it. The mortgage back was a "builder's term mortgage".

I interpret the clause as if it had been expressed: "I warrant, and I acknowledge that you understand, that this is a fully serviced lot."

Whether the provisions in an agreement for sale are superseded by (or, as it is sometimes put, "merged in") the subsequent conveyance depends upon the intention of the parties, expressed or presumed, and is not automatic, applicable in all cases:

The obvious cases where covenants survive the closing are those where the vendor has contracted to build, or complete, a house upon the land conveyed.

There is not to be found in this agreement any language which expressly provides that the parties intended the warranty to survive the closing. The vendor (through her agent) thought the warranty was true, or fulfilled, when the agreement was executed. The purchaser expected to get on closing a deed in proper form conveying the fee simple to it. This it received.

Its solicitor, or Mr. Grella himself, could have ascertained the true facts by a routine inquiry to the Borough engineering department (which Mr. Grella eventually made). On ascertaining the facts, prior to closing, the purchaser could then have said to the vendor: "Make good your warranty to me, or give me an undertaking to do so, else I will refuse to close."

I cannot find, on these facts, circumstances compelling us to find a presumed intention of the parties — which I think must be an intention of *both* parties — that anything further was to be done by the vendor after closing. The purchaser could have protected itself by searches which careful conveyancing required, or by express wording in the deed, or by a warranty or undertaking clearly expressed as surviving the closing. It did none of these things.

With some regret, I conclude that in the absence of fraud by the vendor, the purchaser had no rights after its purchase was closed.

I would therefore allow the appeal with costs, set aside the judgment below, and substitute therefor a judgment dismissing the action with costs. I would not alter the dismissal of the counterclaim without costs. The defendant has her rights under the mortgage.

NOTE

The factors listed in 9 Halsbury, 4th Ed. pp. 220-1 (of which two were referred to by Arnup J.A.) are as follows:

(1) If only a brief period of time elapses between the making of the statement and the formation of the contract, the court may be disposed to hold that the statement is a term of the contract.

(2) Where the party to whom the statement is made makes it clear that he regards the matter as so important that he would not contract without the assurance being given, that is evidence of an intention of the parties that the statement is to be a term of the contract.

(3) Where the party making the statement is stating a fact which is or should be within his own knowledge and of which the other party is ignorant, that is evidence that the statement is intended to be a term of the contract.

(4) Where, subsequent to negotiations, the parties enter into a written contract and that contract does not contain the statement in question, that may point towards the statement being a mere representation, though there have been cases where it has been found that such a preliminary statement constitutes a collateral contract.

(5) Where the party making the statement suggests an independent survey or opinion that may show that no warranty was intended.

(6) It has been said that the maker of a statement can rebut an inference of warranty if he can show that he was innocent of fault in making it, and that it would not be reasonable in the circumstances to hold him bound by it.

The discussion of merger in the case has been reduced substantially.

QUESTIONS

1. Why would Arnup J.A. not have referred to *Dick Bentley v. Harold Smith*?
2. To what extent is it useful to talk of intention?

In *Heilbut, Symons* a warranty is referred to as a "collateral contract". The notion of the warranty being a separate contract is used in the next two cases to reach results that can be regarded as satisfactory. Why was the device of the collateral contract necessary in these cases?

SHANKLIN PIER v. DETEL

[1951] 2 K.B. 854. King's Bench Division.

ACTION.

The plaintiffs were the owners of a pier at Shanklin, in the Isle of Wight, which, during the war, was partly demolished and allowed to fall into disrepair. On July 22, 1946, they entered into a contract with contractors to have the necessary repairs effected and to have the whole pier repainted with two coats of bitumastic or bituminous paint. Under this contract the plaintiffs had, however, the right to vary the specification.

On July 22, 1946, the South Coast director of the defendant company, as a result of an inquiry by the plaintiffs, went to Shanklin with the object of obtaining for his company the contract for the repainting or for the materials for the repainting of the pier. He there saw the managing director of the plaintiff company, and later also the plaintiffs' architect, and told them that certain paint manufactured by the defendants and known as D.M.U. would be suitable for the work. He showed a pamphlet to the architect which stated that two coats of D.M.U. applied to a clean metal surface would keep the underwater surface, top sides, and wind and water line of a ship free from corrosion for over four years. He told the architect that the paint was not subject to creep, suggested that two coats should be used on the pier as a protective coat, and promised him that it should have a life of at least seven to ten years.

On the faith of those statements the plaintiffs caused the specification in their contract with the contractors to be amended by the substitution of two coats of D.M.U. That paint was bought by the contractors from the defendants and applied to the pier, but it proved to be unsatisfactory and lasted only about three months.

The plaintiffs, by their statement of claim, now claimed against the defendants that, in consideration of the plaintiffs' specifying that the contractors should use for repainting the pier two coats of a paint known as D.M.U., manufactured by the defendants, the defendants warranted that the D.M.U. paint would be suitable for repainting the pier, would give a surface impervious to dampness, would prevent corrosion and the creeping of rust, and would have a life of from seven to ten years. The plaintiffs further alleged that, in reliance on that warranty, they duly specified that the contractors should use D.M.U. paint for repainting the pier in lieu of the bituminous paint originally specified; that the contractors bought quantities of the paint from the defendants and used it on the pier; and that, contrary to the warranty, the paint was not suitable for repainting the pier or for the protection of the pier from damp or corrosion or rust, and its life was of a very short duration, with the result that the plaintiffs were put to extra expense amounting to 4,127*l*.

McNair, J. This case raises an interesting and comparatively novel question whether or not an enforceable warranty can arise as between parties other than parties to the main contract for the sale of the article in respect of which the warranty is alleged to have been given. [His Lordship stated the facts set out above and continued:]

The defence, stated broadly, is that no warranty such as is alleged in the statement of claim was ever given and that, if given, it would give rise to no cause of action between these parties. Accordingly, the first question which I have to determine is whether any such warranty was ever given. [His Lordship reviewed the evidence about the negotiations which led to the acceptance by the plaintiffs of two coats of D.M.U. in substitution for the paint originally specified, and continued:]

In the result, I am satisfied that, if a direct contract of purchase and sale of the D.M.U. had then been made between the plaintiffs and the defendants, the correct conclusion on the facts would have been that the defendants gave to the plaintiffs the warranties substantially in the form alleged in the statement of claim. In reaching this conclusion, I adopt the principles stated by Holt, C.J.... that an affirmation at the time of sale is a warranty, provided it appear on evidence to have been so intended.

Counsel for the defendants submitted that in law a warranty could give rise to no enforceable cause of action except between the same parties as the parties to the main contract in relation to which the warranty was given. In principle this submission seems to me to be unsound. If, as is elementary, the consideration for the warranty in the usual case is the entering into of the main contract in relation to which the warranty is given, I see no reason why there may not be an enforceable warranty between A and B supported by the consideration that B should cause C to enter into a contract with A or that B should do some other act for the benefit of A.

Counsel for the defendants, however, relied upon the decision of the Court of Appeal in *Drury v. Victor Buckland Ld.*, [1941] 1 All E.R. 269, and particularly upon the judgment of Scott, L.J. In that case the plaintiff, who had been approached by an agent of the defendants, dealers in refrigerating machines, agreed to purchase such a machine, but, being unable or unwilling to pay forthwith the whole of the purchase price, the deal was put through by the defendants' selling the machine to a finance company, who in turn entered into a hire-purchase agreement with the plaintiff, under which she eventually, when the whole of the hire-purchase instalments had been paid, acquired title to the machine. The machine proving unsatisfactory, the plaintiff sued the defendants, claiming damages for breach of the implied warranty or condition under s. 14, sub-s. 1, of the Sale of Goods Act, 1893.

The claim failed, Scott, L.J., saying: "It was a sale by the Buckland Company [the defendants] to the hire-purchase company. The property passed to them on the terms that they [the defendants] would get paid by the hire-purchase company. Therefore, the claim against them [the defendants] for damages for breach of warranty is a cause of action unsupported by any contract of sale which would carry it". The judgment can readily be understood in relation to its subject-matter, namely, an implied statutory condition or warranty arising out of a contract of sale, and one can well understand it being said that, as there was no contract of sale between the plaintiff and defendants, no such implied warranty or condition could arise between them; but I do not read it as affording any support for the wider proposition for which counsel for the defendants contended.

The same view of the effect of this judgment as I have indicated was, I think, taken by Jones, J., in *Brown v. Sheen and Richmond Car Sales Ld.*, [1950] 1 All E.R. 1102, a case in which the judge entered judgment against a motor car dealer on an express oral warranty given in relation to the purchase of a car, the transaction, as in *Drury's* case, being carried through with the assistance of a finance company. It was here sought to distinguish *Brown's* case on the ground that in the statement of facts in the report in All England Law Reports it was stated that "the plaintiff agreed to buy" the motor car from the defendants, but the pleadings in *Brown's* case, which I have examined, lend no support for suggesting that in that case there was in any legal sense any agreement to sell between the plaintiff and the defendants...

Accordingly, in my judgment the plaintiffs are entitled to recover against the defendants damages for breach of the express warranties alleged.

Judgment for the plaintiffs.

ANDREWS v. HOPKINSON

[1957] 1 Q.B. 229. Queen's Bench Division (England).

[The plaintiff wanted to buy a second-hand car. He went to a used-car lot run by the defendant. There he was shown a 1934 Standard car. When the plaintiff was taken out for a test drive, the defendant said, "It's a good little bus, I would stake my life on it; you will have no trouble with it." The parties agreed on a price of £120. The plaintiff could not pay this and so the deal was financed. The parties followed the standard procedures in such circumstances. The defendant agreed to sell the car to the finance company and the finance company agreed to hire the car to the plaintiff for 18 months giving the plaintiff an option to buy at the end of that period for £1.

Very soon after the plaintiff accepted delivery of the car (after it had been driven about 150 miles) he was involved in an accident. It was proved that the cause of the accident was a defective steering mechanism. The plaintiff suffered serious injuries. He brought an action against the defendant.]

McNair J., reading his judgment, stated the facts substantially as set out above, and continued: On the evidence given before me I am satisfied (1) that the defective condition of the drag-link joint was the cause of the accident; (2) that this condition was of long standing; (3) that at the time when the plaintiff took delivery of the car it was, by reason of these defects, not in good condition and safe and fit for use on a public highway; (4) that this defective condition could have been discovered by any competent mechanic (though probably not by an ordinary owner-driver) without stripping down the steering mechanism, by the simple and recognized method of manually pulling upon the ball pin after jacking up the car for examination; (5) that any motor dealer ought to appreciate that in the case of an old car such as the car in question, one of the most likely places to find excessive and dangerous wear affecting the roadworthiness is in the steering mechanism, and particularly in the drag-link joint where such joint forms part of the steering mechanism; (6) that the defendant had no reason to anticipate that the plaintiff would himself have the car examined by a competent mechanic before taking it on the road, or would himself examine it.

As a result of this accident the car was wrecked and the plaintiff suffered serious injuries involving the fracture of three ribs and a fracture of the left wrist. Happily the fractures united well and there was no residual disability. He was off work for seven or eight weeks. The special damages have been agreed at £245 5s. 6d. and I assess the general damages at the sum of £400.

In these circumstances the plaintiff brings his action against the defendant, basing his claim upon three grounds. He first claims that in the circumstances which I have narrated the defendant warranted that the car was in good condition and reasonably safe and fit for use on the public highway; that he acted on this warranty, and that damage was caused by breach of that warranty. Secondly, he claims that the collision was caused by the negligence of the defendant, particularly by the negligence set out in paragraph 6 of the statement of claim, that the defendant knew, or ought to have known, the said car was defective and therefore dangerous and unfit for use on a highway, and that the defendant failed to take any or sufficient steps to remedy this defect to ensure the car was reasonably safe and fit to use on a public highway; failed to warn the plaintiff that the car was defective and dangerous and unfit to be used on a public highway. Thirdly, by way of amendment made at a late stage of the hearing, the plaintiff relied on the implied warranty similar to that implied in certain cases of sale of goods under section 14(1) of the Sale of Goods Act, 1893.

As to breach of warranty, in the first place it is clear that in law the relationship between the plaintiff and the defendant was not a relationship of seller and purchaser. The hire-purchase transaction evidenced in the documents was a reality and cannot be treated as a mere colourable transaction: see *Drury v. Victor Buckland Ltd.*

Secondly, I am satisfied (1) applying the principle stated by Hold J. in ... *Medina v. Stoughton* (1700), 1 Salk. 210, that if the transaction between the plaintiff and defendant had been in law a sale, the words deposed to by the plaintiff as being the words used by Mr. Hopkinson, junior, could properly be held to be words of warranty, i.e., an affirmation made at the time of sale intended to be a warranty; (2) that the words amounted at least to a warranty that the car was in good condition and reasonably safe and fit for use on a public highway; and (3) that the plaintiff acted upon this warranty in the sense that without it he would not have accepted delivery of the car or entered into the hire-purchase agreement.

On these findings I adopt the reasoning of Jones J. in *Brown v. Sheen and Richmond Car Sales Ltd.* [1950] 1 All E.R. 1102 and follow my own decision in *Shanklin Pier Ltd. v. Detel Products Ltd.*, where I set out at some length the reasons that led me to the conclusion (as they do in this case) that there may be an enforceable warranty between A, the intended purchaser of a car, and B, the motor dealer, supported by the consideration that B should cause the hire-purchase finance company to enter into a hire-purchase agreement with A, the intended purchaser.

It was rather faintly argued that even on these findings the defendant would only be liable for the difference in value between the car as delivered and the car as warranted. Though this, no doubt, may be the prima facie measure of damages in an ordinary case of breach of warranty in the sale of goods, I feel no doubt at all that on the facts of this case the whole of the damages can fairly be considered as loss directly and naturally resulting in the ordinary course of events from the breach of warranty and so recoverable as damages for breach. I hold, accordingly, that as damages for breach of warranty the plaintiff is entitled to judgment for £645 5s. 6d.

Though this conclusion is sufficient to dispose of this action in the plaintiff's favour, it is right that I should also state my views upon the second ground of complaint, namely, negligence.

There was before me abundant evidence that in the case of an old car such as this the danger spot is in the steering mechanism and that this particular defect could have been discovered by a competent mechanic if the car had been jacked up. No such examination was in fact carried out, though the defendant, who had taken the car in part exchange, had had the car in his possession for a week or so. Having regard to the extreme peril involved in allowing an old car with a defective steering mechanism to be used on the road, I have no hesitation in holding that the defendant in the circumstances was guilty of negligence in failing to make the necessary examination, or at least in failing to warn the plaintiff that no such examination had been carried out. The defendant is accordingly also liable for negligence for the like damages.

As to the third ground, namely, the implied warranty, I think it is sufficient to say that I do not feel disposed in this case, where I have decided in favour of the plaintiff on two independent grounds, to examine this head of claim exhaustively.

. . .

Bearing in mind that the statutory implied warranty now embodied in section 14(1) of the Sale of Goods Act, 1893, was merely a modification of the long existing common law in relation to sales, I feel there is much to be said for the view that in a transaction such as the present, which though not in law a transaction of sale between the parties, is closely akin to such a transaction, the court ought to imply such a condition or warranty if any contractual relationship between the parties can in fact be established. I prefer, however, not to rest my judgment on this view.

Judgment for the plaintiff.

QUESTIONS

1. Is the issue in *Andrews v. Hopkinson* the same as in *Dick Bentley v. Harold Smith?*

2. What function is performed by the notion of warranty in each case?

NOTE ON WARRANTIES AND THE SALE OF GOODS ACT

The preceding four cases have dealt with the common law rules regarding warranties in contracts of sale. The law regarding warranties in the narrower category of sales of goods is based on the provisions of The Sale of Goods Act, R.S.O. 1970, c. 421.

13. In a contract of sale, unless the circumstances of the contract are such as to show a different intention, there is,

    (a)   an implied condition on the part of the seller that in the case of a sale he has a right to sell the goods, and that in the case of an agreement to sell he will have a right to sell the goods at the time when the property is to pass;

    (b)   an implied warranty that the buyer will have and enjoy quiet possession of the goods; and

    (c)   an implied warranty that the goods will be free from any charge or encumbrance in favour of any third party, not declared or known to the buyer before or at the time when the contract is made.

14. Where there is a contract for the sale of goods by description, there is an implied condition that the goods will correspond with the description, and, if the sale is by sample as well as by description, it is not sufficient that the bulk of the goods corresponds with the sample if the goods do not also correspond with the description.

15. Subject to this Act and any statute in that behalf, there is no implied warranty or condition as to the quality or fitness for any particular purpose of goods supplied under a contract of sale, except as follows:

    1.   Where the buyer, expressly or by implication, makes known to the seller the particular purpose for which the goods are required so as to show that the buyer relies on the seller's skill or judgment, and the goods are of a description that it is in the course of the seller's business to supply (whether he is the manufacturer or not), there is an implied condition that the goods will be reasonably fit for such purpose, but in the case of a contract for the sale of a specified article under its patent or other trade name there is no implied condition as to its fitness for any particular purpose.

    2.   Where goods are bought by description from a seller who deals in goods of that description (whether he is the manufacturer or not), there is an implied condition that the goods will be of merchantable quality, but if the buyer has examined the goods, there is no implied condition as regards defects that such examination ought to have revealed.

    3.   An implied warranty or condition as to quality or fitness for a particular purpose may be annexed by the usage of trade.

4. An express warranty or condition does not negative a warranty or condition implied by this Act unless inconsistent therewith.

16. – (1) A contract of sale is a contract for sale by sample where there is a term in the contract, express or implied, to that effect.

(2) In the case of a contract for sale by sample, there is an implied condition,

    (a)   that the bulk will correspond with the sample in quality;

    (b)   that the buyer will have a reasonable opportunity of comparing the bulk with the sample; and

    (c)   that the goods will be free from any defect rendering them unmerchantable that would not be apparent on reasonable examination of the sample.

[The equivalent sections in the English Act of 1893 are ss. 12-15. The sections are identical in language.]

You will notice that in s. 13(a) the Act refers to a "condition", while in the remainder of that section the word used is "warranty". We will explore the significance of the term "condition" in Chapter 5, but for our purposes here it is sufficient that the term "condition" refers to a term of the contract, the breach of which gives rise to a right to repudiate the contract, while breach of a warranty gives rise only to a remedy in damages. No simple test can be laid down for determining in any given case whether a term is one or the other. For example, the Act provides:

12(2). Whether a stipulation in a contract of sale is a condition the breach of which may give rise to a right to treat the contract as repudiated or a warranty the breach of which may give rise to a claim for damages but not to a right to reject the goods and treat the contract as repudiated depends in each case on the construction of the contract, and a stipulation may be a condition, though called a warranty in the contract.

(3). Where a contract of sale is not severable and the buyer has accepted the goods or part thereof, or where the contract is for specific goods the property in which has passed to the buyer, the breach of any condition to be fulfilled by the seller can only be treated as a breach of warranty and not as a ground for rejecting the goods and treating the contract as repudiated, unless there is a term of the contract, express or implied, to that effect.

The effect of this subsection is to limit severely the right of the buyer to get out of the contract. The use of the word "condition" in s. 15 does not in practice give any more right than a claim for damages for breach of warranty.

It is not necessary to explore here the provisions of The Sale of Goods Act. The general effect of these sections is to incorporate into every contract of sale certain terms regarding the quality, broadly defined, of the goods being sold. Only one example of the operation of the Act will be given.

The most important of the implied terms are those contained in s. 15. The term implied by s. 15(1) is that the goods must be fit for a particular purpose. But this term requires, first, that the seller is in the business of selling goods of the kind involved and second, that the buyer has relied on the seller's skill and judgment. The buyer may be held to have relied on the seller's skill and judgment even though the buyer has himself extensive knowledge of the trade or goods. In practice, the courts have adopted a generous approach to s. 15(1), but, by way of counter-balance, the reliance of the buyer must be reasonable. An example of the operation of s. 15(1) [s. 14(1) in the English Act] is found in the case of *Wallis v. Russel*, [1902] 1

I.R. 585. An eyewitness account of the trial, held before Lord O'Brien of Kilfenora, the Lord Chief Justice of Ireland (who spoke with a slight lisp) is as follows:

> Mrs. Wallis had brought her action against Messieurs Russell, who were well-known merchants in Cork, in respect of a crab which had been purchased for her supper, and which made her seriously ill. In those days such actions were not common; but Mrs. Wallis happened to be the mother of one of the most original and courageous solicitors in Cork, who at a later date distinguished himself by having his office premises and their garden, situated in the main street of the town of Midleton, declared to be a holding that was partly agricultural or pastoral, and thus entitled to the benefits of the Irish Land Acts. To a mind of such daring an action about a diseased crab would be a trifle. And so the case was launched. There was no doubt about Mrs. Wallis's illness, or about its cause. The whole point was, whether the salesman had warranted the crab to be fit for human consumption. There is a section of the Sale of Goods Act which deals with the matter; and a young lady went into the box to describe her purchase of the crab.
> "I am a companion to Mrs. Wallis," she said. "I went out to buy her some little tasty thing that she might fancy for her tea; and I suddenly thought of a crab. I knew that Russell's had cooked crabs; so I went in there, and asked the shopman for a nice cooked crab, telling him I wanted it for Mrs. Wallis's supper, so as to make known to him the purpose for which it was to be used." Pether pricked up his ears. "You thaid that?" he asked. "Yes, my Lord." "In thothe very wordth?" "Yes, my Lord." Pether reflected a moment. "Remarkable the thrideth education ith taking," he commented. "Go on." The young lady took up her tale.
> "Well, then, when I had told him that, he looked at the crabs, and he selected one and gave it to me. So I, relying on his skill and judgment, took it — "
> "Thtop, thtop!" cried Pether. "You uthed thothe wordth also?" "Yes, my Lord." "Where were you educated?" "At the Ursuline Convent, Blackrock, my Lord." "And thinth when have the Urthuline Thithters included Thection Fourteen of the Thale of Goodth Act in their curriculum?" "I don't know, my Lord; I did not get beyond domestic economy." "Ah-h! That'th where it ith; they teach you to buy food?" "Yes, my Lord." "And they tell you, 'Never buy anything without telling the shopman what it ith for, tho that you can thay you have relied on his thkill and judgment'?" "Yes, my Lord." "What admirable nunth!" said Pether. "Go on!" But his sarcasm went for naught; the young lady's story was implicitly accepted by the jury; and Mrs. Wallis received such comfort as the law could afford her, and set a headline for the example of other persons unfortunate enough to poison themselves with unfit food. (Maurice Healey, *The Old Munster Circuit,* Dublin, 1939, p. 209).

The other sections do not require extensive discussion here. The Ontario Law Reform Commission recommended extensive changes in The Sale of Goods Act and these, in turn, have been the subject of a Green Paper published by the Department of Consumer and Corporate Affairs in 1973. The OLRC and the Green Paper were concerned that, in the case of consumer transactions at least, the seller be unable to contract out of the basic warranty. This was one of the principal problems with the implied terms under The Sale of Goods Act. It is implicit in that Act that the seller can, if he wants to, contract out of any of the warranties provided in s. 15. We will discuss some of the methods by which the courts and the legislature can control the exercise of this power. (Chapter 6, *infra.*)

The Ontario Government in effect amended The Sale of Goods Act by enacting in 1971 the following section as an amendment to The Consumer Protection Act, S.O. 1971, c. 24:

2. – (1) *The Consumer Protection Act* is amended by adding thereto the following section:

4a. — (1) In this section, "consumer sale" means a contract for the sale of goods made in the ordinary course of business to a purchaser for his consumption or use, but does not include a sale,

    (a)   to a purchaser for resale;

    (b)   to a purchaser whose purchase is in the course of carrying on business;

    (c)   to an association of individuals, a partnership or a corporation;

    (d)   by a trustee in bankruptcy, a receiver, a liquidator or a person acting under the order of a court.

(2) The implied conditions and warranties applying to the sale of goods by virtue of *The Sale of Goods Act* apply to goods sold by a consumer sale and any written term or acknowledgement, whether part of the contract of sale or not, that purports to negative or vary any of such implied conditions and warranties is void and, if a term of a contract, is severable therefrom, and such term or acknowledgement shall not be evidence of circumstances showing an intent that any of the implied conditions and warranties are not to apply.

THE SALE OF GOODS ACT AND THIRD PARTIES

The provisions of The Sale of Goods Act only apply to contracts of sales. So far as the ultimate purchase of goods is concerned, the only contract of sale he has made is with the retailer. The retailer may have bought goods from a wholesaler, who may have bought them from the manufacturer, or even from someone else who may have done nothing to them, and that person may have bought them from the manufacturer. The Sale of Goods Act, therefore, gives no direct remedy to the ultimate purchaser against the manufacturer. In many cases this will mean that the ultimate purchaser, who is often a consumer, has no effective remedy against the manufacturer or even the retailer since the retailer may be far less substantial than the manufacturer and not worth suing. There are also strong policy reasons for imposing liability on the manufacturer. The Ontario Law Reform Commission said in its Report on Consumer Warranties and Guarantees in the Sale of Goods:

"It has often been remarked that in the modern marketing milieu it is the manufacturer who plays the dominant role. It is he who is responsible for putting the goods into the stream of commerce and, in most cases, of creating the consumer demand for them by continuous advertising. The retailer is little more than a way station. It is the manufacturer who endows the goods with their characteristics and it is he who determines the type of materials and components that shall be used and who establishes the quality control mechanism. It is also he who determines what express guarantees shall be given to the consumer and who is responsible for the availability of spare parts and the adequacy of servicing facilities. Almost all the consumer's knowledge about the goods is derived from the labels or markings attached to the goods on the sales literature that accompanies them — and these too originate from the manufacturer."

The Ontario Government introduced a bill in 1976, The Consumer Products Warranties Act, which would have allowed a direct action against the manufacturer by the consumer. The problem of a direct action against the manufacturer by the consumer is known as the problem of vertical privity. The reason that the consumer cannot sue the manufacturer is that the consumer has given no consideration for the promise — the implied promise of merchantability, for example — by the manufacturer.

Another similar problem is known as the problem of horizontal privity.

This comes up when, for example, a member of the consumer's family is injured by defective goods. The purchase may have been made by the husband and the injury may have been suffered by his wife or child. The injured person has given no consideration to anyone and so cannot sue anyone in contract. Again the OLRC recommended that the problems of horizontal privity be avoided by broadening the definition of "consumer". The 1976 bill defined "consumer" as follows:

> 1 (1) In this Act,
> (a) 'consumer' means a natural person who is the owner or has the right to possess and use a consumer product...

The 1976 bill died on the order paper and has not, so far, been revived.

It is interesting and to be expected that, once again, the problems caused by the rules regarding third party beneficiaries are having to be avoided by the use of legislation.

The two cases that follow deal with the issue of privity and third party beneficiary contracts in ways that are entirely typical in the common law. Consider how far the devices used by the courts are satisfactory ways of solving the problem. In particular, consider the measure of damages that a plaintiff could recover under each of the various ways that he can put his claim.

McMORRAN v. DOMINION STORES LTD. AND CRUSH INTERNATIONAL LIMITED

(1977), 14 O.R. (2d) 559. Ontario High Court.

Lerner, J.:- This action is for breach of warranty in the sale and negligence in the manufacture of a bottle of carbonated soda-water.

The defendants, Dominion Stores Limited, will be referred to as "Dominion" and Crush International Limited, as "Crush". The breach of warranty is alleged against Dominion as the vendor of a bottle of carbonated soda-water. Crush is alleged to be liable for negligence in the manufacture of this bottle of soda-water. In the third party proceedings, Dominion, if found liable, claims indemnity from Crush.

About noon of March 3, 1973, the plaintiff purchased several bottles of soft drinks including three 26 oz. bottles of carbonated soda-water from a Dominion groceteria located across the street from his home. The plaintiff carried them directly to his apartment in a shopping cart where he placed them on a bedroom shelf. Before dinner that evening, he took two bottles of the soda-water with other bottled beverages to make mixed drinks for his dinner guests. He placed all bottles on a card table in the living-room. Much later that evening, he took the bottle of soda-water in issue from the same shelf, placed it on the same table and held it with his left hand while he began to unscrew the metal crown with the other hand. While twisting the crown there was a loud explosion or noise and the crown flew from the fingers of his right hand, striking and seriously injuring his right eye.

I find that the plaintiff did not mishandle the bottle or crown (ex. 2) from the moment he removed it from the shelf at Dominion to the moment it exploded. Nor is there any evidence that this bottle was subjected to rough or unusual handling while transported from the manufacturer, Crush, to the shelf at Dominion from which the plaintiff removed it.

This carbonated soda-water was manufactured by Crush at the request of Dominion according to a formula approved by Dominion. The beverage consisted of water, carbon dioxide, sodium bicarbonate and citric acid. Crush used new non-refillable glass bottles purchased from a glass bottle manufacturer and crowns from another manufacturer.

. . .

I find on the balance of probabilities that when the plaintiff began to twist the crown on ex. 2, the defective capping allowed the crown to blow off in his hand prematurely before the gas pressure within the bottle had time to gradually dissipate while the crown was being removed. It is significant that the other two bottles of soda-water which he opened similarly did not explode.

Liability of Dominion Stores Limited

The plaintiff's claim against Dominion is in contract, basing his claim for damages on a breach of the implied warranties set out in the *Sale of Goods Act*, R.S.O. 1970, c. 421, s. 15, paras. 1 and 2, which read as follows:

> 15. Subject to this Act and any statute in that behalf, there is no implied warranty or conditions as to the quality or fitness for any particular purpose of goods supplied under a contract of sale, except as follows:
> 1.   Where the buyer, expressly or by implication, makes known to the seller the particular purpose for which the goods are required so as to show that the buyer relies on the seller's skill or judgment, and the goods are of a description that it is in the course of the seller's business to supply (whether he is the manufacturer or not), there is an implied condition that the goods will be reasonably fit for such purpose, but in the case of a contract for the sale of a specified article under its patent or other trade name there is no implied condition as to its fitness for any particular purpose.
> 2.   Where goods are bought by description from a seller who deals in goods of that description (whether he is the manufacturer or not), there is an implied condition that the goods will be of merchantable quality, but if the buyer has examined the goods, there is no implied condition as regards defects that such examination ought to have revealed.

The plaintiff, by implication, made known to Dominion that he intended to remove the crown by hand from the bottle and use its contents. It was also the ordinary or usual use to which, by implication, the plaintiff as buyer would be expected to put the bottle of beverage. The defendant knew that the bottle of soda-water was purchased to use its contents which use would be impossible without removing the crown. Paragraph 1 of s. 15 spells out a warranty of fitness of the bottled beverage for its ordinary purposes and no special communication needed to be made to the seller for that purpose. The warning printed on the crown was not intended to warn the buyer to examine the crown to determine whether it would fly off prematurely in his hand, but was a warning not to accept the bottle for use if the seal was broken because that kind of defect in the seal might allow the pressure of the gas to escape prematurely and leave the liquid without "carbonization" or "flat" and unpalatable after it was opened. From the words of warning an arrow led down to the lower edge of the crown where the seal was located. I find as fact that the warning was not directed to the defect described, *supra*, and located well above the warning words. On the balance of probabilities, the defect in the crown was present when the plaintiff selected the bottle of beverage from the shelf at Dominion's store which therefore brings home liability to this defendant for breach of warranty.

Liability in this type of case, it would seem to me, is long since beyond doubt where the necessary facts are present.

Liability of Crush International Limited

I begin with the finding that the bottle of soda-water left Crush in a defective condition resulting in the plaintiff's injuries. Has the plaintiff satisfied the onus that the defect was caused by the manufacturer's negligence in the application of the crown to the thread on the bottle?

Where the defect arises in the manufacturing process controlled by the defendant, the inference of negligence is practically irresistible: Waddams, *Products Liability* (1974), p. 54. Either the manufacturer's system was at fault or, if the system was sound, then an individual employee must have been negligent.

On the balance of probabilities, the defect was in the sealing of the crown before the bottle left Crush's plant for delivery to Dominion. The question is whether the opportunity of intermediate examination can relieve the manufacturer of liability in negligence.

. . .

Reverting to my finding of facts herein and after considering the warning printed on the crown with arrows pointing at the flange of the seal at the bottom thereof, it is my view that Crush cannot be absolved from liability by applying the proposition of a possible intermediate examination before use by the plaintiff. In my opinion, even a close and meticulous examination of the crown of the bottle by a reasonable, careful and prudent person, while not in any common-sense view within the contemplation of any of the parties, would not have put the plaintiff on notice that the bottle was in a dangerous condition.

In the result, the defendant, Crush, is liable in negligence to the plaintiff for his damages: . . .

Injuries and damages

The plaintiff was struck in the right eye by the crown. He was in hospital for five days with bilateral patches, gradually improved with a diagnosis of a traumatic iritis from this injury with a small irregular pupil in that eye.

. . .

There will therefore be judgment against both defendants in the sum of $14,020.70, and the costs of the action.

Third party proceedings

The defendant, Dominion, claims indemnity from its co-defendant for breach of contract and relies on s. 15 of the *Sale of Goods Act*. The third party statement of defence of Crush denies that the bottle of soda-water sold and delivered to Dominion was unfit, defective and not of merchantable quality. It is unnecessary to recite the facts upon which liability was found for the plaintiff against Crush in the main action.

Laskin, J.A. [as he then was], in *Allan v. Bushnell T.V. Co. Ltd.; Broadcast News Ltd., Third Party* [1968] 1 O.R. 720 at p. 723, 67 D.L.R. (2d) 499 at p. 502 stated:

> . . . there must be a connection of fact or subject-matter between the cause of action upon which the plaintiff sued and the claim of the defendant for redress against the third party . . .

Indemnity will be implied where one defendant is exposed to liability without any fault of his own by the negligent act of a co-defendant, unless the act is clearly illegal in itself.

Dominion having been found liable to the plaintiff for breach of contract pursuant to s. 15 of the *Sale of Goods Act*, Crush has the same legal obligation to Dominion as the latter had to the plaintiff. The negligence of Crush in the manufacture of the bottle of soda-water precipitated the plaintiff's injuries and damages.

The claim of the plaintiff and that of Dominion in the third party proceedings both sound in contract: *Dominion Chain Co. Ltd. v. Eastern Construction Co. Ltd.* (1976), 12 O.R. (2d) 201, 68 D.L.R. (3d) 385, 1 C.P.C. 13 (C.A.).

Dominion will therefore have judgment against Crush for the amounts that it pays the plaintiff for damages and costs in the main action. Dominion will also have the costs of the third party proceedings against Crush.

Judgment for plaintiff.

SIGURDSON v. HILLCREST SERVICE LTD.; ACKLANDS LTD., THIRD PARTY

(1976), 73 D.L.R. (3d) 132. Saskatchewan Queen's Bench.

[The plaintiffs were Mr. and Mrs. Sigurdson and their son, Michael and Christopher. All the plaintiffs were injured in an accident caused by the installation on Mr. Sigurdson's car of a defective brake hose. There was expert evidence that the defects in the hose could not have been discovered except by cutting the hose in half. The plaintiffs sued the service station that had installed the hose. The service station joined the supplier of the hose as a third party.]

Estey J. [after stating the facts, continued]: I take the view that there were no circumstances in the present case which would suggest to an employee of the defendant that the brake hose was or might be defective when it was delivered to the defendant's place of business by the third party. Indeed there was, prior to installation of the brake hose, no test or examination which could be conducted by the defendant which would locate the foreign object short of destruction of the brake hose. Moreover, the operation of the vehicle from May 1st to June 16th suggests in itself that the actual installation of the brake hose was proper. There is therefore in my opinion no negligence on the part of the defendant in either the installation of the break hose or in the failure to inspect such hose prior to installation. As I have held that there is no negligence on the part of the defendant, I dismiss the actions of the plaintiffs Mrs. Sigurdson and her son Christopher.

The liability of the defendant towards the plaintiff Mr. Sigurdson involves other considerations. While I have already held that the defendant's employees were not guilty of negligence the defendant, in so far as the plaintiff Mr. Sigurdson in concerned, is faced with the provision of the *Sale of Goods Act*, R.S.S. 1965, c. 388, s. 16, which reads:

16. Subject to the provisions of this Act and of any Act in that behalf there is no implied warranty or condition as to the quality of fitness for any particular purpose of goods supplied under a contract of sale except as follows:
1. Where the buyer expressly or by implication makes known to the seller the particular purpose for which the goods are required so as to show that the buyer relies on the seller's skill or judgment and the goods are of a description that it is

in the course of the seller's business to supply, whether he be the manufacturer or not, there is an implied condition that the goods shall be reasonably fit for that purpose;

2. Where goods are bought by description from a seller who deals in goods of that description, whether he is the manufacturer or not, there is an implied condition that the goods shall be of merchantable quality:

Provided that if the buyer has examined the goods there shall be no implied condition with regard to defects which such examination ought to have revealed;

3. An implied warranty or condition as to quality or fitness for a particular purpose may be annexed by usage of trade;

Waddams in his text *Products Liability* (1974) suggests that even in the absence of negligence a repairer may be liable to the plaintiff Mr. Sigurdson for breach of the implied warranty as set out in said s. 16 when the author writes at pp. 18-9:

However, insofar as the defect complained of is caused by defective materials supplied by the installer or repairer, there may be liability even in the absence of negligence for breach of an implied warranty that the materials used are reasonably fit.

The said author points out at p. 76 of his text:

... liability for breach of the implied warranties is strict liability in the sense that it is no defence for the seller to show that he exercised reasonable care or that the defect in the goods was undiscoverable.

I am of the view on the facts of the present case that there was by virtue of the *Sale of Goods Act*, an implied warranty or condition that the brake hose would be "reasonably fit" for the purpose for which it was intended. I find that the said brake hose was not "reasonably fit" in that it contained foreign bodies which eventually caused a rupture and brake failure which failure was the cause of the accident.

. . .

My view is that the defendant may successfully recover from its supplier the third party for a breach of warranty, *i.e.*, that the brake hose was defective or not reasonably fit for the purpose for which it was intended. This point is dealt with by Waddams at p. 189 when the author writes:

Although it is doubtful that one held liable for breach of warranty has a claim for contribution against the manufacturer of the defective goods as a joint tortfeasor, he may have a remedy against his own supplier (whether manufacturer or other distributor) for breach of implied warranty.

I therefore award judgment in favour of the defendant against the third party in the amount of the judgment recovered by the plaintiff against the defendant, together with the taxed costs paid by the defendant to the plaintiff.

Judgment for plaintiff.

[There is no indication in the judgment of the disposition of the claim of Michael Sigurdson. It may be presumed that either it was disposed of on the same grounds as that of his brother, or, since he only received scratches, that he had, in any case, not suffered any compensable loss.]

QUESTIONS

1. What reasons might there be to explain why the plaintiffs did not sue the manufacturer of the hose?

2. Could you make an argument in a case like *Sigurdson v. Hillcrest Service* along the lines of the judgment of Lord Denning in *Jackson v. Horizon Holidays*? If you thought that a court might accept such an argument, what would you argue for as damages? Would you want to establish any further facts than were found by Estey J? Would you have to worry about the applicability of the contract rule or the tort rule regarding remoteness of loss?

The technique of implying terms which the Sale of Goods Act uses is one which we will often see being used. Notice that in *Bristol etc. v. Maggs (supra)*, where the deal was upset because the buyer wanted to get a covenant from the purchaser that he would not compete, the law would not imply any such term into the contract of sale of a business. Without such a term the seller could set himself up in business next door to the business he had sold, and, by keeping his old customers, effectively destroy the buyer's business and wipe out whatever advantage the buyer thought he was getting when he bought the goodwill of the seller's business. Can you think of any good reason for this approach to the sale of a business? Why should the maxim, "Caveat Emptor" flourish unrestrictedly in the sale of a business but not in the sale of goods?

The following case is an unusual example of the technique of using a warranty to get a result that the court obviously wanted to reach.

RANGER v. HERBERT A. WATTS (QUEBEC) LTD. ET AL.

[1970] 2 O.R. 225, 10 D.L.R. (3d) 395. Ontario High Court.

Haines, J.:- Peter Jackson Tobacco Limited is a company manufacturing and selling cigarettes under the brand name of "Peter Jackson". They promote the sale of their product by an extensive radio, television, newspaper and poster campaign urging people to switch to Peter Jackson because in any package the purchaser may find a cash certificate worth $1,000 or $10,000. Their advertising assumes a very interesting format of which ex. 2 is an example. In bold letters at the top appears, "Another Ontario P.J. Smoker Has Just Won $10,000". To ensure maximum eye appeal the $10,000 is in red digits, two inches high and ten inches long. Under it is a large photograph of a smiling man who looks as if he has just won $10,000 and printed beside the photograph in readily readable print is the following:

> Mr. George Lustic, 208 Rutherford Drive, Peterborough, Ontario, asked a friend to bring him two packages of Peter Jackson when he came over to visit. What started to be a very quiet evening at home, turned out to be the most exciting one in his life... inside one of the packs was a P.J. cash certificate worth $10,000! (And that's tax-free!)
> Mr. Lustic said that when he first saw the certificate he couldn't believe his eyes! He had to go to the back door and look at in the light! "First I thought it was for $1,000... then I saw it was a $10,000 certificate... then I got so excited, I asked another friend to come over to confirm that it really was for $10,000!"
> When we asked how he would spend this money, Mr. Lustic replied that after he had some work done around his house, and bought a car, he was going to save the rest. Yes, Peter Jackson certainly made Mr. Lustic a very happy man... and can do the same for you!

Underneath in bold type appears, "Some of the Recent $1,000 Winners" and beside it are three photographs of smiling Ontario citizens.

Prominently displayed in the lower section is a large package of king size Peter Jackson filter tipped cigarettes resting on the replicas of a $10,000 and a $1,000 certificate. The certificates appear to be embossed and may be said to resemble somewhat a bank-note. $10,000 is printed horizontally in large print and vertically in smaller print on the edges. In bold print at the bottom is the word "certificate". The poster then concludes in large red print "The Next $1,000 or $10,000 Winner Can Be You". In exceedingly fine print slightly less than one-sixteenth of an inch high appear the words. "In order to win, you must qualify under the rules appearing on the certificate." It is admitted that no such qualification appears in the television and radio advertisements. The defendants do not rely on these words in the poster or in the newspapers as notice of any condition or limitation to prospective purchasers of cigarettes. It also appears that from time to time the photographs of the smiling winners, their winnings and addresses are changed. There is no suggestion these winners are fictitious. They are *bona fide*. The promotion appears to have been quite successful.

However, the cash certificates are not cash certificates at all, and any impression that the smiling people on the posters or the news media have received cash for their certificates is false. The cash certificate is only a ticket entitling the holder to engage in a contest with the prospect of winning the amount mentioned on it. On the back of the certificate appears this message:

$10,000

Serial No. TR-5010

PETER JACKSON CASH AWARD

This offer is open to all residents of Canada 18 years of age or over, except employees of the manufacturers of Peter Jackson cigarettes, their agents, the judging organization and members of their immediate families.

The holder of this Certificate must answer correctly a time-limited, skill-testing question before being awarded any prize. All decisions of the judges in connection with this offer shall be final. This offer is subject to all federal, provincial and local regulations.

To notify us that you are holding a PETER JACKSON Cash Award Certificate, please write to: P.O. Box 6301, Montreal, Quebec, stating your complete name, address, province, telephone number, age and the serial number appearing on this Certificate. Do NOT mail this Certificate. The serial number will then be recorded and the Certificate subsequently verified and registered in your name.

Because of the second paragraph appearing on the certificate the defendant Peter Jackson Tobacco Ltd. engaged the services of Herbert A. Watts (Quebec) Limited whose sole duty is to develop and conduct the contest and report the result to Peter Jackson Tobacco Ltd. who assume full responsibility for the payment of the awards together with the manner and the fairness in which the contest, if any, is conducted.

Ernest Ranger is 47 years of age, a self-employed trucker. He lives in North Bay with his wife and children. He is a modest man of limited education and rather retiring nature. Because it will be important later it should be noted that he cannot read without his glasses and that his wife is deaf in one ear.

For several years he has read the Peter Jackson posters and listened to their radio and television announcements. He says the offer of cash awards "lured" him to smoke Peter Jackson cigarettes, which he usually bought by the carton.

Early in 1968 he purchased a package of Peter Jackson cigarettes and that day opened it and found a $10,000 certificate. It soon became instant news. His children told their friends and soon Mr. Ranger was the subject of conversation in the community and the recipient of a variety of telephone calls. Some of the callers imitated Peter Jackson and then burst out laughing. He knew a few of them and not others. In the meantime Mr. and Mrs. Ranger had read the certificate, sent the necessary information to Box 6301 in Montreal, and waited for what they expected would be a visit from the Peter Jackson people or a telephone call for an appointment.

From this point the evidence assumes the character of a television comedy and reminds one that truth can be stranger than fiction. Earlier in the week Ernest Ranger had broken his glasses and was awaiting a new pair. The day before his driver had rolled over the truck while unloading it necessitating immediate body repairs. On Friday, March 1, 1968, Mr. Ranger worked all day in the welding shop. He came home after 4 o'clock with sore eyes and an aching head. His wife made him a cup of tea and he lay down to rest. The house is a small one. The telephone is in the living-room which at the time was being repaired by the installation of a new ceiling, as a result there was no light in it nor was there any furniture except the television set. The telephone was in its cradle beside the television. Such light that was available in the room came from the television or was reflected from the kitchen. Present in the house were Mrs. Ranger, a teen-aged daughter Maureen, a 12-year-old son Brian, and two teen-age girls who were neighbours. At 5:45 Maureen awakened her father, saying "Jim Munro's wife wants to speak to you." Jim Munro was a truck driver. Arousing himself, Ernest Ranger walked to the living-room, turned down the sound on the television and answered the telephone. It was not Mrs. Munro. It was Jeanne Emelyanov, the judge of the Peter Jackson award promotion, calling. Fortunately, the conversation was taped and after hearing the recording several times in the presence of the witnesses and with the assistance of counsel, an amended transcript was prepared. For more complete appreciation of the transcript, it must be remembered that Mr. Ranger had received several preceding calls from pranksters, and that he was naturally dubious. He was expecting a visit from the Peter Jackson people, and perhaps some indication of the test. He was entirely unprepared for what was to happen. He had no idea he was about to undergo a test of his mathematical skill requiring him to write. He was without his glasses. Finding himself engaged in the so-called test and that a pencil and paper were required, he called loudly to his deaf wife to bring a pencil and paper. He says that with all his children there were always paper and pencils about but none seemed to be readily available. Finally they were secured. The wife took up a position on the other side of the television and its top became an improvised table. No doubt the teen-agers were the audience. As the judge gave him the question he placed his hand over the telephone mouthpiece and repeated it to his wife. The wife copied the question and when the judge asked to have the question read back Mr. Ranger again placed his hand over the receiver and requested his wife to repeat what she had written. Forgetting he was without his glasses his wife kept shoving the piece of paper towards him. Then in his excitement Mr. Ranger started calling back the numbers and factors to the operator only to find he was wrong. The judge became exasperated. She speaks quickly and sharply. Mr. and Mrs. Ranger were excited. The $10,000 was about to vanish. Twelve-year-old Brian grabbed the paper and pencil and started figuring. His mother retrieved the paper. Then the judge threatened to disqualify Mr. Ranger and from then on he says he has only a vague impression of what happened. No better proof of his confusion is required than the transcript which is as follows:

Judge: Mr. Ranger?

Answer: Yes.

Judge: Are you Mr. Ernest Lorenzo Ranger?

Ranger: Right.

Judge: Did you find a Peter Jackson Cash Award Certificate?

Ranger: (Indecipherable) — Speaking.

Judge: Good evening, sir. This is Jeanne Emelyanov calling. I am representing the panel of judges for the manufacturers of Peter Jackson cigarettes. Now, is it convenient for you to give us about 5 minutes of your time on the phone at this time?

Ranger: Yes.

Judge: All right. Thank you. Now, first of all, would you please confirm the serial number appearing on your Certificate?

Ranger: Just a moment please.

Judge: Thank you.

          (Pause)

Ranger: Hello.

Judge: Yes.

Ranger: TR 5010.

Judge: 5010. Fine. Now as the rules clearly stated, Mr. Ranger, this promotion is open to persons 18 years of age or older. Therefore would you mind confirming your age.

Ranger: 45.

Judge: Thank you. Now for our reference we are saying that today is Friday, March 1st, 1968 and it is now ten minutes to six.

Ranger: Yes.

Judge: I would ask you to bear with me if you hear any noise on the telephone connection. The beep signal which you hear periodically indicates that we are taperecording our conversation, so I would ask you to kindly speak clearly and loudly so we can pick it up entirely.

Ranger: Yes. Okay.

Judge: Now, are you or any member of your immediate family employed by the manufacturers of Peter Jackson cigarettes?

Ranger: No.

Judge: By their affiliates, their agents, their advertising agencies or by Herbert A. Watts (Quebec) Limited?

Ranger: No.

Judge: Thank you. Are you employed, Mr. Ranger?

Ranger: Well, self-employed. I'm a truck driver.

Judge:	You are self-employed — self-employed. All right. And, where do you usually buy your Peter Jackson cigarettes, Mr. Ranger?
Ranger:	Oh, well, anywhere handy. I usually buy them by the carton.
Judge:	And you usually buy them by the carton. Fine. Thank you very much. Now in order to conform to the published rules of this promotion, you are now required to correctly answer this skill-testing question. Do you have a pencil and paper handy?
Ranger:	Yes.
Judge:	All right. The question is a mathematical one, Mr. Ranger...
Ranger:	Just a moment please.
	(Pause)
Ranger:	Yes.
Judge:	Yes. The question is a mathematical one, as I was saying. We will read it to you slowly, then to be sure you have taken it down correctly we will ask you to repeat it to us. After that you will have one and a half minutes from the time we say so to calculate the answer. Is that clear?
Ranger:	Yes.
Judge:	All right. Are you ready to take down the question?
Ranger:	Yes.
Judge:	Here it is. Multiply...
Ranger:	Multiply...
Judge:	Twenty-four by six.
Ranger:	Twenty-four by six.
Judge:	Add...
Ranger:	Add...
Judge:	Three hundred and eighty-eight.
Ranger:	Three hundred and eighty-eight.
Judge:	Divide by seven.
Ranger:	Divide by seven.
Judge:	And finally subtract thirty-eight.
Ranger:	And finally subtract thirty-eight.
Judge:	Right. Now would you repeat that to me before you start, please.
Ranger:	(No comment)
Judge:	Mr. Ranger, will you repeat the question to me before you start working on it please?
Ranger:	(Pause) It's... (Pause) I didn't write it down.
Judge:	Would you repeat the question to me, Mr. Ranger?
Ranger:	(more loudly) I didn't write them down, as a —
Judge:	Well, how did you expect to work it out...
Ranger:	(No comment)
Judge:	Hello... Mr. Ranger...
Ranger:	Yes.
Judge:	Would you repeat that question to me. You... You
Ranger:	Oh... I put the twenty-four...
Judge:	Well, I'll repeat it to you now, would you copy it down please.
Ranger:	Yes.
Judge:	Multiply twenty-four by six.
Ranger:	Multiply twenty-four by six.
Judge:	Add three hundred and eighty-eight.
Ranger:	Add three hundred and eighty-eight.
Judge:	Divide by seven.
Ranger:	Divide by seven.
Judge:	Subtract thirty-eight.
Ranger:	And subtract thirty-eight.
Judge:	Now will you repeat it to me please.
Ranger:	Yes. Add twenty...
	(Pause)

Judge: Mr. Ranger, we'll have to disqualify you if you don't read this back to us immediately.

Ranger: Yes... Add twenty-four...

Judge: No, it's multiply...

Ranger: Multiply twenty-four...

Judge: By six.

Ranger: By six.

Judge: Right.

Ranger: Add three eighty-eight.

Judge: Right.

Ranger: Subtract thirty-seven.

Judge: No. Divide by seven.

Ranger: Divide by seven.

Judge: Divide by seven, and subtract...

Ranger: Subtract thirty-eight.

Judge: Have you got it straight now?

Ranger: Yes.

Judge: Or do you want to read it back?

Ranger: No, I think I have it.

Judge: Would you read it again, please, Mr. Ranger?

Ranger: (Pause)

        Add twenty-four by six.

Judge: Multiply.

Ranger: Multiply.

Ranger: Add three eighty-eight.

Judge: Yes.

Ranger: Subtract...

Judge: No, divide...

Ranger: Divide by seven.

Judge: Right.

Ranger: And a... add thirty-eight.

Judge: Subtract.

Ranger: Subtract thirty-eight rather.

Judge: Have you got it straight now, Mr. Ranger?

Ranger: Yes.

Judge: All right, you have one and a half minutes. Go ahead, please.

        (Pause — 75 seconds)

Judge: Fifteen seconds left.

        (Pause — 15 seconds)

Judge: All right, Mr. Ranger, your time is up. May I have your answer?

Ranger: A hundred and fourteen.

Judge: I beg your pardon?

Ranger: A hundred and fourteen.

Judge: No, I'm sorry, sir. A hundred and fourteen is not the right answer. I am very sorry. Thank you very much and good night sir.

As I have said the transcript of the recording shows the obvious state of confusion. Ernest Ranger was not undergoing a test at all. He was acting only as a relay between his wife or son, and while it appears he remembered the numbers correctly he confused the processes as shown by what might be called the last round. Of the four, three were in error. He was not reading from any paper, was repeating either from memory or from what his wife or son told him. The judge corrected his errors, he repeated the corrections, no doubt to the confusion of his wife and son.

Mrs. Jeanne Emelyanov, the judge, quite frankly stated that had she known the true facts she would have adjourned the test. She impressed me as a superior type of person, although somewhat impatient. Unfortunately, her exasperation and threat to disqualify Mr. Ranger even before he started the test were due to her mistaken impression that Mr. Ranger was stalling. Had she conducted the test in the presence of Mr. Ranger no such comedy of errors would have arisen. She would have learned at once that he could not see without his glasses and why he was making so many errors in his answers. She would have discovered she was not testing Mr. Ranger but rather Mr. Ranger's wife and son. The test would have been called off. The simple reason the judge did not discover the true facts was because she elected to conduct the test by telephone and having elected to do so must accept the disabilities accompanying the means. In the result there never has been a test of Mr. Ranger and I so find. Whatever one may call the telephone dialogue it lacked the essential qualities of fairness inherent in any test.

In my opinion it was quite reasonable for Mr. Ranger to expect that someone from the defendants would contact him, verify his possession of the certificate, and make arrangements for the test. It was not fair for the defendants to select at their pleasure the time and means of the test, and conduct it without notice to a contestant at a time and in a manner when the contestant was unable to reasonably participate in it. The defendants have since changed their methods and now give the contestant reasonable notice.

While many theories of liability were advanced by the parties, I think I need deal only with that advanced by the defendants. As I understand their defence it is this. Despite any impression left by their advertising that the purchaser of Peter Jackson cigarettes would get $10,000 on finding a certificate, the *Criminal Code*, s. 179, prevents them paying the money unless the holder answers a skill-testing question. They take the position that the certificate is only an offer by the defendant Peter Jackson Tobacco Ltd. to enter into a contest with the holder and that the holder accepts the offer by notifying the defendants in accordance with para. 3 on the back of the cash award certificate thereby bringing into existence a contract which embodies the terms set forth in para. 2 of the certificate. The defendants submit that the skill-testing question is a reasonable and fair one. In that I agree. Further I find that if Ernest Ranger had been able to see and write on a piece of paper the simple question "Multiply 24 by 6 and to the result add 388 and divide the answer by 7 and subtract 38" he would have got the correct answer. As a trucker hauling and spreading gravel and asphalt by the cubic yard this simple problem could have been done by him had he a pencil and paper and his glasses.

I find the defendants' duty does not end in developing a reasonable skill-testing question. It requires that the test be conducted with essential fairness to the contestant. That includes at least reasonable advance notice, a communication beforehand of the rules by which the test will be conducted, the institution of means whereby the judge can discover that the contestant is in a reasonable condition to engage in the test, and finally to conduct it fairly under the circumstances. I have already found there never was a test of the plaintiff and I have found on the evidence of the judge herself that she would not have conducted the test had she known the true facts. Nothing more need be said.

The question arises as to the remedy. Is the plaintiff entitled to a test or damages? Prior to the commencement of the litigation the plaintiff offered to undergo a test and the defendants refused. Counsel for the defendants quite fairly says that in the event I find against the defendants they do not ask the plaintiff to undergo a test. I agree. In my opinion the defendants by failing to test the plaintiff as I have found repudiated their contract and the plaintiff is entitled to $10,000 damages with costs on a solicitor-and-client basis.

Before leaving this case may I say I wish to leave open for another Court, in the event this matter goes further, the question of whether Peter Jackson Tobacco Ltd. is liable for damages in tort for the manner in which they conducted their advertising campaign. I find the following facts. Peter Jackson Tobacco Ltd. through their advertising led the public to believe that a purchaser of their cigarettes upon finding a certificate would without more than presenting the certificate receive the cash award; that on the strength of this advertising the plaintiff purchased Peter Jackson cigarettes over a long period of time including the cigarettes in question; that the plaintiff had never heard of s. 179 of the *Criminal Code* nor had reason to believe Peter Jackson Tobacco Ltd. would raise s. 179 of the *Criminal Code* as a reason why it would not implement its advertising. It seems to me the time has arrived for an examination of our law upon the obligation of manufacturers and vendors of products to implement their undertaking given in the news media by nation-wide advertising. By such means they stimulate reliance upon the safety and the quality of their products; and in order to stimulate sales offer a host of prizes. To allow a producer to evade the fair implication of his advertising is to permit him to reap a rich harvest of profit without obligation to the purchaser. Should such a manufacturer or sales agency be permitted to create public confidence, promote their sales, and then plead that the criminal law precludes delivery of the premium? By newspaper, radio and television every home has become the display window of the manufacturer, and the stand of every pitchman. By extraordinary skill the printed and spoken word together with the accompanying art form and drama have become an alluring and attractive means of representation of quality and confidence. Honesty in advertising is a concept worthy of re-examination.

In conclusion may I say that at the request of counsel for the defendants I have treated the defendants as one and have drawn no distinction as to their respective roles.

Judgment for plaintiff.

RANGER v. HERBERT WATTS (QUEBEC) LTD. ET AL.

29 D.L.R. (3d) 650, [1971] 3 O.R. 450. Ontario Court of Appeal; Gale C.J.O., MacKay and Brooke JJ.A.

APPEAL from a judgment of Haines, J., [1970] 2 O.R. 225, 10 D.L.R. (3d) 395, allowing plaintiff's action for breach of contract to recover a prize allegedly lost by the unfair procedure adopted by defendant.

The judgment of the Court was delivered orally by

Gale, C.J.O.:- This is an appeal by the defendants from a judgment pronounced by Haines, J., wherein the learned Judge gave judgment in favour of the plaintiff. The respondent was not called upon to make submissions in this matter.

Despite Mr. Cory's very able argument, the Court is not satisfied that there was any error on the part of the trial Judge in regard to his finding. He found that the test, when considered objectively, was not a test as it lacked the essential qualities of fairness. He added [[1970] 2 O.R. 225 at p. 234, 10 D.L.R. (3d) 395 at p. 404]:

> I have already found there never was a test of the plaintiff and I have found that on the evidence of the judge herself that she would not have conducted the test had she known the true facts.

We see no reason to disturb this finding and furthermore we are of the opinion that he was justified in concluding that by failing to test the respondent correctly the appellants repudiated their contract and that the respondent was entitled to $10,000 damages. The appeal must therefore be dismissed with costs.

I should not leave this matter without pointing out that during the argument the question was raised as to the right of the defendant to impose the condition of the skill-testing question when the plaintiff had responded to the defendants' advertising which offered to sell cigarettes with the possibility of receiving in the package a cash award certificate which from the words was apparently exchangeable for money without complying with any further condition.

Mr. Cory contended that without the addition of the skill-testing question requiring more than a minimal degree of skill the appellants' scheme would have been a lottery and any contract entered into accordingly null and void. It seemed perfectly obvious to us that the average member of the public concerned with such advertising and the offer of a cash award would be quite unaware of the lottery laws as they might be applicable to such scheme. It seemed unrealistic that the appellants who seek to induce persons to buy their products in this manner should be able to take refuge in such a defence.

Appeal dismissed.

QUESTIONS

1. What were the terms of the contract in *Ranger v. Herbert Watts*?
2. What term was breached?
3. What interest was the court protecting?
4. Could protection have been afforded in any other way?

NEGLIGENT MISREPRESENTATION

Several recent cases have transformed the law regarding misrepresentations in one important respect. This has occurred through the development of the tort of negligent misrepresentation. To understand the significance of this development some background is desirable.

We assumed at the beginning of this section that a buyer who was induced to buy something by the deliberate misrepresentation of the seller would have a remedy. The remedy is, of course, based on the fact that the seller has been fraudulent. When one person has been defrauded by another, the first person has a choice of relief. He may have the contract set aside and obtain a refund of anything that he has paid. (This is subject to his being able to return anything that he may have obtained from the fraudulent party. This is the normal requirement of *restitutio in integrum* as a condition of rescission. In practice, the courts are more lenient in deciding if rescission is available in cases of fraudulent as opposed to innocent misrepresentation.) The defendant party may, as an alternative (either because he wants to or has to) affirm the contract and sue for damages. His action here is the tort action for deceit.

It is important to understand the economic effects of these remedies. We can explore these effects by taking a specific example:

> A has a painting for sale. He fraudulently represents that it is by Tom Thompson. In fact, it is a copy. B, relying on A's representations, buys the painting. The painting is worth $200. B pays $2,000. If it were a Tom Thompson it would be worth $3,000.

If B rescinds the contract on the ground of fraud, A gives B back $2,000 and B returns the painting. Such a remedy protects B's reliance losses and may also be regarded as making A disgorge his ill-gotten gains. This is exactly the same remedy as for innocent misrepresentation. The only difference is, as we saw from *Redican v. Nesbitt*, that B's claim is not affected by execution of the contract.

If B sues for damages for deceit he gets $1,800, the difference between what he paid and the value of the painting. The economic effect of this is exactly the same as if B had rescinded. The reason for this is that the action for deceit is a tort remedy and tort damages are measured by the reliance interest. If A had warranted that the painting was by Tom Thompson then B can get $1,000, the profit that he would have made had the picture been as promised. This is the normal expectation interest that is protected by the action for breach of contract. We know that B may sometimes have a choice in cases of breach of contract to sue for his expectation losses (the position he would have been in had the contract been performed) or for restitution or reliance losses (the position he would have been in had the contract never been made). In the case of the picture, the important point is that if A is fraudulent, *i.e.*, if B has a tort remedy, then B gets only his reliance losses.

The effect of the decision in *Heilbut, Symons v. Buckleton* was to deny any damages for an innocent misrepresentation. Damages could only be obtained for breach of warranty. The decision of the House of Lords in *Derry v. Peek* (1889), 14 App. Cas. 337 came at the same problem from a different direction. The House of Lords in that case gave a very restricted scope to the action for deceit. It was said that an action for deceit would only lie for a knowingly false representation. The classic statement in that case was that the false statement must be made "knowingly, or without belief in its truth, or recklessly, careless whether it be true or false" (per Lord Herschell). It was made clear in this case that a mere negligent statement would not provide a basis for an action for deceit.

It did not follow logically that there could be no action for negligent (but non-fraudulent) misrepresentation, but because the measure of recovery would have been the same as for fraudulent misrepresentation, it came to be accepted that the law of torts gave no remedy for non-fraudulent misrepresentations. This was established in *LeLievre v. Gould*, [1893] 1 Q.B. 491. It was confirmed by the Court of Appeal (over a vigorous dissent by Denning L.J. (as he then was)) in *Candler v. Crane, Christmas & Co.*, [1951] 2 K.B. 164. So far as any claim for damages was concerned, a prospective plaintiff had either to sue in fraud (a risky venture, given the very restrictive scope of the tort of deceit) or for breach of warranty (or a simple contract). There were two other factors that have to be borne in mind. The first is, that it makes sense to restrict the scope of the tort of deceit. Fraud is, after all, a criminal offence and a very serious accusation to make. The mere fact that an allegation of fraud is made against a businessman could have devastating consequences. The second factor is that the law of torts has never been receptive to the protection of purely economic interests. Generally speaking, a cause of action in tort arises only when there is some physical damage to property or injury to the person of the plaintiff. (See: *Gypsum Carrier Inc. v. The Queen*, (1977), 78 D.L.R. (3d) 175, Federal Court, Trial Division; Collier J.)

We need not consider here whether or not this attitude is justified: it is sufficient for our purposes to note that it existed.

The case that always caused difficulty under the approach that has just been discussed is the following:

> A, an accountant, is employed by B to provide financial statements for a firm owned by B. A knows that C, a prospective investor in the firm, will rely on the statements submitted by A. A prepares the statements negligently, C relies on them and loses his investment.

B could sue A for any losses that he suffered since B had a contract with A. C, however, could not sue A since there was no contract (C was not a party and had given no consideration). Neither could C sue A in tort since A had been negligent but not fraudulent.

All this was changed by the decision of the House of Lords in *Hedley Byrne v. Heller*, [1964] A.C. 465. In that case an advertising agency requested information on a client's credit worthiness from a bank. The agency received a favourable report, and, in reliance on the report, incurred expenses on behalf of the client. The report had been negligently prepared. The House of Lords was prepared to hold that the agency could sue the bank for its negligent misrepresentation.

It is obvious that this development could solve the problem of the shirtless investor who had relied on the negligent accountant. It is also obvious that it can bridge the gap between the remedy for fraud and the remedy for breach of warranty in cases where there is a contract.

The scope of the remedy given in *Hedley Byrne v. Heller* as it has been applied in contracts cases is explored in the following cases. It is clear that development in this area has not yet stopped.

ESSO PETROLEUM CO. LTD. v. MARDON

[1976] Q.B. 801. Court of Appeal (England); Lord Denning M.R., Ormrod and Shaw L. JJ.

Lord Denning M.R. "This is," said the judge, "a tragic story of wasted endeavour and financial disaster." It is a long story starting as long ago as 1961, and finishing in 1967. Since then eight years have been spent in litigation.

In 1961 Esso Petroleum wanted an outlet for their petrol in Southport. They found a vacant site which was very suitable. It was on Eastbank Street, one of the busiest streets of the town. It had already got outline planning permission for a filling station. Esso thought of putting in a bid for the site. But before doing so, they made calculations to see if it would be a paying proposition. They made a careful forecast of the "estimated annual consumption" of petrol. This was the yardstick by which they measured the worth of a filling station. They called it the "e.a.c." In this case they estimated that the throughput of petrol would reach 200,000 gallons a year by the second year after development. This would accrue to their benefit by sales of petrol. In addition, they would get a substantial rental from a tenant. On May 25, 1961, the Esso local representatives recommended the go ahead. They gave the figures, and said: "We feel most strongly that this does genuinely represent a first-class opportunity of gaining representation in the centre of Southport." On that recommendation Esso bought the site and proceeded to erect a service station.

But then something happened which falsified all their calculations. Esso had thought that they could have the forecourt and pumps fronting on to the busy main street. But the Southport Corporation, who were the planning authority, refused to allow this. They insisted that the station should be built "back to front". So that only the showroom fronted on to the main street. The forecourt and pumps were at the back of the site and only accessible by side streets. They could not be seen from the main street. Esso had no choice but to comply with these planning requirements. They built the station "back to front." It was finished early in 1963.

Now at this point Esso made an error which the judge described as a "fatal error." They did not revise their original estimate which they had made in 1961. They still assessed the e.a.c. (estimated annual consumption) of petrol at 200,000 gallons. Whereas they should have made a reappraisal in the light of the building being now "back to front." This adversely affected the site's potential: because passing traffic could not see the station. It would reduce the throughput greatly. The judge found that this "fatal error" was due to want of care on the part of Esso. There can be no doubt about it.

It was under the influence of this "fatal error" that Esso sought to find a tenant for the service station. They found an excellent man, Mr. Philip Lionel Mardon. He was seen by Esso's local manager, Mr. Leitch. Now Mr. Leitch had had 40 years' experience in the petrol trade. It was on his calculations and recommendations that Esso had bought this site and developed it. At the decisive interviews Mr. Leitch was accompanied by the new area manager, Mr. Allen. I will give what took place in the words of the judge:

> "Mr. Mardon was told that Esso estimated that the throughput of the Eastbank Street site, in its third year of operation, would amount to 200,000 gallons a year. I also find that Mr. Mardon then indicated that he thought 100,000 to 150,000 gallons would be a more realistic estimate, but he was convinced by the far greater expertise of, particularly, Mr. Leitch. Mr. Allen is a far younger man and, although on his appointment as manager for the area I am satisfied he made his own observations as to the potentiality of the Eastbank Street site, in the result he accepted Mr. Leitch's estimate. Mr. Mardon, having indicated that he thought that a lower figure would be a more realistic estimate, had his doubts quelled by the experience and the estimate furnished by Mr. Leitch; and it was for that reason, I am satisfied, because of what he was told about the estimated throughput in the third year, that he then proceeded to negotiate for and obtain the grant of a three-year tenancy at a rent of £2,500 a year for the first two years, rising to £3,000 yearly in the last year."

To the judge's summary, I would only add a few questions and answers by Mr. Allen in evidence:

"(Q) Now we know that the person who originally put forward this estimated 200,000 gallons forecast was Mr. Leitch? (A) Yes. (Q) Would somebody have checked Mr. Leitch's figures before they reached you? (A) Oh, very much so.... (Q) You have told my Lord that you accept that, at that interview, ... you might have said that Eastbank was capable of achieving a throughput of 200,000 gallons after the second complete year? (A) Yes. (Q) Would that have been your honest opinion at the time? (A) Most certainly."

All the dealings were based on that estimate of a throughput of 200,000 gallons. It was on that estimate that Esso developed the site at a cost of £40,000: and that the tenant agreed to pay a rent of £2,500, rising to £3,000. A few answers by Mr. Allen will show this:

"(Q) Would you agree that the potential throughput of a station is an important factor in assessing what rent to charge a tenant? (A) Yes.... (Q) The rent would be substantially higher if your estimate was one of 200,000 gallons than if your estimate was one of 100,000 gallons? (A) Generally speaking, that is right.... (Q) You would be able to command a higher rent if the throughput was 200,000 than if it was 100,000? (A) Had it been an estimated throughput of 100,000 gallons, they [Esso] would not have bought it in the first place."

Having induced Mr. Mardon to accept, Mr. Leitch and Mr. Allen sent this telegram to their head office:

"We have interviewed a Mr. Philip Lionel Mardon for tenancy and find him excellent in all respects. We recommend strongly that he be granted tenancy."

So a tenancy was granted to Mr. Mardon. It was dated April 10, 1963, and was for three years at a rent of £2,500 for the first two years, and £3,000 for the third year. It required him to keep open all day every day of the week, including Sunday. It forbade him to assign or underlet.

On the next day Mr. Mardon went into occupation of the service station and did everything that could be desired of him. He was an extremely good tenant and he tried every method to increase the sales and profitability of the service station. Esso freely acknowledge this.

But the throughput was most disappointing. It never got anywhere near the 200,000 gallons. Mr. Mardon put all his available capital into it. It was over £6,000. He raised an overdraft with the bank and used it in the business. He put all his work and endeavour into it. No one could have done more to make it a success. Yet when the accounts were taken for the first 15 months, the throughput was only 78,000 gallons. After paying all outgoings, such as rent, wages and so forth, there was a net loss of £5,800. The position was so serious that Mr. Mardon felt he could not continue. On July 17, 1964, he wrote to Mr. Allen: "I reluctantly give notice to quit forthwith. This is an endeavour to salvage as much as I can in lieu of inevitable bankruptcy." Mr. Allen did not reply in writing, but saw Mr. Mardon. As a result he put in a written report to his superiors recommending that Mr. Mardon's rent should be reduced to £1,000 a year, plus a surcharge according to the amount of petrol sold. Mr. Allen telexed to his superiors on several occasions pressing for a decision. It culminated in a telex he sent on August 28, 1964:

"Unless we hear soon the tenant is likely to resign and we will have difficulty in replacing this man with a tenant of the same high standard."

This brought results. On September 1, 1964, a new tenancy agreement was made in writing. It granted Mr. Mardon a tenancy for one year certain and thereafter determinable on three months' notice. The rent was reduced to £1,000 a year, and a surchage of 1d. to 2d. a gallon, according to the amount sold.

Again Mr. Mardon tried hard to make a success of the service station: but again he failed. It was not his fault. The site was simply not good enough to have a throughput of more than 60,000 or 70,000 gallons. He lost more and more money over it. In order to help him, Esso tried to get another site for him — a "cream" site — so that he could run the two sites in conjunction to offset his losses. But they never found him one. Eventually on January 1, 1966, he wrote to Esso appealing to them to find a solution. He consulted solicitors who wrote on his behalf. But Esso did nothing to help. Quite the contrary. They insisted on the petrol being paid for every day on delivery. On August 28, 1966 (by some mistake or misunderstanding while Mr. Mardon was away), they came and drained his tanks of petrol and cut off his supplies. That put him out of business as a petrol station. He carried on as best he could with odd jobs for customers, like washing cars. Esso had no pity for him. On December 1, 1966, they issued a writ against him claiming possession and £1,133 13s. 9d. for petrol supplied. This defeated him. On March 7, 1967, he gave up the site. He had tried for four years to make a success of it. It was all wasted endeavour. He had lost all his capital and had incurred a large overdraft. It was a financial disaster.

Such being the facts, I turn to consider the law. It is founded on the representation that the estimated throughput of the service station was 200,000 gallons. No claim can be brought under the Misrepresentation Act 1967, because that Act did not come into force until April 22, 1967: whereas this representation was made in April 1963. So the claim is put in two ways. First, that the representation was a collateral warranty. Second, that it was a negligent misrepresentation. I will take them in order.

Collateral warranty

Ever since *Heilbut, Symons & Co. v. Buckleton* [1913] A.C. 30, we have had to contend with the law as laid down by the House of Lords that an innocent misrepresentation gives no right to damages. In order to escape from that rule, the pleader used to allege — I often did it myself — that the misrepresentation was fraudulent, or alternatively a collateral warranty. At the trial we nearly always succeeded on collateral warranty. We had to reckon, of course, with the dictum of Lord Moulton, at p. 47, that "such collateral contracts must from their very nature be rare." But more often than not the court elevated the innocent misrepresentation into a collateral warranty: and thereby did justice — in advance of the Misrepresentation Act 1967. I remember scores of cases of that kind, especially on the sale of a business. A representation as to the profits that had been made in the past was invariably held to be a warranty. Besides that experience, there have been many cases since I have sat in this court where we have readily held a representation — which induces a person to enter into a contract — to be a warranty sounding in damages. I summarised them in *Dick Bentley Productions Ltd. v. Harold Smith (Motors) Ltd.* [1965] 1 W.L.R. 623, 627, when I said:

> "Looking at the cases once more, as we have done so often, it seems to me that if a representation is made in the course of dealings for a contract for the very purpose of inducing the other party to act upon it, and actually inducing him to act upon it, by entering into the contract, that is prima facie ground for inferring that

it was intended as a warranty. It is not necessary to speak of it as being collateral. Suffice it that it was intended to be acted upon and was in fact acted on."

Mr. Ross-Munro, retaliated, however, by citing *Bisset v. Wilkinson* [1927] A.C. 177, where the Privy Council said that a statement by a New Zealand farmer that an area of land "would carry 2,000 sheep" was only an expression of opinion. He submitted that the forecast here of 200,000 gallons was an expression of opinion and not a statement of fact: and that it could not be interpreted as a warranty or promise.

Now I would quite agree with Mr. Ross-Munro that it was not a warranty — in this sense — that it did not *guarantee* that the throughput *would be* 200,000 gallons. But, nevertheless, it was a forecast made by a party — Esso — who had special knowledge and skill. It was the yardstick (the e.a.c.) by which they measured the worth of a filling station. They knew the facts. They knew the traffic in the town. They knew the throughput of comparable stations. They had much experience and expertise at their disposal. They were in a much better position than Mr. Mardon to make a forecast. It seems to me that if such a person makes a forecast, intending that the other should act upon it — and he does act upon it, it can well be interpreted as a warranty that the forecast is sound and reliable in the sense that they made it with reasonable care and skill. It is just as if Esso said to Mr. Mardon; "Our forecast of throughput is 200,000 gallons. You can rely upon it as being a sound forecast of what the service station should do. The rent is calculated on that footing." If the forecast turned out to be an unsound forecast such as no person of skill or experience should have made, there is a breach of warranty. Just as there is a breach of warranty when a forecast is made — "expected to load" by a certain date — if the maker has no reasonable grounds for it: see *Samuel Sanday and Co. v. Keighley, Maxted and Co.* (1922) 27 Com. Cas. 296; or bunkers "expected 600/700 tons": see *Efploia Shipping Corporation Ltd. v. Canadian Transport Co. Ltd. (The Pantanassa)* [1958] 2 Lloyd's Rep. 449, 455-457 by Diplock J. It is very different from the New Zealand case where the land had never been used as a sheep farm and both parties were equally able to form an opinion as to its carrying capacity: see particularly *Bisset v. Wilkinson* [1927] A.C. 177, 183-184.

In the present case it seems to me that there was a warranty that the forecast was sound, that is, Esso made it with reasonable care and skill. That warranty was broken. Most negligently Esso made a "fatal error" in the forecast they stated to Mr. Mardon, and on which he took the tenancy. For this they are liable in damages. The judge, however, declined to find a warranty. So I must go further.

Negligent misrepresentation
Assuming that there was no warranty, the question arises whether Esso are liable for negligent misstatement under the doctrine of *Hedley Byrne & Co. Ltd. v. Heller & Partners Ltd.* [1964] A.C. 465. It has been suggested that *Hedley Byrne* cannot be used so as to impose liability for negligent pre-contractual statements: and that, in a pre-contract situation, the remedy (at any rate before the Act of 1967) was only in warranty or nothing. Thus in *Hedley Byrne* itself Lord Reid said, at p. 483: "Where there is a contract there is no difficulty as regards the contracting parties: the question is whether there is a warranty." And in *Oleificio Zucchi S.p.A. v. Northern Sales Ltd.* [1965] 2 Lloyd's Rep. 496, 519, McNair J. said:

"... as at present advised, I consider the submission advanced by the buyers, that the ruling in [*Hedley Byrne* [1964] A.C. 465] applies as between contracting parties, is without foundation."

As against these, I took a different view in *McInerny v. Lloyds Bank Ltd.* [1974] 1 Lloyd's Rep. 246, 253 when I said:

"... if one person, by a negligent misstatement, induces another to enter into a contract — with himself or with a third person — he may be liable in damages."

In arguing this point, Mr. Ross-Munro took his stand in this way. He submitted that when the negotiations between two parties resulted in a contract between them, their rights and duties were governed by the law of contract and not by the law of tort. There was, therefore, no place in their relationship for *Hedley Byrne*, which was solely on liability in tort. He relied particularly on *Clark v. Kirby-Smith*, [1964] Ch. 506 where Plowman J. held that the liability of a solicitor for negligence was a liability in contract and not in tort, following the observations of Sir Wilfrid Greene M.R. in *Groom v. Crocker*, [1939] 1 K.B. 194, 206. Mr. Ross-Munro might also have cited *Bagot v. Stevens Scanlan & Co. Ltd.*, [1966] 1 Q.B. 197, about an architect; and other cases too. But I venture to suggest that those cases are in conflict with other decisions of high authority which were not cited in them. These decisions show that, in the case of a professional man, the duty to use reasonable care arises not only in contract, but is also imposed by the law apart from contract, and is therefore actionable in tort. It is comparable to the duty of reasonable care which is owed by a master to his servant, or vice versa. It can be put either in contract or in tort: see *Lister v. Romford Ice and Cold Storage Co. Ltd.*, [1957] A.C. 555, 587 by Lord Radcliffe and *Matthews v. Kuwait Bechtel Corporation*, [1959] 2 Q.B. 57. The position was stated by Tindal C.J., delivering the judgment of the Court of Exchequer Chamber in *Boorman v. Brown* (1842), 3 Q.B. 511, 525-526:

"That there is a large class of cases in which the foundation of the action springs out of privity of contract between the parties, but in which, nevertheless, the remedy for the breach, or non-performance, is indifferently either assumpsit or case upon tort, is not disputed. Such are actions against attorneys, surgeons, and other professional men, for want of competent skill or proper care in the service they undertake to render: ... The principle in all these cases would seem to be that the contract creates a duty, and the neglect to perform that duty, or the nonfeasance, is a ground of action upon a tort."

That decision was affirmed in the House of Lords in (1844), 11 Cl. & Fin. 1, when Lord Campbell, giving the one speech, said, at p. 44:

"... wherever there is a contract, and something to be done in the course of the employment which is the subject of that contract, if there is a breach of a duty in the course of that employment, the plaintiff may either recover in tort or in contract."

To this there is to be added the high authority of Viscount Haldane L.C., in *Nocton v. Lord Ashburton*, [1914] A.C. 932, 956:

"... the solicitor contracts with his client to be skilful and careful. For failure to perform his obligation he may be made liable at law in contract or even in tort, for negligence in breach of a duty imposed on him."

That seems to me right. A professional man may give advice under a contract for reward; or without a contract, in pursuance of a voluntary assumption of responsibility, gratuitously without reward. In either case he is under one and the same duty to use reasonable care: see *Cassidy v. Ministry of Health,* [1951] 2 K.B. 343, 359-360. In the one case it is by reason of a term implied by law. In the other, it is by reason of a duty imposed by law. For a breach of that duty he is liable in damages; and those damages should be, and are, the same, whether he is sued in contract or in tort.

It follows that I cannot accept Mr. Ross-Munro's proposition. It seems to me that *Hedley Byrne & Co. Ltd. v. Heller & Partners Ltd.,* properly understood, covers this particular proposition: if a man, who has or professes to have special knowledge or skill, makes a representation by virtue thereof to another — be it advice, information or opinion — with the intention of inducing him to enter into a contract with him, he is under a duty to use reasonable care to see that the representation is correct, and that the advice, information or opinion is reliable. If he negligently gives unsound advice or misleading information or expresses an erroneous opinion, and thereby induces the other side to enter into a contract with him, he is liable in damages. This proposition is in line with what I said in *Candler v. Crane, Christmas & Co.,* [1951] 2 K.B. 164, 179-180, which was approved by the majority of the Privy Council in *Mutual Life and Citizens' Assurance Co. Ltd. v. Evatt,* [1971] A.C. 793. And the judges of the Commonwealth have shown themselves quite ready to apply *Hedley Byrne,* between contracting parties: see in Canada, *Sealand of the Pacific Ltd. v. Ocean Cement Ltd.* (1973), 33 D.L.R. (3d) 625; and in New Zealand, *Capital Motors Ltd. v. Beecham,* [1975] 1 N.Z.L.R. 576.

Applying this principle, it is plain that Esso professed to have — and did in fact have — special knowledge or skill in estimating the throughput of a filling station. They made the representation — they forecast a throughput of 200,000 gallons — intending to induce Mr. Mardon to enter into a tenancy on the faith of it. They made it negligently. It was a "fatal error." And thereby induced Mr. Mardon to enter into a contract of tenancy that was disastrous to him. For this misrepresentation they are liable in damages.

The measure of damages

Mr. Mardon is not to be compensated here for "loss of a bargain." He was given no bargain that the throughput *would* amount to 200,000 gallons a year. He is only to be compensated for having been induced to enter into a contract which turned out to be disastrous for him. Whether it be called breach of warranty or negligent misrepresentation, its effect was *not* to warrant the throughput, but only to induce him to enter the contract. So the damages in either case are to be measured by the loss he suffered. Just as in *Doyle v. Olby (Ironmongers) Ltd.,* [1969] 2 Q.B. 158, 167 he can say: "... I would not have entered into this contract at all but for your representation. Owing to it, I have lost all the capital I put into it. I also incurred a large overdraft. I have spent four years of my life in wasted endeavour without reward; and it will take me some time to re-establish myself."

For all such loss he is entitled to recover damages. It is to be measured in a similar way as the loss due to a personal injury. You should look into the future so as to forecast what would have been likely to happen if he had never entered into this contract: and contrast it with his position as it is now as a result of entering into it. The future is necessarily problematical and can only be a rough-and-ready estimate. But it must be done in assessing the loss.

The new agreement of September 1, 1964

The judge limited the loss to the period from April 1963 to September 1964, when the new agreement was made. He said that from September 1, 1964, Mr. Mardon was carrying on the business "on an entirely fresh basis, of which the negligent misstatement formed no part."

I am afraid I take a different view. It seems to me that from September 1, 1964, Mr. Mardon acted most reasonably. He was doing what he could to retrieve the position, not only in his own interest, but also in the interest of Esso. It was Esso who were anxious for him to stay on. They had no other suitable tenant to replace him. They needed him to keep the station as a going concern and sell their petrol. It is true that by this time the truth was known — that the throughput was very far short of 200,000 gallons — but nevertheless, the effect of the original misstatement was still there. It laid a heavy hand on all that followed. The new agreement was an attempt to mitigate the effect. It was not a fresh cause which eliminated the past. It seems to me that the losses after September 1, 1964, can be attributed to the original misstatement, just as those before.

The company position

The initial capital of £6,270 was not provided by Mr. Mardon personally out of his own bank account. It was provided by a private company in which he and his wife held all the shares. It was suggested that this, in some way, prevented Mr. Mardon from claiming for the loss of it. The judge rejected this suggestion: and so would I. The business of this filling station was undoubtedly the personal business of Mr. Mardon. The money put into it might be obtained by overdraft at the bank or by loan from his own private company — but wherever it came from, it was a loss to him: and he can recover that loss. It is no concern of Esso where it came from: compare *Dennis v. London Passenger Transport Board* [1948] 1 All E.R. 779.

If Mr. Mardon had not been induced to enter into the contract, it is fair to assume that he would have found an alternative business in which to invest his capital. (The judge said so.) It is also fair to assume (as he is a very good man of business) that he would have invested it sufficiently well so that he would not have lost the capital. Nor would he have incurred any overdraft or liabilities that were not covered by his assets. And it may be assumed that he would have made a reasonable return by way of earnings for his own work (in addition to return from his capital). But equally it must be remembered that after March 1967 (when he gave up the site at Southport) he should have been able (if fit) to take other employment or start another business and thus mitigate his loss: and gradually get restored to a position equal to that which he would have had if he had never gone into the Esso business. It would take him some time to do this. So the loss of earnings could only be for a limited number of years.

On this footing, the loss which he has suffered would seem to be as follows (subject to further argument by the parties): Capital loss: cash put into the business and lost, £6,270; overdraft incurred in running the business, £7,774. Loss of earnings to be discussed. There will be interest to be added for a period to be discussed.

Mr. Mardon also claimed damages for having to sell his house to pay off the overdraft. That seems to me too remote and should be compensated by interest on the overdraft. He also suffered in health by reason of all the worry over this disaster, and was off work. That should be compensated by loss of future earnings.

Conclusion

I would like to express my appreciation of the full and careful way in which the judge found the facts and analysed the law. It has been most helpful to the determining of the case. The result is that Mr. Mardon is entitled to substantial damages on his counterclaim. There remains the issues of interest and costs to be discussed. We are also willing to hear further argument on the assessment of damages.

[Ormrod and Shaw L.JJ. wrote judgments agreeing with Lord Denning.]

QUESTIONS

1. Could the approach of either the warranty cases like *Dick Bentley v. Harold Smith* or a case like *Esso v. Mardon* be used to provide a basis for the enforcement of an obligation to bargain in good faith?

2. What would be the remedy provided under each of these approaches for breach of the obligation to bargain in good faith?

NUNES DIAMONDS v. DOM. ELEC. CO.

(1972), 26 D.L.R. (3d) 699. Supreme Court of Canada; Martland, Judson, Spence, Pigeon and Laskin JJ.

[The appellant, plaintiff, was a diamond merchant. He had a contract with the respondent, defendant, under which the defendant supplied burglary protection for the appellant's premises. The contract between the parties limited the defendant's liability for breach of contract to $50. The premises of one Baumgold, another diamond merchant, were broken into and a large quantity of diamonds was stolen. Baumgold's premises were protected by the defendant's system. The alarm had not gone off when the burglary had occurred. It was never determined how the alarm was circumvented. Since the appellant was protected in exactly the same way as Baumgold had been, he became worried that his premises were not burglar-proof. The appellant, therefore, asked someone from the respondent to come and inspect his system. This person (who was never positively identified) said to one of the appellant's employees, "even our own engineers could not go through this system without setting an alarm." The respondent also sent to the appellant copies of letters stating that the system installed at Baumgold's premises had performed its job properly, and that efforts were still being made to solve the burglary. The respondent also undertook to explain (once it knew what had happened) how the Baumgold burlgary had occurred. Before the respondent had fulfilled this undertaking, the appellant's premises were broken into by thieves who circumvented the alarm system, and a large quantity of diamonds was stolen.

An action was brought by the appellant's insurers under their rights of subrogation, in the appellant's name, for damages equal to the total value of the loss (which far exceeded $50). The trial judge and the Ontario Court of Appeal both dismissed the action.]

Pigeon, J. The appellant relies upon the judgment of the House of Lords in *Hedley Byrne & Co. Ltd. v. Heller & Partners Ltd.*, [1964] A.C. 465, in which it was said that there might be, in certain circumstances, a liability for negligent misrepresentation. No finding of negligence was made because it was held that disclaimers of responsibility were sufficient to negative any duty of care which might have existed. The speeches make it clear that it is not every negligent statement which may give rise to a claim in damages. Lord Reid's formulation at p. 486, that is quoted by my brother Spence, was considered by the Privy Council in a recent Australian case, *Mutual Life & Citizens' Assurance Co. Ltd. et al. v. Evatt*, [1971] 1 All E.R. 150, and was the subject of the following observations by Lord Diplock at p. 159:

> This is not the language of statutory codification of the law of tort but of judicial exposition of the reasons for reaching a particular decision on the facts of the case. Read out of the context in which the whole argument in *Hedley Byrne* proceeded, i.e., advice given in the course of a business or profession which involved the giving of skilled, competent and diligent advice, these words are wide enough to sustain the respondent's case in the instant appeal. But in their Lordships' view the reference to "such care as the circumstances require" pre-supposes an ascertainable standard of skill, competence and diligence with which the advisor is acquainted or had represented that he is. Unless he carries on the business or profession of giving advice of that kind he cannot be reasonably expected to know whether any and if so what degree of skill, competence or diligence is called for, and a fortiori, in their Lordships' view, he cannot be reasonably held to have accepted the responsibility of conforming to a standard of skill, competence and diligence of which he is unaware, simply because he answers the enquiry with knowledge that the advisee intends to rely on his answer. This passage should in their Lordships' view be understood as restricted to advisors who carry on the business or profession of giving advice of the kind sought and to advice given by them in the course of that business.

On that view, it was decided that the claimant could not recover the loss suffered by reason of erroneous information negligently given by an insurance company concerning the financial stability of an associated company. Lord Diplock said at pp. 160-1:

> The amendments introduced in the Court of Appeal state the respects in which it is alleged that the company was, and was known by the respondent to be, in a better position that he was to give reliable advice on the subject-matter of his enquiry....
>
> In their Lordships' view these additional allegations are insufficient to fill the fatal gap in the declaration that it contains no averment that the company to the knowledge of the respondent carried on the business of giving advice on investments or in some other way had let it be known to him that they claimed to possess the necessary skill and competence to do so and were prepared to exercise the necessary diligence to give reliable advice to him on the subject-matter of his enquiry. In the absence of any allegation to this effect the respondent was not entitled to assume that the company had accepted any other duty towards him than to give an honest answer to his enquiry nor, in the opinion of their Lordships, did the law impose any higher duty on them.

D.E.P. did not act in any fiduciary or advisory capacity towards Nunes. Its situation was that of a party contracting to supply specified services. The insurance brokers were those who were giving advice to Nunes. By giving them information, D.E.P. did not cease to be a contractor and become an advisor to the appellant on the matter of burglary protection. If it did make an honest, but inaccurate, statement as to the performance of its system it did not thereby assume responsibility for all damage which might thereafter be sustained by the appellant if its system, on his premises, was circumvented.

This is not a case where a person seeks information from another, whose business it is to give such information. It is not a case of misrepresentation leading to the making of a contract. It is a case in which, the parties having mutually established their respective rights and obligations by contract, it is sought to impose upon one of them a much greater obligation than that fixed by the contract by reason of an alleged misrepresentation as to the infallibility of the system which it provides. In essence, the appellant's position is that, although he had agreed to accept the respondent's system for what it was worth, and that the respondent was not to be an insurer, he can now claim in damages because the respondent had subsequently represented that the system could not be circumvented, and such circumvention had occurred.

Furthermore, the basis of tort liability considered in *Hedley Byrne* is inapplicable to any case where the relationship between the parties is governed by a contract, unless the negligence relied on can properly be considered as "an independent tort" unconnected with the performance of that contract, as expressed in *Elder, Dempster & Co., Ltd. v. Paterson, Zochonis & Co., Ltd.,* [1924] A.C. 522 at p. 548. This is specially important in the present case on account of the provisions of the contract with respect to the nature of the obligations assumed and the practical exclusion of responsibility for failure to perform them.

It is an essential basis of the contract between the parties that D.E.P. is not to be in the situation of an insurer. It is in consideration of this stipulation that the charges are established "solely on the probable value of the service", not on the value of the goods intended to be protected. To make the protection company liable, in the case of the failure of its protection system, not for the stipulated nominal damages ($50) but for the full value of the goods to be protected, is a fundamental alteration of the contract.

In my view, the representations relied on by appellant cannot be considered as acts independent of the contractual relationship between the parties. This can be readily verified by asking the question: Would these representations have been made if the parties had not been in the contractual relationship in which they stood? Therefore, the question of liability arising out of those representations should not be approached as if the parties had been strangers, but on the basis of the contract between them. Hence the question should be: May this contract of service be considered as having been turned into the equivalent of a contract of insurance, by virtue of inaccurate or incomplete representations respecting the actual value of the protection service supplied? In my view, there is no doubt that this question should be answered in the negative. There is nothing from which it can properly be inferred that Nunes considered that the contract had been so altered and it is perfectly obvious that D.E.P.'s management never intended to assume such obliations.

Irrespective of my conclusion on that point, I must say that it does not appear to me that Nunes has shown that damages claimed were caused by the statement made and the letters written in October, 1959. In order to support the claim it was suggested that, if not reassured by the statement and the letters as to the value of the protection system, other precautions would have been taken whereby the loss could have been avoided. Those other precautions are: (a) adding another protective device; (b) reducing the inventory; (c) using a bank vault.

Let us see what Nunes' vice-president, D.F. Edminson, said about other protection:

Well after the Baumgold robbery, or call it burglary, we contacted — we made investigations from other protective companies.

Q. Yes? A. To see if they had something to offer, which we could install, something which could give us further protection.

Q. Yes? A. I think this is what was our immediate —

Q. Did you take on any other protection? A. No, we didn't. We considered one other company, but decided not to take them on.

Q. And what was the basis of your decision insofar as you personally were concerned? A. Personally I was satisfied that the company we were considering did not have a central alarm system, and that the Dominion Electric still had a system that was invulnerable, and I was quite satisfied, and it would be just further complicating our systems to install another one, when one was sufficient.

There is nothing in the record from which it could be inferred that this witness was wrong in considering that there was no other system available at the time that would have given effective protection. On the contrary, all the evidence indicates that burglars, clever enough to defeat the D.E.P. system would have, as easily, succeeded in defeating a second system if one had been added. Assuming that on a first attempt to compromise the systems, the burglars had been unsuccessful, the reasonable inference should be that this would have set an alarm which would have been treated as a false alarm, just like the alarm that was registered and reported approximately two weeks before the successful break-in. With respect, the conclusion that a break-in would have been avoided is, in my view, unjustified, it cannot be said to be established on the balance of probabilities. In fact, there is no evidence whatever to support such a conclusion. The only witnesses who gave an expert opinion on that point, Leighton and Grosso, both said that very little or no additional security would be obtained by such means. When insurance broker Curtis was asked what he would have done if Atlee's letter had said that the system had been defeated, he answered: "I certainly would look into every possibility of obtaining additional systems, or a sound system which would satisfy the underwriters in the companies." Edminson's evidence shows that this was done anyway.

The second alternative should be dismissed from consideration entirely because no claim is made on that basis. It is obvious that if the contention is that, without the incorrect information, a lower inventory would have been carried, nothing more than the difference between such reduced inventory and the actual value carried at the time of the burglary could be claimed. No argument was addressed, no figures were submitted on that basis. The claimant no doubt realized that it would have great difficulty in showing that its inventory was larger than its business needs required, or that it would have chosen to restrict its business activities and therefore to reduce its profits, if better informed of the risk of burglary despite the protection system.

As to the use of a bank vault, there is no evidence that the obvious risk involved in daily moving the inventory out of the premises would have been smaller than the risk involved in keeping it in an imperfectly protected safe. In fact, a bank vault was used for a very short time only after the burglary, although several years elapsed before a system with effective protection against circumvention by compromising the line was made available to Nunes.

The proof in this case has shown that for protection against burglary, Nunes really relied on insurance. It was so well protected that after the break-in its insurers paid $67,000 more than the actual cost of its inventory, as found by the trial Judge. This amount being substantially in excess of the additional costs and losses due to the theft, which the trial judge fixed at $22,795.07, Nunes' chartered accountant, Adams, had to negotiate with the Department of National Revenue the allocation of the profit from the "incident" between the taxation years 1960 and 1961. Of course, the existence of indemnity insurance is not a defence available to a tortfeasor. However, this does not necessarily mean that the extent of such protection is not a factor to be borne in mind when considering whether a claimant was really lulled into a false sense of security by misrepresentations as to the value of other protective measures.

The appeal should be dismissed with costs.

[Martland and Judson JJ. agreed with Pigeon J.]

Spence J. [dissenting]. There remains, therefore, the question of whether these representations, which I have found to be misrepresentations, give rise to a cause of action. In this case, no reliance was placed upon any allegation of fraud or deceit and the case must be considered as merely one of innocent misrepresentation.

The general understanding of the decision of the House of Lords in *Derry v. Peek* (1889), 14 App. Cas. 337, was stated to be that there could not be any action for damages for innocent misrepresentation and that fraud in the strictest sense must be alleged and proved. Fraud was said to be either a knowing misstatement of the facts or a statement made recklessly not caring whether it be true or false, and a statement merely made in error and without investigation prior to the making thereof to determine whether it was true or false was not fraud which could give a cause of action.

A series of cases which need not be analysed here followed *Derry v. Peek* and applied that doctrine. However, in *Nocton v. Lord Ashburton*, [1914] A.C. 932, the House of Lords had the opportunity to consider *Derry v. Peek* and to place strict limitations on the extent of the principle there enunciated. The facts in *Nocton v. Ashburton* were that a solicitor had persuaded his client to release part of the security in a mortgage held by the client upon the representation that the balance of the security was more than adequate. The solicitor himself held a subsequent mortgage upon the premises released and, of course, his security was considerably improved by the release of the subject thereof from his client's prior mortgage. The mortgagor defaulted in the payment of the client's mortgage and the security therefor proved most inadequate so that the client Lord Ashburton suffered a very heavy loss and took action against the solicitor Nocton on the basis of the solicitor's misrepresentation. Neville, J., at trial, found that although the misrepresentation was carelessly made it was not fraudulent and relying on *Derry v. Peek*, dismissed the action. The Court of Appeal reversed this finding, held that the representation was fraudulent and therefore held the solicitor liable. The Law Lords, on further appeal, were of the opinion that it was not proper to reverse a finding of fact made as to the non-fraudulent character of the representation by the trial Judge after he had heard the witnesses and considered all the circumstances. They then concluded that *Derry v. Peek* did not apply to all cases of innocent misrepresentation but that, on the other hand, there were cases where misrepresentation although innocent would give rise to a cause of action. Viscount Haldane, the Lord Chancellor, in a lengthy and very carefully considered judgment [at p. 950], accepted as a starting point a statement made by Lord Herschell in the course of his reasons in *Derry v. Peek* wherein Lord Herschell [at p. 360] had carefully excluded from the class,

> "those cases where a person within whose special province it lay to know a particular fact has given an erroneous answer to an inquiry made with regard to it by a person desirous of ascertaining the factor for the purpose of determining his course."

In *Nocton v. Ashburton*, the Court found that the situation between a solicitor and his client was one of those cases. It is true that the major part of the reasons given by the various Law Lords in that case deals with the situation where the representor is in some fiduciary relationship to the representee but that circumstance may be validly explained by saying that that was the situation with which the Law Lords were concerned in that particular case not that a case of fiduciary relationship is the only one within Lord Herschell's carefully enunciated exception which I have quoted above.

There have been a series of cases in which an innocent misrepresentation has been held to give rise to damages following *Nocton v. Ashburton*. Such situations include those between banker and customer. The applicability of the liability under the principle was, however, refused in *Candler v. Crane, Christmas & Co.*, [1951] 2 K.B. 164, a claim made by a person who was then a prospective investor and who was given, by an accountant of the company in which he was considering investing, an erroneous statement of that company's affairs. In that case Denning, L.J., in a very strong dissenting judgment, was in favour of finding liability, saying at p. 178:

> If you read the great cases of *Ashby v. White* (1703), 2 Ld. Raym. 938, *Pasley v. Freeman* (1789), 3 Term. Rep. 51, and *Donoghue v. Stevenson*, [1932] A.C. 562, you will find that in each of them the judges were divided in opinion. On the one side there were the timorous souls who were fearful of allowing a new cause of action. On the other side there were the bold spirits who were ready to allow it if justice so required. It was fortunate for the common law that the progressive view prevailed. Whenever this argument of novelty is put forward I call to mind the emphatic answer given by Pratt, C.J., nearly two hundred years ago in *Chapman v. Pickersgill*, (1762) 2 Wilson 145, 146, when he said: "I wish never to hear this objection again. This action is for a tort: torts are infinitely various; not limited or confined, for there is nothing in nature but may be an instrument of mischief". The same answer was given by Lord Macmillan in *Donoghue v. Stevenson* when he said [at p. 619]: "The criterion of judgment must adjust and adapt itself to the changing circumstances of life. The categories of negligence are never closed". I beg leave to quote those cases and those passages against those who would emphasize the paramount importance of certainty at the expense of justice. It needs only a little imagination to see how much the common law would have suffered if those decisions had gone the other way.

The extent to which the principle should be applied came to a head in *Hedley Byrne & Co. Ltd. v. Heller & Partners Ltd.*, [1964] A.C. 465 (H.L.). There, Hedley Byrne were engaged in business with a company known as Easipower Ltd. and first in August of 1958 turned to their own bankers, the National Provincial Bank, and inquired whether such bankers could inform them in confidence of the financial status of Easipower Ltd. The National Provincial Bank, Piccadilly Office, communicated with its city office, and the representative of the city office telephoned Heller & Partners Ltd. who were the bankers for Easipower Ltd. The officer of the latter company, the respondents, on the day of the call, made an exact note of that telephone request [headnote]:

> "They wanted to know in confidence and without responsibility on our part, the respectability and standing of Easipower Ltd., and whether they would be good for an advertising contract for £8,000 to £9,000. I replied, the company recently opened an account with us. Believed to be respectably constituted and considered good for its normal business engagements...."

Later, in November of the same year, the appellants wrote to their bankers, the National Provincial Bank, at its Piccadilly Branch, asking again that the financial structure and status of Easipower Ltd. be investigated concluding that it would be appreciated if the bank could make its check as exhaustive as it reasonably could. The National Provincial Bank wrote to the respondents Heller & Partners Ltd., a letter headed "Private and Confidential" and reading [headnote]:

> "Dear Sir, We shall be obliged by your opinion in confidence as to the respectability and standing of Easipower Ltd., 27 Albemarle Street, London, W.1, and by stating whether you consider them trustworthy, in the way of business, to the extent of £100,000 per annum advertising contract."

Four days later, the respondent replied:

"CONFIDENTIAL

> "For your private use and without responsibility on the part of this bank or its officials."

"Re E..... Ltd.

> "Respectably constituted company, considered good for its ordinary business engagements. Your figures are larger than we are accustomed to see."

Hedley Byrne & Co. Ltd. proceeded to make contracts for advertising whereby they rendered themselves personally liable for a very large sum and upon the insolvency of Easipower Ltd. suffered a loss of some £17,000. It is to be noted that Heller & Partners Ltd. were not the bankers for and had no connection with Hedley Byrne & Co. and that the advice given to Hedley Byrne & Co. through the National Provincial Bank was given altogether gratuitously and without any situation whereby Heller & Partners Ltd. stood to profit.

It is, of course, apparent from the recital of the facts, that there is no question of fraud or deceit. It was, however, taken as proved that the representation as to the worth of Easipower Ltd. was made carelessly and was in fact a misrepresentation. The action came on for trial before McNair, J., who gave judgment dismissing the action on the ground that the defendant Heller & Partners owed no duty of care to the appellants, saying, in part [quoted by Lord Reid at p. 482]:

> "In my judgment, however, these facts, though clearly relevant on the question of honesty if this had been in issue, are not sufficient to establish any special relationship involving a duty of care even if it was open to me *to extend the sphere of special relationship beyond that of contract and fiduciary relationship.*"

(The italics are my own.)

The Court of Appeal affirmed [[1962] 1 Q.B. 396] the judgment at trial feeling bound by authority and not satisfied that it would be reasonable to impose upon the banker the obligation suggested. All five Law Lords sitting on the appeal to the House of Lords gave judgment. Although they were unanimous in dismissing the appeal upon the ground that the respondent Heller & Partners Ltd. had expressly disclaimed responsibility in exact words when giving the first representation and also the second, the various members of the House of Lords all expressed the view that apart from such disclaimer, the respondents would have been liable. Lord Reid in his reasons referred to Viscount Haldane's using as the base for his judgment in *Nocton v. Ashburton* the speech of Lord Herschell in *Derry v. Peek*, which I have quoted above, and also referred to [at pp. 485-6] Lord Haldane's further statement in *Robinson v. National Bank of Scotland Ltd.,* [1916] S.C. (H.L.) 154 at p. 157, where the Lord Chancellor said:

> "In saying that I wish emphatically to repeat what I said in advising this House in the case of *Nocton v. Lord Ashburton,* [1914] A.C. 932, that it is a great mistake to suppose that, because the principle in *Derry v. Peek,* 14 App. Cas. 337, clearly covers all cases of the class to which I have referred, therefore the freedom of action of the Courts in recognising special duties arising out of other kinds of relationship which they find established by the evidence is in any way affected. I think, as I said in *Nocton's* case, that an exaggerated view was taken by a good many people of the scope of the decision in *Derry v. Peek.* The whole of the doctrines as to fiduciary relationships, as to the duty of care arising from implied as well as express contracts, as to the duty of care arising *from other special relationships which the Courts may find to exist in particular cases,* still remains, and I should be very sorry if any word fell from me which should suggest that the Courts are in any way hampered in recognising that the duty of care may be established when such cases really occur."

(The italics are my own.)

Lord Reid points out that this passage made it clear that Lord Haldane did not think that a duty to take care must be limited to cases of fiduciary relationship in the narrow sense and that Lord Haldane spoke, on the other hand, of "special relationships" and expressed the view that there was no logical stopping place short of all those relationships where it is plain that the party seeking information or advice was trusting the other to exercise such a degree of care as the circumstances required, where it was reasonable for him to do that, and where the other gave the information or advice when he knew or ought to have known that the inquirer was relying on it. Lord Reid continued, at p. 486:

> A reasonable man, knowing that he was being trusted or that his skill and judgment were being relied on, would, I think, have three courses open to him. He could keep silent or decline to give the information or advice sought: or he could give an answer with a clear qualification that he accepted no responsibility for it or that it was given without that reflection or inquiry which a careful answer would require: or he could simply answer without any such qualification. If he chooses to adopt the last course he must, I think, be held to have accepted some responsibility for his answer being given carefully, or to have accepted a relationship with the inquirer which requires him to exercise such care as the circumstances require.

A similar view was expressed by the other Law Lords and I need not make extensive reference to their judgments.

In considering *Hedley Byrne & Co. Ltd. v. Heller & Partners Ltd.,* Schroeder, J.A., in giving reasons for the Court of Appeal for Ontario, quoted the paragraph which I have just quoted and expressed the view that the respondent in this case had followed the first course mentioned by Lord Reid, that is, he had kept silent or declined to give the information. With respect, I must express an opposite conclusion. Although Schroeder, J.A., excepted from his statement the evidence as to the representation made by the so-called technician since he was of the opinion that it could not bind the company, I am of the opinion that the representation made by the general manager in the two letters dated October 25th which I have quoted was much more than refraining from giving any information or advice. The letters contained the bald statement that the equipment had functioned properly and as I have pointed out certainly implied that a further report would be made when the investigation had been completed, an undertaking which the respondent failed to carry out, and in failing to make such further report, by what has been nicknamed an "economy of truth", in fact misrepresented the situation.

I am, therefore, of the opinion that the respondent here adopted not the first course outlined by Lord Reid but the third course outlined by Lord Reid, *i.e.,* that the respondent simply answered without any qualification. As Lord Reid pointed out, a respondent choosing the last course must be held to have accepted some responsibility for his answer being given carelessly or to have accepted a relationship with the inquirer which required him to exercise such care as the circumstances required. Lord Morris of Borth-y-Gest said at pp. 502-3:

> My Lords, I consider that it follows and that it should now be regarded as settled that if someone possessed of a special skill undertakes, quite irrespective of contract, to apply that skill for the assistance of another person who relies upon such skill, a duty of care will arise. The fact that the service is to be given by means of or by the instrumentality of words can make no difference. Furthermore, if in a sphere in which a person is so placed that others could reasonably rely upon his judgment or his skill or upon his ability to make careful inquiry, a person takes it upon himself to give information or advice to, or allows his information or advice to be passed on to, another person who, as he knows or should know, will place reliance upon it, then a duty of care will arise.

Lord Devlin at p. 530, said:

> I shall therefore content myself with the proposition that wherever there is a relationship equivalent to contract, there is a duty of care.

The learned author of Fleming, *The Law of Torts,* in the 4th edition (1971), at p. 564, in referring to *Hedley Byrne v. Heller & Partners,* said:

> The sheet anchor of a duty of care is the speaker's assumption of responsibility for what he says. In other words, the recipient must have had reasonable grounds for believing that the speaker expected to be trusted. There is a world of difference, e.g., between casual statements on social or informal occasions and serious communications made in circumstances warranting reliance. Usually, though by no means exclusively, the latter are encountered in the sphere of business or professional affairs, though not necessarily between persons linked by a contractual or fiduciary tie in the conventional sense.

I am of the view that the learned author, in that statement, properly summarized the effect of *Hedley Byrne v. Heller & Partners,* and I apply the case and that summary to the facts in the present case. Certainly, the inquiries made by the insurance representatives in their letters replied to by the general manager of the respondent on October 26, 1959, and the inquiry made by Miss Geddes to the unnamed technician were not made on social or informal occasions but were serious communications made in circumstances where the representor could have no other view than that his expert opinion was intended to be relied on.

I am personally of the view that under the circumstances which existed in the present case, that is, that the respondent was supplying to the appellant a very important service under a written contract and the inquiry was whether such service was and could be efficiently performed and the representation was that it was so being performed, the decision in *Nocton v. Lord Ashburton* is enough to justify a decision in favour of the appellant. Herein, I think I should note that Addy, J., in his reasons, said [5 D.L.R. (3d) at p. 689]:

> I feel also in the present case that, due to the existence of the contract and also the special knowledge which D.E.P. had, covering the subject-matter of burglar protection systems, a special relation existed between the plaintiff and the defendant. By reason of this D.E.P. would, in my view, be responsible for any misrepresentation pertaining to burglar protection which it negligently made to the plaintiff and which caused damages by inducing the plaintiff to fail to take precautions against burglary which it otherwise would have taken. If, in the ordinary course of business or in professional affairs a person seeks information or advice from another, who is not under contractual obligation to give this advice, in circumstances in which a reasonable man so asked would know that he was being trusted or that his skill or judgment was being relied on, and the person asked chooses to give the information or advice, without clearly so qualifying his answer to show that he does not accept responsibility, then the person replying accepts the legal duty to exercise such care as the circumstances require in making his reply; and, for a failure to exercise that care, an action will lie if damage results...

In so far as that paragraph is a statement of facts, I accept it; in so far as it is a statement of law, I agree with it. In the present case, there was no such express denial of responsibility as was found to have saved Heller & Partners in *Hedley Byrne v. Heller & Partners*. In my opinion, the appellant is entitled to succeed upon the basis of the doctrine outlined in the latter case even if he thought that *Nocton v. Ashburton* did not go far enough to aid it.

Before concluding my consideration of whether the appellant is entitled to succeed on his claim for actionable misrepresentation, I must refer to a case in this Court: *Guay v. Sun Publishing Co.,* [1953] 4 D.L.R. 577, [1953] 2 S.C.R. 216. There, a publishing company in Vancouver had published a news item stating that the appellant's husband and three children had been killed in an automobile accident in Ontario where the husband and three children were then living. No such accident took place and the respondent was unable to get any explanation whatsoever for the publication of the article. The appellant took action for negligence but did not allege either fraud or malice or the existence of any contractual relationship between her and the newspaper. The action was maintained at trial but the Court of Appeal for British Columbia allowed the appeal and that disposition was affirmed in this Court. It is difficult to pick out a *ratio decidendi*. First, it might be pointed out that Cartwright, J., as he then was, giving judgment for himself and for Rinfret, C.J.C., dissenting, simply declined to consider cases as to false misrepresentation with which I have been dealing here being of the view that the case then being considered was analogous to one in which the respondent unintentionally but negligently had struck the appellant or caused some object to strike her and the respondent should have foreseen the probability of the appellant reading the report and suffering injury and therefore the respondent had a duty to check the accuracy of the report before publishing it. Estey, J., admitted that the respondent owed a duty to the appellant to exercise reasonable care to verify the truth of the report but held that the appellant could not succeed upon the evidence because it failed to establish that she suffered physical illness or other injuries consequent upon shock or emotional disturbance caused by the reading of the report. Kerwin, J., as he then was, held that the appellant was not a neighbour of the respondent within the meaning of Lord Atkin's statement in *M'Alister (or Donoghue) v. Stevenson,* [1932] A.C. 562, since she was not a person so closely and directly affected by the publishing of the report that the respondent ought reasonably to have had the appellant in contemplation as being affected injuriously when it was directing its mind to the act of publishing. Whether one agrees with that finding of facts or not the judgment is certainly one on facts. Locke, J., alone gave judgment in reference to the cases as to false though not fraudulent misrepresentations adopting *Le Lievre v. Gould,* [1893] 1 Q.B. 491; *Balden v. Shorter,* [1933] 1 Ch. 427; and *Candler v. Crane, Christmas Co.,* [1951] 2 K.B. 164. Those are all cases which have been directly overruled by the House of Lords in *Hedley Byrne & Co. v. Heller & Partners Ltd., supra.* I am of the opinion that Locke, J., cannot be taken as having given the decision of the Court in this matter and that this Court is now free to adopt the principles outlined in *Hedley Byrne v. Heller & Partners* rather than the earlier narrow view in the cases cited which view has been refuted in *Hedley Byrne v. Heller.*

The question remains whether para. 16 of the agreement between the appellant and the respondent applies. That paragraph reads simply:

16. No conditions, warranties or representations have been made by Dominion Company, its officers, servants or agents other than those endorsed hereon in writing.

That clause is contained in a written contract dated September 26, 1958. By its words, it refers to conditions, warranties or representations which *have been made* and can have no application whatsoever to representations which were made some 13 months after the date of the contract. Addy, J., in giving reasons for judgment at trial, said [at p. 688]:

At the outset, I would like to make it clear that the plaintiff has not, in my view, contracted itself out of its right to claim damages against the defendant, if such damages can be founded on an action in tort. A clause purporting to provide for exclusion of liability for negligence will be strictly interpreted and, even though it might exempt from liability based on a contractual duty, it will not exempt from liability based on the breach of a general duty of care unless the words to that effect are clear and unequivocal.

With that view I agree and have no hesitation in coming to the conclusion that cl. 16 of the agreement between the appellant and the respondent cannot operate as a bar to a claim based on a tortious misrepresentation made many months after the contract which contained such a clause had been executed.

The agreement between the parties is of importance in so far as it established a relationship between them, and thus provided a basis upon which, in the light of subsequent events, the appellant could rightly assess that the negligent misrepresentations of the respondent were made in breach of a duty of care to the appellant. I cannot agree that the mere existence of an antecedent contract foreclosed tort liability under the *Hedley Byrne* principle.

For these reasons, I have come to the conclusion that the appellant is entitled to succeed upon its claim for actionable misrepresentation. A certain amount of time was spent during the argument in this Court and evidently much more in the Court of Appeal for Ontario in discussing the quantum of damages. With respect, I adopt the view stated by Schroeder, J.A., in the sentence [15 D.L.R. (3d) at p. 39]:

> In my opinion, the learned trial Judge was justified in fixing the damages at $303,147.07 on the basis of the evidence which he accepted, and this Court would not be warranted in interfering with his assessment.

I would, therefore, allow the appeal and give judgment for the appellant for that amount with costs throughout.

[Laskin J. agreed with Spence J.]

QUESTIONS

1. The person who would be principally worried about the effectiveness of the burglar alarm would be the plaintiff's insurance company. The letters written by the defendant that were showed to the plaintiff were, in fact, written to the plaintiff's insurance agent. Would the insurers have had a better chance of succeeding had they sued, not under their rights of subrogation (where the action is in form brought by the insured), but in their own names?

2. Would it matter if the policy of insurance between the plaintiff and its insurers had come up for renewal after the letters had been written but before the loss, and the insurance company had taken no steps to reduce the risk of loss or to get a higher premium?

3. Since the action was framed as one brought by the plaintiff himself, would it matter if the contract with the defendant to provide a burglar alarm service had been renewed between the date of the letters and representation and the burglary?

4. Do both judgments show an equal awareness of the fact that the action is between two insurance companies: the plaintiff's under its rights of subrogation, and the defendant's under its liability policy? Should this fact have been considered at all?

PROBLEM

Marcia Peet is an accountant. Harvey Wood has a small manufacturing plant where he employs 15 people to make kitchen gadgets. Harvey wants Marcia to act as his firm's accountant. Harvey has little spare cash and he asks Marcia to do the work as cheaply as possible. Marcia, who needs all the business she can get, agrees. She writes a letter to Harvey in the following terms:

"Dear Harvey,

"This is to set out the terms upon which I agree to act as your accountant.

"1. I will compile, without audit, review or other verification as to accuracy or completeness, financial statements for the year ending 31 Dec. 1977.

"2. To such statements I will add this "Notice to Reader" which, unless unanticipated difficulties are encountered, will be in the following form:

" '*Notice to Reader*

" 'These statements and schedules have been compiled solely for income tax and internal purposes for Harvey Wood Ltd. I have not audited, reviewed or otherwise attempted to verify their accuracy or completeness.'

"3. It is understood and agreed that,

"(a) these financial statements will be used only within the firm and will not be made available to other parties without my agreement; and

"(b) the above users understand the possible limitations on these financial statements, and need not place undue reliance on them because they also have access to further information.

"If these terms are satisfactory please sign and return one copy of this letter.

Yours truly,
Marcia Peet."

Harvey signed one copy of the letter and returned it to Marcia. Marcia duly submitted a financial statement to Harvey showing that the firm had made a profit of $100,000 for the year. Harvey, without Marcia's knowledge or consent, tore off the front page of the statement prepared by Marcia where she had typed in the "Notice to Reader" and showed the statements to Andrea Bloom who subsequently invested $50,000 in the business. Had Marcia reviewed the accounts in the normal way she would have discovered that the profit was only $20,000. This has now all come to light. Is Marcia liable to Andrea?

SEALAND OF THE PACIFIC LTD. v. McHAFFIE LTD.

(1974), 51 D.L.R. (3d) 702. British Columbia Court of Appeal; Farris C.J.B.C., Robertson and Seaton JJ.A.

The judgment of the Court was delivered by

Seaton, J.A.: — Sealand of the Pacific Ltd. ("Sealand") operates an oceanarium at Victoria. It is housed in a vessel that sits low in the water with the display tanks below the surface of the sea.

Late in 1969 Sealand wished to make certain improvements that required increased buoyancy. In addition, it wished to resolve the problem of refraction in the lower part of each tank and to improve the water filtration system. An answer to all of these problems seemed to be the addition of lighter than water material in the bottom of each of the tanks.

Sealand had a meeting on November 10, 1969, with a Mr. Robinson, sales representative of the appellant Ocean Construction Supplies Limited (referred to in the evidence and in these reasons as "Ocean Cement"). Mr. Robinson had many years experience in the cement business and was backed up by Ocean Cement's technical people. His statement that his company had a product that would satisfy Sealand's needs met with immediate acceptance. The material that was unequivocally stated by Mr. Robinson to be suited to the job was called vermiculite or zonolite concrete. He said that its weight would be less than half that of water.

On December 4, 1969, Sealand retained the respondent Robert C. McHaffie Ltd. ("McHaffie Ltd."), naval architects, through discussion with the respondent McHaffie. The work was done in the spring of 1970 by the defendant Frank G. Browne Ltd. It was a complete failure so far as floatation was concerned. Used under these conditions the concrete weighed more than water.

After a lengthy trial, McKay, J., in a carefully reasoned judgment, found Ocean Cement liable and gave judgment against it in the amount of $62,230.83. The actions by Sealand against McHaffie Ltd., Robert C. McHaffie and Frank G. Browne Ltd. were dismissed. Ocean Cement appeals the finding that it is liable, Sealand appeals the dismissal of its action against Mr. McHaffie and McHaffie Ltd., Sealand appeals with regard to the costs of Frank G. Browne Ltd., and Ocean Cement appeals the quantum of damages.

The learned trial Judge found Ocean Cement liable for breach of an express warranty. He found that if there was not an express warranty there was an implied warranty pursuant to the *Sale of Goods Act,* R.S.B.C. 1960, c. 344, s. 20(*a*). In either case the warranty relied on by Sealand was that the product was reasonably fit for the purpose for which it was required. In fact it was wholly unfit. For the reasons given by the learned trial Judge I would conclude that Ocean Cement is liable to Sealand for breach of warranty.

The trial Judge also found Ocean Cement liable in tort and that finding is challenged on the ground that Sealand relied exclusively upon McHaffie Ltd. The evidence does not support that contention. There are some additional problems in a negligence action but I do not think there is to be any purpose in examining them once liability in contract has been established.

It is not necessary to consider the usual role of a naval architect because counsel agree that it was part of this architect's duty to consider the suitability of zonolite concrete. The question is whether that duty was sufficiently discharged by McHaffie Ltd. when it accepted the representations and guarantees made by Ocean Cement through Mr. Robinson. The evidence is that any other inquiries would have disclosed that the use of this product was not a sound engineering procedure. That information would quickly have been given by the company that supplied vermiculite to Ocean Cement.

In addition to Robinson's statements, the architect had a pamphlet. The pamphlet dealt with the use of the product in a different manner and for different purposes, and nothing said in it would tend to comfort one who proposed using vermiculite under water. The instructions in the pamphlet dealt with a shallow pour and did not suggest that it could be poured to a depth of two feet. Inquiry would have revealed that a drying time of months would have been needed under those circumstances. The time recommended by Ocean Cement was hopelessly inadequate.

Sealand had the assurances of Ocean Cement before it asked the architect to consider the suitability of the material. The parties must have intended additional inquiries reaching beyond Ocean Cement. McHaffie Ltd. appreciated that this use of vermiculite concrete was somewhat experimental, and that it was retained to consider the suitability of the product. Under the circumstances McHaffie Ltd. must be taken to have agreed to make inquiries beyond talking to Ocean Cement and looking at the pamphlet. It failed to do so. McHaffie Ltd. is liable to Sealand for breach of its contract.

Sealand also seeks judgment against Mr. McHaffie individually on the basis of a negligent statement, relying on the principle in *Hedley Byrne & Co., Ltd. v. Heller & Partners, Ltd.,* [1964] A.C. 465, [1963] 2 All E.R. 575, [1963] 3 W.L.R. 101. Before dealing specifically with that claim, I shall discuss whether Sealand could recover against McHaffie Ltd. on that principle. There was a contract between Sealand and McHaffie Ltd. The statement was made by an employee of McHaffie Ltd. in carrying out that contract and I think that the duty and the liability ought to be discovered in the contract. If additional duties and liabilities are to be attached, it will have the effect of changing the bargain made by the parties. That would be inappropriate. I agree with the learned trial Judge that the facts here do not meet the test suggested by Pigeon, J., in *J. Nunes Diamonds Ltd. v. Dominion Electric Protection Co.* (1972), 26 D.L.R. (3d) 699 at pp. 727-8, [1972] S.C.R. 769:

Furthermore, the basis of tort liability considered in *Hedley Byrne* is inapplicable to any case where the relationship between the parties is governed by a contract, unless the negligence relied on can properly be considered as "an independent tort" unconnected with the performance of that contract, as expressed in *Elder, Dempster & Co., Ltd. v. Paterson, Zochonis & Co., Ltd.*, [1924] A.C. 522 at p. 548. This is specially important in the present case on account of the provisions of the contract with respect to the nature of the obligations assumed and the practical exclusion of responsibility for failure to perform them.

. . .

In my view, the representations relied on by appellant cannot be considered as acts independent of the contractual relationship between the parties. This can be readily verified by asking the question: Would these representations have been made if the parties had not been in the contractual relationship in which they stood? Therefore, the question of liability arising out of those representations should not be approached as if the parties had been strangers, but on the basis of the contract between them. Hence the question should be: May this contract of service be considered as having been turned into the equivalent of a contract of insurance, by virtue of inaccurate or incomplete representations respecting the actual value of the protection service supplied? In my view, there is no doubt that this question should be answered in the negative. There is nothing from which it can properly be inferred that Nunes considered that the contract had been so altered and it is perfectly obvious that D.E.P.'s management never intended to assume such obligations.

Our duty to follow that decision is not diminished by the fact that the case relied upon, *Elder, Dempster & Co., Ltd. v. Paterson, Zochonis & Co., Ltd.*, [1924] A.C. 522, has not been accepted elsewhere as authority for the proposition for which it won acceptance here: see for example, *Wilson v. Darling Island Stevedoring & Lighterage Co. Ltd.* (1956), 95 C.L.R. 43, particularly the judgment of Fullager, J. at p. 74 *et seq.*, and *Midland Silicones Ltd. v. Scruttons Ltd.*, [1962] A.C. 446.

Now I turn to the claim against Mr. McHaffie. For a statement of part of the principle in *Hedley Byrne* I refer to what Lord Morris of Borth-y-Gest said at pp. 502-3 (A.C.):

My Lords, I consider that it follows and that it should now be regarded as settled that if someone possessed of a special skill undertakes, quite irrespective of contract, to apply that skill for the assistance of another person who relies upon such skill, a duty of care will arise. The fact that the service is to be given by means of or by the instrumentality of words can make no difference.

Here Mr. McHaffie did not undertake to apply his skill for the assistance of Sealand. He did exercise, or fail to exercise, his skill as an employee of McHaffie Ltd. in the carrying out of its contractual duty to Sealand. Further, while Sealand may have chosen to consult McHaffie Ltd. because it had the benefit of Mr. McHaffie's services as an employee, it was with McHaffie Ltd. that Sealand made a contract and it was upon the skill of McHaffie Ltd. that it relied.

An employee's act or omission that constitutes his employer's breach of contract may also impose a liability on the employee in tort. However, this will only be so if there is breach of a duty owed (independently of the contract) by the employee to the other party. Mr. McHaffie did not owe the duty to Sealand to make inquiries. That was a company responsibility. It is the failure to carry out the corporate duty imposed by contract that can attract liability to the company. The duty in negligence and the duty in contract may stand side by side but the duty in contract is not imposed upon the employee as a duty in tort.

I have concluded that the appellant Ocean Cement and the respondent McHaffie Ltd. are liable to the respondent Sealand for the damages caused by the use of this unsuitable material. It is agreed by all counsel that under the circumstances the *Contributory Negligence Act*, R.S.B.C. 1960, c. 74, has no application.

It is submitted that a procedure similar to that envisaged by the *Contributory Negligence Act* ought to be adopted and that liability to make good the loss should be divided between McHaffie Ltd. and Ocean Cement. The foundation for that submission is *Harries, Hall & Kruse v. South Sarnia Properties, Ltd.*, [1929] 2 D.L.R. 821, 63 O.L.R. 597. That decision does not appear to have attracted comment in subsequent decisions and I confess that I do not understand the basis on which the Court thought it appropriate to apportion. What we are here dealing with is liability to the plaintiff, not the liability of the defendants to one another. It may well be that in this case Ocean Cement is obliged to indemnify McHaffie Ltd. for any amount payable by McHaffie Ltd. to Sealand. That is an issue to be determined on the third party proceedings that are not before us.

I am in agreement with the reasoning in *Campbell Flour Mills Co. Ltd. v. Bowes; Campbell Flour Mills Co. Ltd. v. Ellis* (1914), 32 O.L.R. 270, a decision of the Ontario Appellate Division that seems not to have come to the attention of that Division in *Harries, Hall & Kruse, supra*, notwithstanding that two Judges were common to the two cases. The conclusions of Riddell, J., speaking for the Court in *Campbell Flour Mills Co.* are applicable here [at pp. 280-1]:

> In the present case, the plaintiffs had two separate and distinct contracts, the one with the contractors, which was in writing, the other with the architects, which was, as in *Jameson v. Simon*, [1 F. (Ct. of Sess. Cas., 5th Series) 1211] (not in writing but) implied from the employment. The contractors broke their contract when they put bad material into the building; at the same moment the architects broke theirs because they allowed this to be done. Under the circumstances, the damages are the same under either contract; but that is wholly immaterial. The contracts are not the same; and, if judgment were to be obtained in the action against the contractors, it would destroy their contract *quoad hoc*, but it could not affect the contract of the architects — that *non transit in rem judicatam*, but remains a simple contract.
>
> It is true that, if the full amount of the damages were realised out of the contractors, no action (except perhaps for nominal damages) would lie against the architects, but that is on an entirely different principle, namely, that the plaintiffs have suffered no damage from the default of the architects.
>
> The result is, that the plaintiffs are entitled to judgment against both the contractors and the architects, and that is what the judgment in appeal gives them.

Sealand is entitled to judgment for its loss against both Ocean Cement and McHaffie Ltd.

The learned trial Judge assessed damages in the amount of $62,230.83, being the cost of the measures necessarily taken to relieve the problem temporarily and those that will have to be taken in the future to replace the cement with styrofoam.

By an oversight, no allowance was made for the fact that the zonolite cement has not been paid for. It is suggested that the cement is worthless but that overlooks the fact that the award is to put Sealand in the position it would have been in if the cement were as it was represented to be. Sealand should be in that position at the cost originally anticipated. Thus I would deduct from the award of damages the sum of $4,515.94.

The appellant says that the respondent is entitled to the moneys thrown away but not to the cost of replacing the cement with styrofoam. That submission might have validity if this were an action in negligence. It might also have validity if the action were in deceit. But in a case of breach of warranty of fitness where the measure of damages is based upon putting the plaintiff in the position he would have been in, not if the representation had never been made but if the representation had been true, the argument is without foundation.

This is not a case of breach of warranty of quality and thus s. 57(3) of the *Sale of Goods Act* does not apply. In any event that provision is only a *prima facie* rule and in my view does not apply to a breach such as this where special circumstances are communicated to the seller and are thus within the contemplation of the parties. The result of the application of the *Sale of Goods Act* under the circumstances here is to apply to breaches of warranty the same principles as apply at common law to breaches of contract generally.

Subject to the reduction of the amount by reason of the cost of the concrete, a point that was not drawn to the attention of the learned trial Judge, I would not interfere with the amount awarded.

After the order was entered Sealand applied for an order that the costs payable by the then plaintiff to the successful defendants be added to Sealand's costs against Ocean Cement. The learned trial Judge did not deal with the merits of a "Bullock Order" because the application was made too late. In my view the case falls within those in which a Bullock Order ought to be made.

McHaffie Ltd. and McHaffie received one set of costs at trial; they were represented by one counsel on appeal. One has failed, the other has succeeded. Ocean Cement succeeded in a small part of its appeal. Costs of trial taxed by McHaffie Ltd. and McHaffie will be treated as being divisible between them equally. One bill will be taxed by them regarding the appeal and it too will be divided equally. Mr. McHaffie is entitled to his costs (being one-half of the taxed bill) on the trial and appeal. Sealand will tax one bill of costs on the appeal. It will recover from Ocean Cement two-thirds of its costs on trial and appeal, together with two-thirds of the costs it is required to pay to Frank G. Browne Ltd. and Mr. McHaffie. It is entitled to the other one-third of each of those items from McHaffie Ltd. Ocean Cement is entitled to one-fifth of its costs of the appeal from Sealand because of its partial success, the sums found due on taxation to be set off.

Ocean Cement's appeal regarding liability is dismissed. Its appeal as to quantum is allowed to the extent that the amount awarded is reduced to $57,714.89. Sealand's appeal against the dismissal of the action against McHaffie Ltd. is allowed. Sealand's appeal respecting Mr. McHaffie is dismissed. In the result Sealand will have judgment against Ocean Cement and McHaffie Ltd. for $57,714.89.

Since I prepared these reasons, my brother Branca has delivered, for the Court, a judgment in *Northwestern Mutual Ins. Co. v. J.T. O'Bryan & Co. et al., ante,* p. 693. I do not think that there is any conflict between what was said there and what I have said regarding the employee's liability in tort. Thibeau was found liable for the breach of a duty owed by him to Northwestern. That duty to exercise reasonable care arose independently of

O'Bryan's contract. McHaffie was not in breach of any such duty to Sealand.

Appeal allowed in part;
cross-appeal against McHaffie Ltd. allowed;
cross-appeal against McHaffie dismissed.

QUESTIONS

1. Can Sealand recover its full loss from both defendants?
2. Can either defendant sue the other?
3. Are the following provisions of the Negligence Act relevant?
2(1) — Where damages have been caused or contributed to by the fault or neglect of two or more persons, the court shall determine the degree in which each of
such persons is at fault or negligent, and, ... where two or more persons are found
at fault or negligent, they are jointly and severally liable to the person suffering
loss or damage for such fault or negligence, but as between themselves, in the
absence of any contract express or implied, each is liable to make contribution
and indemnify each other in the degree in which they are respectively found to
be at fault or negligent.
3. A tort feasor may recover contribution or indemnity from any other tort feasor
who is, or would if sued have been, liable in respect of the damage to any person
suffering damage as a result of a tort by settling with the person suffering such
damage, and thereafter commencing or continuing action against such other tort
feasor, in which event the tort feasor settling the damage shall satisfy the court
that the amount of the settlement was reasonable, and in the event that the court
finds the amount of the settlement was excessive it may fix the amount at which
the claim should have been settled.
4. Would it make any difference if in the contract with one of the defendants
there was a clause exempting that party from any liability for negligence?

NORTHWESTERN MUTUAL INS. v. J.T. O'BRYAN & CO.

(1974), 51 D.L.R. (3d) 693. British Columbia Court of Appeal; Maclean,
Branca and Carrothers JJ.A.

[The plaintiff had insured a warehouse, known as Plant No. 1, belonging
to Sun Rype Products Ltd., against fire. The plaintiff requested the defendant insurance agency to cancel the insurance since the warehouse was
unsprinklered and vacant. The defendant, Thibeau, was manager of the
defendant's office. The plaintiff wrote to the defendant on January 12, 1970
to have the insurance cancelled. On April 20, 1970 the plaintiff again wrote
to the defendant requesting that the insurance be cancelled. There were
more letters and telephone calls from the plaintiff's representative, one
Trimble, to Thibeau requesting action on the cancellation. On June 8, 1970
Thibeau phoned Trimble to say that the insurance was cancelled as of the
preceding Friday, June 5, 1970.]
The judgment of the court was given by
Branca J.A.: – ... The evidence shows quite conclusively that if O'Bryan
had not complied with the request of Northwestern in deleting the particular risk, Northwestern could and would have cancelled the entire policy and
thus divested itself of the unwanted risk. This evidence was given both by
Beck and Trimble.
A fire occurred at the No. 1 plant on July 13, 1970, and Northwestern
had to pay its proportionate share of that coverage which amounted to
$22,372.86.

Thus briefly it appeared that Northwestern gave certain instructions by letter in January of 1970, to O'Bryan which O'Bryan should have serviced. O'Bryan did not attend to that request as it should have. Other letters were sent and remained unanswered. Finally, Thibeau, who was manager of a production unit promised Trimble on the telephone that he would do something about this matter thus accepting the fact Northwestern relied upon him. He did not reply to that telephone call as he promised.

A further telephone call took place between Trimble and Thibeau and in answer Thibeau told Northwestern that it was off the risk as of Friday. That was not so. Thibeau tried to explain and stated that the telephone call came on a busy Friday afternoon and he went to the insurance record book to check. He checked a record numbered 6A and stated that he found that there was coverage other than the blanket building and equipment policy.

However, the sheet did not refer to the risk in question at all. It is difficult to appreciate how one with the experience of Thibeau could make a mistake of this magnitude. He knew, or should have known, that plant No. 1 was covered for $200,000. The sheet he looked at was for a total coverage of $29,000. He knew, or should have known, that the Sun Rype coverage on plant No. 1 was for a plant situate at Ellis and Roanoak Aves., Kelowna; the sheet he looked at covered a building known as Belgo House on Clement Ave. He knew that the Sun Rype policy in question was written for a term of three years for an exceptionally large sum of money; the sheet he looked at gave coverage for one year. The date of the policy sheet he looked at was May 26, 1969; its expiry date was noted three times as May 31, 1970. One wonders how such an abject careless mistake could be made by a kindergarten child, let alone an experienced insurance manager.

However, that was his incredible excuse.

Northwestern was assured and believed that it was off the risk as of a day long before the fire occurred.

Northwestern, had it known that the information was false and/or inaccurate, could and would have cancelled out its liability without difficulty, in a timely fashion, to avoid its share of a risk under the policy which it reasonably assumed no longer existed, but which in fact did exist.

The learned trial Judge found O'Bryan liable in breach of contract and awarded damages in the sums stated. For the reasons given by the learned trial Judge with which I am in substantial agreement the appeal taken by O'Bryan must fail and is dismissed.

Northwestern appeals against the finding of the learned trial Judge that the evidence did not prove a duty of care on the part of Thibeau towards Northwestern, under the principles enunciated in *Hedley Byrne & Co., Ltd. v. Heller & Partners, Ltd.,* [1963] 2 All E.R. 575; several passages were cited from the reasons of the learned Law Lords who sat on that case. I quote from the judgment of Lord Reid on p. 583 where he stated:

> This passage makes it clear that LORD HALDANE did not think that a duty to take care must be limited to cases of fiduciary relationship in the narrow sense of relationships which had been recognised by the Court of Chancery as being of a fiduciary character. He speaks of other special relationships, and I can see no logical stopping place short of all those relationships where it is plain that the party seeking information or advice was trusting the other to exercise such a degree of care as the circumstances required, where it was reasonable for him to do that, and where the other gave the information or advice when he knew or ought to have known that the inquirer was relying on him. I say "ought to have

known" because in questions of negligence we now apply the objective standard of what the reasonable man would have done.

A reasonable man, knowing that he was being trusted or that his skill and judgment were being relied on, would, I think, have three courses open to him. He could keep silent or decline to give the information or advice sought: or he could give an answer with a clear qualification that he accepted no responsibility for it or that it was given without that reflection or inquiry which a careful answer would require: or he could simply answer without any such qualification. If he chooses to adopt the last course he must, I think, be held to have accepted some responsibility for his answer being given carefully, or to have accepted a relationship with the inquirer which requires him to exercise such care as the circumstances require.

Lord Morris of Borth-y-Gest at p. 594 said as follows:

My Lords, I consider that it follows and that it should now be regarded as settled that if someone possessed of a special skill undertakes, quite irrespective of contract, to apply that skill for the assistance of another person who relies on such skill, a duty of care will arise. The fact that the service is to be given by means of, or by the instrumentality of, words can make no difference. Furthermore if, in a sphere in which a person is so placed that others could reasonably rely on his judgment or his skill or on his ability to make carefuly inquiry, a person takes it on himself to give information or advice to, or allow his information or advice to be passed on to, another person who, as he knows or should know, will place reliance on it, then a duty of care will arise.

Lord Hodson at p. 601 spoke in these words:

I do not think that it is possible to catalogue the special features which must be found to exist before the duty of care will arise in a given case, but since preparing this opinion I have had the opportunity of reading the speech which my noble and learned friend LORD MORRIS OF BORTH-Y- GEST has now delivered. I agree with him that if in a sphere where a person is so placed that others could reasonably rely on his judgment or his skill or on his ability to make careful inquiry such person takes it on himself to give information or advice to, or allows his information or advice to be passed on to, another person who, as he knows, or should know, will place reliance on it, then a duty of care will arise.

In my opinion the facts accepted by the learned trial Judge brought Thibeau, and along with him O'Bryan, directly and squarely within the category of liability formulated in *Hedley Byrne* and with respect to the learned trial Judge, a duty of care did arise on the part of Thibeau towards Northwestern which he, Thibeau, breached by his total lack of care which in turn was the sole cause of the resultant damage to Northwestern.

Thibeau, in the words of Lord Reid, could have kept silent and declined to give the information; in that event Northwestern would have cancelled. Alternatively, Thibeau could have given the information with a reservation that he accepted no liability for its accuracy or otherwise. Had he done so, again Northwestern would have cancelled. In the further alternative, he could, as he did, without any qualification gave the information which Northwestern wanted knowing that Northwestern relied upon him for its accuracy and which was extremely important in the circumstances. The circumstances gave rise to a duty of care.

Counsel for O'Bryan and Thibeau argued strongly in favour of the finding of the learned trial Judge and urged that the evidence did not establish a duty of care and that the evidence, at most, proved only that Thibeau was acting in a friendly way or discharging a kindly act, incidental to their business relationship, which carried with it no legal duty except a duty to be honest. In the alternative he urged that the relationship was a casual one, which invited only a casual reply, in which event there was only an obligation to be honest and in either case he admitted the evidence disclosed that Thibeau was honest although completely mistaken in the information which he passed on.

This was not so. There was nothing casual about the relationship. The information which was wanted started with a letter early in January for information which Thibeau should have given in the ordinary course of business. The requests continued on for a number of months by unanswered letters, telephone calls, telephone messages which were ignored, culminating finally with telephone calls made by Trimble which ended with the information given by Thibeau to Trimble that Northwestern was off the risk.

In my judgment the facts accepted by the learned trial Judge brought Thibeau directly within the class of liability contemplated by *Hedley Byrne*. There resulted a duty of care. That duty of care was breached by the inexcusable negligence of Thibeau that gave rise to damage to Northwestern. The cross-appeal is allowed and there will be judgment against Thibeau in the same sum awarded by the learned trial Judge against O'Bryan.

Appeal dismissed;
cross-appeal allowed.

QUESTIONS

1. What would have happened had the defendant done nothing and the fire had occurred on June 5, 1970?

2. How does the *N.W. Mutual* case differ from *Sealand* in respect of the liability of Thibeau and McHaffie? Suppose that Thibeau was the only shareholder in the company, why do you think that he or McHaffie would have incorporated the companies?

3. Are the reasons for imposing liability here the same as in a case like *Esso v. Mardon* or *Hedley Byrne v. Heller*, itself? If not, is the court justified in doing so?

D. Mistakes

In one sense the problems in the preceding section arose from the fact that one party made a mistake. We did not talk about the mistake as the basis for any remedy: whether the disappointed (mistaken) party had a remedy depended on what was done or said by the other party. The cases in this section are, therefore, in one sense a residuary category. The disappointed party has been driven to use the fact of his mistake alone as the basis for the relief that he wants, since there is nothing else that he can do.

This feature of the law of mistake has a number of important consequences. These include:

1. There is a tremendous variety in the cases in terms of:

(a) the situations where mistake arose,

(b) the consequences of mistake,

(c) the parties who are seeking relief.

2. It is illusory to think that any single approach will offer much of a useful guide to the solutions that have to be found.

3. The remedies that have to be available cover a very wide range. Great care must be taken to work out the appropriate remedy in each case where relief can be given. Once again, the analysis will have to consider the importance of reliance and unjust enrichment as grounds for relief.

The analysis that we shall present is not one that, so far, finds much support in what the courts say that they are doing. It finds much more support in what the courts do. In addition, some very recent Canadian cases indicate that the courts are moving away from the traditional methods of analysis. It is too soon to know how far they will move and where they will eventually end up.

The following check-list is taken from Corbin and offers a convenient list of the factors that must be considered in any case involving a mistake.
Corbin on Contracts, Vol. 3, § 597, p. 582.

Before we consider how it is that we can discover the inducing thought, perhaps mistaken, of a man who has acted, it may be helpful to suggest that his thought and action may be accompanied by a great variety of factors, and that juristic effects will be found to vary with these factors. Some of these many factors, to be discussed in the following sections, will be listed by putting the following questions:

"1. Did both parties, or only one, have a mistaken thought?

"2. Did the mistake induce mutual expressions of agreement; or did it merely induce action by one person toward another? E.g. a payment of money.

"3. If mutual expressions were induced, were they expressions that agreed in meaning, as interpreted by the parties themselves or by third parties?

"4. What was the fact as to which a mistaken thought existed? The possibilities are myriad.

"5. Was the fact of substantial importance?

"6. Did one party know of the other's mistake, or have reason to know it?

"7. Did one party cause the other's mistake, purposely or innocently?

"8. Was the mistaken party negligent?

"9. How soon was the mistake discovered and notice given?

"10. Has either party, or a third party, changed his position, so that restoration of his former position is impossible?

"11. Was the risk of such error assumed by one of the parties, by agreement or by custom?

"12. What remedies are available? Among these are Damages, Restitution, Specific Performance, Rescission, Cancellation, Reformation.

"13. Were there differences between Common Law and Equity, and do they still exist?"

The first group of cases deal with situations where the mistake was made in a written document when the final agreement is alleged not to represent the true agreement. The conventional term for this category is "rectification". Here one party seeks to invoke the equitable jurisdiction of the court to have the agreement rectified; that is, to have it changed to reflect the true agreement of the parties.

U.S.A. v. MOTOR TRUCKS, LTD.

[1924] A.C. 196. Judicial Committee; Lords Birkenhead, Summer, Viscount Haldane, Sir Henry Duke and Duff J.

APPEAL (No. 18 of 1923) from a judgment of the Appellate Division of the Supreme Court of Ontario (April 28, 1922) reversing a judgment of a judge of that Court.

By a contract dated May 18, 1918, the respondent company contracted to machine high-explosive shells for the appellant Government; the contract provided for cancellation by notice in the event of an anticipated termination of the war, and for payments to be made to the respondents thereupon. The payments were to include reimbursement for the cost of buildings, plant, etc., which the respondents had to add to their facilities for the purpose of carrying out the contract. Notice to terminate the contract was given in November, 1918, and the parties thereupon negotiated as to the sum to be paid to the respondents. Ultimately a sum of $1,653,115 was agreed, which included $376,496, being the full amount which the respondents claimed in respect of land and buildings. After deducting from the above total a large sum which had been advanced by the appellant Government to the respondents, together with interest thereon, it was agreed that $637,812 was due to the respondents.

The parties accordingly entered into a formal contract dated October 7, 1919, but not actually signed until November 8. The contract provided that it should supersede the original contract of May 18, 1918, which was thereby terminated, and that the appellant Government should pay to the respondents the sum of $637,812 in full settlement for work and goods delivered and expenses incurred under the original contract; it further provided as follows: "(4.) Title to all property specified in schedule A, hereto annexed and made a part hereof, shall vest in the United States immediately upon execution of this agreement."

The land and buildings were not included in the schedule.

The agreed sum was paid on November 10, 1919, but the respondents subsequently denied the right of the appellant Government to possession of the land and buildings.

The appellant Government brought an action against the respondents in the Supreme Court of Ontario, claiming rectification of the schedule by the inclusion of the land and buildings, and specific performance of the contract as so rectified; alternatively they claimed repayment of the sum paid in respect of the land and buildings.

The trial judge (Kelly J.) found that the intention was that the land and buildings should become the property of the appellant Government. He ordered and declared that the respondents were trustees of the land and buildings for such person as the appellant Government might direct, with rectification of the schedule, the respondents to convey the land accordingly.

On appeal to the Appellate Division the judgment of Kelly J. was reversed and the action dismissed, Meredith C.J. dissenting. The judgments of the majority of the Court were based mainly upon conclusions of fact.

The judgment of their Lordships was delivered by

Earl of Birkenhead... The question which requires the decision of the Board is whether or not it was the intention of the parties that the land and buildings, which had been paid for as claimed without deduction, should be inserted in schedule A and whether, if so, they were omitted therefrom by mutual mistake, so that rectification of an incomplete schedule should be ordered, or whether on the true interpretation of the intentions of the parties the respondents were entitled to receive all that they had expended upon acquiring the land and erecting the building, and, being so compensated, to retain both as their own.

The answer to these questions can only be found by reference to some legal considerations which their Lordships will hereinafter examine. If the parties intended that the lands and buildings should be included in schedule A, so that the omission in the instrument was accidental, rectification ought undoubtedly to be decreed. The Board, therefore, finds it necessary to examine the actions and the words of the parties at the relevant periods. And in enforcing the conclusions which will hereafter be stated their Lordships think it right to make it plain that they have entirely ignored the memorandum of the minutes of the meeting on October 7, 1919. In the opinion of the Board the terms of this memorandum were not admissible and should not have been admitted as evidence.

Their Lordships have reached the conclusion that both the appellants and the respondents intended that the land and buildings should be included in schedule A. That the appellants so intended has not been seriously disputed; and upon this point the Board entertains no doubt. Their Lordships, after giving careful attention to the matter, are no less confident that the respondents clearly understood that the award contemplated the transfer as owners to the United States of the land and buildings for which under its terms that Government had paid the respondents complete and generous compensation.

The reasons which have led their Lordships to a conclusion so clear may be shortly summarized.

[After stating the reasons for the above conclusion, the judgment proceeded:] It remains, therefore, to consider what view in fact and in law must be taken of the respondents' remaining contention that their agreement to part with the ownership of the lands and buildings (in which is implicit their agreement to insert them in the schedule) was produced by an error as to their legal rights under the original contract. Whether they possessed any such rights as those supposed under that contract it is not necessary to consider, for the trial judge found as a fact that those who represented the company were not at any single relevant moment forgetful of any right whatsoever which they may have possessed under that agreement. And their Lordships, so far from quarrelling with this finding, most expressly accept and approve it. Nothing need be added in parting with this contention, except that in all the circumstances it required considerable hardihood to conceive and put it forward.

But even if the company's officials had made a mistake — in the circumstances wholly incredible — such a mistake could not in law have produced any effect upon the rights of the parties. For it is not contended, and could not be, that the mistake was shared by the appellants; and unilateral error, which in such a case as the present would hardly be distinguishable from carelessness, does not afford to the respondents any ground of defence in proceedings such as these.

It was further suggested that the present action involved an attempt to enforce a parol contract inconsistently with the principle of the Statute of Frauds. It is, however, well settled by a series of familiar authorities that the Statute of Frauds is not allowed by any Court administering the doctrines of equity to become an instrument for enabling sharp practice to be committed. And indeed the power of the Court to rectify mutual mistake implies that this power may be exercised notwithstanding that the true agreement of the parties has not been expressed in writing. Nor does the rule make any inroad upon another principle, that the plaintiff must show first that there was an actually concluded agreement antecedent to the instrument which is sought to be rectified; and secondly, that such agreement has been inaccurately represented in the instrument. When this is proved either party may claim, in spite of the Statute of Frauds, that the instrument on which the other insists does not represent the real agreement. The statute, in fact, only provides that no agreement not in writing and not duly signed shall be sued on; but when the written instrument is rectified there is a writing which satisfies the statute, the jurisdiction of the Court to rectify being outside the prohibition of the statute.

The respondents, however, advance still a further point of law. They contend that a plaintiff was not allowed to sue in the old Court of Chancery for the specific performance of a contract with a parol variation. There seems no reason on principle why a Court of equity should not at one and the same time reform and enforce a contract; the matter, however, has been much discussed in the Courts, and the balance of distinguished authority not unequally maintained. But the difficulty, which was almost entirely technical, has been, in the view of the Board, removed by the provisions of the Judicature Act, 1873, s. 24, which are reproduced in s. 16 (*h*) of the Judicature Act of the Province of Ontario, ch. 56 of the Revised Statutes of 1914. This section provides that the Court, which is to administer equity as well as law, is to grant, either absolutely or on such reasonable terms and conditions as it shall deem best, all such remedies as any of the parties may appear to be entitled to in respect of any and every legal and equitable claim properly brought forward by them in such cause or matter, so that, as far as possible, all matters so in controversy between the parties may be completely and finally determined, and all multiplicity of legal proceedings discouraged. . . .

The Board has thought it proper to consider the matters raised in this appeal with some particularity, partly because of the importance of the case, and partly out of respect for the learned judges who took a different view in the Appellate Division. But on analysis the issue has proved to be extremely simple. Both parties intended the lands and buildings to be included in the schedule. These were inadvertently omitted. Rectification must follow unless some exceptional ground for excluding this remedy is advanced. The respondents have attempted only to show that they agreed to the schedule in its intended form by reason of an error as to their existing legal rights. This contention has been rightly negatived on the facts, and would, in any event, be irrelevant in law.

Their Lordships will, therefore, humbly advise His Majesty that this appeal should be allowed, the judgment of the Appellate Division of the Supreme Court set aside with costs, and the judgment of Kelly J. restored. The respondents will pay the costs of the appeal.

PAGET v. MARSHALL

(1884), 28 Ch. D. 255. Chancery Division, England.

[The plaintiff owned a warehouse which consisted of three stores on the first floor (Nos. 48, 49 & 50) and a space on the second floor over the stores. The plaintiff (who occupied No. 48) built a partition between Nos. 48 & 49 on the second floor so that No. 48 had both the first and second floors. The defendant wanted to rent the second and upper floors of the building. He has shown over the building by the plaintiff's brother who pointed out that the second floor over No. 48 was not for rent. When the lease was drawn up and signed it included, by mistake, that part of the second floor over No. 48. The plaintiff sought rectification of the lease as executed to exclude the part of the second floor over No. 48.]

[Note: The judge refers to the second floor as the first floor, in accordance with English usage. The first floor in England is known as the ground floor.]

Bacon, V.C.: In all these cases on the law of mistake it is very difficult to apply a principle, because you have to rely upon the statements of parties interested, and upon not very accurate recollections of what took place between them. But the law I take to be as stated this morning by Mr. *Hemming*. If it is a case of common mistake — a common mistake as to one stipulation out of many provisions contained in a settlement or any other deed, that upon proper evidence may be rectified — the Court has the power to rectify, and that power is very often exercised. The other class of cases is one of what is called unilateral mistake, and there, if the Court is satisfied that the true intention of one of the parties was to do one thing, and he by mistake has signed an agreement to do another, that agreement will not be enforced against him, but the parties will be restored to their original position, and the agreement will be treated as if it had never been entered into. That I take to be the clear conclusion to be drawn from the authorities. The old law is very much as was stated in that very excellent treatise by Mr. *Kerr*, as to which anybody who has read it must be well satisfied with the diligence and industry, the intelligence and sagacity with which he has acquitted himself of his task, but which of course one cannot suppose is an authority upon which I can rely, although I listen to it with interest and respect.

. . . .

Under these circumstances, the facts being as I have stated, am I, because the lease has been executed under seal, demising to the Defendant that which the Plaintiff never meant to let him have, that which the Defendant says he knew at one time the Plaintiff intended to keep for himself, that which he has never claimed at any period prior to the letter — am I to say that the agreement is to be held to be irrevocable? It would be against every principle that regulates the law relating to mistakes, and it would be directly at variance with the proved facts in this case. On the evidence, it looks very like a common mistake. The Defendant, it is true, says in his defence, that he took it on the faith that the first floor of No. 48 was intentionally included in the letter of the 13th of November, 1883. Certainly he never said so until it is said in the defence, which I am looking at now; but he has not said so in his evidence. He has never said that he intended to take that. The argument addressed to me has been this: — "The separation of No. 48 and the blue, is effected solely by means of a brick-on-end partition; and that is easily removed." People building brick-on-end partitions do not mean them to be easily removed, unless there is some purpose to remove them, and here, using the Defendant's own evidence on this occasion, at that time the partition was effectually finished, and the Defendant knew that the Plaintiff intended to reserve it for his own use in his own business. The law being such as I have said, it is not necessary to say anything about how easily you can make holes in a partition, and how you can knock down a partition; you can pull down the front of a house with equal ease if you have proper appliances and proper workmen to do it. The way it is forced on my attention is the reason why the partition was first made, why it was found to be in existence when the Defendant first inspected it, why he knew from that time as well as he knows now that it never was the intention of the Plaintiff that he should have that "magnificent" room which formed one of two rooms which constituted the business place intended by the Plaintiff for his own use, and to which the access was made by one staircase communicating with nothing but the upper room.

But without being certain, as I cannot be certain on the facts before me, whether the mistake was what is called a common mistake — that is, such a common mistake as would induce the Court to strike out of a marriage settlement a provision or limitation — that there was to some extent a common mistake I must in charity and justice to the Defendant believe, because I cannot impute to him the intention of taking advantage of any incorrect expression in this letter. He may have persuaded himself that the letter was right; but if there was not a common mistake it is plain and palpable that the Plaintiff was mistaken, and that he had no intention of letting his own shop, which he had built and carefully constructed for his own purposes.

Upon that ground, therefore, I must say that the contract ought to be annulled. I think it would be right and just and perfectly consistent with other decisions that the Defendant should have an opportunity of choosing whether he will submit, as the Plaintiff asks that he should submit, to have the lease rectified by excluding from it the first floor of No. 48, whether he will choose to take his lease with that rectification, or whether he will choose to throw up the thing entirely, because the object of the Court is, as far as it can, to put the parties into the position in which they would have been if the mistake had not happened. Therefore I give the Defendant an opportunity of saying whether he will or will not submit to rectification. If he does not, then I shall declare that the agreement is annulled. Then we shall have to settle the terms on which it should be annulled. The Plaintiff does not object, if the agreement is annulled, to pay the Defendant any reasonable expenses to which he may have been put by reason of the Plaintiff's mistake; but it must be limited to that. I should like, if it be convenient for counsel or for the parties, to have an answer to the proposition I have made, in order that that may be fully before the persons whom it interests. I may say that I can find no reason for a reduction of the rent. I listened attentively to what Sir *John Ellis* said, and to what Mr. *Farmer* said, and I cannot but think that the rent of £500, if the lease is rectified, ought not, with any show of justice, to suffer any reduction.

Marten, for the Defendant, agreed to strike out the first floor of No. 48 from the lease; the lease in other respects standing as it was executed.

Bacon, V.C.: Then the decree will be, the Defendant electing to have rectification instead of cancellation of the lease, let the lease be rectified by omitting from it all mention of the first floor of No. 48. Then as to the costs of the action, the Plaintiff is not entitled to costs, because he has made a mistake, and the Defendant ought not to have any costs, because his opposition to the Plaintiff's demand has been unreasonable, unjust, and unlawful.

QUESTIONS

1. Are there any reasons for not giving the relief that was asked for in these cases? Specifically, were the expectations that either side had of the deals disappointed, was anyone's reliance defeated?

2. Which of the factors listed by Corbin were relevant here? Are these factors helpful?

These cases indicate that there are cases of mistake where there are very few problems of giving relief. The important point is that the party against whom the relief is sought cannot present a very convincing argument that he is hurt by the granting of any relief. This is because the court says that there was a clear agreement on what the contract was before the final agreement was executed. Cases where there is no such antecedent agreement raise much more difficult problems of giving relief. For example, if the parties have a contract for the sale of animal feed and the purchaser believes that the feed has some particular quality that the feed does not have, he cannot get rectification to have the quality made part of the contractual obligation of the seller unless he can show that the seller promised that the feed has the particular quality the buyer wants. See: *Rose v. Pim*, [1953] 2 Q.B. 450. Of course the line may be hard to draw, but the difficulty of drawing a line does not mean that no line can be drawn.

In *Hobbs v. E. & N. Railway* suppose that, during the negotiations for the sale of the land, Trutch had said to Hobbs, "By land we mean land without the minerals." A claim by E. & N. for rectification would succeed. (This is why on such a claim, evidence of negotiations is *admissible* under the approach of the House of Lords in *Prenn v. Simmonds* (*supra*, section A.)). There might be much more problem in establishing the claim if the evidence of the antecedent agreement to sell land without the minerals was based on factors like the price of the land or Hobbs' knowledge of the general practice of the railway.

There are also examples of simple cases in other areas:

NORWICH UNION v. PRICE

[1934] A.C. 455. Privy Council (N.S.W.); Viscount Sankey L.C., Lords Blanesburgh and Wright, Sir Lancelot Sanderson, Sir Sidney Rowlatt.

[The appellant plaintiffs had insured a cargo of lemons. The insurers were informed that the lemons had been damaged and sold, and they, therefore, paid the insured value to the insured. It was subsequently discovered that the lemons had not been damaged, but were sold because they were ripening. When the insurers paid the claim they took from the insured, the respondent, an assignment of their rights in the goods and the proceeds. The insurers sued to recover what they had paid to the insured.]

Lord Wright: It was ordered in the action that there should first be tried the question whether, on the assumption that the payment was made under a mistake of fact, the moneys paid were recoverable. The Chief Justice stated in his judgment that when the appellants made their agreement of March 25, 1929, there is no doubt they believed that the lemons had been damaged by the collision; he added: "I have no doubt, too, that the defendant was under the same belief." It is not necessary here to consider whether in any subsequent proceeding in this case the respondents will be able to impugn this position. The present proceeding is based on that assumption. The Chief Justice went on to say: "It is clear that the payment of the insurance moneys in consideration of the defendant's agreement to abandon its right to its property and its subrogation of those rights to the plaintiff was based on an underlying assumption by both parties that the lemons had been damaged by a peril insured against, that is, by collision with some submerged object." The Chief Justice accordingly held that at common law the appellants would be entitled to recover as for a payment made under a mistake of fact; but he held that, notwithstanding, the appellants were debarred from recovering because there had been a notice of abandonment given and accepted within the meaning of s. 6, sub-s. 6, of the Australian Marine Insurance Act, 1909, so that a conclusive admission of liability for the loss was constituted as against the appellants. James J. agreed with the Chief Justice; the decision of the trial judge had been to the same effect, and was accordingly affirmed. Davidson J. in the Full Court reached the same conclusion as his colleagues, but for other reasons; he did not agree that the claim was barred by the provisions of the Marine Insurance Act, but he held that the mistake was one of law.

Their Lordships agree with the trial judge and with the majority of the Full Court that for purposes of this appeal the mistake was one of fact and was fundamental to the transaction. On the assumptions on which this appeal proceeds, the misconception under which the payment was made was that there had been a loss by perils insured against; unless that were so, there was no liability under the policy: save for that misconception no payment could have been claimed and no payment would have been made. The facts which were misconceived were those which were essential to liability and were of such a nature that on well-established principles any agreement concluded under such mistake was void in law, so that any payment made under such mistake was recoverable. The mistake, being of the character that it was, prevented there being that intention which the common law regards as essential to the making of an agreement or the transfer of money or property. Thus, in *Kelly v. Solari*, 9 M. & W. 54, where money was paid under a mistake of fact, Baron Parke concludes his well-known statement of the law with these words: "If it (the money) is paid under the impression of the truth of a fact which is untrue, it may, generally speaking, be recovered back, however careless the party paying may have been in omitting to use due diligence to inquire into the fact. In such a case the receiver was not entitled to it, nor intended to have it." The "fact" which Baron Parke is referring to is one "which would entitle the other to the money" if true. The reference to intention is crucial. In the same sense, in *R. E. Jones, Ld. v. Waring & Gillow, Ld.*, [1926] A. C. 670, 696, Lord Sumner says of *Kelly v. Solari*: "The executrix of Solari ought to have known, and probably did, that the company had cancelled the policy and was making a mistake in paying again. If so, there was no real intention on the company's part to enrich her." Lord Sumner had just pointed out that passing of property is a question of intention, and just as much so in the case of a payment of money as in the transfer of a chattel. To the same effect, Lord Shaw in the same case says in respect of mistakes: "The true facts may not have been known to the grantor, or may have been misrepresented with such a result that the mind of the grantor does not go with the transaction at all; his mind goes with another transaction, and he is meaning to give effect to that other transaction, depending on facts different from those which were the true facts." Thus, in the present case the only transaction with which the mind of the appellants went was payment of a claim on the basis of the truth of facts which constituted a loss by perils insured against: they never intended to pay on the basis of facts inconsistent with any such loss by perils insured against. The mistake was as vital as that in *Cooper v. Phibbs* in respect of which Lord Westbury used these words: "If parties contract under a mutual mistake and misapprehension as to their relative and respective rights, the result is, that that agreement is liable to be set aside as having proceeded upon a common mistake." At common law such a contract (or simulacrum of a contract) is more correctly described as void, there being in truth no intention to contract. Their Lordships find nothing tending to contradict or overrule these established principles in *Bell v. Lever Bros., Ld.*

It is true that in general the test of intention in the formation of contracts and the transfer of property is objective; that is, intention is to be ascertained from what the parties said or did. "But proof of mistake affirmatively excludes intention." It is, however, essential that the mistake relied on should be of such a nature that it can be properly described as a mistake in respect of the underlying assumption of the contract or transaction or as being fundamental or basic. Whether the mistake does satisfy this description may often be a matter of great difficulty. Applying these principles to the present case, their Lordships find themselves so far in agreement with the opinions of the Courts below that the money paid is recoverable at common law. That leaves for consideration the point on which the decision went against the appellants, so that this appeal is brought.

It is first necessary to determine precisely what was the transaction of March 25, 1929, the nature of which must be ascertained from the document of that date. The Court below have held that it either constituted or evidenced a notice of abandonment as for a constructive total loss and an acceptance of that notice.

It would seem that a notice of abandonment which is itself a nullity cannot become the basis of rights simply because abandonment has been accepted by the underwriters. It further seems that on general principles mutual mistake will have the same effect in regard to the offer and acceptance of abandonment as in regard to any other contract.

It is unnecessary to repeat what has been said earlier in this judgment as to the effect of mistake, but it seems to follow that just as mistake may render a notice of abandonment a nullity, so in the same way it may render an acceptance of the notice a nullity. In other words, though the goods were in fact lost to the respondents, such a mistake as is here assumed throughout would prevent not only the notice of abandonment but also the acceptance of abandonment from being other than a nullity. No case would then exist for the application of the words of s. 68, sub-s. 6.

Their Lordships have felt it desirable to make some observations on the question of construction out of respect to the opinions expressed in the Courts below, but it is not necessary in this case to express any final opinion. It is enough for the decision of the appeal that in their Lordships' judgment there was here no case of a notice of abandonment or an acceptance of such notice, but it was simply a case of money paid under a mistake of fact, so that the appellants who have paid are entitled to recover.

It follows that their Lordships' judgment is that the appeal should be allowed and the judgment and order appealed from be set aside: the appellants will have the costs of the hearings in the Courts below and of this appeal. They will humbly so advise His Majesty accordingly.

QUESTIONS

1. If this case presents little problem in giving relief, why is this so?
2. Would it matter if the insurer could have easily found out why the lemons were sold before paying on the claim?

The next case is the leading English case on the law of mistake. As such it has frequently been accepted in Canada.

BELL v. LEVER BROTHERS, LTD.

[1932] A.C. 161. House of Lords; Viscount Hailsham, Lords Blanesburgh, Warrington, Atkin and Thankerton.

Lord Atkin. My Lords, this case involves a question of much importance in the formation and dissolution of contracts. The facts are not very complicated, though in the course of eliciting them the legal proceedings have undergone vicissitudes which have made the task of determining the issues more difficult than need be. In 1923 the Niger Company, Ld., was controlled by Lever Brothers, Ld., whom I shall call Levers, who held over 99 per cent. of its shares. The Niger Company dealt in West African produce, including cocoa, and at this time appears to have been making trading losses. To restore the position Levers approached the appellant Bell, who had banking experience, and the appellant Snelling, a chartered accountant, with a view to their taking part in the management of the Niger Company's affairs. In August, 1923, an agreement was made between Levers and Bell, under which Bell entered the service of Levers for a term of five years from November 1, 1923, on the terms of letters of August 8, 1923, which provided that Bell's salary was to be £8000 a year. Levers were to pay the premiums on an endowment policy maturing at the age of sixty for a sum of £16,200. Levers were to appoint and maintain Bell as chairman of the Niger Company during his service. Bell was only to be responsible to the Committee of Control of Lever Brothers and to the shareholders of the Niger Company. In October an agreement was made between Snelling and Levers whereby Snelling was to be in the service of the company for five years from October 1, 1923, on the terms of a letter of September 12, which provided that Snelling was to serve Levers in regard to its West African interests at a salary of £10,000. per annum to March 31, 1925, and £6000. for the remainder of the five years. On September 14 both Bell and Snelling were appointed by the Niger Company directors of the company, and Bell was appointed chairman of the Board. In April, 1924, Snelling was appointed a vice-chairman. The result of the appointments was a success. The Niger Company began to prosper and in July, 1926, the agreements of both Bell and Snelling with Levers were cancelled and new agreements substituted for a further period of five years from July 1, 1926, at the same salaries but with a commission on the profits of the Niger Company. The Niger Company continued to prosper, and in March, 1929, arrangements were concluded for an amalgamation between the Niger Company and its principal trade competitor, the African and Eastern Trade Corporation. The terms of the amalgamation appear to have left no room for Bell or Snelling. It was necessary, therefore, to dispose of the agreements between them and Levers. Mr. D'Arcy Cooper, the chairman of Levers, saw both gentlemen and arranged terms with them which are recorded in two letters of March 19, 1929. [In these letters Levers agreed to pay Bell and Snelling over £30,000 and £20,000, respectively.]

. . .

Both sums were duly paid on May 1, 1929, on which date the two appellants retired from their service with Levers, and from the Boards of the Niger Company and various subsidiary companies to which they had been appointed. Very little attention appears to have been paid at the trial to these subsidiary companies, and there is a scarcity of evidence about them. The position in regard to them may demand further consideration; at present I leave them on one side. The position then is that in March, 1929, the two appellants left the service of Levers with substantial compensation in their pockets and mutual expressions of respect and esteem.

In July, 1929, Levers discovered facts which indicated that their expenditure of £50,000. and their expressions of regard had been misplaced. For the years October to October, 1926-7, 1927-8, and 1928-9, the Niger Company, together with three of its trading competitors, including the African and Eastern Trade Corporation, had been parties to what were called "Pooling Agreements," under which the parties undertook to disclose to one another their dealings in Gold Coast cocoa; not to buy cocoa produced elsewhere without the consent of the Pool Committee; agreed to fix from time to time buying and selling prices and not to sell without consent below the agreed selling price; and made provision for distributing in agreed proportions the proceeds of the pool. It appears to have been considered necessary that the operations of the Niger Company under the pool should be carried out without excessive publicity; and the brokers' contracts for the Niger Company were recorded under initials. In November and December, 1927, the two appellants, at a time when the Pool Committee were lowering the pool purchase price of cocoa, on several occasions sold cocoa short, and closing in a few days at the reduced price made profits. A few days later they bought for the rise and made a small profit. Altogether the dealings resulted in a profit of £1360. The transaction was of course conducted without the knowledge of Levers or any responsible official of the Niger Company. It was carried out in secrecy, and payment of the profit was made by the brokers at the appellants' request in a draft for American dollars. No defence can be offered for this piece of misconduct. The appellants were acting in a business in which their employers were concerned; their interests and their employers' conflicted; they were taking a secret advantage out of their employment, and committing a grave breach of duty both to Levers and to the Niger Company. The jury have found that had the facts been discovered during the service, Levers could and would have dismissed them, and no objection can be taken to this finding.

Having made this discovery it naturally occurred to Levers that instead of spending £50,000. to cancel the two service agreements they might, if they had known the facts, have got rid of them for nothing. They therefore claimed the return of the money from the appellants, as well as the amount of the profits made; and on August 7, 1929, issued the writ in the present action, claiming damages for fraudulent misrepresentation and concealment, an account of the defendants' dealings in cocoa, and repayment of money paid under a mistake of fact.

[At the trial before Wright J. and a jury, the jury found that there had been no fraud on the part of the defendants; that Levers would have dismissed the defendants had their breaches of contract been discovered: that Levers would not have promised to pay the amounts that they paid had they known of the breaches. The judge held that Levers would have been justified in dismissing the defendants. Wright J. gave judgment for Levers. An appeal to the Court of Appeal was unanimously dismissed.]

. . .

Two points present themselves for decision. Was the agreement of March 19, 1929, void by reason of a mutual mistake of Mr. D'Arcy Cooper and Mr. Bell?

Could the agreement of March 19, 1929, be avoided by reason of the failure of Mr. Bell to disclose his misconduct in regard to the cocoa dealings?

My Lords, the rules of law dealing with the effect of mistake on contract appear to be established with reasonable clearness. If mistake operates at all it operates so as to negative or in some cases to nullify consent. The parties may be mistaken in the identity of the contracting parties, or in the existence of the subject-matter of the contract at the date of the contract, or in the qualify of the subject-matter of the contract. These mistakes may be by one party, or by both, and the legal effect may depend upon the class of mistake above mentioned. Thus a mistaken belief by A. that he is contracting with B., whereas in fact he is contracting with C., will negative consent where it is clear that the intention of A. was to contract only with B. So the agreement of A. and B. to purchase a specific article is void if in fact the article had perished before the date of sale. In this case, though the parties in fact were agreed about the subject-matter, yet a consent to transfer or take delivery of something not existent is deemed useless, the consent is nullified. As codified in the Sale of Goods Act the contract is expressed to be void if the seller was in ignorance of the destruction of the specific chattel. I apprehend that if the seller with knowledge that a chattel was destroyed purported to sell it to a purchaser, the latter might sue for damages for non-delivery though the former could not sue for non-acceptance, but I know of no case where a seller has so committed himself. This is a case where mutual mistake certainly and unilateral mistake by the seller of goods will prevent a contract from arising. Corresponding to mistake as to the existence of the subject-matter is mistake as to title in cases where, unknown to the parties, the buyer is already the owner of that which the seller purports to sell to him. The parties intended to effectuate a transfer of ownership: such a transfer is impossible: the stipulation is naturali ratione inutilis. This is the case of *Cooper v. Phibbs* (1867), L.R. 2 H.L. 149, where A. agreed to take a lease of a fishery from B., though contrary to the belief of both parties at the time A. was tenant for life of the fishery and B. appears to have had no title at all. To such a case Lord Westbury applied the principle that if parties contract under a mutual mistake and misapprehension as to their relative and respective rights the result is that the agreement is liable to be set aside as having proceeded upon a common mistake. Applied to the context the statement is only subject to the criticism that the agreement would appear to be void rather than voidable. Applied to mistake as to rights generally it would appear to be too wide. Even where the vendor has no title, though both parties think he has, the correct view would appear to be that there is a contract: but that the vendor has either committed a breach of a stipulation as to title, or is not able to perform his contract. The contract is unenforceable by him but is not void.

Mistake as to quality of the thing contracted for raises more difficult questions. In such a case a mistake will not affect assent unless it is the mistake of both parties, and is as to the existence of some quality which makes the thing without the quality essentially different from the thing as it was believed to be. Of course it may appear that the parties contracted that the article should possess the quality which one or other or both mistakenly believed it to possess. But in such a case there is a contract and the inquiry is a different one, being whether the contract as to quality amounts to a condition or a warranty, a different branch of the law. The principles to be applied are to be found in two cases which, as far as my knowledge goes, have always been treated as authoritative expositions of the law. The first is *Kennedy v. Panama Royal Mail Co.* (1867), L.R. 2 Q.B. 580.

In that case the plaintiff had applied for shares in the defendant company on the faith of a prospectus which stated falsely but innocently that the company had a binding contract with the Government of New Zealand for the carriage of mails. On discovering the true facts the plaintiff brought an action for the recovery of the sums he had paid on calls. The defendants brought a cross action for further calls. Blackburn J., in delivering the judgment of the Court (Cockburn C.J., Blackburn, Mellor and Shee JJ.), said: "The only remaining question is one of much greater difficulty. It was contended by Mr. Mellish, on behalf of Lord Gilbert Kennedy, that the effect of the prospectus was to warrant to the intended shareholders that there really was such a contract as is there represented, and not merely to represent that the company *bonâ fide* believed it; and that the difference in substance between shares in a company with such a contract and shares in a company whose supposed contract was not binding, was a difference in substance in the nature of the thing; and that the shareholder was entitled to return the shares as soon as he discovered this, quite independently of fraud, on the ground that he had applied for one thing and got another. And, if the invalidity of the contract really made the shares he obtained different things in substance from those which he applied for, this would, we think, be good law....

There is, however, a very important difference between cases where a contract may be rescinded on account of fraud, and those in which it may be rescinded on the ground that there is a difference in substance between the thing bargained for and that obtained. It is enough to show that there was a fraudulent representation as to any part of that which induced the party to enter into the contract which he seeks to rescind; but where there has been an innocent misrepresentation or misapprehension, it does not authorize a rescission unless it is such as to show that there is a complete difference in substance between what was supposed to be and what was taken, so as to constitute a failure of consideration. For example, where a horse is bought under a belief that it is sound, if the purchaser was induced to buy a fraudulent representation as to the horse's soundness, the contract may be rescinded. If it was induced by an honest misrepresentation as to its soundness, though it may be clear that both vendor and purchaser thought that they were dealing about a sound horse and were in error, yet the purchaser must pay the whole price unless there was a warranty; and even if there was a warranty, he cannot return the horse and claim back the whole price, unless there was a condition to that effect in the contract: ...

The Court came to the conclusion in that case that, though there was a misapprehension as to that which was a material part of the motive inducing the applicant to ask for the shares, it did not prevent the shares from being in substance those he applied for.

The next case is *Smith v. Hughes* (1871), L.R. 6 Q.B. 597, the well known case as the new and old oats. The action was in the county court, and was for the price of oats sold and delivered and damages for not accepting oats bargained and sold. Cockburn C.J. cites Story on Contracts as follows: "Mr. Justice Story in his work on Contracts (vol. i., s. 516), states the law as to concealment as follows: 'The general rule, both of law and equity, in respect to concealment, is that mere silence with regard to a material fact, which there is no legal obligation to divulge, will not avoid a contract, although it operate as an injury to the party from whom it is concealed.' 'Thus,' he goes on to say (s. 517), 'although a vendor is bound to employ no artifice or disguise for the purpose of concealing defects in the article sold, since that would amount to a positive fraud on the vendee; yet, under the general doctrine of caveat emptor, he is not, ordinarily, bound to disclose every defect of which he may be cognizant, although his silence may operate virtually to deceive the vendee.' 'But,' he continues (s. 518), 'an improper concealment or suppression of a material fact, when the party concealing is legally bound to disclose, and of which the other party has a legal right to insist that he shall be informed, is fraudulent, and will invalidate a contract.' Further, distinguishing between extrinsic circumstances affecting the value of the subject-matter of a sale, and the concealment of intrinsic circumstances appertaining to its nature, character, and condition, he points out (s. 519) that with reference to the latter the rule is 'that mere silence as to anything which the other party might by proper diligence have discovered, and which is open to his examination, is not fraudulent, unless a special trust or confidence exist between the parties, or be implied from the circumstances of the case.' In the doctrine thus laid down I entirely agree."

In a further passage he says: "It only remains to deal with an argument which was pressed upon us, that the defendant in the present case intended to buy old oats, and the plaintiffs to sell new, so the two minds were not ad idem; and that consequently there was no contract. This argument proceeds on the fallacy of confounding what was merely a motive operating on the buyer to induce him to buy with one of the essential conditions of the contract. Both parties were agreed as to the sale and purchase of this particular parcel of oats. The defendant believed the oats to be old and was thus induced to agree to buy them, but he omitted to make their age a condition of the contract. All that can be said is, that the two minds were not ad idem as to the age of the oats; they certainly were ad idem as to the sale and purchase of them. Suppose a person to buy a horse without a warranty, believing him to be sound, and the horse turns out unsound, could it be contended that it would be open to him to say that, as he had intended to buy a sound horse, and the seller to sell an unsound one, the contract was void, because the seller must have known from the price the buyer was willing to give, or from his general habits as a buyer of horses that he thought the horse was sound? The cases are exactly parallel."

Blackburn J. said: "In this case I agree that on the sale of a specific article, unless there be a warranty making it part of the bargain that it possesses some particular quality, the purchaser must take the article he has bought though it does not possess that quality. And I agree that even if the vendor was aware that the purchaser thought that the article possessed that quality, and would not have entered into the contract unless he had so thought, still the purchaser is bound, unless the vendor was guilty of some fraud or deceit upon him, and that a mere abstinence from disabusing the purchaser of that impression is not fraud or deceit; for, whatever may be the case in a court of morals, there is no legal obligation on the vendor to inform the purchaser that he is under a mistake, not induced by the act of the vendor."

The Court ordered a new trial. It is not quite clear whether they considered that if the defendant's contention was correct, the parties were not ad idem or there was a contractual condition that the oats sold were old oats. In either case the defendant would succeed in defeating the claim.

In these cases I am inclined to think that the true analysis is that there is a contract, but that the one party is not able to supply the very thing whether goods or services that the other party contracted to take; and therefore the contract is unenforceable by the one if executory, while if executed the other can recover back money paid on the ground of failure of the consideration.

We are now in a position to apply to the facts of this case the law as to mistake so far as it has been stated. It is essential on this part of the discussion to keep in mind the finding of the jury acquitting the defendants of fraudulent misrepresentation or concealment in procuring the agreements in question. Grave injustice may be done to the defendants and confusion introduced into the legal conclusion, unless it is quite clear that in considering mistake in this case no suggestion of fraud is admissible and cannot strictly be regarded by the judge who has to determine the legal issues raised. The agreement which is said to be void is the agreement contained in the letter of March 19, 1929, that Bell would retire from the Board of the Niger Company and its subsidiaries, and that in consideration of his doing so Levers would pay him as compensation for the termination of his agreements and consequent loss of office the sum of £30,000. in full satisfaction and discharge of all claims and demands of any kind against Lever Brothers, the Niger Company or its subsidiaries. The agreement, which as part of the contract was terminated, had been broken so that it could be repudiated. Is an agreement to terminate a broken contract different in kind from an agreement to terminate an unbroken contract, assuming that the breach has given the one party the right to declare the contract at an end? I feel the weight of the plaintiffs' contention that a contract immediately determinable is a different thing from a contract for an unexpired term, and that the difference in kind can be illustrated by the immense price of release from the longer contract as compared with the shorter. And I agree that an agreement to take an assignment of a lease for five years is not the same thing as to take an assignment of a lease for three years, still less a term for a few months. But, on the whole, I have come to the conclusion that it would be wrong to decide that an agreement to terminate a definite specified contract is void if it turns out that the agreement had already been broken and could have been terminated otherwise. The contract released is the identical contract in both cases, and the party paying for release gets exactly what he bargains for. It seems immaterial that he could have got the same result in another way, or that if he had known the true facts he would not have entered into the bargain. A. buys B.'s horse; he thinks the horse is sound and he pays the price of a sound horse; he would certainly not have bought the horse if he had known as the fact is that the horse is unsound. If B. has made no representation as to soundness and has not contracted that the horse is sound, A. is bound and cannot recover back the price. A. buys a picture from B.; both A. and B. believe it to be the work of an old master, and a high price is paid. It turns out to be a modern copy. A. has no remedy in the absence of representation or warranty. A. agrees to take on lease or to buy from B. an unfurnished dwelling-house. The house is in fact uninhabitable. A. would never have entered into the bargain if he had known the fact. A. has no remedy, and the position is the same whether B. knew the facts or not, so long as he made no representation or gave no warranty. A. buys a roadside garage business from B. abutting on a public thoroughfare: unknown to A., but known to B., it has already been decided to construct a bypass road which will divert substantially the whole of the traffic from passing A.'s garage. Again A. has no remedy. All these cases involve hardship on A. and benefit B., as most people would say, unjustly. They can be supported on the ground that it is of paramount importance that contracts should be observed, and that if parties honestly comply with the essentials of the formation of contracts — i.e., agree in the same terms on the same subject-matter — they are bound, and must rely on the stipulations of the contract for protection from the effect of facts unknown to them.

This brings the discussion to the alternative mode of expressing the result of a mutual mistake. It is said that in such a case as the present there is to be implied a stipulation in the contract that a condition of its efficacy is that the facts should be as understood by both parties — namely, that the contract could not be terminated till the end of the current term. The question of the existence of conditions, express or implied, is obviously one that affects not the formation of contract, but the investigation of the terms of the contract when made. A condition derives its efficacy from the consent of the parties, express or implied. They have agreed, but on what terms. One term may be that unless the facts are or are not of a particular nature, or unless an event has or has not happened, the contract is not to take effect. With regard to future facts such a condition is obviously contractual. Till the event occurs the parties are bound. Thus the condition (the exact terms of which need not here be investigated) that is generally accepted as underlying the principle of the frustration cases is contractual, an implied condition. Sir John Simon formulated for the assistance of your Lordships a proposition which should be recorded: "Whenever it is to be inferred from the terms of a contract or its surrounding circumstances that the consensus has been reached upon the basis of a particular contractual assumption, and that assumption is not true, the contract is avoided: i.e., it is void ab initio if the assumption is of present fact and it ceases to bind if the assumption is of future fact."

I think few would demur to this statement, but its value depends upon the meaning of "a contractual assumption," and also upon the true meaning to be attached to "basis," a metaphor which may mislead. When used expressly in contracts, for instance, in policies of insurance, which state that the truth of the statements in the proposal is to be the basis of the contract of insurance, the meaning is clear. The truth of the statements is made a condition of the contract, which failing, the contract is void unless the condition is waived. The proposition does not amount to more than this that, if the contract expressly or impliedly contains a term that a particular assumption is a condition of the contract, the contract is avoided if the assumption is not true. But we have not advanced far on the inquiry how to ascertain whether the contract does contain such a condition. Various words are to be found to define the state of things which make a condition. "In the contemplation of both parties fundamental to the continued validity of the contract," "a foundation essential to its existence," "a fundamental reason for making it," are phrases found in the important judgment of Scrutton L.J. in the present case. The first two phrases appear to me to be unexceptionable. They cover the case of a contract to serve in a particular place, the existence of which is fundamental to the service, or to procure the services of a professional vocalist, whose continued health is essential to performance. But "a fundamental reason for making a contract" may, with respect, be misleading. The reason of one party only is presumedly not intended, but in the cases I have suggested above, of the sale of a horse or of a picture, it might be said that the fundamental reason for making the contract was the belief of both parties that the horse was sound or the picture an old master, yet in neither case would the condition as I think exist. Nothing is more dangerous than to allow oneself liberty to construct for the parties contracts which they have not in terms made by importing implications which would appear to make the contract more businesslike or more just. The implications to be made are to be no more than are "necessary" for giving business efficacy to the transaction, and it appears to me that, both as to existing facts and future facts, a condition would not be implied unless the new state of facts makes the contract something different in kind from the contract in the original state of facts.

. . .

We therefore get a common standard for mutual mistake, and implied conditions whether as to existing or as to future facts. Does the state of the new facts destroy the identity of the subject-matter as it was in the original state of facts? To apply the principle to the infinite combinations of facts that arise in actual experience will continue to be difficult, but if this case results in establishing order into what has been a somewhat confused and difficult branch of the law it will have served a useful purpose.

I have already stated my reasons for deciding that in the present case the identity of the subject-matter was not destroyed by the mutual mistake, if any, and need not repeat them.

It now becomes necessary to deal with the second point of the plaintiffs — namely, that the contract of March 19, 1929, could be avoided by them in consequence of the non-disclosure by Bell of his misconduct as to the cocoa dealings. Fraudulent concealment has been negatived by the jury; this claim is based upon the contention that Bell owed a duty to Levers to disclose his misconduct, and that in default of disclosure the contract was voidable. Ordinarily the failure to disclose a material fact which might influence the mind of a prudent contractor does not give the right to avoid the contract. The principle of caveat emptor applies outside contracts of sale. There are certain contracts expressed by the law to be contracts of the utmost good faith, where material facts must be disclosed; if not, the contract is voidable. Apart from special fiduciary relationships, contracts for partnership and contracts of insurance are the leading instances. In such cases the duty does not arise out of contract; the duty of a person proposing an insurance arises before a contract is made, so of an intending partner. Unless this contract can be brought within this limited category of contracts uberrimae fidei it appears to me that this ground of defence must fail. I see nothing to differentiate this agreement from the ordinary contract of service; and I am aware of no authority which places contracts of service within the limited category I have mentioned. It seems to me clear that master and man negotiating for an agreement of service are as unfettered as in any other negotiation. Nor can I find anything in the relation of master and servant, when established, that places agreements between them within the protected category.

. . .

The result is that in the present case servants unfaithful in some of their work retain large compensation which some will think they do not deserve. Nevertheless it is of greater importance that well established principles of contract should be maintained than that a particular hardship should be redressed; and I see no way of giving relief to the plaintiffs in the present circumstances except by confiding to the Courts loose powers of introducing terms into contracts which would only serve to introduce doubt and confusion where certainty is essential.

I think therefore that this appeal should be allowed; and I agree with the order to be proposed by my noble and learned friend, Lord Blanesburgh.

[Lords Blanesburgh and Thankerton agreed in the result reached by Lord Atkin.]

Lord Warrington dissented: The learned judge thus describes the mistake invoked in this case as sufficient to justify a Court in saying that there was no true consent — namely, "Some mistake or misapprehension as to some facts.... which by the common intention of the parties, whether expressed or more generally implied, constitute the underlying assumption without which the parties would not have made the contract they did." That a mistake of this nature common to both parties is, if proved, sufficient to render a contract void is, I think, established law.

I will refer to two cases only amongst several in which the principle was acted on. The first is one at common law — namely, *Strickland v. Turner* (1852), 7 Ex. 208. In that case a contract for sale of an annuity, under which the purchase money had been paid, was held to be void at law and the money was ordered to be repaid, on its being discovered that the person on whose life the annuity depended had without the knowledge of either party died before the date of the contract of sale. The parties were treated as having intended to contract on the basis of something of value actually existing, and as this proved not to have been the case the contract failed to be binding.

The other case (*Scott v. Coulson*, [1903] 2 Ch. 249), is an example of the application of the same principle in a Court of equity. A contract for the sale of a policy was set aside on its being discovered that the assured was dead at its date, both parties being in ignorance of that fact. I cite this case for the sake of a passage in the judgment of Vaughan Williams L.J. He says: "If we are to take it that it was common ground that, at the date of the contract for the sale of this policy, both the parties to the contract supposed the assured to be alive, it is true that both parties entered into the contract on the basis of a common affirmative belief that the assured was alive; but as it turned out that there was a common mistake, the contract was one which cannot be enforced. This is so at law; and the plaintiffs do not require to have recourse to equity to rescind the contract, if the basis which both parties recognized as the basis is not true."

This principle, however, is confined to cases in which "the mistake is as to the substance of the whole consideration, going, as it were, to the root of the matter" — *Kennedy v. Panama, &c., Mail Co.* — and does not apply where the mistake is only as to some point, a material point it may be, and even one which may have been the actuating motive of one of the parties, an error as to which does not affect the substance of the whole consideration.

Kennedy v. Panama, &c., Mail Co. is a case in which it was held that the error relied on did not affect the substance of the consideration and the contract in question was accordingly enforced. The contract was one to take shares in a company. The prospectus on the faith of which the plaintiff had applied for shares contained a representation made in good faith that the company had obtained a valuable contract for the carriage of mails. The representation was intended to, and did in fact, induce the plaintiff to apply for shares. It was untrue, for, though at the time the application for shares was made and accepted there were reasonable grounds for expecting that such a contract would be obtained, it was never in fact concluded. It is to be observed that the error did not affect the shares themselves, the subject of the contract impeached; they were, notwithstanding the error, the very thing about which the parties were contracting. All that was affected were the prospects of the company earning profits available for payment of dividends. Accordingly the plaintiff's action brought for the purpose of setting aside the contract and obtaining repayment of his subscription was dismissed.

In *Smith v. Hughes* the result was the same, but for a different reason — namely, that there was no sufficient finding that the mistake was mutual. It was alleged that the vendor was intending to sell and the purchaser intending to buy and believed he was buying old oats, whereas the actual parcel of oats, the subject of the contract, consisted of new oats. The purchasers' claim to be relieved of the contract failed, because the learned judge at the trial did not point out the necessity of finding not only that the purchaser believed the oats were old but that he also believed that the vendor was selling them as old.

This kind of difficulty does not arise in the present case. It is in my opinion clear that each party believed that the remunerative offices, compensation for the loss of which was the subject of the negotiations, were offices which could not be determined except by the consent of the holder thereof, and further believed that the other party was under the same belief and was treating on that footing.

The real question, therefore, is whether the erroneous assumption on the part of both parties to the agreements that the service contracts were undeterminable except by agreement was of such a fundamental character as to constitute an underlying assumption without which the parties would not have made the contract they in fact made, or whether it was only a common error as to a material element, but one not going to the root of the matter and not affecting the substance of the consideration.

With the knowledge that I am differing from the majority of your Lordships, I am unable to arrive at any conclusion except that in this case the erroneous assumption was essential to the contract which without it would not have been made.

It is true that the error was not one as to the terms of the service agreements, but it was one which, having regard to the matter on which the parties were negotiating — namely, the terms on which the service agreements were to be prematurely determined and the compensation to be paid therefor, was in my opinion as fundamental to the bargain as any error one can imagine.

The compensation agreed to be paid was in each case the amount of the full salary for the two years and a half unexpired with the addition in Mr. Bell's case of £10,000. and in Mr. Snelling's of £5000. It is difficult to believe that the jury were otherwise than correct in their answer to the second branch of the group of questions numbered 5 — namely, that had Levers known of the actings of the appellants in regard to the dealings in question they would not have made the agreements now impeached or either of them. It is true that such a finding is not in the strict sense one of fact, but it is an inference which the jury were entitled to draw from the evidence and from all the circumstances of the case, it is one which the learned judge and the Court of Appeal have also drawn, and, if I may say so with respect, it is one I should draw myself. I also agree with the learned judge that looking at the matter from the side of the appellants the existence of an agreement giving them rights which could only be compromised by compensation was in the same way the root and basis of the cancellation agreements.

In my opinion, therefore, assuming that the point was open, the appeal on the main question ought to be dismissed.

As to the question whether the point was open I agree that it is at least doubtful whether mutual mistake as to a fundamental fact was sufficiently pleaded either in the pleading itself or by the particulars subsequently given, but I have no hesitation in coming to the same conclusion as that arrived at by Scrutton and Lawrence L.JJ. — namely, that having regard to the proceedings at the trial effect ought not to be given to a technical objection such as that in question — no further evidence was in my opinion needed or could reasonably be expected to be forthcoming on the question, and no substantial prejudice has been sustained by the defendants.

But, while I think the appeal ought to be dismissed, there is one point which appears to have been overlooked at the trial and in reference to which in my judgment there should, if the appeal were dismissed, be a variation in the order.

The service agreement with Mr. Bell provided that Lord Leverhulme was to take out in the Atlas Assurance Company and Lever Brothers to pay all premiums on an endowment policy on Mr. Bell's life maturing at the age of sixty or previous death for an amount which would provide £1500. per annum or £16,200. at his option. This policy was to belong to him, the premiums being paid by Lever Brothers, notwithstanding the termination of his engagement unless the same should be terminated by him. The cancellation agreement preserved this obligation on the part of Lever Brothers, and if this is set aside the original agreement stands. I cannot think that the conduct of Mr. Bell amounts to a termination by him of the engagement within the meaning of the provision above mentioned, and if the judgment appealed from were to stand provision should be made for the continued payment by Lever Brothers of the premiums, and the repayment to Mr. Bell of any premiums paid by him.

I have purposely avoided dealing with the question whether the appellants were under an obligation as servants to disclose to Lever Brothers their breaches of the service agreements. In the view I take the question is immaterial. If such an obligation existed it would merely afford a further ground for the termination by Lever Brothers of the service agreements, for which such breaches themselves afforded a sufficient ground.

This case seems to me to raise a question as to the application of certain doctrines of common law, and I have therefore not thought it necessary to discuss or explain the special doctrines and practice of Courts of equity in reference to the rescission on the ground of mistake of contracts, conveyances and assignments of property and so forth, or to the refusal on the same ground to decree specific performance, though I think, in accordance with such doctrines and practice, the same result would follow.

[Viscount Hailsham agreed with Lord Warrington.]

[The following poem may be relevant.
"Nine judges in all heard the case that I brought,
And six were for giving me that which I sought.
But, though in support I had easily most,
I suffered the fate of being passed at the post." — *Anon.*]

QUESTIONS

1. What would happen in each of the following situations under the approach of Lord Atkin:
(a) The payment to Bell was an exact actuarial computation of the present value of his salary and anything else that he might have earned during the remaining term of his contract;
(b) The payment consisted of an actuarial computation as in (a) and in addition, £10,000 for the excellent work done by Bell;
(c) Bell knew that Levers did not know of his breach of duty and deliberately said nothing and Bell was paid the amounts determined in (a) or (b);
(d) Bell reasonably believed that Levers knew what he had done and had taken no steps to hide what he had done and was paid amounts determined as in (a) or (b)?

2. To what extent do the preceding questions raise issue of reliance and unjust enrichment? What results would be reached in each case by considering these issues?

3. Do the answers reached by the application of the approach of Lord Atkin coincide with those reached by considering reliance and unjust enrichment? If not can you explain the reason for the discrepancy?

4. A child has asked you to tell her if the following are "fundamentally different" or "different in kind" from each other:
The Sun and Moon
A man and a woman
A good person and a bad person

A "good" contract and a "bad" contract
A contract entered into in the belief that it discharges an obligation under an existing contract and a similar contract where the belief is that the existing contract is a valid contract?
Would you have adequately discharged an obligation to give the child an intelligible response, by saying either "yes" or "no" in each case? If a "yes" or "no" answer will not suffice what kind of answer would? Would Lord Atkin satisfy the child's curiosity?

The next case offers both very different facts and approach from *Bell v. Levers*. There are some questions to bear in mind:

1. To what extent is Denning L.J. justified in saying that *Bell v. Levers* did not deal with the issue of mistake in equity?

2. If *Bell v. Levers* was held to be applicable, what result would follow from the application of that case?

SOLLE v. BUTCHER

[1950] 1 K.B. 671. Court of Appeal, England; Bucknill, Denning and Jenkins L.JJ.

[The parties had been partners in a business that bought houses for renovation. Once renovated and converted into flats the houses were rented. The defendant bought a house, renovated it and leased part of it to the plaintiff. The parties were concerned that the rent charged would not be caught by the Rent Acts. (These acts, originally passed in 1920, prohibited any increase in rent during the term of a tenancy. Rents could be increased with permission at the end of one tenancy and the beginning of another.) The pre-war rent had been £140 p.a. for the flat rented by the plaintiff. The plaintiff undertook to get legal advice on the applicability of the rent acts. After advice had been obtained that the flats were not subject to the pre-war rents, the parties agreed on a rent of £250 p.a. and the plaintiff entered into a 7-year lease. Relations between the parties subsequently deteriorated. The plaintiff brought an action claiming that the maximum rent was £140 and that the overpayment should be returned to him. The county court judge gave judgment for the plaintiff. The defendant appealed.]

Denning L.J. [after holding that the flat was caught by the Rent acts and that the maximum rent that could be charged under those acts was £140, continued:] In this plight the landlord seeks to set aside the lease. He says, with truth, that it is unfair that the tenant should have the benefit of the lease for the outstanding five years of the term at £140. a year, when the proper rent is £250. a year. If he cannot give a notice of increase now, can he not avoid the lease? The only ground on which he can avoid it is on the ground of mistake. It is quite plain that the parties were under a mistake. They thought that the flat was not tied down to a controlled rent, whereas in fact it was. In order to see whether the lease can be avoided for this mistake it is necessary to remember that mistake is of two kinds: first, mistake which renders the contract void, that is, a nullity from the beginning, which is the kind of mistake which was dealt with by the courts of common law; and, secondly, mistake which renders the contract not void, but voidable, that is, liable to be set aside on such terms as the court thinks fit, which is the kind of mistake which was dealt with by the courts of equity. Much of the difficulty which has attended this subject has arisen because, before the fusion of law and equity, the courts of common law, in order to do justice in the case in hand, extended this doctrine of mistake beyond its proper limits and held contracts to be void which were really only voidable, a process which was capable of being attended with much injustice to third persons who had bought goods or otherwise committed themselves on the faith that there was a contract.... Since the fusion of law and equity, there is no reason to continue this process, and it will be found that only those contracts are now held void in which the mistake was such as to prevent the formation of any contract at all.

Let me first consider mistakes which render a contract a nullity. All previous decisions on this subject must now be read in the light of *Bell v. Lever Bros. Ld.* The correct interpretation of that case, to my mind, is that, once a contract has been made, that is to say, once the parties, whatever their inmost states of mind, have to all outward appearances agreed with sufficient certainty in the same terms on the same subject matter, then the contract is good unless and until it is set aside for failure of some condition on which the existence of the contract depends, or for fraud, or on some equitable ground. Neither party can rely on his own mistake to say it was a nullity from the beginning, no matter that it was a mistake which to his mind was fundamental, and no matter that the other party knew that he was under a mistake. A fortiori, if the other party did not know of the mistake, but shared it. The cases where goods have perished at the time of sale, or belong to the buyer, are really contracts which are not void for mistake but are void by reason of an implied condition precedent, because the contract proceeded on the basic assumption that it was possible of performance....

Applying these principles, it is clear that here there was a contract. The parties agreed in the same terms on the same subject-matter. It is true that the landlord was under a mistake which was to him fundamental: he would not for one moment have considered letting the flat for seven years if it meant that he could only charge £140 a year for it. He made the fundamental mistake of believing that the rent he could charge was not tied down to a controlled rent; but, whether it was his own mistake or a mistake common to both him and the tenant, it is not a ground for saying that the lease was from the beginning a nullity. Any other view would lead to remarkable results, for it would mean that, in the many cases where the parties mistakenly think a house is outside the Rent Restriction Acts when it is really within them, the tenancy would be a nullity, and the tenant would have to go; with the result that the tenants would not dare to seek to have their rents reduced to the permitted amounts lest they should be turned out.

Let me next consider mistakes which render a contract voidable, that is, liable to be set aside on some equitable ground. Whilst presupposing that a contract was good at law, or at any rate not void, the court of equity would often relieve a party from the consequences of his own mistake, so long as it could do so without injustice to third parties. The court, it was said, had power to set aside the contract whenever it was of opinion that it was unconscientious for the other party to avail himself of the legal advantage which he had obtained: ...

The court had, of course, to define what it considered to be unconscientious, but in this respect equity has shown a progressive development. It is now clear that a contract will be set aside if the mistake of the one party has been induced by a material misrepresentation of the other, even though it was not fraudulent or fundamental; or if one party, knowing that the other is mistaken about the terms of an offer, or the identity of the person by whom it is made, lets him remain under his delusion and concludes a contract on the mistaken terms instead of pointing out the mistake. . . .

A contract is also liable in equity to be set aside if the parties were under a common misapprehension either as to facts or as to their relative and respective rights, provided that the misapprehension was fundamental and that the party seeking to set it aside was not himself at fault. That principle was first applied to private rights as long ago as 1730 in *Lansdown v. Lansdown* (1730), Mos. 364. There were four brothers, and the second and third of them died. The eldest brother entered on the lands of the deceased brothers, but the youngest brother claimed them. So the two rival brothers consulted a friend who was a local schoolmaster. The friend looked up a book which he then had with him called the Clerk's Remembrancer and gave it as his opinion that the lands belonged to the youngest brother. He recommended the two of them to take further advice, which at first they intended to do, but they did not do so; and, acting on the friend's opinion, the elder brother agreed to divide the estate with the younger brother, and executed deeds and bonds giving effect to the agreement. Lord Chancellor King declared that the documents were obtained by a mistake and by a misrepresentation of the law by the friend, and ordered them to be given up to be cancelled. He pointed out that the maxim ignorantia juris non excusat only means that ignorance cannot be pleaded in excuse of crimes. . . .

If and in so far as those cases were compromises of disputed rights, they have been subjected to justifiable criticism, but, in cases where there is no element of compromise, but only of mistaken rights, the House of Lords in 1867 in the great case of *Cooper v. Phibbs*, affirmed the doctrine there acted on as correct. In that case an uncle had told his nephew, not intending to misrepresent anything, but being in fact in error, that he (the uncle) was entitled to a fishery; and the nephew, after the uncle's death, acting in the belief of the truth of what the uncle had told him, entered into an agreement to rent the fishery from the uncle's daughters, whereas it actually belonged to the nephew himself. The mistake there as to the title to the fishery did not render the tenancy agreement a nullity. If it had done, the contract would have been void at law from the beginning and equity would have had to follow the law. There would have been no contract to set aside and no terms to impose. The House of Lords, however, held that the mistake was only such as to make it voidable, or, in Lord Westbury's words, "liable to be set aside" on such terms as the court thought fit to impose; and it was so set aside.

The principle so established by *Cooper v. Phibbs* has been repeatedly acted on: . . . It is in no way impaired by *Bell v. Lever Bros. Ld.*, which was treated in the House of Lords as a case at law depending on whether the contract was a nullity or not. If it had been considered on equitable grounds, the result might have been different. In any case, the principle of *Cooper v. Phibbs* has been fully restored by *Norwich Union Fire Insurance Society Ld. v. William H. Price, Ld.*

Applying that principle to this case, the facts are that the plaintiff, the tenant, was a surveyor who was employed by the defendant, the landlord, not only to arrange finance for the purchase of the building and to negotiate with the rating authorities as to the new rateable values, but also to let the flats. He was the agent for letting, and he clearly formed the view that the building was not controlled. He told the valuation officer so. He advised the defendant what were the rents which could be charged. He read to the defendant an opinion of counsel relating to the matter, and told him that in his opinion he could charge £250. and that there was no previous control. He said that the flats came outside the Act and that the defendant was "clear." The defendant relied on what the plaintiff told him, and authorized the plaintiff to let at the rentals which he had suggested. The plaintiff not only let the four other flats to other people for a long period of years at the new rentals, but also took one himself for seven years at £250. a year. Now he turns round and says, quite unashamedly, that he wants to take advantage of the mistake to get the flat at £140. a year for seven years instead of the £250. a year, which is not only the rent he agreed to pay but also the fair and economic rent; and it is also the rent permitted by the Acts on compliance with the necessary formalities. If the rules of equity have become so rigid that they cannot remedy such an injustice, it is time we had a new equity, to make good the omissions of the old. But, in my view, the established rules are amply sufficient for this case.

On the defendant's evidence, which the judge preferred, I should have thought there was a good deal to be said for the view that the lease was induced by an innocent material misrepresentation by the plaintiff. It seems to me that the plaintiff was not merely expressing an opinion on the law: he was making an unambiguous statement as to private rights; and a misrepresentation as to private rights is equivalent to a misrepresentation of fact for this purpose: *MacKenzie v. Royal Bank of Canada*, [1934] A.C. 468. But it is unnecessary to come to a firm conclusion on this point, because, as Bucknill L.J. has said, there was clearly a common mistake, or, as I would prefer to describe it, a common misapprehension, which was fundamental and in no way due to any fault of the defendant; and *Cooper v. Phibbs* affords ample authority for saying that, by reason of the common misapprehension, this lease can be set aside on such terms as the court thinks fit.

The fact that the lease has been executed is no bar to this relief. No distinction can, in this respect, be taken between rescission for innocent misrepresentation and rescission for common misapprehension, for many of the common misapprehensions are due to innocent misrepresentation; and *Cooper v. Phibbs* shows that rescission is available even after an agreement of tenancy has been executed and partly performed. The observations in *Seddon v. North Eastern Salt Co. Ld.*, [1905] 1 Ch. 326, have lost all authority since Scrutton L.J., threw doubt on them in *Lever Bros. Ld. v. Bell*, and the Privy Council actually set aside an executed agreement in *Mackenzie v. Royal Bank of Canada*. If and in so far as *Angel v. Jay*, [1911] 1 K.B. 666, decided that an executed lease could not be rescinded for an innocent misrepresentation, it was in my opinion, a wrong decision. It would mean that innocent people would be deprived of their right of rescission before they had any opportunity of knowing they had it. I am aware that in *Wilde v. Gibson* (1848), 1 H.L.C. 605, Lord Campbell said that an executed conveyance could be set aside only on the ground of actual fraud; but this must be taken to be confined to misrepresentations as to defects of title on the conveyance of land.

In the ordinary way, of course, rescission is only granted when the parties can be restored to substantially the same position as that in which they were before the contract was made; but, as Lord Blackburn said in *Erlanger v. New Sombrero Phosphate Co.* (1878), 3 App. Cas. 1218: "The practice has always been for a court of equity to give this relief whenever, by the exercise of its powers, it can do what is practically just, though it cannot restore the parties precisely to the state they were in before the contract." That indeed was what was done in *Cooper v. Phibbs.* Terms were imposed so as to do what was practically just. What terms then, should be imposed here? If the lease were set aside without any terms being imposed, it would mean that the plaintiff, the tenant, would have to go out and would have to pay a reasonable sum for his use and occupation. That would, however, not be just to the tenant.

The situation is similar to that of a case where a long lease is made at the full permitted rent in the common belief that notices of increase have previously been served, whereas in fact they have not. In that case, as in this, when the lease is set aside, terms must be imposed so as to see that the tenant is not unjustly evicted. When Sir John Romilly M.R., was faced with a somewhat similar problem, he gave the tenant the option either to agree to pay the proper rent or to go out: see *Garrard v. Frankel* (1862), 30 Beav. 445; and when Bacon V-C. had a like problem before him he did the same, saying that "the object of the court is, as far as it can, to put the parties into the position in which they would have been in if the mistake had not happened": see *Paget v. Marshall.* If the mistake here had not happened, a proper notice of increase would have been given and the lease would have been executed at the full permitted rent. I think that this court should follow these examples and should impose terms which will enable the tenant to choose either to stay on at the proper rent or to go out.

The terms will be complicated by reason of the Rent Restriction Acts, but it is not beyond the wit of man to devise them. Subject to any observations which the parties may desire to make, the terms which I suggest are these: the lease should only be set aside if the defendant is prepared to give an undertaking that he will permit the plaintiff to be a licensee of the premises pending the grant of a new lease. Then, whilst the plaintiff is a licensee, the defendant will in law be in possession of the premises, and will be able to serve on the plaintiff, as prospective tenant, a notice under s. 7, sub-s. 4, of the Act of 1938 increasing the rent to the full permitted amount. The defendant must further be prepared to give an undertaking that he will serve such a notice within three weeks from the drawing up of the order, and that he will, if written request is made by the plaintiff, within one month of the service of the notice, grant him a new lease at the full permitted amount of rent, not, however, exceeding £250. a year, for a term expiring on September 29, 1954, subject in all other respects to the same covenants and conditions as in the rescinded lease. If there is any difference of opinion about the figures stated in the notice, that can, of course, be adjusted during the currency of the lease. If the plaintiff does not choose to accept the licence or the new lease, he must go out. He will not be entitled to the protection of the Rent Restriction Acts because, the lease being set aside, there will be no initial contractual tenancy from which a statutory tenancy can spring.

In my opinion, therefore, the appeal should be allowed. The declaration that the standard rent of the flat is £140. a year should stand. An order should be made on the counter-claim that, on the defendant's giving the undertakings which I have mentioned, the lease be set aside. An account should be had to determine the sum payable for use and occupation. The plaintiff's claim for repayment of rent and for breach of covenant should be dismissed. In respect of his occupation after rescission and during the subsequent licence, the plaintiff will be liable to pay a reasonable sum for use and occupation. That sum should, prima facie, be assessed at the full amount permitted by the Acts, not, however, exceeding £250. a year. Mesne profits as against a trespasser are assessed at the full amount permitted by the Acts, even though notices of increase have not been served, because that is the amount lost by the landlord. The same assessment should be made here, because the sums payable for use and occupation are not rent, and the statutory provisions about notices of increase do not apply to them. All necessary credits must, of course, be given in respect of past payments, and so forth.

[Bucknill and Jenkins L.JJ. agreed with Denning L.J. in separate judgments.]

QUESTIONS

1. Are there any difficult problems in giving relief here? Was any party's reasonable reliance ignored?

To what extent might there have been unjust enrichment?

Were either party's expectations defeated?

2. Could you have used any part of Lord Atkin's judgment in *Bell v. Levers* to reach the same result?

MAGEE v. PENNINE INSURANCE CO. LTD.

[1969] 2 Q.B. 507, Court of Appeal (England); Lord Denning M.R., Winn and Fenton Atkinson L.JJ.

Lord Denning M.R. In 1961 Mr. Thomas Magee, senior, the plaintiff, aged 58, acquired an Austin car. He signed a proposal form for insurance. In it he said that the car belonged to him. He was asked to give details of his driving licence "and of all other persons who to your present knowledge will drive." These were the details he gave:

(1) "Thomas Magee" — that is himself — "provisional licence aged 58."

(2) "John Magee — that is his elder son — "Police mobile driver, aged 35." He had an annual licence.

(3) "John J. Magee" — that is his younger son — "joiner, aged 18 — provisional licence."

Mr. Magee signed this declaration:

"I ... do hereby declare that the car described is and shall be kept in good condition and that the answers above given are in every respect true and correct and I ... hereby agree that this declaration shall be the basis of the contract of insurance between the company and myself...."

Those details were not written in by Mr. Magee himself. They were written in by Mr. Atkinson at the garage where he got the car. The details unfortunately were completely wrong. Mr. Thomas Magee had never driven a car himself. He had never had a licence, not even a provisional one. He was getting the car really for his son of 18 to drive. And we all know that a young man of 18 has to pay a much higher insurance than a man of 25 or over. This company said they would not have insured a young man of 18.

The judge found that Mr. Thomas Magee, the father, had not been fraudulent. He did not himself fill in the details. They were filled in by Mr. Atkinson, the man at the garage. And then Mr. Thomas Magee signed them. It was Mr. Atkinson who made some mistake or other. But there it was. A misrepresentation was made and on the faith of it being true, the insurance company granted an insurance policy to Mr. Magee.

Thereafter the policy was renewed each year and the premiums were paid. In 1964 that car was replaced by another. The policy was renewed for the new car without anything further being said about the drivers or the ownership. The company assumed, no doubt, that the same details applied.

On April 25, 1965, there was an accident. The younger son, John Magee, was driving the new car at 4 o'clock in the morning. He ran into a shop window. The plate glass was smashed and the car was a complete wreck. The father, Mr. Thomas Magee, put in a claim form, in which he said that the car was £600 in value. That was clearly wrong because the price new was only £547 the year before. The insurers thereupon got their engineer to look at it. On May 12, 1965, the broker wrote to Mr. Thomas Magee a letter, in which he said:

> "... We have today been advised by your insurers that their engineer considers your vehicle is damaged beyond repair. The engineer considers that the pre-accident market value of the vehicle was £410 and they are therefore prepared to offer you this amount, less the £25 accidental damage excess in settlement of your claim. We should be pleased to receive your confirmation that this is acceptable..."

There was no written acceptance, but it was accepted by word of mouth. That seemed to be a concluded agreement whereby the company agreed to pay £385.

But within the next few days the insurance company made further inquiries. One of their representatives saw Mr. Magee and took a statement from him. Then the truth was discovered. Mr. Magee did not drive at all. He had never had a driving licence, not even a provisional one. He said that the car was never his property but was his son's car: and that it was his son, the younger son, who had driven the car and was the only person who had ever driven it. On discovering those facts, the insurance company said they were not liable on the insurance policy.

They had been induced to grant it, they said, by the misrepresentations in the original proposal form; and also by reason of non-disclosure of material facts, namely, that the son aged 18 was normally to be the driver.

Mr. Magee brought an action in the county court in which he claimed the £385. He said it was payable under the insurance policy, or, alternatively, on an agreement of compromise contained in the letter of May 12.

The judge rejected the claim on the policy itself, because the insurance was induced by misrepresentation. He found that the company were entitled to repudiate the policy because of the inaccuracy of Mr. Magee's answers. That finding was not challenged in this court. Mr. Taylor, on behalf of Mr. Magee, admitted that he could not claim on the policy.

But the judge upheld the claim on the letter of May 12. He said it was a binding contract of compromise. I am not so sure about this. It might be said to be a mere quantification of the account which should be paid in case the insurance company were liable: and that it did not preclude them from afterwards contesting liability. But, on the whole, I do not think we should regard it as a mere quantification. The letter contains the important words: "in settlement of your claim," which import that it is to be settled without further controversy. In short, it bears the stamp of an agreement of compromise. The consideration for it was the ascertainment of a sum which was previously unascertained.

But then comes the next point. Accepting that the agreement to pay £385 was an agreement of compromise. Is it vitiated by mistake? The insurance company were clearly under a mistake. They thought that the policy was good and binding. They did not know, at the time of that letter, that there had been misrepresentations in the proposal form. If Mr. Magee knew of their mistake — if he knew that the policy was bad — he certainly could not take advantage of the agreement to pay £385. He would be "snapping at an offer which he knew was made under a mistake": and no man is allowed to get away with that. But I prefer to assume that Mr. Magee was innocent. I think we should take it that both parties were under a common mistake. Both parties thought that the policy was good and binding. The letter of March 12, 1968, was written on the assumption that the policy was good whereas it was in truth voidable.

What is the effect in law of this common mistake? Mr. Taylor said that the agreement to pay £385 was good, despite this common mistake. He relied much on *Bell v. Lever Brothers, Ltd.,* [1932] A.C. 161, and its similarity to the present case. He submitted that, inasmuch as the mistake there did not vitiate that contract, the mistake here should not vitiate this one. I do not propose today to go through the speeches in that case. They have given enough trouble to commentators already. I would say simply this: A common mistake, even on a most fundamental matter, does not make a contract void at law: but it makes it voidable in equity. I analysed the cases in *Solle v. Butcher,* [1950] 1 K.B. 671, and I would repeat what I said there, at p. 693:

> "A contract is also liable in equity to be set aside if the parties were under a common misapprehension either as to facts or as to their relative and respective rights, provided that the misapprehension was fundamental and that the party seeking to set it aside was not himself at fault."

Now applying that principle here, it is clear that, when the insurance company and Mr. Magee made this agreement to pay £385, they were both under a common mistake which was fundamental to the whole agreement. Both thought that Mr. Magee was entitled to claim under the policy of insurance, whereas he was not so entitled. That common mistake does not make the agreement to pay £385 a nullity, but it makes it liable to be set aside in equity.

This brings me to a question which has caused me much difficulty. Is this a case in which we ought to set the agreement aside in equity? I have hesitated on this point, but I cannot shut my eyes to the fact that Mr. Magee had no valid claim on the insurance policy: and, if he had no claim on the policy, it is not equitable that he should have a good claim on the agreement to pay £385, seeing that it was made under a fundamental mistake. It is not fair to hold the insurance company to an agreement which they would not have dreamt of making if they had not been under a mistake. I would, therefore, uphold the appeal and give judgment for the insurance company.

Winn L.J. This appeal has given me pleasure because it has been so well argued by both the counsel who have appeared in it; and, of course, the problem which it presents is not one the solution of which is going to impose frightful actual loss or consequences on the particular individuals or companies who are involved. It is a neat and teasing problem, the difficulty of which is slightly indicated, though by no means established, by the regrettable circumstance that I find myself respectfully having to dissent from the views of my Lord and of my brother Fenton Atkinson L.J. I agree with my Lord that the letter of May 12, 1965, is of very great importance, though I take Mr. Carman's point, that it is not the insurers' letter: it is only what purports to be a report, probably of a telephone conversation, written by the brokers, who were the agents of the plaintiff, Mr. Magee, of what they were told by some representative of the defendant insurance company. I attach importance to it not because of its terms, which may not be an accurate representation of what the insurers had said, but because it contemplates a complete clearance of the whole matter and a termination of the dispute arising out of the claim, in so far as there was any, by return of various documents, which clearly was regarded as the final terminal phase of the matter. Whether or not this could be regarded, on a strict construction, as no more than an offer to fix a figure, which, subject to being liable to pay at all, the insurers were prepared to pay, seems to me to be excluded as a reality by the considerations which I have mentioned. This must have evinced an offer by the insurance company to dispose of the matter by paying £385 in settlement. As I see the matter, it is not a question of whether thereby a contract was formed, since it seems to me it is clear that there was a contract formed by that offer from the insurers and the acceptance of it again through the brokers by Mr. Magee. The question is whether, as my Lord has indicated clearly, that contract is, for one reason or another, invalid and unenforceable by Mr. Magee against the insurers.

I do not desire to take long in expressing my opinion that on the principles of *Bell v. Lever Brothers, Ltd.,* [1932] A.C. 161 applied to the circumstances of this case the contrary conclusion to that which my Lord has expressed is the correct conclusion. It appears to me that the parties were under a misapprehenslon. If there was any misapprehension shared commonly by both Magee and the insurers as to what was the value of any rights that he had against them arising from the insurance policy, that seems to me to have been precisely the subject-matter of the common misapprehension in *Bell v. Lever Brothers, Ltd.* One could pick out and read, and it would be instructive to re-read them many times, several passages from the speech of Lord Atkin, at p. 210, and indeed also from that of Lord Thankerton, at p. 229; but I content myself with the point made by Lord Atkin, when he said, at p. 225: "Various words are to be found to define the state of things which make a condition."; i.e., a condition non-compliance with which will avoid a contract. And he instances, quoting them, the phrases:— " 'In the contemplation of both parties fundamental to the continued validity of the contract', 'a foundation essential to its existence', 'a fundamental reason for making it' " — all of which, as he said, were to be found in the judgment of Scrutton L.J. in the same case; and Lord Atkin said, at p. 226: "The first two phrases appear to me to be unexceptionable." "But" — by contrast, he said — " 'a fundamental reason for making a contract' may, with respect, be misleading." And he goes on to give instances of such misleading assertions or misleading definitions of what is meant by a foundation essential to the contract.

For my part, I think that here there was a misapprehension as to rights, but no misapprehension whatsoever as to the subject-matter of the contract, namely, the settlement of the rights of the assured with regard to the accident that happened. The insurance company was settling his rights, if he had any. He understood them to be settling his rights; but each of them, on the assumption that the county court judge's view of the facts was right, thought his rights against the insurers were very much more valuable than in fact they were, since in reality they were worthless: the insurers could have repudiated — or avoided, that being the more accurate phrase on the basis of the mis-statements which my Lord has narrated.

Lord Thankerton also said, at p. 235:

"The phrase 'underlying assumption by the parties,' as applied to the subject-matter of a contract, may be too widely interpreted so as so [sic] include something which one of the parties had not necessarily in his mind at the time of the contract; in my opinion it can only properly relate to something which both must necessarily have accepted in their minds as an essential and integral element of the subject-matter."

I venture respectfully to contrast that sentence with any such sentence as this:— "which the parties both must necessarily have accepted in their minds as an essential reason, motive, justification or explanation for the making of the contract." In my view the mistake must be a mistake as to the nature or at the very least the quality of the subject-matter and not as to the reason why either party desires to deal with the subject-matter as the contract provides that it should be dealt with.

And Lord Thankerton also said, at p. 236: "I think that it is true to say that in all" the cases — and he is referring to a number of them —

"it either appeared on the face of the contract that the matter as to which the mistake existed was an essential and integral element of the subject-matter of the contract, or it was an inevitable inference from the nature of the contract that all the parties so regarded it."

Since I think there is a most important peripheral implication which might be read into the judgment of this court given today, I want to add only this, that in my opinion in a case such as this there is no rule of law that a warranty given at the inception of a contract of insurance by the terms of the proposal form and its acceptance by the insured is to be embodied or tacitly read into any contract which is made between such a proposer and the insurers in settlement of a claim which he makes under the contract. I do not even think, so far as I am aware, that there is any authority for the proposition that a warranty given in the way I have mentioned is to be implied indefinitely into renewals of the first contract of insurance which is made of which that warranty is an express term as a condition precedent to liability. In every case it must depend on the length of time elapsed, the probability of changes of circumstances, the practicability of adjusting some ages by the addition of a year or more perhaps, and many other considerations, such, for example, as the improbability that the proposer who has called himself the holder of a provisional licence will continue to be either a holder of a provisional licence or a holder of any licence at all indefinitely. He is likely to have been dealt with by the magistrates in one way or another in the time which has elapsed.

For the reasons which I have endeavoured to state quite briefly — though I think there are many other considerations which are relevant to this interesting problem — I find myself, respectfully and diffidently, unable to agree with the judgment of my Lord.

Fenton Atkinson L.J.: Before hearing my Lords' judgments I had been inclined to the view that the letter of May 12 was not an offer to enter into a contract independent of the policy, but merely an offer of quantification of a claim made under a policy, both parties at that stage believing that there was a valid policy under which the insurers could have no answer to a claim. On reflection, I agree that that is an incorrect approach to the case, and I go on to consider the question of mistake, and on that issue I agree with the judgment of my Lord, the Master of the Rolls. It does seem to me that the basic assumption of both parties at the time of the agreement relied upon was that there was a valid enforceable claim under the policy. In fact, Mr. Taylor does not seek here to challenge the finding of the county court judge that the insurers were entitled to repudiate any liability under that policy by reason of the untrue and incorrect statements made in the proposal form in 1961; and, applying in this case the proposition which was accepted by all of their Lordships in *Bell v. Lever Brothers Ltd.*, [1932] A.C. 161, set out in *Chitty on Contracts*, 23rd ed. (1968), para. 207, in these terms:

> "Whenever it is to be inferred from the terms of a contract or its surrounding circumstances that the consensus has been reached on the basis of a particular contractual assumption and that assumption is not true, the contract is avoided."

And to that has to be added the additional rider: "The assumption must have been fundamental to the continued validity of the contract or a foundation essential to its existence." Applying the rule there laid down to the facts of this case, I think it is clear that, when the agreement relied upon by the plaintiff was made, it was made on the basis of a particular and essential contractual assumption, namely, that there was in existence a valid and enforceable policy of insurance, and that assumption was not true. In my view it is the right and equitable result of this case that the insurers should be entitled to avoid that agreement on the ground of mutual mistake in a fundamental and vital matter. I agree that this appeal should succeed on that ground.

Appeal allowed. Judgment to
be entered for appellants.
Leave to appeal refused.

QUESTIONS

1. Was there a mistake in *Fairgrief v. Ellis* (*supra*, Chapter 2, c (iv))?

2. Is that case reconcilable with *Magee v. Pennine*?

3. What would have happened under the approach of each of the judges in *Magee v. Pennine* if the Insurance Co. actually paid Mr. Magee the amount of his loss?

4. Would payment in such a case be distinguishable from the situation in *Norwich Union v. Price*?

5. To what extent are there issues or potential issues of reliance and unjust enrichment here?

6. Refer to the questions at the end of *Bell v. Levers* (*supra*). After reading *Solle v. Butcher* and *Magee v. Pennine* would you change your answers to any of these? If so, which ones and why?

NOTE

The time has come to try to make sense of the problems of mistake as they are raised in these cases. It is clear that to talk about "fundamental assumptions", implied terms, differences in kind or any similar terms is not helpful in showing us what to do. It seems virtually impossible to reconcile *Magee v. Pennine* with *Bell v. Levers*, and just as difficult to do so with *Norwich Union v. Price*, unless we assume that a promise to pay and payment itself are treated in completely different ways. (There may be good reasons for this — possibly hidden in *Fairgrief v. Ellis* — but the judgments do not indicate what it is.)

The first thing to notice about the approach of Lord Atkin is that, in spite of what Lord Denning says in *Solle v. Butcher*, it seems to force us into a clear choice between holding the contract void on the ground of mistake or valid and enforceable in spite of the mistake. Lord Atkin said:

> "My lords, the rule of law dealing with the effect of mistake in contract appear to be established with reasonable clearness. If mistake operates at all, it operates so as to negative or in some cases to nullify consent."

Mistake is then put into the context of offer and acceptance. (This may explain why *Raffles v. Wichelhaus* became a "leading case" on the law of mistake.) Most English commentators pick this up and base their analysis of mistake in these terms.

Closely related to this approach are the terms used by the courts to describe mistake. It is worthwhile to notice the terminology used in this area. Some of the cases use words like "common", "mutual" or "unilateral" to describe mistake. Lord Atkin uses all three in one paragraph. Some commentators use these words, or terms like "bilateral" or "unilateral" (Fridman). Cheshire and Fifoot have made a valiant effort to distinguish all the classes. They define the various words as follows (9th ed., p. 206):

> "In common mistake, both parties make the same mistake. Each knows the intention of the other and accepts it, but each is mistaken about some underlying and fundamental fact. The parties, for example, are unaware that the subject matter of their contract has already perished.
> "In mutual mistake, the parties misunderstand each other and are at cross-purposes. A, for example, intends to offer his Ford Cortina car for sale, but B believes that the offer relates to the Ford Zaphy also owned by A.
> "In unilateral mistake, only one of the parties is mistaken. The other knows, or must be taken to know, of his mistake. Suppose, for instance, that A agrees to buy from B a specific picture which A believes to be a genuine Constable but which in fact is a copy. If B is ignorant of A's erroneous belief, the case is one of mutual mistake, but, if he knows of it, of unilateral mistake."

Cheshire and Fifoot then go on to suggest that there is an agreement in the case of common mistake, but that it is robbed of all efficacy by reason of the mistake. In the other two cases, on the other hand, there is no agreement.

Several recent English cases have adopted either the approach of Cheshire and Fifoot or a variation in which common and mutual are collapsed into one class. Most frequently the terms "common" and "mutual" are used interchangeably.

The problem with all of this is that the terms are not used in any consistent way, and, even if they were, they are not particularly useful in deciding the cases. It is usually said that,

"In mutual or common mistake the error or mistake in order to avoid the contract at law must have been based either upon a fundamental mistaken assumption as to the subject matter of the contract or upon a mistake relating to a fundamental term of the contract." (Thompson J. in *McMaster University v. Wilchar Const. Ltd.*, [1971] 3 O.R. 801, 809.)

The notion that the mistake must be "fundamental" has not helped any analysis of the problem. As we have seen, it is not possible to know what is or is not "fundamental" until one knows why one is asking the question, and even the conclusion that a particular fact was important to one party does not *alone* give any good reason for doing anything in particular. More importantly and seriously, the notion that the mistake must be "fundamental" has led to the denial of relief without any good reason. It is, of course, important that agreements not be lightly upset, but there are mistakes where relief can easily be given even though nothing very fundamental (in the sense used by Thompson J.) has been affected. Relief in a case like *U.S.A. v. Motor Trucks* could be given for a very trivial mistake. Since no one can complain if relief is given there, why worry about the giving of relief? We will see other cases where the same situation exists.

The definition of unilateral mistake by Chesire and Fifoot would indicate that in most cases there would be no reason not to give relief where such a mistake existed. One who knows of the other's mistake can hardly complain if his expectations are defeated: they were unreasonable in the first place. Yet some courts have used the term "unilateral" to indicate those cases where only one party made a mistake (whatever the other may have thought), and have then justified giving no remedy on this basis. Thus in *Riverlate Properties v. Paul*, [1974] 2 All E.R. 656, the English Court of Appeal gave no relief when, by mistake, the cost of repairs under a lease was placed on the lessor and not shared as had been intended. Russell L.J., giving the judgment of the court, said, "It is a case of mere unilateral mistake which cannot entitle the plaintiff to rescission of the lease..." See also, *Imperial Glass Co. Ltd. v. Consolidated Supplies, Ltd.* (1960), 22 D.L.R. (2d) 759.

Recent cases have treated this kind of case in a more useful way. Where one party knows that the other has made a mistake, he will not be allowed to take advantage of it. This solution to the problem of "unilateral mistake" was noted by Bacon V.C. in *Paget v. Marshall*, and has been applied in Ontario. This occurred in the case of *McMaster University v. Wilchar Construction*, [1971] 3 O.R. 801. The plaintiff in this case was attempting to hold the defendant to an agreement to construct a building for the university. To the knowledge of the plaintiff, the defendant had mistakenly submitted its bid without providing an escalator clause. Thompson J. said, (p. 810):

"As a general rule, equity follows the law in its attitude towards contracts which are void by reason of mistake. If the contract is void at common law, equity will also treat it as a nullity. Equity, however, will intervene in certain cases to relieve against the rigours of the common law, even though the mistake would not be operative at law. If, for lack of consensus, no contract comes into existence, there, of course, is nothing to which an equity can attach. It is only in cases where the contract is not void at law that equity may afford relief by declaring the contract voidable. It gives relief for certain types of mistakes which the common law disregards and its remedies are more flexible. Thus, equity does not require the certainty which had led to the narrow common law doctrine of fundamental mistake. It seeks rather the more broad and more elastic approach by attempting to do justice and to relieve against hardship. In equity, to admit of correction, mistake need not relate to the essential substance of the contract, and provided that there is mistake as to the promise or as to some material term of the contract, if the Court finds that there has been honest, even though inadvertent, mistake, it will afford relief in any case where it considers that it would be unfair, unjust or unconscionable not to correct it....

"The type of fraud which affords a cause of action for deceit has been precisely classified, but fraud in the wider sense in which the term is used when stated as a ground for equitable relief, is so infinite in its varieties that the Courts have not attempted to define it: see *Allcard v. Skinner* (1887), 36 Ch. D. 145 at p. 183. Hunter, C.J.B.C., in *Orchardson v. Dominion Bank*, [1923] 2 W.W.R. 958 at p. 961, 32 B.C.R. 348, said: '... new phases of fraud are constantly arising, but all kinds of unfair dealing and unconscionable conduct in matters of contract come within its ken.' Fraud, in a sense to which equity has attached its disapproval, extends to transactions in which the Court is of the opinion that it is unconscientious for a person to avail himself of the legal advantage which he has obtained."

Thompson J., therefore, held that the university could not sue the defendant on the agreement. (This decision was affirmed by the Court of Appeal without written reasons: (1973), 12 O.R. (2d) 512).

This case was followed in *Stepps Investments Ltd. v. Security Capital Corporation* (1976), 14 O.R. (2d) 259 (Ont. H.C.), Grange J. In this case the parties had had an agreement that was conditional on the completion of another between the defendant and a third party. This other agreement fell through. The defendant and the third party then entered into a new agreement. As a result, negotiations were reopened between the plaintiff and defendant. A second agreement was then entered into by the parties. This agreement was the same as the first except that it had been amended so that it was not conditional on the completion of the revived agreement between the defendant and the third party. The plaintiff sued to hold the defendant to the agreement that it signed even though the deal between the defendant and the third party had not been concluded. Grange J. held that, following Cheshire and Fifoot, there was no common or mutual mistake, but a unilateral mistake made by the defendant in signing the second agreement without making sure that it was conditional. Grange J. quoted the passage from *McMaster University v. Wilchar* set out above and then referred to the judgement of Lord Denning in *Solle v. Butcher*. Grange J. concluded (p.272):

"In the circumstances of this case I believe that the plaintiffs should have known of the mistake made by the defendant and I believe it would be equitable accordingly to grant relief to the defendant. It is not unreasonable, in my view, in modern commercial relations, to require the parties, where an important amendment is being made, to ensure that knowledge of such amendment comes to the other side. I do not mean that a party must overcome obtuseness in his opposite number but he must at least give him a real opportunity to appreciate the change. And if the circumstances are such that the amendment might readily be missed he should be particularly reluctant to assume such knowledge. Here the plaintiffs could have resolved the whole problem by a clear reference to the amendment in the correspondence or in the recitals or the operative parts of the agreement itself. It could even have been resolved in a clear, unambiguous, oral conversation with the defendant's solicitors and I cannot find that such a clear and unambiguous conversation ever took place."

In the result he gave the plaintiff the option of rectification in accordance with the defendant's version of the contract or rescission.

A case that has always caused difficulty is the case of *Smith v. Hughes* (1871), L.R. 6 Q.B. 597 (Queen's Bench). This case is almost like *Hadley v. Baxendale* in that it is part of the common law lawyer's cultural heritage. The facts of the case were that the plaintiff offered to sell oats to the defendant. The plaintiff, a farmer, showed the defendant, a trainer of racehorses, a sample of the oats that he had for sale. The parties agreed on a sale of the oats. There was a conflict of evidence on the facts. The defendant contended that he had said that he only wanted to buy *old* oats (new oats being apparently bad for racehorses), and that the plaintiff had said that he was selling *old* oats. The plaintiff denied this. The jury was asked two questions:

1. Was the word "old" used in the conversation between the parties?
2. Did the plaintiff believe that the defendant believed that he (the plaintiff) was contracting to sell old oats?

The jury found for the defendant without answering the questions specifically. The judgment in the court of Queen's Bench agreed that if the first question were answered affirmatively the decision would be right. The judges went on to consider the second question. Blackburn J. said that the crucial distinction was between a belief by the plaintiff that the defendant thought he was getting old oats, and a belief by the plaintiff that the defendant thought that the plaintiff was agreeing to sell the old oats. The court also agreed that the trial judge had not brought out the distinction between these two states of mind of the plaintiff, and so there had to be a new trial.

The importance of the distinction is that in the second case the plaintiff would have had to inform the defendant that he was not contracting to sell old oats. The case is very hard to analyse, but the case appears to fit into the class of cases that we have just been discussing. The plaintiff in *Smith v. Hughes* has no obligation to tell the defendant that he may be making a bad deal, but he has an obligation to tell him that he (the plaintiff) is not offering the deal that the defendant appears to think that he is being offered. The distinction is fine, but can be seen in the following example.

BROOKLIN HEIGHTS HOMES v. MAJOR HOLDINGS

(1977), 17 O.R. (2d) 413, Ontario High Court.

[The parties had agreed on the sale of land for development. One of the costs of development of land is payment to the municipality of "lot levies". This is a charge levied by the municipality to cover the costs of providing services to the development and must be paid before permission to build will be given. The defendant, as vendor of the property undertook to pay "any necessary moneys" to obtain permission to build on the land. The plaintiff, purchaser, subsequently discovered that the lot levies had not been paid and brought an action to recover what he had had to pay and what he would have to pay in the future. The defendant did not intend to pay the lot levies when it gave the undertaking.]

Grange J. said (pp 418-420):

The study of mistake in contracts is, as Professor Waddams says, in its infancy: see Waddams, *Law of Contracts*, p. 211. It is not made easier to understand by the attempts at classification which seems only to lead to greater obscurity. I am not going to attempt another classification here. It is, I think, sufficient for me to say that the Courts will grant relief by way of rectification or avoidance where the agreement has been entered into upon the basis of a common mistake. It is equally the law that the Courts will grant the same relief where only one party is mistaken as to the terms of the contract and his mistake has been accompanied by knowledge thereof or some conduct in the nature of fraud by the non-mistaken party. But clearly neither of those situations exists here. The plaintiff at all times believed the lot levies were paid or would be paid by the defendant. It had no reason to believe and did not believe that the defendant thought otherwise and there is no suggestion of misconduct on its part leading to the defendant's mistake.

The difficulty arises from an attempt to find a third classification of mistake described by some writers with, if I may say so, semantic imprecision as "mutual mistake". This classification of mistake is applied to the situation where both parties are mistaken as to the other's intention. Here it is said — see Cheshire & Fifoot, *Law of Contract*, 9th ed., pp. 225-6, that the test of the validity of the contract is an objective one — whether a reasonable man upon all the evidence would infer a contract in a certain sense. It might perhaps better be said that the test is whether the parties had reached a consensus. Still better it seems to me is to start with Waddams' "initial proposition that reasonable expectations are entitled to protection" — see p. 191 — and deny relief to the mistaken party when his opposite has such expectations. As put by Blackburn, J., in *Smith v. Hughes* (1871), L.R. 6 Q.B. 597 at p. 607:

> If whatever a man's real intention may be, he so conducts himself that a reasonable man would believe that he was assenting to the terms proposed by the other party, and that other party upon that belief enters into the contract with him, the man thus conducting himself would be equally bound as if he had intended to agree to the other party's terms.

and Baggallay, L.J., in *Tamplin v. James* (1880), 15 Ch.D. 215 at pp. 217-8:

> ... where there has been no misrepresentation, and where there is no ambiguity in the terms of the contract, the Defendant cannot be allowed to evade the performance of it by the simple statement that he made a mistake. Were such to be the law the performance of a contract could rarely be enforced upon an unwilling party who was also unscrupulous.

The intention of the non-mistaken party is of importance and may, indeed, in many circumstances be paramount.

Whatever the test and whatever the nature or classification of the mistake of the defendant in the case at bar, I can see no possible relief. The undertaking was not ambiguous, the plaintiff was not mistaken as to its meaning, had a reasonable expectation which is entitled to protection and in no way contributed to the mistake of the defendant. Upon any objective test the plain meaning of the document and the meaning taken from it by the plaintiff could reasonably be inferred....

Accordingly, it follows that the plaintiff will have judgment for the sum of $26,930 together with a declaration that the defendant must pay to the City of Kitchener the lot levies imposed in the future relating to the lands purchased or in the event that the plaintiff shall have paid such lot levies, a declaration that it shall be entitled to repayment thereof from the defendant.

The plaintiff in *Smith v. Hughes* loses if either the defendant reasonably believed that he was selling old oates or if the plaintiff knew that the defendant was under a mistake as to the terms on which the plaintiff was prepared to deal.

See also: *Walton v. Landstock Investments* (1976), 72 D.L.R. (3d) 195 (Ontario Court of Appeal); *Belle River Community Association v. Kaufman* (1977), 15 O.R. (2d) 738 (Ontario High Court, Southey J.)

The Ontario courts' treatment of the problems of mistake (unilateral mistake) avoids many of the problems arising under the traditional analysis. The things that become important are things like knowledge by one party of the mistake of the other, and a belief that one party would be getting an unfair advantage if allowed to enforce the contract. Just as these factors can make the giving of relief easy, so too the absence of knowledge of the mistake may make it clear that no relief should be given. E. & N. Railway made a mistake when they sold land to Hobbs. Precisely because Hobbs did not know of their mistake, he was entitled to hold the railway to its bargain. Analysed in these ways, the problems of "unilateral" mistake become manageable.

The fact remains that cases like *Bell v. Levers* and *Magee v. Pennine* are much more difficult than the ones we have just discussed. The easy cases give us a clue. *U.S.A. v. Motor Trucks* and *Norwich Union v. Price* are easy cases. Why? We have already seen that the following factors are relevant:

1. No one's reliance was defeated by giving relief for the mistake.
2. Had no relief been given, there would have been unjust enrichment of one party.
3. The remedy was precisely appropriate to the relief being sought.

Similarly, the cases like *Hobbs v. E. & N. Railway* where it is clear that no relief can be given (notice the similarity of the reasons of Taschereau J., in dissent, to the offer and acceptance test of *Raffles v. Wichelhaus* and Lord Atkin) show that one cannot lightly set aside agreements when to do so would defeat the reasonable expectations of one party to the agreement. To find a satisfactory approach we have to go outside the cases.

An approach to the problems of mistake along the lines suggested by Corbin is developed by Palmer, *Mistake and Unjust Enrichment*. Palmer suggests that the cases on mistake can be divided into several classes. The basic division is into those cases where the mistaken party could say, "I did not intend to say this", and those where he could say, "I did intend to say this, but this was because I mistakenly believed the facts to be so and so." The broad categories may be subdivided further into, first, cases where there is a misunderstanding between the parties (*e.g. Henkel v. Pape, supra*) and where there is what is termed a mistake in integration. An example of such a case would be *U.S.A. v. Motor Trucks* (*supra*). These kinds of mistake raise comparatively few problems compared with those raised by the cases in the other category. We can subdivide cases in the second category into the following: Mistake in Assumptions and Mistake in Performance. The latter is classically illustrated by the case of the debtor who pays more than he owes. That this has always been an easy case is shown by the fact that it is the paradigm case of the operation of quasi contract: the remedy triggered by unjust enrichment. *Norwich Union v. Price* is a case of mistake in performance. The insurers paid what they did not owe. To have allowed the insured to keep the payment would have resulted in unjust enrichment.

The really difficult cases are the cases of Mistake in Assumptions. As we shall see, there are many cases where there is no easy answer. The fact that this is the case is not an argument in favour of mechanical rules: difficult cases, even more than simple cases, require responsive and sophisticated analytical tools. To see how some of these tools can be used we can look at *Bell v. Levers* and *Magee v. Pennine* in more detail. Both cases can be regarded as examples of mistake in performance. If in both cases the amount paid or agreed to be paid was an exact and only a quantification of an amount believed to be due, then in both cases the debtor would have paid (or would have to pay) more than was due. If actual payment would lead to unjust enrichment, a promise to pay can be no different. The situation in *Norwich Union v. Price* would not be changed if the action were brought on a promise to pay the same amount.

The existence of a promise to pay, however, may make a difference. Argument that the promises in these cases should be enforceable can be made in the following way. The defendant in *Fairgrief v. Ellis* (*supra*, Chap. 2, c.(iv)) made a mistake: he promised to pay more than was due. One reason to hold him to his promise is that when one is settling or agreeing to compromise a disputed claim, there is always the risk that, if taken to court, the claim may turn out to be unfounded (or well-founded). To encourage people to settle (or, perhaps, more accurately, to discourage people from trying to get out of settlements once made) the promise that is a settlement will nearly always be enforced. (For an extreme example, see: *Cook v. Wright* (1861), 1 B. & S. 559, 121 E.R. 822.) Of course, if the amount agreed on is not at one of the extremes of the possible settlement, the justification for setting the agreement aside gets even weaker. If the parties have seen the risk and have allocated it there is no reason to re-allocate it. If, therefore, in either *Bell v. Levers* or *Magee v. Pennine* the promise to pay could be put as a settlement then there is strong pressure to hold the promise enforceable. Of course, in neither case do the facts clearly support this.

These methods of analysis may offer fairly straight-forward solutions to the problems raised by these two cases. *Magee v. Pennine* can probably be more easily analysed in one of these methods than can *Bell v. Levers*. The latter case may have a substantial aspect of mistaken performance but it also has other elements. The knowledge of the parties (particularly of Bell) may be important. The jury held that Bell was not fraudulent, but this does not rule out the possibility that, because Bell must have known that he could have been dismissed for what he did, the case might fit under the kind of fraud mentioned by Thompson J., in *McMaster v. Wilchar*. The extent to which the amount in *Bell v. Levers* is genuine *compensation* for *past* services and not a *quantification* of amounts due, will have an important influence on the extent of the possible unjust enrichment involved. To the extent that *Bell v. Levers* is not a case of mistake in performance, but is closer to a true mistake in assumptions, the case becomes harder to resolve. The complete absence of any suspicion on the part of Levers that Bell had breached his contract of employment prevents the case being regarded as a settlement or compromise. Again, *Bell v. Levers* is complicated by the suspicion that Levers might not have dismissed two successful executives had they found out about what they had done. The existence of this suspicion leads one to doubt that this was a mistake at all. To carry our analysis of *Bell v. Levers* to a conclusion requires more facts than the case gives us.

If the kind of analysis that has just been put forward shows that we need to know more facts about both cases, and that we have to be careful about the lines between the competing categories for analysis, then it is clear that the analysis of Lord Atkin, of Lord Denning and of textbooks like Cheshire and Fifoot is really worse than useless. It blinds us to distinctions that we have to make. It circumscribes the factual enquiry so that we cannot begin to see how the cases might be resolved. Above all, the analysis is unusable. We can never tell by using it what is going to happen in any case that we might have to consider. The difference between the judges in *Magee v. Pennine* is an excellent example of this.

One further problem. It is often said that relief for mistake can only be given for a mistake of fact not of law. The difficulty with this proposition is that it is almost impossible to tell whether any particular mistake falls in one category or the other. For example, relief was given in *Solle v. Butcher* even though the mistake appeared to be on the application of the rent acts to a reconstructed building. In *Jacobs Enterprises Ltd. v. City of Regina* (1964), 44 D.L.R. (2d) 179 the Supreme Court of Canada gave relief where a mistake had been made over the application of a municipal by-law. The court there said that the mistake was not over the interpretation of the by-law — a question of law — but over its existence — a matter of fact. The distinction between mistakes of act and law cannot be wholly ignored but it must be treated with great care.

The problem is again to know when this objection will be raised to deny relief for mistake. In a sense, all cases of compromises or settlements involve mistakes of law and not of fact. The proposition that relief cannot be given for mistake of law, is not confined to compromise cases. Perhaps the best approach to the distinction is along the lines of risk analysis. When the courts deny relief on the ground that the mistaken party made a mistake of law, what they may be saying is that that was the risk that the mistaken party ran in that case. A very large proportion of the mistake of law cases can be justified on this basis. It is clear that it is at the back of the compromise cases and show why in *Solle v. Butcher*, the court would not be bothered about the mistake being a mistake of law.

The remaining cases in this section are variations on the themes that have already been raised. Keep the general questions that we have to ask in mind as you read each case.

SCOTT v. COULSON

[1903] 2 Ch. 249. Court of Appeal (England); Vaughan Williams, Romer and Cozens-Hardy L.JJ.

[The plaintiff owned a policy of life insurance on the life of one A.T. Death. The parties agreed that the plaintiff would assign the contract of life insurance to the defendant. After the agreement had been made but before the actual assignment of the policy was executed, the purchaser, the defendant, obtained information that led him to believe that Death was dead. The plaintiff brought an action to have the agreement and assignment set aside. It was admitted that at the date of the agreement neither party knew that Death was dead.

The trial judge, Kekewich J. gave judgment for the plaintiff.]

[Note: Treat the sale of the policy like a sale of land. The parties first agreed to sell and the formal execution of the assignment took place later.]

Vaughan Williams L.J. On the facts of this case, if one takes those which were found by the learned judge in his judgment, I do not see what room there is for argument on any question of law. If we are to take it that it was common ground that, at the date of the contract for the sale of this policy, both the parties to the contract supposed the assured to be alive, it is true that both parties entered into this contract upon the basis of a common affirmative belief that the assured was alive; but as it turned out that this was a common mistake, the contract was one which cannot be enforced. This is so at law; and the plaintiffs do not require to have recourse to equity to rescind the contract, if the basis which both parties recognised as the basis is not true. Having regard to the evidence, it seems to be clear that the learned judge came to the right conclusion. If it had turned out that the vendors or their agent had requested Coulson to find out whether the assured was dead or alive, and Coulson had come back and said he could not find out, I should have said that, apart from argument, it would have been almost impossible to arrive at the conclusion that both parties entered into the contract upon the basis that the assured was alive. But it turns out that no such inquiry was requested to be made. The only inquiry requested to be made was that contained in Coulson's letter of March 15, 1902, in which he requested inquiry to be made about the assured. Therefore the inference cannot arise which, if it had arisen, would have been fatal to the plaintiffs' contention that this contract was entered into upon the basis that the assured was still alive. If one gets rid of that, what is there left? We have before us the conditions of the proposed sale which were before both parties, in which it certainly seems to be assumed that the assured was still alive.

All I say with regard to the matter is that the material date all through is the date of the contract. If at that date a good contract was entered into, I cannot conceive that it could be rescinded. But it turns out that it was a contract entered into under a common mistake existing at the date of it, and therefore it follows that an assignment executed in pursuance of such a contract cannot be supported.

The learned judge has arrived at a right conclusion, and this appeal must therefore be dismissed, with costs.

Romer L.J. I agree that this appeal must be dismissed. Upon the facts of the case it appears to me that the learned judge came to the right conclusion, namely, that the contract entered into between the parties to the sale and purchase of this policy rested upon the basis of the assured being still alive. It turns out that, before the matter was concluded by assignment to the defendants, the fact upon which the contract was based was not the fact. The defendant Coulson must be taken to have known that the basis upon which the contract had been entered into, and the common belief upon which both parties had acted, did not exist. That was a circumstance which went to the root of the matter, and rendered it improper to insist upon the completion of the contract. What did Coulson do when he received the information leading him to the knowledge or belief that the assured was dead? Did he do what he ought to have done — tell the plaintiffs? Not at all. He allowed the plaintiffs to go on under the old belief, and to execute the assignment on the footing that the old basis continued and that the defendants were entitled to an assignment. I need scarcely say that that was wholly unjustifiable from a legal point of view, and also from an equitable point of view, and none the less so because the defendants apparently thought they were justified in taking the assignment.

Such a transaction cannot be allowed to stand, and therefore this appeal must be dismissed.

[Cozens-Hardy L.J. agreed.]

QUESTIONS

1. Does the reasoning in *Scott v. Coulson* fit into the basic mistake analysis of Lord Atkin? Did the mistake either nullify or negative consent?

2. What precisely were the purchaser's expectations?

3. Were these defeated by the decision?

4. Had the parties allocated the risk of loss (or chance of gain) between themselves? If so, how?

SHERWOOD v. WALKER

(1887), 33 N.W. 919. Supreme Court of Michigan.

Morse, J. Replevin for a cow. Suit commenced in justice's court; judgment for plaintiff; appealed to circuit court of Wayne county, and verdict and judgment for plaintiff in that court. The defendants bring error, and set out 25 assignments of the same.

The main controversy depends upon the construction of a contract for the sale of the cow. The plaintiff claims that the title passed, and bases his action upon such claim. The defendants contend that the contract was executory, and by its terms no title to the animal was acquired by plaintiff. The defendants reside at Detroit, but are in business at Walkerville, Ontario, and have a farm at Greenfield, in Wayne county, upon which were some blooded cattle supposed to be barren as breeders. The Walkers are importers and breeders of polled Angus cattle. The plaintiff is a banker living at Plymouth, in Wayne county. He called upon the defendants at Walkerville for the purchase of some of their stock, but found none there that suited him. Meeting one of the defendants afterwards, he was informed that they had a few head upon their Greenfield farm. He was asked to go out and look at them, with the statement at the time that they were probably barren, and would not breed. May 5, 1886, plaintiff went out to Greenfield, and saw the cattle. A few days thereafter, he called upon one of the defendants with the view of purchasing a cow, known as "Rose 2d of Aberlone." After considerable talk, it was agreed that defendants would telephone Sherwood at his home in Plymouth in reference to the price. The second morning after this talk he was called up by telephone, and the terms of the sale were finally agreed upon. He was to pay five and one-half cents per pound, live weight, fifty pounds shrinkage. He was asked how he intended to take the cow home, and replied that he might ship her from King's cattle-yard. He requested defendants to confirm the sale in writing, which they did by sending him the following letter:

"WALKERVILLE, May 15, 1886.

"*T.C. Sherwood, President, etc.* — DEAR SIR: We confirm sale to you of the cow Rose 2d of Aberlone, lot 56 of our catalogue, at five and a half cents per pound, less fifty pounds shrink. We inclose herewith order on Mr. Graham for the cow. You might leave check with him, or mail to us here, as you prefer.

"Yours, truly,   HIRAM WALKER & SONS."

The order upon Graham inclosed in the letter read as follows:

"WALKERVILLE, May 15, 1886.

"*George Graham*: You will please deliver at King's cattle-yard to Mr. T.C. Sherwood, Plymouth, the cow Rose 2d of Aberlone, lot 56 of our catalogue. Send halter with the cow, and have her weighed.

"Yours truly,   HIRAM WALKER & SONS."

On the twenty-first of the same month the plaintiff went to defendants' farm at Greenfield, and presented the order and letter to Graham, who informed him that the defendants had instructed him not to deliver the cow. Soon after, the plaintiff tendered to Hiram Walker, one of the defendants, $80, and demanded the cow. Walker refused to take the money or deliver the cow. The plaintiff then instituted this suit. After he had secured possession of the cow under the writ of replevin, the plaintiff caused her to be weighed by the constable who served the writ, at a place other than King's cattle-yard. She weighed 1,420 pounds.

When the plaintiff, upon the trial in the circuit court, had submitted his proofs showing the above transaction, defendants moved to strike out and exclude the testimony from the case, for the reason that it was irrelevant and did not tend to show that the title to the cow passed, and that it showed that the contract of sale was merely executory. The court refused the motion, and an exception was taken. The defendants then introduced evidence tending to show that at the time of the alleged sale it was believed by both the plaintiff and themselves that the cow was barren and would not breed; that she cost $850, and if not barren would be worth from $750 to $1,000; that after the date of the letter, and the order to Graham, the defendants were informed by said Graham that in his judgment the cow was with calf, and therefore they instructed him not to deliver her to plaintiff, and on the twentieth of May, 1886, telegraphed plaintiff what Graham thought about the cow being with calf, and that consequently they could not sell her. The cow had a calf in the month of October following....

It appears from the record that both parties supposed this cow was barren and would not breed, and she was sold by the pound for an insignificant sum as compared with her real value if a breeder. She was evidently sold and purchased on the relation of her value for beef, unless the plaintiff had learned of her true condition, and concealed such knowledge from the defendants. Before the plaintiff secured the possession of the animal, the defendants learned that she was with calf, and therefore of great value, and undertook to rescind the sale by refusing to deliver her. The question arises whether they had a right to do so. The circuit judge ruled that this fact did not avoid the sale and it made no difference whether she was barren or not. I am of the opinion that the court erred in this holding. I know that this is a close question, and the dividing line between the adjudicated cases is not easily discerned. But it must be considered as well settled that a party who has given an apparent consent to a contract of sale may refuse to execute it, or he may avoid it after it has been completed, if the assent was founded, or the contract made, upon the mistake of a material fact, — such as the subject-matter of the sale, the price, or some collateral fact materially inducing the agreement; and this can be done when the mistake is mutual....

If there is a difference or misapprehension as to the substance of the thing bargained for; if the thing actually delivered or received is different in substance from the thing bargained for, and intended to be sold, — then there is no contract; but if it be only a difference in some quality or accident, even though the mistake may have been the actuating motive to the purchaser or seller, or both of them, yet the contract remains binding. "The difficulty in every case is to determine whether the mistake or misapprehension is as to the substance of the whole contract, going, as it were, to the root of the matter, or only to some point, even though a material point, an error as to which does not affect the substance of the whole consideration." *Kennedy v. Panama, etc., Mail Co.,* L.R. 2 Q.B. 580, 587. It has been held, in accordance with the principles above stated, that where a horse is bought under the belief that he is sound, and both vendor and vendee honestly believe him to be sound, the purchaser must stand by his bargain, and pay the full price, unless there was a warranty.

It seems to me, however, in the case made by this record, that the mistake or misapprehension of the parties went to the whole substance of the agreement. If the cow was a breeder, she was worth at least $750; if barren, she was worth not over $80. The parties would not have made the contract of sale except upon the understanding and belief that she was incapable of breeding, and of no use as a cow. It is true she is now the identical animal that they thought her to be when the contract was made; there is no mistake as to the identity of the creature. Yet the mistake was not of the mere quality of the animal, but went to the very nature of the thing. A barren cow is substantially a different creature than a breeding one. There is as much difference between them for all purposes of use as there is between an ox and a cow that is capable of breeding and giving milk. If the mutual mistake had simply related to the fact whether she was with calf or not for one season, then it might have been a good sale, but the mistake affected the character of the animal for all time, and for its present and ultimate use. She was not in fact the animal, or the kind of animal, the defendants intended to sell or the plaintiff to buy. She was not a barren cow, and, if this fact had been known, there would have been no contract. The mistake affected the substance of the whole consideration, and it must be considered that there was no contract to sell or sale of the cow as she actually was. The thing sold and bought had in fact no existence. She was sold as a beef creature would be sold; she is in fact a breeding cow, and a valuable one. The court should have instructed the jury that if they found the cow was sold, or contracted to be sold, upon the understanding of both parties that she was barren, and useless for the purpose of breeding, and that in fact she was not barren, but capable of breeding, then the defendants had a right to rescind, and to refuse to deliver, and the verdict should be in their favor.

The judgment of the court below must be reversed, and a new trial granted, with costs of this court to defendants.

[Campbell, C.J., and Champlin, J., concurred.]

Sherwood, J. (*dissenting.*) I do not concur in the opinion given by my brethren in this case. I think the judgments before the justice and at the circuit were right. I agree with my Brother MORSE that the contract made was not within the statute of frauds, and the payment for the property was not a condition precedent to the passing of the title from the defendants to the plaintiff. And I further agree with him that the plaintiff was entitled to a delivery of the property to him when the suit was brought, unless there was a mistake made which would invalidate the contract, and I can find no such mistake. There is no pretense there was any fraud or concealment in the case, and an intimation or insinuation that such a thing might have existed on the part of either of the parties would undoubtedly be a greater surprise to them than anything else that has occurred in their dealings or in the case.

As has already been stated by my brethren, the record shows that the plaintiff is a banker and farmer as well, carrying on a farm, and raising the best breeds of stock, and lived in Plymouth, in the county of Wayne, 23 miles from Detroit; that the defendants lived in Detroit, and were also dealers in stock of the higher grades; that they had a farm at Walkerville, in Canada, and also one in Greenfield in said county of Wayne, and upon these farms the defendants kept their stock. The Greenfield farm was about 15 miles from the plaintiff's. In the spring of 1886 the plaintiff, learning that the defendants had some "polled Angus cattle" for sale, was desirous of purchasing some of that breed, and meeting the defendants, or some of them, at Walkerville, inquired about them, and was informed that they had none at Walkerville "but had a few head left on their farm in Greenfield, and asked the plaintiff to go and see them, stating that in all probability they were sterile and would not breed." In accordance with said request, the plaintiff, on the fifth day of May, went out and looked at the defendants' cattle at Greenfield, and found one called "Rose, Second," which he wished to purchase, and the terms were finally agreed upon at five and a half cents per pound, live weight, 50 pounds to be deducted for shrinkage. The sale was in writing, and the defendants gave an order to the plaintiff directing the man in charge of the Greenfield farm to deliver the cow to plaintiff. This was done on the fifteenth of May. On the twenty-first of May plaintiff went to get his cow, and the defendants refused to let him have her; claiming at the time that the man in charge at the farm thought the cow was with calf, and, if such was the case, they would not sell her for the price agreed upon. The record further shows that the defendants, when they sold the cow, believed the cow was not with calf, and barren; that from what the plaintiff had been told by defendants (for it does not appear he had any other knowledge or facts from which he could form an opinion) he believed the cow was farrow, but still thought she could be made to breed. The foregoing shows the entire interview and treaty between the parties as to the sterility and qualities of the cow sold to the plaintiff. The cow had a calf in the month of October.

There is no question but that the defendants sold the cow representing her of the breed and quality they believed the cow to be, and that the purchaser so understood it. And the buyer purchased her believing her to be of the breed represented by the sellers, and possessing all the qualities stated, and even more. He believed she would breed. There is no pretense that the plaintiff bought the cow for beef, and there is nothing in the record indicating that he would have bought her at all only that he thought she might be made to breed. Under the foregoing facts, — and these are all that are contained in the record material to the contract, — it is held that because it turned out that the plaintiff was more correct in his judgment as to one quality of the cow than the defendants, and a quality, too, which could not by any possibility be positively known at the time by either party to exist, the contract may be annulled by the defendants at their pleasure. I know of no law, and have not been referred to any, which will justify any such holding, and I think the circuit judge was right in his construction of the contract between the parties.

It is claimed that a mutual mistake of a material fact was made by the parties when the contract of sale was made. There was no warranty in the case of the quality of the animal. When a mistaken fact is relied upon as ground for rescinding, such fact must not only exist at the time the contract is made, but must have been known to one or both of the parties. Where there is no warranty, there can be no mistake of fact when no such fact exists, or, if in existence, neither party knew of it, or could know of it; and that is precisely this case. If the owner of a Hambletonian horse had speeded him, and was only able to make him go a mile in three minutes, and should sell him to another, believing that was his greatest speed, for $300, when the purchaser believed he could go much faster, and made the purchase for that sum, and a few days thereafter, under more favorable circumstances, the horse was driven a mile in 2 min. 16 sec., and was found to be worth $20,000, I hardly think it would be held, either at law or in equity, by any one, that the seller in such case could rescind the contract. The same legal principles apply in each case.

In this case neither party knew the actual quality and condition of this cow at the time of the sale. The defendants say, or rather said, to the plaintiff, "they had a few head left on their farm in Greenfield, and asked plaintiff to go and see them, stating to plaintiff that in all probability they were sterile and would not breed." Plaintiff did go as requested, and found there these cows, including the one purchased, with a bull. The cow had been exposed, but neither knew she was with calf or whether she would breed. The defendants thought she would not, but the plaintiff says that he thought she could be made to breed, but believed she was not with calf. The defendants sold the cow for what they believed her to be, and the plaintiff bought her as he believed she was, after the statements made by the defendants. No conditions whatever were attached to the terms of sale by either party. It was in fact as absolute as it could well be made, and I know of no precedent as authority by which this court can alter the contract thus made by these parties in writing, — interpolate in it a condition by which, if the defendants should be mistaken in their belief that the cow was barren, she could be returned to them and their contract should be annulled. It is not the duty of courts to destroy contracts when called upon to enforce them, after they have been legally made. There was no mistake of any material fact by either of the parties in the case as would license the vendors to rescind. There was no difference between the parties, nor misapprehension, as to the substance of the thing bargained for, which was a cow supposed to be barren by one party, and believed not to be by the other. As to the quality of the animal, subsequently developed, both parties were equally ignorant, and as to this each party took his chances. If this were not the law, there would be no safety in purchasing this kind of stock.

. . . .

In this case, if either party had superior knowledge as to the qualities of this animal to the other, certainly the defendants had such advantage. I understand the law to be well settled that "there is no breach of any implied confidence that one party will not profit by his superior knowledge as to facts and circumstances" actually within the knowledge of both, because neither party reposes in any such confidence unless it be specially tendered or required, and that a general sale does not imply warranty of any quality, or the absence of any; and if the seller represents to the purchaser what he himself believes as to the qualities of an animal, and the purchaser buys relying upon his own judgment as to such qualities, there is no warranty in the case, and neither has a cause of action against the other if he finds himself to have been mistaken in judgment.

QUESTIONS

1. Do the judgments disagree on the facts or the law?
2. What would be the effect of giving a remedy here? Would this depend on your view of the facts?
3. Is it relevant that the law has for a long time said that inadequate consideration is no ground for relief?
4. Is the decision just?
5. Would the dissent be just?

In *Wood v. Boynton* (1885), 25 N.W. 42, the Wisconsin Supreme Court gave no relief in a case where a woman sold to a jeweller for $1 a stone which turned out to be a large uncut diamond worth $700. It was found as a fact that the jeweller had no reason to suspect that the stone was a diamond when he bought it. The court said, "There is no pretence of any mistake as to the identity of the thing sold."

QUESTIONS

1. Can there be any satisfactory solution to the problem of *Wood v. Boynton*?
2. To what extent is the law of mistake fulfilling this function of warranty in cases where the buyer seeks a remedy for his disappointment?

If the parties use language that they realize may not adequately deal with a problem that they have forseen they simply leave it up to the court to determine the result should there later be a dispute.

LONDON COUNTY COUNCIL v. BOOT

[1959] 1 W.L.R. 1069 House of Lords.

[The parties had entered into a contract for construction work to be done by the respondent for the appellant. The parties had failed to reach agreement on the application of an escalator clause to the holiday pay of labourers employed by the respondent. The House of Lords held, rejecting the arguments of the respondent, that the clause, as drafted, did not apply to the holiday pay of the labourers so that an increase in that could not be passed onto the appellant.]

Lord Denning, [in referring to the fact that the parties had failed to reach agreement on the scope of the clause, said:]

The London County Council there made it clear that they did not regard holiday credits as coming within the rise-and-fall clause; but the builders' association took a different view. Neither side inserted any words in the contract so as to clear up the difference between them. They left the rise-and-fall clause as it was. It was suggested that on this account there was no consensus ad idem: Your Lordships rejected this suggestion without wishing to hear further argument upon it. There was, to all outward appearances, agreement by the parties on the one thing that really mattered — on the terms that should bind them. In case of difference as to the meaning of those terms, it was for the court to determine it. It does not matter what the parties, in their inmost states of mind, thought the terms meant. They may each have meant different things. But still the contract is binding according to its terms — as interpreted by the court.

[Does this indicate anything about the result in *Raffles v. Wichelhaus* or *Henkel v. Pape*?]

GRIST v. BAILEY

[1966] 2 All E.R. 875. Chancery Division.

[The defendant agreed to sell a house to the plaintiff. The parties believed that the house was occupied by a tenant, who, under the Rent Acts, could not be evicted, and the agreement provided that "the property is sold subject to the existing tenancy thereof." The agreed price was £850. Between the date of the agreement and completion the defendant discovered that the house could be sold with vacant possession. The defendant thereupon refused to complete. The purchaser brought an action for specific performance.]

Goff J.: In these circumstances, the first question which arises is one of law, namely, what is the effect of common mistake? The leading case on this subject is *Bell v. Lever Bros., Ltd.* This, of course, is binding on me and if exhaustive is really fatal to the defendant, since it lays down very narrow limits in which mistake operates to avoid a contract. It was there held that mistake as to the quality of the subject-matter of the contract must be such as to make the actual subject-matter something essentially different from what it was supposed to be — see per Lord Atkin. In that case the plaintiffs sought to recover large sums which they had paid by way of compensation for the determination of certain contracts of service, which, though they did not know it, they were entitled to rescind. The case as pleaded was not one of mutual mistake, and Lord Blanesburgh held it was too late to amend, and Lord Atkin doubted whether amendment was permissible but on the assumption that the pleadings were amended to raise this issue they and Lord Thankerton all agreed that the case must fail. I should have thought that this was more fundamental than any mistake made in the present case, and moreover the examples of the horse, picture, and garage, given by Lord Atkin in his speech would, in my judgment, apply to prevent any mistake as to the nature of the tenancy affecting the property being sufficient to avoid the present agreement.

Counsel for the defendant has argued, however, that there is a wider principle in equity in support of which he quotes Cheshire and Fifoot on *Law of Contract* (5th edn.), p. 184, *Solle v. Butcher*, particularly the judgment of Denning, L.J., and *Huddersfield Banking Co. Ltd. v. Henry Lister & Son, Ltd.*, [1895] 2 Ch. 273, and see also Chitty on *Contracts*, Vol. 1, p. 90, para. 191, and p. 115, para. 254.

In *Solle's* case, as it seems to me, Denning, L.J., clearly drew a distinction between the effect of mistake at law, which, where effective at all, makes the contract void, and in equity where it is a common ground for rescission or for refusing specific performance; and, as it further seems to me, he clearly thought that this was wider than the jurisdiction at law. Denning, L.J., said:

> "The principle so established by *Cooper v. Phibbs* has been repeatedly acted on; see for instance *Earl Beauchamp v. Winn* (1873), L.R. 6 H.L. 223, and *Huddersfield Banking Co., Ltd. v. Henry Lister & Son, Ltd.*. It is in no way impaired by *Bell v. Lever Bros., Ltd.* which was treated in the House of Lords as a case at law depending on whether the contract was a nullity or not. If it had been considered on equitable grounds the result might have been different."

Denning, L.J., laid down the equitable rule in these terms:

> "A contract is also liable in equity to be set aside if the parties were under a common misapprehension either as to facts, or as their relative and respective rights, provided that the misapprehension was fundamental and that the party seeking to set it aside was not himself at fault."

Bucknill, L.J., did not specifically refer to *Bell v. Lever Bros., Ltd.*, but he laid down the principle in similar terms:

> "... there was a mutual mistake of fact on a matter of fundamental importance, namely, as to the identity of the flat with the dwelling-house previously let at a standard rent of £140 a year, and that the principle laid down in *Cooper v. Phibbs* applies."

Counsel for the plaintiff has submitted that there is no difference between law and equity and no case which suggests that *Bell v. Lever Bros.* does not cover the whole field save what he describes as one casual remark of Denning. L.J., in *Solle's* case; and he says, moreover, that Denning, L.J., himself resiled from his earlier view in the later case of *Leaf v. International Galleries*, [1950] 2 K.B. 86.

I cannot accept this interpretation of Denning, L.J.'s judgment, or indeed of *Solle's* case as a whole. It was a carefully considered view of the relevant law and equity, and I do not think that Denning, L.J., resiled from it in any way in the later case. As counsel for the defendant has pointed out, relief in equity was not possible in *Leaf's* case because it was too late; and Denning, L.J., again accepted the equitable view in *Frederick E. Rose (London), Ltd. v. Wm. H. Pim Junr. & Co., Ltd.*, [1953] 2 Q.B. 450 at p. 460, where he said:

> "At the present day, since the fusion of law and equity, the position appears to be that, when the parties to a contract are to all outward appearances in full and certain agreement, neither of them can set up his own mistake, or the mistake of both of them, so as to make the contract a nullity from the beginning. Even a common mistake as to the subject-matter does not make it a nullity. Once the contract is outwardly complete, the contract is good unless and until it is set aside for failure of some condition on which the existence of the contract depends, or for fraud, or on some equitable ground: see *Solle v. Butcher*. Could this contract, then, have been set aside? I think it could, if the parties had acted in time."

Again, in *Oscar Chess, Ltd. v. Williams*, [1957] 1 All E.R. 325 at p. 327, Denning L.J., said:

> "They both believed that the car was a 1948 model, whereas it was only a 1939 one. They were both mistaken and their mistake was of fundamental importance. The effect of such a mistake is this: it does not make the contract a nullity from the beginning, but it does in some circumstances enable the contract to be set aside in equity. If the buyer had come promptly, he might have succeeded in get-

ting the whole transaction set aside in equity on the grounds of this mistake (see *Solle v. Butcher*); but he did not do so, and it is now too late for him to do it; see *Leaf v. International Galleries.*"

Be that as it may, I cannot dismiss what Denning, L.J., said in *Solle's* case as a mere dictum. It was in my judgment the basis of the decision and is binding on me; and, as I have said, I think Bucknill, L.J., took the same view. Whether the mistake in the *Huddersfield Banking* case would have been sufficient at law, Kay, J.'s statement is, I think, further support for the view that there is the equitable jurisdiction.

Then I have to decide first — Was there a common mistake in this case? Secondly — Was it fundamental? Thirdly, perhaps — Was the defendant at fault?

Such being the state of the evidence, in my judgment there was a common mistake — namely, that there was still subsisting a protected tenancy ... and it is to be remembered that the language of cl. 7 of the agreement is "subject to the existing tenancy thereof". In my view, this was nonetheless a common mistake, though the parties may have differed in their belief as to who the tenant was, whether Mrs. or Mr. Brewer, although that may have a bearing on materiality.

Then, was it fundamental? In view of (the plaintiff's agent's) evidence to which I have referred, and the evidence of Mr. Cooper Hurst, a surveyor called on behalf of the defendant, that in his opinion the vacant possession value as at August, 1964, was £2,250, in my judgment it must have been if (the tenant) had no rights under the Rent Acts.

There remains one other point, and that is the condition laid down by Denning, L.J., that the party seeking to take advantage of the mistake must not be at fault. Denning, L.J., did not develop that at all, and it is not, I think with respect, absolutely clear what it comprehends. Clearly, there must be some degree of blameworthiness beyond the mere fault of having made a mistake; but the question is, how much or in what way? Each case must depend on its own facts, and I do not consider that the defendant or her agents were at fault so as to disentitle them to relief.

It was argued that the vendor should know who her tenants are, but this was a case of a long-standing and informal tenancy, the rent under which was paid simply by attendance in the outer office, where it was received by some junior boy or girl, and Mr. Brewer had but recently died.

The result, in my judgment, is that the defendant is entitled to relief in equity, and I do not feel that this is a case for simply refusing specific performance. Accordingly, the action fails, and on the counterclaim I order rescission. It is clear that this being equitable relief may be granted unconditionally or on terms, and counsel on behalf of the defendant, has offered to submit to a condition that the relief I have ordered should be on condition that the defendant is to enter into a fresh contract at a proper vacant possession price, and if required by the plaintiff, I will impose that term.

Action dismissed. Order for rescission on counterclaim.

HYRSKY ET AL. v. SMITH

(1969), 5 D.L.R. (3d) 385. Ontario High Court.

[In May 1959 the parties entered into a contract for the purchase and sale of land. The agreed price was $4,700. The purchasers did not have any search made of the title. A deed was executed in December 1962. In 1966 it was discovered that almost half of the land conveyed by the deed of 1962 had not been owned by the vendor. The purchaser brought an action for rescission on the ground of error in *substantialibus* claiming over $5,000.]

Lieff J.: – ... As to what consititutes an error *in substantialibus* no authority appears to have given a definitive answer. The earlier cases have used the phrase, "total failure of consideration" rather than "error *in substantialibus*" and counsel for the defendant has urged that the latter phrase has the same restricted meaning as the former. Plaintiffs' counsel, on the other hand, submitted that the more recently used phrase is broader in scope than the earlier exception and in fact includes a "total failure of consideration".

The Roman doctrine of *error in substantia* rendered contracts void where there existed mistakes as to quality which related to the substance of the subject-matter of the contract. In *Kennedy v. Panama, etc. Royal Mail Co.* (1867), L.R. 2 Q.B. 580, Blackburn, J., considered the origin of this doctrine and summarized the principle at pp. 587-8 as follows:

> The principle is well illustrated in the civil law, as stated in the Digest, lib. 18, tit. 4. De Contrahendâ Emptione, leges, 9, 10, 11. There, — after laying down the general rule, that where the parties are not at one as to the subject of the contract there is no agreement, and that this applies where the parties have misapprehended each other as to the corpus, as where an absent slave was sold and the buyer thought he was buying Pamphilus and the vendor thought he was selling Stichus, and pronouncing the judgment that in such a case there was no bargain because there was "error in corpore," the framers of the digest moot the point thus: "Inde quaeritur, si in ipso corpore non erretur, sed in substantia error sit, ut, puta, si acetum pro vino veneat, aes pro auro, vel plumbum proargento vel quid aliud argento simile: an emptio et venditio sit;" and the answers given by the great jurists quoted are to the effect, that if there be misapprehension as to the substance of the thing there is no contract; but if it be only a difference in some quality or accident, even though the misapprehension may have been the actuating motive to the purchaser, yet the contract remains binding. Paulus says: "Si aes pro auro veneat, non valet, aliter at que si aurum quidem fuerit, deterius autem quam emptor existimarit: tunc enim emptio valet." Ulpianus, in the eleventh law, puts an example as to the sale of a slave very similar to that of the unsound horse in *Street v. Blay*, 2 B. & Ad. 456. And, as we apprehend, the principle of our law is the same as that of the civil law; and the difficulty in every case is to determine whether the mistake or misapprehension is as to the substance of the whole consideration, going, as it were, to the root of the matter, or only to some point, even though a material point, an error as to which does not affect the substance of the whole consideration.

Consequently, for a contract to be rescinded for mutual mistake, the mistake must go to the root of the contract. In order to constitute an error *in substantialibus*, there must be a mutual fundamental mistake as to the quality of the subject-matter. The application of this principle must, of course, turn upon the facts of each individual case. A practical statement of the test which governs the applicability of the doctrine of fundamental mutual mistake which gives rise to an error *in substantialibus* was put forth by G. H. Treitel in his work, *The Law of Contract*, 2nd ed., p. 179, as follows:

> A thing has many qualities. A car may be black, old, fast and so forth. For any particular purpose one or more of these qualities may be uppermost in the minds of the persons dealing with the thing. Some particular quality may be so important in the minds of the parties that they actually use that quality to *identify* the

thing. If the thing lacks that quality, it is suggested that the parties have made a fundamental mistake, even though they have not mistaken one thing for another, or made a mistake as to the existence of the thing. A practical test for deciding this question is to imagine that one can ask the parties, immediately after they made the contract, what the subject-matter of the contract was. If, in spite of the mistake, they would give the right answer the contract is valid at law.

Having regard to these principles, has the common mistake of the parties as to the quantity of land being conveyed resulted in an error *in substantialibus*? In the case of *De Clerval v. Jones* (1908), 8 W.L.R. 300, the purchaser of land brought an action against the vendor as a result of a mutual mistake by the parties resulting in a substantial deficiency in acreage. The parties were under the mistaken belief that the block of land contained 160.86 acres whereas in fact it contained only 97 acres. Beck, J., thought that the circumstances warranted rescission and he had this to say at pp. 306-7:

> Where there is a mutual mistake, going not necessarily to an essential but to a material, substantial, and important element of the contract, it seems to me that the Court will ordinarily order rescission, even though the contract has been completely executed, if it can do so on equitable terms.
> In the present case I am satisfied that both the plaintiff and Riley, the defendant's agent, were convinced that the land in question comprised approximately at least 160 acres (i.e., they were mutually mistaken as to the quantity), and that, had the plaintiff been aware of the actual deficiency, he would not have entered into the contract. I think that the deficiency being so great it is so material, substantial, and important that the plaintiff is entitled to relief. It is not, however, a case for specific performance; nor, in view of the decision of the Supreme Court of Canada in *Penrose v. Knight*, Cassel's Digest, p. 777, can I order payment of a sum by way of compensation. I think justice will be best achieved by ordering that the contract be rescinded, the defendant re-paying to the plaintiff within a limited time, which I will fix on the settlement of the minutes of judgment, the amount he has received on account of purchase money, with interest, together with the value of the permanent improvements made by the plaintiff (these sums to be ascertained by the clerk of the Court), with the option, however, to the defendant of paying to the plaintiff, by way of compensation for the deficiency, the sum of $504, being the price of 63 acres at $8 per acre.

There is a similar deficiency as to quantity of land in the instant case and there often can be a fine line between quantity and quality. If the mistake as to quantity is so substantial so that in essence it changes the quality of the subject-matter, then a proper case for rescission may exist. In the case at bar, the deficiency approximated one-half of the land purchased and the remanet was unsuitable as a consequence for the purpose for which the purchasers bought the property. I think that on this basis, there can be little doubt that the mistake was so fundamental that the quality and the very identity of the parcel of land which was the subject-matter of the sale had undergone a significant transformation. I believe that if the minds of the parties, upon completion of the sale, had been directed to answer the question, "What was the subject-matter of the agreement?" they would have responded by stating not just a block of land but a parcel of land bearing the specific dimensions set out in the deed.

Counsel for the defendant vendor, however, had urged that the circumstance does not amount to a "total failure of consideration" which he submits is the proper test of an error *in substantialibus*. But what is meant by a "total failure of consideration"? Most of the cases in which Courts have permitted rescission by reason of a total failure of consideration have been situations where the purchaser and vendor of land mistakenly entered into a transaction whereby the purchaser bought land which had all along been his own property, or have been situations analogous thereto: *Bingham v. Bingham* (1748), 1 Ves. Sen. 126, 27 E.R. 934; *Cooper v. Phibbs* (1867), L.R. 2 H.L. 149.

In an Australian case, *Svanosio v. McNamara* (1956), 96 C.L.R. 186, referred to by counsel for the defendant, the plaintiff purchased a hotel and its liquor licence. After the conveyance, the purchaser learned that some of the rooms of the hotel (approximately one-third of the hotel) were situate on adjoining Crown land and he accordingly claimed rescission of the agreement on the ground of common mistake. It was held by the High Court of Australia, on appeal, that only a total failure of consideration could justify rescission and that there could be no rescission for this partial failure of consideration. The Court stated at p. 209:

> There are *dicta* in the cases that relief can be given after the contract has been completed where there is a common mistake upon a material point although there is only a partial failure of consideration... But the proper principle appears to be that, in the case of a completed contract of sale, rescission is only possible on the ground of common mistake where, contrary to the belief of the parties, there is nothing to contract about as in *Bingham v. Bingham* (1748), 1 Ves. Sen. 126 and *Cooper v. Phibbs* (1867), L.R. 2 H.L. 149.

There is little doubt that the cases which have allowed rescission because of a "total failure of consideration" have been limited to only those where there existed a situation, in the words of Cheshire and Fifoot in their text on *The Law of Contract*, 6th ed., p. 187, of *res sua* or *res extincta*. I prefer to think, however, that this aspect of the law in Ontario has broadened in scope with the use of the phrase "error *in substantialibus*" to include not only the aforesaid restricted examples of a total failure of consideration but also what may said to be a virtual failure of consideration. In fact, Dixon, C.J., and Fullagar, J., in the *Svanosio* case, *supra*, at least pay lip service to this possible extension of the principle at pp. 198-9, although it is not reflected in the decision:

> Other statements of the general rule extend the scope of the exception beyond cases of fraud, using various expressions, the general effect of which is, we think, correctly stated by saying that there must be a total failure of consideration or what amounts practically to a total failure of consideration.

I am inclined to believe that the phrase "error *in substantialibus*", used by the Courts today carries the meaning enunciated earlier in these reasons and that is: In equity, a contract is subject to rescission if the parties suffered from a common fundamental misapprehension as to the facts which went to the very root of the contract: *Grist v. Bailey*, [1966] 2 All E.R. 875.

In the case at bar, there were no words of qualification such as "more or less" accompanying the description of the lands in the agreement of purchase and sale and there is a considerable disparity between the quantity of land actually conveyed and the quantity described by the defendant in the deed. Having regard to the fact that this difference amounts to almost one-half of the lands described in the deed, and having regard to the fact that, to the knowledge of the vendor, the purchaser intended to use these lands for investment purposes, the conclusion is inescapable that there existed a common fundamental mistake as to the very quality of the subject-matter of the contract which can be equated to an error *in substantialibus.*

In arriving at this conclusion, I am aware of the policy consideration implicit in the doctrine of *caveat emptor,* as enunciated by Grove, J., in *Clare v. Lamb* (1875), L.R. 10 C.P. 334 at pp. 338-9, as follows:

> In the case of the purchase of an interest in land, the person who sells places at the disposal of the buyer such title-deeds as he possesses and under which he claims. The purchaser has full opportunity for investigating the title of the vendor, and when he takes a conveyance he is assumed to have done so. Considerable inconvenience might result if this were not the rule. Conveyancers may agree upon the title, and, long after the conveyance has been executed, the whole transaction completed, and the proceeds disbursed, the seller might be called upon to return the purchase-money, by reason of some defect of which he had no notice at the time.

To the same effect, see *Allen v. Richardson* (1879), 13 Ch. D. 524 at p. 539, and *Joliffe v. Baker* (1883), 11 Q.B.D. 255 at p. 265. It is true that under our present-day system of conveyancing, the purchaser has ample opportunity to inquire and to inspect before he is compelled to close the transaction and it may be said that execution of the conveyance can be looked upon as a declaration that he is satisfied with the outcome of his investigation. However that may be and notwithstanding the need for certainty and permanence in the law of conveyancing, these policy considerations must yield to the desirability of doing equity where there has been an error *in substantialibus.* For the reasons given above, the plaintiff is entitled to some remedy.

. . .

Only the question of remedy remains. I do not think that this is a proper case for rectification of the deed. McRuer, C.J.H.C., set out the prerequisites of this remedy in *Devald v. Zigeuner,* [1958] O.W.N. 381 at pp. 382-3, 16 D.L.R. (2d) 285 at p. 290, as follows:

> In *Cheshire & Fifoot, Contracts,* 4th ed., p. 185, the essentials for rectification on the basis of mutual mistake were set out as follows: —
> 1. The relief was not granted unless a complete agreement was reached prior to the written instrument which is sought to rectify.
> 2. Both parties must have intended that the exact terms of the alleged prior contract should be reduced to writing, and the intention must have continued unchanged up to the time when the instrument was executed.
> 3. Clear evidence of a mistake common to both parties must be adduced, and the burden of proving this lay on the party who alleged that the instrument ought to be altered.
> 4. The sole purpose of equity's intervention was to cure literal faults and thus to prevent the intention of the parties already clearly revealed in their prior agreement, from being nullified by their failure to express it accurately in the subsequent document.

Also see the judgment of Culliton, C.J.S., in *Bercovici v. Palmer* (1966), 59 D.L.R. (2d) 513, 58 W.W.R. 111, in which may be found a careful review of the principles applicable to rectification. The deed cannot now be made to conform with the common intention of the parties. No question of a mere literal fault in the deed exists. There has been an error *in substantialibus* by both parties and equity will permit in this case nothing less than rescission of the deed. Moreover, having regard to the circumstances, I do not think there were laches on the plaintiffs' part so as to disentitle them to relief.

In the result, therefore, judgment should go on behalf of the plaintiffs rescinding the deed in question. The plaintiffs are also entitled to repayment of $5,387.57 which sum comprises payments made by the plaintiffs of $5,154.77, of $207.40 for taxes, and of $25.40 for legal fees; and also interest at 6% on all moneys expended by the plaintiffs.

The matter of costs caused me some concern because had the plaintiffs searched the title as a prudent purchaser should have done, all of this litigation would never have arisen. For this reason and because the case is somewhat unique, I exercise my discretion and make no order as to costs.

Judgment for plaintiffs.

NOTE

Under the standard practice in real estate deals the purchaser has the chance to search the title, get a survey, and object to any defects that might be disclosed.

QUESTIONS

1. What do you think is meant by an error *in substantialibus*?
2. What do you think that Lieff J. meant by the term?
3. Was any intermediate position possible here?
4. Is the judgment in this case consistent with that of the next case?

AMALGAMATED INVESTMENT AND PROPERTY CO. LTD. v. JOHN WALKER & SONS LTD.

[1976] 3 All E.R. 509. Court of Appeal, Civil Division; Buckley, Lawton L.JJ. and Sir John Pennycuick.

[The defendants wanted to sell a large warehouse. It was advertised as being "for sale for occupation or redevelopment." The plaintiff offered £1,710,000 for the property. This was accepted by the defendants.

Enquiries were made before contract in the ordinary way, and amongst other questions asked was this:

"Although the Purchaser will be making the usual searches and enquiries of the local and planning authorities, the Vendor is asked specifically to state whether he is aware of any order, designation or proposal of any local or other authority or body having compulsory powers involving any of the following..."

Then there are a number of sub-paragraphs, the only relevant one being (iv), which reads: "The designation of the property as a building of special architectual or historic interest." A negative answer was given to that question by the vendors on 14th August.

The formal contract was signed on September 25, 1973. The contract incorporated the Law Society's General Conditions of Sale (1973 Revision) which contained, amongst other provisions, a condition that nothing in the conditions should entitle the vendor to compel the purchaser to accept or the purchaser to compel the vendor to convey (with or without compensation) property which differed substantially from the property agreed to be sold and purchased, whether in quantity, quality, tenure or otherwise, if the purchaser or the vendor respectively would be prejudiced by reason of such difference.

On September 26, 1973, that is the day after the contract, the Department of the Environment wrote a letter to the defendants notifying them that the property, the subject-matter of the contract, had been selected for inclusion in the statutory list of buildings of special architectural or historic interest compiled by the Secretary of State, and that that list was about to be given legal effect.

(The facts of this cannot be recounted here, but they are, as Buckley L.J. said, "rather startling" and are worth reading as an indication of how some governmental decisions are made.)]

Buckley L.J. [after outlining the facts, continued]: ... The judge found as a fact that the value of the property with no redevelopment potential was probably £1,500,000 less than the contract price. So the effect of the building being put into the list was this: that so long as it remained listed and 'listed building consent' could not be obtained, the value of the property was depreciated from the £1,700,000 odd, which was the sale price, to something of the order of £200,000. The judge also found as a fact that the defendants knew at all material times that the purchasers were buying the property for redevelopment.

On 12th December 1973 the plaintiffs issued their writ against the defendants claiming rescission of the agreement on the ground of common mistake, a declaration that the agreement was void and of no effect and a declaration that the agreement was voidable, and an order rescinding the agreement. Those were, of course, alternative remedies. On 14th December the defendants issued a writ against the plaintiffs claiming specific performance of the contract and alternatively a declaration that the plaintiffs had wrongfully repudiated the contract, and forfeiture of the deposit and damages with ancillary relief. Those two actions were consolidated on 19th July 1974, and the action came on with Amalgamated Investment and Property Co. Ltd. as plaintiffs and John Walker & Sons Ltd. as defendants. There was a counterclaim raised by the defendants for the relief sought in their action, specific performance and so forth.

The relevant statutory provisions will be found in the Town and Country Planning Act 1971, ss. 54, 55, 56 and Sch. II; but I do not think that it is necessary for me to refer in detail to any of these.

Plowman V-C held that there was no common mistake. He said:

'In my judgment, however, the issue of mistake does not arise. The relevant event, in my opinion, was the actual listing of the warehouse and not some preliminary step in the process of listing taken within the four walls of the Department, which might or might not result in executive action, although no doubt it probably would.'

He therefore treated the building as having been listed on the day when the list was signed by the head of the relevant branch in the Ministry; that is to say, after the date of the contract. So, on that finding, the contract was not entered into in reliance on any, or under any, common mistake of the parties, for at the time when the contract was entered into the building was not a listed building.

He dealt with the alternative ground of frustration of the contract, which was taken before him, in this way:

'One therefore starts with this (and I quote Lord Radcliffe, [1956] AC 696 at 727) '... frustration is not to be lightly invoked as the dissolvent of a contract'. Let me then try to apply some of the tests proposed by the House of Lords [he is there referring to *Davis Contractors Ltd. v. Fareham Urban District Council,* [1956] AC

696] to the facts of this case. Can it be said that the parties must have made their contract on the footing that the warehouse would not be listed in the future? I can see nothing in the contract to suggest that that must be the case. In my judgment the plaintiffs took the risk under the contract, and it seems to me impossible to maintain that the contract ceased to apply when the property was listed. They could have provided against the risk by an appropriate provision in the contract, but they did not do so. Again, is the contract which the parties made, on its true construction, wide enough to apply to the situation which arose when the property was listed? The answer to that must, in my judgment, be yes, and I can see nothing in the contract to support the contrary view. Would the thing undertaken, if performed, be a different thing from that contracted for ? Or, again, can the plaintiffs say, 'This was not the bargain we made'? (Non haec in foedera veni.) Not in my judgment. The plaintiffs undertook to purchase 33, Commercial Road, and if the purchase is completed, they will have done the very thing which they undertook to do, no more and no less. They took the risk under the contract of the property being listed, and it has turned out badly for them, but as Lord Simonds said, '... it by no means follows that disappointed expectations lead to frustrated contracts".'

So Plowman V-C held that the contract stood and that the purchasers were liable for the full purchase price, and that the contract should be carried out.

It has been contended before us that there was here a common mistake of fact on a matter of fundamental importance, in consequence of which the contract ought to be set aside. Reliance has been placed on the decision of this court in *Solle v. Butcher* and the decision of Goff J. in *Grist v. Bailey.*

Counsel for the plaintiffs says that they bought the property as property which was ripe for development and that the defendants sold on the same basis, and that by reason of the decision to list the property the property was not in fact ripe for development. Therefore he says there was a common mistake as to the nature of the property, and the purchaser is entitled to rescission.

The actual pleading of the common mistake that is alleged is in these terms, to be found in paras 2, 3 and 4 of the statement of claim:

'2. At the time of the execution of the Agreement both the Plaintiff and the Defendant believed that the property was suitable for and capable of being redeveloped, and the said purchase price was determined by the said belief.

'3. Unknown to the Plaintiff and to the Defendant the Department of the Environment had on or before 25th September 1973 selected the property for inclusion in the statutory list of buildings of special architectural or historic interest compiled by the Secretary of State for the Environment.

'4. The selection of the property for inclusion in the said list prevents the property from being suitable for or capable of being redeveloped, or alternatively substantially reduces the potentiality of the said property for redevelopment.'

So the alleged common mistake was that the property was property suitable for and capable of being developed.

For the application of the doctrine of mutual mistake as a ground for setting the contract aside, it is of course necessary to show that the mistake existed at the date of the contract; and so counsel for the plaintiffs relies in that respect not on the signing of the list by the officer who alone was authorised to sign it on behalf of the Secretary of State, but on the decision of Miss Price to include the property in the list. That decision, although in fact it led to the signature of the list in the form in which it was eventually signed, was merely an administrative step in the carrying out of the operations of the branch of the Ministry. It was a personal decision on the part of Miss Price that the list should contain the particular property with which we are concerned. But there was still the possibility that something else might arise before the list was signed. Some communication might have been received from some outside body which threw some light on the qualifications of this building for listing, which might have resulted in its being excluded from the list as it was actually signed. Indeed, the head of the department might himself, had he known of the circumstances, have formed a different opinion from the opinion formed by Miss Price or Miss Price might, I suppose, herself have changed her mind during the time between preparing the list, sending it to the typing pool and eventually laying it before her superior for signature. Although she accepts the responsibility for the decision and says it was her decision, it was (as I say) no more than an administrative step leading to the ultimate signature of the list, just as the obtaining of the information that was eventually included in the report of the investigating officer was an administrative step or the preparation of the report of the investigating officer. It seems to me that it is no more justifiable to point to that date as being the crucial date than it is to point to other earlier dates or later dates. The crucial date, in my judgment, is the date when the list was signed. It was then that the building became a listed building, and it was only then that the expectations of the parties (who no doubt both expected that this property would be capable of being developed, subject always of course to obtaining planning permission, without it being necessary to obtain listed building permission) were disappointed. For myself, I entirely agree with the conclusion which the learned judge reached on this part of the case. In my judgment, there was no mutual mistake as to the circumstances surrounding the contract at the time when the contract was entered into. The only mistake that there was one which related to the expectation of the parties. They expected that the building would be subject only to ordinary town planning consent procedures, and that expectation has been disappointed. But at the date when the contract was entered into I cannot see that there is any ground for saying that the parties were then subject to some mutual mistake of fact relating to the circumstances surrounding the contract. Accordingly, for my part, I think that the learned judge's decision on that part of the case is one which should be upheld.

We have heard an interesting argument whether *Solle v. Butcher*, which I have already mentioned, can stand as good law with *Bell v. Lever Brothers Ltd.* That is not a matter on which I think it is necessary for us to embark, and I do not propose to say anything about it.

I now turn to the alternative argument which has been presented to us in support of this appeal, which is on frustration. Counsel for the plaintiffs has relied on what was said in the speeches in the House of Lords in *Davis Contractors Ltd. v. Fareham Urban District Council*, and it may perhaps be useful if I refer to what was said by Lord Radcliffe:

> 'So, perhaps, it would be simpler to say at the outset that frustration occurs whenever the law recognizes that, without default of either party, a contractual obligation has become incapable of being performed because the circumstances in which performance is called for would render it a thing radically different from that which was undertaken by the contract.'

That is a passage which was referred to by Plowman V-C in the course of his judgment. Then, a little later on, after referring to *Denny, Mott and Dickson Ltd. v. James B. Fraser & Co. Ltd.*, [1944] AC 265, Lord Radcliffe said:

> 'It is for that reason that special importance is necessarily attached to the occurrence of any unexpected event that, as it were, changes the face of things. But, even so, it is not hardship or inconvenience or material loss itself which calls the principle of frustration into play. There must be as well such a change in the significance of the obligation that the thing undertaken would, if performed, be a different thing from that contracted for.'

Now, the obligation undertaken to be performed in this case by the defendants was to sell this property for the contract price and, of course, to show a good title and so forth. The defendants did not warrant in any way that planning permission could be obtained for the development of the property. No doubt both parties considered that the property was property which could advantageously be developed and was property for which planning permission would probably be satisfactorily obtained. But there was no stipulation in the contract to anything of that kind; nor, as I say, was there any warranty on the part of the defendants. I am prepared to assume for the purposes of this judgment that the law relating to frustration of contracts is capable of being applied in the case of a contract for sale of land, though that is not one of the matters which has been debated before us. But, making that assumption I have reached the conclusion that there are not here the necessary factual bases for holding that this contract has been frustrated. It seems to me that the risk of property being listed as property of architectural or historical interest is a risk which inheres in all ownership of buildings. In many cases it may be an extremely remote risk. In many cases it may be a marginal risk. In some cases it may be a substantial risk. But it is a risk, I think, which attaches to all buildings and it is a risk that every owner and every purchaser of property must recognise that he is subject to. The purchasers in the present case bought knowing that they would have to obtain planning permission in order to develop the property. The effect of listing under the sections of the 1971 Act to which I have referred makes the obtaining of planning permission, it may be, more difficult, and it may also make it a longer and more complicated process. But still, in essence, the position is that the would-be developer has to obtain the appropriate planning permissions, one form of permission being the 'listed building permission'. The plaintiffs, when they entered into the contract, must obviously be taken to have known that they would need to get planning permission. They must also, in my judgment, be taken to have known that there was the risk, although they may not have regarded it as a substantial risk, that the building might at some time be listed, and that their chances of obtaining planning permission might possibly be adversely affected to some extent by that, or at any rate their chances of obtaining speedy planning permission. But, in my judgment, this is a risk of a kind which every purchaser should be regarded as knowing that he is subject to when he enters into his contract of purchase. It is a risk which I think the purchaser must carry, and any loss that may result from the maturing of that risk is a loss which must lie where it falls. Moreover, the plaintiffs have not yet established that they will be unable to obtain all the necessary planning permissions, including 'listed building permission'. So it has not yet, I think, been established that the listing of this building has had the drastic effect which the figures I have mentioned suggest that it may have had. It may well turn out to be the case that 'listed building permission' will be obtainable here and the purchasers will be able to carry into effect the development which they desire. For these reasons I reach the conclusion, as I say, that the necessary facts have not been established in this case to found a claim that the contract has been frustrated.

For these reasons, I would dismiss the appeal.

[Lawton L.J. and Sir John Pennycuick agreed with Buckley L.J.]

QUESTIONS

1. What could lawyers for either side have done to improve their client's position?

2. Should the legal effect on the contract of the designation of the building depend on whether the decision is made before or after the contract?

This final section includes some cases which do not fit very well into any of the foregoing categories. The first is *sui generis*:

UPTON-ON-SEVERN RURAL DISTRICT COUNCIL v. POWELL

[1942] 1 All E.R. 220. Court of Appeal (England); Lord Greene M.R., Luxmoore and Goddard L.JJ.

Lord Greene M.R.: The appellant lives at Strensham, and in Nov., 1939, a fire broke out in his Dutch barn; he thereupon telephoned to the police inspector at the Upton police office and told him that there was a fire and asked for the fire brigade to be sent. The police inspector telephoned a garage near to the fire station at Upton, which itself had no telephone, the Upton brigade was informed and immediately went to the fire, where it remained for a long time engaged in putting it out. It so happens that, although the appellant's farm is in the Upton police district, it is not in the Upton fire district. It is in the Pershore fire district, and the appellant was entitled to have the services of the Pershore fire brigade without payment. The Upton fire brigade, on the other hand, was entitled to go to a fire outside its area and, if it did so, quite apart from its statutory rights, it could make a contract that it would be entitled to repayment of its expenses.

The sole question here is whether or not any contract was made by which the Upton fire brigade rendered services on an implied promise to pay for them made by or on behalf of the appellant. It appears that some 6 hours after the arrival of the Upton fire brigade, the officer of the Pershore brigade arrived on the scene, but without his brigade; he pointed out to the Upton officer that it was a Pershore fire, and not an Upton fire, but the Upton fire brigade continued rendering services until the next day when the Pershore fire brigade arrived and took over. In the view that I take in this case, what happened in relation to the arrival of the Pershore officer and his conversation with the Upton officer and the subsequent arrival of the Pershore fire brigade was nothing whatever to do with the issue which we have to decide. The county court judge held that the appellant when he rang up the police inspector, asked for "the fire brigade" to be sent. He also held that the inspector summoned the local Upton fire brigade, which was perfectly natural, and that he took the order as being one for the fire brigade with which he was connected. It appears that neither the appellant, nor the police officer, nor the Upton fire brigade, until it was so informed by the Pershore officer, knew that the appellant's farm was, in fact, not in the Upton area, but was in the Pershore area. The county court judge then goes on to find that the inspector passed on the order and sent his fire brigade, and that was the fire brigade, I have no doubt, which the appellant expected. The county court judge said:

> "The defendant did not know that if he sent for the Pershore fire brigade what advantage he would have obtained. In my view, there is no escape from the legal liability the defendant has incurred. I think he gave the order for the fire brigade he wanted, and he got it."

Now those findings are attacked, because it is said that, as the defendant did not know what fire brigade area he was in, what he really wanted was to get the fire brigade of his area, whatever it might be. It does not seem to me that there is any justification for attacking the finding of the judge on that basis. What the defendant wanted was somebody to put out his fire, and put it out as quickly as possible, and in ringing up the Upton police he must have intended that the inspector at Upton would get the Upton fire brigade; that is the brigade which he would naturally ask for when he rang up Upton. Even apart from that, it seems to me quite sufficient if the Upton inspector reasonably so construed the request made to him, and, indeed, I do not see what other construction the inspector could have put upon that request. It follows, therefore, that on any view the appellant must be treated as having asked for the Upton fire brigade. That request having been made to the Upton fire brigade by a person who was asking for its services, does it prevent there being a contractual relationship merely because the Upton fire brigade, which responds to that request and renders the services, thinks, at the time it starts out and for a considerable time afterwards, that the farm in question is in its area, as the officer in charge appears to have thought? In my opinion, that can make no difference. The real truth of the matter is that the appellant wanted the services of Upton; he asked for the services of Upton — that is the request that he made — and Upton, in response to that request, provided those services. He cannot afterwards turn round and say: "Although I wanted Upton, although I did not concern myself when I asked for Upton as to whether I was entitled to get free services, or whether I would have to pay for them, nevertheless, when it turns out that Upton can demand payment, I am not going to pay them, because Upton were under the erroneous impression that they were rendering gratuitous services in their own area." That, it seems to me, would be quite wrong on principle. In my opinion, the county court judge's finding cannot be assailed and the appeal must be dismissed with costs.

Luxmoore L.J.: I agree.

Goddard L.J.: I agree.

QUESTIONS

1. What did the defendant expect when he made the phone-call to the police station?

2. What did the Upton Fire Brigade expect when it went to the defendant's fire?

BOULTON v. JONES

(1857), 2 H. & N. 564, 157 E.R. 232, Exchequer.

Action for goods sold. Plea. Never indebted.

At the trial before the Assessor of the Court of Passage at Liverpool, it appeared that the plaintiff had been foreman and manager to one Brocklehurst, a pipe hose manufacturer, with whom the defendants had been in the habit of dealing, and with whom they had a running account. On the morning of the 13th January, 1857, the plaintiff bought Brocklehurst's stock, fixtures, and business, and paid for them. In the afternoon of the same day, the defendant's servant brought a written order, addressed to Brocklehurst, for three 50-feet leather hose, 2½ in. The goods were supplied by the plaintiff. The plaintiff's book keeper struck out the name of Brocklehurst and inserted the name of the plaintiff in the order. An invoice was afterwards sent in by the plaintiff to the defendants, who said they knew nothing of him. Upon these facts, the jury, under direction of the Assessor, found a verdict for the plaintiff, and leave was reserved to the defendants to move to enter a verdict for them.

Pollock, C.B. The point raised is, whether the facts proved did not shew an intention on the part of the defendants to deal with Brocklehurst. The plaintiff, who succeeded Brocklehurst in business, executed the order without any intimation of the change that had taken place, and brought this action to recover the price of the goods supplied. It is a rule of law, that if a person intends to contract with A, B cannot give himself any right under it. Here the order in writing was given to Brocklehurst. Possibly Brocklehurst might have adopted the act of the plaintiff in supplying the goods, and maintained an action for their price. But since the plaintiff has chosen to sue, the only course the defendants could take was to plead that there was no contract with him.

Martin, B. I am of the same opinion. This is not a case of principal and agent. If there was any contract at all, it was not with the plaintiff. If a man goes to a shop and makes a contract, intending it to be with one particular person, no other person can convert that into a contract with him.

Bramwell, B. The admitted facts are, that the defendants sent to a shop an order for goods, supposing they were dealing with Brocklehurst. The plaintiff, who supplied the goods, did not undeceive them. If the plaintiff were now at liberty to sue the defendants, they would be deprived of their right of set-off as against Brocklehurst. When a contract is made, in which the personality of the contracting party is or may be of importance, as a contract with a man to write a book, or the like, or where there might be a set-off, no other person can interpose and adopt the contract. As to the difficulty that the defendants need not pay anybody, I do not see why they should, unless they have made a contract either express or implied. I decide the case on the ground that the defendants did not know that the plaintiff was the person who supplied the goods, and that allowing the plaintiff to treat the contract as made with him would be a prejudice to the defendants.

Channell, B. In order to entitle the plaintiff to recover he must shew that there was a contract with himself. The order was given to the plaintiff's predecessor in business. The plaintiff executes it without notifying to the defendants who it was who executed the order. When the invoice was delivered in the name of the plaintiff, it may be that the defendants were not in a situation to return the goods.

Rule absolute.

In *McRae v. Commonwealth Disposals Commission* (1951), 25 A.L.J. 425,
the plaintiff appellant claimed damages from the defendant respondent.
The plaintiff had bought from the defendant what he thought was a
wrecked oil tanker on a reef. There was no oil tanker and no reef at the
place specified by the defendant. The High Court of Australia awarded the
plaintiff damages for his expenses thrown away in going to pick up and salvage the tanker. The defendant argued that since the contract was clearly
entered into under a mistake the contract was void, and it should, therefore
only have to refund the amount paid for the right to salvage. The court held
that there was an implied promise made by the defendant that there was a

tanker to be salvaged and damages could be awarded for breach of this contract.

Such a case would now be regarded as coming under *Hedley Byrne v. Heller*. The remedy would, therefore, not have to be based on any kind of implied contract, but on the misstatement which was relied on in circumstances where such reliance was expected and where the party making the statement had a duty to take care.

REVIEW PROBLEMS

1. *Globe and Mail*, June 30, 1976.

CONTRACT GOES TO FIRM DESPITE MISTAKE IN BID.

Metro Council stuck to its guns yesterday in insisting on awarding a construction contract to a company that doesn't want it. In the process, however, council's executive committee was pointedly reminded that nobody's perfect.

Poole Construction Ltd. of Edmonton is to be awarded a contract to build the Victoria Park garbage-transfer station in accordance with its low bid of $2,836,629.50. Shortly after tenders on the project had been opened, the company asked to withdraw its tender. An executive had entered some figures in the wrong column in calculating estimates for the bid, making the bid $537,988 lower than intended.

Toronto Alderman John Sewell proposed yesterday that council avoid delays and litigation by immediately awarding the contract to the second lowest bidder, Ellis-Don Ltd., which bid $3,129,823.

But he withdrew the suggestion after Metro Solicitor A.P.G. Joy said that, if council awarded the control to Poole, that company would have seven days to sign it. If Poole refused to do this, the Metro executive could immediately award the contract to Ellis-Don, and at the same time consider what it might do to seek compensation.

But, just before yesterday's Council meeting, a quick meeting of the Metro executive committee learned that, in deciding earlier to award Poole a contract for $2,836,020, the executive had been the victim of a typographical error of about $600 by the Metro works department.

QUESTION

Is there a contract? If so, for how much?

2. *Speculands Ltd. v. Adam Vend.*

The following judgment was delivered by Palmer J. in the Supreme Court of Flavelle.

This is an action for rescission of a contract of sale of a 100 acre parcel of land brought by the purchaser. The vendor has counterclaimed for damages.

The agreement was entered into on June 26, 1973, and the sale was to be closed on October 31, 1973. In June 1973 the Ontario legislature passed two acts: The Ontario Planning and Development Act, 1973 and The Parkway Belt Planning and Development Act, 1973. By their respective terms each act came into effect on June 4, 1973. By Regulation made under the latter act (O. Reg. 481/73) all development of (*inter alia*) the land in question was prohibited.

Neither party was aware of this legislation at the time the agreement was signed. The agreed price for the land was $500,000 and the purchaser paid a deposit of $50,000. I find as a fact that the price of $500,000 would only have been paid by the purchaser in the belief that the land could be developed. The development restrictions were discovered by the purchaser on June 30, 1973 during the course of the search for zoning regulations routinely carried out by purchasers after agreement and before closing. Immediately upon making the discovery the purchaser refused to complete the transaction and the defendant subsequently resold the land for $100,000, the agreed market value of land thus restricted in its development potential.

The argument of the purchaser is that the agreement is vitiated by the mistake made by the parties in agreeing to sell land when development — the purpose of the contract — was impossible. Counsel for the plaintiff submits that the law is that where "the very foundation of the agreement" is destroyed, the agreement can be set aside on the ground of mistake.

In my view, in the present instance, "the very foundation of the agreement" has not been destroyed. Though it was, as I have found, well known to the vendor that the purchaser intended to make commercial use of its property by some form of subdivision, the agreement is in no sense made conditional upon the ability of the purchaser to carry out its intention. The "very foundation of the agreement" was that the vendor would sell and the purchaser would buy the property therein described upon the terms therein set out. The only obligations assumed by the vendor were to provide a deed and to join in or consent to any subsequent applications respecting the zoning and to give partial discharges of the mortgage it was taking back under certain circumstances. The only obligation of the purchaser was to pay the cash balance agreed to, execute and give back a mortgage and to pay such mortgage in accordance with its terms. Nothing in legislation affects, in the slightest degree, the abilities of the parties to carry out their respective obligations.

As it was put by counsel for the vendor, a developer in purchasing land is always conscious of the risk that zoning or similar changes may make the carrying out of his intention impossible, or may delay it. He may attempt to guard against risk by the insertion of proper conditions in the contract and thereby persuade the vendor to assume some of the risk. In the present case he has not done so and, indeed, there is no evidence that he has attempted to do so. "The very foundation of the agreement" is not affected and there is no room for the application of the doctrine of mistake.

I regard the case as coming within the well-known case of *Bell v. Levers Bros.*, [1932] A.C. 161. Counsel for the purchaser has argued that recent cases have expanded the scope of the relief for mistake and that the law has changed since 1932. It is worth noting that *Bell v. Levers* was decided in the same year as *Donoghue v. Stevenson*, [1932] A.C. 562 and by courts with substantial overlapping membership, and no one has suggested that the latter case is out of date or subject to criticism.

I therefore conclude that the purchaser is not entitled to relief and that the vendor's action must succeed. I give judgment therefore for the vendor for $400,000 and costs. Since the vendor still has the deposit paid by the purchaser, that amount shall be taken into account.

PROBLEM

The purchaser has appealed. The ground of appeal is that the trial judge erred in holding that the mistake made by the parties affords no ground for relief.

Prepare a factum for one side on the appeal.

E. Frustration

In the cases on mistake we looked at cases where the agreement the parties had in fact made turned out to be quite different from that which they thought they had made. These were cases which we classified as mistake in assumptions. The cases in this section are analytically very similar to those. Here the mistake only comes to light after the parties have had a contract for some time. The question as presented here is whether this offers a basis for discharging the parties from any further performance. Obviously, if both agree, the contract will be rescinded. Where one party does not agree, the courts have to decide if there is an excuse for non-performance so that the contract will be discharged. As you read the cases consider the following questions:

1. What is the stated basis for giving or denying relief?
2. How far would an analysis based on the following factors take one towards a solution
   (a) the prevention of unjust enrichment;
   (b) the protection of reliance;
   (c) the allocation of risk made by the parties;
   (d) the practice in the particular area of commercial activity involved.
3. What problems are there in reaching flexible and fair results?

The first case in this section is one that is always regarded as the "leading case" in this area. If age were everything it would certainly qualify on that ground. The case did not start life as a leading case. It appears to have been forgotten for over 150 years until it was revived in a note by a Serjeant Williams to Saunders' Reports. These reports were a collection of late seventeenth century cases. *Paradine v. Jane* was paraphrased by Williams in a note to the case of *Walton v. Waterhouse* (1684), 2 Williams Saunders 420; 85 E.R. 1233. These notes were published in 1802. It was frequently referred to throughout the nineteenth century. See, *e.g.,* Blackburn J. in *Taylor v. Caldwell (infra)*.

For a discussion of the case and its history see: Gilmore, *The Death of Contract*.

Paradine v. Jane was regarded as the foundation of the idea that contractual liability was not only strict, it was absolute. This means that there could be no excuse for a failure to perform a contractual obligation. The remaining cases in this section show that the courts cannot live with that and that ways to excuse people must be found.

PARADINE v. JANE

(1647), Aleyn. 26; 82 E.R. 897.

Debt.

In debt the plaintiff declares upon a lease for years rendring rent at the four usual feasts; and for rent behind for three years, ending at the Feast of the Annunciation, 21 Car. brings his action; the defendant pleads, that a certain German prince, by name Prince Rupert, an alien born, enemy to the King and kingdom, had invaded the realm with an hostile army of men; and with the same force did enter upon the defendant's possession, and him expelled, and held out of possession from the 19 of July 18 Car. till the Feast of the Annunciation, 21 Car. whereby he could not take the profits; whereupon the plaintiff demurred, and the plea was resolved insufficient.

. . .

3. It was resolved, that the matter of the plea was insufficient; for though the whole army had been alien enemies, yet he ought to pay his rent. And this difference was taken, that where the law creates a duty or charge, and the party is disabled to perform it without any default in him, and hath no remedy over, there the law will excuse him. As in the case of waste, if a house be destroyed by tempest, or by enemies, the lessee is excused ... but when the party by his own contract creates a duty or charge upon himself, he is bound to make it good, if he may, notwithstanding any accident by

inevitable necessity, because he might have provided against it by his contract. And therefore if the lessee covenant to repair a house, though it be burnt by lightning, or thrown down by enemies, yet he ought to repair it. Now the rent is a duty created by the parties upon the reservation, and had there been a covenant to pay it, there had been no question but the lessee must have made it good, notwithstanding the interruption by enemies, for the law would not protect him beyond his own agreement, no more than in the case of reparations; this reservation then being a covenant in law, and whereupon an action of covenant hath been maintained (as Roll said) it is all one as if there had been an actual covenant. Another reason was added, that as the lessee is to have the advantage of casual profits, so he must run the hazard of casual losses, and not lay the whole burthen of them upon his lessor; ... that though the land be surrounded, or gained by the sea, or made barren by wildfire, yet the lessor shall have his whole rent: and judgment was given for the plaintiff.

TAYLOR v. CALDWELL

(1863), 3 B. & S. 826; 122 E.R. 309. Queen's Bench.

[An agreement was made between the parties that the plaintiff would have the use of the Surrey Gardens and Music Hall on four days during the summer of 1861. The defendant was the owner of the Music Hall. The agreement provided for the following programme of entertainment:]

"Agreement between Messrs. Caldwell & Bishop, of the one part, and Messrs. Taylor & Lewis of the other part, whereby the said Caldwell & Bishop agree to let, and the said Taylor & Lewis agree to take, on the terms hereinafter stated, The Surrey Gardens and Music Hall, Newington, Surrey, ... for the purpose of giving a series of four grand concerts and day and night fêtes at the said Gardens and Hall on those days respectively at the rent or sum of £100 for each of the said days. The said Caldwell & Bishop agree to find and provide at their own sole expense, on each of the aforesaid days, for the amusement of the public and persons then in the said Gardens and Hall, an efficient and organized military and quadrille band, the united bands to consist of from thirty-five to forty members; al fresco entertainments of various descriptions; coloured minstrels, fireworks and full illuminations; a ballet or divertissement, if permitted; a wizard and Grecian statues; tight rope performances; rifle galleries; air gun shooting; Chinese and Parisian games; boats on the lake, and (weather permitting) aquatic sports, and all and every other entertainment as given nightly during the months and times above mentioned. And the said Caldwell & Bishop also agree that the before mentioned united bands shall be present and assist at each of the said concerts, from its commencement until 9 o'clock at night; that they will, one week at least previous to the above mentioned dates, underline in bold-type in all their bills and advertisements that Mr. Sims Reeves and other artistes will sing at the said gardens on those dates respectively, and that the said Taylor & Lewis shall have the right of placing their boards, bills and placards in such number and manner (but subject to the approval of the said Caldwell & Bishop) in and about the entrance to the said gardens, and in the said grounds, one week at least previous to each of the above mentioned days respectively, all bills so displayed being affixed on boards. And the said Caldwell & Bishop also agree to allow dancing on the new circular platform after 9 o'clock at night, but not before. And the said Caldwell & Bishop also agree not to allow the firework display to take place till a ¼ past 11 o'clock at night. And, lastly, the said Caldwell & Bishop agree that the said Taylor & Lewis shall be entitled to and shall be at liberty to take and receive, as and for the sole use and property of them the said Taylor & Lewis, all moneys paid for entrance to the Gardens, Galleries and Music Hall and firework galleries, and that the said Taylor & Lewis may in their own discretion secure the patronage of any charitable institution in connection with the said concerts. And the said Taylor & Lewis agree to pay the aforesaid respective sum of 100l. in the evening of the said respective days by a crossed cheque, and also to find and provide, at their own sole cost, all the necessary artistes for the said concerts, including Mr. Sims Reeves, God's will permitting."

[*NOTE*: This is apparently the only case containing an entire theatrical programme. Mr. Sims Reeves (1818-1900) was a famous Victorian singer who took such care of his voice that he would refuse to sing if there was any danger of harming his voice. Whether he would sing or not at any particular function was always uncertain. A wise impressario would, therefore, never promise that he would sing. See: Pollock, *For My Grandson*.]

[Less than one week before the first performance the music hall was destroyed by fire. The plaintiff sued for damages for breach of contract.]

The judgment of the court was given by

Blackburn J.: After the making of the agreement and before the first day on which a concert was to be given, the Hall was destroyed by fire. This destruction, we must take it on the evidence, was without the fault of either party, and was so complete that in consequences the concerts could not be given as intended. And the question we have to decide is whether, under these circumstances, the loss which the plaintiffs have sustained is to fall upon the defendants. The parties when framing their agreement evidently had not present to their minds the possibility of such a disaster, and have made no express stipulation with reference to it, so that the answer to the question must depend upon the general rules of law applicable to such a contract.

There seems no doubt that where there is a positive contract to do a thing, not in itself unlawful, the contractor must perform it or pay damages for not doing it, although in consequence of unforeseen accidents, the performance of his contract has become unexpectedly burthensome or even impossible. The law is so laid down in 1 Roll. Abr. 450, Condition (G), and in the note (2) to *Walton v. Waterhouse* (2 Wms. Saund. 421 a. 6th ed.), and is recognised as the general rule by all the Judges in the much discussed case of *Hall v. Wright* (1859) (E.B. & E. 746). But this rule is only applicable when the contract is positive and absolute, and not subject to any condition either express or implied: and there are authorities which, as we think, establish the principle that where, from the nature of the contract, it appears that the parties must from the beginning have known that it could not be fulfilled unless when the time for the fulfillment of the contract arrived some particular specified thing continued to exist, so that, when entering into the contract, they must have contemplated such continuing existence as the foundation of what was to be done; there, in the absence of any express or implied warranty that the thing shall exist, the contract is not to be construed as a positive contract, but as subject to an implied condition that the parties shall be excused in case, before breach, performance becomes impossible from the perishing of the thing without default of the contractor.

There seems little doubt that this implication tends to further the great object of making the legal construction such as to fulfill the intention of those who entered into the contract. For in the course of affairs men in making such contracts in general would, if it were brought to their minds, say that there should be such a condition.

Accordingly, in the Civil law, such an exception is implied in every obligation of the class which they call obligatio de certo corpore. The rule is laid down in the Digest, lib. XLV., tit. 1, de verborum obligationibus, l. 33. "Si Stichus certo die dari promissus, ante diem moriatur: non tenetur promissor." The principle is more fully developed in l. 23. "Si ex legati causa, aut ex stipulatû hominem certum mihi debeas: non aliter post mortem ejus tenearis mihi, quam si per te steterit, quominus vivo eo eum mihi dares: quod ita fit, si aut interpellatus non dedisti, aut occidisti eum." The examples are of contracts respecting a slave, which was the common illustration of a certain subject used by the Roman lawyers, just as we are apt to take a horse; and no doubt the propriety, one might almost say necessity, of the implied condition is more obvious when the contract relates to a living animal, whether man or brute, than when it relates to some inanimate thing (such as in the present case a theatre) the existence of which is not so obviously precarious as that of the live animal, but the principle is adopted in the Civil law as applicable to every obligation of which the subject is a certain thing. The general subject is treated of by Pothier, who in his Traité des Obligations, partie 3, chap. 6, art. 3, § 668 states the result to be that the debtor corporis certi is freed from his obligation when the thing has perished, neither by his act, nor his neglect, and before he is in default, unless by some stipulation he has taken on himself the risk of the particular misfortune which has occurred.

Although the Civil law is not of itself authority in an English Court, it affords great assistance in investigating the principles on which the law is grounded. And it seems to us that the common law authorities establish that in such a contract the same condition of the continued existence of the thing is implied by English law.

There is a class of contracts in which a person binds himself to do something which requires to be performed by him in person; and such promises, e.g. promises to marry, or promises to serve for a certain time, are never in practice qualified by an express exception of the death of the party; and therefore in such cases the contract is in terms broken if the promisor dies before fulfillment. Yet it was very early determined that, if the performance is personal, the executors are not liable; *Hyde v. The Dean of Windsor* (Cro. Eliz. 552, 553). See 2 Wms. Exors. 1560, 5th ed., where a very apt illustration is given. "Thus," says the learned author, "if an author undertakes to compose a work, and dies before completing it, his executors are discharged from this contract: for the undertaking is merely personal in its nature, and, by the intervention of the contractor's death, has become impossible to be performed." For this he cites a dictum of Lord Lyndhurst in *Marshall v. Broadhurst* (1 Tyr. 348, 349), and a case mentioned by Patteson J. in *Wentworth v. Cock* (10 A. & E. 42, 45-46). In *Hall v. Wright*, Crompton J., in his judgment, puts another case. "Where a contract depends upon personal skill, and the act of God renders it impossible, as, for instance, in the case of a painter employed to paint a picture who is struck blind, it may be that the performance might be excused."

It seems that in those cases the only ground on which the parties or their executors, can be excused from the consequences of the breach of the contract is, that from the nature of the contract there is an implied condition of the continued existence of the life of the contractor, and, perhaps in the case of the painter of his eyesight.

. . .

It may, we think, be safely asserted to be now English law, that in all contracts of loan of chattels or bailments if the performance of the promise of the borrower or bailee to return the things lent or bailed, becomes impossible because it has perished, this impossibility (if not arising from the fault of the borrower or bailee from some risk which he has taken upon himself) excuses the borrower or bailee from the performance of his promise to redeliver the chattel.

The great case of *Coggs v. Bernard* (1703) (1 Smith's L. C. 171, 5th ed.; 2 L. Raym. 909) is now the leading case on the law of bailments, and Lord Holt, in that case, referred so much to the Civil law that it might perhaps be thought that this principle was there derived direct from the civilians, and was not generally applicable in English law except in the case of bailments; but the case of *Williams v. Lloyd* (W. Jones, 179), above cited, shews that the same law had been already adopted by the English law as early as The Book of Assizes. The principle seems to us to be that, in contracts in which the performance depends on the continued existence of a given person or thing, a condition is implied that the impossibility of performance arising from the perishing of the person or thing shall excuse the performance.

In none of these cases is the promise in words other than positive, nor is there any express stipulation that the destruction of the person or thing shall excuse the performance; but that excuse is by law implied, because from the nature of the contract it is apparent that the parties contracted on the basis of the continued existence of the particular person or chattel. In the present case, looking at the whole contract, we find that the parties contracted on the basis of the continued existence of the Music Hall at the time when the concerts were to be given; that being essential to their performance.

We think, therefore, that the Music Hall having ceased to exist, without fault of either party, both parties are excused, the plaintiffs from taking the gardens and paying the money, the defendants from performing their promise to give the use of the Hall and Gardens and other things. Consequently the rule must be absolute to enter the verdict for the defendants.

Rule absolute.

QUESTIONS

1. Is the rule laid down in *Paradine v. Jane* good law after *Taylor v. Caldwell*?
2. What is the effect of the judgment on the insurance protection each party should obtain?
3. To what extent is the power of the court to imply terms into contracts, a device used by the court to justify any conclusion it thinks just? Did the parties think through what would happen if the music hall should burn down? If not, what basis is there for implying any terms into the contract?

KRELL v. HENRY

[1903] 2 K.B. 740. Court of Appeal (England); Vaughan Williams, Romer and Stirling L.JJ.

[The plaintiff had agreed to rent rooms to the defendant for the purpose of viewing the coronation processions of Edward VII on June 26 and 27, 1902. The agreed rent was £75. The defendant paid £25 as a deposit. The balance was payable on June 24th 1902. On that day the King was taken ill with appendicitis and the processions were cancelled. (This was one of the first successful operations for appendicitis and it made the operation very popular. The coronation took place on August 9th 1902.) The defendant refused to pay the balance of the £75. The plaintiff sued. The trial judge (Darling J.) dismissed the action. The plaintiff appealed.]

Vaughan Williams L.J. read the following written judgment: — The real question in this case is the extent of the application in English law of the principle of the Roman law which has been adopted and acted on in many English decisions, and notably in the case of *Taylor v. Caldwell*. That case at least makes it clear that "where, from the nature of the contract, it appears that the parties must from the beginning have known that it could not be fulfilled unless, when the time for the fulfillment of the contract arrived, some particular specified thing continued to exist, so that when entering into the contract they must have contemplated such continued existence as the foundation of what was to be done; there, in the absence of any express or implied warranty that the thing shall exist, the contract is not to be considered a positive contract, but as subject to an implied condition that the parties shall be excused in case, before breach, performance becomes impossible from the perishing of the thing without default of the contractor." Thus far it is clear that the principle of the Roman law has been introduced into the English law. The doubt in the present case arises as to how far this principle extends. The Roman law dealt with obligationes de certo corpore. Whatever may have been the limits of the Roman law, the case of *Nickoll v. Ashton*, [1901] 2 K.B. 126, makes it plain that the English law applies the principle not only to cases where the performance of the contract becomes impossible by the cessation of existence of the thing which is the subject-matter of the contract, but also to cases where the event which renders the contract incapable of performance is the cessation or non-existence of an express condition or state of things, going to the root of the contract, and essential to its performance.

It is said, on the one side, that the specified thing, state of things, or condition the continued existence of which is necessary for the fulfilment of the contract, so that the parties entering into the contract must have contemplated the continued existence of that thing, condition, or state of things as the foundation of what was to be done under the contract, is limited to things which are either the subject-matter of the contract or the condition or state of things, present or anticipated, which is expressly mentioned in the contract. But, on the other side, it is said that the condition or state of things need not be expressly specified, but that it is sufficient if that condition or state of things clearly appears by extrinsic evidence to have been assumed by the parties to be the foundation or basis of the contract, and the event which causes the impossibility is of such a character that it cannot reasonably be supposed to have been in the contemplation of the contracting parties when the contract was made. In such a case the contracting parties will not be held bound by the general words which, though large enough to include, were not used with reference to a possibility of a particular event rendering performance of the contract impossible.

I do not think that the principle of the civil law as introduced into the

English law is limited to cases in which the event causing the impossibility of performance is the destruction or non-existence of some thing which is the subject-matter of the contract or of some condition or state of things expressly specified as a condition of it. I think that you first have to ascertain, not necessarily from the terms of the contract, but, if required, from necessary inferences, drawn from surrounding circumstances recognised by both contracting parties, what is the substance of the contract, and then to ask the question whether that substantial contract needs for its foundation the assumption of the existence of a particular state of things. If it does, this will limit the operation of the general words, and in such case, if the contract becomes impossible of performance by reason of the non-existence of the state of things assumed by both contracting parties as the foundation of the contract, there will be no breach of the contract thus limited.

Now what are the facts of the present case? The contract is contained in two letters of June 20 which passed between the defendant and this plaintiff's agent, Mr. Cecil Bisgood. These letters do not mention the coronation, but speak merely of the taking of Mr. Krell's chambers, or, rather, of the use of them, in the daytime of June 26 and 27, for the sum of £75., £25. then paid, balance £50. to be paid on the 24th. But the affidavits, which by agreement between the parties are to be taken as stating the facts of the case, shew that the plaintiff exhibited on his premises, third floor, 56A, Pall Mall, an announcement to the effect that windows to view the Royal coronation procession were to be let, and that the defendant was induced by that announcement to apply to the housekeeper on the premises, who said that the owner was willing to let the suite of rooms for the purpose of seeing the Royal procession for both days, but not nights, of June 26 and 27. In my judgment the use of the rooms was let and taken for the purpose of seeing the Royal procession. It was not a demise of the rooms, or even an agreement to let and take the rooms. It is a licence to use rooms for a particular purpose and none other. And in my judgment the taking place of those processions on the days proclaimed along the proclaimed route, which passed 56A, Pall Mall, was regarded by both contracting parties as the foundation of the contract; and I think that it cannot reasonably be supposed to have been in the contemplation of the contracting parties, when the contract was made, that the coronation would not be held on the proclaimed days, or the processions not take place on those days along the proclaimed route; and I think that the words imposing on the defendant the obligation to accept and pay for the use of the rooms for the named days, although general and unconditional, were not used with reference to the possibility of the particular contingency which afterwards occurred.

It was suggested in the course of the argument that if the occurrence, on the proclaimed days, of the coronation and the procession in this case were the foundation of the contract, and if the general words are thereby limited or qualified, so that in the event of the non-occurrence of the coronation and procession along the proclaimed route they would discharge both parties from further performance of the contract, it would follow that if a cabman was engaged to take some one to Epsom on Derby Day at a suitable enhanced price for such a journey, say £10., both parties to the contract would be discharged in the contingency of the race at Epsom for some reason becoming impossible; but I do not think this follows, for I do not think that in the cab case the happening of the race would be the foundation of the contract. No doubt the purpose of the engager would be to go to see the Derby, and the price would be proportionately high; but the cab had no special qualifications for the purpose which led to the selection of the cab for this particular occasion. Any other cab would have done as well. Moreover, I think that, under the cab contract, the hirer, even if the race went off, could have said, "Drive me to Epsom; I will pay you the agreed sum; you have nothing to do with the purpose for which I hired the cab," and that if the cabman refused he would have been guilty of a breach of contract, there being nothing to qualify his promise to drive the hirer to Epsom on a particular day. Whereas in the case of the coronation, there is not merely the purpose of the hirer to see the coronation procession, but it is the coronation procession and the relative position of the rooms which is the basis of the contract as much for the lessor as the hirer; and I think that if the King, before the coronation day and after the contract, had died, the hirer could not have insisted on having the rooms on the days named. It could not in the cab case be reasonably said that seeing the Derby race was the foundation of the contract, as it was of the licence in this case. Whereas in the present case, where the rooms were offered and taken, by reason of their peculiar suitability from the position of the rooms for a view of the coronation procession, surely the view of the coronation procession was the foundation of the contract, which is a very different thing from the purpose of the man who engaged the cab — namely, to see the race — being held to be the foundation of the contract.

Each case must be judged by its own circumstances. In each case one must ask oneself, first, what, having regard to all the circumstances, was the foundation of the contract? Secondly, was the performance of the contract prevented? Thirdly, was the event which prevented the performance of the contract of such a character that it cannot reasonably be said to have been in the contemplation of the parties at the date of the contract? If all these questions are answered in the affirmative (as I think they should be in this case), I think both parties are discharged from further performance of the contract. I think that the coronation was the foundation of this contract, and that the non-happening of it prevented the performance of the contract; and, secondly, I think that the non-happening of the procession, to use the words of Sir James Hannen in *Baily v. De Crespigny* (1869), L.R. 4 Q.B. 180, was an event "of such a character that it cannot reasonably be supposed to have been in the contemplation of the contracting parties when the contract was made, and that they are not to be held bound by general words which, though large enough to include, were not used with reference to the possibility of the particular contingency which afterwards happened." The test seems to be whether the event which causes the impossibility was or might have been anticipated and guarded against. It seems difficult to say, in a case where both parties anticipate the happening of an event, which anticipation is the foundation of the contract, that either party must be taken to have anticipated, and ought to have guarded against, the event which prevented the performance of the contract. In both *Jackson v. Union Marine Insurance Co.* (1873), L.R. 8 C.P. 572 and *Nickoll v. Ashton* the parties might have anticipated as a possibility that perils of the sea might delay the ship and frustrate the commercial venture: in the former case the carriage of the goods to effect which the charterparty was entered into; in the latter case the sale of the goods which were to be shipped on the steamship which was delayed. But the Court held in the former case that the basis of the contract was that the ship would arrive in time to carry out the contemplated commercial venture, and in the latter that the steamship would arrive in time for the loading of the goods the subject of the sale.

I wish to observe that cases of this sort are very different from cases where a contract or warranty or representation is implied, such as was implied in *The Moorcock* (1889), 14 P.O. 64, and refused to be implied in *Hamlyn v. Wood*, [1891] 2 Q.B. 488. But *The Moorcock* is of importance in the present case as shewing that whatever is the suggested implication — be it condition, as in this case, or warranty or representation — one must, in judging whether the implication ought to be made, look not only at the words of the contract, but also at the surrounding facts and the knowledge of the parties of those facts. There seems to me to be ample authority for this proposition. Thus in *Jackson v. Union Marine Insurance Co.*, in the Common Pleas, the question whether the object of the voyage had been frustrated by the delay of the ship was left as a question of fact to the jury, although there was nothing in the charterparty defining the time within which the charterers were to supply the cargo of iron rails for San Francisco, and nothing on the face of the charterparty to indicate the importance of time in the venture; and that was a case in which, as Bramwell B. points out in his judgment at p. 148, *Taylor v. Caldwell* was a strong authority to support the conclusion arrived at in the judgment — that the ship not arriving in time for the voyage contemplated, but at such time as to frustrate the commercial venture, was not only a breach of the contract but discharged the charterer, though he had such an excuse that no action would lie....

I myself am clearly of opinion that in this case, where we have to ask ourselves whether the object of the contract was frustrated by the non-happening of the coronation and its procession on the days proclaimed, parol evidence is admissible to shew that the subject of the contract was rooms to view the coronation procession, and was so to the knowledge of both parties. When once this is established, I see no difficulty whatever in the case. It is not essential to the application of the principle of *Taylor v. Caldwell* that the direct subject of the contract should perish or fail to be in existence at the date of performance of the contract. It is sufficient if a state of things or condition expressed in the contract and essential to its performance perishes or fails to be in existence at that time. In the present case the condition which fails and prevents the achievement of that which was, in the contemplation of both parties, the foundation of the contract, is not expressly mentioned either as a condition of the contract or the purpose of it; but I think for the reasons which I have given that the principle of *Taylor v. Caldwell* ought to be applied. This disposes of the plaintiff's claim for £50. unpaid balance of the price to be paid for the use of the rooms. The defendant at one time set up a cross-claim for the return of the 25l. he paid at the date of the contract. As that claim is now withdrawn it is unnecessary to say anything about it. I have only to add that the facts of this case do not bring it within the principle laid down in *Stubbs v. Holywell Ry. Co.* (1867), L.R. 2 Ex. 311; that in the case of contracts falling directly within the rule of *Taylor v. Caldwell* the subsequent impossibility does not affect rights already acquired, because the defendant had the whole of June 24 to pay the balance, and the public announcement that the coronation and processions would not take place on the proclaimed days was made early on the morning of the 24th, and no cause of action could accrue till the end of that day. I think this appeal ought to be dismissed.

[Romer and Stirling L.JJ. agreed with Vaughan Williams L.J.]

[*NOTE*: The cancellation of the coronation procession and other festivities planned at this time led to a rush of cases on frustration. Compare *Krell v. Henry* and *Herne Bay Steamboat Co. v. Hutton*, [1903] 2 K.B. 683, Court of Appeal (England), where a contract for the hire of a boat to take people to see the naval review at Spithead was not held to have been frustrated by the cancellation of the review.

QUESTIONS

1. What difficulties do you see in "unwinding" the transaction in these cases?

2. What is the basis for the distinction between the agreement sued upon and the case of the cab hired for Derby Day? Can you defend the different results?

3. What would be the most satisfactory solution to cases of this kind?

CAPITAL QUALITY HOMES LTD. v. COLWYN CONSTRUCTION LTD.

(1975), 9 O.R. (2d) 617. Ontario Court of Appeal; Evans, Jessup and Brooke JJ.A.

Evans, J.A.: — The defendant Colwyn Construction Limited appeals from the judgment of the Honourable Mr. Justice Keith granting the plaintiff recovery from the defendant of the sum of $13,980 being the return of a deposit paid by the plaintiff pursuant to an agreement for sale between the parties relative to certain undeveloped land in the City of Windsor.

The trial proceeded on an agreed statement of facts which was presented orally to the Court by counsel and which may be briefly summarized as follows: Under an agreement dated January 5, 1969, the plaintiff, purchaser, agreed to purchase from the defendant, vendor, 26 building lots each comprising parts of lots within a registered plan of subdivision. The date fixed for closing was July 30, 1970. Both parties were aware that the purchaser was buying building lots for the purpose of erecting a home on each lot with the intention of selling the several homes by way of separate conveyances. Under the terms of the agreement it was entitled to a conveyance of a building lot upon payment of $6,000 and, upon full payment, to 26 separate deeds of conveyance each representing one building lot. It is agreed that no demand for any conveyance was made prior to the date of closing.

When the sale agreement was executed the designated land was not within an area of subdivision control and not subject to any restriction limiting the right to convey. On June 27, 1970, certain amendments [1970, c. 72, s. 1] to the *Planning Act*, R.S.O. 1960, c. 296, came into effect whereby these lands came under the provisions of what is now s. 29 of the *Planning Act*, R.S.O. 1970, c. 349, which in certain circumstances restricts an owner's right to convey and makes necessary the obtaining of a consent from the relevant committee of adjustment designated in the amending legislation. In the absence of such consent no interest in part of a lot within a registered plan of subdivision can be conveyed.

The vendor was accordingly precluded from conveying the 26 building lots in 26 separate deeds without proper consents and while a conveyance to the purchaser of all lots in one deed may have been permissible, the purchaser in any event would be unable to reconvey individual building lots to prospective home buyers as it had intended without complying with the restrictive provisions of the new legislation.

This substantial change in the law, prohibiting and restricting conveyancing of the lands, 33 days prior to the anticipated closing date, resulted in some discussion between the parties relative to possible postponement of the closing date in order to devise some method of circumventing the restrictions to which the lands were now subject. No arrangement was made to extend closing. On the agreed date of closing the purchaser insisted that the vendor deliver conveyances for each individual building lot with the consents necessary to effectually transfer the lots. The vendor insisted that it was the responsibility of the purchaser to obtain the necessary consents. On the closing date the balance of the agreed purchase price was tendered by the solicitors for the purchaser but no conveyances were forthcoming in the mode contemplated by the agreement. It is common ground that the purchaser would not withdraw its demand for 26 individual conveyances with consents attached and that the vendor did not provide such conveyances. Following failure to close on the agreed date, the purchaser contended that the vendor was in default and on August 5, 1970, repudiated the agreement and made demand upon the vendor for the return of the balance of the deposit.

Although the statement of facts agreed to by counsel does not state that the relatively short period of time, 33 days, between the effective date of the amending legislation and the stipulated closing date made impossible the obtaining of the necessary consents, the argument indicated that such was the understanding and I have accordingly assumed that the time factor was so limited that the parties were in agreement that it would have been impossible to process the applications for consents prior to the closing date.

The trial Judge stated in his reasons [[1973] 3 O.R. 651 at p. 655, 37 D.L.R. (3d) 671 at p. 675] that he did not consider it necessary to deal with the "theory of commercial frustration" which was argued before him and proceeded to found his judgment on the narrow ground "that the vendor could not deliver separate and effective conveyances for each building lot as it was required to do under the express terms of the agreement without having first secured the consent required under the *Planning Act*". He went on to hold that the vendor was not justified in its default and that the purchaser was entitled to repudiate the contract and recover its deposit.

Accordingly, I propose to deal with this appeal on the basis of the argument advanced before us, *i.e.*, on the doctrine of frustration and its applicability to contracts involving the sale and purchase of land.

Turning now to the argument advanced on the appeal, the appellant, vendor, submitted that the supervening legislation which restricted transfer of the lots was a burden falling upon the purchaser. The argument was that upon execution of an agreement for the sale of land the purchaser became the equitable owner of the lands and any amending legislation which affected either zoning or alienation of land was a burden to be assumed by the purchaser. Accordingly, the purchaser was in error in attempting to repudiate the agreement and could not recover the deposit paid.

The respondent, purchaser, took the position that the effect of the new legislation was to make impossible the fulfilment of the terms of the contract; that there was a failure of consideration and that equity would not force the purchaser to take something fundamentally different from that for which it had bargained.

The vendor also argued that the obligation to obtain the consent of the committee of adjustment rested upon the purchaser. I do not agree. Unless otherwise provided in the agreement of sale the vendor is required to convey a marketable title in fee simple. There was no provision in the instant agreement which would permit the vendor to escape from that normal obligation.

That default alone was sufficient to entitle the purchaser to the return of its deposit.

The issues for determination, as I apprehend them, are:

(1)   Does the doctrine of impossibility of performance of a contract, *i.e.*, frustration, have any application when the contract is for the purchase and sale of land?

(2)   Assuming that frustration is applicable to agreements for sale of land, does the factual situation in this case permit the doctrine to be invoked?

(3)   Assuming that (1) and (2) are both answered in the affirmative what results flow therefrom?

In order to show the birth and development of the doctrine of frustration it is necessary to recall that the common law exacted strict performance of contractual obligations. A promise demanded performance and if performance became impossible, no matter what the reason, the defaulting party was liable in damages. *Paradine v. Jane* (1647), Aleyn 26, 82 E.R. 897, restated the principle and it is alleged that the justification for imposing such onerous obligations was that if contracting parties voluntarily entered into absolute and unconditional agreements they cannot complain if their lack of foresight in failing to provide against all contingencies created hardships to them.

English Courts, prior to *Taylor et al. v. Caldwell et al.* (1863), 3 B. & S. 826, 122 E.R. 309, followed the rule that impossibility of performance of a contract did not relieve the party unable to perform from liability in damages. Subsequently, that rigid rule was relaxed and contracts were held to be terminated and the parties discharged when the events which denied fulfilment of the contract were caused by some circumstance beyond the control of the contracting parties. In *Taylor et al. v. Caldwell, supra*, the subject-matter of the contract was destroyed before the date upon which performance was required. Blackburn, J., held that when a music-hall which was rented for the purpose of holding concerts, was accidentally destroyed by fire prior to the concerts being held, the owner was discharged from his contract and not liable in damages. The common law doctrine of contract was uncompromising in its insistence on performance and if a party could not actually perform an act because some event made it physically impossible, then specific performance could not be ordered but the party failing would be liable in damages for non-performance. The breakthrough by Blackburn, J., was accomplished by holding that a contract is not to be construed as absolute if the contracting parties from the beginning must have known that its fulfilment depended upon the continued existence of some peculiar thing and therefore must have realized that this continuing existence was the foundation of the bargain. He held that the contract is "subject to an implied condition that the parties shall be excused in case, before breach, performance becomes impossible from the perishing of the thing without default of the contractor". He implied a term or condition into the contract. The doctrine of impossibility of performance or as it is now generally called, the doctrine of frustration, developed rapidly, particularly in commercial contracts and English Courts sought to do justice by holding that a contract was discharged when some catastrophic event occurred, the result of which was to destroy the very basis of the contract.

Krell v. Henry, [1903] 2 K.B. 740 (C.A.), dealt with a hire of premises to view a coronation subsequently cancelled and the Court held that the view of the coronation procession was the foundation of the contract and the non-happening of it prevented the performance of the contract. *Marshall v. Glanvill et al.*, [1917] 2 K.B. 87, was concerned with a contract of employment and the liability of the employee to compulsory military service was held to determine the contract.

In all these commercial contract cases in which the principle is referred to as "frustration of the adventure" the Court has implied into the contract a term or condition because the contract itself does not provide for the supervening act which produces the frustration. Lord Sumner in *Cheong Yne Steamship Co. Ltd. v. Hirji Mulji et al.*, [1926] 1 W.W.R. 917, [1926] A.C. 497, referred to the doctrine of frustration as "a device by which the rules as to absolute contracts can be reconciled with a special exception which justice demands". The legal effect of the frustration of a contract does not depend upon the intention of the parties, or their opinions or even knowledge as to the event that has brought about the frustration, but upon its occurrence in such circumstances as to show it to be inconsistent with the further prosecution of the adventure. On the contrary, it seems that when the event occurs, the meaning of the contract must be taken to be, not what the parties did intend (for they had neither thought nor intention regarding it) but that which the parties, as fair and reasonable men, would presumably have agreed upon if, having such possibility in view, they had made express provision as to their several rights and liabilities in the event of its occurrence: *Dahl v. Nelson et al.* (1880), 6 App. Cas. 38.

The supervening event must be something beyond the control of the parties and must result in a significant change in the original obligation assumed by them. The theory of the implied term has been replaced by the more realistic view that the Court imposes upon the parties the just and reasonable solution that the new situation demands.

Lord Radcliffe in *Davis Contractors Ltd. v. Fareham Urban District Council*, [1956] A.C. 696 at pp. 728-9, stated:

> So perhaps it would be simpler to say at the outset that frustration occurs whenever the law recognizes that without default of either party a contractual obligation has become incapable of being performed because the circumstances in which performance is called for would render it a thing radically different from that which was undertaken by the contract. Non haec in foedera veni. It was not this that I promised to do.

The development of the doctrine briefly referred to above is traced with considerable detail in Chesire & Fifoot, *Law of Contracts*, 7th ed. (1969), at p. 506, and following. The *Law Reform (Frustrated Contracts) Act*, 1943 (U.K.), c. 40, defined the position of the parties in England when a contract is discharged by frustration and set out those particular contracts to which the Act did not apply.

The controversial question that is still undecided by the House of Lords is whether the doctrine of frustration can be applied to a lease of land. Cases involving the destruction of a chattel, the subject of the contract, as in *Howell v. Coupland* (1876), 1 Q.B.D. 258, or the destruction of a music-hall, the existence of which was the foundation of the contract as in *Taylor et al. v. Caldwell et al., supra,* or those cases in which the performance of the contract has become illegal because of some supervening legislation are to be distinguished from land leases which are considered to be more than contracts, since they create estates in land which give rise to proprietary rights in addition to purely personal rights as found in all commercial contracts. In the development of the modern law of contracts an increasingly wider conception of the doctrine of frustration as a ground of discharge of commercial contracts came into operation but the English Courts have consistently held that the doctrine of frustration has no application when the contract creates an estate in land.

In *Cricklewood Property & Investment Trust, Ltd. v. Leighton's Investment Trust, Ltd.,* [1945] A.C. 221, Lord Russell of Killowen and Lord Goddard held to the view that the doctrine of frustration cannot apply to a demise of real property. Viscount Simon, L.C., and Lord Wright took the position that the doctrine is modern and flexible and ought not to be restricted by an arbitrary formula. Lord Porter expressed no opinion on the question. The case involved a building lease for a term of 99 years. The war of 1939 broke out and restrictions imposed by the Government made it impossible for the building to be proceeded with at that time. The Court unanimously held that the doctrine, even if it were capable of application to a lease, did not apply as the compulsory suspension of building did not strike at the root of the transaction since the lease had 90 years to run from the date the restriction was imposed and therefore the interruption in performance was likely to last only a small fraction of the term.

In *Cricklewood Property & Investment Trust, Ltd. v. Leighton's Investment Trust, Ltd., supra,* the trial Judge would have held the contract to be discharged, had he not been convinced that there was clear authority that the doctrine of frustration could not be applied to a demise of real property. The Court of Appeal affirmed his judgment on the ground that frustration was not applicable. It was only when the case was considered in the House of Lords that some doubt was cast upon the earlier cases which had come to be regarded as authoritative. Viscount Simon, L.C., defined "frustration" as [at p. 228]

> ... the premature determination of an agreement between parties, lawfully entered into and in course of operation at the time of its premature determination, owing to the occurrence of an intervening event or change of circumstances so fundamental as to be regarded by the law both as striking at the root of the agreement, and as entirely beyond what was contemplated by the parties when they entered into the agreement.

He was of the opinion that the doctrine could apply to a lease of land although he considered that the instances in which it could be successfully invoked were very rare. He stated that the Court of Appeal was in error in concluding that the authorities held that a lease cannot in any circumstances be ended by frustration.

In *Matthey v. Curling,* [1922] 2 A.C. 180, Atkin, L.J., in a dissenting judgment in the Court of Appeal, at p. 183, observed at pp. 199-200:

> ... it does not appear to me conclusive against the application to a lease of the doctrine of frustration that the lease, in addition to containing contractual terms, grants a term of years. Seeing that the instrument as a rule expressly provides for the lease being determined at the option of the lessor upon the happening of certain specified events, I see no logical absurdity in implying a term that it shall be determined absolutely on the happening of other events — namely, those which in an ordinary contract work a frustration.

Lord Simon adopted the above passage as exactly expressing his view. Lord Wright agreed with Lord Simon and pointed out that the doctrine of frustration is not subject to being constricted by an arbitrary formula.

In *Hillingdon Estates Co. v. Stonefield Estates, Ltd.*, [1952] 1 All E.R. 853, [1952] Ch. 627, a contract for the sale of land was involved. The contract was executed in 1938 and the lands were intended to be used for a building development. In 1948, some 10 years after the contract was entered into, the County Council expropriated the lands. The purchasers, to whom no conveyance of the legal estate had yet been made, brought action claiming that the foundation of the contract was the development of the land, that development had been frustrated by the expropriation and that therefore the contract was extinguished. The vendors counterclaimed for specific performance on the contract. Vaisey, J., dismissed the action and granted specific performance. He pointed out that the expropriation raised no obstacle to the conveyance of the legal estate and held that the contract, far from being frustrated, could and should be carried out and stated at p. 856:

> The complete absence of authority does rather suggest to my mind that the doctrine of frustration does not operate normally in the case of contracts for the sale of land.

The learned Judge referred to the long delay involved and balanced the vendor's right to payment of the purchase price against the purchaser's right to receive the expropriation compensation. This case was criticized by Professor Laskin, now Laskin, C.J.C., in *Special Lectures, Law Society of Upper Canada* (1960), p. 400, who pointed out that specific performance was not available since the vendor was unable to give title on closing.

Vaisey, J., seemed to be of the view that the purchasers were no worse off than they would have been if they had completed their contract before the compulsory taking occurred. In his opinion if they had not delayed completion of the contract the property would have been transferred to the purchasers from whom it would then have been expropriated. The result is that one is left in some doubt whether the long delay in completion of the contract and also the fact that a substantial part of the payment sought to be recovered represented interest may have had some bearing upon the decision since these factors affected the equities between the parties. For these reasons I believe the case can be distinguished.

There can be no frustration if the supervening event results from the voluntary act of one of the parties or if the possibility of such event arising during the term of the agreement was contemplated by the parties and provided for in the agreement. In the instant case the planning legislation which supervened was not contemplated by the parties, not provided for in the agreement and not brought about through a voluntary act of either party. The factor remaining to be considered is whether the effect of the planning legislation is of such a nature that the law would consider the fundamental character of the agreement to have been so altered as to no longer reflect the original basis of the agreement. In my opinion the legislation destroyed the very foundation of the agreement. The purchaser was purchasing 26 separate building lots upon which it proposed to build houses for resale involving a reconveyance in each instance. This purpose was known to the vendor. The lack of ability to do so creates a situation not within the contemplation of the parties when they entered into the agreement. I believe that all the factors necessary to constitute impossibility of performance have been established and that the doctrine of frustration can be invoked to terminate the agreement.

The doctrine of frustration has been applied to commercial contracts since *Taylor et al. v. Caldwell et al., supra*. In *Cricklewood v. Leighton's, supra*, Viscount Simon, L.C., and Lord Wright held against the accepted view that leases were outside the doctrine since a lease in addition to being a contract creates an estate in the land demised for the period of the agreed term. I adopt the reasoning of Viscount Simon, L.C., and his conclusion that there is no binding authority precluding the application of the doctrine of frustration to contracts involving the lease of lands. I am also in accord with his observations that the doctrine is flexible and ought not to be restricted by any arbitrary formula. I see no reason why the doctrine cannot be logically extended to contracts involving the purchase and sale of land. If the supervening event makes the contract incapable of fulfilment as contemplated by the parties, then it appears to me illogical and unreasonable to contend that the fundamental object of the contract can be effected because the equitable interest in the land has passed to the purchaser....

I adopt the reasoning of Lord Simon in *Cricklewood v. Leighton's, supra*, and accept his conclusion that there is no binding authority in England precluding the application of the doctrine of frustration to contracts involving a lease of land. I believe the situation to be the same in Ontario and I am unable to distinguish any difference between leases of land and agreements for the sale of land, so far as the application of the doctrine is concerned. Each is more than a simple contract. In the former an estate in land is created while in the latter an equitable estate arises. There does not appear to be any logical reason or binding legal authority which would prohibit the extension of the doctrine to contracts involving land.

If the factual situation is such that there is a clear "frustration of the common venture" then the contract, whether it is a contract for the sale of land or otherwise, is at an end and the parties are discharged from further performance and the adjustment of the rights and liabilities of the parties are left to be determined under the *Frustrated Contracts Act*. In my opinion, on the facts of this case, the contract was frustrated; the doctrine was applicable and should be invoked with the result that both parties are discharged from performance of the contract and the purchaser is entitled to recover the full amount paid as it is not claimed that the vendor incurred any expenses in connection with the performance of the contract, prior to frustration, which would entitle it to retain a portion of the money paid as provided for in s. 3(2) of the *Frustrated Contracts Act*. Accordingly, the vendor must refund to the purchaser the balance of the deposit money, that is, $13,980.

The judgment below is affirmed and the appeal is dismissed with costs.

Appeal dismissed.

QUESTIONS

1. Does the judgment acknowledge the same concerns as did the judgment in *Amalgamated Investments v. John Walker* (*supra*)?

2. Contracts to rent rooms to view coronation processions are fairly rare. Contracts to sell land for development are, on the other hand, very common. To what extent does this fact justify (or force) a different method of analysis?

Many of the leading cases on frustration are discussed in the judgment of Evans J.A. in *Capital Quality Homes v. Colwyn Construction Ltd.* Some further examples of the kinds of problems that can come up are:

1. The parties had made a contract under which the defendants agreed to sell to the plaintiffs some Finnish timber. The invariable practice in the Finnish timber trade was for the timber to be carried directly from Finland; no stocks were normally kept in England. The outbreak of war in 1914 made the shipment of Finnish timber impossible.
The Court of Appeal in England in *Blackburn Bobbin Co. Ltd. v. Allen*, [1918] 2 K.B. 467 held that the defendants were liable for breach of contract since there was "nothing to show that the plaintiff contemplated... that the sellers should continue to have the ordinary facilities for dispatching the timber from Finland." This was a matter which to the plaintiffs was wholly immaterial.

2. The seller had agreed with the buyer to sell Sudanese groundnuts, and to ship them during November/December 1956 from the Sudan to Hamburg. Shipping arrangements were made in October 1956. In November 1956, the Suez Canal was blocked. The seller failed to make the shipment. The buyer claimed damages.
The House of Lords in *Tsakiroglou v. Noblee Thorl G.m.b.H.*, [1962] A.C. 93, held that shipment by South Africa rather than the Suez Canal would not have made the carriage so expensive that the contract would have been something quite different from that which the parties had contemplated. The sellers were therefore liable for breach of contract.
The contract contained a "force majeure" clause in the following terms: "In case of prohibition of import or export, blockade or war, epidemic or strike, and in all cases of force majeure preventing the shipment within the time fixed, or the delivery, the period allowed for shipment or delivery shall be extended by not exceeding two months. After that, if the case of force majeure be still operating, the contract shall be cancelled."
This was held to be inapplicable since nothing had prevented shipment. All that had happened was that the cost of carriage was now far higher than the sellers had expected.

3. In *The Eugenia*, [1964] 2 Q.B. 226, the Court of Appeal in England held that a contract for the charter of a ship to carry iron and steel goods from the Black Sea to India was not frustrated by the same closing of the Suez Canal. The charterers had picked up the ship in Genoa and the contract was for the ship to go from there to the Black Sea and then to India and back. It was proved that the total time via the Cape of Good Hope would have been 138 days and via Suez 105 days. This difference in a voyage for the carriage of non-perishable goods was held not to justify the charterers in regarding the contract as at an end.

The problem for the charterers was that the ship had gone to Port Said when the canal was already closed and had got trapped there for 2 1/2 months. If the contract could have been held to be frustrated, the obligation of the charterers to pay for the ship during that time would be at an end. If not, the charterers would have to keep paying. The fact that the ship was trapped was not a frustrating event since that came about through the charterers' own act of entering into a "dangerous zone" without the consent of the owners.

4. Particular problems have arisen with leases. Some of these are mentioned by Evans J.A. in *Capital Quality Homes v. Colwyn Construction.* The Ontario Court of Appeal in *Merkur v. Shoom*, [1954] 1 D.L.R. 85, had held that a lease could not be frustrated, though it is not possible to tell from the judgment whether the court meant that frustration can never arise in a case of a lease since the only kind of recognizable frustration would be the disappearance of the estate created by the lease or, that even if frustration of the object of the transaction could occur its application in regard to leases was ruled out as a matter of law.
In any case, *Merkur v. Shoom* will have to be reconsidered in the light of *Capital Quality Homes v. Colwyn Construction.*

Part IV of the *Landlord and Tenant Act*, R.S.O. 1970, c. 236, s. 88 now provides in relation to residential tenancies that:

> The doctrine of frustration of contract applies to tenancy agreements and the *Frustrated Contracts Act* applies thereto.

QUESTIONS

1. Owner has two ships registered in Vancouver under the Canada Shipping Act. Both ships are chartered to Margaret and Maureen respectively. The Canadian Government, acting under statutory authority, tells owner that one of his ships is to be requisitioned, but he can nominate the one. The requisition will frustrate the contract in each case. If owner nominates the ship chartered to Margaret, can she sue? and, if so, for what?
2. Would it matter if owner was operating one of the ships himself, and nominated the one chartered to Margaret?

SAINSBURY LTD. v. STREET

[1972] 3 All E.R. 1126. Queen's Bench Division.

[The defendant was a farmer. The plaintiff was a grain dealer. The defendant had planted barley on his land. On July 1, 1970, he agreed to sell 275 tons of barley to the plaintiff. This was before the harvest and, since it could not be known how much the crop would be, the parties agreed on a yield of 1.5 tons/acre. The contract price was £20/ton. That year the harvest in England and the U.S. was poor and throughout July and August the price of barley was rising rapidly. The defendant's total crop only came to 140 tons. He sold 100 tons to another grain dealer for £27/ton keeping about 40 tons for himself. The plaintiff bought barley against the contract at £30/ton, and sued the defendant for breach of contract.]

MacKenna J. [after stating the facts, continued]: ... I am prepared to assume, consistently with the plaintiffs' abandonment of their claim for damages for the tonnage not in fact produced, that it was an implied condition of the contract that if the defendant, through no fault of his, failed to produce the stipulated tonnage of his growing crop, he should not be required to pay damages. It seems a very reasonable condition, considering the risks of agriculture and the fact that the crop was at the contract date still growing. But a condition that he need not deliver any if, through some misfortune, he could not deliver the whole is a very different one, and in my opinion so unreasonable that I would not imply it unless compelled to do so by authority. The way in which the parties chose the more or less conventional figure of 30 cwt per acre as the estimated yield of the crop is, I think, an additional reason in this case against the implication. If they had intended that a failure to achieve this optimistic tonnage would mean the end of the contract for both of them, they would have gone about the business of estimating yield in a much more cautious manner. Counsel for the defendant argued that it was reasonable that the defendant should be freed of all his obligations under the contract if without his fault he failed to produce the whole tonnage. 275 tons (5 per cent more or less) set an upper limit to the quantity which the plaintiffs could be compelled to take. It was reasonable, he said, that there should be a lower limit to the amount which the defendant could be compelled to deliver. In a year when the defendant's yield was high market prices would probably be low and it would be a benefit to the plaintiffs not to be required to take more than an agreed tonnage at the contract price fixed in advance. In a year when the yield was low, as in the present case, it would be a benefit to the defendant if he were free to disregard his contract and to sell his crop to some other buyer at the higher market price. The contract should, if possible, be construed as giving him this freedom. I am not persuaded by the argument. The upper limit of 275 tons might in the circumstances of a particular case be beneficial to both parties. But even if it could be beneficial only to the buyer that is no reason for implying a term that the same figure shall serve as a lower limit to the seller's obligation to deliver, so that his failure to reach that figure, if blameless, would release him from the contract.

I must now consider the three authorities which counsel for the defendant put before me in support of his argument. The first was *Howell v Coupland* (1874), L.R. 9 Q.B. 462, a decision of the Court of Queen's Bench, upheld by the Court of Appeal (1876), 1 Q.B. 258. This is the headnote in the report of the decision of the Court of Queen's Bench:

> 'Plaintiff and defendant entered into an agreement in March, whereby defendant agreed to sell and plaintiff to purchase "200 tons of regent potatoes grown on land belonging to defendant in W., at rate of £3. 10s. 6d. per ton, to be delivered in September or October, and paid for as taken away." In March defendant had sixty-eight acres ready for potatoes, which were sown, and were amply sufficient to grow more than 200 tons in an average year; but in August the potato blight appeared and the crop failed, so that the [defendant] was able to deliver only 80 tons. The plaintiff having brought an action for the non-delivery of the other 120 tons: — *Held*, that the contract was for a portion of a specific crop, and was within the principle of *Taylor v. Caldwell*, and the contract must be taken to be subject to the implied condition that the parties shall be excused, if, before breach, performance becomes impossible from the perishing of the thing without default in the contractor.'

Blackburn J gave his reasons for the decision:

> The principle of *Taylor v. Caldwell*, which was followed in *Appleby v. Myers*

(1867), L.R. 2 C.P. 651, in the Exchequer Chamber, at all events, decides that where there is a contract with respect to a particular thing, and that thing cannot be delivered owing to it perishing without any default in the seller, the delivery is excused. Of course, if the perishing were owing to any default of the seller, that would be quite another thing. But here the crop failed entirely owing to the blight, which no skill, care, or diligence of the defendant could prevent... But the contract was for 200 tons of a particular crop in particular fields, and therefore there was an implied term in the contract that each party should be free if the crop perished. The property and risk had clearly not been transferred under the terms of this contract, so that the consequence of the failure of the crop is, that the bargain is off so far as the 120 tons are concerned.'

It is clear from the statement of the facts in the headnote that the case raised no question about the seller's obligation to deliver the potatoes which he had in fact produced, and clear from the last sentence quoted from the judgment of Blackburn J that it gives no support to the view that the bargain was off both as to the 120 tons and the 80. There is nothing in the judgments of the Court of Appeal which touches this question.

After the decision of *Howell v Coupland* the Sale of Goods Act 1893 was passed. Its relevant provisions are contained in the following sections:

'5 ... (2)There may be a contract for the sale of goods, the acquisition of which by the seller depends upon a contingency which may or may not happen...

'6. Where there is a contract for the sale of specific goods, and the goods without the knowledge of the seller have perished at the time when the contract is made, the contract is void.

'7. Where there is an agreement to sell specific goods, and subsequently the goods, without any fault on the part of the seller or buyer, perish before the risk passes to the buyer, the agreement is thereby avoided...

'61 ... (2)The rules of the common law, including the law merchant, save in so far as they are inconsistent with the express provisions of this Act, and in particular the rules relating to the law of principal and agent and the effect of fraud, misrepresentation, duress or coercion, mistake, or other invalidating cause, shall continue to apply to contracts for the sale of goods.'

The rule in *Howell v Coupland* is, I think, preserved by s 5(2). If I am wrong in that view, because the growing of a crop cannot be considered the 'acquisition' of goods within the meaning of that section, then it is preserved by s 61(2). I do not think it is preserved by ss 6 or 7. These sections are, in my opinion, dealing with goods existing, and a crop not yet grown does not answer either description. I quote a passage from the judgment of Atkin LJ in *Re Wait*, [1927] 1 Cl. 606, which was the next case cited by counsel for the defendant:

'The case of *Howell v. Coupland* would now be covered either by s. 5, sub-s. 2, of the Code or, as is suggested by the learned authors of the last two editions of Benjamin on Sale, ... by s. 61, sub-s. 2, of the Code.'

The decision in *Wait's* case does not touch the question which I have to decide, and I pass from it to the third case cited by counsel for the defendant, *Barrow, Lane & Ballard Ltd v Phillip Phillips & Co Ltd*, [1929] 1 K.B. 574, a decision of Wright J in which he applied s 6 of the Sale of Goods Act 1893 to the following facts. The plaintiffs had sold the defendants goods described as '700 bags marked E.C.P. and known as Lot 7 of Chinese ground nuts in shell then lying at the National Wharves in London'. Unknown to either party there were not 700 bags then lying at the wharves but only 591, as the wharfingers or their servants had abstracted 109. The contract of sale was made on 11th October 1927. On 12th October the sellers gave the buyers a delivery order for the 700 bags and the buyers gave bills of exchange for the price. Between 11th October and 6th December more bags were abstracted, but there were still just enough to meet two delivery orders totalling 150 bags sent by the sellers to the warehouse on 6th or 7th December. All the rest had gone. The sellers sued the buyers on the bills for the price of 591 bags. The buyers admitted liability for the 150 actually delivered but disputed liability for the balance. The buyers won. The following passage gives the reason for the decision:

> 'Does the case come within s. 6 of the Sale of Goods Act, so that it would be the same as if the whole parcel had ceased to exist? In my judgment it does. The contract here was for a parcel of 700 bags, and at the time when it was made there were only 591 bags. A contract for a parcel of 700 bags is something different from a contract for 591 bags, and the position appears to me to be in no way different from what it would have been if the whole 700 bags had ceased to exist. The result is that the parties were contracting about something which, at the date of the contract, without the knowledge or fault of either party, did not exist. To compel the buyer in those circumstances to take 591 bags would be to compel him to take something which he had not contracted to take, and would in my judgment be unjust.'

If there had been no misfortune the sellers could not have compelled the buyers to take 591 bags in lieu of 700. That was not the buyers' contract. Their obligation was to take 700 bags and nothing less. Section 6 should not be so construed as to oblige them to take the lesser quantity. There are two steps in this reasoning. First there is the construction of the contract, which is held not to impose any obligation on the buyers to accept less than 700 bags. The second step is the construction of s 6. Neither part of the decision compels me to decide the present case in favour of the defendant. Because the contract in that case did not oblige the buyers to accept less than 700 bags is no reason why the implied condition in this case, which excuses the defendant from making full delivery, should be construed as excusing him from delivering the lesser quantity in fact produced if the plaintiffs were willing to accept it. The meaning of s 6 cannot affect the present case.

A passage in Benjamin on Sale is relevant:

> 'It was not decided in *Howell v. Coupland* whether the seller might have refused delivery of the 80 tons which he in fact delivered. Blackburn, J., and Quain, J., seemed to have thought that he was liable to deliver what he could... On the other hand, in *Lovatt v. Hamilton* (1839), 5 M&W. 639, where goods were sold "to arrive" by a particular ship, and only a small part arrived in that ship, the Court of Exchequer held that the buyers were not entitled to it, as the contract was entire for the whole quantity... But this was a case of condition precedent; and it is arguable that, as the seller's excuse under s. 7 is a privilege operating by way of condition subsequent..., he should not be entitled to excuse himself to an extent more than is necessary. The question is one of the presumed intention of the parties. Where the subject-matter of the sale is such an indivisible whole as a number of volumes forming one work, the intention would doubtless be that the seller should be wholly discharged. The case of a mere quantity of specific goods is not so clear.'

I have four comments to make on this passage: (1) I would distinguish *Lovatt v Hamilton*, on the language of the contract which provided for the sale of '50 tons of palm oil, to arrive per Mansfield, at £32. per ton... In case of non-arrival, or the vessels not having so much in after delivery of former contracts, this contract to be void.' The ship had only 7 tons in after delivery of former contracts. It was held that the buyers were not entitled to these 7 tons. The case is, I think, distinguishable. It is one thing to hold that where a contract provides that it shall be void in a certain case, this means that it shall be wholly inoperative, which is the decision in *Lovatt's case*. It is another to hold that the failure of an implied condition must always operate to discharge the whole contract, which I am in effect asked to hold.

(2) I have already expressed the view that s 7 of the Sale of Goods Act 1893 is not the relevant section in a case like *Howell v Coupland*. The excuse is given to the seller either by a condition of the kind referred to in s 5 (2) of the Sale of Goods Act 1893 or by one implied under some provision of the common law preserved by s 61 (2).

(3) The condition which excuses the defendant can be cast either in the form of a condition precedent to the existence of an obligation to deliver, or in the form of a condition subsequent to the existence of such an obligation determining the same, without affecting the substance of the matter. 'He shall be under an obligation to deliver in the future if he produces...' would be in form a condition precedent. 'He is under an obligation to deliver in the future but that obligation shall be discharged if he does not produce...' would be in form a condition subsequent. The difference is a matter of words, not of substance: see Williston on Sales. For this reason I should not wish to rest anything, in this case at least, on the distinction between the two kinds of condition.

(4) What is said in this passage about the presumed intention of the parties seems to me very relevant in determining what condition shall be implied. It should be a condition which will give effect to the presumed intention of reasonable men. In the case which the writer supposes it would be unreasonable to compel the buyer to accept delivery of the odd volume. This difficulty could be met in one of two ways, either by implying a condition in cases of that kind that the contract shall be wholly discharged, or by implying a condition in such cases, or indeed in all cases when the seller is excused, that the buyer shall have an option of accepting part delivery. The United States Sales Act cited in Williston on Sales expressly allows the buyer, in case of deterioration or partial destruction of the subject-matter of a sale or contract to sell, to require such performance as remains possible.

So much for the authorities, which do not, I think, oblige me to decide this case in the defendant's favour. Therefore my judgment will be for the plaintiffs for £1,050.

PROBLEMS

1. Would the problem be simplified by the following provision of the U.C.C.?
"§ 2-615. Except so far as a seller may have assumed a greater obligation and subject to the preceding section on substituted performance:
"(a)   Delay in delivery or non-delivery in whole or in part by a seller who complies with paragraphs (b) and (c) is not a breach of his duty under a contract for sale if performance as agreed has been made impracticable by the occurrence of a contingency the non-occurrence of which was a basic assumption on which the contract was made or by compliance in good faith with any applicable foreign or domestic governmental regulation or order whether or not it later proves to be invalid.
"(b)   Where the causes mentioned in paragraph (a) affect only a part of the seller's capacity to perform, he must allocate production and deliveries

among his customers but may at his option include regular customers not then under contract as well as his own requirements for further manufacture. He may so allocate in any manner which is fair and reasonable.

"(c)   The seller must notify the buyer seasonably that there will be delay or non-delivery and, when allocation is required under paragraph (b), of the estimated quota thus made available for the buyer."

2. Is it relevant that under the Sale of Goods Act, the plaintiff would not have had to buy the defendant's crop.

"29(1) Where the seller delivers to the buyer a quantity of goods less than he contracted to sell, the buyer may reject them, but if the buyer accepts the goods so delivered, he shall pay for them at the contract rate."

3. Suppose that the total crop that was expected to be grown on Farmer's land is 400 tons and Farmer reasonably needed half for his own purposes. Farmer agrees to sell 200 tons to Dealer in circumstances similar to those in *Sainsbury v. Street*. The total crop is only 250 tons. How much can Farmer keep without being liable for breach of contract?

4. To what extent do the economics of these transactions indicate who should bear what risk?

APPLEBY v. MYERS

(1867), L.R. 2 C.P. 651. Exch. Ch.

[The facts are taken from the headnote.

The plaintiffs contracted to erect certain machinery on the defendant's premises at specific prices for particular portions, and to keep it in repair for two years, — the price to be paid upon the completion of the whole. After some portions of the work had been finished, and others were in the course of completion, the premises with all the machinery and materials thereon were destroyed by an accidental fire.]

June 21. The judgment of the Court (Martin, B., Blackburn, J., Bramwell, B., Shee and Lush, JJ.), was delivered by

Blackburn, J. This case was partly argued before us at the last sittings; and the argument was resumed and completed at the present sittings.

Having had the advantage of hearing the very able arguments of Mr. Holl and Mr. Hannen, and having during the interval had the opportunity of considering the judgment of the Court below, there is no reason that we should further delay expressing the opinion at which we have all arrived, which is, that the judgment of the Court below is wrong, and ought to be reversed.

The whole question depends upon the true construction of the contract between the parties. We agree with the Court below in thinking that it sufficiently appears that the work which the plaintiffs agreed to perform could not be performed unless the defendant's premises continued in a fit state to enable the plaintiffs to perform the work on them; and we agree with them in thinking that, if by any default on the part of the defendant, his premises were rendered unfit to receive the work, the plaintiffs would have had the option to sue the defendant for this default, or to treat the contract as rescinded, and sue on a quantum meruit. But we do not agree with them in thinking that there was an absolute promise or warranty by the defendant that the premises should at all events continue so fit. We think that where, as in the present case, the premises are destroyed without fault on either side, it is a misfortune equally affecting both parties; excusing both from further performance of the contract, but giving a cause of action to neither.

Then it was argued before us, that, inasmuch as this was a contract of that nature which would in pleading be described as a contract for work, labour, and materials, and not as one of bargain and sale, the labour and materials necessarily became the property of the defendant as soon as they were worked into his premises and became part of them, and therefore were at his risk. We think that, as to a great part at least of the work done in this case, the materials had not become the property of the defendant; for, we think that the plaintiffs, who were to complete the whole for a fixed sum, and keep it in repair for two years, would have had a perfect right, if they thought that a portion of the engine which they had put up was too slight, to change it and substitute another in their opinion better calculated to keep in good repair during the two years, and that without consulting or asking the leave of the defendant. But, even on the supposition that the materials had become unalterably fixed to the defendant's premises, we do not think that, under such a contract as this, the plaintiffs could recover anything unless the whole work was completed. It is quite true that materials worked by one into the property of another become part of that property. This is equally true, whether it be fixed or movable property. Bricks built into a wall become part of the house; thread stitched into a coat which is under repair, or planks and nails and pitch worked into a ship under repair, become part of the coat or the ship; and therefore, generally, and in the absence of something to shew a contrary intention, the bricklayer, or tailor, or shipwright, is to be paid for the work and materials he has done and provided, although the whole work is not complete. It is not material whether in such a case the non-completion is because the shipwright did not choose to go on with the work ... or because in consequence of a fire he could not go on with it ... But, though this is the primâ facie contract between those who enter into contracts for doing work and supplying materials, there is nothing to render it either illegal or absurd in the workman to agree to complete the whole, and be paid when the whole is complete, and not till then: and we think that the plaintiffs in the present case had entered into such a contract. Had the accidental fire left the defendant's premises untouched, and only injured a part of the work which the plaintiffs had already done, we apprehend that it is clear the plaintiffs under such a contract as the present must have done that part over again, in order to fulfil their contract to complete the whole and "put it to work for the sums above named respectively." As it is, they are, according to the principle laid down in *Taylor v. Caldwell*, excused from completing the work; but they are not therefore entitled to any compensation for what they have done, but which has, without any fault of the defendant, perished. The case is in principle like that of a shipowner who has been excused from the performance of his contract to carry goods to their destination, because his ship has been disabled by one of the excepted perils, but who is not therefore entitled to any payment on account of the part-performance of the voyage, unless there is something to justify the conclusion that there has been a fresh contract to pay freight pro ratâ.

On the argument, much reference was made to the Civil law. The opinions of the great lawyers collected in the Digest afford us very great assistance in tracing out any question of doubtful principle; but they do not bind us: and we think that, on the principles of English law laid down in *Cutter v. Powell* (1795), 6 T.R. 320, ... the plaintiffs, having contracted to do an entire work for a specific sum, can recover nothing unless the work be done, or it can be shewn that it was the defendant's fault that the work was incomplete, or that there is something to justify the conclusion that the parties have entered into a fresh contract.

We think, therefore, as already said, that the judgment should be reversed.

Judgment reversed.

NOTE

Blackburn J. makes references to the case of *Cutter v. Powell*. This is a reference to what is known as the "entire contract rule." Briefly stated, this is that a party who does not perform an entire contract — in *Cutter v. Powell* serving as an officer on a ship for a voyage from the West Indies to Liverpool — cannot sue for any part of the contract that he may have performed. The cases are further discussed in Chapter 5, s. C.

FIBROSA SPOLKA AKCYJNA v. FAIRBAIRN LAWSON COMBE BARBOUR LTD.

[1943] A.C. 32 (House of Lords). Viscount Simon L.C., Lords Atkin, Russell, Macmillan, Wright, Roche and Porter.

APPEAL from the Court of Appeal.

The facts as stated by **Viscount Simon L.C.** were as follows: The respondents were a limited company carrying on at Leeds the business of manufacturing textile machinery, and by a contract in writing dated July 12, 1939, the respondents agreed to supply the appellants, a Polish company, of Vilna, with certain flax-hackling machines as therein specified and described, at a lump-sum price of £4800. The machines were of a special kind. The place of erection of the machinery was not mentioned in the contract, but it was agreed that it was the intention of the parties that it was to be erected at Vilna. By the terms of the contract, delivery was to be in three to four months from the settlement of final details. The machines were to be packed and delivered by the respondents c.i.f. Gdynia, the services of a skilled monteur to superintend erection were to be provided by the respondents and included in the price, and payment was to be made by cheque on London, one-third of the price (£1600.) with the order and the balance (£3200.) against shipping documents. By cl. 7 of the conditions of sale attached to the contract: ". . . . . Should dispatch be hindered or delayed by your instructions, or lack of instructions, or by any cause whatsoever beyond our reasonable control including strikes, lock-outs, war, fire, accidents. . . . a reasonable extension of time shall be granted. . . ." By cl. 10 provisions were made for dispatch and possible storage pending dispatch.

On July 18, 1939, the appellants paid to the respondents £1000. on account of the initial payment of £1600. due under the contract. On September 1, 1939, Germany invaded Poland and on September 3 Great Britain declared war on Germany. On September 7, the appellants' agents in England wrote to the respondents: "Owing to the outbreak of hostilities, it is now quite evident that the delivery of the hackling machines on order for Poland cannot take place. Under the circumstances we shall be obliged if you will kindly arrange to return our initial payment of £1000. at your early convenience." To this request, the respondents replied on the next day refusing to return the sum and stating that "considerable work has been done upon these machines and we cannot consent to the return of this payment. After the war the matter can be reconsidered." There was further correspondence between the parties or their agents which failed to produce agreement, and on May 1, 1940, the appellants issued a writ and by their statement of claim alleged that the respondents had broken the contract by refusing to deliver the machines, while the appellants "are and have at all material times been ready and willing to take delivery of the said machinery and to pay for the same." The prayer of the claim was (*a*) for damages for breach of contract, (*b*) for specific performance or, alternatively, return of the £1000. with interest, and (*c*) for further or other relief. The substantial defence of the respondents was that the contract had been frustrated by the German occupation of Gdynia in September, 1939, and that in these circumstances the appellants had no right to the return of the £1000. Tucker J. dismissed the action on March 7, 1941, and the Court of Appeal affirmed his decision on May 15, 1941. The appellants appealed to the House of Lords.

Lord Wright. My Lords, the claim in the action was to recover a prepayment of £1000. made on account of the price under a contract which had been frustrated. The claim was for money paid for a consideration which had failed. It is clear that any civilized system of law is bound to provide remedies for cases of what has been called unjust enrichment or unjust benefit, that is to prevent a man from retaining the money of or some benefit derived from another which it is against conscience that he should keep. Such remedies in English law are generically different from remedies in contract or in tort, and are now recognized to fall within a third category of the common law which has been called quasi-contract or restitution. The root idea was stated by three Lords of Appeal, Lord Shaw, Lord Sumner and Lord Carson, in *R.E. Jones, Ld. v. Waring & Gillow, Ld.*, [1926] A.C. 670, which dealt with a particular species of the category, namely, money paid under a mistake of fact. Lord Sumner referring to *Kelly v. Solari* (1841), 9 M.W. 54, where money had been paid by an insurance company under the mistaken impression that it was due to an executrix under a policy which had in fact been cancelled, said: "There was no real intention on the company's part to enrich her." Payment under a mistake of fact is only one head of this category of the law. Another class is where, as in this case, there is prepayment on account of money to be paid as consideration for the performance of a contract which in the event becomes abortive and is not performed, so that the money never becomes due. There was in such circumstances no intention to enrich the payee. This is the class of claims for the recovery of money paid for a consideration which has failed. Such causes of action have long been familiar and were assumed to be commonplace by Holt C.J. in *Holmes v. Hall* in 1704. Holt C.J. was there concerned only about the proper form of action and took the cause of the action as beyond question. He said: "If A give money to B to pay to C upon C's giving writings, etc., and C will not do it, indebit will lie for A against B for so much money received to his use. And many such actions have been maintained for earnests in bargains, when the bargainor would not perform, and for premiums for insurance, when the ship, etc., did not go the voyage." The Chief Justice is there using earnest as meaning a prepayment on account of the price, not in the modern sense of an irrevocable payment to bind their bargain, and he is recognizing that the indebitatus assumpsit had by that time been accepted as the appropriate form of action in place of the procedure which had been used in earlier times to enforce these claims such as debt, account or case.

By 1760 actions for money had and received had increased in number and variety. Lord Mansfield C.J., in a familiar passage in *Moses v. Macferlan* (1760), 2 Bun. 1005, sought to rationalize the action for money had and received, and illustrated it by some typical instances. "It lies," he said, "for money paid by mistake; or upon a consideration which happens to fail; or for money got through imposition (express, or implied;) or extortion; or oppression; or an undue advantage taken of the plaintiff's situation, contrary to laws made for the protection of persons under those circumstances. In one word, the gist of this kind of action is, that the defendant, upon the circumstances of the case, is obliged by the ties of natural justice and equity to refund the money." Lord Mansfield prefaced this pronouncement by observations which are to be noted. "If the defendant be under an obligation from the ties of natural justice, to refund; the law implies a debt and gives this action [sc. indebitatus assumpsit] founded in the equity of the plaintiff's case, as it were, upon a contract ('quasi ex contractu' as the Roman law expresses it)". Lord Mansfield does not say that the law implies a promise. The law implies a debt or obligation which is a different thing. In fact, he denies that there is a contract; the obligation is as efficacious as if it were upon a contract. The obligation is a creation of the law, just as much as an obligation in tort. The obligation belongs to a third class, distinct from either contract or tort, though it resembles contract rather than tort. This statement of Lord Mansfield has been the basis of the modern law of quasi-contract, notwithstanding the criticisms which have been launched against it. Like all large generalizations, it has needed and received qualifications in practice. There is, for instance, the qualification that an action for money had and received does not lie for money paid under an erroneous judgment or for moneys paid under an illegal or excessive distress. The law has provided other remedies as being more convenient. The standard of what is against conscience in this context has become more or less canalized or defined, but in substance the juristic concept remains as Lord Mansfield left it.

The gist of the action is a debt or obligation implied, or, more accurately, imposed, by law in much the same way as the law enforces as a debt the obligation to pay a statutory or customary impost. This is important because some confusion seems to have arisen though perhaps only in recent times when the true nature of the forms of action have become obscured by want of user. If I may borrow from another context the elegant phrase of Viscount Simon L.C. in *United Australia, Ld. v. Barclays Bank, Ld.*, [1914] A.C. 1, there has sometimes been, as it seems to me, "a misreading of technical rules, now happily swept away." The writ of indebitatus assumpsit involved at least two averments, the debt or obligation and the assumpsit. The former was the basis of the claim and was the real cause of action. The latter was merely fictitious and could not be traversed, but was necessary to enable the convenient and liberal form of action to be used in such cases. This fictitious assumpsit or promise was wiped out by the Common Law Procedure Act, 1852. As Bullen and Leake (Precedents of Pleading, 3rd ed., p. 36) points out, this Act, by s. 3, provided that the plaintiff was no longer required to specify the particular form of action in which he sued, and by s. 49 that (inter alia) the statement of promises in indebitatus counts which there was no need to prove were to be omitted; "the action of indebitatus assumpsit," the authors add, "is [that is by 1868] virtually become obsolete." Lord Atkin in the *United Australia* case, after instancing the case of the blackmailer, says: "The man has my money which I have not delivered to him with any real intention of passing to him the property. I sue him because he has the actual property taken." He adds: "These fantastic resemblances of contracts invented in order to meet requirements of the law as to forms of action which have now disappeared should not in these days be allowed to affect actual rights." Yet the ghosts of the forms of action have been allowed at times to intrude in the ways of the living and impede vital functions of the law. Thus in *Sinclair v. Brougham*, [1914] A.C. 398, Lord Sumner stated that "all these causes of action [sc. for money had and received] are common species of the genus assumpsit. All now rest, and long have rested, upon a notional or imputed promise to repay." This observation, which was not necessary for the decision of the case, obviously does not mean that there is an actual promise of the party. The phrase "notional or implied promise" is only a way of describing a debt or obligation arising by construction of law. The claim for money had and received always rested on a debt or obligation which the law implied or more accurately imposed, whether the procedure actually in vogue at any time was debt or account or case or indebitatus assumpsit. Even the fictitious assumpsit disappeared after the Act of 1852. I prefer Lord Sumner's explanation of the cause of action in *Jones's* case. This agrees with the words of Lord Atkin which I have just quoted, yet serious legal writers have seemed to say that these words of the great judge in *Sinclair v. Brougham* closed the door to any theory of unjust enrichment in English law. I do not understand why or how. It would indeed be a reductio ad absurdum of the doctrine of precedents. In fact, the common law still employs the action for money had and received as a practical and useful, if not complete or ideally perfect, instrument to prevent unjust enrichment, aided by the various methods of technical equity which are also available, as they were found to be in *Sinclair v. Brougham.*

Must, then, the court stay its hand in what would otherwise appear to be an ordinary case for the repayment of money paid in advance on account of the purchase price under a contract for the sale of goods merely because the contract has become impossible of performance and the consideration has failed for that reason? The defendant has the plaintiff's money. There was no intention to enrich him in the events which happened. No doubt, when money is paid under a contract it can only be claimed back as for failure of consideration where the contract is terminated as to the future. Characteristic instances are where it is dissolved by frustration or impossibility or by the contract becoming abortive for any reason not involving fault on the part of the plaintiff where the consideration, if entire, has entirely failed, or where, if it is severable, it has entirely failed as to the severable residue, as in *Rugg v. Minett* (1809), 11 East 210. The claim for repayment is not based on the contract which is dissolved on the frustration but on the fact that the defendant has received the money and has on the events which have supervened no right to keep it. The same event which automatically renders performance of the consideration for the payment impossible, not only termi-

nates the contract as to the future, but terminates the right of the payee to
retain the money which he has received only on the terms of the contract
performance. In *Hirji Mulji v. Cheong Yue Steamship Co., Ld.*, [1926] A.C.
497, Lord Sumner who has done so much in his judgments to elucidate the
meaning and effect of frustration, contrasts rescission of a contract by one
party on the ground of breach by the other party, which depends on election by the former, with frustration, which operates automatically apart
from either party's election. He finds, however, a similarity in the respect
that rights and wrongs which have come already into existence remain,
though the contract is ended as regards obligations de futuro. But the contract is in neither case wiped out, or avoided ab initio. The right in such a
case to claim repayment of money paid in advance must in principle, in my
judgment, attach at the moment of dissolution. The payment was originally
conditional. The condition of retaining it is eventual performance. Accordingly, when that condition fails, the right to retain the money must simultaneously fail. It is not like a claim for damages for breach of the contract
which would generally differ in measure and amount, nor is it a claim under
the contract. It is in theory and is expressed to be a claim to recover money,
received to the use of the plaintiff....
It is clear that the failure of consideration need not be attributable to
breach of contract or misconduct on the part of the defendant, as the cases
I have cited and many others show. Impossibility of performance or frustration is only a particular type of circumstance in which a party who is disabled from performing his contract is entitled to say that the contract is terminated as to the future, and in which repayment of money paid on
account of performance may be demanded.

These principles, however, only apply where the payment is not of such a
character that by the express or implied terms of the contract it is irrecoverable even though the consideration fails. The contract may exclude the
repayment. An illustration of this is afforded by advance freight which by
English law is not recoverable if the delivery of the goods is prevented by
the act of God, perils of the seas or other excepted cause which excludes an
action of damages. In *Allison v. Bristol Marine Insurance Co.*, Lord Selborne
stated it to be "the peculiar rule of English mercantile law, that an advance
on account of freight to be earned ... is, in the absence of any stipulation to
the contrary, an irrevocable payment at the risk of the shipper of the
goods." So, indeed, the law had been laid down by Saunders C.J. in *Anon.*
(Case 271) in 1682 and has remained ever since ... The irrecoverable nature
of the payment is there determined by custom or law, unless the contract
provides for the contrary. In other cases likewise a particular contract may
effectively make a prepayment irrecoverable. In the present case the payment is not made irrecoverable by any custom or rule of law, or by any
express or implied terms of the contract. It was paid on account of the
price. It was not paid out-and-out for the signing of the contract. When the
sellers were disabled to perform the contract by the shipment to Gdynia
becoming illegal, the ordinary rules of law and the authorities to which I
have referred show that the sum of £1000. paid in advance of the price was
recoverable by the appellants in the present action.

The court below have held themselves bound to reach the contrary decision only on the authority of certain cases, generally known as the
"coronation cases," in particular *Blakeley v. Muller & Co.*, [1903] 2 K.B.

670, reported in a note to *Civil Service Co-operative Society, Ld. v. General Steam Navigation Co.,* [1903] 2 K.B. 656, and *Chandler v. Webster*. These cases dealt with agreements for the hiring of rooms from which to view the procession on the coronation of King Edward VII. It had been held in *Krell v. Henry,* that the mere use of the rooms on the appointed day was only part of the consideration for the agreed payment, and that an essential part of the consideration was the opportunity of viewing the procession. That was the object or basis of the contract in contemplation of both parties. When the procession could not take place, the contract, it was held, became abortive or was frustrated. There was no decision in that case on whether money paid in advance was recoverable. In *Blakeley v. Muller & Co.* the prepayment had fallen due before the frustration supervened. A Divisional Court held that the hirer, who had paid in advance, could not recover back the money. They did not discuss the principles or authorities to which I have referred on the right to recover money paid for a consideration which has failed. I take the ratio decidendi from the judgment of Channell J., because in the next case of that type, the *Civil Service Co-operative Society* case, Lord Halsbury L.C., sitting in the Court of Appeal, quoted a long passage from it and added that he concurred with every word of it. The reasoning of Channell J., as I understand his judgment, was that the loss must remain where it was at the time of the abandonment, because it was impossible to import into a contract a condition which the parties might have imported but had not, and that under *Taylor v. Caldwell* and *Appleby v. Myers* (cases of impossibility), all that was said was that the parties were excused from further performance, not that anything that was done under the contract was void. In the former case, the claim was for damages, in the latter it was on a quantum meruit for partial performance of an entire consideration. Each claim failed. Neither was a claim for money had and received. Channell J. instanced the case of advance freight under the charterparty. I have already explained that rule, which in Lord Selborne's view is peculiar. I have also explained my view that the right to repayment of advance payments as money had and received to the plaintiff's use is not a claim under the contract or for further performance of the contract of for damages, but a claim outside the contract. The ground of the claim is that the contract has been dissolved as to future performance and hence that the consideration has failed. The Court of Appeal, however, dismissed the claim for the money, following *Blakeley v. Muller & Co.* When shortly afterwards the same question on similar facts again came before a differently constituted Court of Appeal, in *Chandler v. Webster*, Collins M.R. discussed the matter more elaborately, but he still ignored the principles and authorities on the action for money had and received to which I have referred, though the claim was to recover as on a total failure of consideration. He indeed discussed the case from that point of view. The hirer was claiming to recover what he had paid in advance and was resisting a counterclaim for the balance which was by the contract payable before the date when the procession became impossible. He ought, in my opinion, to have succeeded on both issues, but by the judgment of the Court of Appeal he failed on both. The reasoning of the Master of the Rolls may, I think, fairly be summarized to be that impossibility through the fault of neither party leaves the parties where they were but relieves them from further performance, and that it is only if the contract is wiped out altogether that money paid under it would have to be repaid as on a failure of consideration, but that the only effect of impossibility is to release the parties from further performance. The rule, he said, is arbitrary, but it is really impossible to work or adjust with any exactitude what the rights of the parties in the event should be. I hesitate to criticize the ruling of so great a lawyer as the Master of the Rolls, but I cannot concur in these propositions. I need scarcely repeat my reasons for doing so, which are apparent from what I have already said. The claim for money had and received is not, in my opinion, a claim for further performance of the contract. It is a claim outside the contract. If the parties are left where they are, one feature of the position is that the one who has received the prepayment is left in possession of a sum of money which belongs to the other. The frustration does not change the property in the money, nor is the contract wiped out altogether, but only the future performance. I may add that the difficulty emphasized by the Master of the Rolls that such a claim involves constructing a hypothetical contract by supposing what terms the parties would have arrived at if they contemplated the future impossibility does not arise, but I do not think that this way of envisaging the matter accords with the true position. In my opinion, the contract is automatically terminated as to the future because at that date its further performance becomes impossible in fact in circumstances which involve no liability for damages for the failure on either party. When the court holds a contract to be thus terminated, it is simply giving appropriate effect to the circumstances of the case, including the actual contract and its meaning applied to the event. It is this view which is involved in Lord Sumner's phrase in *Hirji Mulji v. Cheong Yue Steamship Co., Ld.* "It" [sc. the doctrine of frustration] "is really a device, by which the rules as to absolute contracts are reconciled with a special exception which justice demands." He combined with this a reference to what has been generally accepted by English law, that the rule is explained in theory as a condition or term of the contract implied by the law ab initio. No one who reads the reported cases can ignore how inveterate is this theory or explanation in English law. I do not see any objection to this mode of expression so long as it is understood that what is implied is what the court thinks the parties ought to have agreed on the basis of what is fair and reasonable, not what as individuals they would or might have agreed. "It is," said Lord Sumner, "irrespective of the individuals concerned, their temperaments and failings, their interest and circumstances." The court is thus taken to assume the role of the reasonable man, and decides what the reasonable man would regard as just on the facts of the case. The hypothetical "reasonable man" is personified by the court itself. It is the court which decides. The position is thus somewhat like the position in the cases in which the court imports a term in a contract on the basis of what is reasonable. As frustration is automatic, so equally the claim for money had and received here follows automatically.

   Chandler v. Webster had bound subsequent Courts of Appeal . . . The decision reached in *Chandler v. Webster* is criticized by Williston on Contracts: s. 1954, p. 5477: see, too, s. 1974, p. 5544, and has not been followed in most of the States of America. Nor is it adopted in the Restatement of the Law of Contract by the American Law Institute, s. 468, pp. 884, et seq. Indeed, the law of the United States seems to go beyond the mere remedy of claims for money had and received and allow the recovery of the value of the benefit of any part performance rendered while performance was possible. Such and similar claims should be recognized in any complete system of law, but it is not clear how far they have been admitted in English law.

.   .   .

I ought to notice, in order to reject, an argument of Mr. Holmes that the House should not reverse or depart from a doctrine which has stood since 1904 and has been followed in several cases by the Court of Appeal and acted upon on practical affairs. The doctrine, however, has been severely criticized by writers both in this country and elsewhere and has been treated as open to review by this House, as recently as 1923 in the *Cantiare* case, [1924] A.C. 226. If the doctrine is, as I think it clearly is, wrong and unjust, it is the duty of this House exercising its function of finally declaring the law, to reverse it, unless there are very special circumstances... On the other hand, ... the House has recently overruled a decision which had been acted on in frequent practice for 27 years. I may in conclusion add a reference to a very learned article by Professor Buckland, in Harvard Law Review, vol. xlvi., p. 1281. He concludes by observing that, whatever the merits or demerits of *Chandler v. Webster* and other cases which he considers in that article, the Roman law cannot be made responsible for the rules laid down in them. In my judgment the appeal should be allowed.

[Only the judgment of Lord Wright is reproduced here. The others all wrote judgments agreeing in allowing the appeal.]

THE FRUSTRATED CONTRACTS ACT

R.S.O. 1970, c. 185.

1. In this Act,
(*a*)   "contract" includes a contract to which the Crown is a party;
(*b*)   "court" means the court or arbitrator by or before whom a matter falls to be determined;
(*c*)   "discharged" means relieved from further performance of the contract. R.S.O. 1960, c. 157, s. 1.

2. — (1) This Act applies to any contract that is governed by the law of Ontario and that has become impossible of performance or been otherwise frustrated and the parties to which for that reason have been discharged.

(2) This Act does not apply,
(*a*)   to a charterparty or a contract for the carriage of goods by sea, except a time charterparty or a charterparty by way of demise;
(*b*)   to a contract of insurance; or
(*c*)   to a contract for the sale of specific goods where the goods, without the knowledge of the seller have perished at the time the contract was made, or where the goods, without any fault on the part of the seller or buyer, perished before the risk passed to the buyer. R.S.O. 1960, c. 157, s. 2, *amended.*

3. — (1) The sums paid or payable to a party in pursuance of a contract before the parties were discharged,
(*a*)   in the case of sums paid, are recoverable from him as money received by him for the use of the party by whom the sums were paid; and
(*b*)   in the case of sums payable, cease to be payable.

(2) If, before the parties were discharged, the party to whom the sums

were paid or payable incurred expenses in connection with the performance of the contract, the court, if it considers it just to do so having regard to all the circumstances, may allow him to retain or to recover, as the case may be, the whole or any part of the sums paid or payable not exceeding the amount of the expenses, and, without restricting the generality of the foregoing, the court, in estimating the amount of the expenses, may include such sum as appears to be reasonable in respect of overhead expenses and in respect of any work or services performed personally by the party incurring the expenses.

(3) If, before the parties were discharged, any of them has, by reason of anything done by any other party in connection with the performance of the contract, obtained a valuable benefit other than a payment of money, the court, if it considers it just to do so having regard to all the circumstances, may allow the other party to recover from the party benefited the whole or any part of the value of the benefit.

(4) Where a party has assumed an obligation under the contract in consideration of the conferring of a benefit by any other party to the contract upon any other person, whether a party to the contract or not, the court, if it considers it just to do so having regard to all the circumstances, may, for the purposes of subsection 3, treat any benefit so conferred as a benefit obtained by the party who has assumed the obligation.

(5) In considering whether any sum ought to be recovered or retained under this section by a party to the contract, the court shall not take into account any sum that, by reason of the circumstances giving rise to the frustration of the contract, has become payable to that party under any contract of insurance unless there was an obligation to insure imposed by an express term of the frustrated contract or by or under any enactment.

(6) Where the contract contains a provision that upon the true construction of the contract is intended to have effect in the event of circumstances that operate, or but for the provision would operate, to frustrate the contract, or is intended to have effect whether such circumstances arise or not, the court shall give effect to the provision and shall give effect to this section only to such extent, if any, as appears to the court to be consistent with the provision.

(7) Where it appears to the court that a part of the contract can be severed properly from the remainder of the contract, being a part wholly performed before the parties were discharged, or so performed except for the payment in respect of that part of the contract of sums that are or can be ascertained under the contract, the court shall treat that part of the contract as if it were a separate contract that had not been frustrated and shall treat this section as applicable only to the remainder of the contract. R.S.O. 1960, c. 157, s. 3.

QUESTIONS

1. Would the application of the act have avoided the problems in the following cases:

(a) *Appleby v. Myers;*
(b) *Fibrosa;*
(c) *Krell v. Henry;*
(d) *Taylor v. Caldwell;*
(e) *Capital Quality v. Colwyn Construction?*

2. If the act would not directly solve any of these problems, could you use the

analogy of the act to solve them? In other words, to what extent is the purpose of the act, the purpose of the law generally, and hence a guide to what courts can do?

On this issue generally, see: Landis, *Statutes and the Sources of Law* (*infra*, Chapter 8).

F. Third Parties and Mistakes

The fact which distinguishes these cases from those that we have already discussed is that in these cases the rights of third parties have intervened after the mistake was made.

These cases represent two traditional classes of mistake. The first class are cases of "*non est factum*". This refers to a class where the mistake was made by someone who signed a document under the belief that he was signing something else. The phrase, "*non est factum*", is a contraction of the Latin tag: "*Hoc scriptum non est factum meum*" — "This writing is not my deed". This was a plea allowed by the common law whenever an action was brought on a sealed document. The word "deed" is used because in any action in the early common law any document was likely to have been sealed. Now, of course, there is no requirement that the writing be a deed: the defence is available in any case of a signed writing. One of the few defences allowed under the common law to an action on a deed was the defence that the maker had not known what he was signing. In a society where many people were illiterate, it would happen that one man would execute a deed without being able to know what it said. If he had had it incorrectly read over to him, he could later avoid liability on it. Much of the history of the law in this area is discussed in the judgments.

The second class are cases where X, by fraud, induces A to sell him something. X then sells the thing to B, from whom it is claimed by A. The courts have then to decide if A or B has the better claim to the thing.

PRUDENTIAL TRUST CO. LTD. v. CUGNET

(1956), 5 D.L.R. 2d 1. Supreme Court of Canada. Taschereau, Locke, Cartwright, Fauteux and Nolan JJ.

The facts are taken from the judgment of **Cartwright J.**

APPEAL from a judgment of the Saskatchewan Court of Appeal, [1955] 4 D.L.R. 18, affirming a decision of Graham J., 11 W.W.R. (N.S.) 634, dismissing appellant's application for a declaration of title to certain mines and minerals by virtue of a transfer thereof by respondent.

On January 26, 1951, the respondent Edmond G. Cugnet, hereinafter called "Cugnet Senior" signed and sealed a document whereby he conveyed an undivided one-half interest in all petroleum, natural gas and related hydrocarbons in and under two quarter-sections owned by him to Prudential Trust Co. Ltd., hereinafter called "Prudential", and granted to that company an option to acquire upon the termination of an existing petroleum and natural gas lease a petroleum and natural gas lease covering the said lands for a term of 99 years from January 26, 1951, on the same terms as those contained in the existing lease except that the cash rental was to be 25 cents per acre. Cugnet Senior was induced to sign this document by the fraudulent representation made to him by one Edward Hunter that it contained only the grant of an option. Cugnet Senior is literate, has had experience in buying and selling properties, has been successful, and, in his own words, has "lots of money". He signed the document without reading it. He does not suggest that any thing was done to prevent him reading it but appears to have been anxious to return without delay to the game of cards which had been interrupted by Hunter's arrival. He had not met Hunter previously. Hunter took the document away with him but 2 or 3 weeks later Cugnet Senior received a copy of it together with a cheque for $64 the amount of the consideration which he had agreed to accept. He did not read this copy until some months later when his son, the respondent Raymond A. Cugnet, called his attention to its contents. In the meantime the copy had been hanging up on a spike in the kitchen at the home of Cugnet Senior. Prudential in taking the conveyance was acting as bare trustee for Amigo Petroleums Ltd. During February, 1951, the last-mentioned company transferred the one-half interest and the option to one Nickle who, in turn, transferred them for value to the appellant Canuck Freehold Royalties Ltd., hereinafter called "Canuck" for which Prudential holds as bare trustee. Canuck had no notice or knowledge of the fraud practised by Hunter.

Nolan J.... At trial it was contended on behalf of the appellants that the evidence adduced on behalf of the respondents did not establish a plea of *non est factum* as to the documents in question and that the transaction between Hunter, in the name of the appellant Prudential, and the respondent Edmond Cugnet was voidable and not void and that the appellant Canuck Freehold Royalties Ltd. was a *bonâ fide* purchaser for value without notice and was entitled to the interest in the lands in question specified in the assignment and to a transfer of an undivided one-half interest in the petroleum and natural gas within, upon or under the said lands. In the alternative, the appellants contended that the appellant Canuck Freehold Royalties Ltd. was entitled to the option as specified in the assignment.

The respondents took the position that the transaction was not merely voidable, but void *ab initio*, and that a plea of *bonâ fide* purchaser for value was of no assistance to the appellant Canuck Freehold Royalties Ltd. They further contended that in any event, irrespective of misrepresentation, there was no *consensus ad idem* between the parties and no agreement between them, or that the agreement, if any, was void for uncertainty.

The learned trial Judge, who was favourably impressed with the evidence of the respondent Edmond Cugnet, found that he never intended to complete the assignment and transfer, as they now appear in the record, and relied on the misrepresentation of Hunter that the documents he was asked to sign constituted only the granting of an option. Hunter was not called as a witness at the trial, his whereabouts being unknown. The learned trial Judge further found that the respondent Edmond Cugnet was mistaken as to the nature and character of the assignment and transfer and that this mistake was induced by the fraudulent misrepresentation of Hunter, the agent of the appellant Prudential. In the result, the learned trial Judge held that the plea of *non est factum* was established and that the documents were void.

With respect to the submission on behalf of the appellants that Canuck Freehold Royalties Ltd. was a purchaser for value without notice of the fraud inducing the signing of the documents, the learned trial Judge held, while the evidence supported this submission, the rights of Canuck Freehold Royalties Ltd. were invalid and unenforceable because the documents were void. Further, the learned trial Judge refused to give effect to the submission on behalf of the appellants that in any event Canuck Freehold Royalties Ltd. was entitled to the rights under the option granted by the respondent Edmond Cugnet and contained in the assignment, on the ground that the whole transaction, as evidenced by the documents, was void and the documents themselves were in a like position. The judgment of the learned trial Judge, dismissing the action of the appellants, declared the assignment and transfer were void and of no effect and that they be delivered up to the respondent Edmond Cugnet for cancellation, and directed that the caveat and certificate of *lis pendens* be vacated.

From that judgment an appeal was taken to the Court of Appeal and by a unanimous judgment the appeal was dismissed on the ground that the plea of *non est factum*, as found by the learned trial Judge, must be sustained. The Court of Appeal granted special leave to appeal from that judgment to this Court.

In the Courts below the appellants relied on *Howatson v. Webb*, [1907] 1 Ch. 537; affd [1908] 1 Ch. 1....

The appellants contend, on the authority of *Howatson v. Webb,* that, while the respondent Edmond Cugnet was indifferent and careless as to what he signed, nevertheless he is bound by what he did sign and cannot successfully maintain a plea of *non est factum.*

The respondents rely on *Carlisle & Cumberland Banking Co. v. Bragg,* [1911] 1 K.B. 489...

In order to determine the effectiveness of the plea of *non est factum* as applied to the facts of this case, it is necessary to examine the authorities.

The old cases on misrepresentation as to the contents of a deed were based upon the illiterate character of the person to whom the deed was read over, and on the fact that an illiterate man was treated as being in the same position as a blind man: Sheppard's Touchstone, 8th ed., vol. 1, p. 56.

An early instance of the application of the plea is to be found in *Thoroughgood's Case*, 2 Co. Rep. 9a, where it was held that a deed executed by an illiterate person does not bind him, if read falsely either by the grantee or a stranger; (2) that an illiterate man need not execute a deed before it is read to him in a language which he understands, but if the party executes without desiring it to be read, the deed is binding; (3) that if an illiterate man execute a deed which is falsely read, or the sense declared differently from the truth, it does not bind him.

It appears in more recent cases that the application of the plea has been extended beyond the earlier cases, which turned upon the question of illiteracy or blindness.

This extension is well illustrated in *Foster v. Mackinnon,* L.R. 4 C.P. 704, where the facts were that the defendant had been induced to put his name upon the back of a bill of exchange, making himself liable as endorser, on the fraudulent representation of the acceptor that he was signing a guarantee. The bill got into the hands of a *bona fide* holder for value, who sued the defendant as endorser, and the result of the action was that the defendant, having signed the document without knowing it was a bill and under the belief that it was a guarantee, and not having been guilty of any negligence in so signing it, was held not liable on the endorsement. Byles J. at p. 711 said: "It seems plain, on principle and on authority, that, if a blind man, or a man who cannot read, or who for some reason (not implying negligence) forbears to read, has a written contract falsely read over to him, the reader misreading to such a degree that the written contract is of a nature altogether different from the contract pretended to be read from the paper which the blind or illiterate man afterwards signs; then, at least if there be no negligence, the signature so obtained is of no force. And it is invalid not merely on the ground of fraud, where fraud exists, but on the ground that the mind of the signer did not accompany the signature; in other words, that he never intended to sign, and therefore in contemplation of law never did sign, the contract to which his name is appended.". . .

The question for determination is whether the principle contained in *Carlisle & Cumberland Banking Co. v. Bragg*, [1911] 1 K.B. 489, or that contained in the earlier case of *Howatson v. Webb*, [1908] 1 Ch. 1, should be applied to the facts of this case.

It is to be observed, as was pointed out by the Court of Appeal in the present case, that in *Howatson v. Webb, supra*, the misrepresentation was made by a solicitor and that the defendant, also a solicitor, should have realized that he was signing a mortgage and not a transfer. Halsbury, 3rd ed., vol. 11, p. 360, note (*o*), also makes reference to the fact that the defendant was a solicitor and could not have been misled if he had read the document, but chose to execute it without doing so. When the defendant Webb asked what the deeds were that he had been asked to sign he was told that they were just deeds transferring the Edmonton property. In fact one deed was a mortgage, but it is to be remembered that in England a mortgage operates as a conveyance and is a transfer of property by way of mortgage. The Court may have been influenced by the fact that the document signed by Webb was not of a character "wholly different" from what was represented to him.

The principle contained in *Carlisle & Cumberland Banking Co. v. Bragg, supra*, was approved in this Court in *Minchau v. Busse*, [1940] 2 D.L.R. 282. Sir Lyman P. Duff C.J.C. said at p. 294: "The law is stated in the most satisfactory way in the judgment of Buckley L.J. in *Carlisle & Cumberland Banking Co. v. Bragg*, [1911] 1 K.B. 489 at p. 495."

In my view, while the respondent Edmond Cugnet knew that he was dealing with his petroleum and natural gas rights, the representation made to him was as to the nature and character of the document and not merely as to its contents. It was represented to be an option to grant a petroleum and natural gas lease, when in fact, it contained an assignment and transfer to the appellant Prudential of an undivided one-half interest in the petroleum and natural gas rights of the respondent Edmond Cugnet in the lands in question in the action.

Applying the principle contained in *Carlisle & Cumberland Banking Co. v. Bragg, supra*, as I do, I have come to the conclusion that the mind of the respondent Edmond Cugnet did not go with his hand and that the plea of *non est factum* has been established.

It was contended on behalf of the appellant Prudential, in the alternative, that, in any event, the appellant Canuck Freehold Royalties Ltd. was entitled to the option contained in the document in question, which, on the evidence, the respondent Edmond Cugnet agreed to grant and for which he received payment.

With this contention I am unable to agree. The option is predicated upon the assignment and transfer to the appellant Prudential of an undivided one-half interest in the petroleum and natural gas upon or under the lands in question. It is an option given jointly by the respondent Edmond Cugnet and the appellant Prudential to grant a petroleum and natural gas lease to the appellant Prudential or its nominee.

Moreover, the option provided that, in addition to the share of the production to which the appellant Prudential, or its nominee, will become entitled as lessee under the terms of any lease obtained under the option, the appellant Prudential shall be entitled to its share of production reserved by the respondent Edmond Cugnet and the appellant Prudential as lessors under such lease.

In my view, if the assignment of the one-half interest is void, then that portion of the document granting the option cannot be severed and falls with the rest of the transaction.

Having come to the conclusion that the plea of *non est factum* has been established and that the whole transaction is void, it is unnecessary to consider the other points raised in argument on the appeal.

I would dismiss the appeal with costs.

[Taschereau and Fauteux JJ. concurred with Nolan J.]

Locke J.: — ... It is my opinion that the result of the authorities was correctly stated in the *Bragg* case. To say that a person may be estopped by careless conduct such as that in the present case, when the instrument is not negotiable, is to assert the existence of some duty on the part of the person owing to the public at large, or to other persons unknown to him who might suffer damage by acting upon the instrument on the footing that it is valid in the hands of the holder. I do not consider that the authorities support the view that there is any such general duty, the breach of which imposes a liability in negligence. I think the validity of the contention may be tested by asking whether, in a case such as this, an action for damages would lie at the suit of Canuck Freehold Royalties Ltd. against Edmund Cugnet. The answer to that question must, in my opinion, be in the negative: *Bank of Ireland v. Evans Trustees* (1885), 5 H.L.C. 389, 10 E.R. 950, Parke B. at p. 410; the *Swan* case, 7 H & N at p. 650. If, indeed, there were such a duty, I think, for the reason pointed out by Channel B. in the *Swan* case, that such an action would fail since the proximate cause of the damage was the fraudulent act of Hunter.

For these reasons, it is my opinion that the appeal should fail and be dismissed with costs.

Cartwright J. (dissenting): — The question raised for decision in this appeal is which of two innocent parties is to suffer for the fraud of a third....

In upholding the respondent's plea of *non est factum* the learned trial Judge distinguished the case at bar from *Howatson v. Webb*, [1907] 1 Ch. 537; [1908] 1 Ch. 1, on the ground that the misrepresentation was in the latter as to the contents of the document and in the former as to the nature and character of the document. I must confess that I find difficulty in discerning a difference between a conveyance of a half-interest in the oil and gas under specified lands and the grant of an option to obtain a 99-year lease of such oil and gas which is greater or more fundamental than the difference between a reconveyance by a bare trustee of the legal estate in specified land to the beneficial owner thereof and a mortgage of such land containing a personal covenant to pay. The following words of Warrington J.

might well be applied in the case at bar; in [1907] 1 Ch. at pp. 547-8, that learned Judge said: "But it seems to me that these dicta contained in the judgments clearly point to this, that if a man knows that the deed is one purporting to deal with his property and he executes it, it will not be sufficient for him, in order to support a plea of non est factum, to shew that a misrepresentation was made to him as to the contents of the deed. The deed in the present case is not of a character so wholly different from that which it was represented to be as to come within the principle within which Lord Hatherley held that the case before him did not fall."

It is clear that Cugnet Senior knew that the deed which he was executing was one purporting to deal with the petroleum and natural gas under two correctly specified quarter-sections owned by him. On the assumption that a distinction can validly be drawn between the facts in *Howatson v. Webb, supra,* and those in *Carlisle & Cumberland Banking Co. v. Bragg,* [1911] 1 K.B. 489, it is my view that on its facts the case at bar falls within the class of cases of which the former is an example.

If, however, it be assumed that the Courts below were right in holding that the document of January 26, 1951, was entirely different in nature from what Cugnet Senior believed it to be, it is my opinion that in signing and sealing the document without reading it he was guilty of such negligence that as between himself and Canuck, which gave valuable consideration on the strength of the deed which he had in fact signed and sealed, he must bear the loss.

The general principle was stated as follows by Lord Halsbury sitting in the Court of Appeal in *Henderson & Co. v. Williams,* [1895] 1 Q.B. 521 at pp. 528-9: "I think that it is not undesirable to refer to an American authority, which, I observe, was quoted in the case of *Kingsford v. Merry, Root v. French* in which, in the Supreme Court of New York, Savage C.J. makes observations which seem to me to be well worthy of consideration. Speaking of a bonâ fide purchaser who has purchased property from a fraudulent vendee and given value for it, he says: 'He is protected in doing so upon the principle just stated, that when one of two innocent persons must suffer from the fraud of a third, he shall suffer, who, by his indiscretion, has enabled such third person to commit the fraud. A contrary principle would endanger the security of commercial transactions, and destroy that confidence upon which what is called the usual course of trade materially rests.' "

In *Farquharson Bros. & Co. v. C. King & Co.,* [1902] A.C. 325 at pp. 331-2, Lord Halsbury L.C. presiding in the House of Lords reaffirmed the above passage and pointed out that in the case then before the House the Court of Appeal had fallen into error through disregarding the words "who, by his indiscretion".

A branch of the principle so stated is the rule that, generally speaking, a person who executes a document without taking the trouble to read it is liable on it and cannot plead that he mistook its contents, at all events, as against a person who acting in good faith in the ordinary course of business has changed his position in reliance on such document. But it is said that the plea of *non est factum* operates as an exception to this salutary rule. That this is so in the case of a blind or illiterate person may be taken to be established by *Thoroughgood's Case* (1583), 2 Co. Rep. 9a, 76 E.R. 408, but whether the exception extends to an educated person who is not blind is a question which was treated by Sir G. Mellish L.J. in *Hunter v. Walters* (1871), L.R. 7 Ch. 75, and by Warrington J. and the Court of Appeal in *Howatson v. Webb, supra,* as being still open. In the former case at pp. 86-7, Mellish L.J. says:

> "Now, I am of opinion that there is evidence that both *Hunter* and *Darnell* were induced by the fraud of *Walters* to execute that deed; but the mere circumstance that they were induced to execute it by fraud does not make it a void deed in point of law. But it is said that there is something more than this, and that where a deed is procured by an actual false representation respecting the contents of the deed itself, or respecting the legal effect of the deed, there the deed is not only voidable, but is actually void at law, and, being void, the parties are in the same position as if it had never been executed at all. Thence, no doubt, it would follow, that Mr. *Walters* never got any estate in these premises at all, and therefore that an equitable mortgage by him would be altogether invalid.
>
> "Now, in my opinion, it is still a doubtful question at law, on which I do not wish to give any decisive opinion, whether, if there be a false representation respecting the contents of a deed, a person who is an educated person, and who might, by very simple means, have satisfied himself as to what the contents of the deed really were, may not, by executing it negligently be estopped as between himself and a person who innocently acts upon the faith of the deed being valid, and who accepts an estate under it."

This passage is quoted by Warrington J. in *Howatson v. Webb* and in the Court of Appeal, [1908] 1 Ch. at pp. 3-4, Farwell L.J. says: "I think myself that the question suggested, but not decided, by Mellish L.J. in that case will some day have to be determined, viz., whether the old cases on misrepresentation as to the contents of a deed were not based upon the illiterate character of the person to whom the deed was read over, and on the fact that an illiterate man was treated as being in the same position as a blind man: see *Thoroughgood's Case* (1582), 2 Rep. 9a, and Sheppard's Touchstone, p. 56; and whether at the present time an educated person, who is not blind, is not estopped from availing himself of the plea of non est factum against a person who innocently acts upon the faith of the deed being valid."

While he does not refer specifically to the question suggested by Mellish L.J., Buckley L.J. gives an answer to it in *Carlisle v. Bragg,* [1911] 1 K.B. at p. 496, where, speaking of the plea of *non est factum,* he says: "I do not think myself that cases of this kind are to be confined to the blind and illiterate. Blindness and illiteracy constitute a state of things of which the equivalent for this purpose may under certain circumstances be predicated of persons who are neither blind nor illiterate. If a document were presented to me written in Hebrew or Syriac, I should for the purposes of that document be both blind and illiterate — blind in the sense that, although I saw some marks on the paper, they conveyed no meaning to my mind, and illiterate as regards the particular document, because I could not read it. It seems to me that the same doctrine applies to every person who is so placed as that he is incapable by the use of such means as are open to him of ascertaining, *or* is by false information deceived in a material respect as to, the contents of the document which he is asked to sign."

With the greatest respect, it appears to me that instead of the word "or" which I have italicized in this passage the word "and" ought to have been used. In a case where the deed in question has in fact been executed by the person raising the plea it is of the essence of the plea of *non est factum* that such person shall have been deceived as to its contents. I do not, of course, suggest that Buckley L.J. used the word "or" by inadvertance, for it seems clear that Bragg was capable by the use of such means as were open to him of ascertaining the contents of the document which he was asked to sign. All that he had to do was to read it.

An anxious consideration of all the authorities referred to by counsel and in the Courts below has brought me to the conclusion that, insofar as *Carlisle v. Bragg* decides that the rule that negligence excludes a plea of *non est factum* is limited to the case of negotiable instruments and does not extend to a deed such as the one before us, we should refuse to follow it. I do not read the judgment of Sir Lyman P. Duff C.J.C. in *Minchau v. Busse,* [1940] 2 D.L.R. 282, and particularly his reference at p. 294 to the judgment of Buckley L.J. as binding us to follow everything that was decided in *Carlisle v. Bragg.*

In my view the effect of the decisions prior to *Carlisle v. Bragg* is accurately summarized in Cheshire & Fifoot on Contract, 4th ed., pp. 206-7, as follows: "The rule before 1911 was that if A., the victim of the fraud of C., was *guilty of negligence* in executing a written instrument different in kind from that which he intended to execute, then he was estopped as against innocent transferees from denying the validity of the written contract."

That rule was, I think, laid down by Byles J. delivering the unanimous judgment of the Court in *Foster v. Mackinnon,* L.R. 4 C.P. 704, as being applicable to all written contracts. It appears to me that the Court of Appeal in *Carlisle v. Bragg* misinterpreted the following passage in the judgment of Byles J. at p. 712:

> "Nevertheless, this principle, when applied to negotiable instruments, must be and is limited in its application. These instruments are not only assignable, but they form part of the currency of the country. A qualification of the general rule is necessary to protect innocent transferrees for value. If, therefore, a man write his name across the back of a blank bill-stamp, and part with it, and the paper is afterwards improperly filled up, he is liable as endorser. If he write it across the face of the bill, he is liable as acceptor, when the instrument has once passed into the hands of an innocent endorsee for value before maturity, and liable to the extent of any sum which the stamp will cover.
> "In these cases, however, the party signing knows what he is doing: the endorser intended to endorse, and the acceptor intended to accept, a bill of exchange to be thereafter filled up, leaving the amount, the date, the maturity, and the other parties to the bill undetermined.
> "But, in the case now under consideration, the defendant, according to the evidence, if believed, and the finding of the jury, never intended to endorse a bill of exchange at all, but intended to sign a contract of an entirely different nature. It was not his design, and, if he were guilty of no negligence, it was not even his fault that the instrument he signed turned out to be a bill of exchange."

This does not say that the rule, that the signer if guilty of negligence will be estopped from denying the validity of a document as against a purchaser for value in good faith, is confined to the case of negotiable instruments; but rather that a person who knows he is signing a negotiable instrument cannot deny its validity to a holder in due course although he was guilty of no negligence in affixing his signature.

It may be said that the term negligence is inappropriate because it presupposes a duty owed by Cugnet Senior to Canuck, but in the passages quoted the term is, I think, used as meaning that lack of reasonable care in statement which gives rise to an estoppel. As it was put by Sir William Anson in an article on *Carlisle & Cumberland Banking Co. v. Bragg* in 28 L.Q. Rev. 190 at p. 194: "And further, there seems some confusion between the negligence which creates a liability in tort, and the lack of reasonable care in statement which gives rise to an estoppel. Bragg might well have been precluded by carelessness from resisting the effect of his written words, though the Bank might not have been able to sue him for negligence."

On the facts in the case at bar it cannot be doubted that Cugnet Senior failed to exercise reasonable care in signing the document in question. He executed a deed which he knew dealt with the oil and gas under his property without reading it, relying on the statements as to its contents made by Hunter who was a stranger to him. It does not appear that anything was done to prevent his reading the document. He chose to sign it unread rather than to absent himself for a few more minutes from the game of cards. His conduct, in my opinion, precludes him from relying on the plea of *non est factum* as against Canuck which purchased relying on the deed, in good faith, for value, and without notice or knowledge of any circumstances affecting the validity of the deed.

The terms of the deed appear to me to be sufficiently clear and I think that the plea that it is void for uncertainty must be rejected.

In the result I would allow the appeal with costs throughout and direct that judgment be entered for the relief claimed in the amended statement of claim.

SAUNDERS v. ANGLIA BUILDING SOCIETY

[1970] 3 All E.R. 961. House of Lords; Lords Reid, Hodson, Dilhorne, Wilberforce and Pearson.

[Mrs. Gallie was 78 in 1962. She had a nephew, Wally Parkin to whom she had planned to leave her estate. She owned a house where she lived. She had had a mortgage but that had been paid off. When the mortgage was paid off, she gave the deeds to her nephew saying that the house was his, but that she wanted to live there for the rest of her life. Parkin and a friend, Lee, together with a solicitor's managing clerk, arranged to borrow money for Lee on the security of Mrs. Gallie's house. A deed was prepared under which Mrs. Gallie was to sell her house to Lee for £3,000 (which sum was not to be paid) and then Lee could mortgage the property. Parkin asked Mrs. Gallie to sign the document. She had broken her glasses and could not read. She asked Lee what the deed was for. He said that it was a deed of gift to Parkin. She said that she would be happy to help her nephew and she understood that she could live in the house rent free. Lee borrowed money on the deed from a building society (now the Anglia Building Society) and gave a mortgage. He used the proceeds to pay off his debts. Lee defaulted on the mortgage and the building society sought to recover possession. Mrs. Gallie sought a declaration that she was not bound by the deed to Lee.

The trial judge, Stamp J. made these findings of fact:

"... I find as a fact that [the plaintiff] did not read the document, that [the first defendant] represented it to her as a deed of gift to Mr. Parkin and that [the plaintiff] executed it in the belief that that was what it was. I also find as a fact that [the plaintiff] had no idea that the document took the form of a conveyance on sale from her to [the first defendant] and that a sale or gift to him was something which she did not and would not for one moment have contemplated."

On this basis he gave judgment for the plaintiff, Mrs. Gallie. The building society appealed.

In the Court of Appeal (where the case was reported as *Gallie v. Lee*, [1969] 1 All E.R. 1062) a judgment was given by Lord Denning M.R. Lord Denning observed that the result reached by the trial judge would be most unjust for the effect would be to give Parkin, the nephew, Mrs. Gallie's house under her will free of any claims. Lord Denning then made a very full summary of the law and concluded:

"After all this long discussion, I would endeavour to state the principle. It seems to me to be this. Whenever a man of full age and understanding, who can read and write, signs a legal document which is put before him for signature — by which I mean a document which, it is apparent on the face of it, is intended to have legal consequences — then, if he does not take the trouble to read it but signs it as it is, relying on the word of another as to its character or contents or effect, he cannot be heard to say that it is not his document. By his conduct in signing it he has represented, to all those into whose hands it may come, that it is his document; and once they act on it as being his document, he cannot go back on it, and say that it was a nullity from the beginning. If his signature was obtained by fraud, or under the influence of mistake, or something of the kind, he may be able to avoid it up to a point — but not when it has come into the hands of one who has in all innocence advanced money on the faith of its being his document, or otherwise has relied on it as being his document.

"My brethren think that we are not at liberty to adopt this principle. It is contrary, they say, to previous authorities in this court. I do not agree. There is no case against it save *Carlisle and Cumberland Banking Co. v. Bragg*, [1911] 1 K.B. 489, and that is inconsistent with many others. It can, therefore, be disregarded. But even if there were authorities against it, they are only to be found in this court, and not in the House of Lords. We are, of course, bound by the decisions of the House, but I do not think we are bound by prior decisions of our own, or at any rate, not absolutely bound. We are not fettered as it was once thought. It was a self imposed limitation; and we who imposed it can also remove it. The House of Lords have done it. So why should not we do likewise? We should be just as free, no more and no less, to depart from a prior precedent of our own, as in like case in the House of Lords or a judge of first instance. It is very, very rare that we will go against a previous decision of our own, but if it is clearly shown to be erroneous, we should be able to put it right.

"I propose, therefore, to apply the principle which I have stated. In consonance with it, I am quite clear that the plaintiff cannot in this case say that the deed of assignment was not her deed. She signed it without reading it, relying on the assurance of the first defendant that it was a deed of gift to Mr. Parkin. It turned out to be a deed of assignment to the first defendant. But it was obviously a legal document. She signed it; and the building society advanced money on the faith of its being her document. She cannot now be allowed to disavow her signature.

"I would allow the appeal and enter judgment for the building society".

Russell and Salmon L.JJ. agreed in the result with Lord Denning. The Court of Appeal refused leave to appeal. The House of Lords gave leave. Mrs. Gallie died before the appeal and the action was maintained by her executrix. Lee took no part in the appeal. The House of Lords dismissed the appeal. Only the judgment of Lord Wilberforce is reproduced. The others agreed in the result.]

Lord Wilberforce. My Lords, the present case is fairly typical of many where a person, having signed and had witnessed his signature to a formal legal document, contends that the fact of signing should not bind him to the effect of it. Such situations, in many legal systems, are regulated by the requirement of execution before a notary who, if he is competent and honest, as he usually is, can do much to ensure that the signer understands and intends what he is doing. In other systems, such as ours, dependence has to be placed on the level of education and prudence of the signer and on the honesty and competence of his professional adviser. But as, inevitably, these controls are sometimes imperfect, the law must provide some measure of relief. In so doing it has two conflicting objectives: relief to a signer whose consent is genuinely lacking (I expand on this later); and protection to innocent third parties who have acted on an apparently regular and properly executed document. Because each of these factors may involve questions of degree or shading any rule of law must represent a compromise and must allow to the court some flexibility in application.

The plea of non est factum has a long history. In mediaeval times, when contracts were made by deeds, and the deed had a kind of life in the law of its own, illiterate people who either could not read, or could not understand, the language in which the deed was written, were allowed this plea (that is what 'non est factum' is — a plea); the result of it, if successful, was that the deed was not their deed. I think that three things can be said about the early law. First, that no definition was given of the nature or extent of the difference which must exist between what was intended and what was done — whether such as later appeared as the distinction between 'character' and 'contents' or otherwise. (See *Thoroughgood's Case, Thoroughgood v. Cole* (1582), 2 Co Rep 9a, when the decision was based on the reading of the deed 'in other words than in truth it is', and the sixteenth century case recorded in Keilwey — difference between one acre and two acres. See also the nineteenth century note C to *Whelpdale's Case* (1604), 5 Co Rep 119a, referring to the inconsistency of the cases: *Shulter's Case* (1611), 12 Co Rep 90 — of a man aged 115 years.) Secondly, these cases are for the most part as between the original parties to the deed, or if a third party is concerned (e g *Thoroughgood's Case*) he is a successor to the estate granted. Thirdly, there is some indication that the plea was not available where the signer had been guilty of a lack of care in signing what he did; there is no great precision in the definition of the disabling conduct. If Fleta is to be relied on, there was an exception of negligentia or imperitia — see Holdsworth.

In the nineteenth century, the emphasis had shifted toward the consensual contract, and the courts, probably unconscious of the fact, had a choice. They could either have discarded the whole doctrine on which non est factum was based, as obsolete, or they could try to adapt it to the prevailing structure of contract ('these cases apply to deeds; but the principle is equally applicable to other written contracts' — *Foster v. Mackinnon* (1869), LR 4 CP 704 at 712). They chose the course of adaptation, and, as in many other fields of the law this process of adaptation has not been logical, or led to a logical result. The modern version still contains some fossilised elements.

We had traced, in arguments at the bar, the emergence of the distinction, which has come to be made between a difference (of intention from result) of character, which may render a document void, and a difference of contents which at most makes it voidable. As it emerged it was expressed as being between the actual contents, on the one hand, and its legal effect on the other (see per Bayley B). Here 'actual contents' evidently means 'character'. In this form it was taken into the leading case of *Foster v. Mackinnon*. In the well-known passage from the judgment of the court, Byles J used the words 'to such a degree that the written contract is of a nature altogether different from the contract pretended to be read', and later in his conclusion: 'He was deceived, not merely as to the legal effect, but as to the *actual contents* of the instrument.' The language used may have been imperfect; but I think that the courts were groping for the test of what should enable a man to say that the document was not his document, his consent no consent, the contract no contract. It was really the language used in the second leading case of *Howatson v. Webb*, [1907] I Ch. 537, which has given rise to difficulty. There, in a judgment of Warrington J, which has carried much conviction and authority, we find that, although the judgment of Byles J in *Foster v Mackinnon* is quoted, the use of the word 'contents' is switched to mean what the deed actually (as a matter of detail) contains, and contrasted with what is called its legal character, 'The misrepresentation was as to the contents of the deed, and not as to the character and class of the deed'.

The distinction, as restated, is terminologically confusing and in substance illogical, as the judgments in the Court of Appeal demonstrate. On the one hand, it cannot be right that a document should be void through a mistake as to the label it bears, however little this mistake may be fundamental to what the signer intends; on the other hand, it is not satisfactory that the document should be valid if the mistake is merely as to what the document contains, however radical this mistake may be and however cataclysmic its result.

The existing test, or at least its terminology, may be criticised, but does it follow that there are no definable circumstances in which a document to which a man has put his signature may be held to be not his document, and so void rather than merely voidable? The judgment of Lord Denning MR seems at first sight to suggest that there are not and that the whole doctrine ought to be discarded, but a closer reading shows that he is really confining his observations to the plainest, and no doubt commonest, cases where a man of full understanding and capacity forbears, or negligently omits, to read what he has signed. That, in the present age, such a person should be denied the non est factum plea I would accept; so to hold follows in logical development from the well-known suggested question of Mellish LJ in *Hunter v Walters* (1871), 7 Ch App 75, and from what was said by Farwell LJ in *Howatson v Webb*. But there remains a residue of difficult cases. There are still illiterate or senile persons who cannot read, or apprehend, a legal document; there are still persons who may be tricked into putting their signature on a piece of paper which has legal consequences totally different from anything they intended. Certainly the first class may in some cases, even without the plea, be able to obtain relief, either because no third party has become involved, or, if he has, with the assistance of equitable doctrines, because the third party's interest is equitable only and his conduct such that his rights should be postponed (see *National Provincial Bank of England v Jackson* (1886), 33 Ch D 1 and cf *Hunter v Walters* (1871), 7 Ch

App at 89). Certainly, too, the second class may in some cases fall under the heading of plain forgery, in which event the plea of non est factum is not needed, or indeed available (cf *Swan v North British Australasian Co Ltd* (1863), 2 H & C 175) and in others be reduced if the signer is denied the benefit of the plea because of his negligence. But accepting all that has been said by learned judges as to the necessity of confining the plea within narrow limits, to eliminate it altogether would, in my opinion, deprive the courts of what may be, doubtless on sufficiently rare occasions, an instrument of justice.

How, then, ought the principle, on which a plea of non est factum is admissible, to be stated? In my opinion, a document should be held to be void (as opposed to voidable) only when the element of consent to it is totally lacking, i.e., more concretely, when the transaction which the document purports to effect is essentially different in substance or in kind from the transaction intended. Many other expressions or adjectives could be used — 'basically' or 'radically' or 'fundamentally'. In substance, the test does not differ from that which was applied in the leading cases of *Thoroughgood's Case* and *Foster v Mackinnon*, except in moving from the character/contents distinction to an area better understood in modern practice.

To this general test it is necessary to add certain amplifications. First, there is the case of fraud. The law as to this is best stated in the words of the judgment in *Foster v Mackinnon* where it is said that a signature obtained by fraud:

> '... is invalid not merely on the ground of fraud, where fraud exists, but on the ground that the mind of the signer did not accompany the signature; in other words, that he never intended to sign, and therefore in contemplation of law never did sign, the contract to which his name is appended.'

In other words, it is the lack of consent that matters, not the means by which this result was brought about. Fraud by itself may do no more than make the contract voidable.

Secondly, a man cannot escape from the consequences, as regards innocent third parties, of signing a document if, being a man of ordinary education and competence, he chooses to sign it without informing himself of its purport and effect. This principle is sometimes found expressed in the language that 'he is doing something with his estate' (*Hunter v Walters, Howatson v Webb*) but it really reflects a rule of common sense on the exigency of busy lives.

Thirdly, there is the case where the signer has been careless, in not taking ordinary precautions against being deceived. This is a difficult area. Until 1911 the law was reasonably clear; it had been stated plainly in *Foster v Mackinnon* that negligence — ie carelessness — might deny the signer the benefit of the plea. Since *Bragg's* case was decided in 1911 (*Carlisle and Cumberland Banking Co v Bragg*, [1911] 1 K.B. 489) the law has been that, except in relation to negotiable instruments, mere carelessness is not disabling; there must be negligence arising from a duty of care to the third person who ultimately relies on the document. It does not need much force to demolish this battered precedent. It is sufficient to point to two major defects in it. First, it confuses the kind of careless conduct which disentitles a man from denying the effect of his signature with such legal negligence as entitles a person injured to bring an action in tort. The two are quite different things in standard and scope. Secondly, the judgment proceeds on a palpable misunderstanding of the judgment in *Foster v Mackinnon*; for Byles J, so far from confining the relevance of negligence to negotiable instruments (as *Bragg's* case suggests),clearly thought that the signer of a negotiable instrument would be liable, negligence or no negligence, and that negligence was relevant in relation to documents other than negotiable instruments; e.g., (as in the actual case before him) to a guarantee.

In my opinion, the correct rule, and that which in fact prevailed until *Bragg's* case, is that, leaving aside negotiable instruments to which special rules may apply, a person who signs a document, and parts with it so that it may come into other hands, has a responsibility, that of the normal man of prudence, to take care what he signs, which, if neglected, prevents him from denying his liability under the document according to its tenor. I would add that the onus of proof in this matter rests on him, i.e., to prove that he acted carefully and not on the third party to prove the contrary. I consider therefore that *Carlisle and Cumberland Banking Co v Bragg* was wrong, both in the principle it states and in its decision, and that it should no longer be cited as an authority for any purpose.

The preceding paragraphs contemplate persons who are adult and literate: the conclusion as to such persons is that, while there are cases in which they may successfully plead non est factum, these cases will, in modern times, be rare. As to persons who are illiterate, or blind, or lacking in understanding, the law is in a dilemma. On the one hand, the law is traditionally, and rightly, ready to relieve them against hardship and imposition. On the other hand, regard has to be paid to the position of innocent third parties who cannot be expected, and often would have no means, to know the condition or status of the signer. I do not think that a defined solution can be provided for all cases. The law ought, in my opinion, to give relief if satisfied that consent was truly lacking but will require of signers even in this class that they act responsibly and carefully according to their circumstances in putting their signature to legal documents.

This brings me to the present case. The plaintiff was a lady of advanced age, but, as her evidence shows, by no means incapable physically or mentally. It certainly cannot be said that she did not receive sympathetic consideration or the benefit of much doubt from the judge as to the circumstances in which the assignment was executed. But accepting all of this, I am satisfied, with Russell LJ, that she fell short, very far short, of making the clear and satisfactory case which is required of those who seek to have a legal act declared void and of establishing a sufficient discrepancy between her intentions and her act. I am satisfied to adopt, without repetition, the analysis of the facts which appears in the judgment of Russell LJ as well as that of my noble and learned friend, Lord Pearson.

I would dismiss the appeal.

PROBLEM

Lear, an 80-year-old farmer, has a daughter Ophelia, who is a stock-broker. Lear's principal asset is his farm. Ophelia is anxious to make a quick fortune and needs to raise $100,000 in a hurry. She therefore induces her father to sign a document which she represents as an application for fire insurance. The document is, in fact, a mortgage of the farm to Lilly White Trust Co., who advance $100,000 to Ophelia. The money has been lost and the Trust Co. want to realize on their security.

What facts would each side have to prove to obtain judgment,

a)   if the law is as in *Prudential Trust v. Cugnet,*
b)   if the law is as in *Saunders v. Anglia?*
If the development of the law has been a continued expansion of the legally relevant, which decision represents the more developed stage in the law?
What is the law in Ontario?

The next case raises a common problem in mistake. The problem is, in part, caused by the common law rules in regard to property. An owner who has had a chattel stolen from him may bring an action in conversion against anyone who deals with the thing in a way inconsistent with the owner's right. The fact that the purchaser who is ultimately sued is an innocent third party (in full: a bona fide third party purchaser for value without notice) does not provide any defence. Where the goods have not been stolen but have been obtained through some kind of contract, the courts have had to decide which of two innocent parties must suffer for the fraud of a third party.

Many of the problems of the English law of mistake are caused by the fact that cases like *Lewis v. Averay* are put into the general heading of mistake. There it is said that a mistake of identity (e.g., A deals with B but thinks that B is C) makes the contract void. This fits in well with the mistake analysis in *Bell v. Levers* in terms of offer and acceptance, but it plays havoc with the development of a sensible approach to mistake. We saw in cases like *Saunders v. Anglia* how unwilling the courts are to give relief for mistake when the rights of a third party have intervened. This is what one would expect. Since this is also what one would expect in cases like *Lewis v. Averay*, Lord Denning's approach is much preferable to that of many of the cases he discusses. *Lewis v. Averay* therefore is another case where almost every argument points towards the denial of relief for mistake. The failure of the traditional analysis to realize the difference between the two and three party cases is one of its principal defects.

LEWIS v. AVERAY

[1971] 3 All E.R. 907. Court of Appeal; Lord Denning M.R., Phillimore and Megaw L.JJ.

Lord Denning MR. This is another case where one of two innocent persons has to suffer for the fraud of a third. It will no doubt interest students and find its place in the textbooks.

Mr Lewis is a young man who is a postgraduate student of chemistry. He lives at Clifton near Bristol. He had an Austin Cooper motor car. He decided to sell it. He put an advertisement in the newspaper offering it for £450. On 8th May 1969, in reply to the advertisement, a man — I will simply call him the 'rogue', for so he was — telephoned and asked if he could come and see the car. He did not give his name. He said he was speaking from Glamorganshire in Wales. Mr Lewis said that he could come and see it. He came in the the evening to Mr Lewis's flat. Mr Lewis showed him the car which was parked outside. The rogue drove it and tested it. He said that he liked it. They then went along to the flat of Mr Lewis's fiancée, Miss Kershaw (they have since married). He told them that he was Richard Green and talked much about the film world. He led both of them to believe that he was the well-known film actor, Richard Greene, who played Robin Hood in the 'Robin Hood' series. They talked about the car. He asked to see the log book. He was shown it and seemed satisfied. He said he would like to buy the car. They agreed a price of £450. The rogue wrote out a cheque for £450 on the Beckenham branch of the Midland Bank. He signed it 'R A Green'. He wanted to take the car at once. But Mr Lewis was not willing for him to have it until the cheque was cleared. To hold him off Mr Lewis said that there were one or two small jobs he would like to do on the car before letting him have it, and that would give time for the cheque to be cleared. The rogue said: 'Don't worry about those small jobs. I would like to take the car now.' Mr Lewis said: 'Have you anything to prove that you are Mr Richard Green?' The rogue thereupon brought out a special pass of admission to Pinewood Studios, which had an official stamp on it. It bore the name of Richard A Green and the address, and also a photograph which was plainly the photograph of this man, who was the rogue. On seeing this pass, Mr Lewis was satisfied. He thought that this man was really Mr Richard Greene, the film actor. By that time it was 11.00 pm. Mr Lewis took the cheque and let the rogue have the car and the log book and the Ministry of Transport test certificate. Each wrote and signed a receipt evidencing the transaction. Mr Lewis wrote:

> 'Received from
> Richard A Green
> 59 Marsh Rd,
> Beckenham
> Kent
> the sum of £450 in return for Austin Cooper "S" Reg No. AHT 484B chassis No. CA257—549597
>
> > Signed Keith Lewis.'

The rogue wrote: 'Received log-book No. 771835 and M.O.T. for Mini Cooper "S" No. AHT 484B R A Green.'

Next day, 9th May 1969, Mr Lewis put the cheque into the bank. A few days later the bank told him it was worthless. The rogue had stolen a cheque book and written this £450 on a stolen cheque.

Meanwhile, whilst the cheque was going through, the rogue sold the car to an innocent purchaser. He sold it to a young man called Mr Averay. He was at the time under 21. He was a music student in London at the Royal College of Music. His parents live at Bromley. He was keen to buy a car. He put an advertisement in the Exchange and Mart, seeking a car for £200. In answer he had a telephone call from the rogue. He said that he was speaking from South Wales. He said that he was coming to London to sell a car. Mr Averay arranged to meet him on 11th May 1969. The rogue came with the car. Young Mr Averay liked it, but wanted to get the approval of his parents. They drove it to Bromley. The parents did approve. Young Mr Averay agreed to buy it for £200. The rogue gave his name as Mr Lewis. He handed over the car and log book to young Mr Averay. The log book showed the owner as Mr Lewis. In return Mr Averay, in entire good faith, gave the rogue a cheque for £200. The rogue signed this receipt:

> 'Sale of Cooper S to A. J. Averay. Received £200 for the Cooper S Registration No. AHT 484B, the said car being my property absolutely, there being no hire-

purchase charges outstanding or other impediment to selling the car.

Signed Keith Lewis
May 13th 1969.'

A fortnight later, on 29th May 1969, Mr Averay wanted the workshop manual for the car. So his father on his behalf wrote to the name and address of the seller as given in the log book, that is, to Mr Lewis. Then, of course, the whole story came to light. The rogue had cashed the cheque and disappeared. The police have tried to trace him, but without success.

Now Mr Lewis, the original owner of the car, sues young Mr Avery. Mr Lewis claims that the car is still his. He claims damages for conversion. The judge found in favour of Mr Lewis and awarded damages of £330 for conversion.

The real question in the case is whether on 8th May 1969 there was a contract of sale under which the property in the car passed from Mr Lewis to the rogue. If there was such a contract, then even though it was voidable for fraud, nevertheless Mr Averay would get a good title to the car. But if there was no contract of sale by Mr Lewis to the rogue — either because there was, on the face of it, no agreement between the parties, or because any apparent agreement was a nullity and void ab initio for mistake, then no property would pass from Mr Lewis to the rogue. Mr Averay would not get a good title because the rogue had no property to pass to him.

There is no doubt that Mr Lewis was mistaken as to the identity of the person who handed him the cheque. He thought that he was Richard Greene, a film actor of standing and worth; whereas in fact he was a rogue whose identity is quite unknown. It was under the influence of that mistake that Mr Lewis let the rogue have the car. He would not have dreamed of letting him have it otherwise.

What is the effect of this mistake? There are two cases in our books which cannot, to my mind, be reconciled the one with the other. One of them is *Phillips v Brooks*, [1919] 2 K.B. 243, where a jeweller had a ring for sale. The other is *Ingram v Little*, [1961] 1 Q.B. 31, where two ladies had a car for sale. In each case the story is very similar to the present. A plausible rogue comes along. The rogue says that he likes the ring, or the car, as the case may be. He asks the price. The seller names it. The rogue says that he is prepared to buy it at that price. He pulls out a cheque book. He writes or prepares to write, a cheque for the price. The seller hesitates. He has never met this man before. He does not want to hand over the ring or the car not knowing whether the cheque will be met. The rogue notices the seller's hesitation. He is quick with his next move. He says to the jeweller, in *Phillips v Brooks*: 'I am Sir George Bullough of 11 St. James' Square; or to the ladies in *Ingram v Little*: 'I am P. G. M. Hutchinson of Stanstead House, Stanstead Road, Caterham'; or to Mr Lewis in the present case: 'I am Richard Greene, the film actor of the Robin Hood series'. Each seller checks up the information. The jeweller looks up in the directory and finds there is a Sir George Bullough at 11 St James's Square. The ladies check up too. They look at the telephone directory and find there is a 'P. G. M. Hutchinson of Stanstead House, Stanstead Road, Caterham'. Mr Lewis checks up too. He examines the official pass of the Pinewood Studios and finds that it is a pass for 'Richard A. Green' to the Pinewood Studios with this man's photograph on it. In each case the seller feels that this is sufficient confirmation of the man's identity. So he accepts the cheque signed by the rogue and lets him have the ring, in the one case, and the car and log book in the other two cases. The rogue goes off and sells the goods to a third person who buys them in entire good faith and pays the price to the rogue. The rogue disappears. The original seller presents the cheque. It is dishonoured. Who is entitled to the goods? The original seller or the ultimate buyer? The courts have given different answers. In *Phillips v Brooks Ltd* the ultimate buyer was held to be entitled to the ring. In *Ingram v Little* the original seller was held to be entitled to the car. In the present case the deputy county court judge has held the original seller entitled.

It seems to me that the material facts in each case are quite indistinguishable the one from the other. In each case there was, to all outward appearance, a contract; but there was a mistake by the seller as to the identity of the buyer. This mistake was fundamental. In each case it led to the handing over of the goods. Without it the seller would not have parted with them.

This case therefore raises the question: what is the effect of a mistake by one party as to the identity of the other? It has sometimes been said that, if a party makes a mistake as to the identity of the person with whom he is contracting, there is no contract, or, if there is a contract, it is a nullity and void, so that no property can pass under it. This has been supported by a reference to the French jurist Pothier; but I have said before, and I repeat now, his statement is no part of English law. I know that it was quoted by Viscount Haldane in *Lake v Simmons,* [1927] A.C. 487 at 501, and as such, misled Tucker J in *Sowler v Potter,* [1940] 1 K.B. 271 into holding that a lease was void whereas it was really voidable. But the statement by Pothier has given rise to such refinements that it is time it was dead and buried altogether.

For instance, in *Ingram v Little* the majority of the court suggested that the difference between *Phillips v Brooks* and *Ingram v Little* was that in *Phillips v Brooks* the contract of sale was concluded (so as to pass the property to the rogue) before the rogue made the fraudulent misrepresentation, whereas in *Ingram v Little* the rogue made the fraudulent misrepresentation before the contract was concluded. My own view is that in each case the property in the goods did not pass until the seller let the rogue have the goods.

Again it has been suggested that a mistake as to the identity of a person is one thing; and a mistake as to his attributes is another. A mistake as to identity, it is said, avoids a contract; whereas a mistake as to attributes does not. But this is a distinction without a difference. A man's very name is one of his attributes. It is also a key to his identity. If then, he gives a false name, is it a mistake as to his identity? or a mistake as to his attributes? These fine distinctions do no good to the law.

As I listened to the argument in this case, I felt it wrong that an innocent purchaser (who knew nothing of what passed between the seller and the rogue) should have his title depend on such refinements. After all, he has acted with complete circumspection and in entire good faith; whereas it was the seller who let the rogue have the goods and thus enabled him to commit the fraud. I do not, therefore, accept the theory that a mistake as to identity renders a contract void.

I think the true principle is that which underlies the decision of this court in *King's Norton Metal Co Ltd v Eldridge, Merrett & Co Ltd* and of Horridge J in *Phillips v Brooks Ltd.*, which has stood for these last 50 years. It is this:

when two parties have come to a contract — or rather what appears, on the face of it, to be a contract — the fact that one party is mistaken as to the identity of the other does not mean that there is no contract, or that the contract is a nullity and void from the beginning. It only means that the contract is voidable, that is, liable to be set aside at the instance of the mistaken person, so long as he does so before third parties have in good faith acquired rights under it.

Applied to the cases such as the present, this principle is in full accord with the presumption stated by Pearce LJ and also by Devlin LJ in *Ingram v Little*. When a dealing is had between a seller like Mr Lewis and a person who is actually there present before him, then the presumption in law is that there is a contract, even though there is a fraudulent impersonation by the buyer representing himself as a different man than he is. There is a contract made with the very person there, who is present in person. It is liable no doubt to be avoided for fraud but it is still a good contract under which title will pass unless and until it is avoided. In support of that presumption, Devlin LJ quoted, not only the English case of *Phillips v Brooks,* but other cases in the United States where:

'The Courts hold that if A appeared in person before B, impersonating C, an innocent purchaser from A gets the property in the goods against B.'

That seems to me to be right in principle in this country also.

In this case Mr Lewis made a contract of sale with the very man, the rogue, who came to the flat. I say that he 'made a contract' because in this regard we do not look into his intentions, or into his mind to know what he was thinking or into the mind of the rogue. We look to the outward appearances. On the face of the dealing, Mr Lewis made a contract under which he sold the car to the rogue, delivered the car and the log book to him, and took a cheque in return. The contract is evidenced by the receipts which were signed. It was, of course, induced by fraud. The rogue made false representations as to his identity. But it was still a contract, though voidable for fraud. It was a contract under which this property passed to the rogue, and in due course passed from the rogue to Mr Averay, before the contract was avoided.

Altough I very much regret that either of these good and reliable gentlemen should suffer, in my judgment it is Mr Lewis who should do so. I think the appeal should be allowed and judgment entered for the defendant.

Phillimore LJ. I share the regret expressed by Lord Denning MR. I think that the law was conveniently stated by Pearce LJ, in the course of his judgment in *Ingram v Little,* to which reference has already been made. He said this:

'Each case must be decided on its own facts. The question in such cases is this, Has it been sufficiently shown in the particular circumstances that, contrary to the prima facie presumption [and I would emphasise those words], a party was not contracting with the physical person to whom he uttered the offer, but with another individual whom (to the other party's knowledge) he believed to be the physical person present. The answer to that question is a finding of fact.'

Now, in that particular case the Court of Appeal, by a majority and in the very special and unusual facts of the case, decided that it had been sufficiently shown in the particular circumstances that, contrary to the prima facie presumption, the lady who was selling the motor car was not dealing with the person actually present. But in the present case I am bound to say that I do not think that there was anything which could displace the prima facie presumption that Mr Lewis was dealing with the gentleman present there in the flat — the rogue. It seems to me that when, at the conclusion of the transaction, the car was handed over, the log book was handed over, the cheque was accepted and the receipts were given, it is really impossible to say that a contract had not been made. I think this case really is on all fours with *Phillips v Brooks Ltd,* which has been good law for over 50 years. True the contract was induced by fraud, and Mr Lewis, when he discovered that he had been defrauded, was entitled to avoid it; but in the meanwhile the rogue had parted with the property in this motor car which he had obtained to Mr Averay, who bought it bona fide without any notice of the fraud, and accordingly he thereby, as I think, acquired a good title. This action was in my judgment one which was bound to fail. I think the judge was wrong in the decision to which he came and this appeal must be allowed.

Megaw LJ. For myself, with very great respect, I find it difficult to understand the basis, either in logic or in practical considerations, of the test laid down by the majority of the court in *Ingram v Little.* That test is I think accurately recorded in the headnote:

'... where a person physically present and negotiating to buy a chattel fraudulently assumed the identity of an existing third person, the test to determine to whom the offer was addressed was how ought the promisee to have interpreted the promise...'

The promisee, be it noted, is the rogue. The question of the existence of a contract and therefore the passing of property, and therefore the right of third parties, if this test is correct, is made to depend on the view which some rogue should have formed, presumably knowing that he is a rogue, as to the state of mind of the opposite party, to the negotiation, who does not know that he is dealing with a rogue.

However that may be, and assuming that the test as so stated is indeed valid, in my view this appeal can be decided on a short and simple point. It is the point which was put at the outset of his argument by counsel for the defendant. The well-known textbook on the Law of Contract, Cheshire and Fifoot, deals with the question of invalidity of a contract by virtue of unilateral mistake, and in particular unilateral mistake relating to mistaken identity. The learned editors describe what in their submission are certain facts that must be established in order to enable one to avoid contract on the basis of unilateral mistake by him as to the identity of the opposite party. The first of those facts is that at the time when he made the offer he regarded the identity of the offeree as a matter of vital importance. To translate that into the facts of the present case, it must be established that at the time of offering to sell his car to the rogue, Mr Lewis regarded the identity of the rogue as a matter of vital importance. In my view, counsel for the defendant is abundantly justified, on the notes of the evidence and on the findings of the learned judge, in his submission that the mistake of Mr Lewis went no further than a mistake as to the attributes of the rogue. It was simply a mistake as to the creditworthiness of the man who was there present and who described himself as Mr Green. I should say that I think that the learned judge may possibly have been to some extent misled, because he seems to have assumed that the evidence given by the lady who is now Mrs Lewis and who was then Mr Lewis's fiancée was of some assistance. The learned judge refers in many places to 'they saw' or 'they thought'. That is all very well, if there were evidence that Mr Lewis himself heard or knew the same things as his fiancée heard or knew, or if she, having heard, for example, the name of Mr Green when he first arrived, had mentioned that fact to Mr Lewis. But there was no such evidence, and therefore all that the learned judge recites about what Miss Kershaw heard and thought appears to me, with great respect, not to assist in this matter. When one looks at the evidence of Mr Lewis himself, it is, I think, clear, as counsel for the defendant submits, that there was not here any evidence that would justify the finding that he, Mr Lewis, regarded the identity of the man who called himself Mr Green as a matter of vital importance.

I agree that the appeal should be allowed.

Appeal allowed.

The cases discussed by Lord Denning in *Lewis v. Averay* were, as he indicated, hard to reconcile. It was said, for example, that a mistake as to identity makes the contract void (with the result that the owner can sue the innocent purchaser) while a mistake as to attributes makes it voidable only (so that the innocent purchaser can keep the thing). This is justified in conceptual terms by saying that A cannot accept an offer which he knows is made to B, and so in such a case there can be no contract. Yet if A has merely represented that he has credit where, in fact, he has none, then a contract can be formed. As Lord Denning said, "These fine distinctions do no good to the law." It is hard to see where the distinction would be really useful. A valiant attempt to explain and justify the conflicting decisions is made by Côté, *An Introduction to the Law of Contract*, pp. 137, 138, where he says:

"Error as to the identity of one or both the parties makes the purported contract a complete nullity.

"Giving effect to that rule where it is applicable is easy; what is difficult is to know when it applies. What is the difference between error of identity making a contract void, and error as to mere attributes which does not? At first we all think we know what we mean by a man's identity, but the more one pursues its exact meaning the more elusive it becomes. To a considerable extent the difference between identity and attributes is one of degree, but it is still a real difference even then, for ten hairs do not make a beard. And apart from that there is a further distinction for many people are alike in appearance and temperament without being the same person. What motivates a person to deal with one entity or identity and not another may well be one or a number of that other person's attributes, such as good reputation or solvency, but his motives and his intent to deal or not deal are not the same thing. The basic problem therefore is to distinguish one who intended to deal only with a certain other person, from one who intended to deal with anyone possessing certain attributes. That test is all the more difficult to apply because the distinction is one which hardly ever can have been present in the mind of the person mistaken. The crux of the matter is that he was confused, and his mental state hard to unravel.

"It has been persuasively argued that the only true distinction is confusion of two entities. It is said that the error is merely one as to attributes unless one can point out two distinct entities, the one the other party intended to deal with, and the one he in fact dealt with instead. If that test is not satisfied, it is said that the "victim" had only one person in mind, the person with whom he dealt, even though he may have thought he had a name and attributes very different from what he in fact had.

"That test appears to be basically correct..."

QUESTIONS

1. To what extent is Lord Denning, in rejecting the kind of analysis put forward by Côté, moving towards a solution similar to that reached in *Saunders v. Anglia*?

2. Do the following provisions of The Sale of Goods Act offer any useful analogy:

25. (1) Where a person having sold goods continues or is in possession of the goods or of the documents of title to the goods, the delivery of transfer by that person, or by a mercantile agent acting for him, of the goods or documents of title under a sale, pledge or other disposition thereof to a person receiving the goods or documents of title in good faith and without notice of the previous sale, has the same effect as if the person making the delivery or transfer were expressly authorized by the owner of the goods to make the delivery or transfer.

(2) Where a person having bought or agreed to buy goods obtains, with the consent of the seller, possession of the goods or the documents of title to the goods, the delivery or transfer by that person, or by a mercantile agent acting for him, of the goods or documents of title, under a sale, pledge or other disposition thereof to a person receiving the goods or documents of title in good faith and without notice of any lien or other right of the original seller in respect of the goods, has the same effect as if the person making the delivery or transfer were a mercantile agent in possession of the goods or documents of title with the consent of the owner.

(3) Subject to subsection 5, subsection 2 does not apply to goods the possession of which has been obtained by a buyer under a security agreement whereby the seller retains a security interest within the meaning of The Personal Property Security Act, and the rights of the parties shall be determined by that Act.

(4) In this section, "mercantile agent" means a mercantile agent having, in the customary course of his business as such agent, authority either to sell goods or to consign goods for the purpose of sale, or to buy goods, or to raise money on the security of goods.

NOTE

The effect of a delivery or transfer by a mercantile agent in possession of the goods with the consent of the owner is governed by The Factors Act, R.S.O. 1970, c. 156, which provides:

2. — (1) Where a mercantile agent is, with the consent of the owner, in possession of goods or of the documents of title to goods, a sale, pledge or other disposition of the goods made by him when acting in the ordinary course of business of a mercantile agent is, subject to this Act, as valid as if he were expressly authorized by the owner of the goods to make the disposition, if the person taking under it acts in good faith and has not at the time thereof notice that the person making it has not authority to make it.

(4) For the purposes of this Act, the consent of the owner shall be presumed in the absence of evidence to the contrary.

A NOTE ON SECURED TRANSACTIONS

When a buyer cannot afford to pay for what he wants to buy, he may be able to borrow money from another to pay the seller. The lender may wish to keep title to the thing bought so that he may have some security for the loan. The typical mortgage of real estate is such a case. The same arrangement can be made with regard to chattels. The buyer gets possession of the chattel — that is, after all, why he wants to buy the thing — and the lender has title. A buyer in such a position, because he has possession, can have the appearance of ownership. Cases where a buyer has sold the thing to a third party have been problems for years.

In Ontario, a lender who wants to protect his interest in the thing would have to register his interest in it under The Personal Property Security Act, R.S.O. 1970, c. 344, to protect himself from the claims of third party purchasers. That Act provides in s. 9:

> Except as otherwise provided by this or any other Act, a security agreement [meaning an agreement that creates or provides for a security interest] is effective according to its terms between the parties to it and against third parties.

The Act goes on to provide that the security interest is only effective against third parties when the lender either has possession of the collateral or has registered the agreement.

The Sale of Goods Act provides that the P.P.S.A. governs cases that would otherwise come under s. 25(2). Registration of the security interest under the P.P.S.A. is deemed to give notice to subsequent purchasers of the claim of the secured party. Failure to comply with the P.P.S.A. has the effect of leaving the rights of the parties to be decided by s. 25(2) of The Sale of Goods Act.

Cases that come under s. 25(1) of The Sale of Goods Act can also come under The Bills of Sale Act, R.S.O. 1970, c. 44. The operative section of that Act is:

> 3. Every sale of goods, not accompanied by an immediate delivery and followed by an actual and continued change of possession of the goods sold, shall be evidenced by a writing signed by the seller, and such writing is a bill of sale under this Act, and such bill of sale, accompanied by an affidavit of an attesting witness thereto of the due execution of the bill of sale and an affidavit of the buyer that the sale is bona fide and for good consideration, as set forth in the bill of sale, and not for the purpose of holding or enabling the buyer to hold the goods mentioned therein against the creditors of the seller, shall be registered as provided by this Act; otherwise the sale is void as against the creditors of the seller and as against subsequent buyers and mortgagees in good faith.

A buyer who wishes to protect himself from the consequences of a sale that would come under s. 25(1) must comply with The Bills of Sale Act to do so.

The English method of financing is known as "hire-purchase". The form of the transaction is a lease of the thing. The "rent" includes part of the purchase price and a financing charge. There is no system of registration in England. The form of the transaction in Ontario does not matter: the P.P.S.A. applies to a lease where that is used for the purposes of maintaining a security interest.

It is interesting to note the following provisions of the Civil Code of Quebec:

> Article 1487. The sale of a thing which does not belong to the seller is null, subject to the exceptions declared in the three next following articles. The buyer may recover damages of the seller, if he were ignorant that the thing did not belong to the latter.
>
> Article 1488. The sale is valid if it be a commercial matter, or if the seller afterwards become owner of the thing.
>
> Article 1489. If a thing lost or stolen be bought in good faith in a fair or market, or at a public sale, or from a trader dealing in similar articles, the owner cannot reclaim it, without reimbursing to the purchaser the price he has paid for it.

Article 1490. If the thing lost or stolen be sold under the authority of law, it cannot be reclaimed.

There have been other attempts to get around the distinction between void and voidable contracts upon which the cases rest.

Devlin L.J. (as he then was) in *Ingram v. Little*, [1961] 1 Q.B. 31 said in a strong dissenting judgment:

> "There can be no doubt, as all this difference of opinion shows, that the dividing line between voidness and voidability, between fundamental mistake and incidental deceit, is a very fine one. That a fine and difficult distinction has to be drawn is not necessarily any reproach to the law. But need the rights of the parties in a case like this depend on such a distinction? The great virtue of the common law is that it sets out to solve legal problems by the application to them of principles which the ordinary man is expected to recognise as sensible and just; their application in any particular case may produce what seems to him a hard result, but as principles they should be within his understanding and merit his approval. But here, contrary to its habit, the common law, instead of looking for a principle that is simple and just, rests on theoretical distinctions. Why should the question whether the defendant should or should not pay the plaintiff damages for conversion depend upon voidness or voidability, and upon inferences to be drawn from a conversation in which the defendant took no part? The true spirit of the common law is to override theoretical distinctions when they stand in the way of doing practical justice. For the doing of justice, the relevant question in this sort of case is not whether the contract was void or voidable, but which of two innocent parties shall suffer for the fraud of a third. The plain answer is that the loss should be divided between them in such proportion as is just in all the circumstances. If it be pure misfortune, the loss should be borne equally; if the fault or imprudence of either party has caused or contributed to the loss, it should be borne by that party in the whole or in the greater part. In saying this, I am suggesting nothing novel, for this sort of observation has often been made. But it is only in comparatively recent times that the idea of giving to a court power to apportion loss has found a place in our law. I have in mind particularly the Law Reform Acts of 1935, 1943 and 1945, that dealt respectively with joint tortfeasors, frustrated contracts and contributory negligence. These statutes, which I believe to have worked satisfactorily, show a modern inclination towards a decision based on a just apportionment rather than one given in black or in white according to the logic of the law. I believe it would be useful if Parliament were now to consider whether or not it is practicable by means of a similar act of law reform to provide for the victims of a fraud a better way of adjusting their mutual loss than that which has grown out of the common law."

QUESTIONS

1. Suppose that the rogue in *Lewis v. Averay* had stolen the car from the plaintiff,
   (a)   could Lord Denning have handled the case in the same way; or,
   (b)   should Lord Denning have done so?
2. Suppose that the person in the position of Averay when the car had been stolen, spent £200 in fixing up the car, is there any way in which he can be protected?
3. What is to stop the court from apportioning the loss? Again, refer to Landis, *Statutes and the Sources of Law* (*infra.* Chap. 8).
4. To what extent do the cases similar to *Lewis v. Avery*, forward, ignore, or frustrate the approach of the law that is indicated in the Sale of Goods Act as it applies to these problems?
5. To what extent should reform of the law in this area come by statute or by court decisions? What are the features of each method of law-making that bear on this question?

CHAPTER 5

THE EFFECT OF NON-PERFORMANCE BY THE PLAINTIFF

The focus of this chapter is on those situations where the party suing for breach of contract has not performed that which the contract required him to do. The cases cover a range of situations from those where the plaintiff's failure to perform gives the defendant an excuse for his non-performance to those where the defendant's breach gives the plaintiff an excuse for his non-performance. We will also have to deal with the cases where, even though the plaintiff has not performed and he has no excuse, it is felt that he should nevertheless have a remedy.

A. Excuses for the Defendant's Non-Performance: Herein of Conditions.

(1) The Effect of Express Conditions

Up to now we have been principally concerned with promises. One party promises to do something for another and does not do so, and is then sued for damages for breach. Suppose that A and B are negotiating over the purchase and sale of a house. A may agree to buy from B if he is able to sell his present house. A may not be prepared to make an unequivocal promise to B since he has only partial control over the sale of his own house, and to promise to buy B's house before he has sold his own might be unwise. A may therefore want to make the purchase of B's house *conditional* on the sale of his own. The sale of A's house may, therefore, be said to be a condition of the contract between A and B. The term condition may be used to refer to a state of events, the existence or non existence of which will have some operative legal consequence on the duties of the parties to a contract. The term "express condition", "refers to an *explicit contractual provision* which provides either: (1) that a party to the contract is not obliged to perform one or more of his duties thereunder unless some state of events occurs or fails to occur; or (2) that *if* some state of events occurs or fails to occur, the obligation of a party to perform one or more of his duties thereunder is suspended or terminated." (Fuller and Eisenberg, p. 664.)

The event referred to may lie within the control of one party or it may not. If it does not, the party may be expected to make its occurrence or non-occurrence a condition. Thus A may be most unwilling to leave the sale of his present house as an irrelevant matter in the contract he makes with B. Similarly if, in the same example, it is important to A that a change in the zoning of the land be made, he may want to make that change a condition, since B would usually be most unwilling to promise that the change would be made, and without the change the price that A would be prepared to pay would be far lower. The use of conditions is, therefore, a very important tool for the person drafting contracts. It is easy to see how one side, by making some act of the other a *condition* of any obligation of his own, may insulate himself somewhat from the hazards of an action for damages for breach.

PYM v. CAMPBELL

(1856), 6 El. & Bl. 370, 119 E.R. 903, Queen's Bench; Lord Campbell C.J., Erle and Crompton JJ.

[The defendants agreed to purchase from the plaintiff for £800, three-eights parts of the benefits to accrue from an invention of the plaintiff's. The agreement was contained in a written document. It was proved that the plaintiff orally agreed to allow his "crushing, washing and amalgamating machine" to be inspected by two engineers appointed by the defendants. One engineer approved the machine, the other did not. The defendants thereupon declined to proceed with the deal. The plaintiff sued on the written agreement. The defendants pleaded the oral arrangement. The jury found a verdict for the defendants. The plaintiff obtained a rule *nisi*.]

Erle J. I think that this rule ought to be discharged. The point made is that this is a written agreement, absolute on the face of it, and that evidence was admitted to shew it was conditional: and if that had been so it would have been wrong. But I am of opinion that the evidence shewed that in fact there was never any agreement at all. The production of a paper purporting to be an agreement by a party, with his signature attached, affords a strong presumption that it is his written agreement; and, if in fact he did sign the paper animo contrahendi, the terms contained in it are conclusive, and cannot be varied by parol evidence: but in the present case the defence begins one step earlier: the parties met and expressly stated to each other that, though for convenience they would then sign the memorandum of the terms, yet they were not to sign it as an agreement until Abernethie was consulted. I grant the risk that such a defence may be set up without ground; and I agree that a jury should therefore always look on such a defence with suspicion: but, if it be proved that in fact the paper was signed with the express intention that it should not be an agreement, the other party cannot fix it as an agreement upon those so signing. The distinction in point of law is that evidence to vary the terms of an agreement in writing is not admissible, but evidence to shew that there is not an agreement at all is admissible.

Crompton J. I also think that the point in this case was properly left to the jury. If the parties had come to an agreement, though subject to a condition not shewn in the agreement, they could not shew the condition, because the agreement on the face of the writing would have been absolute, and could not be varied: but the finding of the jury is that this paper was signed on the terms that it was to be an agreement if Abernethie approved of the invention, not otherwise. I know of no rule of law to estop parties from shewing that a paper, purporting to be a signed agreement, was in fact signed by mistake, or that it was signed on the terms that it should not be an agreement till money was paid, or something else done. When the instrument is under seal it cannot be a deed until there is a delivery; and when there is a delivery that estops the parties to the deed; that is a technical reason why a deed cannot be delivered as an escrow to the other party. But parol contracts, whether by word of mouth or in writing, do not estop. There is no distinction between them, except that where there is a writing it is the record of the contract...

[T]he parties may not vary a written agreement; but they may shew that they never came to an agreement at all, and that the signed paper was never intended to be the record of the terms of the agreement; for they never had agreeing minds. Evidence to shew that does not vary an agreement, and is admissible.

Lord Campbell C.J. I agree. No addition to or variation from the terms of a written contract can be made by parol: but in this case the defence was that there never was any agreement entered into. Evidence to that effect was admissible; and the evidence given in this case was overwhelming. It was proved in the most satisfactory manner that before the paper was signed it was explained to the plaintiff that the defendants did not intend the paper to be an agreement till Abernethie had been consulted, and found to approve of the invention; and that the paper was signed before he was seen only because it was not convenient to the defendants to remain. The plaintiff assented to this, and received the writing on those terms. That being proved, there was no agreement.

(Wightman J., not having heard the whole argument, gave no opinion.)

Rule discharged.

TURNEY v. ZHILKA

[1959] S.C.R. 578. Supreme Court of Canada; Taschereau, Locke, Cartwright, Martland and Judson JJ.

[Zhilka agreed to purchase property from Turney, "Providing the property can be annexed to the Village of Streetsville and a plan is approved by the Village Council for subdivision."

Neither party agreed to fulfil this condition and neither party expressly reserved a power of waiver.

Zhilka made some enquiries of the Village Council but made little progress and received little encouragement, and the prospects of annexation were, on the evidence, remote. Later, Zhilka purported to waive this condition on the ground that it was solely for his benefit and was severable, and he sued for specific performance without reference to the condition.]

Judson J.: The learned trial judge found that the condition was one introduced for the sole benefit of the purchaser and that he could waive it.

I have doubts whether this inference may be drawn from the evidence adduced in this case, but, in any event, the defence falls to be decided on broader grounds. The cases on which the judgment is founded are *Hawksley v. Outram*, [1892] 3 Ch. 359, and *Morrell v. Studd*, [1913] 2 Ch. 648. In the first case a purchaser of a business stipulated in the contract of sale that he should have the right to carry on under the old name and that the vendors would not compete within a certain area. A dispute arose whether one of the vendors, who had signed the contract of sale under a power of attorney from another, had acted within his power. The purchaser then said that he would waive these rights and successfully sued for specific performance. In the second case, the contract provided that the purchaser should pay a certain sum on completion and the balance within two years. He also promised to secure the balance to the vendor's satisfaction. The purchaser raised difficulties about the performance of this promise, and the vendor said that he would waive it and take the purchaser's unsecured promise. It was held that he was entitled to do so. All that waiver means in these circumstances is that one party to a contract may forego a promised advantage or may dispense with part of the promised performance of the other party which is simply and solely for the benefit of the first party and is severable from the rest of the contract.

But here there is no right to be waived. The obligations under the contract, on both sides, depend upon a future uncertain event, the happening of which depends entirely on the will of a third party — the Village council. This is a true condition precedent — an external condition upon which the existence of the obligation depends. Until the event occurs there is no right to performance on either side. The parties have not promised that it will occur. In the absence of such a promise there can be no breach of contract until the event does occur. The purchaser now seeks to make the vendor liable on his promise to convey in spite of the non-performance of the condition and this to suit his own convenience only. This is not a case of renunciation or relinquishment of a right but rather an attempt by one party, without the consent of the other, to write a new contract. Waiver has often been referred to as a troublesome and uncertain term in the law but it does at least presuppose the existence of a right to be relinquished.

[The action was dismissed with costs.]

BEAUCHAMP ET AL. v. BEAUCHAMP ET AL.

(1973), 2 O.R. 43. Court of Appeal.

The judgment of the Court was delivered orally by

Gale, C.J.O.: — On April 13, 1971, the appellants signed an offer to purchase certain lands in the Township of Gloucester for the sum of $15,500 in cash. I emphasize that the purchasers were to pay cash and nothing else, in the form of a deposit of $500, and the balance on closing. The closing was to take place on July 1st. The agreement also had the following condition included in it:

> This sale is conditional for a period of 15 days from date of acceptance of same upon the Purchaser or his Agent being able to obtain a first mortgage in the amount of Ten Thousand Dollars ($10,000.00) bearing interest at the current rate otherwise, this offer shall be null and void and all deposit monies shall be returned to the Purchaser without interest or any other charge. This offer is also conditional for a period of 15 days from date of acceptance of same upon the Purchaser or his Agent being able to secure a second mortgage in the amount of $2,500.00 for a period of five (5) years, bearing interest at the current rate, otherwise, this offer shall be null and void and all deposit monies returned to the Purchaser without interest or any other charge.

The appellants were able to arrange for a first mortgage of $12,000 and, on April 28, 1971, as found by the trial Judge, they caused a notice in the following form to be delivered to the respondents:

> This is to notify you that the condition specified on the agreement of purchase and sale between Mr. Vianney Beauchamp and Carmen Beauchamp herein called the Vendors and Mr. Ronald Beauchamp and Pauline Beauchamp herein called the Purchasers has been met. The transaction will therefore close as per the agreement.

The Judge also found that there was an anticipatory breach by the respondents which excused the appellants from the need to make formal tender. However, he dismissed the appellant's action for specific performance, holding that the respondents were excused from completing the sale on the ground that the condition which I have quoted was a condition precedent which had not been strictly complied with by the appellants' arranging of a first mortgage of $10,000 and a second mortgage of $2,500.

We point out, as did the trial Judge, that the condition was solely for the protection of the appellants, and all the respondents were interested in was receiving the sum of $15,500 in cash. The notice to which I have referred brought home to the respondents the fact that payment of the $15,500 in cash would be made and that the appellants had met the condition referred to in the offer, or, alternatively, were waiving it.

In those circumstances, we are of the view that the learned trial Judge erred in declining to order specific performance. Counsel for the respondents relied upon the cases of *Turney et al. v. Zhilka*, [1959] S.C.R. 578, 18 D.L.R. (2d) 447, and *Aldercrest Developments Ltd. v. Hunter et al.*, [1970] 2 O.R. 562, 11 D.L.R. (3d) 439, for the proposition that a true condition precedent cannot be waived, even though it is in favour of one party only and the fulfilment of the condition is completely within the control of that one party. We do not think that those cases are appropriate to the circumstances here; they are distinguishable, as the condition herein is not such as is dealt with in those cases.

The appeal will therefore be allowed and judgment given for specific performance, with costs to the appellants throughout.

Appeal allowed.

[An appeal to the Supreme Court of Canada was dismissed without hearing the respondents' arguments. The court consisted of Laskin C.J.C., Martland, Judson, Spence and Dickson JJ. See (1974), 40 D.L.R. (3d) 160.]

QUESTION

Why was the condition in *Beauchamp* not "such as [was] dealt with" in *Turney* (*supra*)?

BARNETT v. HARRISON

(1975), 57 D.L.R. (3d) 225. Supreme Court of Canada; Laskin C.J.C., Martland, Judson, Ritchie, Spence, Pigeon, Dickson, Beetz and de Grandpré JJ.

[An agreement for the purchase by Barnett of lands owned by Harrison contained the following clause:

If this offer is accepted by the vendors, the contract of purchase and sale will be subject to the condition that the necessary approvals of the Ontario Municipal Board and the Town of Stoney Creek to the site plan and proposed changes in zoning, and any approval of the Committee of Adjustment or Planning Board required are given. The applications for and all matters and appearances relating to such approval shall be prepared by and at the expense of the purchaser but may be brought in the names of the vendors. The vendors agree and undertake to give all help and co-operation required by the purchaser and to execute all necessary documents and make all attendances necessary (without costs to the purchaser) to assist in and facilitate the obtaining of the approvals and registrations required by the purchaser. *It is agreed between the parties that the Application and hearing before the Ontario Municipal Board shall be completed on or before the 30th day of September, 1968* (without the decision necessarily having been made). Provided however, if any adjournment results from opposition beyond the control of the purchaser, then the said date for completion of the application and hearing shall be extended to the 31st day of January, 1969 at the latest. Provided further, that the purchaser shall within two months after all Municipal approvals have been granted, cause an appointment to be obtained for a hearing before the Ontario Municipal Board. *In the event that these conditions are not complied with, then notwithstanding anything herein contained, the agreement of purchase and sale shall be null and void and the deposit monies returned to the purchaser.*

Barnett made "assiduous efforts" to obtain the requisite approvals, but the Town was processing his application in a "lethargic way" by the Town planning authorities. On September 30, Barnett "in a last minute attempt to save the agreement gave notice to Harrison that he waived the conditions referred to above. Harrison replied that as the conditions had not been fulfilled, the agreement was "null and void". Barnett sued for specific performance.]

Dickson J.: ... This case raises once again the question whether a contracting party may waive a condition of the contract on the ground it is intended only for his benefit, and then bring an action for specific performance. ...

There can be no doubt on the evidence that the purchaser seriously planned and assiduously sought approval of a major housing development. The approval, a future uncertain event, was entirely dependent upon the will of third parties, the Town of Stoney Creek, the Planning Board, the Minister and the Ontario Municipal Board. The factual infrastructure of this case may differ in detail from *Turney and Turney v. Zhilka* and is perhaps more analogous to that of the two later cases which came before the Court; in *F.T. Developments Ltd. v. Sherman et al., supra,* the offer was conditional upon the purchaser obtaining rezoning on a specified (M-5) zoning basis. I do not think, however, it can be very seriously questioned that the general principle laid down in *Turney and Turney v. Zhilka* applies.

The Court was invited by counsel for the appellant to reappraise the rule in *Turney and Turney v. Zhilka* if that case was found to be controlling. Counsel cited a number of American and English authorities which support the broad proposition that a party to a contract can waive a condition that is for his benefit. Despite the support elsewhere for such a general proposition, I am of the view the rule expressed in *Turney and Turney v. Zhilka* should not be disturbed for several reasons. First, the distinction made in *Turney and Turney v. Zhilka* between (i) the manifest right of A to waive default by B in the performance of a severable condition intended for the benefit of A, and (ii) the attempt by A to waive his own default or the default of C, upon whom depends the performance which gives rise to the obligation, *i.e.,* the true condition precedent, seems to me, with respect, to be valid. Second, when parties, as here, aided by legal advisors, make a contract subject to explicit conditions precedent and provide therein specifically that in the event of non-compliance with one or more of the conditions, the contract shall be void, the Court runs roughshod over the agreement by introducing an implied provision conceding to the purchaser the right to waive compliance. In the instant case the conditions for water and sewer requirements were expressed to be subject to waiver at the option of the purchaser but the conditions respecting site plan and zoning were not; if all of these various conditions were to be placed on the same footing, the Court would be simply rewriting the agreement. Third, if the purchaser is to be put in the position of being able to rely on the conditions precedent or to waive them, depending on which course is to his greater benefit, the result may be that the purchaser has been given an option to purchase, for which he has paid nothing; if the property increases in value, the purchaser waives compliance and demands specific performance but if property declines in value, the purchaser does not waive compliance and the agreement becomes null and void in accordance with its terms. It is right to say that this opportunity to select against the vendors will not arise in every case. The zoning changes or other contingency, the subject-matter of the condition precedent, may be approved by the third party or otherwise satisfied within the purchase. He will not be permitted purposely to fail to perform his obligations in order to avoid the contract. But even when, as here, no question of bad faith arises, approvals may not be forthcoming within the prescribed time, and the vendors, whose lands have been tied up for 20 months, can be in the position where they do not know until the final day whether or not the purchaser will waive compliance and whether or not the sale will be completed. If what has been termed an agreement of purchase and sale is to be in reality an option, the purchaser will take the benefit of the appreciation in land value during the intervening months but if the agreement takes effect in accordance with its terms the vendors will have that benefit. I can see no injustice to the purchaser if the contract terms prevail and possible injustice to vendors if they do not. Fourth, application of the rule in *Turney and Turney v. Zhilka* may avoid determination of two questions which can give rise to difficulty (i) whether the condition precedent is for the benefit of the purchaser alone or for the joint benefit and (ii) whether the conditions precedent are severable from the balance of the agreement. I am inclined to the view in the present case that they are not. Finally, the rule in *Turney and Turney v. Zhilka* has been in effect since 1959, and has been applied many times. In the interests of certainty and predictability in the law, the rule should endure unless compelling reason for change be shown. If in any case the parties agree that the rule shall not apply, that can be readily written into the agreement. *Genern Investments Ltd. v. Back et al.* (1969), 3 D.L.R. (3d) 611, [1969] 1 O.R. 694, and *Dennis v. Evans* (1972), 23 D.L.R. (3d) 625, [1972] 1 O.R. [affd 27 D.L.R (3d) 680*n*, [1972] 3 O.R. 228*n*], are examples of cases in which the contract expressly provided that a condition could be waived by the party for whose benefit it had been inserted.

[The case of *Beauchamp et al. v. Beauchamp et al.* was cited by counsel for the appellant. There,] the vendors refused to close on the ground the condition precedent had not been strictly complied with but the position was untenable. The patent purpose of the condition was to afford the purchasers an opportunity of raising the moneys with which to complete the purchase; in this they were successful and so advised the vendors timeously. It was of no importance whatever that the funds required by the purchasers came from a first mortgage for $12,000 rather than a first mortgage for $10,000 and a second mortgage for $2,500. That case should, I think, be regarded as one in which the condition precedent was satisfied and not as one in which it was waived.

I would dismiss the appeal with costs.

[Judson, Martland, Ritchie, Pigeon, Beetz, and de Grandpré JJ., concurred in the judgment of Dickson J.]

Laskin C.J.C., dissenting: I pass now to a consideration of *Turney and Turney v. Zhilka* and to the principle on which it was based. The condition in that case, upon which the suit for specific performance foundered, was one fixed by the contract without reference to any obligation of performance being placed on either the vendor or the purchaser. The relevant condition read as follows: "Providing the property can be annexed to the Village of Streetsville and a plan is approved by the Village Council for subdivision." Judson, J., speaking for this Court read this provision as depending (to use his words) "entirely on the will of a third party". That is not the present case, it being quite clear under the contract (even apart from the evidence of the vendors) that it was the purchaser who was to prepare and seek approval of a site plan, and of necessary rezoning, in order to carry out his apartment project which was the known and particularized use to which the land was to be put. Since the obligation to proceed with a site plan and to seek rezoning was expressly put on the purchaser, and since, on the evidence, the condition was one exacted by him solely for his benefit, there is a marked difference between the present case and *Turney and Turney v. Zhilka.*

The issue raised by *Turney and Turney v. Zhilka* and by the cases that have followed it, such as the *F.T. Developments* case and the *O'Reilly* case, appears to me to require a proper understanding of the phrase "true condition precedent" which was used by Judson, J., in *Turney and Turney v. Zhilka.*

A condition which is characterized as a condition precedent may be one in which both parties have an interest and yet it may be subject to waiver at the suit of one only of the parties. That is because their interest in it may not be the same. The condition may be for the protection of one party only in the sense that it is solely for his benefit, but it may be important to the other party in the sense that he is entitled to know the consequence of its performance or waiver by the date fixed for its performance so that he may, if he is the vendor, either collect his money or be free to look for another purchaser. It would, in my view, be a mistake to move from the fact that both parties have an interest in the performance or non-performance of a condition of the contract to the conclusion that the condition cannot therefore be waived at the suit of the one party for whose sole benefit the condition was introduced into the contract. Some of the submissions made here, especially on the re-argument of the appeal, failed to draw this distinction which, to me, is a vital one.

Another distinction that appears to me to be vital is one that is clear upon a comparison of the relevant conditions in *Turney and Turney v. Zhilka* and in the present case. The fact that the conduct or action of a third party is involved in the proper performance of a condition does not on that ground alone make it a "true condition precedent" which cannot be waived. Thus, to take a homely example, the fact that a purchaser may make it a condition of completion that he be able to obtain mortgage financing within a fixed period does not, in my opinion, preclude him from waiving the condition and paying in cash, provided, of course, he makes his election to waive the condition within the period fixed by the contract: see *Scott v. Rania*, [1966] N.Z.L.R. 527. In principle, there is no difference between the foregoing situation and one where the duty of one of the parties to the contract arises only upon the act of a third party, as for example, the obligation to pay money upon the certificate of an architect or engineer. Of course, the obligor is not likely to make the payment unless the certificate is provided, but the fact that he could insist on its production does not mean that he could not waive this condition of his duty to pay.

There is a parallel situation where title defects are involved. It is unquestionable that a purchaser may choose to accept the subject property notwithstanding an impediment to perfect title upon whose removal he could insist: see *Bennett v. Fowler* (1840), 2 Beav. 302. As Cardozo, J., put it in *Catholic Foreign Mission Society of America v. Oussani* (1915), 215 N.Y. 1 at p. 8:

> ... a buyer in such circumstances is not bound to rescind. He may waive the condition, and accept the title though defective. If he does, the seller may not refuse to convey because the buyer could not have been compelled to waive.

The same point of principle was made much earlier by Lopes, L.J., in *Hawksley v. Outram*, [1892] 3 Ch. 359 at p. 378, when he said, in respect of certain non-competition provisions in a contract for the sale of a business, that "it is perfectly clear that they are provisions intended solely for the benefit of the purchaser; the purchaser, therefore, is at liberty to relinquish them, and, if he does so, it is immaterial whether he could have successfully insisted on them".

The principle operates in favour of a vendor as well as in favour of a purchaser. *Morrell v. Studd & Millington*, [1913] 2 Ch. 648, is illustrative. There it was held that a vendor could waive a provision that the balance of the purchase price be secured to his satisfaction and could sue the purchaser for specific performance after forgoing that provision which was one solely for his benefit.

In this class of case, whether it be action or conduct by one of the parties that is involved or action or conduct of a third party, what is important is whether that action or conduct is a condition of an obligation of one of the parties only or of both. If of one only, there is no reason why he should not be able to offer performance of his own obligation or duty without insisting on the condition and then call on the other to perform his side of the bargain.

What has sometimes complicated the application of this principle are cases which involved not the performance of a concluded contract but rather the question whether there was a concluded contract. *Lloyd v. Nowell*, [1895] 2 Ch. 744, is referred to by *Fry on Specific Performance*, 6th ed. (1921), at pp. 175 and 461 to point up the distinction. Thus, where a transaction was subject to "the preparation by my solicitor and completion of a formal contract", it could not be said that the vendor could waive this provision and create a contract by his unilateral act. Nor could a purchaser do so under a similar provision respecting the preparation of a formal contract by his solicitor: see *Von Hatzfeldt-Wildenburg v. Alexander*, [1912] 1 Ch. 284.

I take *Turney and Turney v. Zhilka* to have involved, as a matter of construction, a condition which was applicable to the duty of both parties. As Judson, J., put it, at p. 450 D.L.R., p. 583 S.C.R., "the obligations under the contract, *on both sides*, depends upon a future uncertain event, the happening of which depends entirely on the will of a third party — the village council". (The emphasis is mine.) It is on this basis only that it can be said, as Judson, J., did, that there was here a "true condition precedent", that is one external to the obligations of both parties and one where the contract did not give the carriage of the matter to either one of the parties so as to provide a basis for contending that it was for his benefit alone and could be waived by him. This construction of a condition involving some action of a third party is not a necessary one: see, for example, *Funke v. Paist et al.* (1947), 52 A. 2d 655 (Pa.), and *Richardson v. Snipes* (1959), 330 S.W. 2d 381 (Tenn.), holding required zoning approvals to be conditions of the duty of the purchaser only and hence open to waiver by him. Nevertheless, there can be no doubt that, in particular situations of which *Turney and Turney v. Zhilka* is illustrative, a provision for rezoning or redevelopment consent may be construed as one for the mutual advantage or benefit of both of the parties to a contract of sale of land and hence not open to unilateral waiver. This was the result reached in the recent English case of *Heron Garage Properties Ltd. v. Moss et al.*, [1974] 1 All E.R. 421. There is one point in that case which also calls for consideration here and that is the fact that the date of completion is geared to the obtaining of planning consent or zoning approval, thus raising the question of the severability of the provision which the purchaser purported to waive. I will return to this point later in these reasons...

It may be noted that the situation in the *F.T. Developments* case was different from that in *Turney and Turney v. Zhilka* in that there the very offer of the purchaser was made conditional upon obtaining the rezoning while in the latter there was a concluded contract, performance of which depended upon a certain condition, but this difference did not enter into the Court's assessment of the issue. However, Cartwright, C.J.C., did not find it necessary to decide whether the condition could be unilaterally waived because on the evidence and findings of fact there was no waiver declared until after the time for closing had passed.

I would not myself have found any consonance between the condition in the *F.T. Developments* case and that in *Turney and Turney v. Zhilka*. Even less of a consonance appears to me to exist between the condition in *Turney and Turney v. Zhilka* and that in the *O'Reilly* case, *supra*. In the latter case, a purchaser had agreed to buy Lot 7 in a certain area from a vendor, and the contract included a provision as to the purchaser being able to purchase Lot 8 from a third party on terms and conditions satisfactory to the purchaser and prior to a named date. On the question whether this was a condition for the purchaser's sole benefit and open to waiver by him, the British Columbia Court of Appeal so held in reversal of the trial Judge. This Court, again speaking through Judson, J., held that *Turney and Turney v. Zhilka* and the *F.T. Developments* case governed the legal issue. It was his view, to quote his words, that "the vendor in the present appeal had no enforceable contract without performance of the condition. Neither had the purchaser." In short, the view was taken that the provision as to the purchase of Lot 8 was a condition of the duty of performance of both the vendor and the purchaser. I cannot so read the provision which, on its face, seems so clearly to be directed to the duty of the purchaser and not to any duty or interest of the vendor. Being, in my opinion, for the purchaser's benefit alone, it was one which he could forgo in asserting a claim to specific performance against the vendor. The provision was there to enable the purchaser to defend against the vendor if it was unperformed and not *vice versa*.

I cannot but think that if the condition in the present case and the condition in the *O'Reilly* case are not instances of conditions which can be waived by the one party to whose duty of performance they go, there can hardly be any case in which waiver can be lawfully effected short of an express provision therefor in the contract of sale. No doubt this is a salutary procedure, but the law of contract has long ago ceased to depend on exact expression of every consequence of a contractual provision.

An examination of the case law in England, in Australia, in New Zealand and in the United States discloses no differentiation in applicable principle between those provisions where action of a third party is involved and those where only the action of the opposite party is involved so far as concerns the right of waiver of a provision which is found to be for the benefit of one party only. Of course, a party cannot base a claim for performance by the opposite party of a conditional obligation on his own failure to perform, unless it can be said that the failure relates to a mere promise rather than to the condition; but, even as to a condition to which a party is obliged in favour of the opposite party, the latter may elect to enforce the contract rather than rescind upon breach of the condition.

The present case, in a sense, shows the opposite side of the coin because if the provision in question is solely for the benefit of a party who decides to renounce that benefit, there is then no impediment to calling for the opposite party's performance provided the provision waived is not tied in with other terms from which it cannot be extricated by way of unilateral relinquishment. What the earlier observation shows, however, is that failure to perform a condition does not necessarily mean that there is no contract to enforce since the innocent party may elect to keep it alive.

The High Court of Australia in *Maynard v. Goode et al.* (1926), 37 C.L.R. 529, was met with a submission that a provision in a contract of sale of land that the Crown postpone payment of rent due to it was a "true condition precedent" as being for the benefit of both parties to the contract. The fact that action by a third party, the Crown, was involved, did not prevent the Court from concluding, as had the trial Judge, that the provision was open to waiver as being for the sole benefit of the vendor in that case. The matter was considered at great length by Hutchison, J., of the Supreme Court of New Zealand in *Donaldson et al. v. Tracy et al.*, [1951] N.Z.L.R. 684, in terms of a distinction drawn by counsel between a "pure" condition (the "true condition precedent" under another formula) depending on the action of a third party and provisions that were merely promises or undertakings. The case arose out of an accepted offer for the purchase of a hotel property and of the hotel business. In the offer the purchaser stipulated for the approval of the Licensing Commission and also that it not recommend any other licensed premises within a two-mile radius. The Commission did in fact approve a licence within that area but the purchaser sought to waive this provision and sued for specific performance when the vendor contended that the contract was no longer binding. The purchaser obtained a decree.

Two points emerge from the judgment and, although they have already been made, they are worth repeating. First, to use the words of the Court at p. 691:

> Where there is a failure of a condition, I think on principle, that it does not make any difference whether the failure is due to the action of a party or to the action of an outsider, as far as regards the right of the other party to waive the condition if it is solely for his benefit.

Second, that a condition is for the sole benefit of the party who purports to waive it may be shown by evidence of surrounding circumstances. Hutchison, J., was of opinion that on the face of the contested provision it was for the benefit of the purchaser, a conclusion fortified by the observation that the vendor would suffer no prejudice if the particular condition was not in the contract.

A similar approach with similar results runs through American case law. I may refer first to 17A C.J.S., pp. 688-90, which brings into relation the position of a party who may waive rights to which he is entitled and who may also elect not to take advantage of a breach by the opposite party. A line of authorities supporting waiver of a provision for rezoning approval will be found in American Law Reports Annotated (1961), 76 ALR 2d 1204. I will refer in detail to only one modern American case, *Godfrey Co. v. Crawford et al.* (1964), 126 N.W. 2d 495 (Wis.), because it bears also on the "null and void" contention previously canvassed in these reasons.

The case involved an accepted offer to purchase certain land and it had a completion date of March 1, 1963. The contract provided that the purchaser should be joined by the vendors and by owners of adjacent premises to petition the municipal council for rezoning to permit a certain development, such petition to be filed on or before January 3, 1963, "and in the event the petition for rezoning is denied or cannot be consummated on or before March 1, 1963 ... this offer to purchase shall become null and void and all monies paid hereunder shall be returned to the buyer". Prior to March 1, 1963, the purchaser advised the vendors of a waiver and of a readiness to complete the purchase on the completion date. In affirming dismissal of a demurrer to the purchaser's action for specific performance, the Court made some observations which I reproduce and adopt here, as follows (at pp. 497-8):

> We agree with defendants' contention that the provision in the contract, that it was to become null and void upon the failure to consummate the zoning revision by March 1st, is obviously for the protection of the sellers as well as the buyer. It is for the protection of the buyer because nonfulfillment of the zoning revision cancels its liability on the contract and enables it to recover any prior payments made on the purchase price. It is for the protection of the sellers because such nonfulfillment also terminates their liability on the contract and leaves them free to immediately sell the premises to someone else. Without such a provision the sellers might well have their property tied up for a long period of time should a court find that time was not of the essence with respect to accomplishing the zoning revision. If at the end of such time the buyer defaulted the sellers in the meantime could have lost an opportunity of an advantageous sale to someone else. . . .
>
> The fact that this particular provision is held to be for the benefit of the sellers as well as the buyer, however, does not in itself preclude the buyer from waiving prior to March 1, 1963, the condition that the zoning revision be consummated by March 1, 1963. This is because it is alleged in the amended complaint that the zoning change was for the protection of the buyer and the general rule is that a party to a contract can waive a condition that is for his benefit. . . .
>
> By permitting the buyer to waive the condition with respect to zoning revision, providing such waiver occurs prior to the specified cut-off date of March 1, 1963, there is no interference with the protection afforded sellers by the provision in the contract that, if the zoning revision is not consummated by that date, the contract is rendered null and void. The prior waiver has the same effect as a consummated zoning revision insofar as the rights of the sellers are concerned. In either event the buyer is absolutely obligated to pay the balance of purchase

price on the closing date of March 1, 1963. The sellers have no protectable interest in whether or not the zoning revision has been consummated as such, but only in knowing on March 1, 1963, that either (1) the buyer is absolutely bound to immediately pay the balance of purchase price, or (2) the contract is at an end and they are immediately free to sell to someone else.

In view of the foregoing we hold that plaintiff buyer did have the right prior to March 1, 1963, to waive the contract provision with respect to the consummation of the zoning revision by that date. By so doing we do not consider that we have rewritten or reformed the agreement of the parties, but have merely given effect to the well-recognized principle that a party may waive a provision inserted in a contract for his benefit. Defendant sellers contend that such a construction will do violence to their rights, because they relied to their detriment in agreeing to sell to the corporate defendant contingent upon no zoning revision having occurred by March 1, 1963. The answer to this contention is that the contract clause which defendants claim to have relied upon was always open to the contingency that the courts would construe it as we have done. They acted at their peril in so acting as not to protect themselves against such a contingency.

The most potent argument advanced by defendants is the fact that the contract between plaintiff and the individual defendants specifically authorized plaintiff to waive title defects, but is entirely silent with respect to its right to waive the consummation of the desired zoning revision. In a close case where the scales are somewhat evenly balanced between one interpretation and another, this might well be the decisive factor in arriving at the court's decision. We do not consider, however, that this is such a close case. Defendants have failed to point out any way in which the defendant sellers' protection is weakened in the slightest degree by the interpretation adopted by this court.

Having had the benefit of seeing the reasons prepared by my brother Dickson before completing my own, I would underline two of the points of difference between us. I do not view waiver as involving a rewriting of an agreement any more than I regard estoppel of a party from insisting upon a term of an agreement as a rewriting thereof. A party that is entitled to a range of benefits under an agreement does not rewrite it against the opposite party by forgoing some of those benefits. Second, I find nothing offensive or prejudicial in the fact that a vendor may not know until completion date whether the contract will be performed according to its very terms or whether there will be a waiver so as to give the purchaser a choice to opt out or to insist on performance by the vendor. This is not an uncommon situation in contracts and depends simply on their terms.

In the result, while recognizing the basis upon which *Turney and Turney v. Zhilka* proceeded, I do not find that it precludes a contrary conclusion in the present case, and I would, accordingly, allow the appeal, set aside the judgments below and enter a decree of specific performance in favour of the purchaser with costs throughout.

[Spence J. agreed with Laskin C.J.C.]

QUESTION

Would Harrison have had any rights if Barnett's efforts to secure the approvals had been half-hearted?

See: *Metropolitan Trust v. Pressure Concrete Services* (1973), 37 D.L.R. 3d 649, and *Aldercrest Developments Ltd. v. Hunter*, [1970] 2 O.R. 562 (C.A.).

[In *Schuler v. Wickman*, [1973] 2 All E.R. 39 (reproduced above, on another point), the parties had provided, in clause 7(b), of a contract that it was to be a "condition of (the) agreement" that the respondent should send a salesman to visit certain named firms at least once a week. The salesman did not always fulfil the obligation under the contract and the appellant contended that it could terminate the agreement. The House of Lords, (Lord Wilberforce dissenting) held that the use of the word "condition" created a presumption that it indicated a term of the contract, the breach of which, however small, would give rise to a right to repudiate. But, in the circumstances, it was held that this was so unreasonable that the parties could not have intended it, and therefore the appellant was not entitled to repudiate the agreement.]

Lord Reid said (p. 45): Schuler maintain that the use of the word 'condition' is in itself enough to establish this intention. No doubt some words used by lawyers do have a rigid inflexible meaning. But we must remember that we are seeking to discover intention as disclosed by the contract as a whole. Use of the word 'condition' is an indication — even a strong indication — of such an intention but it is by no means conclusive. The fact that a particular construction leads to a very unreasonable result must be a relevant consideration. The more unreasonable the result the more unlikely it is that the parties can have intended it, and if they do intend it the more necessary it is that they shall make that intention abundantly clear.

Clause 7(b) requires that over a long period each of the six firms shall be visited every week by one or other of two named representatives. It makes no provision for Wickman being entitled to substitute others even on the death or retirement of one of the named representatives. Even if one could imply some right to do this, it makes no provision for both representatives being ill during a particular week. And it makes no provision for the possibility that one or other of the firms may tell Wickman that they cannot receive Wickman's representative during a particular week. So if the parties gave any thought to the matter at all they must have realised the probability that in a few cases out of the 1,400 required visits a visit as stipulated would be impossible. But if Schuler's contention is right failure to make even one visit entitles them to terminate the contract however blameless Wickman might be. This is so unreasonable that it must make me search for some other possible meaning of the contract. If none can be found then Wickman must suffer the consequences. But only if that is the only possible interpretation.

If I have to construe cl 7 standing by itself then I do find difficulty in reaching any other interpretation. But if cl 7 must be read with cl 11 the difficulty disappears. The word 'condition' would make any breach of cl 7(b), however excusable, a material breach. That would then entitle Schuler to give notice under cl 11(a)(i) requiring the breach to be remedied. There would be no point in giving such a notice if Wickman were clearly not in fault but if it were given Wickman would have no difficulty in shewing that the breach had been remedied. If Wickman were at fault then on receiving such a notice they would have to amend their system so that they could shew that the breach had been remedied. If they did not do that within the period of the notice then Schuler would be entitled to rescind.

In my view, that is a possible and reasonable construction of the contract and I would therefore adopt it. The contract is so obscure that I can have no confidence that this is its true meaning but for the reasons which I have given I think that it is the preferable construction. It follows that Schuler were not entitled to rescind the contract as they purported to do. So I would dismiss this appeal....

Lord Wilberforce:... My Lords, with two qualifications, this case is one of interpretation of the written agency or distributorship agreement between the appellants and the respondents dated 1st May 1963, in particular of cl 7(b) of that agreement....

The second legal issue which arises I would state in this way: whether it is open to the parties to a contract, not being a contract for the sale of goods, to use the word 'condition' to introduce a term, breach of which ipso facto entitles the other party to treat the contract at an end.

The proposition that this may be done has not been uncriticised. It is said that this is contrary to modern trends which focus interest rather on the nature of the breach, allowing the innocent party to rescind or repudiate whenever the breach is fundamental, whether the clause breached is called a condition or not: that the affixing of the label 'condition' cannot pre-empt the right of the court to estimate for itself the character of the breach. Alternatively it is said that the result contended for can only be achieved if the consequences of a breach of a 'condition' (sc, that the other party may rescind) are spelt out in the contract. In support of this line of argument reliance is placed on the judgment of the Court of Appeal in *Hong Kong Fir Shipping Co Ltd v Kawasaki Kisen Kaisha Ltd*, [1962] 2 Q.B. 26.

My Lords, this approach has something to commend it: it has academic support. The use as a promissory term of 'condition' is artificial, as is that of 'warranty' in some contexts. But in my opinion this use is now too deeply embedded in English law to be uprooted by anything less than a complete revision. I shall not trace the development of the term through 19th century cases, many of them decisions of Lord Blackburn, to the present time; this has been well done by academic writers. I would only add that the *Hong Kong Fir* case, even if it could, did not reverse the trend. What it did decide, and I do not think that this was anything new, was that although a term (there a 'seaworthiness' term) was not a 'condition' in the technical sense, it might still be a term breach of which if sufficiently serious could go to the root of the contract. Nothing in the judgments as I read them casts any doubt on the meaning or effect of 'condition' where that word is technically used.

The alternative argument, in my opinion, is equally precluded by authority. It is not necessary for parties to a contract, when stipulating a condition, to spell out the consequences of breach: these are inherent in the (assumedly deliberate) use of the word (*Suisse Atlantique Société D'Armement Maritime SA v NV Rotterdamsche Kolen Centrale*, [1967] 1 A.C. 361, per Lord Upjohn).

It is on this legal basis, as to which I venture to think that your Lordships are agreed, that this contract must be construed. Does cl 7(b) amount to a 'condition' or a 'term'? (to call it an important or material term adds, with all respect, nothing but some intellectual assuagement). My Lords, I am clear in my own mind that it is a condition, but your Lordships take the contrary view. On a matter of construction of a particular document, to develop the reasons for a minority opinion serves no purpose. I am all the more happy to refrain from so doing because the judgments of Mocatta J,

Stephenson LJ, and indeed of Edmund Davies LJ on construction, give me complete satisfaction and I could in any case add little of value to their reasons. I would only add that, for my part, to call the clause arbitrary, capricious or fantastic, or to introduce as a test of its validity the ubiquitous reasonable man (I do not know whether he is English or German) is to assume, contrary to the evidence, that both parties to this contract adopted a standard of easygoing tolerance rather than one of aggressive, insistent punctuality and efficiency. This is not an assumption I am prepared to make, nor do I think myself entitled to impose the former standard on the parties if their words indicate, as they plainly do, the latter. I note finally, that the result of treating the clause, so careful and specific in its requirements, as a term is, in effect, to deprive the appellants of any remedy in respect of admitted and by no means minimal breaches. The arbitrator's finding that these breaches were not 'material' was not, in my opinion, justified in law in the face of the parties' own characterisation of them in their document: indeed the fact that he was able to do so, and so leave the appellants without remedy, argues strongly that the legal basis of his finding — that cl 7(b) was merely a term — is unsound.

I would allow this appeal.

QUESTIONS

1. How could you make the parties' intention clearer?
2. Would or should it matter whether you could or could not make that intention clearer?
3. After having read the cases in this section, draft appropriate clauses in the following situations:
   (a)   The purchaser of land wants to make an offer to purchase conditional on,
       (i)   his obtaining satisfactory financing
      (ii)   an inspection of the premises by a professional inspector and a satisfactory report from him.
      (You must consider what you think the solicitor for the vendor would refuse to allow.)
   (b)   Schuler wants to make sure that Wickman visits potential customers at least once a week and in a way that is likely to maximize the effectiveness of such visits. Schuler wants to be able to terminate the arrangement if Wickman does not do all that he can to comply with this term.

(2) The Technique of Implying a Condition

In section (1), above, the parties had at least provided expressly that the occurrence of some state of affairs was to be a "condition" of their contract. We have seen that even in such cases, the Courts have a wide discretion which they must exercise when the proposed state of affairs does not materialize (see *Beauchamp, Barnett,* and *Schuler,* above).

Sometimes the parties do not provide even this minimum guidance to the Court. It is then up to the Court to determine the effect of the non-occurrence of those events. The same factors which influence the Courts in interpreting and construing contracts, in deciding when to imply terms, in deciding whether or not there is consideration and in determining the effect of express conditions can be expected to influence the Courts' decisions in the cases in this section. What are those factors?

Perhaps a more accurate description of the judicial process here is to regard the Courts as deciding what the effect of the non-occurrence of some event should be, and then deciding, in light of the first decision, how the contractual terms are to be classified. Consider whether or not this description is accurate as you read the cases. Is the matter of any practical significance?

The following are some classic statements on the power of the court to imply terms in contracts:

1. *Bowen L.J.*: "I believe if one were to take all the cases, and there are many, of implied warranties or covenants in law, it will be found that in all of them the law is raising an implication from the presumed intention of the parties, with the object of giving to the transaction such efficacy as both parties must have intended that at all events it should have. In business transactions such as this, what the law desires to effect by the implication is to give such business efficacy to the transaction as must have been intended at all events by both parties who are business men.... The question is what inference is to be drawn where the parties are dealing with each other on the assumption that the negotiations are to have some fruit, and where they say nothing about the burden of this unseen peril, leaving the law to raise such inferences as are reasonable from the very nature of the transaction." (*The Moorcock* (1889) 14 P.D. 64, 68, 70.)

2. *Scrutton L.J.*: "A term can only be implied, if it is necessary in the business sense to give efficacy to the contract, *i.e.*, if it is such a term that it can confidently be said that if at the time the contract was being negotiated some one had said to the parties: 'What will happen in such a case?' they would both have replied: 'Of course so and so will happen; we did not trouble to say that; it is too clear.' " (*Reigate v. Union Manufacturing Co.*, [1918] 1 K.B. 592, 605.)

3. *McKinnon L.J.*: "I recognize that the right or duty of a Court to find the existence of an implied term or implied terms in a written contract is a matter to be exercised with care; and a Court is too often invited to do so upon vague and uncertain grounds. Too often also such an invitation is backed by the citation of a sentence or two from the judgment of Bowen L.J. in *The Moorcock*. They are sentences from an extempore judgment as sound and sensible as all the utterances of that great judge; but I fancy that he would have been rather surprised if he could have foreseen that these general remarks of his would come to be a favourite citation of a supposed principle of law, and I even think that he might sympathize with the occasional impatience of his successors when *The Moorcock* is so often flushed for them in that guise.

"For my part, I think that there is a test that may be at least as useful as such generalities. If I may quote from an essay which I wrote some years ago, I then said: 'Prima facie that which in any contract is left to be implied and need not be expressed is something so obvious that it goes without saying; so that, if, while the parties were making their bargain, an officious bystander were to suggest some express provision for it in their agreement, they would testily suppress him with a common "Oh, of course!" ' " (*Shirlaw v. Southern Foundries* [1939] 2 K.B. 206, 227.)

4. *Lord Pearson*: "An unexpressed term can be implied, if and only if the court finds that the parties must have intended that term to form part of their contract: It is not enough for the court to find that such a term would have been adopted by the parties as reasonable men if it had been suggested to them: it must have been a term that went without saying, a term neces-

sary to give business efficacy to the contract, a term which although tacit, formed part of the contract which the parties made for themselves."
(*Trollope & Colls Ltd. v. N.W. Regional Hospital Board* [1973] 2 All E.R. 260, 268.)

QUESTIONS

1. How would you use any of these quotations in a case in which you were counsel?
— as telling you what you should ask a witness?
— as an argument on a point of law before the judge?
— as an argument that a certain question asked by the other side was inadmissible?
2. If you did not like the decision that a trial judge came to in a case where you had used one of these quotations, would you feel free to raise the issue before the Court of Appeal?

KINGSTON v. PRESTON

(1773), 2 Dougl. 689; 99 E.R. 437. King's Bench; Reported in the report of the argument in *Jones v. Barkley*.

[The defendant promised to employ the plaintiff for a year so that the latter could learn the defendant's business. At the end of the year the defendant agreed to transfer his business to the plaintiff and to the defendant's nephew. The plaintiff promised to give security for the payment of £250 per month to the defendant. The plaintiff sued the defendant on his promise to transfer the business. The defendant alleged, and the plaintiff admitted, that the plaintiff had given and could give no security for the payment of £250 per month (and so could not perform his part of the bargain).]
— In delivering the judgment of the Court, **Lord Mansfield** expressed himself to the following effect: There are three kinds of covenants: 1. Such as are called mutual and independant, where either party may recover damages from the other, for the injury he may have received by a breach of the covenants in his favour, and where it is no excuse for the defendant, to allege a breach of the covenants on the part of the plaintiff. 2. There are covenants which are conditions and dependant, in which the performance of one depends on the prior performance of another, and, therefore, till this prior condition is performed, the other party is not liable to an action on his covenant. 3. There is also a third sort of covenants, which are mutual conditions to be performed at the same time; and, in these, if one party was ready, and offered, to perform his part, and the other neglected, or refused, to perform his, he who was ready, and offered, has fulfilled his engagement, and may maintain an action for the default of the other; though it is not certain that either is obliged to do the first act. — His Lordship then proceeded to say, that the dependance, or independance, of covenants, was to be collected from the evident sense and meaning of the parties, and, that, however transposed they might be in the deed, their precedency must depend on the order of time in which the intent of the transaction requires their performance. That, in the case before the Court, it would be the greatest injustice if the plaintiff should prevail: the essence of the agreement was, that the defendant should not trust to the personal security of the plaintiff, but, before he delivered up his stock and business, should have good security for the payment of the money. The giving such security, therefore, must

necessarily be a condition precedent. — Judgment was accordingly given for the defendant, because the part to be performed by the plaintiff was clearly a condition precedent.

BOONE v. EYRE

(1777), 1 H. Bl. 273; 126 E.R. 160. Reported in a note to the argument in *Duke of St. Albans v. Shore.*

Covenant on a deed, whereby the plaintiff conveyed to the defendant the equity of redemption of a plantation in the West Indies, together with the stock of negroes upon it, in consideration of 500l. and an annuity of 160l. per annum for his life; and covenanted that he had a good title to the plantation, was lawfully possessed of the negroes, and that the defendant should quietly enjoy. The defendant covenanted, that the plaintiff well and truly performing all and every thing therein contained on his part to be performed, he the defendant would pay the annuity. The breach assigned was the non-payment of the annuity. Plea, that the plaintiff was not, at the time of making the deed, legally possessed of the negroes on the plantation, and so had not a good title to convey.

To which there was a general demurrer.

Lord Mansfield. — The distinction is very clear, where mutual covenants go to the whole of the consideration on both sides, they are mutual conditions, the one precedent to the other. But where they go only to a part, where a breach may be paid for in damages, there the defendant has a remedy on his covenant, and shall not plead it as a condition precedent. If this plea were to be allowed, any one negro not being the property of the plaintiff would bar the action.

Judgment for the plaintiff.

These cases make it clear that sometimes performance by one party will be a condition of performance by the other; and sometimes such performance will not be. The next case attempts to say when one party will be discharged from further performance when the other party has not performed his part of the bargain.

HONG KONG FIR v. KAWASAKI KISEN KAISHA LTD.

[1962] 2 Q.B. 26. Court of Appeal (England); Sellers, Upjohn, and Diplock L.JJ.

[The plaintiffs bought a ship and chartered it to the defendants. Under the terms of the charter-party, the owners promised that the vessel was "in every way fitted for ordinary cargo service", and that they would "maintain her in a thoroughly efficient state in hull and machinery during service." The charterers promised to pay hire but were excused if the ship was in port for repairs. The ship sailed for Liverpool in February 1957. She was to go to Newport News, Va., to pick up coal to take to Osaka. The voyage was a catalogue of disasters: decrepit machinery, incompetent and insufficient crew. The ship reached Osaka on May 25. She was not ready for sea again until September 15. Between Liverpool and Osaka she was at sea for 8½ weeks, and off hired for 5 weeks. To get to Osaka £21,000 had to be spent. She needed 15 more weeks and £37,500 to get her ready for sea once she reached Osaka.

"On June 5 and 6 and July 27 the charterers wrote repudiating the charter and claiming damages for breach of contract; on August 8 and 12 the owners wrote intimating that they would treat the contract as cancelled by the charterers' wrongful repudiation and claim damages. On September 11 the charterers wrote again repudiating the charter and the owners formally accepted that repudiation on September 13.

"On November 8, 1957, the owners issued a writ against the charterers claiming damages for wrongful repudiation of the charterparty. The charterers alleged breaches by the plaintiffs of clauses 1, 2 and 3 of the charterparty in that, inter alia, the vessel was unseaworthy by reason of the condition of her machinery, that the owners had failed to exercise due diligence to make her seaworthy and fitted for the voyage and also that the description in the charterparty of the vessel's steaming capacity was inaccurate; alternatively, they alleged that the charterparty was frustrated by reason of the breakdowns and repairs and delays consequent thereon; the charterers also counterclaimed for damages."

The trial judge, Salmon J., held that the shipowners were entitled to damages for breach of contract. The charterer appealed. Only the judgment of Diplock L.J. is reproduced. The others agreed in the result.]

Diplock L.J. The contract, the familiar "Baltime 1939" charter, and the facts upon which this case turns have been already stated in the judgment of Sellers L.J., who has also referred to many of the relevant cases. With his analysis of the cases, as with the clear and careful judgment of Salmon J., I am in agreement, and I desire to add only some general observations upon the legal questions which this case involves.

Every synallagmatic contract contains in it the seeds of the problem: in what event will a party be relieved of his undertaking to do that which he has agreed to do but has not yet done? The contract may itself expressly define some of these events, as in the cancellation clause in a charterparty; but, human prescience being limited, it seldom does so exhaustively and often fails to do so at all. In some classes of contracts such as sale of goods, marine insurance, contracts of affreightment evidenced by bills of lading and those between parties to bills of exchange, Parliament has defined by statute some of the events not provided for expressly in individual contracts of that class; but where an event occurs the occurrence of which neither the parties nor Parliament have expressly stated will discharge one of the parties from further performance of his undertakings, it is for the court to determine whether the event has this effect or not.

The test whether an event has this effect or not has been stated in a number of metaphors all of which I think amount to the same thing: does the occurrence of the event deprive the party who has further undertakings still to perform of substantially the whole benefit which it was the intention of the parties as expressed in the contract that he should obtain as the consideration for performing those undertakings?

This test is applicable whether or not the event occurs as a result of the default of one of the parties to the contract, but the consequences of the event are different in the two cases. Where the event occurs as a result of the default of one party, the party in default cannot rely upon it as relieving himself of the performance of any further undertakings on his part, and the innocent party, although entitled to, need not treat the event as relieving him of the further performance of his own undertakings. This is only a specific application of the fundamental legal and moral rule that a man should not be allowed to take advantage of his own wrong. Where the event occurs as a result of the default of neither party, each is relieved of the further performance of his own undertakings, and their rights in respect of undertakings previously performed are now regulated by the Law Reform (Frustrated Contracts) Act, 1943.

This branch of the common law has reached its present stage by the normal process of historical growth, and the fallacy in Mr. Ashton Roskill's contention that a different test is applicable when the event occurs as a result of the default of one party from that applicable in cases of frustration where the event occurs as a result of the default of neither party lies, in my view, from a failure to view the cases in their historical context. The problem: in what event will a party to a contract be relieved of his undertaking to do that which he has agreed to do but has not yet done? has exercised the English courts for centuries, probably ever since assumpsit emerged as a form of action distinct from covenant and debt and long before even the earliest cases which we have been invited to examine; but until the rigour of the rule in *Paradine v. Jane* was mitigated in the middle of the last century by the classic judgments of Blackburn J. in *Taylor v. Caldwell* and Bramwell B. in *Jackson v. Union Marine Insurance Co. Ltd.*, (1874), L.R. 10 C.P. 125, it was in general only events resulting from one party's failure to perform his contractual obligations which were regarded as capable of relieving the other party from continuing to perform that which he had undertaken to do.

In the earlier cases before the Common Law Procedure Act, 1852, the problem tends to be obscured to modern readers by the rules of pleading peculiar to the relevant forms of action — covenant, debt and assumpsit — and the nomenclature adopted in the judgments, which were mainly on demurrer, reflects this. It was early recognised that contractual undertakings were of two different kinds: those collateral to the main purpose of the parties as expressed in the contract and those which were mutually dependent so that the non-performance by one party of an undertaking of this class was an event which excused the other party from the performance of his corresponding undertaking. In the nomenclature of the eighteenth and early nineteenth centuries undertakings of the latter class were called "conditions precedent" and a plaintiff under the rules of pleading had to aver specially in his declaration his performance or readiness and willingness to perform all those contractual undertakings on his part which constituted conditions precedent to the defendant's undertaking for non-performance of which the action was brought. In the earliest cases such as *Pordage v. Cole* (1669), 1 Wms. Saund. 319, and *Thorpe v. Thorpe* (1701), 12 Mod. 455, the question whether an undertaking was a condition precedent appears to have turned upon the verbal niceties of the particular phrases used in the written contract and it was not until 1773 that Lord Mansfield, in the case which is a legal landmark, *Boone v. Eyre*, swept away these arid technicalities. "The distinction," he said, "is very clear, *where mutual covenants go to the whole of the consideration on both sides, they are mutual conditions, the one precedent to the other. But where they go only to a part, where a* breach may be paid for in damages, there the defendant has a remedy on his covenant, and shall not plead it as a condition precedent."

This, too, was a judgment on demurrer, but the principle was the same when the substance of the matter was in issue. Other phrases expressing the same idea were used by other judges in the cases which have already been cited by Sellers L.J., and I would only add to his comments upon them that when it is borne in mind that until the latter half of the nineteenth century the only event that could be relied upon to excuse performance by one party of his undertakings was a default by the other party, no importance can be attached to the fact that in occasional cases, and there may be others besides *Freeman v. Taylor* (1831), 8 Bing. 124, the court has referred to the object or purpose of the party not in default rather than to the object or purpose of the contract, for the relevant object or purpose of the party not in default is that upon which there has been a consensus ad idem of both parties as expressed in the words which they have used in their contract construed in the light of the surrounding circumstances.

The fact that the emphasis in the earlier cases was upon the breach by one party to the contract of his contractual undertakings, for this was the commonest circumstance in which the question arose, tended to obscure the fact that it was really the event resulting from the breach which relieved the other party of further performance of his obligations; but the principle was applied early in the nineteenth century and without analysis to cases where the event relied upon was one brought about by a party to a contract before the time for performance of his undertakings arose but which would make it impossible to perform those obligations when the time to do so did arrive: for example... It was not, however, until *Jackson v. Union Marine Insurance Co. Ltd.* that it was recognised that it was the happening of the event and not the fact that the event was the result of a breach by one party of his contractual obligations that relieved the other party from further performance of his obligations.

"There are the cases," said Bramwell B. (p. 147), "which hold that, where the shipowner has not merely broken his contract, but has so broken it that the condition precedent is not performed, the charterer is discharged: ... Why? Not merely because the contract is broken. If it is not a condition precedent, what matters it whether it is unperformed with or without excuse? Not arriving with due diligence, or at a day named, is the subject of a cross-action only. But not arriving in time for the voyage contemplated, but at such a time that it is frustrated, is not only a breach of contract, but discharges the charterer. And so it should, though he has such an excuse that no action lies."

Once it is appreciated that it is the event and not the fact that the event is a result of a breach of contract which relieves the party not in default of further performance of his obligations, two consequences follow. (1) The test whether the event relied upon has this consequence is the same whether the event is the result of the other party's breach of contract or not, as Devlin J. pointed out in *Universal Cargo Carriers Corporation v. Citati*, [1957] 2 Q.B. 401. (2) The question whether an event which is the result of the other party's breach of contract has this consequence cannot be answered by treating all contractual undertakings as falling into one of two separate categories: "conditions" the breach of which gives rise to an event which relieves the party not in default of further performance of his obligations, and "warranties" the breach of which does not give rise to such an event.

Lawyers tend to speak of this classification as if it were comprehensive, partly for the historical reasons which I have already mentioned and partly because Parliament itself adopted it in the Sale of Goods Act, 1893, as respects a number of implied terms in contracts for the sale of goods and has in that Act used the expressions "condition" and "warranty" in that meaning. But it is by no means true of contractual undertakings in general at common law.

No doubt there are many simple contractual undertakings, sometimes express but more often because of their very simplicity ("It goes without saying") to be implied, of which it can be predicated that every breach of such an undertaking must give rise to an event which will deprive the party not in default of substantially the whole benefit which it was intended that he should obtain from the contract. And such a stipulation, unless the parties have agreed that breach of it shall not entitle the non-defaulting party to treat the contract as repudiated, is a "condition." So too there may be other simple contractual undertakings of which it can be predicated that *no* breach can give rise to an event which will deprive the party not in default of substantially the whole benefit which it was intended that he should obtain from the contract; and such a stipulation, unless the parties have agreed that breach of it shall entitle the non-defaulting party to treat the contract as repudiated, is a "warranty."

There are, however, many contractual undertakings of a more complex character which cannot be categorised as being "conditions" or "warranties," if the late nineteenth-century meaning adopted in the Sale of Goods Act, 1893, and used by Bowen L.J. in *Bentsen v. Taylor, Sons & Co.,* [1893] 2 Q.B. 274, be given to those terms. Of such undertakings all that can be predicated is that some breaches will and others will not give rise to an event which will deprive the party not in default of substantially the whole benefit which it was intended that he should obtain from the contract; and the legal consequences of a breach of such an undertaking, unless provided for expressly in the contract, depend upon the nature of the event to which the breach gives rise and do not follow automatically from a prior classification of the undertaking as a "condition" or a "warranty." For instance, to take Bramwell B.'s example in *Jackson v. Union Marine Insurance Co. Ltd.* itself, breach of an undertaking by a shipowner to sail with all possible dispatch to a named port does not necessarily relieve the charterer of further performance of his obligation under the charterparty, but if the breach is so prolonged that the contemplated voyage is frustrated it does have this effect.

In 1874 when the doctrine of frustration was being foaled by "impossibility of performance" out of "condition precedent" it is not surprising that the explanation given by Bramwell B. should give full credit to the dam by suggesting that in addition to the express *warranty* to sail with all possible dispatch there was an implied *condition precedent* that the ship should arrive at the named port in time for the voyage contemplated. In *Jackson v. Union Marine Insurance Co. Ltd.* there was no breach of the express warranty; but if there had been, to engraft the implied condition upon the express warranty would have been merely a more complicated way of saying that a breach of a shipowners's undertaking to sail with all possible dispatch may, but will not necessarily, give rise to an event which will deprive the charterer of substantially the whole benefit which it was intended that he should obtain from the charter. Now that the doctrine of frustration has matured and flourished for nearly a century and the old technicalities of pleading "conditions precedent" are more than a century out of date, it does not clarify, but on the contrary obscures, the modern principle of law where such an event *has* occurred as a result of a breach of an express stipulation in a contract, to continue to add the now unnecessary colophon "Therefore it was an implied *condition* of the contract that a particular kind of breach of an express *warranty* should not occur." The common law evolves not merely by breeding new principles but also, when they are fully grown, by burying their progenitors.

As my brethren have already pointed out, the shipowners' undertaking to tender a seaworthy ship has, as a result of numerous decisions as to what can amount to "unseaworthiness," become one of the most complex of contractual undertakings. It embraces obligations with respect to every part of the hull and machinery, stores and equipment and the crew itself. It can be broken by the presence of trivial defects easily and rapidly remediable as well as by defects which must inevitably result in a total loss of the vessel.

Consequently the problem in this case is, in my view, neither solved nor soluble by debating whether the shipowner's express or implied undertaking to tender a seaworthy ship is a "condition" or a "warranty." It is like so many other contractual terms an undertaking one breach of which may give rise to an event which relieves the charterer of further performance of his undertakings if he so elects and another breach of which may not give rise to such an event but entitle him only to monetary compensation in the form of damages. It is, with all deference to Mr. Ashton Roskill's skilful argument, by no means surprising that among the many hundreds of previous cases about the shipowner's undertaking to deliver a seaworthy ship there is none where it was found profitable to discuss in the judgments the question whether that undertaking is a "condition" or a "warranty"; for the true answer, as I have already indicated, is that it is neither, but one of that large class of contractual undertakings one breach of which may have the same effect as that ascribed to a breach of "condition" under the Sale of Goods Act, 1893, and a different breach of which may have only the same effect as that ascribed to a breach of "warranty" under that Act. The cases referred to by Sellers L.J. illustrate this...

What the judge had to do in the present case, as in any other case where one party to a contract relies upon a breach by the other party as giving him a right to elect to rescind the contract, and the contract itself makes no express provision as to this, was to look at the events which had occurred as a result of the breach at the time at which the charterers purported to rescind the charterparty and to decide whether the occurrence of those events deprived the charterers of substantially the whole benefit which it was the intention of the parties as expressed in the charterparty that the charterers should obtain from the further performance of their own contractual undertakings.

One turns therefore to the contract, the Baltime 1939 charter, of which Sellers L.J. has already cited the relevant terms. Clause 13, the "due diligence" clause, which exempts the shipowners from responsibility for delay or loss or damage to goods on board due to unseaworthiness, unless such delay or loss or damage has been caused by want of due diligence of the owners in making the vessel seaworthy and fitted for the voyage, is in itself sufficient to show that the mere occurrence of the events that the vessel was in some respect unseaworthy when tendered or that such unseaworthiness had caused some delay in performance of the charterparty would not deprive the charterer of the whole benefit which it was the intention of the parties he should obtain from the performance of his obligations under the contract — for he undertakes to continue to perform his obligations notwithstanding the occurrence of such events if they fall short of frustration of the contract and even deprives himself of any remedy in damages unless such events are the consequence of want of due diligence on the part of the shipowner.

The question which the judge had to ask himself was, as he rightly decided, whether or not at the date when the charterers purported to rescind the contract, namely, June 6, 1957, or when the shipowners purported to accept such rescission, namely, August 8, 1957, the delay which had already occurred as a result of the incompetence of the engine-room staff, and the delay which was likely to occur in repairing the engines of the vessel and the conduct of the shipowners by that date in taking steps to remedy these two matters, were, when taken together, such as to deprive the charterers of substantially the whole benefit which it was the intention of the parties they should obtain from further use of the vessel under the charterparty.

In my view, in his judgment — on which I would not seek to improve — the judge took into account and gave due weight to all the relevant considerations and arrived at the right answer for the right reasons.

NOTE ON TERMINOLOGY

The effect of an express condition in a contract can, as we have seen, bring a contractual obligation to an end or suspend such an obligation until the condition is satisfied. The feature common to a case like *Pym v. Campbell* and the *Hong Kong Fir Case* is that the obligation to perform either never arose or may be terminated. This possible effect on the obligation is why the *Hong Kong Fir Case* is put under the heading of "implied conditions." Since the effect of the event could have been to bring one party's obligation to an end, we could say that the question was whether the shipowner breached an implied condition of the contract. Such reasoning would put this case in the same line of cases as *Taylor v. Caldwell*. As we saw, to talk of implied terms is not helpful. The actual test suggested by Diplock L.J. is, of course, independent of any notion that the courts can only give relief in this kind of case through the implication of terms. It is better to use the term "condition" to refer to cases where there is an express clause in the agreement that may have a suspensive or determinative effect on the obligation. The effect of the *Hong Kong Fir Case* is simply that there may be an event which will bring the obligation to perform to an end. We do not have to refer to this as a condition of any kind.

The use of terms like condition is further complicated by the Sale of Goods Act. That act regards a condition as an important term of the contract. Thus condition is distinguished from warranty in the following way:

> "12(2). Whether a stipulation in a contract of sale is a condition the breach of which may give rise to a right to treat the contract as repudiated or a warranty the breach of which may give rise to a claim for damages but not to a right to reject the goods and treat the contract as repudiated depends in each case on the construction of the contract, and a stipulation may be a condition, though called a warranty in the contract."

Such an approach excludes the kind of test found in the *Hong Kong Fir Case*, since the only test is whether the *term* is sufficiently important that a breach of it should be considered as discharging one party from his obligation. You will find examples of this approach to the problem in the cases, and even in the textbooks. For example, Fridman, *The Law of Contract*, says (p. 272):

> "The more modern analysis of the court in the *Hong Kong Fir Case* does invite greater uncertainty, as well as greater flexibility. For this reason, in a commercial context, it may be less desirable, even though it might be more intelligible, valid and descriptive of the law."

The difficulty with the approach of the Sale of Goods Act is that it is never easy to classify the terms of the contract into conditions, warranties and representations. Secondly, the process of classification itself cannot offer any answers to the actual cases. Any such classification tends to be result-selective: if the court believes that one party should be discharged, then the term breached can be called a condition.

Of course, the parties may not have taken the trouble to spell out exactly what express conditions they want in the agreement. There is then always the problem of interpretation to determine what the parties meant or what agreement they will be held to. We saw this happening in *Schuler v. Wickman*. Similarly an event can have a suspensive or determinative effect even though not expressly stated to be a condition. This is just what one would expect and does not touch on the basic problems of cases like *Hong Kong Fir*.

In *Cehave N.V. v. Bremer*, [1975] 3 All E.R. 739, the English Court of Appeal rejected the exclusive application of s. 12(2) in cases under the Sale of Goods Act and held that the test was whether the breach was, in the context of the contract, so serious as to discharge one party from further performance. Lord Denning M.R. said (p. 747):

> "The task of the court can be stated simply in the way in which Upjohn LJ stated it (in the *Hong Kong Fir Case*, [1962] 2 Q.B. 26, 64). First, see whether the stipulation on its true construction, is a condition strictly so called, that is a stipulation such that, for any breach of it, the other party is entitled to treat himself as discharged. Second, if it is not such a condition, then look to the extent of the actual breach which has taken place. If it is such as to go to the root of the contract, the other party is entitled to treat himself as discharged; but, otherwise, not. To this may be added an anticipatory breach. If the one party, before the day on which he is due to perform his part, shows by his words or conduct that he will not perform it in a vital respect when the day comes, the other party is entitled to treat himself as discharged."

The next case is another example of this problem.

JACOB AND YOUNGS v. KENT

(1921), 129 N.E. 889. New York Court of Appeals.

Cardozo J. The plaintiff built a country residence for the defendant at a cost of upwards of $77,000, and now sues to recover a balance of $3,483.46, remaining unpaid. The work of construction ceased in June, 1914, and the defendant then began to occupy the dwelling. There was no complaint of defective performance until March, 1915. One of the specifications for the plumbing work provides that —

"All wrought-iron pipe must be well galvanized, lap welded pipe of the grade known as 'standard pipe' of Reading manufacture."

The defendant learned in March, 1915, that some of the pipe, instead of being made in Reading, was the product of other factories. The plaintiff was accordingly directed by the architect to do the work anew. The plumbing was then encased within the walls except in a few places where it had to be exposed. Obedience to the order meant more than the substitution of other pipe. It meant the demolition at great expense of substantial parts of the completed structure. The plaintiff left the work untouched, and asked for a certificate that the final payment was due. Refusal of the certificate was followed by this suit.

The evidence sustains a finding that the omission of the prescribed brand of pipe was neither fraudulent nor willful. It was the result of the oversight and inattention of the plaintiff's subcontractor. Reading pipe is distinguished from Cohoes pipe and other brands only by the name of the manufacturer stamped upon it at intervals of between six and seven feet. Even the defendant's architect, though he inspected the pipe on arrival, failed to notice the discrepancy. The plaintiff tried to show that the brands installed, though made by other manufacturers, were the same in quality, in appearance, in market value, and in cost as the brand stated in the contract — that they were, indeed, the same thing, though manufactured in another place. The evidence was excluded, and a verdict directed for the defendant. The Appellate Division reversed, and granted a new trial.

We think the evidence, if admitted, would have supplied some basis for the inference that the defect was insignificant in its relation to the project. The courts never say that one who makes a contract fills the measure of his duty by less than full performance. They do say, however, that an omission, both trivial and innocent, will sometimes be atoned for by allowance of the resulting damage, and will not always be the breach of a condition to be followed by a forfeiture.... The distinction is akin to that between dependent and independent promises, or between promises and conditions. Anson on *Contracts* (Corbin's Ed.) § 367; Williston on *Contracts*, § 842. Some promises are so plainly independent that they can never by fair construction be conditions of one another.... Others are so plainly dependent that they must always be conditions. Others, though dependent and thus conditions when there is departure in point of substance, will be viewed as independent and collateral when the departure is insignificant.... Considerations partly of justice and partly of presumable intention are to tell us whether this or that promise shall be placed in one class or in another. The simple and the uniform will call for different remedies from the multifarious and the intricate. The margin of departure within the range of normal expectation upon a sale of common chattels will vary from the margin to be expected upon a contract for the construction of a mansion or a "skyscraper". There will be harshness sometimes and oppression in the implication of a condition when the thing upon which labor has been expended is incapable of surrender because united to the land, and equity and reason in the implication of a like condition when the subject-matter, if defective, is in shape to be returned. From the conclusion that promises may not be treated as dependent to the extent of their uttermost minutiae without a sacrifice of justice, the progress is a short one to the conclusion that they may not be so treated without a perversion of intention. Intention not otherwise revealed may be presumed to hold in contemplation the reasonable and probable. If something else is in view, it must not be left to implication. There will be no assumption of a purpose to visit venial faults with oppressive retribution.

Those who think more of symmetry and logic in the development of legal rules than of practical adaptation to the attainment of a just result will be troubled by a classification where the lines of division are so wavering and blurred. Something, doubtless, may be said on the score of consistency and certainty in favor of a stricter standard. The courts have balanced such considerations against those of equity and fairness, and found the latter to be the weightier. The decisions in this state commit us to the liberal view, which is making its way, nowadays, in jurisdictions slow to welcome it. *Dakin & Co. v. Lee*, [1916] 1 K.B. 566, 579. Where the line is to be drawn between the important and the trivial cannot be settled by a formula. "In the nature of the case precise boundaries are impossible." 2 Williston on *Contracts*, § 841. The same omission may take on one aspect or another according to its setting. Substitution of equivalents may not have the same significance in fields of art on the one side and in those of mere utility on the other. Nowhere will change be tolerated, however, if it is so dominant or pervasive as in any real or substantial measure to frustrate the purpose of the contract.... There is no general license to install whatever, in the builder's judgment, may be regarded as "just as good".... The question is one of degree, to be answered, if there is doubt, by the triers of the facts... and, if the inferences are certain, by the judges of the law.... We must weigh the purpose to be served, the desire to be gratified, the excuse for deviation from the letter, the cruelty of enforced adherence. Then only can we tell whether literal fulfillment is to be implied by law as a condition. This is not to say that the parties are not freed by apt and certain words to effectuate a purpose that performance of every term shall be a condition of recovery. That question is not here. This is merely to say that the law will be slow to impute the purpose, in the silence of the parties, where the significance of the default is grievously out of proportion to the oppression of the forfeiture. The willful transgressor must accept the penalty of his transgression.... For him there is no occasion to mitigate the rigor of implied conditions. The transgressor whose default is unintentional and trivial may hope for mercy if he will offer atonement for his wrong....

In the circumstances of this case, we think the measure of the allowance is not the cost of replacement, which would be great, but the difference in value, which would be either nominal or nothing. Some of the exposed sections might perhaps have been replaced at moderate expense. The defendant did not limit his demand to them, but treated the plumbing as a unit to be corrected from cellar to roof. In point of fact, the plaintiff never reached the stage at which evidence of the extent of the allowance became necessary. The trial court had excluded evidence that the defect was unsubstantial, and in view of that ruling there was no occasion for the plaintiff to go farther with an offer of proof. We think, however, that the offer, if it had been made, would not of necessity have been defective because directed to difference in value. It is true that in most cases the cost of replacement is the measure. The owner is entitled to the money which will permit him to complete, unless the cost of completion is grossly and unfairly out of proportion to the good to be attained. When that is true, the measure is the difference in value. Specifications call, let us say, for a foundation built of granite quarried in Vermont. On the completion of the building, the owner learns that through the blunder of a subcontractor part of the foundation has been built of granite of the same quality quarried in New Hampshire. The measure of allowance is not the cost of reconstruction. "There may be omissions of that which could not afterwards be supplied exactly as called for by the contract without taking down the building to its foundations, and at the same time the omission may not affect the value of the building for use or otherwise, except so slightly as to be hardly appreciable."... The rule that gives a remedy in cases of substantial performance with compensation for defects of trivial or inappreciable importance has been developed by the courts as an instrument of justice. The measure of the allowance must be shaped to the same end.

The order should be affirmed, and judgment absolute directed in favor of the plaintiff upon the stipulation, with costs in all courts.

McLaughlin J. I dissent. The plaintiff did not perform its contract. Its failure to do so was either intentional or due to gross neglect which, under the uncontradicted facts, amounted to the same thing, nor did it make any proof of the cost of compliance, where compliance was possible.

. . .

I am of the opinion the trial court was right in directing a verdict for the defendant. The plaintiff agreed that all the pipe used should be of the Reading Manufacturing Company. Only about two-fifths of it, so far as appears, was of that kind. If more were used, then the burden of proving that fact was upon the plaintiff, which it could easily have done, since it knew where the pipe was obtained. The question of substantial performance of a contract of the character of the one under consideration depends in no small degree upon the good faith of the contractor. If the plaintiff had intended to, and had, complied with the terms of the contract except as to minor omissions, due to inadvertence, then he might be allowed to recover the contract price, less the amount necessary to fully compensate the defendant for damages caused by such omissions.... But that is not this case. It installed between 2,000 and 2,500 feet of pipe, of which only 1,000 feet at most complied with the contract. No explanation was given why pipe called for by the contract was not used, nor that any effort made to show what it would cost to remove the pipe of other manufacturers and install that of the Reading Manufacturing Company. The defendant had a right to contract for what he wanted. He had a right before making payment to get what the contract called for. It is no answer to this suggestion to say that the pipe put in was just as good as that made by the Reading Manufacturing Company, or that the difference in value between such pipe and the pipe made by the Reading Manufacturing Company would be either "nominal or nothing". Defendant contracted for pipe made by the Reading Manufacturing Company. What his reason was for requiring this kind of pipe is of no importance. He wanted that and was entitled to it. It may have been a mere whim on his part, but even so, he had a right to this kind of pipe, regardless of whether some other kind, according to the opinion of the contractor or experts, would have been "just as good, better, or done just as well". He agreed to pay only upon condition that the pipe installed were made by that company and he ought not to be compelled to pay unless that condition be performed.... The rule, therefore, of substantial performance, with damages for unsubstantial omissions, has no application....

What was said by this court in *Smith v. Brady*, 17 N.Y. 173, is quite applicable here:

> "I suppose it will be conceded that every one has a right to build his house, his cottage or his store after such a model and in such style as shall best accord with his notions of utility or be most agreeable to his fancy. The specifications of the contract become the law between the parties until voluntarily changed. If the owner prefers a plain and simple Doric column, and has so provided in the agreement, the contractor has no right to put in its place the more costly and elegant Corinthian. If the owner, having regard to strength and durability, has contracted for walls of specified materials to be laid in a particular manner, or for a given number of joists and beams, the builder has no right to substitute his own judgment or that of others. Having departed from the agreement, if performance has not been waived by the other party, the law will not allow him to allege that he has made as good a building as the one he engaged to erect. He can demand payment only upon and according to the terms of his contract, and if the conditions on which payment is due have not been performed, then the right to demand it does not exist. To hold a different doctrine would be simply to make another contract, and would be giving to parties an encouragement to violate their engagements, which the just policy of the law does not permit." (17 N.Y. 186, 72 Am. Dec. 442).

I am of the opinion the trial court did not err in ruling on the admission of evidence or in directing a verdict for the defendant.

For the foregoing reasons I think the judgment of the Appellate Division should be reversed and the judgment of the Trial Term affirmed.

Hiscock C.J. and Hogan and Crane JJ., concur with Cardozo J.

Pound and Andrews JJ., concur with McLaughlin J.

QUESTIONS

1. Is Cardozo doing here what he did in *Wood v. Lucy (supra)*?

2. Is the issue raised in this case the same as that in *Peevyhouse v. Garland Coal (supra)*? If it is what does that say about the approach of both courts?

3. What does McLaughlin J. mean by "right" when he says, "The defendant had a right to contract for what he wanted. He had a right before making payment to get what the contract called for".

4. Is his view of what the defendant could get by way of damages consistent with the attitude of the courts to damages and to specific performance as an alternative to damages?

B. Excuses for the Plaintiff's Non-Performance

In this section, we shall examine cases in which the plaintiff sues in respect of the defendant's breach even though the plaintiff himself has not performed his obligations under the contract in full before commencing suit.

The plaintiff claims that some "act" of the defendant released plaintiff from the full performance which would otherwise be required of plaintiff before suit could be brought.

What sort of considerations should influence a Court in deciding whether or not a plaintiff is released? The practical difficulties which face a lawyer advising a party in this sort of case are also illustrated in this section. When can a lawyer safely advise the client that there is no need to complete? What can a lawyer do to protect a client who wishes to escape, at the least possible cost, from a deal which now appears onerous?

CORT v. THE AMBERGATE RAILWAY CO.

(1851), 17 Q.B. 127; 117 E.R. 1229.

[The parties had made a contract under which the plaintiff would manufacture and sell to the defendant railway chairs for the building of the defendant's railway. The total amount of the chairs was about 4,000 tons. The defendant accepted about 1,800 tons (costing £12,000). Subsequently the defendants gave notice to the plaintiff that they would not take any more chairs. The plaintiff sued for damages for breach of the contract to take the full 4,000 tons. The defendant argued that the plaintiff had not proved that he was ready and willing to deliver the chairs.]

Lord Campbell C.J., on a later day of the term (June 4th), delivered the judgment of the Court.

Next we have to consider whether the plaintiffs were entitled to a verdict on the issue whether they were ready and willing to execute and perform the said contract according to the said conditions and stipulations, in manner and form, &c.; and on the issue whether the defendants did refuse to accept or receive the residue of the chairs, or prevent or discharge the plaintiffs from supplying the said residue, and from the further execution and performance of the said contract. It is not denied that, if the defendants would have regularly accepted and paid for the chairs, the plaintiffs would have gone on regularly making and delivering them according to the contract; the objection is that, although the plaintiffs were desirous that the contract should be fully performed, yet, after receiving the notice that the company did not wish to have any more chairs, and would not accept any more, they ceased to make any more, insomuch that the residue which the company are alleged to have refused to accept never were made. The defendants contend that, as the plaintiffs did not make and tender the residue of the chairs, they cannot be said to have been ready and willing to perform the contract; that the defendants cannot be charged with a breach of it; that, after the notice from the defendants, which in truth amounted to a declaration that they had broken and thenceforward renounced the contract, the plaintiffs, if they wished to have any redress, were bound to buy the requisite quantity of the peculiar sort of iron suited for these railway chairs, to make the whole of them according to the pattern, with the name of the company upon them, and to bring them to the appointed places of delivery and tender them to the defendants, who, from insolvency, had abandoned the completion of the line for which the chairs were intended, desiring that no more chairs might be made, and declaring, in effect, that no more should be accepted or paid for. We are of opinion, however, that the jury were fully justified upon the evidence in finding that the plaintiffs were ready and willing to perform the contract, although they never made and tendered the residue of the chairs. In common sense the meaning of such an averment of readiness and willingness must be that the noncompletion of the contract was not the fault of the plaintiffs, and that they were disposed and able to complete it if it had not been renounced by the defendants. What more can reasonably be required by the parties for whom the goods are to be manufactured? If, having accepted a part, they are unable to pay for the residue, and have resolved not to accept them, no benefit can accrue to them from a useless waste of materials and labour, which might possibly enhance the amount of damages to be awarded against them.

Upon the last issue, was there not evidence that the defendants refused to accept the residue of the chairs? If they had said, "Make no more for us, for we will have nothing to do with them," was not that refusing to accept or receive them according to the contract? But the learned counsel for the defendants laid peculiar stress upon the words "nor did they prevent or discharge the plaintiffs from supplying the said residue" of the chairs "and from the further execution and performance of the said contract." We consider the material part of the allegation which the last plea traverses to be, that the defendants refused to receive the residue of the chairs. But, assuming that the whole must be proved, we think there is evidence to shew that the defendants did prevent and discharge the plaintiffs from supplying the residue of the chairs, and from the further execution of the contract. It is contended that "prevent" here must mean an obstruction by physical force; and, in answer to a question from the Court, we were told it would not be a preventing of the delivery of goods if the purchaser were to write, in a letter to the person who ought to supply them, "Should you come to my house to deliver them, I will blow your brains out." But may I not reasonably say that I was prevented from completing a contract by being desired not to complete it? Are there no means of preventing an act from being done, except physical force or brute violence? Again, we are told there can be no "discharge" by a corporation unless by deed under the corporate seal. Of a discharge in one sense of the word this is true. A discharge is sometimes used as equivalent to a release, which must be under seal... But we conceive that, in the allegation traversed by the last plea, discharge only means, like prevent, that the act of the defendants was the cause of the residue of the chairs not being delivered, and of the contract not being further executed or performed. Taking the language employed in its natural and reasonable sense, there was abundant evidence to support the finding of the last issue for the plaintiffs.

It is averred, however, that there are express authorities to shew that there could be no readiness and willingness to perform the contract unless all the chairs were finished and tendered; that to prevent must be by positive physical obstruction, and that there can be no discharging unless by instrument under seal....

Upon the whole, we think we are justified, on principle and without trenching on any former decision, in holding that, when there is an executory contract for the manufacturing and supply of goods from time to time, to be paid for after delivery, if the purchaser, having accepted and paid for a portion of the goods contracted for, gives notice to the vendor not to manufacture any more as he has no occasion for them and will not accept or pay for them, the vendor having been desirous and able to complete the contract, he may, without manufacturing and tendering the rest of the goods, maintain an action against the purchaser for breach of contract; and that he is entitled to a verdict on pleas traversing allegations that he was ready and willing to perform the contract, that the defendant refused to accept the residue of the goods, and that he prevented and discharged the plaintiff from manufacturing and delivering them.

We are likewise of opinion that, in this case, the damages are not excessive, as the jury were justified in taking into their calculation all the chairs which remained to be delivered, and which the defendants refused to accept. They were all included in the declaration and in the issues joined:

the time mentioned in the proposal for the delivery of some of them had arrived before the notice was given; but the time of delivery was not of the essence of the contract; and the obligation was still incumbent upon the defendants to accept the whole of the residue.

The rule must therefore be discharged.

Rule discharged.

HOCHSTER v. DE LA TOUR

(1853), 2 El. & Bl. 678; 118 E.R. 922.

[On April 12, 1852 the defendant agreed to employ the plaintiff as a courier to travel in Europe. The engagement was to begin on June 1, 1852. On May 11, 1852 the defendant told the plaintiff that he had changed his mind and would not need his services. The plaintiff commenced this action on May 22. It was argued on behalf of the defendant that the action had been brought too soon, that there could be no breach before June 1.]

Lord Campbell C.J. now delivered the judgment of the Court.

On this motion in arrest of judgment, the question arises, Whether, if there be an agreement between A. and B., whereby B. engages to employ A. on and from a future day for a given period of time, to travel with him into a foreign country as a courier, and to start with him in that capacity on that day, A. being to receive a monthly salary during the continuance of such service, B. may, before the day, refuse to perform the agreement and break and renounce it, so as to entitle A. before the day to commence an action against B. to recover damages for breach of the agreement; A. having been ready and willing to perform it, till it was broken and renounced by B. The defendant's counsel very powerfully contended that, if the plaintiff was not contented to dissolve the contract, and to abandon all remedy upon it, he was bound to remain ready and willing to perform it till the day when the actual employment as courier in the service of the defendant was to begin; and that there could be no breach of the agreement, before that day, to give a right of action. But it cannot be laid down as a universal rule that, where by agreement an act is to be done on a future day, no action can be brought for a breach of the agreement till the day for doing the act has arrived. If a man promises to marry a woman on a future day, and before that day marries another woman, he is instantly liable to an action for breach of promise of marriage.... If a man contracts to execute a lease on and from a future day for a certain term, and, before that day, executes a lease to another for the same term, he may be immediately sued for breaking the contract... So, if a man contracts to sell and deliver specific goods on a future day, and before the day he sells and delivers them to another, he is immediately liable to an action at the suit of the person with whom he first contracted to sell and deliver them ... One reason alleged in support of such an action is, that the defendant has, before the day, rendered it impossible for him to perform the contract at the day: but this does not necessarily follow; for, prior to the day fixed for doing the act, the first wife may have died, a surrender of the lease executed might be obtained, and the defendant might have repurchased the goods so as to be in a situation to sell and deliver them to the plaintiff. Another reason may be, that, where there is a contract to do an act on a future day, there is a relation constituted between the parties in the meantime by the contract, and that they impliedly promise that in the meantime neither will do any thing to the prejudice of the other inconsistent with that relation. As an example, a man and woman engaged to marry are affianced to one another during the period between the time of the engagement and the celebration of the marriage. In this very case, of traveller and courier, from the day of the hiring till the day when the employment was to begin, they were engaged to each other; and it seems to be a breach of an implied contract if either of them renounces the engagement. ... The declaration in the present case, in alleging a breach, states a great deal more than a passing intention on the part of the defendant which he may repent of, and could only be proved by evidence that he had utterly renounced the contract, or done some act which rendered it impossible for him to perform it. If the plaintiff has no remedy for breach of the contract unless he treats the contract as in force, and acts upon it down to the 1st June 1852, it follows that, till then, he must enter into no employment which will interfere with his promise "to start with the defendant on such travels on the day and year," and that he must then be properly equipped in all respects as a courier for a three months' tour on the continent of Europe. But it is surely much more rational, and more for the benefit of both parties, that, after the renunciation of the agreement by the defendant, the plaintiff should be at liberty to consider himself absolved from any future performance of it, retaining his right to sue for any damage he has suffered from the breach of it. Thus, instead of remaining idle and laying out money in preparations which must be useless, he is at liberty to seek service under another employer, which would go in mitigation of the damages to which he would otherwise be entitled for a breach of the contract. It seems strange that the defendant, after renouncing the contract, and absolutely declaring that he will never act under it, should be permitted to object that faith is given to his assertion, and that an opportunity is not left to him of changing his mind. If the plaintiff is barred of any remedy by entering into an engagement inconsistent with starting as a courier with the defendant on the 1st June, he is prejudiced by putting faith in the defendant's assertion: and it would be more consonant with principle, if the defendant were precluded from saying that he had not broken the contract when he declared that he entirely renounced it. Suppose that the defendant, at the time of his renunciation, had embarked on a voyage for Australia, so as to render it physically impossible for him to employ the plaintiff as a courier on the continent of Europe in the months of June, July and August 1852: according to decided cases, the action might have been brought before the 1st June; but the renunciation may have been founded on other facts, to be given in evidence, which would equally have rendered the defendant's performance of the contract impossible. The man who wrongfully renounces a contract into which he has deliberately entered cannot justly complain if he is immediately sued for a compensation in damages by the man whom he has injured: and it seems reasonable to allow an option to the injured party, either to sue immediately, or to wait till the time when the act was to be done, still holding it as prospectively binding for the exercise of this option, which may be advantageous to the innocent party, and cannot be prejudicial to the wrongdoer. An argument against the action before the 1st of June is urged from the difficulty of calculating the damages: but this argument is equally strong against an action before the 1st of September, when the three months would expire. In either case, the jury in assessing the dam-

ages would be justified in looking to all that had happened, or was likely to
happen, to increase or mitigate the loss of the plaintiff down to the day of
trial. We do not find any decision contrary to the view we are taking of this
case.

.   .   .

If it should be held that, upon a contract to do an act on a future day, a
renunciation of the contract by one party dispenses with a condition to be
performed in the meantime by the other, there seems no reason for requiring that other to wait till the day arrives before seeking his remedy by
action: and the only ground on which the condition can be dispensed with
seems to be, that the renunciation may be treated as a breach of the contract.

Upon the whole, we think that the declaration in this case is sufficient. It
gives us great satisfaction to reflect that, the question being on the record,
our opinion may be reviewed in a Court of Error. In the meantime we must
give judgment for the plaintiff.

Judgment for plaintiff.

NOTE

In *Frost v. Knight* (1872), L.R. 7 Exch. 111, the decision in *Hochster v. De La Tour*
was approved. In *Frost v. Knight*, the plaintiff sought damages for breach of promise
of marriage. The parties had agreed to marry on the death of the defendant's father.
The defendant, before his father's death, said that he would not marry the plaintiff.
The plaintiff immediately sued. Cockburn C.J., in giving judgment said:

"The law with reference to a contract to be performed at a future time, where the
party bound to performance announces prior to the time his intention not to perform it, as established by the cases of *Hochster v. De la Tour*... may be thus stated. The promisee, if he pleases, may treat the notice of intention as inoperative,
and await the time when the contract is to be executed, and then hold the other
party responsible for all the consequences of non-performance: but in that case
he keeps the contract alive for the benefit of the other party as well as his own;
he remains subject to all his own obligations and liabilities under it, and enables
the other party not only to complete the contract, if so advised, notwithstanding
his previous repudiation of it, but also to take advantage of any supervening circumstance which would justify him in declining to complete it.

"On the other hand, the promisee may, if he thinks proper, treat the repudiation
of the other party as a wrongful putting an end to the contract, and may at once
bring his action as on a breach of it; and in such action he will be entitled to such
damages as would have arisen from the non-performance of the contract at the
appointed time, subject, however, to abatement in respect of any circumstances
which may have afforded him the means of mitigating his loss."

This is usually regarded as the classic statement of the law. He went on to say:

"The contract having been thus broken by the promisor, and treated as broken
by the promisee, performance at the appointed time becomes excluded, and the
breach by reason of the future non-performance becomes virtually involved in
the action as one of the consequences of the repudiation of the contract; and the
eventual non-performance may therefore, by anticipation, be treated as a cause
of action, and damages be assessed and recovered in respect of it, though the
time for performance may yet be remote.

"It is obvious that such a course must lead to the convenience of both parties;
and though we should be unwilling to found our opinion on grounds of convenience alone, yet the latter tend strongly to support the view that such an action
ought to be admitted and upheld. By acting on such a notice of the intention of
the promisor, and taking timely measures, the promisee may in many cases avert,
or at all events materially lessen, the injurious effects which would otherwise flow

from the non-fulfilment of the contract; and in assessing the damages for breach of performance, a jury will of course take into account whatever the plaintiff has done, or has had the means of doing, and, as a prudent man, ought in reason to have done, whereby his loss has been, or would have been, diminished.

"It appears to us that the foregoing considerations apply to the case of a contract the performance of which is made to depend on a contingency, as much as to one in which the performance is to take place at a future time; and we are, therefore, of opinion that the principle of the decision of *Hochster v. De la Tour* is equally applicable to such a case as the present."

Cockburn, C.J. further said that allowing the plaintiff to sue immediately would reduce the damages suffered by the plaintiff since she would become less marriageable as she got older.

DALRYMPLE v. SCOTT

(1892), 19 O.A.R. 477. Ontario Court of Appeal; Hagarty C.J.O., Burton, Osler, and Maclennan JJ.A.

[The defendants had agreed to sell flour to the plaintiff. The agreement was made in letters and telegrams between the parties; the defendants' offer was accepted by the plaintiffs on March 27, 1890. On April 15, 1890 the defendants wrote to the plaintiffs "cancelling the order" of the plaintiffs. The defendants were held to have had no right to do this. Nothing further occurred after the letter of April 15, until the action was commenced in June, 1890.

The trial judge held that there was no contract and dismissed the action. This was reversed by the Queen's Bench Division. The defendant appealed.]

Osler J.A. In the case at bar, the plaintiffs declare upon the contract and aver the performance of it on their part according to its original terms; that is to say, they aver that they duly demanded the delivery of the flour, and that they were always ready and willing to accept and pay for the same. They say nothing about the renunciation or repudiation of the contract by the defendants, or of their having adopted or acted upon such repudiation. The Divisional Court appears to have regarded their "taking no further action in respect of the contract" as a sufficient acting upon the refusal of the defendants to perform it to bring the case within the rule, but with all deference, I think that cannot be so. All that can be said is, that the plaintiffs had taken no notice of the defendants' attempted rescission of the contract. They had done nothing to interfere with the performance of it on their part according to its original terms. They might, notwithstanding the defendants' notice, have demanded its performance at the proper time, and they did nothing to shew that they did not intend to do so. Their statement of claim, on the contrary, shews that they are proceeding as upon a breach of the contract at the time fixed for the performance; and they allege, as they were in that view bound to allege and prove, a performance of conditions precedent on their part, one of which at least was a demand for the delivery of the flour. But they proved no demand, and seem to have relied upon the fact of their not having made one as evidence that they had adopted the defendants' notice as a breach of their contract, or else that not having retracted their notice, it was evidence of a continued refusal on their part to perform it, so as to dispense with the performance of conditions precedent on their part.

The case of *Frost v. Knight*, L. R. 7 Exch. 111, is entirely opposed to this.

[Osler J.A. quoted the judgment of Cockburn C.J. in that case that is reproduced, *supra*.]

Clearly, what the plaintiffs have done here is to adopt the first of the two alternatives shewn to be open to them. They have treated the defendants' notice of intention to break their contract as inoperative, and have chosen to await the time when the contract was to be executed, and then in an action for breach of the contract at that time to attempt to hold the defendants responsible without proof of performance of the conditions precedent on their part.

[Hagarty C.J.O. and Burton J.A. agreed with Osler J.A.]

[Maclennan J.A. dissented.]

———————

Re-read at this point: *White and Carter (Councils) Ltd. v. McGregor*, [1962] A.C. 413; House of Lords. (Reproduced, *supra*, Chap. 1.)

PROBLEMS

1. Suppose that the following conversation takes place:
Sarah, "I know that I promised that I would have 100 cartons of paper ready for you at the end of the month, but I am afraid that it looks as if I can't make it."
Dick, "This is really serious for me, I have several orders to fill for which I need that paper. I shall have to go and find someone else and I expect you to pay the difference."
Can Dick sue Sarah for breach of contract at this point?
2. Suppose now that Dick replies to Sarah as follows:
Dick, "I really need that paper; I have a lot riding on what I can produce in the next few weeks. Please do what you can to meet my order."
Sarah: "O.K. I'll do what I can, but I am not optimistic."
A week later, Dick believes that there is almost no chance that Sarah can perform her contract with him. Can Dick safely go out to obtain an alternative supply? What steps can he take to make it safe for him to do so?

BRITISH AND BENNINGTONS LTD. v. NORTH WESTERN CACHAR TEA CO. LTD.

[1923] A.C. 48. House of Lords; Lords Atkinson, Sumner, Buckmaster, Wrenbury and Carson.

[The parties had entered into a contract in Sept. 1919 for the sale of tea by the respondents to the appellants. The contract provided that the teas purchased were to be delivered to a bonded warehouse in London. There was heavy congestion in the Port of London in 1920 and ships carrying the tea covered by the contract were diverted away from London. The buyers ultimately attempted to reject the tea because it had not been delivered in London within a reasonable time as, they argued, the contract required.

The dispute went to arbitration and the arbitrator made an award in favour of the sellers. He found that the buyers had repudiated the contract by letters written on July 15 and 28, 1920. He also found that a reasonable time for delivery had not expired by July 28, 1920. He awarded damages to the sellers, and stated a case for the court.]

Lord Atkinson ... The sellers, in order to sustain this award, must take their stand on the written contract. And if the buyers had not repudiated it, and had been suing for some breach of it, I did not understand it to be contended that at the time of the alleged breach they were ready and willing to deliver the goods. Lord Abinger, in *De Medina v. Norman* (1842), 9 M. & W. 820, 827 laid down that the words, "readiness and willingness," used in such a connection, imply not only the disposition but the capacity to perform the contract. But the point has been urged by the respondents, and was much relied upon by the Court of Appeal, that when a buyer, before breach of a contract for the sale of goods, repudiates it, as was held by the arbitrator the appellants on July 28, 1920, did in this case, and that repudiation is accepted and acted upon by the seller, as it evidently was in this case, the seller is relieved from the performance of all conditions precedent, including the condition of being ready and willing at the date of repudiation to deliver the goods. In *Jones v. Barkley* (1781), 2 Doug. K. B. 684, Lord Mansfield says: "Take it on the reason of the thing. The party must shew he was ready; but, if the other stops him on the ground of an intention not to perform his part, it is not necessary for the first to go farther, and do a nugatory act. Here, the draft was shewn to the defendant for his approbation of the form, but he would not read it, and, upon a different ground, namely, that he means not to pay the money, discharges the plaintiffs." . . .

The case of *Cort v. Ambergate, &c., Ry. Co.* is something to the same effect. There the plaintiffs contracted with the defendant company to manufacture and from time to time supply to them certain goods, called railway chairs, to be paid for after delivery. The defendant company were by the plaintiffs supplied with, accepted, and paid for a certain portion of these goods. The defendant company then gave the plaintiffs notice not to manufacture any more chairs as they, the company, had no need for them, and would neither accept nor pay for them. The plaintiffs were desirous and able to manufacture the chairs and complete the supply. It was held that the plaintiffs were entitled, without manufacturing or tendering the rest of the chairs, to maintain an action against the purchasers, the defendant company, for breach of contract, and that the proof of this notice enabled the plaintiffs to recover on a count alleging readiness and willingness to perform the contract, and that the defendant company's refusal to accept the goods absolved them from supplying them.

Lord Campbell, in delivering judgment, said: "The defendants contend that, as the plaintiffs did not make and tender the residue of the chairs, they cannot be said to have been ready and willing to perform the contract." He then points out that the defendants had in effect declared that they would not accept or pay for any more of the chairs than they had already received. He then said "that the jury were fully justified upon the evidence in finding that the plaintiffs were ready and willing to perform the contract, although they never made and tendered the residue of the chairs. In common sense the meaning of such an averment of readiness and willingness must be that the noncompletion of the contract was not the fault of the plaintiffs, and that they were disposed and able to complete it if it had not been renounced by the defendants. What more can reasonably be required by the parties for whom the goods are to be manufactured?"

In *Braithwaite v. Foreign Hardwood Co.*, [1905] 2 K.B. 543, the contract provided for the sale of rosewood in the year 1903 to be delivered at Hull in instalments during the year. While the first consignment was on the sea the buyers repudiated the contract and refused to accept the rosewood, on the ground that the seller had committed a breach of a collateral contract not to supply rosewood to any person in the trade other than the buyers during the year 1903. When the bill of lading was tendered to the buyers for the first consignment they refused to accept it or to pay for the rosewood covered by it. The seller sold this rosewood and claimed from the buyers, as damages for their refusal to accept, the difference between the contract price and the price at which it was sold. The second consignment was treated in the same manner. The buyers subsequently discovered that some portion of the first consignment, though none of the second, was of an inferior quality, which would be compensated for by an allowance of 6 per cent. The seller having sued the buyers for damages for not accepting the rosewood, the defendants pleaded: (1.) that the purchase was subject to this collateral agreement; and (2.) that they were entitled to repudiate the contract on the ground that the shipments of rosewood tendered under the contract were not of a good, sound and merchantable quality. The learned judge who tried the case found that the collateral agreement never existed, that the repudiation was wrongful, and that it was accepted by the plaintiff as final; but he also found that the first consignment was not according to contract, and that it would have entitled the defendants to repudiate the whole of the consignment had they not previously repudiated. It was this obligation to prove that the first consignment was not of inferior quality that the plaintiff was relieved from establishing. The Master of the Rolls (Sir Richard Henn Collins as he then was) said, [1905] 2 K.B. 543, 552: "The defendants are not in a position now, by reason of their after-acquired knowledge, to set up a defence which they previously elected not to take. We must in such a case look to see whether, at the time of each alleged breach, each side was ready and willing to perform the conditions of the contract which it lay upon them to perform, and there was clearly a breach by the defendants, for they had by their own act absolved the plaintiff from the performance of the conditions of the contract." As Lord Mansfield says (1781), 2 Doug. K.B. 684, 694: "The party must shew he was ready; but, if the other stops him on the ground of an intention not to perform his part, it is not necessary for the first to go farther, and do a nugatory act."

In *In re Bayley-Worthington and Cohen's Contract*, [1909] 1 Ch. 648, 664, Parker J. (as he then was) says: "In my opinion the repudiation of the contract by the purchaser relieved the vendors during such time as the purchaser insisted on repudiation from proceeding with their part of the bargain." ...

I am therefore of opinion that the purchasers, having on July 28, 1920, wrongfully repudiated their contract, the sellers were not, in order to recover damages for breach of this contract, bound to prove that they were ready and willing on that day to deliver the teas at London. No distinction can be drawn between the three cases. The answer to the question submitted by the arbitrator is therefore that the amounts awarded should stand.

[The other law Lords agreed in the result reached by Lord Atkinson.]

PROBLEMS

1. By contract dated July 1, Mary promised to sell goods to Tom. She promised to deliver on October 1. On September 1, Tom tells Mary that he will not accept delivery of the goods. Mary does nothing. Mary sues for breach of contract on September 15. On September 30, the goods that Mary would have delivered to Tom are destroyed by fire so that she could not have performed her contract with Tom

before January 2. Assume that the goods tendered on January 2 could be refused by Tom. Is Tom liable to Mary?

2. Bruce agreed to paint Ted's house. The contract was a standard one that Bruce used for all his work. It provided that, while Ted must determine colour and quality of the paint, in the absence of any specification of maker by him, Bruce could use paint manufactured by anyone. Bruce always used paint made by Coverall Ltd. Unknown to Bruce, Ted owned shares in a competing paint manufacturer called Glosheen Ltd. Ted had expected Bruce to use paint by Glosheen. After Bruce had put on the first of two coats, Ted found that Bruce had used Coverall paint. Ted said that he would pay for what had been done, but that he would not let Bruce do any more. Bruce immediately stopped the work and sued Ted for breach. When the action came on for trial Ted discovered that Bruce had planned to use paint of quality inferior to that specified by Ted.

Does this fact give Ted any defence to the action brought by Bruce?

Many contracts provide for performance to take place over a period of time. Thus in contracts of sale the delivery of the goods may be made over a period. Payment may be made for each delivery or at some other time. These kinds of contracts have always caused problems. The question is to know what to say to a client when the party with whom the client is dealing has not complied with the contract. The Sale of Goods Act provides:

> "30(2) Where there is a contract for the sale of goods to be delivered by stated instalments that are to be separately paid for and the seller makes defective deliveries in respect of one or more instalments or fails to deliver one or more instalments or the buyer neglects or refuses to take delivery of or pay for one or more instalments, it is a question in each case depending on the terms of the contract and the circumstances of the case whether the breach of contract is repudiation of the whole contract or whether it is a severable breach giving rise to a claim or compensation but not to a right to treat the whole contract as repudiated."

The position at common law would be the same both in cases of sales before the Act and in cases outside the Act. This is not to suggest that the act or common law rules are always easy to apply.

In *Bettini v. Gye* (1876), 1 Q.B.D. 183, the plaintiff, an opera singer, sued for damages for breach of contract when he was not allowed to perform an engagement he had been promised. The defendant argued that the plaintiff had breached the contract by missing a week of rehearsals before the opening. The court held that this was not a breach that would entitle the defendant to regard the contract as at an end and that, therefore, the defendant was liable for breach.

In *Poussard v. Spiers* (1876), 1 Q.B.D. 410, the plaintiff, also an opera singer, sued for breach of her engagement. She had missed the opening night's performance and the next three nights. The defendant was held to be entitled to regard his obligation at an end by reason of her breach. The court in this case consisted of two (out of three) of the judges who decided *Bettini v. Gye*.

The cases appear to make important exactly what one would expect: opening night is more important than rehearsals. In *Bettini v. Gye*, the plaintiff had agreed not to sing in England for three months before the engagement that he had with the defendant. There was then reliance and a partly executed contract.

C. Restitution in the Event of the Plaintiff's Breach

In some cases, a plaintiff may sue although the plaintiff has breached the contract without excuse. The plaintiff admits that the defendant is entitled to damages, but claims to have conferred on the defendant before the breach occurred benefits greater than the defendant's damages.

Two cases are typical: the plaintiff has made a payment in advance to the defendant, and has then defaulted; or the plaintiff has begun to perform, by supplying work or goods to the defendant, before breach.

It is accepted that the plaintiff cannot sue "in contract", since the plaintiff has not performed the obligations required and has not been excused from their performance. But it is clear that, in some cases, the plaintiff can bring a restitution action, claiming the value of the benefits in defendant's hands over and above defendant's damages.

Some of the difficulties involved in bringing such actions are canvassed in this section.

HOWE v. SMITH

(1884), 27 Ch. D. 89. Court of Appeal, England; Cotton, Bowen and Fry L.JJ.

Fry L.J. On the 24th of March, 1881, the Defendant and Plaintiff entered into an agreement in writing, by which the Defendant agreed to sell and the purchaser agreed to buy certain real estate for £12,500, of which £500 was in the contract stated to have been paid on the signing of the agreement as a deposit and in part payment of the purchase-money. The contract provided for the payment of the balance on the 24th of April, 1881, and it further provided by the 8th condition that if the purchaser should fail to comply with the agreement the vendor should be at liberty to resell the premises, and the deficiency on such second sale thereof, with all expenses attending the same, should be made good by the defaulter and be recoverable as liquidated damages.

The Plaintiff, the purchaser, did not pay the balance of his purchase-money on the day stipulated, and he has been guilty of such delay and neglect in completing that, according to our judgment already expressed, he has lost all right to the specific performance of the contract in equity.

The question then arises which has been argued before us, although not before Mr. Justice *Kay*, whether or not the Plaintiff is entitled to recover the £500 paid on the signing of the contract.

The £500 was paid, in the words of the contract, as "a deposit and in part payment of the purchase-money." What is the meaning of this expression? The authorities seem to leave the matter in some doubt.

.   .   .

These authorities appear to afford no certain light to answer the inquiry whether, in the absence of express stipulation, money paid as a deposit on the signing of a contract can be recovered by the payer if he has made such default in performance of his part as to have lost all right to performance by the other party to the contract or damages for his own non-performance.

Money paid as a deposit must, I conceive, be paid on some terms implied or expressed. In this case no terms are expressed, and we must therefore inquire what terms are to be implied. The terms most naturally to be implied appear to me in the case of money paid on the signing of a contract to be that in the event of the contract being performed it shall be brought into account, but if the contract is not performed by the payer it shall remain the property of the payee. It is not merely a part payment, but is then also an earnest to bind the bargain so entered into, and creates by the fear of its forfeiture a motive in the payer to perform the rest of the contract.

The practice of giving something to signify the conclusion of the contract, sometimes a sum of money, sometimes a ring or other object, to be repaid or redelivered on the completion of the contract, appears to be one of great antiquity and very general prevalence. It may not be unimportant to observe as evidence of this antiquity that our own word "earnest" has been supposed to flow from a Phoenician source through... the Greeks, the *arra* or *arrha* of the Latins, and the *arrhes* of the French. It was familiar to the law of Rome, ...

Taking these early authorities into consideration, I think we may conclude that the deposit in the present case is the earnest or *arrha* of our earlier writers; that the expression used in the present contract that the money is paid "as a deposit and in part payment of the purchase-money," relates to the two alternatives, and declares that in the event of the purchaser making default the money is to be forfeited, and that in the event of the purchase being completed the sum is to be taken in part payment.

Such being my view of the nature of the deposit, it appears to me to be clear that the purchaser has lost all right to recover it if he has lost both his right to specific performance in equity and his right to sue for damages for its non-performance at law. That the purchaser has by his delay lost all rights to specific performance we have already decided. It remains to inquire whether he has also lost all right to sue for damages for its non-performance.

.   .   .

But in my opinion there has been such default as justifies the vendor in treating the contract as rescinded; it affords the vendor an alternative remedy, so that he may either affirm the contract and sell under this clause or rescind the contract and sell under his absolute title. If he acts under the clause, he must bring the deposit into account in his claim for the deficiency: if he sell as owner, he may retain the deposit, but loses his claim for the deficiency under the clause in question.

For these reasons I conclude that the appeal must be dismissed, with costs.

[Cotton and Bowen L.JJ. agreed with Fry L.J.]

DIES v. BRITISH AND INTERNATIONAL MINING AND FINANCE CORP. LTD.

[1939] 1 K.B. 724. King's Bench Division.

Stable J. The facts, so far as they are material, are not in dispute, and no evidence was called by either side except as to the meaning of certain French words and as to the amount of damages, if any, recoverable by the defendant corporation against the plaintiffs. The facts may shortly be summarized as follows: Mr. Quintana, the plaintiff, being minded to buy a large quantity of Mauser rifles and the appropriate ammunition, entered into a contract with the defendant corporation, the terms of which are set out in the two letters dated November 14, 1936. For the purposes of the present action the second letter may be ignored. Subsequently this contract was either varied or a new contract was substituted in its place, it matters not which, but in the result the terms of the contract which it is accepted was ultimately made between the parties are to be found in the three letters.

The contract was a contract governed by the law of England. The language employed by the contracting parties was French. The translations of the contractual letters into the English language have been agreed, with the exception of certain words the meanings of which are in dispute and which were the subject-matter of evidence called before me. In substance, the contract provided for the sale by the defendant corporation to Mr. Quintana of a number of Mauser rifles and a quantity of ammunition at the price of £270,000. The goods were stated in the contract to be destined for Turkey. Delivery was to be made by December 15, 1936, which date was extended by mutual agreement, and it appears for the mutual convenience of both of the contracting parties, to January 15, 1937.

As regards the price, £100,000. was paid on or about November 14, 1936, and the plaintiff, Mr. Quintana, was to provide for the balance of the purchase price by means of an irrevocable credit to be opened in favour of the defendant corporation with a bank in Prague, and perhaps, after the quantity of the rifles sold was increased, by a further cash payment of £100,000. and the enlargement of the credit. This latter point is not very clear and is in any event immaterial. The transaction was complicated by the fact that the original contract of November 14 was for the sale of 10,000 units at a price of £135,000., a unit consisting of one rifle and 1000 rounds of the appropriate ammunition. By the letter of December 19, 1936, the quantity of the goods sold was increased to 20,000 units, and the price was correspondingly doubled. No other material alteration was made in the terms of the contract. Mr. Quintana paid to the corporation the sum of £100,000. and no more, and it is this sum or part of this sum that the plaintiffs claim to be entitled to recover in this action.

Notwithstanding the fact that he had made this substantial payment, for reasons which have not been disclosed to me Mr. Quintana was unable to take delivery of any of the rifles or ammunition sold to him. It is admitted in the statement of claim that the contract was broken by Mr. Quintana in that he never paid the additional £100,000. or opened the additional credit of £35,000., and was never ready or willing to take delivery. A certain amount of reticence has been observed as to the causes or circumstances which occasioned this breach, but the breach itself is admitted. By a letter dated February 4, 1937, the defendant corporation, as they were lawfully entitled to do in view of the breach or breaches of contract by Mr. Quintana going to the root of the contract, elected to treat the contract as being at an end in the sense that it ceased to impose any obligation of further performance on either party. As from the letter of February 4, 1937, the right of the defendant corporation was to sue Mr. Quintana, the other contracting party, for the damages they had sustained by reason of his breach of contract, and their obligation to deliver the goods was at an end.

[Stable J. discussed the terms of the contract and an argument that the defendant was entitled, under the contract, to keep at least the £13,500 as liquidated damages. He held that the defendant was not entitled to do this.]

The matter has to be decided, in my judgment, not on any express or implied term contained in the contract, but on the principle of law applicable where the contract itself is silent, except in so far as the intention of the parties can be ascertained from the designation used to indicate the nature of the sum that was paid. On this basis the plaintiffs' contention can, I think, be fairly summarized as follows: Where there is a contract for the sale of goods, and a part payment for the goods is made, but no goods are delivered or tendered by reason of the default of the buyer, the seller's only remedy is to recover damages for the default, while the buyer, notwithstanding that it is by reason of his default that the contract has not been performed, is entitled to recover the purchase price that he has paid, subject possibly to the right of the seller to set off against that claim the damages to which he can establish his title.

In support of this contention a number of authorities were cited to me. The form of declaration or count which it was said embraced a claim of this nature was the old common count for money had and received. A considerable amount of discussion centred round the precise area of legal right covered by an action framed in this particular way. No doubt in the earlier stages of our law, when forms of action were few in number and restricted in their scope, no person obtained a remedy in the common-law Courts of this country unless he could bring his particular grievance within the ambit of some recognized form of pleading. The result was that the existence of a right depended on the existence of some recognized writ or form of pleading in which the claim could be comprised. It was therefore the object of the pleader, and to some extent of the Courts, in cases where it was found that the then existing forms were too narrow to meet the changing conditions of life, to devise new forms or adapt old ones so that just claims should not fall to the ground by reason of the defects of the system rather than any lack of merit in the litigant. Under these circumstances the count for money had and received came into being, and was developed and expanded by Lord Mansfield. I was referred to a number of cases in which the origin and the ambit of this particular remedy were discussed, and in particular the celebrated opinion of Lord Sumner in the case of *Sinclair v. Brougham*, [1914] A.C. 398. Lord Sumner pointed out that the basis of the action was an implied or notional or fictitious promise to pay. The actual decision in *Sinclair v. Brougham* on this particular point was that a depositor who had banked with a company carrying on a banking business that was wholly ultra vires could not recover that money in any action based on a notional promise to repay, inasmuch as, if there had been an express promise in fact, it would have been ultra vires, and a notional promise could not have any greater efficacy than that of the real promise, if real promise there had been....

In the present case, neither by the use of the word "deposit" or otherwise, is there anything to indicate that the payment of £100,000. was intended or was believed by either party to be in the nature of a guarantee or earnest for the due performance of the contract. It was part payment of the price of the goods sold and was so described.

On behalf of the defendant corporation it was contended that on the true construction of the contract the part payment was agreed to be regarded as an earnest for the performance of the contract, inasmuch as, since the clause which I have already read provided for the return of a part of the payment to the plaintiffs in one event only, it must have been the intention of the parties that in every other event the money was to be retained by the defendant corporation.

I do not so construe the contract. The clause, in my judgment, deals with one situation, and one situation only — namely, the frustration of the performance of the contract. It was, as I have already said, designed to confer on the defendant corporation certain rights additional to the rights which the law alone in the absence of agreement would have given in the event of the performance of the contract being frustrated. Beyond that field its implications ought not to be extended, and the doctrine "expressum facit cessare tacitum" has no application. The argument under this head is double-edged, since it might be argued on behalf of the plaintiffs that, as the contract expressly conferred on the corporation the right in one event to retain £13,500., it cannot have been intended that in another event they were to have the right of retaining £100,000.

It was said further that the rule which under certain circumstances enables a purchaser in default to recover a payment or part payment of the purchase price is a rule applicable to the sale of land only and must not be extended to the sale of goods, but no authority for this latter proposition was cited to me, and I was referred to certain passages in the Seventh Edition of Benjamin on Sale, at pp. 989, 994 and 995, which state the rule as being of general application.

At p. 989 the principle is summarized in these words: "In ordinary circumstances, unless the contract otherwise provides, the seller, on rescission following the buyer's default, becomes liable to repay the part of the price paid."

If this passage accurately states the law as, in my judgment, it does where the language used in a contract is neutral, the general rule is that the law confers on the purchaser the right to recover his money, and that to enable the seller to keep it he must be able to point to some language in the contract from which the inference to be drawn is that the parties intended and agreed that he should.

The argument on behalf of the defendant corporation was supported by the submission that the action for money had and received would not lie, since on the present facts the only possible basis was a total failure of consideration, which basis was ruled out by the fact that it was the purchaser who had made default....

I was, however, quite satisfied that in the present case the foundation of the right, if right there be, is not a total failure of consideration. There was no failure of consideration, total or partial. It was not the consideration that failed but the party to the contract.

This objection, in my judgment, really goes to a question of form and not of substance, for if under the present circumstances there is a right in the buyer to recover a payment he has made in part, it is wholly immaterial in point of form whether the basis of right depends on a total failure of consideration, or something else. In my judgment, the real foundation of the right which I hold exists in the present case is not a total failure of consideration but the right of the purchaser, derived from the terms of the contract and the principle of law applicable, to recover back his money....

In the result I find that the plaintiffs have a right of action for the recovery of the £100,000.

The defendants, on the other hand, are, or may be, entitled to damages.

It appears that the defendants had not actually got the commodities which they had agreed to sell, but intended to obtain them from an arms factory in Czecho-Slovakia at a price which would have shown them a substantial profit on the transaction. The evidence before me, which consisted of a statement in writing dated August 25, 1938, by a Mr. Kantor, a director of the Bank in Prague, is insufficient to enable me to quantify the damage. In the first place it dealt with the situation on the footing that the breach had taken place on or about December 20, 1936. In my judgment, the correspondence makes it clear that there was no breach until January 15, 1937. Mr. Pritt argued that the damage must be assessed in accordance with the provisions of s. 50, sub-s. 3, of the Sale of Goods Act. I am satisfied that the section has no application to the facts of the present case. In my judgment, that sub-section applies where the seller actually has the goods which he has contracted to sell, and has no application to the case where the seller has not acquired the goods he has sold before the contract goes off. A section regulating the assessment of damages cannot be construed so as to impose on the seller the obligation of buying the goods after the sale has gone off.

In my judgment, the true measure of damages is the loss of profit that the sellers would have made on the deal. This is measured by the difference between the price at which they could have bought and the contract price. There must also be brought into account such incidental expenses as delivery charges and the cost of sending the goods to the port to be selected by the buyers, an obligation which fell on the sellers.

Moreover, I think the possibility of their being unable to obtain this particular class of commodity, or except at an enhanced price, is a factor which, if there is available evidence on the point, must be considered.

The precise form which the order must take will have to be considered. There must be an inquiry to ascertain the damage, and, when this figure has been arrived at, if it is less than the sum of £100,000., the defendant corporation will have to pay the balance to the plaintiffs. If the damages are more than £100,000. the claim will be extinguished to the extent of £100,000 by the money which the defendant corporation have in their hands, and judgment will be entered for the defendant corporation for the balance. Mr. Pritt suggested that the £100,000. should carry interest, but I do not think that this is a case in which interest ought to be allowed. It is true that the defendant corporation has had the £100,000. Equally, it is hoped that Mr. Quintana has had the use of the money which he will have to pay to the defendant corporation in damages.

Judgment for the plaintiffs on the claim.

SUMPTER v. HEDGES

[1898] 1 Q.B. 673. Court of Appeal (England); A.L. Smith, Chitty and Collins L.JJ.

APPEAL from the judgment of Bruce J. at the trial before him without a jury.

The action was for work done and materials provided. The plaintiff, a builder, had contracted with the defendant to build upon the defendant's land two houses and stables for the sum of £565. The plaintiff did part of the work, amounting in value to about £333., and had received payment of part of the price. He then informed the defendant that he had no money, and could not go on with the work. The learned judge found that he had abandoned the contract. The defendant thereupon finished the buildings on his own account, using for that purpose certain building materials which the plaintiff had left on the ground. The judge gave judgment for the plaintiff for the value of the materials so used, but allowed him nothing in respect of the work which he had done upon the buildings.

A. L. Smith L.J. In this case the plaintiff, a builder, entered into a contract to build two houses and stables on the defendant's land for a lump sum. When the buildings were still in an unfinished state the plaintiff informed the defendant that he had no money, and was not going on with the work any more. The learned judge has found as a fact that he abandoned the contract. Under such circumstances, what is a building owner to do? He cannot keep the buildings on his land in an unfinished state for ever. The law is that, where there is a contract to do work for a lump sum, until the work is completed the price of it cannot be recovered. Therefore the plaintiff could not recover on the original contract. It is suggested however that the plaintiff was entitled to recover for the work he did on a quantum meruit. But, in order that that may be so, there must be evidence of a fresh contract to pay for the work already done. With regard to that, the case of *Munro v. Butt* (1858), 8 E. & B. 738, appears to be exactly in point. That case decides that, unless the building owner does something from which a new contract can be inferred to pay for the work already done, the plaintiff in such a case as this cannot recover on a quantum meruit. In the case of *Lysaght v. Pearson* (reported only in the *Times*, 3 March, 1879), to which we have been referred, the case of *Munro v. Butt* does not appear to have been referred to. There the plaintiff had contracted to erect on the defendant's land two corrugated iron roofs. When he had completed one of them, he does not seem to have said that he abandoned the contract, but merely that he would not go on unless the defendant paid him for what he had already done. The defendant thereupon proceeded to erect for himself the second roof. The Court of Appeal held that there was in that case something from which a new contract might be inferred to pay for the work done by the plaintiff. That is not this case. In the case of *Whitaker v. Dunn* (1887), 3 T.L.R. 602, there was a contract to erect a laundry on defendant's land, and the laundry erected was not in accordance with the contract, but the official referee held that the plaintiff could recover on a quantum meruit. The case came before a Divisional Court, consisting of Lord Coleridge C.J. and myself, and we said that the decision in *Munro v. Butt* applied, and there being no circumstances to justify an inference of a fresh contract the plaintiff must fail. My brother Collins thinks that that case went to the Court of Appeal, and that he argued it there, and the Court affirmed the decision of the Queen's Bench Division. I think the appeal must be dismissed.

Chitty L.J. I am of the same opinion. The plaintiff had contracted to erect certain buildings for a lump sum. When the work was only partly done, the plaintiff said that he could not go on with it, and the judge has found that he abandoned the contract. The position therefore was that the defendant found his land with unfinished buildings upon it, and he thereupon completed the work. That is no evidence from which the inference can be drawn that he entered into a fresh contract to pay for the work done by the plaintiff. If we held that the plaintiff could recover, we should in my opinion be overruling *Cutter v. Powell* (1795), 6 T.R. 320, and a long series of cases in which it has been decided that there must in such a case be some evidence of a new contract to enable the plaintiff to recover on a quantum meruit. There was nothing new in the decision in *Pattinson v. Luckley*, but Bramwell B. there pointed out with his usual clearness that in the case of a building erected upon land the mere fact that the defendant remains in possession of his land is no evidence upon which an inference of a new contract can be founded. He says: "In the case of goods sold and delivered, it is easy to shew a contract from the retention of the goods; but that is not so where work is done on real property." I think the learned judge was quite right in holding that in this case there was no evidence from which a fresh contract to pay for the work done could be inferred.

[Collins, L.J. agreed.]

QUESTIONS

1. Why is *Lysaght v. Pearson* not the same as *Sumpter v. Hedges*?
2. What do you think would be "evidence of a fresh contract to pay for the work already done"? Could such evidence be inferred? If so, what kind of things do you think would lead the court to draw such an inference?

DAKIN AND CO. LTD. v. LEE

[1916] 1 K.B. 566. Court of Appeal (England); Lord Cozens-Hardy M.R., Pickford and Warrington L.JJ.

Lord Cozens-Hardy M.R. This is an appeal from a decision of the Divisional Court reversing the finding of the official referee in a dispute between builders and a building owner. The building owner was a lady who was engaged in school work, and whose house required certain alterations and improvements.

A specification was prepared in August, 1913, by which the builders agreed to do a great deal. They were to examine the roof and renew the decayed parts of it and the gutter pipes, to repair the gutters and rainwater pipes in the roof over the conservatory, to examine the main roof, to underpin, where necessary, the piers and walls of the conservatory, and rebuild any portions where found necessary, to repair or renew the wood staircase, to take down the bay window and rebuild it, to reconstruct the arches over the first and second floor windows, to alter the porch roof, to repair the basement area window, to cut out the cracks in the flank wall, to excavate as required and underpin the flank wall and chimney breasts with solid Portland cement concrete base, the concrete underpinning to be composed of one part of Portland cement concrete to six parts of clean Thames ballast, to test and examine the drains, to take down the brick arches in the back elevation, to alter the front gate, and to do a number of other things. It will be observed that one of the matters which is mentioned more than once is the underpinning of a wall, which was to be done with solid Portland cement concrete base. The work was finished — and when I say this I do not wish to prejudice matters, but I cannot think of a better word to use at the moment.

There were then disputes, as I have said, between the building owner and the builders. An action was commenced by the builders and referred to the official referee, and the official referee heard arguments extending over some seven or eight days, and he went twice to look at the house. He has made a finding to the effect that the obligation on the plaintiffs was to put down concrete 4 feet in depth throughout the part to be underpinned; I am not quite sure whether that is true. There is, in the specification itself, no clause binding them to put concrete to the depth of 4 feet. It is true that, in the letter of even date which enclosed the estimate for doing the work comprised in the specification, it is said that the estimate was on the basis of concrete being 4 feet deep; but there is not an express contract that the concrete should be of that depth. However, the offical referee has found that the plaintiffs were under the obligation to put down 4 feet of concrete, and the builders swore at the trial that 4 feet of concrete had in fact been put in. The official referee went to the house on two occasions and tested it, and he has found as a fact "that in no parts was there the contract depth, 1 foot 7 inches to 2 feet was the average depth." He also said "It is immaterial that the plaintiffs considered and that the defendant considered the depth to be safe." He has also found that the builders put in two solid columns 4 inches in diameter when, according to the specification, they were to be 5 inches in diameter, hollow; but that is a trivial matter, and so trivial that I do not propose to say another word about it. He then says that certain rolled steel joists ought to have been bolted to caps and to each other, and that this was quite ignored. That may or may not have been a matter of importance. Lastly, he finds that the concrete was not properly mixed.

In these circumstances it has been argued before us that, in a contract of this kind to do work for a lump sum, the defect in some of the items in the specification, or the failure to do every item contained in the specification, puts an end to the whole contract, and prevents the builders from making any claim upon it; and therefore, where there is no ground for presuming any fresh contract, he cannot obtain any payment. The matter has been treated in the argument as though the ommission to do every item perfectly was an abandonment of the contract. That seems to me, with great respect, to be absolutely and entirely wrong. An illustration of the abandonment of a contract which was given from one of the authorities was that of a builder who, when he had half finished his work, said to the employer "I cannot finish it, because I have no money," and left the job undone at that stage. That is an abandonment of the contract, and prevents the builder, therefore, from making any claim, unless there be some other circumstances leading to a different conclusion. But to say that a builder cannot recover from a building owner merely because some item of the work has been done negligently or inefficiently or improperly is a proposition which I should not listen to unless compelled by a decision of the House of Lords. Take a contract for a lump sum to decorate a house; the contract provides that there shall be three coats of oil paint, but in one of the rooms only two coats of paint are put on. Can anybody seriously say that under these circumstances the building owner could go and occupy the house and take the benefit of all the decorations which had been done in the other rooms without paying a penny for all the work done by the builder, just because only two coats of paint had been put on in one room where there ought to have been three?

I regard the present case as one of negligence and bad workmanship, and not as a case where there has been an omission of any one of the items in the specification. The builders thought apparently, or so they have sworn, that they had done all that was intended to be done in reference to the contract; and I suppose the defects are due to carelessness on the part of some of the workmen or of the foreman: but the existence of these defects does not amount to a refusal by them to perform part of the contract; it simply shows negligence in the way in which they have done the work. Thus, in regard to the rolled steel joists they have not apparently bolted them together in some particular way, the precise nature of which I confess I do not understand.

Then what is the result? It seems to me that the result is that the builders are entitled to recover the contract price, less so much as it is found ought to be allowed in respect of the items which the official referee has found to be defective. There is no finding by the referee as to what the precise figures should be, and, unless they are agreed, the matter must go back to him to decide what ought to be allowed in respect of the concrete not being 4 feet and the wrong joining of the rolled steel joists, and what, if anything, ought to be allowed in respect of the concrete not having been properly mixed.

The appeal substantially fails and must be dismissed; but the case must go back, if necessary, to the official referee to find what allowance ought to be made from the sum to be paid the builders in respect of those items. The appellant must pay the costs of this appeal.

QUESTIONS

1. Would it matter if the builder in a case like *Dakin v. Lee* deliberately breached the contract?

2. Suppose that Builder agreed to renovate Owner's house using copper pipe for all bath and sink drains. Builder uses plastic pipe rather than copper. It is proved to the court that plastic pipe is as good as copper and that the quality of the work done was excellent. Owner refuses to pay. Builder sues relying on *Dakin v. Lee*. How will the amount that Builder can get be determined? How will the amount that Owner can claim as damages be determined? How well are each party's expectations being protected? Could this be achieved in more efficient ways? What is the court's role in this kind of dispute?

BLAKE v. SHAW

(1853), 10 U.C.Q.B. 180.

Assumpsit on the common counts. *Pleas* — Non-assumpsit, payment, and set-off.

At the trial, before Sullivan, J., at Niagara, it was proved on behalf of the plaintiff that the defendant was a merchant in St. Catharines, in large business; that the plaintiff was in his service as a clerk, from the 13th of November, 1848, till the 20th of September, 1850, and that his service was worth from £75. to £100. a year, besides his board; that in September, 1850, the plaintiff went to California, and that by his instructions a relative of his afterwards went to the defendant to demand payment of his wages: that the defendant said he would not pay until he saw the plaintiff himself, who would be more in want of his wages when he returned than at that time. This witness swore that she had herself lent the plaintiff £35. when he went away.

On the defence it was sworn, by Shaw, the defendant, that he had agreed with the plaintiff about the 15th of November, 1848, to pay him £60. a year; that in September, 1850, he left the defendant's service without notice or permission, and sent his sister-in-law to the defendant with an order. The defendant swore that he had paid the plaintiff more than his wages for the first year, and that he told his sister-in-law if he wished to settle he must come himself, for that he did not believe he owed him anything. He swore that the plaintiff agreed with him to serve by the year. The defendant admitted that he offered to give £25. and costs to settle this suit, but not because it was a balance due.

A fellow clerk of the plaintiff swore that he knew nothing of the plaintiff's intention to leave; he went with the permission of the defendant to a fair in the neighbourhood, and never returned; the witness recommended him to come back, but the plaintiff said he had got tired of working at £60. a year. This clerk swore that if he were to leave in the same manner, he should expect to lose his wages.

The learned judge ruled that, although it appeared by the evidence that there might be a balance of £45. due to the plaintiff on account of his current year's wages, yet that he was not entitled to sue for it, being hired for a year, and having left without permission before the year had ended.

The jury gave a verdict for the plaintiff for £25.

Robinson, C.J., delivered the judgment of the court.

We have no doubt that upon the evidence the verdict given in this cause was against the law, which is clear that where a clerk or other person hired for a year, departs without consent before the year is up, he forfeits his wages, and cannot recover for the part of the year that he has served. And in this case the footing on which the parties were is plain. It was not merely a constructive hiring for a year, but an actual contract of that kind; and courts of justice have expressed themselves strongly on the importance to society of enforcing such engagements, by making parties bear the legal consequences of breaking them. The only room for a doubt whether we may not properly decline to grant a new trial is, that there was certainly no misdirection. The jury were not misled; and it may be said, and perhaps thought, that the verdict is consistent with justice, and ought not therefore to be disturbed. But, as was remarked by the court in the case of *Farrant v. Olmius,* cited by Mr. Eccles, "If that argument were to prevail, it would encourage juries to commit a breach of duty, by finding verdicts contrary to law, and would enable them to set aside the contracts of mankind."

The jury, we think it probable, awarded the plaintiff £25. in this case, because it was sworn that the defendant, while this action was pending, offered that sum, if the action were dropped, at the same time contending that he was under no obligation to pay anything. The very object of such offer is to stop a law suit, and when the party to whom it is made rejects it, and will persevere in his action; he should derive no advantage from having refused it; but as he has thought proper to insist on his supposed legal right, in the hope of compelling the defendant to pay more, he should be left to abide by the proper legal result of that action.

We are of opinion that there ought to be a new trial without costs.

Rule absolute.

HAMILTON v. RAYMOND

(1853), 2 U.C.C.P. 392.

[The plaintiff had agreed with the defendant that he would build a house and barn for the defendant. The plaintiff did about two-thirds of the work before abandoning it. The defendant then finished the work. It was provided in the agreement that the plaintiff should complete the work by August 10 1851. The plaintiff sued to recover the value of what he had done.]

Macaulay, C.J. — The question is not, whether the performance of the work is a condition precedent to the plaintiff's right to be paid the £90., as if he had declared specially therefor upon the agreement, without averring performance of the work at or after the 10th of August, or any excuse for not performing it; but it is whether, having performed a great portion of the work without being paid, he can recover the value thereof, as for work, labour, and materials, furnished at the defendant's request, although the plaintiff's part of the agreement was not executed at the day, nor completed at any time afterwards....

The inference from all these authorities seems to me to be, that if the contract is entire and still executory, the plaintiff cannot recover under the first count for work, labour, and materials, until it is executed, unless the time be past and the non-completion of the work was prevented by, or the fault of, the defendant, and not of the plaintiff.

Here the work was not finished by the day appointed but Lucas Godwin, as well as the terms of the agreement, (having a penalty after the day) shew that the day or time was not the essence of the contract.

Still, not being completed at the day, it continued and was executory after the day. The defendant was willing and desirous that the plaintiff should go on and finish it, without any default on the defendant's part, for I do not consider any delay on the plaintiff's part for want of lumber material in this action, if time was not conditional or of the essence of the agreement, whatever its importance might be in a cross-action for non-performance of the work at the day. It rests then upon the consideration whether the agreement remained executory at the time the action was brought. If the defendant had refused to accept or take possession of these buildings in an unfinished state, or until finished, but assented to the plaintiff's going on and completing the contract, the defence would certainly be a good one. But it appears, that after the plaintiff's default, the defendant took possession, availed himself of the work done by the plaintiff, sold or appraised the premises to another, and that the defendant, or his agent as then holding under him, not only assumed and occupied the building, but did additional work thereto and towards the completion thereof. The defendant also paid a large part of the price after the day.

Under these circumstances, I am disposed to think that the special agreement was terminated by the default of the plaintiff and the possession taken by, and subsequent conduct of the defendant, so that the door was opened to the implied assumpsit, a promise by defendant to pay plaintiff what the work so accepted was worth, and on which implied promise this action is founded. Otherwise the plaintiff, owing to the defendant's acts, will be precluded from recovering anything from what he did and from hereafter finishing the work so as to entitle himself to the whole sum.

It seems the just rule that the plaintiff should recover what his work, labour, and materials were worth, being compensated *pro rata* according to the value of the work done, as compared with the whole work valued at £90., and that any claim of the defendant's to enforce the penalty or to recover damages for disappointment, delay, and consequential damage, should form the subject of a cross-action.

[The leading English case is *Cutter v. Powell* (1795), 6 T.R. 320; 101 E.R. 573, K.B., where Lord Kenyon C.J. refused to allow any claim by the widow of a ship's officer for part of his pay earned on a voyage from Jamaica to Liverpool. The officer had been promised £31-10-0 for the voyage but he died after completing about ⅔ of it. It was held that the defendant's obligation to pay only arose when the officer had completed the voyage.

Compare this with *Britton v. Turner* (1834), 6 N.H. 481 where a quantum meruit claim was allowed in similar circumstances.]

QUESTIONS

1. If you were an unscrupulous employer what would you do to cut your employment costs?

2. Why do you think that an employee should be in a worse position than a building contractor?

See now: Apportionment Act, (R.S.O. 1970, c. 23)

3. All rents, annuities, dividends, and other periodical payments in the nature of income, whether reserved or made payable under an instrument in writing or otherwise, shall, like interest on money lent, be considered as accruing from day to day, and are apportionable in respect of time accordingly.

BRIGHT v. GANAS
(1936), 189 Atl. 427.

Sloan, Judge. The plaintiff, Paul Ganas, sued the defendant, Robert S. Bright, executor of James G. Darden, deceased, on an alleged testamentary contract for the sum of $20,000. The judgment being for the plaintiff for $8,990, the defendant appeals.

The first count of the declaration set up an oral agreement between the plaintiff and James G. Darden, entered into the month of May, 1929, whereby the plaintiff was to live with Darden, at the latter's newly purchased home at Cambridge, Md., as a servant, and, in consideration of the plaintiff's so continuing with Darden during his life-time, the plaintiff was to receive on Darden's death "out of his estate" the sum of $20,000; but that Darden died without having made provision for the plaintiff in his will (dated September 14, 1931), which was admitted to probate and recorded in Dorchester county; that Darden accepted the services of the plaintiff which were faithfully rendered, and so continued to November 18, 1933, when Darden died. The second count was "for work done and materials furnished" at decedent's request.

Paul Ganas, the plaintiff, a native of Greece, at the age of thirteen, came to this country about twenty-seven years ago, whither he had been preceded by his father, then engaged in the restaurant business at Roanoke, Va. He worked at various places principally as a waiter, finally going to Washington, where he became acquainted with Col. James G. Darden, a picturesque and mysterious character, who lived luxuriously and seemed to be supplied with plenty of money, though we are not informed as to the nature or size of his estate. Col. Darden settled in Cambridge in 1929, where he bought a house, and in May of that year engaged Ganas as a servant or man of all work, more or less personal in its nature, and there Ganas continued until Darden's death in November, 1933 at about the age of sixty-eight. According to Ganas, he gave up a job as a waiter in a Washington hotel, which paid him from a hundred and fifty to two hundred dollars a month, to enter the employ of Darden, on the promise that he would receive out of Darden's estate, at the latter's death, twenty thousand dollars. He was not permitted to testify to this under the Evidence Act (Code, art. 35, § 3), and every time he disclosed the terms of his agreement it was, on motion, stricken out, except in two instances when it got in without objection. He had witnesses, however, who could and did testify to the agreement. . . . Col. Darden was ill for several months continuously to the day of his death. So far as he knew, during that time, the plaintiff was serving him faithfully, and assisted in nursing him. On or about the last day of August, 1933, Mrs. Darden had left her husband's room late at night (the plaintiff was downstairs at the time), and had gone to her room, where she there found on her bed an envelope containing a letter addressed to her by the plaintiff. It would serve no worthy purpose to quote it or to even summarize its contents, except to say that this plaintiff had designs on his employer's wife, which he was intent on revealing to her. She testified that the next morning she took the letter to her mother, who lived in Cambridge, asked her to read it, and asked her advice. She told Dr. Wolfe, her husband's physician (since deceased), about it, and he advised her against telling her husband. She said, "I wanted to that night, but I knew he could not stand it." Asked on cross-examination, "You spoke of locking your door after the burial. There was never any effort on Paul's part to follow this up was there?" she answered, "He did not have a chance. I had someone near me all the time." About two hours after Col. Darden's funeral she showed Mr. Bright, the executor, the letter and told him the plaintiff must get out of the house. He being told by Mr. Bright that he must leave, he rebelled, and the next day he was told by his attorney he had to go, and then did.

The plaintiff must have had some conception of the gravity and consequences of his offense, for on the envelope containing the letter he wrote: "If I lose my job by this note — at least I would gain my peace of mind —." When asked at the trial what led him to write·the letter he gave a long, incoherent, unresponsive answer, which showed no reason or excuse for writing it, and that it was inspired by moral depravity or a disordered, disorderly mind, with no conception of the proprieties, especially when his employer, who seemed to be fond of him, and whose confidence was thus betrayed, was so ill that his physician forbade any communication with him on the subject. This record discloses no excuse or justification for the plaintiff's behavior. He is the one who offended against all the rules of propriety and decency, and he ought to pay the penalty instead of reaping a reward. There was nothing in the wife's conduct inviting such an outburst from the plaintiff. If this act of the plaintiff was such as to justify his immediate and summary discharge, if his employer had known of the incident, then, in our opinion, it is as available to the executor as a defense, as it would have been to the decedent in his lifetime.

. . . As we have indicated, this is one entire contract, and the plaintiff was entitled to the full consideration of his contract or none of it. . . . On the theory of an entire contract, if the act of unfaithfulness and disloyalty here charged against the plaintiff was sufficient to warrant his immediate discharge by his employer, had it been known to him, then his right to compensation has been forfeited, for it cannot be assumed that the employer would not have done the thing that common decency and loyalty to his wife would have required him to do.

... In this case the violation of the agreement by the plaintiff was so flagrant, unjustified, and inexcusable as to justify his discharge, and, if by it he earned his discharge, then he cannot recover.

... The plaintiff, having shown without contradiction an express contract he was not entitled to recover on a quantum meruit under the second count, as the jury was instructed it might do under the only prayer, the third, granted the plaintiff.

CHAPTER 6

THE CONTROL OF CONTRACT POWER

A. Introduction

The institution of contract may be regarded as the grant to individuals of the right to make decisions for themselves for all kinds of things. There is nothing inevitable about contract: it is possible to imagine a society without private contract. The question which we will be investigating in this chapter will be the kind of controls that can be used to prevent the abuse of contract power. We shall see that the law adopts all kinds of methods to prevent abuse of contract power: interpretation, unconscionability, illegality are all used to prevent parties from doing things that courts or legislatures think that they should not be doing. It will be important to see just which method is being used in each case. Sometimes the courts are devious and even dishonest in the way they exercise this control. At other times they are open and unblushing in saying that a particular agreement is offensive and will not be enforced.

Re-read here, Fuller and Eisenberg, "The Role of Contract in the Ordering Processes of Society". (Reproduced *supra*.)

We offer here the views of a marxist lawyer who had some interesting things to say about contract.

RENNER, THE INSTITUTIONS OF PRIVATE LAW AND THEIR SOCIAL FUNCTION.

[Karl Renner was born in 1870. On the abdication of the Emperor Charles I in November 1918, he became the head of the provisional Austrian Government. He was the first Chancellor of the Austrian Republic (1919-1920). As the Second World War was ending (April 1945), Renner became Premier and Minister of Foreign Affairs in the provisional government. In December 1945 he was elected President. He died in 1950.

The Introduction by Professor Kahn-Freund is very famous and it is all worth reading. We have only included one third of it (pp. 1-16).

The second extract is taken from Renner's work itself (pp. 104-122). It is only part of a longer discussion of contract.

Footnotes are omitted.

Renner's work was originally published in 1906.]

INTRODUCTION
By O. Kahn-Freund, LL.M., Dr. Jur.

Karl Renner's work on the Institutions of Private Law and their Social Function is an attempt to utilise the Marxist system of sociology for the construction of a theory of law. As a statement and formulation of an important aspect of Marxist doctrine and as a highly original contribution to jurisprudence the book has for many years been well known on the Continent. It is now, for the first time, made accessible to the English speaking world.

I

Renner's work is concerned with the sociology of law, and, more particularly, with the impact of economic forces and social changes upon the functioning of legal institutions. The legal institutions which he examines are those which are classified as belonging to the sphere of "private law": ownership in land and movable property, contracts of various types, mortgage and lease, marriage and succession. "Public law", which includes the organisation of the state and of local government bodies is outside the purview of his analysis.

It is one of the tasks of a sociology of law to explore the social forces which bring about the creation of legal norms and institutions and changes in the positive law. Renner's work does not deal with this aspect of the inter-relation between law and society. It does not investigate the problem how and why legal principles like that of the freedom of contract or of the owner's unfettered right of disposition come into being at a given stage of social development. He pre-supposes the stability and relative immutability of legal institutions such as property and contract, and he asks: how is it possible that, given unchanged norms, unchanged conceptions of ownership and sale, contract and debt, mortgage and inheritance, their social function can nevertheless undergo a profound transformation? How is it possible that — to take the most prominent example and the central theme of Renner's work — as a legal institution "property" can mean the same thing, say, in 1750 and in 1900, and yet in the latter year produce economic and social effects almost diametrically opposed to those it had in the former? How can one account for the functional transformation of a norm which remains stable? What, in particular, is the technique used by a developing capitalist society in order to adapt pre-capitalist and early capitalist legal conceptions to the needs of high capitalism without changing those conceptions themselves? How does society use the institutions of the law, what does it make of them, how does it group and re-group them? How does it put them to new services without transforming their normative content? How, in particular, has property been able to become the legal framework of a capitalist economy?

II

It will be seen that Renner postulates the normative "purity" of all legal institutions. It is impossible to understand his analysis without realising that he belongs to the positivist school of legal thought. In his view the legal norm is indifferent towards its social function, the economic effect extraneous to the definition of a legal concept. Institutions such as property, contract, succession by inheritance, are "neutral", "colourless", "empty frames", they are neither "feudal", nor "capitalist", nor "socialist". Their juridical analysis cannot teach us anything about their social or economic effect. Renner insists that the place which legal institutions occupy in society is a matter for the economist, for the political scientist, for the sociologist. A lawyer may be interested in it during his leisure hours, but he must not allow this interest to intrude upon his work, no more than the botanist as such may be concerned with the economic use to which others put the plants he studies under the microscope. Renner rejects the sociological or functional method of interpreting positive law itself. He is uninfluenced by and opposed to those trends of legal thought represented by jurists such as

Ihering or the American realists who urge the judge and the lawyer to be aware of, and take into account, the social purposes of the legal norms which he applies, and to interpret them in their light.

No consistent positivist can ever admit that the normative content of legal institutions can be influenced by their function, by the factual results of their application. The "functional transformation" of legal institutions which Renner examines in his work is not — he emphasises it again and again — a transformation of these institutions themselves as part of the positive law.

It is not necessarily inherent in the positivist doctrine that the legal norm should be understood as a command or as an imperative. Kelsen, for example, holds that the logical structure of the legal norm is that of a hypothetical judgment. Renner, however, adheres to the view of the majority of continental positivists (which was also the view of Austin), that every norm is an imperative. Whatever the formulation in which it appears in codes, statutes, or decress, it can, according to this doctrine, never be more than a command addressed by one individual to another. Renner insists that the law can neither control nature nor regulate man's relation to nature. The technical progress of mankind, the development of productivity is achieved "under the eye of the law, but not by means of the law". Nor does Renner admit that the law can ever fully control human associations and "groups", though he agrees that it may enhance their efficiency. Even where it purports to issue its commands to collective bodies, it can ultimately enforce them against individuals only. Similarly, the "collective" will which pretends to be embodied in legislation is, on ultimate analysis, the will of those individuals who enforce it. Whether they are able to do so, and how, is not determined by the law, but by "the social conditions prevailing at that particular historical period".

Renner's conception of the law as a series of imperatives addressed by one individual to another is of profound significance for the whole of his theory. It goes without saying that these relations between individual "wills" which are alone capable of being moulded by the law exist in a social and in a natural environment. They derive their social meaning from the influence which this environment exercises upon them and which they in turn exercise upon society as a whole. It is, however, just this mutual impact which lies beyond the province of the law, as understood by positivism. "The lever which the law uses upon social facts is too short to control them. Legal ties are mere threads compared with the Herculean power of natural life. Yet this Hercules stretches his limbs so gradually and imperceptibly, that the threads do not suddenly snap in all places."

Legislation is thus not seen as the prime mover of social change. It is, at best, a response of the law to a change which has already taken place in the womb of society. On this important point dialectical Marxism agrees with representatives of the historical school such as Savigny and Maine, albeit on very different grounds. Social and economic developments, transformations of the substratum which affect people's lives, are not, as a rule, brought about by the law, nor do they necessarily change the law itself. They do not occur by leaps and bounds. "The social substratum knows evolution only, not revolution" Revolutions, i.e. political revolutions, take place in the normative sphere. They may — and often do — lay the normative foundation for new evolutionary developments in society. They make room for social change, but they are not its *causa causans*. The belief that one can transform society by "decree" is stigmatised by Renner as a superstition, as "idolatry of legislation", "decretinism", and it is, in his view, a common characteristic of successful revolutions. He argues that it betrays a misapprehension of the social rôle of law as such and an over-estimation of its effectiveness.

It is inherent in Renner's approach — and he is at pains expressly to point out — that the crude formula which reduces the relation between economy and law to one of cause and effect does not meet the case. He refuses to describe the complex interdependence between the relations of production and consumption on the one side and the institutions of the law on the other by means of the simple architectural image of substructure and superstructure. In so far as the economic and legal systems of a given society can be understood in terms of cause and effect at all, changes in the economic relations are often the result of legal developments, though it is far more usual to find that a transformation of the economic system ultimately produces a change in the law. However — and this is one of Renner's cardinal arguments — not only does such a change never occur automatically (i.e. without a political development), it also invariably occurs after a time lag, which may have to be measured in centuries. During this time lag norms which, at an earlier period of history, may have been a true mirror of social relations, may cease to be an adequate expression of factual conditions. In extreme cases an institution may survive as part of the law, but lose all its social functions, a phenomenon — called *desuetudo* — of which English legal history offers examples (e.g. military tenure which had long ceased to be a living institution when it was formally abolished in the 17th century). As a rule, however, there is not a disappearance but a transformation of the social function. An institution may be put to the service of a variety of economic objectives: to-day the ownership of land serves the provision of dwelling room no less than of agriculture or factory production. One economic effect may be produced by the alternative application of a variety of legal techniques: the provision of dwelling houses for the working and lower middle classes may be effectuated through the mechanism of the building society mortgage or through that of the lease.

Much more important, however, is the fact that under the conditions of modern capitalism economic results can only be achieved through the simultaneous operation of a multitude of legal institutions. Ownership taken by itself is incapable of serving the organisation of modern industry. It can do so only with the aid of a number of satellite or complementary institutions: company law and patent law, the contract of sale and the contract of employment. A simple economic process often corresponds to a whole group of legal categories. The subservience of many legal categories to one economic process is what Renner calls their economic function.

All economic processes, however, are themselves part and parcel of the social processes of "production" and "reproduction", of the maintenance of the human species. Legal institutions can and must be understood as the tools used by society in achieving this ultimate aim. They are cogs in the mechanism of the production, consumption and distribution of the social product. This is what Renner calls their social function.

A simple photographic picture of a given society at a given stage of its development will fail to reveal the manner in which legal concepts and institutions are used and grouped for economic and social purposes. Society must always be viewed as a process, a dialectical process. Hence it is, as it were, a cinematographic picture which the sociologist has to envisage. Only thus will he discern the laws which determine the grouping and re-grouping of legal institutions, the sequence of uses to which they are put and of arrangements into which they enter. Society handles the institutions of the law in much the same way as a child handles his bricks. It uses the same bricks all the time — or for a long time, — to-day to build a manor house, to-morrow to build a factory, and the day after to build a railway station. The number of bricks is limited: the manor house may have to be pulled down to make way for the factory. But — this is Renner's positivist axiom — the bricks remain the same. The law provides the bricks. What society makes of them, is none of the lawyer's business. The legal institution is a rigid abstract, a congeries of crystallised imperatives, and, owing to its very rigidity and abstract nature, a "fetish" in the Marxist sense, like the "commodity" concept of the economist. Renner builds the tenets of positivism into the structure of the Marxist system, and thus succeeds in extending the Marxist doctrine to the theory of law. The discrepancy between the normative content of the law (which is static) and its economic and social function (which is dynamic) is the key to its dialectical development. This development can be summarised as the functional transformation of the untransformed norm.

The ultimate end of society, and hence the ultimate social function of the law, is the maintenance of the species. The maintenance of the species requires the organisation of society. Society organises itself in three different ways: it allocates to the individuals who are its members the work which is needed for production and reproduction, the power to command which is necessary to keep the organisation in being, and the factual "detention", the "having" of all things, movable and immovable. By its very nature every human society must have an "order of labour", an "order of power", an "order of goods". No matter whether it is a primitive tribe in Central Africa or a modern industrial community, whether it is feudal or capitalist or socialist, society must keep production and reproduction going, it must establish a hierarchy of subordination (and relations of co-ordination too), and it cannot dispense with a distribution of the handling and having of goods among its members. Lawyers may talk about corporate entities, public or private, but ultimately it is always an individual and an individual only who works, who commands, and who "possesses" (in the sense of the Roman detention) a thing.

All this would be commonplace, had it not been for the curious illusion created by capitalist society that it could live without an order of labour and of goods, and partly without an order of power. The legal order of feudalism deliberately allocated the control of land and goods, established the hierarchy of power, and imposed the duty to work in accordance with the social functions of possession, power, and labour. The function of the legal institutions corresponded to their normative structure. Capitalist society, however, pretended to be able to forego a functional organisation of possession and of labour. It covered the order of goods with a legal concept of property defined in the abstract, it avoided, in the name of personal freedom, a legal formulation of the duty to work. "*De jure* bourgeois society has no order of goods and no order of labour." Property was protected, whoever be the owner, and whatever be the purpose of ownership. Compulsion to work was — seemingly — abolished. Society pretended to abdicate in favour of the will of the individual. Yet, behind the smokescreen of abstract norms, behind the legal system of *a priori* categories, like "person", "property", "liberty", there was concealed an order of labour, of power, of goods, no less determined, no less purposeful than that of feudalism. But the laws which constituted the order of goods and of labour were not expressed, they appeared not as legal norms, for they were the economic "laws" governing capitalist production, distribution, and consumption. Society rules over production, distribution, and consumption whether it does so openly by express norms and through institutions such as feudal tenure and villeinage or under the guise of the law of property and free employment. The law of property is an order of detention which conceals its own objectives. It is — *sub specia historiae* — an ephemeral order, one of many such orders that have appeared in the course of the centuries. It is also part of an order of labour and of an order of power: the "imperatives" issued by the factory owner to his workers by virtue of his ownership of the plant take the place of the express norms which regulated the labour of the serf. The law of succession to property and those parts of company law which deal with the appointment of directors belong to the order of power no less than the law of feudal investiture which they replace.

The analysis of the social function of property and of its transformation in the course of the history of capitalism is the most important part of Renner's investigation.

III

Since the positivist assumption is one of the cornerstones of this analysis, it is useful to reflect on the question how far the structure of the Anglo-American common law precludes an application of the positivist doctrine. To what extent, in other words, is Renner's analysis without validity for a capitalist society whose legal system differs from any Continental system as fundamentally as does the English common law?

It would be quite fruitless — and it is not the purpose of this Introduction — to examine the validity of the positivist tenets. During the forty years which have elapsed since Renner wrote the first edition of his work the positivist theory of law has been subjected to the most searching criticism, both in Europe and in America. To repeat the arguments which have been advanced in favour of a functional approach to law itself would be equivalent to kicking at a door that is already open. Suffice it to remind the reader that, whatever be its logical merits, the positivist theory fails to yield a practical guidance to the judge, to the advocate, to the administrator. Positivism is a utopia. The law is neither consistent nor self-sufficient. Whatever theorists may say and whatever he himself may think and say, the judge constantly recurs to an analysis, articulate or inarticulate, of the moral, social, economic function and effect of the rules and principles he applies, and of his own decision. The task of the law-maker and that of the law-finder cannot be kept in watertight compartments, and judges have always acted and will always act on the celebrated principle of the Swiss Civil Code of 1912 that, in the absence of a statutory or customary norm, the judge must decide "in accordance with the rule he would lay down if he were the legislator".

One cannot, however, dispose of positivism simply by stating that it is a utopia. Like other utopias it has its place in the history of human ideas, a place which is (at least partly) determined by the social and political environment in which it arose. Is it simply a response to the needs of capitalism? Is it the outcome of conditions peculiar to the European Continent?

Every legal system requires an element of ideological unity. However much one may be aware that the application of the legal norm is, in many cases, a policy-making process, one cannot dispense with a principle which links one decision with another, which raises the judicial act beyond the level of the realm of sheer expediency. Without such a principle the practical lawyer cannot operate, without it the law cannot command the respect of the public. The fiction of logical consistency, however threadbare it may look to the critical eyes of our generation, did once provide this unifying principle. It does so still — up to a point — and it does so both on the Continent and in the common-law jurisdictions of the British Empire and of the United States. There is, however, an important difference between the place which this fiction occupies in continental legal thought and the rôle it plays in the common law world.

In a systematised legal structure such as the *Usus Modernus Pandectarum* and the modern Continental Codes legal institutions such as ownership, sale, marriage, appear as part and parcel of a self-contained logical entity, of an intricate network of major and minor premises. It is the task of the jurist, of the legal scholar, to analyse and re-analyse the normative content of the law, to make the logical network more and more refined and pliable. It is the function of the judge to find his decision with the help of the intellectual tools which the "science of the law" has put at his disposal. Every new factual situation must somehow be fitted into the existing system. That system is comprehensive and without "gaps". It stands firm like a rock, be it even in the midst of a turbulent sea of social change.

The conceptualist school of thought was, on the Continent, the dominant variety of positivism in the 19th century. It postulated the logical consistency of the legal system as a whole. The judicial process, it insisted, is of a strictly deductive nature. The norm which the judge applies is, in its view, incapable of being transformed by the process of application. Hence, the judicial decision itself can in no sense be considered as a source of law. It must justify itself exclusively by the process of deduction from abstract premises on which it is based.

Although this conceptualist doctrine has for many decades been discarded by the majority of continental scholars, it has left as its legacy the fiction of systematic consistency as the primary element of ideological unity in the law.

In this country and in the whole common-law world, the place of the systematic fiction is taken to a considerable extent by the fiction of historical continuity. Every decision appears in the cloak of a mere application or adaptation of pre-existing "principles" laid down in earlier judicial pronouncements. Where historical continuity and systematic consistency are in conflict, it is the former which prevails, and it prevails even where the question at stake is the interpretation of a statute. If law can be called a science, it is, in this country, an empirical not a speculative science. It is an answer — primarily — to the question: "what was done previously?", not a logical process untrammelled by previous attempts to grapple with a similar situation. The positivist utopia has its place in a systematic as well as in a casuistic legal structure, but, in the latter, the logical fiction will be pushed into the background by the historical fiction.

It is necessary to bear this in mind in reading Renner's analysis. But it is also necessary to remember what are the historical causes and events which account for this difference, and to avoid two all too frequent misapprehensions.

It is not, as is sometimes argued, the codification of the law which gives rise to the idea of systematic consistency. Germany before 1900 was the Mecca of "legal science". It paved the way for the Code which came into force that year, the Code was its fruit, not its root. On the other hand, large parts of Land Law, of Commercial Law, of Administrative Law, and of Criminal Law have been codified in England, but the "principle of precedent" continues to dominate these branches of law to such an extent that the highest Court had occasion to remind the lower instances that there was — after all — a codification. Codification does not necessarily engender "scientific" legal thought (as Bentham erroneously assumed), a code can be survived by the fiction of historical continuity. While, therefore, the inherent connection between conceptual positivism and codification must not be overrated, it must be understood that in Renner's analysis the terms "law" and "written law" are largely synonymous. He does not draw a distinction between "*droit*" and "*loi*", between "*Recht*" and "*Gesetz*". The Austrian Civil Code had been in force for almost a century (since 1811), the German Civil Code had just seen the light of day when he wrote his book. In the background of his thought there was the "*ratio scripta*", Justinian's Corpus Juris. What Renner says about the stability of the norm in the face of a changing social substratum would not have been said, or not have been said that way, if customary and judge-made law had been within the scope of his analysis. Where the courts are openly recognised as law-making agencies, it is difficult, if not impossible to maintain the fiction that the norm is stable and unaffected by social change. Every case "*primae impressionis*" is a living refutation of that fiction.

Systematic positivism is, in this country, sometimes associated with the influence of Roman Law. To some extent this too is a misunderstanding. It is quite true that the systematic grouping of positive norms as "legal institutions" and the definition of these institutions (ownership, obligation, sale, hire, pledge, etc.) was one of the great contributions of the Roman mind to human civilisation. It is equally true that, as Ihering has formulated it, it was the Romans who succeeded in "precipitating" legal conceptions out of the multitude of legal norms, and in building up an "alphabet" of legal concepts which is the pre-condition and indispensable tool of scientific legal thought. Nevertheless, no one who has endeavoured to compare the method of the common lawyer with that of the Roman jurist and of the 19th century continental legal scholar can fail to agree with Buckland and McNair "that there is more affinity between the Roman jurist and the common lawyer than there is between the Roman jurist and his modern civilian successor". "Both the common lawyer and the Roman jurist avoid generalisations and, so far as possible, definitions. Their method is intensely casuistic. ... That is not the method of the Pandectist. For him the law is a set of rules to be deduced from a group of primary principles, the statement of which constitutes the '*Allgemeiner Teil*' of his structure." The conceptual method which implies the "purity" of the norm and which claims to be capable of establishing and enforcing a *judicium finium regundorum* between "norm" and "substratum" is not inherent in Roman Law. It is the heritage of the *Usus Modernus Pandectarum*, of the "Roman common law" influenced by natural law concepts and by Germanic customs and developed on the Continent since the Middle Ages.

Neither codification nor the influence of Roman Law can account for the difference between the Continental and the Anglo-Saxon types of positivism. The axiom that the law is a logical system, self-sufficient, comprehensive, without "gaps", arose on the Continent as a response to the needs of the growing civil service state. Max Weber has demonstrated how the continental monarchies from the 16th to the 19th centuries availed themselves of the systematised structure of legal conceptions built up by the scholarly expositors of the Roman Law. The rigid frame-work of positive legal concepts made for unity of administration, it also facilitated the smooth operation and the supervision of the administration of the law by a judicial and administrative civil service, a civil service which was scattered over wide areas, but subject to a centralised control. It is not, of course, suggested that the growth of systematic positivism on the Continent can be entirely explained by a simple formula like this. Many factors, the influence of natural law not being the least of them, have contributed to the development of this particular type of what Weber calls the "formal rationality" of the law. It cannot, however, be denied that the social structure of the legal profession on the Continent and, above all, the political structure of the absolute monarchies were the "prime movers" in the creation of this unique phenomenon of a "logical utopia" in the law.

None of the sociological and political factors which, on the Continent, made for systematisation and for the restriction of judicial discretion to a minimum was present in this country, not, at any rate, since the middle of the 17th century.

In this country the unification of the law had been the work of the medieval monarchy operating largely through the common law courts. It is impossible to over-emphasise the historical importance of this fact. What was a problem still to be solved on the Continent at the inception of the capitalist era — the creation of a uniform law — was, in England, an accomplished achievement. Systematisation was very largely unnecessary, because it was not required in order to overcome the chaos of local laws and customs. Of all the important jurisdictions of Europe, England was the only one to emerge from the Middle Ages with a "*common* law". The heritage of feudalism in this country was a unified body of institutions and rules which, while lacking in logic, were nevertheless capable of being intellectually absorbed and — above all — capable of being applied throughout the country. The lawyer did not need the Ariadne thread of systematic thought to help him to grope his way through a labyrinth of "*Stadtrechte*", of "*coutumes*", etc.

Moreover — and Max Weber's sociological analysis has made this convincingly clear — the thought-processes of the common law can and should be understood as the outcome of the needs and habits of a legal profession organised in gilds and preserving the structure and the power of a medieval vocational body. The modern continental systems were developed in the universities by legal scholars for the use of officials. English law evolved as a series of gild rules for the use and guidance of the members and apprentices of the Inns of Court. It was due to political factors, to the failure of the absolute monarchy in England, to the aristocratic structure of the body politic in the 18th century, that the administration of the law remained in the hands of the lawyers' guilds. With some exaggeration one might say that it was the Revolution of 1688, not the refusal to "receive" Roman Law that, in this country, sealed the fate of systematic legal science in the continental sense.

The common law was developed by that branch of the legal profession whose main interest lies in litigation. It was, until well into the 19th century (and, to a degree, it still is), a series of rules of conduct for practising advocates, a comprehensive answer to the question: "how do I behave in court?" It was a body of practical and technical craft-rules, handed down from master to apprentice, and designed to instruct the advocate in the art of raising and defending claims. This largely accounts for its "empirical", for its casuistic as opposed to the continental logical and systematic method. The craftsman asks: "how has this — or a similar — case been handled before?" He is not very much concerned with the question, whether the answer is capable of being fitted into an abstract system. It is, of course, easy to over-emphasise the contrast between the two methods. Logical deduction was never absent from the thought-processes of English judges and advocates, and precedents have played and are playing an important and rapidly increasing rôle on the Continent. We are merely concerned with a basic difference in outlook and with the historical factors which account for this difference.

The contrast between the methods of thought of university trained and gild trained lawyers may also serve as an explanation for the essentially "remedial" or "procedural" structure of English legal ideas. English law does not pose and answer the question: "what are the legal guarantees for the freedom of the individual from arbitrary arrest?" It is content to ask: "in what circumstances will you, the barrister, be able to obtain for your client a writ of *habeas corpus* or a judgment for damages on the ground of false imprisonment?" From a practical point of view there is no difference between these two types of question. Nevertheless the contrast between the two formulations reveals the gulf between thought processes influenced by natural law and orientated towards a systematic structure of rights and duties, and a method of argument whose primary pre-occupation is with remedies, not with rights, with procedural form, not with juridical substance. It will be seen that the difference in approach to the law of property can and must be explained as a similar divergence in method rather than in practical results. It is not so much in the practical operation of legal institutions as in the intellectual machinery which promotes that operation that systematic and historical positivism, the continental and the Anglo-Saxon methods, are divided.

The foregoing remarks are not intended to give a comprehensive account of the methodological difference between the two types of legal thought, even less to give a full explanation of its causes. What they are designed to demonstrate is that it is not an inherent feature of capitalism as such to give rise to either systematic or historical positivism. That the continental method of approach was not adopted in England, that the principle of precedent (in its English form) did not take root on the Continent, has its social causes. But these causes must be found in the structure of the body politic, not in the economic and social function of legal institutions. The rising middle classes were interested in what Max Weber calls the "calculability of chances". They were inclined to press for a development of the law which permitted their lawyers to predict the outcome of disputes. There is no doubt that the needs of capitalism promoted the "formal rationality" of the law, i.e. the decision of each individual case in accordance with a rational thought process, not in accordance with ethical imperatives, expediency or political maxims. This formal rationality, however, is a common characteristic of systematic and of historical positivism. As long as the judge proceeds on lines which can be predicted, it is irrelevant to the lawyer's client whether the argument is empirical or speculative, based on precedent or on general principles. "Modern capitalism can equally flourish and show identical traits under legal orders which not only possess widely different norms and legal institutions, but whose ultimate formal principles of structure are as widely divergent from each other as possible." "There is not inherent in capitalism as such any decisive motive for favouring that form of rationalisation of the law which, since the rise of Romanist University education, has remained a characteristic of the continental occident."

The contrast between the continental legal systems and English law lies far more in "ultimate formal principles of structure" than in positive "norms and institutions". The practical results are very often identical, where the lines of reasoning which lead up to them are as divergent as possible. Renner's analysis is concerned with the function of legal institutions, and especially with the adaptation of the property concept to an almost infinite variety of social and economic uses. Whether and to what extent lawyers choose to clothe the practical operation of these institutions in general formulae is largely irrelevant for an analysis of this kind. English law has never developed a fixed and rounded definition of property, but, from the point of view of a sociological investigation, it matters little whether the owner claims his property by virtue of a *rei vindicatio* arising from the institution of ownership as such or whether he avails himself of an action for conversion or of detinue arising from the right to possession and being in its origin and structure a species of a delictal claim. It is only a question of legal technique whether I ask: "what are the conditions for the acquisition of ownership?" or: "who is the proper plaintiff, who is the proper defendant in an action for conversion?" From the point of view of the function of the institution of property it is irrelevant whether I devise a systematic set of principles culminating in the monumental pronouncement: "*En fait de meubles, la possession vaut titre,*" or whether I am content to say that, as against a defendant who has given value in good faith, the plaintiff is, in certain circumstances, estopped from pleading a title better than that of the defendant's alleged predecessor. The difference is very important for those who learn the law and those who teach it. It is equally important for those who apply it. It is of next to no account for those whose interests are involved.

A continental lawyer and an English lawyer engaged in a conversation upon the law of succession on death will find it very difficult to understand the "thought processes" of their partner. The Englishman will take it for granted that there must be a "personal representative", an administrator or executor, who as such has no beneficial interest in the deceased's estate at all, has merely powers and duties, but no rights of enjoyment. He will fail to appreciate what his colleague means when he speaks about an "heir" or "heirs" in whom the estate vests *ipso facto*, who is (or are) liable for the debts of the deceased, and entitled to keep the residue. Nevertheless, if they forget their legal techniques and look at the practical results with the eyes of their clients, they will soon be convinced, that English law — without saying so — embodies the principle of "heirship" no less than French law which defines an "*héritier*" and a "*légataire universel*" or German law which defines an "*Erbe*". Two bankruptcy specialists, one from the Continent and the other from England, will soon discover that it is not very relevant from a practical point of view whether the law gives an abstract definition of insolvency or enumerates a catalogue of types of conduct — known as "acts of bankruptcy" — which indicate an individual's inability to pay his debts.

The institutions of property, of heirship, of bankruptcy, and innumerable others exist — perhaps in a somewhat inarticulate fashion — on this side of the Channel as on the other. The normative content of the institutions varies in detail, not in fundamentals. Their social and economic functions are similar.

The language of Renner's analysis appears to envisage continental institutions only, its substance applies in this country as much or as little as it applies in its country of origin. The capitalist environment of the law favours the positivist approach. Whether positivism is more of the systematic or of the empirical variety may affect the degree to which legal institutions adapt their normative content to changes in their social environment. It does not affect the relevance and validity of Renner's question: given a set of legal institutions, how can they change their functions without changing their norms?

Chapter II, Section ii. THE DEVELOPMENT OF CAPITALIST PROPERTY AND THE LEGAL INSTITUTIONS COMPLEMENTARY TO THE PROPERTY NORM

I. PROPERTY AND THE CONTRACT OF EMPLOYMENT

The subject-matter of the property-norm is generally an occupied item of nature, a corporeal thing. In its natural form it is technically subservient to man. In so far as it is not ready to be consumed, it is at first raw material or working tool, and in this form it enters the process of production.

The character mask of the property-subject is that of a person owning material goods. At the stage of simple commodity production the owner is at the same time a worker who enjoys the benefits of his labour. All economic character masks which later become distinct from each other, are still united within the same individual. The law which declares this individual "free" from all others, thereby gives him legal personality.

Side by side with the person who is also property-owner, there is the person who, equally free, possesses nothing. Formerly his character mask was that of beggar, he then develops into the legal type of pauper which soon becomes that of worker.

The Spanish beggars of the Middle Ages formed a chevaleresque order, they wore berets, daggers and guitars, they lived on the surplus product of the owners on the strength of the legal title conferred upon them by the Gospel. Since Paradise, labour has been the curse of possessions, but poverty gives a truly divine right to idleness. As we see, it was pleasant and honourable to be a beggar, and this character mask has been preserved till the present day in the venerable figure of the begging friar. But now the day of the lay-beggar is over, the poor are compelled to work; "pauper" and "worker" were still synonymous in the time of Adam Smith. They enter the guild-master's workshop to obtain access to consumer goods. "Capitalist production only then really begins... when each individual capital employs simultaneously a comparative large number of labourers.... The workshop of the medieval master handicraftsman is simply enlarged" (*Capital* i, p. 311). A larger number of workmen is engaged, and property which hitherto has fulfilled only the function of detention, suddenly assumes new functions.

a. Property Becomes Power of Command

Journeymen and apprentices used to live in the master's household. Their relation was in the nature of a subjection determined by public law, on the lines of the Germanic *patria potestas*, which served the purposes of education, training and mastery of the craft, and whose function therefore was to ensure the continuity of the working population. This relationship was abolished by the mere force of facts; it was replaced by the private contracts of *do ut facias*. The old regulation of labour is dissolved, and for a while there is no new regulation.

But the property-object (*res*) as it develops into and assumes the functions of capital, itself inaugurates a process of education for the owner no less than for the dispossessed. "We saw in a former chapter, that a certain minimum amount of capital was necessary, in order that the number of labourers simultaneously employed... might suffice to liberate the employer himself from manual labour, convert him from a small master into a capitalist, and thus formally to establish capitalist production.... We also saw that, at first, the subjection of labour to capital was only a formal result of the fact that the labourer, instead of working for himself, works for and consequently under the capitalist. By the co-operation of numerous wage-labourers, the sway of capital develops into a requisite for carrying on the labour process itself, into a real requisite of production. That a capitalist should command on the field of production, is now as indispensable as that a general should command on the field of battle.... The work of directing, superintending and adjusting, becomes one of the functions of capital, from the moment that labour under the control of capital, becomes co-operative. Once a function of capital it acquires special characteristics" (*Capital* i, pp. 320-1).

What is the essence of this power of command? It is based on contract. But so was the relation of the feudal lord to his vassal, yet this was essentially of a public nature. An element of domination is without doubt implied in this system of superordination and subordination, and in spite of the form of contract it remains essentially a system of power.

The question is whether this control is still in essence the Germanic medieval *mundium*, that reflection of paternal power. Is it established in favour of the ruled or of the ruling, is it a government of protection or of exploitation? What are its essential features? "The directing motive, the end and aim of capitalist production, is to extract the greatest possible amount of surplus-value, and consequently to exploit labour-power to the greatest possible extent.... The control exercised by the capitalist is not only a special function, due to the nature of the social labour-process, and peculiar to that process, but it is, at the same time, a function of the exploitation of a social labour-process, and is consequently rooted in the unavoidable antagonism between the exploiter and the living and labouring raw material he exploits.... Moreover, the co-operation of wage-labourers is entirely brought about by the capital that employs them. Their union into one single productive body and the establishment of a connexion between their individual functions, are matters foreign and external to them, are not their own act, but the act of the capital that brings and keeps them together. Hence the connexion existing between their various labours appears to them, ideally, in the shape of a pre-conceived plan of the capitalist, and practically in the shape of the authority of the same capitalist, in the shape of the powerful will of another, who subjects their activity to his aims" (ibid. pp. 321-2).

In the eyes of the law, the property-subject is related to the object only, controlling matter alone. But what is control of property in law, becomes in fact man's control of human beings, of the wage-labourers, as soon as property has developed into capital. The individual called owner sets the tasks to others, he makes them subject to his commands and, at least in the initial stages of capitalist development, supervises the execution of his commands. The owner of a *res* imposes his will upon *personae*, autonomy is converted into heteronomy of will.

Capital extends its scale, it expands beyond the sphere of the capitalist's personal control. "Just as at first the capitalist is relieved from actual labour,... so now, he hands over the work of direct and constant supervision, ... to a special kind of wage labourer.... The work of supervision becomes their established and exclusive function" (ibid. i, p. 322).

We see that the right of ownership thus assumes a new social function. Without any change in the norm, below the threshold of collective consciousness, a *de facto* right is added to the personal absolute domination over a corporeal thing. This right is not based upon a special legal provision. It is the power of control, the power to issue commands and to enforce them. The inherent urge of capital to beget constantly further capital provides the motive for this *imperium*.

This power of control is a social necessity, but at the same time it is profitable to the owners — it establishes a rule not for the purpose of protection but for the purpose of exploitation, of profit.

The subordination of the workers which at the same time effects their mutual co-ordination, is a corresponding phenomenon. Is this co-ordination also based on contract? The workers are not asked whether their neighbour appeals to them, yet they are forced into close proximity and in this way they become united into an association of workers. What is it that brings about this passive association of the workers? What is it that correlates their functions and shapes them into a unified productive body? There is no doubt that these workers who contribute partial operations form a compulsory association according to all rules of legal doctrine.

This association receives its individuality from the capital that collects the workers in one place and keeps them there. Just as the law is the norm for the citizens, so the plan, the plan of production, is the abstract and impersonal norm for this compulsory association, supported by the ultimate and most concrete authority of the capitalist, the power of an alien will. Supervision is delegated to special functionaries, and thus relations of superordination and subordination are made into an organic whole.

Thus the institution of property leads automatically to an organisation similar to the state. Power over matter begets personal power. "It is not because he is a leader of industry that a man is a capitalist; on the contrary, he is a leader of industry because he is a capitalist. The leadership of industry is an attribute of capital, just as in feudal times the functions of general and judge were attribute of landed property" (ibid. i, p. 323).

We see that even at the first stage of capitalism, that of co-operation, the old microcosm is replaced by a new one which derives its unity from capital, which here is the aggregate of the technical means of production, i.e. objects of ownership. These new organisations bring about a gradual transformation of man and matter, without any norm imposed by the state.

b. Property Assumes the Function of Organisation

Industrial progress develops co-operation into primitive manufacture. The differentiation of labour is reflected in the labour product. "The commodity, from being the individual product of an independent artificer, becomes the social product of a union of artificers, each of whom performs one, and only one, of the constituent partial operations" (pp. 328-9). "Individual" "private" property creates "unions of artificers" without regard to their wishes, without leave from the authorities; it lessens their personal freedom, and debases their inherited skill to the continuous performance of partial operations. Such property encroaches upon the division of labour which has existed for centuries, on the one hand combining crafts that formerly were separated, on the other hand dissolving formerly undifferentiated crafts into individual partial operations.

"... its final form is invariably the same — a productive mechanism whose parts are human beings" (p. 329). "... each workman becomes exclusively assigned to a partial function, ... and for the rest of his life his labour power is turned into the organ of this detail function" (ibid. p. 330).

Property increasingly fulfils the function of capital, encroaching in actual fact on that freedom which in the eyes of the law is universal, by assigning to every individual a specific and strictly differentiated social function. As its subject-matter is concentrated into a microcosm or macrocosm of goods, property concentrates the workers and at the same time differentiates their work, it appropriates specialised labour to each of its constituent parts and it thus converts the labourer into an organ of capital for the whole of his life-time. Further, Marx shows that: "Manufacture, in fact, produces the skill of the detail labourer, by reproducing, and systematically driving to an extreme within the workshop, the naturally developed differentiation of trades, which is found ready to hand in society at large. On the other hand, the conversion of fractional work into the life calling of one man, corresponds to the tendency shown by earlier societies, to make trades hereditary ... to petrify them into castes.... Castes and guilds arise from the action of the same natural law, that regulates the differentiation of plants and animals into species and varieties, except that, when a certain degree of development has been reached, the heredity of castes and the exclusiveness of guilds are ordained as a law of society" (ibid. i, p. 331).

The evolution of the property object gives to property the power to create separate species within the *genus homo*, a power like that of an Egyptian king who establishes castes; yet the lawyer does not take cognisance of this supreme power. The evolution of property develops its special "hierarchy of labour-powers" (*Capital* i, p. 342), but this is a hierarchy for which no Canon Law has been developed by the experts.

The division of labour within the workshop, brought about by the system of manufacture, is established by the control of the employer who is the capitalist, at the very same time as free competition leads to an automatic and anarchic general division of labour within society among the employers. Therefore the owners and the dispossessed are organised according to two contrasting principles. "The division of labour in the workshop implies concentration of the means of production in the hands of one capitalist; the division of labour in society implies their dispersion among many independent producers of commodities.... Division of labour within the workshop implies the undisputed authority of the capitalist over men, that are but parts of a mechanism that belongs to him. The division of labour within the society brings into contact independent commodity-producers, who acknowledge no other authority but that of competition" (ibid. i, p. 349). "The same bourgeois mind which praises division of labour in the workshop, life-long annexation of the labourer to a partial operation, and his complete subjection to capital as being an organisation of labour that increases its productiveness... denounces with equal vigour every conscious attempt to socially control and regulate the process of production, as an inroad upon such sacred things as the rights of property.... It is very characteristic that the enthusiastic apologists of the factory system have nothing more damning to urge against a general organisation of the labour of society, than that it would turn all society into one immense factory.... In a society with capitalist production, anarchy in the social division of labour and despotism in that of the workshop are mutual conditions the one of the other" (ibid. p. 350).

We see that two "societies" are superimposed here, as they were in the feudal period. Compulsory associations according to factory law, the "copy-holders" of capital, form the base, the free market communities of owners form the higher stratum and above all stands the bureaucracy governed by the law of administration. We are reminded of old times when the peasant lived according to manorial law, the owner of an allodium according to land law and the vassal according to feudal law.

c. Property Dissolves the Old Social Order

The evolution of property does not rest, it is like a Chronos who devours — other people's children. The system of manufacture which as yet has no knowledge of machinery develops into the factory system (machinofacture). The property-object now absorbs not only physical but also intellectual labour, for it employs the brain worker. Just as muscular power is embodied in the labour-product, as it must be embodied if a tangible object is to achieve citizenship in the world of commodities, so the inventor's genius must be materialised, it must be embodied in the machine. And since this world is ruled by private property, the machine is forced into the Caudian forks, into the service of capitalism — it must become an object of property and in this capacity a value which begets surplus value. And were not the owners of the manufacturing enterprises entitled to appropriate the results of science? Had they not first dissolved muscular labour into mechanical functions, degrading man to a machine, so that later on he should learn to make machines?

Whereas during the period of manufacture, the traditional simple means of production, the legal '*res*' confronted labour-power as ruling capital, large scale industry separated scientific labour from manual labour, embodying the former in the machine, a concrete object of property. It is industry on a large scale "which makes science a productive force distinct from labour and presses it into the service of capital" (*Capital* i, p. 355). Our inventors of genius were foolish to imagine that labour-saving machines would diminish the suffering of mankind. No doubt it should have been so, for the machine really does save labour. How could the result have been different? But then — the machine became property, an object of ownership, and consequently assumed social functions at once. Would these be new functions, as the *res* was of a new kind?

"In its specific capitalist form... manufacture is but a particular method ... of augmenting at the expense of the labourer the self-expansion of capital.... It increases the social productive power of labour... for the benefit of the capitalist instead of for that of the labourer.... It creates new conditions for the lordship of capital over labour" (ibid., p. 359).

The organisation of the control of labour by property had not been perfected. Artisans skilled in their trades still opposed their reduction to detailed functions of the productive mechanism. "Order was wanting in manufacture and 'Arkwright created order' " (*Capital* i, p. 362). The worker was still a master of labour, the labour process was centred around him, and the finished raw material, the tools which he employed, were means to an end. The inanimate property-object did not yet completely rule over the work of flesh and blood, "order was wanting". But now the *res* is transformed into the machine, into the automaton. "The automaton itself is the subject, and the workmen are merely conscious organs, co-ordinate with the unconscious organs of the automaton, and together with them, subordinated to the central moving-power" (ibid. p. 419).

Lo and behold! paradise grows out of chaos. "In these spacious halls the benignant power of steam summons around him his myriads of willing menials" (ibid. i, p. 419).

"In handicrafts and manufacture, the workman makes use of a tool, in the factory the machine makes use of him.... In manufacture the workmen are parts of a living mechanism. In the factory we have a lifeless mechanism independent of the workman, who becomes his mere living appendage.... Every kind of capitalist production... has this in common, that it is not the workman that employs the instruments of labour, but the instruments of labour that employ the workman. But it is only in the factory system that this inversion for the first time acquires technical and palpable reality. By means of its conversion into an automaton, the instrument of labour confronts the labourer, during the labour-process, in the shape of capital, of dead labour, that dominates, and pumps dry, living labour-power. The separation of the intellectual powers of production from the manual labour, and the conversion of those powers into the might of capital over labour, is, as we have already shown, finally completed by modern industry erected on the foundation of machinery" (ibid. pp. 422-3).

The kind of subject-matter which is the object of the property-norm is irrelevant to the legal definition of property. One object is as good as another. The norms which make up the institution of property are neutral like an algebraic formula, for instance the formula of acceleration. But if one factor in this formula of acceleration is the avalanche, everybody is crushed, and if one factor in the property-norm which makes a person the owner of a thing, is the machine, generations are devoured. The development of machinery abolished the technical foundation for the division of labour which manufacture had brought about. Its typical hierarchy of specialised labourers was consequently replaced by a tendency to equalise labour, or to level it down in the mechanised factory.

The artisan guarded the skill of his craft as his own "mystery"; his qualified and specialised labour was his social power, his pride, his bread. In comparison with this, the instruments of labour had scarcely any social significance. Albrecht Duerer's study was not very different from the workshop of a master house-painter. The worker of the manufacturing period was still an individualised worker, though capital in its initial stages made him join a co-operating group. Now capital blots out every individual trait, moral as well as technical. "Thus we see that machinery, while augmenting the human material that forms the principal object of capital's exploiting power, at the same time raises the degree of exploitation" (ibid. i, p. 392). "Taking the exchange of commodities as our basis, our first assumption was that capitalist and labourer met as free persons.... But now the capitalist buys children and young persons under age. Previously, the workman sold his own labour-power, which he disposed of nominally as a free agent. Now he sells wife and child. He has become a slave dealer" (ibid. p. 393).

This piece of property called the machine, this organism of property-objects called the factory, are substituted, though only temporarily, for another legal institution, they take over the functions of paternal and conjugal power.

The evolution of property makes the *res* in the owner's hand "into systematic robbery of what is necessary for the life of the workman" (ibid. p. 426), it converts the property-object, machine, "the instrument of labour" into "a competitor of the workman himself" (ibid. p. 430), and into a powerful weapon of war for the repression of periodical revolts committed by workers against the autocracy of capital (ibid. p. 432), leading to "the economical paradox, that the most powerful instrument for shortening labour-time, becomes the most unfailing means for placing every moment of the labourer's time and that of his family, at the disposal of the capitalist for the purpose of expanding the value of his capital" (ibid. p. 406).

Now we understand the implications of the general power of disposal which the legislator has given to the owner, we understand what it means that a person should have an all-embracing right over a corporeal object. But we are still far from our goal, for we have considered the *res* only at a certain stage, that of production, and only in a special form of economy. We adopt Marx's concise description of one function fulfilled by this legal institution:

"The technical subordination of the workman..., the peculiar composition of the body of workpeople..., give rise to a barrack discipline which... fully develops this before mentioned labour of overlooking.... The factory code in which capital formulates, like a private legislator, and at his own good will, his autocracy over his workpeople, unaccompanied by that division of responsibility, in other matters so much approved of by the bourgeoisie... is but the capitalist caricature of that social regulation of the labour process which becomes requisite in co-operation on a great scale, and in the employment in common, of instruments of labour and especially of machinery. The place of the slave driver's lash is taken by the overlooker's book of penalties" (*Capital* i, pp. 423-4).

At this stage it is useful to realise the original implications of the institution of property: it is not a mere order of goods. It is just in respect of the deliberate planned social distribution of goods that it first abdicates. It merely protects him who has possession by virtue of an unassailable title, but it does not distribute goods according to a plan. Contrast with this the law of property of the feudal epoch. How richly diversified was its catalogue of *jura in rem*. The property law of bourgeois society leaves the order of the goods to the goods themselves. It is only thus that they become commodities and capital, only thus that they organise themselves and accumulate in accordance with the specific laws of capitalist circulation. At this stage we see already that this anonymous and anarchical regulation of "goods" becomes control over men in their capacity as potential labour. We also see that in our time this factual regulation of "goods" presumes to dictate the social regulation of power and labour. We see further that this regulation of power and labour remains concealed to the whole of bourgeois legal doctrine which is aware of nothing but its most formal, general and extraneous limitations, viz. its foundation on the contract of employment.

Wage labour is a relation of autocracy with all the legal characteristics of despotism. The factory is an establishment with its own code with all the characteristics of a legal code. It contains norms of every description, not excluding criminal law, and it establishes special organs and jurisdiction. Labour regulations and the conventions valid within economic enterprises deserve just as well to be treated as legal institutions as the manorial law of the feudal epoch. This, too, was based upon private rule, upon the will of a Lord, one manorial custom differing from another only in details. Even if this difference had been so fundamental as to exclude all understanding and exposition on a common basis — and this cannot even be imagined — these institutions would still remain an integral part of the legal system of that period. The same applies to factory law, the general regulations of labour in economic enterprises. No exposition of our legal order can be complete without it, it regulates the relations of a large part of the population. If material differences were to prevent a general exposition, there would still remain the fundamental problem of the intrinsic nature of this right.

d. Property Becomes Control over Strangers

Once we have raised this question, all the fictions of bourgeois legal doctrine disappear, above all the distinction between public and private law. The right of the capitalist is delegated public authority, conferred indiscriminately upon the person who will use it for his own benefit. The employment relationship is an indirect power relationship, a public obligation to service, like the serfdom of feudal times. It differs from serfdom only in this respect, that it is based upon contract, not upon inheritance. No society has yet existed without a regulation of labour peculiar to it, the regulation of labour being as essential for every society as the digestive tract for the animal organism. The period of simple commodity production when in fact the working *persona*, the instruments of labour and the labour product merged into one another, was the only period in which the process of production and reproduction, the very life process of society, was independent of social consciousness. As an individual process, it remained private, not revealing any underlying correlations of power and labour. The co-operative labour-process, however, is social; in its very essence it cannot be private. The contents of the right have assumed a public nature, though legal doctrine still conceives of it in terms of private law.

During Karl Marx's life-time the capitalist is still in full control, legislative, executive and judiciary, of his enterprise. His power contains all the elements of state absolutism, mitigated only by the fact that it is founded upon a contract which can be dissolved by notice. Up to this period capital knows no "separation of powers". This purely legal limitation, however, becomes illusory, as soon as we conceive of capitalists and wage labourers confronting each other as classes. If we accept this, it becomes evident at once that the worker, though he can exchange one individual capitalist for another, cannot escape from the Capitalist. There is no doubt that in the sphere of production the bourgeoisie as a class has absolute control of the non-propertied classes as far as the law is concerned. Restrictions of their power in fact are imposed only by bourgeois self-interest and fear of the "subjects of steam power". Such is the position at the height of capitalist development.

Since no society can live without the eternal and natural necessity of labour, it is a naive conception that any society could exist without a regulation of labour, an organised power of disposal over the whole of its available labour-power. It is exclusively the merit of Marx to have discovered this hidden regulation of labour within bourgeois society, to have explored its nature and to have analysed its functions. The "natural laws" of society which normally achieve this regulation within capitalist society are sufficient only so long as labour-power remains actually chained to the *res*.

If a revolt of the workers loosens these chains, society throws off its mask of torpor. It suddenly becomes conscious of its mission to regulate labour. Then it applies direct and authoritative measures of coercion against labour in the form of laws. "In the ordinary run of things, the labourer can be left to the 'natural laws' of 'production' " (ibid. i, p. 761). But whenever these laws fail, bourgeois legislation has recourse to direct force outside the economic field. So, above all, at the stage of primitive accumulation. It was only upon the completion of the capitalist order of economy that the wage-regulating laws were repealed. "They were an absurd anomaly, since the capitalist regulated his factory by private legislation" (ibid. p. 764). The machine was Lycurgus, Draco and Solon at the same time, it converted labour into the actual appendage of capital, its psychological embodiment, just as a building is an appendage of an estate in the eyes of the law. Occasionally the capitalist, that psychological incarnation of capital, even unblushingly asserts the proprietary rights of capital over labour-power" (ibid. p. 587). "I allow that the workers are not a property, not the property of Lancashire and the masters; but they are the strength of both; they are the mental and trained power which cannot be replaced for a generation; the mere machinery which they work might much of it beneficially be replaced, nay improved, in a twelvemonth. Encourage or allow (!) the working power to emigrate, and what of the capitalist?" (Potter, quoted by Marx, ibid. p. 588). Capital demands no less than that public authority should maintain the labour which it has appropriated, even if, owing to lack of raw material, the machines stand idle. It demands that the state should store labour in the work-houses, capital's general public reserve dumps. If ever labour remembers its personal freedom in fields where it is manifest even to the most stupid brain that work is a function of the social body (e.g. in the railway industry or the provision trade), if labour makes use of this freedom by strike, then the bourgeoisie makes labour a military institution or replaces free labour by a labour organisation on military lines, achieving a direct socialisation of labour.

New functions thus accrue to the legal character "person" who also has the economic character "proprietor". Now he regulates labour, ruling and exploiting. Property, from a mere title to dispose of material objects, becomes a title to power, and as it exercises power in the private interest, it becomes a title to domination.

At the same time the free person, the labourer with no property, becomes a subject *sui generis*, as history does not repeat itself. Among all those who have the power and are destined to be his master, he may choose the master who most appeals to him, but as a class the subjects are chained to the class of the masters.

We see that property at the stage of simple commodity production endows the worker with the detention of his means of production, making man the master of matter. Now property changes its function without a corresponding change in the law. It gives the legal detention of the means of production to the individuals who do not perform any labour, making them thus the masters of labour. Property automatically takes over the function of regulating power and labour, and it becomes a private title to domination. The law endows this non-worker with the legal detention of the means of production, but in any society only the worker can actually hold them, as he must have them in his hands in order to work with them. Thus the law, by means of a complementary institution, the contract of service, takes actual detention away from the owner. The worker may mind the machine, but he must pay the price of submitting himself to exploitation. A permanent state of war between legal and actual detention is thus established.

2. THE MOST RECENT DEVELOPMENT OF PROPERTY AND LABOUR

A generation and a half have passed away since the death of Karl Marx, two generations since the first publication of *Das Kapital*. Yet his analysis of the transformation of property not only gives a complete picture of the phase which it had reached in his days, it extends much further. Nevertheless, contemporary development, which has by no means remained static, has overtaken Marx's analysis and again transformed the substratum of the norms. Above all, much has matured which at the time of Marx could only be seen in its initial stages. These two generations, however, have changed the world of norms much more than the world of the substratum. Although exposition and explanation of this transformation of norms is beyond the scope of this enquiry, we endeavour to outline it briefly in order to achieve a clearer understanding.

"The most surprising fact is the lack of social observation. Millions of people live among changing conditions, they daily feel their practical impacts, yet their theoretical implications do not become conscious to them. They think in concepts of a by-gone generation."

In order to illustrate this transformation, as well as the contradictions implied in our social order, we consider the following two examples.

Upon its enclosed state there stands the manor house of the old noble family, and the peasant's farm is surrounded by his own land. Property is distinctly fenced off, notice-boards announce that it is "private" and that

"trespassers will be prosecuted". In contrast, let us consider the most striking example of modern development, a privately owned railway. We enter
the station hall, but though this is registered property like the manor and
the farm, it does not even come into our minds that we have entered somebody else's property. No one enquires who is the owner, his identity has
become a matter of indifference. We go to the booking office. There, the
lawyers assure us, we conclude a contract for a *facere*, not for a *dare*. But
nobody else thinks of it in this way. We get our ticket which the other party
is obliged to give us, there is no trace of bargaining, of freedom of contract,
of conditions and terms; published bye-laws fix everything in advance. We
board the train and do not think for a split second that we have hired Mr.
X.'s private vehicle, though lawyers may still construe it in this way. We
know that we have acquired the privilege, conferred upon us by public law,
to make use of a public utility, against payment of the usual fee which is
also fixed or confirmed by public law, and that we have thus submitted ourselves to the public regulations of the bye-laws. The owner, Mr. X., has no
significance whatever in any of these proceedings and more than that, he
remains outside the sphere of our consciousness.

In the first case the substratum and the norm coincide at least as regards
the main aspect. One's own property is clearly distinguished from that of
other persons, property appears as what it is: as private. In the second case,
on the other hand, property has become everybody's own; the owner himself, if he books a ticket for a journey, is now like a stranger. As far as the
economic and social function of the *res* is concerned, the legal owner has
become completely irrelevant. Yet he continues to perform an invisible part
with which we shall have to deal later on.

In this instance it has become evident that private property has been
transformed into a public utility, though it has not become public property.
The old peasant farm and the old manor are nothing of the kind. This
example leads us to suspect that rights of ownership have outgrown the limitations of private law. In this particular case this is so evident that even the
law takes cognisance of it, by creating a number of norms, public and private, which convert property into a public utility. The private character of
property has been forced into the background by complementary institutions of public law.

But these new norms, which, as we have stressed repeatedly, belong to
another branch of research, could not accomplish more than to give a precise legal form to what had existed in the world of facts long before they
intervened. The specific features of a public utility were established in the
substratum before the norm got hold of them. In innumerable other cases
this change within the substratum has not been recognised or admitted,
though property indeed advertises its new character of a public utility. The
cobbler's shop advertises itself as a "shoe-repairing service", thus declaring
that the whole public acquires the right to its services against payment of
the scheduled fee. This kind of shop sign is more than a joke, thousands of
similar signs express a new public opinion vis-à-vis a gradual creation of
new law. It is the profession of lawyers to disregard and deny this; for this
very purpose they have been led for years through the labyrinth of Roman
Law. But let us leave the cobbler. We give our soiled linen to a laundering
establishment and get their receipt in exchange. The two contracting parties, as a rule, do not even know each other's name, they never see each

other. It is a mere fiction that a private "contract" is here agreed on, though it might be so "construed". A peasant farm adjoining that mentioned in our example above may have become a dairy and thus an establishment that owes to the public certain services against payment of specified and advertised fees. The transformation of private property into public utility is completed in form as well, as soon as the licensing authorities make it obligatory to serve everybody and to exhibit a tariff of charges. But even without this, public opinion regards every owner of such an establishment as under a legal obligation. Private property has now become accessible to everyone, it is put at everybody's disposal. I think that this change is remarkable enough. During the war this already existing trend of development has suddenly become strikingly apparent. The sovereign owner of private property has suddenly, by one stroke of the pen, been converted into a subject who has public duties. The landowner must cultivate his land or some other person seizes it for cultivation, he must sell, he must charge the controlled price instead of the market price, he must dispatch his corn to the railway or mill, and so forth.

All of a sudden it becomes apparent to us that property has developed into public utility.

This is an indication of the trend of the future development of legislation. It will not only shamefacedly hint at this new character of property by complementary institutions, the norm itself will openly reveal it, and all property-units which to-day already have become the substratum of public utility, will accordingly become establishments of public law. This is the first unavoidable step towards nationalisation of private property. Even more striking is the development which has taken place at the other pole of society, that of labour. It was not in vain that the workers, thrown together by the capitalists into compulsory associations, were in revolt for fifty years. According to Marx, and in fact during his life-time, the capitalist hired the individual worker on the labour market for a wage that was individually agreed and took him into the workshop. The labour relation in its entirety was based upon individual regulation. But to-day the position is different, thanks to a century of struggle.

The prospective employee registers with a labour exchange, which is either a private establishment or run by the state, a municipality or a trade union. He is assigned to a job by rote. This state of affairs is unintelligible in an economy based upon freedom of contract, which can explain it no more than pure science can explain the working of a typewriter, which is a technical product. If the worker is accepted, at terms which are fixed beforehand and scarcely mentioned, he goes on the job. Formerly based upon contract, the labour relationship has now developed into a "position", just as property has developed into public utility. If a person occupies a "position", this means that his rights and duties are closely circumscribed, the "position" has become a legal institution in character much like the fee of feudal times. The "position" comprises the claim to adequate remuneration (settled by collective agreement or works rule), the obligation to pay certain contributions (for trade unions and insurance), the right to special benefits (sickness, accident, old age, death) and finally certain safeguards against loss of the position or in case of its loss.

What is the meaning of this development from the contract of employment to the position of work and service? The private contract, by means of the complementary institutions of collective agreement, labour exchanges, social insurance and the like, has become an institution of public law. It is still largely determined by the private will of the individuals concerned, yet this influence is continually decreasing, and the state element is almost of greater importance than the private element, the collective element more important than the individual element. It predominates today, when the job is becoming the "established position". The development of the law gradually works out what is socially reasonable. Labour, in fact, never is and never was a merely private affair, it has always been public service. Only an economic science unrelated to the state has transformed and disfigured the social necessity of labour into the private pleasure of individual capitalists and workers whose relations are established by acts of exchange.

Yet it is true that this development to "establishment" and "position" has affected only a part of property and labour and even this only partially. The fundamental character of society is undergoing a process of change. The ultimate direction of this change is clearly determined and its results are unequivocal, but they have neither undergone theoretical analysis, nor have they entered common consciousness. Human society, unconscious or only half conscious of its own needs, drags itself forward, driven on by obscure urges. The achievements of the second half of the century, at which we have here been able only to hint, are so predominantly a change of norms that they need special exposition.

3. PROPERTY AND CONTRACTS OF ALIENATION

At the stage of simple commodity production, the city-dwelling owner's way of life is no longer one of closed domestic economics. Not only does he sell occasional surplus products but he works with a view to selling his produce. Even at this period the contracts of alienation are the complementary legal institutions for this method of economy.

But he sells only his own produce, he owns the means of production as his patrimony and as a rule, as an agriculturist, he produces even his raw material. The sale of his produce is nothing but the short final stage of his own long labours. From a modern point of view we would say that the sale serves mainly to realise the wage for his labour. If it were permissible to apply the later category of wage to this earlier period, we could briefly say that alienation is essentially realisation of the wage and that price is only wage in disguise. This is the function of alienation. But it is not wage only that is realised.

Renner discusses contracts, as Kahn-Freund observes, as a positivist. One characteristic of positivism is that, according to that view of law, a statement of what the law is, is logically unconnected with any idea of what the law should be. The positivist believes that it is confusing to mix up any idea of what law should be with any attempt to understand what the law is. This particular dispute is at the heart of a great dispute between rival schools of legal philosophy. It might be easier for us if the dispute remained at the level of abstract propositions. However, that cannot be so since the dispute touches the foundations of any approach to law.

It is worthwhile, therefore, to consider how far the judgments that we have examined accept or reject the positivist analysis. We have had difficulty throughout the course in discovering any rational purpose behind some of the judgments. The question is whether this difficulty is caused because some judges adopt a positivist attitude to the law.

The other obvious question to ask is whether the rejection (or apparent rejection) of a positivist analysis leads to better solutions to the problems presented by the cases. It is clear that people like Fuller have rejected the idea that one can understand the law without asking what it is for. We also know that judges are much more likely than not to reach the right results. We have seen them doing this both by a correct and satisfactory method of reasoning and by a process of reasoning that seems to make the right result more a matter of chance.

What is clear from all the cases and from the fact that there is more than one way to look at law, is that one cannot be indifferent to the process of reasoning that the judge undertakes. If we think that to be (at least, formally) unconcerned about purpose is dangerous, then we have to be suspicious of theoretical analyses of law that suggests that this is possible. If we think that purposes must be considered we have to worry about whose purposes, about the relation between competing purposes and about the power and duty of the court to make judgments about social values. The material in this chapter raises these issues at a very basic level.

The following extracts and cases are here because they illustrate very well the problem that a failure to be aware of underlying philosophical premises causes. The extracts from Kessler, Macneil and Havighurst point out some practical considerations that have to be borne in mind when one is trying to decide how far one party should be free to control another through contract. The cases show that, while the courts are, on the whole, aware of the same practical concerns, they seldom articulate them and feel compelled to justify the results they reach on quite different grounds. This leads to great confusion and causes us much greater difficulty in trying to understand the cases than would be the case if the courts were honest. We shall see that sometimes they are honest and that when this happens things fit neatly into place and the results are easily understood.

In understanding the cases by realizing that the courts are not always honest, you are, of course, doing nothing that is new. At this stage in the course, it is necessary to raise this problem again and very explicitly since these problems we are going to examine are among the most important current problems in the law. In addition, legislation has been introduced that has significantly altered the common law approach to the problems and we have to be aware of what we are trying to do if we are going to make much sense of what the legislature has done.

Further readings:
Fuller, *The Morality of Law*, Rev. Ed. 1969.
Weiler, "Two Models of Judicial Decision-Making" (1968), 46 Can. Bar Rev. 407.
Weiler, "Legal Values and Judicial Decision-Making" (1970), 48 Can. Bar Rev. 1.
Weiler, *In the Last Resort, A Critical Study of the Supreme Court of Canada,* 1974.
Holmes, "The Path of the Law" (1897), 10 Harv. L.R. 461.
Cohen, "Transcendental Nonsense and the Functional Approach" (1935), 35 Col. L.R. 809.
Llewellyn, *The Bramble Bush* (1930).
Fuller, "American Legal Realism" (1934), 82 U. Pa. L.R. 429.

KESSLER, "CONTRACTS OF ADHESION — SOME THOUGHTS ABOUT FREEDOM OF CONTRACT"

(1943), 43 Col. L.R. 629.

With the development of a free enterprise system based on an unheard of division of labor, capitalistic society needed a highly elastic legal institution to safeguard the exchange of goods and services on the market. Common law lawyers, responding to this social need, transformed "contract" from the clumsy institution that it was in the sixteenth century into a tool of almost unlimited usefulness and pliability. Contract thus became the indispensable instrument of the enterpriser, enabling him to go about his affairs in a rational way. Rational behavior within the context of our culture is only possible if agreements will be respected. It requires that reasonable expectations created by promises receive the protection of the law or else we will suffer the fate of Montesquieu's Troglodytes, who perished because they did not fulfill their promises. This idea permeates our whole law of contracts, the doctrines dealing with their formation, performance, impossibility and damages.

Under a free enterprise system rationality of the law of contracts has still another aspect. To keep pace with the constant widening of the market the legal system has to place at the disposal of the members of the community an ever increasing number of typical business transactions and regulate their consequences. But the law cannot possibly anticipate the content of an infinite number of atypical transactions into which members of the community may need to enter. Society, therefore, has to give the parties freedom of contract; to accommodate the business community the ceremony necessary to vouch for the deliberate nature of a transaction has to be reduced to the absolute minimum. Furthermore, the rules of the common law of contract have to remain *Jus dispositivum* — to use the phrase of the Romans; that is, their application has to depend on the intention of the parties or on their neglect to rule otherwise. (If parties to a contract have failed to regulate its consequences in their own way, they will be supposed to have intended the consequences envisaged by the common law). Beyond that the law cannot go. It has to delegate legislation to the contracting parties. As far as they are concerned, the law of contract has to be of their own making.

Thus freedom of contract does not commend itself for moral reasons only; it is also an eminently practical principle. It is the inevitable counterpart of a free enterprise system. As a result, our legal lore of contracts reflects a proud spirit of individualism and of *laissez faire*. This is particularly true for the axioms and rules dealing with the formation and interpretation of contracts, the genuineness and reality of consent. Contract — the language of the cases tells us — is a private affair and not a social institution. The judicial system, therefore, provides only for their interpretation, but the courts cannot make contracts for the parties. There is no contract without assent, but once the objective manifestations of assent are present, their author is bound. A person is supposed to know the contract that he makes. "A mere offer imposes no duty of action upon the offeree; there is no obligation to accept or reject or to take any notice of it." (Prosser, "Delay in Acting on an Application for Insurance" (1935) 3 U. of Chi. L.

Rev. 39, 45.) If an offeror does not hear from the offeree about the offer, he is free to make inquiries or to withdraw his offer, but he cannot regard silence as an acceptance. Either party is supposed to look out for his own interests and his own protection. Oppressive bargains can be avoided by careful shopping around. Everyone has complete freedom of choice with regard to his partner in contract, and the privity-of-contract principle respects the exclusiveness of this choice. Since a contract is the result of the free bargaining of parties who are brought together by the play of the market and who meet each other on a footing of social and approximate economic equality, there is no danger that freedom of contract will be a threat to the social order as a whole. Influenced by this optimistic creed, courts are extremely hesitant to declare contracts void as against public policy "because if there is one thing which more than another public policy requires it is that men of full age and competent understanding shall have the utmost liberty of contracting, and that their contracts when entered into freely and voluntarily shall be held sacred and shall be enforced by Courts of justice." (Sir G. Jessel, M.R., in *Printing and Numerical Registering Co. v. Sampson*, L. R. 19 Eq. 462, 465 (1875).)

The development of large scale enterprise with its mass production and mass distribution made a new type of contract inevitable — the standardized mass contract. A standardized contract, once its contents have been formulated by a business firm, is used in every bargain dealing with the same product or service. The individuality of the parties which so frequently gave color to the old type contract has disappeared. The sterotyped contract of today reflects the impersonality of the market. It has reached its greatest perfection in the different types of contracts used on the various exchanges. Once the usefulness of these contracts was discovered and perfected in the transportation, insurance, and banking business, their use spread into all other fields of large scale enterprise, into international as well as national trade, and into labour relations. It is to be noted that uniformity of terms of contracts typically recurring in a business enterprise is an important factor in the exact calculation of risks. Risks which are difficult to calculate can be excluded altogether. Unforseeable contingencies affecting performance, such as strikes, fire, and transportation difficulties can be taken care of. The standard clauses in insurance policies are the most striking illustrations of successful attempts on the part of business enterprises to select and control risks assumed under a contract. The insurance business probably deserves credit also for having first realized the full importance of the so-called "juridical risk", the danger that a court or jury may be swayed by "irrational factors" to decide against a powerful defendant. Ingenious clauses have been the result. Once their practical utility was proven, they were made use of in other lines of business. It is highly probable that the desire to avoid juridical risks has been a motivating factor in the widespread use of warranty clauses in the machine industry limiting the common law remedies of the buyer to breach of an implied warranty of quality and particularly excluding his right to claim damages. The same is true for arbitration clauses in international trade. Standardized contracts have thus become an important means of excluding or controlling the "irrational factor" in litigation. In this respect they are a true reflection of the spirit of our time with its hostility to irrational factors in the judicial process, and they belong in the same category as codifications and restatements.

In so far as the reduction of costs of production and distribution thus achieved is reflected in reduced prices, society as a whole ultimately benefits from the use of standard contracts. And there can be no doubt that this has been the case to a considerable extent. The use of standard contracts has, however, another aspect which has become increasingly important. Standard contracts are typically used by enterprises with strong bargaining power. The weaker party, in need of the goods or services, is frequently not in a position to shop around for better terms, either because the author of the standard contract has a monopoly (natural or artificial) or because all competitors use the same clauses. His contractual intention is but a subjection more or less voluntary to terms dictated by the stronger party, terms whose consequences are often understood only in a vague way, if at all. Thus, standardized contracts are frequently contracts of adhesion; they are *à prendre ou à laisser*. Not infrequently the weaker party to a prospective contract even agrees in advance not to retract his offer while the offeree reserves for himself the power to accept or refuse; or he submits to terms or change of terms which will be communicated to him later. To be sure, the latter type of clauses regularly provide for a power to disaffirm, but as a practical matter they are acquiesced in frequently, thus becoming part of the "living law". Lastly, standardized contracts have also been used to control and regulate the distribution of goods from producer all the way down to the ultimate consumer. They have become one of the many devices to build up and strengthen industrial empires.

And yet the tremendous economic importance of contracts of adhesion is hardly reflected in the great texts on contracts or in the Restatement. As a matter of fact, the term "contract of adhesion" or a similar symbol has not even found general recognition in our legal vocabulary. This will not do any harm if we remain fully aware that the use of the word "contract" does not commit us to an indiscriminate extension of the ordinary contract rules to all contracts. But apparently the realization of the deepgoing antinomies in the structure of our system of contracts is too painful an experience to be permitted to rise to the full level of our consciousness. Consequently, courts have made great efforts to protect the weaker contracting party and still keep "the elementary rules" of the law of contracts intact. As a result, our common law of standardized contracts is highly contradictory and confusing, and the potentialities inherent in the common law system for coping with contracts of adhesion have not been fully developed. The law of insurance contracts furnishes excellent illustrations. Handicapped by the axiom that courts can only interpret but cannot make contracts for the parties, courts had to rely heavily on their prerogative of interpretation to protect a policy holder. To be sure many courts have shown a remarkable skill in reaching "just" decisions by construing ambiguous clauses against their author even in cases where there was no ambiguity. Still, this round about method has its disadvantages as the story of the treatment of warranties in life insurance contracts strikingly demonstrates. Courts, when protecting an innocent policy holder against the harshness of the doctrine, did not state clearly that as a matter of public policy an insurance company cannot avoid liability merely because of the falsity of a statement which has been labelled "warranty". They felt that freedom of contract prevented them from saying so. Instead they disguised as "interpretation" their efforts to change warranties into representations. But this makeshift solution tempted insurance companies to try the usefulness of "warranties" again and again.

Society had thus to pay a high price in terms of uncertainty for the luxury of an apparent homogeneity in the law of contracts. Finally, the legislature had to step in. In many jurisdictions warranties have been put on the same footing with representations; in fire insurance, legislation has even prescribed the contents of the standard policy. No such need has arisen with regard to contracts for reinsurance. Here parties of equal skill and bargaining power are dealing with another.

Although the episode of warranties, because of the intervention of legislation, belongs largely to the past, another well known controversy still lacks a satisfactory solution. Courts have been unable to agree as to who shall bear the risk of "loss without insurance" caused by an unreasonable delay on the part of an insurance company in issuing a policy of insurance for which application has been made. Here again the pious myth that the law of contracts is of one cloth has stood in the path of progress. The courts, because of their reliance on and preoccupation with "interpretation", were lacking experience in handling this situation.

Most courts have felt rather strongly that a recovery in contract is out of the question. According to a "thoroughly established principle of the law of contracts within the field of which insurance largely lies, an application for insurance is a bare offer and therefore imposes no liability upon the insurance company until it is accepted. Nor does it "afford a basis for any liability by reason of delay in accepting it or the want of care in dealing with it". A decision of the Connecticut Supreme Court has summed up the arguments against an implied contract in the most persuasive form:

> It is of course true that failure to act upon it may, in such a case as this, cause loss to the applicant or to those to be named beneficiaries in the policy, against which he expected to secure protection. That situation is not, however, peculiar to the insurance law; for example, one may make an offer to buy goods which he needs at a certain price, having reason to believe the price will advance, and may incur loss through the failure of the one to whom it is made to act upon the offer within a reasonable time. (*Swentusky v. Prudential Ins. Co.*, 116 Conn., 526, 534 (1933).)

To fortify the argument we are told that an implied promise for future action would be unsupported by consideration. "No legal benefit moved from the applicant to it by reason of the offer, and any detriment which the applicant suffers is not one which was contemplated by the terms of the offer or its acceptance". This is all the more true, courts assure us, since the applicant does not agree not to seek insurance elsewhere and is at liberty to withdraw his offer any time before acceptance.

The argument that a recovery in contract would be "contrary to the well settled principles of contract law" has influenced almost the whole of legal literature, particularly since applications typically contain a provision to the effect that the company shall incur no liability under the application until it has been approved by the home office and a formal policy issued and delivered. Besides, we are informed, the assumption of an implied promise to act promptly "ignores actuality". "If a court should hold that a contract to decide expeditiously on the proposal did exist, it is believed that, within a short time, all insurance companies doing business in that jurisdiction would incorporate in their applications stipulations expressly negativing any such promise." (Funk, "The Duty of an Insurer to Act Promptly on Applications" (1927) 75 U. of Pa. L. Rev. 207, 214.)

And yet, although most courts subscribe to this doctrine, the majority still allows recovery by the back door, so to speak. They regard recovery *ex contractu* as impossible, but at the same time allow recovery *ex delictu*. The failure of an insurance company to take prompt action — according to these decisions — amounts to the breach of a general duty towards the public to act without undue delay on applications for acceptable risks. The courts are sure that the policy of insurance cannot be treated like any other contract. The state, by granting a franchise to the insurance company, by regulating and supervising its business, recognizes the great social importance of insurance business; it is, therefore, in the public interest that applications for acceptable risks shall not be unduly delayed. Thus the courts pay merely lip service to the dogma that the common law of contracts governs insurance contracts. With the help of the law of torts they nullify those parts of the law of contracts which in the public interest are regarded as inapplicable. Disguised as tort law the courts recognized a liability for *culpa in contrahendo* thus making new law with regard to the formation of insurance contracts. This approach enables them to disregard the clause in the application by means of which the company attempted to avoid liability prior to the delivery of the policy. No wonder that this line of reasoning has been sharply criticized not only for its inconsistency but also for undermining legal certainty and the stability of the insurance business. To impose upon an insurance company, because it acts under franchise from the state, a duty to act promptly on an application

> would be to open a field of legal liability the limits of which we cannot encompass, and which would go far to introduce chaos in the entire business of insurance, indeed, would almost necessarily reach out into the field of other specially chartered corporations occupying not dissimilar relations to the public, as banks, utility companies, and the like. Public interest more requires that stability of the insurance business which is necessary to guard the great body of persons who enter into relations with it for their own protection and that of those dependent upon them, than it does that certain individuals should be saved the loss which may result by adherence to established legal principles. (*Swentusky v. Prudential Ins. Co.,* 116 Conn. 526, 532 (1933).)

This line-up of arguments brings out clearly the basic issue with which the courts in the insurance cases are confronted. It is: can the unity of the law of contracts be maintained in the face of the increasing use of contracts of adhesion? The few courts which allow recovery in contract and the many which allow recovery in tort feel more or less clearly that insurance contracts are contracts of adhesion, and try to protect the weaker contracting party against the harshness of the common law and against what they think are abuses of freedom of contract. The courts denying recovery, on the other hand, cling to the belief that an application for insurance is not different from any other offer, and they are convinced that efforts to build up by trial and error a dual system of contract law must inevitably undermine the security function of all law, particularly since courts are ill equipped to decide whether and to what extent an insurance contract has compulsory features.

To be sure, the task of building up a multiple system of contract law is eminently difficult, particularly since courts are not commissions which are able to examine carefully the ramifications of the problem involved, and can see only the narrow aspect of the total problem which comes up for litigation. Equally difficult is the job of determining whether and to what extent a contract, for instance that of insurance, is a contract of adhesion. Still, the predicament to which an applicant for insurance is exposed by an unreasonable delay in handling his application is deserving of more serious consideration than the assertion that in case of unreasonable delay the applicant can withdraw his offer and apply elsewhere. The denial of liability may very well put a premium on inefficiency. It is submitted that in this respect the attitude of the courts which allow the applicant to recover as if he were insured is more realistic, provided the risk was acceptable and the insurance company, in dealing with the application, deviated from its standard pattern of behavior, on which the applicant could reasonably rely. There has been no evidence that the insurance business has been unable to adjust itself to the new law created by the decisions allowing recovery. This is not surprising since deviations from the standard practice in handling applications which result in "loss without insurance" are the exception.

The idea implicit in the cases which allow recovery seems very fruitful indeed. In dealing with standardized contracts courts have to determine what the weaker contracting party could legitimately expect by way of services according to the enterpriser's "calling", and to what extent the stronger party disappointed reasonable expectations based on the typical life situation. It can hardly be objected that the resulting task of rewriting, if necessary, the contents of a contract of adhesion is foreign to the function of common law courts; the judge-made law in the field of constructive conditions is amply proving the opposite and refutes the contention that a contract implied in fact does not differ from an express contract except that the intention of the party is circumstantially proved.

The task of adjusting in each individual case the common law of contracts to contracts of adhesion has to be faced squarely and not indirectly. This is possible only if courts become fully aware of their emotional attitude with regard to freedom of contract. Here lies the main obstacle to progress, particularly since courts have an understandable tendency to avoid this crucial issue by way of rationalizations. They prefer to convince themselves and the community that legal certainty and "sound principles" of contract law should not be sacrificed to dictates of justice or social desirability. Such discussions are hardly profitable.

To be sure "case law and the feeling of justice are certainly not synonymous" (M. Cohen, *Positivism and the Limits of Idealism in the Law*, Proceedings of the Sixth International Congress of Philosophy (1927) 469, 470.) it is just to obey the laws of which one does not approve. But it is equally true that the rules of the common law are flexible enough to enable courts to listen to their sense of justice and to the sense of justice of the community. Just as freedom of contract gives individual contracting parties all the needed leeway for shaping the law of contract according to their needs, the elasticity of the common law, with rule and counterrule constantly competing, makes it possible for courts to follow the dictates of "social desirability". Whatever one may think about the possibility of separating the "law that is" from the "law that ought to be", this much is certain: In the development of the common law the ideal tends constantly to become the practice. And in this process the ideal of certainty has constantly to be weighed against the social desirability of change, and very often legal certainty has to be sacrificed to progress. The inconsistencies and contradictions within the legal system resulting from the uneven growth of the law and from conflicting ideologies are inevitable.

It is not even profitable to spend "the energy of counsel, the money of clients and the time and analysis of judges" (Douglas, "Vicarious Liability and Administration of Risk, I" (1929) 38 Yale L. J. 584, 594.) in discussing the problems presented by contracts of adhesion in terms of established legal principles and to proclaim that recovery is "contrary to the well settled principles of contract law". This approach tries to create the impression that the rules concerning the formation of contracts are a closed and harmonious system. But this is hardly the case. The doctrine of consideration, for instance, more than any other doctrine, is in a constant process of evolution, full of contradictions and inconsistencies. It has responded to the belief in freedom of contract, as the pepper corn theory of consideration illustrates. It can also be used to protect a creditor against the risk of economic duress of his debtor (*Foakes v. Beer*). Diametrically opposed social policies have thus been defended in the name of consideration. Furthermore, the harshness of the rule of *Thorne v. Deas*, (4 Johns. 84 (N.Y. 1809). It is difficult to believe that the efforts on the part of some courts [*e.g., Comfort v. McCorkle*, 149 Misc. 826, 268 N.Y. Supp. 192 (1933)] to reconcile §§ 45 and 90 of the Restatement by limiting the application of promissory estoppel to charitable subscriptions and promises to make gifts (non-commercial cases) will be successful in the long run.) which seems to support the theory of the courts which deny liability in contract, is mitigated by a counter rule which is constantly gaining in strength and has found expression in Section 90 of the Restatement. Even the mere risk of reliance has been regarded sufficient consideration, a doctrine which comes in handy here to offset the argument that the applicant could have withdrawn his application and applied for insurance elsewhere. It is true that acceptance of the application can hardly be inferred from silence for an unreasonable length of time since the standard clause in the application expressly warns the applicant that the company shall incur no liability under the application until it has been approved and a formal policy has been issued and delivered. But is this clause sufficiently unequivocal to negative not only an acceptance by silence but also an implied collateral promise (as it is technically called) to take prompt action on an application for an acceptable risk? More serious is the argument that the assumption of an implied promise to act promptly is unrealistic because insurance companies, once subjected to such an implied promise, would immediately negative it by express stipulation in the policy. But is this argument not begging the question? The crucial problem is not whether insurance companies would insert such a clause but whether they could do so with impunity.

Thus, technical doctrines of the law of contracts cannot possibly provide the courts with the right answers. They convince only those courts which are already convinced. For instance, which consideration doctrine the court is going to choose as the correct one depends upon its attitude with regard to freedom of contract. All the technical doctrines resorted to by the courts in the insurance cases denying liability are in the last analysis but rationalizations of the court's emotional desire to preserve freedom of contract. Even the cases which hold the insurance company liable in tort pay tribute to the dogma; otherwise it would have been unnecessary constantly to emphasize that the plaintiff is not seeking recovery in contract. The freedom of contract dogma is the real hero or villain in the drama of the insurance cases, but it prefers to remain in the safety of the background if possible, leaving the actual fighting to consideration and to the host of other satellites — all of which is very often confusion to the audience which vaguely senses the unreality of the atmosphere.

Still, the tort cases are a constant though indirect challenge to the claims of the freedom of contract dogma. They keep alive the question whether or not the "received ideas" on freedom of contract which form the background of the insurance cases represent a cultural lag.

The individualism of our rules of contract law, of which freedom of contract is the most powerful symbol, is closely tied up with the ethics of free enterprise capitalism and the ideals of justice of a mobile society of small enterprisers, individual merchants and independent craftsmen. This society believed that individual and cooperative action left unrestrained in family, church and market would not lessen the freedom and dignity of man but would secure the highest possible social justice. It was firmly convinced of a natural law according to which the individual serving his own interest was also serving the interest of the community. Profits can be earned only by supplying consumable commodities. Freedom of competition will prevent profits from rising unduly. The play of the market if left to itself must therefore maximize net satisfactions. Justice within this framework has a very definite meaning. It means freedom of property and of contract, of profit making and of trade. Freedom of contract thus receives its moral justification. The "prestablized harmony" of a social system based on freedom of enterprise and perfect competition sees to it that the "private autonomy" of contracting parties will be kept within bounds and will work out to the benefit of the whole.

With the decline of the free enterprise system due to the innate trend of competitive capitalism towards monopoly, the meaning of contract has changed radically. Society, when granting freedom of contract, does not guarantee that all members of the community will be able to make use of it to the same extent. On the contrary, the law, by protecting the unequal distribution of property, does nothing to prevent freedom of contract from becoming a one-sided privilege. Society, by proclaiming freedom of contract, guarantees that it will not interfere with the exercise of power by contract. Freedom of contract enables enterprisers to legislate by contract and, what is even more important, to legislate in a substantially authoritarian manner without using the appearance of authoritarian forms. Standard contracts in particular could thus become effective instruments in the hands of powerful industrial and commercial overlords enabling them to impose a new feudal order of their own making upon a vast host of vassals. This spectacle is all the more fascinating since not more than a hundred years ago contract ideology had been successfully used to break down the last vestiges of a patriarchal and benevolent feudal order in the field of master and servant (*Priestley v. Fowler*). Thus the return back from contract to status which we experience today was greatly facilitated by the fact that the belief in freedom of contract has remained one of the firmest axioms in the whole fabric of the social philosophy of our culture.

The role played by contract in the destruction of the institutional framework of capitalistic society is constantly obscured to the lawyer by the still prevailing philosophy of law which neglects to treat contract as the most important source of law. According to conventional theory contract is only a convenient label for a number of "operative facts" which have the consequences intended by the parties if the law so ordains. In this respect the great philosophers of natural law thought quite differently: society, in proclaiming freedom of contract — according to their teaching — has delegated to individual citizens a piece of sovereignty which enables them to participate constantly in the law making process. Freedom of contract means that the state has no monopoly in the creation of law. The consent of contracting parties creates law also. The lawmaking process is decentralized. As a result, law is not an order imposed by the state from above upon its citizens; it is rather an order created from below. This was a realistic insight. Unwarranted, however, was the optimistic belief that capitalism meant a permanent advance over the preceding social system, feudalism, because of the fact that contract and not status had become the chief means of social integration. Nor can we subscribe to the thesis of natural law philosophers that the progress in any society towards freedom is to be measured by the extent to which all political relations can be reduced to contract, "the perfect form of obligation".

In the happy days of free enterprise capitalism the belief that contracting is law making had largely emotional importance. Law making by contract was no threat to the harmony of the democratic system. On the contrary it reaffirmed it. The courts, therefore, representing the community as a whole, could remain neutral in the name of freedom of contract. The deterioration of the social order into the pluralistic society of our days with its powerful pressure groups was needed to make the wisdom of the contract theory of the natural law philosophers meaningful to us. The prevailing dogma, on the other hand, insisting that contract is *only* a set of operative facts, helps to preserve the illusion that the "law" will protect the public against any abuse of freedom of contract. This will not be the case so long as we fail to realize that freedom of contract must mean different things for different types of contracts. Its meaning must change with the social importance of the type of contract and with the degree of monopoly enjoyed by the author of the standardized contract.

MACNEIL, CONTRACTS, EXCHANGE TRANSACTIONS AND RELATIONS
2d Ed. 1978, pp. 445-447 (Chapter 4).

(E) CONTRACTS OF ADHESION

"Contracts of adhesion" is a term now commonly used to describe certain kinds of form contracts. Its use reflects a developing recognition in the legal system of differences between contracts of adhesion and non-adhesion contracts and a consequent willingness of the courts to regulate the former more stringently than the latter. It is therefore worth exploring the characteristics of the archetypical situations in which contracts of adhesion come into existence.

First, at least some aspects of the transaction are not unique but are standardized in nature, permitting the planning of them on a mass production basis by printing forms.

Second, one of the parties is in a position unilaterally to cause the use of a particular form without the other party's having effective power to modify it.

Third, the form was prepared primarily for the benefit of the party causing it to be used.

Fourth, the standardized portions of the form are, at least at the time of "agreement," likely to be left unexamined or not to be understood by the party adhering to it.

One of the countless examples of transaction in which contracts of adhesion are used is the sale of a new automobile. The situation was well described by Judge Francis in the well-known case of *Henningsen v. Bloomfield Motors, Inc.*, 32 N.J. 358, 161 A.2d 69, 87 (1960):

> The warranty before us is a standardized form designed for mass use. It is imposed upon the automobile consumer. He takes it or leaves it, and he must take it to buy an automobile. No bargaining is engaged in with respect to it. In fact, the dealer through whom it comes to the buyer is without authority to alter it; his function is ministerial — simply to deliver it. The form warranty is not only standard with Chrysler but, as mentioned above, it is the uniform warranty of the Automobile Manufacturers Association. Members of the Association are: General Motors, Inc., Ford, Chrysler, Studebaker-Packard, American Motors (Rambler), Willys Motors, Checker Motors Corp., and International Harvester Company. Automobile Facts and Figures (1958 Ed., Automobile Manufacturers Association) 69. Of these companies, the "Big Three" (General Motors, Ford, and Chrysler) represented 93.5% of the passenger-car production for 1958 and the independents 6.5%. [Cit.]. And for the same year the "Big Three" had 86.72% of the total passenger vehicle registrations. [Cit.].

In a later case Judge Francis described contracts of adhesion involving consumer finance, *Unico v. Owen*, 50 N.J. 101, 110, 232 A.2d 405, 410 (1967):

> The consumer-credit market is essentially a process of exchange, the general nature of which is shaped by the objectives and relative bargaining power of each of the parties. In consumer goods transactions there is almost always a substantial differential in bargaining power between the seller and his financer, on the one side, and the householder on the other. That difference exists because generally there is a substantial inequality of economic resources between them, and of course, that balance in the great mass of cases favors the seller and gives him and his financer the power to shape the exchange to their advantage. Their greater economic resources permit them to obtain the advice of experts; moreover, they have more time to reflect about the specific terms of the exchange prior to the negotiations with the consumer; they know from experience how to strengthen their own position in consumer-credit arrangements; and the financer-creditor is better able to absorb the impact of a single imprudent or unfair exchange.

The last three elements of the pure contract of adhesion are not necessarily always present whenever a standard form is utilized in the establishment of a contractual relationship. Many a standard form is used for reasons other than the unilateral insistence of one of the parties that it should be used. For example, the Worth Street Rules set out standard forms which are widely used in the sales of grey goods (unfinished cloth as it comes from the loom.) They are used not because one party is in a position unilaterally to insist upon their use, but because their use has become the mutually accepted custom of both sellers and buyers in the grey goods market. Much the same thing might be said of the American Institute of Architects Standard Agreements with which we shall deal subsequently. (This is not to suggest that such a form cannot be unilaterally imposed, but only that it commonly is not.)

Closely related to the second element of the typical contract of adhesion is the third, the fact that the form was prepared primarily for the benefit of the party causing it to be used. Here again there are many forms in widespread use in which the interests of all parties to the form were considered in its drafting. Both the Worth Street Rules and the AIA Standard Agreements are examples of this type of form. It is fairly safe generalization to say that such relatively balanced forms come about only when there is at least some degree of equality of bargaining power between the parties or collectives of the parties, such as trade associations or perhaps consumer groups. With respect to consumer transactions such power may be exercised on behalf of the consumers by the government through statute or administrative law, an example of which was seen in the materials relating to insurance in sub-section (1), supra. (The political processes, of course, preclude the government from being a single-minded bargaining agent on behalf of one group such as consumers. Thus such statutory or administrative provisions are likely at least in part to be the result of compromises somewhat different from those made, for example, by a retailers trade association in negotiating a standard form agreement with a wholesalers trade association.)

Standard forms may also be used in situations lacking the fourth element of contracts of adhesion, the likelihood that one (or often both) party is not familiar with its content. Building Contractors and Owners (usually through their agent, the Architect) often know AIA or similar form contracts backwards and forwards. The same thing can be said of experts who use Worth Street contracts and experienced government contractors whose knowledge of the Federal Procurement Regulations and the Armed Services Procurement Regulations and government contract forms may exceed that of the government officials with whom they deal. Moreover, even the most untutored consumer often knows some of the standardized content of contracts which he enters.

HAROLD C. HAVIGHURST, THE NATURE OF PRIVATE CONTRACT

pp. 113-118.

More extensive in their operation are the policies directed toward an egalitarian purpose. Such policies are counteractants to superior bargaining power or other circumstance that places one party to the contract in a position to fix the terms without any participation by the other. They rest upon the view that justice and the interests of society are furthered when the law to some extent ranges itself upon the side of the party who for some reason or another is unable properly to safeguard his own interests. At times these manifestations appear more as tendencies than as admitted policies, but I shall call them "policies."

Business firms often draw up elaborate forms to be used in all dealings of the same kind, and these have been called "contracts of adhesion." Occasionally the law-conscious individual, if he insists, may obtain an interlineation in his favor. But in most instances, if he wants to do business, he must adhere. The equalizing process is not confined to instances where such forms are used, but nowadays contracts of adhesion are often thought to call for it.

Egalitarian policies operate in two situations. These are often found in conjunction, but it will serve the purpose of clarity, I believe, if we consider them separately. The first is represented principally by the contracts to which I referred in the second lecture whereby the common man obtains what he needs for his family enterprise. These are the deals in which the ignorant, the necessitous, or the irresponsibly optimistic may be induced by the sharp uncommon man to assent to the harsh term by virtue of which, when literally applied, the consequence of even a trifling default is disastrous. These are the transactions in which the contract provides for the penalties and the forfeitures that equity is supposed to abhor.

It must be admitted that courts have never consistently granted relief from unconscionable provisions of this character. They have not always had patience with the frailties I have mentioned. The remedies the creditor has reserved for himself, the penalties he has prescribed — to which the weaker party has given nominal assent — have at times no doubt appeared to judges as wholesome. Furthermore, the actual damages upon default are hard to prove. Juries may be oversympathetic for the plight of the defaulter and undersympathetic with the exasperations to which the dispensers of easy credit are subjected. Strong measures are called for, or contracts will not be performed. This was a nineteenth century point of view, and it has had its adherents in other periods. Today, however, the drift is in the direction of strengthening the policy that affords relief.

Certain patterns for preventing forfeiture have long been well established. The equity of redemption for mortgaged property and relief from the penalty provision of a bond are so imbedded in the legal fabric that today it is quite well understood that such instruments do not have the meaning which the words express. In drafting them the safest way to obtain the intended effect is to state what is not intended.

The other situation in which a policy of equalization is sometimes applied is not concerned with default by the party who does not participate in drawing up the terms. Indeed this party may not even enter into any undertaking for the future. These contracts define the duties of the party who prepares them, and the natural tendency is to narrow legal duties to the point where the party who adheres is deprived of a day in court. The policy evoked is designed to preserve the day in court.

This policy is not so old as the one directed against unconscionable forfeitures. The practices against which it is directed are ordinarily found when business is conducted upon such a scale that individualized dealing is impracticable. In order to see how a contract of adhesion comes into being in this situation we must first look to the factors that determine the verbal dimensions of the contract.

Whenever parties who know and trust each other enter into a transaction or relation, a few words to make plain the specificities are ordinarily all in the way of a contract that is needed. Quite apart from any catalogue of terms, each one, if he has had any experience in similar matters, will have a fairly clear idea of what he expects from the other party in a course of events that does not veer too far from the usual, and a fairly clear idea of what the other party expects from him. Each one is willing to accommodate himself within reasonable limits to a fixed idea of the other and to compromise in the unusual event that fixed ideas should conflict. Neither anticipates any difficulty. Law is far from their thoughts.

This pleasant state of affairs, however, does not always exist. If the relation is to extend over a period and the parties are uncertain about what the future holds, if they have reason to expect the unexpected, they may not, even when they know and trust each other, be confident of their ability to meet all contingencies in a spirit of peace and friendship. It may seem desirable to try to anticipate what may happen and to make specific provision for everything that can be foreseen. The lawyer properly encourages this state of mind. In my first lecture I mentioned the contribution of the profession to the cause of peace. "Nip controversy before it even buds!" is good advice.

Yet, though an elaborate contract is drawn, it is not with a view to litigation. Unless either imagination or expression proves inadequate there will be no controversy, and even if differences should arise, the parties expect to be able to resolve them.

It is only when a party is dealing with someone he does not know and trust that he begins to think about the law and to feel that for legal reasons he needs a contract of many words. In a deal in which credit is extended no words, however voluminous, will take the place of an investigation, but the need of which I am now speaking has nothing to do with credit. The drawer of the contract is not concerned about the other party's performance nor with his own legal remedies. His worry is that the other party will prove to be an evil person, that the other party will trump up a lawsuit against him.

This is not an idle fear. Fraudulent lawsuits are common. Some persons will commit arson or even murder with a view to establishing an insurance claim. Others may be honest, but they are neurotic and easily moved without provocation to pursue an aggressive course of action.

A business that deals with many customers or suppliers or employees or holders of dealer franchises or tenants does not ordinarily find it feasible to conduct a thorough investigation in each case of character and emotional stability. Furthermore, if the dealing is expected to extend over a long period, character and emotional stability, unexceptionable at the time, may later suffer deterioration. It is far simpler to require adhesion to a contract that commits the business legally to a performance far less than it expects to render, to hedge promises about with conditions that it does not expect to insist upon, unless the other party proves to be evil or unstable. If carefully prepared, the contract, supplemented by verbal assurances, may yield the advantage of raising the expectations necessary to induce the desired performance and at the same time insulate against legal liability.

Such a course cannot always be characterized as sharp dealing. These are not harsh terms imposed in every instance by reason of superior bargaining power. The business may be quite competitive. But informed, intelligent and well-balanced people are not as a rule too much concerned about the extent of the legal pressures available in the event of dispute. In deciding with whom they will deal they are apt to take more account of the attractiveness of other terms and of the company's reputation for fair dealing.

For the business enterprise, then, good judgment prompts elimination, as far as possible, of the legal hazard. If a few are constrained to deal elsewhere because the proposition is not attractive from a legal standpoint, they are probably the litigious-minded people and their loss is good riddance.

I have several wealthy neighbors who apparently are obsessed with worry about burglars. They have great iron fences surrounding their properties and fierce dogs. When the fierce dogs bark behind the iron fences, the evil person bent upon intrusion tends to be dissuaded. For the business enterprise, possessed of assets and obsessed with worry about evil litigants, the contract of adhesion is a great iron fence. The business may not have fierce dogs, but it has lawyers — lawyers who keep the fences in repair and lawyers who make appropriate noises when prospective litigants approach. The evil person bent upon a lawsuit tends to be dissuaded.

However, as you readily see, there is here a problem. The iron fence that excludes the bad man also excludes the good. And a man who sincerely believes that his claim is just may sometimes be regarded by the enterpriser as evil. The contract of adhesion, though conceived in a worthy cause, has the effect of depriving every adherent of a day in court.

The question is: To what extent is this deprivation of public concern?

In many situations, in my opinion, it is not a matter of concern; and the reason is that there is no real need for legal enforcement. The non-legal pressures are ample to insure performance. Many firms in their dealing lean over backward to preserve good will and to keep the peace. They pursue a course epitomized in the slogan, "The customer is always right." When a claim is denied, it is more certain that it had no substance than if, there having been no contract spelling out the terms, it had been dismissed in a court of law.

But in the first two situations described in my second lecture where legal pressures attain maximum importance, the power of one party to deprive the other of a day in court *is* a matter of public concern. In these instances the need is for enforcement against the stronger party, and he is the one in a position to prepare the contract of adhesion — to build the iron fence. Here it has been necessary to impose limitations upon freedom of contract.

First among the principal situations in which legal enforcement is advantageous, you will remember, is the one found in a class of dealing that lends itself easily to fly-by-night operation. The best example is the insurance business. Here, when contract is completely free, the contract of adhesion, filled with multifarious conditions and warranties, utterly destroys the day in court of the policyholder or his beneficiary; and, as I have said, the non-legal sanctions are entirely inadequate. Prior to legislative intervention, the courts did much to preserve a vestige of judicial remedy by remaking the contract through construction. But nowadays, in life insurance, in accident and health insurance, and in fire insurance the terms of the contracts are largely prescribed by law.

The big and respected companies, having with the help of public regulation achieved conscience and consciousness of the benefits of public esteem, support such legislation. They recognize that if there were no restrictions upon contract terms, although they themselves would either write fair contracts or in any event adopt a liberal policy in paying claims, fly-by-night operation would take some of their business and tend to give the whole insurance industry a bad name.

It may be interesting to note that automobile insurance has taken a different course. This kind of insurance came upon the scene after the business had attained responsibility and had become jealous of its public standing. In the case of this kind of insurance the companies themselves have co-operated with each other in preparing contract language and they have adopted forms whose terms do not destroy the policyholder's day in court. For this kind of insurance, the requirement that forms must be approved by the insurance commissioner may help to keep companies in line, but the legislatures have not yet deemed it necessary to prescribe standard forms.

The second situation I mentioned in which legal enforcement is essential is one in which the contracting parties are subject to unequal competitive pressures. It is typified by the contract by which the powerful enterpriser obtains the co-operation of the small man. In the labor field generally collective bargaining, fostered by limitations upon contract freedom of a kind I have yet to discuss, has redressed the imbalance. But there are other relations involving disparate competitive pressures in which organization of those in the weaker position has not been and perhaps cannot be achieved.

The most obvious example of such a relation is that between the large manufacturer of nationally advertised products and its sales agencies. In some businesses of this kind, dealers frequently are deprived of a needed day in court. Contracts of adhesion still commit the manufacturer to a performance far less than he expects to render, and in the event of controversy the dealer's only hope is for a drastic judicial distortion of the contract language. In the automobile business, however, an act of Congress and laws in a number of states have limited the power of the manufacturer, no matter how the contract reads, to terminate the agency at will. It has provided for the automobile dealer a day in court.

It is more than probable that in the future we shall see an increased number of prescribed terms of this character. In England statutes have already appeared establishing for leases provisions which cannot be varied by agreement. Several British writers who have taken the position that the present contract law is inadequate have in mind that there are still many kinds of dealing in which one of the parties is in a position to fix the terms without any participation by the other. If this is true in England, it cannot be otherwise in the United States.

On these first two classes of limitations upon freedom of contract I have dwelt long; and perhaps I can justify the extent of the discussion upon the ground that the more legal the subject is, the greater is its difficulty. However, the controls of contract-in-fact, which make up the third class in my enumeration, have a far greater impact upon business and upon life, and they cut deeper into freedom.

The controversy over freedom of contract beginning in the late nineteenth century and extending through the period of the New Deal generated all of its heat in connection with legislation imposing restrictions of this kind. The great constitutional cases were concerned with them — hours of work, child labor, minimum wage, discrimination in hiring and firing based upon union membership, and others.

I have spoken of the limitations in this class as controls of contract-in-fact; and I should like to take a moment to make the point that, although such legislation may occasionally have some slight significance in the matter of the legal enforcement of the contract, its effect in this regard, when it exists at all, is only incidental. In the case of a contract prohibited by social legislation, of which the employment of child labor is an example, the question of contract enforcement practically never arises. Such statutes aim by prescribing penalties to prevent the use of the contract in a way or upon terms thought to be socially undesirable, It is true that a minimum wage statute, permitting a suit by an underpaid employee for what he should have been paid, and for penalties, suggests an overlapping with the second class of limitations; but such a suit is important principally because of the penalties.

The denial of enforcement of contracts in restraint of trade has no doubt some significance. But for making antitrust policy effective, reliance has been placed upon criminal penalties, injunctions, cease and desist orders and private actions for triple damages. Without these, the mere recognition of a defense to a contract action based upon a violation could not make a visible dent upon monopolistic practices. For this, experience prior to the Sherman Act affords ample proof. Contracts in restraint of trade, it is to be remembered, have been unenforceable in Anglo-American law for more than five centuries.

What, then, are the purposes of the limitations in this category? Once we gain an understanding of contract-in-fact as an instrument of power, a subject which I tried to develop in my first lecture, it is fairly easy to see, I think, why its use has been restricted.

The restrictions relate to the uses of contract to build power and also to exercise it.

As to the building of power, restrictions have been imposed upon contract both in order to prevent the growth of private concentrations of economic power and to facilitate them. In fields of business in which it has seemed possible to maintain competition, the effort has been through the antitrust laws to prevent price-fixing and the formation of great integrated organizations dominating the market. But combinations of employees in labor unions have been encouraged. Such organizations are exempt from antitrust laws and the use of private power to stop them has itself been stopped by placing severe limitations upon the employer's freedom of contract.

The purpose, of course, in all of these efforts has been to maintain a power balance, to iron out those great inequalities in bargaining power that enable one party to impose his will upon the other.

The law does not write the terms of the labor agreement, but in this field it is plain that there is only a qualified freedom of contract. Having trained great antagonists in a way to provide some assurance that neither one will destroy or even very seriously injure the other, the Government brings them together and keeps them together, saying: "Bargain! You do not have to agree. Fight a little if you feel like it. But don't fight too long or hurt anybody else very much, or something will happen to you! And it will be better for both of you if you never find out what it is!"

The power of these great organizations on both sides is subject to abuse in relation to the individual, and I suppose that the system cannot be called ideal. A priori one might doubt that it would work to keep enterprise going. Even with experience we have fears about the next time. But it *has* worked. The great antagonists do usually agree, and if they fight, they eventually settle. If at first they are hard and tough, the rigors of the inconclusive struggle eventually lead to what Rabelais called the "pudding time." They become tired of fighting; they yield to Government pressure; in the fullness and the softness of the "pudding time," great antagonists reach agreement.

Another reason for imposing limitations upon contract-in-fact is to prevent its use by monopolistic power to exact what the traffic will bear in fields of enterprise where it is impossible to maintain competition. Few, among even the most dedicated economic liberals, would leave contract free when these circumstances prevail. There have been clashes; but they have occurred, not over the theory of regulation, but over alleged oppression by the administrative agencies that do the job of regulating.

There is also, as every schoolboy knows — at least every high school boy — , the need to limit contract in order to preserve health, safety and morals. Contract is not to be used as an instrument of power to bring pressure to do what may prove harmful to the doer. Things a person — child, woman or man — may do to himself, others may not through contract require him to do. It is said that the law clerks of Justice Brandeis used to work sixteen hours in a day to glean material for an "economic brief" showing that it was harmful to health to work more than eight hours in a day. But these law clerks worked for the same reason that law students work — not under compulsion but out of sheer enthusiasm for the task. Such activity is healthful. It is not comparable to long hours of labor induced by economic need.

It is true that in our society every contract is not to be proscribed whenever judges, legislators or administrators believe that its terms are unfair or unjust or in any degree opposed to the public interest. Just as there must be "freedom for the thought that we hate," so there must also be, in a measure, freedom for the contract that we hate. Otherwise all private autonomy in the economic field is destroyed. But the invasion of economic liberty by government must run deeper than curbs upon free speech. For the inducements of contract are more powerful than the incitements of speech, and when these inducements threaten serious harm there is usually a clear and present danger that the harm will come about.

Before leaving health, safety, and morals, I must remark again upon the black sheep — Chance — whom you have doubtless seen hanging about, and who I am sure, would feel slighted if he were not included among the blights upon the public morals. He has never enjoyed the shelter of the Constitution, but apparently he has never needed it.

At this point I wish to consider briefly another class of limitations upon contract which I did not list. I refer to economic controls. I am not sure that these fall within our subject. So long as Government taxes and spends to do a policeman's job, or even to do an economic doctor's job, or even to do a welfare job, its actions affect the terms of contracts, just as Nature and the actions of other men affect the terms of contracts, by creating the situation in which the parties deal. Whatever one may think about government's proper sphere, these are not curbs upon liberty of contract. But when the power to spend is used simply and exclusively to support the price of agricultural commodities I see no real difference between that and any other form of price control.

This kind of limitation fills me with a vague disquiet which I have difficulty in accounting for. I suppose these supports can be justified. If an undispersible concentration of power in the form of a natural monopoly justifies a maximum price, an uncementable dispersion of power may justify a minimum price. But I cannot say that this thought makes me entirely comfortable. Perhaps I am jealous because the economist here takes the business away from the lawyer. Perhaps I am troubled because I cannot think of an appropriate figure of speech. In any event I do not see this as a wonderful system.

This brings us to the fourth and final category of limitations — the stifling of contract by involuntary status duties. Here I use "status" to refer to all duties in the creation of which the uncoerced will of the individual has no part. Slavery and peonage provide obvious illustrations; the duty of a man drafted for military service is another.

The law in respect to involuntary status does not in terms prohibit the making of promises; but insofar as custom and coercion serve the purposes of enterprise, power and peace, and insofar as they have vitality and represent the "living law," there is no need for contract. In the realm of activity to which they apply they make contract impossible. To the extent that contract is crowded out, there is no freedom of contract.

If the order of the classes of limitations were arranged historically this last one would come first. Involuntary status duties resting upon kinship represent the oldest way of obtaining co-operation for the enterprise. The meaning of status, as I use the term here, is very close, I think, to the meaning attached to the word by Sir Henry Maine when he said that the movement of the progressive societies has hitherto been a movement from status to contract. From the conception of status he excluded all relationships which are the "immediate or remote result of agreement."

Both those who have used Maine's observation as an idea weapon and those who have denounced it have invariably regarded it as relating to all kinds of limitations upon freedom of contract. Yet when we adhere to Maine's own definition of status, I cannot see that the famous pronouncement has a bearing upon any of the limitations except those in this fourth class. I am skeptical in general of attempts to formulate historical "laws." But if I understand Maine correctly, developments in the twentieth century have not as yet revealed a reversal of the trend which he noted.

Although this movement hitherto from involuntary status to contract, as I said, suggests that this category of limitation should be listed first, I have chosen to list it last. The reason is that in my list the classes of limitations are arranged in the order of the depth to which they cut into freedom of contract. The limitations in this last class cut the deepest, and they are in truth deadly. If involuntary status duties are numerous in a society, it will approach the condition of the ant society of which I spoke in the Introduction.

The first three classes of limitations I have discussed are not only consistent with a free society, but they are needed in order to maintain it. The imposition of involuntary status duties, on the other hand, unless narrowly confined, will quickly destroy freedom. Even in the great wartime emergency, you will remember, we did not conscript a labor force.

———————

As these extracts have suggested, the issues involved in controlling contract power are complex and important. Once again, direct solutions are likely to be most effective. To illustrate that such an approach is possible, the following case is included at this point. We will return to this problem later in the chapter.

MORRISON v. COAST FINANCE LTD.

(1965), 55 D.L.R. (2d) 710. B.C. Court of Appeal; Davey, Sheppard and Bull JJ.A.

Davey, J.A.: — The appellant Morrison, an old woman 79 years of age, and a widow of meagre means, was persuaded by two men, Lowe and Kitely, to borrow $4,200 from the respondent Coast Finance Ltd. on a first mortgage on her home for that amount and interest to maturity and to lend the proceeds to them so that Lowe could repay $915 that he owed the finance company, and he and Kitely could pay the other respondent company $2,302 for two automobiles they were buying from it for resale. The proceeds of the loan were applied accordingly and the balance was repaid at once to the finance company and automobile company, respectively, by way of prepayment of monthly instalments, insurance premiums, and costs. The mortgage was to be repaid at the rate of $300 a month, which was to be secured from payments to be made by Lowe at the finance company's office on her account by way of repayment of the money lent to him and Kitely. She had no other means of repaying the money, and the house was her only substantial asset. She had no independent advice, although the evidence shows she wanted and asked for help. Lowe and Kitely failed to pay the appellant. She commenced action to have the mortgage set aside as having been procured by undue influence and as an unconscionable bargain made between persons in an unequal position. She did not join Lowe and Kitely as defendants to the action.

The learned trial Judge dismissed the action on the grounds that the relationship between the parties was not such as to create a presumption of undue influence, and that none had been proven; that there was nothing in the terms of the mortgage to make it an unconscionable transaction. In my respectful opinion that learned trial Judge took too narrow a view of the appellant's case on the second ground.

Appellant's principal submission before us on this second ground was that, not only the mortgage, but the whole transaction was unconscionable; that it was unconscionable for Lowe and Kitely and the two companies to have the appellant mortgage her home in order to secure the money to lend to Lowe and Kitely to enable them to pay off the finance company and buy the two cars from the automobile company. This case is somewhat sketchily, but sufficiently, set up in the pleadings: see *Nocton v. Lord Ashburton*, [1914] A.C. 932, headnote (2). Counsel told us he took this point below, and respondents' counsel made only a qualified denial. It is apparent that the learned trial Judge and respondents' counsel did not appreciate the full scope of appellant's case on this point.

The equitable principles relating to undue influence and relief against unconscionable bargains are closely related, but the doctrines are separate and distinct. The finding here against undue influence does not conclude the question whether the appellant is entitled to relief against an unconscionable transaction. A plea of undue influence attacks the sufficiency of consent; a plea that a bargain is unconscionable invokes relief against an unfair advantage gained by an unconscientious use of power by a stronger party against a weaker. On such a claim the material ingredients are proof of inequality in the position of the parties arising out of the ignorance, need or distress of the weaker, which left him in the power of the stronger, and proof of substantial unfairness of the bargain obtained by the stronger. On proof of those circumstances, it creates a presumption of fraud which the stronger must repel by proving that the bargain was fair, just and reasonable: *Earl of Aylesford v. Morris* (1873), L.R. 8 Ch. 484, *per* Lord Selborne, L.C., at p. 491; or perhaps by showing that no advantage was taken: see *Harrison v. Guest* (1855), 6 De G. M. & G. 424 at p. 438, 43 E.R. 1298; affirmed (1860), 8 H.L.C. 481 at pp. 492-3, 11 E.R. 517. In *Fry v. Lane*

(1888), 40 Ch. D. 312, Kay, J., accurately stated the modern scope and application of the principle and discussed the earlier authorities upon which it rests. At p. 322 he said:

> The result of the decisions is that where a purchase is made from a poor and ignorant man at a considerable undervalue, the vendor having no independent advice, a Court of Equity will set aside the transaction.
>
> This will be done even in the case of property in possession, and *à fortiori* if the interest is reversionary.
>
> The circumstances of poverty and ignorance of the vendor, and absence of independent advice, throw upon the purchaser, when the transaction is impeached, the onus of proving, in *Lord Selborne's* words, that the purchase was "fair, just, and reasonable."

The finance company was engaged in the business of financing automobile purchases and lending money on mortgages. The other respondent company was an automobile dealer. They shared adjoining offices, employed the same solicitor, and had a common office manager, one Crawford, who in the final stages of this transaction acted for both companies. The president, director, and owner of half the shares of the finance company was a director of the automobile company, and with his wife controlled it. The finance company financed most of the automobile company's paper.

There can be no doubt about the inequality in the position of the appellant on one side and the respondent companies and Lowe and Kitely on the other. The question is whether the transaction was so unfair that it creates a presumption of overreaching by the respondents.

The learned trial Judge approached this question as if it was a simple case of the appellant borrowing money from the finance company for her own purposes — that is to say to lend it to Lowe and Kitely. Accordingly he looked to see if the terms of the mortgage were unconscionable. If that were the true scope of the inquiry, I would agree with his conclusion, for although the rate of interest is high and the mortgage does not state the effective rate of interest as required by the *Interest Act*, R.S.C. 1952, c. 156, s. 6, the rate of interest is not so high as to be exorbitant for a loan up to 100% of the value of the security, as this was.

But this was not a simple loan of that kind. It was a loan to the appellant to advance the interests of the companies as well as Lowe and Kitely by providing her with money to lend to Lowe and Kitely to enable them to carry out their arrangements with the companies. Crawford made certain that the proceeds of the loan reached the two respondent companies. The appellant, Lowe and Kitely, did not retain one cent of the money advanced, although the two men got delivery of the two automobiles they bought with the money.

The extreme folly of this old woman mortgaging her home in order to borrow money which she could not repay out of her own resources, for the purpose of lending it to the two men, who were comparative strangers, is self-evident. It would have been bad enough if there had been any prospect of profit, but there was no expectation of reward and no real security. The amount to be paid back to her was exactly the amount of her mortgage to the finance company. The respondent companies knew the essential facts, and undertook the preparation of the documents for the transaction. For them to take advantage of her obvious ignorance and inexperience in order to further their respective businesses raises a presumption of fraud within the above authorities. The distinction between the case which the learned trial Judge considered, and that which arises on the evidence was neatly put by appellant's counsel. He said it would not be wrong for a bank to lend money to an old and ignorant person, upon usual banking terms, for his own purposes, but quite wrong to lend him money on those terms so that he might lend it to an impecunious debtor from whom the bank intended to recover it in payment of a bad debt.

There is supporting evidence of gross overreaching by the respondent companies. They received the application for the loan, not from the appellant, but from Lowe or Kitely, who, with them, were to benefit by it. Without having seen the appellant, Crawford obtained a valuation of her home and instructed the companies' solicitor to prepare the mortgage. He first met her when she came to the companies' office with Lowe, Kitely, and Lowe's friend, Ivy Patton, just before signing the mortgage. She was alone with persons expecting to benefit by her folly. He took them to the respondents' solicitor to sign the papers, where he must have heard the appellant say to Lowe, when she learned the amount of the mortgage, "Frank, that is more than I agreed to lend you". He must have heard the appellant ask the solicitor, "Should I sign this?", showing that she felt the need for advice, and the solicitor inform her that he could not advise her without knowing more of her arrangements with her friends. Crawford does not admit hearing these things, but he does not deny that he did so, and he must have heard them since the solicitor says Crawford was within 3 ft. of the appellant at the counter.

After the mortgage had been signed Crawford escorted the party back to his office, where he had a cheque for the proceeds of the mortgage made out to the appellant and had her endorse and hand it to Lowe or Kitely; then he secured it from them, and it was deposited to the account of the automobile company, out of which Lowe's debt of $915 to the finance company was paid. This money was thereby disbursed and distributed the day before the mortgage was registered, a course so unusual that it excites suspicion. Significant also is the fact that, either late that day or the next, Crawford drew a promissory note from Lowe to the appellant for the amount of the mortgage and had Lowe sign it. At the same time he drew a conditional sales agreement between Lowe and Kitely and the automobile company for the two cars they had bought, and caused the automobile company to assign its vendor's interest to the appellant, notwithstanding Lowe and Kitely had earlier paid the purchase price in full from the proceeds of the loan. The companies were turning over to this inexperienced, unprotected old woman, as the sole security for a loan she was making to advance the interests of Lowe and Kitely and themselves, a security of questionable value. I cannot believe that the law is so deficient that it cannot reach and remedy such a gross abuse of overwhelming inequality between the parties.

Probably the whole transaction ought to be set aside, but that cannot be done as Lowe and Kitely are not before us, and the automobiles sold to them are likely worthless and irrecoverable. That has troubled me. On reflection, I have concluded that it will be sufficient to set aside the mortgage, without requiring the appellant to repay the money, since, as was intended, that part which was not immediately repaid to or retained by the finance company was immediately returned on other accounts to the companies, who were acting in concert. That will allow the sale of the automobiles and the payment of Lowe's debt to stand. The automobile company loses nothing and justice will be done to the finance company by requiring the appellant as a condition of relief to transfer to it Lowe's promissory note and the conditional sales agreement that the companies secured for her.

I should add that the companies called only their solicitor and his student-at-law, and did not call Crawford or any other officer, and made no attempt to prove that the whole transaction was fair, just and reasonable.

In view of the tenor of this judgment and the criticism of the companies, I should add that the criticism does not extend to their solicitor or his student. The evidence does not indicate that the solicitor knew that the money the appellant was borrowing was in the main to be at once returned to the companies on transactions between them and Lowe and Kitely. So far as he knew this was a simple routine loan by the finance company. The facts known by the two companies and their participation in the proceeds of the mortgage made it their duty to see that the appellant received independent advice, but the knowledge possessed by the solicitor was not sufficient to impose that duty upon him, and he is not to be criticized for not doing so. But I think it would have been better if he had told her to consult another solicitor instead of telling her he could not advise her.

In conclusion the way in which the form for maker on the mortgage was completed must be deprecated. The solicitor certified that the appellant mortgagor was personally known to him, which was not the case. He established her identity to his satisfaction by putting certain questions to her. He should have required some one personally known to him to identify her under oath and have so certified on the appropriate form. The loose practice followed in this case facilitates impersonation and forgery of documents of title of which we have had a recent example.

Contrary to the rules the exhibits are printed in numerical order instead of chronological. The respective solicitors ought not to have accepted or approved the book in that form, nor should the Registrar have settled it. In similar cases we have deprived the successful party of a substantial part of his costs, but because of the incidence of such an order, I think we ought not to do so here.

I would allow the appeal accordingly.

[Sheppard and Bull JJ.A. agreed in the result.]

B. Standard Form Contracts

(1) The "Ticket" Cases

We have already seen several illustrations of problems which can arise when one party asserts that certain written terms are "the terms of the bargain" and the other party asserts that they are not (Battle of the Forms, *supra*). Those cases involved businessmen who were expected to recognize, at least, that the writing on one of their forms would constitute "the contract"; (indeed, each tried hard to assure that his own form would govern).

The problem becomes more acute when one party asserts that the terms of the contract are the ones it has "imposed" on the other party by posting them or by printing them on a ticket or invoice. Courts are, of course, concerned that the "other party" have a chance to see these terms so that he at least knows the terms on which the first party proposes to do business.

However concerns of fairness and of the possible abuse of the strength which the party who imposes the terms possesses weigh heavily with the Courts. To the extent that the terms sought to be imposed do not reflect the expectations that a reasonable "other party" might have in that type of transaction (checking a coat, parking a car), the Courts can be expected to resile from enforcing them fully against the "victim". The Courts' approach in such cases shows a dogged determination to prevent injustice which might occur if internal legal logic were allowed to run unchecked.

PARKER v. THE SOUTH EASTERN RAILWAY CO.

(1877), 2 C.P.D., 416. C. A.; Mellish, Baggallay and Bramwell L.JJ.

ACTIONS against the South Eastern Railway Company for the value of bags and their contents lost to the plaintiffs respectively by the negligence of the company's servants.

The plaintiff in each case had deposited a bag in a cloak-room at the defendants' railway station, had paid the clerk 2*d.*, and had received a paper ticket, on one side of which were written a number and a date, and were printed notices as to when the office would be opened and closed, and the words "See back." On the other side were printed several clauses relating to articles left by passengers, the last of which was, "The company will not be responsible for any package exceeding the value of £10." In each case the plaintiff on the same day presented his ticket and demanded his bag, and in each case the bag could not be found, and had not been since found. Parker claimed £24 10*s.* as the value of his bag, and Gabell claimed £50 16*s.* The company in each case pleaded that they had accepted the goods on the condition that they would not be responsible for the value if it exceeded 10*l.*; and on the trial they relied on the words printed on the back of the ticket, and also on the fact that a notice to the same effect was printed and hung up in the cloak-room. Each plaintiff gave evidence and denied that he had seen the notice, or read what was printed on the ticket. Each plaintiff admitted that he had often received such tickets, and knew there was printed matter on them, but said that he did not know what it was. Parker said that he imagined the ticket to be a receipt for the money paid by him; and Gabell said he supposed it was evidence of the company having received the bag, and that he knew that the number on it corresponded with a number on his goods.

Parker's case was tried at Westminster on the 27th of February, 1876, before Pollock, B.; and Gabell's case was tried at Westminster on the 15th of November, 1876, before Grove, J. The questions left in each case by the judge to the jury were: 1. Did the plaintiff read or was he aware of the special condition upon which the articles were deposited? 2. Was the plaintiff, under the circumstances, under any obligation, in the exercise of reasonable and proper caution, to read or make himself aware of the condition?

The jury in each case answered both questions in the negative, and the judge thereupon directed judgment to be entered for the plaintiff for the amount claimed, reserving leave to the defendants to move to enter judgment for them.

In Parker's case the defendants moved to enter judgment, and also obtained from the Common Pleas Division an order nisi for a new trial, on the ground of misdirection. The order was discharged, and the motion was refused by the Common Pleas Division.

The defendants appealed.

In Gabell's case the defendants applied to the Common Pleas Division for an order nisi for a new trial on the ground of misdirection, but the Court refused to grant the order. The defendants then moved for judgment and also obtained from the Court of Appeal an order nisi for a new trial, on the ground of misdirection.

The cases were heard together.

. . .

F. Pollock (Prentice, Q.C. with him), for Parker. Suppose that the company had put on the ticket that if the goods were not redeemed within twenty-four hours they would be forfeited, or could not be redeemed except on payment of £5; would that have bound the plaintiff? It is no answer that that would be unreasonable, if the ticket is said to constitute a contract; nor is a depositor obliged to know what would be reasonable. To say that he is at his peril obliged to read this ticket, is to say that the general law of bailments is so absurd that a bailor must expect special conditions. No one can be expected to know that a receipt or a mere voucher given in order to secure the return of the article to the proper person contains special conditions. The questions were rightly put to the jury, and the verdict ought to stand.

Bremner, in reply. If the companies are for 2*d.* to incur indefinite liabilities they will shut up the cloak-rooms. It is admitted that the terms specified on the ticket are reasonable, and it is needless to speculate on what would be the consequence if the terms were unreasonable. The depositor had plenty of time to read what was printed, and if he did not he must take the consequences.

April 25. The following judgments were delivered.

Mellish, L.J. In this case we have to consider whether a person who deposits in the cloak-room of a railway company, articles which are lost through the carelessness of the company's servants, is prevented from recovering, by a condition on the back of the ticket, that the company would not be liable for the loss of goods exceeding the value of 10*l.* It was argued on behalf of the railway company that the company's servants were only authorized to receive goods on behalf of the company upon the terms contained in the ticket; and a passage from Mr. Justice Blackburn's judgment in *Harris v. Great Western Ry. Co.* (1876), 1 Q. B. D. 515, 533, was relied on in support of their contention: "I doubt much — inasmuch as the railway company did not authorize their servants to receive goods for deposit on any other terms, and as they had done nothing to lead the plaintiff to believe that they had given such authority to their servants so as to preclude them from asserting, as against her, that the authority was so limited — whether the true rule of law is not that the plaintiff must assent to the contract intended by the defendants to be authorized, or treat the case as one in which there was no contract at all, and consequently no liability for safe custody." I am of opinion that this objection cannot prevail. It is clear that the company's servants did not exceed the authority given them by the company. They did the exact thing they were authorized to do. They were authorized to receive articles on deposit as bailees on behalf of the company, charging 2*d.* for each article, and delivering a ticket properly filled up to the person leaving the article. This is exactly what they did in the present cases, and whatever may be the legal effect of what was done, the company must, in my opinion, be bound by it. The directors may have thought, and no doubt did think, that the delivering the ticket to the person depositing the article would be sufficient to make him bound by the conditions contained in the ticket and if they were mistaken in that, the company must bear the consequence.

The question then is, whether the plaintiff was bound by the conditions contained in the ticket. In an ordinary case, where an action is brought on a written agreement which is signed by the defendant, the agreement is proved by proving his signature, and, in the absence of fraud, it is wholly immaterial that he has not read the agreement and does not know its contents. The parties may, however, reduce their agreement into writing, so that the writing constitutes the sole evidence of the agreement, without signing it; but in that case there must be evidence independently of the agreement itself to prove that the defendant has assented to it. In that case, also, if it is proved that the defendant has assented to the writing constituting the agreement between the parties, it is, in the absence of fraud, immaterial that the defendant had not read the agreement and did not know its contents. Now if in the course of making a contract one party delivers to another a paper containing writing, and the party receiving the paper knows that the paper contains conditions which the party delivering it intends to constitute the contract, I have no doubt that the party receiving the paper does, by receiving and keeping it, assent to the conditions contained in it, although he does not read them, and does not know what they are....

Now, I am of opinion that we cannot lay down, as a matter of law, either that the plaintiff was bound or that he was not bound by the conditions printed on the ticket, from the mere fact that he knew there was writing on the ticket, but did not know that the writing contained conditions. I think there may be cases in which a paper containing writing is delivered by one party to another in the course of a business transaction, where it would be quite reasonable that the party receiving it should assume that the writing contained in it no condition, and should put it in his pocket unread. For instance, if a person driving through a turnpike-gate received a ticket upon paying a toll, he might reasonably assume that the object of the ticket was that by producing it he might be free from paying toll at some other turnpike-gate, and might put it in his pocket unread. On the other hand, if a person who ships goods to be carried on a voyage by sea receives a bill of lading signed by the master, he would plainly be bound by it, although afterwards in an action against the shipowner for the loss of goods, he might swear that he had never read the bill of lading, and that he did not know that it contained the terms of the contract of carriage, and that the shipowner was protected by the exceptions contained in it. Now the reason why the person receiving the bill of lading would be bound seems to me to be that in the great majority of cases persons shipping goods do know that the bill of lading contains the terms of the contract of carriage; and the shipowner, or the master delivering the bill of lading, is entitled to assume that the person shipping goods has that knowledge. It is, however, quite possible to suppose that a person who is neither a man of business nor a lawyer might on some particular occasion ship goods without the least knowledge of what a bill of lading was, but in my opinion such a person must bear the consequences of his own exceptional ignorance, it being plainly impossible that business could be carried on if every person who delivers a bill of lading had to stop to explain what a bill of lading was.

Now the question we have to consider is whether the railway company were entitled to assume that a person depositing luggage, and receiving a ticket in such a way that he could see that some writing was printed on it, would understand that the writing contained the conditions of contract, and this seems to me to depend upon whether people in general would in fact, and naturally, draw that inference. The railway company, as it seems to me, must be entitled to make some assumptions respecting the person who deposits luggage with them: I think they are entitled to assume that he can read, and that he understands the English language, and that he pays such attention to what he is about as may be reasonably expected from a person in such a transaction as that of depositing luggage in a cloak-room. The railway company must, however, take mankind as they find them, and if what they do is sufficient to inform people in general that the ticket contains conditions, I think that a particular plaintiff ought not to be in a better position than other persons on account of his exceptional ignorance or stupidity or carelessness. But if what the railway company do is not sufficient to convey to the minds of people in general that the ticket contains conditions, then they have received goods on deposit without obtaining the consent of the persons depositing them to the conditions limiting their liability. I am of opinion, therefore, that the proper direction to leave to the jury in these cases is, that if the person receiving the ticket did not see or know that there was any writing on the ticket, he is not bound by the conditions; that if he knew there was writing, and knew or believed that the writing contained conditions, then he is bound by the conditions, that if he knew there was writing on the ticket, but did not know or believe that the writing contained conditions, nevertheless he would be bound, if the delivering of the ticket to him in such a manner that he could see there was writing upon it, was, in the opinion of the jury, reasonable notice that the writing contained conditions.

I have lastly to consider whether the direction of the learned judge was correct, namely, "Was the plaintiff, under the circumstances, under any obligation, in the exercise of reasonable and proper caution, to read or to make himself aware of the condition?" I think that this direction was not strictly accurate, and was calculated to mislead the jury. The plaintiff was certainly under no obligation to read the ticket, but was entitled to leave it unread if he pleased, and the question does not appear to me to direct the attention of the jury to the real question, namely, whether the railway company did what was reasonably sufficient to give the plaintiff notice of the condition.

On the whole, I am of opinion that there ought to be a new trial.

. . .

Bramwell, L.J. It is clear that if the plaintiffs in these actions had read the conditions on the tickets and not objected, they would have been bound by them. No point was or could be made that the contract was complete before the ticket was given. If then reading the conditions they would have been bound, it follows that had they been told they were the conditions of the contract and invited to read them, and they had refused, saying they were content to take them whatever they might be, then also they would be bound by them. So also would they be if they were so told, and made no answer, and did nothing; for in that case they would have tacitly said the same thing, viz., that they were content to take them, whatever they might be. It follows, further, that if they knew that what was on the tickets was the contract which the defendants were willing to enter into, they, the plaintiffs, would be bound, though not told they were the conditions; for it cannot make a difference that they were not told what by the hypothesis they knew already. We have it, then, that if the plaintiffs knew that what was printed was the contract which the defendants were willing to enter into, the plaintiffs, not objecting, are bound by its terms, though they did not inform themselves what they were. The plaintiffs have sworn that they did not know that the printing was the contract, and we must act as though that was true and we believed it, at least as far as entering the verdict for the defendants is concerned. Does this make any difference? The plaintiffs knew of the printed matter. Both admit they knew it concerned them in some way, though they said they did not know what it was; yet neither pretends that he knew or believed it was not the contract. Neither pretends he thought it had nothing to do with the business in hand; that he thought it was an advertisement or other matter unconnected with his deposit of a parcel at the defendants' cloak-room. They admit that, for anything they knew or believed, it might be, only they did not know or believe it was, the contract. Their evidence is very much that they did not think, or, thinking, did not care about it. Now they claim to charge the company, and to have the benefit of their own indifference. Is this just? Is it reasonable? Is it the way in which any other business is allowed to be conducted? Is it even allowed to a man to "think," "judge," "guess," "chance" a matter, without informing himself when he can, and then when his "thought," "judgment," "guess," or "chance" turns out wrong or unsuccessful, claim to impose a burthen or duty on another which he could not have done had he informed himself as he might? Suppose the clerk or porter at the cloak-room had said to the plaintiffs, "Read that, it concerns you," and they had not read it, would they be at liberty to set up that though told to read they did not, because they thought something or other? But what is the difference between that case and the present? Why is there printing on the paper, except that it may be read? The putting of it into their hands was equivalent to saying, "Read that." Could the defendants practically do more than they did? Had they not a right to suppose either that the plaintiffs knew the conditions, or that they were content to take on trust whatever is printed? Let us for the moment forget that the defendants are a caput lupinum — a railway company. Take any other case — any case of money being paid and a paper given by the receiver, or goods bought on credit and a paper given with them ... Has not the giver of the paper a right to suppose that the receiver is content to deal on the terms in the paper? What more can be done? Must he say, "Read that?" As I have said, he does so in effect when he puts it into the other's hands. The truth is, people are content to take these things on trust. They know that there is a form which is always used — they are satisfied it is not unreasonable, because people do not usually put unreasonable terms into their contracts. If they did, then dealing would soon be stopped. Besides, unreasonable practices would be known. The very fact of not looking at the paper shews that this confidence exists. It is asked: What if there was some unreasonable condition, as for instance to forfeit £1000 if the goods were not removed in forty-eight hours? Would the depositor be bound? I might content myself by asking: Would he be, if he were told "our conditions are on this ticket," and he did not read them. In my judgment, he would not be bound in either case. I think there is an implied understanding that there is no condition unreasonable to the knowledge of the party tendering the document and not insisting on its being read — no condition not relevant to the matter in hand. I am of opinion, therefore, that the plaintiffs, having notice of the printing, were in the same situation as though the porter had said, "Read that, it concerns the matter in hand;" that if the plaintiffs did not read it, they were as much bound as if they had read it and had not objected.

The difficulty I feel as to what I have written is that it is too demonstrative. But, put in practical language, it is this: The defendants put into the hands of the plaintiff a paper with printed matter on it, which in all good sense and reason must be supposed to relate to the matter in hand. This printed matter the plaintiff sees, and must either read it, and object if he does not agree to it, or if he does read it and not object, or does not read it, he must be held to consent to its terms; therefore, on the facts, the judges should have directed verdicts for the defendants.

The second question left, in my opinion, should not have been left, and was calculated to mislead the jury. It might equally have been put if the plaintiffs had been told that the conditions of the contract were on the ticket, and had been asked to read them. It would then manifestly have been a question of law, and so it is now. Besides, by its terms it was calculated to mislead the jury. The question was, whether the plaintiff was under any obligation, in the exercise of reasonable and proper caution, to read the ticket. Obligation to whom? Not to himself, as people sometimes say, for there is no such duty, or if any, he may excuse himself from performing it. If it means whether a reasonably and properly cautious person might omit to read it, I say Yes. At least I hope so. Such a person might well take the matter on trust, but then he ought to be content to take the consequences of so doing. But he has no right, having omitted to inform himself, and having had the means of doing so, to make a claim which he might have fairly made had he had no such means of informing himself. The question possibly means "obligation to the defendants." That is, had the plaintiff a right to omit to do so, and then make his claim? I repeat that the same question might be put if he were told that the print contained the conditions of the contract, and then it would obviously be a question of law as it is now. The question is imperfect. The question whether of law or fact is, "Can a man properly omit to inform himself, being able to do so, and then justly claim, when he could not have claimed if he had informed himself?" The latter part of the question is left out.

...I am of opinion, therefore, that the judgment should be reversed, and be given for the defendants. If not, though I think the question one of law, still, if it is of fact, it has not been left to the jury, and there should be a new trial. The possible question of fact is that set forth in the judgment of the Lord Justice Mellish, with a perusal of which he has favoured me. But I repeat I think it is a question of law. I also think the verdict against evidence, and that on that ground there should be a new trial. No one can read the evidence of the plaintiffs in this case without seeing the mischief of encouraging claims so unconscientious as the present.

Orders absolute for new trials.

QUESTIONS

1. What are the conflicting principles that the court sees here?

2. Do you think that they are satisfactorily resolved by Mellish L.J. or Bramwell L.J.?

3. What do you think that Bramwell L.J. means when he says, " It is clear that if the plaintiffs in these actions had read the conditions and not objected, they would have been bound by them."? What would the plaintiffs have been told if they had objected?

4. Outline specifically the points that under each of the judgments should be covered in a proper charge to the jury. (Even if we do not use juries in such cases now, the trial judge would have to ask himself the same questions.) Assume that each side has raised all relevant arguments.

NOTE

In *J. Spurling Ltd. v. Bradshaw*, [1956] 2 All E.R. 121 (Court of Appeal, England) Denning L.J. dealt with an exemption clause in a contract between the plaintiff, a warehouseman, and the defendant, the owner of 8 casks of orange juice. The plaintiff had sued for his charges, and the defendant had counterclaimed for negligence in the storage of the casks since nearly all the juice had been lost before the casks had been picked up. In upholding a decision of the trial judge who had held that the exemption clause would protect the plaintiff, he said:

"This brings me to the question whether this clause was part of the contract. Counsel for the defendant urged us to hold that the plaintiffs did not do what was reasonably sufficient to give notice of the conditions within *Parker v. South Eastern Ry. Co.* I agree that the more unreasonable a clause is, the greater the notice which must be given of it. Some clauses which I have seen would need to be printed in red ink on the face of the document with a red hand pointing to it before the notice could be held to be sufficient. The clause in this case, however, in my judgment, does not call for such exceptional treatment, especially when it is construed, as it should be, subject to the proviso that it only applies when the warehouseman is carrying out his contract and not when he is deviating from it or breaking it in a radical respect. So construed, the judge was, I think, entitled to find that sufficient notice was given. It is to be noticed that the landing account on its face told the defendant that the goods would be insured if he gave instructions; otherwise they were not insured. The invoice, on its face, told him they were warehoused "at owner's risk". The printed conditions, when read subject to the proviso which I have mentioned, added little or nothing to those explicit statements taken together. Next it was said that the landing account and invoice were issued after the goods had been received and could not therefore be part of the contract of bailment: but the defendant admitted that he had received many landing accounts before. True he had not troubled to read them. On receiving this account, he took no objection to it, left the goods there, and went on paying the warehouse rent for months afterwards. It seems to me that by the course of business and conduct of the parties, these conditions were part of the contract. "In these circumstances, the plaintiffs were entitled to rely on this exempting condition. I think, therefore, that the counterclaim was properly dismissed, and this appeal also should be dismissed."

HEFFRON v. IMPERIAL PARKING CO. ET AL.

(1974), 3 O.R. (2d) 722; Evans, Brooke and Estey JJ.A.

The judgment of the Court was delivered by

Estey, J.A.: — This is an appeal from a judgment pronounced by His Honour Judge Shortt in the County Court of the Judicial District of York on March 29, 1973, wherein the plaintiff was awarded $1,251.92 as damages for the loss of an automobile left by the respondent with the appellants, the operators of a parking lot, together with costs.

The respondent on October 10, 1970, parked his motor vehicle in the parking lot of the appellants in downtown Toronto paying the evening flat rate charge and receiving in return a ticket whereon there was printed:

No. 49801

PARKING CONDITIONS

we are not responsible for theft or damage of car or contents, however caused

IMPERIAL PARKING CO.

237 Victoria Street — 364-4611

Corner Bond & Dundas Sts.

Open 8.00 a.m. — 12.00 p.m.

At the request of the appellants' attendant the respondent left the keys in the automobile. The lot was marked with three signs on which the same message was set out as appeared on the ticket. The learned trial Judge came to the conclusion "that the defendants took reasonable steps under the circumstances to draw the conditions of parking to the plaintiff's attention even though, as he admitted, he had not read the parking ticket but merely slipped it into his pocket". In addition to these signs there was a sign announcing the hours in which the parking lot was open and which were the same as set out on the ticket described above. I can find no reason to disturb the learned trial Judge's conclusion that the appellant had taken all reasonable measures to communicate to the respondent the parking conditions including the hours of operation.

The respondent returned to the parking lot about one hour after it had closed and was unable to locate his car. Three days later it was discovered abandoned in a damaged condition. The evidence is that when the car was left with the appellants by the respondent it contained some personal property of the respondent including clothing, a tape player and an electric razor; there is no evidence to indicate that the tape player was affixed to or formed part of the car. These items of personal property were not in the car when it was recovered.

There was evidence indicating that the appellants operated a parking garage across the street from the parking lot in question and that it was a normal practice for the attendant when leaving the lot at midnight to take the keys of any cars remaining on the lot to the office of the parking garage across the street which was operated by the appellant. The keys to the respondent's car were not found in either the kiosk on the parking lot or in the office of the parking garage.

The appellants called no evidence to describe or explain any of the events which occurred. The attendant on duty at the parking lot was not called to give evidence and the only evidence presented by the defence was that of the manager of the appellants who testified to some of the normal practices followed in the operation of the appellants' parking lots. This witness was asked on this point:

Q. What was the procedure with regard to keys left for cars with respect to cars that hadn't been picked up at the time the attendant left the lot? A. The procedure now?

Q. No. Then. A. The keys were taken out of the car and taken — we have a parking garage across the street directly next to the Imperial Theatre and the cars are — we ask the people to pick up their keys at the parking garage. We have a man posted there until 2:00 a.m.

Q. Were any keys ever left in the cars or in the kiosk at that time?

A. Sometimes the — if the attendant would go out for coffee or something.

Q. No. I mean when he closed the lot. A. I honestly can't say.

.   .   .

BY THE COURT: Q. Just a moment. I am not clear. How would the customer know if he came back at one o'clock? A. There is a note left on the car, sir.

Q. That he should go across to the parking lot? A. "Please pick up your keys at the parking garage…"

Q. You mentioned that you have a lot in the immediate vicinity that is open until two o'clock? A. Yes. We have a man posted until 2:00 a.m.

Q. So you retain custody of the car and the keys by taking the keys over to the other lot, is that right? A. If the keys are left in the cars. If there are any cars on the parking lot left with keys, we try to do that.

The learned trial Judge in granting judgment in favour of the respondent stated:

> The mere disappearance of the car does not of necessity import theft nor am I convinced that the admitted damage was done before the car left the parking lot. It would be going too far in view of "the magic words" to say that the defendant must negative negligence. It is, however, in my opinion, clearly necessary for the bailee to lead evidence to negative a fundamental breach or deviation from the contract of bailment which would render inoperative the exculpatory words: see *Williams & Wilson Ltd. v. OK Parking Ltd.*, [1971] 2 O.R. 151, 17 D.L.R. (3d) 243.

The appellant relies upon the decision of this Court in *Samuel Smith & Sons Ltd. v. Silverman*, [1961] O.R. 648, 29 D.L.R. (2d) 98, in support of its submission that the exculpatory condition in the ticket together with the same message in the signs posted on the parking lot are sufficiently broad in their terms to exonerate the appellant even when the damage occurred through negligence of the appellant, its servants or a third party. The appellant also submits that it is under no onus or obligation to advance any explanation for the non-delivery of the respondent's automobile and since the respondent was unable to show that its loss was occasioned by a fundamental breach of the contract by the appellant, the respondent's action should be dismissed. The appellant alternatively submits that the respondent in parking his automobile on the appellant's premises is a mere licensee and consequently, no bailment arose and therefore no duty in the appellants to explain the loss.

In the *Samuel Smith* case the parties conceded and the Court proceeded on the basis that at least where the parking lot operator has asked the motorist to leave the keys in the car so that it may be moved around the parking lot for the convenience of the operator "that this is a true case of bailment". In that case and the one before this Court the principal argument made was that the terms of the contract excluded liability in the parking lot operator. Neither in the *Samuel Smith* case nor in this case was evidence led by the parking lot operator to explain the disappearance of the automobile. Much of the discussion in the *Samuel Smith* case dealt with the communication of the ticket conditions to the car owner and the only direct reference in the judgment to the effect of the limiting conditions on the ticket is found in the concluding portion of the judgment at p. 652 O.R., p. 102 D.L.R.:

The words printed on the ticket and the signs in question are not susceptible of this criticism. The clear declaration that the defendant was not to be responsible for theft or damage of car or contents *however caused*, is sufficiently broad in its terms to extend to a case where the damage occurred through the negligence either of the defendant or his servants, or the negligence or carelessness of a third party whether lawfully on the premises or not.

The Court thereupon concluded that the exclusionary clause applied to the claim of the plaintiff. The applicability of the doctrine of fundamental breach was apparently not advanced and in any case was not dealt with by the Court.

In another line of cases a relationship different from bailment was found to arise between the parties to such a transaction as parking a car in a parking lot. In *Ashby v. Tolhurst*, [1973] 2 All E.R. 837, Lord Greene, M.R., found that a somewhat similar transaction resulted in the establishment of a licence relationship and not a bailment relationship. This Court followed and applied the *Ashby* judgment in *Palmer v. Toronto Medical Arts Building Ltd.*, [1960] O.R. 60, 21 D.L.R. (2d) 181. The trial Judge had found that the plaintiff was a mere licensee and that there was no bailment of his automobile. In any case he found that any bailment which may have arisen was gratuitous bailment and without gross negligence no liability arose in the parking lot owner. As in *Ashby v. Tolhurst*, the Court found in the circumstances of the case the car had not been delivered to the defendants for safe custody but only for "parking" and nothing more. A circumstance of significance mentioned by Schroeder, J.A., speaking for the Court in the *Palmer* case at p. 69 O.R., pp. 187-8 D.L.R., was the lack of a ticket system:

> The fact that there was no system of giving a card or parking ticket to the persons using this parking lot has vital significance and should have suggested to the plaintiff the absence of any arrangement for supervision or control over the cars left on the lot, since no person was required to surrender a ticket or produce any other form of identification when removing his car.

In that case the surrender of keys to an attendant was an unusual occurrence brought about by a heavy snowfall that morning which made the usual practice of car parking by its owner impossible. The attendant made it clear to the plaintiff that he could, if he wished, retain control over his car or he could remove it to some other parking lot or accept the attendant's offer extended as a voluntary courtesy to park the car for him when space became available. Sir Wilfrid Greene, M.R., in the *Ashby* case, *supra*, at p. 840, mentions a further circumstance which indicates the relationship which arises in law between the parties to such a transaction:

> The first thing to do is to examine the nature of the relationship between the parties, a matter upon which the character of the ground is, I think, not without importance, but the most important element is the document itself. It describes the place in which the car is to be left as a "car park," and the document is described as a "car park ticket." I myself regard those words as being in one sense, in a real sense, I think, the most important part of the document, because they indicate the nature of the rights which the proprietor of the car is going to get. "Car park ticket,": you take a ticket in order to park you [sic] car, and parking your car means, I should have thought, leaving your car in a place. If you park your car in the street, you are liable to get into trouble with the police. On the other hand, you are entitled to park your car in places indicated by the police or the appropriate authorities for the purpose. Parking a car is leaving a car and, I should have thought, nothing else. The right, therefore, which this document starts off by giving on its face is a right to park the car.

In that case the plaintiff locked his car and did not leave the keys with the attendant.

The respective characteristics of the bailment and the licence relationships are guides to the application of the appropriate relationship to the case at hand. Bailment has been defined as "a delivery of personal chattels in trust, on a contract, express or implied, that the trust shall be duly executed, and the chattels redelivered in either their original or an altered form, as soon as the time or use for, or condition on which they were bailed, shall have elapsed or been performed": *Bacon's Abridgement*, adopted in *Re S. Davis & Co., Ltd.*, [1945] Ch. 402 at p. 405. A licence on the other hand is simply the grant of such authority to another to enter upon land for an agreed purpose as to justify that which otherwise would be a trespass and its only legal effect is that the licensor until the licence is revoked is precluded from bringing an action for trespass. Romer, L.J., speaking at p. 844 in the *Ashby* case, *supra*, distinguished a bailment from all other relationships when he stated: "... in order that there shall be a bailment there must be a delivery by the bailor, that is to say, he must part with his possession of the chattel in question".

While no single fact may be of controlling importance in the isolation and categorization of the relationship between the parties to this appeal, the combination of the following factors favour the relationship of bailor-bailee, rather than licensor-licensee:

(a) The owner of the car delivered the keys and therefore the control over the movement of his automobile to the attendant at the attendant's request;

(b) the parking ticket had a serial number which would indicate that the surrender of the specific ticket would be necessary in order to obtain delivery from the attendant of the automobile;

(c) the provision of the attendant raises a reasonable inference that he is supplied by the owner of the business for more than the mere function of receiving money upon the parking of the car;

(d) the parking lot closed, according to the conditions announced on the ticket and signs, at midnight and no conditions were imposed concerning the removal of cars prior thereto;

(e) the notice of a closing hour reasonably infers an active operation of the parking lot rather than a passive allotment of parking stations from which the car owner could at any time, day or night, unilaterally withdraw his parked vehicle, and

(f) the practice of the parking lot owner (although unknown to the owner of the car) was to place the keys left in automobiles at the end of the day in the office of the appellants' car parking garage across the road.

In my view, the special circumstances of this case, which I have summarized above, indicate that there was no mutual intention of a mere parking of the car by the respondent owner on the appellants' lot without any action required by the appellants beyond the collection of the fee. The appellants did not hold out a single identified unit of parking space for the exclusive use of the respondent nor did the appellants represent to the respondent that there would be identified a small rectangular island of land somewhere in the appellants' parking lot on which either the respondent or the appellants would place the respondent's vehicle as an alternative to leaving it at the side of the street. The ticket system, the hours of operation, the operating habits of the appellants, including the disposition of car keys at the close of business, and the stipulation that the keys be left in the car so as to enable the appellants to place and move the car at their convenience anywhere within the appellants' parking facility, all indicate a relationship quite different from that of a licence passively granted by the appellant as licensor to the respondent. In the *Ashby* case, *supra*, the car was placed by its owner in a designated spot and locked and the keys were left by the owner with the parking lot supervisor. Here the respondent surrendered and the appellant accepted (indeed required) control of this valuable and highly mobile item of property. I therefore conclude that there was a delivery of possession by the respondent to the appellants of the automobile under a contract of bailment.

The exculpatory clause I have set out above and observe that it is in words identical with those appearing on the ticket which came before this Court in *Mitchell v. Silverman*, [1952] O.W.N. 130, where Robertson, C.J.O., in an oral judgment found that the contract between the parties excluded any liability in the parking lot operator and placed no burden on that operator to account for the missing automobile. The appellant has submitted that should it be found that it was a bailee the exculpatory terms of the contract relieve it from any liability including negligence of the appellant's servants. The respondent in turn has argued that by reason of the fundamental breach of the contract of bailment by the appellant the contract has been terminated including the exculpatory term and the appellant is therefore liable to the respondent for damages thereby occasioned.

Linked inextricably with the answer to the question of applicability of the exempting clause in any such transaction, is the determination of what onus, if any, lies upon the bailee once the bailor proves non-delivery. Lord Denning in *J. Spurling Ltd. v. Bradshaw*, [1956] 1 W.L.R. 461 at p. 466, stated:

> A bailor, by pleading and presenting his case properly, can always put on the bailee the burden of proof. In the case of non-delivery, for instance, all he need plead is the contract and a failure to deliver on demand. That puts on the bailee the burden of proving either loss without his fault (which, of course, would be a complete answer at common law) or, if it was due to his fault, it was a fault from which he is excused by the exempting clause...

Vide also *Woolmer v. Delmer Price Ltd.*, [1955] 1 Q.B. 291 at p. 294. The onus in the case of a licence relationship is of course quite different and the licensor is not ordinarily called upon to discharge any burden or onus other than to demonstrate that he has honoured the existence of the licence.

We are left, therefore, with the unexplained disappearance of the respondent's automobile and the last question remaining to be answered is whether the exculpatory clause exonerates the appellants notwithstanding the appellants' complete failure to explain the cause of disappearance, or whether the clause ceased to operate upon the happening of the unexplained loss of the automobile by reason of a breach of a fundamental term of the contract. At one time it was clear that loss by the bailee of the subject of the bailment without any demonstration of the cause was a fundamental breach going to the root of the contract: *Karsales (Harrow), Ltd. v. Wallis*, [1956] 2 All E.R. 866 at p. 868.

The doctrine of fundamental breach came under review in the House of

Lords judgments in *Suisse Atlantique Société d'Armement Maritime S.A. v. N.V. Rotterdamsche Kolen Centrale*, [1967] 1 A.C. 361. Lord Reid, Viscount Dilhorne and Lord Upjohn found no rule in the common law prohibiting the contracting out of liability for breach of a fundamental term of the contract. Lord Hodson concluded that as a matter of construction an exculpatory clause would be normally construed as not applicable to escape liability for a breach of a fundamental term going to the root of a contract.

Lord Wilberforce found the law to be that when the contractual intention of the parties is ascertained and did not embrace the events amounting to a breach of a fundamental term, the events must be outside the exculpatory clause which would therefore not apply. His Lordship added that in those circumstances for a Court to apply the exculpatory clause to exonerate the guilty party would be to convert the basic covenants of the contract into a "mere declaration of intention". Shortly thereafter Lord Denning M.R., speaking in *Mendelssohn v. Normand, Ltd.*, [1969] 2 All E.R. 1215 at p. 1218, said of the *Suisse Atlantique* judgments: "It was there said to be all a matter of construction", and that the earlier contract doctrine restricting the operation of the exculpatory clauses to the performance of the contract in the stipulated manner and not extending to the violation of the terms thereof in a fundamental sense, is "in no way diminished in authority by Suisse Atlantique...".

This Court applied the substance of the doctrine of fundamental breach in a not dissimilar manner in *R. G. McLean Ltd. v. Canadian Vickers Ltd. et al.*, [1971] 1 O.R. 207, 15 D.L.R. (3d) 15, where a contract clause purporting to limit a vendor's liability to the replacement of parts and to the repair of a printing machine and to exclude any liability for direct or indirect loss, was found to be inapplicable in the circumstances where the machine failed entirely to perform in the manner contemplated by the parties. Whether this result is obtained by applying the doctrine of fundamental breach as a matter of contract construction or as an independent principle of law, it is clear that the phenomenon is alive and prospering in the law of this Province.

On the facts now before this Court the question is whether the parties to this car parking transaction contemplated that upon the delivery of the complete possession and control over the car, the operator of the parking lot would be free to maintain silence and escape any liability upon his failure to deliver the car to the respondent on surrender of the appropriate serial parking ticket? To answer the question in the affirmative one must find that the owner, on surrendering his car to the lot operator upon payment of the requested fee for this service, thereupon accepted the implied condition that the operator could, when closing or at the end of the day, leave the car and its keys unprotected and available to any thief or joyrider who might happen upon the lot. Such an assumption would make meaningless the purpose of parking a car off the highway on a lot supervised by an attendant and equipped with a kiosk from which the lot and the properties placed thereon could be supervised. Furthermore, the issue of a serially numbered ticket upon delivery of possession of the car would either be a meaningless ritual or, worse still, a practice intended to induce a false sense of security. Such an interpretation is denied by the strongest inference by the appellant itself whose president in evidence partially excerpted above detailed the steps followed at the end of the day for safeguarding the keys of automobiles still on the parking lot. It should be emphasized that the basic transaction here was on quite a different basis than the transaction in *Ashby v. Tolhurst*, [1937] 2 All E.R. 837, and *Palmer v. Toronto Medical Arts Building Ltd.*, [1960] O.R. 60, 21 D.L.R. (2d) 181. In neither of these cases was the owner of the car required as a term of the transaction to leave the keys in the car for the convenience and presumably the greater profit of the operator. In the former case the keys were not left in the car and in the latter case the keys were taken by the attendant as a gratuitous courtesy offered to the owner to park his car when the lot had been cleared of snow.

In a recent decision of this Court, *Bata v. City Parking Canada Ltd.* (1973), 2 O.R. (2d) 446, 43 D.L.R. (3d) 190, Schroeder, J.A., sitting alone on an appeal from the Small Claims Court, applied the *Ashby* and *Palmer* cases rather than the *Samuel Smith & Sons Ltd. v. Silverman*, [1961] O.R. 648, 29 D.L.R. (2d) 98, line of reasoning by reason of the peculiar wording of the ticket given by the operator to the owner of the automobile. The ticket emphasized the charges were for "parking space only" and similar wording appeared on signs on the premises. The actual wording in all instances was "charges are for use of parking space only". For that reason the Court found the relationship to be that of licence rather than bailment and, in my view, is clearly distinguishable from the facts now before us.

But there is a further circumstance in this case which requires examination to completely dispose of this transaction and the rights and obligations of the parties therein. As stated earlier, both the signs on the lot and the ticket referred to the closing of the lot at 12:00 p.m., which the parties agreed in this instance means midnight. When the appellants asked the respondent to leave the keys in the car there arose the clearest implied duty in the appellants to take reasonable steps at the close of business to retain custody of the keys in a manner appropriate to the need of the respondent to recover his car and the necessity of protecting the keys and the car from loss. The appellants are unable to explain what became of the keys. They were never located in either the kiosk on the lot or in the appellants' parking garage across the road. Thus, the keys were either stolen during the day or after the lot closed. In either case the appellants must fail, in the first instance as bailee of the keys and the car for the reasons I have outlined earlier, and in the second instance for breach of duty to exercise reasonable care to safeguard the keys after the closing of the lot. This latter understanding and the duty arising therefrom are entirely unrelated to the exculpatory term set out in the parking ticket. It could not be otherwise as the law would then be unable to imply a duty to exercise reasonable care in the second stage of the custodial arrangement. I adopt the words of Devlin, J., in *Firestone Tyre & Rubber Co. Ltd. v. Vokins & Co. Ltd.*, [1951] 1 Ll. Rep. 32 at p. 39: "It is illusory to say: "We promise to do a thing, but we are not liable if we do not do it'." Alternatively, if the exculpatory clause were to apply throughout the transaction breach of the primary, albeit an applied term, of the arrangement is as fundamental to the parties as failure to redeliver to the owner the subject of the bailment during the term of the bailment. In any case, the term of the bailment may expire but the consequential duty to make reasonable provision for the return of the keys to the owner continues. The appellants upon the unexplained failure to deliver are, therefore, faced with a fundamental breach of the contract of bailment during the term thereof or breach of duty with respect to the disposition of the keys to the automobile after the term of the bailment. The appellants have not, and presumably cannot, relate the non-delivery to either time period and I know of no principle of law requiring the respondent to do so as plaintiff in order to recover his damages.

There was some evidence that the ignition of the car was faulty prior to the disappearance of the car from the appellants' lot but in any event there is no evidence to dispel the ordinary explanation that the keys were used to improperly remove the automobile.

Finally, we turn to the question of the contents of the automobile which, when the car was subsequently recovered in a damaged condition, were not in the car. This personal property consisted of some tools, clothing, and a radio and tape player for which the respondent claimed in all $308.10, calculated on the basis of the value of the goods at the time of loss. These goods were generally of a type which one might reasonably be expected to carry in an automobile. The evidence does not indicate whether these articles were located in the trunk or the body of the car. However, once the keys fall into the hands of a person intent upon stealing the automobile it makes no difference whether the personal property mentioned above is located in the trunk or inside the car.

Laidlaw, J.A., in dealing with a similar claim in *Brown v. Toronto Auto Parks Ltd.*, [1955] O.W.N. 456, [1955] 2 D.L.R. 525, found neither actual nor constructive knowledge in the bailee of the presence of a quantity of books in the car and, hence, the contract of bailment did not extend to cover the books in the car. On the facts in the case before this Court the goods are not of such an unusual nature that would not reasonably be expected to be regularly found in an automobile and it, therefore, is not unreasonable for a parking lot operator to assume that a great many of the cars left in his custody will contain this kind of personal property in reasonable quantity. On this basis I conclude that the items mentioned above were constructively included in the bailment arrangement and were properly included in the claims made by the respondent.

For these reasons I would dismiss the appeal with costs but in so doing wish to add that the Court was greatly assisted in the disposition of this matter by the thorough and detailed analysis of the authorities presented by both counsel.

Appeal dismissed.

THORNTON v. SHOE LANE PARKING

[1971] 1 All E.R. 686. Court of Appeal (England); Lord Denning M.R., Megaw and Willmer L.JJ.

Lord Denning MR. In 1964 Mr Thornton, the plaintiff, who was a freelance trumpeter of the highest quality, had an engagement with the BBC at Farringdon Hall. He drove to the City in his motor car and went to park it at a multi-storey automatic car park. It had only been open a few months. He had never gone there before. There was a notice on the outside headed 'Shoe Lane Parking'. It gave the parking charges, 5s for two hours, 7s 6d for three hours, and so forth; and at the bottom: 'ALL CARS PARKED AT OWNERS RISK'. The plaintiff drove up to the entrance. There was not a man in attendance. There was a traffic light which showed red. As he drove in and got to the appropriate place, the traffic light turned green and a ticket was pushed out from the machine. The plaintiff took it. He drove on into the garage. The motor car was taken up by mechanical means to a floor above. The plaintiff left it there and went off to keep his appointment with the BBC. Three hours later he came back. He went to the office and paid the charge for the time that the car was there. His car was brought down from the upper floor. He went to put his belongings into the boot of the car; but unfortunately there was an accident. The plaintiff was severely injured. The judge has found it was half his own fault, but half the fault of Shoe Lane Parking Ltd, the defendants. The judge awarded him £3,637 6s 11d.

On this appeal the defendants do not contest the judge's findings about the accident. They acknowledge that they were at fault, but they claim that they are protected by some exempting conditions. They rely on the ticket which was issued to the plaintiff by the machine. They say that it was a contractual document and that it incorporated a condition which exempts them from liability to him. The ticket was headed 'Shoe Lane Parking'. Just below there was a 'box' in which was automatically recorded the time when the car went into the garage. There was a notice alongside: 'Please present this ticket to cashier to claim your car.' Just below the time, there was some small print in the left hand corner which said: 'This ticket is issued subject to the conditions of issue as displayed on the premises.' That is all.

The plaintiff says that he looked at the ticket to see the time on it, and put it in his pocket. He could see there was printing on the ticket, but he did not read it. He only read the time. He did not read the words which said that the ticket was issued subject to the conditions as displayed on the premises. If the plaintiff had read those words on the ticket and had looked round the premises to see where the conditions were displayed, he would have had to have driven his car on into the garage and walked round. Then he would have found, on a pillar opposite the ticket machine, a set of printed conditions in a panel. He would also have found, in the paying office (to be visited when coming back for the car) two more panels containing the printed conditions. If he had the time to read the conditions — it would take him a very considerable time — he would read this:

'CONDITIONS

'The following are the conditions upon which alone motor vehicles are accepted for parking: —
'1. The customer agrees to pay the charges of [the defendants]...
'2. The Customer is deemed to be fully insured at all times against all risks (including, without prejudice to the generality of the foregoing, fire, damage and theft, whether due to the negligence of others or not) and the [defendants] shall not be responsible or liable for any loss or misdelivery of or damage of whatever kind to the Customer's motor vehicle, or any articles carried therein or thereon or of or to any accessories carried thereon or therein *or injury to the Customer* or any other person *occurring when the Customer's motor vehicle is in the Parking Building howsoever that loss, misdelivery, damage or injury shall be caused*; and it is agreed and understood that the Customer's motor vehicle is parked and permitted by the [defendants] to be parked in the Parking Building in accordance with this Licence entirely at the Customer's risk...'

There is a lot more. I have only read about one-tenth of the conditions. The important thing to notice is that the defendants seek by this condition to exempt themselves from liability, not only for damage to the car, but also for injury to the customer howsoever caused. The condition talks about insurance. It is well known that the customer is usually insured against damage to the car; but he is not insured against damage to himself. If the condition is incorporated into the contract of parking, it means that the plaintiff will be unable to recover any damages for his personal injuries which were caused by the negligence of the company.

We have been referred to the ticket cases of former times from *Parker v South Eastern Ry Co* to *McCutcheon v David MacBrayne Ltd*, [1964] 1 All E.R. 430. They were concerned with railways, steamships and cloakrooms where booking clerks issued tickets to customers who took them away without reading them. In those cases the issue of the ticket was regarded as an *offer* by the company. If the customer took it and retained it without objection, his act was regarded as an *acceptance* of the offer: ... These cases were based on the theory that the customer, on being handed the ticket, could refuse it and decline to enter into a contract on those terms. He could ask for his money back. That theory was, of course, a fiction. No customer in a thousand ever read the conditions. If he had stopped to do so, he would have missed the train or the boat.

None of those cases has any application to a ticket which is issued by an automatic machine. The customer pays his money and gets a ticket. He cannot refuse it. He cannot get his money back. He may protest to the machine, even swear at it; but it will remain unmoved. He is committed beyond recall. He was committed at the very moment when he put his money into the machine. The contract was concluded at that time. It can be translated into offer and acceptance in this way. The offer is made when the proprietor of the machine holds it out as being ready to receive the money. The acceptance takes place when the customer puts his money into the slot. The terms of the offer are contained in the notice placed on or near the machine stating what is offered for the money. The customer is bound by those terms as long as they are sufficiently brought to his notice beforehand, but not otherwise. He is not bound by the terms printed on the ticket if they differ from the notice, because the ticket comes too late. The contract has already been made: see *Olley v Marlborough Court Ltd*, [1949] 1 K.B. 532. The ticket is no more than a voucher or receipt for the money that has been paid (as in the deckchair case, *Chapelton v Barry Urban District Council*, [1940] 1 K.B. 532), on terms which have been offered and accepted before the ticket is issued. In the present case the offer was contained in the notice at the entrance giving the charges for garaging and saying 'at owners risk', i e at the risk of the owner so far as damage to the car was concerned. The offer was accepted when the plaintiff drove up to the entrance and, by the movement of his car, turned the light from red to green, and the ticket was thrust at him. The contract was then concluded, and it could not be altered by any words printed on the ticket itself. In particular, it could not be altered so as to exempt the company from liability for personal injury due to their negligence.

Assuming, however, that an automatic machine is a booking clerk in disguise, so that the old fashioned ticket cases still apply to it, we then have to go back to the three questions put by Mellish LJ in *Parker v South Eastern Ry Co*, subject to this qualification: Mellish LJ used the word 'conditions' in the plural, whereas it would be more apt to use the word 'condition' in the singular, as indeed Mellish LJ himself did at the end of his judgment. After all, the only condition that matters for this purpose is the exempting condition. It is no use telling the customer that the ticket is issued subject to some 'conditions' or other, without more; for he may reasonably regard 'conditions' in general as merely regulatory, and not as taking away his rights, unless the exempting condition is drawn specifically to his attention. (Alternatively, if the plural 'conditions' is used, it would be better prefaced with the word 'exempting', because the exempting conditions are the only conditions that matter for this purpose.) Telescoping the three questions, they come to this: the customer is bound by the exempting condition if he knows that the ticket is issued subject to it; or, if the company did what was reasonably sufficient to give him notice of it. Counsel for the defendants admitted here that the defendants did not do what was reasonably sufficient to give the plaintiff notice of the exempting condition. That admission was properly made. I do not pause to enquire whether the exempting condition is void for unreasonableness. All I say is that it is so wide and so destructive of rights that the court should not hold any man bound by it unless it is drawn to his attention in the most explicit way. It is an instance of what I had in mind in *J Spurling Ltd v Bradshaw*. In order to give sufficient notice, it would need to be printed in red ink with a red hand pointing to it, or something equally startling.

However, although reasonable notice of it was not given, counsel for the defendants said that this case came within the second question propounded by Mellish LJ, namely that the plaintiff 'knew or believed that the writing contained conditions'. There was no finding to that effect. The burden was on the defendants to prove it, and they did not do so. Certainly there was no evidence that the plaintiff knew of this exempting condition. He is not, therefore, bound by it. Counsel for the defendants relied on a case in this court last year, *Mendelssohn v Normand Ltd*, [1970] 1 Q.B. 177. Mr Mendelssohn parked his car in the Cumberland Garage at Marble Arch and was given a ticket which contained an exempting condition. There was no discussion as to whether the condition formed part of the contract. It was conceded that it did. That is shown by the report. Yet the garage company were not entitled to rely on the exempting condition for the reasons there given. That case does not touch the present, where the whole question is whether the exempting condition formed part of the contract. I do not think it did. The plaintiff did not know of the condition, and the defendants did not do what was reasonably sufficient to give him notice of it.

I do not think the defendants can escape liability by reason of the exempting condition. I would, therefore, dismiss the appeal.

[Megaw and Willmer L.JJ. agreed.]

QUESTIONS AND PROBLEMS

1. The University of Toronto uses the following clause on the back of its parking ticket.

"Neither the University of Toronto nor any of its employees is responsible for thefts of, or damage to, vehicles or contents, however caused, while parked on University property."

Do you think that this clause is effective to exempt the University for liability? Could you draft a better clause?

2. Is it (a) possible, and (b) practicable to draft a clause that would exempt, by way of notice, anyone from liability for personal injuries?

Consider specifically the following situations:

Spectators at a hockey rink;

Occupants of a car on a parking lot;

Spectators at a rock concert.

If you answer both questions in the affirmative, draft such a clause. If you think that it is not practicable, justify that conclusion.

3. Consider the following problem:

Peter parks his car on the parking lot operated by Alice. There are signs in large letters on the lot saying, "Charges are for use of parking space only" and "Cars parked at owner's risk. For conditions see back of ticket". Peter gets a ticket when he drives in but does not read it. On the back is the following clause, "This lot is closed from 2.00 a.m. to 8.00 a.m. No car can be removed during that time". Peter returns at 2.10 a.m. to find the lot locked up and a heavy gate across the entrance. Peter is forced to take a cab home, costing $50.00 and is unable to make an important early meeting the next day. Has he any remedy against Alice?

4. How useful is the analysis of the problem on the basis of offer and acceptance? Does such an analysis represent a concern for any of the values that might be thought to be important?

5. Would Lord Denning have treated a claim based on the theft of Mr. Thornton's trumpet from the car in the same way?

(2) Signed Contracts (In general, contracts in writing)

(a) *The Problem in the Courts*

(1) *Introduction*

One of the problems with the "ticket cases" was the issue whether or not one side had received adequate notice of the terms on which the contract was made. When a contract is signed, the normal rule is that the person signing is bound by all the terms on the signed contract whether he had notice of them or not. Signing disposes conclusively of the issue of notice. The case that is usually cited in support of this proposition is the case of *L'Estrange v. Graucob, Ltd.*, [1934] 2 K.B. 394 (Court of Appeal, England). There Scrutton L.J. referred to the judgment of Mellish L.J. in *Parker v. S.E. Railway Co.* (*supra*), where it was said,

> "In an ordinary case, where an action is brought on a written agreement which is signed by the defendant, the agreement is proved by proving his signature, and, in the absence of fraud, it is wholly immaterial that he has not read the agreement and does not know the contents."

Scrutton then said much the same thing in a sentence that has been frequently quoted:

> "When a document containing contractual terms is signed, then, in the absence of fraud, or I will add, misrepresentation, the party signing is bound, as it is wholly immaterial whether he has read the document or not." (p. 403)

The cases that follow go on from here, so to speak. The concerns that motivated courts to get around the problem of the exemption clause in the ticket cases apply to the signed contract, and we shall be concerned to see how well the courts do the job of policing the exercise of contract power.

A number of fairly simple techniques are available. These include, first, the technique of construing any exemption clause very narrowly. For example in *Wallis v. Pratt*, [1911] A.C. 394, the respondent, defendant, sold seed to the appellant, plaintiff. The seed was supposed to be "common English Sainfoin". The contract of sale contained a clause that "the seller gives no warranty express or implied as to growth, description or any other matter". The seed was accepted by the buyer but turned out to be the seed of a different plant. The buyer claimed damages for breach of contract. (The buyer could not reject the seed since he had accepted it: Sale of Goods Act, s. 12(3).) The House of Lords held that the exemption clause did not apply since it was a condition of the contract that the seed be "common English Sainfoin" (s. 15). This term remained a condition even though the buyer had lost the right to repudiate the contract. This technique is obviously capable of rendering many exemption clauses ineffective.

A second technique is finding that the exemption clause is inconsistent with other terms of the contract. Thus in a number of cases the courts have held an exemption clause ineffective if at the time the contract is made an employee of the party seeking to rely on the clause has orally assured the other that he or she does not have to worry or that the clause is more limited in scope than it is in fact. (See: *Curtis v. Chemical Cleaning & Dyeing Co.*, [1951] 1 K.B. 805 and *Mendelssohn v. Normand Ltd.*, [1970] 1 Q.B. 177, [1969] 2 All E.R. 1215.) In the latter case, the plaintiff had parked his car in the defendant's garage. He wanted to lock his car but was told by the attendant that he could not do so. He told the attendant that there were valuables in the car. The attendant promised to lock up the car. The valuables disappeared. The contract contained two clauses. One, that the defendant accepted no liability for loss and, two, that the terms could only be varied if done so in writing and signed by the defendant's manager. Lord Denning found no problem in holding the defendant liable. He said:

> "[The plaintiff] relies on the conversation which Mr. Mendelssohn had with the attendant. The man promised to lock up the car. In other words, he promised to see that the contents were safe. He did not do so. Instead he left the car unlocked. It was probably he who took the suitcase himself. What is the effect of such a promise? It was not within the actual authority of the attendant to give it but it was within his ostensible authority. He was there to receive cars on behalf of the garage company. He had apparent authority to make a statement relating to its custody. Such a statement is binding on the company. It takes priority over any printed condition. There are many cases in the books when a man has made, by word of mouth, a promise or a representation of fact, on which the other party acts by entering into the contract. In all such cases the man is not allowed to repudiate his representation by reference to a printed condition, see *Couchman v. Hill*, [1947] 1 K.B. 554; *Curtis v. Chemical Cleaning and Dyeing Co.* [1951] 1 K.B. 805; and *Harling v. Eddy*, [1951] 2 K.B. 739; nor is he allowed to go back on his promise by reliance on a written clause, see *City and Westminster Properties (1934) Ltd. v. Mudd*, [1959] Ch. 129, 145 by Harman J. The reason is because the oral promise or representation has a decisive influence on the transaction — it is the very thing which induces the other to contract — and it would be most unjust to allow the maker to go back on it. The printed condition is rejected because it is repugnant to the express oral promise or representation. As Devlin J. said in *Firestone Tyre and Rubber Co. Ltd. v. Vokins & Co. Ltd.*, [1951] 1 Lloyd's Rep. 32, 39: It is illusory to say: 'We promise to do a thing, but we are not liable if we do not do it!' To avoid this illusion, the law gives the oral promise priority over the printed clause."

Again it can easily be seen that this kind of approach gives the court a wide power to undo whatever the draftsman of the contract may have intended.

There are a number of minor techinques that are also available, *e.g.* if there is any ambiguity in the clause it will be resolved against the party relying on the clause. This is sometimes dignified by a Latin tag as the "*contra proferentem*" rule. Many of these techniques have been used for many years in cases of insurance, where the insurer sought to avoid payment on a policy in circumstances where the court thought that payment should be made.

The courts have also been particularly hostile to attempts to obtain exemption from liability for negligence. Perhaps they feel that since negligence requires fault, it is improper that anyone should not be liable when he has been guilty of fault. What has often been suggested as the proper response to the case where exemption from negligence is in issue is the following:

1. If the clause expressly exempts one party from negligence, then effect must be given to that clause; however,

2. if there is no mention of negligence, then the issue is whether the words are wide enough, in their ordinary meaning, to cover negligence; but,

3. even if the words are wide enough, the court must consider whether liability can be imposed on some other ground or not. If liability can be imposed on some other ground, then that clause will not cover liability for negligence. By finding some other ground the courts are not denying *all* effect to the clause.

These rules will be referred to in the cases that follow. The principal focus in those cases is, however, on other methods of dealing with the problems facing the courts. The first two cases provide an example of a judicial approach to exemption clauses that appears to ride roughshod over the contract in issue. The questions that we shall consider are how far this is proper exercise of judicial power and how we can tell when the courts are going to respond in this way and when they won't. The remaining cases show what happens when the basis for interference is forgotten and, by way of contrast, what happens when the basis is remembered and made the express justification for the decision.

As you read the cases keep the following questions in mind:

1. What purpose does the clause in question serve?

2. Have the parties agreed to an allocation of risk that can be insured against?

3. To what extent is there an imbalance of bargaining power?

4. To what extent has this imbalance resulted in the ability of one side to impose terms on the other?

5. Should one distinguish between cases involving merchants only and those involving consumers?

(2) The Problem Outlined

YEOMAN CREDIT v. APPS

[1962] 2 Q.B. 508. Court of Appeals (England); Holroyd Pearce, Harman and Davies L.JJ.

APPEAL from Judge Baxter sitting at Bow County Court.

The following statement of facts is taken from the judgment of Holroyd Pearce L.J.: By a hire-purchase agreement, dated April 21, 1959, the plaintiffs, Yeoman Credit Ltd., a finance company, hired to the defendant, Henry Joseph Apps, a secondhand 1954 Ford motor-car sold to them by Goodbody Motors Ltd., dealers. The cash price of the car was £495 and the hire-purchase price £574, there being an initial instalment of £125 with 30 monthly instalments of £14 19s. 1d. The agreement provided that the hirer should keep the car licensed and insured. Clause 3 provided: "If the hirer shall duly make the said payments and strictly observe and perform all the terms and conditions on his part herein contained he shall thereupon have the option of purchasing the goods for the sum of £1 but until such option to purchase shall have been exercised the goods shall remain the absolute property of the owner and the hirer shall not have any right or interest in the same other than that of hirer under this agreement," and in the details of payments the hire charges were stated to be £78 12s. 6d. and the hire-purchase price the total of cash price and hire charges plus £1 purchase fee. Clauses 4 and 5 contained provisions for determination of the agreement.

By clause 8: "No warranty whatsoever is given by the owner as to the age, state or quality of the goods or as to fitness for any purpose and any implied warranties and conditions are also hereby expressly excluded except such as are implied by section 9 (1) of the Hire-Purchase Act, 1938 of applicable." At the time of signing the agreement the defendant signed a delivery receipt attached to it and addressed to the plaintiffs in these terms: "I hereby acknowledge having examined and taken delivery of the goods described in the schedule to the within written hire-purchase agreement between us and am satisfied as to their condition and their fitness for the purpose or purposes required."

The defendant had been introduced to Goodbody, the dealer, in April, 1959, and, late at night when it was dark, Goodbody had brought the car to his house and asked him to have a run in it. It being dark, the defendant had not been able to examine the car. They went for a short ride. Goodbody drove the car at what the defendant described as a steady pace. The defendant noticed that the windows were cracked: he pointed that out, and Goodbody said that he would have the car overhauled and the windows replaced and new tyres, or better tyres, exchanged for the defective tyres which were then on the car. They went to a house at which the defendant was introduced to one Marx, and Goodbody and Marx persuaded him to agree to take the car at a cash price of £495 and to sign the hire-purchase agreement. The defendant paid the initial instalment of £125 then and there to Goodbody. On May 5 the car was delivered to the defendant. Goodbody brought it round at night and left it outside the house. No repairs at all had been done; it was in exactly the same condition as it was when the defendant signed the agreement. The county court judge accepted the evidence that "the article delivered to Mr. Apps was a 1954 Zephyr car in an unusable, unroadworthy and unsafe condition requiring an expenditure of at least £70, and possibly £100 to £120 to put it into a reasonable roadworthy condition."

According to the defendant's account of what happened thereafter: "That month I got copy of agreement. I had had the car by that time. I had been able to drive it — very poor. I telephoned finance company in the West End. They said they would put me through to London office. Put through to a man. He said I would have to go to Goodbody. I rang up finance company over twenty times. I took car to Mr. Watson" — that was about the middle of May — "He did some work for me. I had not been able to use it. I had tried. Took me 1½ hours to go three to four miles. Brake, clutch, steering terrible. Watson repaired it so that I could get it back to Goodbody. I tried to return it to him. He was away. I took it home. Again rang the finance company. They told me to take it to Goodbody. I paid some instalments. I hoped Goodbody would bear half the expense of repair."

The defendant in fact paid the three instalments due on May 21, June 21 and July 21, 1959. The judge found he had made some complaints to the owners about the condition of the car, but not as many complaints as he claimed to have made. He failed to pay instalments due on August 21 and September 21. Accordingly, on October 9 the plaintiffs determined the hiring under clause 4 of the agreement on the ground of the defendant's failure to pay the instalments. A collector went to the defendant's house, taking with him a notice of termination. He had a discussion with the defendant who told him that as the car was not roadworthy, he could take it away. As the car would not go, the collector had it towed away. The car was resold by the plaintiffs just as it was for £210.

The plaintiffs claimed against the defendant for £29 18s. 2d., arrears of rental instalments; they also claimed £87 10s. 10d. damages for depreciation and £76 6s. 6d. damages for disrepair and loss of profit, alternatively, £163 17s. 4d. damages for breach of contract. The defendant counterclaimed for £170, the initial payment and the three rental instalments paid by him, as sums paid by him to the plaintiffs the consideration for which had wholly failed. The county court judge dismissed the plaintiffs' claim and, holding that there had been a total failure of consideration for the payments, gave judgment for the defendant on the counterclaim.

The plaintiffs appealed.

Holroyd Pearce L.J. This is the plaintiffs' appeal from a judgment of Judge Baxter at Bow County Court. He dismissed the plaintiffs' claim for arrears of instalments due under a hire-purchase agreement and for damages. He gave judgment for the defendant on the counterclaim for £170, being the first payment and three monthly instalments of hire paid by him under the agreement. The judge held that there had been a total failure of consideration for those payments.

[His Lordship stated the facts set out above, observed that, unfortunately, Goodbody was now insolvent so that the loss which in the event was caused by him must fall on others and that it was clear, as the county court judge found, that the agreement between the defendant and Goodbody was not an agreement with Goodbody Motors Ltd. as agent for the plaintiffs but that the defendant relied on Goodbody himself, and continued:] By a letter to the defendant, dated November 5, 1959, the plaintiffs claimed various amounts, the total of which was £193 15s. 6d. which sum was claimed in the action. The judge found that if the plaintiffs were entitled to anything, they were entitled to only £29 18s. 2d., being the two instalments in arrear, plus £30 damages for breach of the agreement.

So much of the appeal as is against that finding has been abandoned, and the plaintiffs here ask for judgment for £59 18s. 2d. On that part of the case the defendant's counsel argues (rightly, I think) that there is no evidence on which the judge could find damages proved even to the extent of £30, since he had held that the sum payable under clause 7 (5) by way of liquidated damages for depreciation was a penalty, and therefore irrecoverable.

. . . .

Whether there has been a breach of a fundamental condition of the agreement is a question of degree depending on the facts. Such a breach is different in weight and gravity from breaches of condition which would come within the exemption. It may be, as in *Pollock & Co. v. Macrae* (and in the present case) an accumulation of defects which, taken singly, might well have been within the exemption clause, but taken en masse constitute such a non-performance or repudiation of breach going to the root of the contract as disentitles the owners to take refuge behind an exception clause intended only to give protection to those breaches which are not inconsistent with and not destructive of the whole essence of the contract. One would not lightly come to the conclusion that mere defects in repair, even though numerous, amount to breach of a fundamental condition of the contract.

But in this case I accept the finding of the judge on the facts "that the plaintiffs were in breach of a fundamental term of the contract to hire a motor-car suitable for use on the highway and cannot rely on the exemption clause." There was, to use the words of Lord Dunedin, "such a congeries of defects as to destroy the workable character of the machine." I cannot, however, with all respect, agree with the judge that there was a total failure of consideration. The defendant was plainly entitled to reject the car, to accept the plaintiff's repudiation of the contract by their delivery of such a car, and to rescind the contract. Had he done so, there would have been a total failure of consideration, and he would have recovered the sums paid. But, as the judge found, he made no serious effort to return the car. He kept it for five or six months, and approbated the contract by paying three instalments. He intended (to quote his evidence) "to keep the car, and hoped Goodbody would pay half the cost." He tried to find out from the plaintiffs what he could do to make Goodbody carry out the work. In those circumstances he was at that stage continuing with the agreement while protesting against the state of the car which was due to a breach of condition by the plaintiffs. This is not a case like *Rowland v. Divall*, [1923] 2 K.B. 500, where title was lacking, and the defendant never had lawful possession. Here the defendant had the possession of the car and its use, such as it was. In evidence he said: "That month I got copy of agreement. I had had the car by that time. I had been able to drive it — very poor." Admittedly the use was of little (if any) value, but in my view that use, coupled with possession, and his continuance of the hiring agreement with the intention of keeping the car and getting Goodbody to pay half the repairs, debars the defendant from saying that there was a total failure of consideration.

On the amount of the defendant's damages, the judge said: "If I had thought the defendant was only entitled to set off or recover damages, I would have assessed these at £100. This would cover not only the cost of remedying the defects already discovered by Mr. Watson, and putting the car in a condition which conformed with the plaintiffs' obligations, but also making some allowance for the possibility, indeed the likelihood, that further examinations might disclose a need for overhaul and further expense."

The defendant, therefore, kept the car, and was entitled to £100 damages to make good the car for the use for which he was paying, and which he had an ultimate right to buy which he has now lost. In my view that is damage which he has suffered, and to which he is entitled. On this point the judge said: "Later, however, owing to the strong view he had formed about the condition of the vehicle, and his inability to get satisfaction from either the dealer or the plaintiffs, the defendant declined to make further payments. Stereotyped formal reminders were sent, but he still failed to pay. The defendant tells me that he rang the plaintiff company telling them that the car was not roadworthy, that he was not going to pay any more, and that they could take the car away. The plaintiffs have no record of this, but I think some such remark was made to some officer of the plaintiffs. The defendant made no serious effort to return the car, and I do not think I can find that he terminated the hiring as he was entitled to do under clause 5 of the agreement."

That seems to show that the defendant allowed the August instalment to fall due before he sought to repudiate the agreement. In my view he is, therefore, liable for the August instalment. Thereafter he rejected the car. Was he entitled to do so? Had this been a sale of goods on instalment payments, he could not, of course, have done so after payment of instalments and acceptance of the goods. Had this been a simple hiring, say, of a gas stove which did not work at all, and which the owners, after frequent requests over some months, had declined to put in order, he would have been entitled to reject it and end the hiring since the owner's breach was a continuing one. The owner's conduct would constitute a continuing repudiation. This hire-purchase agreement was, at the material time, more analogous to a simple hiring than to a purchase. It had a contingent option to purchase of which the defendant might have availed himself in two years time; but in September the defendant could, as a hirer refuse to go on with the transaction since the plaintiffs, in spite of repeated requests, were still consistently refusing to honour their obligations.

The defendant, therefore, is entitled to £100 damages; but he must pay the instalment that fell due on August 21, namely, £14 19s. 1d.

[Harman and Davies L.JJ. gave judgment to the same effect.]

CANADIAN-DOMINION LEASING CORP. LTD. v. SUBURBAN SUPERDRUG LTD.

(1966), 56 D.L.R. (2d) 43. Alberta Supreme Court, Appellate Division; Smith C.J.A., Kane and McDermid JJ.A.

The judgment of the Court was delivered by

Kane, J.A.: — This is an appeal from the judgment of Gardiner, D.C.J., dismissing with costs the appellant's claim for arrears of rent under an agreement in writing dated November 23, 1962, whereby the appellant leased a Berg Selector to the respondent for a term of 5 years in consideration of the respondent agreeing to pay rent of $48.99 every 3 months during the term; and for interest on the arrears.

The appellant is engaged in the business of leasing commercial and industrial equipment to commercial and industrial stores. The respondent carries on a general drug-store business at Edmonton.

In November, 1962, and it would appear on the 7th of that month, one Nye, a representative of W. H. Galaugher & Associates Ltd., called upon Sam Hardin, the president of the respondent. He wished to interest Hardin in a Berg Selector unit. Mr. Hardin stated he would like to see the selector in operation and Nye had one outside Hardin's store in his parked automobile. He brought the selector into the store and demonstrated it to Hardin.

This unit is a motion type showcase designed for the display for sale of small items of jewellery and small giftware. It works on a chain driven motor operated arrangement on an automatic principle with a series of trays revolving. The automatic principle of it is that it revolves, stops each

10 seconds, then runs again for a few seconds and stops again, and so on, so each tray in turn becomes visible through a window to a prospective customer as he stands in front of the machine. Mr. Hardin stated that " The idea is a gimmick type idea" to attract attention and present the largest amount of this type of merchandise in the smallest amount of floor space. The unit is 30 ins. in width.

Mr. Hardin testified he leased the selector because it opened a new avenue of sales, that he was particularly struck with the motion of the selector and the small amount of floor space it required.

Following the demonstration on November 7th, the respondent signed certain documents which Nye had with him to the knowledge and consent of the appellant.

Under one of these, the respondent requested the appellant to purchase from the Galaugher company one Berg Selector and agreed upon acceptance of this request by the appellant to lease the selector from the appellant. Under another such document the respondent as lessee executed a lease of the selector from the appellant as lessor. The lease was for a term of 5 years on a monthly rental of $16.33. The respondent delivered to Nye four cheques, each payable to the appellant in the amount of $48.99 dated respectively November 7, 1962, February 7th, May 7th and August 7, 1963, covering the first year's rental. The selector was then left with the respondent on November 7th.

The lease I have referred to is a one sheet document. On the front under the heading "Terms and Conditions of Lease" appear paragraphs numbered 1 to 4. Under para. 4 appear the following words: "See reverse side for additional terms and conditions which are part of this lease." Under those words appears the further sentence, "The undersigned agree to all the terms and conditions set forth above *and on the reverse side hereof,* and in witness thereof hereby execute this lease."

The documents bear date as to execution by the respondent of November 7, 1962, and of execution by the appellant, November 23, 1962. Such execution was made at the bottom of the front of the sheet. On the reverse side of this sheet there are printed cls. 5 to 24 inclusive.

About 5 or 6 days after November 7th, the motor stopped running and accordingly the selector stopped operating automatically. The respondent was able to operate the selector manually for a few days; then it stopped working completely. The respondent wrote the Galaugher company immediately. It did not communicate with appellant. The Galaugher company sent an electrical contractor, Mr. Souch, who replaced the motor with another at no cost to the respondent. The unit then operated for about 2 or 3 weeks; then it broke down. Mr. Hardin was not sure whether after the second breakdown Mr. Souch, whom he called, replaced or fixed the motor. He thought it was replaced. In any event, whether it was replaced or repaired, the selector then operated for about 3 or 4 weeks when it broke down again. Hardin then had the selector put in the basement of the store. He testified that he wrote to the Galaugher company, told it that he could not make the selector operate and informed it that Mr. Souch was of the opinion the motor was not suitable for the job. He further stated that he asked the Galaugher company to remove it or to let him know where he could send it. He testified that the selector worked "really good" for about 6 weeks altogether, but when it did not operate it was a detriment in that it took up 30 ins. of floor space, serving no other purpose than a counter top.

The four cheques above mentioned were duly paid although the selector only operated for a very short time. The respondent refused to pay any further amounts. The appellant then commenced this action claiming $783.84 as balance of rental and interest at the rate of 2% per month on unpaid rentals. The trial Judge found that the selector was far from being reasonably fit and suitable for the purpose for which it was intended and that in fact it had to be completely discarded by the respondent. He dismissed the appellant's action and directed that after payment of the amount owing to the respondent under the judgment (this would be the taxed costs), the appellant might have the selector.

The appellant contends there was no evidence before the trial Judge from which he could reasonably find that the selector was not reasonably fit and suitable for its purposes.

It was also contended on behalf of the appellant that the trial Judge was in error in holding there was an implied warranty that the selector was reasonably fit for the purpose for which it was hired because,

(a) this implied warranty was never intended to apply to a person in the position of the respondent, it not being an owner in possession of the selector;

(b) the appellant was not in the position of an owner in possession but relied on the respondent's selection of the chattel to be hired.

The appellant refers to para. 2 of the lease which reads as follows:

2. SELECTION OF EQUIPMENT. Lessee has requested the equipment of the type and quantity specified above and has selected the supplier named above. Lessor agrees to order such equipment from said supplier but shall not be liable for performance of this lease or damages if for any reason the supplier delays or fails to fill the order. Lessee shall accept such equipment if delivered in good repair and hereby authorizes lessor to insert the serial numbers of each item of equipment so delivered. Any delay in delivery shall not affect the validity of this lease.

(c) The respondent should not be permitted to raise defects in the selector at this time.

The appellant refers to para. 12 of the lease which reads as follows:

12. NOTICE OF DEFECTS. Unless lessee gives lessor written notice of each defect or other proper objection to an item of equipment within five (5) business days after receipt thereof it shall be conclusively presumed as between lessee and lessor that the item of equipment was delivered in good repair and that lessee accepts it as an item of equipment described in this lease.

(d) The combined effect of paras. 12 and 18 of the lease are sufficient to exclude the implied warranty.

Paragraph 12 has been set out above. Paragraph 18 reads as follows:

18. ENTIRE AGREEMENT. This instrument constitutes the entire agreement between lessor and lessee. No agent or employee of the supplier is authorized to bind lessor to this lease, to waive or alter any term or condition printed herein or add any provision hereto. Except as provided in paragraph 3 hereof a provision may be added hereto or a provision hereof may be altered or varied only by a writing signed and made part hereof by an authorized officer of lessor. Waiver by lessor of any provision hereof in one instance shall not constitute a waiver as to any other instance.

(e) The effect of para. 4 of the lease is sufficient in itself to exclude an implied warranty.

Paragraph 4 reads as follows:

4. WARRANTIES. Lessor makes no representations or warranty (express, implied, statutory or otherwise) as to any matter whatsoever, including without limitation, the condition of the equipment, its merchantability or its fitness for any particular purpose. Lessor agrees that to the extent permitted by law any representation or warranty by the manufacturer or supplier of the equipment is for the benefit of both lessee and lessor and may be enforced jointly or separately.

In my view, the appellant in the circumstances of this case cannot rely on the exemption clauses in the lease.

The respondent was entitled to receive a selector capable of self-propulsion for, at the very least, a reasonable time. What it received was a selector which within a matter of just a few days ceased to operate by self-propulsion because the motor was defective. When that motor was replaced the selector operated for only another short period. When the second motor was either replaced or repaired, the selector operated for another very short period of time. After this third breakdown, the selector was put into the basement of the respondent's store. It was of no use to the respondent for the purposes for which he had agreed to rent it.

Karsales (Harrow) Ltd. v. Wallis, [1956] 2 All E.R. 866, was a case in which the defendant had inspected a Buick automobile, found it to be in good condition, and entered into a hire-purchaser agreement. The car was left by the seller outside the defendant's garage at night. When the defendant inspected it the following morning, he found it to be in deplorable condition and incapable of self-propulsion. It was held by the Court of Appeal that the car delivered was not the car contracted to be taken and that there was a fundamental breach of contract which disentitled the plaintiff from relying on the exception clause in the contract, which clause read as follows:

3(g) No condition or warranty that the vehicle is roadworthy or as to its age, condition or fitness for any purpose is given by the owner or implied herein.

In the *Karsales* case, Denning, L.J. (now Lord Denning), said (at pp. 868-9):

The law about exempting clauses, however, has been much developed in recent years, at any rate about printed exempting clauses, which so often pass unread. Notwithstanding earlier cases which might suggest the contrary, it is now settled that exempting clauses of this kind, no matter how widely they are expressed, only avail the party when he is carrying out his contract in its essential respects. He is not allowed to use them as a cover for misconduct or indifference or to enable him to turn a blind eye to his obligations. They do not avail him when he is guilty of a breach which goes to the root of the contract. It is necessary to look at the contract apart from the exempting clauses and see what are the terms, express or implied, which impose an obligation on the party. If he has been guilty of a breach of those obligations in a respect which goes to the very root of the contract, he cannot rely on the exempting clauses.

In the same case Parker, L.J. (now Lord Chief Justice), said (at p. 871):

Accordingly, Mutual Finance, Ltd., and their assignees, the plaintiffs, said (in effect) that it does not matter what is delivered so long as it bears the appellation of a "Buick" car as described in the agreement, and that the hirer is bound to take it. In my judgment, however extensive the exception clause may be, it has no application if there has been a breach of a fundamental term.

Parker, L.J., further stated (at p. 871):

Applying that to the facts of this case, it seems to me that the vehicle delivered in effect is not properly described (as the agreement describes it) as a motor vehicle, "Buick", giving the chassis and engine number. By that I am not saying that every defect in a car which renders it for the moment unusable on the road amounts to a breach of a fundamental term; but where, as here, a vehicle is delivered incapable of self-propulsion except after a complete overhaul and in the condition referred to by my Lord, it seems to me that it is abundantly clear that there was a breach of a fundamental term and that accordingly the exceptions in cl. 3 (g) do not apply.

In *Astley Industrial Trust, Ltd. v. Grimley*, [1963] 2 All E.R. 33, it was held that a finance company which had let on hire-purchase a Bedford tipper, was in the circumstances under an obligation as to the fitness of the tipping lorry, such obligation being that it was a lorry of the make specified, and a tipper, and a motor vehicle capable of self-propulsion along a road and of receiving and carrying materials. It was also held that no breach of the fundamental terms and implied conditions had been proved. The contract under consideration contained a provision as follows:

3. The hirer's acceptance of delivery of the vehicle shall be conclusive that he has examined the vehicle and found the same to be complete and in good order and condition and in every way satisfactory to him. Except where it is implied by the Hire-Purchase Acts, 1938 and 1954 the [finance company] give no warranty as to the state or quality of the vehicle, and, save as aforesaid, any warranty as to description, repair, quality or fitness for any purpose is hereby excluded.

In his judgment Pearson, L.J. (now Lord Pearson), said (p. 44):

In my view the finance company are not entitled to say that they had no obligation at all under the agreement as to the fitness of the vehicle for the first defendant's purpose. They were letting on hire to him a Bedford tipper, and it had to be a Bedford tipper, i.e. a lorry of that make, and a tipper. It had to be an automobile, capable of self-propulsion along a road, and it had to be capable of receiving and carrying and tipping loads of materials. The condition or fundamental term is to be implied in this case, as it was in the *Karsales* case and in the *Apps* case [*Yeoman Credit Ltd. v. Apps*, [1961] 2 All E.R. 281].

In the same case Upjohn, L.J., who agreed with the judgment of Pearson, L.J., said, speaking of implied conditions, warranties or stipulations relating to hiring, whether simple hire or hire-purchase (at p. 46):

First, there is an implied stipulation that the vehicle hired corresponds with the description of the vehicle contracted to be hired, or to put it in another way, the lender must lend that which he contracts to lend and not something which is essentially different. Thus, as my Lord has pointed out, a tipping lorry plainly hired for use as such must be capable of self-propulsion to a reasonable degree and must have a rear compartment capable of being mechanically tipped.
This implied stipulation is a fundamental implied term and breach of it at once gives the hirer the right, if he desires to do so, to treat the contract as repudiated. Furthermore, being a fundamental term the lender cannot by clauses of exclusion or exception, however widely phrased, exclude liability for this fundamental term for the simple reason that the law will not permit one of the contracting parties to escape liability for failure to deliver that which he has contracted to lend by delivery of something which is essentially different. The question whether or not the motor vehicle delivered complies with this fundamental obligation of the lender is very largely a question of fact and degree and must depend on the circumstances of each case.

A very helpful article appears in Cheshire and Fifoot, *Law of Contract*,

6th ed. In the introductory paragraph of that article at pp. 116-7 the authors
state:

> In a number of cases, now extending over many years, judges have ruled from
> time to time that no exempting clause, however wide, may protect a party who
> has broken the basic duties created by the very nature and character of the con-
> tract. A variety of language has been used to describe this over-riding considera-
> tion. The words "fundamental term" are, perhaps, most often on judicial lips.
> But this phrase, in so far as it suggests that the courts are only adding a further
> term to those already expressed or implied in the contract, is misleading. The
> essential assumption is that the party at fault has done more than break a term of
> the contract, however important this may be: he has failed to satisfy the very
> purpose for which the contract was designed and he may no longer rely on one of
> its component parts. If this were not the essence of the doctrine, it could not be
> used, as it is, to cancel an exemption clause in whatever language it may be draft-
> ed. A more appropriate title, it is therefore suggested, is "the doctrine of the fun-
> damental obligation."

With respect, I agree with Bastin, J. (*Schmidt v. International Harvester
Co. of Canada Ltd.* (1962), 38 W.W.R. 180 at p. 183), when he said that to
invoke the principle in the *Karsales* case there must be proved a breach of
contract of a flagrant nature.

Both *Yeoman Credit v. Apps* and *Canadian Dominion Leasing v. Suburban
Superdrug* involved claims by finance companies. Parties in the position of
finance companies have always sought to insulate themselves from the consequences of the buyer's disappointment. They want the buyer to look to
his seller, while they force the buyer to pay them that which he has promised to pay. Most of the cases that are like these two (and there are many)
have, in effect, given to the buyer the defences that he would have had if
sued by the seller. Again it is useful to see this being done directly.

The following case shows that the common law can deal with this issue
quite satisfactorily.

FEDERAL DISCOUNT CORP. v. ST. PIERRE

(1962), 32 D.L.R. (2d) 86. Ontario Court of Appeal.

[The plaintiff sued on a promissory note signed by the defendants (husband and wife). The note had been given by the defendants to the vendor of
a home knitting machine, Fair Isle Knitting Ltd. and endorsed by Fair Isle
to the plaintiff. Fair Isle operated, in conjunction with another company,
Yarncraft Ltd., a scheme under which purchasers of knitting machines from
Fair Isle were offered contracts by Yarncraft for the sale of knitted products made by the purchasers. The scheme and its advertising were designed
to indicate that profits easily sufficient to pay the purchase price of the
machine could be earned. The defendant raised as a defence to the action
brought by the plaintiff the argument that the relationship between the
plaintiff, Fair Isle and Yarncraft was so close that the plaintiff was not entitled to sue as a holder in due course of the note. The defendant also
counter-claimed for an amount due from Yarncraft for goods sold to it. The
Division Court (the former Small Claims Court) had dismissed the
plaintiff's action. The plaintiff appealed.]

Kelly J.A.: On this appeal the plaintiff contended that it was a holder in due course of the note sued upon; that there was no evidence to support the finding that the plaintiff had at the time of negotiation notice of any defect of title of the payee; that there was no evidence the plaintiff knew anything of the specific transaction opposed to the general conduct of the business of its predecessor in title; and that as between the original parties there was no ground which would entitle the defendants to rescission of the contract of purchase.

The rights which accrue to a holder in due course of a bill of exchange are unique and distinguishable from the rights of an assignee of a contract which does not fall within the description of a bill of exchange. The assignee of a contract, unlike the holder in due course of a bill of exchange, takes subject to all the equities between the original parties, which have arisen prior to the date of notice of the assignment to the party sought to be charged.

The special privileges enjoyed by a holder in due course of a bill of exchange are quite foreign to the common law and have their origin in the law merchant.

There is little difficulty in appreciating how trade between merchants required that he who put into circulation his engagement to pay a specified sum at a designated time and place knowing that it was the custom of merchants to regard such paper much as we do our paper currency, should be held to the letter of his obligation and be prevented from setting up defences which might derogate from the apparently absolute nature of his obligation.

At first the customs prevailing amongst merchants as to bills of exchange extended only to merchant strangers trafficking with English merchants; later they were extended to inland bills between merchants trafficking with one another within England; then to all persons trafficking and finally to all persons trafficking or not.

Thus in time the particular conditions which were recognized as prevailing amongst merchants became engrafted onto the law generally applicable and came to be looked on as arising from the document itself rather than from the character of the parties dealing with the document. It is significant, however, that the transition did not affect the legal position as to one another of immediate parties and that as between any two immediate parties, maker and payee, or endorser and endorsee, none of the extraordinary conditions otherwise attaching to the bill, serve to affect adversely the rights and obligations existing between them as contracting parties. The document itself becomes irreproachable and affords special protection to its holder only, when at some stage of its passage from payee or acceptor to holder, there has been a *bona fide* transaction of trade with respect to it wherein the transferee took for value and without any notice of circumstances which might give rise to a defence on the part of the maker. Unless the ultimate holder or some earlier holder has acquired the instrument in the course of such a transaction the earlier tainting circumstances survive and the holder seeking to enforce payment of it must, on the merits, meet any defence which would have been available to the maker. Thus it appears that the peculiar immunity which the holding of a bill of exchange brings to the holder in due course arises not from the original nature of the document itself but from the quality which had been imparted to it by at least some one transfer of it. It follows that the transfer which is alleged to have given such a special character to the bill of exchange should be subject to more than a casual examination and that the true nature of that transaction be discovered.

There can be no doubt that everyday commercial life demands that the integrity of bills of exchange be recognized and that those acquiring them in good faith should not be required unnecessarily to make inquiries to establish their authenticity. Courts quite properly have refused to recognize that constructive notice has any place in the law of negotiable instruments: *London Joint Stock Bank v. Simmonds*, [1892] A.C. 201 at p. 221. Any attempt to weaken the provisions of a valid bill of exchange duly launched into the stream of commercial life, should be avoided. To do so, however, does not require that a prospective purchaser of a bill of exchange who has knowledge of certain circumstances about the seller's business which puts him on inquiry can by avoiding making inquiries or drawing reasonable inferences from the circumstances known to him, improve his position beyond that which it would have been had he made the enquiries he should have made or drawn the inference he should have drawn. This is not charging the holder with constructive notice and does not go beyond the standard of conduct laid down by the House of Lords in *Earl of Sheffield v. London Joint Stock Bank* (1888), 13 App. Cas. 333.

It is not necessary for the support of ordinary commercial transactions that the holder of a bill of exchange should under all circumstances be permitted to shield himself behind the guise of a holder in due course and attempt to separate his character as holder in due course from the debilitating effect of facts and circumstances actually known to him at the time he acquired the bill or which were reasonably inferable from facts and circumstances which were brought to his knowledge.

In the examination of any transfer to decide if it constituted the transferee a holder in due course the plaintiff's actual involvement with the transferor will be a major factor; on this account the whole relationship between the plaintiff and its transferor must be examined and considered.

With the growth of the sale of household and personal goods on the extended payment plan, the promissory note, the conditional sales contract and the finance company have become inseparable parts of the procedure whereby the merchant realizes immediately cash from the extended obligation of the purchaser from him. The very existence of the seller's business depends on his ability to convert into cash these obligations and the finance company, standing ready and willing to buy them, has become not only an essential part of retail selling on the time payment plan but is in effect a department of the seller's business, exercising a measure of control over the seller's sales by the requirements laid down with regard to the negotiable paper proposed to be purchased.

In the course of this development an attempt has been made to project into the field of household law the law merchant originally designed for dealings between merchants. The fiction has been permitted to flourish that the finance company is a foreign and independent agency. When it does acquire the contracts which it was incorporated to buy and which it arranged to purchase before the contracts actually came into existence it attempts to shield itself behind the protection of the law merchant which can apply only, if at all, to one of the documents constituting the arrangement between the seller and the buyer; at the same time it takes unto itself all the advantages that can be drawn from the transaction out of which the note arose. It is beyond question that the promissory note is included in the documents required to be signed by the purchaser for the express purpose of enabling the finance company to avoid defences which would otherwise be available to the maker against his vendor and any assignee of his purchase obligation.

The plaintiff was in the business of discounting notes: it was its practice and policy where any note had relationship to a conditional sales contract that the conditional sales contract should also be purchased and assigned to it: when a dealer first approached the plaintiff with a view to having the plaintiff discount notes which were to arise from the dealer's sales, the plaintiff investigated the applicant as to its financial stability, moral responsibility and various other aspects which would qualify the applicant to be a dealer "with the plaintiff"; the plaintiff was interested in knowing the possible volume of the business of the dealer as in the words of the witness McGarry, the plaintiff's Credit and Collection Manager, "It's got to be worthwhile before you can go into business with them". It was also well known to the plaintiff that Fair Isle and Yarncraft were companies having the same principals and officers.

The plaintiff was informed of the manner in which Fair Isle intended to conduct its selling campaign for the distribution of home knitting machines and was told by Turack, an officer of both Fair Isle and Yarncraft, "What we were doing in the other company" (Yarncraft). In fact the form of purchase order, questionnaire, conditional sales contract, and application for home knitting contract which were used in the approach to the female defendant were shown to the plaintiff company at the inception of the dealings between the plaintiff and Fair Isle. The purpose of the incorporation of two distinct companies, Fair Isle Knitting (Ontario) Limited and Yarncraft Industries Limited, was stated by Turack to be that one, Fair Isle, would sell knitting machines in conjunction with the giving of home knitting contract by the other, Yarncraft, and that the operation of Yarncraft and its home knitting contracts was something to facilitate the sale of home knitting machines by Fair Isle.

The plaintiff was fully aware of the general course of operation employed by Fair Isle and Yarncraft in their dealings with the purchasers such as the defendants. The words which were impressed by rubber stamp on exs. 24 and 25, "Note — payments must be made when due, regardless of the amount earned from knitting", proved beyond a shadow of a doubt that the plaintiff knew that the purchasers of home knitting machines would be or at least could have been left with the impression which was in the mind of the female defendant, that is, that the moneys to meet the instalments of purchase-price would be forthcoming from earnings under the home knitting contract.

According to the evidence of Barber, the association of the home knitting contract with the sale of home knitting machine was one of the reasons why the plaintiff dealt with Fair Isle because the plaintiff "felt that if a person could make money, sell their material back to Yarncraft Industries, they would be able to pay for the machine".

The course of dealings between the plaintiff and the officers of Fair Isle indicates a relationship much more intimate than that of endorsee or endorser in a normal commercial transaction. The company selling the home knitting machines in conjunction with the awarding by its associate of home knitting contracts and the plaintiff who made possible the operations of the seller by buying the purchaser's instalment obligation were more nearly engaged in one business, each one in the conduct of its particular phase being useless without the association of the other. To pretend that they were so separate that the transfer of each note constituted an independent commercial transaction not affected by the pre-existing arrangements between them would, in my view, be to permit the form to prevail over the substance.

My view of the relationship of the plaintiff and its endorser of the note sued upon is reinforced by the evidence as to the arrangement between the plaintiff and Fair Isle, which resulted in the writing of a letter of March 17, 1959, ex. 13. The conduct of the plaintiff and Fair Isle leading up to the despatch of this letter is of itself of such an extraordinary nature as to require no comment other than to say that it indicates a relationship somewhat beyond what would be expected of a financial institution and a merchant dealing in the ordinary course of business. Even granting that the plaintiff did not have actual notice of facts the knowledge of which would have prevented it from becoming a holder in due course, the transfer of the note to it by Fair Isle fell short of being the type of business transaction between two parties, dealing with respect to the note in complete good faith, which would have imparted to the note the power to endow with the character of holder in due course, one becoming a holder with complete knowledge of its history and the complete facts of the relationship between the maker and the payee.

There appear to be no Canadian cases which have held that the business relationship between a dealer and a finance company is an element to be considered in deciding finance company's claim to be a holder in due course; the question has been dealt with by American Courts in this manner and I would adopt the reasoning of the Judges who decided these cases: *Buffalo Industrial Bank v. De Marzio* (1937), 296 N.Y. Supp. 783; *Commercial Credit Co. v. T. F. Childs* (1940), 128 A.L.R. 726; *Taylor et ux. v. Atlas Security Co.* (1923), 249 S.W. 746.

Under the circumstances of this case I can find no error in the conclusion arrived at by the trial Judge, namely, that the plaintiff was not a holder in due course of the promissory note sued upon in this action.

[In the result, the plaintiff was allowed to succeed in its action on the note, but because the plaintiff could not sue as a holder in due course, the defendant's counterclaim was upheld.]

NOTE

The problems raised by the case of *Federal Discount v. St. Pierre* are now covered by statute. Amendments to both the Bills of Exchange Act, R.S.C. 1970, 1st supp. c.4, ss. 188-192, and the Consumer Protection Act, S.O. 1971, c. 24, s. 1, have made it possible for a consumer to raise the kind of defences raised in this case. These will be examined later in the chapter.

SUISSE ATLANTIQUE SOCIETE D'ARMEMENT MARITIME S.A. v. N.V. ROTTERDAMSCHE KOLEN CENTRALE

[1967] A.C. 361. House of Lords; Viscount Dilhorne, Lords Reid, Hodson, Upjohn and Wilberforce.

Viscount Dilhorne. My Lords, this appeal is from a decision of the Court of Appeal (Sellers, Harman and Diplock L.JJ.) dismissing an appeal by the appellants from a decision by Mocatta J. on a consultative case in relation to a dispute between the parties which has arisen in connection with the charter of a vessel from the appellants.

On December 21, 1956, the respondents agreed to charter a vessel from the appellants for the carriage of coal from the United States to Europe. That charter was to remain in force "for a total of two years consecutive voyages" (clause 23 of the charterparty). The vessel had "with all possible dispatch" to "sail and proceed" to a port in the United States and there load on each voyage a cargo of coal "and being so loaded, shall therewith proceed with all possible dispatch" to a port in Europe (clause 1). She had to be loaded at a specified rate per running day and, if she was detained beyond the loading time, the charterers were to pay $1,000 a day demurrage. In computing the loading time, detention of the vessel in consequence of the happening of certain events was to be disregarded (clause 3). Similarly if she was detained longer than was required to unload her at the stipulated rate per day and that was not due to strikes, etc., or other causes beyond the control of the charterers, the charterers who were to discharge the cargo were to pay demurrage at the rate of $1,000 a day.

On September 16, 1957, the appellants regarded themselves as entitled to treat the charterparty as repudiated by reason of the respondents' delays in loading and discharging the vessel. This was not accepted by the respondents and on October 8, 1957, it was agreed, without prejudice to this dispute, that from thence-forward the charterparty would be carried out.

Between October 16, 1957, and the end of the charter the vessel made eight round voyages. The appellants contended that she ought reasonably to have completed each round voyage in 30 or 37 days including loading and unloading. On this basis eight voyages would have taken 240 or 296 days. In fact they took 511 and the difference, the appellants alleged, was due to delays in loading and unloading for which the respondents were responsible. The result was, so the appellants alleged, that the vessel did not make as many voyages as she should have done with the result that they were deprived of the freights they would have earned on 9 or alternatively 6 voyages. On this basis, after giving credit for the demurrage payments received by them, they claimed $772,866.92 and alternatively $476,490.92 from the respondents.

This claim went to arbitration and, at the request of the appellants, the arbitrators stated the following questions in the form of a consultative case:

> "(A) (i) The claimants are entitled to recover (subject to giving credit for the demurrage payments received by them) any damages suffered by them by reason of the respondents having failed to load and discharge the vessel within the lay-days whereby the charterparty was (if so proved) rendered less profitable to the claimants by consequent loss of voyages or voyage time.
> "(ii) Upon the assumption that such loss of profitability resulted from the respondents having deliberately (i.e., with the wilful intention of limiting the number of

contractual voyages) failed to load and/or discharge the vessel; (a) With such ordinary dispatch as the circumstances permitted, or (b) within the laydays, the claimants are entitled to recover any damages suffered by the claimants through the charterparty having been rendered less profitable as aforesaid subject to giving credit for the demurrage payments received by them and for any such despatch money as would have been earned by the respondents.

"(B) If the answer to any of the questions under ('A') be 'Yes,' the payment by the respondents and acceptance by the claimants of demurrage in respect of those periods when the laydays were exceeded preclude the claimants from recovering any damages otherwise recoverable by them in accordance with such answer or answers."

Before Mocatta J. it was agreed that he should confine his decision to answering questions A (i) and (ii) and that the words "or voyage time" at the end of A (i) added nothing.

Mr. MacCrindle for the appellants submitted to your Lordships, as he had in the courts below, that the appellants had under the charterparty a contractual right to the number of voyages which would be performed if both parties complied with their obligations; and, secondly, that the appellants' claim for the loss of freight on the voyages which should have been performed was not limited to the demurrage payments.

· · ·

Lord Reid. My Lords, I am satisfied that for the reasons given by your Lordships this appeal could not succeed on any of the grounds submitted to the Court of Appeal and to your Lordships at the first hearing of this appeal. But at the end of his opening address counsel for the appellant put forward a new contention based on there having been a fundamental breach of contract by the respondents. Normally this House would not permit a new question of that character to be argued. But this is a consultative case stated by arbitrators and the appellants could still raise such a new question before the arbitrators. So in order to avoid delay and expense your Lordships adjourned the hearing on terms as to costs and ordered the parties to lodge supplementary cases dealing with this new contention. I only intend to deal with the new question argued at the second hearing.

The case arises out of a charterparty for two years' consecutive voyages made on December 21, 1956, between the appellants, the owners, and the respondents, the charterers. After a dispute the parties made a further agreement on October 8, 1957, to perform the charterparty for the remainder of the two-year period. The purpose of the charterparty was that on each voyage the vessel should proceed in ballast to an Atlantic port in the United States and there load coal to be carried to a port in the Netherlands. During this remaining part of the two years the vessel only made eight voyages and she spent some 380 days in ports of loading or discharge. There was provision for payment of demurrage with wide exceptions of causes of delay beyond the control of the charterer. But the respondents have admitted liability to pay demurrage for some 150 days. The complaint of the appellants is that by reason of the failure of the respondents to perform their contractual obligations to load and discharge within the laydays the appellants have been deprived of the freight which would have been earned on the additional voyages which would have been performed had there not been this delay for which the respondents are responsible. They claim that six or nine more voyages would have been performed within the period if the respondents had fulfilled their obligations and they estimate their loss from that cause at $875,000 or alternatively $580,000. The respondents' answer is that the appellants are only entitled to demurrage at the agreed rate of $1,000 per day and they have paid some $150,000 as demurrage.

The new contention submitted by the appellants is that the breaches of contract which caused these delays amounted to fundamental breach or breach going to the root of the contract so that at some time during the currency of the agreement the appellants would have been entitled to treat the breaches as a repudiation, to terminate or rescind the contract and to claim damages at common law. It is, I think, clear that if they did have that right they must be held to have elected not to treat the breaches as repudiatory. But they argue that nevertheless the fact that there was a fundamental breach prevents the respondents from relying on the demurrage clause as limiting their responsibility.

So the first question must be whether these delays can be regarded as involving fundamental breach. If so, it is for the arbitrators, at least in the first instance, to decide whether there was fundamental breach. The respondents deny that these breaches are capable of being regarded as amounting to fundamental breach. General use of the term "fundamental breach" is of recent origin and I can find nothing to indicate that it means either more or less than the well known type of breach which entitles the innocent party to treat it as repudiatory and to rescind the contract. The appellants allege that the respondents caused these delays deliberately (i.e., with the wilful intention of limiting the number of contractual voyages). They do not allege fraud or bad faith. This allegation would appear to cover a case where the charterers decided that it would pay them better to delay loading and discharge and pay the resulting demurrage at the relatively low agreed rate, rather than load and discharge more speedily and then have to buy more coal and pay the relatively high agreed freight on the additional voyages which would then be possible. If facts of that kind could be proved I think that it would be open to the arbitrators to find that the respondents had committed a fundamental or repudiatory breach. One way of looking at the matter would be to ask whether the party in breach has by his breach produced a situation fundamentally different from anything which the parties could as reasonable men have contemplated when the contract was made. Then one would have to ask not only what had already happened but also what was likely to happen in future. And there the fact that the breach was deliberate might be of great importance.

If fundamental breach is established the next question is what effect, if any, that has on the applicability of other terms of the contract. This question has often arisen with regard to clauses excluding liability, in whole or in part, of the party in breach. I do not think that there is generally much difficulty where the innocent party has elected to treat the breach as a repudiation, bring the contract to an end and sue for damages. Then the whole contract has ceased to exist including the exclusion clause, and I do not see how that clause can then be used to exclude an action for loss which will be suffered by the innocent party after it has ceased to exist, such as loss of the profit which would have accrued if the contract had run its full term. But that is not the situation in the present case, where in my view the appellants elected that the contract should continue in force.

Where the contract has been affirmed by the innocent party, at first sight the position is simple. You must either affirm the whole contract or rescind the whole contract: you cannot approbate and reprobate by affirming part of it and disaffirming the rest — that would be making a new contract. So the clause excluding liability must continue to apply. But that is too simple and there is authority for two quite different ways of holding that, in spite of affirmation of the contract as a whole by the innocent party, the guilty party may not be entitled to rely on a clause in it. One way depends on construction of the clause. The other way depends on the existence of a rule of substantive law.

As a matter of construction it may appear that the terms of the exclusion clause are not wide enough to cover the kind of breach which has been committed. Such clauses must be construed strictly and if ambiguous the narrower meaning will be taken. Or it may appear that the terms of the clause are so wide that they cannot be applied literally: that may be because this would lead to an absurdity or because it would defeat the main object of the contract or perhaps for other reasons. And where some limit must be read into the clause it is generally reasonable to draw the line at fundamental breaches. There is no reason why a contract should not make a provision for events which the parties do not have in contemplation or even which are unforeseeable, if sufficiently clear words are used. But if some limitation has to be read in it seems reasonable to suppose that neither party had in contemplation a breach which goes to the root of the contract. Then the true analysis seems to me to be that the whole contract, including the clause excluding liability, does survive after election to affirm it, but that that does not avail the party in breach. The exclusion clause does not change its meaning; as a matter of construction it never did apply and does not after election apply to this type of breach, and therefore is no answer to an action brought in respect of this type of breach.

But applying a strict construction to these clauses is not sufficient to exclude them in all cases of fundamental breach. It cannot be said as a matter of law that the resources of the English language are so limited that it is impossible to devise an exclusion clause which will apply to at least some cases of fundamental breach without being so widely drawn that it can be cut down on any ground by applying ordinary principles of construction. So, if there is to be a universal rule that, no matter how the exclusion clause is expressed, it will not apply to protect a party in fundamental breach, any such rule must be a substantive rule of law nullifying any agreement to the contrary and to that extent restricting the general principle of English law that parties are free to contract as they may see fit.

There is recent authority for the existence of such a rule of law but I cannot find support for it in the older authorities. Most of them arose out of deviation from the contractual voyage or similar breaches of contracts of carriage by land. Any deviation has always been regarded as a breach going to the root of the contract, and it was held in these earlier cases that, if the consignor's goods were lost after there had been a deviation, the shipowner could not rely on clauses excluding or limiting his liability. The reasons given for this varied but I do not think that it is useful now to examine them in detail because it was made clear in the speeches in this House in *Hain Steamship Co. Ltd.* v. *Tate & Lyle Ltd.*, [1936] 2 All E.R. 597, that there is no special rule applicable to deviation cases: the ordinary principles of the law of contract must be applied. The special feature of these cases is that the consignor's goods were lost before he knew of the deviation and therefore before he had any opportunity to elect whether or not to treat it as bringing the contract to an end. When he learns of the deviation and of the subsequent loss of his goods there is hardly room for any election, but the fact that he sues for their value could be treated as an election to terminate the contract by reason of and immediately after the deviation.

Among the reasons given in the earlier cases I do not find any reliance on any rule of law that a party guilty of a breach going to the root of the contract can never rely on clauses excluding his liability. And I do not think that the decision in *Tate & Lyle's* case assists us. There the owners of the goods had known of the deviation and had elected to waive it before the goods were lost. The breach was not a continuing breach and it did not cause the loss of the goods. In this case the breach, if it was a fundamental breach, was a continuing breach and it did cause the loss of which the appellants complain.

I think that *Smeaton Hanscomb* v. *Sassoon I. Setty, Son & Co. (No. 1),* [1953] 2 All E.R. 1471, can be regarded as the first of the series of recent cases dealing with fundamental breach. There the question was whether a claim by the buyer was barred by a clause in the contract "any claim must be made within 14 days from the final discharge of the goods." Devlin J. said (p. 1473):

> "It is no doubt a principle of construction that exceptions are to be construed as not being applicable for the protection of those for whose benefit they are inserted if the beneficiary has committed a breach of a fundamental term of the contract; and that a clause requiring the claim to be brought within a specified period is to be regarded as an exception for this purpose... I do not think that what is a fundamental term has ever been closely defined. It must be something, I think, narrower than a condition of the contract, for it would be limiting the exceptions too much to say that they applied only to breaches of warranty. It is, I think, something which underlies the whole contract so that, if it is not complied with, the performance becomes something totally different from that which the contract contemplates."

It is true that Lord Devlin says that he is applying a principle of construction but I think that he is really applying a substantive rule of law. He does not reach his conclusion by construing the clause in its context: there is no statement of any reason why the apparently general terms of this particular clause must be cut down or limited so as to make it only applicable to claims in respect of breaches which do not go to the root of the contract or which are not breaches of fundamental terms. And it does not appear to me to be obvious that some canon of construction would require a limitation of the apparently general terms of this clause.

The next case is *Karsales (Harrow) Ltd.* v. *Wallis,* [1956] 2 All E.R. 866, There the contract provided that — "No condition or warranty that the vehicle is roadworthy," or "as to its age, condition or fitness for any purpose is given by the owner or implied herein." Lord Denning said (p. 868):

> "Notwithstanding earlier cases which might suggest the contrary, it is now settled that exempting clauses of this kind, no matter how widely they are expressed, only avail the party when he is carrying out his contract in its essential respects. He is not allowed to use them as a cover for misconduct or indifference or to enable him to turn a blind eye to his obligations. They do not avail him when he is guilty of a breach which goes to the root of the contract."

And Parker L.J. said (p. 871):

"But, in my judgment, however extensive the exception clause may be, it has no application if there has been a breach of a fundamental term."

This is a clear statement of a rule of law. If it is right, it would be irrelevant that on its true construction an exempting clause must be held to be intended to apply to the breach in question, and that it is not so wide in its terms that as a matter of construction in its context its applicability must be limited. It must mean that the law does not permit contracting out of common law liability for a fundamental breach. I think that I should go on to examine the rest of the series of recent cases, but, under the present practice of the Court of Appeal with regard to the binding character of any of its own decisions, it was hardly to be expected that this statement of the law would not be followed. I should add that I cannot deduce from the authorities cited in *Karsales* that the proposition stated in the judgments could be regarded as in any way settled law.

In *Sze Hai Tong Bank Ltd.* v. *Rambler Cycle Co. Ltd.*, [1959] A.C. 576, I think that the ground of decision was that "The clause must therefore be limited and modified to the extent necessary to enable effect to be given to the main object and intent of the contract." applying *Glynn* v. *Margetson & Co.*, [1893] A.C. 351. But in delivering the judgment of the Board Lord Denning made some observations about deliberate breach. He said, [1959] A.C. 576, 587:

"And they deliberately disregarded one of the prime obligations of the contract. No court can allow so fundamental a breach to pass unnoticed under the cloak of a general exemption clause"

and later (p. 588):

"The self-same distinction runs through all the cases where a fundamental breach has disentitled a party from relying on an exemption clause. In each of them there will be found a breach which evinces a deliberate disregard of his bounden obligations."

Then he cited *Bontex Knitting Works Ltd.* v. *St. John's Garage*, [1943] 2 All E.R. 690; *Alexander* v. *Railway Executive*, [1951] 2 K.B. 882, and *Karsales (Harrow) Ltd.* v. *Wallis* and added ([1959] A.C. 576, 589):

"In each of those cases it could reasonably be inferred that the servant or agent deliberately disregarded one of the prime obligations of the contract. He was entrusted by the principal with the performance of the contract on his behalf: and his action could properly be treated as the action of his principal. In each case it was held that the principal could not take advantage of the exemption clause. It might have been different if the servant or agent had been merely negligent or inadvertent."

Yeoman Credit Ltd. v. *Apps* was another case of hire-purchase of a car with an exemption clause similar to that in *Karsales*. Holroyd Pearce L.J. quoted the passages from the judgments in *Karsales* to which I have referred, and later on in his judgment he referred to:

"such a non-performance or repudiation or breach going to the root of the contract as disentitles the owners to take refuge behind an exception clause intended only to give protection to those breaches which are not inconsistent with and not destructive of the whole essence of the contract."

Charterhouse Credit Ltd. v. *Tolly*, [1963] 2 Q.B. 683, was a similar case but with more complicated facts. It had been argued that the exemption clause was not sufficiently clear to be given effect. Donovan L.J. said (p. 702):

"I do not find it necessary to determine the true construction of this clause, for even if it bears the construction contended for by the finance company, I am of the opinion that it is of no avail to it in this case. As has been often said in recent years, a fundamental breach of contract, that is, one which goes to its very root, disentitles the party in breach from relying on the provisions of an exempting clause."

and he gives *Karsales* as his authority.

There was a finding that the hirer had elected to treat the contract as still on foot and it was argued that therefore he must be as much bound by the exemption clause as by any other clause. On this matter Donovan L.J. said (p. 704):

"The point is, apparently, free from direct authority, but, on principle, the election by the hirer of one remedy for the fundamental breach, instead of another remedy, ought, as I see it, to make no difference to the ineffectiveness of an exempting clause in face of such a breach. However this may be, two decisions of the House of Lords exist where one party to a contract elected to treat it as still subsisting despite a fundamental breach by the other, and succeeded in obtaining damages for such breach despite the existence in the contract of an exempting clause similar to clause 5 here. One is *Pollock & Co. v. Macrae*, [1922] S.C (H.L.) 192, and the other *Wallis, Son & Wells* v. *Pratt & Haynes*, [1911] A.C. 394. The contention I am now considering was not specifically raised in either case, but it is impossible to think that, if valid, it would have been overlooked not only by the parties sued, but by all the courts before which the two cases came."

Upjohn L.J. said (p. 709):

"The authorities establish that where there is a breach of a fundamental term the person in breach cannot rely on clauses of exclusion to protect him as against the other party. But the company said with some force that that is so, no doubt, when the innocent party treats the contract as repudiated, but that if he elects to affirm the contract, then he must take the benefit of the contract subject to all its provisions, including a clause of exclusion, and he can no longer plead that the finance company, though in breach of a fundamental term, cannot rely on a clause of exclusion. That is not, I think, an easy question, and there appears to be no authority where the matter has been expressly decided. If I am right in the analysis of this fundamental term, that it really stems from the fact that the finance company must lend that which it contracts to lend and not something which is essentially different, it seems to me that the principle must apply whether it is a case of repudiation accepted by the hirer or whether he affirms the contract and sues for damages."

This was substantially repeated by him in *Astley Industrial Trust Ltd.* v. *Grimley*, [1963] 2 All E.R. 33, 46. My noble and learned friend gave the example of a contract for delivery of a tractor and delivery instead of Suffolk Punch horses. I would be inclined to think that that was not delivery under the contract at all, but that it was an offer of a new contract on terms to be implied.

I do not think that either of the two cases to which Lord Donovan referred is of assistance in this connection. In each it was held that on a true construction the exempting clause was not wide enough to apply to the breach. In *Pollock & Co.* v. *Macrae* Lord Dunedin said:

"Such conditions to be effectual must be most clearly and unambiguously expressed, as is always necessary in cases where a well-known common law liability is sought to be avoided."

Then he referred to *London & North Western Railway Co.* v. *Neilson*, [1922] 2 A.C. 263, and continued:

"Reading the clauses in this light, I am of opinion that, although they excuse from damage flowing from the insufficiency of a part or parts of the machinery, they have no application to damage arising when there has been total breach of contract by failing to supply the article truly contracted for."

In *Wallis, Son & Wells* v. *Pratt & Haynes* an inferior variety of seed was delivered but the buyer did not discover this until it was too late to reject the goods: so he sued for damages. The contract included the clause "sellers give no warranty express or implied" but it was held that this was not wide enough in its terms to apply to breach of a condition. In neither case was there any question of cutting down of limiting the application of a clause apparently wide enough to apply to the breach. Both really turned on pure construction.

In *U.G.S. Finance Ltd.* v. *National Mortgage Bank of Greece and National Bank of Greece, S.A.*, [1964] 1 Lloyd's Rep. 446, the question related to a condition to the effect that interest coupons were forfeited if not presented within six years. Lord Denning repeated in substance what he had said in *Karsales* and added:

"The doctrine does not depend on the customer electing to disaffirm the contract. Usually he has no option open to him. The contract has been broken irretrievably before he gets to know of it, and the only course for him is to sue for the breach. So the point does not very often arise. But even if he does get to know of it, in time to affirm or disaffirm, he can still treat the contract as in being, and sue for the breach (without being defeated by the exemption clause) provided always that the breach itself is continuing to operate and cause damage to him."

A different view was expressed by Pearson L.J.:

"As to the question of 'fundamental breach', I think there is a rule of construction that normally an exception or exclusion clause or similar provision in a contract should be construed as not applying to a situation created by a fundamental breach of the contract. This is not an independent rule of law imposed by the court on the parties willy-nilly in disregard of their contractual intention. On the contrary it is a rule of construction based on the presumed intention of the contracting parties. It involves the implication of a term to give to the contract that business efficacy which the parties as reasonable men must have intended it to have. This rule of construction is not new in principle but it has become prominent in recent years in consequence of the tendency to have standard forms of contract containing exceptions clauses drawn in extravagantly wide terms, which would produce absurd results if applied literally."

If this new rule of law is to be adopted, how far does it go? In its simplest form it would be that a party is not permitted to contract out of common law liability for a fundamental breach. If that were right then a demurrage clause could not stand as limiting liability for loss resulting from a fundamental breach: and the same would apply to any clause providing for liquidated damages. I do not suppose that anyone has intended that this rule should go quite so far as that. But I would find it difficult to say just where the line would have to be drawn.

In my view no such rule of law ought to be adopted. I do not take that view merely because any such rule is new or because it goes beyond what can be done by developing or adapting existing principles. Courts have often introduced new rules when, in their view, they were required by public policy. In former times when Parliament seldom amended the common law, that could hardly have been avoided. And there are recent examples although, for reasons which I gave in *Shaw* v. *Director of Public Prosecutions,* [1962] A.C. 220, I think that this power ought now to be used sparingly. But my main reason is that this rule would not be a satisfactory solution of the problem which undoubtedly exists.

Exemption clauses differ greatly in many respects. Probably the most objectionable are found in the complex standard conditions which are now so common. In the ordinary way the customer has no time to read them, and if he did read them he would probably not understand them. And if he did understand and object to any of them, he would generally be told he could take it or leave it. And if he then went to another supplier the result would be the same. Freedom to contract must surely imply some choice or room for bargaining.

At the other extreme is the case where parties are bargaining on terms of equality and a stringent exemption clause is accepted for a quid pro quo or other good reason. But this rule appears to treat all cases alike. There is no indication in the recent cases that the courts are to consider whether the exemption is fair in all the circumstances or is harsh and unconscionable or whether it was freely agreed by the customer. And it does not seem to me to be satisfactory that the decision must always go one way if, e.g., defects in a car or other goods are just sufficient to make the breach of contract a fundamental breach, but must always go the other way if the defects fall just short of that. This is a complex problem which intimately affects millions of people and it appears to me that its solution should be left to Parliament. If your Lordships reject this new rule there will certainly be a need for urgent legislative action but that is not beyond reasonable expectation.

I have no doubt that exemption clauses should be construed strictly and I think that this case must be decided by considering whether there is any ground for adopting any but the natural meaning of the demurrage clause. Having provided for the calculation of the laydays and for extension of the laydays when delays are caused by various events for which the charterer is not responsible, clause 3 of the charterparty continues:

> "If longer delayed charterer to pay $1,000 U.S. currency payable in the same manner as the freight per running day (or pro rata for part thereof) demurrage, if sooner dispatched vessel to pay charterer or his agents $500 U.S. currency per day (or pro rata for part thereof) dispatch money for lay time saved."

It is impossible to hold that these words are not wide enough to apply to the circumstances of the present case, whether or not there was fundamental breach. So the only question is whether there is any reason for limiting their scope. The authorities are against the appellants, but, even putting them aside, I can find no such reason. The appellants chose to agree to what they now say was an inadequate sum for demurrage, but that does not appear to me to affect the construction of this clause. Even if one assumes that the $1,000 per day was inadequate and was known to both parties to be inadequate when the contract was made, I do not think that it can be said that giving to the clause its natural meaning could lead to an absurdity or could defeat the main object of the contract or could for any other reason justify cutting down its scope. If there was a fundamental breach the appellants elected that the contract should continue and they did so in the knowledge that this clause would continue. On the whole matter I am of opinion that this appeal fails and that the questions should be answered as my noble and learned friend proposes.

. . .

Lord Wilberforce. My Lords, I agree that the present appeal, in so far as it is based upon the reasons advanced in the original case lodged by the appellants, must fail and I do not find it necessary to add to the reasons for so finding given by Mocatta J. and the Court of Appeal. It is only upon the submissions contained in the appellants' supplementary case that I desire to add some observations, since these involve some issues of general importance in the law of contract.

The nature of the appellants' contentions can most conveniently be seen from the answer which they suggest should be given to the questions stated in the consultative case. To the first question (which is whether the owners can recover damages suffered by reason of the respondents having failed to load and discharge the vessels within laydays, whereby the charterparty was rendered less profitable to the owners by consequent loss of voyages or voyage time) the appellants suggest the qualified answer "Yes, if the detention of the vessel was a deviation from, or a repudiation or fundamental breach of, the charterparty. Otherwise, no." And they suggest that the same answer should be given to the second question which is based upon the assumption that such loss of profitability resulted from the respondents having deliberately (i.e., with the wilful intention of limiting the number of contractual voyages) failed to load and/or discharge the vessel within the laydays.

In amplification of this, the appellants submit that the qualification appearing in the suggested answer would apply, first, if the detention of the vessel caused by the respondents' breaches of contract was in the aggregate so long as to frustrate the commercial purpose of the charterparty, or, secondly, if that detention was deliberate, in the special sense used in the consultative case. Whether either of these situations existed would be for the arbitrators to find. I am prepared to deal with the submissions of law so made upon the assumption that it is open to the arbitrators so to find that they might do so.

The appellants' main argument in law is formulated as follows: First, they say that a breach of contract which goes to the root of the contract or which conflicts with its main purpose is a deviation from or a repudiation or fundamental breach of such contract. Secondly, they contend that exceptions clauses do not apply to breaches which are deviations from or repudiations or fundamental breaches of the contract. These propositions contain in themselves implicitly or explicitly several distinct lines of argument. It is necessary to separate the strands before attempting to examine them.

It is convenient first to segregate the reference to what is sometimes (and conveniently) described as the main purpose rule. This is a rule of construction, a classic statement of which is found in Lord Halsbury's speech in *Glynn* v. *Margetson & Co.*: it can be summed up in his words:

> "Looking at the whole of the instrument, and seeing what one must regard, as its main purpose, one must reject words, indeed whole provisions, if they are inconsistent with what one assumes to be the main purpose of the contract."

The decision in that case was that printed words in a document intended to be used in a variety of contracts of affreightment between a variety of ports ought to be restricted so as to be consistent with the purpose of the particular charterparty which was for a voyage from Malaga to Liverpool. There is no difficulty as to this, and I shall consider in due course whether it has any application to the relevant clause (i.e., the demurrage clause) in the contract.

Next for consideration is the argument based on "fundamental breach" or, which is presumably the same thing, a breach going "to the root of the contract." These expressions are used in the cases to denote two quite different things, namely, (i) a performance totally different from that which the contract contemplates, (ii) a breach of contract more serious than one which would entitle the other party merely to damages and which (at least) would entitle him to refuse performance or further performance under the contract.

Both of these situations have long been familiar in the English law of contract; and it will have to be considered whether the conception of "fundamental breach" extends beyond them. What is certain is that to use the expression without distinguishing to which of these, or to what other, situations it refers is to invite confusion.

The importance of the difference between these meanings lies in this, that they relate to two separate questions which may arise in relation to any contract. These are (as to (i)) whether an "exceptions" clause contained in the contract applies as regards a particular breach and (as to (ii)) whether one party is entitled to elect to refuse further performance.

The appellants, in their submission that exceptions clauses do not apply to "fundamental breaches" or "repudiations" confuse these two questions. There is in fact no necessary coincidence between the two kinds of (so-called fundamental) breach. For, though it may be true generally, if the contract contains a wide exceptions clause, that a breach sufficiently serious to take the case outside that clause, will also give the other party the right to refuse further performance, it is not the case, necessarily, that a breach of the latter character has the former consequence. An act which, apart from the exceptions clause, might be a breach sufficiently serious to justify refusal of further performance, may be reduced in effect, or made not a breach at all, by the terms of the clause.

The present case is concerned with the application of what may be said (with what justice will be later considered) to be an exceptions clause to a possible type of "fundamental breach." I treat the words "exceptions clause" as covering broadly such clauses in a contract as profess to exclude or limit, either quantitatively or as to the time within which action must be taken, the right of the injured party to bring an action for damages. Such a clause must, ex hypothesi, reflect the contemplation of the parties that a breach of contract, or what apart from the clause would be a breach of contract, may be committed, otherwise the clause would not be there; but the question remains open in any case whether there is a limit to the type of breach which they have in mind. One may safely say that the parties cannot, in a contract, have contemplated that the clause should have so wide an ambit as in effect to deprive one party's stipulations of all contractual force: to do so would be to reduce the contract to a mere declaration of intent. To this extent it may be correct to say that there is a rule of law against the application of an exceptions clause to a particular type of breach. But short of this it must be a question of contractual intention whether a particular breach is covered or not and the courts are entitled to insist, as they do, that the more radical the breach the clearer must the language be if it is to be covered. As Lord Parmoor said in *Cunard Steamship Co. Ltd.* v. *Buerger*, [1927] A.C. 1, in relation to exception clauses:

> "[they] do not apply when...loss or damage has occurred outside the route or voyage contemplated by the parties when they entered the contract of carriage, unless the intention that such limitations should apply is expressed in clear and unambiguous language."

And in *The Cap Palos* Atkin L.J. similarly said:

> "I am far from saying that a contractor may not make a valid contract that he is not to be liable for any failure to perform his contract, including even wilful default; but he must use very clear words to express that purpose..."

In application to more radical breaches of contract, the courts have sometimes stated the principle as being that a "total breach of the contract" disentitles a party to rely on exceptions clauses. This formulation has its use so long as one understands it to mean that the clause cannot be taken to refer to such a breach but it is not a universal solvent: for it leaves to be decided what is meant by a "total" breach for this purpose — a departure from the contract? but how great a departure?; a delivery of something or a performance different from that promised? but how different? No formula will solve this type of question and one must look individually at the nature of the contract, the character of the breach and its effect upon future performance and expectation and make a judicial estimation of the final result.

A few illustrations from three groups of decided cases may explain how the courts have dealt with this problem.

(i) Supply of a different article: As long ago as 1838, where the contract provided for the supply of peas, but beans were delivered, Lord Abinger C.B. explained the difference between this case and a breach of "condition": "The contract is to sell peas, and if he sends him anything else in their stead, it is a non-performance of it." (*Chanter* v. *Hopkins* (1838), 4 M. & W. 339, 404). This was followed (after the Sale of Goods Act, 1893), in *Pinnock Brothers* v. *Lewis & Peat Ltd.*, [1923] 1 K.B. 690 (copra cake) and Pearson L.J. accepted the principle, while modernising the illustration (chalk for cheese) in *U.G.S. Finance Ltd.* v. *National Mortgage Bank of Greece and National Bank of Greece, S.A..* Since the contracting parties could hardly have been supposed to contemplate such a mis-performance, or to have provided against it without destroying the whole contractual substratum, there is no difficulty here in holding exception clauses to be inapplicable.

(ii) Hire purchase cases: In several recent decisions, the courts have been able to hold wide exception clauses inapplicable by finding that what was delivered was totally different from that promised. Such are *Karsales (Harrow) Ltd.* v. *Wallis* and *Charterhouse Credit Co. Ltd.* v. *Tolly*. These cases, and others, follow the judgment of Devlin J. in *Smeaton Hanscomb & Co.* v. *Sassoon I. Setty & Co. (No. 1)* where he expressed the test as being whether there was a performance totally different from that contemplated by the contract. In some of these cases difficult questions of fact have arisen in deciding whether there is the total difference, or merely a serious breach of contract, as can be seen by comparing the *Karsales* case with *Astley Indus-*

trial Trust Ltd. v. *Grimley* and some doubt may be felt whether the right result on the facts was reached in *Charterhouse Credit Co. Ltd.* v. *Tolly:* but the principle is well in line with that of the cases mentioned under (i).

(iii) Marine cases relating to deviation: There is a long line of authority the commencement of which is usually taken from the judgment of Tindal C.J. in *Davis* v. *Garrett* (1830), 6 Bing. 716, which shows that a shipowner who deviates from an agreed voyage, steps out of the contract, so that clauses in the contract (such as exceptions or limitation clauses) which are designed to apply to the contracted voyage are held to have no application to the deviating voyage. The basis for the rule was explained in *Stag Line Ltd.* v. *Foscolo, Mango & Co.*, [1932] A.C. 328, by Lord Russell of Killowen in these terms:

> "it was well settled before the Act [of 1924] that an unjustifiable deviation deprived a ship of the protection of exceptions. They only applied to the contract voyage."

In *The Cap Palos* Atkin L.J. had applied this principle to contracts generally, adopting for this purpose the formulation of Scrutton L.J. in *Gibaud* v. *Great Eastern Railway Company*, [1921] 2 K.B. 435:

> "The principle is well-known, and perhaps *Lilley* v. *Doubleday* (1881), 7 Q.B.D. 510, is the best illustration, that if you undertake to do a thing in a certain way, or to keep a thing in a certain place, with certain conditions protecting it, and have broken the contract by not doing the thing contracted for in the way contracted for, or not keeping the article in the place in which you have contracted to keep it, you cannot rely on the conditions which were only intended to protect you if you carried out the contract in the way which you had contracted to do it."

The words "intended to protect you" show quite clearly that the rule is based on contractual intention.

The conception, therefore, of "fundamental breach" as one which, through ascertainment of the parties' contractual intention, falls outside an exceptions clause is well recognised and comprehensible. Is there any need, or authority, in relation to exceptions clauses, for extension of it beyond this? In my opinion there is not. The principle that the contractual intention is to be ascertained — not just grammatically from words used, but by consideration of those words in relation to commercial purpose (or other purpose according to the type of contract) — is surely flexible enough, and though it may be the case that adhesion contracts give rise to particular difficulties in ascertaining or attributing a contractual intent, which may require a special solution, those difficulties need not be imported into the general law of contract nor be permitted to deform it.

The only new category of "fundamental breach" which in this context I understand to have been suggested in one of "deliberate" breaches. This most clearly appears in the Privy Council case of *Sze Hai Tong Bank Ltd.* v. *Rambler Cycle Co. Ltd.* The decision itself presents no difficulty and seems to have been based on construction: it was that an exceptions clause referring to "discharge" of the goods did not apply to a discharge wholly outside the contract, a case I would have thought well within the principle of the "deviation" cases. But the appellants rely on one passage in the judgment of the Board which seems to suggest that "deliberate" breaches may, of themselves, form a separate category, citing three previous English decisions. Two of them *Alexander* v. *Railway Executive* and *Karsales (Harrow) Ltd.* v.

Wallis (on which I have already commented) are straightforward cases of "total departure" from what is contractually contemplated and present no difficulty. The third *Bontex Knitting Works Ltd.* v. *St. John's Garage* does not appear to be based on the deliberate character of the breach. The decision may be justified on the basis that there was a breach of contract equivalent to a deviation, but if it goes beyond this I would regard it as of doubtful validity. The "deliberate" character of a breach cannot, in my opinion, of itself give to a breach of contract a "fundamental" character, in either sense of that word. Some deliberate breaches there may be of a minor character which can appropriately be sanctioned by damages: some may be, on construction, within an exceptions clause (for example, a deliberate delay for one day in loading). This is not to say that "deliberateness" may not be a relevant factor: depending on what the party in breach "deliberately" intended to do, it may be possible to say that the parties never contemplated that such a breach would be excused or limited: and a deliberate breach may give rise to a right for the innocent party to refuse further performance because it indicates the other party's attitude towards future performance. All these arguments fit without difficulty into the general principle: to create a special rule for deliberate acts is unnecessary and may lead astray.

I now come to the facts of the present case. First, it is necessary to decide what is the legal nature of the demurrage clause: is it a clause by which damages for breach of the contract are agreed in advance, a liquidated damages clause as such provisions are commonly called, or is it, as the appellants submit, a clause limiting damages? If it is the latter, the appellants are evidently a step nearer the point when they can invoke cases in which clauses of exception, or exemption, do not apply to particular breaches of contract. The appellants' strongest argument here rests upon the discrepancy which they assert to exist between the demurrage rate of $1,000 per diem and the freight rate for which the charterparty provides. The extent of the discrepancy is said to be shown by the difference between the appellants' claim for lost freight (which is of the order of $900,000 on one calculation and $600,000 on another) and the amount which they would receive under the demurrage provision, which is approximately $150,000. So, the argument runs, the $1,000 per diem cannot be a pre-estimate of damage: it must be a limit in the charterer's favour.

I am unable to accept this. Leaving aside that the figures quoted for lost freight represent merely the owners' claim, it must be borne in mind that the $1,000-a-day figure has to cover a number of possible events. There might have been delay for one day or a few days beyond the laytime, in which case the owners might, and probably would, lose nothing in the way of freight and only suffer through increased overheads in port. Even if a case were to arise where freight was lost, over a period of two years circumstances might well change which would affect adversely the owners' anticipated rate of profit. So I am far from satisfied that any such discrepancy has been shown between the agreed figure and reality as requires the conclusion that the clause is not what on its face it purports to be — particularly when one bears in mind that each side derives an advantage from having the figure fixed and so being assured of payment without the expense and difficulty of proof.

The form of the clause is, of course, not decisive, nor is there any rule of law which requires that demurrage clauses should be construed as clauses of liquidated damages; but it is the fact that the clause is expressed as one agreeing a figure, and not as imposing a limit: and as a matter of commercial opinion and practice demurrage clauses are normally regarded as liquidated damage clauses. . . .

The clause being, then, one which fixes, by mutual agreement, the amount of damages to be paid to the owners of the vessel if "longer detained" than is permitted by the contract, is there any reason why it should not apply in the present case in either of the assumed alternatives, i.e., either that the aggregated delays add up to a "frustrating" breach of contract, or that the delays were "deliberate" in the special sense? In answering these questions it is necessary to have in mind what happened. It appears that there was an initial dispute between the owners and the charterers in which the owners claimed that they were entitled to treat the charterers as having repudiated the charterparty. This dispute was resolved by an agreement on October 8, 1957, under which the charterers agreed to pay an agreed sum as demurrage, leaving it to arbitration to decide whether the owners' claim was correct and, if so, what damages they should recover. It was further agreed that the charterparty should be performed for the remainder of the agreed two-year period. The manner in which it was performed is set out in a schedule to the consultative case. There were eight voyages in all, the last terminating on March 7, 1959, three days before the termination date. It is as regards these eight voyages that it is claimed that the delays in question occurred. During the whole of the period, although the periods spent in port on either side of the Atlantic (in fact at Rotterdam and, in every case but the first, Newport News) must have been known to the owners, who must also have been in a position to ascertain the availability of cargo and of loading and discharging facilities, the owners took no steps which would indicate that they regarded the charterparty as repudiated: they did not sail their vessel away but allowed it to continue with further voyages and took demurrage at the agreed rate for the delays. So there is no question here of any termination of the contract having taken place. Is there, then, any basis upon which the owners can escape from their bargain as regards detention of the vessel? In my opinion there is not. The arbitrators can (on the assumptions required) only find that the breach of contract falls within one, or other, or both of the two stated categories, namely, that they "frustrate the commercial purpose of the charterparty," or that the delays were "deliberate" (in the special sense). In either case, why should not the agreed clause operate? Or what reason is there for limiting its application to such delays as fall short of such as "frustrate the commercial purpose" or such as are not "deliberate"? I can see no such reason for limiting a plain contractual provision, nor is there here any such conflict between the demurrage clause and the main purpose of the contract as to bring into play the doctrine of *Glynn* v. *Margetson & Co.* On a consideration of the nature of this clause, together with the events which took place, and in particular the fact that the owners did not during its currency put an end to the contract, I reach the conclusion that the owners are clearly bound by it and can recover no more than the appropriate amount of demurrage.

. . .

On the whole case, I would dismiss the appeal.

Appeal dismissed.

[Viscount Dilhorne, Lords Hodson and Upjohn agreed with the result reached by Lords Reid and Wilberforce.]

QUESTIONS

1. Suppose that the owners of the ship had, in the words of Lord Reid, "elected to treat the breach as a repudiation, bring the contract to an end and sue for damages", what would have happened? Specifically, what would have been the measure of damages?

2. How do you determine under Lord Reid's approach when the owners would have had the right to treat the breach as a repudiation? Is Lord Reid proposing some test that is different from that offered by Diplock L.J. in *Hong Kong Fir*?

3. Lord Wilberforce said, "One may safely say that the parties cannot, in a contract, have contemplated that the clause should have so wide an ambit as in effect to deprive one party's stipulations of all contractual force: to do so would be to reduce the contract to a mere declaration of intent. To this extent it may be correct to say that there is a rule of law against the application of an exceptions clause to a particular type of breach." How does one determine when this rule of law applies? Is this another side of the issue discussed by Cardozo C.J. in *Wood v. Lucy*?

HARBUTT'S PLASTICINE v. WAYNE TANK CO. LTD.

[1970] 1 All E.R. 225. Court of Appeal (England); Lord Denning M.R.,
Widgery and Cross L.JJ.

[The plaintiffs owned and operated a factory making plasticine. The defendants undertook to install a heated pipe that would carry stearine—the raw material of plasticine—from a heated tank to the place where it would be processed. The defendants installed a pipe made of a plastic called durapipe. The pipe was installed and an employee of the defendants switched on the heating coil. The durapipe melted and the stearine in it caught fire and the factory was destroyed. The plaintiffs' insurers paid the plaintiffs' losses and then, acting under their right of subrogation, sued the defendants. The trial judge found that the fire was caused by the fact that the use of durapipe was completely unsuitable for a heated pipe. He said that it should have been made of stainless steel. He said,

'In breach of their contract the defendants designed, supplied and erected a system which was thoroughly — I need not abstain from saying *wholly* — unsuitable for its purpose, incapable of carrying it out unless drastically altered, and certain to result not only in its own destruction but in considerable further destruction and damage... the supply of the useless and dangerous durapipe, coupled with the useless thermostat was a breach of the basic purpose which might be described as total, going to the root of the contract.']

Lord Denning (after stating the facts, continued): That is a plain finding that the defendants were guilty of a fundamental breach.

The construction of cl 15. Prima facie, therefore, the defendants are liable in damages for breach of contract — damages which the judge has assessed at £146,581. But the defendants say that their liability is limited to only £2,330 by reason of a condition of the contract. The contract was in writing and incorporated a set of printed conditions. The condition relied on by the defendants is in cl 15 (which deals with the liability of the defendants for accidents and damage *before* the installation has been taken over by the plaintiffs — which is, of course, this case). But I must set out cll 13 and 16 too.

'13. Time of taking over. The plant shall be deemed to have been taken over by you when erection is completed or on completion of test on site when included or one calendar month after it shall have been put into commercial use (whichever may be the earlier): Provided that in any case the plant shall be deemed to have been taken over at the expiration of two calendar months after we shall have given you written notice that it is complete, unless in the meanwhile tests shall have been made showing that it does not comply with the terms of the contract. The time of taking over shall not be delayed on account of additions, minor omissions or defects which do not materially affect the commercial use of the plant.

'15. Liability for accidents and damage. Until the goods shall have been taken over, or be deemed to have been taken over under Clause 13, our *sole* liability for accidents and damage is as follows: (1) We will indemnify you against direct damage or injury to your property or persons or that of others caused by the negligence of ourselves or of our servants, but *not otherwise,* to the extent of repairing the damage to property or compensating personal injury, provided that such damage or injury is not caused or does not arise wholly or partially from your acts or omissions or the acts or omissions of others, or is not due to circumstances over which we have no reasonable control, *provided always* that *our total liability* for loss, damage or injury *shall not exceed the total value of the contract.* (2)We will indemnify you against claims and actions brought against you by persons in our employ on the site under, and subject to the provisions of, the Workmen's Compensation Act, 1925, or other statute in force at the time dealing with employer's liability for injuries sustained by employees. We will not be liable for loss due to stoppage of machinery or for any other damage loss or injuries of any kind whatsoever. After such taking over all liability on our part for accidents and damage ceases.

'16. General liability and maintenance guarantee. Save as provided in Clause 8, in lieu of any warranty condition or liability implied by law, our liability in respect of any defect in or failure of the goods supplied, or for any loss injury or damage attributable thereto, is limited to making good by replacement or repair defects which, under proper use, appear therein and arise solely through faulty design, materials, or workmanship, within a period of twelve calendar months after such goods have been taken over or been deemed to have been taken over under Clause 13: Provided always that such defective parts are promptly returned free to our works unless otherwise arranged. The repaired or new parts will be delivered free within Railway Company's free delivery area and, in the case of goods not of our manufacture, you are entitled only to such benefits as we may receive under any guarantee given to us in respect thereof.'

I find these conditions difficult to construe, but I am inclined to agree with the judge's view of them, which I take to be this: cl 15 deals with the liability of the contractors, the defendants, *before* takeover, and, in particular, with their liability for the 'negligence' of themselves or their servants. During that time — before takeover, their men will be in and about the place, and may by their negligence do damage to somebody or something. The contractors will be liable *in tort* for the damage. Clause 15 is designed to limit their liability for it to the amount of the contract. Clause 16 deals with the liability of the contractors, the defendants, *after* takeover, and in particular for their liability for "faulty design, materials or workmanship". At that time their men will have left the place, but there may be defects in the design or materials which cause damage. The contractors will be liable *in contract* for the damage, see *Bagot v Stevens Scanlan & Co.,* [1966] 1 Q.B. 197. Clause 16 is designed to limit the liability to replacement or repair.

Seeing that those are the broad lines of the two clauses, I would be inclined to read cl 15 as the judge did, namely, as limited to accidents and damage done in the course of carrying out the work of erection, eg lorries running away, workmen dropping tools, and so forth. The *sole* liability of the defendants for *such* accidents and damage is when they are caused by the negligence of themselves or their servants, but *not otherwise,* ie not when they are caused by the negligence of sub-contractors or third persons, nor when they happen without negligence on the part of anyone. On this reading of cl 15 it does not apply to damage done by breach of contract, such as faulty design. It does not, therefore, cover this case.

But I am by no means confident of this interpretation of cl 15. So far I am not prepared to base my judgment on it, as the judge did. But I do think that it is a possible interpretation, and, as such, it means at least that cl 15 is ambiguous. If it is ambiguous, then on all the authorities, it does not avail the defendants. They cannot, by a printed clause like this, exclude or limit their liability, unless the words are clear and unambiguous.

Fundamental breach. Assuming that cl 15 does, in terms, purport to limit the liability of the defendants, the next question is whether the defendants were guilty of a fundamental breach of contract which disentitled them from relying on it. I eschew in this context the word "repudiation" because it is applied so differently in so many different contexts, as Lord Wright explained in *Heyman v. Darwins Ltd.*, [1942] A.C. 356. There was no repudiation in this case by the defendants — not, at any rate, in its proper sense of denying they are bound by the contract. The defendants have always acknowledged the contract. All that has happened is that they have broken it. If they have broken it in a way that goes to the very root of it, then it is a fundamental breach. If they have broken it in a lesser way, then the breach is not fundamental.

In considering the consequences of a fundamental breach, it is necessary to draw a distinction between a fundamental breach which still leaves the contract open to be performed and a fundamental breach which itself brings the contract to an end.

(i) *The first group.* In cases where the contract is still open to be performed, the effect of a fundamental breach is this: it gives the innocent party, when he gets to know of it, an option either to *affirm* the contract or to disaffirm it. If he elects to *affirm* it, then it remains in being *for the future* on both sides. Each has a right to sue for damages for *past or future* breaches. If he elects to disaffirm it (ie accepts the fundamental breach as determining the contract), then it is at an end from that moment. It does not continue into the future. All that is left is the right to sue for past breaches or for the fundamental breach, but there is no right to sue for *future* breaches.

(ii) *The second group.* In cases where the fundamental breach itself brings the contract to an end, there is no room for any option in the innocent party. The present case is typical of this group. The fire was so disastrous that it destroyed the mill itself. If the fire had been accidental, it would certainly have meant that the contract was frustrated and brought to an end by a supervening event; just as in the leading case in 1861, when the Surrey Music Hall was burnt down, see *Taylor v. Caldwell.* At the time of the fire at this mill, the cause of it was not known. It might have been no one's fault. In that case the contract would plainly have been frustrated. It would have been automatically at an end, so far as the future was concerned, with no option on either side. Does it make any difference because, after many years, the cause of the fire has been found? It has been found to be the fault of the defendants. I cannot think that this makes any difference. The contract came to an end when the mill was burnt down. It came to an end by a frustrating event, without either side having an election to continue it. It is not to be revived simply because it has been found to be the fault of one of the parties. All that happens is that the innocent party can sue the guilty party for the breach.

All that I have said thus far is so obvious that it needs no authority. But now I come to the great question. When a contract is brought to an end by a fundamental breach by one of the parties, can the guilty party rely on an exclusion or limitation clause so as to avoid or limit his liability for the breach? I propose to take first the group of cases when the fundamental breach does not automatically bring the contract to an end, but it has to be accepted by the innocent party as doing so. Such a case was *Karsales (Harrow) Ltd. v. Wallis* where the hirer, on discovering the fundamental breach, at once rejected the car. In this group it is settled that, once he accepts it the innocent party can sue for the breach and the guilty party cannot rely on the exclusion or limitation clause. That clearly appears from the speeches in the House of Lords in *Suisse Atlantique Société d'Armement Maritime SA v NV Rotterdamsche Kolen Centrale.* Lord Reid said:

> 'If fundamental breach is established, the next question is what effect, if any, that has on the applicability of other terms of the contract. This question has often arisen with regard to clauses excluding liability, in whole or in part, of the party in breach. I do not think that there is generally much difficulty where the innocent party has elected to treat the breach as a repudiation, bring the contract to an end and sue for damages. Then the whole contract has ceased to exist, including the exclusion clause, and I do not see how that clause can then be used to exclude an action for loss which will be suffered by the innocent party after it has ceased to exist, such as loss of the profit which would have accrued if the contract had run its full term.'

And by Lord Upjohn:

> '... the principle on which one party to a contract cannot rely on the clauses of exception or limitation of liability inserted for his sole protection ... [is that] if there is a fundamental breach accepted by the innocent party, the contract is at an end; the guilty party cannot rely on any special terms in the contract.'

When their Lordships said the contract 'is at an end', they meant, of course, for the future. Such an ending disentitles the guilty party from relying on an exclusion clause in respect of the breach.

Such then is established as law when there is a 'fundamental breach accepted by the innocent party', that is, when the innocent party has an *election* to treat the contract as at an end and does so. The position must, I think, be the same when the defendant has been guilty of such a fundamental breach that the contract is *automatically* at an end without the innocent party having an election. The innocent party is entitled to sue for damages for the breach and the guilty party cannot rely on the exclusion or limitation clause: for the simple reason that he, by his own breach, has brought the contract to an end; with the result that he cannot rely on the clause to exempt or limit his liability for that breach. ...

The one question in this case is, therefore: were the defendants guilty of a fundamental breach which brought the contract to an end? for, if so, they cannot rely on the limitation clause. It was suggested that, in order to determine whether a breach is fundamental or not, one must look at the quality of it, and not at the results. I do not accept this suggestion. It is not the breach itself which counts so much, but the event resulting from it. A serious breach may have slight consequences. A trivial breach grave ones. Take this very case. The specification of durapipe was, no doubt, a serious breach; but it would not have done much harm if it had been discovered in time and replaced by stainless steel. In that event the plaintiffs could not repudiate the contract or treat it as at an end. But it did, in fact, do great harm because of the consequences. The results were so grave as to bring the contract to an end. One must, therefore, look not only at the breach but also at the results of it. Diplock LJ made that clear in *Hong Kong Fir Shipping Co. Ltd. v. Kawasaki Kisen Kaisha Ltd.*, when he pointed out that it is the '*the event resulting from the breach* which relieved the other party of further performance of his obligations'.

So I come to the question: were the breaches by the defendants and the consequences of them so fundamental as to bring the contract to an end, and thus disentitle the defendants to rely on the limitation clause? The learned judge thought that they were. I agree with him. I think that the case is very like *Pollock & Co. v. Macrae* except that instead of 'a congeries of defects' there is 'a congeries of faults'. The words of Lord Dunedin are applicable. 'Now, when there is such a congeries of defects as to destroy the workable character of the machine, I think this amounts to a total breach of contract' which prevents the suppliers from relying on the conditions.

Before leaving this part of the case, I would just like to say what, in my opinion, is the result of the *Suisse Atlantique* case, It affirms the long line of cases in this court that when one party has been guilty of a fundamental breach of the contract, that is, a breach which goes to the very root of it, and the other side accepts it, so that the contract comes to an end — or if it comes to an end anyway by reason of the breach — then the guilty party cannot rely on an exception or limitation clause to escape from his liability for the breach.

If the innocent party, on getting to know of the breach, does not accept it, but keeps the contract in being (as in *Charterhouse Credit Co. Ltd. v. Tolly*) then it is a matter of construction whether the guilty party can rely on the exception or limitation clause, always remembering that it is not to be supposed that the parties intended to give a guilty party a blanket to cover up his own misconduct or indifference, or to enable him to turn a blind eye to his obligations. The courts may reject, as matter of construction, even the widest exemption clause if it:

> '... would lead to an absurdity, or because it would defeat the main object of the contract or perhaps for other reasons. And where some limit must be read into the clause, it is generally reasonable to draw the line at fundamental breaches,'

per Lord Reid. So, in the name of construction, we get back to the principle that, when a company inserts in printed conditions an exception clause purporting to exempt them from all and every breach, that is not readily to be construed or considered as exempting them from liability for a fundamental breach; for the good reason that it is only intended to avail them when they are carrying out the contract in substance; and not when they are breaking it in a manner which goes to the very root of the contract.

Replacement or indemnity. A question was raised on the measure of damages. The plaintiffs were not allowed to rebuild the old mill (which was five storeys high) for use as a factory. They had to put up a new factory of two storeys. But it had no more accommodation. Are they entitled to the actual cost of replacement? or are they limited to the difference in value of the old mill before and after the fire?

The figures were agreed:

	Cost of Reinstatement £	Difference in Value £
Buildings	67,973	42,538
Stock	17,324	17,324
Loss of Profit	21,000	21,000
Plant & Machinery	40,284	35,923
	146,581	116,785

The defendants said that it should be the difference in value before and after the fire.... The plaintiffs said that it should be the cost of replacement....

The destruction of a building is different from the destruction of a chattel. If a secondhand car is destroyed, the owner only gets its value; because he can go into the market and get another secondhand car to replace it. He cannot charge the other party with the cost of replacing it with a new car. But, when this mill was destroyed, the plaintiffs had no choice. They were bound to replace it as soon as they could, not only to keep their business going, but also to mitigate the loss of profit (for which they would be able to charge the defendants). They replaced it in the only possible way, without adding any extras. I think they should be allowed the cost of replacement. True it is they got new for old, but I do not think the wrongdoer can diminish the claim on that account. If they had added extra accommodation or made extra improvements, they would have to give credit. But that is not this case.

I think the judge was right on this point.

Interest. The plaintiffs received considerable sums from their insurance company soon after the fire: £50,000 within eight weeks, and so forth. Are those to be taken into account in awarding interest? The plaintiffs say that the court should ignore the fact that they were insured, or have received insurance moneys, and should give them full interest as if they had paid the cost of replacement out of their own pocket or borrowed money for the purpose. I think this goes too far. In assessing damages, we ignore, of course, the fact that the plaintiffs are insured. But, in awarding interest, it is different. An award of interest is discretionary. It seems to me that the basis of an award of interest is that the defendant has kept the plaintiff out of his money; and the defendant has had the use of it himself. So he ought to compensate the plaintiff accordingly. This reasoning does not apply when the plaintiff has not been kept out of his money but has in fact been indemnified by an insurance company. I do not think that the plaintiff should recover interest for himself on the money when he has not been kept out of it. The receipt from the insurance company should go in relief of the defendants. The wind should be tempered to the shorn lamb. The judge did relieve the defendants somewhat, but he did not do it very scientifically. I would prefer to ask him to reassess it. He should take the date when the defendants ought in all the circumstances to have paid the sum awarded (such as the letter before action or the writ) and make them pay interest from that date, but he should take into account the fact that the plaintiffs had already received substantial sums from the insurance company; and award interest on the balance only. That would be, I expect, a great deal less than the £26,385 which he did award.

I would, therefore, remit this question of interest to the judge, but otherwise affirm his decision in its entirety.

Widgery L.J.: ... We have had our attention drawn to the decision of the House of Lords in *Suisse Atlantique Société v NV Rotterdamsche Kolen Centrale*, and it is not disputed that if the defendants committed a fundamental breach of the contract, which the plaintiffs accepted as amounting to a repudiation thereof, the result has been to put an end to the whole contract and deprive the defendants of the protection of cl 15. As Lord Reid said:

'If fundamental breach is established, the next question is what effect, if any, that has on the applicability of other terms of the contract. This question has often arisen with regard to clauses excluding liability, in whole or in part, of the party in breach. I do not think that there is generally much difficulty where the innocent party has elected to treat the breach as a repudiation, bring the contract to an end and sue for damages. Then the whole contract has ceased to exist including the exclusion clause...'

Counsel for the defendants contends that this is in substance a claim in negligence and that the defendants were guilty of no breach of contract save only that their duty to take care arose under the contract as well as at common law. He disputes that the defendants admitted fault in specifying durapipe was itself a breach of contract, because he contends that this was an experimental installation, in which errors were to be expected, and that it was the intention of the parties that the defendants should have the right to correct errors appearing at the final test. Hence it is contended that such design errors did not amount to a breach of contract unless they remained uncorrected after the equipment had been finally tested and handed over. I think that this might well have been the intention of the parties but it finds no place in the contract documents and I can see no sufficient material on which such a term could have been implied or assumed to have been incorporated by variation. Accordingly, it seems to me that the defendants were in breach of the contract when they completed the installation on 5th February since that installation was not reasonably suitable for its purpose and they had strictly no right to remove their difficulty by substituting stainless steel for durapipe and thus departing from another agreed term of the bargain.

If, however, these matters had come to light before the fire, this breach would not have been a fundamental one entitling the plaintiffs to determine the contract. The substitution of stainless steel for durapipe at that stage would have cost perhaps £150 and caused a delay of a few days. The plaintiffs could have had this work done by another contractor at the defendants' expense, but could not have set the whole contract aside. It is the fact that the defect was not discovered, thus providing the opportunity for the tapes to be energised and left unattended with the resultant fire, which has deprived the plaintiffs of the benefit of the work.

Counsel for the defendants further contends that in deciding whether a breach is a fundamental one it is necessary to look at the quality of the act which constitutes the breach rather than at the consequences which in fact flow from it. He says that if someone had chanced to visit the factory in the late evening of 5th February and had discovered that the pipes were overheating, the fire would have been avoided and no fundamental breach of contract would have occurred. The mere fact that the consequences of Mr Duncan's negligence proved to be so serious cannot, he argues, turn the defendants' breach into a fundamental one.

On this aspect of the case the plaintiffs rely on *Hong Kong Fir Shipping Co. Ltd. v Kawasaki Kisen Kaisha Ltd.*, where Diplock LJ said:

'Every synallagmatic contract contains in it the seeds of the problem: in what event will a party be relieved of his undertaking to do that which he has agreed to do but has not got done?... The test whether an event has this effect or not has been stated in a number of metaphors all of which I think amount to the same thing: does the occurrence of the event deprive the party who has further undertakings still to perform of substantially the whole benefit which it was the intention of the parties as expressed in the contract that he should obtain as the consideration for performing those undertakings? This test is applicable whether or not the event occurs as a result of the default of one of the parties to the contract, but the consequences of the event are different in the two cases. Where the event occurs as a result of the default of one party, the party in default cannot rely on it as relieving himself of the performance of any further undertakings on his part and the innocent party, although entitled to, need not treat the event as relieving him of the performance of his own undertakings... Where the event occurs as a result of the default of neither party, each is relieved of the further performance of his own undertakings...'

Diplock LJ continued:

'Once it is appreciated that it is the event and not the fact that the event is a result of a breach of contract which relieves the party not in default of further performance of his obligations, two consequences follow: (i) The test whether the event relied on has this consequence is the same whether the event is the result of the other party's breach of contract or not...'

Adopting this analysis it follows that the first step is to see whether an 'event' has occurred which has deprived the plaintiffs of substantially the whole benefit which they were to obtain under the contract. The fire was such an event because not only did it destroy the equipment installed by the defendants, but it also destroyed the factory, thus making replacement impracticable. The fire was caused by the defendants' breach of contract and the plaintiffs say that the contract is at an end on this account. It appears to follow from Diplock LJ's reasoning that if the event which occurs as a result of the defendants' breach is an event which would have frustrated the contract had it occurred without the fault of either party, then the breach is a fundamental breach for present purposes. In the present case the plaintiffs must be treated as having accepted the breach as a repudiation of the contract, since they had no alternative but to do so. In my judgment, therefore, the defendants are not entitled to rely on the limit of liability in cl 15.

I must now turn to the issues raised as to the measure of damage. The distinction between those cases in which the measure of damage is the cost of repair of the damaged article, and those in which it is the diminution in value of the article, is not clearly defined. In my opinion each case depends on its own facts, it being remembered, first, that the purpose of the award of damages is to restore the plaintiff to his position before the loss occurred, and secondly, that the plaintiff must act reasonably to mitigate his loss. If the article damaged is a motor car of popular make, the plaintiff cannot charge the defendant with the cost of repair when it is cheaper to buy a similar car on the market. On the other hand, if no substitute for the damaged article is available and no reasonable alternative can be provided, the plaintiff should be entitled to the cost of repair. It was clear in the present case that it was reasonable for the plaintiffs to rebuild their factory, because there was no other way in which they could carry on their business and retain their labour force. The plaintiffs rebuilt their factory to a substantially different design, and if this had involved expenditure beyond the cost of replacing the old, the difference might not have been recoverable, but there is no suggestion of this here. Nor do I accept that the plaintiffs must give credit under the heading of 'betterment' for the fact that their new factory is modern in design and materials. To do so would be the equivalent of forcing the plaintiffs to invest their money in the modernising of their plant which might be highly inconvenient for them. Accordingly, I agree with the sum allowed by the trial judge as the cost of replacement.

On the issue with regard to interest I agree with what has been said by Lord Denning MR and I agree with the order proposed by him.

[Cross L.J. gave a judgment to the same effect.]

QUESTIONS

1. What does it mean to say that the contract is "brought to an end"?
2. If the parties are free to allocate the risk of loss in cases where, apart from such allocation, the contract would be frustrated, why are they not free to allocate the risk of loss in cases where the "frustration" is brought about by the fault of one party?
3. Why should the court think that it can make a better allocation of the risk than the parties?
4. Does this case come within any of the classes discussed by Lord Wilberforce in *Suisse Atlantique*? In other words, is this a case of the delivery of peas instead of beans?

NOTE

When Wayne Tank was sued by Harbutt's Plasticine (actually by the latter's insurers under their rights of subrogation), Wayne Tank called on their insurers to defend them. Wayne Tank had two policies of insurance. The first was their primary insurance. This was placed with Employers' Liability Corporation. Wayne Tank also had a second policy. This is known as "umbrella insurance" and was intended to act as reserve insurance to cover whatever was not covered by the primary insurance. When the loss occurred at Harbutt's Plasticine and Wayne Tank was held liable for the loss, the loss was in fact paid by the reserve insurer (Insurance Co. of North America). The reserve insurer contended that the loss should have been paid by the primary insurer, and so the Insurance Company of North America sued Employers' Liability Corp. (The action was in the name of Wayne Tank, since the action was brought by the Ins. Co. of North America under their rights of subrogation.)

The policy that Wayne Tank had had with Employers' Liability contained an exclusion of liability clause:

"The company will not indemnify the Insured in respect of liability consequent upon... (5) death injury or damage caused by the nature or condition of any goods or the containers thereof sold or supplied by or on behalf of the Insured...'

The Court of Appeal held in *Wayne Tank v. Employers' Liability*, [1973] 3 All E.R. 825, that this clause was effective to protect the primary insurers from liability. There is no direct relation between the clause in the agreement between Wayne Tank and Harbutt's Plasticine and the clause in their insurance policy. However, it does seem likely that Wayne Tank sought to limit *their* liability because their insurance coverage was limited. The long-term effect of the decision in *Harbutt's Plasticine v. Wayne Tank* would then be to expose Wayne Tank's reserve insurer to far higher risks than this kind of insurance is designed to bear. The effect of this might lead to the cancellation of this coverage. (An increase in premium is possible but still leaves the insurer with an unknown risk).

The issue is then whether one can easily justify the decision in *Harbutt's Plasticine v. Wayne Tank* given the insurance coverage that the parties had arranged. One insurance company will have to bear the loss. The question is whether the right one had to bear the loss. If the risk is wrongly allocated by the court what are the economic effects of this?

LINTON v. C.N.R.

(1974), 49 D.L.R. (3d) 548. Supreme Court of Canada; Full Court.

Ritchie, J.: — This is an appeal from a judgment of the Appellate Division of the Supreme Court of Alberta, Smith, C.J.A., dissenting, which affirmed the judgment rendered at trial by Mr. Justice Lieberman and dismissed the appellant's claim for damages resulting from the alleged negligence of the respondent in delaying the delivery of a telegram containing the appellant's reduced tender for the construction of a bridge on the Alaska Highway.

The facts are not in dispute and have been made the subject of an agreed statement by the parties which discloses that the Department of Public Works had called for tenders on the construction of the bridge in question which were required to be made either by letter in writing or a telegram delivered to the Department in Vancouver. Telex messages were unacceptable and tenders were to close whether by way of original bid or alteration thereof by 11 o'clock, Vancouver time, on April 10, 1969. It further appears that the appellant, who had entered a bid, obtained a revised price for the steel on the evening of April 9th which enabled him to reduce his bid by $27,000 and there seems no doubt that if this bid had been received by the Department before 11 a.m. on April 10th, the contract would have been awarded to the appellant.

What in fact occurred was that Mr. Linton, the president of the appellant company, dispatched a telegram at the respondent's office in Fort Nelson, B.C., containing his revised bid with instructions that it should be sent to Vancouver on a rush basis, and owing to admitted negligence on the part of the defendant's servants, the message did not arrive until one hour after the close of tenders so that the contract was awarded elsewhere.

It is of significance that the appellant's telegram was made out on his company's notepaper and that the usual form ordinarily filled in by persons sending telegrams was not used.

The facts are fully set forth in the judgment of the Appellate Division, which is now reported in 24 D.L.R. (3d) 410, [1972] 3 W.W.R. 321, and I accordingly feel relieved of the necessity of recounting them in more detail.

The respondent invoked the provisions of certain orders of the Railway Commissioners for Canada as relieving it of all liability for the delay in transmission and it becomes necessary to consider the relevant orders. In the first place, Order 162 of March 30, 1916, which is reproduced at pp. 420-1 of 24 D.L.R. (3d), contained the following opening paragraphs:

> "**It Is Ordered** that the conditions of the telegraph forms used by telegraph companies subject to the jurisdiction of the Board on which messages to be transmitted are to be written, be, and they are hereby, approved as follows, namely:
> 'It is agreed between the sender of the message on the face of this form and this Company that said Company shall not be liable for damages arising from failure to transmit or deliver, or for any error in the transmission or delivery of any unrepeated telegram, whether happening from negligence of its servants or otherwise, or for delays from interruptions in the working of its lines, for errors in cypher or obscure messages, or for errors from illegible writing, beyond the amount received for sending the same.' "
>
> .   .   .

The argument advanced on behalf of the appellant hinges on the construction to be placed upon the first paragraph of Order 162 and particularly upon the inclusion in Order 49274 and Order T-40 of the opening words of that paragraph which read:

> It is agreed between the *sender of the message on the face of this form* and this Company that said Company shall not be liable for damages arising from failure to transmit or deliver, or for any error in the transmission or delivery of...

The italics are my own.

The appellant construes this language to mean that the terms and conditions in question can only be effective if they are set out in full on the reverse side of the form on which the message is to be transmitted and it is accordingly contended that where, as in this case, the message was written on the appellant's own notepaper with nothing on the reverse side of it, the respondent cannot rely on any of the limitations of liability prescribed in Order 49274.

In my view the words "the sender of the message on the face of this form and this Company" as they occur in Order 162 designate the parties to an agreement which becomes binding upon any person who sends a message on a form upon the reverse side of which certain "terms and conditions" are printed, but these words of themselves cannot be described as either "terms" or "conditions" and it is clear from the wording of Order 49274 that it was not the "form" referred to in Order 162 which was given the force of law as part of the *Railway Act* upon due publication in the *Canada Gazette*, but rather the "terms and conditions" contained on the reverse side thereof, and these "terms and conditions" thus became a part of the law of Canada whether endorsed on the reverse side of the form used by the sender or not.

It is not disputed that the telegram in question was an "unrepeated telegram" and it follows from the above that the respondent was relieved

> ... for damages arising from failure to transmit or deliver, or for any error in the transmission or delivery of any unrepeated telegram, whether happening from negligence of its servants or otherwise, or for delays from interruptions in the working of its lines...

For all these reasons, as well as for those set forth in the reasons for judgment of Mr. Justice Allen, I would dismiss this appeal with costs.

Since writing the above I have had the opportunity of reading the reasons for judgment prepared for delivery by the Chief Justice and Mr. Justice Spence, both of whom appear to take the view that the delay in delivering the "telegraph message" here in question and its ultimate delivery in telex form, which the company's agent at Port George had been told was unacceptable to the addressee, constituted a "fundamental breach of the contract" which no exemption clause could excuse.

The Chief Justice, in referring to the exemption clause contained in the relevant Order of the Commission [at p. 551, *supra*] observes:

> It is to me a rather monstrous proposition, if it is seriously advanced, that Parliament in its legislation authorized total immunity from liability to be conferred upon a carrier which, under its cover, could decide when and if it would send a requested telegram.

I think I should say that I am unable to construe the agreed statement of facts as affording any basis for advancing such a proposition and no such construction has in any way contributed to the conclusion which I have reached.

My understanding of the facts as disclosed by the statement is that the delay in the delivery of the message and the mistake in delivering it in telex form were due to negligence on the part of the respondent's servants. A telegraph message was dispatched and through negligence it arrived an hour late and in the wrong form.

There is, in my view, a wide difference between negligent performance of a contract and fundamental breach. Cases such as *Karsales (Harrow), Ltd. v. Wallis,* [1956] 2 All E.R. 866, where the defendant had agreed to purchase a car which was in excellent condition and was delivered one which was virtually a wreck, exemplify the kind of situation in which a breach going to the root of the contract may exclude reliance on an exemption clause. Under such circumstances it can be said that the contract has not been performed at all, whereas the present case is one of negligent performance.

The case of *Suisse Atlantique Société D'Armement Maritime S.A. v. N.V. Rotterdamsche Kolen Centrale,* [1966] 2 All E.R. 61, is one of many authorities indicating that although in cases of ambiguity an exemption clause is to be strictly construed against the party relying on it, it is nevertheless to be given full force and effect if the language in which it is drafted is sufficiently clear to leave no doubt as to its meaning.

Clauses providing for exemption for negligence in the performance of a contract are not rare and the terms and conditions which Order 49274 of the Board of Transport Commissioners prescribes for the transmission of "telegraph messages" by telegraph companies appear to me to be unambiguous in this regard. By the first of these terms it is stipulated that

> ... the said Company shall not be liable for damages arising from failure to transmit or deliver, or for any error in the transmission or delivery of any unrepeated telegram, whether happening from negligence of its servants or otherwise...

It does not appear to me that this phraseology is capable of any other meaning than that one of the terms on which the company accepts "telegraph messages" is that it will not be responsible for damages arising from the negligence of its servants if the message is in the form of an "unrepeated telegram" as it was in this case. In my view, if there were any doubt as to what was meant, it is resolved by reference to the provisions of the succeeding term of the conditions adopted by the Board's Order. That term reads:

> To guard against error, the Company will repeat back any telegram for an extra payment of one-half the regular rate; and, in that case, the Company shall be liable for damages suffered by the sender to an extent not exceeding $200.00, due to the negligence of the Company in the transmission or delivery of the telegram.

This must, in my view, mean that the company is not liable for damages due to negligence in the transmission of a telegram unless it is dispatched after the making of an extra payment of one-half of the regular rate, and the intention of the Board is made even more explicit by the next term of the conditions which provides that "correctness in the transmission and delivery of the message can be ensured by contract in writing…".

As I have indicated, in my opinion, the terms and conditions to which I have referred expressly exempt the defendant company from liability for any damages which the plaintiff may have suffered arising from error in the transmission and delivery of the telegraph message which Mr. Linton handed to the defendant's employee at Fort Nelson on April 10, 1969.

[Martland, Judson, Pigeon and De Grandpré, JJ. concur with Ritchie J.]

Spence J. dissenting: The terms and conditions as approved by the Board under its General Order 162 which were prescribed by Order 49274 commence with the words: "It is ordered that the conditions of the telegraph forms used by telegraph companies subject to the jurisdiction of the Board be and they are hereby approved as follows". And then the first paragraph commences with the words "It is agreed between the sender of the message on the face of this form and this company…". Surely, therefore, what the Board did by Order 49274 was to prescribe conditions and those conditions were that the sender of the telegram and the company should agree in a certain manner and that it is a proper inference that that agreement should be communicated to the sender by reference to the form setting out the terms and conditions.

. . .

In para. 19 of the agreed statement of facts it was agreed that "unless the limitation of liability is effective in the circumstances, the Defendant is liable to the Plaintiff for such loss and damage as may be established by the Plaintiff on an assessment of damages or agreed upon between the parties". The respondent, therefore, has agreed that the limitations and conditions do deprive the plaintiff of remedies to which it would be entitled at common law. Allen, J.A., in giving reasons for the majority in the Appellate Division, said: "Obviously the intent of Order 49274 was that the Board itself would prescribe the terms and conditions of what might be termed a statutory contract…". In interpreting that contract, the well-established rule as to the interpretation of contracts cutting down common law rights must be considered.

Byles, J., said in *R. v. Morris* (1867), L.R. 1 C.C.R. 90 at p. 94: "… to construe a statute in conformity with the common law, rather than against it, except where or so far as the statute is plainly intended to alter the course of the common law." This was a sound rule.

Coleridge, J., in *R. v. Benjamin Scott* (1856), 25 L.J.M.C. 128 at p. 133, said:

> How, then, upon general principles are we to proceed in a seeming conflict between the common law and these provisions of the statute? Not, I apprehend,

by assuming at once that there is a real conflict, and sacrificing the common law, but by carefully examining whether the two may not be reconciled, and full effect be given to both.

In *National Assistance Board v. Wilkinson,* [1952] 2 Q.B. 648, Devlin, J., said at p. 661:

> It is a well-established principle of construction that a statute is not to be taken as effecting a fundamental alteration in the general law unless it uses words that point unmistakably to that conclusion.

In the present case, if the words of Order 49274 were given the broad interpretation which the Courts below have given to them, there would be a very material derogation of the appellant's common law rights. The words do not require such an interpretation and, in fact, may be considered to be quite ambiguous. The evil which the Order was intended to cure was not one which affects the appellant's situation but rather the position of a person who telephones in to the telegraph office a message; and as I have said it was sufficient to constitute the receiving clerk as the agent of that sender who had used the telephone in order to place upon him the limitations of the Order. On the other hand, it was not so necessary to have those limitations apply to a person who attended the office unless that person was notified by use of the form, or even by the words of the receiving clerk, that the sending of the telegram entailed this very serious limitation on the liabilities of the telegraph company.

I am, therefore, of the opinion that Order 49274 of the Board of Railway Commissioners and in the same fashion Order T-40 of the Canadian Transport Board should be interpreted to leave free of the limitation a sender who has attended the telegraph company's office and who has not been notified and is unaware of any limitations on the ordinary common law rights he would have as against the telegraph company.

I am also concerned with the application of a further doctrine in contract law. This subject was referred to by the Chief Justice during the argument but neither counsel chose to develop it. I quote from Cheshire and Fifoot, *Law of Contract,* 6th ed. (1964), at p. 116:

> In a number of cases, now extending over many years, judges have ruled from time to time that no exempting clause, however wide, may protect a party who has broken the basic duties created by the very nature and character of the contract. A variety of language has been used to describe this over-riding consideration. The words "fundamental term" are, perhaps, most often on judicial lips. But this phrase, in so far as it suggests that the courts are only adding a further term to those already expressed or implied in the contract, is misleading. The essential assumption is that the party at fault has done more than break a term of the contract, however important this may be: he has failed to satisfy the very purpose for which the contract was designed and he may no longer rely on one of its component parts.

One of the outstanding examples of such a case is *Karsales (Harrow), Ltd. v. Wallis,* [1956] 1 W.L.R. 936, a decision of the English Court of Appeal. There, Denning, L.J., said at pp. 940-1:

> Notwithstanding earlier cases which might suggest the contrary, it is now settled that exempting clauses of this kind, no matter how widely they are expressed, only avail the party when he is carrying out his contract in its essential respects. He is not allowed to use them as a cover for misconduct or indifference or to enable him to turn a blind eye to his obligations. They do not avail him when he

is guilty of a breach which goes to the root of the contract. The thing to do is to look at the contract apart from the exempting clauses and see what are the terms, express or implied, which impose an obligation on the party. If he has been guilty of a breach of those obligations in a respect which goes to the very root of the contract, he cannot rely on the exempting clauses.... The principle is sometimes said to be that the party cannot rely on an exempting clause when he delivers something "different in kind" from that contracted for, or has broken a "fundamental term" or a "fundamental contractual obligation", but these are, I think, all comprehended by the general principle that a breach which goes to the root of the contract disentitles the party from relying on the exempting clause.

A similar view was adopted by the Appellate Division of the Supreme Court of Alberta in *Canadian-Dominion Leasing Corporation Ltd. v. Suburban Superdrug Ltd.* (1966), 56 D.L.R. (2d) 43, 56 W.W.R. 396, and the British Columbia Supreme Court in *Lightburn v. Belmont Sales Ltd. et al.* (1969), 6 D.L.R. (3d) 692, 69 W.W.R. 734, and as well by the Court of Appeal for Ontario in *R. G. McLean Ltd. v. Canadian Vickers Ltd.* (1970), 15 D.L.R. (3d) 15, [1971] 1 O.R. 207. It is true that those are cases in which an exemption clause in the contract is construed and the result where the Courts refuse to apply such exemption clause. What we are concerned with here is an exemption which, it is alleged, was granted by an order of the then Board of Railway Commissioners. As I have pointed out, however, that exemption was, in the view of Allen, J.A., granted by the insertion of a statutory clause in a contract and, therefore, it is an exemption clause in a contract despite the fact that it originated in an order of the Board.

Upon the agreed statement of facts in the present case, the appellant, through its president, Mr. Linton, had attended the office of the respondent and there informed the clerk of the necessity of having this telegram delivered at the addressee's place of business not later than 11:00 a.m. on the day on which it was being sent and that such a course was possible because of the hour's variation in time between Fort George and Vancouver. The defendant agreed to send the message on a rush basis and the defendant through its employee undertook to deliver that message by telegram not later than 11:00 a.m. on that day. Despite that agreement made in full knowledge of all the circumstances by the representative of the telegraph company, the message was not marked "Rush". Although it was sent from the Fort George office immediately, it was delayed for some time in the Alberta office because the clerk had miscounted the words. When the clerk being called upon by the Alberta office made a proper count of the words, he again assured Mr. Linton that the message would be delivered on time in the manner instructed. When the message finally arrived at the office of the addressee, it was not within that time but over an hour later. In addition, it was not on an ordinary telegraph form but was on a telex form, although the receiving clerk had been warned that a telex would not be accepted by the addressee.

Under these circumstances, I am of the opinion that there was a complete failure to carry out the contract on the part of the respondent. The doctrine of fundamental breach, or a breach going to the root of the contract, would be more accurate, would apply and therefore the respondent is unable to avail itself of the exempting provisions appearing in the Order of the Board and set out on the reverse side of the form, if the latter had been used. For this reason also, I would allow the appeal.

In the result, the appeal should be allowed and the case should be returned to the Supreme Court of Alberta so that the damages may be assessed failing the agreement of the parties. The appellant is entitled to its costs throughout.

[Dickson and Beetz JJ. concur with Spence J.]

Laskin, C.J.C. (dissenting): — I agree with my brother Spence both in his reasons and in his conclusions, but I wish to add some observations of my own on a ground, one of those taken by my brother Spence, which in my view is of itself sufficient to establish the respondent's liability. The comedy of errors of the respondent's employees in handling a simple telegram message is admitted in the agreed statement of facts, but all of them are alleged to be of no consequence because of the exemptions from liability endorsed upon the usual telegram forms, pursuant to prescribed orders of the federal regulatory agencies successively authorized to regulate telegram traffic.

In fact, the message which the appellant wished to send was not put on one of those forms when submitted to the respondent's employee for transmission. Assuming this to be immaterial to the force of the exemption provisions, the respondent's claim to exoneration fails because it did not send a telegram (which would be delivered as a sealed message) but sent an open telex message which was received in that form and could not therefore be accepted as a tender for a Government construction job on which the appellant was bidding. This was so far a departure from what the respondent (through its employees) had undertaken to do as to disentitle it to rely on the exemption provisions.

Counsel for the respondent, in argument before this Court on this aspect of the case, conceded that his reliance on the exemption clause would take him to the point of denying any liability even if a sender's message, written out on an authorized form, was deliberately destroyed or thrown aside by an employee of the respondent. The sending of the telex message in this case had, for the sender, the same effect as if it had been torn up or simply ignored. I repeat, for convenience here, the exemption clause upon which the respondent relies. It reads as follows:

> It is agreed between the sender of the message on the face of this form and this Company that the said Company shall not be liable for damages arising from failure to transmit or deliver, or for any error in the transmission or delivery of any unrepeated telegram, whether happening from negligence of its servants or otherwise, or for delays from interruptions in the working of its lines, for errors in cypher or obscure messages, or for errors from illegible writing, beyond the amount received for sending the same.

Two points arise for consideration on the facts of this case, taken in the light of the foregoing clause: first, whether as a matter of law or of construction the exemption clause applies to the admitted default of the respondent that occurred; and, second, if the answer is in the negative (as I think it must be), whether the situation is affected by the fact that the exemption clause in question is a promulgation of the federal regulatory agency empowered to prescribe it. I propose to deal with the second question first and, as a base, I point out that the clause aforesaid was promulgated in virtue of the authority vested in the Board of Transport Commissioners of Canada, as the regulatory agency was then called (it is now the Canadian Transport Commission), under s. 348 of the *Railway Act,* R.S.C. 1927, c. 170, which is now, with an immaterial change, s. 322 of the *Railway Act,* R.S.C. 1970, c. R-2. This last-mentioned provision reads as follows:

322(1) No contract, condition, by-law, regulation, declaration or notice made or given by the company, impairing, restricting or limiting its liability in respect of any traffic shall, except as hereinafter provided, relieve the company from such liability, unless the class of contract, condition, by-law, regulation, declaration or notice has been first authorized or approved by order or regulation of the Commission.

(2) The Commission may, in any case, or by regulation, determine the extent to which the liability of the company may be so impaired, restricted or limited.

(3) The Commission may by regulation prescribe the terms and conditions under which any traffic may be carried by the company.

I find nothing in s. 322 that in any way excludes the operation of judicial rules of construction or principles of law in the determination of the question whether the respondent herein may rely on the exemption clause. Section 322(3) (in the same words as its predecessor s. 348 (3)) envisages that traffic will be carried, that telegrams will be transmitted; and, indeed, as a common carrier, the respondent is obliged in the course of its business to accept telegram messages for transmission to their intended recipients. It is to me a rather monstrous proposition, if it is seriously advanced, that Parliament in its legislation authorized total immunity from liability to be conferred upon a carrier which, under its cover, could decide when and if it would send a requested telegram.

I would not read the words in s. 322(1) "impairing, restricting or limiting its liability" as authorizing complete immunity of the kind I am considering, and, subject to what follows in these reasons, I do not regard any orders of the regulatory agency as giving *carte blanche* to a carrier to take or refuse or to ignore messages tendered for transmission. Their orders are no more immune from construction than are bilaterally bargained contract terms.

The main question then is what is the scope of the exculpatory provision relied on by the respondent. We have here a standard contract, a contract of adhesion from which the appellant is powerless to depart and which, at least so far as the particular exempting provision is concerned, is equally binding upon the respondent. I do not think that these circumstances provide any good reason to qualify the rule of strict construction which has ordinarily been applied to exculpatory provisions. This is one side of the equation which must be considered when an issue arises whether upon a breach of contract the offending party is none the less entitled to rely upon an exemption clause. The other side has to do with the character of the breach, whether it is a breach which would ordinarily give rise only to damages, or a breach which is a breach of a term entitling the innocent party to terminate or (assuming there is a difference here), whether it is a breach which is in essence a complete denial or departure from the contract. A decision on this phase of the matter is in truth non-segregable from the exercise of determining the reach of the exculpatory provision. It has, however, spawned a line of cases in England under which a fundamental breach is, as a matter of law, a ground for excluding the application of exemption clauses: see, for example, *Karsales (Harrow), Ltd. v. Wallis,* [1956] 2 All E.R. 866. This emphasis on the character of the breach was negated by the House of Lords in *Suisse Atlantique Société D'Armement Maritime S.A. v. N.V. Rotterdamsche Kolen Centrale,* [1966] 2 All E.R. 61, which emphasized rather the construction side of the equation.

The interaction of the foregoing two approaches makes it possible to say of an exculpatory clause, construed to cover the event which is relied upon to escape it, that it prevents that event from being a breach of contract. The ultimate situation that arises here is a complete negation of any obligation which the transaction may have appeared to contemplate, but that is a result which, in my view, can hardly be reached where the parties have not been trifling and did have reciprocal obligations in view. A *fortiori*, it is not a result which is open in this case where the terms of the transaction have been prescribed under statutory authorization. There must be a residue of obligation that is not cancelled out by concurrent exemption; otherwise, it is illusory to speak of a contract: *cf.* Treitel, *Law of Contract*, 3rd ed. (1970), pp. 188ff.

In the present case, the respondent through its employees undertook to send a telegram. None was sent, nor was there even an attempt to send one which was aborted by difficulties of one sort or another. The situation goes beyond mere negligence on the part of the respondent's employees. There is, moreover, no ground in the agreed statement of facts upon which it might be urged that the appellant was content to have a message sent in any form or manner chosen by the respondent's employees. It was of the highest importance to the appellant that a telegram be sent. In these circumstances, I find the exemption provision inapplicable, and hence I would allow the appeal as proposed by my brother Spence.

[Beetz J. also concurred with Laskin C.J.C.]

QUESTIONS

1. Should it have made any difference if the origin of the exemption clause was statutory and not consensual?

2. Is the approach of the majority consistent with that of the English Court of Appeal in *Harbutt's Plasticine v. Wayne Tank*?

3. How does one know when an obligation has been, to use the words of Laskin C.J.C., "completely negated", so that the allocation of risk worked out by the parties (or even by one party) is ineffective? What reasons are there for taking such a view in the ordinary commercial case?

The next case does not raise the problem of the effectiveness of an exemption clause in quite the same way as the cases we have just looked at. However, the issue of risk allocation and the powers of the parties (or one party) to determine the allocation in advance is the crux of the case. As you read the case consider how many of the same issues as were present in the last few cases are relevant here.

TOEPFER v. CONTINENTAL GRAIN

[1974] 1 Lloyd's Rep. 11. Court of Appeal (England); Lord Denning M.R., Cairns and Roskill L.JJ.

[The plaintiff agreed to buy wheat from the defendant. The contract of sale contained the following clause:

"Quality: No. 3 Hard Amber Durum Wheat of U.S. origin quality/condition final at loading as per official certificate."

The buyer sold to sub-buyers. These contracts contained the same clauses. The contracts were all standard forms used in the grain trade. The wheat shipped under the contract was inspected and found to be of the contract quality. An inspection certificate was given by the U.S. inspector in Wisconsin. The buyers paid the seller, the sub-buyers paid the buyers. The wheat was later found to be of poorer quality than it was supposed to be. The dispute went to arbitration in London (as provided for in the standard form contracts). The umpire held for the sellers. The arbitration Board of Appeal stated a case for the opinion of the court. The trial judge agreed with the umpire and Board of Appeal that the certificate was final. The buyers appealed.]

Lord Denning M.R. (after stating the fact, continued): In giving their decision the Board of Appeal expressed their sympathy with the buyers. In a significant passage they said:

> ... There was no suggestion that the Grain Inspection Certificates had been obtained by fraud or mistake but it was clear that the Certificates had been issued as a result of an error by the Inspector... the Inspector had been "negligent". We feel unable however to make our Award without expressing our own disquiet at the effect thereof. It seems to us commercially harsh that a buyer should be left without remedy as the result of a negligent certification which is accepted by all interested parties including the issuing authority to be in error. Had we felt free to do so we would have allowed the appeal. It is however our duty to decide this Appeal according to the law as we understand it....

So the Board of Appeal held that according to law the certificate was final. But they felt it was exceedingly hard on the buyers to have to put up with this wheat which was not up to contract and yet have no recompense.

I will see later whether there is any means of compensating the buyers, but meanwhile the question is whether, as between buyers and sellers, the certificate was final.

The first point taken by the buyers was that the certificate was only final as to "quality". It was not final, they said, as to the "description" of the goods. The error here they said was an error in the description and not as to quality. We were treated to a learned discussion on the difference between "quality" and "description". We were referred to cases on sale of goods and to the provisions of the statute. I confess that I found the discussion unhelpful. The "description" of goods often includes a statement of their quality. Thus "new-laid eggs" contains both quality and description all in one. "Quality" is often part of the description. In this very case the word "hard" is a word both of quality and of description. If a certificate is final as to the quality "hard", it is final as to that description also. The quality and description cannot be separated. Finality as to one means finality as to the other. But in any case, on a matter of this kind, the commercial arbitrators are much better Judges than any lawyers. Their interpretation of the word "quality" in this contract, though not binding on the Court, is of the highest value. In their findings, the Board of Appeal specifically said:

> Insofar as it is a question of fact we find that the word "quality" in relation to Durum Wheat refers both to the grade and the sub-class of such Wheat.

I hold therefore that this certificate, in certifying that this wheat was "No. 3 Hard Amber Durum Wheat" was certifying the quality of the wheat. It was expressly agreed to be final. It is binding on both buyers and sellers unless there is some reason for overthrowing it.

It is said: This certificate was made under a mistake. The Department of Agriculture in the United States have admitted it. They have reprimanded the inspector. They have issued "a formal corrective action" to him. The inspector himself admitted that he made a mistake. On this ground it is said that the certificate is not binding.

Apart altogether from authority, I am clearly of opinion that a mistake by the certifier, even when afterwards admitted by him to be a mistake, does not invalidate the certificate. It remains binding as between seller and buyer and all down the chain. The Board of Appeal in their award set out the commercial reasons which support this view:

> The commercial purpose of the provisions [for an official certificate to be final as to quality]... is to avoid disputes as to quality and to achieve finality in this respect once a proper certificate of inspection had been issued and tendered. A further reason... is that differences of opinion are otherwise to be expected among persons experienced in the grain trade in countries outside the United States and Canada as to the correct grading (including both the grade and sub-class) of consignments of U.S. or Canadian grain and such differences would otherwise give rise to numerous disputes.

It must be remembered that numerous persons act on the faith of the certificate, such as the buyers, sub-buyers, bankers lending money and so forth. Good sense requires that the finality of the clause should be upheld by arbitrators and the Courts in full. It is not open to the arbitrator himself to say afterwards: "I have made a mistake".

These commercial considerations are borne out by legal principles. I tried to summarize them in the recent case of *Arenson v. Arenson*, [1973] 2 Lloyd's Rep. 104 at p. 107; [1973] 2 W.L.R. 553 at p. 559:

> ... Whenever two persons agree together to refer a matter to a third person for decision, and further agree that his decision is to be final and binding upon them, then, so long as he arrives at his decision honestly and in good faith, the two parties are bound by it. They cannot re-open it for mistake or error on his part of for any reason other than for fraud or collusion...

Those words are appropriate here. There is no suggestion of fraud or collusion. It is a case of a mistake or error. Mr. Staughton referred us to *Dean v. Prince*, [1953] Ch. 590, [1954] Ch. 409, and *Wright v. Frodoor*, [1967] 1 W.L.R. 506, where it was said that a certificate or valuation can be set aside, not only for fraud, but also for a material mistake or miscarriage, at any rate if it appears on the face of the certificate or is admitted by the certifier. Mr. Staughton relied in particular on what Mr. Justice Harman said in *Dean v. Prince* at p. 593. I do not think those cases and those observations apply to a case like the present. They apply at most to contracts which are still executory and a party comes to a Court of equity asking for them to be specifically enforced. They do not apply to contracts which have been executed, as here, contracts for the sale of goods which have been delivered. In such cases the parties, and all those down the chain, are entitled to regard the certificate as final. It cannot be upset, as between them, for mistake of the certifier.

I return now to the significant passage which I have read, in which the Board of Appeal said that it was "commercially harsh that a buyer should be left without remedy as the result of a negligent certificate." I do not think he is left without a remedy. He has no remedy against the seller, but he may well have a remedy against the negligent certifier. We looked at this question in *Arenson v. Arenson,[1973] 2 Lloyd's Rep. 104; [1973] 2 W.L.R. 553.* We were referred to authorities in the Courts of the United States. These show that, in that country, a certificate cannot, as between the parties, be set aside for mistake of the certifier, see *Sanitary Farm v. Gammel*, (1952) 195 F. 2d. 106: but the negligent certifier is liable in damages to the party injured by his negligence, see *Gammel v. Ernst & Ernst*, (1955) in the United States. This may not yet be the law in this country but powerful voices think that it should be, see *Sutcliffe v. Thackrah*, [1973] 2 Lloyd's Rep. 115; [1973] 1 W.L.R. 888. In the present case, however, the certificate was given in the United States where there does seem to be a remedy. In that country the buyers may obtain a remedy for the "commercially harsh" result.

Returning, however, to the present case as between buyer and seller, I have no doubt that the umpire, the Board of Appeal and the Judge were entirely right. I would dismiss this appeal.

[Cairns and Roskill L.JJ. agreed in dismissing the appeal.]

QUESTIONS

1. Could you apply what Lord Denning says about the need for the certificate of the inspector to be binding for reasons of commercial convenience to the facts of *Harbutt's Plasticine v. Wayne Tank*?

2. Could you now draft a concise statement of the reasons why the courts have developed and apply the doctrine of fundamental breach, taking into consideration the cases from *Yeoman Credit v. Apps* on?

3. If you could not do so (or would find it difficult to do so) say why. If you could do so, draft the statement.

It can be said that the cases in this chapter so far have been examples of problems that have not found a very satisfactory solution in the judgments. As always when this happens, the question must be, "Where do we go from here?" The cases that follow begin to show what a solution might look like and how the courts' power to review might function.

(3) Penalties and Forfeitures

The problems that we had with the last group of cases were that it was difficult, if not impossible to know why the courts interfered with the contracts that they considered. This interference makes it clear that the old shibboleth that the courts do not make contracts for the parties is no longer a valid principle. The next few cases raise the issue of the basis of the courts' interference with contracts in a narrower and much more ancient area. In all of the cases we have just looked at, one party has attempted to limit his responsibility for defective performance. The finance company wants to avoid any arguments about the quality of a car or display cabinet, a manufacturer wants to limit his responsibility for consequential loss arising from breach. In each case the clause in question was put in the contract to deal with some of the problems that might arise if things went wrong. It is just as likely, however, that a draftsman may want to make sure that, if the other side breaches the contract, his client can expect to recover a fixed amount of money for breach. We saw that the problems of calculating damages are not always easy or predictable. In an effort to avoid these problems a draftsman might stipulate in a contract of sale that, in the event of breach by the seller, the seller should pay the buyer $1,000/day. We saw just such a clause in *Suisse Atlantique*. The traditional problem the courts have faced here is that one party may stipulate that the other shall pay exorbitant damages in the event of breach. For a very long time (several centuries) the courts of equity have exercised a supervisory function over these clauses.

An exorbitant sum is called a "penalty" and, traditionally, penalties are not recoverable. A variation on this is the stipulation for a large deposit, the deposit to be forfeited on default. Excessive deposits or forfeitures also come under the protective jurisdiction of the courts of equity.

As you read the next few cases consider the reasons (stated or unstated) for interference by the courts. We are always faced with the problem of knowing how far we as draftsmen can go in any particular case, and from that point of view it is important to see what guidance the courts give.

DUNLOP TYRE COMPANY LTD. v. NEW GARAGE & MOTOR CO. LTD.

[1915] A.C. 79. House of Lords; Lords Dunedin, Atkinson, Parker and Parmore.

July 1. **Lord Dunedin.** My Lords, the appellants, through an agent, entered into a contract with the respondents under which they supplied them with their goods, which consisted mainly of motor-tyre covers and tubes. By this contract, in respect of certain concessions as to discounts, the respondents bound themselves not to do several things, which may be shortly set forth as follows: not to tamper with the manufacturers' marks; not to sell to any private customer or co-operative society at prices less than the current price list issued by the Dunlop Company; not to supply to persons whose supplies the Dunlop Company had decided to suspend; not to exhibit or to export without the Dunlop Company's assent. Finally, the agreement concluded (clause 5), "We agree to pay to the Dunlop Pneumatic Tyre Company, Ltd. the sum of 5*l.* for each and every tyre, cover or tube sold or offered in breach of this agreement, as and by way of liquidated damages and not as a penalty."

The appellants, having discovered that the respondents had sold covers and tubes at under the current list price, raised action and demanded damages. The case was tried and the breach in fact held proved. An inquiry was directed before the Master as to damages. The Master inquired, and assessed the damages at 250*l.*, adding this explanation: "I find that it was left open to me to decide whether the 5*l.* fixed in the agreement was penalty or liquidated damages. I find that it was liquidated damages."

The respondents appealed to the Court of Appeal, when the majority of that Court, Vaughan Williams and Swinfen Eady L.JJ., held, Kennedy L.J. dissenting, that the said sum of 5*l.* was a penalty, and entered judgment for the plaintiffs for the sum of 2*l.* as nominal damages. Appeal from that decision is now before your Lordships' House.

My Lords, we had the benefit of a full and satisfactory argument, and a citation of the very numerous cases which have been decided on this branch of the law. The matter has been handled, and at no distant date, in the Courts of highest resort. I particularly refer to the *Clydebank Case*, [1905] A.C. 6, in your Lordships' House and the cases of *Public Works Commissioner* v. *Hills*, [1906] A.C. 368, and *Webster* v. *Bosanquet*, [1912] A.C. 394, in the Privy Council. In both of these cases many of the previous cases were considered. In view of that fact, and of the number of the authorities available, I do not think it advisable to attempt any detailed review of the various cases, but I shall content myself with stating succinctly the various propositions which I think are deducible from the decisions which rank as authoritative: —

1. Though the parties to a contract who use the words "penalty" or "liquidated damages" may prima facie be supposed to mean what they say, yet the expression used is not conclusive. The Court must find out whether the payment stipulated is in truth a penalty or liquidated damages. This doctrine may be said to be found passim in nearly every case.

2. The essence of a penalty is a payment of money stipulated as in terrorem of the offending party; the essence of liquidated damages is a genuine covenanted pre-estimate of damage (*Clydebank Engineering and Shipbuilding Co.* v. *Don Jose Ramos Yzquierdo y Castaneda*).

3. The question whether a sum stipulated is penalty or liquidated damages is a question of construction to be decided upon the terms and inherent circumstances of each particular contract, judged of as at the time of the making of the contract, not as at the time of the breach.

4. To assist this task of construction various tests have been suggested, which if applicable to the case under consideration may prove helpful, or even conclusive. Such are:

(*a*) It will be held to be penalty if the sum stipulated for is extravagant and unconscionable in amount in comparison with the greatest loss that could conceivably be proved to have followed from the breach. (Illustration given by Lord Halsbury in *Clydebank Case.*)

(*b*) It will be held to be a penalty if the breach consists only in not paying a sum of money, and the sum stipulated is a sum greater than the sum which ought to have been paid (*Kemble* v. *Farren*, 6 Bing. 141). This though one of the most ancient instances is truly a corollary to the last test. Whether it had its historical origin in the doctrine of the common law that when A. promised to pay B. a sum of money on a certain day and did not do so, B. could only recover the sum with, in certain cases, interest, but could never recover further damages for non-timeous payment, or whether it was a survival of the time when equity reformed unconscionable bargains merely because they were unconscionable... is probably more interesting than material.

(*c*) There is a presumption (but no more) that it is penalty when "a single lump sum is made payable by way of compensation, on the occurrence of one or more or all of several events, some of which may occasion serious and others but trifling damage" (Lord Watson in *Lord Elphinstone* v. *Monkland Iron and Coal Co.*, 11 App. Cas. 332).

On the other hand:

(*d*) It is no obstacle to the sum stipulated being a genuine pre-estimate of damage, that the consequences of the breach are such as to make precise pre-estimation almost an impossibility. On the contrary, that is just the situation when it is probable that pre-estimated damage was the true bargain between the parties.

Turning now to the facts of the case, it is evident that the damage apprehended by the appellants owing to the breaking of the agreement was an indirect and not a direct damage. So long as they got their price from the respondents for each article sold, it could not matter to them directly what the respondents did with it. Indirectly it did. Accordingly, the agreement is headed "Price Maintenance Agreement," and the way in which the appellants would be damaged if prices were cut is clearly explained in evidence by Mr. Baisley, and no successful attempt is made to controvert that evidence. But though damage as a whole from such a practice would be certain, yet damage from any one sale would be impossible to forecast. It is just, therefore, one of those cases where it seems quite reasonable for parties to contract that they should estimate that damage at a certain figure, and provided that figure is not extravagant there would seem no reason to suspect that it is not truly a bargain to assess damages, but rather a penalty to be held in terrorem.

The argument of the respondents was really based on two heads. They overpressed, in my judgment, the dictum of Lord Watson in *Lord Elphinstone's Case*, reading it as if he had said that the matter was conclusive, instead of saying, as he did, that it raised a presumption, and they relied strongly on the case of *Willson v. Love*, [1896] 1 Q.B. 626.

Now, in the first place, I have considerable doubt whether the stipulated payment here can fairly be said to deal with breaches, "some of which" — I am quoting Lord Watson's words — "may occasion serious and others but trifling damage." As a mere matter of construction, I doubt whether clause 5 applies to anything but sales below price. But I will assume that it does. None the less the mischief, as I have already pointed out, is an indirect mischief, and I see no data on which, as a matter of construction, I could settle in my own mind that the indirect damage from selling a cover would differ in magnitude from the indirect damage from selling a tube; or that the indirect damage from a cutting-price sale would differ from the indirect damage from supply at a full price to a hostile, because prohibited, agent. You cannot weigh such things in a chemical balance. The character of the agricultural land which was ruined by slag heaps in *Elphinstone's Case*, was not all the same, but no objection was raised by Lord Watson to applying an overhead rate per acre, the sum not being in itself unconscionable.

I think *Elphinstone's Case* or rather the dicta in it, do go this length, that if there are various breaches to which one indiscriminate sum to be paid in breach is applied, then the strength of the chain must be taken at its weakest link. If you can clearly see that the loss on one particular breach could never amount to the stipulated sum, then you may come to the conclusion that the sum is penalty. But further than this it does not go; so, for the reasons already stated, I do not think the present case forms an instance of what I have just expressed.

On the whole matter, therefore, I go with the opinion of Kennedy L.J., and I move your Lordships that the appeal be allowed, and judgment given for the sum as brought out by the Master, the appellants to have their costs in this House and in the Courts below.

[The other judges agreed in the result.]

H.F. CLARKE LTD. v. THERMIDAIRE CORP. LTD.

(1974), 54 D.L.R. (3d) 385. Supreme Court of Canada.

Laskin, C.J.C.: — There are three points in this appeal, which concerns the enforceability, under an exclusive distributorship contract, of covenants against competition during the currency of the contract and for three years after its lawful termination. The first point relates to the validity of the covenants by reason of their alleged unlimited scope. Secondly, there is an important issue, which in my opinion is the main issue, whether the formula fixing damages for breach of the covenant in the specified post-contract period establishes the measure of liquidated damages or is in reality a penalty against which relief must be given. The third point relates to certain products which, on the appellant's contention, should not be taken into account in assessing damages. Although the appellant also questioned the reference as to damages, directed by the trial Judge and affirmed by the Court of Appeal, it being its contention that the assessment should be by a Judge of the Supreme Court of Ontario, I would not interfere with this direction if the right to damages should be confirmed by this Court.

The contract which is the subject of this litigation was dated January 14, 1966, and as amended shortly thereafter, it constituted the appellant, as from January 1, 1966, the exclusive distributor of the respondent's products (as defined) in a specified area of Canada, embracing the larger part of Canada from Ontario to the west coast and including the Northwest Territories and part of Quebec but excluding the eastern part of Quebec and the four Atlantic Provinces. This contract replaced an earlier one under which the two covenants against competition, one respecting competition during the currency of the contract, and the second respecting competition during the three-year period after termination or cancellation of the contract showed one marked variation from the successor covenants. Article 7 of the first contract of January 20, 1964, provided as follows:

> 7. *Sale of Competitive Products*
> Distributor undertakes and agrees that during the currency of this Agreement and for a period of three (3) years after the termination hereof, as herein provided, neither it nor any company affiliated or associated with it shall sell competitive products in the Territory.

In the contract out of which this litigation arises, the references to the three-year period and to the territory were left out, and the paragraph, numbered 7 as before, was in these words:

> 7. *Sale of Competitive Products*
> Clarke undertakes and agrees that during the currency of this Agreement, neither it nor any company associated or affiliated with it shall manufacture, sell, cause to be manufactured or sold, products competitive to Thermidaire products.

Neither art. 14 of the first contract nor its successor art. 15 of the second contract, in restraining competition for three years after termination or cancellation made any reference to its operation in the territory of the distributorship. The two articles were substantially the same in their relevant particulars, and it is enough to reproduce the one that is in issue here. It reads as follows:

> 15. *Termination of Agreement by Clarke:* In the event of the termination or cancellation of this Agreement by, or caused by, Clarke, either by reason of its non-renewal by Clarke or by reason of any default on the part of Clarke or by reason of any violation or non-fulfilment of the conditions of this contract by Clarke and not remedied by Clarke as laid down in Section 12, including the grounds for termination specified in paragraph 19 hereof, Clarke further undertakes and agrees that neither it nor any company affiliated or associated with it will produce, sell or cause to be produced or sold, directly or indirectly, products competitive with Thermidaire Products for a period of three (3) years after the date of termination or cancellation. In the event of breach by Clarke of this covenant pertaining to competitive products, Clarke shall pay to Thermidaire by way of liquidated damages an amount equal to the gross trading profit realized through the sale of such competitive products.

Although neither of the covenants against competition referred to a territorial limitation on their ambit and rectification was sought on the ground of mutual mistake, the trial Judge found them enforceable without granting rectification, it being his view that there was no mutual mistake, In the Court of Appeal, whose reasons were delivered by Brooke, J.A., the cross-appeal as to rectification was allowed and the operation of the two covenants was qualified by including therein the words "in the Territory".

I am not disposed to interfere with the view on rectification taken by the Court of Appeal, but I do not think that the relief was necessary in view of the definition in the contract of the territory within which the distributorship was to operate. It seems to me that, in the absence of any indications in the covenants against competition that they were to operate outside the distributorship territory, reasonable construction would limit them to that territory. I do not find it compelling today to view the covenants against competition as if they were detached provisions and to seek thereby a basis of invalidation, especially when no claim was made by the covenantee for a wider application than the distributorship territory.

I need not embark here on any discussion of whether the two covenants, either as rectified or as limited by construction to operation only in the distributorship territory, are invalid as in the unreasonable restraint of trade. Both the trial Judge and the Court of Appeal found them to be reasonable *inter partes* and consonant with the public interest, and this conclusion was not questioned by the appellant save by reading the covenants as being unlimited in territorial ambit. In failing on this point they fail also in any challenge to the covenants as being in unreasonable restraint of trade.

This brings me to the second and, as I said, the main point in the appeal. The trial Judge found, and the Court of Appeal confirmed, that the appellant Clarke had broken the contract during its currency by selling competitive products other than those of the respondent and that it had also broken the covenant against post-contract competition. These findings, and as well a finding that the respondent was entitled to terminate the contract before it had run its five-year period, were not contested in this Court by the appellant.

At the time the parties hereto commenced their business relationship the appellant was in the business of selling boilers in western Canada. The respondent from 1958 on concentrated on the manufacture and sale of water treatment products; and in agreeing to give the appellant the exclusive distributorship of its products in the defined territory it necessarily excluded itself from sales therein and thus depended on the appellant to keep its name and its reputation before the public in the territory. The appellant was not only precluded by the contract between the parties from selling products in the territory competitive to those of the respondent but was also subject to other supporting contractual obligations, such as being required to give the respondent upon request its list of customers, and various provisions respecting advertising and packaging.

It was the appellant which initiated suit, claiming damages for wrongful termination of the contract on January 19, 1967, by the respondent and the latter counterclaimed for damages under the covenants against competition. The action was brought on March 9, 1967, the statement of claim was delivered on April 10, 1967 and the defence and counterclaim on April 25, 1967. The appellant discontinued its action on April 29, 1968, and the trial of the counterclaim began on September 19, 1971, well after the expiry of the three-year period within which the post-contract covenant against competition was effective. The respondent did not seek an interim or interlocutory injunction, which it might have done promptly and thus avoided the running of some of the damages which it claimed in its suit. Its explanation, which is far from satisfactory, was that there was a serious question whether there was a breach of the agreement by the appellant and, even if there was a breach, whether it was not remedied. The prayer for relief in the counterclaim did ask for an injunction but, of course, by the time the action came on for trial there was no longer any basis for one. None the less, it was obvious from the record that the appellant continued to sell competitive products other than those of the respondent after the contract was terminated and thus put itself at the risk, which indeed materialized, of being called to account under the formula for post-contract damages. Notwithstanding this, no interlocutory injunction was sought by the respondent.

No question arises here as to the entitlement of the respondent to damages for breach of the covenant against competition during the currency of the contract (the covenant in this respect being enforceable), such damages being the loss suffered by the respondent by reason of sales by the appellant of products competitive with those of the respondent and not purchased from the respondent. The formula for assessing damages for breach of art. 15, the post-contract covenant, was however attacked as constituting a penalty rather than a measure of liquidated damages. It was accepted by counsel for the respective parties that the damages under the prescribed formula, namely, the gross trading profit realized by the covenantor on the sale of competitive products, would be about $200,000. Counsel for the appellant pointed to the very modest, almost inconsequential, profits of the respondent for the ten-year period 1961 to 1970 inclusive. Indeed, it was contended that were it not for an interest free loan to the respondent by its president, there would have been a loss over the ten-year period of some $86,000 if a realistic rate of interest had to be paid for the loan. To support its contention of the extravagance of the formula as a measure of liquidated damages, counsel for the appellant noted (although not accepting the sum as properly based) that the respondent had, in the alternative, claimed some $92,000 as the amount of its actual loss of net profit over the three-year post-contract period.

The trial Judge concluded that the formula of gross trading profit as the measure of liquidated damages was a business-like and reasonable one, but this conclusion was associated with an apparent belief that the damages according to this formula would be small. The Court of Appeal accepted, as did counsel, that they would reach $200,000, but it held none the less that the formula, in the circumstances, was "one designed for the determination of liquidated damages in the truest sense and . . . therefore enforceable".

Although there was only brief consideration in the reasons of the trial Judge of the issue whether the provision for liquidated damages (so termed by the parties in their contract) was not in substance a penalty and hence unenforceable, the Court of Appeal addressed itself to this issue at some length. I think it important to appreciate that we are dealing here with a not very usual case (so far as reported decisions go) where the pre-estimate of damages was not a fixed sum (as was the situation in the leading English case of *Dunlop Pneumatic Tyre Co., Ltd. v. New Garage & Motor Co., Ltd.,* [1915] A.C. 79) but was based upon a formula which when applied necessarily yielded a result far in excess of loss of net profits. Gross trading profit, in the words of the trial Judge, "means the difference between the net selling prices of the goods and their laid down cost", the laid down cost being the seller's invoice price plus transportation charges to put the goods on the purchaser's shelves. In the words of the Court of Appeal, "the term 'gross trading profit' is profit after cost of sales but before costs customarily deducted to determine net profit".

The contract in this case was lawfully terminated by the respondent on January 19, 1967 and the three-year post-contract covenant against competition ran from that date. The appellant admitted in a letter from its president, dated January 16, 1967, that as late as June, 1966, it had sold competitive products covered by the agreement and not purchased from the respondent, and it promised to desist from this "hereafter". The trial Judge, obviously by inadvertent error, referred to June 30, 1967 (instead of to June, 1966) as the end period to which the admission referred. In fact, the appellant did not desist after termination of the contract, and there is evidence that from January 1, 1967 to January 31, 1969, the gross trading profit of the appellant was $177,161.20, consisting of $78,739.80 for 1967, $93,609.25 for 1968 and $4,812.15 for the one month of 1969, the appellant having in 1969 changed its year end from December 31st to January 31st.

I take the judgment of the Ontario Court of Appeal to be based on the fact that the parties had fixed the formula of gross trading profit after a mutual consideration of the difficulty of establishing compensation for a probably substantial loss, having regard to the factors to be considered, if there was a breach of the post-contract covenant not to compete. The extent of the loss, by reason of the formula, would vary directly with the length of time, up to the three-year limit, over which the breach would continue. In his reasons in the Court of Appeal, Brooke, J.A., assessed the matter as follows [9 C.P.R. (2d) 203 at pp. 216-7, 33 D.L.R. (3d) 13 at pp. 25-6, [1973] 2 O.R. 57]:

> The disproportion of gross trading profit and net profit and the financial position of Thermidaire were known by the parties when this agreement was struck. No doubt net profit was considered inappropriate as a measure of damage or loss since its application would involve charging all the costs of advertising, promotion and administration used to put down Thermidaire in a prohibited competitive venture. As to the true object of the provision, Mr. Deeks stated that the formula was used because of the serious difficulties involved in calculating not only simple loss of profit through the prohibited competition, but also the loss of things of value, of real value, which the parties well understood. This included such matters as the loss of the past value of previous years of advertising by Clarke of the Thermidaire products, the loss of present and future worth of advertising by Thermidaire by reason of Clarke's active competition and, of course, the loss of the value of product identification, product integrity and the loss of customers and, of importance, the name and reputation of the product in the market-place. If the effect in terms of loss of present and future sales because of adverse advertising and competitive sales suffered by a company which had placed its entire reliance upon the conduct of its exclusive agent was properly a part of the parties' consideration, perhaps the difficulty encountered by the witness Anderson in his attempt to establish the loss limited to Thermidaire's net profit reflects the difficulties which the parties foresaw in any effort to assess the real loss which would be sustained by Thermidaire in the event of a breach. It is clear to me that the learned trial Judge accepted the evidence of Mr. Deeks as worthy of belief and entirely reasonable in these circumstances.

Does the formula represent a genuine attempt by the parties to pre-estimate the loss as best they could within their special knowledge of the circumstances? It is true that the amount that may eventually be assessed may be large, but this was forseeable when the contract was entered upon. Equally clear was the fact that the loss in terms of both profits and value, as above-mentioned, would also be large. Indeed, the longer the competition was carried on within the prohibited period the greater would be the loss, and the more successful the competition, the greater was the probability that Thermidaire would suffer substantial and permanent damage in the light of the various factors above-mentioned. Losses such as loss of product identification, loss of the benefits of advertising through the operations of its exclusive agent throughout a large territory are among the imponderables for the appraisal which this clause was intended to provide. To have fixed a lump sum as a measure of Thermidaire's damages would have been a haphazard measure at best and, in all the circumstances, the employment of a formula geared to sales of competitive products during the prohibited period was adopted by two keen business firms as the best method of determining the loss resulting from a breach of the covenant — a covenant into which they entered with their eyes open.

When is the amount of recovery in such circumstances extravagant as opposed to actual probable loss? The fact that the estimated loss of net profit, $92,000, is something a little less than half of the possible recovery of $200,000 in circumstances like these is not by itself proof of extravagance. The figures may be large, but I am not persuaded that they are unrealistic or extravagant. The parties knew and appreciated these factors and chose this method to establish compensation for a loss, the amount of which was difficult to determine and, no doubt, very costly to establish. I am convinced that they agreed upon a method which they both regarded as one which would lead to a fair and just determination of Thermidaire's damages and losses in the event of a breach of the covenant.

If all that was involved in determining whether the parties had agreed on a measure of liquidated damages or on a penalty was the intention of those parties, there could be no quarrel with the result reached at trial and on appeal. Indeed, if that was the case it is difficult to conceive how any penalty conclusion could ever be reached when businessmen or business corporations, with relatively equal bargaining power, entered into a contract which provided for payment of a fixed sum or for payment pursuant to a formula for determining damages, in case of a breach of specified covenants, including a covenant not to compete. The law has not, however, developed in this way in common law jurisdictions; and the power to relieve against what a Court may decide is a penalty is a recognized head of equity jurisdiction. Of course, the Court will begin by construing the contract in which the parties have objectively manifested their intentions, and will consider the surrounding circumstances so far as they can illuminate the contract and thus aid in its construction. It seems to me, however, that if, in the face of the parties' assertion in their contract that they were fixing liquidated damages, the Court concludes that a penalty was provided, it would be patently absurd to say that the Court was giving effect to the real intention of the parties when the Court's conclusion was in disregard of that intention as expressed by the parties.

What the Court does in this class of case, as it does in other contract situations, is to refuse to enforce a promise in strict conformity with its terms. The Court exercises a dispensing power (which is unknown to the civil law of Quebec) because the parties' intentions, directed at the time to the performance of their contract, will not alone be allowed to determine how the prescribed sum or the loss formula will be characterized. The primary concern in breach of contract cases (as it is in tort cases, albeit in a different context) is compensation, and judicial interference with the enforcement of what the Courts regard as penalty clauses is simply a manifestation of a concern for fairness and reasonableness, rising above contractual stipulation, whenever the parties seek to remove from the Courts their ordinary authority to determine not only whether there has been a breach but what damages may be recovered as a result thereof.

The Courts may be quite content to have the parties fix the damages in advance and relieve the Courts of this burden in cases where the nature of the obligation upon the breach of which damages will arise, the losses that may reasonably be expected to flow from a breach and their unsusceptibility to ready determination upon the occurrence of a breach provide a base upon which a pre-estimation may be made. But this is only the lesser half of the problem. The interference of the Courts does not follow because they conclude that no attempt should have been made to predetermine the damages or their measure. It is always open to the parties to make the predetermination, but it must yield to judicial appraisal of its reasonableness in the circumstances. This becomes a difficult question of judgment, especially in a case like the present one involving a covenant not to compete which engages the reputation and the vicarious presence of the covenantee in the territorial area of the covenant as well as the products which are the subject of the covenant.

In the present case the formula of gross trading profit was not defined, but in the general understanding of the term as adopted by the Courts below [it] departs markedly from any reasonable approach to recoverable loss or actual loss since all the elements of costs and expenses which would be taken into account to arrive at net profit are excluded from consideration. It is of considerable significance on this aspect of the matter to note how the respondent, in putting its best foot forward to show its actual loss, made up its estimated loss of net profits of $92,017, which is less than half of the sum, in fact about 40%, which would be its recoverable damages under the contract formula of gross trading profits.

Evidence of the estimated loss of net profits over the three-year period in question was given on behalf of the respondent by one Anderson, a chartered accountant and member of a firm which was auditor for the respondent. His calculations are set out in an exhibit, ex. 72, which shows sales for each of the three years 1967 to 1969 inclusive and cost of sales. The difference between these sums was the gross profit in an amount of $110,270 from which were deducted expenses of warehousing (a minor expense), commissions, office and travel expenses, leaving a net of $92,017 as the loss of profit. Anderson agreed, when cross-examined on his calculations, that they were based on four assumptions put to him by counsel for the appellant, as follows:

> Q. Then the validity of your figures as estimates depends on four assumptions: the first, that Thermidaire would have sold all that Clarke did; the second, that Clarke's sales figures for water chemical treatment material are the correct sales figures; that your figures for Thermidaire's cost of sales are correct; and that your estimate as to how selling and administrative expenses would have increased with increased sales.
> A. That is correct.

Anderson's evidence was that Clarke's gross trading profit for the three-year period amounted to $239,449.05, consisting of $78,739.80 in 1967, $93,609.25 in 1968 and $67,100 in 1969. By contrast, the appellant's net profit for the three-year period in respect of sales of competitive products appears to have been insignificant, if indeed there was any at all. There was a net loss of over $17,000 in 1967 and a net gain of some $18,000 in 1968. There was no net gain figure for 1969, but taking $67,100 as the gross trading profit for that year (as Anderson's evidence showed) the net profit, on any reasonable assessment of deductible expenses, could not have been very large. The respondent Thermidaire's gross trading profit during this period, if it had sold the units or products that Clarke had sold in the same period would have been $110,270, and this is the sum shown on ex. 72. The reason for the disparity between the gross trading profits of the appellant and of the respondent, referable to the same and to the same number of items, was that the respondent was a wholesaler selling through a distributor, the appellant, which sold direct to the consumer at retail prices. There could be no affinity between the respective profits of the two firms in respect of products which the appellant did in fact sell and those that the respondent might have sold in the same market during the three-year period because the respondent would be selling at wholesale prices and the appellant at retail prices which would involve a considerable distributor's or resale mark-up, as, for example, a 47% mark-up in 1968 as noted by Anderson in his evidence. (The mark-ups for 1967 and 1969, estimated by Anderson, were 52% and 45% respectively, and he regarded the mark-ups for the three years as reasonable.) Thus, their respective costs were different and their respective selling and administrative expenses were different.

Anderson's figures for Thermidaire's projected sales for 1967 to 1969 inclusive were the figures for Clarke's actual retail sales in that period less the resale mark-up. To take 1967, by way of illustration, Clarke's retail sales in that year of Thermidaire products had a value of $159,667.83, which less the mark-up left the sum of $102,154. From this sum Anderson deducted Thermidaire's cost of sales to arrive at gross profit and then deducted expenses to arrive at net profit for the year. His formula for determining cost of sales was based on an examination of the respondent's financial statements for the years 1967 to 1969 and a finding that the cost was a certain percentage of the selling price, namely, 30.37% for 1967 and until September, 1968 and 24.65% for the remainder of 1968 and for all of 1969. The lower percentage was because the respondent began to sell its own manufactured products in October, 1968. The percentages were applied to the retail sale figures of the appellant's sales (not deducting the resale mark-up) and thus a figure was obtained of the estimated cost of sales.

The estimated net profit loss of $92,017 was vigorously attacked by the appellant, and with some justification. For example, there appears to have been some dispute as to whether Anderson's calculations were based solely on so-called competitive products or included others that were not differentiated in the appellant's financial statements. I need say no more about it here other than that it represented an estimate that was as favourable as such an exercise could be to the party that commissioned it. Because of the views of the Courts below that gross trading profits were recoverable it was unnecessary for them to inquire into the merit of the sum put forward as the estimated loss of net profits.

I think it well to emphasize that the estimated actual loss of $92,017 and the estimated loss of gross trading profits of $239,449.05 are sums which relate to the entire three-year post-contract period during which the covenant not to compete was operative. Had the Court been called upon [to] deal with the question of liquidated damages or penalty at or shortly after the time that the contract was lawfully terminated neither the actual loss nor the gross trading profits would have been in any substantial figure, a result that would be fortified, and indeed secured, if an interlocutory injunction had been sought and granted. No such injunction was, however, even sought, and hence the continuation of the breach to the end of the post-contract covenant period yielded the high figures to which reference has been made.

Had a single sum been fixed as a pre-estimate in the amount of some $200,000, it is impossible to think that the Court would not have concluded that an *in terrorem* penalty had been fixed at the time of the contract. Moreover, to regard that sum as being equally claimable for a breach that lasted for a short time as well as for a breach which continued over the entire covenant period would be an unreasonable conclusion. The question that arises here however is whether the same appreciation should prevail in a case where the quantum of damages, actually suffered or claimable, depends on the length of time over which the covenantor continues to be in breach of its covenant.

Should the respondent here be faulted then because it did not seek an interim injunction when it filed its counterclaim on April 25, 1967, some three months after it terminated the contract, or because it did not thereafter seek an interlocutory injunction until trial through which to stanch the flow of damages measured by gross trading profits? There is no doubt that a covenantee cannot have both an injunction during the covenant period and damages based on a breach of covenant for the entire period where they are based on a formula. There is case law holding that where a fixed sum is stipulated as the liquidated damages upon a breach, the covenantee cannot have both the damages and an injunction but must elect between the two remedies: see *General Accident Assurance Corp. v. Noel*, [1962] 1 K.B. 377; *Wirth & Hamid Fair Booking Inc. et al. v. Wirth* (1934), 192 N.E. 297. I do not however read these cases as excluding damages for past loss by reason of the breach, but only as precluding recovery of the liquidated amount referable to breach in the future which that amount was designed to cover and against which an injunction has been granted. By not seeking an interim or interlocutory injunction, the respondent gives some support to the proposition that it was more profitable to it to let the default of the appellant continue. On the other hand, the appellant accepted the risk of being held liable for gross trading profits by continuing to be in breach for the entire post-contract period of the covenant's operation.

In this state of affairs, I think the proper course is to look at the situation (as in fact it was at the time of the trial) as one where each party was content to have the issue of liquidated damages or penalty determined according to the consequences of a breach over the entire period of the covenant. The appellant cannot, of course, escape liability for at least the damages which a Court would fix if called upon to do so. Should it be so called upon in this case by a holding that to allow recovery of gross trading profits would be to impose a penalty and not to give compensation in a situation where calculation of damages is difficult and incapable of precise determination? I would answer this question (and I do it after anxious consideration) in the affirmative.

I do not ignore a factor or factors in connection with breach of a covenant not to compete that are not as easily measured in dollars as are gross trading profits and net profits but which none the less have a value. These entered into the consideration of the Ontario Court of Appeal, and they were mentioned in Anderson's evidence, as follows:

> Q. Now I want you to make two assumptions before answering the question I am going to put to you. The first assumption is, assume that Thermidaire properly terminated Exhibit 3 for cause, and secondly, assume that Clarke sold products competitive with Thermidaire products during the three year period. In your opinion what harm would Thermidaire suffer as a result of Clarke's competition during that three year period, assuming he did compete?
>
> A. During the three year period he would suffer lost profits, because without that competition presumably he would have had more sales, with very few additional costs, inasmuch as he would have had access to an established market, that had been vacated. Now after the three year period the loss would continue because he doesn't have a group of customers that he might otherwise have had, and this loss is virtually incalculable — it would be very, very difficult to calculate without having more information.
>
> Q. Well, what additional information would assist you in making such a calculation?
>
> A. Information out of the books of H. F. Clarke Co. Ltd., product analysis, customer analysis — this type of information — so that we would know perhaps where we would be selling where we are not now, or where Thermidaire would be selling where it is not now — so that profit margin and so on could be actually computed; these factors would help.
>
> Q. Well, with this information, even with this information, how would you describe the task of calculating the dollar value of the harm done as you have described it?
>
> A. Very, very difficult.
>
> Q. Are there any intangibles in such a calculation?
>
> A. Yes, there are. The basic intangibles are, what harm has been done to Thermidaire for the lack of its name being before the public, its stature in the market place — this type of injury. I would say it would be an exceedingly difficult task to arrive with any degree of certainty at a figure.

When regard is had, on the one hand, to the market situation with which the respondent had to contend before the appellant became its distributor, and, on the other hand, to the position of the distributor as itself an already known firm in that market, the respondent is undoubtedly entitled to an allowance for what it has termed loss of product identification and goodwill and for depreciation of its customer and trade relations during the three-year period of unlawful competition by the appellant. This allowance cannot, however, be assessed on the basis that ignores completely the existence of the appellant. Whatever it may turn out to be, as related to and as in addition to the estimated net profit loss of $92,017, in my opinion it cannot, because of the difficulty of putting a figure on it, lend the necessary support to make the gross trading profits of $239,449.05 an acceptable measure of liquidated damages.

I regard the exaction of gross trading profits as a penalty in this case because it is, in my opinion, a grossly excessive and punitive response to the problem to which it was addressed; and the fact that the appellant subscribed to it, and may have been foolish to do so, does not mean that it should be left to rue its unwisdom. *Snell's Principles of Equity*, 27th ed. (1973), at p. 535 states the applicable doctrine as follows:

> The sum will be held to be a penalty if it is extravagant and unconscionable in amount in comparison with the greatest loss that could conceivably be proved to have followed from the breach.

This proposition comes from a statement by Lord Halsbury in the House of Lords in *Clydebank Engineering & Shipbuilding Co. Ltd. et al. v. Don José Ramos Yzquierdo y Castaneda et al.,* [1905] A.C. 6 at p. 10, and was reiterated by Lord Dunedin in *Dunlop Pneumatic Tyre Co., Ltd. v. New Garage & Motor Co., Ltd.,* [1915] A.C. 79 at p. 87. I do not think that it loses its force in cases where there is difficulty of exact calculation or pre-estimation when the stipulation for liquidated damages, as in this case, is disproportionate and unreasonable when compared with the damages sustained or which would be recoverable through an action in the Courts for breach of the covenant in question: see 25 Corp. Jur. Sec., § 108, pp. 1051 *et seq.* The fact that the highest amount put forward by the respondent as its actual loss was $92,017 is plainly indicative of the disproportion that resides in the exaction of gross trading profits of $239,449.05.

But this ignores the other factors

I would characterize the exaction of gross trading profits for a three-year period as a penalty and not as giving rise to a sum claimable as compensation by way of liquidated damages. The respondent is, however, entitled to recover its provable damages for the breach of covenant, and I would direct a reference to the Master at Toronto, Ontario to enable it to make its proof of all elements entering into such damages.

The appellant urged in this Court, as it did below, that sales of certain products ought not to be taken into account because they were not Thermidaire products within the terms of the contract. On this point I am in agreement with the Courts below which rejected this submission.

In the result, I would allow the appeal on what I have called the main issue, set aside the judgments below and in their place I would direct judgment for the respondent for damages for breach of the covenants not to compete with a reference to the Master at Toronto, Ontario, to ascertain the damages. The appellant should have its costs in this Court and in the Ontario Court of Appeal. The respondent should have the costs of the trial and of the reference as ordered by the trial Judge.

Martland, J. (dissenting): — I am in agreement with the unanimous reasons of the Court of Appeal for Ontario delivered by Brooke, J.A. [9 C.P.R. (2d) 203, 33 D.L.R. (3d) 13, [1973] 2 O.R. 57] and, accordingly, I would dismiss the appeal with costs.

Judson and Spence, JJ., concur with Laskin, C.J.C.

Dickson, J., concurs with Martland, J.

QUESTIONS

1. The substance of the judgment of the Ontario Court of Appeal is made clear from the extract quoted by Laskin C.J.C. Do you think that the Supreme Court of Canada and the Ontario Court of Appeal have the same view of:
   a) the law
   b) the reasons for the exercise of the power of the courts to review agreements of this kind?

2. What is wrong with the agreement in this case that would justify the decision of the majority of the S.C.C.?

3. Does Laskin's judgment in *Clarke v. Thermidaire* take the same justification for interference as his judgment in *Linton v. C.N.R.?*

STOCKLOSER v. JOHNSON

[1954] 1 Q.B. 476. Court of Appeal (England).

[The plaintiff agreed to purchase quarry equipment from the defendant. The contract provided that the payment of the purchase price should be made by instalments, and that should the purchaser be in default in making any payment for 28 days, the vendor, the defendant, should be entitled to rescind the contract, keep the instalments already paid and retake possession of the equipment. The plaintiff defaulted and sued for the return of the instalments paid. The trial judge allowed the plaintiff's claim in respect of part of the equipment but not in respect of another part. The defendant appealed and the plaintiff cross-appealed.]

Denning L.J. There was acute contest as to the proper legal principles to apply in this case. On the one hand, Mr. Neil Lawson urged us to hold that the buyer was entitled to recover the instalments at law. He said that the forfeiture clause should be ignored because it was of a penal character; and once it was ignored, it meant that the buyer was left with a simple right to repayment of his money on the lines of *Dies v. British and International Mining and Finance Corporation,* subject only to a cross-claim for damages. In asking us to ignore the forfeiture clause, Mr. Lawson relied on the familiar tests which are used to distinguish between penalties and liquidated damages, and said that these tests had been applied in cases for the repayment of money...

There is, I think, a plain distinction between penalty cases, strictly so called, and cases like the present.

It is this: when one party seeks to exact a penalty from the other, he is seeking to exact payment of an extravagant sum either by action at law or by appropriating to himself moneys belonging to the other party.... The claimant invariably relies, like Shylock, on the letter of the contract to support his demand, but the courts decline to give him their aid because they will not assist him in an act of oppression...

In the present case, however, the seller is not seeking to exact a penalty. He only wants to keep money which already belongs to him. The money was handed to him in part payment of the purchase price and, as soon as it was paid, it belonged to him absolutely. He did not obtain it by extortion or oppression or anything of that sort, and there is an express clause — a forfeiture clause, if you please — permitting him to keep it. It is not the case of a seller seeking to enforce a penalty, but a buyer seeking restitution of money paid. If the buyer is to recover it, he must, I think, have recourse to somewhat different principles from those applicable to penalties, strictly so called.

On the other hand, Mr. Beney urged us to hold that the buyer could only recover the money if he was able and willing to perform the contract, and for this purpose he ought to pay or offer to pay the instalments which were in arrear and be willing to pay the future instalments as they became due...

I think that this contention goes too far in the opposite direction. If the buyer was seeking to re-establish the contract, he would of course have to pay up the arrears and to show himself willing to perform the contract in the future, just as a lessee, who has suffered a forfeiture, has to do when he seeks to re-establish the lease. So, also, if the buyer were seeking specific performance he would have to show himself able and willing to perform his part. But the buyer's object here is not to re-establish the contract. It is to get his money back, and to do this I do not think that it is necessary for him to go so far as to show that he is ready and willing to perform the contract.

I reject, therefore, the arguments of counsel at each extreme. It seems to me that the cases show the law to be this: (1) *When there is no forfeiture clause.* If money is handed over in part payment of the purchase price, and then the buyer makes default as to the balance, then, so long as the seller keeps the contract open and available for performance, the buyer cannot recover the money; but once the seller rescinds the contract or treats it as at an end owing to the buyer's default, then the buyer is entitled to recover his money by action at law, subject to a cross-claim by the seller for damages: see ... *Dies v. British and International Co.;* Williams on Vendor and Purchaser, 4th ed., p. 1006. (2) *But when there is a forfeiture clause or the money is expressly paid as a deposit (which is equivalent to a forfeiture clause),* then the buyer who is in default cannot recover the money at law at all. He may, however, have a remedy in equity, for, despite the express stipulation in the contract, equity can relieve the buyer from forfeiture of the money and order the seller to repay it on such terms as the court thinks fit. That is, I think, shown clearly by the decision of the Privy Council in *Steedman v. Drinkle,* [1916] A.C. 275, where the Board consisted of a strong three, Viscount Haldane, Lord Parker and Lord Sumner.

The difficulty is to know what are the circumstances which give rise to this equity, but I must say that I agree with all that Somervell L.J. has said about it, differing herein from the view of Romer L.J. Two things are necessary: first, the forfeiture clause must be of a penal nature, in this sense, that the sum forfeited must be out of all proportion to the damage, and, secondly, it must be unconscionable for the seller to retain the money. Inasmuch as the only case in which this jurisdiction has been exercised is *Steedman v. Drinkle,* I have examined the record and would draw attention to the circumstances of that case. The agreement was in effect a hire-purchase agreement of land. The purchase-money was payable by instalments over six years, completion to be at the end of the six years, and meanwhile the purchasers were to be let into possession of the land as tenants with the instalments ranking as rent. In case of default the vendor was at liberty to cancel the contract and retain the payments which had been made. The purchasers paid the first instalment and went into possession, but they failed to pay the second instalment which was due at the end of the first year. The value of the land had risen greatly during that year and the vendor seized upon the purchaser's default as giving him the opportunity to rescind the contract. Without previous warning, the vendor gave notice cancelling the contract. The purchasers at once tendered the amount due but the vendor refused to accept it. The purchasers issued a writ for specific performance and meanwhile remained in possession of the land taking the crops off it. They failed to get specific performance in the first court, then succeeded in the Court of Appeal, but failed again in the Privy Council on the ground that time was expressly of the essence of the contract. Nevertheless, the Privy Council relieved the purchasers from forfeiture of the sums already paid. The purchasers would no doubt have to give credit for the crops they had taken from the land during the three years or more that they had been in possession, but subject to that credit they would get their money back.

In the later case of *Mussen v. Van Dieman's Land Co.* [1938] Ch. 253, Farwell J. said that the whole basis of the decision in *Steedman v. Drinkle* was that the purchasers were ready and willing to perform the contract; but I think that that is much too narrow an explanation. Readiness and willingness is essential in specific performance, and in relief from forfeiture of leases, but not in relief from forfeiture of sums paid. The basis of the decision in *Steedman v. Drinkle* was, I think, that the vendor had somewhat sharply exercised his right to rescind the contract and retake the land, and it was unconscionable for him also to forfeit the sums already paid. Equity could not specifically enforce the contract, but it could and would relieve against the forfeiture.

In the course of the argument before us Somervell L.J. put an illustration which shows the necessity for this equity even though the buyer is not ready and willing to perform the contract. Suppose a buyer has agreed to buy a necklace by instalments, and the contract provides that, on default in payment of any one instalment, the seller is entitled to rescind the contract and forfeit the instalments already paid. The buyer pays 90 per cent of the price but fails to pay the last instalment. He is not able to perform the contract because he simply cannot find the money. The seller thereupon rescinds the contract and retakes the necklace and resells it at a higher price. Surely equity will relieve the buyer against forfeiture of the money on such terms as may be just.

Again, suppose that a vendor of property, in lieu of the usual 10 per cent. deposit, stipulates for an initial payment of 50 per cent. of the price as a deposit and a part payment; and later, when the purchaser fails to complete, the vendor resells the property at a profit and in addition claims to forfeit the 50 per cent. deposit. Surely the court will relieve against the forfeiture. The vendor cannot forestall this equity by describing an extravagant sum as a deposit, any more than he can recover a penalty by calling it liquidated damages.

These illustrations convince me that in a proper case there is an equity of restitution which a party in default does not lose simply because he is not able and willing to perform the contract. Nay, that is the very reason why he needs the equity. The equity operates, not because of the plaintiff's default, but because it is in the particular case unconscionable for the seller to retain the money. In short, he ought not unjustly to enrich himself at the plaintiff's expense. This equity of restitution is to be tested, I think, not at the time of the contract, but by the conditions existing when it is invoked. Suppose, for instance, that in the instance of the necklace, the first instalment was only 5 per cent. of the price; and the buyer made default on the second instalment. There would be no equity by which he could ask for the first instalment to be repaid to him any more than he could claim repayment of a deposit. But it is very different after 90 per cent. has been paid. Again, delay may be very material. Thus in *Mussen's* case the court was much influenced by the fact that the purchaser had allowed nearly six years to elapse before claiming restitution. He had already had a good deal of land conveyed to him and, during his six years delay, values had so greatly changed that it may be that he had had his money's worth. At any rate, it was not unconscionable for the defendant to retain the money.

Applying these principles to the present case, even if one regards the forfeiture clause as of a penal nature — as the judge did and I am prepared to do — nevertheless I do not think that it was unconscionable for the seller to retain the money. The buyer seems to have gambled on the royalties being higher than they were. He thought that they would go a long way to enable him to pay the instalments; but owing to bad weather they turned out to be smaller than he had hoped and he could not find the additional amount necessary to pay the instalments. The judge summarized the position neatly when he said that the purchaser "is in the position of a gambler who has lost his stake and is now saying that it is for the court of equity to get it back for him." He said, "if it is a question of what is unconscionable, or, to use a word with a less legal flavour, unfair, I can see nothing whatever unfair in the defendant retaining the money." With that finding of the judge I entirely agree and think that it disposes of the purchaser's claim to restitution. . . .

Romer L.J. It appears to me that it is an essential foundation for the purchaser's contention to the effect that clause 5 of the agreement of April 6, 1950, and the corresponding clause (clause 6) of the agreement of June 24, 1950, operated as penalties, from which he is entitled to be relieved, that he should be able to establish that on the true construction of those clauses the vendor would be entitled, on the default of the purchaser in paying an instalment, not only to retain the instalments which had been previously paid but also to recover from the purchaser the royalties which he had received from the hirers of the plant. I say this because where A agrees to sell an income-producing asset to B by deferred payments, and it is expressly provided in the contract that if B (who is allowed to enter into immediate possession) defaults in payment of an instalment, A may rescind, and thereupon B shall forfeit the instalments which he has paid but shall be entitled to retain the income which he has received, no question of a penalty can arise — and a fortiori where profits and instalments are likely to be equated to the extent which my Lord has indicated in his judgment; and the position is the same if a bargain to that effect is implicit in the contract although not introduced into it by express language. It is only if a purchaser, on default, forfeits to the vendor both past instalments and past profits of an income-producing asset that he can be regarded as entering the area of jurisdiction which the purchaser is seeking to invoke in the present case.

What, then, was the position in this regard under the relevant clauses in the two agreements? In my opinion it is quite plain that, on the vendor rescinding by reason of the purchaser's default, the ensuing forfeiture was to operate only on past instalments of the purchase moneys and that the purchaser was to be left in undisturbed possession of the royalties which he had previously received. The purchaser's contention to the contrary was entirely based on the provision in the clauses that, if the vendor elected to "rescind," he was to be entitled again to enter into enjoyment of the hiring agreements and the fruits thereof "as though" the agreements between vendor and purchaser "had never been executed." The argument is that if the agreements had never been executed the vendor would have been entitled to all the profits of the hiring agreements and that the object of the clauses was to restore these profits to him on rescission. In my judgment the judge was quite right in rejecting this argument, which involves the conception of rescission ab initio, with the result, inter alia, that the vendor would be

APPEL TÉLÉPHONIQUE
PHONE CALL

Date.. Heure
                                           Time........................

A
To..

DURANT VOTRE ABSENCE
WHILE YOU WERE OUT

M..

de
of..

No. de téléphone
Phone..

A téléphoné Telephoned	☐	Appelez-le S.V.P. Please call	☐
Est venu vous voir Called to see you	☐	Doit rappeler Will call again	☐
Voudrait vous voir Wants to see you	☐	A répondu à votre appel Returned your call	☐

MESSAGE..

....

....

....

Opératrice
Operator..

FORM NO. 24B

BOND PRINTERS & STATIONERS LTD.

automatically deprived of any accrued rights arising from the indemnities contained in the first and second agreement. It is quite clear to me that the contemplated "rescissions" were not to operate retrospectively and that the "fruits" of the hiring agreements which the vendor was "again" (a word not without significance) to enjoy were confined to future profits.

On this view of the matter, as I have already indicated, no question of penalties or relief therefrom arises and the plaintiff's claim against the defendant wholly fails; with the result that the defendant's appeal should be allowed and the cross-appeal should be dismissed. Out of deference, however, to the argument which was addressed to us on the assumption that the forfeiture clause in each agreement constituted a penalty, or something in the nature of a penalty, I should like to deal with the question of whether the purchaser could have successfully sought the intervention of equity, in relation to the contractual results of these provisions, if the profit-producing quality of the properties to which I have referred had not existed. The matter was considered by the late Farwell J. in *Mussen's* case, but before referring further to that case it would be convenient to consider the point as one of principle.

Generally speaking, courts of equity have never interfered with contracts merely by reason of their being improvident. "The Chancery," as Lord Nottingham said in *Maynard v. Moseley,* (1676) 3 Swanst. 651, 655 "mends no man's bargain." To this rule exceptions were made, notably in favour of expectant heirs and borrowers, to whom equity manifested some tenderness, on the supposition that the sale or mortgaging of their inheritances or properties was usually induced by the pressure of financial need. Such persons were regarded as being to some extent at the mercy of persons who were willing, on terms, to enter into financial relations with them, and the court frequently intervened so as to relieve them from the strict letter of their obligations upon such conditions as it considered fair and just. The equity of redemption which mortgagors have enjoyed for over 300 years had its origin in this exceptional jurisdiction and may be taken as an example of it.

In general, however, as I have said, people were expected to abide by their contracts, and if a man made a foolish or improvident one so much the worse for him. The question, then, is whether a purchaser who freely and voluntarily negotiates and executes a contract of sale upon terms that the price is to be paid by instalments and that, on default by him of payment of any instalment, the vendor may rescind the contract and retain any instalments previously paid, is entitled to relief in equity if he finds himself unable to comply with his bargain. It is to be observed that, in such a case, no element of pressure or duress exists and no question of the purchaser acting under the stress of economic necessity; both parties to the contract are on terms of bargaining equality with each other, the one desiring to exchange cash for property, the other desiring to exchange property for cash. I confess that, in these circumstances, I am unable to see what ground there is for interference by a court of equity if it ultimately turns out that the terms on which these exchanges are mutually agreed operate hardly on either vendor or purchaser. If one of the terms which the vendor requires is disagreeable to the purchaser he is under no compulsion to accept it; he can either keep his money and forgo the property or he can purchase a similar property from some other vendor who is more tolerant in his approach to the conditions of sale.

If a man agrees to buy property by instalments which he will forfeit to the vendor if he cannot continue them to completion, he knows perfectly well the risk which he is taking and I do not know what right he has to appeal to equity if that risk does in fact ripen into actuality....

Pausing then at this point, it appears to me that the cases establish that if a purchaser defaults in punctual payment of instalments of purchase-money the court will, in a proper case, relieve the purchaser from his contractual liability to forfeit instalments (apart from the deposit) already paid to the extent of giving him a further chance and further time to pay the money which is in arrear if he is able and willing to do so; but the cases do not, in my judgment, show that the court will relieve such a purchaser to any further extent than this....

There is, in my judgment, nothing inequitable per se in a vendor, whose conduct is not open to criticism in other respects, insisting upon his contractual right to retain instalments of purchase-money already paid. In my judgment, there is no sufficient ground for interfering with the contractual rights of a vendor under forfeiture clauses of the nature which are now under consideration, while the contract is still subsisting, beyond giving a purchaser who is in default, but who is able and willing to proceed with the contract, a further opportunity of doing so; and no relief of any other nature can properly be given, in the absence of some special circumstances such as fraud, sharp practice or other unconscionable conduct of the vendor, to a purchaser after the vendor has rescinded the contract.

My brother Denning in his judgment has referred to the hypothetical case which was suggested during the argument of a purchaser who buys a pearl necklace on terms that the purchase price is to be payable by instalments and that the vendor is to be entitled to get the necklace back and retain all previous payments if the purchaser makes default in the punctual payment of any instalment, even the final one. It would certainly seem hard that the purchaser should lose both the necklace and all previous instalments owing to his inability to pay the last one. But that is the bargain into which the purchaser freely entered and the risk which he voluntarily accepted. The court would doubtless, as I have already indicated, give him further time to find the money if he could establish some probability of his being able to do so, but I do not know why it should interfere further; nor would it be easy to determine at what point in his failure to pay the agreed instalments the suggested equity would arise. In any event I venture to suggest that it is extremely unlikely that such a case would occur in practice; for a purchaser who had paid, say, nine-tenths of the agreed price for the necklace would have little difficulty in borrowing the remaining one-tenth on the security of his interest therein....

I have dealt with this question at, I am afraid, some length because it is an important one and because we heard considerable argument on at least some aspects of it. It does not in truth arise in the present case because, on the facts and on the true construction of the agreements between the plaintiff and the defendant, nothing in the nature of a penalty (or indeed of a forfeiture in any real sense) enters into the picture. I would, however, like to point out that the plaintiff could not, in my opinion, invoke any equitable jurisdiction or remedy in the present case. Even after the defendant rescinded he invited the plaintiff to make some proposal for the belated fulfilment of his obligations, but without any response from the plaintiff, who never made the slightest attempt to remedy his default. But, further, although it appears that he received a sum of £4,000 from Canada he paid none of it towards the discharge of his obligations to the defendant, but diverted it all elsewhere; and conduct of that kind is a poor qualification in a suitor for equitable relief....

[Somerville J. gave a judgment to the same effect as Denning L.J.]

GISVOLD v. HILL

(1963), 37 D.L.R. (2d) 606. British Columbia Supreme Court

[The plaintiffs agreed to sell their house to the defendants who agreed to pay $17,500. The defendants failed to pay the price on closing. The parties used a standard form agreement prepared by the Vancouver Real Estate Board but no agent was involved. The defendants paid $1 as a deposit. The plaintiffs subsequently sold the house for $17,900.]

Aikins J.... The plaintiffs were under no obligation to pay a real estate agent's commission on the sale to the defendants, but, on the second sale, that is the sale in May, they became liable for a commission of $700 and they paid this commission. The plaintiffs assert that this sum of $700 is an expense of the second sale and that they, therefore, only received a net of $17,200 out of the total proceeds of $17,900 and that they thereby suffered a loss of $300 as a result of the failure of the defendants to pay the purchase price of $17,500.

The measure of damages is, I think, the difference between the contract-price and the market value of the property at the time when the transaction should have been completed by payment of the balance of the purchase-price. Under the terms of the interim agreement, that date was March 25, 1960. The resale price of $17,900, in my opinion, is the only evidence of the market value of the property following the default of the defendants. On the face of it there was no loss to the plaintiffs and the plaintiffs actually gained $400 on the resale. The loss of $300 claimed by the plaintiffs is valid only if the damages are to be computed by taking the contract-price of $17,500 and deducting the net proceeds received by the plaintiffs after allowing them to deduct as an expense of sale the $700 expended by them in order to effect the sale of $17,900.

The proper rule as to the measure of damages is I think, correctly stated in *Mayne & McGregor on Damages*, 12th ed., para. 472, as follows:

> The true analysis is this. The seller recovers the full contract price less the *net* market value of the property left on his hands, *i.e.*, the amount at which a resale has been or could be made deducting therefrom the costs of resale. Thus the expenses to be looked at are not those of the abortive sale but those of the resale, or, where there has been no resale, the estimated cost of a resale.

In the particular circumstances of this case, there being no commission payable on the aborted sale and the commission properly paid on the resale whereby the plaintiffs mitigated their damages, the plaintiffs would, in the absence of any agreement precluding recovery, be entitled to the $300 damages claimed.

In the present case, by the interim agreement, the parties to this action agreed as follows:

> It is understood that time shall be of the essence hereof, and unless the balance

of the cash payment is paid and a formal agreement entered into within the time mentioned to pay the balance, the owner may (at his option) cancel this agreement, and in such event the amount paid by the purchaser shall be absolutely forfeited to the owner as liquidated damages.

On the defendants refusing to pay the balance of the purchase-price and repudiating the agreement, the plaintiffs had two courses open to them. First, they could have proceeded against the defendants to enforce the agreement and recover the purchase-price which the defendants agreed to pay. Secondly, and in the alternative, they had the right to cancel the agreement and to retain the deposit as liquidated damages. The plaintiffs did not make any election to cancel the agreement by any formal action, that is by any form of notification of cancellation to the defendants, but I think they must be held to have elected to cancel the agreement because by selling the house in question to persons other than the defendants, the plaintiffs put it beyond their power to carry out their part of the agreement with the defendants. The position, therefore, put simply, is this: the plaintiffs by their conduct have elected to treat the agreement as cancelled and they have retained the amount of one dollar paid by the defendants as a deposit on account of the proposed purchase-price.

The interim agreement, with reference to the forfeiture of the monies paid by the purchasers (the defendants), uses the words, "shall be absolutely forfeited to the owner as liquidated damages". If it were not set out in the agreement that the monies forfeited would be forfeited as liquidated damages there would be no problem, the plaintiffs would be entitled to such damages as they could prove and the defendants would be entitled to credit the forfeited deposit against the amount of such damages. If by the use of the words which I have quoted, the plaintiffs are to be taken to have agreed by fixing or liquidating the damages in the amount of the forfeited deposit to have given up any claim for damages in excess of this amount, then, by agreement, the defendants' liability is limited to the amount forfeited. If, on the other hand, the words used on proper construction thereof, do not show that the plaintiffs agreed that the amount forfeited to them as liquidated damages would be all the damages to which they would be entitled, notwithstanding that their actual loss might be greater, then neither the defendants' liability to pay damages or the plaintiffs' right to recover damages is limited thereby.

In addition to the problem of construing the clause which I have quoted from the interim agreement, there is a further issue which arises and which was argued. In most cases in which it is necessary to consider whether the sum of money stated to be liquidated damages and to be either forfeited to, or recovered by one party to an agreement from the other, the issue is whether the amount agreed upon is unreasonably large in relation to the loss and is, therefore, a penalty, and whether or not relief should be given to the party penalized. In the instant case the situation as argued for the plaintiffs, is the reverse of the usual one. It is submitted by counsel for the plaintiffs that the sum of one dollar, the only money actually paid by the defendants, is unreasonably small in relation to the loss, and that the plaintiffs are thereby penalized and should have relief.

There are, therefore, two problems. First, does the clause in the agreement which I have quoted and which uses the words "as liquidated damages" mean that the parties have by agreement liquidated or fixed the damages in advance of breach and that the plaintiffs are bound thereby regardless of the actual damage? Secondly, if it does mean this then is the amount so disproportionately small as to penalize the persons to whom it is forfeited, that is the plaintiffs, and are they entitled to any relief?

. . .

My conclusion is that the parties by using the particular words "as liquidated damages", by agreement fixed or liquidated the damages and that they are bound thereby, unless as is argued for the plaintiffs, the sum of one dollar agreed upon is to be considered a penalty against the plaintiffs and they are entitled to relief.

This brings me to the second question that was argued, namely, is the amount of one dollar agreed upon as liquidated damages so disproportionately small in relation to the probable loss that it should be considered a penalty against the plaintiffs, and, if so, are they entitled to relief? The learned author of the twelfth edition of *Mayne & McGregor on Damages* at para. 251, writing about the peculiar situation of the stipulated sum to be paid or forfeited being disproportionately small in relation to the loss, says:

> Occasionally however, the situation may arise where the stipulated sum is disproportionately small in relation to the probable loss. Here it is still true that the stipulated sum is disproportionate to, and cannot be said to be a genuine pre-estimate of, the probable loss; but it cannot realistically be called a penalty in the conventional sense of an extravagant and unconscionable sum fixed *in terrorem*. The only manner in which it might be said that a sum substantially smaller than the probable loss could be a penalty is in relation not to the party paying but to the party to be paid the sum: he has agreed to accept as compensation for breach a completely inadequate amount, which is thus fixed *in terrorem of him* and penalises *him*. Yet the possibilities of oppression from an unconscionably large agreed sum are greater than in the case of an agreement for an amount less than the probable loss, and the courts have not been astute to see oppression where a party has agreed to cut down on his prima facie rights, as is clear from the many limitation of liability clauses which are daily upheld in the courts. A small agreed sum of this type is indeed akin to a clause limiting the extent in damages of a party's liability; it differs from such a clause only in that it does not represent a ceiling beyond which the recoverable damages cannot rise but forms the exact amount that may be recovered even if in the result the actual damage is less than the stipulated figure.

In *Cellulose Acetate Silk Co. v. Widnes Foundry (1925), Ltd.*, [1933] A.C. 20, the House of Lords had to consider this problem. In this case the defendants agreed to deliver and erect an acetone recovery plant for the plaintiff within a limited time and to pay £20 a week as a penalty for each week's delay. Much greater damage could have been expected from delay in completion and in fact was suffered by the plaintiff. The plaintiff sought to recover its actual damage, maintaining that the agreed sum was a penalty and should be disregarded. It was found that the sum of £20 a week was not a pre-estimate of the damage, but that by agreeing to this amount as a weekly penalty to be paid by the defendant, the plaintiff had agreed that the defendants' liability for delay would be limited to this amount. The decision turns in large part on the course of negotiations between the parties and the question with which I am concerned was left open. Lord Atkin said at p. 26:

> For these reasons I think the Silk Company are only entitled to recover £20. a week as agreed damages; and that the decision of the Court of Appeal was correct and should be affirmed. In these circumstances I find it unnecessary to con-

sider what would be the position if this were a penalty. It was argued by the appellants that if this were a penalty they would have an option either to sue for the penalty or for damages for breach of the promise as to time of delivery. I desire to leave open the question whether, where a penalty is plainly less in amount than the prospective damages, there is any legal objection to suing on it, or in a suitable case ignoring it and suing for damages.

Counsel for the plaintiffs did not refer me to any case which seemed to me to be directly in point and I have been unable to find any decision dealing with the question left open by the House of Lords.

Regardless of whether or not in appropriate circumstances a sum of money stated to be liquidated damages and which is disproportionately small in relation to the probable loss may be regarded as a penalty, and relief given to the party to whom the sum is to be paid by allowing him to recover his actual loss, and I do not purport to decide this question, the circumstances of the present case are not in my opinion such as to justify any such relief being given. In the present case the parties entered into a binding agreement to sell and purchase. The parties agreed to a deposit of one dollar. It was stipulated that time should be of the essence. The plaintiffs and the defendants agreed that if the defendants did not make the payment they agreed to make on the agreed date then the plaintiffs would have the right to cancel the agreement and in such event that the deposit would be forfeited as liquidated damages. The interim agreement was dated March 16th and the cash payment of the balance was to be made on the 25th day of the same month. This is a comparatively short period, 9 days only, and I cannot conceive that the parties, if they had directed their minds consciously to the question of what loss the plaintiffs might suffer if the purchase-price was not paid at the end of the 9-day period, would have come to the conclusions that the value of the house would fluctuate in any substantial amount over such a short time, and that there might be substantial damages. In these circumstances, on the plaintiffs exercising their right, given to them by the agreement, of electing to cancel and retain the house and forfeit the deposit, I do not think it can be said that the forfeiture of the deposit of one dollar as liquidated damages is unreasonable. It is also an important circumstance of this case that the plaintiffs on default by the defendants were not left in the position that the only thing they could do was forfeit the one dollar deposit. The plaintiffs had an election, they did not have to accept the one dollar, they could, if they had seen fit to do so, have sued to enforce the agreement. In these circumstances the plaintiffs must be held to their bargain. The plaintiffs' action is accordingly dismissed with costs.

QUESTIONS

1. Does the case of *Gisvold v. Hill* offer an alternative solution to the problem faced by the draftsman who wants to limit his client's liability in the event of breach?

2. Should the parties be put free to determine the application of the following issues to their case:

  (a) The application of the rules in *Hadley v. Baxendale*;
  (b) The right to an equitable remedy;
  (c) The exclusion of the effect of The Limitations Act;
  (d) The abandonment of the right to sue at all?

3. What would happen if Canner in the problem in Chap. 1, B. stipulated that for every ton which Farmer sold elsewhere he should pay Canner $50? It can be

accepted that this is a genuine attempt to fix a figure for Canner's losses in these circumstances.

4. Builder agrees to construct a house for Owner for $40,000. The date of completion is to be October 1. The contract provides that if the house is completed before that date Owner will pay a bonus of $10,000. The time allowed for completion is reasonable and a fair price for the house would be $50,000.

5. Contractor agrees with the Ontario Government to build a bridge on a new highway. The highway is planned as an important new link between Toronto and Hamilton. The Government is concerned that all work be completed on schedule, and that, for example, the opening (which is planned to occur before the next election) not be delayed because one bridge is not finished. The contract provides that Contractor shall pay $1,000 per day for every day taken to complete the bridge beyond the day fixed for completion.

Consider the following situations:
(a) Contractor is 10 days late;
(b) Contractor is 50 days late;
(c) Contractor abandons the bridge which is finished by another 100 days late.
Can the Government recover the agreed damages in each of these cases?

Would your answers to any of the above questions and problems be different if you:
(a) adopted Laskin's view in *Clarke v. Thermidaire;*
(b) adopted the view of the Ontario Court of Appeal;
(c) adopted the view of Denning L.J. in *Stockloser v. Johnson;*
(d) adopted the view of Romer L.J. in that case?

A Tentative Solution

LLEWELLYN, THE COMMON LAW TRADITION

pp. 362-371

19. *The Form or Boiler-Plate "Agreement"*

(Footnotes are at end of article.)

I know of few "private" law problems which remotely rival the importance, economic, governmental, or "law"-legal, of the form-pad agreement; and I know of none which has been either more disturbing to life or more baffling to lawyers.

The impetus to the form-pad is clear, for any business unit: by standardizing terms, and by standardizing even the spot on the form where any individually dickered term appears, one saves all the time and skill otherwise needed to dig out and record the meaning of variant language; one makes check-up, totaling, follow-through, etc., into routine operations; one has duplicates (in many colors) available for the administration of a multidepartment business; and so on more. The content of the standardized terms accumulates experience, it avoids or reduces legal risks and also confers all kinds of operating leeways and advantages, all without need of either consulting counsel from instance to instance or of bargaining with the other parties. Not to be overlooked, either, is the tailoring of the crude misfitting hand-me-down pattern of the "general law" "in the absence of agreement" to the particular detailed working needs of your own line of business — whether apartment rentals, stock brokerage, international grain trade, installment selling of appliances, flour milling, sugar beet raising, or insurance. It would be a heart-warming scene, a triumph of private attention to what is essentially private self-government in the lesser transactions of life or in those areas too specialized for the blunt, slow tools of the legislature — if only all businessmen and all their lawyers would be reasonable.

But power, like greed, if it does not always corrupt, goes easily to the head. So that the form-agreements tend either at once or over the years, and often by whole lines of trade, into a massive and almost terrifying jug-handled character; the one party lays his head into the mouth of a lion — either, and mostly, without reading the fine print, or occasionally in hope and expectation (not infrequently solid) that it will be a sweet and gentle lion. The more familiar instances, perhaps, are the United Realtors' Standard Lease, almost any bank's collateral note or agreement, almost any installment sale form, an accident insurance policy, a steamship ticket, a beet sugar refinery contract with a farmer or a flour miller's with its customer; or, on a lesser scale, the standard nonwarranty given by seed companies or auto manufacturers. In regard to such, one notes four things: (1) sometimes language which seems at first sight horrifying may have good human and economic stimulus; thus, suits for loss of crop before a farmer jury are pretty terrible things to face for the price of a few bags of seed; and (2) there are crooked claims and there are irrationally unreasonable ones — each with its jury risk — as well as solid ones; and only a clause which in law bars the claim absolutely can free an outfit like an insurance company to deal fairly though "in its discretion" with the latter class. On the other hand, (3) boiler-plate clauses can and often do run far beyond any such need or excuse, sometimes (thus, as early as our *Lake v. Columbus Ins. Co.,* Ohio, 1844, above, pp. 69 f., and distressingly today in, e.g., the cheap furniture business) involving flagrant trickery; and (4) not all "dominant" parties are nice lions, and even nice lions can make mistakes.

There is a fifth and no less vital thing to note: Where the form is drawn with a touch of Mr. Dooley's "gentlemanly restraint," or where, as with the overseas grain contracts or the Pacific Coast dried fruit contracts or the Worth Street Rules on textiles, two-fisted bargainers on either side have worked out in the form a balanced code to govern the particular line or trade or industry, there is every reason for a court to assume both fairness and wisdom in the terms, and to seek in first instance to learn, understand, and fit both its own thinking and its action into the whole design. Contracts of this kind (so long as reasonable in the net) are a road to better than official-legal regulation of our economic life; indeed, they tend to lead into the setting up of their own quick, cheap, expert tribunals.

·   ·   ·

Such is the background of a phenomenon which has been gaining in importance for more than a century, its well-done pieces tending, as stated, to slide off out of court or "legal" notice because of dispute avoidance, ready adjustment, or arbitration. For the work of official law that has been unfortunate. It has tended to keep out of the familiar law books, where they might stir imitation and imagination of other lawyers, the balanced type of boiler-plate. It has tended also to keep away from the appellate courts enough contact with the balanced type of form to let that type grow into a recognized pattern and a welcomed standard against which hog-drafting can be spotted, measured, and damned, so that the two different approaches and technique-lines of construction which are needed could be made articulate and reserved each to its appropriate sphere[1] Instead, the material which has come into court and into the American books has been in the main the jug-handled, mess-making stuff. What, then, of that?

For the courts, the story is quick to tell, though the cases must run into the thousands, and with no reckonability anywhere in sight. Unpredictably, they read the document for what it says, drop a word about freedom of contract, or about opportunity to read or improvident use of the pen, or about powerlessness of the court to do more than regret, or the like, and proceed to spit the victim for the barbecue. With equal unpredictability, they see the lopsided document as indecent, and evade it:

> A court can "construe" language into patently not meaning what the language is patently trying to say. It can find inconsistencies between clauses and throw out the troublesome one. It can even reject a clause as counter to the whole purpose of the transaction. It can reject enforcement by one side for want of "mutuality," though allowing enforcement by the weaker side because "consideration" in some other sense is present. Indeed, the law of agreeing can be subjected to divers modes of employment, to make the whole bargain or a particular clause stick or not stick according to the status of the party claiming under it: as when, in the interest of the lesser party, the whole contract is conditioned on some presupposition which is held to have failed. The difficulty with these techniques of ours is threefold. First, since they all rest on the admission that the clauses in question are permissible in purpose and content, they invite the draftsman to recur to the attack. Give him time, and he will make the grade. Second, since they do not face the issue, they fail to accumulate either experience or authority in the needed direction: that of marking out for any given type of transaction what the *minimum decencies* are which a court will insist upon as essential to an enforceable bargain of a given type, or as being inherent in a bargain of that type. Third, since they purport to construe, and do not really construe, nor are intended to, but are instead tools of intentional and creative misconstruction, they seriously embarrass later efforts at true construction, later efforts to get at the true meaning of those wholly legitimate contracts and clauses which call for their meaning to be got at instead of avoided. The net effect is unnecessary confusion and unpredictability, together with inadequate remedy, and evil persisting that calls for remedy. Covert tools are never reliable tools.[2]

It is plain that the effect of such work on "Words and Phrases" and the like can be pretty awful. Above all, the sound impulse for fairness — better, against outrage — fails to *cumulate* into any effective or standard techniques, except in a very few areas such as life and fire insurance. Moreover, such techniques as the above are, for the most part (the "repugnancy" idea is a striking exception), mere dodge or artifice, ready to prove embarrassing if taken seriously tomorrow in a case of a different flavor. Thus, knocking out an auto manufacturer's enforcement of a power-clause in an agency contract on the ground that the bargain lacks consideration or "mutuality" can lead (and has) to conferring at-will termination power on the same manufacturer, so to speak by operation of court.

What, now, have the scholars added? They began, so far as my reading goes, by making the matter worse. The Story passage on nominal consideration which was quoted at page 166 is typical of the all-or-nothing approach which was applied, as well, to contract formation; the "classical" law of offer and acceptance may have made it tricky to accept those offers which their "master" was supposed to shape with fiendish ingenuity to keep the deal from being closed, but once one was cleanly closed — as by an accepting signature on a form — the "classical" approach to what has been "assented to" was equally formal, rigid, and devoid of contact with the facts of life. Up until 1925 or 1930, except for a luggage check or so, the classrooms of the country honored the problem by ignoring it, by quiet assump-

tion that signature means assent, and, should one of the tough cases cross
the mind, then, whenever "consideration" could be technically established,
pilloried the "inadequate analysis" of judges who were finding in absence of
"mutuality" a way of protecting the signer-upper whose nose was firmly in
the dirt. The matter paralleled the harshness of the keen-eyed scholar on
those more labored forms of misconstruction of "description" in a sales
contract which courts have (irregularly) used to work out an undercover
law of substantial compliance in cases where such a rule is needed.

But no one was able to come up with any practicable *general* line of remedy. The New York model lease-form was disregarded. Insurance was
partly under legislative and/or administrative control — as in due course
were, for instance, the agreements of bond issue trustees; and efforts were
being made to slightly clean up the installment selling abuses by way of legislation — but no such attack had any general application. Everyone with
sense did agree that the bargained-out form-contract was a device of value,
of singular promise.

But even where the form moved into the shockingly outrageous, there
was not too much general operating help to be had from going at the matter
bluntly by way of reality of assent to the boiler-plate material, because
among those terms which plainly are in fact assented to only one time in a
thousand there are still many which are sound particularizations of the deal
to the business, very useful and wholly within reason; and those ought to be
sustained and applied. A workable guide for courts must offer some wherewithal to sort such out from the clauses of oppression or outrage, some
wherewithal to sustain the one, reject the other. As suggested above, the
court's own lines remained almost equally blind on this; they tended (save
in regard to the infrequent "repugnancy" concept) to strike down the whole
deal in order to prevent enforcement of the obnoxious clause. The following
passage of mine from 1939 was entirely abreast of the thought of the day.
Note the almost complete absence of available *measures* and traditional
support to allow an appellate court to justify to its own conscience that
remodeling of the agreement which is so often called for:

> The crude but effective ax-work of centuries past on forfeit of security can serve
> as precedent and impetus, but the examination of the standardized contract of a
> particular modern line of trade to distinguish clauses serving the better function-
> ing of the work from those inspired by the sole interest of the higher contracting
> party (to paraphrase Demogue . . .) is not a task for which a common-law judge's
> equipment has peculiarly fitted him.
>
> Nor do I think it will ever so fit him fully. But what it does fit him for is to see
> that there is such a distinction; to see that free contract presupposes free bargain,
> and that free bargain presupposes free bargaining; and that where bargaining is
> absent in fact, the conditions and clauses to be read into a bargain are not those
> which happen to be printed on the unread paper, but are those which a sane man
> might reasonably expect to find on that paper. The background of trade practice
> gives a first indication; the line of authority rejecting unreasonable practice
> offers the needed corrective. The distinction involved, even when applied to the
> testing of a standardized printing, is a simple one, and one which responds rather
> readily to the trained intuition of a case-law judge for what is *too* unfair. Courts
> have taken distinctions much like it, as Prausnitz shows, for instance, in regard to
> what kind of policy an oral contract for insurance called for. It is a distinction,
> too, which makes sense in the reading of people's actions. It offers a wherewithal
> for striking out utterly unreasonable clauses, while yet leaving a due presumption

in favor of an expert's knowledge of what the conditions of his trade may be calling for. Courts' business is not the making of detailed contracts for parties; but courts' business is eminently the marking out of the limits of the permissible, and the reading of fair understanding, and the adaptation to the modern form-pad bargain of older rules based on the individualized *writings* of an earlier day — and still applicable to such writings.[3]

What the story shows thus far is first, scholars persistently off-base while judges grope over well-nigh a century in irregular but dogged fashion for escape from a recurring discomfort of imbalance that rests on what is in fact substantial *non*agreement despite perfect semblance of agreement. We have then thirty-five years or so while scholars slowly wake up and launch a type of general inquiry, comparative study, diagnosis, and analysis which develops a depth and a perspective hard for judicial case-by-case experience to rival. Yet thus far the scholars are still sticking in the bark of the job: they cannot come to grips with effective *measures*: while the appellate judges, still irregularly, but somewhat less so, are slowly getting (as a class) a little clearer about the net ideals of avoiding indecency and preserving at least a color of balance, in form-pad deals.

In truth, judicial work had set up, here and there, the lines along which scholars might have builded a road out. There was first the heritage from Tudor days of *loan* as a transaction-type which had an iron essence that neither form nor formula could reach — so in regard to contracting away the equity of redemption; so in regard to masking usury. The same basic approach underlay the view of the contract for common carriage as one which did not admit of the carrier's contracting out of liability for negligence. The picture is one of this or that transaction-type as having, I say, an essence which contains a minimum of balance, a core without which the type fails of being: a "principal" or a "partner," for instance, must "take the burdens with the benefits." (1) The doctrine of "repugnancy" sees the type-transaction intended, and kills off the clause which will not square with the iron core; (2) the doctrine of illusory promise and the vaguish manipulation of "mutuality" see balance as of the essence, fail to find it, and so find no transaction achieved at all; (3) the Cardozo approach sees the arrangement as unmistakably intended, balance as of the essence, and so reads the balance in.[4] The first and third ways of work are effectively curative, and offer mutually complementary, and general, patterns.

Here, as I see it, was the scholar's proper field: the searching out and assembly of a battery of such techniques, perhaps with needed invention thrown in. That, as the first job. Second, the examination of half a dozen or a dozen major transaction-types, to locate, describe, and test proper specifications for an iron core of each. I am not, mind you, speaking of such transaction-types as are set up by the Uniform Sales Act or Uniform Partnership Act with regard to most of their provisions, all effective only "unless otherwise agreed," but of basic unavoidables like the partnership gain-loss or the sales sell-buy combinations, or the delivery-on-shipment inherent aspect of a c.i.f. contract.

This open and inviting field is still substantially unoccupied. In regard to contracts for the sale of goods, one effort which may have some small promise has been made, in the Uniform Commercial Code. The lines of approach are three, in combination. First, "Every contract or duty... imposes an obligation of good faith in its performance or enforcement"

(§1-203), and good faith, in regard to sales, includes "in the case of a merchant... the observance of reasonable commercial standards of fair dealing
in the trade" (§ 2-103(1)(b)). Second, under Section 2-302

> (1) If the court as a matter of law finds the contract or any clause of the contract
> to have been unconscionable at the time it was made, the court may refuse to
> enforce the contract, or it may enforce the remainder of the contract without the
> unconscionable clause, or it may so limit the application of any unconscionable
> clause as to avoid any unconscionable result.
> (2) When it is claimed or appears to the court that the contract or any clause
> thereof may be unconscionable, the parties shall be afforded a reasonable oppor-
> tunity to present evidence as to its commercial setting, purpose, and effect to aid
> the court in making the determination.

There seems to me to be some possibility that these provisions may lead
appellate courts into a machinery for striking down where striking down is
needed, without getting in the way of reasonable construction of the reasonable, and without need for wholly upsetting the deal in order to escape a
particular obnoxious result. Especially would there seem to be hope of this
because the Code itself provides without need of clause for the more usual
type of protection which has needed in sales cases to be arranged by contract: thus, for example, for excuse (§§ 2-615, 2-616) or substituted performance (§ 2-614) on failure of presupposed conditions (shipping facilities,
strikes, destruction of plant, etc.) or on impairment of expectation of performance (§ 2-609) (slow pay, successive deficient deliveries, etc.). And the
Code provides without need of clause for such commercially needed good
faith remedies as partial acceptance (§ 2-601(c)) or an informal covering
purchase (§ 2-712) or resale (§ 2-706). It is possible, it may even be likely,
that the fairly drawn statutory coverage of such matters will set for a court a
standard against which to judge when an unbalanced clause on the same
subject, or on any other, moves out into what may shock conscience and
good faith.

At best, however, in our system an approach by statute seems to me,
dubious, uncertain, and likely to be both awkward in manner and deficient
or spotty in scope. And the true answer to the whole problem seems, amus-
ingly, to be one which could occur to any court or any lawyer, at any time,
as readily as to a scholar who had spent a lifetime on the subject — though
I doubt if it could occur to anyone without the inquiry and analysis in
depth which we owe to the scholarly work.

The answer, I suggest, is this: Instead of thinking about "assent" to
boiler-plate clauses, we can recognize that so far as concerns the specific,
there is no assent at all. What has in fact been assented to, specifically, are
the few dickered terms, and the broad type of the transaction, and but one
thing more. That one thing more is a blanket assent (not a specific assent)
to any not unreasonable or indecent terms the seller may have on his form,
which do not alter or eviscerate the reasonable meaning of the dickered
terms. The fine print which has not been read has no business to cut under
the reasonable meaning of those dickered terms which constitute the dominant and only real expression of agreement, but much of it commonly
belongs in.

The queer thing is that where the transaction occurs without the fine
print present, courts do not find this general line of approach too hard to
understand: thus in the cases Prausnitz gathers, in regard to what kind of

policy an oral contract for insurance contemplates; nor can I see a court having trouble, where a short memo agrees in due course to sign "our standard contract," in rejecting an outrageous form as not being fairly within the reasonable meaning of the term. The clearest case to see is the handing over of a blank check: no court, judging as between the parties, would fail to reach for the circumstances, in determining whether the amount filled in had gone beyond the reasonable.

Why, then, can we not face the fact where boiler-plate is present? There has been an arm's-length deal, with dickered terms. There has been accompanying that basic deal another which, if not on any fiduciary basis, at least involves a plain expression of confidence, asked and accepted, with a corresponding limit on the powers granted: the boiler-plate is assented to en bloc, "unsight, unseen," on the implicit assumption and to the full extent that (1) it does not alter or impair the fair meaning of the dickered terms when read alone, and (2) that its terms are neither in the particular nor in the net manifestly unreasonable and unfair. Such is the reality, and I see nothing in the way of a court's operating on that basis, to truly effectuate the only intention which can in reason be worked out as common to the two parties, granted good faith. And if the boiler-plate party is not playing in good faith, there is law enough to bar that fact from benefiting it. We had a hundred years of sales law in which any sales transaction with explicit words resulted in two several contracts for the one consideration: that of sale, and the collateral one of warranty. The idea is applicable here, for better reason: any contract with boiler-plate results in *two* several contracts: the *dickered* deal, and the collateral one of *supplementary* boiler-plate.

Rooted in sense, history, and simplicity, it is an answer which could occur to anyone.

---

1. Such a development is a possibility only. Thus in England, even though balanced form-contracts have been frequent in the courts because of the practice of appeal from the arbitration tribunals of the trades, the courts have been very slow to develop the two different conscious manners of construction which are required for health.

2. From my review in 52 Harv. L. Rev. 700, 702-703 (1939), of Prausnitz, The Standardization of Commercial Contracts in English and Continental Law (1937).

3. Review of Prausnitz, cited above, at 704.

4. Moran v. Standard Oil Co., 211 N.Y. 187, 105 N.E. 217 (1914), opened the ball, reading in a promise to employ for five years to balance the agent's promise to work. Wood v. Duff-Gordon, 222 N.Y. 88, 118 N.E. 214 (1917), applied the same method to what appears to have otherwise been a fair contract, in favor of the contract-drafter, who had left out his own promise — which he then later needed, to serve as consideration. The first agreement was tailor-made, the second may have been. But the approach is perfect for the handling of one phase of boiler-plate.

GILLESPIE BROTHERS v. ROY BOWLES

[1973] 1 All E.R. 193. Court of Appeal (England); Lord Denning M.R., Buckley and Orr L.JJ.

Lord Denning MR. On 7th March 1969 a small parcel containing three gold watches was stolen at London Airport, at Heathrow. Who is to bear the loss? It may fall on one or other of three persons. Either (a) the owners of the watches; or (b) the forwarding agents; or (c) the carriers. I will describe them in turn.

(a) The *owners* of the watches were the plaintiffs, Gillespie Brothers & Co. Ltd, who carry on business in the City of London. They ordered the watches from Swiss manufacturers. The watches were for resale to buyers in Jamaica. The parcel containing the watches was sent by air from Basle to London Airport. It was to be sent on to Jamaica. It arrived at Heathrow on 26th February 1969. It was placed in the customs warehouse in bond. Customs duty would not be payable — provided that a trans-shipment bond was given to the customs.

(b) The *forwarding agents* were the third party, Rennie Hogg Ltd. As soon as the parcel arrived at Heathrow, the owners asked the forwarding agents to arrange for the trans-shipment and to put the parcel on the first flight to Jamaica. On 6th March 1969 the forwarding agents gave to the customs authorities a trans-shipment bond in their own name. They filled in a trans-shipment shipping bill. They named themselves as exporters and also as the firm conveying the goods to the export flight. The customs passed it as sufficient. They taped and sealed the parcel ready for collection. It was the duty of the *forwarding agents* to collect the parcel from the bonded warehouse and take it to their office, which was only a mile away; and thence to take it to the export shed for the flight to Jamaica.

(c) The *carriers* were the defendants, Roy Bowles Transport Ltd. The forwarding agents did not have their own vans and drivers. They hired them from the carriers. This particular van and driver was hired on a monthly basis. During the period of hire it was exclusively at the disposal of the forwarding agents. On the morning of 7th March 1969 the driver drove the van to the import shed of the bonded warehouse. He went to an office and got from a pigeon-hole the Rennie Hogg papers, that is, the cleared papers relating to the various goods being dealt with by the forwarding agents. Amongst them were the papers for the parcel of three watches. The parcel was of such high value that it was in a security cage. The warehousemen got it out and handed it to the driver. He put the parcel in the back of his van and covered it up. He went back to sign the book. He signed it, came back, closed the van and drove to the office of the forwarding agents a mile away. When he got there, he looked for the parcel and found it was missing. It had been stolen whilst he was signing the book.

The judge held that the driver had been at fault. He ought to have locked up the van before going back to sign. Although the driver was engaged in work for the forwarding agents, nevertheless the driver remained the servant of the carriers... It was the carriers who, by their servant, had taken the parcel into their charge, and they were under a duty to take reasonable care of it... There were two contracts underlying these transactions.

1. *The contract between the owners and the forwarding agents*

First, there was the contract between the owners of the goods and the forwarding agents. It was made by correspondence on 27th February 1969. The owners asked the forwarding agents to arrange the trans-shipment.

The position of a forwarding agent was described by Rowlatt J in *Jones v European & General Express Co.* (1920), 26 Com. Cas. 296. They usually act as agents for the owners of the goods in arranging transport. But in this case there was one activity which they conducted as principals. They themselves were, by the usage of the trade, responsible for the trans-shipment of the goods from the customs warehouse to their office, and thence to the export shed for Jamaica. They employed the carriers as sub-contractors to execute this activity.

The correspondence shows that the forwarding agents, in their contract with the owners, made this stipulation:

> "All goods carried or business undertaken is subject to the Standard Terms and Conditions of the Institute of Shipping and Forwarding Agents obtainable on application.'

Among those conditions were conditions to the effect that all goods were carried *subject to the conditions stipulated by carriers into whose possession or custody the goods may pass*; that the forwarding agents were not liable for loss or damage to goods unless it happened whilst the goods were in their actual custody; and that in no case should the liability of the forwarding agents exceed a sum of £50 per ton. In view of those conditions, the owners did not sue the forwarding agents. They preferred to sue the carriers in tort.

2. *The contract between the forwarding agents and the carriers*

There was the contract between the forwarding agents and the carriers. This was made by a telephone conversation on 8th August 1968. The forwarding agents hired a three ton van, with a driver, from the carriers on a month-to-month basis. The forwarding agents used this van and driver much as if it was their own, telling him where to go, what to collect, and so forth. It was in pursuance of this contract that the driver of the van collected the parcel in this case. The correspondence shows that the carriers made their contract with the forwarding agents 'subject to the conditions of the Road Haulage Association'. They sent copies of this to the forwarding agents from time to time.

Under the conditions of the Road Haulage Association, the carriers were liable for loss or damage to goods in terms equivalent to the liability of a common carrier. Condition 11 says:

> 'Subject to these Conditions the Carrier shall be liable for any loss, or misdelivery of or damage to goods occasioned during transit unless the Carrier shall prove that such loss, misdelivery or damage has arisen from...'

There follow in (*a*) to (*j*) several exceptions, such as, act of God, act of foreign enemy, act or omission of consignor, inherent vice, insufficient packing, nearly all of which are defences available to a common carrier.

But the conditions go on to stipulate for a limitation of liability. Condition 12 says:

> 'Subject to these Conditions, the liability of the Carrier in respect of any one consignment shall in any case be limited: (I) where the loss or damage however sustained is in respect of the whole of the consignment to a sum at the rate of £800 per ton... Provided that: (*a*) nothing in this clause shall limit the Carrier's liability below the sum of £10 in respect of any one consignment...'

3. *Can the limitation be avoided?*

If the carrier were sued by the customer who contracted with him, he would, no doubt, rely on the limitation; but in this case he is sued not by the contracting party, but by the owners of the goods. As against an owner, the carrier has difficulty in setting up the limitation, because of *Scruttons Ltd v Midland Silicones Ltd*, [1962] A.C. 446. That case proceeds on the broad proposition that, on a contract of carriage, the conditions only apply as between the two parties to the contract. If an injured person can frame an action in tort — not between those two parties — the conditions, it is said, do not apply. That proposition is fair enough when it is a contract for the carriage of passengers, who do not usually insure their own safety by land or sea. But it has been the source of much trouble when applied to the carriage of goods. It has been the common practice of carriers — by land, sea or air — to make conditions limiting their liability to specific sums; and to leave the goods owner to insure if he wants greater cover. Carriers base their charges, and the insurers calculate their premiums, on the footing that the limitation is valid and effective between all concerned. The law should support this course of trade and uphold the limitation. But it has not done so. The effectiveness of the conditions was seriously undermined by *Scruttons Ltd v Midland Silicones Ltd.* So in consequence many efforts have been made to get around the decision. One way is by inserting a clause expressly to protect persons who handle the goods (such as stevedores) saying that the carrier is their agent. Such a clause has, however, been held ineffective by the Court of Appeal in New Zealand in *A N Satterthwaite & Co Ltd v New Zealand Shipping Co Ltd, The Eurymedon*, [1972] 2 Lloyd's Rep 544. Another way is by holding that the owner of the goods (if he is not a party to the contract) is bound by the conditions if he impliedly consented to them as being in the usual form... Yet another way is by way of international convention, which is made law by statute. Thus, in the schedule to the Carriage of Goods by Sea Act 1971, it is provided (art IV bis, para I):

'The defences and limits of liability provided for in these Rules shall apply in any action against the carrier in respect of loss or damage to goods covered by a contract of carriage whether the action be founded in contract or in tort.'

Finally, there is the way to be found in the conditions of the Road Haulage Association, which we have before us today. To these conditions I now turn.

4. *The road haulage conditions*

'I. *Definitions*

'In these Conditions the following expressions shall have the meanings hereby respectively assigned to them, that is to say:- "*Trader*" shall mean the customer who contracts for the services of the Carrier. [It means, therefore, in this case, the forwarding agent.]...

'3. *Parties and Sub-Contracting*

'(1) Where the Trader is not the owner of some or all of the goods in any consignment he shall be deemed for all purposes to be the agent of the owner or owners.

'(2) The Carrier may employ the services of any other carrier for the purposes of fulfilling the Contract...

'(3) The Carrier enters into the Contract for and on behalf of himself and his servants, agents, and sub-contractors and his sub-contractors servants, agents, and sub-contractors; all of whom shall be entitled to the benefit of the Contract and shall be under no liability whatsoever to the Trader or anyone claiming through him in respect of the goods in addition to or separately from that of the Carrier under the Contract.

'(4) The Trader shall save harmless and keep the Carrier indemnified against all claims or demands whatsoever by whomsoever made in excess of the liability of the Carrier under these conditions.'

That indemnity at cl 3 (4) is the one here relied on by the carrier. It is designed to enable the carrier (when he is sued by the owner of the goods) to come down on the trader, i e the forwarding agents, for indemnity. If the words of cl 3 (4) are given their ordinary meaning, they clearly cover this case. The words 'all claims or demands whatsoever' are certainly wide enough.

5. *The ruling in Canada Steamship Lines Ltd v R* [1952] A.C. 192.

But the forwarding agents deny that the carriers can pray in aid the indemnity clause. They say that the carriers were by their servants guilty of negligence; and that they cannot get indemnity for their own negligence. They say that an indemnity clause is to be treated in the same way as an exemption clause. They rely on the ruling, numbered (iii), of the Privy Council in *Canada Steamship Lines Ltd v R*:

> 'If the words used are wide enough [in their ordinary meaning, to cover negligence on the part of the servants of the proferens]... the existence of a possible head of damage other than that of negligence is fatal to the *proferens...*'

Taking that ruling literally, the forwarding agents explored the possibility of other heads of damage. They put forward five possible heads of damage other than that of negligence. (1) The carriers might, without negligence, be faced with a claim for conversion. There might be two rival claimants to the goods. If the carriers handed them to one, they might be held liable to the other in conversion. (2) The carriers might have got a sub-contractor to carry the goods for them. The carriers might, without negligence on their part, be liable for the negligence of the sub-contractor. (3) The goods might be liquids which leaked and caused damage to the vehicle of a sub-contractor; and the carriers might be liable to the sub-contractor. (4) The carriers might have a claim brought against them for negligence and resist it successfully — and get an order for costs against the claimant — and must be able to recover them because the claimant had no money to pay them. (5) The carriers might be called on to pay customs duty or air hire charges.

The judge considered those five possible heads. He held that those numbered 1, 2, 4 and 5 were possible heads of damage, other than negligence and that, applying the Privy Council ruling, the existence of them was 'fatal' to the claim for indemnity.

I can well see that the judge felt obliged to explore all those five heads. He had before him the explicit words of the Privy Council in the *Canada Steamship* case... So explicit were the words of the Privy Council that I felt myself, at first, that we ought to explore all those five heads. I considered the many authorities cited by counsel, and I actually went so far as to prepare a judgment differing from the judge on them. But it proved so long and so tedious that I have discarded it. And I am glad to find that Buckley and Orr LJJ have not now discussed those five heads either.

In justification of this course, I would make this comment on the Privy Council ruling. It was based in terms on the words of Lord Greene MR in *Alderslade v Hendon Laundry Ltd* [1945] K.B. 189. But those words have recently come under review in *Hollier v Rambler Motors (AMC) Ltd* [1972] 2 Q.B. 71; and this court there issued a warning against taking Lord Greene MR's words au pied de la lettre. It actually overruled two of the cases on which he relied. I would issue a like warning about the Privy Council ruling. Taken at its face value, it assumes that the words of an exempting clause are wide enough, in their ordinary meaning, to cover negligence; but then lays down an artificial rule by which the court is compelled to depart from their ordinary meaning. It says: 'The existence of a possible head of damage other than that of negligence is *fatal*'. Such compulsion is not a rule of construction. It is a rule of law. I would quote against it the words of Salmon LJ in *Hollier v Rambler Motors (AMC) Ltd*:

> 'If it were so extended, it would make the law entirely artificial by ignoring that rules of construction are merely our guides and not our masters; in the end you are driven back to construing the clause in question to see what it means.'

I would suggest, therefore, that we should not apply the Privy Council ruling in its full force. We should not explore in depth 'other possible heads'. The correct proposition, as I have always understood it, is this: even though the words of a clause are wide enough in their ordinary meaning to exclude liability for negligence, nevertheless if it is apparent that sufficient content can be given to them without doing so (as in the case of a common carrier), then they will be given that content only. They will not be held to cover negligence. So stated, however, the forwarding agents may still rely on it. Condition II puts a liability on the carrier equivalent to a common carrier. So they may still say that the indemnity clause should not be held to cover the negligence of the carrier himself.

6. *What is the justification?*

But, even so, I say to myself: this indemnity clause, in its ordinary meaning, is wide enough to cover the negligence of the carrier himself. Why should not effect be given to it? What is the justification for the courts, in this or any other case, departing from the ordinary meaning of the words? If you examine all the cases you will, I think, find that at bottom it is because the clause (relieving a man from his own negligence) is unreasonable, or is being applied unreasonably in the circumstances of the particular case. The judges have, then, time after time, sanctioned a departure from the ordinary meaning. They have done it under the guise of 'construing' the clause. They assume that the party cannot have intended anything so unreasonable. So they construe the clause 'strictly'. They cut down the ordinary meaning of the words and reduce them to reasonable proportions. They use all their skill and art to this end. Thus they have repeatedly held that words do not exempt a man from negligence unless it is made clear beyond doubt; nor entitle a man to indemnity from the consequences of his own negligence... Even when the words are clear enough to ordinary mortals, they have made fine distinctions between the *kind* of loss and the *cause* of loss; so that, if a clause exempts from 'any loss' it is not sufficient, but if the magic words 'however caused' are added, it is... Likewise, they have regularly disallowed exemption clauses where sufficient content can be given to them without exempting negligence: see *Hollier v Rambler Motors (AMC) Ltd*. Nor will the words of an exemption clause normally be held to apply to a situation created by a fundamental breach of contract: see *UGS Finance Ltd v National Mortgage Bank of Greece and National Bank of Greece SA*. [1964] 1 Lloyd's Rep. 446, per Pearson LJ, which was approved by the House of Lords in *Suisse Atlantique Sociéte d'Armement Maritime SA v NV Rotterdamsche Kolen Centrale*. The time may come when this process of 'construing' the contract can be pursued no further. The words are too clear to permit of it. Are the courts then powerless? Are they to permit the party to enforce his unreasonable clause, even when it is so unreasonable, or applied so unreasonably, as to be unconscionable? When it gets to this point, I would say, as I said many years ago, '... there is the vigilance of the common law which, while allowing freedom of contract, watches to see that it is not abused'... It will not allow a party to exempt himself from his liability at common law when it would be quite unconscionable for him to do so.

7. Reasonableness

But none of that applies to the present case, because this clause, as I see it, when given its ordinary meaning, is perfectly fair and reasonable. When a clause is reasonable and is reasonably applied, it should be given effect according to its terms. I know that the judges hitherto have never confessed openly to the test of reasonableness. But it has been the driving force behind many of the decisions. And now it has the backing of the Law Commissions of England and Wales, and of Scotland. I venture to suggest that the words of such a clause (be it an exemption clause, or a limitation clause, or an indemnity clause) should be construed in the same way as any other clause. It should be given its ordinary meaning, that is, the meaning which the parties understood by the clause and must be presumed to have intended. The courts should give effect to the clause according to that meaning, provided always (and this is new) that it is reasonable as between the parties and is applied reasonably in the circumstances of the particular case.

There is a line of authority which supports that proposition. It was common in the last century for a carrier or a warehouseman to give notice that he 'will not be responsible for loss or damage' to goods worth more than £10, or, as the case might be, unless the value was declared and an increased charge paid. Such clauses did not contain the magic words 'however caused' or any similar words. On such a clause in 1841 the Court of Exchequer held that those words did not exempt the carrier from liability for the negligence of his servants... But in the following year (1842) under a statute which said that no common carrier 'shall be liable for the loss of or injury' to property above the value of £10 unless the value was declared and an increased charge paid, the Court of Queen's Bench held that those words were valid and effective to exempt the carrier from liability for the negligence of his servants... The view of the Queen's Bench judges prevailed. Since that time it has been always accepted that such a stipulation in a contract, or a statute, must be given its ordinary meaning, namely, that unless the value is declared and an increased charge paid, the carrier is exempt from liability for loss or damage, even though it is caused by the negligence of his servants.

.   .   .

What then is the justification for upholding such a clause? It does not include the magic words 'however caused', or their equivalent. The only justification, as I see it, is that such a clause, when given its ordinary meaning, is in the words of Scrutton LJ.'an eminently reasonable clause': see *Gibaud v Great Eastern Railway Co*. When such a clause is *agreed on*, and is *reasonable*, it should be given effect according to its terms. No one surely can dispute that proposition.

Conclusion

Apply this first to the limitation clause (cl 12) in the Road Haulage Conditions. It says '... the liability of the Carrier in respect of any one consignment shall in any case be limited' to £10. That limitation applies, even though it does not say 'however caused'. So with many limitation clauses in carriage by land, sea and air, often contained in contracts, and sometimes in statutes. They are all valid. They apply even though the carrier, by his servants, is negligent. This is because they are reasonable.

Apply it next to the indemnity clause (cl 3 (4)) in the road haulage conditions. It gives the carriers an indemnity against 'all claims or demands whatsoever by whomsoever made in excess of the liability of the Carrier under these conditions'. Those words, in their ordinary meaning — especially the word 'whatsoever' — are wide enough to cover negligence. I next ask: is this indemnity clause, when given that meaning, reasonable as between the parties? The answer is: yes, it is. Under the road haulage conditions, the carrier stipulates that his liability shall be limited to £10 in respect of any one consignment, leaving the owner of the goods to insure for any excess above that sum. The indemnity clause is inserted so as to make that limitation effective. It is perfectly fair to put the responsibility on to the forwarding agents. They have been employed by the owner of the goods to make the necessary arrangements for him. They should see that the owner of the goods has insured the goods (as he probably has) or they themselves should take out an insurance to cover the goods. But all we have to decide is whether the indemnity clause avails the carriers against the forwarding agents. I think it does. I am glad to find that in 1961 in *L Harris (Harella) Ltd v Continental Express Ltd,* [1961] 1 Lloyd's Rep. 251, Paull J held such a clause to be good. I agree with him. I would allow the appeal accordingly.

[Buckley and Orr L.JJ. agreed in the result.]

LEVISON v. PATENT STEAM CARPET CLEANING CO. LTD.

[1977] 3 W.L.R. 90. Court of Appeal, England; Lord Denning M.R., Orr L.J. and Sir David Cairns.

[The plaintiff had a valuable Chinese carpet that needed cleaning. The defendant picked the carpet up from the plaintiff's home and took it away. It disappeared and was presumed to be stolen. The plaintiff signed a form which contained the following terms:

"2(a) The maximum value of any carpet, rug or tapestry delivered to the company for any purpose whatsoever shall if the area thereof exceed four square yards be deemed to be £2 per square yard, and if the area does not exceed four square yards shall be deemed to be £10."

"5. All merchandise is expressly accepted at the owner's risk and owners are recommended either to insure such merchandise in such manner as to cover them whilst in the company's hands or to instruct the company to insure it as their agents in such sum and in such manner at their cost as they shall specify."

The area of the carpet was 20 sq. yds.

The plaintiff sued for the value of the carpet. The county court judge gave judgment for the plaintiff for £900. The defendant appealed.]

Lord Denning M.R. (with whom the others agreed), after stating the facts, continued:

Inequality of bargaining power

The conditions were on the back of a standard form. The customer was asked to sign them without being given an opportunity of considering them or taking objection to them. It is a classic instance of superior bargaining power, to which Lord Diplock drew attention in *Instone v. A. Schroeder Music Publishing Co. Ltd.* [1974] 1 W.L.R. 1308, 1316:

"This [standard form of contract] is of comparatively modern origin. It is the result of the concentration of particular kinds of business in relatively few hands … The terms … have not been the subject of negotiation between the parties to it, or approved by any organisation representing the interests of the weaker party. They have been dictated by that party whose bargaining power, either exercised alone or in conjunction with others providing similar goods or services, enables him to say: 'If you want these goods or services at all, these are the only terms on which they are obtainable. Take it or leave it.' "

I would only add that in this case — as in many others — the weaker party is not even told "Take it or leave it." He is simply presented with a form to sign, and told "Sign here"; and so he does. Then, later on, when the goods are lost or damaged, the form is produced: and the stronger party says: "You have no claim. Look at the conditions on the form. You signed it and are bound by those conditions! The law is settled by *L'Estrange v. F. Graucob Ltd.* [1934] 2 K.B. 394.' "

In such circumstances as here the Law Commission in 1975 recommended that a term which exempts the stronger party from his ordinary common law liability should not be given effect except when it is reasonable: see The Law Commission and the Scottish Law Commission Report, Exemption Clauses, Second Report, (1975) (August 5, 1975) Law Com. No. 69 (H.C. 605), pp. 62, 174; and there is a bill now before Parliament which gives effect to the test of reasonableness. This is a gratifying piece of law reform: but I do not think we need wait for that bill to be passed into law. You never know what may happen to a bill. Meanwhile the common law has its own principles ready to hand. In *Gillespie Bros. & Co. Ltd. v. Roy Bowles Transport Ltd.* [1973] Q.B. 400, 416, I suggested that an exemption or limitation clause should not be given effect if it was unreasonable, or if it would be unreasonable to apply it in the circumstances of the case. I see no reason why this should not be applied today, at any rate in contracts in standard forms where there is inequality of bargaining power. In this case I would apply it in this way: take the limitation clause 2(a). In some circumstances that clause might be reasonable. But it would not in the present case be reasonable to allow the cleaning company to rely on it. They knew that they were to collect a heavy Chinese carpet which was worth a lot of money. To limit liability to £40 (without a word of warning) would, I think, be most unreasonable.

So also with clause 5. It was not reasonable for the cleaning company to stipulate that all the merchandise should be "at the owner's risk" unless they did a great deal more to see that the customer was protected. At the very least they ought to have drawn the clause specifically to the customer's attention: and made it clear that he ought to insure against loss or damage to it. But they did nothing at all to protect him or warn him. I do not think the cleaning company can rely on this clause. They ought to have insured themselves, and not leave it to the customer to do so.

I may be wrong, however, in applying the test of reasonableness. So I would go on to consider the other means which have been used by the courts to get round the injustice of these exemptions and limitation clauses.

Strict construction

One means is by construing the clauses "strictly" so as to cut it down to reasonable proportions. But these clauses are not susceptible to that treatment. …

Fundamental breach

The other means of getting round the injustice of these exemption or limitation clauses is by means of the doctrine of fundamental breach. I will not today go through the history of that doctrine or the precise legal theory on which it rests. It is well established as both counsel acknowledged. It certainly applies in standard form contracts where there is inequality of bargaining power....

I would hold, therefore, that the doctrine of fundamental breach, as it was enunciated by this court in many cases, still applies in standard form contracts where there is inequality of bargaining power. If a party uses his superior power to impose an exemption or limitation clause on the weaker party, he will not be allowed to rely on it if he has himself been guilty of a breach going to the root of the contract. In other cases, the court will, whenever it can, construe the contract so that an exemption or limitation clause only avails the party when he is carrying out the contract in substance: and not when he is breaking it in a manner which goes to the very root of the contract: ...

The burden of proof

This brings me to the crux of the case. On whom is the burden of proof? Take the present case. Assuming that clause 2(a) or clause 5, or either of them, limits or exempts the cleaners from liability for negligence: but not for a fundamental breach. On whom is the burden to prove that there was fundamental breach?

Upon principle, I should have thought that the burden was on the cleaners to prove that they were not guilty of a fundamental breach. After all, Mrs. Levison does not know what happened to it. The cleaners are the ones who know, or should know, what happened to the carpet, and the burden should be on them to say what it was....

It is, therefore, a moot point for decision. On it I am clearly of opinion that, in a contract of bailment, when a bailee seeks to escape liability on the ground that he was not negligent or that he was excused by an exception or limitation clause, then he must show what happened to the goods. He must prove all the circumstances known to him in which the loss or damage occurred. If it appears that the goods were lost or damaged without any negligence on his part, then, of course, he is not liable. If it appears that they were lost or damaged by a slight breach — not going to the root of the contract — he may be protected by the exemption or limitation clause. But, if he leaves the cause of loss or damage undiscovered and unexplained — then I think he is liable: because it is then quite likely that the goods were stolen by one of his servants; or delivered by a servant to the wrong address; or damaged by reckless or wilful misconduct; all of which the offending servant will conceal and not make known to his employer. Such conduct would be a fundamental breach against which the exemption or limitation clause will not protect him.

The cleaning company in this case did not show what happened to the carpet. They did not prove how it was lost. They gave all sorts of excuses for non-delivery and eventually said it had been stolen. Then I would ask: By whom was it stolen? Was it by one of their own servants? Or with his connivance? Alternatively, was it delivered by one of their servants to the wrong address? In the absence of any explanation, I would infer that it was one of these causes. In none of them would the cleaning company be protected by the exemption or limitation clause.

Conclusion

I think the judge was quite right in holding that the burden of proof was on the cleaning company to exclude fundamental breach. As they did not exclude it, they cannot rely on the exemption or limitation clauses. I would, therefore, dismiss this appeal.

TILDEN RENT-A-CAR COMPANY v. CLENDENNING

Ontario Court of Appeal. April 8 1978 (unreported as of 1 May 1978),
Dubin, Lacourciere and Zuber JJ.A.

[Appeal by the plaintiff from a judgment dismissing its claim for damages arising out of an accident causing damage to a car rented by the defendant. The rest of the facts appear from the judgment of Dubin J.A.]

Dubin J.A.:- Upon his arrival at Vancouver airport, Mr. Clendenning, a resident of Woodstock, Ontario, attended upon the office of Tilden Rent-A-Car Company for the purpose of renting a car while he was in Vancouver. He was an experienced traveller and had used Tilden Rent-A-Car Company on many prior occasions. He provided the clerk employed at the airport office of Tilden Rent-A-Car Company with the minimum information which was asked of him, and produced his American Express credit card. He was asked by the clerk whether he desired additional coverage, and, as was his practice, he said "yes". A contract was submitted to him for his signature, which he signed in the presence of the clerk, and he returned the contract to her. She placed his copy of it in an envelope and gave him the keys to the car. He then placed the contract in the glove compartment of the vehicle. He did not read the terms of the contract before signing it, as was readily apparent to the clerk, and in fact he did not read the contract until this litigation was commenced, nor had he read a copy of a similar contract on any prior occasion.

The issue on the appeal is whether the defendant is liable for the damage caused to the automobile while being driven by him by reason of the exclusionary provisions which appear in the contract.

On the front of the contract are two relevant clauses set forth in box form. They are as follows:

"*15 COLLISION DAMAGE WAIVER* BY CUSTOMERS INITIALS "J.C." *In consideration of the payment of 2.00 per day customers liability for damage to rented vehicle including windshield is limited to NIL.* But notwithstanding payment of said fee, customer shall be fully liable for all collision damage if vehicle is used, operated or driven in violation of any of the provisions of this rental agreement or off highways serviced by federal, provincial, or municipal governments, and for all damages to vehicle by striking overhead objects.

"16 I, the undersigned have read and received a copy of above and reverse side of this contract

"Signature of customer or employee of customer "John T. Clendenning" (Emphasis added.)

On the back of the contract in particularly small type and so faint in the customer's copy as to be hardly legible, there are a series of conditions, the relevant ones being as follows:

"6. The customer agrees not to use the vehicle in violation of any law, ordinance, rule or regulation of any public authority.

"7. The customer agrees that the vehicle will not be operated:

"(a) By any person who has drunk or consumed any intoxicating liquor, whatever be the quantity, or who is under the influence of drugs or narcotics;"

The rented vehicle was damaged while being driven by Mr. Clendenning in Vancouver. His evidence at trial, which was accepted by the trial judge, was to the effect that in endeavouring to avoid a collision with another vehicle and acting out of a sudden emergency, he drove the car into a pole. He stated that although he had pleaded guilty to a charge of driving while impaired in Vancouver, he did so on the advice of counsel, and at the time of the impact he was capable of the proper control of the motor vehicle. This evidence was also accepted by the trial judge.

Mr. Clendenning testified that on earlier occasions when he had inquired as to what added coverage he would receive for the payment of $2. per day, he had been advised that "such payment provided full nondeductible coverage". It is to be observed that the portion of the contract reproduced above does provide that "in consideration of the payment of $2. per day customers liability for damage to rented vehicle including windshield is limited to nil".

A witness called on behalf of the plaintiff company gave evidence as to the practice of the company in drawing attention of the conditions in the contract to its customers. He stated that unless inquiries were made, nothing was said by its clerks to the customer with respect to the exclusionary conditions. He went on to state that if inquiries were made, the clerks were instructed to advise the customer that by the payment of the $2. additional fee the customer had complete coverage "unless he were intoxicated, or unless he committed an offence under the *Criminal Code* such as intoxication".

Mr. Clendenning acknowledged that he had assumed, either by what had been told to him in the past or otherwise, that he would not be responsible for any damage to the vehicle on payment of the extra premium unless such damage was caused by reason of his being so intoxicated as to be incapable of the proper control of the vehicle, a provision with which he was familiar as being a statutory provision in his own insurance contract.

The provisions fastening liability for damage to the vehicle on the hirer, as contained in the clauses hereinbefore referred to, are completely inconsistent with the express terms which purport to provide complete coverage for damage to the vehicle in exchange for the additional premium. It is to be noted, for example, that if the driver of the vehicle exceeded the speed limit even by one mile per hour, or parked the vehicle in a no parking area, or even had one glass of wine or one bottle of beer, the contract purports to make the hirer completely responsible for all damage to the vehicle. Indeed, if the vehicle at the time of any damage to it was being driven off a federal, provincial or municipal highway, such as a shopping plaza for instance, the hirer purportedly would be responsible for all damage to the vehicle.

Mr. Clendenning stated that if he had known of the full terms of the written instrument, he would not have entered into such a contract. Having regard to the findings made by the trial judge, it is apparent that Mr. Clendenning had not in fact acquiesced to such terms.

It was urged that the rights of the parties were governed by what has come to be known as "the rule in *L'Estrange v. F. Graucob, Limited*", [1934] 2 K.B. 394, and in particular the following portion from the judgment of Scrutton L.J., at p. 403:

> "In cases in which the contract is contained in a railway ticket or other unsigned document, it is necessary to prove that an alleged party was aware, or ought to

have been aware, of its terms and conditions. These cases have no application when the document has been signed. *When a document containing contractual terms is signed then, in the absence of fraud, or, I will add, misrepresentation, the party signing it is bound, and it is wholly immaterial whether he has read the document or not.*"
(Emphasis added.)

In the same case Maugham, L.J. added at p. 406:

> "There can be no dispute as to the soundness in law of the statement of Mellish L.J. in *Parker v. South Eastern Ry. Co.*, 2 C.P.D. 416, 421, which has been read by my learned brother, to the effect that where a party has signed a written agreement it is immaterial to the question of his liability under it that he has not read it and does not know its contents. That is true in any case in which the agreement is held to be an agreement in writing.
>
> "There are, however, two possibilities to be kept in view. The first is that it might be proved that the document, though signed by the plaintiff, was signed in circumstances which made it not her act. That is known as the case of Non est factum."

And at p. 407:

> " Another possibility is that the plaintiff might have been induced to sign the document by misrepresentation."

Consensus ad idem is as much a part of the law of written contracts as it is of oral contracts. The signature to a contract is only one way of manifesting assent to contractual terms. However, in the case of *L'Estrange v. F. Graucob, Limited, supra*, there was in fact no *consensus ad idem*. Miss L'Estrange was a proprietor of a cafe. Two salesmen of the defendant company persuaded her to order a cigarette machine to be sold to her by their employer. They produced an order form which Miss L'Estrange signed without reading all of its terms. Amongst the many clauses in the document signed by her, there was included a paragraph, with respect to which she was completely unaware, which stated "any express or implied condition, statement, or warranty, statutory or otherwise not stated herein is hereby excluded". In her action against the company she alleged that the article sold to her was unfit for the purposes for which it was sold and contrary to The Sale of Goods Act. The company successfully defended on the basis of that exemption clause.

Although the subject of critical analysis by learned authors (see, for example, Spencer, "Signature, Consent, and the Rule in *L'Estrange v. Graucob*, [1973] Cambridge Law Review 104), the case has survived, and it is now said that it applies to all contracts irrespective of the circumstances under which they are entered into, if they are signed by the party who seeks to escape their provisions.

Thus, it was submitted that the ticket cases, which in the circumstances of this case would afford a ready defence for the hirer of the automobile, are not applicable.

As is pointed out in Waddams, *The Law of Contracts*, p. 191:

> "From the 19th century until recent times an extraordinary status has been accorded to the signed document that will be seen in retrospect, it is suggested, to have been excessive."

The justification for the rule in *L'Estrange v. F. Graucob, Limited, supra*, appears to have been founded upon the objective theory of contracts, by which means parties are bound to a contract in writing by measuring their conduct by outward appearance rather than what the parties inwardly meant to decide. This, in turn, stems from the classic statement of Blackburn J. in *Smith v. Hughes* (1871), L.R. 6 Q.B. 597 at p. 607:

> "I apprehend that if one of the parties intends to make a contract on one set of terms, and the other intends to make a contract on another set of terms, or, as it is sometimes expressed, if the parties are not *ad idem*, there is no contract, unless the circumstances are such as to preclude one of the parties from denying that he has agreed to the terms of the other. The rule of law is that stated in *Freeman v. Cooke* (1848), 2 Ex. 654, 154 E.R. 652. *If, whatever a man's real intention may be, he so conducts himself that a reasonable man would believe that he was assenting to the terms proposed by the other party, and that other party upon that belief enters into the contract with him, the man thus conducting himself would be equally bound as if he had intended to agree to the other party's terms."* (Emphasis added.)

Even accepting the objective theory to determine whether Mr. Clendenning had entered into a contract which included all the terms of the written instrument, it is to be observed that an essential part of that test is whether the other party entered into the contract in the belief that Mr. Clendenning was assenting to all such terms. In the instant case, it was apparent to the employee of Tilden-Rent-A-Car that Mr. Clendenning had not in fact read the document in its entirety before he signed it. It follows under such circumstances that Tilden-Rent-A-Car cannot rely on provisions of the contract which it had no reason to believe were being assented to by the other contracting party.

As stated in Waddams, *The Law of Contracts*, p. 191:

> "One who signs a written document cannot complain if the other party reasonably relies on the signature as a manifestation of assent to the contents, or ascribes to words he uses their reasonable meaning. But the other side of the same coin is that only a reasonable expectation will be protected. If the party seeking to enforce the document knew or had reason to know of the other's mistake the document should not be enforced."

In ordinary commercial practice where there is frequently a sense of formality in the transaction, and where there is a full opportunity for the parties to consider the terms of the proposed contract submitted for signature, it might well be safe to assume that the party who attaches his signature to the contract intends by so doing to acknowledge his acquiescence to its terms, and that the other party entered into the contract upon that belief. This can hardly be said, however, where the contract is entered into in circumstances such as were present in this case.

A transaction, such as this one, is invariably carried out in a hurried, informal manner. The speed with which the transaction is completed is said to be one of the attractive features of the services provided.

The clauses relied on in this case, as I have already stated, are inconsistent with the overall purpose for which the contract is entered into by the hirer. Under such circumstances, something more should be done by the party submitting the contract for signature than merely handing it over to be signed.

In an analogous situation Lord Devlin in the case of *McCutcheon v. David MacBrayne Ltd.*, [1964] 1 W.L.R. 125, commented as follows at pp. 132-4:

> "It would be a strangely generous set of conditions in which the persistent reader,

after wading through the verbiage, could not find something to protect the carrier against 'any loss... wheresoever or whensoever occurring'; and condition 19 by itself is enough to absolve the respondents several times over for all their negligence. *It is conceded that if the form had been signed as usual, the appellant would have had no case.* But, by a stroke of ill luck for the respondents, it was upon this day of all days that they omitted to get Mr. McSporran to sign the conditions. What difference does that make?

"*If it were possible for your Lordships to escape from the world of make-believe which the law has created into the real world in which transactions of this sort are actually done, the answer would be short and simple. It should make no difference whatever. This sort of document is not meant to be read, still less to be understood. Its signature is in truth about as significant as a handshake that marks the formal conclusion of a bargain.*

"Your Lordships were referred to the dictum of Blackburn J. in *Harris v. Great Western Railway Co.* (1876) 1 Q.B.D. 515, 530. The passage is as follows: 'And it is clear law that where there is a writing, into which the terms of any agreement are reduced, the terms are to be regulated by that writing. And though one of the parties may not have read the writing, yet, in general, he is bound to the other by those terms; and that, I apprehend, is on the ground that, by assenting to the contract thus reduced to writing, he represents to the other side that he has made himself acquainted with the contents of that writing and assents to them, and so induces the other side to act upon that representation by entering into the contract with him, and is consequently precluded from denying that he did make himself acquainted with those terms. But then the preclusion only exists when the case is brought within the rule so carefully and accurately laid down by Parke B., in delivering the judgment of the Exchequer in *Freeman v. Cooke* (1848), 2 Ex. 654, that is, if he 'means his representation to be acted upon, and it is acted upon accordingly: or if, whatever a man's real intentions may be, he so conduct himself that a reasonable man would take the representation to be true, and believe that it was meant that he should act upon it, and did act upon it as true.'

"If the ordinary law of estoppel was applicable to this case, it might well be argued that the circumstances leave no room for any representation by the sender on which the carrier acted. I believe that any other member of the public in Mr. McCutcheon's place — and this goes for lawyers as well as for laymen — would have found himself compelled to give the same sort of answers as Mr. McCutcheon gave; and I doubt if any carrier who serves out documents of this type could honestly say that he acted in the belief that the recipient had 'made himself acquainted with the contents.' But Blackburn J. was dealing with an unsigned document, a cloakroom ticket. Unless your Lordships are to disapprove the decision of the Court of Appeal in *L'Estrange v. F. Graucob Ltd.*, [1934] 2 K.B. 394 (C.A.) — and there has been no suggestion in this case that you should — the law is clear, without any recourse to the doctrine of estoppel, that a signature to a contract is conclusive." (Emphasis added.)

An analysis of the Canadian cases, however, indicates that the approach in this country has not been so rigid. In the case of *Colonial Investment Co. of Winnipeg, Man. v. Borland*, [1911] 1 W.W.R. 171 at p. 189, Beck J. set forth the following propositions:

"*Consensus ad idem* is essential to the creation of a contract, whether oral, in writing or under seal, subject to this, that as between the immediate parties (and merely voluntary assigns) apparent — as distinguished from real — consent will on the ground of estoppel effect a binding obligation unless the party denying the obligation proves:

"(1) That the other party knew at the time of the making of the alleged contract that the mind of the denying party did not accompany the expression of his consent; or

"(2) Such facts and circumstances as show that it was not reasonable and natural for the other party to suppose that the denying party was giving his real consent and he did not in fact give it;"

In commenting on the *Colonial Investment Co. of Winnipeg, Man. v. Borland* case, Spencer, in the article above cited, observes at p. 121:

"It is instructive to compare a Canadian approach to the problem of confusing documents which are signed but not fully understood."

And at p. 122 the author concludes his article with the following analysis:

"Policy considerations, but of different kinds, no doubt lay behind both the Canadian and the English approaches to this problem. The Canadian court was impressed by the abuses which would result — and, in England, have resulted — from enabling companies to hold ignorant signatories to the letter of sweeping exemption clauses contained in contracts in standard form. The English courts, however, were much more impressed with the danger of furnishing an easy line of defence by which liars could evade contractual liabilities freely assumed. It would be very dangerous to allow a man over the age of legal infancy to escape from the legal effect of a document he has, after reading it, signed, in the absence of any express misrepresentation by the other party of that legal effect. Forty years later, most lawyers would admit that the English courts made a bad choice between two evils...."

The significance of the circumstances under which a contract is entered into is noted by Taschereau J. in *The Provident Savings Life Assurance Society of New York and Mowat and Another* (1902), 32 S.C.R. 147, as follows at p. 162:

"As remarked by Mr. Justice MacLennan (27 O.A.R. 675):
" 'The case of a formal instrument like the present, prepared and executed, after a long negotiation, and correspondence delivered and accepted, and acted upon for years, is wholly different from the cases relating to railways and steamship and cloak-room tickets, in which it has been held that conditions qualifying the principal contract of carriage or bailment, not sufficiently brought to the attention of the passenger or bailor are not binding upon him. Such contracts are usually made in moments of more or less haste and confusion and stand by themselves.' "

I see no real distinction in contracts such as these, where the signature by itself does not truly represent an acquiescence of unusual and onerous terms which are inconsistent with the true object of the contract, and the ticket cases. This point was made by Beck J.A. in *Can. Bk. Commerce v. Foreman*, [1927] 2 D.L.R. 530, at p. 537 where he stated:

"Personally I have a very strong opinion, which is not to the full extent shared by other members of the Court and expressed in *Gray-Campbell Ltd. v. Flynn*, [1923] 1 D.L.R. 51, 18 Alta. L.R. 547, and for which I see some support in some circumstances in *Ball v. Gutschenritter*, [1925] 1 D.L.R. 901, at p. 908 (and see also *Jadis v. Porte* (1915), 23 D.L.R. 713, 8 Alta. L.R. 489) — *the opinion that when a contract of a common type contains special onerous and unusual provisions it is the duty of the party in whose interest such provisions are inserted to see that they are effectively called to the attention of the other party under the penalty of their being held not binding upon the latter party* but I think that would not ordinarily affect the residue of the contract and consequently the question does not arise in the present case. The only special provision which the bank needs to invoke, and which is of that special character that it alters the rights of the parties, is that permitting the giving of time to the debtor etc.; but this I would not place under the category of special provisions of an onerous or special character but would consider to be such a provision as the ordinary layman would suppose to express the law independently of a special provision." (Emphasis added.)

The same point of view was expressed by Lord Denning in the case of *Jaques v. Lloyd D. George & Partners Ltd.*, [1968] 1 W.L.R. 625, at p. 630:

> "The principles which in my opinion are applicable are these: When an estate agent is employed to find a purchaser for a business or a house, the ordinary understanding of mankind is that the commission is payable out of the purchase price when the matter is concluded. If the agent seeks to depart from that ordinary and well-understood term, then he must make it perfectly plain to his client. He must bring it home to him such as to make sure he agrees to it. When his representative produces a printed form and puts it before the client to sign, he should explain its effect to him, making it clear that it goes beyond the usual understanding in these matters. In the absence of such explanation, a client is entitled to assume that the form contains nothing unreasonable or oppressive. If he does not read it and the form is found afterwards to contain a term which is wholly unreasonable and totally uncertain, as this is, then the estate agent cannot enforce it against the innocent vendor."

In commenting on *Jaques v. Lloyd D. George & Partners Ltd., supra,* and on the case of *O'Connor Real Estate Ltd. v. Flynn* (1969), 3 D.L.R. (3d) 345, 11 D.L.R. (3d) 559, in 49 Can. Bar Rev., Professor Waddams makes the following observations at p. 590:

> "These cases suggest that there is a special onus on the supplier to point out any terms in a printed form which differ from what the consumer might reasonably expect. If he fails to do so, he will be guilty of a 'misrepresentation by omission', and the court will strike down clauses which 'differ from the ordinary understanding of mankind' or (and sometimes this is the same thing) clauses which are 'unreasonable or oppressive'. If this principle is accepted, the rule about written documents might be restated as follows: the signer is bound by the terms of the document if, and only if, the other party believes on reasonable grounds that those terms truly express the signer's intention. This principle retains the role of signed documents as a means of protecting reasonable expectations; what it does not allow is that a party should rely on a printed document to contradict what he knows, or ought to know, is the understanding of the other party. Again this principle seems to be particularly applicable in situations involving the distribution of goods and services to consumers, though it is by no means confined to such situations."

In modern commercial practice, many standard form printed documents are signed without being read or understood. In many cases the parties seeking to rely on the terms of the contract know or ought to know that the signature of a party to the contract does not represent the true intention of the signer, and that the party signing is unaware of the stringent and onerous provisions which the standard form contains. Under such circumstances, I am of the opinion that the party seeking to rely on such terms should not be able to do so in the absence of first having taken reasonable measures to draw such terms to the attention of the other party, and, in the absence of such reasonable measures, it is not necessary for the party denying knowledge of such terms to prove either fraud, misrepresentation or *non est factum.*

In the case at bar, Tilden Rent-A-Car took no steps to alert Mr. Clendenning of the onerous provisions in the standard form of contract presented by it. The clerk could not help but have known that Mr. Clendenning had not in fact read the contract before signing it. Indeed the form of the contract itself with the important provisions on the reverse side and in very small type would discourage even the most cautious customer from endeavouring to read and understand it. Mr. Clendenning was in fact unaware of the exempting provisions. Under such circumstances, it was not open to Tilden Rent-A-Car to rely on those clauses, and it was not incumbent on Mr. Clendenning to establish fraud, misrepresentation or *non est factum*. Having paid the premium, he was not liable for any damage to the vehicle while being driven by him.

As Lord Denning stated in *Neuchatel Asphalte Co. Ltd. v. Barnett*, [1957] 1 W.L.R. 356, at p. 360:

"We do not allow printed forms to be made a trap for the unwary."

In this case the trial judge held that "the rule in *L'Estrange v. Graucob*" governed. He dismissed the action, however, on the ground that Tilden Rent-A-Car had by their prior oral representations misrepresented the terms of the contract. He imputed into the contract the assumption of Mr. Clendenning that by the payment of the premium he was "provided full non-deductible coverage unless at the time of the damage he was operating the automobile while under the influence of intoxicating liquor to such an extent as to be for the time incapable of the proper control of the automobile". Having found that Mr. Clendenning had not breached such a provision, the action was dismissed.

For the reasons already expressed, I do not think that in the circumstances of this case "the rule in *L'Estrange v. Graucob*" governed, and it was not incumbent upon Mr. Clendenning to prove misrepresentation.

In any event, if "the rule in *L'Estrange v. Graucob*" were applicable, it was in error, in my respectful opinion, to impute into the contract a provision which Tilden Rent-A-Car had not in fact represented as being a term of the contract.

As was stated in *Canadian Indemnity Company v. Okanagan Mainline Real Estate Board et al.*, [1971] S.C.R. 493, at p. 500:

"A party who misrepresents, albeit innocently, the contents or effect of a clause inserted by him into a contract cannot rely on the clause in the face of his misrepresentation: ...."

Under such circumstances, absent the exclusionary provisions of the contract, the defendant was entitled to the benefit of the contract in the manner provided without the exclusionary provisions, and the action, therefore, had to fail.

In the result, therefore, I would dismiss the appeal with costs.

[Zuber J.A. agreed with Dubin J.A.]

Lacourcière J.A: (dissenting): I have had the advantage of reading the reasons for judgment prepared for release by my brother Dubin, which relieves me of the obligation of setting out the facts in this appeal, which are not really in dispute, or the relevant clauses of the contract. In my view the printing is not difficult to read, and the presence of conditions on the reverse side of the signed contract is brought to the signatory's attention in a very clear way.

It is not in dispute that the respondent violated two conditions of the contract: he drove the company's vehicle into a post, after drinking an unrecalled quantity of alcohol between 11.30 p.m. and 2 a.m. He was given a breathalyzer test, indicating a police officer's belief, on reasonable and probable grounds, that he had committed an offence of driving a motor vehicle while his ability to drive was impaired by alcohol or after having consumed alcohol in such quantity that the proportion of alcohol in his blood exceeded the penal limit. On the advice of counsel he pleaded guilty to a charge of impaired driving. I have set this out only to show that the respondent's violation of the contractual conditions was not a mere technical breach of an admittedly strict clause.

In the wisdom of the common law there has been a traditional distinction with respect to standard form contracts between the position of a person who signed the contract and the one who did not do so. In the absence of duress, fraud or misrepresentation — and subject to the defence of *non est factum* — the former was bound by the printed conditions, even if he or she did not read them. *L'Estrange v. F. Graucob, Limited*, [1934] 2 K.B. 394. The non-signatory was also bound if that person knew of the existence of the conditions; in the absence of knowledge, the question of the notice given by the other party became important. The distinction rests clearly on that essential prerequisite of a contract, *consensus ad idem*. The signatory is legally bound by the plain meaning of the words to which he has given assent, whereas the non-signatory should not be deemed to have assented to unknown printed conditions, unless he was given notice of their existence. See H.B. Sales (1953) 16 Mod. L.R. 318, "Standard Form Contracts".

The respondent, a frequent user of rented vehicles, could not recall what was said at the Tilden counter before he signed the agreement and initialled the collision damage waiver clause. He was aware that the contract contained writing on the back, but he claims that his attention was never drawn to the printed conditions until the action was brought against him.

After careful examination of the evidence, I am unable to agree with the learned trial Judge's conclusion that Tilden's counter clerk misrepresented the contract. The evidence of all witnesses concerning the common practice at a car rental counter had minimal probative value, and was probably inadmissible by reason of the parol evidence rule, in addition to being, at best, secondary evidence of what passed between the parties before the signing of the written contract.

I am therefore in agreement with Dubin J.A. that the learned trial Judge was in error when he imported into the contract an assumption made by the respondent concerning the extent and import of the exemption clause relating to alcohol, on the basis of tenuous and doubtful evidence. Once the respondent, not claiming fraud or duress, admitted having signed the contract, the onus was on him to prove by a preponderance of acceptable evidence that the conditions were misrepresented to him. In my view, this onus was not met by the respondent. The appellant has accordingly shown reversible error in the trial below.

Although the above would be sufficient to dispose of the appeal, I feel bound to express my view on the submission made on behalf of the respondent that the contract contained such unusual and onerous exculpatory terms that the respondent is not bound by them unless the appellant proves that reasonable measures were taken to draw them to his attention.

.   .   .

Lord Denning... in *John Lee & Son (Grantham), Ltd. and Others v. Railway Executive*, [1949] 2 All E.R. 581 at 584, in referring to an unreasonably onerous term in a standard form contract referred to the "vigilance of the common law which, while allowing freedom of contract, watches to see that it is not abused."

Lord Denning repeated the above words in *Gillespie Brothers & Co. Ltd. v. Roy Bowles Transport Ltd.*, [1973] Q.B. 400 at 415-6 where he talked of unreasonableness amounting to unconscionability. However, that case involved an attempt by a party to exempt himself from his liability at common law, which is not the situation in the present case. Furthermore Lord Buckley, while agreeing with Lord Denning in the result, disagreed with his approach and stated at p. 421:

> "It is not in my view the function of a court of construction to fashion a contract in such a way as to produce a result which the court considers that it would have been fair or reasonable for the parties to have intended. The court must attempt to discover what they did in fact intend."

Some attempts at exemption from common law liability may merit the harsh words of Lord Denning. But the common law has traditionally refused to strike down contractual 'standard form' conditions unless the terms are "so unreasonable as to amount to fraud, or manifestly irrelevant to the object of the contract". *Gibaud v. Great Eastern Ry.*, [1920] 2 K.B. 426.

The traditional attitude, with which I respectfully agree, has been for judges to avoid the difficult task of deciding the issue of 'reasonableness' of clauses in businesses which compete freely in the market place for consumer support.

. . . .

In this contract of bailment of a vehicle for a fixed remuneration, the customer is normally bound to take reasonable care of the vehicle, and is liable for damages caused by his negligence. This is subject to collision insurance: the customer is responsible for the deductible amount, $100 or $200 depending on location. By the payment of an additional premium, this liability of the customer is eliminated with this proviso:

> "... notwithstanding payment of said fee, customer shall be fully liable for all collision damage if vehicle is used, operated or driven in violation of any of the provisions of this rental agreement or off highways serviced by federal, provincial, or municipal governments, and for all damages to vehicle by striking overhead objects."

The clause is undoubtedly a strict one. It is not for a court to nullify its effect by branding it unfair, unreasonable and oppressive. It may be perfectly sound and reasonable from an insurance risk viewpoint, and may indeed be necessary in the competitive business of car rentals, where rates are calculated on the basis of the whole contract. On this point, see the majority judgment delivered by Lord Wilberforce in *New Zealand Shipping Co. Ltd. and A.M. Satterthwaite & Co. Ltd.*, [1975] A.C. 154 at 169, where it was held that the court must give effect to the clear intent of a commercial document.

I am of the view that, even if the respondent's signature is not conclusive, the terms of the contract are not unusual, oppressive or unreasonable and are binding on the respondent. I would therefore allow the appeal with costs, set aside the judgment below and in lieu thereof substitute a judgment for the amount of the agreed damages and costs.

QUESTION

Is it relevant that commercials for companies like Tilden advertise the speed and efficiency of their operations at airports?

McCUTCHEON v. DAVID MacBRAYNE, LTD.

[1964] 1 W.L.R. 125. House of Lords; Lords Reid, Hodson, Guest, Devlin and Pearce.

[Only the judgment of Lord Devlin is reproduced. Lord Devlin retired on January 10, 1964. This judgment was delivered on January 21, 1964.]

Lord Devlin. My Lords, when a person in the Isle of Islay wishes to send goods to the mainland he goes into the office of MacBrayne (the respondents) in Port Askaig which is conveniently combined with the local post office. There he is presented with a document headed "conditions" containing three or four thousand words of small print divided into 27 paragraphs. Beneath them there is a space for the sender's signature which he puts below his statement in quite legible print that he thereby agrees to ship on the conditions stated above. The appellant, Mr. McCutcheon, described the negotiations which preceded the making of this formidable contract in the following terms:

"Q. Tell us about that document; how did you come to sign it? A. You just walk in the office and the document is filled up ready and all you have to do is to sign your name and go out. Q. Did you ever read the conditions? A. No. Q. Did you know what was in them? A. No."

There are many other passages in which Mr. McCutcheon and his brother-in-law, Mr. McSporran, endeavour more or less successfully to appease the forensic astonishment aroused by this statement. People shipping calves, Mr. McCutcheon said (he was dealing with an occasion when he had shipped 36 calves), had not much time to give to the reading. Asked to deal with another occasion when he was unhampered by livestock, he said that people generally just tried to be in time for the boat's sailing; it would, he thought, take half a day to read and understand the conditions and then he would miss the boat. In another part of his evidence he went so far as to say that if everybody took time to read the document, "MacBrayne's office would be packed out the door." Mr. McSporran evidently thought the whole matter rather academic because, as he pointed out, there was no other way to send a car.

There came a day, October 8, 1960, when one of the respondents' vessels was negligently sailed into a rock and sank. She had on board a car belonging to Mr. McCutcheon which he had got Mr. McSporran to ship for him, and the car was a total loss. It would be a strangely generous set of conditions in which the persistent reader, after wading through the verbiage, could not find something to protect the carrier against "any loss ... wheresoever or whensoever occurring"; and condition 19 by itself is enough to absolve the respondents several times over for all their negligence. It is conceded that if the form had been signed as usual, the appellant would have had no case. But, by a stroke of ill luck for the respondents, it was upon this day of all days that they omitted to get Mr. McSporran to sign the conditions. What difference does that make?

If it were possible for your Lordships to escape from the world of make-believe which the law has created into the real world in which transactions of this sort are actually done, the answer would be short and simple. It should make no difference whatever. This sort of document is not meant to be read, still less to be understood. Its signature is in truth about as significant as a handshake that marks the formal conclusion of a bargain.

Your Lordships were referred to the dictum of Blackburn J. in *Harris v. Great Western Railway Co.* (1876), 1 Q.B.D. 515. The passage is as follows: "And it is clear law that where there is a writing, into which the terms of any agreement are reduced, the terms are to be regulated by that writing. And though one of the parties may not have read the writing, yet, in general, he is bound to the other by those terms; and that, I apprehend, is on the ground that, by assenting to the contract thus reduced to writing, he represents to the other side that he has made himself acquainted with the contents of that writing and assents to them, and so induces the other side to act upon that representation by entering into the contract with him, and is consequently precluded from denying that he did make himself acquainted with those terms. But then the preclusion only exists when the case is brought within the rule so carefully and accurately laid down by Parke B., in delivering the judgment of the Exchequer in *Freeman v. Cooke* (1848), 2 Exch. 654, that is, if he "means his representation to be acted upon, and it is acted upon accordingly: or if, whatever a man's real intentions may be, he so conduct himself that a resonable man would take the representation to be true, and believe that it was meant that he should act upon it, and did act upon it as true.' "

If the ordinary law of estoppel was applicable to this case, it might well be argued that the circumstances leave no room for any representation by the sender on which the carrier acted. I believe that any other member of the public in Mr. McCutcheon's place — and this goes for lawyers as well as for laymen — would have found himself compelled to give the same sort of answers as Mr. McCutcheon gave; and I doubt if any carrier who serves out documents of this type could honestly say that he acted in the belief that the recipient had "made himself acquainted with the contents." But Blackburn J. was dealing with an unsigned document, a cloakroom ticket. Unless your Lordships are to disapprove the decision of the Court of Appeal in *L'Estrange v. F. Graucob Ltd.*, [1934] 2 K.B. 394 — and there has been no suggestion in this case that you should — the law is clear, without any recourse to the doctrine of estoppel, that a signature to a contract is conclusive.

This is a matter that is relevant to the way in which the respondents put their case. They say that the previous dealings between themselves and the appellant, being always on the terms of their "risk note," as they call their written conditions, the contract between themselves and the appellant must be deemed to import the same conditions. In my opinion, the bare fact that there have been previous dealings between the parties does not assist the respondents at all. The fact that a man has made a contract in the same form 99 times (let alone three or four times which are here alleged) will not of itself affect the hundredth contract in which the form is not used. Previous dealings are relevant only if they prove knowledge of the terms, actual and not constructive, and assent to them. If a term is not expressed in a contract, there is only one other way in which it can come into it and that is by implication. No implication can be made against a party of a term which was unknown to him. If previous dealings show that a man knew of and agreed to a term on 99 occasions there is a basis for saying that it can be imported into the hundredth contract without an express statement. It may or may not be sufficient to justify the importation, — that depends on the circumstances; but at least by proving knowledge the essential beginning is made. Without knowledge there is nothing.

It is for the purpose of proving knowledge that the respondents rely on the dictum of Blackburn J. which I have cited. My Lords, in spite of the great authority of Blackburn J., I think that this is a dictum which some day your Lordships may have to examine more closely. It seems to me that when a party assents to a document forming the whole or a part of his contract, he is bound by the terms of the document, read or unread, signed or unsigned, simply because they are in the contract; and it is unnecessary and possibly misleading to say that he is bound by them because he represents to the other party that he has made himself acquainted with them. But if there be an estoppel of this sort, its effect is, in my opinion, limited to the contract in relation to which the representation is made; and it cannot (unless of course there be something else on which the estoppel is founded besides the mere receipt of the document) assist the other party in relation to other transactions. The respondents in the present case have quite failed to prove that the appellant made himself acquainted with the conditions they had introduced into previous dealings. He is not estopped from saying that, for good reasons or bad, he signed the previous contracts without the slightest idea of what was in them. If that is so, previous dealings are no evidence of knowledge and so are of little or no use to the respondents in this case.

I say "of little or no use" because the appellant did admit that he knew that there were some conditions, though he did not know what they were. He certainly did not know that they were conditions which exempted the respondents from liability for their own negligence, though I suppose, if he had thought about them at all, he would have known that they probably exempted the respondents from the strict liability of a carrier. Most people know that carriers exact some conditions and it does not matter in this case whether Mr. McCutcheon's knowledge was general knowledge of this sort or was derived from previous dealings. Your Lordships can therefore leave previous dealings out of it ask yourselves simply what is the position of a man who, with that amount of general knowledge, apparently makes a contract into which no conditions are expressly inserted?

The answer must surely be that either he does not make a contract at all because the parties are not ad idem, or he makes the contract without the conditions. You cannot have a contract subject to uncommunicated conditions the terms of which are known only to one side.

It is at this point, I think, that their Lordships in the Second Division fell into error. The Lord Justice-Clerk said: "It is, I think, well settled that, if A contracts with B for the carriage by B of A's goods in the knowledge, gained through previous experience of similar transactions, that B carries goods subject to conditions, A is bound by these conditions under this later contract, if it is of a similar nature to those which have gone before, in the absence of agreement or information to the contrary. This applies even if A, knowing that there are conditions, does not take the trouble to ascertain precisely what these conditions are." Similarly Lord MacIntosh said: "In these circumstances, I am of opinion, following what I understand to be the law as laid down in *Parker v. South Eastern Railway Co.,* and particularly by Baggallay L.J., that the pursuer being aware, by reason of his own previous experience and of that of the agent who happened to be acting for him in the present transaction, that goods were carried on the defenders' vessels subject to certain conditions, and having been given no reason to think that these conditions were not still operative on October 8, 1960, was bound by the conditions, although, as was proved to have been the case, he had never at any time acquainted himself with their purport."

My Lords, I think, with great respect, that this is to introduce a new and fundamentally erroneous principle into the law of contract. There can be no conditions in any contract unless they are brought into it by expression, incorporation or implication. They are not brought into it simply because one party has inserted them into similar transactions in the past and has not given the other party any reason to think that he will not want to insert them again. The error is based, I think, on a misunderstanding of what are commonly called the ticket cases; I say this because the single authority cited for the proposition is one of the leading ticket cases, *Parker v. South Eastern Railway Co.* The question in these cases is whether or not the passenger has accepted the ticket as a contractual document. If he knows that it contains conditions of some sort, he must know that it is meant to be contractual. If he accepts it as a contractual document, then prima facie (I am not dealing with questions of reasonable notice) he is bound by the conditions that are printed on it or incorporated in it by sufficient reference to some other document, whether he has inquired about them or not. That is all that Baggallay L.J. is saying in *Parker v. South Eastern Railway Co.*

In the present case there is no contractual document at all. There is not so much as a peg on which to hang any terms that are not expressed in the contract nor a phrase which is capable of expansion. It is as if the appellant had been accepted as a passenger without being given a ticket at all. There is, then, no special contract and the contract is the ordinary one which the law imposes on carriers. As Baggallay L.J. said: "This clearly would be the nature of the contract if no ticket were delivered, as occasionally happens."

If a man is given a blank ticket without conditions or any reference to them, even if he knows in detail what the conditions usually exacted are, he is not, in the absence of any allegation of fraud or of that sort of mistake for which the law gives relief, bound by such conditions. It may seem a narrow and artificial line that divides a ticket that is blank on the back from one that says "For conditions see time-tables," or something of that sort, that has been held to be enough notice. I agree that it is an artificial line and one that has little relevance to everyday conditions. It may be beyond your Lordships' power to make the artificial line more natural; but at least you can see that it is drawn fairly for both sides and that there is not one law for individuals and another for organisations that can issue printed documents. If the respondents had remembered to issue a risk note in this case, they would have invited your Lordships to give a curt answer to any complaint by the appellant. He might say that the terms were unfair and unreasonable, that he had never voluntarily agreed to them, that it was impossible to read or understand them and that anyway if he had tried to negotiate any change the respondents would not have listened to him. The respondents would expect him to be told that he had made his contract and must abide by it. Now the boot is on the other foot. It is just as legitimate, but also just as vain, for the respondents to say that it was only a slip on their part, that it is unfair and unreasonable of the appellant to take advantage of it and that he knew perfectly well that they never carried goods except on conditions. The law must give the same answer: they must abide by the contract they made. What is sauce for the goose is sauce for the gander. It will remain unpalatable sauce for both animals until the legislature, if the courts cannot do it, intervenes to secure that when contracts are made in circumstances in which there is no scope for free negotiation of the terms, they are made upon terms that are clear, fair and reasonable and settled independently as such. That is what Parliament has done in the case of carriage of goods by rail and on the high seas.

I have now given my opinion on the main point in the case and the one on which the respondents succeeded below. On the other points on which the respondents failed below and which they put forward again as grounds for dismissing the claim, I have nothing to add to what your Lordships have already said. In my opinion, the appeal should be allowed.

BRITISH CRANE HIRE CORPORATION LTD. v. IPSWICH PLANT HIRE LTD.,

[1974] 1 All E.R. 1059. Court of Appeal (England); Lord Denning M.R., Megaw L.J. and Sir Eric Sachs.

[The parties were both in the crane rental business. The defendants needed a crane in a hurry. The plaintiffs agreed to supply one. The crane got stuck in a marsh. There was an argument that the defendants were negligent but there was doubt on this. The plaintiffs argued that, in any case, the defendants were bound by a term in their standard agreement. The defendants had not signed the agreement in this case, and there was insufficient evidence to show a course of dealing. The trial judge gave judgment for the plaintiffs. The defendants appealed.]

Lord Denning M.R. (after stating the facts, continued):

In *Hollier v. Rambler Motors (AMC) Ltd*, [1972] 2 Q.B. 71, 76, Salmon LJ said he knew of no case —

'in which it has been decided or even argued that a term could be implied into an oral contract on the strength of a course of dealing (if it can be so called) which consisted at the most of three or four transactions over a period of five years.'

That was a case of a private individual who had had his car repaired by the defendants and had signed forms with conditions on three or four occasions. The plaintiff there was not of equal bargaining power with the garage company which repaired the car. The conditions were not incorporated.

But here the parties were both in the trade and were of equal bargaining power. Each was a firm of plant hirers who hired out plant. The defendants themselves knew that firms in the plant-hiring trade always imposed conditions in regard to the hiring of plant; and that their conditions were on much the same lines. The defendants' manager, Mr. Turner (who knew the crane), was asked about it. He agreed that he had seen these conditions or similar ones in regard to the hiring of plant. He said that most of them were, to one extent or another, variations of a form which he called 'the Contractors' Plant Association form'. The defendants themselves (when they let out cranes) used the conditions of that form. The conditions on the plaintiffs' form were in rather different words, but nevertheless to much the same effect. He was asked one or two further questions which I would like to read:

'*Q.* If it was a matter of urgency, you would hire that machine out, and the conditions of hire would no doubt follow? *A.* They would.

'*Q.* Is it right that, by the very nature of your business, this is not something that happens just once a year, nor does it happen every day either, but it happens fairly regularly? *A.* It does.

'*Q.* You are well aware of the condition that it is the hirer's responsibility to make sure that soft ground is suitable for a vehicle or machine? *A.* It is; it is also the owner's responsibility to see that the machine is operated competently.

Then the judge asked:

'*Q.* But it is the hirer's job to see what in relation to the ground? *A.* That suitable timber was supplied for the machine to operate on in relation to the soft ground.'

Then counsel asked:

'*Q.* And in fact it is the hirer's job to recover the crane from the soft ground, if it should go into it? *A.* If the crane sank overnight of its own accord, I dare say it would be.'

From that evidence it is clear that both parties knew quite well that conditions were habitually imposed by the supplier of these machines: and both parties knew the substance of those conditions. In particular that, if the crane sank in soft ground it was the hirer's job to recover it; and that there was an indemnity clause. In these circumstances, I think the conditions on the form should be regarded as incorporated into the contract. I would not put it so much on the course of dealing, but rather on the common understanding which is to be derived from the conduct of the parties, namely, that the hiring was to be on the terms of the plaintiffs' usual conditions.

As Lord Reid said in *McCutcheon v. David MacBrayne Ltd,* quoting from the Scottish textbook Gloag on Contract:

'The judicial task is not to discover the actual intentions of each party; it is to decide what each was reasonably entitled to conclude from the attitude of the other.'

It seems to me that, in view of the relationship of the parties, when the defendants requested this crane urgently and it was supplied at once — before the usual form was received — the plaintiffs were entitled to conclude that the defendants were accepting it on the terms of the plaintiffs' own printed conditions — which would follow in a day or two. It is just as if the plaintiffs had said, 'We will supply it on our usual conditions', and the defendants said, 'Of course, that is quite understood'.

[Lord Denning held the defendants liable for the loss, and dismissed the appeal.]

[Megaw L.J. and Sir Eric Sachs agreed.]

HENNINGSEN v. BLOOMFIELD MOTORS, INC.

(1960), 161 A. 2d 69. Supreme Court of New Jersey.

The opinion of the court was delivered by

Francis, J. Plaintiff Claus H. Henningsen purchased a Plymouth automobile, manufactured by defendant Chrysler Corporation, from defendant Bloomfield Motors, Inc. His wife, plaintiff Helen Henningsen, was injured while driving it and instituted suit against both defendants to recover damages on account of her injuries. Her husband joined in the action seeking compensation for his consequential losses. The complaint was predicated upon breach of express and implied warranties and upon negligence. At the trial the negligence counts were dismissed by the court and the cause was submitted to the jury for determination solely on the issues of implied warranty of merchantability. Verdicts were returned against both defendants and in favor of the plaintiffs. Defendants appealed and plaintiffs cross-appealed from the dismissal of their negligence claim. The matter was certified by this court prior to consideration in the Appellate Division.

The facts are not complicated, but a general outline of them is necessary to an understanding of the case.

On May 7, 1955 Mr. and Mrs. Henningsen visited the place of business of Bloomfield Motors, Inc., an authorized De Soto and Plymouth dealer, to look at a Plymouth. They wanted to buy a car and were considering a Ford or a Chevrolet as well as a Plymouth. They were shown a Plymouth which appealed to them and the purchase followed. The record indicates that Mr. Henningsen intended the car as a Mother's Day gift to his wife. He said the intention was communicated to the dealer. When the purchase order or contract was prepared and presented, the husband executed it alone. His wife did not join as a party.

The purchase order was a printed form of one page. On the front it contained blanks to be filled in with a description of the automobile to be sold, the various accessories to be included, and the details of the financing. The particular car selected was described as a 1955 Plymouth, Plaza "6", Club Sedan. The type used in the printed parts of the form became smaller in size, different in style, and less readable toward the bottom where the line for the purchaser's signature was placed. The smallest type on the page appears in the two paragraphs, one of two and one-quarter lines and the second of one and one-half lines, on which great stress is laid by the defense in the case. These two paragraphs are the least legible and the most difficult to read in the instrument, but they are most important in the evaluation of the rights of the contesting parties. They do not attract attention and there is nothing about the format which would draw the reader's eye to them. In fact, a studied and concentrated effort would have to be made to read them. De-emphasis seems the motive rather than emphasis. More particularly, most of the printing in the body of the order appears to be 12 point block type, and easy to read. In the short paragraphs under discussion, however, the type appears to be six point script and the print is solid, that is, the lines are very close together.

The two paragraphs are:

"The front and back of this Order comprise the entire agreement affecting this purchase and no other agreement or understanding of any nature concerning same has been made or entered into, or will be recognized. I hereby certify that no credit has been extended to me for the purchase of this motor vehicle except as appears in writing on the face of this agreement.

"I have read the matter printed on the back hereof and agree to it as a part of this order the same as if it were printed above my signature. I certify that I am 21 years of age, or older, and hereby acknowledge receipt of a copy of this order."

On the right side of the form, immediately below these clauses and immediately above the signature line, and in. 12 point block type, the following appears:

"CASH OR CERTIFIED CHECK ONLY ON DELIVERY."

On the left side, just opposite and in the same style type as the two quoted clauses, but in eight point size, this statement is set out:

"This agreement shall not become binding upon the Dealer until approved by an officer of the company."

The two latter statements are in the interest of the dealer and obviously an effort is made to draw attention to them.

The testimony of Claus Henningsen justifies the conclusion that he did not read the two fine print paragraphs referring to the back of the purchase contract. And it is uncontradicted that no one made any reference to them, or called them to his attention. With respect to the matter appearing on the back, it is likewise uncontradicted that he did not read it and that no one called it to his attention.

The reverse side of the contract contains 8½ inches of fine print. It is not as small, however, as the two critical paragraphs described above. The page is headed "Conditions" and contains ten separate paragraphs consisting of 65 lines in all. The paragraphs do not have headnotes or margin notes denoting their particular subject, as in the case of the "Owner Service Certificate" to be referred to later. In the seventh paragraph, about two-thirds of the way down the page, the warranty, which is the focal point of the case, is set forth. It is as follows:

"7. It is expressly agreed that there are no warranties, express or implied, *made* by either the dealer or the manufacturer on the motor vehicle, chassis, of parts furnished hereunder except as follows.

" 'The manufacturer warrants each new motor vehicle (including original equipment placed thereon by the manufacturer except tires), chassis or parts manufactured by it to be free from defects in material or workmanship under normal use and service. Its obligation under this warranty being limited to making good at its factory any part or parts thereof which shall, within ninety (90) days after delivery of such vehicle *to the original purchaser* or before such vehicle has been driven 4,000 miles, whichever event shall first occur, be returned to it with transportation charges prepaid and which its examination shall disclose to its satisfaction to have been thus defective; *this warranty being expressly in lieu of all other warranties expressed or implied, and all other obligations or liabilities on its part,* and it neither assumes nor authorizes any other person to assume for it any other liability in connection with the sale of its vehicles.....' " (Emphasis ours.)

After the contract had been executed, plaintiffs were told the car had to be serviced and that it would be ready in two days. According to the dealer's president, a number of cars were on hand at the time; they had come in from the factory about three or four weeks earlier and at least some of them, including the one selected by the Henningsens, were kept in the back of the shop for display purposes. When sold, plaintiffs' vehicle was not "a serviced car, ready to go." The testimony shows that Chrysler Corporation sends from the factory to the dealer a "'New Car Preparation Service Guide" with each new automobile. The guide contains detailed instructions as to what has to be done to prepare the car for delivery. The dealer is told to "Use this form as a guide to inspect and prepare this new Plymouth for delivery." It specifies 66 separate items to be checked, tested, tightened or adjusted in the course of the servicing, but dismantling the vehicle or checking all of its internal parts is not prescribed. The guide also calls for delivery of the Owner Service Certificate with the car.

This Certificate, which at least by inference is authorized by Chrysler, was in the car when released to Claus Henningsen on May 9, 1955. It was not made part of the purchase contract, nor was it shown to him prior to the consummation of that agreement. The only reference to it therein is that the dealer "agrees to promptly perform and fulfill all terms and conditions of the owner service policy." The Certificate contains a warranty entitled "Automobile Manufacturers Association Uniform Warranty." The provisions thereof are the same as those set forth on the reverse side of the purchase order, except that an additional paragraph is added by which the dealer extends that warranty to the purchaser in the same manner as if the word "Dealer" appeared instead of the word "Manufacturer".

The new Plymouth was turned over to the Henningsens on May 9, 1955. No proof was adduced by the dealer to show precisely what was done in the way of mechanical or road testing beyond testimony that the manufacturer's instructions were probably followed. Mr. Henningsen drove it from the dealer's place of business in Bloomfield to their home in Keansburg. On the trip nothing unusual appeared in the way in which it operated. Thereafter, it was used for short trips on paved streets about the town. It had no servicing and no mishaps of any kind before the event of May 19. That day, Mrs. Henningsen drove to Asbury Park. On the way down and in returning the car performed in normal fashion until the accident occurred. She was proceeding north on Route 36 in Highlands, New Jersey, at 20-22 miles per hour. The highway was paved and smooth, and contained two lanes for northbound travel. She was riding in the right-hand lane. Suddenly she heard a loud noise "from the bottom, by the hood." It "felt as if something cracked." The steering wheel spun in her hands; the car veered sharply to the right and crashed into a highway sign and a brick wall. No other vehicle was in any way involved. A bus operator driving in the left-hand lane testified that he observed plaintiffs' car approaching in normal fashion in the opposite direction; "all of a sudden [it] veered at 90 degrees … and right into this wall." As a result of the impact, the front of the car was so badly damaged that it was impossible to determine if any of the parts of the steering wheel mechanism or workmanship or assembly were defective or improper prior to the accident. The condition was such that the collision insurance carrier, after inspection, declared the vehicle a total loss. It had 468 miles on the speedometer at the time.

The insurance carrier's inspector and appraiser of damaged cars, with 11 years of experience, advanced the opinion, based on the history and his examination, that something definitely went "wrong from the steering wheel down to the front wheels" and that the untoward happening must have been due to mechanical defect or failure; "something down there had to drop off or break loose to cause the car" to act in the manner described.

As has been indicated, the trial court felt that the proof was not sufficient to make out a *prima facie* case as to the negligence of either the manufacturer or the dealer. The case was given to the jury, therefore, solely on the warranty theory, with results favorable to the plaintiffs against both defendants.

II.

The Effect of the Disclaimer and Limitation of Liability Clauses on the Implied Warranty of Merchantability.

Judicial notice may be taken of the fact that automobile manufacturers, including Chrysler Corporation, undertake large scale advertising programs over television, radio, in newspapers, magazines and all media of communication in order to persuade the public to buy their products. As has been observed above, a number of jurisdictions, conscious of modern marketing practices, have declared that when a manufacturer engages in advertising in order to bring his goods and their quality to the attention of the public and thus to create consumer demand, the representations made constitute an express warranty running directly to a buyer who purchases in reliance thereon. The fact that the sale is consummated with an independent dealer does not obviate that warranty.

. . .

In view of the cases in various jurisdictions suggesting the conclusion which we have now reached with respect to the implied warranty of merchantability, it becomes apparent that manufacturers who enter into promotional activities to stimulate consumer buying may incur warranty obligations of either or both the express or implied character. These developments in the law inevitably suggest the inference that the form of express warranty made part of the Henningsen purchase contract was devised for general use in the automobile industry as a possible means of avoiding the consequences of the growing judicial acceptance of the thesis that the described express or implied warranties run directly to the consumer.

In the light of these matters, what effect should be given to the express warranty in question which seeks to limit the manufacturer's liability to replacement of defective parts, and which disclaims all other warranties, express or implied? In assessing its significance we must keep in mind the general principle that, in the absence of fraud, one who does not choose to read a contract before signing it, cannot later relieve himself of its burdens ... and in applying that principle, the basic tenet of freedom of competent parties to contract is a factor of importance. But in the framework of modern commercial life and business practices, such rules cannot be applied on a strict, doctrinal basis. The conflicting interests of the buyer and seller must be evaluated realistically and justly, giving due weight to the social policy evinced by the Uniform Sales Act, the progressive decisions of the courts engaged in administering it, the mass production methods of manufacture and distribution to the public, and the bargaining position occupied by the ordinary consumer in such an economy. This history of the law shows that legal doctrines, as first expounded, often prove to be inadequate under the impact of later experience. In such case, the need for justice has stimulated the necessary qualifications or adjustments...

In these times, an automobile is almost as much a servant of convenience for the ordinary person as a household utensil. For a multitude of other persons it is a necessity. Crowded highways and filled parking lots are a commonplace of our existence. There is no need to look any farther than the daily newspaper to be convinced that when an automobile is defective, it has great potentiality for harm.

No one spoke more graphically on this subject than Justice Cardozo in the landmark case of MacPherson v. Buick Motor Co., 217 N.Y. 382, 111 N.E. 1050, 1053, L.R.A.1916F, 696 (Ct.App.1916):

> "Beyond all question, the nature of an automobile gives warning of probable danger if its construction is defective. This automobile was designed to go 50 miles per hour. Unless its wheels were sound and strong, injury was almost certain. It was as much a thing of danger as a defective engine for a railroad... The dealer was indeed the one person of whom it might be said with some approach to certainty that by him the car would not be used... Precedents drawn from the days of travel by stagecoach do not fit the conditions of travel to-day. The principle that the danger must be imminent does not change, but the things subject to the principle do change. They are whatever the needs of life in a developing civilization require them to be."

In the 44 years that have intervened since that utterance, the average car has been constructed for almost double the speed mentioned; 60 miles per hour is permitted on our parkways. The number of automobiles in use has multiplied many times and the hazard to the user and the public has increased proportionately. The Legislature has intervened in the public interest, not only to regulate the manner of operation on the highway but also to require periodic inspection of motor vehicles and to impose a duty on manufacturers to adopt certain safety devices and methods in their construction. R.S. 39:3-43 et seq., N.J.S.A. It is apparent that the public has an interest not only in the safe manufacture of automobiles, but also, as shown by the Sales Act, in protecting the rights and remedies of purchasers, so far as it can be accomplished consistently with our system of free enterprise. In a society such as ours, where the automobile is a common and necessary adjunct of daily life, and where its use is so fraught with danger to the driver, passengers and the public, the manufacturer is under a special obligation in connection with the construction, promotion and sale of his cars. Consequently, the courts must examine purchase agreements closely to see if consumer and public interests are treated fairly.

What influence should these circumstances have on the restrictive effect of Chrysler's express warranty in the framework of the purchase contract? As we have said, warranties originated in the law to safeguard the buyer and not to limit the liability of the seller or manufacturer. It seems obvious in this instance that the motive was to avoid the warranty obligations which are normally incidental to such sales. The language gave little and withdrew much. In return for the delusive remedy of replacement of defective parts at the factory, the buyer is said to have accepted the exclusion of the maker's liability for personal injuries arising from the breach of the warranty, and to have agreed to the elimination of any other express or implied warranty. An instinctively felt sense of justice cries out against such a sharp bargain. But does the doctrine that a person is bound by his signed agreement, in the absence of fraud, stand in the way of any relief?

In the modern consideration of problems such as this, Corbin suggests that practically all judges are "chancellors" and cannot fail to be influenced by any equitable doctrines that are available. And he opines that "there is sufficient flexibility in the concepts of fraud, duress, misrepresentation and undue influence, not to mention differences in economic bargaining power" to enable the courts to avoid enforcement of unconscionable provisions in long printed standardized contracts. 1 Corbin on Contracts (1950) § 128, p. 188. Freedom of contract is not such an immutable doctrine as to admit of no qualification in the area in which we are concerned. As Chief Justice Hughes said in his dissent in Morehead v. People of State of New York ex rel. Tipaldo, 298 U.S. 587, 627, 56 S.Ct. 918, 930, 80 L.Ed. 1347, 1364 (1936):

> "We have had frequent occasion to consider the limitations on liberty of con-
> tract. While it is highly important to preserve that liberty from arbitrary and
> capricious interference, it is also necessary to prevent its abuse, as otherwise it
> could be used to override all public interests and thus in the end destroy the very
> freedom of opportunity which it is designed to safeguard."

That sentiment was echoed by Justice Frankfurter in his dissent in United States v. Bethlehem Steel Corp., 315 U.S. 289, 326, 62 S.Ct. 581, 599, 86 L.Ed. 855, 876 (1942):

> "It is said that familiar principles would be outraged if Bethlehem were denied
> recovery on these contracts. But is there any principle which is more familiar or
> more firmly embedded in the history of Anglo-American law than the basic doc-
> trine that the courts will not permit themselves to be used as instruments of ine-
> quity and injustice? Does any principle in our law have more universal applica-
> tion than the doctrine that courts will not enforce transactions in which the
> relative positions of the parties are such that one has unconscionably taken
> advantage of the necessities of the other?
> "These principles are not foreign to the law of contracts. Fraud and physical
> duress are not the only grounds upon which courts refuse to enforce contracts.
> The law is not so primitive that it sanctions every injustice except brute force and
> downright fraud. More specifically, the courts generally refuse to lend themselves
> to the enforcement of a 'bargain' in which one party has unjustly taken advan-
> tage of the economic necessities of the other...."

The traditional contract is the result of free bargaining of parties who are brought together by the play of the market, and who meet each other on a footing of approximate economic equality. In such a society there is no danger that freedom of contract will be a threat to the social order as a whole. But in present-day commercial life the standardized mass contract has appeared. It is used primarily by enterprises with strong bargaining power and position. "The weaker party, in need of the goods or services, is frequently not in a position to shop around for better terms, either because the author of the standard contract has a monopoly (natural or artificial) or because all competitors use the same clauses. His contractual intention is but a subjection more or less voluntary to terms dictated by the stronger party, terms whose consequences are often understood in a vague way, if at all." Kessler, "Contracts of Adhesion — Some Thoughts About Freedom of Contract," 43 Colum.L.Rev. 629, 632 (1943); Ehrenzweig, "Adhesion Contracts in the Conflict of Laws," 53 Colum.L.Rev. 1072, 1075, 1089 (1953). Such standardized contracts have been described as those in which one predominant party will dictate its law to an undetermined multiple rather than to an individual. They are said to resemble a law rather than a meeting of the minds. Siegelman v. Cunard White Star, 221 F.2d 189, 206 (2 Cir. 1955).

Vold, in the recent revision of his Law of Sales (2d ed. 1959) at page 447, wrote of this type of contract and its effect upon the ordinary buyer:

"In recent times the marketing process has been getting more highly organized than ever before. Business units have been expanding on a scale never before known. The standardized contract with its broad disclaimer clauses is drawn by legal advisers of sellers widely organized in trade associations. It is encountered on every hand. Extreme inequality of bargaining between buyer and seller in this respect is now often conspicuous. Many buyers no longer have any real choice in the matter. They must often accept what they can get though accompanied by broad disclaimers. The terms of these disclaimers deprive them of all substantial protection with regard to the quality of the goods. In effect, this is by force of contract between very unequal parties. It throws the risk of defective articles on the most dependent party. He has the least individual power to avoid the presence of defects. He also has the least individual ability to bear their disastrous consequences."

The warranty before us is a standardized form designed for mass use. It is imposed upon the automobile consumer. He takes it or leaves it, and he must take it to buy an automobile. No bargaining is engaged in with respect to it. In fact, the dealer through whom it comes to the buyer is without authority to alter it; his function is ministerial — simply to deliver it.

The form warranty is not only standard with Chrysler but, as mentioned above, it is the uniform warranty of the Automobile Manufacturers Association. Members of the Association are: General Motors, Inc., Ford, Chrysler, Studebaker-Packard, American Motors, (Rambler), Willys Motors, Checker Motors Corp., and International Harvester Company. Automobile Facts and Figures (1958 Ed., Automobile Manufacturers Association) 69. Of these companies, the "Big Three" (General Motors, Ford, and Chrysler) represented 93.5% of the passenger-car production for 1958 and the independents 6.5%. Standard & Poor (Industrial Surveys, Autos, Basic Analysis, June 25, 1959) 4109. And for the same year the "Big Three" had 86.72% of the total passenger vehicle registrations. Automotive News, 1959 Almanac (Slocum Publishing Co., Inc.) p. 25.

The gross inequality of bargaining position occupied by the consumer in the automobile industry is thus apparent. There is no competition among the car makers in the area of the express warranty. Where can the buyer go to negotiate for better protection? Such control and limitation of his remedies are inimical to the public welfare and, at the very least, call for great care by the courts to avoid injustice through application of strict common-law principles of freedom of contract. Because there is no competition among the motor vehicle manufacturers with respect to the scope of protection guaranteed to the buyer, there is no incentive on their part to stimulate good will in that field of public relations. Thus, there is lacking a factor existing in more competitive fields, one which tends to guarantee the safe construction of the article sold. Since all competitors operate in the same way, the urge to be careful is not so pressing. See "Warranties of Kind and Quality," 57 Yale L.J. 1389, 1400 (1948).

Although the courts, with few exceptions, have been most sensitive to problems presented by contracts resulting from gross disparity in buyer-seller bargaining positions, they have not articulated a general principle condemning, as opposed to public policy, the imposition on the buyer of a skeleton warranty as a means of limiting the responsibility of the manufacturer. They have endeavored thus far to avoid a drastic departure from age-old tenets of freedom of contract by adopting doctrines of strict construction, and notice and knowledgeable assent by the buyer to the attempted exculpation of the seller. 1 Corbin, supra, 337; 2 Harper & James, supra, 1590; Prosser, "Warranty of Merchantable Quality," 27 Minn.L.Rev. 117, 159 (1932). Accordingly to be found in the cases are statements that disclaimers and the consequent limitation of liability will not be given effect if "unfairly procured,"

. . .

Basically, the reason a contracting party offering services of a public or *quasi*-public nature has been held to the requirements of fair dealing, and, when it attempts to limit its liability, of securing the understanding consent of the patron or consumer, is because members of the public generally have no other means of fulfilling the specific need represented by the contract. Having in mind the situation in the automobile industry as detailed above, and particularly the fact that the limited warranty extended by the manufacturers is a uniform one, there would appear to be no just reason why the principles of all of the cases set forth should not chart the course to be taken here.

It is undisputed that the president of the dealer with whom Henningsen dealt did not specifically call attention to the warranty on the back of the purchase order. The form and the arrangement of its face, as described above, certainly would cause the minds of reasonable men to differ as to whether notice of a yielding of basic rights stemming from the relationship with the manufacturer was adequately given. The words "warranty" or "limited warranty" did not even appear in the fine print above the place for signature, and a jury might well find that the type of print itself was such as to promote lack of attention rather than sharp scrutiny. The inference from the facts is that Chrysler placed the method of communicating its warranty to the purchaser in the hands of the dealer. If either one or both of them wished to make certain that Henningsen became aware of that agreement and its purported implications, neither the form of the document nor the method of expressing the precise nature of the obligation intended to be assumed would have presented any difficulty.

But there is more than this. Assuming that a jury might find that the fine print referred to reasonably served the objective of directing a buyer's attention to the warranty on the reverse side, and, therefore, that he should be charged with awareness of its language, can it be said that an ordinary layman would realize what he was relinquishing in return for what he was being granted? Under the law, breach of warranty against defective parts or workmanship which caused personal injuries would entitle a buyer to damages even if due care were used in the manufacturing process. Because of the great potential for harm if the vehicle was defective, that right is the most important and fundamental one arising from the relationship. Difficulties so frequently encountered in establishing negligence in manufacture in the ordinary case make this manifest. 2 Harper & James, supra, §§ 28.14, 28.15; Prosser, supra, 506. Any ordinary layman of reasonable intelligence, looking at the phraseology, might well conclude that Chrysler was agreeing to replace defective parts and perhaps replace anything that went wrong because of defective workmanship during the first 90 days or 4,000 miles of operation, but that he would not be entitled to a new car. It is not unreasonable to believe that the entire scheme being conveyed was a proposed remedy for physical deficiencies in the car. *In the context* of this warranty, only the abandonment of all sense of justice would permit us to hold that, as a matter of law, the phrase "its obligation under this warranty being limited to making good at its factory any part or parts thereof" signifies to an ordinary reasonable person that he is relinquishing any personal injury claim that might flow from the use of a defective automobile. Such claims are nowhere mentioned. The draftsmanship is reflective of the care and skill of the Automobile Manufacturers Association in undertaking to avoid warranty obligations without drawing too much attention to its effort in that regard. No one can doubt that if the will to do so were present, the ability to inform the buying public of the intention to disclaim liability for injury claims arising from breach of warranty would present no problem.

In this connection, attention is drawn to the Plymouth Owner Certificate mentioned earlier. Obviously, Chrysler is aware of it because the New Car Preparation Service Guide sent from the factory to the dealer directs that it be given to the purchaser. That certificate contains a paragraph called "Explanation of Warranty." Its entire tenor relates to replacement of defective parts. There is nothing about it to stimulate the idea that the intention of the warranty is to exclude personal injury claims....

The task of the judiciary is to administer the spirit as well as the letter of the law. On issues such as the present one, part of that burden is to protect the ordinary man against the loss of important rights through what, in effect, is the unilateral act of the manufacturer. The status of the automobile industry is unique. Manufacturers are few in number and strong in bargaining position. In the matter of warranties on the sale of their products, the Automotive Manufacturers Association has enabled them to present a united front. From the standpoint of the purchaser, there can be no arms length negotiating on the subject. Because his capacity for bargaining is so grossly unequal, the inexorable conclusion which follows is that he is not permitted to bargain at all. He must take or leave the automobile on the warranty terms dictated by the maker. He cannot turn to a competitor for better security.

Public policy is a term not easily defined. Its significance varies as the habits and needs of a people may vary. It is not static and the field of application is an ever increasing one. A contract, or a particular provision therein, valid in one era may be wholly opposed to the public policy of another. ... Courts keep in mind the principle that the best interests of society demand that persons should not be unnecessarily restricted in their freedom to contract. But they do not hesitate to declare void as against public policy contractual provisions which clearly tend to the injury of the public in some way....

Public policy at a given time finds expression in the Constitution, the statutory law and in judicial decisions. In the area of sale of goods, the legislative will has imposed an implied warranty of merchantability as a general incident of sale of an automobile by description. The warranty does not depend upon the affirmative intention of the parties. It is a child of the law; it annexes itself to the contract because of the very nature of the transaction.... The judicial process has recognized a right to recover damages for personal injuries arising from a breach of that warranty. The disclaimer of the implied warranty and exclusion of all obligations except those specifically assumed by the express warranty signify a studied effort to frustrate that protection. True, the Sales Act authorizes agreements between buyer and seller qualifying the warranty obligations. But quite obviously the Legislature contemplated lawful stipulations (which are determined by the circumstances of a particular case) arrived at freely by parties of relatively equal bargaining strength. The lawmakers did not authorize the automobile manufacturer to use its grossly disproportionate bargaining power to relieve itself from liability and to impose on the ordinary buyer, who in effect has no real freedom of choice, the grave danger of injury to himself and others that attends the sale of such a dangerous instrumentality as a defectively made automobile. In the framework of this case, illuminated as it is by the facts and the many decisions noted, we are of the opinion that Chrysler's attempted disclaimer of an implied warranty of merchantability and of the obligations arising therefrom is so inimical to the public good as to compel an adjudication of its invalidity. See 57 Yale L.J., supra, at pp. 1400-1404; proposed Uniform Commercial Code, 1958 Official Text, § 202.

QUESTIONS

1. How does the approach taken in these cases differ from that in the earlier ones in this section?
2. Do you think that this is a preferable approach?

The following extract is part of a paper that we looked at earlier in Chapter 2.

MACAULAY, "THE STANDARDIZED CONTRACTS OF UNITED STATES AUTOMOBILE MANUFACTURERS"

[In this part of the paper Professor Macaulay examines the relationship between the automobile manufacturers and their customers. Notice particularly the way in which legislation operates and the response of the manufacturers to the problems they faced. Footnotes are at end of article.]

iii. *The Manufacturers and Their Customers*

a. Description of the Relationship

37. The manufacturers' goals concerning their customers are simple: they want to sell all of the new cars they possibly can. The products are heavily advertised, and people are urged to buy new cars while their old ones still have useful life as machines. Models generally are changed in appearance each year to create a demand for something new. The manufacturer strives to build an image for its products of quality, safety and reliability. Since a manufacturer's ideal customer will buy a new car to replace his old one every year or every other year, manufacturers are concerned about the continuing good-will and continuing loyalty of car buyers. The context in which the manufacturers have pursued their goals has changed over time. Since the Second World War, the United States has become more and more a nation of people who live great distances from their places of employment and shopping areas. At the same time there has been a decrease in the amount and quality of public transportation. Great amounts of government funds have gone into a network of roads to support this pattern of living. The private passenger car has become a "necessity." Judged by the way they

used automobiles in the post Second World War period, most Americans
formerly believed that their cars were safe and reliable. However, more
recently complaints about unreliability and poor repairs have become more
frequent and more loud.

b. The Changing Legal Context: The Statutes and Cases

aa. Introduction

38. When an automobile is sold, what obligations concerning safety and
reliability are assumed by or imposed on the manufacturer? To what extent
are American automobile manufacturers selling safety and reliability in
their advertising, and to what extent do they pass through the terms of sales
contracts the risk of danger and unreliability on to the people who buy their
cars? To what extent have the courts and legislatures influenced the allocation of these risks? At the outset, one must observe that under the law of the
various states it is still possible for an individual to sell his used car to
another "as is," so that the buyer assumes the risk of any defects (UCC § 2-
316 (3) (a)). An uncharitable observer might describe the practices of the
American automobile manufacturers as an attempt to create strong expectations of safety and quality but to limit legal liability at the same time to an
"as is" sale. There has been a change in the law in many states over the past
20 years; the trend has been to limit the manufacturers' power to avoid liability for unsafe automobiles although its responsibility for unreliability not
likely to cause accidents is less clear. Moreover, when one takes into
account the practices of the manufacturers, the situation is even more complex.

Suppose an owner of a new automobile is injured in an accident involving his car; suppose his car is damaged in an accident; or suppose his car
will not function reliably. The owner believes that his physical or economic
injury was caused by a defect in the automobile. What legal remedies might
he seek? He could attempt to recover for the manufacturer's negligence in
designing or building the car; he could attempt to hold the manufacturer
responsible for promising that the car would be safe and reliable; and, since
the mid-1960's in many states, he could seek to recover for his physical injuries under a developing liability without fault theory.

bb. The Tort of Negligence

39. At least theoretically, the owner's negligence suit would face two
great problems. First, it is very difficult to prove that a manufacturer failed
to act reasonably in making any particular automobile since it is almost
impossible to recreate the events surrounding the building of any one of the
hundreds of automobiles produced daily on an assembly line. Second, it is
often impossible to show that damage to the car or to a person was caused
by a defective part rather than by some intervening factor completely out of
the control of the manufacturer. For example, suppose a car leaves the road
and crashes. After the event, we can find broken parts. Did they break causing the accident or did the driver's inattention cause the accident that
caused the parts to break? While one cannot be sure of the explanation,
before the 1960's, negligence suits were not a major problem for the manufacturers.

cc. Warranty, Disclaimers and Absolute Liability

(I) Before 1960: Liability Limited by Contract

40. The law of the United States has long offered another theory of liability which avoids the problem of proving fault. Typically, a purchaser of goods can sue for breach of contract – a breach of warranty – on the theory of an express or implied obligation that goods supplied under a contract will be suited for their normal functions and will have at least the quality typical of such items. While the origins of this liability rest on implied contract, it is now codified into statute in almost all states (UCC § 2-313 – 2-315). However, historically, this obligation ran only to a party to the sales contract, one in "privity" with the buyer. The manufacturers once attempted to avoid liability by using this doctrine. They sold their products to their dealers who, in turn, sold them to consumers. Thus the consumers were not in privity with the manufacturer-dealer contract, and the manufacturer was not in privity with the dealer-consumer contract. The privity doctrine has been slowly dying, but any consumer seeking to sue a manufacturer had to be prepared to argue that his case came within one of its many exceptions. Moreover, sellers and buyers could disclaim the warranty obligation by contract (Uniform Sales Act § 71). Before 1960, all American manufacturers used a uniform warranty clause prepared by the Automobile Manufacturers Association. Most of the clause talked about a guarantee which was being given to the customer by the manufacturer. In essence, the manufacturer promised to repair the car until a specified period of time had elapsed or until the car had been driven a stated distance. The customer did receive a remedy not imposed by the law – repair of defects. However, in 23 words buried in a 154 word sentence, the uniform clause stated that "this warranty... (is) expressly in lieu of all other warranties expressed or implied and of all other obligations or liabilities on its part..." Thus, while the customer got a limited right to repairs, he paid a high price in exchange. He lost a right to damages for personal injury or injury to the car caused by its defects and a right to return an unreliable car and recover what he paid for it – all remedies which he would have had if the contract had said nothing. In the words which emphasized what the customer was given, a great deal was being taken away.

(2) After 1960: New Warranty Disclaimers and Liability Imposed by Government

41. During the early 1960's, two developments prompted the manufacturers to cease using the Automobile Manufacturers Association clause and to write their own warranties in a slightly different way. First, during the late 1950's and early 1960's, almost all American states adopted the Uniform Commercial Code. The Code raises questions about the ability of a manufacturer of an advertised consumer product to disclaim all warranties or to limit the remedies available for breach of warranty. Under one plausible reading of the Code, a manufacturer cannot create reasonable expectations of quality and reliability by advertising or representations at the point of sale while warding off legal responsibility by disclaimers or limitations of remedy that are written and presented so as to minimize the chance that the consumer will understand the risks that are being imposed upon him.[1] For example, under this view, Ford could not advertise the high quality of its vehicles and, then, by language hidden in the fine print of a form contract which was understandable only to some lawyers, so disclaim and limit its liability that it was selling its cars "as is" and "with all faults." However, a

contrary reading is also possible. Under this interpretation of the Code, the question is a matter of form. If certain key words are used and the provisions are not too outrageously hidden, warranties may be disclaimed and remedies sharply limited.[2] The meaning of the UCC will remain open until the highest courts in at least several states address the question. The manufacturers' lawyers took the second interpretation of the UCC, and they were prompted to do what they could to protect the manufacturers by redrafting the form contracts which their dealers used in sales of automobiles.

42. The second development that prompted changes in automobile warranties has received a great deal of attention in legal journals. Appellate courts in several states expressed disapproval of the manufacturers' uniform warranty clause. The highest court of Massachusetts commented that this "is not the kind of agreement which commends itself to the sense of justice of the court."

Then, in *Henningsen v. Bloomfield Motors* (and *Chrysler Corporation*), the Supreme Court of NEW JERSEY found the manufacturers' warranty practices to be against the public policy of that state. The court objected to the fact that all American manufacturers used a single clause, that the clause was hidden from all but the most cautious who had the ability to translate legal language, and that the clause disclaimed a liability which the court implied ought to be assumed by the producers. In sum, the opinion implicitly charged the automobile manufacturers with dealing dishonestly with the public in order to be free to put dangerous vehicles on the road.

43. In order to deal with the set-back of the *Henningsen* case, to meet the challenge of an increase in the coverage offered by the Ford Motor Company warranty, and to gain some competitive advantage in marketing its cars, Chrysler Corporation then announced a greatly expanded warranty on all of its cars. The warranty offered customers a guarantee of some parts up to five years, but still, in terms, disclaimed any liability beyond repair or replacement of defective parts. The other manufacturers followed this lead. The new warranties of the four manufacturers differed in wording and in detail but there are some common elements. All gave a warranty from the manufacturer to the consumer; they no longer attempted to use privity as a defense. All continued to disclaim liability for personal injuries and consequential damages such as lost profits caused by not being able to use the car. For example, Chrysler's warranty stated that this "warranty is the only warranty applicable to passenger cars manufactured by Chrysler Corporation and is expressly in lieu of any warranties otherwise implied by law (including, but not limited to, implied warranties of merchantability or fitness for a particular purpose). The remedies under this warranty shall be the only remedies available to any owner thereof or other person..." This statement still could be overlooked by consumers who were not alerted to look for it, and one can question whether most consumers would have understood its legal effect even if they did read the warranty carefully enough to find it. The legal effect of all this effort at redrafting was limited in about one-third of the states during the mid-and late-1960's, when the highest courts in those jurisdictions adopted a rule of liability without fault covering defective consumer products which caused physical harm. In these states the disclaimers apply only to purely economic harm such as damage to the vehicle.

c. Manufacturers' Practices: The Law in Action

44. A study of the litigation involving those injured by automobiles who sought to recover from the manufacturers and of the settlement practices of the manufacturers concluded that in the typical case the manufacturer did not assert its rights under the disclaimer as a defense. The only question really in issue was whether or not a defect in the automobile caused the injury. If there was evidence that it had, the manufacturer was willing to settle despite its legal right to assert the assumption of risk defense or to assert that there was no proof of negligence in making the car. Litigation centered around the causation issue, too. Even in the landmark *Henningsen* case, Chrysler had not raised the disclaimer as a defense; the appellate court raised it on its own motion. At the trial, Chrysler relied on a hospital record on which it was stated that *Mrs. Henningsen* had said that she had lost control of the car because her hand slipped on the steering wheel. Apparently, the manufacturers are moved by public relations considerations to deny that their cars are defective, and they are constrained by these same considerations not to be put in a public posture of saying that even though our car was defective and hurt a buyer, we will hide behind an obscure and technically worded clause to evade liability. The clause has been used when there was a claim of consequential damages. It always could be asserted where public relations considerations were outweighed by some other factor, and it might have an impact on settlement negotiations.

45. A study of the administration of the expanded warranties shows that consumers have had difficulty in many instances in getting the repairs which are promised to them. The warranties were advertised widely in the mid-1960's and may have created expectations in the minds of new-car buyers far beyond the literal words used by the manufacturers. Dealers have reason to make repairs without charge in order to gain customer good-will which might aid the dealer when a customer next was in the market for a new car. While such good-will could also aid the manufacturer, it could be very costly. Moreover, some dealers who did not have enough service business to keep their mechanics busy might solve this problem by making unnecessary repairs if they could freely bill the manufacturer for them. The manufacturers control this process by a complex system governing payment of dealers for claimed warranty repairs. Most questions are covered in a detailed book of regulations given to the dealer – if the claim is not authorized by regulation, the manufacturer will not reimburse the dealer for the work, and, as a result, dealers usually are careful not to make repairs unless they are clearly authorized. In the case of some expensive repairs, the dealer must notify the manufacturer before the work is begun and a manufacturer's representative must inspect the car and authorize the work. Moreover, many dealers claim that the manufacturer reimburses them for warranty work at a rate lower than that usually charged customers. This, too, provides an incentive to refuse to do warranty work, to do it quickly and not too carefully, or to delay doing it as long as non-warranty work is available to occupy a dealer's staff of mechanics.

46. How far can the legal system aid a consumer in getting repairs? At the outset, one must note that the expectations of many consumers are based on advertising which creates the impression that far more responsibility is being assumed by the manufacturer than the literal words of the warranty do assume. Often, the warranty coverage is not clearly presented to

the customer when he is negotiating for the purchase of the car (although some manufacturers and some dealers do make great efforts to make the obligation clear). Secondly, the document which, as a practical matter, controls the extent of warranty coverage is the book of regulations sent by the manufacturer to the dealer, a book which the customer almost never sees. It is likely that the automobile-buyer does have a legally enforceable contract right to the guarantee made by the warranty for replacement or repair of defective parts. Moreover, it is likely that the coverage of that warranty obligation would be construed by a court in light of a customer's reasonable expectations based on the language of the warranty as read in the light of the manufacturer's advertising rather than its regulations sent to dealers. Nonetheless, the new-car buyer faces real difficulty in asserting these rights. Most warranty repairs, although involving significant amounts to the purchaser, still involve too little to make litigation worthwhile in view of the costs of suing a manufacturer. The one clearly effective remedy would be a right to rescind, return the car and obtain a refund of the purchase price. However, the express terms of the warranty bar this remedy and this limitation has yet to be overturned as unconscionable, if, indeed, it is.

d. Safety and Reliability as a Public Issue

47. All of this concerns individual complaints about particular vehicles. On another level, automobile safety became a general public issue in the United States and thus the government became interested in regulation of automobile safety and reliability. Hearings were held before the United States Senate to look into charges that automobiles were generally unsafe. These hearings received wide publicity. The manufacturers made a number of modifications in their designs to better their positions as they appeared before Congress. But these efforts did not succeed. Legislation was passed creating an administrative agency and setting a procedure for framing safety standards for all automobiles sold in the United States. Although controversy continues about whether or not these standards are adequate and about the nature of the enforcement tactics pursued by the agency, there is no doubt that the manufacturers are far more concerned about safety and reliability than in the past. From an era where injured buyers had few if any rights against the automobile manufacturers, we have come to a time when not only are private rights being expanded, but the very design of the automobile has become a matter in which the government has come to assume a responsibility to protect the buyer.

---

1. Put as briefly as possible, the argument would be that statements about quality and reliability are "affirmations of fact" "which relate to the goods and become part of the basis of the bargain" and, therefore, create an express warranty (UCC § 2-313 (1) (a)). Even if a buyer could not point to specific statements, unless effectively disclaimed, there is also an implied warranty of merchantability (UCC § 2-314 (1)), which would require that a new automobile be of such quality and reliability as to "pass without objection in the trade under the contract description..." (UCC § 2-314 (2) (a)). Exclusion or modification of warranties is covered in UCC § 2-316. Express warranties and disclaimers are to be construed when possible as consistent but where such a construction is "unreasonable," "negation or limitation is inoperative." To "exclude or modify the implied warranty of merchantability or any part of it, the language must mention merchantability and in case of a writing must be conspicuous." "A term or clause is conspicuous when it is so written that a rea-

sonable person against whom it is to operate ought to have noticed it... Language in the body of a form is 'conspicuous' if it is in larger or other contrasting type or color..." (UCC § 1-201 (10)). The Official Comment to UCC § 2-316 explains that the section "seeks to protect a buyer from unexpected and unbargained language of disclaimer by... permitting the exclusion of implied warranties only by conspicuous language or other circumstances which protect the buyer from surprise (no. 1)." One could argue that language of disclaimer should be deemed to be "conspicuous" only if as a matter of fact it does protect a buyer from surprise. Thus, a clause reading, "There is no implied warranty of merchantability" would not necessarily serve as an effective disclaimer even though it were printed in slightly larger type or a contrasting color. This might be the case where a reasonable person could have failed to notice the clause as, for example, where the clause was part of a lengthy and complex document customarily used in a manner to discourage reading before signing. Moreover, even if a consumer-buyer ought to have noticed such a clause, it seems likely that a high percentage of consumers would have no idea of the meaning of the statement: "There is no implied warranty of merchantability", particularly when presented as part of a clause purporting to grant consumers valuable rights in the context of the purchase of a product widely advertised to be of high quality and reliability. See *Whitford,* The Functions of Disclosure Regulation in Consumer Transactions: 1973 Wis.L.Rev. 400, 420, 425, 449. Such a taking away of rights in the guise of granting something when done by a national advertiser could well be deemed by a court to be "unconscionable" under UCC § 2-302. The Official Comment to that section states that its principle is "the prevention of oppression and unfair surprise (no. 1)."

Attempts to grant a warranty but to limit the remedy for breach are governed by UCC § 2-719. Generally, one can warrant his goods but limit the remedy to replacement or repair of any that are defective. However, the statute does provide: "Consequential damages may be limited or excluded unless the limitation or exclusion is unconscionable. Limitation of consequential damages for injury to the person in the case of consumer goods is prima facie unconscionable but limitation of damages where the loss is commercial is not" (UCC § 2-719 (3)). Automobile warranties are worded as if only a limited warranty is being given. However, a court might well find that actually a full warranty is being given but that an attempt is being made to limit the remedy to replacement or repair at the option of the manufacturer. Despite the words used by the automobile companies, there is no such thing as a warranty of replacement or repair. Rather there is a warranty of *quality* (either an express one or an implied one of merchantability or fitness for a particular purpose) and *remedies* of replacement or repair. The manufacturers' purported disclaimers are, in substance, remedy limitations subject to UCC § 2-719 (3). If the manufacturer's clause were read as involving a limitation, it would be *prima facie* unconscionable where a defect in the car had caused injury to the person. See *Matthews v. Ford Motor Co.,* 479 F.2d 399 (4 Cir. 1973).

2. This argument would first emphasize that the manufacturers are careful to create no express warranties. UCC § 2-313 (2) says that "a statement purporting to be merely the seller's opinion or commendation of the goods does not create a warranty." Advertising which commends the goods should not be deemed part of the basis of the bargain; the bargain is reflected solely by the written contract of sale. Second, implied warranties of merchantability are effectively disclaimed by conspicuous language which mentions merchantability (UCC § 2-316 (2)). Section 1-201 (10) says: "Language in the body of a form is 'conspicuous' if it is in larger or other contrasting type or color..." Automobile manufacturers almost always print a statement that "there is no implied warranty of merchantability" in larger type face, and thus they effectively disclaim the warranty. A court should not find such a disclaimer unconscionable under § 2-302 because the Code itself specifically authorizes such a limitation of risk in the words quoted from § 1-201 (10). Moreover, the language of the disclaimer is just that – a disclaimer. There is no reason to construe it as a limitation of remedy subject to § 2-719. In sum, the Code authorizes a certain form

of achieving a purpose, and the legislatures which passed the Code have found that the use of the form of language mentioning merchantability in larger or contrasting type adequately balances the interests of manufacturers and consumers.

C. Exemption Clauses and Third Parties

In the *Henningsen Case*, the plaintiff sued both the dealer and the manufacturer. The court in that case disposed of the problem of the direct action by the plaintiff against Chrysler by holding that the dealer was simply the agent of Chrysler. The contract when made was therefore between the plaintiff and Chrysler. This part of the judgment was omitted in the extract given above. A court that was more bothered by the problems of vertical privity than the Supreme Court of New Jersey might have had some problem with this direct action if it was based on contractual liability, *i.e.*, liability for breach of the implied warranties of the Sale of Goods Act. We have seen how the problems of vertical and horizontal privity can undercut the effectiveness of even the implied warranties that the Sale of Goods Act gives. The same problem comes up with exemption clauses. An exemption clause that may protect one party to a contract from claims by the other may not protect the first party from claims by third parties. A clause that may protect one party may not protect people who work for that party. For example a clause that protects a carrier may not protect the carrier's employees or subcontractors. If every case involved the same issue as *Henningsen*, we might be quite happy that the doctrine of consideration was here seeming to work well. The trouble is, of course, that few cases raise the issues of *Henningsen*. Where the contracting parties have properly allocated the risk of loss and have arranged insurance on that basis, it may make no sense for the allocation to be upset by the application of the rules of privity. The following cases raise these problems:

SCRUTTONS v. MIDLAND SILICONES LTD.

[1962] A.C. 462. House of Lords; Viscount Simonds, Lords Reid, Keith, Morris and Denning.

[The respondent plaintiffs sued the appellant defendants, for damage to a drum of pump fluid belonging to them. In their defence the appellants admitted the negligence complained of, but claimed that they were entitled to limit their liability to the same extent as were United States Lines, the carriers under a bill of lading on the terms of which the respondents were the consignees of the drum.

At all material times the appellants were employed by United States Lines as their stevedores in London under a stevedoring contract dated August 16, 1952. That contract contained the following provision: "Ship, Cargo and Property Claims. The stevedores are to be fully responsible for any damage to the vessel or other property and any damage to or loss of cargo while being handled or stowed, unshipped or delivered, or while in stowage, if damage caused by any negligence of themselves or their servants. The stevedores to have such protection as is afforded by the terms, conditions and exceptions of the bills of lading westbound and eastbound." There was a further provision: "Liability for Declared Value Including Ad Valorem Packages. For an additional charge of ¼ per cent. on the total of the stevedores' discharging, loading and tallying accounts (excluding direct expenses and management fund charge) and stevedores agree to effect an insurance policy on Lloyds to cover any damage or loss of cargo on which a value in excess of $500 per package has been declared." The respondents were not at any time aware of the existence or of the terms of the stevedoring contract.

On March 26, 1957, Dow Corning Corporation of New York shipped the drum in question on the American Reporter for carriage from New York to London under a bill of lading by which the drum was consigned to the respondents. The respondents were the owners of the drum, having bought it on c.i.f. terms under a contract made on February 4, 1957, and having received the bill of lading on April 1, 1957.

The shipper did not declare the value of the drum to the carrier, and its value was not inserted in the bill of lading. The drum was dealt with as ordinary cargo, both by the carriers and the appellants. It was duly carried to London. The appellants duly discharged the ship and put the drum in a shed. The respondents sent a truck to take delivery of the drum. The appellants were lowering the drum onto the truck when they negligently dropped it and some of the contents worth considerably more than $500 was lost. The respondents sued the appellants for the full value.]

Viscount Simonds. My Lords, the facts in this case are not in dispute. They are fully and accurately stated in the judgment of the learned trial judge, Diplock J., and I do not think it necessary to restate them. I come at once to the question of law which arises upon them.

The question is whether the appellants, a well-known firm of stevedores, who admittedly by their negligence caused damage to certain cargo consigned to the respondents under a bill of lading of March 26, 1957, can take advantage of a provision for limitation of liability contained in that document. In judgments, with which I entirely agree and to which, but for the importance of the case, I should not think it necessary to add anything, the learned judge and the Court of Appeal have unanimously answered the question in the negative.

The appellants' claim to immunity (for so I will call it for short) was put in a number of different ways, but I think that I do no injustice to the able argument of their counsel if I say that he rested in the main on the well-known case of *Elder, Dempster & Co. Ltd. v. Paterson, Zochonis & Co. Ltd.,* [1924] A.C. 522, contending that that is an authority binding this House to decide in his favour.

Let me, then, get rid shortly of some of the other arguments advanced on behalf of the appellants.

In the first place, I see no reason for saying that the word "carrier" either in the bill of lading or in the United States Carriage of Goods by Sea Act, 1936 (which the bill of lading incorporated) means or includes a stevedore. This is a proposition which does not admit of any expansion. A stevedore is not a carrier according to the ordinary use of language and, so far from the context supplying an extended meaning to the latter word, the contrary is indicated, as Hodson L.J. points out, by clause 17 of the bill of lading which authorizes the carrier or master to appoint stevedores.

Then, to avert the consequences which would appear to follow from the fact that the stevedores were not a party to the contract conferring immunity on the carriers, it was argued that the carriers contracted as agents for the stevedores. They did not expressly do so: if then there was agency, it was a case of an agent acting for an undisclosed principal. I am met at once by the difficulty that there is no ground whatever for saying that the carriers were contracting as agent either for this firm of stevedores or any other stevedores they might employ. The relation of the stevedores in this case to the carriers was that of independent contractors. Why should it be assumed that the carriers entered into a contract of affreightment or into any part of it as agents for them?

Next it was urged that there was an implied contract between the cargo owners, the respondents, and the stevedores that the latter should have the benefit of the immunity clause in the bill of lading. This argument presents, if possible, greater difficulties. When A and B have entered into a contract, it is not uncommon to imply a term in order to give what is called "business efficacy" to it — a process, I may say, against the abuse of which the courts must keep constant guard. But it is a very different matter to infer a contractual relation between parties who have never entered into a contract at all. In the present case the cargo owners had a contract with the carrier which provided amongst other things for the unloading of their cargo. They knew nothing of the relations between the carrier and the stevedores. It was no business of theirs. They were concerned only to have the job done which the carriers had contracted to do. There is no conceivable reason why an implication should be made that they had entered into any contractual relation with the stevedores.

But, my Lords, all these contentions were but a prelude to one which, had your Lordships accepted it, would have been the foundation of a dramatic decision of this House. It was argued, if I understood the argument, that if A contracts with B to do something for the benefit of C, then C, though not a party to the contract, can sue A to enforce it. This is independent of whether C is A's undisclosed principal or a beneficiary under a trust of which A is trustee. It is sufficient that C is an "interested person." My Lords, if this is the law of England, then, subject always to the question of consideration, no doubt, if the carrier purports to contract for the benefit of the stevedore, the latter can enforce the contract. Whether that [premise] is satisfied in this case is another matter, but, since the argument is advanced, it is right that I should deal with it.

Learned counsel for the respondents met it, as they had successfully done in the courts below, by asserting a principle which is, I suppose, as well established as any in our law, a "fundamental" principle, as Lord Haldane called it in *Dunlop Pneumatic Tyre Co. Ltd. v. Selfridge & Co. Ltd.,* [1915] A.C. 847, an "elementary" principle, as it has been called times without number, that only a person who is a party to a contract can sue upon it. "Our law," said Lord Haldane, "knows nothing of a jus quaesitum tertio arising by way of contract." Learned counsel for the respondents claimed that this was the orthodox view and asked your Lordships to reject any proposition that impinged upon it. To that invitation I readily respond. For to me heterodoxy, or, as some might say, heresy, is not the more attractive because it is dignified by the name of reform. Nor will I easily be led by an undiscerning zeal for some abstract kind of justice to ignore our first duty, which is to administer justice according to law, the law which is established for us by Act of Parliament or the binding authority of precedent. The law is developed by the application of old principles to new circumstances.

Therein lies its genius. Its reform by the abrogation of those principles is the task not of the courts of law but of Parliament. Therefore I reject the argument for the appellants under this head and invite your Lordships to say that certain statements which appear to support it in recent cases such as *Smith and Snipes Hall Farm Ltd. v. River Douglas Catchment Board*, [1949] 2 K.B. 500, and *White v. John Warwick & Co. Ltd.*, [1953] 1 W.L.R. 1285, must be rejected. If the principle of jus quaesitum tertio is to be introduced into our law, it must be done by Parliament after a due consideration of its merits and demerits. I should not be prepared to give it my support without a greater knowledge than I at present possess of its operation in other systems of law.

[Lords Reid, Keith and Morris agreed with Viscount Simonds. Lord Denning dissented.]

[Compare the language of Viscount Simonds in this case with his language in *Shaw v. D.P.P.*, [1962] A.C. 220, 226:

> My Lords, as I have already said, the first count in the indictment is "Conspiracy to corrupt public morals," and the particulars of offence will have sufficiently appeared. I am concerned only to assert what was vigorously denied by counsel for the appellant, that such an offence is known to the common law, and that it was open to the jury to find on the facts of this case that the appellant was guilty of such an offence. I must say categorically that, if it were not so, Her Majesty's courts would strangely have failed in their duty as servants and guardians of the common law. Need I say, my Lords, that I am no advocate of the right of the judges to create new criminal offences? I will repeat well-known words: "Amongst many other points of happiness and freedom which your Majesty's subjects have enjoyed there is none which they have accounted more dear and precious than this, to be guided and governed by certain rules of law which giveth both to the head and members that which of right belongeth to them and not by any arbitrary or uncertain form of government." These words are as true today as they were in the seventeenth century and command the allegiance of us all. But I am at a loss to understand how it can be said either that the law does not recognise a conspiracy to corrupt public morals or that, though there may not be an exact precedent for such a conspiracy as this case reveals, it does not fall fairly within the general words by which it is described. I do not propose to examine all the relevant authorities. That will be done by my noble and learned friend. The fallacy in the argument that was addressed to us lay in the attempt to exclude from the scope of general words acts well calculated to corrupt public morals just because they had not been committed or had not been brought to the notice of the court before. It is not thus that the common law has developed. We are perhaps more accustomed to hear this matter discussed upon the question whether such and such a transaction is contrary to public policy. At once the controversy arises. On the one hand it is said that it is not possible in the twentieth century for the court to create a new head of public policy, on the other it is said that this is but a new example of a well-established head. In the sphere of criminal law I entertain no doubt that there remains in the courts of law a residual power to enforce the supreme and fundamental purpose of the law, to conserve not only the safety and order but also the moral welfare of the State, and that it is its duty to guard it against attacks which may be the more insidious because they are novel and unprepared for. That is the broad head (call it public policy if you wish) within which the present indictment falls. It matters little what label is given to the offending act. To one of your Lordships it may appear an affront to public decency, to another considering that it may succeed in its obvious intention of provoking libidinous desires it will seem a corruption of public morals. Yet others may deem it aptly described as the creation of a public mischief or the undermining of moral conduct. The same act will not in all ages be

regarded in the same way. The law must be related to the changing standards of life, not yielding to every shifting impulse of the popular will but having regard to fundamental assessments of human values and the purposes of society. Today a denial of the fundamental Christian doctrine, which in past centuries would have been regarded by the ecclesiastical courts as heresy and by the common law as blasphemy, will no longer be an offence if the decencies of controversy are observed. When Lord Mansfield, speaking long after the Star Chamber had been abolished, said that the Court of King's Bench was the custos morum of the people and had the superintendency of offences contra bonos mores, he was asserting, as I now assert, that there is in that court a residual power, where no statute has yet intervened to supersede the common law, to superintend those offences which are prejudicial to the public welfare. Such occasions will be rare, for Parliament has not been slow to legislate when attention has been sufficiently aroused. But gaps remain and will always remain since no one can foresee every way in which the wickedness of man may disrupt the order of society. Let me take a single instance to which my noble and learned friend Lord Tucker refers. Let it be supposed that at some future, perhaps, early, date homosexual practices between adult consenting males are no longer a crime. Would it not be an offence if even without obscenity, such practices were publicly advocated and encouraged by pamphlet and advertisement? Or must we wait until Parliament finds time to deal with such conduct? I say, my Lords, that if the common law is powerless in such an event, then we should no longer do her reverence. But I say that her hand is still powerful and that it is for Her Majesty's judges to play the part which Lord Mansfield pointed out to them.

QUESTIONS

1. What values are being forwarded by the decision in *Scruttons v. Midland Silicones*?
2. What devices are available to reach the opposite result in that case?
3. What values are being forwarded in *Shaw v. D.P.P.*?
4. What limitations on the approach of the House of Lords in *Shaw v. D.P.P.* might one expect from the fact that Shaw was being prosecuted for a crime?
5. Would one expect the court to be more flexible in a contract case or in a criminal case?

THE NEW ZEALAND SHIPPING CO. LTD. v. A.M. SATTERTHWAITE & CO. LTD.

[1974] 1 All E.R. 1015. Privy Council; Lords Wilberforce, Hodson, Viscount Dilhorne, Simon and Salmon.

Lord Wilberforce delivered the majority opinion. The facts of this case are not in dispute. An expensive drilling machine was received on board the ship 'Eurymedon' at Liverpool for trans-shipment to Wellington pursuant to the terms of a bill of lading no 1262 dated 5th June 1964. The shipper was the maker of the drill, Ajax Machine Tool Co Ltd ('the consignor'). The bill of lading was issued by agents for the Federal Steam Navigation Co Ltd ('the carrier'). The consignees were the respondents, AM Satterthwaite & Co Ltd of Christchurch, New Zealand ('the consignee'). For several years before 1964 the appellants, The New Zealand Shipping Co Ltd ('the stevedore'), had carried out all stevedoring work in Wellington in respect of the ships owned by the carrier, which was a wholly owned subsidiary of the stevedore. In addition to this stevedoring work the stevedore generally acted as agent for the carrier in New Zealand; and in such capacity as general agent (not in the course of their stevedoring functions) the stevedore received the bill of lading at Wellington on 31st July 1964. Clause 1 of the bill of lading, on the construction of which this case turns, was in the same terms as bills of lading usually issued by the stevedore and its associated companies in respect of ordinary cargo carried by its ships from the United Kingdom to New Zealand. The consignee became the holder of the bill of lading and owner of the drill prior to 14th August 1964. On that date the drill was damaged as a result of the stevedore's negligence during unloading.

At the foot of the first page of the bill of lading the following words were printed in small capitals:

'IN ACCEPTING THIS BILL OF LADING THE SHIPPER, CONSIGNEE AND THE OWNERS OF THE GOODS, AND THE HOLDER OF THIS BILL OF LADING, AGREE TO BE BOUND BY ALL OF ITS CONDITIONS, EXCEPTIONS AND PROVISIONS WHETHER WRITTEN, PRINTED OR STAMPED ON THE FRONT OR BACK HEREOF.'

On the back of the bill of lading a number of clauses were printed in small type. It is only necessary to set out the following:

'1. This Bill of Lading shall have effect (*a*) subject to the provisions of any legislation giving effect to the International Convention for the unification of certain rules relating to Bills of Lading dated Brussels, 25th August, 1924, or to similar effect which is compulsorily applicable to the contract of carriage evidenced hereby and (*b*) where no such legislation is applicable as if the Carriage of Goods by Sea Act 1924, of Great Britain and the Rules scheduled thereto applied hereto and were incorporated herein. Nothing herein contained shall be deemed to be a surrender by the Carrier of any of his rights or immunities or an increase of any of his responsibilities or liabilities under the provisions of the said legislation or Act and Rules (as the case may be) and the said provisions shall not (unless and to the extent that they are by law compulsorily applicable) apply to that portion of the contract evidenced by this Bill of Lading which relates to forwarding under Clause 4 hereof. If anything herein contained be inconsistent with or repugnant to the said provisions, it shall to the extent of such inconsistency or repugnance and no further be null and void...

'It is hereby expressly agreed that no servant or agent of the Carrier (including every independent contractor from time to time employed by the Carrier) shall in any circumstances whatsoever be under any liability whatsoever to the Shipper, Consignee or Owner of the goods or to any holder of this Bill of Lading for any loss or damage or delay of whatsoever kind arising or resulting directly or indirectly from any act neglect or default on his part while acting in the course of or in connection with his employment and, without prejudice to the generality of the foregoing provisions in this Clause, every exemption, limitation, condition and liberty herein contained and every right, exemption from liability, defence and immunity of whatsoever nature applicable to the Carrier or to which the Carrier is entitled hereunder shall also be available and shall extend to protect every such servant or agent of the Carrier acting as aforesaid and for the purpose of all the foregoing provisions of this Clause the Carrier is or shall be deemed to be acting as agent or trustee on behalf of and for the benefit of all persons who are or might be his servants or agents from time to time (including independent contractors as aforesaid) and all such persons shall to this extent be or be deemed to be parties to the contract in or evidenced by this Bill of Lading...

'11. The Carrier will not be accountable for goods of any description beyond £100 in respect of any one package or unit unless the value thereof shall have been stated in writing both on the Broker's Order which must be obtained before shipment and on the Shipping Note presented on shipment and extra freight agreed upon and paid and Bills of Lading signed with a declaration of the nature and value of the goods appearing thereon. When the value is declared and extra freight agreed as aforesaid the Carrier's liability shall not exceed such value or pro rata on that basis in the event of partial loss or damage.'

No declaration as to the nature and value of the goods having appeared in the bill of lading, and no extra freight having been agreed on or paid, it was acknowledged by the consignee that the liability of the carrier was accordingly limited to £100 by the application of cl II of the bill of lading. Moreover, the incorporation in the bill of lading of the rules scheduled to the Carriage of Goods by Sea Act 1924 meant that the carrier and the ship were discharged from all liability in respect of damage to the drill. Unless suit was brought against them within one year after delivery. No action was commenced until April 1967, when the consignee sued the stevedore in negligence, claiming £880 the cost of repairing the damaged drill.

The question in the appeal is whether the stevedore can take the benefit of the time limitation provision. The starting point, in discussion on this question, is provided by the House of Lords decision in *Scruttons Ltd v Midland Silicones Ltd.* There is no need to question or even to qualify that case insofar as it affirms the general proposition that a contract between two parties cannot be sued on by a third person even though the contract is expressed to be for his benefit. Nor is it necessary to disagree with anything which was said to the same effect in the Australian case of *Wilson v Darling Island Stevedoring & Lighterage Co Ltd*, [1956] 1 Lloyd's Rep. 346. Each of these cases was dealing with a simple case of a contract the benefit of which was sought to be taken by a third person not a party to it, and the emphatic pronouncements in the speeches and judgments were directed to this situation. But *Midland Silicones* left open the case where one of the parties contracts as agent for the third person: in particular Lord Reid's speech spelt out, in four propositions, the prerequisites for the validity of such an agency contract. There is of course nothing unique to this case in the conception of agency contracts: well-known and common instances exist in the field of hire-purchase, of bankers' commercial credits and other transactions. Lord Reid said this:

'I can see a possibility of success of the agency argument if (first) the bill of lading makes it clear that the stevedore is intended to be protected by the provisions in it which limit liability, (secondly) the bill of lading makes it clear that the carrier, in addition to contracting for these provisions on his own behalf, is also contracting as agent for the stevedore that these provisions should apply to the stevedore, (thirdly) the carrier has authority from the stevedore to do that, or perhaps later ratification by the stevedore would suffice, and (fourthly) that any difficulties about consideration moving from the stevedore were overcome. And then to affect the consignee it would be necessary to show that the provisions of the Bills of Lading Act 1855, apply.'

The question in this appeal is whether the contract satisfies these propositions.

Clause 1 of the bill of lading, whatever the defects in its drafting, is clear in its relevant terms. The carrier, on his own account, stipulates for certain exemptions and immunities: among these is that conferred by art III!(6) of the Hague Rules which discharges the carrier from all liability for loss or damage unless suit is brought within one year after delivery.

In addition to these stipulations on his own account, the carrier as agent for (inter alios) independent contractors stipulates for the same exemptions.

Much was made of the fact that the carrier also contracts as agent for numerous other persons; the relevance of this argument is not apparent. It cannot be disputed that among such independent contractors, for whom, as agent, the carrier contracted, is the appellant company which habitually acts as stevedore in New Zealand by arrangement with the carrier and which is, moreover, the parent company of the carrier. The carrier was, indisputably, authorised by the stevedore to contract as its agent for the purposes of cl 1. All of this is quite straightforward and was accepted by all of the learned judges in New Zealand. The only question was, and is, the fourth question presented by Lord Reid, namely that of consideration.

It was on this point that the Court of Appeal differed from Beattie J, holding that it had not been shown that any consideration for the shipper's promise as to exemption moved from the promisee, i e the stevedore.

If the choice, and the antithesis, is between a gratuitous promise, and a promise for consideration, as it must be, in the absence of a tertium quid, there can be little doubt which, in commercial reality, this is. The whole contract is of a commercial character, involving service on one side, rates of payment on the other, and qualifying stipulations as to both. The relations of all parties to each other are commercial relations entered into for business reasons of ultimate profit. To describe one set of promises, in this context, as gratuitous, or nudum pactum, seems paradoxical and is prima facie implausible. It is only the precise analysis of this complex of relations into the classical offer and acceptance, with identifiable consideration, that seems to present difficulty, but this same difficulty exists in many situations of daily life, eg sales at auction; supermarket purchases; boarding an omnibus; purchasing a train ticket; tenders for the supply of goods; offers of reward; acceptance by post; warranties of authority by agents; manufacturers' guarantees; gratuitous bailments; bankers' commercial credits. These are all examples which show that English law, having committed itself to a rather technical and schematic doctrine of contract, in application takes a practical approach, often at the cost of forcing the facts to fit uneasily into the marked slots of offer, acceptance and consideration.

In their Lordships' opinion the present contract presents much less difficulty than many of those above referred to. It is one of carriage from Liverpool to Wellington. The carrier assumes an obligation to transport the goods and to discharge at the port of arrival. The goods are to be carried and discharged, so the transaction is inherently contractual. It is contemplated that a part of this contract, viz discharge, may be performed by independent contractors — viz the stevedore. By cl 1 of the bill of lading the shipper agrees to exempt from liability the carrier, his servants and independent contractors in respect of the performance of this contract of carriage. Thus, if the carriage, including the discharge, is wholly carried out by the carrier, he is exempt. If part is carried out by him, and part by his servants, he and they are exempt. If part is carried out by him and part by an independent contractor, he and the independent contractor are exempt. The exemption is designed to cover the whole carriage from loading to discharge, by whomsoever it is performed: the performance attracts the exemption or immunity in favour of whoever the performer turns out to be. There is possibly more than one way of analysing this business transaction into the necessary components; that which their Lordships would accept is to say that the bill of lading brought into existence a bargain initially unilateral but capable of becoming mutual, between the shippers and the stevedore, made through the carrier as agent. This became a full contract when the stevedore performed services by discharging the goods. The performance of these services for the benefit of the shipper was the consideration for the agreement by the shipper that the stevedore should have the benefit of the exemptions and limitations contained in the bill of lading. The conception of a 'unilateral' contract of this kind was recognised in *Great Northern Railway Co v Witham* and is well established. This way of regarding the matter is very close to, if not identical to, that accepted by Beattie J in the Supreme Court; he analysed the transaction as one of an offer open to acceptance by action such as was found in *Carlill v Carbolic Smoke Ball Co* But whether one describes the shipper's promise to exempt as an offer to be accepted by performance or as a promise in exchange for an act seems in the present context to be a matter of semantics. The words of Bowen LJ in *Carlill v Carbolic Smoke Ball Co*, '... why should not an offer be made to all the world which is to ripen into a contract with anybody who comes forward and performs the condition?' seem to bridge both conceptions: he certainly seems to draw no distinction between an offer which matures into a contract when accepted and a promise which matures into a contract after performance and, though in some special contexts (such as in connection with the right to withdraw) some further refinement may be needed, either analysis may be equally valid. On the main point in the appeal, their Lordships are in substantial agreement with Beattie J.

The following other points require mention:

1. In their Lordships' opinion, consideration may quite well be provided by the stevedore, as suggested, even though (or if) it was already under an obligation to discharge to the carrier. (There is no direct evidence of the existence or nature of this obligation, but their Lordships are prepared to assume it.) An agreement to do an act which the promisor is under an existing obligation to a third party to do, may quite well amount to valid consideration and does so in the present case: the promisee obtains the benefit of a direct obligation which he can enforce. This proposition is illustrated and supported by *Scotson v Pegg* which their Lordships consider to be good law.

2. The consignee is entitled to the benefit of, and is bound by, the stipulations in the bill of lading by his acceptance of it and request for delivery of the goods thereunder. This is shown by *Brandt v Liverpool, Brazil and River Plate Steam Navigation Co Ltd*, [1924] 1 K.B. 575, and a line of earlier cases. The Bills of Lading Act 1855, s 1 (in New Zealand the Mercantile Law Act 1908, s 13) gives partial statutory recognition to this rule, but, where the statute does not apply, as it may well not do in this case, the previously established law remains effective.

3. The stevedore submitted, in the alternative, an argument that, quite apart from contract, exemptions from, or limitation of, liability in tort may be conferred by mere consent on the part of the party who may be injured. As their Lordships consider that the stevedore ought to succeed in contract, they prefer to express no opinion on this argument: to evaluate it requires elaborate discussion.

4. A clause very similar to the present was given effect by a United States District Court in *Carle and Montanari Inc v. American Export Isbrandtsen Lines Inc*, [1968] 1 Lloyd's Rep. 260. The carrier in that case contracted, in an exemption clause, as agent for, inter alios, all stevedores and other independent contractors, and although it is no doubt true that the law in the

United States is more liberal than ours as regards third party contracts, their Lordships see no reason why the law of the Commonwealth should be more restrictive and technical as regards agency contracts. Commercial consideration should have the same force on both sides of the Pacific.

In the opinion of their Lordships, to give the stevedore the benefit of the exemptions and limitations contained in the bill of lading is to give effect to the clear intentions of a commercial document, and can be given within existing principles. They see no reason to strain the law or the facts in order to defeat these intentions. It should not be overlooked that the effect of denying validity to the clause would be to encourage actions against servants, agents and independent contractors in order to get round exemptions (which are almost invariable and often compulsory) accepted by shippers against carriers, the existence, and presumed efficacy, of which is reflected in the rates of freight. They see no attraction in this consequence.

Their Lordships will humbly advise Her Majesty that the appeal be allowed and the judgment of Beattie J restored. The consignee must pay the costs of the appeal and in the Court of Appeal.

[Viscount Dilhorne and Lord Simon dissented on the ground (broadly) that *Scruttons v. Midland Silicone* applied.]

[Lord Simon concluded his judgment by saying,]

In so concluding I must not be taken to be doubting that a suitably drawn instrument could bring a consignor and a stevedore into a relationship of obligation and meet Lord Reid's five conditions in such a way that a stevedore could claim the benefit of an exemption clause even against a consignee. In this connection I note that the clause instantly in question appeared in bills of lading before the *Midland Silicones* case and was not drawn in the light of that case. Alternatively, no doubt, exemption could in practice be secured by a suitably drawn indemnity clause. Finally, there seems no reason to question that, as Turner P thought, a bill of lading could, if appropriately drafted, contain an offer giving rise to a unilateral contract with a stevedore.

QUESTION

To what extent is a court justified in saying to a litigant, "If you had only had a very good lawyer to advise you from the very beginning, you would have had no problems in arranging your affairs as you wanted. Since you did not have a lawyer of any kind, we have no obligation to help you achieve the results that you wanted."

––––––––––

In *Calkins and Burke Ltd. v. Far Eastern Steamship Co.* (1976), 72 D.L.R. (3d) 625, Schultz J. of the B.C. Supreme Court applied *Scruttons v. Midland Silicones* to hold stevedores liable for loss due to their negligence in spite of an exemption clause in the contract between the plaintiff and the carrier. The judge distinguished the *N.Z. Shipping Co. Ltd. Case* on the facts: *i.e.*, that the carrier had no authority to contract on behalf of the stevedore.

The Quebec Court of Appeal in *Ceres Stevedoring Co. Ltd. v. Eisen und Metall A.G.* (1976), 72 D.L.R. (3d) 660 applied the *N.Z. Shipping Co. Ltd. Case* to protect a stevedore from liability.

Both courts referred to a decision of the Supreme Court of Canada, *C.G.E. v. Pickford-Black Ltd.*, [1971] S.C.R. 41, 14 D.L.R. (3d) 372, which had followed *Scruttons v. Midland Silicones*. Schultz J. said, p. 635:

"Neither the judgment of the House of Lords, nor that of the Privy Council, while often of strong persuasive value is binding upon a trail judge in British Columbia. On the other hand, a judgment of the Supreme Court of Canada is determinative of the law in Canada".

Owen J.A. in the Quebec Court of Appeal simply said that he preferred to follow the *N.Z. Shipping Co. Ltd. Case* and implied that it, being later than the *C.G.E. Case*, should govern. The Law Society Gazette (Vol. XI, No. 2, June 1977, p. 135), quotes the following statement from *Cardozo*:

"A fruitful parent of injustice is the tyranny of concepts. They are tyrants rather than servants when treated as real existences and developed with merciless disregard of consequences to the limit of their logic." (*The Paradoxes of Legal Science* (1928) p. 61.)

QUESTION

What is the law in Canada?

D. Unconscionability

We saw in *Morrison v. Coast Finance* that the courts would relieve people from the consequences of bargains that were unfair and where there was disparity of bargaining power. The law has developed considerably since 1965 and it is now possible to speak of the general ground of unconscionability. The problems in the cases in this section is to know how far the courts are going to go in relieving people from unfair bargains.

There are a number of specific problems that we have to worry about. These include the following:

(a) What is the basis for the courts' interference?

(b) What factors are important in triggering the courts' concern?

(c) What limits are being set on freedom of contract?

Underlying these issues is one of much more fundamental importance. The process of adjudication is characterized by the way in which the parties participate. This participation involves the right to present proofs and reasoned arguments. As we have seen throughout the course, there is a very close relationship between facts and rules. We cannot know if we are justified in applying a rule in any particular situation, until we have enough facts to be able to know if its application is sensible. Rules that ignore relevant facts are not likely to be satisfactory. These issues have been at the bottom of many of the problems we have looked at in this course and in this chapter. In *Harbutt's Plasticine v. Wayne Tank* we saw that, with more facts, the decision begins to be harder to defend. In *Henningsen v. Bloomfield Motors* the court's investigation of a wide range of facts led to a satisfactory result. Generally it is true that the development of the law has been characterized by the expansion of the legally relevant.

However, there is a point where we have to worry about this expansion. If the court investigates too many facts, a number of things happen:

(a) It becomes harder for the court to get accurate facts, and the chance of getting the wrong facts increases.

(b) A tremendous burden is placed on the parties. Fact-finding and presentation is at their expense.

(c) Courts are tempted to find facts on their own. This has the potential for seriously undermining the whole process of adjudication since these facts cannot be argued about by the parties.

(d) Courts find themselves making very broad and basic decisions of social values that should, perhaps, be made by some other institutions in our society.

The cases in this section have, therefore, much to show about the problems of proper role of the courts in fact-finding and policy-making. Once we get into this kind of problem, we have to raise the issue whether or not the courts are the best kind of body to make some of the reforms that seem to be required. This leads us naturally to investigate the role of legislation as providing solutions to some of the contract problems the courts have had to worry about.

LLOYDS BANK v. BUNDY

[1974] 3 All E.R. 757, Court of Appeal (England); Lord Denning M.R., Cairns L.J. and Sir Eric Sachs.

Lord Denning MR. Broadchalke is one of the most pleasing villages in England. Old Herbert Bundy was a farmer there. His home was at Yew Tree Farm. It went back for 300 years. His family had been there for generations. It was his only asset. But he did a very foolish thing. He mortgaged it to the bank. Up to the very hilt. Not to borrow money for himself, but for the sake of his son. Now the bank have come down on him. They have foreclosed. They want to get him out of Yew Tree Farm and to sell it. They have brought this action against him for possession. Going out means ruin for him. He was granted legal aid. His lawyers put in a defence. They said that when he executed the charge to the bank he did not know what he was doing; or at any rate the circumstances were such that he ought not to be bound by it. At the trial his plight was plain. The judge was sorry for him. He said he was a 'poor old gentleman'. He was so obviously incapacitated that the judge admitted his proof in evidence. He had a heart attack in the witness box. Yet the judge felt he could do nothing for him. There is nothing, he said, 'which takes this out of the vast range of commercial transactions'. He ordered Herbert Bundy to give up possession of Yew Tree Farm to the bank.

Now there is an appeal to this court. The ground is that the circumstances were so exceptional that Herbert Bundy should not be held bound.

1. *The events before December 1969*

Herbert Bundy had only one son, Michael Bundy. He had great faith in him. They were both customers of Lloyds Bank at the Salisbury branch. They had been customers for many years. The son formed a company called MJB Plant Hire Ltd. It hired out earth-moving machinery and so forth. The company banked at Lloyds too at the same branch.

In 1961 the son's company was in difficulties. The father on 19th September 1966 guaranteed the company's overdraft for £1,500 and charged Yew Tree Farm to the bank to secure the £1,500. Afterwards the son's company got further into difficulties. The overdraft ran into thousands. In May 1967 the assistant bank manager, Mr Bennett, told the son the bank must have further security. The son said his father would give it. So Mr Bennett and the son went together to see the father. Mr Bennett produced the papers. He suggested that the father should sign a further guarantee for

£5,000 and to execute a further charge for £6,000. The father said that he would help his son as far as he possibly could. Mr Bennett did not ask the father to sign the papers there and then. He left them with the father so that he could consider them overnight and take advice on them. The father showed them to his solicitor, Mr Trethowan, who lived in the same village. The solicitor told the father the £5,000 was the utmost that he could sink in his son's affairs. The house was worth about £10,000 and this was half his assets. On that advice the father on 27th May 1969 did execute the further guarantee and the charge, and Mr Bennett witnessed it. So at the end of May 1967 the father had charged the house to secure £7,500.

2. *The events of December 1969*

During the next six months the affairs of the son and his company went from bad to worse. The bank had granted the son's company an overdraft up to a limit of £10,000, but this was not enough to meet the outgoings. The son's company drew cheques which the bank returned unpaid. The bank were anxious. By this time Mr Bennett had left to go to another branch. He was succeeded by a new assistant manager, Mr Head. In November 1969 Mr Head saw the son and told him that the account was unsatisfactory and that he considered that the company might have to cease operations. The son suggested that the difficulty was only temporary and that his father would be prepared to provide further money if necessary.

On 17th December 1969 there came the occasion which, in the judge's words, was important and disastrous for the father. The son took Mr Head to see his father. Mr Head had never met the father before. This was his first visit. He went prepared. He took with him a form of guarantee and a form of charge filled in with the father's name ready for signature. There was a family gathering. The father and mother were there. The son and the son's wife. Mr Head said that the bank had given serious thought whether they could continue to support the son's company. But that the bank were prepared to do so in this way. (i) The bank would continue to allow the company to draw money on overdraft up to the existing level of £10,000, but the bank would require the company to pay ten per cent of its incomings into a separate account. So that ten per cent would not go to reduce the overdraft. Mr Head said that this would have the effect 'of reducing the level of borrowing'. In other words, the bank was cutting down the overdraft. (ii) The bank would require the father to give a guarantee of the company's account in a sum of £11,000 and to give the bank a further charge on the house of £3,500, so as to bring the total charge to £11,000. The house was only worth about £10,000, so this charge for £11,000 would sweep up all that the father had.

On hearing the proposal, the father said that Michael was his only son and that he was 100 per cent behind him. Mr Head produced the forms that had already been filled in. The father signed them and Mr Head witnessed them there and then. On this occasion, Mr Head, unlike Mr Bennett, did not leave the forms with the father; nor did the father have any independent advice.

It is important to notice the state of mind of Mr Head and of the father. Mr Head said in evidence:

> '[The father] asked me what in my opinion Company was doing wrong and Company's position. I told him. I did not explain Company's accounts very fully as I had only just taken over ... [The son] said Company had a number of bad

debts. I wasn't entirely satisfied with this. I thought the trouble was more deep-seated... I thought there was no conflict of interest. I would think the [father] relied on me implicitly to advise him about the transaction as Bank Manager... I knew he had no other assets except Yew Tree Cottage.'

The father said in evidence:

'Always thought Mr Head was genuine. I have always trusted him... No discussion how business was doing that I can remember. I simply sat back and did what they said.'

The solicitor, Mr Trethowan, said of the father:

'[The father] is straightforward. Agrees with anyone... Doubt if he understood all that Mr Head explained to him.'

So the father signed the papers. Mr Head witnessed them and took them away. The father had charged the whole of his remaining asset, leaving himself with nothing. The son and his company gained a respite. But only for a short time. Five months later, in May 1970, a receiving order was made against the son. Thereupon the bank stopped all overdraft facilities for the company. It ceased to trade. The father's solicitor, Mr Trethowan, at once went to see Mr Head. He said he was concerned that the father had signed the guarantee.

In due course the bank insisted on the sale of the house. In December 1971 they agreed to sell it for £7,500 with vacant possession. The family were very disappointed with this figure. It was, they said, worth much more. Estate agents were called to say so. But the judge held that it was a valid sale and that the bank can take all the proceeds. The sale has not been completed, because the father is still in possession. The bank have brought these proceedings to evict the father.

3. *The general rule*

Now let me say at once that in the vast majority of cases a customer who signs a bank guarantee or a charge cannot get out of it. No bargain will be upset which is the result of the ordinary interplay of forces. There are many hard cases which are caught by this rule. Take the case of a poor man who is homeless. He agrees to pay a high rent to a landlord just to get a roof over his head. The common law will not interfere. It is left to Parliament. Next take the case of a borrower in urgent need of money. He borrows it from the bank at high interest and it is guaranteed by a friend. The guarantor gives his bond and gets nothing in return. The common law will not interfere. Parliament has intervened to prevent moneylenders charging excessive interest. But it has never interfered with banks.

Yet there are exceptions to this general rule. There are cases in our books in which the courts will set aside a contract, or a transfer of property, when the parties have not met on equal terms, when the one is so strong in bargaining power and the other so weak that, as a matter of common fairness, it is not right that the strong should be allowed to push the weak to the wall. Hitherto those exceptional cases have been treated each as a separate category in itself. But I think the time has come when we should seek to find a principle to unite them. I put on one side contracts or transactions which are voidable for fraud or misrepresentation or mistake. All those are governed by settled principles. I go only to those where there has been inequality of bargaining power, such as to merit the intervention of the court.

4. *The categories*

The first category is that of 'duress of goods'. A typical case is when a man is in a strong bargaining position by being in possession of the goods of another by virtue of a legal right, such as, by way of pawn or pledge or taken in distress. The owner is in a weak position because he is in urgent need of the goods. The stronger demands of the weaker more than is justly due, and he pays it in order to get the goods. Such a transaction is voidable. He can recover the excess... To which may be added the cases of 'colore officii', where a man is in a strong bargaining position by virtue of his official position or public profession. He relies on it so as to gain from the weaker — who is urgently in need — more than is justly due... In such cases the stronger may make his claim in good faith honestly believing that he is entitled to make his demand. He may not be guilty of any fraud or misrepresentation. The inequality of bargaining power — the strength of the one versus the urgent need of the other — renders the transaction voidable and the money paid to be recovered back...

The second category is that of the 'unconscionable transaction'. A man is so placed as to be in need of special care and protection and yet his weakness is exploited by another far stronger than himself so as to get his property at a gross undervalue. The typical case is that of the 'expectant heir'. But it applies to all cases where a man comes into property, or is expected to come into it, and then being in urgent need another gives him ready cash for it, greatly below its true worth, and so gets the property transferred to him.... Even though there be no evidence of fraud or misrepresentation, nevertheless the transaction will be set side: see *Fry v Lane* (1888), 40 Ch. D. 312, 322 where Kay J said:

> 'The result of the decisions is that where a purchase is made from a poor and ignorant man at a considerable undervalue, the vendor having no independent advice, a Court of Equity will set aside the transaction.'

This second category is said to extend to all cases where an unfair advantage has been gained by an unconscientious use of power by a stronger party against a weaker: see the cases cited in 17 Halsbury's Laws of England 3rd p. 682, and in Canada, *Morrison v Coast Finance Ltd* and *Knupp v Bell* (1968), 67 D.L.R. (2d) 256.

The third category is that of 'undue influence' usually so called. These are divided into two classes as stated by Cotton LJ in *Allcard v Skinner* (1887), 36 Ch. D. 145, 171. The first are these where the stronger has been guilty of some fraud or wrongful act — expressly so as to gain some gift or advantage from the weaker. The second are those where the stronger has not been guilty of any wrongful act, but has, through the relationship which existed between him and the weaker, gained some gift or advantage for himself. Sometimes the relationship is such as to raise a presumption of undue influence, such as parent over child, solicitor over client, doctor over patient, spiritual adviser over follower. At other times a relationship of confidence must be proved to exist. But to all of them the general principle obtains which was stated by Lord Chelmsford LC in *Tate v Williamson* (1866), 2 Ch. App. 55, 61:

> 'Wherever the persons stand in such a relation that, while it continues, confidence is necessarily reposed by one, and the influence which naturally grows out of that confidence is possessed by the other, and this confidence is abused, or the influence is exerted to obtain an advantage at the expense of the confiding party, the person so availing himself of his position will not be permitted to retain the

advantage, although the transaction could not have been impeached if no such confidential relation had existed.'

The fourth category is that of 'undue pressure'. The most apposite of that is *Williams v Bayley* (1866), L.R.1.H.L. 200, where a son forged his father's name to a promissory note, and, by means of it, raised money from the bank of which they were both customers. The bank said to the father, in effect: 'Take your choice — give us security for your son's debt. If you do take that on yourself, then it will all go smoothly; if you do not, we shall be bound to exercise pressure.' Thereupon the father charged his property to the bank with payment of the note. The House of Lords held that the charge was invalid because of undue pressure exerted by the bank. Lord Westbury said:

'A contract to give security for the debt of another, which is a contract without consideration, is, above all things, a contract that should be based upon the free and voluntary agency of the individual who enters into it.'

Other instances of undue pressure are where one party stipulates for an unfair advantage to which the other has no option but to submit. As where an employer — the stronger party — had employed a builder — the weaker party — to do work for him. When the builder asked for payment of sums properly due (so as to pay his workmen) the employer refused to pay unless he was given some added advantage. Stuart V-C said:

'Where an agreement, hard and inequitable in itself, has been exacted under circumstances of pressure on the part of the person who exacts it this Court will set it aside':

See . . .; *D & C Builders Ltd v Rees.*

The fifth category is that of salvage agreements. When a vessel is in danger of sinking and seeks help, the rescuer is in a strong bargaining position. The vessel in distress is in urgent need. The parties cannot be truly said to be on equal terms. The Court of Admiralty have always recognised that fact. The fundamental rule is:

'If the parties have made an agreement, the Court will enforce it, unless it be manifestly unfair and unjust; but if it be manifestly unfair and unjust, the Court will disregard it and decree what is fair and just.'

See *Akerblom v Price* (1881), 7 Q.B.D. 129, 133 per Brett LJ applied in a striking case, *The Port Caledonia and The Anna*, [1903] P. 184, when the rescuer refused to help with a rope unless he was paid £1,000.

5. The general principles

Gathering all together, I would suggest that through all these instances there runs a single thread. They rest on 'inequality of bargaining power'. By virtue of it, the English law gives relief to one who, without independent advice, enters into a contract on terms which are very unfair or transfers property for a consideration which is grossly inadequate, when his bargaining power is grievously impaired by reason of his own needs or desires, or by his own ignorance or infirmity, coupled with undue influences or pressures brought to bear on him by or for the benefit of the other. When I use the word 'undue' I do not mean to suggest that the principle depends on proof of any wrongdoing. The one who stipulates for an unfair advantage may be moved solely by his own self-interest, unconscious of the distress he is bringing to the other. I have also avoided any reference to the will of the one being 'dominated' or 'overcome' by the other. One who is in extreme need may knowingly consent to a most improvident bargain, solely to relieve the straits in which he finds himself. Again, I do no mean to suggest that every transaction is saved by independent advice. But the absence of it may be fatal. With these explanations, I hope this principle will be found to reconcile the cases. Applying it to the present case, I would notice these points.

(I) The consideration moving from the bank was grossly inadequate. The son's company was in serious difficulty. The overdraft was at its limit of £10,000. The bank considered that their existing security was insufficient. In order to get further security, they asked the father to charge the house — his sole asset — to the uttermost. It was worth £10,000. The charge was for £11,000. That was for the benefit of the bank. But not at all for the benefit of the father, or indeed for the company. The bank did not promise to continue the overdraft or to increase it. On the contrary, they required the overdraft to be reduced. All that the company gained was a short respite from impending doom.

(2) The relationship between the bank and the father was one of trust and confidence. The bank knew that the father relied on them implicitly to advise him about the transaction. The father trusted the bank. This gave the bank much influence on the father. Yet the bank failed in that trust. They allowed the father to charge the house to his ruin.

(3) The relationship between the father and the son was one where the father's natural affection had much influence on him.

(4) He would naturally desire to accede to his son's request. He trusted his son. There was a conflict of interest between the bank and the father. Yet the bank did not realise it. Nor did they suggest that the father should get independent advice. If the father had gone to his solicitor — or to any man of business — there is no doubt that any one of them would say: 'You must not enter into this transaction. You are giving up your house, your sole remaining asset, for no benefit to you. The company is in such a parlous state that you must not do it.'

These considerations seem to me to bring this case within the principles I have stated. But, in case that principle is wrong, I would also say that the case falls within the category of undue influence of the second class stated by Cotton LJ in *Allcard v Skinner*. I have no doubt that the assistant bank manager acted in the utmost good faith and was straightforward and genuine. Indeed the father said so. But beyond doubt he was acting in the interests of the bank — to get further security for a bad debt. There was such a relationship of trust and confidence between them that the bank ought not to have swept up his sole remaining asset into their hands — for nothing — without his having independent advice. I would therefore allow this appeal.

Cairns LJ. I have had some doubt whether it was established in this case that there was such a special relationship between the defendant and the bank as to give rise to a duty on the part of the bank, through Mr Head, to advise the defendant about the desirability of his obtaining independent advice. In the end, however, for the reasons given by Sir Eric Sachs in the judgment which he is about to deliver and which I have had the opportunity of reading, I have reached the conclusion that in the very unusual circumstances of this case there was such a duty. Because it was not fulfilled, the guarantee can be avoided on the ground of undue influence. I therefore agree that the appeal should be allowed, the judgment for the plaintiff set aside and judgment entered for the defendant.

Sir Eric Sachs. At trial in the county court a number of complex defences were raised, ranging from non est factum, through undue influence and absence of consideration to negligence in, and improper exercise of, the bank's duty when contracting for the sale of the relevant property. It is thus at the outset appropriate to record that in this court no challenge has been offered to any of the conclusions of the learned county court judge on law or on fact save as regards one aspect of one of the defences — appropriately pleaded as undue influence. As regards that defence, however, it is clear that he vitally misapprehended the law and the points to be considered and that moreover he apparently fell into error — as his own notes disclose — on an important fact touching that issue. In the result this court is thus faced with a task that is far from being easy.

The first and most troublesome issue which here falls for consideration is whether on the particular and somewhat unusual facts of the case the bank was, when obtaining his signatures on 17th December 1969, in a relationship with the defendant that entailed a duty on their part of what can for convenience be called fiduciary care. (The phrase 'fiduciary care' is used to avoid the confusion with the common law duty of care — a different field of our jurisprudence.)

As was pointed out in *Tufton v. Sperni*, [1952] 2 T.L.R. 516, 522, the relationships which result in such a duty must not be circumscribed by reference to defined limits; it is necessary to —

> 'refute the suggestion that, to create the relationship of confidence, the person owing a duty must be found clothed in the recognizable garb of a guardian trustee, solicitor, priest, doctor, manager, or the like.'

Everything depends on the particular facts, and such a relationship has been held to exist in unusual circumstances as between purchaser and vendor, as between great uncle and adult nephew, and in other widely differing sets of circumstances. Moreover, it is neither feasible nor desirable to attempt closely to define the relationship, or its characteristics, or the demarcation line showing the exact transition point where a relationship that does not entail that duty passes into one that does (cf Ungoed-Thomas J in *Re Craig*, [1971] Ch. 95, 104.)

On the other hand, whilst disclaiming any intention of seeking to catalogue the elements of such a special relationship, it is perhaps of a little assistance to note some of those which have in the past frequently been found to exist where the court had been led to decide that this relationship existed as between adults of sound mind. Such cases tend to arise where someone relies on the guidance or advice of another, where the other is aware of that reliance and where the person on whom reliance is placed obtains, or may well obtain, a benefit from the transaction or has some other interest in it being concluded. In addition, there must, of course, be shown to exist a vital element which in this judgment will for convenience be referred to as confidentiality. It is this element which is so impossible to define and which is a matter for the judgment of the court on the facts of any particular case.

[Confidentiality], a relatively little used word, is being here adopted, albeit with some hesitation, to avoid the possible confusion that can arise through referring to 'confidence'. Reliance on advice can in many circumstances be said to import that type of confidence which only results in a common law duty to take care — a duty which may co-exist with but is not coterminous with that of fiduciary care. 'Confidentiality' is intended to convey that extra quality in the relevant confidence that is implicit in the phrase 'confidential relationship' (cf per Lord Chemsford LC in *Tate v. Williamson* (1866), 2 Ch. App. 55, 62, Lindley LJ in *Allcard v. Skinner* (1887), 36 Ch. D. 145, 181, and Wright J in *Morley v. Loughnan*, [1893] 1 Ch. 736, 751) and may perhaps have something in common with 'confiding' and also 'confidant' when, for instance, referring to someone's 'man of affairs'. It imports some quality beyond that inherent in the confidence that can well exist between trustworthy persons who in business affairs deal with each other at arm's length. It is one of the features of this element that once it exists, influence naturally grows out of it (cf Evershed MR in *Tufton v. Sperni*, following Lord Chelmsford LC in *Tate v. Williamson*).

It was inevitably conceded on behalf of the bank that the relevant relationship can arise as between banker and customer. Equally, it was inevitably conceded on behalf of the defendant that in the normal course of transactions by which a customer guarantees a third party's obligations, the relationship does not arise. The onus of proof lies on the customer who alleges that in any individual case the line has been crossed and the relationship has arisen.

Before proceeding to examine the position further, it is as well to dispose of some points on which confusion is apt to arise. Of these the first is one which plainly led to misapprehension on the part of the learned county court judge. Undue influence is a phrase which is commonly regarded — even in the eyes of a number of lawyers — as relating solely to occasions when the will of one person has become so dominated by that of another that, to use the learned county court judge's words, 'the person acts as the mere puppet of the dominator'. Such occasions, of course, fall within what Cotton LJ in *Allcard v. Skinner* described as the first class of cases to which the doctrine on undue influence applies. There is, however, a second class of such cases. This is referred to by Cotton LJ as follows:

'In the second class of cases the Court interferes, not on the ground that any wrongful act has in fact been committed by the donee, but on the ground of public policy, and to prevent the relations which existed between the parties and the influence arising therefrom being abused.'

It is thus to be emphasised that as regards the second class the exercise of the court's jurisdiction to set aside the relevant transaction does not depend on proof of one party being 'able to dominate the other as though a puppet' (to use the words again adopted by the learned county court judge when testing whether the defence was established) nor any wrongful intention on the part of the person who gains a benefit from it, but on the concept that once the special relationship has been shown to exist, no benefit can be retained from the transaction unless it has been positively established that the duty of fiduciary care has been entirely filfilled. To this second class, however, the learned judge never averted and plainly never directed his mind.

It is also to be noted that what constitutes filfilment of that duty (the second issue in the case now under consideration) depends again on the facts before the court. It may in the particular circumstances entail that the person in whom confidence has been reposed should insist on independent advice being obtained or ensuring in one way or another that the person being asked to execute a document is not insufficiently informed of some factor which could affect his judgment. The duty has been well stated as being one to ensure that the person liable to be influenced has formed 'an independent *and informed* judgment', or to use the phraseology of Lord Evershed MR in *Zamet v. Hyman*, [1961] 3 All ER 933, 938, 'after full, free *and informed* thought'. (The italics in each case are mine.) As to the difficulties in which a person may be placed and as to what he should do when there is a conflict of interest between him and the person asked to execute a document, see *Bank of Montreal v. Stuart*, [1911] A.C. 120, 139.

Stress was placed in argument for the bank on the effect of the word 'abused' as it appears in the above cited passage in the judgment of Cotton LJ and in other judgments and textbooks. As regards the second class of undue influence, however, that word in the context means no more than that once the existence of a special relationship has been established, then any possible use of the relevant influence is, irrespective of the intentions of the persons possessing it, regarded in relation to the transaction under consideration as an abuse — unless and until the duty of fiduciary care has been shown to be filfilled or the transaction is shown to be truly for the benefit of the person influenced. This approach is a matter of public policy.

One further point on which potential confusion emerged in the course of the helpful addresses of counsel stemmed from submissions to the effect that Mr. Head, the assistant bank manager, should be cleared of all blame in the matter. When one has to deal with claims of breach of either common law or fiduciary care, it is not unusual to find that counsel for a big corporation tends to try and focus the attention of the court on the responsibility of the employee who deals with the particular matter rather than on that of the corporation as an entity. What we are concerned with in the present case is whether the element of confidentiality has been established as against the bank; Mr. Head's part in the affair is but one link in a chain of events. Moreover, when it comes to a question of the relevant knowledge which will have to be discussed later in this judgment, it is the knowledge of the bank and not merely the personal knowledge of Mr. Head that has to be examined.

Having discussed the nature of the issues to which the learned county court judge should have directed his mind, it is now convenient to turn to the evidence relating to the first of them — whether the special relationship has here been shown to exist at the material time.

Counsel for the bank stressed the paucity of the evidence given by the defendant as to any reliance placed by him on the bank's advice — and, a fortiori, as to its quality. In cases of the type under consideration the paucity, or sometimes absense, of such evidence may well occur; moreover such evidence, if adduced, can be suspect. In the present case it is manifest that at the date of the trial the defendant's recollection of what happened was so minimal as to be unreliable, though not the slightest attack was made on his honesty. Indeed, his condition at trial was such that his sketchy proof was admitted into evidence. The learned judge's reference to him as 'poor old Mr. Bundy' and to his 'obvious incapacity' are in point on this aspect of the matter. It is not surprising in such a case for the result to depend on the success of the cross-examination of some witness called for the party against whom the special relationship is pleaded.

Prime reliance was accordingly placed by counsel for the defendant on answers given by Mr. Head when under cross-examination by junior counsel for the defendant. In the forefront came an answer which, unfortunately, was misapprehended by the learned judge, who thus came to make a vitally erroneous entry in his notebook. That answer as amended, after trial and judgment, in the notes before us, with the assent of the judge, is agreed to have been: 'I would think the defendant relied on me implicitly to advise him about the transaction as Bank Manager.' It is to be observed that in the judge's original note there is to be found the following, which was erased when the above quoted answer was substituted: 'Q. Defendant relied on you to advise *Company* as to the position in the transaction? A. No.' (The italicising of the word 'Company' is mine — to emphasise the distinction between the answer as noted and the answer now agreed to have been given.)

In the face of that vital answer, counsel for the bank found it necessary to submit that the words 'as bank manager' were intended to confine the reliance to the explaining of the legal effect of the document and the sums involved as opposed to more general advice as a confidant. I reject that submission. Taking Mr. Head's evidence as a whole, it seems plain that the defendant was, for instance, worried about, considered material, and asked questions about the company's affairs and the state of its accounts; and was thus seeking and being given advice on the viability of the company as a factor to be taken into account. (The vital bearing of this factor on the wisdom of the transaction is discussed later in this judgment.) Moreover, the answer to the judge followed immediately after: 'Q Conflict of interest? A No, it didn't occur to me at that time. I always thought there was no conflict of interest.' That question and answer (which was in itself immediately preceded by questions on the company's viability) do more than merely indicate a failure on the part of Mr. Head to understand the position; they indicate that at that stage of the cross-examination the questions being addressed to Mr. Head related to the wider issue of the wisdom of the transaction.

Moreover what happened on 17th December 1969 has to be assessed in the light of the general background of the existence of the long-standing relations between the Bundy family and the bank. It not infrequently occurs in provincial and country branches of great banks that a relationship is built up over the years, and in due course the senior officials may become trusted counsellors of customers of whose affairs they have an intimate knowledge. Confidential trust is placed in them because of a combination of status, goodwill and knowledge. Mr. Head was the last of a relevant chain of those who over the years had earned or inherited, such trust whilst becoming familiar with the finance and business of the Bundys and the relevant company; he had taken over the accounts from Mr. Bennett (a former assistant manager at Salisbury) of whom the defendant said: 'I always trusted him.'

The fact that the defendant may later have referred to Mr. Head as being 'straight' is not inconsistent with this view — see also the statement of Mr. Trethowan, that: 'Defendant is straightforward. Agrees with anyone.' Indeed more than one passage in the defendant's evidence is consistent with Mr. Head's vital answer as to the implicit reliance placed on his advice.

It is, of course, plain that when Mr. Head was asking the defendant to sign the documents, the bank would derive benefit from the signature, that there was a conflict of interest as between the bank and the defendant, that the bank gave him advice, that he relied on that advice, and that the bank knew of the reliance. The further question is whether on the evidence concerning the matters already recited there was also established that element of confidentiality which has been discussed. In my judgment it is thus established. Moreover reinforcement for that view can be derived from some of the material which it is more convenient to examine in greater detail when considering what the resulting duty of fiduciary care entailed.

What was required to be done on the bank's behalf once the existence of that duty is shown to have been established? The situation of the defendant in his sitting-room at Yew Tree Farm can be stated as follows. He was faced by three persons anxious for him to sign. There was his son Michael, the overdraft of whose company had been, as is shown by the correspondence, escalating rapidly; whose influence over his father was observed by the judge — and can hardly not have been realised by the bank; and whose ability to overcome the difficulties of his company was plainly doubtful, indeed its troubles were known to Mr. Head to be 'deep-seated'. There was Mr. Head, on behalf of the bank, coming with the documents designed to protect the bank's interest already substantially made out and in his pocket. There was Michael's wife asking Mr. Head to help her husband.

The documents which the defendant was being asked to sign could result, if the company's troubles continued, in the defendant's sole asset being sold, the proceeds all going to the bank, and his being left penniless in his old age. That he could thus be rendered penniless was known to the bank — and in particular to Mr. Head. That the company might come to a bad end quite soon with these results was not exactly difficult to deduce (less than four months later, on 3rd April 1970, the bank were insisting that Yew Tree Farm be sold).

The situation was thus one which to any reasonably sensible person, who gave it but a moment's thought, cried aloud the defendant's need for careful independent advice. Over and above the need any man has for counsel when asked to risk his last penny on even an apparently reasonable project, was the need here for informed advice as to whether there was any real chance of the company's affairs becoming viable if the documents were signed. If not, there arose questions such as, what is the use of taking the risk of becoming penniless without benefiting anyone but the bank; is it not better both for you and your son that you, at any rate, should still have some money when the crash comes; and should not the bank at least bind itself to hold its hand for some given period? The answers to such questions could only be given in the light of a worthwhile appraisement of the company's affairs — without which the defendant could not come to an *informed judgment* as to the wisdom of what he was doing.

No such advice to get an independent opinion was given; on the contrary, Mr. Head chose to give his own views on the company's affairs and to take this course, though he had at trial to admit: 'I did not explain the company's affairs very fully I had only just taken over.' (Another answer that escaped entry in the learned judge's original notes.)

On the above recited facts, the breach of the duty to take fiduciary care is manifest. It is not necessary for the defendant to rely on another factor tending to show such a breach. The bank knew full well that the defendant had a well-known solicitor of standing. Mr. Trethowan, who usually advised him on important matters, including the previous charge signed in May 1969, only seven months earlier. Indeed, on that occasion the bank seems very properly to have taken steps which either ensured that Mr. Trethowan's advice was obtained or at least assumed it was being obtained. It is no answer that Mr. Head, relatively a newcomer to the Bundy accounts at the Salisbury branch, may not personally have known these matters; it is the bank's knowledge that is material. Incidentally, Mr. Head discussed the relevant accounts with his manager.

The existence of the duty and its breach having thus been established, there remains the submission urged by counsel for the bank that whatever independent advice had been obtained the defendant would have been so obstinately determined to help his son that the documents would anyway have been signed. The point fails for more than one reason, of which it is sufficient to mention two. First, on a question of fact it ignores the point that the independent advice might well have been to the effect that it would benefit the son better in the event of an almost inevitable crash if his father had some money left after it occurred — advice which could have affected the mind of the defendant. Secondly, once the relevant duty is established, it is contrary to public policy that benefit of the transaction be retained by the person under the duty unless he positively shows that the duty of fiduciary care has been fulfilled: there is normally no room for debate on the issue as to what would have happened had the care been taken.

It follows that the county court judgment cannot stand. The learned judge having failed to direct his mind to a crucial issue and to important evidence supporting the defendant's case thereon, at the very least the latter is entitled to an order for a new trial. That would produce as an outcome of this appeal a prolongation of uncertainties affecting others beside the defendant, who still resides at Yew Tree Farm, and could hardly be called desirable even if one left out of account the latter's health and financial position. In my judgment, however, a breach by the bank of their duty to take fiduciary care has, on the evidence, as a whole been so affirmatively established that this court can and should make an order setting aside the guarantee and the charge of 17th December 1969.

I would add that Mr. Head was, of course, not guilty of any intentional wrongful act. In essence what happened was that having gone to Yew Tree Farm 'in the interests of the bank' (as counsel for the bank stressed more than once), he failed to apprehend that there was a conflict of interest as between the bank and the defendant, that he should have insisted on the obvious need for independent advice. In addition, it was unfortunate that he was — through some absence of relevant information from Mr. Bennett (who had previously dealt with the relevant accounts) — not aware of the way Mr. Trethowan had come to advise the defendant as regards the May 1969 guarantee and charge. Though I have not founded any part of this judgment on that facet of the case, I am yet inclined to view the bank's failure to suggest that Mr. Trethowan be consulted when they were pursuing their quest for the defendant's signature in such a potentially disastrous situation, as open to criticism and as something that might of itself have led to an adverse decision against the bank in this particular case.

The conclusion that the defendant has established that as between himself and the bank the relevant transaction fell within the second category of undue influence cases referred to by Cotton LJ in *Allcard v. Skinner* is one reached on the single issue pursued on behalf of the defendant in this court. On that issue we have had the benefit of cogent and helpful submissions on matter plainly raised in the pleadings. As regards the wider areas covered in masterly survey in the judgment of Lord Denning MR, but not raised arguendo, I do not venture to express an opinion — though having some sympathy with the views that the courts should be able to give relief to a party who has been subject to undue pressure as defined in the concluding passage of his judgment on that point.

There remains to mention that counsel for the bank whilst conceding that the relevant special relationship could arise as between banker and customer, urged in somewhat doom-laden terms that a decision taken against the bank on the facts of this particular case would seriously affect banking practice. With all respect to that submission, it seems necessary to point out that nothing in this judgment affects the duties of a bank in the normal case where it is obtaining a guarantee, and in accordance with standard practice explains to the person about to sign its legal effect and the sums involved. When, however, a bank, as in this case, goes further and advises on more general matters germane to the wisdom of the transaction, that indicates that it may — not necessarily must — be crossing the line into the area of confidentiality so that the court may then have to examine all the facts, including, of course, the history leading up to the transaction, to ascertain whether or not that line has, as here, been crossed. It would indeed be rather odd if a bank which vis-à-vis a customer attained a special relationship in some ways akin to that of a 'man of affairs' — something which can be a matter of pride and enhance his local reputation — should not where a conflict of interest has arisen as between itself and the person advised be under the resulting duty now under discussion. Once, as was inevitably conceded, it is possible for a bank to be under that duty, it is, as in the present case, simply a question for 'meticulous examination' of the particular facts to see whether that duty has arisen. On the special facts here it did arise and it has been broken.

The appeal should be allowed.

Appeal allowed; judgment below set aside. Judgment for defendant on claim and counterclaim. Legal charge and guarantee dated 17th December 1969 set aside; documents to be delivered up for cancellation. Leave to appeal to the House of Lords refused.

QUESTIONS

1. What was the most important fact in the case under Lord Denning's approach?

2. What was the most important fact in the case under the approach of Sir Eric Sachs?

As you read the next case consider if it makes any difference which of the two approaches in *Lloyds Bank v. Bundy* is adopted.

Notice the range of facts considered by Sachs L.J. He says:

"It not infrequently occurs in provincial and country branches of great banks that a relationship is built up over the years, and in due course the senior officials may become trusted counsellors of customers of whose affairs they have an intimate knowledge. Confidential trust is placed in them because of a combination of status, goodwill and knowledge."

There is no evidence that this fact was proved to the court. Sachs L.J. presumably took judicial notice of it. It is probably true, but its truth was not tested in the normal way.

This kind of fact raises difficult problems for lawyers:

1. Could you draft a letter to be sent to the managers and loan officers of a bank explaining what they should do in the light of this case?

2. You are counsel for a person in the position of Mr. Bundy. What do you do to show the court that, for example, the banks invite trust and confidence? Would you put in photographs of marble banking halls, copies of advertisements in the press or radio and T.V. commercials?

3. As counsel for a bank how could you counter such tactics? Can you say that banks do not invite trust?

Sachs L.J. makes important the notion of fiduciary care. The general idea of a fiduciary obligation is briefly outlined in the following cases. They illustrate the background against which that kind of duty must be seen. Notice that when the courts enforce a fiduciary obligation they do so because the relationship is one whose integrity the law wants to protect. The idea of a fiduciary obligation is found in many areas of the law. The cases here refer only to the obligation arising out of that relation of principal and agent. It also arises between the directors of a corporation and the corporation and, of course, between a trustee and the beneficiary of the trust. The notion of fiduciary obligation is one of the most significant developments of the Court of Chancery. There is also a very wide range of remedies available to protect the relationship.

REGIER v. CAMPBELL-STUART

[1939] Ch. 766. Chancery Division.

[The plaintiff wanted to buy a house. The plaintiff's son requested the defendant, a real estate dealer, to find her a house in London. The defendant found a suitable house, known as "The Red House". The particulars of sale listed the price as £4,250. However, the defendant, through his brother-in-law, one Brown, bought it for £2,000. The defendant purported to buy the house from Brown for £4,500. The defendant then told the plaintiff that he had bought it for £4,500 and the plaintiff agreed to buy it for £5,000, giving the defendant a commission of £500. When the plaintiff found out what had happened she sued for damages for fraud and for an accounting.]

Farwell J. [having stated the facts:] It has been argued by counsel for the defendant, who has conducted this case on behalf of his client with moderation and ability, that the fact that the defendant told the plaintiff, before she entered into the contract, that he himself was the vendor of the property, was sufficient to determine his agency for her. I cannot doubt that at any rate up to that time there did exist the relationship of principal and agent between the plaintiff and the defendant. No doubt the scope of that agency was limited. What the defendant had undertaken to do for the son of the plaintiff, who was acting on her behalf throughout, was to provide particulars of any houses of which he should hear and think suitable for the purpose which the plaintiff had in mind and which she had communicated to him. He was an agent to that extent. Of course, he was not an agent for the purpose of signing any contract of the plaintiff's or doing more than assisting in the way I have mentioned, but that there was the relationship of principal and agent to that limited extent I think is quite plain.

When the relationship of principal and agent exists, the agent may terminate that relationship by himself selling to his principal property which belongs to him so long as the principal knows that the property does in fact belong to the agent and that the agent is intending to sell his own property. But that must, in my judgment, be limited to this extent, that it is the duty of every agent to act honestly and faithfully towards his principal, and, if he conceals most material facts from his principal and by means of a fraud obtains an advantage for himself by purporting to sell or by selling property which is his own, then the duty which lies upon him is not put an end to by such a contract, and he remains liable to account for any secret profit which he has made as the result of the transactions between himself and the principal.

In the present case I am satisfied that the whole of this transaction between the plaintiff and the defendant and Harold Brown was in fact a contrivance for the purpose of enabling the defendant to obtain a handsome profit as the result of his dealing with the house and in the hope, I think the very lively hope, that the profit would be obtained from the plaintiff who had, through her son, conveyed to him information as to the nature of the house which she desired to buy, which knowledge the defendant was making use of for that purpose.

In those circumstances it follows that the plaintiff is entitled to the relief which she seeks. I do not think that it is necessary in this rather unhappy and sordid story to travel through it at any greater length. The facts as I find them in this case are in a very small compass and, in my judgment, lead to the only possible result, that the plaintiff is entitled to recover from the defendant whatever profit the defendant made as a result of the dealings which he had in connection with this lease between himself and the plaintiff. I propose to direct that an account be taken of all profit obtained by the defendant without the plaintiff's knowledge or consent in his capacity as agent for the plaintiff. The defendant must pay the costs of the action.

McLEOD v. SWEEZEY

[1944] 2 D.L.R. 145. Supreme Court of Canada; Rinfret C.J.C., Kerwin, Hudson, Taschereau and Rand JJ.

[The plaintiffs had staked mining claims in Northern Manitoba in 1923. They believed they had found asbestos. They did not have the money to maintain their claims. In 1937 the defendant (a prospector with a high reputation) became interested in these claims. The parties drew up an agreement under which the defendant was to prospect and stake the claims and the plaintiffs were to say where the claims were and pay the costs of recording the claims. They agreed to divide any profits: 25% to the defendant, and 75% to the plaintiffs. The defendant was also given authority to dispose of the claims. The defendant went out to examine the claims. He reported that there was nothing there. The defendant some time later went back and staked claims in the area. These claims turned out to have valuable chrome and the defendant was given a substantial share in the profits to be made from the claims. The plaintiffs sued for their share of the benefits that the defendant had obtained.]

Rand J. gave the judgment of the court (and after stating the facts continued):

The trial judgment [[1943] 1 D.L.R. 471] declared the defendant to hold all of these interests as to 75% of them under a constructive trust in favour of the plaintiffs, and in respect of cash received by Sweezey, the plaintiffs recovered the proportion that should have been paid over to them. On appeal that judgment was reversed [[1943] 4 D.L.R. 391]; and the plaintiffs bring the controversy here.

The first question that arises is this: what was the precise undertaking of the defendant? Was it, as contended by him, merely an employment of his labour to stake the described claims without the benefit of his judgment on them or of the area in which they were to be found? I do not think so. The plaintiffs had special knowledge of mineral indications in this limited field off the beaten track of prospectors, and it was of value to them. To disclose that information meant to give up once and for all any advantage they thereby held; all would then be at large; and they did what they thought necessary to protect themselves accordingly. The obligation assumed by the defendant was what they took in return and it was all that remained to them.

They had bargained for his mature judgment and for that not only on the possibility of asbestos. The expression in the memorandum agreement. "asbestos mineral claims." was description of what had been originally staked. The plaintiffs desired an expert opinion on those claims in the totality of their possibilities and not on one of them only. That, therefore, was the measure of the defendant's duty as the fiduciary of the plaintiffs in acting upon the disclosure of all the plaintiffs had of value; he undertook to apply his experience to everything found in the area of the claims and, on the strength of the opinion so formed, to stake, if that was called for, and to advise the plaintiffs of that opinion. There was no such thing in the mining law as an "asbestos mineral claim." A claim staked and recorded covered all minerals except a few specifically reserved by the statute. He, therefore, owed to the plaintiffs the utmost good faith in his examination of the structure, formation, and other evidence of the land to which he was directed, and a duty to give them an unreserved account of what he had found and what, in his judgment, the mineral prospect was.

The trial Judge has found that he failed to observe that duty. Instead, he deliberately misled the plaintiffs into discarding the claims as prospects by falsely misrepresenting as to asbestos, and concealing as to other minerals, his own judgment of them.

Trueman J.A. conceded the existence of a fiduciary relation but treated the original undertaking as at an end in October upon the report of the defendant and acquiescence in it by the plaintiffs. I find difficulty in following this reasoning. That acquiescence was induced by fraud. How can a termination of such a relation so brought about be held to be effective while the fraud still operates?] The fraud continued to have effect both on the plaintiffs in their acceptance of the misrepresentation of opinion and on the defendant in his acquisition and capitalization of the claims, and the original duty remained ... I agree, therefore, that as to any interest held by him, acquired through the conversion and realization of property which he obtained through information gained in the course of the service he undertook, the defendant holds it as a constructive trustee and that he is liable to account to the plaintiffs for their share of the monies received in cash.

[The appeal was therefore allowed.]

JIRNA v. MR. DONUT

(1973), 40 D.L.R. (3d) 303. Supreme Court of Canada; Martland, Judson, Ritchie, Spence and Laskin JJ.

[The plaintiff was a franchisee of the defendant. He operated three outlets for "Mister Donut" in Toronto. The business was profitable. During the negotiation for the franchise, the defendant assured the plaintiff that one of the benefits of the franchise operation were the savings possible in purchasing supplies in large quantities. The franchise agreement that was signed by the parties provided that:

"7. The Company shall sell to the Dealer and the Dealer shall buy from the Company, or from such sources as the Company may first approve in writing, any and all ingredients and commodities which may form any part of the whole of any end product of food or beverage made, sold or consumed on the Dealer's Premises, ... " and,

"16.... The relationship between the parties is only that of independent contractors. No partnership, joint venture or relationship of principal and agent is intended."

The plaintiff subsequently discovered that the suppliers of the ingredients that he needed (and from whom he was required to buy) were giving kick-backs to the defendant. The plaintiff sued to recover these.

The trial judge, Stark J. gave judgment for the plaintiff. During the course of his judgment he said (1970), 13 D.L.R.(3d) 645, 654:

"In view of the close relationship between the parties and in view of the assurances made to the plaintiff, surely the plaintiff in entrusting complete powers of purchase of supplies to the defendant was entitled to expect that the defendant in exercising that power and insisting upon the high quality which the manufactured product required would still endeavour to obtain the supplies at the most favourable price on behalf of the franchisee that could be arranged. Far from that, it allowed its own interest to prevail and the prices paid by the franchisees were certainly higher than they should have paid, at least to the extent of the secret rebate.

"In other words, it appears to me that the close association of the franchisor and the franchisee in this case has created what must be construed as a fiduciary relationship and that the actions of the defendant constitute what can best be described as "constructive fraud". I use the term as it was best outlined by Viscount Haldane, L.C., in *Nocton v. Lord Ashburton*, [1914] A.C. 932 at p. 954, in this language:

"'But when fraud is referred to in the wider sense in which the books are full of the expression, used in Chancery in describing cases which were within its exclusive jurisdiction, it is a mistake to suppose that an actual intention to cheat must always be proved. A man may misconceive the extent of the obligation which a Court of Equity imposes on him. His fault is that he has violated, however innocently because of his ignorance, an obligation which he must be taken by the Court to have known, and his conduct has in that sense always been called fraudulent, even in such a case as a technical fraud on a power. It was thus that the expression 'constructive fraud' came into existence. The trustee who purchases the trust estate, the solicitor who makes a bargain with his client that cannot stand, have all for several centuries run the risk of the word fraudulent being applied to them. What it really means in this connection is, not moral fraud in the ordinary sense, but breach of the sort of obligation which is enforced by a Court that from the beginning regarded itself as a Court of conscience.'

"Again, at p. 955:

"'But side by side with the enforcement of the duty of universal obligation to be honest and the principle which gave the right to rescission, the Courts, and especially the Court of Chancery, had to deal with the other cases to which I have referred, cases raising claims of an essentially different character, which have often been mistaken for actions of deceit. *Such claims raise the question whether the circumstances and relations of the parties are such as to give rise to duties of particular obligation which* have not been fulfilled...

Such a special duty may arise from the circumstances and relations of the parties. These may give rise to an implied contract at law or to a fiduciary obligation in equity.'

(Italics Mine.)

"It must of course be recognized that in a situation such as this, if a purely business relationship exists, the mere fact that the plaintiff places greater confidence upon the defendant than he should is not in itself sufficient to transform the arrangement into one of a fiduciary nature. In this case, however, as I have already pointed out, the relationship is much closer and much more intimate than in a simpler form of business relationship. Moreover, in view of the representations which the defendant made at the outset, it was well aware of the confidence and trust which the plaintiff was imposing upon it in the matter of the purchase of supplies. This was recognized by Reardon, J., in *Broomfield v. Kosow* (1965), 212 N.E. 2d 556 at p. 560, a decision of the Supreme Judicial Court of Massachusetts where he used this language:

"'... the plaintiff alone, by reposing trust and confidence in the defendant, cannot thereby transform a business relationship into one which is fiduciary in nature. The catalyst in such a change is the defendant's knowledge of the plaintiff's reliance upon him.'"

The Court of Appeal allowed the appeal. Plaintiff appealed to the Supreme Court of Canada. The judgment of the Court was delivered by

Martland, J.: — The facts in this case are fully stated in the judgments in the Courts below.

The appellant's claim as against the respondent, as framed in its statement of claim, is, essentially, a claim based upon fraud, within the definition stated in *Derry v. Peek* (1889), 14 App. Cas. 337. Neither of the Courts below has found that there was liability on the part of the respondent under the principles stated in that case, and, although it was argued in this Court, I am not prepared to find that there was a cause of action based upon legal fraud.

The learned trial Judge found in favour of the appellant on the ground that the close association between the parties created what must be construed as a fiduciary relationship and that the actions of the respondent could best be described as "constructive fraud", as defined in *Nocton v. Lord Ashburton,* [1914] A.C. 932. This finding was made, notwithstanding the fact that the parties had, themselves, defined their relationship, in the agreements made between them, as follows:

> "The relationship between the parties is only that of independent contractors. No partnership, joint venture or relationship of principal and agent is intended."

The Court of Appeal allowed the respondent's appeal, holding that it must give full effect to the express intention of the terms of the agreement made between the parties on equal footing and at arm's length.

I am in agreement with the reasons and conclusions of the Court of Appeal and would only add that para. 7 of the agreements between the parties does not assist the appellant in its claim to recover secret profits, commissions or rebates received by the respondent in respect of products which the appellant bought from firms approved by the respondent. That paragraph is, so far as relevant, in these terms:

> "The Company shall sell to the Dealer and the Dealer shall buy from the Company, or from such sources as the Company may first approve in writing, any and all ingredients and commodities which may form any part or the whole of any end product of food or beverage made, sold, or consumed on the Dealer's Premises, including by way of illustration but not by limitation, doughnut flours, doughnut sugars, toppings, fillings, frostings, flavorings, shortenings, milk, cream, ice cream and other dairy products, coffee, tea, chocolate and other non-alcoholic beverages..."

It was not contended that the respondent used its position under this paragraph to make it impossible or even difficult for the appellant to carry on a profitable business. That would have raised other considerations which do not arise here because, on the evidence, the appellant's franchise has been profitable, albeit not as profitable as it expected. It is unnecessary to go into detail on the price comparisons, some favourable and some unfavourable to the appellant, relating to various products purchased from approved sources and also available elsewhere. There is no commitment under para. 7 to see that prices on individual products are similar or competitive; and the fact that the respondent, under largely pre-existing arrangements with suppliers, profited under this paragraph through the franchises to the appellant does not alone give rise to any enforceable claim in the appellant to recover the profit.

I would dismiss the appeal with costs.

McKENZIE v. BANK OF MONTREAL

(1975), 55 D.L.R. (3d) 641. Ontario High Court.

[The plaintiff, a middle-aged widow became friends with one Lawrence. They became engaged, but never married. In 1968 the plaintiff and Lawrence purchased a farm in joint tenancy. The bulk of the purchase price was supplied by the plaintiff. In 1969 the plaintiff bought a new car. She raised half the purchase price on a trade-in and the balance was borrowed by Lawrence from the defendant bank. The car was registered in the plaintiff's name. Unknown to the plaintiff, Lawrence gave the bank a chattel mortgage on the plaintiff's car. The bank had lent large sums to Lawrence and was becoming concerned over his failure to repay them. In March 1970, the bank repossessed the plaintiff's car. The manager refused to give it back to the plaintiff until Lawrence paid what he owed to the bank. In April 1970, the bank signed default judgments against Lawrence. The plaintiff had still no knowledge of Lawrence's involvement with the bank. She was not a customer of the bank. In May 1970, the plaintiff, at the request of Lawrence, went to the bank to sign some papers. The bank's credit manager, Warwick, told the plaintiff where to sign. but did not tell her that she was signing a mortgage of the farm (as she was). She also paid the bank $2,000 that she had borrowed to help Lawrence. After she had signed she got back the keys to her car.

The plaintiff brought an action against the bank seeking to have the mortgage set aside.]

Stark J. (after stating the facts, continued:)

With the knowledge that the bank possessed, there was surely some duty resting upon the bank, either to require that she obtain independent advice or at the least to ensure that full disclosure be made to her of Lawrence's heavy debts with the bank, of his failure to keep up mortgage payments and taxes on the farm, and therefore of the unlikelihood that the farming venture could ever succeed. These explanations were never attempted, on the bank's own admission; and in any event, could never have been delivered in the few minutes allotted for the signing of the necessary papers.

It must be remembered that the only thought uppermost in the plaintiff's mind and the only purpose in her attendance at the bank, was the recovery of her motor-car. Her keys were handed over to her only after all the papers had been signed; and this withholding of her car placed the bank in a very strong and unfair bargaining position.

The leading authority of *Nocton v. Ashburton (Lord)* (1914), 83 L.J. Ch. 784, places very high the duty of persons who are acting in confidential relationships. There the House of Lords recognized the doctrine of obligation to exercise care by persons in particular situations, who are doing acts which may injure the property or persons of others. At p. 790, the Lord Chancellor used this language:

> "Although liability for negligence in word has in material respects been developed in our law differently from liability for negligence in act, it is none the less true that a man may come under a special duty to exercise care in giving information or advice."

It appears to me that in the case at bar, under the peculiar facts of the case, the bank was under a special duty to the plaintiff not to dismiss the matter as a mere formality but to provide the plaintiff with the necessary information or advice, or to see that she obtained it. Had the bank not been personally interested in the result, the advice would have been quite different....

Particularly in point is the recent decision of *Lloyds Bank Ltd. v. Bundy*, [1974] 3 All E.R. 757. It is true that in that case, the defendant Bundy was a customer of the bank and in the case at bar the plaintiff was not. But the principles enunciated in that case are applicable here. Special circumstances existed there, which imposed a duty of fiduciary care upon the bank: and in the case at bar, the special circumstances which I have outlined, placed a similar duty upon the bank. Whether the case at hand be regarded as one of misrepresentation, in that the signing of the documents was much more than a mere formality, or whether the bank used the pressure of the possession of the motor-car to obtain a benefit for itself, it would be strange indeed if the Courts could find no relief. As Lord Denning put it in the *Lloyds Bank* case at p. 763:

> "There are cases in our books in which the courts will set aside a contract, or a transfer of property, when the parties have not met on equal terms, when the one is so strong in bargaining power and the other so weak that, as a matter of common fairness, it is not right that the strong should be allowed to push the weak to the wall. Hitherto those exceptional cases have been treated each as a separate category in itself. But I think the time has come when we should seek to find a principle to unite them. I put on one side contracts or transactions which are voidable for fraud or misrepresentation or mistake. All those are governed by

settled principles. I go only to those where there has been inequality of bargaining power, such as to merit the intervention of the court."

Lord Denning then divides into four the various categories of such cases, into any one of which it appears to me the case at bar might fall. He says the first category is that of "duress of goods". At p. 763:

> "A typical case is when a man is in a strong bargaining position by being in possession of the goods of another by virtue of a legal right, such as, by way of pawn or pledge or taken in distress. The owner is in a weak position because he is in urgent need of the goods."

At p. 764 he writes:

> "This second category is said to extend to all cases where an unfair advantage has been gained by an unconscientious use of power by a stronger party against a weaker:"

The third category he mentions is that of "undue influence"; and under this category he cites the general principle as laid down by Lord Chelmsford in *Tate v. Williamson* (1866), 2 Ch. App. 55 at p. 61:

> "Wherever the persons stand in such a relation that, while it continues, confidence is necessarily reposed by one, and the influence which naturally grows out of that confidence is possessed by the other, and this confidence is abused, or the influence is exerted to obtain an advantage at the expense of the confiding party, the person so availing himself of his position will not be permitted to retain the advantage, although the transaction could not have been impeached if no such confidential relation had existed."

The fourth category discussed by Lord Denning is that of "undue pressure". Here Lord Denning adopts the language of Lord Westbury in the case of *Williams v. Bayley* (1866), L.R. 1 H.L. 200:

> "A contract to give security for the debt of another, which is a contract without consideration, is, above all things, a contract that should be based upon the free and voluntary agency of the individual who enters into it."

In the case at hand the plaintiff was being asked to give a contract providing security for the debts of Lawrence, and the only real consideration for the contract was the return to her of her car which had been wrongfully seized.

Finally, Lord Denning deals with a fifth category which is not applicable here. Then, at p. 765, he continues:

> "Gathering all together, I would suggest that through all these instances there runs a single thread. They rest on "inequality of bargaining power". By virtue of it, the English law gives relief to one who, without independent advice, enters into a contract on terms which are very unfair or transfers property for a consideration which is grossly inadequate, when his bargaining power is grievously impaired by reason of his own needs or desires, or by his own ignorance or infirmity, coupled with undue influences or pressures brought to bear on him by or for the benefit of the other. When I use the word "undue" I do not mean to suggest that the principle depends on proof of any wrongdoing. The one who stipulates for an unfair advantage may be moved solely by his own self-interest, unconscious of the distress he is bringing to the other. I have also avoided any reference to the will of the one being "dominated" or "overcome" by the other. One who is in extreme need may knowingly consent to a most improvident bargain, solely to relieve the straits in which he finds himself. Again, I do not mean to suggest that every transaction is saved by independent advice. But the absence of it may be fatal."

Of course, the bank officials were acting in the interests of the bank; they were anxious to obtain valuable security for a bad debt. Ordinarily they would have had no special duty towards the plaintiff who was not their customer; but their special knowledge of Lawrence's affairs and of his crooked dealings fixed them with an obligation towards the plaintiff to ensure that the plaintiff in mortgaging her farm was really doing what she wished to do and with full knowledge of the probable consequences.

I find therefore that the mortgage signed by the plaintiff cannot be allowed to stand, at least in so far as she is concerned. In my view, her default judgment against Lawrence as to her sole ownership of the farm, is not binding against the bank. Consequently, being a joint tenant of the farm by registration, she is entitled to one-half of the proceeds, plus interest, of the amount presently standing in Court.

I turn now to the seizure of the plaintiff's motor-car. This was wrongful on the part of the defendant and its servants and agents, since any proper investigation of its title would have disclosed that the registration and ownership of the car from the time of its purchase and continuously thereafter, was always in the plaintiff's name. Moreover, even after being informed of their error, the bank continued in possession for a period of some three months. The car was seized without any prior notification to her, and her first knowledge of the seizure was when she observed it being removed from the office premises where she worked. She was embarrassed and mortified; and for the three months that followed was without use of her car and with the necessity of explaining its absence to her friends. Even when the bank did learn of its error, it would not release the car until the cash payment of $2,000 was made by the plaintiff. I consider that she is entitled to damages which I assess at $2,000, being both general and exemplary or punitive damages, covering the loss of use of her car, and covering also the damages for the embarrassment as well as the inconvenience to which she was made subject and covering also any physical injury to the vehicle.

Accordingly, the plaintiff is entitled to recover these sums from the defendants, together with her costs of these proceedings which should be taxed on the Supreme Court scale.

Judgment for the plaintiff therefore in the amount of one-half the amount of the moneys presently standing in Court, together with interest, plus judgment for the sum of $2,000, and the costs of these proceedings.

Judgment for plaintiff.

[The judgment of Stark J. was affirmed in the Ontario Court of Appeal (Brooke, Houlden and Blair JJ.A) (1976), 70 D.L.R. (3d) 113. The judgment was given orally by Houlden J.A. who said (p. 114):

"We think that there was evidence on which the trial Judge could find that there was an obligation on the bank to ensure that the plaintiff knew what she was signing, and what the effect of the document would be. Considering the bank's wrongful detention of the plaintiff's automobile, the bank's knowledge of the crooked dealings of Lawrence, the bank's obtaining of a substantial judgment against Lawrence which was unsatisfied, and Warwick's representation to the plaintiff that the documents were mere formalities, we think that there was inequality of bargaining power in this case, and the bank failed to meet the obligation that rested on it to see that the plaintiff was aware of what she was doing when she executed the mortgage: *Lloyds Bank Ltd. v. Bundy,* [1974] 3 All E.R. 757."]

QUESTION

Could you now draft a letter to bank managers summarizing the effect of *Lloyds Bank v. Bundy* and *McKenzie v. Bank of Montreal* on the conduct of their job.

In much the same way as the courts' power to relieve against penalties and forfeitures can be seen as part of the courts' general power to police individual terms in the agreement, so the power of the courts to strike down covenants in restraint of trade (as is done in the next two cases) is again an aspect of its wide power to control unconscionability.

The two cases that follow show that the courts' power to control covenants in restraint of trade is very old, and has been exercised for several centuries. As always, we are concerned with the basis for the power and the circumstances where it might be applied.

The third case, *Schroeder v. Macaulay,* may possibly be seen as an expansion of the power to control covenants in restraint of trade and an equation of that power with the general power to control unconscionability.

SHERK v. HORWITZ

[1972] 2 O.R. 451. Ontario High Court.

Donohue, J.: —This action was tried before me at St. Catharines on November 15, 16, 18 and 19, 1971. It is an action for an injunction to restrain the defendant until July 31, 1976, from carrying on the practice of medicine or surgery in any of its branches on his own account or in association with any other person or persons, or corporation, or in the employ of any such person or persons, or corporation, within the said City of St. Catharines or within five miles of the limits thereof. There is also a claim for damages.

The background of the case is as follows. The plaintiffs, and in particular Boyce E. Sherk, were the founders of the medical clinic named herein. This began in 1951 and by 1967 had grown to the stage where some eight physicians and surgeons were carrying on group practice. Dr. Sherk describes himself and his co-plaintiff Dr. Rogers as specialists in general surgery. Dr. Daugavietis was said to be a specialist in internal medicine. There were about five general practitioners in the group in 1968.

The defendant Horwitz was born in 1926 in South Africa and after undergraduate work in that country he did graduate work in England for five years and emerged from this as a specialist in obstetrics and gynaecology and practised in Rhodesia from 1958 to 1961 when he immigrated to Canada. By the summer of 1967 he had been practising his specialty in the City of Toronto for six years. It appears that his Toronto practice was meagre in terms of money earned. He ascribes this to the difficulty of obtaining hospital beds in Toronto, he having had privileges only at the Toronto General Hospital which was some 15 miles from the area of his practice.

As a result of an advertisement published in the medical press by the plaintiffs, the defendant got in touch with Dr. Sherk and a meeting took place between them in St. Catharines in May, 1967.

As to what agreement was reached between the defendant and Dr.

Sherk, there is dispute on some points. It is clear, however, that the defendant was invited to come to St. Catharines to work in the clinic and that he was to be paid 60% of his billings and in any case not less than $12,000 per year.

By July 1, 1967, the defendant had closed off his Toronto practice and started work at the clinic. He states that on July 12, 1967, the business manager of the clinic presented to him the agreement which is ex. 3 at trial and requested that he sign the same. The defendant states that the restrictive covenant set out in para. 3 of said exhibit was never mentioned to him previous to said July 12, 1967. Such covenant reads as follows:

> Should the employment of the Party of the Second Part by the Parties of the First Part terminate for any reason whatsoever, the Party of the Second Part COVENANTS AND AGREES that he will not carry on the practice of medicine or surgery in any of its branches on his own account or in association with any other person or persons, or corporation, or in the employ of any such person or persons or corporation within the said City of St. Catharines or within five miles of the limits thereof for a period of five years (5) thereafter.

It appears that the defendant was busy. His income on the 60% of billings basis rose steadily from about $25,000 in the second year to about $35,000 in the third year and on a projected basis for 1971-72 it would have been about $45,000

In May or June, 1971, the defendant expressed some dissatisfaction over certain matters of procedure and lack of nursing help and other matters. Whatever the truth or otherwise of these complaints. I do not think that they were not negotiable with Dr. Sherk nor were they the real cause of the defendant leaving the clinic, which he did on August 31, 1971, and at once entered into practice on his own in the said City of St. Catharines.

I find that the defendant signed the agreement, ex. 3, being well aware of the restrictive covenant therein and that he was under no duress or at any disadvantage in so doing. The agreement was supported by the mutual promises of the plaintiffs and in any event, it was under seal. Were it not for other aspects of this case, I would hold that it was binding on the defendant and the plaintiffs were entitled to the injunction which they seek.

The first other aspect of the matter which, in my view, renders the covenant unenforceable is the public interest.

In the few years that the defendant worked in the clinic he has treated some thousands of patients, for example 2,800 in his last year, nearly all female since his specialty is in this field. I think it fair to find that in the modern practice of obstetrics, the visits to the obstetrician begin fairly early in pregnancy and continue until after delivery. These patients, some of whom no doubt consulted the defendant before he withdrew from the clinic, are part of the public who, having confidence in the defendant, are entitled to have the benefit of his continuing care. Two such patients gave evidence at the trial, indicating that they had confidence in the defendant and wished to continue with his services. It is plain from the evidence that while in the clinic he confined himself to obstetrics and gynaecology and the only other persons in the clinic who were doing obstetrics were one or two of the general practitioners and there was no other specialist in gynaecology in the clinic. We can assume, therefore, that practically all of the defendant's work in the clinic was related to his specialty and this means that there is a large body of people who look to him for care in this field. I do not think that these people should be deprived of his services as they would be bound to be if he were obliged to stay five miles beyond the limits of the City of St. Catharines until 1976. In my view, no answer is to be found in saying that these people, who were formerly treated by the defendant, can easily find another specialist. Choosing a physician or surgeon is not akin to commercial transactions.

In this case also there is a further element for consideration. Dr. J. J. Fraser is a specialist in obstetrics practising in Thorold, Ontario, and he is a member of a medical clinic consisting of six general practitioners and himself and has been chief of obstetrics at St. Catharines General Hospital. He testified that there is a definite shortage of obstetricians in St. Catharines; that a proper proportion would be one obstetrician for 10,000 of population and St. Catharines has only seven for a population of 130,000. Similar evidence was given by Dr. D. F. Donovan, a specialist in obstetrics and gynaecology practising in St. Catharines.

Now the reasonableness of the covenant is to be judged as to the time it was entered into. Obviously in 1967 there was plenty of room for a specialist in obstetrics and gynaecology in St. Catharines from the very fact that the plaintiffs went seeking one. I think, therefore, that what Drs. Fraser and Donovan say about the need for obstetricians in the area in 1971 would be equally applicable to the situation in 1967.

In his evidence Dr. Sherk stated that the purpose of the restrictive covenant here was to protect the clinic from the "enterprising doctor". In Trietel, *Law of Contract,* 3rd ed. (1970), it is stated at p. 388:

> The reasonableness of the restraint must be established by the person who seeks to enforce the contract; it is then up to the party resisting enforcement to establish that the restraint is contrary to the public interest.

I will deal later with the plaintiffs' burden of establishing the reasonableness of the contract and continue with the burden on the defendant here, *i.e.,* whether this covenant is injurious to the public interest.

In my view, the public interest is the same as public policy.

In the *Harvard Law Review,* vol. 42 (1929), p. 76, Professor Winfield, then of St. John's College, Cambridge, England, at p. 92, defines public policy as: "'a principle of judicial legislation or interpretation founded on the current needs of the community.'" He goes on to say that:

> ... this signifies that the interests of the whole public must be taken into account; but it leads in practice to the paradox that in many cases what seems to be in contemplation is the interest of one section only of the public, and a small section at that.

The same author goes on to point out that courses of action permitted at one time are now forbidden on grounds of public policy such as the purchase of commissions in the army, and the consideration of public policy may change not only from century to century but from generation to generation and even in the same generation. And, further [at p. 95]:

> This variability of public policy is a stone in the edifice of the doctrine, and not a missile to be flung at it.... The march of civilization and the difficulty of ascertaining public opinion at any given time make it essential.

This author goes on to say at p. 97 that in ascertaining what is public policy at any time, one guide that Judges are certain to employ whenever it is available is statutory legislation *in pari materia.*

It will, therefore, be apposite to consider how statute law in the Province of Ontario affects medical care for the residents of this Province. To a considerable extent the evidence of Dr. Sherk shows how the implementation of the *Health Services Insurance Act,* which was passed in 1967 [1968-69 (Ont.), c. 43 (now R.S.O. 1970, c. 200)] has affected the medical practitioners. He stated that the problem of unpaid medical bills has virtually ceased to exist. The financial side of medical practice has been greatly improved.

Now the beneficial purpose of this legislation is to provide the widest medical care for the residents of the Province. Clearly this is in the public good. And I think it follows that the public are entitled to the widest choice in the selection of their medical practitioners.

In the light of this modern development, ex. 26 at the trial may have some special significance where in May, 1971, a resolution of the council of the Ontario Medical Association was passed as follows:

RESOLVED that the Ontario Medical Association disapproves the concept of restrictive covenants in the contracts of one physician with another.

A further feature to be considered is whether a restrictive covenant between medical people tends to further limit the right of the public to deal with a profession which has a strong monopoly position. I believe that it does and I think that to widen that monopoly would be injurious to the public.

The whole picture of medical care in Ontario has greatly changed in the years since 1952 where in *Mills et al. v. Gill,* [1952] O.R. 257, [1952] 3 D.L.R. 27, 16 C.P.R. 46, a restrictive covenant was upheld and, as Professor Winfield has said, changes in considerations of public policy can take place in a generation.

Turning now to the reasonableness of this covenant in 1967, it is to be noted that it reads:

Should the employment of the Party of the Second Part by the Parties of the First Part terminate for any reason whatsoever, the Party of the Second Part COVENANTS AND AGREES that he will not carry on the practice of medicine or surgery in any of its branches on his own account or in association with any other person or persons, or corporation, or in the employ of any such person or persons or corporation, within the said City of St. Catharines or within five miles of the limits thereof for a period of five years (5) thereafter.

It is plain from this that Dr. Horwitz could have been discharged at any time even after many years of service and would still be bound by his covenant. I consider this to be far too wide than was needed to protect the interest of the plaintiffs and I hold the covenant unenforceable on this ground.

On behalf of the defendant a number of other defences were raised which require findings of fact on my part.

. . .

It was said by Evershed, J., in *Routh et al. v. Jones,* [1947] 1 All E.R. 179 at p. 181, that what a covenantee is entitled to protection against is "competition flowing... from the intimacies and knowledge of the master's business acquired by the servant from the circumstances of his employment". It is difficult to discern what intimacies and knowledge the defendant acquired here. Dr. Sherk did not suggest that there were any secret processes in the work of himself and his co-plaintiffs that the defendant could have acquired. In fact, Dr. Sherk made it quite plain that what he objected to was that the defendant got to know the patients coming to the clinic and by reason of that acquaintance some of them followed the defendant when he left the clinic.

Secondly, the defendant argues that because the three plaintiffs were specialists in fields other than the defendant's specialty, they had no interest to protect. I find as a fact that Dr. Sherk and Dr. Rogers largely confined themselves to general surgery and Dr. Daugavietis was a specialist in internal medicine. I further find as a fact that one or two of the general practitioners in the clinic did some obstetrics. It is obvious, therefore, that the broad covenant which prohibits the defendant from practising any kind of medicine or surgery which would include obstetrics would mainly help the general practitioners in the clinic who did obstetrics but who are not parties to the contract. On this point, I would hold that the restraint is too broad and is not severable.

In this action there is a counterclaim for unpaid salary. I am satisfied that there would be no dispute about this but if there were, a reference can be had to the Master at St. Catharines.

The question of damages gives me some concern. The real threat of this action was to enforce the covenant. This, in my findings, fails on the ground of public policy and the further grounds of being unreasonable and too wide. For breaching or abandoning a contract which I have found to be unenforceable; I do not think I can award any damages to the plaintiffs. But, in any event, I would assess such damages at $7,500. Likewise, the matter of costs troubles me. However, the defendant has succeeded on the main issue and the action will, therefore, be dismissed with costs.

Action dismissed.

[Note: The case was affirmed, [1973] 1 O.R. 360, but on different grounds.]

QUESTIONS

1. Could you draft a clause which would have given the plaintiff what he wanted? Or, at least, as much as the law would allow?
2. What is the basis for the court's interference here?
3. What facts does the court consider in reaching its conclusion?

ESSO PETROLEUM CO. LTD. v. HARPER'S GARAGE (STOURPORT) LTD.

[1968] A.C. 269. House of Lords; Lords Reid, Morris, Hodson, Pearce and Wilberforce. (Only the judgment of Lord Reid is reproduced here.)

February 23, 1967. **Lord Reid.** My Lords, the appellants are a large company whose most important product is Esso petrol, most of which is sold by them to garages and filling stations for resale to the public. The respondent company own two garages: They contracted with the appellants under what are known as solus agreements and bound themselves for the periods of those agreements, inter alia, to sell at their garages Esso petrol and no other. When cheaper "cut price" petrol came on the market they began to sell it and ceased to sell Esso petrol. The appellants then raised two actions, now consolidated, to prevent this: they sought injunctions to restrain the respondents from buying otherwise than from them any motor fuel for resale at these garages. On March 17, 1955, Mocatta J. granted an injunction, but on appeal the Court of Appeal set aside this order on the ground that the ties in these agreements were in restraint of trade and were unenforceable. The appellants now maintain first that these ties were not in restraint of trade and secondly that, if they were, they were in the circumstances valid and enforceable.

The earlier agreement related to the Corner Garage, Stourport, and was to remain in force for 21 years from July 1, 1962. But, as the case with regard to it is complicated by there being a mortgage in security for money lent by the appellants to the respondents, I shall first consider the second agreement which related to the Mustow Green Garage near Kidderminster. This agreement was to remain in force for four years and five months from July 1, 1963. It appears that the appellants had a similar agreement with the previous owners of that garage and that this period was chosen because it was the unexpired period of that earlier agreement.

The main provisions of the Mustow Green agreement are that while it remained in force the respondents agreed to buy from the appellants their total requirements of motor fuels for resale at that garage and agreed to keep it open at all reasonable hours for the sale of Esso motor fuels and Esso motor oils, and in return the appellants agreed to sell to the respondents at their wholesale schedule price at the time of delivery, and to allow a rebate from that price of one penny farthing per gallon payable quarterly. There were a number of other provisions with regard to advertising, service at the garage, etc., which I shall not specify because they do not appear to me to assist in determining the questions at issue. But there are two other provisions which I must notice. If the respondents wished to dispose of the garage they were not to do so except to a person who agreed to be substituted for them for all purposes of this agreement. If the agreement is otherwise unobjectionable, I do not think that this provision can invalidate it, because it was only by some such means that the appellants could ensure that their petrol would continue to be sold at this garage for the full period of the agreement. The other is a provision for retail price maintenance which the appellants at that time inserted in all their numerous tieing agreements with garages and filling stations. Shortly before the present action was raised the appellants intimated that they would not enforce this clause against any of their tied customers. The respondents were in favour of retail price maintenance and their original defence was that this change of policy by the appellants entitled them to rescind the whole agreement for the tie. This defence was rejected by Mocatta J. and it has not been maintained before your Lordships.

So I can now turn to the first question in this appeal — whether this agreement is to be regarded in law as an agreement in restraint of trade. The law with regard to restraint of trade is of ancient origin. There are references to it in the Year Books and it seems to have received considerable attention in the time of Queen Elizabeth I. But the old cases lie within a narrow compass. It seems to have been common for an apprentice or a craftsman to agree with his master that he would not compete with him after leaving his service, and also for a trader who sold his business to agree that he would not thereafter compete with the purchaser of his business. But no early case was cited which did not fall within one or other of these categories. And even in recent times there have been surprisingly few reported cases falling outside these categories in which restraint of trade has been pleaded: we were informed by counsel that there are only about 40 English cases which can be traced. On the other hand, there is an immense body of authorities with regard to the two original categories. I have not found it an easy task to determine how far principles developed for the original categories have been or should be extended.

The most general statement with regard to restraint of trade is that of Lord Parker in *Attorney-General of the Commonwealth of Australia v. Adelaide Steamship Co. Ltd.*, [1913] A.C. 781, 794. He said:

> "Monopolies and contracts in restraint of trade have this in common, that they both, if enforced, involve a derogation from the common law right in virtue of which any member of the community may exercise any trade or business he pleases and in such manner as he thinks best in his own interests."

But that cannot have been intended to be a definition: all contracts in restraint of trade involve such a derogation but not all contracts involving such a derogation are contracts in restraint of trade. Whenever a man agrees to do something over a period he thereby puts it wholly or partly out of his power to "exercise any trade or business he pleases" during that period. He may enter into a contract of service or may agree to give his exclusive services to another: then during the period of the contract he is not entitled to engage in other business activities. But no one has ever suggested that such contracts are in restraint of trade except in very unusual circumstances, such as those in *Young v. Timmins,* (1831), 1 Cr. & J. 331, where the servant had agreed not to work for anyone else but might have been given no work and received no remuneration for considerable periods and thus have been deprived of a livelihood: the grounds of judgment may not now be correct but I think that the case was rightly decided.

That Lord Parker cannot have intended those words to be a definition is I think made clear by a passage lower on the same page of the report:

> "Contracts in restraint of trade were subject to somewhat different considerations. There is little doubt that the common law in the earlier stages of its growth treated *all*" (my italics) "such contracts as contracts of imperfect obligation, if not void for all purposes; they were said to be against public policy in the sense that it was deemed impolitic to enforce them."

He certainly never supposed that all contracts which by obliging a man to act in one way (for example, as a servant) prevented him from doing other things had ever been held to be of imperfect obligation or against public policy.

The leading case of *Nordenfelt v. Maxim Nordenfelt Guns & Ammunition Co. Ltd.*, [1894] A.C. 535, fell within the old categories, and it may be misleading to take the well-known passages out of context and try to apply them to cases of quite different nature. Lord Macnaghten said:

> "The public have an interest in every person's carrying on his trade freely: so has the individual. All interference with individual liberty of action in trading, and all restraints of trade of themselves, if there is nothing more, are contrary to public policy, and therefore void."

By "interference" he meant interference to which the individual had agreed by contract but I am sure that he did not mean to include all cases in which one party had "interfered" with the liberty of another by getting him to agree to give his whole time to the other party's affairs. He had said:

"In the age of Queen Elizabeth all restraints of trade, whatever they were, general or partial, were thought to be contrary to public policy, and therefore void."

So he only had in mind the two original kinds of case. There was no need in *Nordenfelt's* case to attempt to define other classes of case to which the doctrine of restraint would apply.

If a contract is within the class of contracts in restraint of trade the law which applies to it is quite different from the law which applies to contracts generally. In general unless a contract is vitiated by duress, fraud or mistake its terms will be enforced though unreasonable or even harsh and unconscionable, but here a term in restraint of trade will not be enforced unless it is reasonable. And in the ordinary case the court will not remake a contract: unless in the special case where the contract is severable, it will not strike out one provision as unenforceable and enforce the rest. But here the party who has been paid for agreeing to the restraint may be unjustly enriched if the court holds the restraint to be too wide to be enforceable and is unable to adjust the consideration given by the other party.

It is much too late now to say that this rather anomalous doctrine of restraint of trade can be confined to the two classes of case to which it was originally applied. But the cases outside these two classes afford little guidance as to the circumstances in which it should be applied. In some it has been assumed that the doctrine applies and the controversy has been whether the restraint was reasonable. And in others where one might have expected the point to be taken it was not taken, perhaps because counsel thought that there was no chance of the court holding that the restraint was too wide to be reasonable. . . .

The main argument submitted for the appellant on this matter was that restraint of trade means a personal restraint and does not apply to a restraint on the use of a particular piece of land. Otherwise, it was said, every covenant running with the land which prevents its use for all or for some trading purposes would be a covenant in restraint of trade and therefore unenforceable unless it could be shown to be reasonable and for the protection of some legitimate interest. It was said that the present agreement only prevents the sale of petrol from other suppliers on the site of the Mustow Green Garage: It leaves the respondents free to trade anywhere else in any way they choose. But in many cases a trader trading at a particular place does not have the resources to enable him to begin trading elsewhere as well, and if he did he might find it difficult to find another suitable garage for sale or to get planning permission to open a new filling station on another site. As the whole doctrine of restraint of trade is based on public policy its application ought to depend less on legal niceties or theoretical possibilities than on the practical effect of a restraint in hampering that freedom which it is the policy of the law to protect.

It is true that it would be an innovation to hold that ordinary negative covenants preventing the use of a particular site for trading of all kinds or of a particular kind are within the scope of the doctrine of restraint of trade. I do not think they are. Restraint of trade appears to me to imply that a man contracts to give up some freedom which otherwise he would have had. A person buying or leasing land had no previous right to be there at all, let alone to trade there, and when he takes possession of that land subject to a negative restrictive covenant he gives up no right or freedom which he previously had. I think that the "tied house" cases might be explained in this way, apart from *Biggs v. Hoddinott*, [1898] 2 Ch. 307, where the owner of a freehouse had agreed to a tie in favour of a brewer who had lent him money. Restraint of trade was not pleaded. If it had been, the restraint would probably have been held to be reasonable. But there is some difficulty if a restraint in a lease not merely prevents the person who takes possession of the land under the lease from doing certain things there, but also obliges him to act in a particular way. In the present case the respondents before they made this agreement were entitled to use this land in any lawful way they chose, and by making this agreement they agreed to restrict their right by giving up their right to sell there petrol not supplied by the appellants.

In my view this agreement is within the scope of the doctrine of restraint of trade as it had been developed in English law. Not only have the respondents agreed negatively not to sell other petrol but they have agreed positively to keep this garage open for the sale of the appellants' petrol at all reasonable hours throughout the period of the tie. It was argued that this was merely regulating the respondent's trading and rather promoting than restraining his trade. But regulating a person's existing trade may be a greater restraint than prohibiting him from engaging in a new trade. And a contract to take one's whole supply from one source may be much more hampering than a contract to sell one's whole output to one buyer. I would not attempt to define the dividing line between contracts which are and contracts which are not in restraint of trade, but in my view this contract must be held to be in restraint of trade. So it is necessary to consider whether its provisions can be justified.

But before considering this question I must deal briefly with the other agreement tying the Corner Garage for 21 years. The rebate and other advantages to the respondents were similar to those in the Mustow Green agreement but in addition the appellants made a loan of £7,000 to the respondents to enable them to improve their garage and this loan was to be repaid over the 21 years of the tie. In security they took a mortgage of this garage. The agreement provided that the loan should not be paid off earlier than at the dates stipulated. But the respondents now tender the unpaid balance of the loan and they say that the appellants have no interest to refuse to accept repayment now, except in order to maintain the tie for the full 21 years.

The appellants argue that the fact that there is a mortgage excludes any application of the doctrine of restraint of trade. But I agree with your Lordships in rejecting that argument. I am prepared to assume that, if the respondents had not offered to repay the loan so far as it is still outstanding, the appellants would have been entitled to retain the tie. But, as they have tendered repayment, I do not think that the existence of the loan and the mortgage puts the appellants in any stronger position to maintain the tie than they would have been in if the original agreements had permitted repayment at an earlier date. The appellants must show that in the circumstances when the agreement was made a tie for 21 years was justifiable.

It is now generally accepted that a provision in a contract which is to be regarded as in restraint of trade must be justified if it is to be enforceable, and that the law on this matter was correctly stated by Lord Macnaghten in the *Nordenfelt* case. He said:

"... restraints of trade and interference with individual liberty of action may be

justified by the special circumstances of a particular case. It is a sufficient justification, and indeed it is the only justification, if the restriction is reasonable —
reasonable, that is, in reference to the interests of the parties concerned and reasonable in reference to the interests of the public, so framed and so guarded as
to afford adequate protection to the party in whose favour it is imposed, while at
the same time it is in no way injurious to the public."

So in every case it is necessary to consider first whether the restraint went
farther than to afford adequate protection to the party in whose favour it
was granted, secondly whether it can be justified as being in the interests of
the party restrained, and, thirdly, whether it must be held contrary to the
public interest. I find it difficult to agree with the way in which the court
has in some cases treated the interests of the party restrained. Surely it can
never be in the interest of a person to agree to suffer a restraint unless he
gets some compensating advantage, direct or indirect. And Lord Macnaghten said: "... of course the quantum of consideration may enter into
the question of the reasonableness of the contract."

Where two experienced traders are bargaining on equal terms and one
has agreed to a restraint for reasons which seem good to him the court is in
grave danger of stultifying itself if it says that it knows that trader's interest
better than he does himself. But there may well be cases where, although the
party to be restrained has deliberately accepted the main terms of the contract, he has been at a disadvantage as regards other terms: for example
where a set of conditions has been incorporated which has not been the
subject of negotiation — there the court may have greater freedom to hold
them unreasonable.

I think that in some cases where the court has held that a restraint was
not in the interests of the parties it would have been more correct to hold
that the restraint was against the public interest. For example, in *Kores
Manufacturing Co. Ltd. v. Kolok Manufacturing Co. Ltd.*, [1959] Ch. 108, the
parties had agreed that neither would employ any man who had left the service of the other. From their own points of view there was probably very
good reason for that. But it could well be held to be against the public interest to interfere in this way with the freedom of their employees. If the parties chose to abide by their agreement an employee would have no more
right to complain than the Mogul Company had in the *Mogul* case, [1892]
A.C. 25. But the law would not countenance their agreement by enforcing
it. And in cases where a party, who is in no way at a disadvantage in bargaining, chooses to take a calculated risk, I see no reason why the court
should say that he has acted against his own interests: but it can say that
the restraint might well produce a situation which would be contrary to the
public interest.

Again, whether or not a restraint is in the personal interests of the parties, it is I think well established that the court will not enforce a restraint
which goes further than affording adequate protection to the legitimate
interests of the party in whose favour it is granted. This must I think be
because too wide a restraint is against the public interest. It has often been
said that a person is not entitled to be protected against mere competition. I
do not find that very helpful in a case like the present. I think it better to
ascertain what were the legitimate interests of the appellants which they
were entitled to protect and then to see whether these restraints were more
than adequate for that purpose.

What were the appellants' legitimate interests must depend largely on what was the state of affairs in their business and with regard to the distribution and sale of petrol generally. And those are questions of fact to be answered by evidence or common knowledge. In the present case restraint of trade was not pleaded originally and the appellants only received notice that it was to be raised a fortnight before the trial. They may have been wise in not seeking a postponement of the trial when the pleadings were amended. But the result has been that the evidence on this matter is scanty. I think however that it is legitimate to supplement it from the considerable body of reported cases regarding solus agreements and from the facts found in the Report of the Monopolies Commission of July, 1965.

When petrol rationing came to an end in 1950 the large producers began to make agreements, now known as solus agreements, with garage owners under which the garage owner, in return for certain advantages, agreed to sell only the petrol of the producer with whom he made the agreement. Within a short time three-quarters of the filling stations in this country were tied in that way and by the dates of the agreements in this case over 90 per cent had agreed to ties. It appears that the garage owners were not at a disadvantage in bargaining with the large producing companies as there was intense competition between these companies to obtain these ties. So we can assume that both the garage owners and the companies thought that such ties were to their advantage. And it is not said in this case that all ties are either against the public interest or against the interests of the parties. The respondents' case is that the ties with which we are concerned are for too long periods.

The advantage to the garage owner is that he gets a rebate on the wholesale price of the petrol which he buys and also may get other benefits or financial assistance. The main advantages for the producing company appear to be that distribution is made easier and more economical and that it is assured of a steady outlet for its petrol over a period. As regards distribution, it appears that there were some 35,000 filling stations in this country at the relevant time, of which about a fifth were tied to the appellants. So they only have to distribute to some 7,000 filling stations instead of to a very much larger number if most filling stations sold several brands of petrol. But the main reason why the producing companies want ties for five years and more, instead of ties for one or two years only, seems to be that they can organise their business better if on the average only one-fifth or less of their ties come to an end in any one year. The appellants make a point of the fact that they have invested some £200 millions in refineries and other plant and that they could not have done that unless they could foresee a steady and assured level of sales of their petrol. Most of their ties appear to have been made for periods of between five and 20 years. But we have no evidence as to the precise additional advantage which they derive from a five-year tie as compared with a two-year tie or from a 20-year tie as compared with a five-year tie.

The Court of Appeal held that these ties were for unreasonably long periods. They thought that, if for any reason the respondents ceased to sell the appellants' petrol, the appellants could have found other suitable outlets in the neighbourhood within two or three years. I do not think that that is the right test. In the first place there was no evidence about this and I do not think that it would be practicable to apply this test in practice. It might happen that when the respondents ceased to sell their petrol, the appellants would find such an alternative outlet in a very short time. But, looking to the fact that well over 90 per cent of existing filling stations are tied and that there may be great difficulty in opening a new filling station, it might take a very long time to find an alternative. Any estimate of how long it might take to find suitable alternatives for the respondents' filling stations could be little better than guesswork.

I do not think that the appellants' interest can be regarded so narrowly. They are not so much concerned with any particular outlet as with maintaining a stable system of distribution throughout the country so as to enable their business to be run efficiently and economically. In my view there is sufficient material to justify a decision that ties of less than five years were insufficient, in the circumstances of the trade when these agreements were made, to afford adequate protection to the appellants' legitimate interests. And if that is so I cannot find anything in the details of the Mustow Green agreement which would indicate that it is unreasonable. It is true that if some of the provisions were operated by the appellants in a manner which would be commercially unreasonable they might put the respondents in difficulties. But I think that a court must have regard to the fact that the appellants must act in such a way that they will be able to obtain renewals of the great majority of their very numerous ties, some of which will come to an end almost every week. If in such circumstances a garage owner chooses to rely on the commercial probity and good sense of the producer, I do not think that a court should hold his agreement unreasonable because it is legally capable of some misuse. I would therefore allow the appeal as regards the Mustow Green agreement.

But the Corner Garage agreement involves much more difficulty. Taking first the legitimate interests of the appellants, a new argument was submitted to your Lordships that, apart from any question of security for their loan, it would be unfair to the appellants if the respondents, having used the appellants' money to build up their business, were entitled after a comparatively short time to be free to seek better terms from a competing producer. But there is no material on which I can assess the strength of this argument and I do not find myself in a position to determine whether it has any validity. A tie for 21 years stretches far beyond any period for which developments are reasonably foreseeable. Restrictions on the garage owner which might seem tolerable and reasonable in reasonably foreseeable conditions might come to have a very different effect in quite different conditions: the public interest comes in here more strongly. And, apart from a case where he gets a loan, a garage owner appears to get no greater advantage from a 20-year tie than he gets from a five-year tie. So I would think that there must at least be some clearly established advantage to the producing company — something to show that a shorter period would not be adequate — before so long a period could be justified. But in this case there is no evidence to prove anything of the kind. And the other material which I have thought it right to consider does not appear to me to assist the appellant here. I would therefore dismiss the appeal as regards the Corner Garage agreement.

I would add that the decision in this case — particularly in view of the paucity of evidence — ought not, in my view, to be regarded as laying down any general rule as to the length of tie permissible in a solus agreement....

But I must not be taken as expressing any opinion as to the validity of ties for periods mid-way between the two periods with which the present case is concerned.

[Appeal allowed in part.]

QUESTIONS

1. The economic effect of a decision such as this must be considerable. Did Lord Reid have enough information to make such a decision?

2. If he did not have enough information what should he have done? Does this case raise issues similar to those raised by *I.N.S. v. A.P.*?

In *Stephens v. Gulf Oil Canada Ltd.* (1976), 11 O.R. (2d) 129, the Ontario Court of Appeal upheld an arrangement under which Gulf had an irredeemable 10-year mortgage (and coterminous tie) and a right of first refusal to buy the land on which a service station was located. Howland J.A. said that the mortgage to Gulf could not be considered oppressive or unconscionable.

There is evidence that the effect of the decision in *Esso v. Harper's Garage* was to encourage oil companies to open up their own gas stations and have them run by employees. The result is that there are almost no independent gas dealers left in business.

SCHROEDER v. MACAULAY

[1974] 3 All E.R. 618. House of Lords; Lords Reid, Dilhorne, Diplock, Simon and Kilbrandon.

Lord Reid. My Lords, the appellants are publishers of music. The respondent is a writer of songs. On 12th July 1966 they entered into a somewhat elaborate agreement under which the appellants engaged the exclusive services of the respondent for a term of five years which in a certain event was to be extended to ten years. In 1970 the respondent raised the present action claiming a declaration that the agreement is contrary to public policy and void. He also made various alternative claims which your Lordships have found it unnecessary to consider. Plowman J. made the declaration claimed and his decision was affirmed by the Court of Appeal.

In 1966 the respondent was aged about 21. He and a Mr. McLeod had collaborated in writing a few songs, but it appears that none of them had been published. He obtained an interview with Mr. Schroeder who, with Mrs. Schroeder, controls an American music publishing corporation with world wide connections. The appellant company is a subsidiary of the corporation. The respondent wished to get a different kind of contract but agreed to sign this agreement which is in the appellants' standard form with a few alterations.

It is not disputed that the validity of the agreement must be determined as at the date when it was signed and it is therefore unnecessary to deal with the reasons why the respondent now wishes to be freed from it. The law with regard to the validity of agreements in restraint of trade was fully considered by this House in *Esso Petroleum Co Ltd v Harper's Garage* and I do not intend to restate the principles there set out or to add to or modify what

I said myself. I think that in a case like the present case two questions must be considered. Are the terms of the agreement so restrictive that either they cannot be justified at all or that they must be justified by the party seeking to enforce the agreement? Then, if there is room for justification, has that party proved justification — normally by shewing that the restrictions were no more than what was reasonably required to protect his legitimate interests. In this case evidence on the second question was scanty and I turn first to the terms of the agreement. The agreement contains 17 clauses. It must of course be read as a whole and we must consider the cumulative effect of the restrictions contained therein. I think it best to set it out in full omitting only those parts which deal with performing rights, because neither party founded on them in argument, and some formal matters. The relevant parts are as follows:

'1. Subject as hereinafter mentioned this Agreement shall remain in force for a period of FIVE (5) years from the date hereof (hereinafter called 'the said term').

'2. (a) The Publisher engages the exclusive services of the Composer and the Composer will render the same to the Publisher during the said term. (b) The Composer shall obey and comply with all lawful orders and directions in relation to his services hereunder given to him by the Publisher and shall use his best endeavours to promote the interests of the Publisher. (c) The Composer will not during the said term directly or indirectly work for render services or be affiliated to or be interested in or connected with any person firm or corporation engaged in the music publishing business other than the Publisher nor will he during the said term carry on or be concerned in whether alone or in partnership any music publishing business. (d) The Composer will not divulge to any person except as may be required by the Publisher any confidential information relating to the business of the Publisher.

'3. (a) The Composer HEREBY ASSIGNS to the Publisher the full copyright for the whole world in each and every original musical composition and/or lyric including but without prejudice to the generality of the foregoing the title words and music thereof written/or composed created or conceived by the Composer alone or in collaboration with any other person or persons and whether in his own name or under a nom-de-plume at any time during the said term or at any time prior to the date hereof insofar as such latter compositions and/or lyrics are still owned or controlled by the Composer directly or indirectly... (b) In this Agreement references to musical works and/or lyrics shall include the part or parts hereof (if separate and divisible) written composed created or conceived by the Composer...

'4. Where a musical composition and/or lyric to which this Agreement applies is a 'work of joint authorship' as defined by Section 11 of the Copyright Act 1956, the Composer will procure that his co-author or co-authors as the case may be will join with him in doing such acts and things and executing such deeds and documents as may be necessary to vest the copyright in the said work in the Publisher.

'5. In respect of each work hereinbefore referred to the copyrights in which has been assigned by the Composer and his collaborators (if any), the Publisher will pay to the Composer and his collaborators (if any); (a) on all piano copies sold and paid for (after the first 500 copies) in the United Kingdom of Great Britain and Northern Ireland and Eire a royalty of 10% of the marked selling price; (b) 50% of all net royalties received by the Publishers in respect of mechanical reproduction of the said works and of all net synchronisation fees; (c) in the event of the said works being published in any country outside the United Kingdom and Eire, 50% of the net royalties received by the Publisher from persons authorised to publish the said works in such foreign territories.

'6. (a) Fees in respect of performing rights shall be divided as to 50% to the Composer and his collaborators (if any) (hereinafter referred to as 'the Composer's Share') and 50% to the Publisher... (c) If the Composer shall be or become a member of P.R.S. and while he remains such member all performing fees shall be divided between the parties hereto in accordance with P.R.S. rules for the time being in force subject to the agreement of the parties hereinbefore contained varying the divisions as permitted by such rules so that 50% of such fees are for the Composer and his collaborators (if any) and 50% for the Publisher...

'8. (a) The Publisher shall pay the sum of £50 to the Composer, which shall be a general advance against royalties payable by the Publisher under this Agreement and to be recouped therefrom but in no case shall the Publisher be entitled to the return of any part of such sums. Upon the recoupment by the Publisher of said general advance payment of Fifty (£50) Pounds, the Publisher agrees to pay another Fifty (£50) Pounds, which is to be treated as a general advance as described herein. This same procedure shall continue throughout the said term hereof; i.e. as each general advance of Fifty (£50) Pounds is recouped in full by the Publisher, the Publisher shall pay to the Composer the sum of Fifty (£50) Pounds, etcetera. (b) The Publisher will render to the Composer semi annually statements showing the amount of royalties due to the Composer as at 31st December and 30th June in each year. Such statements shall be delivered within 60 days of the relevant date and shall be accompanied by a remittance for such sum (if any) as may be shown to be due to the Composer.

'9. (a) If during the said term the total of the Composer's royalties hereunder and all advances thereon (if any) shall equal or exceed £5000 then this agreement shall automatically be extended for a further period of FIVE (5) years and for the purpose of this Agreement the said period of FIVE (5) years shall be deemed to be included in and be part of the said term. (b) The Publisher may at any time during the said term terminate this Agreement by giving to the Composer one month's written notice to that effect. Such termination shall be without prejudice to the rights of the parties in respect of any antecedent breach of this Agreement and the Publisher's obligation to pay royalties hereinbefore provided for.

'10. (a) The Composer will forthwith submit to the Publisher every composition and/or lyric written and/or composed created or conceived by him alone or in collaboration. The Composer warrants to the Publisher that the copyright in all such works will pass to the Publisher free from any adverse claims or rights from any third party and that all such works submitted to the Publisher will be original work of the Composer and his collaborators (if any), (b) The Composer will indemnify the Publisher against all claims damages and demands and against all costs incurred in the institution or defence of any actions or proceedings relating to the said works submitted to the Publisher...

'12. (a) The Composer will execute a standard song writer's Agreement in respect of each and every work the subject of this Agreement. Such song writer's Agreement shall be in the form annexed hereto and initialled by the parties (hereinafter referred to as 'the song writer's Agreement'). (b) For the avoidance of doubt it is agreed that any assignment required under Clauses 4 or 12 hereof shall be in the form of the song writer's Agreement.

'13. In the event of any breach of the terms or conditions of this Agreement by the Composer the Publisher shall be entitled to suspend and withhold payment of royalties (including the general advances provided for in para. 8 hereinabove) until such breach has been remedied. If the Composer shall fail to remedy any such breach within One month of written notice by the Publisher requiring him so to do all royalties then or thereafter due under this Agreement shall cease to be or shall not become (as the case may be) payable...

'15. For the avoidance of any possible doubt and without in any way limiting the assignment hereinbefore contained it is hereby declared that the copyright hereby assigned includes: (a) the right to renew and extend the copyright and the ownership of such renewed and extended copyright. (b) the right to make and publish new adaptations and arrangements and to make such additions adaptations and alterations in and to the words and/or music as the Publisher may desire and to provide and translate the lyric thereof in any and all languages of the world.

'16. (a) The Publisher shall have the right to assign this Agreement and all rights and obligations hereunder to any person firm or corporation and shall also have the right to assign any or all rights in a particular work. (b) The Composer will not assign his rights under this Agreement without the Publisher's prior written consent.

'17. The Composer will at the Publisher's request at any time during the said term or thereafter execute any other document and do all other acts or things which may hereafter be required for vesting in the Publisher the rights and benefits hereby expressed to be assigned and conferred.'

Clauses 1 and 9(a) determine the duration of the agreement. It was to last for five years in any event and for ten years if the royalties for the first five years exceeded £5,000. There is little evidence about this extension. Five thousand pounds in five years appears to represent a very modest success, and so if the respondent's work became well known and popular he would be tied by the agreement for ten years. The duration of an agreement in restraint of trade is a factor of great importance in determining whether the restrictions in the agreement can be justified but there was no evidence as to why so long a period was necessary to protect the appellants' interest. Clause 2 requires the respondent to give the exclusive services to and obey all lawful orders of the appellants. It is not very clear what this means. Read in conjunction with cl 2(c) it probably does not prevent him from doing non-musical work so long as that does not interfere with his obligations to the appellants. I do not attach importance to this clause as being at all unduly restrictive. Clause 3 is of importance but I shall return to it later. Clauses 5 to 8 deal with remuneration. Some parts are not very clear but it was not argued that this was an unreasonable basis for the remuneration of a composer unknown when the agreement was made. Claude 9(b) entitles the appellants to terminate the agreement but there is no corresponding provision in favour of the respondent. I shall have to deal with this later. Clause 10(b) could be rather oppressive but no serious objection was taken to it and the same may be said of cl 13. Clause 16 appears to me to be important. There may sometimes be room for an argument that although on a strict literal construction restrictions could be enforced oppressively, one is entitled to have regard to the fact that a large organisation could not afford to act oppressively without damaging the goodwill of its business. But the power to assign leaves no room for that argument. We cannot assume that an assignee would always act reasonably.

The public interest requires in the interests both of the public and of the individual that everyone should be free so far as practicable to earn a livelihood and to give to the public the fruits of his particular abilities. The main question to be considered is whether and how far the operation of the terms of this agreement is likely to conflict with this objective. The respondent is bound to assign to the appellants during a long period the fruits of his musical talent. But what are the appellants bound to do with those fruits? Under the contract nothing. If they do use the songs which the respondent composes they must pay in terms of the contract. But they need not do so. As has been said they may put them in a drawer and leave them there. No doubt the expectation was that if the songs were of value they would be published to the advantage of both parties. But if for any reason the appellants chose not to publish them the respondent would get no remuneration and he could not do anything. Inevitably the respondent must take the risk of misjudgment of the merits of his work by the appellants. But that is not the only reason which might cause the appellants not to publish. There is no evidence about this so we must do the best we can with common knowledge. It does not seem fanciful and it was not argued that it is fanciful to suppose that purely commercial consideration might cause a publisher to refrain from publishing and promoting promising material. He might think it likely to be more profitable to promote work by other composers with whom he had agreements and unwise or too expensive to try to publish and popularise the respondent's work in addition. And there is always the possibility that less legitimate reasons might influence a decision to not to publish the respondent's work.

It was argued that there must be read into this agreement an obligation on the publisher to act in good faith. I take that to mean that he would be in breach of contract if by reason of some oblique or malicious motive he refrained from publishing work which he would otherwise have published. I very much doubt this but even if it were so it would make little difference. Such a case would seldom occur and then would be difficult to prove.

I agree with the appellants' argument to this extent. I do not think that a publisher could reasonably be expected to enter into any positive commitment to publish future work by an unknown composer. Possibly there might be some general undertaking to use his best endeavours to promote the composer's work. But that would probably have to be in such general terms as to be of little use to the composer.

But if no satisfactory positive undertaking by the publisher can be devised, it appears to me to be an unreasonable restraint to tie the composer for this period of years so that his work will be sterilised and he can earn nothing from his abilities as a composer if the publisher chooses not to publish. If there had been in cl 9 any provision entitling the composer to terminate the agreement in such an event the case might have had a very different appearance. But as the agreement stands not only is the composer tied but he cannot recover the copyright of the work which the publisher refuses to publish.

It was strenuously argued that the agreement is in standard form, that it has stood the test of time, and that there is no indication that it ever causes injustice. Reference was made to passages in the speeches of Lord Pearce and Lord Wilberforce in the *Esso* case with which I wholly agree. Lord Pearce said:

> 'It is important that the court, in weighing the question of reasonableness, should give full weight to commercial practices and to the generality of contracts made freely by parties bargaining on equal terms.'

Later Lord Wilberforce said:

> 'The development of the law does seem to show, however, that judges have been able to dispense from the necessity of justification under a public policy test of reasonableness such contracts or provisions of contracts as, under contemporary conditions, may be found to have passed into the accepted and normal currency of commercial or contractual or conveyancing relations. That such contracts have done so may be taken to show with at least strong prima force that, moulded under the pressures of negotiation, competition and public opinion, they have assumed a form which satisfies the test of public policy as understood

by the courts at the time, or, regarding the matter from the point of view of the trade, that the trade in question has assumed such a form that for its health or expansion it requires a degree of regulation.'

But those passages refer to contracts 'made freely by parties bargaining on equal terms' or 'moulded under the pressures of negotiation, competition and public opinion'. I do not find from any evidence in this case, nor does it seem probable, that this form of contract made between a publisher and an unknown composer has been moulded by any pressure of negotiation. Indeed, it appears that established composers who can bargain on equal terms can and do make their own contracts.

Any contract by which a person engages to give his exclusive services to another for a period necessarily involves extensive restriction during that period of the common law right to exercise any lawful activity he chooses in such manner as he thinks best. Normally the doctrine of restraint of trade has no application to such restrictions: they require no justification. But if contractual restrictions appear to be unnecessary or to be reasonably capable of enforcement in an oppressive manner, then they must be justified before they can be enforced.

In the present case the respondent assigned to the appellants 'the full copyright for the whole world' in every musical composition 'composed created or conceived' by him alone or in collaboration with any other person during a period of five or it might be ten years. He received no payment (apart from an initial £50) unless his work was published and the appellants need not publish unless they chose to do so. And if they did not publish he had no right to terminate the agreement or to have any copyrights re-assigned to him. I need not consider whether in any circumstances it would be possible to justify such a one-sided agreement. It is sufficient to say that such evidence as there is falls far short of justification. It must therefore follow that the agreement so far as unperformed is unenforceable.

I would dismiss this appeal.

Viscount Dilhorne. My Lords, I have had the advantage of reading the speech of my noble and learned friend, Lord Reid, in draft. I agree with it and for the reasons he gives, I too, would dismiss this appeal.

Lord Diplock. My Lords, the contract under consideration in this appeal is one whereby the respondent accepted restrictions on the way in which he would exploit his earning power as a song-writer for the next ten years. Because this can be classified as a contract in restraint of trade the restrictions that the respondent accepted fell within one of those limited categories of contractual promises in respect of which the courts still retain the power to relieve the promisor of his legal duty to fulfil them. In order to determine whether this case is one in which that power ought to be exercised, what your Lordships have in fact been doing has been to assess the relative bargaining power of the publisher and the song-writer at the time the contract was made and to decide whether the publisher had used his superior bargaining power to exact from the song-writer promises that were unfairly onerous to him. Your Lordships have not been concerned to enquire whether the public have in fact been deprived of the fruit of the song-writer's talents by reason of the restrictions, nor to assess the likelihood that they would be so deprived in the future if the contract were permitted to run its full course.

It is, in my view, salutory to acknowledge that in refusing to enforce provisions of a contract whereby one party agrees for the benefit of the other party to exploit or to refrain from exploiting his own earning-power, the public policy which the court is implementing is not some 19th century economic theory about the benefit to the general public of freedom of trade, but the protection of those whose bargaining power is weak against being forced by those whose bargaining power is stronger to enter into bargains that are unconscionable. Under the influence of Bentham and of laissez-faire the courts in the 19th century abandoned the practice of applying the public policy against unconscionable bargains to contracts generally, as they had formerly done to any contract considered to be usurious; but the policy survived in its application to penalty clauses and to relief against forfeiture and also to the special category of contracts in restraint of trade. If one looks at the reasoning of 19th century judges in cases about contracts in restraint of trade one finds lip service paid to current economic theories but if one looks at what they said in the light of what they did, one finds that they struck down a bargain if they thought it was unconscionable as between the parties to it, and upheld it if they thought that it was not.

So I would hold that the question to be answered as respects a contract in restraint of trade of the kind with which this appeal is concerned is: was the bargain fair? The test of fairness is, no doubt, whether the restrictions are both reasonably necessary for the protection of the legitimate interests of the promisee and commensurate with the benefits secured to the promisor under the contract. For the purpose of this test all the provisions of the contract must be taken into consideration.

My Lords, the provisions of the contract have already been sufficiently stated by my noble and learned friend, Lord Reid. I agree with his analysis of them and with his conclusion that the contract is unenforceable. It does not satisfy the test of fairness as I have endeavoured to state it. I will accordingly content myself with adding some observations directed to the argument that because the contract was in a 'standard form' in common use between music publishers and song-writers, the restraints that it imposes on the song-writer's liberty to exploit his talents must be presumed to be fair and reasonable.

Standard forms of contracts are of two kinds. The first, of very ancient origin, are those which set out the terms on which mercantile transactions of common occurrence are to be carried out. Examples are bills of lading, charterparties, policies of insurance, contracts of sale in the commodity markets. The standard clauses in these contracts have been settled over the years by negotiation by representatives of the commercial interests involved and have been widely adopted because experience has shown that they facilitate the conduct of trade. Contracts of these kinds affect not only the actual parties to them but also others who may have a commercial interest in the transactions to which they relate, as buyers or sellers, charterers or shipowners, insurers or bankers. If fairness or reasonableness were relevant to their enforceability the fact that they are widely used by parties whose bargaining power is fairly matched would raise a strong presumption that their terms are fair and reasonable.

The same presumption, however, does not apply to the other kind of standard form of contract. This is of comparatively modern origin. It is the result of the concentration of particular kinds of business in relatively few hands. The ticket cases in the 19th century provide what are probably the first examples. The terms of this kind of standard form of contract have not been the subject of negotiation between the parties to it, or approved by any organisation representing the interests of the weaker party. They have been dictated by that party whose bargaining power, either exercised alone or in conjunction with other providing similar goods or services, enables him to say: 'If you want these goods or services at all, these are the only terms on which they are obtainable. Take it or leave it.'

To be in a position to adopt this attitude towards a party desirous of entering into a contract to obtain goods or services provides a classic instance of superior bargaining power. It is not without significance that on the evidence in the present case, music publishers in negotiating with song-writers whose success has been already established do not insist on adhering to a contract in the standard form they offered to the respondent. The fact that the appellants' bargaining power vis-à-vis the respondent was strong enough to enable them to adopt this take-it-or-leave it attitude raises no presumption that they used it to drive an unconscionable bargain with him, but in the field of restraint of trade it calls for vigilance on the part of the court to see that they did not.

Lord Simon of Glaisdale. My Lords, I have had the advantage of reading in draft the speeches prepared by my noble and learned friends, Lord Reid and Lord Diplock. I agree with them and I would therefore dismiss this appeal.

Lord Kilbrandon. My Lords, I have had the advantage of reading the speeches prepared by my noble and learned friends, Lord Reid and Lord Diplock. I agree with their conclusions, and like them would dismiss this appeal.

Appeal dismissed.

QUESTIONS

1. Lord Diplock divides standard form contracts into two classes.
(a) Was there any evidence led concerning the validity of this classification?
(b) Does this classification bind future courts?
(c) Is it right? To what extent is the power to impose terms necessarily dependant on monopoly power? Do Kessler and Havighurst in the extracts at the beginning of this chapter support Lord Diplock's conclusions?
2. Redraft the contract in *Schroeder v. Macaulay* to give the publisher what it needs.
3. Would counsel for Schroeder weaken or strengthen his case by showing that Schroeder's standard form is essentially standard throughout the industry in cases of unknown composers?

Many of the factual assumptions of the House of Lords are challenged by Trebilcock, "The Doctrine of Inequality of Bargaining Power: Post-Benthamite Economics in the House of Lords" (1976), 26 U.T.L.J. 359.

Trebilcock states that in the U.K. in 1975-76 there were 428 music publishers: 276 record and tape manufacturers/distributors/ importers and 54 independent record producers. All the evidence, both in the U.K. and elsewhere, indicates a highly competitive market.

E. The Legislative Response

We have so far concentrated almost entirely on the development of the law of contract through the courts. The impact of legislation in this area is growing and may be expected to increase still further in the future. There has, of course, been legislation in regard to contracts for a long time. The Statute of Frauds is 300 years old, and the Sale of Goods Act has been in force, in England at least, for nearly 85 years. The impact of legislation like this has been minimal on basic contract doctrine. All of the provisions of the Sale of Goods Act that appear to offer some protection to the buyer can be contracted out of, and the Act never attempted to do more than codify the existing law. The U.C.C., on the other hand, has had far more of an impact on the basic rules of contracts and these have been modified where the Code applies (e.g., § 2-207 and the Battle of the Forms).

Legislative development in Canada is beginning to have an impact on the basic rules of contracts. We shall examine the possible impact of legislation in tracing the problems that can arise in the case of a simple, common consumer transaction: the purchase of a used car.

Allcars Ltd. is a company owned by Sarah and Bruce Ovlov. The company is in the business of selling used cars. To get set up in business the Ovlov's had to have the company incorporated under the Ontario Business Corporations Act. They also had to obtain licences to carry on a business from the City of Toronto and the Ontario Ministry of Revenue (under the Retail Sales Tax Act). Since the business of Allcars was the buying and selling of used cars, the company and all its sales-people had to be registered under the Motor Vehicle Dealers Act, R.S.O. 1970, c. 475 (formerly The Used Car Dealers Act). That Act provides:

> 1. In this Act...
> (cb) 'motor vehicle dealer' means a person who carries on the business of buying or selling motor vehicles, whether for his own account or the account of any other person, or who holds himself out as carrying on the business of buying or selling motor vehicles.
> . . .
> 3. (1) No person shall,
> (a) carry on business as a motor vehicle dealer unless he is registered under this Act; or
> (b) act as a salesman of or on behalf of a motor vehicle dealer unless he is registered as a salesman of such dealer and such dealer is registered as a motor vehicle dealer under this Act.
> . . .
> 4. A motor vehicle dealer shall not retain the services of a salesman who is not registered under this Act.

These sections make sure that anyone who is involved in the new or used car business comes under the Act. There are criminal penalties provided for violation of the Act. These are:

> 33. — (1) Every person who, knowingly,
> (a)   furnishes false information in any application under this Act or in any statement or return required to be furnished under this Act or the regulations;
> (b)   fails to comply with any order, direction or other requirement made under this Act; or
> (c)   contravenes any provision of this Act or the regulations,

and every director or officer of a corporation who knowingly concurs in such furnishing, failure or contravention is guilty of an offence and on summary conviction is liable to a fine of not more than $2,000 or to imprisonment for a term of not more than one year, or to both.

(2) Where a corporation is convicted of an offence under subsection 1, the maximum penalty that may be imposed upon the corporation is $25,000 and not as provided therein...."

The Act goes on to control the conduct of motor vehicle dealers.

5. — (1) An applicant is entitled to registration or renewal of registration by the Registrar except where,

(a)   having regard to his financial position, the applicant cannot reasonably be expected to be financially responsible in the conduct of his business; or

(b)   the past conduct of the applicant affords reasonable grounds for relief that he will not carry on business in accordance with law and with integrity and honesty; or

(c)   the applicant is a corporation and,

    (i)   having regard to its financial position, it cannot reasonably be expected to be financially responsible in the conduct of its business, or

    (ii)   the past conduct of its officers or directors affords reasonable grounds for belief that its business will not be carried on in accordance with law and with integrity and honesty; or

(d)   the applicant is carrying on activities that are, or will be, if the applicant is registered, in contravention of this Act or the regulations.

(2) A registration is subject to such terms and conditions to give effect to the purposes of this Act as are consented to by the applicant, imposed by the Tribunal or prescribed by the regulations.

6. — (1) Subject to section 7, the Registrar may refuse to register an application where in the Registrar's opinion the applicant is disentitled to registration under section 5.

(2) Subject to section 7, the Registrar may refuse to renew or may suspend or revoke a registration for any reason that would disentitle the registrant to registration under section 5 if he were an applicant, or where the registrant is in breach of a term or condition of the registration.

7. — (1) Where the Registrar proposes to refuse to grant or renew a registration or proposes to suspend or revoke a registration, he shall serve notice of his proposal, together with written reasons therefor, on the applicant or registrant....

The power given to the Registrar under these two sections to control the used car business is extensive. Obviously, the penalty for fraud by a used car dealer is far more serious than for the ordinary person, since cancellation of registration puts the dealer out of business. The ways in which the Registrar can exercise this power and the procedures that must be followed before registration can be cancelled or refused, involve several aspects of administrative law. The details of this do not concern us here. What is important is that the power to cancel a dealer's registration is a very potent one. Thus in one case where a dealer had, in violation of Regulation 19(2) under the Motor Vehicle Dealers Act, turned back the odometers on 48 cars for a total of over 1,000,000 miles, the Court of Appeal suspended the dealer's registration for three months. The case came to the Court of Appeal on appeal from the Commercial Registration Appeal Tribunal. The Tribunal had, in effect, put the dealer on probation, by ordering that the dealer's registration would be suspended if the dealer did not behave himself. The Court of Appeal said: (*Re Registrar of Used Car Dealers and Rowe Motors Ltd.* (1972), 31 D.L.R. (3d) 35, 38-40).

"The powers of this Court on an appeal of this kind are set out in s. 19 of The Used Car Dealers Act, and in part s-s. (3) of s. 19 provides:

(3)... the court may confirm or alter the decision of the Tribunal or direct the Registrar or the Tribunal to do any act the Registrar or the Tribunal is authorized to do under this Act and as the court considers proper, and the court may substitute its opinion for that of the Registrar and the Tribunal and may exercise the same powers as it exercises on an appeal from a judge of the High Court sitting without a jury.

"At first reading this would appear to confer upon this Court very broad powers indeed. However, the circumstances under which this Court exercises its jurisdiction on an appeal from a Judge of the High Court sitting without a jury are well known and the principles on which the jurisdiction is exercised have been settled for many years. In so far as they are relevant to the circumstances of this appeal, the principle is, and we apply it here, that we ought not to interfere with an exercise of the discretionary power by the Tribunal from which the appeal is brought unless we are satisfied that that discretion has been exercised on a wrong principle. In this case, we are so satisfied.

"In our view, the statute and the Regulations were passed in the interest of, and for the protection of, the public. Their enforcement, in our view, would be greatly hampered by a decision which in effect imposed a penalty of 'probation' with terms, which for practical purposes have no meaning at all, in a case where very serious offences, numerous in themselves, and, it seems to us, obviously important to the public, were shown to have been committed by the dealership whose registration is under question.

"Some analogy and assistance is gained from the decision of Chief Justice Robertson in *Re Securities Act and Morton*, [1946] O.R. 492, [1946] 3 D.L.R. 724, cited to us on this appeal, but in another connection. At p. 494 O.R., p. 726 D.L.R., Robertson, C.J.O., said:

'The Commission is to suspend or cancel a registration where, in its opinion, such action is in the public interest: s. 10. A registered broker or salesman has no vested interest that is to be weighed in the balance against the public interest. I have no doubt the Commission will, on proper occasions, give consideration to the possible serious consequences of taking away a man's livelihood, and of making the business of a broker or salesman a precarious occupation. Such considerations may have their proper place in determining what is in the public interest. It is, however, the public interest that is to be served by the Commission, and not private interests or the interests of any profession or business, in the exercise of the Commission's powers of suspension or cancellation of the registration of any broker or salesman.'

"We have, in this case, given anxious consideration to what the late Chief Justice referred to as 'the possible serious consequences of taking away a man's livelihood', and we have further given consideration to the effect on the persons employed in, or associated with the business. It would appear that two members of the family of Mr. Rowe are employed in the business and three others are members of its board of directors. In addition, it appears to have six employees in what is described as its garage, and some 10 men who might otherwise be unemployed, who are employed on an average of three days a week to drive cars from one location to another. Notwithstanding this, it is the opinion of all members of the Court that if this appeal had been brought before us as it should have been, in April or May of this year, in other words within a reasonable time after the transcript of evidence was available, it would have been proper on our part to set aside the order of the Tribunal and to impose a suspension of the registration of both the company and Mr. Rowe for a period of six months. However, the appeal was not brought properly forward and Mr. Charlton candidly says that he cannot put to us any legitimate excuse for this being the case. In the circumstances, therefore, we have decided in the exercise of our discretion, that the appropriate period of suspension should be three months and that in order to give the dealer a reasonable opportunity to arrange his affairs with this in mind, the period of suspension will commence on November 15, 1972.

"In view of the order which we are making, we do not find it necessary to decide whether, having regard to its statutory powers quoted above, the Tribunal has the power to make the kind of order which it made.

"The appeal will therefore be allowed and the order of the Tribunal will be set aside and in lieu thereof there will be substituted an order that the registration of Robert Rowe Motors Limited as a dealer and Robert Hugh Rowe as a salesman be suspended for a period of three months commencing November 15, 1972."

The various purchasers from Rowe Motors Ltd. may have had actions against it for breach of warranty or fraud, but the chances of any action being brought or, if brought, being successful, would have been so low that no effective deterrent would have existed. On the other hand, the threat of loss of livelihood may be a far more effective deterrent. The requirement of licensing or registration is a very common requirement now, and provides the possibility of very effective control of any form of activity.

There are various other problems that face the car dealer. The Act requires a bond in the amount of $5,000 to be supplied by a dealer before the dealer can be registered. The bond may be declared forfeited by the Registrar under s. 7 of the Regulations:

7. The Registrar may declare any bond mentioned in section 3 forfeited,
(a) where a motor vehicle dealer, including any member of a partnership, in respect of whose conduct the bond has been conditioned, has been convicted of,
(i)   an offence under the Act, or
(ii)   an offence involving fraud or theft or conspiracy to commit an offence involving fraud or theft under the *Criminal Code* (Canada), and the conviction has become final.
(b) where proceedings by or in respect of a motor vehicle dealer, including any member of a partnership, in respect of whose conduct the bond has been conditioned, have been taken under the *Bankruptcy Act* (Canada), either by way of assignment or by petition, or where proceedings have been taken by way of winding up, and in the case of a petition, a receiving order under the *Bankruptcy Act* (Canada), or a winding-up order has been made, and the order has become final.
(c) where a judgment based on a finding of fraud has been given against a motor vehicle dealer, including any member of a partnership, in respect of whose conduct the bond has been conditioned and the judgment has become final; or
(d) where judgment has been given against a motor vehicle dealer, including any member of a partnership, in respect of whose conduct the bond has been conditioned, on any claim arising out of a transaction involving a motor vehicle, other than a judgment against the motor vehicle dealer in favour of a salesman or other motor vehicle dealer, and the judgment has remained unsatisfied for a period of ninety days,
and thereupon the amount thereof becomes due and owing by the person bound thereby as a debt due the Crown in right of Ontario.

These provisions increase the possible penalty that may be incurred by a motor vehicle dealer by helping to ensure that people who have claims against the dealer have at least some of his assets to go against.

Once the dealer is set up in business and has obtained his registration, he has to make some sales. Typically he does this by advertising. The common law attitude to advertising is fairly casual. Generally, what is said in an advertisement is regarded as a "mere puff" and is not part of the contract. There is, of course, nothing to prevent an advertisement being regarded as part of the contract (as in *Carlill v. Carbolic Smoke Ball* (*supra*) or *Lefkowitz v. Great Minneapolis Surplus Store* (*supra*) but those are exceptional cases. More recently in Ontario, what was said in advertisements has been used as a factor in imposing liability (*Ranger v. Herbert Watts Ltd.* (*supra*) and *Babcock v. Servacar Ltd.*, [1970] 1 O.R. 125). The test is now probably going to be that laid down in *Heilbut, Symons v. Buckleton* (*supra*) as interpreted by Lord Denning in *Dick Bentley Productions Ltd. v. Harold Smith Motors Ltd.* (*supra*).

Modern statutory developments, however, have probably made the common law rules regarding advertising of much less importance. The Motor Vehicle Dealers Act gives power to make regulations in respect of:

35....
(j)   prescribing the information that motor vehicle dealers and salesman shall disclose respecting the history of any class or classes of motor vehicles.
(k)   prohibiting prescribed alterations of motor vehicles or any part thereof and requiring disclosure of prescribed alterations not prohibited;
(l)   governing contracts for the sale and purchase of motor vehicles; ... "

The following regulations have been made in respect of advertising;

18. (1) Every advertisement placed by or on behalf of a motor vehicle dealer shall identify the name under which the motor vehicle dealer is registered and the address of the premises from which he is authorized to operate.
(2) No motor vehicle dealer shall advertise or offer for sale any motor vehicle that has been used as a taxicab or police cruiser, without making such disclosure in the advertisement or the offer for sale.
(3) No motor vehicle dealer shall refer in any advertisement or offer for sale of a motor vehicle to the motor vehicle as being a company car, an executive car, or a demonstrator unless such car was used by the motor vehicle dealer in the course of his normal operation and had been acquired by the motor vehicle dealer as a new automobile."

The Business Practices Act, S.O. 1974, c. 131, controls advertising by making certain kinds of advertising claims "unfair practices". The Act covers much more than just advertising claims, and we shall see later what its direct effect is on individual contracts that might be made by a customer for the purchase of a used car. The Act provides:

2. For the purposes of this Act, the following shall be deemed to be unfair practices,
(a)   a false, misleading or deceptive consumer representation including, but without limiting the generality of the foregoing,
      (i)   a representation that the goods or services have sponsorhsip, approval, performance characteristics, assessories, uses, ingredients, benefits or quantities they do not have,
      (ii)   a representation that the person who is to supply the goods or services has sponsorship, approval, status, affiliation or connection he does not have,
      (iii) a representation that the goods are of a particular standard, quality, grade, style or model, if they are not,
      (iv)   a representation that the goods are new, or unused, if they are not or are reconditioned or reclaimed, provided that the reasonable use of goods to enable the seller to service, prepare, test and deliver the goods for the purpose of sale shall not be deemed to make the goods used for the purposes of this subclause,

(v)   a representation that the goods have been used to an extent that is materially different from the fact,

(vi)   a representation that the goods or services are available for a reason that does not exist,

(vii)   a representation that the goods or services have been supplied in accordance with a previous representation, if they have not,

(viii)   a representation that the goods or services or any part thereof are available to the consumer when the person making the representation knows or ought to know they will not be supplied,

(ix)   a representation that a service, part, replacement or repair is needed, if it is not,

(x)   a representation that a specific price advantage exists, if it does not,

(xi)   a representation that misrepresents the authority of a salesman, representative, employee or agent to negotiate the final terms of the proposed transaction,

(xii)   a representation that the proposed transaction involves or does not involve rights, remedies or obligations if the representation is false or misleading,

(xiii)   a representation using exaggeration, innuendo or ambiguity as to a material fact or failing to state a material fact if such use or failure deceives or tends to deceive,

(xiv)   a representation that misrepresents the purpose or intent of any solicitation of or any communication with a consumer; ... "

The Act defines "consumer representation" as follows:

1. (c) "consumer representation" means a representation, statement, offer, request or proposal,

(i)   made respecting or with a view to the supplying of goods or services, or both, to a consumer, or

(ii)   made for the purpose of or with a view to receiving consideration for goods or services, or both, supplied or purporting to have been supplied to a consumer; ... "

The Act provides that anyone who engages in an unfair practice as defined above is guilty of an offence and liable to a fine of $2,000 or imprisonment for one year. (A corporation may be fined $25,000). This Act is modelled fairly closely on the Uniform Consumer Sales Practices Act in the U.S.

Criminal liability for deceptive advertising is also imposed under federal legislation. This legislation is more often used to punish those who make deceptive advertisements. *Combines Investigation Act* R.S.C. 1970, c. C-23 (as amended);

36 – (1) No person shall, for the purpose of promoting, directly or indirectly, the supply or use of a product or for the purpose of promoting, directly or indirectly, any business interest, by any means whatever,

(a)   make a representation to the public that is false or misleading in a material respect;

(b)   make a representation to the public in the form of a statement, warranty or guarantee of the performance, efficacy or length of life of a product that is not based on an adequate and proper test thereof, the proof of which lies upon the person making the representation;

(c)   make a representation to the public in a form that purports to be

(i)   a warranty or guarantee of a product, or

(ii)   a promise to replace, maintain or repair an article or any part thereof or to repeat or continue a service until it has achieved a special result if such form of purported warranty or guarantee or promise is materially misleading or if there is no reasonable prospect that it will be carried out; or

(d)   make a materially misleading, representation to the public concerning the price at which a product or like products have been, are or will be ordinarily sold; and for the purposes of this paragraph a representation as to price is deemed to refer to the price at which the product has been sold by sellers generally in the relevant market unless it is clearly specified to be the price at which the product has been sold by the person by whom or on whose behalf the representation is made.

(2) For the purposes of this section and section 36.1, a representation that is

(a)   expressed on an article offered or displayed for sale, its wrapper or container,

(b)   expressed on anything attached to, inserted in or accompanying an article offered or displayed for sale, its wrapper or container, or anything on which the article is mounted for display or sale,

(c)   expressed on an in-store or other point-of-purchase display,

(d)   made in the course of in-store, door-to-door or telephone selling to a person as ultimate user, or

(e)   contained in or on anything that is sold, sent, delivered, transmitted or in any other manner whatever made available to a member of the public,

shall be deemed to be made to the public by and only by the person who caused the representation to be so expressed made or contained and, where that person is outside Canada, by

(f)   the person who imported the article into Canada, in a case described in paragraph (a), (b) or (e) and

(g)   the person who imported the display into Canada, in a case described in paragraph (c).

(3) Subject to subsection (2), every one who, for the purpose of promoting, directly or indirectly, the supply or use of a product or any business interest, supplies to a wholesaler, retailer or other distributor of a product any material or thing that contains a representation of a nature referred to in subsection (1) shall be deemed to have made that representation to the public.

(4) In any prosecution for a violation of this section, the general impression conveyed by a representation as well as the literal meaning thereof shall be taken into account in determining whether or not the representation is false or misleading in a material respect.

(5) Any person who violates subsection (1) is guilty of an offence and is liable

(a)   on conviction on indictment, to a fine in the discretion of the court or to imprisonment for five years or to both; or

(b)   on summary conviction, to a fine of twenty-five thousand dollars or to imprisonment for one year or to both."

The Act goes on to deal with specific situations like double-ticketing (it is an offence to charge more than the lowest price shown), pyramid selling and bait-and-switch selling. There have been frequent prosecution under this legislation. It is an offence of strict liability: *mens rea* is not necessary. It has been held to be a violation of this section when a car dealer advertised "free 100 gallons of gas with every purchase" but only made the offer to those who bought at the list price.

In addition to these controls on advertising, there is more legislation that deal directly with the quality of the thing being sold. Thus The Highway Traffic Act provides:

58b. – (1) No person shall sell a used motor vehicle unless,

(a)   on the delivery of the vehicle to the purchaser, the seller gives to the purchaser a safety standards certificate that was issued upon an inspection that was completed in respect of the motor vehicle not more than thirty days before the date of the delivery of the used motor vehicle to the purchaser; or

(b)   the seller forwards to the Ministry the notice required under subsection 2 of section 9 together with the current number plates and permit issued with respect to the motor vehicle.

The Highway Traffic Act contains a number of provisions designed to make sure that cars are properly inspected. Thus R.R.O. 1970, Reg. 410 made under the Act sets out in considerable detail the criteria to be used when inspecting a car. The Act itself provides that inspections may only be made by certain people:

58c – (1) No person other than a licensee, or a person authorized in writing by a licensee shall issue a safety standards certificate.

The Act also controls the mechanics who have to sign the certificates:

58e – (1) No person shall sign a vehicle inspection record as mechanic or certify in a safety standards certificate that a vehicle complies with the standards of equipment and performance prescribed in the regulations unless he is registered by the Director as a motor vehicle inspection mechanic in a motor vehicle inspection station...

A mechanic can lose his registration if he misbehaves in the issuance of safety certificates. The Act provides:

58e – (3)... the Director may refuse to register a motor vehicle inspection mechanic where, in his opinion,

(a)   the past conduct of the mechanic affords reasonable grounds for belief that the mechanic will not act as a motor vehicle inspection mechanic in accordance with the law and with honesty and integrity; or

(b)   the mechanic is not competent to act as a motor vehicle inspection mechanic.

58f. The Director may revoke the registration of a motor vehicle inspection mechanic where,

(a)   the registrant or the licensee has made a false statement in the application for registration of the registrant or in a safety standards certificate or in any report, document or other information required to be furnished by this Act or the regulations or any other Act or regulation that applies to the registrant;

(b)   any inspection performed under the authority of his registration is incompetently performed by the registrant; or

(c)   the registrant does not comply with the Act or the regulations.

There is a Director of Vehicle Inspection Standards appointed to oversee the issuance of licences and the conduct of licensees and mechanics. Licences have to be obtained annually and may be cancelled or the Director may refuse to renew. As we have seen this can be a very effective form of control.

The Highway Traffic Act was substantially amended in 1973 (S.O. 1973, c. 167). This amendment shows what can happen when the legislature decides to get tough. The former s. 58 of the Act (R.S.O. 1970, c. 202) provided:

58 – (1)... Every dealer in used motor vehicles, before he enters into a contract to sell a used motor vehicle, shall give to the purchaser a certificate of mechanical fitness as prescribed by the regulations that is duly completed and signed by the dealer.

A fine of $300 was provided if any false statements were made in a certificate or for any violation of s. 58(1). However, these provisions were ineffective to ensure that inspections were properly carried out. The 1973 amendments, therefore, brought the issuance of certificates of mechanical fitness under control as tight as that over motor vehicle dealers. The office of the Director was set up and the requirements of a licence and registration established. The fine for violation of the Act was increased to $500.

The effect of these provisions of the Highway Traffic Act is, presumably, to ensure that only mechanically fit used cars are sold. If a purchaser of a used car wants to put it on the road, the car has to have passed a test of mechanical fitness. The obligation on the dealer is therefore imposed in the interests of increasing safety on the roads. It is one more restriction that the used car dealer has to observe.

It will be seen that the public law controls on the conduct of the used car business can have a very significant impact on the way in which the business is conducted. This will have some effect on the role of contracts in the business. If advertising is scrupulously honest then there will be fewer cases of disappointed buyers. If the dealer stands to lose his livelihood if he cheats one customer, he may refrain from cheating any. The legislation, however, does provide direct controls on the contracts that dealers may make.

The Business Practices Act, lists in s. 2, as we have seen, certain unfair practices. The Act goes on to provide:

"2. For the purpose of this Act, the following shall be deemed to be unfair practices,...

(b)   an unconscionable consumer representation made in respect of a particular transaction and in determining whether or not a consumer representation is unconscionable there may be taken into account that the person making the representation or his employer or principal knows or ought to know,

    (i)   that the consumer is not reasonably able to protect his interests because of his physical infirmity, ignorance, illiteracy, inability to understand the language of an agreement or similar factors,

    (ii)   that the price grossly exceeds the price at which similar goods or services are readily available to like consumers,

    (iii)   that the consumer is unable to receive a substantial benefit from the subject-matter of the consumer representation,

    (iv)   that there is no reasonable probability of payment of the obligation in full by the consumer,

    (v)   that the proposed transaction is excessively one-sided in favour of someone other than the consumer,

    (vi)   that the terms or conditions of the proposed transaction are so adverse to the consumer as to be inequitable,

    (vii)   that he is making a misleading statement of opinion on which the consumer is likely to rely to his detriment,

    (viii)   that he is subjecting the consumer to undue pressure to enter into the transaction;

(c)   such other consumer representations under clause a as are prescribed by the regulations made in accordance with section 16.

3. (1) No person shall engage in an unfair practice.

(2) A person who performs one act referred to in section 2 shall be deemed to be engaging in an unfair practice.

4. (1) Subject to subsection 2, any agreement, whether written, oral or implied, entered into by a consumer after a consumer representation that is an unfair practice and that induced the consumer to enter into the agreement,

(a) may be rescinded by the consumer and the consumer is entitled to any remedy therefor that is at law available, including damages; or

(b) where rescission is not possible because restitution is no longer possible, or because rescission would deprive a third party of a right in the subject-matter of the agreement that he has acquired in good faith and for value, the consumer is entitled to recover the amount by which the amount paid under the agreement exceeds the fair value of the goods or services received under the agreement or damages, or both.

(2) Where the unfair practice referred to in subsection 1 comes within clause b of section 2, the court may award exemplary or punitive damages.... "

The provisions of s. 2(b) are in addition to those in s. 2(a) which cover deceptive "consumer representations".

A used car dealer, therefore, whose salesman has been careless in "puffing up" the qualities of a car may find that the customer may rescind the contract under s. 4. The Act is too new for there to have been many cases under it, and there are, so far, no reported cases. The right to repudiate given by s. 4 is wider than that given in equity, since rescission under s. 4 is only restricted where restitution is no longer possible, i.e., where the goods are lost or damaged, or when the rights of a third party have intervened. In addition, even though rescission may not be possible, damages may be awarded. The act also extends the scope of the defence of unconscionability by the provisions of s. 2(b). A price disparity alone is sufficient to have the contract rescinded. Section 4 (1)(a) also gives the consumer a remedy in damages as well as the right to rescind. This would presumably protect the consumer's reliance interest as well as his restitutionary one.

If we return to our example of Allcars Ltd. and the Ovlovs we can explore the act in more detail. Allcars advertised a 1976 AMC Gremlin for sale on its lot. Hope Springs came to the lot looking for a used car. The agreement that she signed was the standard form adopted by the Toronto Automobile Dealers Association. (The entire agreement is reproduced in Appendix 2, #8. The Motor Vehicle Dealers Act Regulations specify what information must be shown on the order. Section 16(2) of the Regulations provides:

Where a used motor vehicle is sold, the sales or purchase order shall show,

(a) the name and address of the purchaser;

(b) the date of sale;

(c) the make of vehicle;

(d) the model year;

(e) the manufacturer's serial number;

(f) the body type;

(g) the licence plate number;

(h) the sale price;

(i) an itemized list of the cost of all extra equipment sold to the purchaser and to be installed by the motor vehicle dealer according to the agreement made at the time of sale;

(j) the total sale price;

(k) the down payment or deposit, if any;

(l) the balance to be paid by the purchaser;

(m) an itemized list of the cost of other charges for which the purchaser is responsible such as insurance and licence fees;

(n) if the balance is to be financed, the information that a lender is required to give to a borrower, before giving the credit, under section 36 of *The Con-*

sumer Protection Act, together with a notation that the said section has been complied with;

(o)   the recorded odometer reading at the time of sale; and

(p)   an itemized list of any repairs to be effected and the cost thereof, if any.)

The agreed price was $3,900.00. Hope had no trade in and agreed to pay the whole amount in cash. With tax, this came to $4,173.00. The agreement contained the following terms:

"2. ACKNOWLEDGEMENT OF CONDITIONS: The purchaser acknowledges having read the conditions printed on the reverse side hereof and agrees that the same are hereby incorporated by reference and shall constitute part of this agreement as fully as if printed on the face of the agreement and above the Purchaser's signature.

WARRANTIES

"3. There are no warranties or representations by the dealer with respect to the motor vehicle described herein or affecting the rights of the parties, other than those set out in any applicable legislation and in the case of a new motor vehicle, provided in the new car warranty given by the manufacturer and/or the dealer. No other warranty agreement or representation made hereto, nor any modification hereof, shall be binding upon the dealer or his assigns unless endorsed hereon in writing."

The normal effect of such clauses and the signing of the agreement has already been discussed. However the efficacy of such clauses is now considerably affected by statute.

First, The Consumer Protection Act was amended in 1971 (S.O. 1971, c. 24) to provide:

44a. — (1) In this section, "consumer sale" means a contract for the sale of goods made in the ordinary course of business to a purchaser for his consumption or use, but does not include a sale,

(a)   to a purchaser for resale;

(b)   to a purchaser whose purchase is in the course of carrying on business;

(c)   to an association of individuals, a partnership or a corporation;

(d)   by a trustee in bankruptcy, a receiver, a liquidator or a person acting under the order of a court.

(2) The implied conditions and warranties applying to the sale of goods by virtue of *The Sale of Goods Act* apply to goods sold by a consumer sale and any written term or acknowledgement, whether part of the contract of sale or not, that purports to negative or vary any of such implied conditions and warranties is void and, if a term of a contract, is severable therefrom, and such term or acknowledgement shall not be evidence of circumstances showing an intent that any of the implied conditions and warranties are not to apply.

Any attempt to exclude the implied terms of The Sale of Goods Act would therefore be ineffective. Second, if the salesman who was employed by Allcars had been too generous in his praise of the car, then what he too said may become part of the contract. This is in spite of the final sentence of clause 3 of the conditions. The Business Practices Act provides:

s.4(8) This section notwithstanding any agreement or waiver to the contrary.

The provisions of s. 2 that we looked at earlier are sufficient to make any misleading statement by a salesman sufficient to be an "unfair practice" entitling the purchaser to the remedies provided by s. 4.

The position of the purchaser is further strengthened by another provision of the Motor Vehicle Dealers Act Regulations which provides:

20. — (1) All funds received by a motor vehicle dealer prior to the delivery of the motor vehicle shall be deemed to be trust funds.

(2) For the purposes of subsection 1, every motor vehicle dealer shall maintain a ledger account into which shall be entered the names and addresses of all persons from whom trust funds are obtained with details of the amounts retained and a record of all disbursements therefrom.

(3) Every motor vehicle dealer shall maintain in respect of all funds that come into his hands in trust a separate trust account clearly designated as "The Motor Vehicle Dealers Act Trust Account" in a chartered bank, loan or trust company, or Province of Ontario Savings Office and into which he shall deposit such funds and every motor vehicle dealer shall, at all times, keep such funds secure and make disbursements from such trust account in accordance with the terms of the trust.

(4) Where funds are paid, whether by way of deposit, down payment or otherwise, on account of an undelivered motor vehicle, the motor vehicle dealer shall retain such funds in trust for the purchaser until,

(a) the motor vehicle is delivered;
(b) the contract is mutually cancelled; or
(c) direction or authority is received from the Registrar concerning disbursements."

If Hope should pay the purchase price but leave the car with Allcars for servicing or repairs, then the provisions of s. 20 should ensure that she can get her money back should she rescind, even though Allcars may be bankrupt. As trust funds, her money would not be available to the general creditors of Allcars Ltd.

Not all purchasers can afford to pay cash for the car. Many purchasers of used cars are financed by banks, finance companies, credit unions and the like. The buyer borrows money, often on the security of the car, and promises to pay the balance in instalments.

The points to notice in such an agreement are that the contract is between the dealer as the seller and the buyer. The seller immediately assigns the agreement to the finance company, who advance the purchase price to the dealer. The agreement will also contain provisions respecting the liability of the seller to the finance company. The seller will usually agree to be responsible for the debt incurred by the buyer unless the agreement specifically provides that the assignment is "without recourse". In all cases, however, the seller is liable for breach of any warranties in connection with the sale.

Not all financing arrangements are made by contract in this way. The seller may agree to finance the purchase and may then, without notice to the buyer, discount the promissory note that is signed by the buyer and assign the conditional sales agreement to a finance company. There is then, at common law, no privity between the purchaser and the finance company.

Some recent legislation has focussed on the issue of disclosure. The lender is obliged to state what is the rate of interest that is being charged. The Consumer Protection Act provides:

36. Except as provided in section 37, every lender shall furnish to the borrower, before giving the credit, a clear statement in writing showing,

(a) the sum,
    (i) expressed as one sum in dollars and cents, actually received in cash by the borrower, plus insurance or official fees, if any, actually paid by the lender, or

    (ii)   where the lender is a seller, being the amount of the cash price of the goods or services, including any insurance or official fees;

(b)   where the lender is a seller, the sums, if any, actually paid as a down payment or credited in respect of a trade-in, or paid or credited for any other reason;

(c)   where the lender is a seller, the amount by which the sum stated under subclause ii of clause a exceeds the sum stated under clause b;

(d)   the cost of borrowing expressed as one sum in dollars and cents;

(e)   the percentage that the cost of borrowing bears to the sum stated,

    (i)   under subclause i of clause a, where the lender is not a seller, or

    (ii)   under clause c, where the lender is a seller,

expressed as an annual rate applied to the unpaid balance thereof from time to time, calculated and expressed in the manner prescribed by the regulations;

(f)   the amount, if any, charged for insurance;

(g)   the amount, if any, charged for official fees; and

(h)   the basis upon which additional charges are to be made in the event of default....

39. A borrower is not liable to pay a lender as the cost of borrowing any sum in excess of the sum shown in the statement required by section 36 or 37 in respect of the transaction.

The Consumer Protection Act is supplemented by federal legislation of various kinds. The Bank Act, for example, governs the activities of the Chartered Banks. This legislation has only an indirect influence on the contract between the lender and borrower. More significant has been developments that have extended the consumer's right to raise defences based on the quality of the goods against the finance company as well as the seller. This has, in effect, destroyed the protection afforded a finance company that had merely taken an assignment of the conditional sales contract and that had sought to claim as a holder in due course of the promissory note signed by the purchaser. Section 191 of the Bills of Exchange Act provides, for example:

> Notwithstanding any agreement to the contrary, the right of a holder of a consumer bill or consumer note... to have the whole or any part thereof paid by the purchaser or any party signing to accommodate the purchaser is subject to any defence or right of set-off, other than counter-claim, that the purchaser would have had in an action by the seller on the consumer bill or consumer note.

The position reached by this section was, as we have seen, also reached at common law by Kelly J.A. of the Ontario Court of Appeal in *Federal Discount Corp. Ltd. v. St. Pierre* (1967), 32 D.L.R. (2d) 86.

Similar provisions dealing specifically with assignments are found in the Consumer Protection Act, as amended by S.O. 1971, c. 24, s. 1:

> s. 42(a) (1) The assignee of any rights of a lender has no greater rights than and is subject to the same obligations, liabilities and duties as the assignor, and the provisions of this Act apply equally to such assignee.
>
> (2) Notwithstanding subsection 1, a borrower shall not recover from or be entitled to set off against, an assignee of the lender an amount greater than the balance owing on the contract at the time of the assignment....

This is why in any financing arrangement there will be a promise on the part of the seller of a car to indemnify the finance company if the seller should breach any of the implied warranties in the sale or be liable under the Business Practices Act.

Of more direct contractual significance is The Unconscionable Transactions Relief Act, R.S.O. 1970.

1. In this Act,

(a) "Cost of the loan" means the whole cost to the debtor of money lent and includes interest, discount, subscription, premium, dues, bonus, commission, brokerage fees and charges, but not actual lawful and necessary disbursements made to a registrar of deeds, a master of titles, a clerk of a county or district court, a sheriff or a treasurer of a municipality;

(b) "court" means a court having jurisdiction in an action for the recovery of a debt or money demand to the amount claimed by a creditor in respect of money lent;

(c) "creditor" includes the person advancing money lent and the assignee of any claim arising or security given in respect of money lent;

(d) "debtor" means a person to whom or on whose account money lent is advanced and includes every surety and endorser or other person liable for the repayment of money lent or upon any agreement or collateral or other security given in respect thereof;

(e) "money lent" includes money advanced on account of any person in any transaction that, whatever its form may be, is substantially one of money-lending or securing the repayment of money so advanced and includes and has always included a mortgage within the meaning of *The Mortgages Act.*

2. Where, in respect of money lent, the court finds that, having regard to the risk and to all the circumstances, the cost of the loan is excessive and that the transaction is harsh and unconscionable, the court may,

(a)   reopen the transaction and take an account between the creditor and the debtor;

(b)   notwithstanding any statement or settlement of account or any agreement purporting to close previous dealings and create a new obligation, reopen any account already taken and relieve the debtor from payment of any sum in excess of the sum adjudged by the court to be fairly due in respect of the principal and the cost of the loan;

(c)   order the creditor to repay any such excess if the same has been paid or allowed on account by the debtor;

(d)   set aside either wholly or in part or revise or alter any security given or agreement made in respect of the money lent, and, if the creditor has parted with the security, order him to indemnify the debtor.

3. The powers conferred by section 2 may be exercised,

(a)   in an action or proceeding by a creditor for the recovery of money lent;

(b)   in an action or proceeding by the debtor notwithstanding any provision or agreement to the contrary, and notwithstanding that the time for repayment of the loan or any instalment thereof has not arrived;

(c)   in an action or proceeding in which the amount due or to become due in respect of money lent is in question.

4. — (1) In addition to any right that a debtor may have under this or any other Act or otherwise in respect of money lent, he may apply for relief under this Act to a judge of the county or district court of the county or district in which he resides, and the judge on the application may exercise any of the powers of the court under section 2.

(2) Where an application is made under subsection 1, the judge may, if he sees fit, at any time before disposing of the application, by order remove the proceedings into the Supreme Court.

(3) When an order is made under subsection 2, the clerk of the county or district court shall forthwith transmit the papers in the case to the proper office of the Supreme Court in the county or district in which the application was made.

(4) When the papers have been received in the proper office of the Supreme Court, the application is *ipso facto* removed into the Supreme Court and shall be heard and determined by a judge of the Supreme Court in chambers, and the judge on the application may exercise any of the powers of the court under section 2 or he may direct an issue.

(5) An appeal lies to the Court of Appeal from any order made under subsection 1 or 4.

5. Nothing in this Act affects the rights of a *bona fide* assignee or holder for value without notice, or derogates from the existing powers or jurisdiction of any court.

Unlike The Business Practices Act, this Act gives the court a discretion to re-make the deal for the parties. An example of how the Act operates is provided by the following case:

COLLINS v. FOREST HILL INVESTMENT CORP. LTD.

(1967), 63 D.L.R. (2d) 429. Ontario County Court.

[The plaintiffs, husband and wife, wanted to refinance the mortgage on their house. They heard a commercial for the defendant offering mortgages. They called a representative of the defendant, one Newton, and had a meeting with him. He agreed to advance them $1,500 to pay off the existing mortgage and taxes. They signed a new mortgage for $2,450 at 7%. The trial judge found that Newton had never explained to the plaintiffs what was going on, and that they had no idea what a bonus on a mortgage was. However, the judge rejected an argument that the mortgage was void on the ground of *non est factum*, and that Newton owed the plaintiffs any fiduciary obligation. The following documents are referred to in the judgment: Exhibit 1, a card filled out by Newton after the initial call. Exhibit 2, an application addressed to defendants for a loan of $1,500 and an offer to give a mortgage of $2,450, the difference being described "collateral advantage, legal fees, and commission, etc." Exhibit 3 was the "collateral advantage" agreement, Exhibit 4 was an acknowledgement that the amount owing was $2,450 and Exhibit 5 was the mortgage. The judge found that Ex. 4 was not signed in blank.]

Willmott Co. Ct. J.: ... The transaction would be regarded as harsh and unconscionable in equity, independently of The Unconscionable Transactions Relief Act, R.S.O. 1960, c. 410, since an experienced money-lender was taking advantage of the limited education and experience of the plaintiffs: See *Longley v. Barbrick* (1962), 36 D.L.R. (2d) 672. Although the bonus was greater there, the same principle applies. The evidence of Alexander Gromansky, real estate appraiser with Gibson Willoughby Limited, clearly shows that at the time of this transaction, a first mortgage loan of $1,500 at 8% or 8½% or 9% without any bonus, was obtainable on the plaintiffs' property. The plaintiffs' credit record was good. Houses such as the plaintiffs' sell readily at low prices in any market, and there would have been no difficulty in realizing the security. There was clear evidence of "overreaching", which is sometimes called "equitable fraud". Although the facts would not support rescission, a Court of equity, independently of statute, would have reopened the mortgage account and allowed the plaintiffs to redeem on reasonable terms.

As against the mortgage, the plaintiffs are entitled to the same relief under the statute.... An unjustified or excessive bonus or excessive interest rate alone can make a transaction harsh and unconscionable. The evidence clearly shows that the lowest possible calculation of the mortgagee's profit under this transaction, as a rate of interest per annum, is 23.07%, and it can be stated at as high as 42.05%. Assuming the figure of 23.07% to be correct, it is not far short of three times the rate at which a loan could have been obtained elsewhere.... Looking at the matter from another angle, a bonus of $950 on a loan of $1,500 is a profit of 63.3% to which interest at 7% would be added. From either point of view, such terms in a first mortgage loan are harsh and unconscionable.

... On the other hand, the solicitors' fees for the transaction were not deducted from the advance. According to Newton's evidence, these fees amounted to $75 and should be added to the advance and the total of $1,575 without any bonus, should bear interest at 8½%. The mortgage account should be reopened and recalculated on this basis, as against the defendant company. Costs will be dealt with later.

Although the defendant Newton was the architect of the whole structure, there is no evidence that he acted, in relation to the plaintiffs, other than as an officer or agent of the defendant company. He did not, as it appears, purport to act on behalf of the plaintiffs. Exhibit 2, completed during the interview of October 7th, is an application addressed to the defendant company. No fraud or misrepresentation has been brought home to him, but he personally imposed the unconscionable terms, although on behalf of the company. In the result, the action must be dismissed as against him.

The defendant Ann King appears in the evidence to have taken the mortgage for value, in good faith, and without notice of the facts entitling the plaintiffs to demand that the mortgage account be reopened. The only thing that might have "put her on notice" was the sale of the mortgage at a discount within such a short time after it was made. However, she was not, it seems, engaged in buying mortgages. This was an isolated transaction and she does not appear to have been aware of the nature or course of the mortgage market. The mortgage contained an unequivocal statement that the amount of principal was $2,450, and ex. 4 contained an unequivocal acknowledgement to the same effect. She did not see ex. 3 and was not told about the bonus. She cannot be blamed for believing that the original loan had been one of $2,450. Thus, unless the plaintiffs' equity or statutory right is enforceable against her, even as a purchaser for value in good faith and without notice, she is entitled to enforce the mortgage for its full stated amount, under the well-known rule that the purchaser of a chose in action at a discount may enforce it in full against the debtor.

Notwithstanding the good faith of the defendant Ann King, as assignee of the mortgage, she would, subject to the questions of estoppel and laches, take the mortgage subject to the equities. The right to rescission arising from circumstances existing at the time of making the mortgage would be such an equity.

. . .

In the present case, the plaintiffs not only executed the mortgage, ex. 5, which contained an acknowledgement of receipt of $2,450. They also signed ex. 4, in which they expressly achnowledged that the full amount of $2,450 and interest from October 15, 1959, was owing.

As against the mortgagee, these acknowledgements would not have any effect, but the assignee taking in good faith, for value without notice, had a better equity than the equity of the plaintiffs, and is protected by the statutory rule as well as by the rule in equity apart from the statute.

After becoming aware, on reading ex. 1, of the effect of the mortgage, the plaintiffs continued to make monthly payments, at first to the mortgagee and then to the assignee, for over four years, without making any objection.

They took no action until they learned that Newton and the mortgagee had got into trouble over other mortgages. They cannot be estopped by such payments, since Ann King did not change her position relying on them. She had already changed her position relying on the mortgage and on ex. 4. However, the acts of the plaintiffs in continuing to make payments without complaint not only to the mortgagee but also to the assignee are evidence, as against the assignee, of both laches and an election not to try to rescind or reopen the mortgage account, and go to strengthen the position of the assignee. In the result the plaintiffs' claim against the assignee must fail.

If the plaintiffs had not been bound by estoppel and laches, their right against the assignee would appear to have been preserved by s. 5 of The Unconscionable Transaction Relief Act, but in the circumstances that section preserves the rights of the defendant Ann King.

The action must be dismissed against her with costs. Her counsel claims costs as between solicitor and client, under a clause in the mortgage which entitles the mortgagee to recover "all costs, charges and expenses [between solicitor and client] which may be incurred in taking, recovering, and keeping possession of the said lands, and of negotiating this loan, investigating title, and registering the mortgage and other necessary deeds, and generally in any other proceedings taken, in connection with or to realize this security". Under another clause, the assigns of the mortagee are given all the advantages, etc., given to the mortgagee. A claim of this kind was considered by Manson, J., in *Manufacturer's Life Ins. Co. v. Independent Investment Co. Ltd.*, [1939] 4 D.L.R. 811n, 54 B.C.R. 5, and he decided that costs as between solicitor and client were payable *ex contractu* to the mortgagee and could not be denied. It is regretted that the same conclusion appears to be inescapable here and judgment should go accordingly.

The amount due to Mrs. Ann King is based on the following computation: Balance of principal due as of the date of the issue of her writ on July 2, 1964, $1,413.16. To this sum is added interest compounded semi-annually at 7% to July 2, 1967, of $323.95 making in all, $1,737.11. The defendant Ann King will have judgment against the plaintiffs for $1,737.11.

On the basis of a revised principal sum of $1,575 with interest at 8½% compounded semi-annually with monthly payments of $30 for five years, the total amount payable by the plaintiffs as mortgagors amounts to $1,963.28 of which $388.28 is interest.

The plaintiffs have made 52 payments of $30 for a total of $1,560. Their unpaid balance of $403.28 will be set off against the amount payable by Forest Hill Investments Ltd. to the plaintiff.

The defendant company's charter was cancelled on November 8, 1966, pending this action, but by s. 326a [enacted 1962-63, c. 24, s. 12] of The Corporations Act, R.S.O. 1960, c. 71, the company continues in existence for the purpose of the completion of these proceedings.

By virtue of s. 2(d) of The Unconscionable Transactions Relief Act, the defendant company should be orderd to indemnify the plaintiffs against all liability to the defendant Ann King under the mortgage over and above the amount found due as above, including the defendant Ann King's costs in this action, since it was reasonable for the plaintiffs to add her as a defendant. Judgment accordingly. The question of costs, other than those of Ann King, is reserved for further submission by counsel.

On the question of costs after hearing the submission of the respective counsel the costs will be disposed of as follows:

1. The action of the plaintiffs against J. Newton must be dismissed but owing to his participation and the fact that it was not unreasonable for the plaintiffs to join him as a defendant the dismissal will be without costs.

2. The plaintiffs will have their costs against the defendant Forest Hill Investment Corporation Ltd.

3. Ann King on her mortgage action will have judgment for payment, possession and foreclosure for the amount set out in the reasons for judgment, namely, $1,737.11. There will be a stay of execution on this judgment for 60 days.

4. The mortgagee Ann King will have her costs on a party-and-party basis on this mortgage action up to August 16, 1965.

5. The plaintiffs' action against Ann King as the assignee of the mortgage must fail. This action is dismissed against her with costs on a solicitor-and client basis.

6. The plaintiffs Samuel P. Collins and Elsie Collins will be indemnified by Forest Hill Investment Corporation Ltd. for the costs of the mortgagee Ann King on a solicitor-and-client basis, and for her costs as plaintiff in her mortgage foreclosure action.

         Order accordingly.

In Canada, most of the statutory changes that bear directly on the law of contracts affect "consumer" transactions. The political pressure that led to such measures has been obvious for some time. It was also clear that the need to protect consumers was great. We have seen constant efforts by the courts to do so in cases like *Yeoman Credit v. Apps*, (*supra*) and *Henningson v. Bloomfield Motors* (supra). The use in contracts between businesses of the devices used to redress the imbalance of bargaining power in consumer transactions lead, as we have seen, to some serious problems. It might cause similar problems to import the provisions of acts like The Business Practices Act into all transactions. Nevertheless, there is an increasing need to protect some businesses from others. The position of the franchisee, for example, may be very weak compared with that of the franchisor, and legislation may be expected to redress this imbalance. There is already some legislation in Alberta on this topic: The Franchises Act, S.A. 1971, c. 38 (as amended).

UNIFORM COMMERCIAL CODE, § 2-302

The U.C.C. gives the court a wide power to review any contract for unconscionability. § 2-302 reads:

§ *2-302. Unconscionable Contract or Clause*

(1) If the court as a matter of law finds the contract or any clause of the contract to have been unconscionable at the time it was made the court may refuse to enforce the contract, or it may enforce the remainder of the contract without the unconscionable clause, or it may so limit the application of any unconscionable clause as to avoid any unconscionable result.

(2) When it is claimed or appears to the court that the contract or any

clause thereof may be unconscionable the parties shall be afforded a reasonable opportunity to present evidence as to its commercial setting, purpose and effect to aid the court in making the determination.

Official Comment

Prior Uniform Statutory Provision: None.
Purposes:

1. This section is intended to make it possible for the courts to police explicitly against the contracts or clauses which they find to be unconscionable. In the past such policing has been accomplished by adverse construction of language, by manipulation of the rules of offer and acceptance or by determinations that the clause is contrary to public policy or to the dominant purpose of the contract. This section is intended to allow the court to pass directly on the unconscionability of the contract or particular clause therein and to make a conclusion of law as to its unconscionability. The basic test is whether, in the light of the general commercial background and the commercial needs of the particular trade or case, the clauses involved are so one-sided as to be unconscionable under the circumstances existing at the time of the making of the contract. Subsection (2) makes it clear that it is proper for the court to hear evidence upon these questions. The principle is one of the prevention of oppression and unfair surprise (Cf. Campbell Soup Co. v. Wentz, 172 F. 2d 80, 3d Cir. 1948) and not of disturbance of allocation of risks because of superior bargaining power....

2. Under this section the court, in its discretion, may refuse to enforce the contract as a whole if it is permeated by the unconscionability, or it may strike any single clause or group of clauses which are so tainted or which are contrary to the essential purpose of the agreement, or it may simply limit unconscionable clauses so as to avoid unconscionable results.

3. The present section is addressed to the court, and the decision is to be made by it. The commercial evidence referred to in subsection (2) is for the court's consideration, not the jury's. Only the agreement which results from the court's action on these matters is to be submitted to the general triers of the facts.

The problems that have had to be solved by legislation have required a very varied approach. Sometimes the legislation has made certain conduct criminal. In other cases, the obtaining of a licence has been made a pre-requisite to carrying on certain businesses. Legislation has given the aggrieved party a direct remedy against the other party; it has specified the information to be provided in certain transactions, and it has given other subsidiary remedies, like the provision for payment for a car to be treated as trust funds. Any proposals for further legislation must consider all the techniques that are available. As you review those cases where something was wrong with the law of contract, consider how best to solve the problem. Is the matter one that can best be solved by the courts? Could one, for example statutorily overrule *Gilbert Steel v. University Construction*? Is § 2-302 necessary if one were to accept Llewellyn's argument about standard forms? If legislation is necessary, is the criminal law to be the primary means of control, or should it only be used as a back-up force? What kind of discretion should the court be given? To what extent can the problem be solved by requiring that notice (with certain specified information) be given by one party to the other? Is the technique of requiring registration or a licence one that should be more or less used?

CHAPTER 7

THE STATUTE OF FRAUDS

Introduction

The Statute of Frauds was passed in 1677. Its purpose was the "prevention of many fraudulent practices which are commonly endeavoured to be upheld by perjury and subornation of perjury". The method of achieving this was the requirement that certain kinds of transactions had to be supported by some kind of writing. This technique has been adopted by legislatures or authorities in ancient Babylon and Soviet Russia, by African customary law and the Code Napoléon. In the common law world, the act of Charles II has been almost universally copied. The Ontario Act (R.S.O. 1970, c. 444) contains 11 sections, but of these only a few are of concern to most lawyers. The principal sections are:

> 4. No action shall be brought whereby to charge any executor or administrator upon any special promise to answer damages out of his own estate, or whereby to charge any person upon any special promise to answer for the debt, default or miscarriage of any other person, or to charge any person upon any agreement made upon consideration of marriage, or upon any contract or sale of lands, tenements or hereditaments, or any interest in or concerning them, or upon any agreement that is not to be performed within the space of one year from the making thereof, unless the agreement upon which the action is brought, or some memorandum or note thereof is in writing and signed by the party to be charged therewith or some person thereunto by him lawfully authorized....
>
> 6. No special promise made by a person to answer for the debt, default or miscarriage of another person, being in writing and signed by the party to be charged therewith, or by some other person by him thereunto lawfully authorized, shall be deemed invalid to support an action or other proceeding to charge the person by whom the promise was made by reason only that the consideration for the promise does not appear in writing, or by necessary inference from a written document.
>
> 7. No action shall be maintained whereby to charge a person upon a promise made after full age to pay a debt contracted during infancy or upon a ratification after full age of a promise or simple contract made during infancy, unless the promise or ratification is made by a writing signed by the party to be charged therewith or by his agent duly authorized to make the promise or ratification.
>
> 8. No action shall be brought whereby to charge a person upon or by reason of a representation or assurance made or given concerning or relating to the character, conduct, credit, ability, trade or dealings of any other person, to the intent or purpose that such other person may obtain money, goods or credit thereupon, unless the representation or assurance is made by a writing signed by the party to be charged therewith....

The original statute contained section 17 dealing with contracts for the sale of goods. This is now found in The Sale of Goods Act (R.S.O. 1970, c. 421):

> 5. (1) A contract for the sale of goods of the value of $40 or more is not enforceable by action unless the buyer accepts part of the goods so sold and actually receives them, or gives something in earnest to bind the contract or in part payment, or unless some note or memorandum in writing of the contract is made and signed by the party to be charged or his agent in that behalf.
>
> (2) This section applies to every such contract notwithstanding that the goods

may be intended to be delivered at some future time, or may not at the time of the contract be actually made, procured, or provided, or fit or ready for delivery, or some act may be requisite for the making or completing thereof, or rendering them fit for delivery.

(3) There is an acceptance of goods within the meaning of this section when the buyer does any act in relation to the goods that recognizes a pre-existing contract of sale, whether there is an acceptance in performance of the contract or not.

It is obvious that a statute passed at any date takes its purpose and method of achieving that purpose from the views and ideas that are current at that time. To understand the Statute of Frauds, we must note briefly the features of the legal system in 1677. Until *Slade's Case* in 1602 and the triumph of the action of assumpsit, the law of contracts had been heavily biased in favour of defendants. A defendant who could, for example, "wage his law" was in a very strong position compared with the plaintiff who would not even get the facts before the trier of fact. This bias was largely reversed by the action of assumpsit. Now the plaintiff could get his case before the jury and the jury was far less subject to judicial control than it was subsequently to become. The courts were only beginning to consider granting a new trial when the verdict was against the evidence, and the close review of the charge to the jury that we see in nineteenth-century cases was unknown.

The reason for this position was explained in *Bushel's Case* (1670), Vaughan 135, 124 E.R. 1006. There Vaughan C.J. explained that a jury could properly decide upon its own knowledge, not just on the evidence. A jury that decided a case dishonestly could be punished by attaint. By this procedure, the original jury's verdict was tested by a second jury, this time of 24 men, and if this jury disagreed with the first, the verdict of the first was set aside and the jurors were subject to heavy punishment. The first jury was regarded as having committed perjury since, as they were deciding on the basis of their own knowledge, a false verdict must have meant that they were false to their oaths to decide on the facts as they knew them. The punishment was imprisonment and forfeiture of all their goods. Since only the members of the jury were subject to attaint, and since it would be no defence to them that they had followed the direction of the judge, it followed that they must be free to disregard his charge. However, by 1670 the punishment of attaint was obsolete and the effect of *Bushel's Case* was to leave the jury free of all control. In addition, the law took the view that anyone interested in the outcome of litigation would obviously give perjured evidence and was, therefore, incompetent as a witness. A further complicating factor was the extreme litigiousness of the English during the sixteenth and seventeenth centuries. People were aggressive and aggressiveness took the form of frequent litigation.

The problem that faced the law was how to ensure that the jury would be somewhat controlled in what it could do. This meant that it would have to be limited in what it could hear. There were two ways by which this could be achieved. The first was the reform of the law of evidence. The second was by requiring that the parties take some steps to reduce their agreements to a form so that their content and authenticity could be easily established. The first of these methods was obviously beyond the capacity of the lawyers of the seventeenth century. In fact reform of the law of evidence took over 200 years to achieve and even now is unfinished. The second was adopted and resulted in the Statute of Frauds.

As will be seen, the Statute of Frauds does some surprising things and is fairly obviously inappropriate now. However, we should be fair to those who drafted it and understand that it is unlikely, to say the least, that legislation passed 300 years ago to deal with problems that existed at that time, would work well now. If this is so, then the fault is ours not theirs; we are the ones who should change. The drafters could not have foreseen what might happen. It should also be remembered that in 1677, the law of contract was in a very primitive state. The law was wholly case-law at that time; this was the first statute dealing with contracts in general.

(For further discussion of the origin of the Statute see: Simpson, *A History of the Common Law of Contract*, Chap. XIII; Holdsworth, *History of English Law*, Vol. 6, pp. 379-397.)

Section 4 of the Act can be broken down into the following parts:

No action shall be brought
(a) whereby to charge any executor or administrator upon any special promise to answer damages out of his own estate, or
(b) whereby to charge any person upon any special promise to answer for the debt, default or miscarriage of any other person, or
(c) to charge any person upon any agreement made upon consideration of marriage, or
(d) upon any contract or sale of lands, tenements or hereditaments, or any interest in or concerning them, or
(e) upon any agreement that is not to be performed within the space of one year from the making thereof,

unless the agreement upon which the action is brought, or some memorandum or note thereof is in writing and signed by the party to be charged therewith or some person thereunto by him lawfully authorized.

We shall deal with each clause by reference to the above letters.

Clauses (a) and (b) can be conveniently dealt with together.

Clause (b) is the general clause and is often referred to as the "suretyship section". Clause (a) is the special case of an executor promising to answer for the debt of another person, in this case the deceased. Few cases have come up under clause (a) and we may confine our investigation to clause (b). The drafting of the clause is not very effective and there are major difficulties in the cases that have come up. The word "special" is used in both clauses (a) and (b) but it has no significance now, whatever it might once have had. The phrase, "debt, default or miscarriage" has been held to cover liability under contract and in tort. Thus a promise to pay for tortious damage done could come "within the statute" — the phrase used to describe those cases where the promise is held to be unenforceable by reason only of s. 4 (or s. 17). The tendency of courts from at least the beginning of the nineteenth century has been to restrict the scope of agreements that come within it. The broadening of the scope of clause (b) is therefore unusual. A typical case is the following:

D owes C money. S promises C that if D does not pay him, S will do so.

This case would be within the statute and S's promise would only be enforceable by C if s. 4 is complied with. However, if the promise is made to D himself, then the statute does not apply. Thus the defendant, in *Eastwood v. Kenyon* (1840), 11 Ad. & El. 438; 113 E.R. 482 (*supra*), in the example, S, made the promise to pay to D, the plaintiff, and not to the person whom D was indebted. This promise was held to be outside the statute.

In the famous case of *Mountstephen v. Lakeman* (1871), L.R. 7 Q.B. 196

(aff'd. L.R. 7 H.L. 17), the defendant, Lakeman, was chairman of a Local Board of Health. It was suggested to the plaintiff, Mountstephen, that he should connect some houses to the main sewer. The plaintiff wanted to know how he would be paid, and the following conversation took place:

> Lakeman: "What objection have you to make in the connection?"
> Mountstephen: "I have none, if you or the board will order the work or become responsible for payment."
> Lakeman: "Go on, Mountstephen, and do the work and I will see you paid."

The board refused to pay and so the plaintiff sued the defendant. The defendant pleaded the statute. [Note: Rule 145 of the Ontario Rules of Practice requires that a defendant who is relying on the Statute of Frauds must specifically plead the statute in his defence. This is an exception to the general rule that the pleadings involve allegation of fact and not law.] The court held that the defendant's promise was not within the statute as there was no other debtor — the board not having authorized the work it was not liable. The defendant's promise was not a promise to answer for another's debt, and so the plaintiff could sue on the oral promise.

These examples are fairly straightforward and the cases can be justified by a close reading of the statute. More difficult problems can come up in the following case which is taken from Fuller and Eisenberg, *Basic Contract Law*, at pp. 1008-1009:

> Manley Minus owes Cherie Claim $1000. Minus gives Claim a mortgage on Blackacre to secure this debt. Thereafter Minus conveys Blackacre to Palfrey Pawn, subject to the mortgage but with a promise by Minus that he will discharge the mortgage and thus release Pawn's land of the mortgage lien. Minus fails to pay the debt and Claim brings a suit to foreclose the mortgage on Blackacre. To save his land, Pawn orally promises Claim that if Claim will give up the suit, he, Pawn, will stand back of Minus's debt. Claim discontinues the suit. Pawn refuses to honor his promise. Claim sues Pawn on the oral agreement. Pawn pleads the Statute of Frauds, asserting that his promise was a promise to answer for the debt of another, namely Minus. A well-established line of authorities would hold the promise not within the Statute and would render judgment for Claim.

The usual way of explaining the result in this case is to say that when Pawn promises to pay the debt owed to Claim, he was only doing so to save his own property and that therefore his promise is outside the statute. There is nothing in the words of the section to support this interpretation. It could be argued that the purpose of the formal requirements of the statute is concern for the *cautionary* function. When someone in the position of Pawn promises to pay another's debt and does so to protect his own interest, then that function is already adequately protected and that therefore the added protection of the statute is not necessary. The difficulty with this rationalization is that the statute is generally regarded as protecting the *evidentiary* function. (Such a purpose could be inferred from the origin of the statute.) This conclusion is supported by the rule that even if the creditor should give consideration for the surety's promise, the promise is within the statute and unenforceable unless in writing. What we see here is that there are competing purposes behind the statute and until we can be clear as to how those are going to be used, we cannot be sure what will happen. The result in the example is sometimes referred to as the "main purpose rule". The statute will not apply where the main purpose of the surety's promise is to protect his own property or his own interests.

The courts have another way to avoid the application of clause (b) in those cases where the creditor is promised his money by both of the other parties. In some cases it may not be clear whether one party is a debtor and the other his surety or both parties are debtors. For example, the supplier of goods to a small incorporated business may require from the owner of the company a promise to pay the debts incurred by the business. It will not always be clear whether the owner is acting only as a surety for his company's debts or is promising to pay as a principal debtor in any event. The result in any case will depend much on the attitude of the court and also on the knowledge of the creditor of the relationship between the other parties.

Problem: C lends money to D on the oral promise of S to be surety. All parties know that D is a minor and that he, therefore, cannot be sued for the debt. Can C sue S?

Clause (c), the "marriage section", is of comparatively slight importance. It does not require that any promise to marry must be in writing to be enforceable, since any engagement the contract consists in the mutual promises to marry. This clause does catch the promise, say, by a father to pay his son $10,000 on the latter's marriage. A promise by both sets of parents to pay the couple $10,000 on their marriage is outside the statute since the parents are each promising to pay and the consideration is then in the mutual promises. The marriage is then the occasion for the payment not the consideration.

See: *Tweddle v. Atkinson (supra).*

Clause (d), brings within the statute all contracts for the sale of land. (It is generally accepted that the words "contract *or* sale of lands" should have read, "contract *for* sale of lands".) It has been held that this includes promises to devise lands by will as well as contracts for the exchange of land for something else. It does not matter what the value of the interest in land might be. Contracts and conveyances of interests in land are also covered by the first three sections of the Act. Under these sections all conveyances have to be made by deed (subject to certain exceptions) and all leases, except those for less than three years, have to be by deed.

The courts have generally regarded as interests in land the kind of rights that would be generally thought to relate to real property. These would include the fee simple, life estate and easement, but might not include all cases of licences, *e.g.*, an agreement to let someone have a particular seat in a theatre.

There is one large exception to the rule requiring contracts for the sale of land to be in writing which has been developed by the courts of equity. This is the doctrine of part performance. This aspect of the interpretation of the statute was discussed by the Supreme Court of Canada in *Deglman v. Guaranty Trust Co.*, [1954] 3 D.L.R. 785 (*supra*). The position taken by the Supreme Court of Canada in that case is consistent with the general view of the courts, and is summed up in the judgment of Rand J. To be "part performance" sufficient to avoid the effects of the statute, the acts must be uniquely referable to the contract that has been alleged. The most common example is the purchaser's taking possession of the land. This fact was held to offer evidence of the contract that was independent of the oral contract.

However, the House of Lords in *Steadman v. Steadman*, [1974] 2 All E.R. 977, held, by a majority, that part performance would be available in a wider range of cases than had been thought to be the case. In this case a husband and wife had orally agreed that the wife would release her interest in the family home for a promise by the husband to pay her £1500 and that he would immediately pay £100 in respect of arrears of maintenance. The promise to pay the arrears of maintenance in this way was approved by the magistrates' court. The husband paid £100 in accordance with the agreement, but the wife refused to execute a transfer of her interest in the house. The wife argued that the promise was not in writing and was therefore unenforceable and that there had been no part performance. (The statutory provision equivalent to s. 4 of the Ontario Statute of Frauds is s. 40 of the Law of Property Act, 1925, but the sections are in substance the same.)

     Lord Reid said (p. 981)

> "The argument for the wife, for which there is a good deal of authority, is that no act can be relied on as an act of part performance unless it relates to the land to be acquired and can only be explained by the existence of a contract relating to the land. But let me suppose a case of an oral contract where the consideration for the transfer of the land was not money but the transfer of some personal property or the performance of some obligation. The personal property is then transferred or the obligation is performed to the knowledge of the owner of the land in circumstances where there can be no restitutio in integrum. On what rational principle could it be said that the doctrine of part performance is not to apply? And we were not referred to any case of that kind where the court had refused to apply it. The transfer of the personal property or the performance of the obligation would indicate the existence of a contract but it would not indicate that the contract related to that or any other land.
>
> "I think that there has been some confusion between this supposed rule and another perfectly good rule. You must not first look at the oral contract and then see whether the alleged acts or part performance are consistent with it. You must first look at the alleged acts of part performance and see whether they prove that there must have been a contract and it is only if they do so prove that you can bring in the oral contract.
>
> "A thing is proved in civil litigation by shewing that it is more probably true than not; and I see no reason why there should be any different standard of proof here. If there were what would the standard be? The only other recognised standard of proof is beyond reasonable doubt but why should that apply here?
>
> "I am aware that it has often been said that the acts relied on must necessarily or unequivocally indicate the existence of a contract. It may well be that we should consider whether any prudent reasonable man would have done those acts if there had not been a contract but many people are neither prudent nor reasonable and they might often spend money or prejudice their position not in reliance on a contract but in the optimistic expectation that a contract would follow. So if there were a rule that acts relied on as part performance must of their own nature unequivocally shew that there was a contract, it would be only in the rarest case that all other possible explanations could be excluded.
>
> "In my view, unless the law is to be divorced from reason and principle, the rule must be that you take the whole circumstances, leaving aside evidence about the oral contract, and see whether it is proved that the acts relied on were done in reliance on a contract: that will be proved if it is shewn to be more probable than not.
>
> "Authorities which seem to require more than that appear to be based on an idea, never clearly defined, to the effect that the law of part performance is a rule of evidence rather than an application of an equitable principle. I do not know on what ground any court could say that, although you cannot produce the evidence required by the Statute of Frauds, some other kind of evidence will do instead. But I can see that if part performance is simply regarded as evidence

then it would be reasonable to hold not only that the acts of part performance must relate to the land but that they must indicate the nature of the oral contract with regard to the land. But that appears to me to be a fundamental departure from the true doctrine of part performance."

The House of Lords, therefore, held that the wife's promise was enforceable.

It remains to be seen what the ultimate effect of *Steadman v. Steadman* will be. The original interference of the court of equity was to prevent the statute being used to permit frauds rather than to prevent them. The equitable doctrine of part performance is a striking example of what one might regard as a purposive interpretation of a statute. Similarly, the courts have refused to allow the statute to be used "to prevent the Court of Equity from giving relief in a case of a plain, clear and deliberate fraud" (*Haigh v. Kaye* (1872), L.R. 7 Ch. App. 469 per James L.J. at p. 474). A recent example of the operation of the principle that "the Statute of Frauds cannot be used as an engine of fraud" is *Bannister v. Bannister*, [1948] 2 All E.R. 133 (C.A.). The defendant sold properties to the plaintiff on the plaintiff's oral promise that the defendant could live rent free in a particular cottage for as long as she liked. After the property had been conveyed (by a deed containing no reference to the earlier oral agreement), disagreement arose between the parties and the plaintiff claimed possession of the cottage. Defendant pleaded the oral agreement, while the plaintiff relied on the English equivalent of s. 4 which required such an agreement to be in a written and signed form. The Court of Appeal held (*inter alia*), that it was fraudulent on the plaintiff's part to insist on the absolute nature of the conveyance in an attempt to defeat the defendant's beneficial interest. Such "hiding behind the statute" was not to be permitted: the plaintiff was held to be a constructive trustee of the property for the defendant, and he was required to hold the property on the terms of the oral agreement.

Section 5 of *The Sale of Goods Act*, which replaced s. 17 of the original statute and requires that a contract for the sale of goods of more than $40 must be in writing, incorporates the doctrine of part performance by providing that no writing is necessary if the buyer accepts the goods and actually receives them, or gives some deposit or part payment. The original statute provided that writing was only necessary in contracts for the sale of goods for £10 or more. The translation of £10 into $40 ignores the effect of inflation over 300 years. The U.C.C. in § 2.201 has a writing requirement in cases of sales over $500, though £10 in 1677 is probably more like $1,000 – 2,000 now.

Clause (e) appears to be fairly straightforward, but once again, the apparent failure of the draftsman to think things through has led to some extraordinary results. The purpose of this clause we may assume was to prevent undue reliance on the memory of witnesses by requiring some permanent record of the agreement. If this purpose were to be consistently followed, one might have expected concern for such related matters as the Statute of Limitations (first passed in 1623) and for agreements which might run for more than one year, though capable of being performed in one year. It was suggested soon after the statute was passed that the outcome might depend on what happened. However, a "wait and see" policy in regard to contract could hardly work if disputes arose within a few months of the making of the agreement. A second attempt at a solution was to have regard to the time expected by the parties for performance. But again this solution will not work since in the case of contracts of uncertain duration (*e.g.*, a contract to support someone until death) it is impossible to translate the expected term into years. The solution that the courts have finally adopted is to consider what could have happened. The test is therefore whether the contract could be performed within one year or not. If the contract could be so performed then the contract is not within the statute. A contract, therefore, to employ a man for the rest of his life is not within the statute, even though the employee might live for forty years. What about a contract to employ the same person for 10 years, is that within the statute? It is true that the man could die within the year, and so come within reasoning similar to that in the earlier example. If this reasoning had been accepted by the courts, it would be hard to think of any contract that would be within the statute. The distinction between the two cases is that the first contract is fully performed by the employee's death, while the second is not *performed* until the ten-year term is up, though it may be *discharged* by the employee's death before the term is up. This interpretation of the statute results in a curious reversal of the arguments that one might expect from each side. An employer sued by his employee who raises the defence of the statute may seek to argue that the employee has a far more secure position than the latter might have expected. Similarly an employee may be forced to argue that there was no fixed term for the contract. (For judicial comment on this, see Du Parcq. L.J. in *Adams v. Union Cinemas Ltd.,* [1939] 3 All E.R. 136.) The courts have also had to deal with contracts where the term may be for, say, two years, but both sides may have an option to terminate on six months' notice. Is such a contract within the statute? In *Hanau v. Ehrlich*, [1912] A.C. 39, the House of Lords held that the contract was within the statute. Where one party may perform within the year but the other's obligation cannot be so performed, the courts have held that the contract is without the statute. However, a similar contract where one party's obligation is of indefinite duration is within the statute and unenforceable.

The statute requires that the "agreement... or some memorandum or note thereof" be in writing. What is a sufficient memorandum or note under the statute? A signed offer is sufficient since the statute does not require that the agreement be in writing. A document is "signed" within the meaning of the statute if the party's name appears in printed form. An actual "signature" is not required. The note must be sufficiently precise to enable the court to understand the contract. However complete accuracy is not necessary. Section 6 specifies that in the case of an agreement coming within clause (b), the note need not show the consideration for the promise. This is an important concession since, in contracts of guarantee, the consideration is seldom stated. A sufficient "note" may be obtained from more than one piece of paper, provided that it can be shown that the pieces relate to the same agreement. A memorandum may fail to satisfy the statute because it does not correctly set out the agreement. Thus we have the paradox that parol evidence of the oral agreement may be used to impugn a memorandum when the oral agreement itself could not be sued upon because of the statute! This statement is, however, subject to the parol evidence rule which may operate to prevent any challenge to the written agreement if the court concludes that it does represent the agreement, *i.e.*, that the contract is integrated.

Difficulties largely of a conceptual kind have arisen over the issue of whether an agreement within the statute can be rectified. If the purpose of the statute is to prevent the jury from having too wide a discretion then rectification presents no problems since the jury is not involved in the issue, rectification being an equitable remedy. The general rule accepted now is that the fact that the contract is within the statute does not, of itself, prevent rectification. However, the result in any particular case may depend on what term is sought to be rectified, and on the parties' reliance on the contract. Rectification will not usually be allowed when the only purpose of rectification will be to supply a memorandum satisfying the statute.

So far we have largely been discussing the application of the statute when the contract is executory. It is one thing to say that because of distrust of oral evidence a contract within the statute is not enforceable when neither party has done anything in reliance on the contract. It is another to say that the oral contract is of absolutely no effect if caught by the statute so that no remedy is available to either party, when there has been a serious change of position by one party.

It will be remembered that in *Deglman v. Guaranty Trust Co.*, [1954] 3 D.L.R. 785 (*supra*), the Supreme Court of Canada, after holding that the agreement was within the statute and unenforceable, went on to allow the plaintiff's claim for a *quantum meruit*. The justification for this is that the remedy given is not based on the unenforceable contract but on an obligation implied in law. The difference would be in the measure of the plaintiff's recovery. In an action on the contract, the normal measure of damages would be the expectation interest — the value of the thing promised. The measure in an action in *quasi* contract would be the extent to which the other side would be unjustly enriched. The oddness of this analysis is that the oral agreement has to be proved to show that the plaintiff's performance was not gratuitous, and the plaintiff will be able to adduce evidence of the value of the property that he was promised. (Note that in the *Deglman* case, the plaintiff had not adduced such evidence since the claim was for a decree of specific performance and the lower courts had granted the decree.) There is a certain inconsistency in allowing proof of an oral contract for one purpose but not for another. As a practical matter, the results from the point of view of the plaintiff may be very similar, particularly if the value of the defendant's performance is known.

The case of *Boone v. Coe* (1913), 154 S.W. 900, (*supra*), is an illustration of the fact that, while an action of quasi-contract may be available when the defendant has been unjustly enriched, it may not be available when there has been no such enrichment. In other words, the statute may have little practical effect when the restitution interest is being protected, but much more effect when only the reliance interest is jeopardized. This distinction should not, however, be uncritically accepted. A very strong case may be made for wider protection even when the contract is within the statute. The Restatement II provides:

§ 217A. "A promise which the promisor should reasonably expect to induce action or forbearance on the part of the promisee or a third person and which does induce the action or forbearance is enforceable notwithstanding the Statute of Frauds if injustice can be avoided only by enforcement of the promise. The remedy granted for breach is to be limited as justice requires".

There may, therefore, be various ways around the statute when the restitution and reliance interests are involved. A plaintiff may also be able to make a strong argument for the protection of his expectation interest, *i.e.*, that which was promised by the defendant in his oral contract, particularly when the plaintiff has performed his part of the agreement. The fact of performance is strong independent evidence of the contract. One problem with this argument is that there is internal evidence in the statute that would suggest that part performance is not a panacea. The statute provided in s. 17 (the sale of goods section) that part performance would take the contract out of the statute. No such provision exists in respect of s. 4. However, as we have seen, the court of equity developed the doctrine of part performance in regard to contracts of land. After *Steadman v. Steadman* the way seems open for a development of the doctrine of part performance as a more general way of getting around the statute. One problem remains. Since the doctrine of part performance was an equitable remedy, the usual remedy when it was applied was an equitable one, *e.g.*, specific performance. It was not usually possible or (since the doctrine principally came up in land transactions) desirable to seek common law damages. When the scope of the doctrine of part performance is widened, this problem will have to be faced.

It was said in regard to contracts coming with s. 4(e) that in certain circumstances it may be important whether one party's obligation may be performed within the year or not, whatever may be the limit for performance of the other party's obligation. There are cases holding that actual performance by one party of his obligation may take the agreement out of the statute, and allow an action on the oral contract for the promised return obligation. Perhaps the courts feel that they have taken so many liberties with that part of the statute that a few more won't hurt!

Section 4 of the statute and s. 5 of The Sale of Goods Act say, respectively, that, "no action shall be brought..." and "a contract... is not enforceable by action...". What do these phrases mean? Suppose the following facts:

A promises to build a swimming pool for B. B promises to give A a lot suitable for a summer cottage. These promises are oral. A performs and B conveys the lot. A subsequently argues that the pool was worth $5,000 and the lot only $2,000. A argues that under the statute the oral agreement is unenforceable and so he should be able to sue on a quantum meruit.

It is well established that A will not succeed. The proof of the oral agreement will defeat A's claim since the statute does not prevent the agreement being used as a defence by B. Upon proof by B that he paid the agreed price for the work done by A, A has no basis for his claim that B was unjustly enriched.

A more difficult problem would arise if, on the same facts, A discovers halfway through his work on the pool that the promise of B to convey the lot is unenforceable. Can A then stop work and sue on a quantum meruit? Suppose that B says that he is quite prepared to convey the lot, can he be compelled to sign a sufficient memorandum?

QUESTIONS

1. What assumptions are made by the legislatures of jurisdictions that retain the Statute of Frauds?

2. To what extent are these assumptions justified?

3. How are the answers to questions 1 and 2 relevant:

(a) to a lawyer asked to represent one party to a dispute;

(b) to courts presented with a plea of the Statute of Frauds in any particular litigation;

(c) to a legislature considering questions of whether, and if so how, the Statute of Frauds should be reformed?

CHAPTER 8

ILLEGAL CONTRACTS

Introduction

If a court were ever called upon to enforce a contract whereby A promised to pay B $100,000 if B killed A's husband, it might be expected that the court would feel some reluctance in giving judgment for B. Such a contract would be held to be against public policy and void. The courts have always asserted a power to refuse to enforce contracts on the grounds that they are against public policy or that their enforcement would be an abuse of the process of the court. The cases in this chapter raise questions about the extent to which the courts can, do and should curtail the rights of parties whose contractual relations appear to involve breaches of public policy generally or of specific legislative enactments. The number of these cases may be expected to be large given the very widespread regulation of so many commercial activities now. As you read the cases consider the following points:

1. Are contracts which are executory treated differently from those which are partly executed?
2. When a statute is the basis for the determination of illegality, to what extent is the choice of which remedial approach to use dependent ultimately on legislative intent?
3. In the case of partly executed agreements found void due to illegality, will the court step in with quasi-contractual remedies to restore the status quo anti?
4. Is the making of the contract itself an illegal act which would render a party criminally liable or could the contract that was made possibly have been performed in a lawful manner?
5. Are both parties to an illegal contract equally at fault, and if so what effect does that have on a court's approach to remedies?
6. What are the non-statutory policies which motivate the courts to restrict the freedom of contracting?
7. If a contractual clause exceeds permissible limits set by a statute, must a court invalidate the whole clause, or can it enforce the obligations of the contract to the extent not made illegal by the statute?
8. Similarly, if one clause of a contract is illegal should this make the whole contract illegal and unenforceable or is the contract "divisible" so that it is enforceable without the illegal clause?

JAMES McCAULEY LANDIS, STATUTES AND THE SOURCES OF LAW

(1965), 2 Harvard Journal of Legislation, 7

[1899-1964. In 1932, when Mr. Landis wrote this article, he had been for four years Professor of Legislation at Harvard Law School and was destined to enter public service as a member of the FTC and coauthor of the Securities Act of 1933. Thereafter he served as chairman of both the SEC, 1935-37, and the CAB, 1946-47. However, those who speak of him as Dean Landis remember him best as Dean of the Harvard Law School from 1937 to 1946.

A chief point of departure between nineteenth- and twentieth-century theories of law lies in the emphasis placed upon the judge as a creative artist in the making of law. This, in turn, has pointed inquiry to the sources of judicial law-making. With the rise of the social sciences, there has developed an insistence that those sources should be as far-flung as that immense empire. The traditional method of handling legal materials, however, feeds too much upon itself and offers strenuous resistance to such interpenetration. New techniques are thus demanded for the exploration of other than the customary sources, but the extent to which these materials should be employed for the judicial development of law remains a perplexing problem.

Though, perhaps, the major portion of the law is now skeletonized between the covers of the statute book, little beyond mere recognition of that fact has altered the present approach to law. Such efforts as have concerned themselves with the treatment of this material have, for the most part, centred about the development of a science of statutory interpretation. But even here the results have been disappointing. There still arises a certain unhappiness among judges, to say the least, when they find themselves compelled to dispose of cases upon the basis of governing statutes. Instead of attempting to acquire a better understanding of the relationship that courts should bear to modern legislatures, the avowed tools of interpretation are still the pious canons of an early age developed to guide courts in the interpretation of very primitive legislative mandates. Here and there one finds a plea that recognizes more adequately the function of a legislative assembly and the creative qualities intrinsic to the judicial process. Obviously the increasing scope of legislative activity has only made the need for further advancement of the subject of statutory interpretation more imperative.

Beyond the accepted boundaries that can be accorded to statutory interpretation, however, lies a more neglected but more significant field. This concerns the place that statutes are to occupy in the ultimate processes of law-making by judges. Certainly statutes can never embrace within their sweep all human activity that law is called upon to order. Even the latitudinarian methods of statutory interpretation evolved by civilian theorists — sometimes gossamer-like in their fineness and subtlety and so scarcely able to withstand the rough and ready tumble of actual legal administration — have failed to net the interstices so tightly as to confine the judicial process merely to textual construction. However, to admit the existence of wide areas for legal administration beyond the direct governance of statutes is not to assume that statutes have no part in the solution of problems impossible to bring within the reach of their terms.

I

Historically statutes have never played such a confined role in the development of English law. Instead, much of what is ordinarily regarded as "common law" finds its sources in legislative enactment. The flexible instrument of conspiracy, both in its criminal and civil aspects, has a definite statutory origin. Doctrines that surround the enforcement of the labor contract in its manifold aspects have grown out of a statute-born policy. One needs only recall such legislation as the Statute of Frauds or the Statute of Limitations to conjure up a vast body of law springing from parliamentary enactment and yet independent of its terms, even interpretatively applied. English and American land law responds to the same tests and reveals upon analysis that many of its germinating ideas have a statutory origin. The American doctrine of common-law statutes is in itself testimony to this concept of the statute as a nursing mother of the law. It is small wonder, therefore, that common-law courts at an early stage developed the doctrine of the equity of the statute. To ascribe its origin, as latterday judges and commentators have done, to the poor draftsmanship of the early statutes which naturally excused judges in extending them beyond their terms, is to ignore the nature of the tasks that then confronted the judiciary. It assumes a refined conception of the separation of powers alien to English political life until the time of Anne. But more than this, it fails to recognize that law had then to be made in some fashion, and that as sure sources for its making lay in the policies outlined by a parliament as in the customs of a people.

The doctrine of the equity of the statute was a double-edged device. As Plowden so sagely observed, merely knowing the letter of the statute does not mean that you know its sense, "for sometimes the Sense is more confined and contracted than the Letter, and sometimes it is more large and extensive." Under its authority exceptions dictated by sound policy were written by judges into loose statutory generalizations, and, on the other hand, situations were brought within the reach of the statute that admittedly lay without its express terms. No apology other than the need for a decent administration of justice was indulged in by judges who invoked its aid. Definite principles, therefore, as to the circumstances which would justify extending statutes to cover cases beyond the scope of their language seem never to have been evolved. Rather there was simply the urge to do equity and so mould the law to conform more closely to its recognized aims.

The cases in which judges resorted to the equity of the statute do, however, reveal several recurring factors. Legislation of an early date is often special in character, applying, like the judgment of a court, to a particular situation brought to the attention of Parliament. The modern concept of wide and generalized legislative powers was of slow growth. Statutes would thus be restricted in their application to designated individuals or be limited in their incidence to a named locality. But the same mischief, to use Coke's favorite phrase, would call for like treatment in like situations, and the recognition of this fact led judges to extend the remedies or restrictions of the special act to other persons and other localities similarly circumstanced. Behind this treatment of special legislation lay the revolutionizing idea that "when the Words of a Statute enact one Thing, they enact all other Things which are in a like Degree." Such a concept obviously carried the principle of the equity of the statute beyond that of merely transmuting special into general legislation. Enabling judges to distill from a statute its basic purpose, they could then employ it to slough off the archaisms in their own legal structure. Even general legislation could thus be made to yield a meaning for law beyond its expressed operative effect. The class of situations to which the statutory remedy was expressly made applicable were but illustrative of other analogous cases that deserved to be governed by the same principle. The extension of one remedy beyond its recognized common-law area by the statute justified judges in giving another remedy the same expansive effect. The imposition of liability in a defined series of circumstances was not exhaustive, but offered a reason for fastening liability upon similar conduct.

The leavening influence of this principle in the development of early common law has still to be adequately explored. Its significance, though clearly appreciated by the early writers even up to the time of Coke, has been largely obscured by later commentators like Blackstone, who, like the social contract theorists, held to the faith of a full-fledged system of common law. The rise of equity, permeating law with ideas originating within a coordinate judicial system, has undoubtedly served to obscure the significance of this early attitude toward legislation as one of the major dynamic forces in the law's development. But the present-day importance of ancient statutes is ample evidence of the weight that should be accorded to the method of their treatment in the early law. The essence of that method lay in the recognition by judges that behind the formal fiat of the statute lay an aim that challenged their sympathetic attention, and that the appropriate exercise of judicial power permitted courts to advance ends so emphatically asserted.

Later generations were to imprint a feebler *non possumus* upon the judicial process. The reasons for this professed self-abnegation of power seem extrinsic rather than intrinsic to the nature of law. The eighteenth century as a whole marks a recession from the earlier periods of pronounced major legislative activity. The same century, with characteristic abstract rationalism, attached to the growing fact of the separation of powers an important doctrinal validity. This, in turn, theoretically divorced legislative powers from the judiciary, and led as a matter of logical verity to the conception of judges as passive agents, impotent to do otherwise than merely "find" law. Even the vigor of Lord Mansfield's injection of moral concepts into the law led to rebellion when his personality was removed from the scene. Furthermore, the conception of the common law as a fully matured system, so entrancingly portrayed by Blackstone, naturally lent force to the view that changes in that ideally self-sufficient system should not be lightly countenanced. Under such influences not only was it impossible for the technique of equitable statutory construction to survive, but there developed the antagonistic maxim that statutes in derogation of the common law should be strictly construed.

The first half of the nineteenth century saw a heightening of these influences. The analytical theories of jurisprudence that then held sway served to emphasize the nature of the judicial process as limited to the mere finding of law. The mechanistic evolutionary concepts of the historical jurists required them to oppose all legislation that sought to tamper with the germinal verities that they found inherent in the common law. Added to this was the reaction naturally engendered in a conservative judiciary by the increasing popular demands for reform. The reformers, under the inspiration of Bentham's guidance, turned to legislation as the means of accomplishing their desires, and when the Reform Bill of 1832 brought achievement within their grasp, the attitude of the judiciary, already enunciated in stern maxims, must unconsciously have stiffened.

America, on the other hand, reveals these trends closing in upon its law much later in point of time. The difficulty of bodily transplanting English common law into an alien soil necessitated its modification to meet the new conditions that were there encountered, and thus developed a flexible temper toward its content. With legislation, after the Revolution, a chief agency for the development of law, statutes were readily regarded as sources of law.

Indeed, for a time, the doctrine of the equity of the statute held considerable sway in American courts. It was elevated to the position of a juristic principle under the term "construction" as contrasted with "interpretation" by Francis Lieber in his immortal treatise on hermeneutics. The later professed rejection of such a principle seems, however, to be the result of factors not unlike those that prevailed in England. The extension of the suffrage and the Jacksonian insistence upon wide popular participation in government generated hostility upon the part of the more conservative guardians of the law, which was immeasurably heightened by the dysnomy of democratic legislative methods. In addition to this, juristic conceptions of the passive nature of the judicial process gained sustenance from the erection of the doctrine of the separation of powers into a constitutional maxim, and, with true American faddism for fashions of thinking, achieved an ascendancy that only now is beginning to be threatened. Finally, general contentment with the wide scope of judicial review exercised since the Fourteenth Amendment has robbed legislatures of much of their opportunity to mark out the aims of law, and has generated in the profession something of contempt for the legislative process.

II

Courts to-day have avowedly rejected as part of their technique the doctrine of the equity of the statute. Whatever significance statutes possess to govern results, they achieve by virtue of being interpreted to include the particular situation. Under the guise of interpretation, however, much is accomplished that upon analysis reveals the court as true to the more ancient doctrine of the equitable application of statutes. The results of such dissembling are doubly unfortunate. They discredit the conception that there is any science of interpretation; but they also prevent the development of an appropriate juristic approach towards statutes as a source of "common law." Obviously there is something intrinsic in the attitude toward legislation that was once phrased by reference to the equity of the statute, that cannot be exorcised from the law. To confine to interpretation the judicial development of law from legislation will not suffice; an approach must be made to the problem of the place that statutes should occupy in judicial administration in terms other than hermeneutic theories as to the meaning of legislative enactments.

Certain factors peculiar to modern life make the problem more pressing. Both the profession and the schools are now demanding something more adequate than the traditional method of developing law purely from earlier judicial precedents. Even though the process permits a slow infiltration of wisdom from other branches of sociological effort, some more open liaison is required. Legislation, too, is assuming both a volume and a creative aspect of purpose that makes it impossible to ignore. But at the same time civilization is achieving a complexity that outstrips this effort to embrace its multitudinous activity by rules, while the traditional attitude of courts toward the legislative process insists upon confining that process to the making of rules. Changes in attitude, points of departure, germinating principles — these the judicial process reserves to itself and places beyond the scope of legislative power. On the other hand, the last few decades have seen the steady development of better methods of legislation. Not only has there been progress in the art of draftsmanship, but the growing use of experts and the committee system, itself tending toward an empiric efficiency, has meant much in the advancement of legislative method. A realization of this fact has already made for greater reliance upon the legislative process as an aid to statutory interpretation. Also, there is a growing comprehension that wide modifications have been effected by recent legislation in the structural content of the law. The realization of their full significance is far from complete, for effort is now bent only towards unearthing and classifying the mass of materials dormant in our statute books. Clearly these factors negative the possibility of relegating the legislative process to the role of mere rule-making and of confining the relationship between courts and legislatures merely to the interpretation of statutes.

One well recognized field exists where statutes have been commonly relied upon by courts to determine whether certain types of conduct are to be regarded as tortious. Legislatures in striking at action deemed by them to be undesirable often fail to think beyond the imposition of a criminal penalty for pursuing forbidden acts. The very prohibition, however, carries with it a judgment of culpability. Courts have generally recognized this fact, and have enlarged the area of tort liability by giving the statute the effect of attaching culpability to action in disregard of the statute. The different theories expounded by commentators as to the particular significances to be attached to such statutes need not here detain one; it is the use made of this legislation that holds import. The relevance of the legislature's judgment as to the desirability of particular conduct is obvious. In the unfettered choice open to a heterogeneous assembly the pressure of the various interests making for or against penalizing certain action finds a ready reflection. What remains for the judicial process in such cases is the extent to which the indirect pressure of civil liability shall be employed to compel conformance to the legislative rule.

Legislation in this field is only permitted by courts to exercise a limited function, that of crystallizing recognized principles of liability into more rigid rules to cover recurring type situations. A more extensive use of like statutory material can fairly ask indulgence. The statutory rule may have picked out for reprobation only a limited number of examples from a wide field of not essentially dissimilar instances; but unless the enacted rule covers the particular type of conduct in issue, the traditional technique ignores the legislative treatment of analogous cases. The reasons for this neglect are difficult to grasp. The method of judicial evaluation of the conflicting claims which finally results in the enunciation of a rule has only very generalized and indefinite standards to guide it. Reliance is placed in the main upon particulars which consist of analogous cases decided by other courts, and which consequently reflect only a limited contact with the problem. The judgments of legislatures as expressed in statutory rules often represent a wider and more comprehensive grasp of the situation and yet are practically neglected.

When the highest tribunal of England in 1868 decided that the landowner who artificially accumulates water upon his premises is absolutely liable for damage caused by its escape, that judgment had an enormous influence throughout Anglo-American law. True, the rule evolved was supposed to possess a rational basis in the earlier common-law treatment accorded wild animals. But we are sufficiently mature to recognize that there are differences between rattlesnakes and reservoirs, and to realize that the ultimate wisdom of such a judgment must rest upon the question of how well it distributes the unavoidable losses incident to the pursuit of a particular industrial occupation. Had Parliament in 1868 adopted a similar rule, no such permeating results to the general body of Anglo-American law would have ensued. And this would be true, though the act had been preceded by a thorough and patient inquiry by a Royal Commission into the business of storing large volumes of water and its concomitant risks, and even though the same Lords who approved Mr. Fletcher's claim had in voting "aye" upon the measure given reasons identical with those contained in their judgments. Such a statute would have caused no ripple in the processes of adjudication either in England or on the other side of the Atlantic, and the judicial mind would have failed to discern the essential similarity between water stored in reservoirs, crude petroleum stored in tanks, and gas and electricity confined and maintained upon the premises — surely an easier leap than that from wild animals to reservoirs.

The arguments adduced for neglecting such statutory material generally do little more than pour contempt upon the legislative process. Legislation is presumed immune to "principle"; its judgments represent merely the political pressure of a special class; it is both ignorant and perverse. Criticisms such as these, of course, have substance, but statutes are of all types. The task of distinguishing between the deliberate and the *ad hoc* pronouncements of a legislature is not too difficult. A course of legislation dealing continuously with a series of instances can be made to unfold a principle of action as easily as the sporadic judgments of courts. Deliberate and conscientious preferment of competing claims can be shown to underly the enacted rule, while the wide generality of such a choice can be evidenced by the legislation of other jurisdictions. Only jejune conceptions of both the judicial and the legislative process stand in the way of the appropriate use of such statutory material.

III

Another field, somewhat less apparent, reveals courts giving effects to statutes far beyond their express terms. Doctrines of common law dealing with the relationship between individuals will often be seen to hinge upon a conception as to the position that one party is to occupy in our social structure. This becomes solidified into a concept of status. But obviously status has no meaning apart from its incidents. These incidents, often so numerous as to escape description, have a varying importance in shaping the nucleus of a status. The alteration of some of them possesses no importance beyond the change itself; the alteration of others, however, may call for a radical revision of the privileges or disabilities that have generally been attached to a particular status. The common-law incidents of status, that in their origin have themselves been of empiric growth, must then give way before the new aims deducible from such a basic alteration.

Changes of this nature are commonly the product of legislation. The statutes that express them rarely directly make or alter a status as such; nor do the statutes often see the seamlessness of the pattern that they seek to change. The task of modifying the existing body of the law to fit the structural changes must of necessity be left to courts with the hope that given an end they will mould substantive doctrine to make it effective. Such was the method pursued in the married women's legislation of the last century. The statutes themselves were quite terse, generally granting to married women merely powers to hold and convey property and to sue and be sued. Obviously they swept away the contradictory common-law limitations, but their terms did not directly control numerous allied questions. The resolution of these demanded consideration of how far the change made by the statutes in one incident of the status should affect doctrine developed under a different conception of the married woman's position in society.

The incidental results of the married women's acts are to be seen in decisions dealing with such questions as the liability of the husband for the torts of his wife, his responsibility for crimes committed by her in his presence, their joint liability for conspiracy, the survival of the common-law estate by the entirety, the husband's right to alimony and support, and his duty of support. The statutory grant to the wife of the power to sue, though admittedly concerned with her rights against third persons, has been an important factor in determining what torts committed by one spouse against the property or person of another should give rise to a right of compensation. The specific results that courts have reached in these cases need not here be detailed. It is the method that is significant. There has been general recognition that the married women's acts embodied principles which were of wider import than the statutes in terms expressed and thus necessitated remoulding common-law doctrines to fit the statutory aims. Judgments that sought to retain older common-law limitations hostile to the aim of the statutes were overruled by subsequent legislation, more attuned to the principles of the married women's acts than the courts that professed to be controlled by "principle." The result is an impressive edifice of law resting upon statute and yet not depending upon the express terms of the statutes for its content.

A similar development can be seen in bastardy law. In the early nineteenth century American states quite generally sought to alleviate the unfortunate position that the common law accorded the illegitimate child as a *filius nullius*. These statutes generally made him the heir of his mother, while some states provided means for the subsequent legitimation of children born out of wedlock. In terms the statutes did not touch the nature of such children as "children" within the terms of a will, nor were they correlated with the contemporaneous wrongful death acts that gave "children" and "parents" reciprocal rights for compensation for injuries resulting in death. The course of decision in these two situations is worth elaborating.

Statutes which allow the illegitimate child to inherit from its mother, in terms apply only to the situation upon intestacy. Whether the illegitimate child should take as a "child" under a will rested theoretically upon the intent of the testator. That intent was fashioned for testators by courts imbued with a morality which rigorously excluded the illegitimate child. That morality found its expression in the common-law concept that the bastard had no inheritable blood. This the statutes swept away, and so they should have been given the effect of throwing into the discard an interpretative attitude based upon that policy. With some exceptions, the statutes were so utilized, and courts either adopted the presumption that the illegitimate child is to be considered the "child" of the parent from whom he has inheritable rights or, throwing aside any presumption, sought to give effect to the true intent of the testator by inquiry into the *de facto* relationship as to the particular child.

American wrongful death acts commonly provide that a "child" may maintain an action for the death of its "parent" and *vice versa*, or else give the personal representative of the deceased a right to sue for the benefit of the next of kin. The latter type of act plainly draws upon principles of intestate distribution in order to fix the incidence of the injury caused by death, and distributes compensation in accordance with such a general plan. Changes in the principles of intestate distribution, whether made prior or subsequent to the death statute, should therefore carry through into the distribution of compensation effected by the death acts. Thus legislation giving the illegitimate child inheritable rights should make him one of the "next of kin" entitled to compensation by the death statute. Such a result has almost uniformly been reached by the courts. But strangely enough courts have on occasion shrunk from designating illegitimate children as "children" in death statutes that framed their plans of distributive compensation in such language. Here, as distinct from the problem of interpreting "children" in testamentary dispositions, considerations of *de facto* relationships play no part, and the issue turns only upon legal and moral conceptions of the reciprocal duty of support. The illegitimate child statutes have definitely moulded these relationships, and only adherence to doctrine, now devoid of substance, can be adduced for failing to carry out the principle of this legislation.

Another illustration of statutes indirectly effecting relational changes concerns the responsibility of trade-unions for torts committed by their members. Both broad social considerations and the bias of our law would seem to have made for a rule that would impose a real liability upon union funds, but for years the dry logic of the common law made against such a result. When in the Taff Vale and Coronado cases trade-unions were finally made responsible for the conduct of their members, great emphasis was placed upon the fact that legislatures, ignoring the attitude of the common law, had been consistently affixing responsibilities and granting privileges to trade-unions as such. The status that legislation had accorded trade-unions was thus generally carried over into the law. These decisions have been explained as being derived from the statutes by the interpretative process or as being dictated by considerations wholly independent of the course of legislation. But mere interpretation is incapable of furnishing an adequate basis for the results, while the very different treatment accorded the same problem in the absence of a similar legislative background illustrates the significance of the statutes. Here again legislation afforded more than a rule; it revealed a governing attitude which was not exhausted but merely illustrated by particular instances.

IV

Apart from statutes more acutely defining norms of conduct and legislation affecting status, various other instances occur of the employment of statutes to alter the fixed approach that adjudication grown conceptual has taken to various problems. Statutes may tend to affix a value to a claim that as yet has failed to gain any judicial recognition. The tendency of the statute, however, is to define that value by reference to a series of circumstances that transmute it into a right. But the circumstances are rarely exhaustive, so that courts are called upon to determine whether, outside of its statutory field of recognition, the interest is to receive any protection.

A typical example of such a process is to be seen in the handling of wrongful death statutes by American courts. The common law's refusal to recognize death as a compensable injury seems to have been no "more profound than the absence of a remedy when a man's body was hanged and his goods confiscated for the felony." The doctrine had only a precarious foothold in American common law when wrongful death acts generally swept it aside. But admiralty jurisdiction is at points unamenable to state legislation, and so the issue was presented as to how far such values, widely recognized on land, could claim recognition at sea. Judges, awake to the purport of this legislative movement, eagerly seized upon principles derivable from "natural equity" and "consonant . . . with the benign spirit of English and American legislation on the subject" to mould admiralty law to conform with the trend of civilized thought. But the Supreme Court of the United States, turning its back on what it conceived to be a non-judicial technique, overturned these decisions and insisted that admiralty law must draw its content from the obsolete doctrines of the common law.

The subsequent history of this problem illustrates the waste attendant upon such an attitude toward the judicial process. The Supreme Court only permitted the maintenance under state statutes of an action for wrongful death, either in the state courts, or by a libel *in personam* in the federal courts, where the tort occurred within the jurisdictional waters of a state or involved vessels subject to the same or substantially similar jurisdictional control. Accidental features, wholly foreign to the intrinsic merits of imposing liability, thus governed results. Finally Congress intervened with its own wrongful death-at-sea act.

But the lesson seems always to need re-learning. In 1924 the Court was called upon to decide whether an action for wrongful death was maintainable in the Canal Zone. The Panama Code contained merely the customary formulation of the civil-law principle of liability for damage caused by fault. A thorough understanding of the sources of this provision would have yielded a definite answer in favor of the claimant, but both the majority and minority of the Court turned to the common law for a solution. The minority, speaking through Mr. Justice Holmes, insisted that the wrongful death statutes, in force in every American state, not only repudiated basis of the older common-law doctrine but were in themselves the juridical material in the light of which the Code provision should be given a meaning adequate to modern needs. The majority, insisting that common law could not be altered by principles derivable only from legislation, engrafted upon Canal Zone law a doctrine then rejected by every civilized jurisdiction. The decision was immediately repudiated by congressional action, with the net result that one known plaintiff was sacrificed to a theory that made the common law consistent only to its own archaisms.

A similar neglect of the significance to be attached to legislation permeates another field. The common law's insistence that "dying without issue" should be interpreted to mean an indefinite rather than a definite failure of issue is traceable to the fact that by such a construction it would convert the estate of the first taker into a fee tail, consistently with conceptions of the devolution of property natural to a society where primogeniture prevailed. American legislation, based upon more democratic ideas of the distribution of realty, quite generally substituted the fee simple for the fee tail. The conversion of a fee tail into a fee simple by force of the statute not only robbed the phrase "dying without issue" of its otherwise accepted meaning; it invalidated on the ground of remoteness any gift over made to depend upon an indefinite failure of issue. Obviously such legislation required a reversal of the older canons of construction, but judges continued to recite the ancient rubrics until supplementary statutes directly rejected their mouldering learning. The point can be made clearer by comparing the common-law treatment of bequests of personalty made upon such a contingency. Because of the absence of fee tails in personalty and the consequent remoteness of the gift over, the presumption that dying without issue meant an indefinite failure of issue readily yielded to a different interpretation. The statutes, by abolishing fee tails, in this respect likened realty to personalty, and the liberality that attached to the construction of gifts of personalty should naturally have been carried over to similar gifts of realty. The extraordinary fact is that no such result ensued, but that new rules of interpretation had to be positively imposed by statute.

One may contrast with these cases the attitude of the quasi-civil Scotch law in dealing with salmon fishing in Scotch rivers. From early times Scotch legislation, with the object of securing the free passage of spawning salmon up the rivers, had prohibited the erection of certain obstacles which would prevent unimpeded access to and from the spawning grounds. The statutes only expressly restricted particular modes of fishing. But Scotch courts, drawing from this legislation a principle of free passage against interruption by fixed works placed in the rivers, evolved from the statutes prohibitions against fishing devices the use of which violated such a principle. An ingenious type of weir would thus fall under the ban "although not particularly prohibited by any act of parliament." The House of Lords, giving the same effect to this type of legislation, recognized that the Scotch technique was nothing more than their own older "equity of the statute."

In the handling of the American uniform acts something of this quality occasionally appears. The very fact that such legislation supposedly only restates the common law and that it seeks to comprehend within its four corners the entire law upon the subject, makes it yield more readily to this type of treatment. Courts thus with little hesitation refer to sections of the Negotiable Instruments Law to illustrate a principle in the same way in which cases are commonly adduced to guide decision. Even the consciousness that legislation is being used in a somewhat novel manner is missing. But where the rule enunciated by the Act differs rather radically from earlier common-law authority, there is more hesitation in so employing it. Instead of correlating the law in situations not directly governed by the statute to correspond with the basic conceptions of the Act, the mere fact that the Act has for a good reason repudiated an earlier common-law rule is a ground for taking the bad rather than the good as a premise. The desirable approach would call for an even more extensive reliance upon such statutory material, and would demand correlation of the various uniform commercial acts in an effort to unearth guiding principles.

Differences of degree will always present themselves in any consideration of the extent to which values created by statute should be recognized in fields not directly governed by legislation. But a thorough understanding of the process underlying the statute will often give a clue as to the influence that it deserves. "Mischiefs," as Coke said, are often responsible for legislative action and are the key to its meaning. The consequences of the mischief may only have been appreciated by the legislature in a limited field and patent abuses alone eliminated. But thorough understanding of the statute enables one to pierce through the specific remedial measures to a concern with the causative influences that made action necessary. On the other hand, statutes may represent merely a rectification of the existing pattern of the law without striking at its deeper assumptions. Yet even rectifications, sufficiently abundant, may, like the empiric process of adjudication, spell out an attitude of more moment than the manifestations themselves, and thus bring into being a policy calling for a fuller realization.

Distinctions of this nature cannot be formulated into rules. Their discovery, however, follows upon a thorough acquaintance with the whole sweep of the legislative process. Instead of treating statutory materials in an isolated fashion, care and imagination in handling them, such as is customary in dealing with judicial precedents, may produce fruitful results. Coordinating existing legal institutions with statutory aims surely is as significant as correlating them with conceptions spun from the odds and ends of judicial logic. And like judge-made law, the territorial relevance of statutes is not to be too closely circumscribed. The comparative technique is important to a perception of their wider import. Judges alive to the necessity of making law adequate to the needs of a new continent did not hesitate to draw upon the "benign spirit of English legislation."

V

The interplay between legislation and adjudication has been generally explored from the standpoint of interpretation. The function of the legislature as, in essence, a supreme court of appeal constantly busying itself with correcting the aberrations of the judicial process has been largely ignored. Cases, so far as their doctrinal content go, are overruled at almost every legislative session. The deeper import of such action has yet to be appreciated. A decent respect for the legislative process would strike a more favorable balance between legislative and judicial development of law.

One phase of the problem assumes importance especially in a nation with forty-eight coordinate but common legal systems. One jurisdiction faced with the same problem earlier decided by another jurisdiction has to weigh the significance to be attached to a statute repudiating the judicial solution made of the problem. To the narrow traditionalist the statute itself is a datum which reinforces the fact that the overruled decision is evidence of the common law, and so error perpetuates itself. But the simplicity of such a conception of the common law is slowly passing. A better understanding now exists of the nature of the judicial process and the nicety of the choices that sway judgment and thus result in law. Plainly, then, the statute is pertinent. Bench and bar have been prone to neglect this aspect of legislation. Cases are relied upon as authoritative without cognizance of the fact that in the jurisdiction that gave them birth they have already been repudiated. An editorial criticism of a decision is relied upon as an excuse for refusing to follow it, while the judgment of a legislature overturning its effect is neglected. Judicial reversals avowedly based upon the social inexpediency of the earlier conclusion stifle its germinating powers, but the same sober judgment of a representative assembly merely adds virulence to the poison of judicial unwisdom. Indeed, at times the process portrays a fantasy more than fit for a new Erewhon.

This has not always been true. When in 1863 the Supreme Judicial Court of Massachusetts had to determine whether a general devise operated to execute a power of appointment vested in the testator, the Court turned its back upon the common-law authorities that refused to accord the devise such an effect. Instead, awake to the inequities of the common-law rule and conscious of its abrogation by the Wills Act of 1837, the Court chose the legislative solution, convinced that "the rule of the English statute appears to us the wiser and safer rule." Similarly New York, where the statutory revisers had already incorporated the rule of the Wills Act but applied it in terms only to realty, extended the statutory doctrine to cover dispositions of personalty. Needless legislation had to be evoked in other states to overturn decisions of their courts, whose traditionalism had led them to adhere to the common-law rule.

An illustration of the same technique may be drawn from the Judicial Committee of the Privy Council. Equity courts had refused, in the absence of an express command, to regard a power of appointment as exclusionary, and had further hampered its exclusionary use by the development of the doctrine of illusory appointments. The whole equitable doctrine had come in for bitter criticism by English chancellors. First by a badly conceived statute, drafted by Lord St. Leonards, and later in 1874 by additional legislation, Parliament swept away the doctrine of illusory and exclusionary appointments. In 1885 the Privy Council was required to determine what rule as to such appointments should govern in Lower Canada. No Canadian authorities or Canadian legislation bore upon the issue, while the English legislation concerned only the United Kingdom. Applying the traditional technique, the Privy Council would have engrafted upon Lower Canada a system that the next legislature would have been called upon to abrogate. Instead, it refused to be "bound by a course of English decisions which have been swept away by the legislature as fraught with inconvenience and mischief... and thereby introduce into Lower Canada all those difficulties and inconveniences which it required the force of an Act of Parliament in England to remove."

Characteristics of the modern legislative process serve to increase the importance of such a technique. Judicial councils exist with the function of acting as ministries of justice to call to the attention of the legislature weaknesses in existing judge-made law. Their recommendations, when translated into statutes, ought to possess great persuasive value. Expert legislative draftsmen are commonly attached to legislatures, their counsels operating to prevent the unfortunate incidents that characterized the legislation of early democratic assemblies. In the light of changes that modern juristic thinking has wrought in the nature and sources of law, judicial precedents are assuming a less coercive quality. If it be true that law reflects and should reflect experience rather than logic, legislation born of such an urge demands careful and sympathetic consideration.

VI

The present attitude responsible for our cavalier treatment of legislation is certain to be a passing phenomenon. The consciousness that the judicial and legislative processes are closely allied both in technique and in aims will inevitably make for greater interdependence in both. The beginnings of such a movement are already clearly discernible in the process of statutory interpretation where courts, returning to an earlier attitude, seek to interpret expressions of policy in the light of the manifold circumstances responsible for the statutory formulation. Grammatical interpretation is giving way to functional construction. The distrust of legislative intervention is subsiding with the important advances made in the mechanics of law-making. Our prevailing philosophy makes us less certain that we have seized upon universals, and the search for pragmatical truth carries us naturally to seek for wisdom in the many sources of experience. Black-letter learning has rarely been characteristic of the legislative process, and its importance to adjudication is disappearing with the rise of the social scientific method. And the consciousness that that method, though often in its crudest form, underlies legislation makes for tolerance with the product.

Circumstances militating against a freer use of statutory materials, apart from the passing juridical conception that negates the creative qualities intrinsic in the judicial process, are chiefly technical. The methods of statute-making still fail fully to disclose the operative forces behind legislation. Adequate records that give the lineage of a statute are, for the most part, non-existent. Often the assurance that respectable impulses have underlain its passage is wanting. Doubt may exist as to whether there has been a thorough exploration of the issues upon which choices have been made. Under the pressure of the legislative mechanics of an earlier generation, statutes have been stripped of everything save normative and compulsory provisions. Reasons for the legislature's action, once incorporated in unwieldy preambles, have been eliminated or expressed only in an incidental fashion where sterile judicial technique forbids their examination. Though the older preamble hardly offers the solution, some means of formulating in an authoritative manner the conceptions of policy upon which the statute is based are necessary. Statute books, too, are encumbered with a mass of detailed administrative regulation that tends to bring the entire process into contempt.

Finally, the profession and the schools are at fault for not affording the bench better technical aids. These United States present a most extraordinary laboratory for comparative legislative study. But while the precedents of even our *nisi prius* courts are carefully catalogued, analyzed, and weighed, no scientific concern is manifested over our constantly accumulating legislation. Texts and source-books thread their way through the welter of our decisions, throwing off statutes as excrescences upon the body of the law. Under the impulse of great law-teaching a national attitude toward the common law has arisen to counter-balance the centrifugal forces of our many states. But even the idea that the same spirit can control legislative law is wanting. The task of its development promises to be a chief concern of to-morrow.

PEARCE v. BROOKS

[1866] L.R. 1 Ex. 213. Exchequer Court; Pollock C.B., Martin, Pigott and Bramwell B.B.

DECLARATION stating an agreement by which the plaintiffs agreed to supply the defendant with a new miniature brougham on hire, till the purchase money should be paid by instalments in a period which was not to exceed twelve months; the defendant to have the option to purchase as aforesaid, and to pay 50*l.* down; and in case the brougham should be returned before a second instalment was paid, a forfeiture of fifteen guineas was to be paid in addition to the 50*l.*, and also any damage, except fair wear. Averment, that the defendant returned the brougham before a second instalment was paid, and that it was damaged. Breach, nonpayment of fifteen guineas, or the amount of the damage. Money counts.

Plea 3, to the first count, that at the time of making the supposed agreement, the defendant was to the knowledge of the plaintiffs a prostitute, and that the supposed agreement was made for the supply of a brougham to be used by her as such prostitute, and to assist her in carrying on her said immoral vocation, as the plaintiffs when they made the said agreement well knew, and in the expectation by the plaintiffs that the defendant would pay the plaintiffs the moneys to be paid by the said agreement out of her receipts as such prostitute. Issue.

The case was tried before Bramwell, B., at Guildhall, at the sittings after Michaelmas Term, 1865. It then appeared that the plaintiffs were coachbuilders in partnership, and evidence was given which satisfied the jury that one of the partners knew that the defendant was a prostitute; but there was no direct evidence that either of the plaintiffs knew that the brougham was intended to be used for the purpose of enabling the defendant to prosecute her trade of prostitution; and there was no evidence that the plaintiffs expected to be paid out of the wages of prostitution.

The learned judge ruled that the allegation in the plea as to the mode of payment was immaterial, and he put to the jury the following questions: 1. Did the defendant hire the brougham for the purpose of her prostitution? 2. If she did, did the plaintiffs know the purpose for which it was hired? The jury found that the carriage was used by the defendant as part of her display, to attract men; and that the plaintiffs knew it was supplied to be used for that purpose. They gave nothing for the alleged damage.

On this finding, the learned judge directed a verdict for the defendant, and gave the plaintiffs leave to move to enter a verdict for them for the fifteen guineas penalty.

M. Chambers, Q.C., in Hilary Term, obtained a rule accordingly, on the ground that there was no evidence that the plaintiffs knew the purpose for which the brougham was to be used; and that if there was, the allegation in the plea that the plaintiffs expected to be paid out of the receipts of defendant's prostitution was a material allegation, and had not been proved:

Digby Seymour, Q.C., and *Beresford,* shewed cause. No direct evidence could be given of the plaintiffs' knowledge that the defendant was about to use the carriage for the purpose of prostitution; but the fact that a person known to be a prostitute hires an ornamental brougham is sufficient ground for the finding of the jury.

[BRAMWELL, B. At the trial I was at first disposed to think that there was no evidence on this point, and I put it to the jury, that, in some sense, everything which was supplied to a prostitute is supplied to her to enable her to carry on her trade, as, for instance, shoes sold to a street walker; and that the things supplied must be not merely such as would be necessary or useful for ordinary purposes, and might be also applied to an immoral one; but that they must be such as would under the circumstances not be required, except with that view. The jury, by the mode in which they answered the question, shewed that they appreciated the distinction; and on reflection I think they were entitled to draw the inference which they did. They were entitled to bring their knowledge of the world to bear upon the facts proved. The inference that a prostitute (who swore that she could not read writing) required an ornamental brougham for the purposes of her calling, was as natural a one as that a medical man would want a brougham for the purpose of visiting his patients; and the knowledge of the defendant's condition being brought home to the plaintiffs, the jury were entitled to ascribe to them also the knowledge of her purpose.]

Upon the second point, the case of *Bowry v. Bennett* (1808), 1 Camp. 348, falls short of proving that the plaintiff must intend to be paid out of the proceeds of the illegal act. The report states that the evidence of the plaintiffs' knowledge of the defendant's way of life was "very slight;" and Lord Ellenborough appears to have referred to the intention as to payment not as a legal test, but as a matter of evidence with reference to the particular circumstances of the case. The goods supplied there were clothes; without other circumstances there would be nothing illegal in selling clothes to a known prostitute; but if it were shewn that the seller intended to be paid out of her illegal earnings, the otherwise innocent contract would be vitiated. Neither is *Lloyd v. Johnson* (1798), 1 Bos. & P. 340, cited in the note to the last case, an authority for the plaintiffs, for there part of the contract would have been innocent, and all that the Court says is, that it cannot "take into consideration which of the articles were used by the defendant to an improper purpose, and which were not;" they had no materials for doing so. The present case rather resembles the case of *Crisp v. Churchill,* (1794) cited in *Lloyd v. Johnson* 1 Bos. & P. at p. 340, where the plaintiff was not allowed to recover for the use of lodgings let for the purpose of prostitution.

Pollock, C.B. We are all of opinion that this rule must be discharged. I do not think it is necessary to enter into the subject at large after what has fallen from the bench in the course of the argument, further than to say, that since the case of *Cannan v. Bryce* (1819), 3 B. & Ald. 179, cited by Lord Abinger in delivering the judgment of this Court in the case of *M'Kinnell v. Robinson* (1838), 3 M. & W. 434, and followed by the case in which it was cited, I have always considered it as settled law, that any person who contributes to the performance of an illegal act by supplying a thing with the knowledge that it is going to be used for that purpose, cannot recover the price of the thing so supplied. If, to create that incapacity, it was ever considered necessary that the price should be bargained or expected to be paid out of the fruits of the illegal act (which I do not stop to examine), that proposition has been overruled by the cases I have referred to, and has now ceased to be law. Nor can any distinction be made between an illegal and an immoral purpose; the rule which is applicable to the matter is, *ex turpi causá non oritur actio*, and whether it is an immoral or an illegal purpose in which the plaintiff has participated, it comes equally within the terms of that maxim, and the effect is the same; no cause of action can arise out of either the one or the other. The rule of law was well settled in *Cannan v. Bryce*; that was a case which at the time it was decided, I, in common with many other lawyers in Westminster Hall, was at first disposed to regard with surprise. But the learned judge (then Sir Charles Abbott) who decided it, though not distinguished as an advocate, nor at first eminent as a judge, was one than whom few have adorned the bench with clearer views, or more accurate minds, or have produced more beneficial results in the law. The judgment in that case was, I believe, emphatically *his* judgment; it was assented to by all the members of the Court of King's Bench, and is now the law of the land. If, therefore, this article was furnished to the defendant for the purpose of enabling her to make a display favourable to her immoral purposes, the plaintiffs can derive no cause of action from the bargain. I cannot go with Mr. Chambers in thinking that everything must be found by a jury in such a case with that accuracy from which ordinary decency would recoil. For criminal law it is sometimes necessary that details of a revolting character should be found distinctly and minutely, but for civil purposes this is not necessary. If evidence is given which is sufficient to satisfy the jury of the fact of the immoral purpose, and of the plaintiffs' knowledge of it, and that the article was required and furnished to facilitate that object, it is sufficient, although the facts are not expressed with such plainness as would offend the sense of decency. I agree with my Brother Bramwell that the verdict was right, and that the rule must be discharged.

Martin, B. I am of the same opinion. The real question is, whether sufficient has been found by the jury to make a legal defence to the action under the third plea. The plea states first the fact that the defendant was to the plaintiffs' knowledge a prostitute; second, that the brougham was furnished to enable her to exercise her immoral calling; third, that the plaintiffs expected to be paid out of the earnings of her prostitution. In my opinion the plea is good if the third averment be struck out; and if, therefore, there is evidence that the brougham was, to the knowledge of the plaintiffs, hired for the purpose of such display as would assist the defendant in her immoral occupation, the substance of the plea is proved, and the contract was illegal. When the rule was moved I did not clearly apprehend that the evidence went to that point; had I done so, I should not have concurred in granting it. It is now plain that enough was proved to support the verdict.

As to the case of *Cannan v. Bryce*, I have a strong impression that it has been questioned to this extent, that if money is lent, the lender merely handing it over into the absolute control of the borrower, although he may have reason to suppose that it will be employed illegally, he will not be disentitled from recovering. But, no doubt, if it were part of the contract that the money should be so applied, the contract would be illegal.

Pigott, B. I am of the same opinion. I concurred in granting the rule, not on any doubt as to the law, but because it did not seem clear whether the evidence would support the material allegations in the plea. Upon this point, I think that the jury were entitled to call in aid their knowledge of the usages of the day to interpret the facts proved before them. If a woman, who is known to be a prostitute, wants an ornamental brougham, there can be very little doubt for what purpose she requires it. Then the principle of law expressed in the maxim which my Lord has cited governs the case. It cannot be necessary that the plaintiffs should look to the proceeds of the immoral act for payment; the law would indeed be blind if it supported a contract where the parties were silent as to the mode of payment, and refused to support a similar contract in the rare case where the parties were imprudent enough to express it. The plaintiffs knew the woman's mode of life, and where the means of payment would come from, and to require the proposed addition to the rule would be to make it futile. As to the expressions of Lord Ellenborough which have been relied on, I think they were only meant to give an illustration of what would be evidence of the plaintiffs' participation in the immoral act, and that we are not overruling anything that he has laid down.

Bramwell, B. I am of the same opinion. There is no doubt that the woman was a prostitute; no doubt to my mind that the plaintiffs knew it; there was cogent evidence of the fact, and the jury have so found. The only fact really in dispute is for what purpose was the brougham hired, and if for an immoral purpose, did the plaintiffs know it? At the trial I doubted whether there was evidence of this, but, for the reasons I have already stated, I think the jury were entitled to infer, as they did, that it was hired for the purpose of display, that is, for the purpose of enabling the defendant to pursue her calling, and that the plaintiffs knew it.

That being made out, my difficulty was, whether, though the defendant hired the brougham for that purpose, it could be said that the plaintiffs let it for the same purpose. In one sense, it was not for the same purpose. If a man were to ask for duelling pistols, and to say: "I think I shall fight a duel to-morrow," might not the seller answer: "I do not want to know your purpose; I have nothing to do with it; that is your business: mine is to sell the pistols, and I look only to the profit of trade." No doubt the act would be immoral, but I have felt a doubt whether it would be illegal; and I should still feel it, but that the authority of *Cannan v. Bryce, M'Kinnell v. Robinson* concludes the matter. In the latter case the plea does not say that the money was lent on the terms that the borrower should game with it; but only that it was borrowed by the defendant, and lent by the plaintiff "for the purpose of the defendant's illegally playing and gaming therewith." The case was argued by Mr. Justice Crompton against the plea, and by Mr. Justice Wightman in support of it; and the considered judgment of the Court was delivered by Lord Abinger, who says (p. 441): "As the plea states that the money for which the action is brought was lent for the purpose of illegally playing and gaming therewith, at the illegal game of 'Hazard,' this money cannot be recovered back, on the principle, not for the first time laid down, but fully settled in the case of *Cannan v. Bryce*. This principle is that the repayment of money, lent for the express purpose of accomplishing an illegal object, cannot be enforced." This Court, then, following *Cannan v. Bryce*, decided that it need not be part of the bargain that the subject of the contract should be used unlawfully, but that it is enough if it is handed over for the purpose that the borrower shall so apply it. We are, then, concluded by authority on the point; and, as I have no doubt that the finding of the jury was right, the rule must be discharged.

With respect, however, to the allegation in the plea, which, as I have said, need not be proved, and which I refused to leave to the jury, I desire that it may not be supposed we are overruling anything that Lord Ellenborough has said. It is manifest that he could not have meant to lay down as a rule of law that there would be no illegality in a contract unless payment were to be made out of the proceeds of the illegal act, and that his observation was made with a different view. In the case of the hiring of a cab, which was mentioned in the argument, it would be absurd to suppose that, when both parties were doing the same thing, with the same object and purpose, it would be a lawful act in the one, and unlawful in the other.

Pollock, C.B. I wish to add that I entirely agree with what has fallen from my Brother Martin, as to the case of *Cannan v. Bryce*. If a person lends money, but with a doubt in his mind whether it is to be actually applied to an illegal purpose, it will be a question for the jury whether he meant it to be so applied; but if it were advanced in such a way that it could not possibly be a bribe to an illegal purpose, and afterwards it was turned to that use, neither *Cannan v. Bryce*, nor any other case, decides that his act would be illegal. The case cited rests on the fact that the money was borrowed with the very object of satisfying an illegal purpose.

Rule discharged.

QUESTIONS

1. What does the person in the position of the plaintiff have to know before he falls into the problem the plaintiff faced:

(a) That the purchaser is a prostitute;
(b) That the carriage will be used by a prostitute in the course of her trade;
(c) That the carriage is one that a prostitute is likely to use in her trade;
(d) That the carriage is subsequently used by a prostitute?

2. Suppose that a prostitute wants to buy (on time) the following:

(a) clothes
(b) cosmetics
(c) furniture

or to rent an apartment. Would you expect the courts to take the same view as that adopted in *Pearce v. Brooks*?

3. Would the result in *Pearce* have been different if the parties had agreed on the same terms as indicated in the judgment above, but the defendant had refused to pay the initial £50 deposit and the plaintiffs had been suing in respect of that amount? Would it matter that the plaintiffs had, in reliance on the contract, "customized" the carriage?

4. Suppose that after paying the £50 down payment, the defendant refused to make any of the further instalment payments required by the contract and that, as well, she refused to return the carriage. Would the plaintiffs succeed:

(a) in an action for instalments owing;
(b) in an action for the return of the brougham?

5. How do courts answer such questions as those raised by *Pearce* or by questions 1-4 above?

HOLMAN v. JOHNSON

(1775), 1 Co p 341; 98 E.R. 1120. Queen's Bench.

Assumpsit for goods sold and delivered: plea non assumpsit and verdict for the plaintiff. Upon a rule to shew cause why a new trial should not be granted, Lord Mansfield reported the case, which was shortly this: the plaintiff who was resident at, and an inhabitant of, Dunkirk, together with his partner, a native of that place, sold and delivered a quantity of tea, for the price of which the action was brought, to the order of the defendant, knowing it was intended to be smuggled by him into England: they had, however, no concern in the smuggling scheme itself, but merely sold this tea to him, as they would have done to any other person in the common and ordinary course of their trade.

Mr. Mansfield, in support of the rule, insisted, that the contract for the sale of this tea being founded upon an intention to make an illicit use of it, which intention and purpose was with the privity and knowledge of the plaintiff, he was not entitled to the assistance of the laws of this country to recover the value of it.

Lord Mansfield. — There can be no doubt, but that every action tried here must be tried by the law of England; but the law of England says, that in a variety of circumstances, with regard to contracts legally made abroad, the laws of the country where the cause of action arose shall govern. — There are a great many cases which every country says shall be determined by the laws of foreign countries where they arise. But I do not see how the principles on which that doctrine obtains are applicable to the present case. For no country ever takes notice of the revenue laws of another.

The objection, that a contract is immoral or illegal as between plaintiff and defendant, sounds at all times very ill in the mouth of the defendant. It is not for his sake, however, that the objection is ever allowed; but it is founded in general principles of policy, which the defendant has the advantage of, contrary to the real justice, as between him and the plaintiff, by accident, if I may so say. The principle of public policy is this; ex dolo malo non oritur actio. No Court will lend its aid to a man who founds his cause of action upon an immoral or an illegal act. If, from the plaintiff's own stating or otherwise, the cause of action appears to arise ex turpi causâ, or the transgression of a positive law of this country, there the Court says he has no right to be assisted. It is upon that ground the Court goes; not for the sake of the defendant, but because they will not lend their aid to such a plaintiff. So if the plaintiff and defendant were to change sides, and the defendant was to bring his action against the plaintiff, the latter would then have the advantage of it; for where both are equally in fault, potior est conditio defendentis.

The question therefore is, whether, in this case, the plaintiff's demand is founded upon the ground of any immoral act or contract, or upon the ground of his being guilty of any thing which is prohibited by a positive law of this country. — An immoral contract it certainly is not; for the revenue laws themselves, as well as the offences against them, are all positivi juris. What then is the contract of the plaintiff? It is this: being a resident and inhabitant of Dunkirk, together with his partner, who was born there, he sells a quantity of tea to the defendant, and delivers it at Dunkirk to the defendant's order, to be paid for in ready money there, or by bills drawn personally upon him in England. This is an action brought merely for goods sold and delivered at Dunkirk. Where then, or in what respect is the plaintiff guilty of any crime? Is there any law of England transgressed by a person making a complete sale of a parcel of goods at Dunkirk, and giving credit for them? The contract is complete, and nothing is left to be done. The seller, indeed, knows what the buyer is going to do with the goods, but has no concern in the transaction itself. It is not a bargain to be paid in case the vendee should succeed in landing the goods, but the interest of the vendor is totally at an end, and his contract complete by the delivery of the goods at Dunkirk.

To what a dangerous extent would this go if it were to be held a crime. If contraband clothes are bought in France, and brought home hither; or if glass bought abroad, which ought to pay a great duty, is run into England; shall the French tailor or the glass-manufacturer stand to the risk or loss attending their being run into England? Clearly not. Debt follows the person, and may be recovered in England, let the contract of debt be made where it will; and the law allows a fiction for the sake of expediting the remedy. Therefore, I am clearly of opinion, that the vendors of these goods are not guilty of any offence, nor have they transgressed against the provisions of any Act of Parliament.

I am very glad the old books have been looked into. The doctrine Huberus lays down, is founded in good sense, and upon general principles of justice. I entirely agree with him. He puts the general case in question, thus: tit. De Conflictu Legum, 1 2, pag. 539. "In certo loco merces quaedam prohibitae sunt. Si vendantur ibi, contractus est nullus. Verum, si merx eadem alibi sit vendita, ubi non erat interdicta, emptor condemnabitur, quia, contractus inde ab initio validus fuit." Translated, it might be rendered thus: In England, tea, which has not paid duty, is prohibited; and if sold there the contract is null and void. But if sold and delivered at a place where it is not prohibited, as at Dunkirk, and an action is brought for the price of it in England, the buyer shall be condemned to pay the price; because the original contract was good and valid. — He goes on thus: "Verum si merces venditae in altero loco, ubi prohibitae sunt essent tradendae, jam non fieret condemnatio, quia repugnaret hoc juri et commodo reipublicae quae merces prohibuit." Apply this in the same manner. — But if the goods sold were to be delivered in England, where they are prohibited; the contract is void, and the buyer shall not be liable in an action for the price, because it would be an inconvenience and prejudice to the State if such an action could be maintained.

The gist of the whole turns upon this; that the conclusive delivery was at Dunkirk. If the defendant had bespoke the tea at Dunkirk to be sent to England at a certain price; and the plaintiff had undertaken to send it into England, or had had any concern in the running it into England, he would have been an offender against the laws of this country. But upon the facts of the case, from the first to the last, he clearly has offended against no law of England. Therefore, let the rule for a new trial be discharged.

The three other Judges concurred.

QUESTIONS

1. Is the process by which the court reaches its conclusion here, the same as that used by the *Pearce* court?

2. Would you expect a modern court to be as sympathetic as *Lord Mansfield* was in this case?

Cf. Reggazoni v. Sethia, [1958] A.C. 301 where the House of Lords held that a contract for the sale of jute bags from India to South Africa was void as being against *English* public policy when the performance of the contract involved violating a prohibition by the government of India against trade with South Africa. At that time South Africa was still a member of the Commonwealth.

In *Beresford v. Royal Insurance*, [1938] A.C. 586, the House of Lords disallowed a claim under a policy of life insurance where the insured committed suicide. The policy contained a clause expressly covering death by suicide. The insured killed himself 5 minutes before the policy was due to expire for non-payment of the premium. The court applied the principle that "no system of jurisprudence can with reason include amongst the benefits which it enforces rights directly resulting to the person asserting them from the crime of that person." (*Cleaver v. Mutual Reserve Fund Life Assoc.*, [1892] 1 Q.B. 156).

ROGERS v. LEONARD

(1973), 39 D.L.R. (3d) 349, 1 O.R. (2d) 57.

Haines, J.: — This is an action for damages arising out of the alleged breach of an agreement for sale of certain lands situate in the Oakwood Park area of the community of Grand Bend, in Huron County, Ontario.

The facts which give rise to this action are as follows: The plaintiffs, Fred Rogers and his wife Mary Lee, are residents of Grosse Point, a suburb of Detroit, Michigan, and were friends of people from Grosse Point, the Finks, who had property in Grand Bend, Ontario.

In the month of July, 1971, the plaintiffs were invited by the Finks to spend a week-end with them in Grand Bend. At this time it came to the attention of the Rogers, who were interested in acquiring vacation property in the area, that the defendant, Mrs. Sarah Leonard, owned a cottage in Oakwood Park which had not been used for some years. A meeting was arranged between the plaintiffs and the defendant by Mrs. Fink, a long-time friend of the defendant.

This meeting took place on July 25, 1971, in the London home of Mrs. Leonard. Also present at the meeting were Chris Panos and Sue Fink Panos, at whose wedding the plaintiff, Fred Rogers, had been best man. The proposed purchase was discussed, and the meeting concluded with Mrs. Leonard stating that she would discuss the matter of the purchase with her husband and her lawyer and friends.

A second meeting was arranged for the week-end of August 7, 1971. There is some dispute as to whether this meeting took place on Saturday, August 7th or Sunday, August 8th. However, for reasons set out below, I find that the second meeting took place on Sunday, August 8th, in London at Mrs. Leonard's home where the plaintiffs and Sue and Chris Panos, who were also present, were served luncheon by the defendant's maid. At this meeting Mrs. Leonard announced that she had decided to sell the cottage, known as Clois de Bois, for the sum of $15,000 cash, despite the advice of her lawyer and friends who felt the property was worth more. Mrs. Leonard demanded an instantaneous acceptance or refusal of the offer and the plaintiffs accepted, whereupon Chris Panos, at the request of the defendant who wished to have the agreement embodied in writing, drew up a memorandum dated "8-7-71" which reads as follows:

> Mrs. Sarah Leonard has agreed to sell her property to Fred and Mary Lee Rogers for the sum of $15,000.00 (fifteen thousand) in cash located know (*sic*) as Clois de Bois in Oakwood on this date August 7, 1971. This note is to let it be known until the official papers are drawn up.

I will refer to this memorandum as "the agreement". The agreement is signed by the plaintiffs and the defendant, and witnessed by Susan F. Panos and Chris Panos.

Mrs. Leonard suggested to the plaintiffs that they use her lawyer, Mr. Huron Davidson of London, and promised to speak to her friend, Mr. Allyn Taylor, the chairman of the board of Canada Trust, with respect to mortgage financing. She then telephoned her caretaker, one James Cutting, and advised him that she had sold the cottage called Clois de Bois to the plaintiffs. Mr. Cutting was instructed to meet the plaintiffs at the cottage and to show them all the necessary electrical, water and heating systems, and afterwards to turn the key over to them. The plaintiffs met Mr. Cutting that evening and the same evening returned to Grosse Point, Michigan.

On or about August 9th, Mrs. Leonard contacted her lawyer, Mr. David-son, and Mr. Taylor of Canada Trust, both of whom contacted Mr. Rogers by telephone. It was agreed that the property should be appraised by Canada Trust and Mr. Rogers sent a $50 appraisal fee. Mr. Davidson subsequently wrote to Rogers stating that it might be better if Mr. Rogers could obtain an independent solicitor so that he could have a fresh approach to the question of title, and a new solicitor, Mr. George Mitchell, was subsequently retained. Rogers also arranged to have the cottage professionally cleaned.

On Saturday, August 14th, a third meeting took place between the plaintiffs and the defendant at Clois de Bois, the defendant having expressed the desire to meet the Rogers' children. The defendant also wished, in accordance with an understanding reached the previous Sunday, to remove certain objects from the cottage, the purchase price of which was to have included the contents. Mrs. Leonard was accompanied by a friend, one Dr. Wilcox, who pressed her to take several objects she was unwilling to remove, and whom she more than once reminded that she had sold the cottage and contents. She was also accompanied by a plumber who was to determine the location of a new well to be installed. There was no indication at this time that the defendant would repudiate the transaction.

However, on August 16th, Mr. Rogers received a telephone call from Mr. Mitchell indicating that he was withdrawing from the transaction. Mr. Rogers was required to retain another solicitor, Mr. Girones, his present counsel.

Following a conversation between Girones and Davidson, Davidson informed Rogers by letter dated August 17, 1971, that he was of the opinion that the agreement did not constitute a contract to purchase, and that Mrs. Leonard took this position and requested that Rogers return the key to Clois de Bois. This was confirmed by an undated letter postmarked August 17, 1971, from Sarah Leonard to Rogers, indicating that she would not complete the transaction because the agreement had been signed on Sunday, the Lord's Day. By letter dated August 18, 1971, the $50 appraisal fee was returned by Canada Trust.

Mr. Rogers then wrote to both Mr. Davidson and the defendant indicating that he was ready, willing and able to complete the transaction. On September 15, 1971, the plaintiffs issued a writ for specific performance of the agreement and in the alternative, damages for breach of contract.

There is a counterclaim for possession of the property, and for damages or, in the alternative, occupation rent, the plaintiffs having gone into possession pursuant to an alleged oral agreement with Mrs. Leonard on August 8th, and having remained in possession to date despite the defendant's request that they return the key to the premises.

While it is clear that at the time the agreement was made, the property in question had a value, exclusive of contents, in excess of $30,000, counsel for the defendant does not allege impropriety or undue influence on the part of the plaintiffs, nor incapacity on the part of the defendant. Indeed, the plaintiffs at no time suggested a purchase price, and the defendant, in suggesting the figure of $15,000, had the benefit of the advice of her husband and lawyer, which she saw fit to ignore.

The defendant was an elderly woman of means who was desirous of settling her affairs. As she retained two cottages adjacent to Clois de Bois, she was anxious to have as neighbours compatible persons who were family friends of the Finks. The cottage had not been used for some two years, and I think that there is no question that the defendant knew what she was doing in offering to sell her property for $15,000 cash.

Nevertheless, between August 14th and August 17th, the defendant changed, or was induced to change, her mind. She complained vaguely of dead trees cut down and of dogs running on the property. There is evidence that the defendant was harassed by neighbours and friends and that she asked the plaintiffs to wait until things died down, and told them that they might have the cottage the following year.

Be that as it may, the defendant now seeks to rely upon the following legal defences: (1) that the agreement does not satisfy the requirements of the *Statute of Frauds*, R.S.O. 1970, c. 444; (2) that it is illegal as having been signed on a Sunday contrary to s. 4 of the *Lord's Day Act*, R.S.C. 1970, c. L-13; and (3) that the agreement is in contravention of s. 29 of the *Planning Act*, R.S.O. 1970, c. 349.

The first defence, that the agreement does not fulfil the requirements of the *Statute of Frauds*, was not seriously maintained or argued by the defendant, and in view of my findings with respect to the other defences, I do not consider it necessary to decide whether the agreement fails for non-compliance with the statute.

I will discuss the remaining defences in turn.

The agreement is void as having been signed on a Sunday

Before considering the applicable law, it is necessary to determine whether the agreement was in fact executed on a Sunday. Neither of the plaintiffs can recall whether they met with Mrs. Leonard on Saturday, August 7th or Sunday, August 8th, but rather rely on the fact that the agreement is dated "8-7-71", and upon the repetition of that date in the body of the agreement.

The witness, Chris Panos, inserted the date "8-7-71" in the top right-hand corner of the document after consulting a wrist calendar. The balance of the document was dictated by the defendant, who presumably was also of the impression that the date was August 7th.

In my opinion, however, the agreement was signed on Sunday, August 8th, and in so finding I am influenced by the following facts. Chris Panos testified that the only basis for saying that he believed that the agreement was signed on Saturday was the date "8-7-71" which he inserted in the top right-hand corner of the agreement. He took this date from a small one-month calendar attached to his wrist watch band and admitted that he could have misread the calendar, stating that he is now in doubt whether the agreement was signed on Saturday or Sunday. Susan Panos gave evidence in chief that she believed that the agreement was signed in Mrs. Leonard's home on a Sunday.

Fred Rogers admitted in cross-examination that he drove from Grosse Point, Michigan to Mrs. Leonard's home in London, and thence to Oakwood where he took possession of the cottage and back to Grosse Point all in the same day. There is no question, therefore, of the Rogers having been in Canada on both Saturday, August 7th and Sunday, August 8th. On Tuesday, August 10th, Fred Rogers wrote two letters, the first to one, Fred Walker, wherein he states that he was in Grand Bend on Sunday hoping to meet Walker, and the second to Mrs. Leonard, thanking her for the delightful lunch on Sunday.

Then there is the evidence of Joan Newton, Mrs. Leonard's housekeeper, who could pinpoint Sunday, August 8th as being the date of the Rogers' and Panos' visit to London, because Mrs. Leonard had asked her to work Sunday to prepare dinner for the guests. Mrs. Newton always had Sunday and only Sunday off, and prevailed upon Mrs. Leonard to allow her to prepare the food on Saturday so that it could be served by the maid on Sunday. Mrs. Newton remained in the home all day Saturday preparing the food, and testified that the guests did not arrive on that day. Mrs. Newton was off on Sunday and not in the house.

I have no doubt that the plaintiffs were ignorant of the provisions of the *Lord's Day Act*, and did not realize that it was illegal to enter into an agreement for the sale of land on a Sunday. Mrs. Leonard, on the other hand, was, by her own evidence, quite aware that one could not dispose of property on a Sunday, and knowingly breached the statute on the basis that she was "dealing with friends".

The plaintiffs argue that they were innocent parties throughout and that the defendant, having knowingly proceeded contrary to the statute, should not be allowed to take advantage of her own illegality.

The plaintiffs further maintain that the intent of the *Lord's Day Act* is to prevent the carrying on on Sundays of the business of selling land, and that the Act was passed for the protection of persons who purchase from those engaged in the business of selling land on Sundays, which persons may then invite, or decline to take advantage of, its provisions. In support of these submissions, the plaintiffs rely on *Aconley et al. v. Willart Holdings Ltd.* (1964), 47 D.L.R. (2d) 146, 49 W.W.R. 46, and *Sidmay Ltd. et al. v. Wehttam Investments Ltd.*, [1967] 1 O.R. 508, 61 D.L.R. (2d) 358 (Ont. C.A.) [aff'd [1968] S.C.R. 828, 69 D.L.R. (2d) 336].

In my view the plaintiffs have failed to distinguish between a contract which is illegal in its formation as being prohibited by statute, and a contract which, although *ex facie* lawful, is illegally performed in that one or both parties fail to perform the contract as required by statute. In the latter case the Courts distinguish between the innocent and guilty parties and, while the guilty party is afforded no remedy, the innocent party is allowed to recover damages for breach of contract.

In the former case, however, where the contract as formed is forbidden by statute, it is totally void and cannot be specifically enforced; nor can an action for damages for breach of contract be founded upon it, notwithstanding that it is the defendant who has breached the law and who seeks to set up his own illegality.

The principles upon which the Court refuses to act are stated by Lord Mansfield in *Holman v. Johnson* (1775), 1 Cowp. 341 at p. 343, 98 E.R. 1120, as follows:

> The objection, that a contract is immoral or illegal as between plaintiff and defendant, sounds at all times very ill in the mouth of the defendant. It is not for his sake, however, that the objection is ever allowed; but it is founded in general principles of policy, which the defendant has the advantage of, contrary to the real justice, as between him and the plaintiff, by accident, if I may say so. The principle of public policy is this: *ex dolo malo non oritur actio*. No Court will lend its aid to a man who founds his cause of action upon an immoral or an illegal act. If, from the plaintiff's own stating or otherwise, the cause of action appears to arise *ex turpi causa*, or the transgression of a positive law of this country, there the Court says he has no right to be assisted. It is upon that ground the Court goes; not for the sake of the defendant, but because they will not lend their aid to such a plaintiff.

In *Re Mahmoud and Ispahani*, [1921] 2 K.B. 716, it was provided by statute that no person should buy or sell certain items, including linseed oil, unless licensed to do so. The plaintiff, who had a licence, sold to the defendant a quantity of linseed oil, having inquired of the defendant prior to entering into the contract whether he had a licence and having been assured that the defendant was indeed licensed under the statute. The defendant, who did not in fact have a licence, refused to accept delivery of the oil, and when sued by the plaintiff, sought to defend on the ground that the contract was illegal. According to Scrutton, L.J., at p. 729:

> As I understand, two reasons are given why in this case the Court should enforce this contract. First of all, it is said that the Court will not listen to a person who says, "Protect me from my own illegality." In my view the Court is bound, once it knows that the contract is illegal, to take the objection and to refuse to enforce the contract, whether its knowledge comes from the statement of the party who was guilty of the illegality, or whether its knowledge comes from outside sources. The Court does not sit to enforce illegal contracts. There is no question of estoppel; it is for the protection of the public that the Court refuses to enforce such a contract.
>
> The other point is that, where a contract can be performed lawfully or unlawfully, and the defendant without the knowledge of the plaintiff elects to perform it unlawfully, he cannot plead its illegality. That in my view does not apply to a case where the contract sought to be enforced is altogether prohibited, and in this case to contract with a person who had no licence was altogether prohibited. It was not that the plaintiff might lawfully contract with the defendant and chance his getting the licence before the plaintiff delivered the goods. The contract was absolutely prohibited; and in my view, if an act is prohibited by statute for the public benefit, the Court must enforce the prohibition, even though the person breaking the law relies upon his own illegality.

In the present case, s. 4 of the *Lord's Day Act*, R.S.C. 1970, c. L-13, reads as follows:

> 4. It is not lawful for any person on the Lord's Day, except as provided herein, or in any provincial Act or law in force on or after the 1st day of March 1907, to sell or offer for sale or purchase any goods, chattels, or other personal property, or any real estate, or to carry on or transact any business of his ordinary calling, or in connection with such calling, or for gain to do, or employ any other person to do, on that day, any work, business, or labour.

This section clearly prohibits entering into an agreement for the sale of land on a Sunday. *Ciz v. Hauka* (1953), 108 C.C.C. 349, 11 W.W.R. (N.S.) 433, 61 Man. R. 370; *Neider v. Carda of Peace River District Ltd.*, [1972] S.C.R. 678, 25 D.L.R. (3d) 363, [1972] 4 W.W.R. 513, and *Perry v. Anderson* (1970), 12 D.L.R. (3d) 414, are authority for the proposition that agreements for the sale of land entered into on a Sunday are illegal and consequently void.

The plaintiffs rely on the *Aconley* case, *supra*, as constituting an exception to the principle that a contract, the formation of which is forbidden by statute, is illegal and void, and as authority for the proposition that the state of mind of parties to an illegal contract is relevant to the question of recovery of damages for breach thereof. In the *Aconley* case the parties, following negotiations of more than one month's duration, settled the terms of a contract for the sale of the plaintiff's land to the defendant company. A written agreement was drawn up by one of the plaintiff's solicitors, executed by the plaintiffs, and delivered to the defendant's solicitor for execution by the defendant on Friday, February 8th at which time the defendant's solicitor stated that the agreement would be signed on that date. In fact, however, the agreement was executed by one of the defendant's signing officers on Saturday, February 9th, and by the other signing officer on Sunday, February 10th. On Saturday, February 9th, the defendant had delivered lumber to the property in question. The defendant subsequently refused to complete the transaction and, as a defence to the plaintiffs' action for specific performance, pleaded s. 4 of the *Lord's Day Act*.

In holding the plaintiffs entitled to specific performance, Smith, J., expressed the opinion that, on its facts, the case was distinguishable from *Mahmoud, supra,* and that where the plaintiffs had no reason to suspect that the agreement was executed on Sunday, it would constitute a miscarriage of justice to permit the defendant to successfully plead the *Lord's Day Act.*

However, Smith, J., then went on to state that he was not basing his decision on this ground, but rather on the existence, prior to Sunday, February 10th, of an agreement between the parties which did not depend on the written agreement for its enforceability. The terms of this agreement had been settled before February 10th, and its existence was evidenced by the defendant's having partially performed the contract by delivering lumber to the premises on February 9th.

Without agreeing with Smith, J., concerning the applicability of s. 4 of the *Lord's Day Act* to the circumstances of the *Aconley* case, I find that the present case is quite distinguishable. The plaintiffs, while they did not appreciate the significance of selling land on a Sunday, were present at the home of Mrs. Leonard on Sunday, August 8th when she, and they, executed the memorandum. They, unlike the plaintiffs in the *Aconley* case, had full knowledge of the fact which constituted the illegality, in this case that the contract was signed on a Sunday.

I cannot agree with the plaintiffs that s. 4 was intended to protect purchasers from those engaged in the business of selling land on Sundays. The provision, it seems clear, is dictated by considerations of public policy. Nor, in my opinion, does the *Sidmay* case, *supra,* support the proposition that a contract prohibited by statute can be specifically enforced or form the basis for an action for damages by an innocent plaintiff for whose protection the statute was passed against a defendant who pleads his own illegality. On the contrary, Laskin, J.A., states at pp. 534-5 O.R., pp. 384-5 D.L.R.:

> It would be my view that whether or not a plaintiff is within the class of those for whose benefit an illegalizing statute has been passed, he cannot have the aid of the Court to enforce any executory portion of a transaction that is caught by the statute, even though it is the defendant's act or omission that has caused the illegality: see *Chai Sau Yin v. Liew Kwee Sam,* [1962] A.C. 304.

Rather, the case states the proposition that a plaintiff is entitled to seek the aid of the Courts to recover property which has passed under an illegal contract, or for relief from his bargain without being obliged to make restitution for benefits received thereunder, if he is not equally at fault with the other party in breaching a statute which was passed to protect the class of persons of which he is a member.

Therefore, the agreement of August 8, 1971, is illegal and void by reason of s. 4 of the *Lord's Day Act*, and no suit may be brought to enforce it, nor will the Courts recognize any cause of action founded upon it.

The agreement is void as being in contravention of the Planning Act

The defendant was, on August 8, 1971, and is now, the registered owner of Parts 1, 2 and 3 of Lot 11 and Block B, Registered Plan No. 27 for the Township of Stephen in the County of Huron.

The defendant alleges that, because the land which was the subject of the agreement for sale is Part 3 only of Lot 11 and Block B, it cannot, by virtue of s. 29(4) of the *Planning Act*, be conveyed and an agreement for its sale cannot be entered into without the consent of the Huron Land Division Committee. Furthermore, according to the defendant's contention, s. 29(7) of the *Planning Act* renders the agreement illegal and void because it does not expressly provide that the agreement is conditional upon the obtaining of such consent.

It is clear that neither the plaintiffs nor the defendant had any knowledge of the provisions of the *Planning Act* at the time of the execution of the agreement. As soon as the plaintiffs became aware that the defendant intended to rely upon the *Planning Act* as a defence to their action for specific performance, they applied for the consent required by s. 29(4)(*d*) of the *Planning Act* to the Huron Land Division Committee, which dismissed their application on the ground that it did not conform with the draft official plan. All appeals from this decision have now been exhausted. At all stages of the proceedings and appeals, the defendant, through her counsel, opposed the plaintiffs' application. The plaintiffs accordingly elected damages for breach of contract in lieu of specific performance of the agreement.

The relevant provisions of the *Planning Act* are as follows:

> 29(4) Where land is within a plan of subdivision registered before or after the coming into force of this section, no person shall convey a part of any lot or block of the land by way of a deed or transfer, or grant, assign or exercise a power of appointment with respect to a part of any lot or block of the land, or mortgage or charge a part of any lot or block of the land, or enter into an agreement of sale and purchase of a part of any lot or block of the land or enter into any agreement that has the effect of granting the use of or right in a part of any lot or block of the land directly or by entitlement to renewal for a period of twenty-one years or more unless,...
>
> (*d*) a consent is given to convey, mortgage or charge the land or grant, assign or exercise a power of appointment with respect to the land or enter into an agreement with respect to the land....
>
> (7) An agreement, conveyance, mortgage or charge made, or a power of appointment granted, assigned or exercised in contravention of this section or a predecessor thereof does not create or convey any interest in land, but this section does not affect an agreement entered into subject to the express condition contained therein that such agreement is to be effective only if the provisions of this section are complied with.

The combined effect of these sections is to prohibit a party from entering into an agreement for the sale of land without first obtaining the consent of the committee of adjustments, unless there is inserted in the agreement an express condition that the agreement is to be effective only if the provisions of s. 29 are complied with. Failing such provision, the agreement "does not create or convey any interest in land".

It is the plaintiffs' submission that the parties to the action could enter into the agreement since it is evident that such agreement was conditional upon, and contemplated compliance with the *Planning Act* and all applicable legislation, and that the conditional nature of the contract is evidenced by the words "this note is to let it be known until all the official papers are drawn up".

. . . .

The parties never having heard of the *Planning Act*, it is difficult to imagine how compliance therewith could have been contemplated. In my opinion, a mere statement of intent contained in the agreement that all official papers are to be drawn up, and a general intention to comply with all legal formalities cannot constitute an express condition within the meaning of s. 29(7).

As a result the agreement, by virtue of s. 29(7), creates no interest in land and is illegal and void and no rights can flow from it.

. . .

The question remains whether the plaintiffs are entitled to recover the sum of $108.65 for labour and materials expended in cleaning the cottage after taking possesion.

As a general rule a party may not invoke the aid of the Courts to recover property transferred or money expended pursuant to an illegal transaction, the legal maxim being *in pari delicto potior est conditio defendentis.* While there are exceptions to this rule, I cannot see that the plaintiffs, who are not among a class for whose benefit the statute was passed, and who, to succeed would be forced to rely on the illegal contract, fall within these exceptions.

The plaintiffs rely on *Lauff v. Cooney*, [1960] O.W.N. 481. However, the instant case is again distinguishable by reason of the plaintiffs' knowledge of the fact which constituted the illegality, whereas in the *Lauff* case the purchaser was ignorant of such facts. According to Thompson, J., at p. 482 of the report:

> This, then, being a contract tainted with illegality the general answer was that no rights flowed therefrom. Such a contract was not specifically enforceable, nor could an action for damages for its breach follow. The rights of the parties, and the obligations of the parties, were generally speaking governed by the maxim, *ex turpi causa non oritur actio*, which in the case of illegality of a contract applied with full force. The law, however, had recognized and given effect to certain exceptions upon occasion. This case fell within one of those exceptions.
> Where the illegality was unknown to one of the parties, that is where he had no knowledge of the illegality, then he was not *particeps criminis* or *in pari delicto* with another party who had such knowledge. In such a case knowledge did not mean knowledge of the law, nor was reference made to ignorance of the law which might make a contract illegal, because the law imputed to all persons within its purview a knowledge of its provisions. The reference, rather, was to ignorance of some fact making illegal a contract which would upon the facts known to the party be a legal contract if those facts were in fact established and correct.

I must therefore dismiss the plaintiffs' action for damages and for recovery of the sum of $108.65. I do so with regret, as the plaintiffs have at all times proceeded in good faith and with a genuine intent to comply with all laws. The defendant on the other hand, knowingly breached the *Lord's Day Act*, only to rely on her own illegal breach, and actively opposed the plaintiffs in their attempt to comply with the *Planning Act* by obtaining the consent of the Land Division Committee to severance. While the defendant is entitled at law to succeed on the basis of the technical defences set out, her actions throughout have been characterized by gross bad faith, and in view of this I dismiss the plaintiffs' action without costs.

I will now deal with the defendant's counterclaim for possession of the premises which the plaintiffs still occupy, and for damages in the amount of $2,000, or in the alternative, the sum of $2,000 as occupation rent.

Despite the defendant's contention that the key to the cottage was given to the plaintiffs for the purpose of inspection only, I find that the defendant agreed orally with the plaintiffs on Sunday, August 8th that they should enter into possession of the premises pending completion of the transaction, and that she telephoned her caretaker, James Cutting, and instructed him to show the premises to the plaintiffs and afterwards to turn the keys over to them. The defendant consented to the plaintiffs' occupation until, by Davidson's letter of August 17, 1971, the plaintiffs were requested to return the key to the premises.

I will deal first with the countercalim for possession. The general rule, as stated above, is that a party may not seek the aid of the Courts to recover property or benefits which have passed under an illegal contract. However, by way of exception to this rule, a party may enforce the recovery of property if he can frame his action in such a way that he is not required to rely upon the illegal contract.

Therefore, in so far as the defendant's counterclaim for possession is based upon her registered ownership of the property in question, she is entitled to recover possession: *Mistry Amar Singh v. Kulubya*, [1963] 3 All E.R. 499.

The defendant also counterclaims for damages in the amount of $2,000, presumably for unlawful possession, and, in the alternative, for occupation rent in the sum of $2,000.

While I have been unable to find any cases which deal specifically with a claim for occupation rent or damages against persons in possession under an illegal contract (in *Mistry Amar Sangh, supra*, the plaintiff abandoned his claim for rents), the Courts have aided parties to illegal transactions in the recovery of property or chattels which have passed thereunder. The test is set out in *Taylor v. Chester* (1869), L.R. 4 Q.B. 309 at 314:

> The true test for determining whether or not the plaintiff and the defendant were in pari delicto, is by considering whether the plaintiff could make out his case otherwise than through the medium and by the aid of the illegal transaction to which he was himself a party.

In *Bowmakers, Ltd. v. Barnet Instruments, Ltd.*, [1945] K.B. 65, it is stated at p. 71:

> In our opinion, a man's right to possess his own chattels will as a general rule be enforced against one who, without any claim of right, is detaining them, or has converted them to his own use, even though it may appear either from the pleadings, or in the course of the trial, that the chattels in question came into the defendant's possession by reason of an illegal contract between himself and the plaintiff, provided that the plaintiff does not seek, and is not forced, either to found his claim on the illegal contract or to plead its illegality in order to support his claim.

However, without considering whether it would be possible for the defendant to frame her counterclaim so as not to be forced to rely upon the illegal agreement, the defendant has in fact sought to rely upon the illegality of the agreement in maintaining her claim for damages and occupation rent, stating that because the agreement is void, the plaintiffs have no right to be in possession of the premises. This being so, the following principle stated by Lindley, L.J., in *Scott v. Brown, Doering, McNab & Co.; Slaughter & May v. Brown, Doering, McNab & Co.*, [1892] 2 K.B. 724 at p. 728, applies:

> Ex turpi causa non oritur actio. This old and well-known legal maxim is founded in good sense, and expresses a clear and well-recognised legal principle, which is not confined to indictable offences. No Court ought to enforce an illegal contract or allow itself to be made the instrument of enforcing obligations alleged to arise

out of a contract or transaction which is illegal, if the illegality is duly brought to the notice of the Court, and if the person invoking the aid of the Court is himself implicated in the illegality. It matters not whether the defendant has pleaded the illegality or whether he has not. If the evidence adduced by the plaintiff proves the illegality the Court ought not to assist him.

With respect to the claim for occupation rent I note that to maintain an action for use and occupation, it is necessary to show that the occupation was under a contract, express or implied. There is obviously no express contract in the present case, and before the Court will imply a contract, the plaintiff must establish that the defendant occupies the premises with his consent: *Zalev v. Harris* (1924), 27 O.W.N. 197 (C.A.). *Quaere*, whether the defendant in the instant case is bound by the pleadings to the effect that the plaintiffs took possession of the property without the consent of the defendant.

Furthermore, the presumption from which, upon proof of possession of land with the consent of another, the law implies a contract in favour of the other that reasonable remuneration will be paid for use and occupation, may be rebutted, and it can be argued that the circumstances of this case are such that the law will not imply such a contract, as it is obvious that a landlord and tenant relationship was never contemplated. The law is clear that where a prospective purchaser under a valid agreement of purchase and sales goes into possession pending completion, the vendor cannot succeed in an action for use and occupation: *Temple v. McDonald* (1865), 6 N.S.R. 155 (C.A.).

In the present case, of course, we do not have a valid agreement, but the agreement, while void, is nevertheless evidence of the terms under which the plaintiffs took possession.

Finally, the defendant refers to *Laczko v. Patterson et al.*, [1972] 1 O.R. 100, 22 D.L.R. (3d) 288, in support of the submission on behalf of the defendant that she is entitled to interest at 5% per annum on the principal sum of $15,000 from August 8, 1971, to the date of the plaintiff's delivering up of possession. In *Laczko*, the purchasers under an agreement of purchase and sale entered into possession of the premises pending completion of the transaction, which event occurred approximately one year later. The vendor brought an action for occupation rent which was dismissed at trial. On appeal the vendor was allowed to amend his claim to assert a claim based on the equitable principle that in equity a purchaser in possession of an estate and retaining the purchase price is liable to the vendor for interest on the unpaid purchase price in the absence of an agreement to the contrary. This rule is more fully set out in *International R. Co. v. Niagara Parks Commission*, [1941] 3 D.L.R. 385 at pp. 394-5, [1941] A.C. 328, [1941] 2 W.W.R. 338:

> The equitable rule was established many years before the decision in *Birch v. Joy* [3 H.L.C. 565, 10 E.R. 222] which was decided in 1852. The true rule is that if in cases where Courts of Equity would grant specific performance the purchaser obtains possession of the subject-matter of the contract before the payment of the purchase-price he must in the absence of express agreement to the contrary pay interest on his purchase-money as from the date when he gets possession until the date of payment because it would be inequitable for him to have the benefit of possession of the subject-matter of the contract and also of the purchase money.

The principle, therefore, applies only where the Courts would grant specific performance.

The defendant admits that this principle might not apply if the defendant were in default under the agreement, but maintains that there can be no default as the agreement is null and void. It should be obvious to the defendant that if the Court will decline to exercise its equitable jurisdiction to aid a defaulting vendor in his claim for interest on the purchase price, so also will it refuse to assist a party who relies on her own illegality in seeking to escape from her obligations under an agreement of purchase and sale.

For the foregoing reasons the plaintiffs' action is dismissed without costs. The defendant's counterclaim for possession is allowed without costs, but in other respects it is dismissed without costs. In my respectful opinion the defendant has dealt harshly and unfairly with the plaintiffs who have at all times acted in good faith. To prevent a repetition of similar conduct on the part of the defendant, especially with respect to the plaintiffs vacating the premises and removing their personal possessions and fixtures, I direct that my judgment do not issue for a period of six weeks from the date of these reasons.

Action dismissed; counterclaim allowed in part.

THE LORD'S DAY ACT

R.S.C. 1970, c. L-13.
Offences and Penalties

12. Any person who violates any of the provisions of this Act is for each offence liable, on summary conviction, to a fine of not less than one dollar and not exceeding forty dollars, together with the cost of prosecution.

13. Every employer who authorizes or directs anything to be done in violation of this Act, is for each offence liable, on summary conviction, to a fine not exceeding one hundred dollars and not less than twenty dollars, in addition to any other penalty prescribed by law for the same offence.

14. Every corporation that authorizes, directs, or permits its employees to carry on any part of the business of such corporation in violation of this Act, is liable, on summary conviction before two justices of the peace, for the first offence, to a penalty not exceeding two hundred and fifty dollars and not less than fifty dollars, and, for each subsequent offence, to a penalty not exceeding five hundred dollars and not less than one hundred dollars, in addition to any other penalty prescribed by law for the same offence.

In *Neider v. Carda* (1972), 25 D.L.R. (3d) 363, the Supreme Court of Canada (Martland, Ritchie, Hall, Spence and Laskin JJ.) held a contract for the sale of land which had been made on a Sunday void. The transaction was executed. The Alberta Land Titles Act provided, s. 67, that any sale made on a Sunday was "utterly void".

QUESTIONS

1. Are any matters that should legitimately concern the court not acknowledged in *Rogers*?

2. Suppose that the transaction on Sunday August 8, 1971, had been a conveyance to the Rogers rather than an agreement to convey. Suppose as well that in December of 1974 the Rogers conveyed (on a Monday), to Evelyn and Walter Lauren. Suppose that in January of 1976, Mrs. Leonard sued the Laurens and the Rogers for a declaration that the 1971 conveyance was void. Would she succeed?

KIRIRI COTTON CO. LTD. v. DEWANI

[1960] A.C. 192. Judicial Committee of the Privy Council.

The following facts are taken from the judgment of the Judicial Committee: The plaintiff (respondent) Ranchhoddas Keshavji Dewani was an Indian merchant living at Kampala in Uganda. The defendants (appellants) were the Kiriri Cotton Co. Ltd., which owned a block of flats in Salisbury Road, Kampala. The plaintiff claimed the sum of 10,000 shillings as money received by the defendant company for the use of the plaintiff. The High Court of Uganda (Lyon J.) gave judgment for the plaintiff for that amount, with costs. The Court of Appeal for Eastern Africa (O'Connor P., Forbes J.A. and Keatinge J.) affirmed the decision. The defendant company appealed to Her Majesty in Council.

The facts were simple. The plaintiff came to Kampala in March, 1953, and looked for somewhere to live. At the end of May, 1953, he took a flat in Salisbury Road, but he had to pay 10,000 shillings premium. He now said that that premium was illegal because it was in contravention of the Rent Restriction Ordinance, and he claimed the return of it.

The oral evidence was so short that it could be set out in full. Only the plaintiff gave evidence. He said:

> "I came to Kampala, Uganda, in 1953 — March. I lived with a brother for 1½ months. I took a flat but I had to pay key money. I was searching for some time.
> "I got a flat at Kololo but after 2-3 days I had to leave as I had trouble with a co-tenant. Then I got in touch with C.B. Patel, after having difficulty. I borrowed 10,000/- from the company as my brother was a director."
> Cross-examination: "I paid the money by borrowing the money."

It was apparent from that evidence, as the trial judge said, that during the negotiations for the flat the plaintiff was at a disadvantage. He was having difficulty in obtaining accommodation — and he only got the flat by paying a premium of 10,000 shillings, which he borrowed for the purpose. He took it under a sublease dated September 17, 1953. This was prepared by lawyers. It contained provisions whereby the defendant company, in consideration of the sum of 10,000/- paid by the plaintiff by way of premium, subleased to him Flat No. 1 on the first floor for residence only, having three rooms, one kitchen, one bathroom and one lavatory. The term was seven years and one day from May 31, 1953. The rent was 300/- a month payable monthly in advance. And there were several covenants on either side.

The Rent Restriction Ordinance, 1949, of Uganda, provided by section 3(2): "Any person whether the owner of the property or not who in consideration of the letting or subletting of a dwelling-house ... to a person asks for, solicits or receives any sum of money other than rent ... shall be guilty of an offence and liable to a fine not exceeding Shs. 10,000 or imprisonment for a period not exceeding six months or to both such fine and imprisonment: ..."

Dec. 14. The judgment of their Lordships was delivered by **Lord Denning,** who stated the facts set out above, and continued: Their Lordships desire to point out at once that neither party thought they were doing anything illegal. The lease was for more than seven years and it was thought that, on a lease for that length of time, there was nothing wrong in asking for a premium or receiving it.

This was an easy mistake to make, as will be seen if one reads section 3(1) and (2) of the Rent Restriction Ordinance:

> 3. — (1) No owner or lessee of a dwelling-house or premises shall let or sublet such dwelling-house or premises at a rent which exceeds the standard rent.
> (2) Any person whether the owner of the property or not who in consideration of the letting or subletting of a dwelling-house or premises to a person asks for, solicits or receives any sum of money other than rent or any thing of value whether such asking, soliciting or receiving is made before or after the grant of a tenancy shall be guilty of an offence and liable to a fine not exceeding Shs. 10,000 or imprisonment for a period not exceeding six months or to both such fine and imprisonment:
> Provided that a person acting bona fide as an agent for either party to an intended tenancy agreement shall be entitled to a reasonable commission for his services:
> And provided further that nothing in this section shall be deemed to make unlawful the charging of a purchase price or premium on the sale, grant, assignment or renewal of a long lease of premises where the term or unexpired term is seven years or more.

Anyone reading the last proviso to that section — without more — might well think that a premium could be charged on the lease of this flat for seven years and one day. He would readily assume that the word "premises" included a flat. But he would be wrong. For if he took pains to look back to the definition section 2, he would find that in this Ordinance, the word "premises" refers only to business premises and not to residential flats at all. And so this proviso does not apply to this flat — because by the very terms of the sublease it was let "for residence only." Their Lordships ought perhaps to set out the material words of the definition clause which produces this result — it says that " 'dwelling-house' means any building or part of a building let for human habitation as a separate dwelling" and " 'premises' means any building or part of a building let for business, trade or professional purpose or for the public service."

It was owing to the failure of the lawyers to refer to those definitions — or at any rate to appreciate the importance of them — that the mistake arose.

Their Lordships also think it right to point out that there was no evidence to show whether the premium of 10,000/- was extortionate or not. Their Lordships were told that no standard rent had been fixed for this flat because it was a new flat. It is obvious that if the standard rent were to be fixed at, say, 450/- a month for seven years, there would be nothing extortionate in a premium of 10,000/- down and a rent of 300/- a month thereafter: for it would come in the long run to much about the same.

Nevertheless, no matter whether the mistake was excusable or inexcusable, or the premium fair or extortionate, the fact remains that the landlord received a premium contrary to the provisions of the Ordinance: and the question is whether the tenant can recover it back — remembering always that there is nothing in the Uganda Ordinance, comparable to the English Acts, enabling a premium to be recovered back.

It is clear that in the present case the illegal transaction was fully executed and carried out. The money was paid. The lease was granted. It was and still is vested in the plaintiff. In order to recover the premium, therefore, the plaintiff must show that he was not in pari delicto with the defendant. That was, indeed, the way he put his claim in the pleadings. After setting out the lease, the payment of the premium and the entry into occupation, the statement of claim proceeded simply to say: "By virtue of the provisions of subsection (2) of section 3 of the Rent Restriction Ordinance, the receipt of the said sum of Shs. 10,000 by the defendant from the plaintiff... was illegal but the plaintiff is entitled to recover the same since he (the plaintiff) was not in pari delicto with the defendant.

"The plaintiff claims the sum of Shs. 10,000 as money received by the defendant for the use of the plaintiff."

The issue thus becomes: Was the plaintiff in pari delicto with the defendant? Mr. Elwyn Jones, for the appellant, said they were both in pari delicto. The payment was, he said, made voluntarily, under no mistake of fact, and without any extortion, oppression or imposition, and could not be recovered back. True, it was paid under a mistake of law, but that was a mistake common to them both. They were both equally supposed to know the law. They both equally mistook it and were thus in pari delicto. In support of this argument the appellant referred to such well-known cases as *Harse v. Pearl Life Assurance Co.*, [1904] 1 K.B. 558; *William Whiteley Ltd. v. The King* (1909), 26 T.L.R. 19; *Evanson v. Crooks* (1911), 28 T.L.R. 123; and particularly to *Sharp Brothers & Knight v. Chant*, [1917] 1 K.B. 771.

Their Lordships cannot accept this argument. It is not correct to say that everyone is presumed to know the law. The true proposition is that no man can excuse himself from doing his duty by saying that he did not know the law on the matter. Ignorantia juris neminem excusat. Nor is it correct to say that money paid under a mistake of law can never be recovered back. The true proposition is that money paid under a mistake of law, by itself and without more, cannot be recovered back. James L.J. pointed that out in *Rogers v. Ingham* (1876), 3 Ch. D. 351, 355. If there is something more in addition to a mistake of law — if there is something in the defendant's conduct which shows that, of the two of them, he is the one primarily responsible for the mistake — then it may be recovered back. Thus, if as between the two of them the duty of observing the law is placed on the shoulders of the one rather than the other — it being imposed on him specially for the protection of the other — then they are not in pari delicto and the money can be recovered back; see *Browning v. Morris* (1778), 2 Cowp. 790, 792, by Lord Mansfield. Likewise, if the responsibility for the mistake lies more on the one than the other — because he has misled the other when he ought to know better — then again they are not in pari delicto and the money can be recovered back; see *Harse v. Pearl Life Assurance Co.*, [1904] 1 K.B. 558, 564, by Romer L.J. These propositions are in full accord with the principles laid down by Lord Mansfield relating to the action for money had and received. Their Lordships have in mind particularly his judgment in *Smith v. Bromley* (1760), 2 Doug. 696 in notis, which he delivered when he sat at Guildhall in April, 1760: and his celebrated judgment three or four weeks later, on May 19, 1760, in *Moses v. Macferlan* (1760), 2 Burr. 1005, when he sat in banco. Their Lordships were referred to some cases 30 or 40 years ago where disparaging remarks were made about the action for money had and received: but their Lordships venture to suggest that these were made under a misunderstanding of its origin. It is not an action on contract or imputed contract. If it were, none such could be imputed here, as their Lordships readily agree. It is simply an action for restitution of money which the defendant has received but which the law says he ought to return to the plaintiff. This was explained by Lord Wright in *Fibrosa Spolka Akcyjna v. Fairbairn Lawson Combe Barbour Ltd.*, [1943] A.C. 32. All the particular heads of money had and received, such as money paid, under a mistake of fact, paid under a consideration that has wholly failed, money paid by one who is not in pari delicto with the defendant, are only instances where the law says the money ought to be returned.

In applying these principles to the present case, the most important thing to observe is that the Rent Restriction Ordinance was intended to protect tenants from being exploited by landlords in days of housing shortage. One of the obvious ways in which a landlord can exploit the housing shortage is by demanding from the tenant "key-money." Section 3(2) of the Rent Restriction Ordinance was enacted so as to protect tenants from exploitation of that kind. This is apparent from the fact that the penalty is imposed only on the landlord or his agent and not upon the tenant. It is imposed on the person who "asks for, solicits or receives any sum of money," but not on the person who submits to the demand and pays the money. It may be that the tenant who pays money is an accomplice or an aider and abettor (see *Johnson v. Youden* and section 3 of the Rent Restriction (Amendment) Ordinance, 1954), but he can hardly be said to be in pari delicto with the landlord. The duty of observing the law is firmly placed by the Ordinance on the shoulders of the landlord for the protection of the tenant: and if the law is broken, the landlord must take the primary responsibility. Whether it be a rich tenant who pays a premium as a bribe in order to "jump the queue," or a poor tenant who is at his wit's end to find accommodation, neither is so much to blame as the landlord who is using his property rights so as to exploit those in need of a roof over their heads.

Seeing then that the parties are not in pari delicto, the tenant is entitled to recover the premium by the common law: and it is not necessary to find a remedy given by the Ordinance, either expressly or by implication. The omission of a statutory remedy does not, in cases of this kind, exclude the remedy by money had and received. That is amply shown by the numerous cases to which their Lordships were referred, such as those arising under the statutes against usury, lotteries and gaming, in which there was no remedy given by the statute but nevertheless it was held that an action lay for money had and received. It was accepted, too, by Parker J. in his considered judgment in *Green v. Portsmouth Stadium Ltd.*, [1950] 1 K.B. 544: and his decision was only reversed by the Court of Appeal because they thought the statute there was of a different kind. It was not intended to protect bookmakers from the demands of race-course owners, but was rather for the regulation of race-courses. There was nothing in that case to show that the plaintiff was not in pari delicto with the defendants.

Their Lordships find themselves in full agreement with the judgment of the High Court of Uganda and of the Court of Appeal for Eastern Africa, and will humbly advise Her Majesty that this appeal should be dismissed. The appellant must pay the costs.

KINGSHOTT v. BRUNSKILL

[1953] O.W.N. 133. Ontario Court of Appeal; Laidlaw, Roach and
Aylesworth JJ.A.

An appeal by the plaintiff from a judgment of Cochrane Co. Ct. J., of the
County Court of the County of Peel, dismissing the action.

The judgment of the Court was delivered by

Roach J.A. [after stating the nature of the appeal]: — The facts of this
case are simple but it raises an important question under The Farm Products Grades and Sales Act, R.S.O. 1950, c. 130, and the regulations passed
thereunder.

The plaintiff operates a fruit and market garden on 34 acres of land in
the county of Peel. On that land he has a small apple orchard. He is not a
large producer of apples and his main income is derived from the operation
of greenhouses. In the fall of 1950 he had harvested his apple crop and the
apples were stored on his premises. Among these apples were 846 bushels of
Spy and Delicious apples. They were in bushel baskets. No effort had been
made by him to grade or sort them, although there was no mixture of the
two varieties in any basket. In harvesting the apples the plaintiff had taken
the empty baskets and marked some of them "Fancy Delicious" and the
others of them "Fancy Grade Spies". It was stated in evidence that the
usual practice is to mark the baskets or hampers with the name and quality
of the variety which the producer intends, after grading, that those hampers
shall contain. The hampers were then sent out to the orchard and the apples
were picked direct from the tree and placed in the appropriate hampers.
The plaintiff had no intention of offering those apples for sale to the public
until they were first graded in compliance with the regulations passed under
the Act.

The defendant resides on land about one mile distant from the plaintiff's
premises. His main business is the growing and marketing of apples and
purchasing apples from other apple growers, grading them and marketing
them.

On 14th December the defendant came to the plaintiff's premises and
inquired whether or not the plaintiff would sell his Spy apples. The plaintiff
replied that he would not sell the Delicious and Spies separately and that if
he sold them he wanted to sell the whole lot. It was apparent to the defendant that the apples had not been graded. After some preliminary discussion, the defendant entered into a contract with the plaintiff to purchase the
apples at $1.10 per bushel and paid the plaintiff a deposit of $25. As the
learned trial judge said in his reasons, there was no warranty, express or
implied. The defendant inspected the apples and simply bought what he
saw in the premises where they were stored. Under the terms of the contract
it was the defendant's obligation to remove the apples. From time to time
he removed quantities of them to his own premises, graded them and sold
them. By April 1951 there were still some hampers of apples which the
defendant had not yet removed. The plaintiff requested the defendant to
remove them because he needed the space, and when the defendant delayed
removing them the plaintiff sent them over to the defendant's premises.
During the course of the removal by the defendant he paid the plaintiff on
account the further sum of $200. When the last of the apples had been
delivered by the plaintiff to the defendant, the defendant called an inspec-

tor appointed under the regulations and the inspector marked the last consignment of delivery with a detention order, as he was permitted to do under the regulations. Notice of that detention order was given to the plaintiff. The defendant, alleging that of the total quantity of apples received by him there were certain defective apples, computed the balance that he owed to the plaintiff and sent him a cheque for $619.80, being the amount which the defendant considered represented the balance owing by him. This cheque was marked "in full payment for apples". This cheque was not accepted by the plaintiff but was returned to the defendant. The plaintiff thereupon sued the defendant for the sum of $719.60, which sum was made up of $705.60, being the balance owing for the apples, plus $14.00, being the value of hampers which the defendant had not returned to the plaintiff.

The defendant pleaded that the apples had not been graded, packed or marked in accordance with The Farm Products Grades and Sales Act and the regulations passed thereunder and in particular, regulation 3(a), (c), (d), (f) and (g), and that the sale of the apples was thereby prohibited by statute and illegal. The learned trial judge gave effect to that plea and it is with some regret that I feel myself constrained to agree with that decision.

Section 2(1) of the statute authorizes the Minister of Agriculture, subject to the approval of the Lieutenant-Governor in Council, to make certain regulations respecting farm products as defined in the statute. Farm products as there defined include fruit. The regulations that the Minister may make as aforesaid include regulations,

"(a) establishing grades and classes for any farm product;

"(b) providing for the inspection, grading, packages and packing, marketing, handling, shipping, transporting, advertising, purchasing and selling of farm products within Ontario;".

Pursuant to the authority contained in the statute, regulations were made and they are known as Regulations 87 (1 C.R.O. 1950, p. 431). Regulation 3 thereof provides in part as follows:

"No person shall pack, transport, ship, advertise, sell, offer for sale or have in possession for sale any produce,

"(a) unless the produce has been graded, packed and marked in accordance with the provisions of the Act and these regulations;

"(b) which is below the minimum grade for the produce but this provision shall not apply to produce for an establishment [establishment is defined in Regulation 1 as including any plant, factory or premises where produce is canned, preserved or otherwise processed];

"(c) where the faced or shown surface falsely represents the contents;

"(d) in a package unless the package is properly filled and packed;

"(f) in a package which has been previously marked unless the marks are completely removed;

"(g) which is so immature or so diseased or otherwise affected as to be unfit for human consumption;".

By s. 8 of the statute every person who contravenes any of the provisions of the Act or the regulations is guilty of an offence and liable on summary conviction to the penalties therein set out.

It must be concluded that the main object of the statute and the regulations passed thereunder is the protection of the public. The penalty authorized by the statute is imposed wholly for the protection of the public. Therefore, if the sale here in question was forbidden by the regulations, then it was illegal and notwithstanding that the defendant resold the apples after having graded them and made a profit thereby, the plaintiff cannot recover in an action for the price of those apples...

I have looked in vain for any provision in the regulations that would exempt the plaintiff in the circumstances of this case from their application. It is not difficult to conceive a case in which a farmer who has a small orchard on his farm may have neither the manpower nor the equipment necessary to grade and pack the product of his orchard, in accordance with the regulations. His neighbour, with a much larger orchard and specializing in the growing of fruit, has the necessary help and equipment for the grading and packing of the produce not only of his own orchard but of others in the neighbourhood. It would seem not unreasonable that the first of those two farmers should be permitted to sell his whole crop of fruit to the second of those two farmers, who, having the necessary help and equipment, could grade it and pack it in accordance with the regulations before offering it for sale to the public. The regulations, however, do not appear to provide for such a case. There is no provision in the regulations that would exempt the first of those two farmers in that hypothetical case from compliance with the regulations. The Court cannot read into the regulations exemptions which might appear to the Court to be justifiable in a given set of circumstances.

For these reasons the appeal must be dismissed with costs.

QUESTIONS

1. To what extent were the purposes behind the legislation in each of the last three cases forwarded by the decision in the case?

2. Would the answer to this question give you wholly satisfactory answers to the cases?

3. Was there any rule of law that *required* the two Ontario courts to reach the result that they did?

SIDMAY LTD. v. WEHTTAM

(1967), 61 D.L.R. (2d) 358. Ontario Court of Appeal; Kelly, Wells and Laskin JJ.A.

APPEAL from a judgment of Grant, J., [1966] 1 O.R. 457, 54 D.L.R. (2d) 194, declaring that a certain mortgage given upon real estate was illegal and void by reason of the mortgagee's failure to register in accordance with the Provisions of the *Loan and Trust Corporations Act* (Ont.).

Kelly, J.A.: — The appellant Wehttam Investments Ltd. (Wehttam) appeals from the judgment of Grant, J., dated November 4, 1965, declaring void and unenforceable a mortgage dated May 8, 1964, made between the respondent Sidmay Ltd. (Sidmay) as mortgagor and Wehttam as mortgagee, the respondents Joseph M. Gordon and Bernard Benjamin having joined therein as covenantors. This document will be referred to as the "impugned mortgage".

While the parties do not agree as to some of the amounts involved, these differences are not pertinent to the matters in issue in this appeal: there is no dispute as to the relevant facts.

The personal respondents had for some years been actively engaged in the promotion and building of housing accommodation; and by themselves or through the medium of companies they controlled they had on previous occasions obtained loans from Wehttam for purposes similar to the purposes for which they sought funds purported to be secured by the impugned mortgage.

On May 5, 1964, Wehttam addressed a letter (ex. 2) to Sidmay and the personal respondents which confirmed an agreement whereby Wehttam would lend money as a building loan for the erection of 56 units (two-storey maisonettes) in six buildings on land in the letter described. The amount of the loan was to be $308,250; the term, six months from May 1, 1964; interest was to be calculated monthly at the rate of 12% per annum on the whole of the loan and be payable at the time of each advance, notwithstanding that the total loan amount had not been advanced; the principal amount was to become due and be payable on November 1, 1964, and the borrowers were to have the privilege of prepaying all or any part of the loan before the maturity date but such prepayments were not to reduce the payments of interest above provided; the security was to be a first mortgage on a parcel of land on the east and west sides of Claridge Road, more particularly described in Instrument 165987 Burlington, and the several personal guarantees of Joseph M. Gordon and Bernard Benjamin. The letter also set out other conditions in regard to insurance, legal inspection and appraisal costs, mortgage advances and other matters, none of which are of significance to the issues before this Court.

Although there were other arrangements with respect to the said lands in which all or some of the parties to this action were involved, it is sufficient for the purpose of this appeal to say that eventually the impugned mortgage came into existence, was registered after having been duly executed by Sidmay as mortgagor and the personal respondents as covenantors and the moneys secured by it (save as to an inconsequential amount) were advanced to or upon the direction of Sidmay and the personal respondents. It is admitted by the respondents that the moneys secured were repayable according to the tenor of the mortgage and that the mortgage was in all respects regular, unless the mortgage be void upon the grounds upon which the respondents sought to have it so declared in this action.

The sole ground of illegality alleged as voiding the impugned mortgage, is that the appellant, not being registered as a loan company under the provisions of the *Loan and Trust Corporations Act*, R.S.O. 1960, c. 222 (the Act) had, in the making of the loan to Sidmay, contravened the provisions of s. 133 of the Act which section reads as follows:

> 133(1) No incorporated body or person acting in its behalf, other than a registered corporation and a person duly authorized by it to act in its behalf, shall undertake or transact in Ontario the business of a loan corporation or of a loaning land corporation or of a trust company.
>
> (2) Any setting up or exhibiting of a sign or inscription containing the name of the corporation, or any distribution or publication of any proposal, circular, card, advertisement, printed form or like document in the name of the corporation, or any written or oral solicitation on the corporation's behalf shall, both as to the corporation and as to the person acting or purporting to act on its behalf, be deemed undertaking the business of the corporation within the meaning of this section.
>
> (3) Any promoter, organizer, manager, director, officer, collector, agent, employee or person who undertakes or transacts any business of a corporation that is not registered under this Act is guilty of an offence.

The respondents alleged that Wehttam being an incorporated company, constituted, authorized or operated for the purpose of lending money on real estate or that and any other purpose, made a series of loans on the security of real estate, each of which was related to the other in such a manner as to be incapable of being described as isolated transactions and therefore that the series constituted the carrying on of business. It is not necessary to consider whether the impugned mortgage was an isolated transaction or a step in the carrying on of business since Wehttam concedes that, if the provisions of the Act are applicable to a business in the conduct of which occurred transactions of a type which took place between it and Sidmay, that transaction when taken in conjunction with others of a similar nature into which it had entered with Sidmay and other borrowers, would constitute the carrying on of the prohibited business.

Since Wehttam, without conceding that it was required to be registered, admits that it was not registered, the questions which present themselves for consideration by reason of this attack on the impugned mortgage, are as follows:

(a) Did Wehttam contravene s. 133 by carrying on the business of a loan corporation?

(b) If, by the making of the loan in question or by any other of its operations, Wehttam was carrying on the business of a loan corporation, is the impugned mortgage null and void for illegality?

The decision under appeal has had a drastic and perhaps unexpected result for Wehttam, but it need hardly be emphasized that the effect of that decision if upheld will be to hamper seriously a large part of the conveyancing work in Ontario. A solicitor in examining a title to land derived from a mortgagee corporation not registered under the Act could not safely pass the title until exhaustive inquiries had been made to discover, not only the nature of the transaction which gave rise to the mortgage, but the general conduct of the business of the corporate mortgagee: and to accept the title he would be bound to satisfy himself that despite the particular mortgage, considered in concert with other mortgage transactions in which the corporation had engaged, the corporate mortgagee had not been at the particular time undertaking or transacting the business of a loan corporation, something that no examination of the records of any one registry office, no matter how exhaustive, would conclusively disclose.

Granted that the effect which a decision of this Court may have on others than the parties to the action is not a valid ground for tempering the judgment of the Court, yet the unfavourable consequences which will result from the universal application of the principle under which the impugned mortgage was declared null and void demand that, in the public interest, this Court, unless compelled to do so by authorities which are so clear and unambiguous that they defy distinction, should not arrive at a conclusion the effect of which will interfere with the rights and remedies accorded to parties by the ordinary law of contract, particularly when such interference will have such an impact upon a substantial area of the financial life of the community: see *St. John Shipping Corp. v. J. Rank Ltd.*, [1956] 3 All E.R. 683 at p. 690:

> If a contract has as its whole object the doing of the very act which the statute prohibits, it can be argued that you can hardly make sense of a statute which forbids an act and yet permits to be made a contract to do it; that is a clear implica-

tion. But unless you get a clear implication of that sort, I think that a court ought to be very slow to hold that a statute intends to interfere with the rights and remedies given by the ordinary law of contract. Caution in this respect is, I think, especially necessary in these times when so much of commercial life is governed by regulations of one sort or another which may easily be broken without wicked intent. Persons who deliberately set out to break the law cannot expect to be aided in a court of justice, but it is a different matter when the law is unwittingly broken. To nullify a bargain in such circumstances frequently means that in a case — perhaps of such triviality that no authority would have felt it worth while to prosecute — a seller, because he cannot enforce his civil rights, may forfeit a sum vastly in excess of any penalty that a criminal court would impose; and the sum forfeited will not go into the public purse but into the pockets of someone who is lucky enough to pick up the windfall or astute enough to have contrived to get it. It is questionable how far this contributes to public morality.

I propose to consider first the submission on behalf of the respondent that Wehttam, at the time of and in the making of the loan to Sidmay on the security of the impugned mortgage, was contravening the provisions of s. 133 of the Act in that it, being an unregistered incorporated body, was undertaking or transacting in Ontario the business of a loan corporation....

The various types of bodies now capable of inclusion in the very broad definition of the term "corporation" in the Act, which in earlier days were the subject-matter of separate enactments, have, in their function, little in common. Trust companies have come to be looked upon as a source of funds for mortgage loans, but this phase of the business of trust companies is almost accidental, certainly not fundamental. Dissimilarities are readily apparent between the function of a building society and a loan or trust company. While the earlier loan companies Acts may have been intended to encourage their loaning activities to help in the development of the country, the incorporation into a single Act of the provisions of the Acts as to building societies, loan companies and trust companies, in my view indicates that the purpose of that Act was to exercise a form of control over the incorporation and operation of corporations which lend to the public funds drawn from a wide clientele of depositors, debenture holders and other persons in a creditor relationship to the corporation to the end that some measure of protection may be offered to those who entrust, or are exposed to solicitation to entrust their funds to the corporation. In seeking for a legislative purpose for bringing such diverse operations under the same umbrella, the recognizable common denominator is the intention to protect the money of the public, deposited with, loaned or entrusted to or invested in the corporations made subject to the provisions of the Act for the purpose of enabling the corporation to lend such money mainly on the security of mortgages on real estate. The provision with respect to minimum capital, limitation on borrowing powers fixed by relation to paid-up capital, restriction on the type or size of loans entitled to be made, provisions for the furnishing of financial information, description of the type of security to be accepted for loans, are indicative of an intention to afford protection to those whose money, in one form or another, comes into the hands of a corporation which proposes to invest that money, in its own name and which holds itself out as engaged in the business of lending that money. None of the provisions of the Act are appropriate for the protection of a borrower. Other legislation, notably the *Unconscionable Transactions Relief Act*, R.S.O.

1960, c. 410, is calculated directly to advance the interests of the borrower. All the protection provisions of the Act become meaningless when an attempt is made to apply them to a company which is engaged in lending only its own money on security which it deems adequate for its own protection and which has not sought or received its funds as a result of an invitation to or solicitation from the public or any element thereof.

The inappropriateness of the Act to a company such as Wehttam becomes even more apparent when an attempt is made to apply its provisions to a company which by its charter is prohibited from extending to the public any invitation to subscribe for its shares or securities.

If the intent and purpose of the Act be the protection of the money of those of the public who become shareholders, security holders, creditors or *cestuis que trust* of the lending agency, the interpretation of the statute in a manner which would permit a borrower of funds who admits he has received them, to retain them to the prejudice of the persons in whose interest the statute was enacted, would be detrimental, not beneficial, to the very persons for whose protection the legislation was enacted.

It would be equally absurd, though it would necessarily follow from the interpretation urged by the respondents, that a borrower from a registered loan corporation could resist repayment of a loan made by the loan corporation because the amount loaned exceeded two-thirds of the value of the real estate upon which it was secured contrary to the provisions of s. 133(3) of the Act. In my opinion, the words used by the Legislature in framing s. 133, even when read without the assistance of the realization of the over-all purpose of the Legislature in enacting the statute in which they appear, would not extend to make illegal an otherwise legal transaction merely because at the time of making the loan the lender was contravening the prohibition with respect to undertaking or transacting the business of a loan company. Greater difficulty might have been encountered in rationalizing the apparently all-embracing provisions of the Act with the impossibility of applying them universally were it not for the inclusion in the Act itself of s. 2(1) in the following terms:

> 2(1) This Act applies, according to its context, to every corporation within the meaning of this Act.

The effect of this section combined with the directives in the *Interpretation Act*, R.S.O. 1960, c. 191, require that the whole of the Act be construed in a manner which will make its provisions as effective as possible to achieve the purpose for which the Act is designed. Any extension of the application of the Act beyond the class of corporations to which its operative provisions are applicable cannot be supported by giving to the words of s. 1(*h*) a meaning which disregards the import of s. 2(1).

I therefore conclude that, taking into consideration the intent and object of the Act and the nature of the corporation to which its provisions are relevant, the definition of "loan corporation" contained in s. 1(*h*) must be interpreted as if it read, " 'Loan corporation' means an incorporated company, association or society, to which according to the context of the Act the provisions of this Act are applicable, constituted, authorized or operated for the purpose of lending money on the security of real estate or for that and any other purpose, but does not include a chartered bank, an insurance corporation, a loaning land corporation, a trust company, or an investment company registered under the Investment Contracts Act."

Even if I had been satisfied that Wehttam had been at the relevant times operating a business in contravention of s. 133(1), in my opinion this would not have served to make illegal the mortgage transaction in question. I have come to this conclusion for two principal reasons: first, I find in the Act itself indications of precise and deliberate avoidance of any reference to interference with contractual obligations incurred in the course of a prohibited business. It is not without significance that s. 133(3) which specifically creates a punishable offence, carefully avoids the imposition of any penalty on the corporation which transacts the business and imposes the burden of the offence on the promoter, organizer, manager, director, officer, collector, agent, employee or person who undertakes or transacts the business of the corporation. This is completely consistent with the overriding intention of the Act to afford every possible protection to the funds of the depositors and a reluctance to place any burden on the corporation which would adversely affect those funds. Second, the underlying purpose of the Act to afford greater security to the depositors, creditors and security holders of the corporation would be defeated if its assets become depleted by the inability to recover from the borrower the money lent on the security of real estate.

To permit a borrower to retain the amount of the loan made to it from the funds entrusted to such corporation for investment would produce exactly the opposite of the result sought to be obtained by the Act; and, again, to rely on the provisions of s. 133, dealing with the transaction of business, to nullify a particular contract, appears to me to be so out of keeping with the intention of the Legislature as to compel the adoption of any alternative construction which will preserve the legality of the borrower's undertaking to repay the money received by him as the result of his request for an advance to him by way of loan. It is my opinion that this statute, read as a whole, must be interpreted as indicating an intention not to affect the validity of any contractual obligation arising from a loan made on the security of real estate even if that loan were made in the course of a business, the transaction of which by an unregistered corporation is prohibited.

Assuming, contrary to the conclusion already reached, that the transaction in question is illegal due to it being a prohibited one because entered into by an unregistered loan corporation, the law applicable to the situation then prevailing would be as set out in the following passage from the judgment of Tucker, J., in *Cohen v. J. Lester Ltd.*, [1938] 4 All E.R. 188. In that case the Court had before it a contract which the *Moneylenders Act*, 1927 (U.K.), c. 21, made unenforceable. In considering the relevance to an unenforceable contract of the consequences attending upon an illegal contract, Tucker, J., adopted and approved the statement of Parker, J., in *Lodge v. National Union Inv. Co. Ltd.*, [1907] 1 Ch. 300 [pp. 191-2]:

> It is to be observed that in that case the transaction in question was one which was an illegal one because it is expressly so stated by the Money-lenders Act, 1900, s. 2 — that is, a moneylending transaction by an unregistered moneylender is illegal. The action was brought claiming a declaration that the contracts and transactions were illegal and void against the plaintiff, asking for the delivery up of the assignments, bills of exchange and securities, and repayment of the sum of £150 due on the bills, or, alternatively, certain declarations. Parker, J., as he then was, pointed out in his judgment, at p. 306:
> "The usual rule is that in the case of a transaction void for illegality neither party can take any proceedings against the other party for the restoration of any prop-

erty or for the repayment of any money which has been transferred or paid in the course of the illegal transaction. To this rule, however, there are exceptions, one of them being in favour of the persons for whose protection the illegality of the contract has been created, and in the authorities I have mentioned it has been held that in the case of loan transactions void under the Act of 1900 the borrower is within that exception. The illegality of the transaction, therefore, does not preclude the plaintiff from maintaining this action. The defendants, however, maintain that, this being an appeal to the equitable jurisdiction of the court, the plaintiff can be put upon terms and not allowed to assert any equity unless he himself is prepared to do equity by repaying the £1,075 less the £150 paid for the privilege of renewing the bills, and certain sums which they are willing to allow him to deduct which I need not refer to in detail."

Then Parker, J., proceeds to decide that that contention on the part of the defendants is a good one, and that the plaintiff can get back the security only on payment of the money due. That proceeds on the basis that the application was an appeal to the equitable jurisdiction of the court, that it was an application by somebody who was a party to an illegal contract, who, ordinarily speaking, would not have been heard to come into court at all, but who, by reason of the exceptions in the provisions in the statute in question, being a statute passed for the benefit of the protection of borrowers, was entitled in that case to come to the court, but, if he did so, could come to the court only on certain terms. That is the position with regard to an illegal contract.

While it is true that this case held that the principles applicable to relief from an illegal contract including the return of security in respect thereof were distinguishable from the principles applicable to an unenforceable contract, there is no disagreement with the statement of the law made by Parker, J., in *Lodge v. National Union Investment Co. Ltd., supra.*

At first sight the cases decided with respect to money-lending contracts appear to present some inconsistency. But it must be borne in mind that cases decided in England in three different periods were governed by entirely different considerations. The basis for these differences have been succinctly stated by Lord Radcliffe, in *Kasumu et al. v. Baba-Egbe*, [1956] 3 All E.R. 266 at p. 271:

> According to medieval ideas, the taking of usury involved the sin of avarice. It was not the lending of money or the circumstances in which it was lent that were the material matter, but the obtaining of profit from the use of money. When medieval conceptions began gradually to give way before the impulse of commercial and industrial activity, the sin of avarice turned into the offence of usury; but the usury prohibited was no longer the lending of money at profit but the lending of money at a rate of profit greater than that permitted by the statute. What the law penalized and made void was a particular kind of grasping contract; and it was evidently felt by equity judges at any rate that they were doing nothing that contravened the policy of the Acts if they insisted that the price of their remedies should be the return of the principal money and a reasonable rate of interest, so long as no effect was given to those elements of the loan in which the usury itself consisted.
>
> But the Usury Acts disappeared in 1854, and much of the Moneylenders Act, 1900, and the Moneylenders Act, 1927, is directed to enforcing measures of control that have no concern with the intrinsic nature of the contract made.

The *Money-lenders Act* of 1900 approached the problem in two ways: first, by s. 1 the Courts were empowered to reform contracts made by the parties in order to relieve the borrower from the payment of any sum in excess of that adjudged to be fairly due in respect of such principal, interest and charges as the Court, having regard to the risk and all the circumstances, may adjudge to be reasonable: second, by imposing requirements as to the registration of the money-lender, the carrying on of business in his registered name, and the furnishing of copies of documents to the borrower, resulting in illegality of any contract made contrary to the requirements of the statute.

The *Moneylenders Act* of 1927 added to but did not supersede the Act of 1900; s. 6 of the Act of 1927 provides that, in the absence of a specified note or memorandum, the contract shall be unenforceable.

It was held in *Victorian Daylesford Syndicate v. Dott*, [1905] 2 Ch. 624, and in *Bonnard v. Dott*, [1906] 1 Ch. 740, that transactions by money-lenders who did not conform to the requirements of the Act of 1900 were void for illegality. In *Lodge v. National Union Investment Co. Ltd., supra*, Parker, J., considered he would be justified in the circumstances of that case in treating the decisions under the usury Acts as authorities for what he should do in a case which arose under the *Money-lenders Act* of 1900. In line with this view he imposed terms on the plaintiff as the price of granting the relief from the burden of the illegal contract. In 1956 Lord Radcliffe had occasion to discuss the *Lodge* case in *Kasumu et al. v. Baba-Egbe, supra*, an appeal to the Privy Council from the West African Court of Appeal, involving a transaction allegedly unenforceable under the Nigerian Moneylenders Ordinance, an enactment having provisions similar to s. 6 of the *Moneylenders Act* of 1927. In the course of his speech, Lord Radcliffe made the following comment [p. 270]:

> *Lodge v. National Union Investment Co., Ltd.* [*supra*] was a decision of a great equity lawyer, and it has stood as a decision since the year 1906. Nevertheless, it cannot be treated as having established any wide general principle that governs the action of courts in granting relief in moneylending cases.

Cohen v. J. Lester Ltd., supra, dealt with a contract held to be unenforceable under the Act of 1927: what it decided was that where a statute declares a contract to be unenforceable, not illegal, the Court will not impose any terms as a condition of giving the borrower the benefit of the unenforceability of the contract. Lord Radcliffe in *Kasumu et al. v. Baba-Egbe*, commented upon the impossibility of transferring the principle which guided the Courts in dealing with claims based on the usury Acts to claims for relief arising out of transactions rendered void or unenforceable by the system of regulation under the *Moneylenders Act*.

In the case before us the attack is upon the legality of the contract and if it be held to be illegal the result would be that the Courts would not lend their aid with respect to any remedy arising out of the illegal contract unless the respondents can bring themselves within the class of person for the benefit of whom the debilitating legislation was enacted. The respondents in this action are not of the class for whose benefit the Act was enacted and therefore cannot come within the exception to the general rule. Even though innocent and ignorant they were parties to an executed illegal contract and *ex turpi causa non oritur actio*. Under the circumstances of this case it is doubtful that they are entitled even to sympathy on the basis of innocence and ignorance. The respondents were not mere amateurs in borrowing money on the security of real estate any more than the appellant was an amateur lender; by reason of prior dealings the respondents must have been fully aware at the time of the transaction of the nature of

Wehttam's business as they were when the action was instituted and can only be assumed to have been ready to permit the appellant to perform fully its part of the bargain and to accept the advances of substantial sums of money in an illegal transaction. In such circumstances when the parties have bargained at arm's length and have each performed, the Court may properly leave them where they are.

In an endeavour to escape the rule which would have denied them access to the Courts, counsel for the respondents advanced an ingenious argument. It was submitted that access to the Courts is denied only where the rights sought to be enforced or the relief secured must depend on an illegal contract; that an action for a declaratory judgment as to the invalidity of a mortgage due to illegality did not constitute resort to the Courts in reliance on an illegal transaction and therefore does not fall within the class of actions where the Court will refuse to assist the parties.

In support of this proposition there was cited the case of *Chapman v. Michaelson*, [1908] 2 Ch. 612; affd [1909] 1 Ch. 238. This was a case decided under the Act of 1900 wherein the Court declared a contract to be illegal and void without imposing any terms on the plaintiff as the price of granting the relief claimed. Due to the peculiar facts of this case I consider that no principle of general application supporting the proposition of counsel for the respondents can be extracted from it and that it should be considered only as an authority to be followed when the identical situation comes before the Court. The defendant, a money-lender, lent one Loyd £2,000 on the security of a mortgage upon a contingent life interest under the will of Baron Overstone. The mortgage was made to the defendant under a name other than that under which he was registered as a money-lender, a contravention of the requirements of the *Money-lenders Act*, 1900; shortly after the mortgage was given a receiving order was made against Loyd, who thereupon brought forward a scheme of arrangement under which he proposed that all his property which would become divisible amongst his creditors if he were adjudged bankrupt, should vest in Chapman as trustee to be administered by Chapman in satisfaction and discharge of all the encumbrances created by Loyd (particulars of which were set out in a schedule) and in payment to all unsecured creditors, with the balance if any payable to Loyd. It was admitted that the transaction between Loyd and the defendant was a transaction entered into in the course of the defendant's business as a money-lender and had been made not in his registered name. The defendant, however, submitted (1) that the plaintiff should not have the declaration he asked without going on to ask what would be in the ordinary course ancillary relief, and (2) the Court should impose terms on the plaintiff at the price at which he should be allowed to purchase this declaration. Since it was necessary that Chapman, in order to discharge his duties as trustee, should be able to rely on a decision of the Court as to the legality or illegality of the transaction, it was held that Chapman could properly come before the Court to seek the declaration: but it was pointed out that the declaration of the Court did not deal with the relevant rights of the parties consequent upon the declaration. In that case the plaintiff who was not a party to the illegal loan, had no direct personal interest in supporting or attacking the contract which was declared to be illegal and was not seeking to benefit by any relief ancillary to the declaration he sought. The respondents here have failed to bring themselves within the four corners of that decision: they have a direct personal interest in the declaration sought and the prayer in their statement of claim does not end with the request for a declaration as to the illegality of the contract but goes on to ask for consequential relief. While the attention of the learned trial Judge was directed mainly to the question of the determination of the illegality of the mortgage, it was not the sole question before the Court and the learned trial Judge was not, by amendment of the pleadings or by action of counsel for the respondents, relieved from the consideration of the other issues raised by the prayer of the statement of claim: he was never placed in the exact position of the Court in *Chapman v. Michaelson, supra.*

The present case proceeded to trial and was heard on issues raised by the pleadings: this is an appeal from the judgment rendered after that trial and the respondents cannot now change the position upon which they submitted their right to the trial Judge. True, counsel for the respondents during the course of his argument before this Court, when he was discussing *Chapman v. Michaelson* stated that he was then abandoning claims (b) and (c) in para. 25 of the statement of claim (those claiming the consequential relief), but the nature of this action and its dissimilarity from the peculiar facts of *Chapman v. Michaelson* persist despite the belated attempt to remodel it to meet the specifications of the authority quoted. Further, I do not consider that anything in *Chapman v. Michaelson* is authority for the proposition that a party to an illegal contract may come to the Court for a declaration of illegality unless he is able to qualify as belonging to the class for the benefit of which the contracts were made to be illegal. To be able to invoke the Court's aid in the gaining of relief from the consequences of their conduct in the contract freely made, the respondents must demonstrate that they are of the class in whose favour an exception is made to the general rule of non-access to the Courts. The respondents are not of this class and so are not entitled to the relief they seek by having the contract voluntarily made declared to be illegal.

Another instance in which a Court declared a contract void without imposing conditions is to be found in *Steinberg v. Cohen*, 64 O.L.R. 545, [1930] 2 D.L.R. 916. That was a case where the plaintiff sought to have declared void a mortgage given to stifle a prosecution: the Court's attitude in determining that case may be gathered from two comments from the judgments of Riddell, J.A. at p. 547: "... the evidence discloses as unsavoury and discreditable a story as (I hope) has ever been told in a court of justice." [p. 550] "There was a glaring conspiracy to defeat the ends of justice, participated in by the plaintiff, the defendant, Alderman Gitlin, Bob Cohen and perhaps the solicitor..." I cannot consider the conclusion of the Court with respect to that case a suitable guide for the determination of the case which is now before the Court since under no view of the facts can they be held parallel to the situation the Court dealt with in *Steinberg v. Cohen, supra.*

If, however, I am in error and the respondents are to be held properly to be a member of the classes in whose favour the exception to the rule is applicable, this would be a proper case for the Court, in return for the exercise of the Court's power to relieve the respondents against the contract they made, to impose conditions which would, so far as possible, restore the parties to the *status quo ante*: the repayment of the sum advanced to the respondents and interest thereon according to the terms of the contract they made should be imposed as a condition of any relief.

My conclusions on the assumption that the contract should be held to be illegal can be summarized as follows:

1. There is a general rule that the Court will not render assistance to the enforcing of any rights of parties to an illegal contract unless the party claiming relief before the Court can bring itself within the class of persons for whose protection the illegality of the contract was created.

2. The respondents in this case are not persons for whose protection the prohibition in the *Loan and Trust Corporations Act* was enacted.

3. If I am incorrect in this and a proper case is made out for appeal to the assistance of the Court for relief from the illegal contract, the Court should impose as a term of its intervention repayment by the respondents to Wehttam of the sum of money received by the corporate respondent from Wehttam pursuant to the arrangements made by the respondents and Wehttam, together with interest thereon as provided in the contract made by the parties to and incorporated in the impugned mortgage.

At this point I would draw attention to what must be a clerical error in the formal judgment of November 4, 1965. The concluding words of para. 1 read "are void and unenforceable and doth order and adjudge the same accordingly". I have already noted the distinction between a contract void for illegality and a contract which is unenforceable. On the facts of this case I fail to see any ground alleged upon which the mortgage could be held to be unenforceable if it be not void. Although the judgment follows the prayer in the statement of claim, in my view even if the finding that the mortgage was void had stood, it would not be proper for the formal judgment also to have declared the mortgage to be unenforceable. That is something different from and slightly less than void. The double declarations are, I believe, inconsistent.

Although I have discussed the rights of the parties, alternatively, on the assumption that the mortgage is illegal and therefore void, as I have already stated, I do not consider the mortgage void: I would allow the appeal with costs, set aside the judgment below and direct the entry of judgment dismissing the action of the respondents in all respects save with respect to the following — if the parties are unable to agree upon the amount properly payable under the said mortgage there should be a reference to the Master to determine such amount. The appellant should have the costs of the action and the costs of the reference should he in the discretion of the Master taking the accounts.

Wells, J.A., agrees with Kelly, J.A.

[Laskin J.A. wrote a separate judgment concurring with his brethren for the reasons given by Kelly J.A. His judgment concluded as follows:]

Laskin J.A. ... [It] seems to me that the facts of this case come within the principle, which I endorse, expressed in s. 601 of the American Law Institute, *Restatement of the Law of Contracts*, p. 1116. It is headed "Recovery on an Illegal Bargain Because of the Effect of Refusal" and is in the following terms:

> If refusal to enforce or to rescind an illegal bargain would produce a harmful effect on the parties for whose protection the law making the bargain illegal exists, enforcement or rescission, whichever is appropriate, is allowed.

The first illustration given of this principle is that of a bank which is forbidden by statute to invest in real estate mortgages, and the statute makes it criminal to do so. The bank nevertheless invests in such mortgages. Action, it is said, can be maintained on the mortgage debt and to foreclose the mortgage, since otherwise creditors and shareholders of the bank, for whose protection the statute is enacted, would be injured. The analogical aptness of this illustration is clear.

There is, I am aware, a logical difficulty created by referring to a transaction as void where it involves a purported transfer of title to property. If truly void, then no title passes; and if possession has been taken by the transferee should the Court not permit the transferor to recover it? If in the case of a mortgage where title is passed by a deed, the mortgagor retains possession, does the fact that the transaction is void mean that the mortgagor can freely ignore the existence or registration of the mortgage? I think that "void" in this connection cannot mean that the law does not help either party, but rather that the law leaves them, or any one of them, where they are as a result of their transaction and the Court will refuse to aid either or one of them in a suit between them unless the case is brought within some exception. There are difficulties even with this view, because in a case where title and possession are separated, there will be uncertainty in a third party as to how far he can safely deal for the title or the possession of the property. I need not pursue this matter any further in this case but a useful discussion will be found in Wade, *Legal Status of Property Transferred under an Illegal Transaction* (1946), 41 Ill. L. Rev. 487; and *cf.* Glanville L. Williams, *Legal Effect of Illegal Contracts* (1942), 8 Camb. L.J. 51.

Appeal allowed.

PROBLEMS

1. A and B entered into an arrangement for the use by A of a truck owned by A but which was to be licensed in B's name since A could not get a licence to operate a truck. The licensing authorities required that the truck be registered in B's name. A transferred the truck to B.

(a) Before the arrangement had been put into operation, A repented and sought to get his truck back. Can he do so?

(b) After the arrangement had been in operation for some time, A sought to get his truck back. Can he do so?

(c) A had possession of the truck in pursuance of the arrangement. B now seeks to get possession. Can he do so?

2. Do you think that it would make any difference if B had assured A that what the parties proposed to do was perfectly legal?

3. Suppose that the truck was owned by B but transferred by him to A so that A could get the licence and operate it, and that only the owner of a truck could get a licence. Can B recover the truck?

ST. JOHN SHIPPING CORP. v. JOSEPH RANK LTD.

[1957] 1 Q.B. 267. Queen's Bench Division.

ACTION.

The plaintiffs, St. John Shipping Corporation, were a body incorporated under the laws of Panama and owners of the vessel *St. John*, registered in Panama and a "load line vessel not registered in the United Kingdom" within the meaning of section 57 of the Merchant Shipping (Safety and Load Line Conventions) Act, 1932. The vessel's summer load line corresponded to a mean draft of 27 ft. 8⅞ ins. and her winter load line to a mean draft 27 ft. 1⅞ ins. The vessel was chartered by a charterparty dated London, October 18, 1955, by the plaintiffs to Gilbert J. McCaul & Co. Ltd., English charterers, to load 9,700 tons of 2240 lbs. of heavy grain at one safe port, U.S. Gulf, for carriage to London, Avonmouth or Birkenhead, one port only, and deliver the same always afloat agreeable to bills of lading, on being paid freight in cash in British sterling at discharging port.

The defendants, Joseph Rank Ltd., were holders of a bill of lading in respect of 28 parcels of wheat on which the freight due was £18,893 4s. 0d. They paid £16,893 4s. 0d. but withheld the balance of £2,000. The plaintiffs sued for the balance.

The following statement of facts was agreed between the parties.

The goods on which the plaintiffs claimed the balance of freight were loaded on the vessel at Mobile, Alabama, in November, 1955, and were carried by the vessel to Birkenhead pursuant to a bill of lading dated November 2, 1955, whereof the defendants were indorsees to whom the property in the goods passed upon or by reason of such indorsement. The vessel completed loading and sailed from Mobile at 9.30 a.m. on November 2, 1955. On completion of loading the vessel's mean draft, according to a certificate of inspection issued by National Cargo Bureau Inc., dated November 2, 1955, was 27 ft. 8½ ins. The vessel then called at Port Everglades, Florida, for bunkers. She arrived at Port Everglades at 5.30 p.m. on November 5, and sailed at 1.30 a.m. on November 6, having taken on board 600 tons of bunkers. By virtue of the bunkers so taken on board the vessel's mean draft on her departure from Port Everglades was increased to about 28 ft. 7 ins. thereby causing the vessel's summer load line to become submerged by about 10 inches. On November 8 the vessel crossed latitude 36° north and thereby passed into the winter zone, having at all times previously been in the summer zone. The vessel was thereafter throughout in the winter zone and on November 22 she reached the River Mersey. Upon entering the winter zone the vessel's winter load line was submerged by about 16 inches. In the course of the vessel's passage up the River Mersey the master caused the vessel's forepeak tank to be filled for the purpose of trimming the vessel. The capacity of the tank was about 140 tons and the effect of filling the same was to increase the vessel's arrival draft by about 2 ft. 8 ins. On arrival at Birkenhead the vessel's mean draft was about 28 ft. 1 in. and the vessel was accordingly laden below her winter marks by about 11 inches.

Proceedings were thereafter instituted against the master in a court of summary jurisdiction held at Wallasey wherein the master was charged with an offence under sections 44 and 57 of the Merchant Shipping (Safety and Load Line Conventions) Act, 1932, in respect of the vessel being overloaded at Birkenhead, and on November 28, 1955, the master was fined the sum of £1,200. Evidence was tendered in the proceedings that the vessel's deadweight scale was out of date. The vessel loaded in fresh water at Mobile and it was accordingly necessary to load by reference to the vessel's deadweight scale.

In the present action the plaintiffs claimed the amount of freight withheld by the defendants on their parcel. Another receiver also withheld freight to the amount of £295 8s. 10d. The total thus withheld was withheld in consultation with and at the request of the charterers and was the equivalent to freight on about 427 tons of cargo, which tonnage was equivalent to the overall additional cargo on board the vessel by reason whereof the ves-

sel was found to be loaded below her winter marks on arrival at Birkenhead.

The Governments of the United States of America and of Panama ratified or acceded to the International Load Line Convention, 1930, in the
years 1932 and 1936 respectively, and the United States of America and
Panama are "countries to which the Load Line Convention applies" within
the meaning of the Act of 1932 by virtue of declarations made by Order in
Council pursuant to section 65 of the Act.

It was agreed that (a) in event of the parties agreeing the text of any
material legislation of the U.S.A. and/or Panama the court should be free
to construe the same and expert evidence as to the effect of such foreign law
should be dispensed with; (b) in the event of the parties not having agreed
the text of any such material legislation either party should be at liberty to
adduce evidence at the trial with regard to the same.

By their defence the defendants alleged that the plaintiffs had performed
the charter in an illegal manner, by so loading the ship as to submerge or
allow to be submerged her load line by about 11 inches while in part of the
United Kingdom, namely, Birkenhead, contrary to the provisions of the
Merchant Shipping (Safety and Load Line Conventions) Act, 1932. They
accordingly claimed that the plaintiffs were not entitled to the sum claimed
or any part thereof.

The plaintiffs, in reply, contended that the matters relied on by the
defendants afforded no ground of defence in point of law to the claim made
against them.

.   .   .

Oct. 29. **Devlin J.** read the following judgment: The continued depreciation of the pound is beginning to take effect on the criminal law. A maximum fine which at the time when Parliament fixed it would have been
regarded as a sharp disincentive (if the word was then in use) may now
prove to be little or no deterrent. In 1932 Parliament enacted the Merchant
Shipping (Safety and Loadline Conventions) Act, 1932, which, inter alia, by
sections 44 and 57, made it an offence to load a ship so that her loadline
was submerged. The temptation to overload a freighter and so to submerge
her marks is, of course, that the more she carries the more she will earn for
the same expenditure on the voyage. So Parliament, when prescribing a fine
as the punishment for an offence against section 44 related it to the earning
capacity of the ship. The maximum fine was not to exceed the court's estimate of the extent to which the earning capacity of the ship was, or would
have been, increased by reason of the submersion; and was also not to
exceed £100 for every inch or fraction of an inch by which the loadline was
submerged. I suppose that in 1932 £100 was considered an outside figure of
earning capacity per inch, but freights now are very different from what
they were then.

When the master of the plaintiffs' ship *St. John* was prosecuted at Birkenhead under the Act and, on November 28, 1955, found to have overloaded his ship by more than 11 inches, he was fined the maximum of
£1,200; but the amount of cargo by which the ship was overloaded was 427
tons and the extra freight earned was £2,295. So the ship came very well out
of this situation; and she and other ships will doubtless continue to come
very well out of similar situations until the Act of 1932 is amended.

I can see that it is a situation that must cause some concern to cargo owners whose property is at risk. The ship was carrying a cargo of about 10,000 tons of grain from Mobile, Alabama, U.S.A., to Birkenhead. The defendants held a bill of lading for about 3,500 tons of this quantity on which the freight due was nearly £19,000. The defendants, apparently in association with the charterers, decided that some additional punishment should be inflicted on the plaintiffs, and that it should take the form of withholding the £2,295 extra freight. The defendants have withheld £2,000, for which sum they are being sued in this action; and another cargo owner has withheld £295 and is being sued for it in an action that depends on this one.

This is the explanation of how this dispute has arisen. But I, of course, have not got to decide whether the defendants are morally justified in trying to make good deficiencies in the criminal law; nor is any justification of that sort put forward in the case. The defendants' case in law is that since the plaintiffs performed the contract of carriage, evidenced by the bill of lading, in such a way as to infringe the Act of 1932, they committed an illegality which prevents them from enforcing the contract at all; the defendants say they were not obliged to pay any freight, and so cannot be sued for the unpaid balance. If this is right, and if all the consignees had exerted to the full their legal powers, the effective penalty for the plaintiffs' misdeed would have been the loss of the whole freight of more than £50,000.

I do not, of course, regard an offence against the Act of 1932 as a trivial matter, particularly if it is committed deliberately, and if the safety of lives at sea is involved. It is an offence for which the master of a British ship (the plaintiffs' ship was registered in Panama) could be imprisoned. The agreed statement of facts, on which this case is being tried, does not say that the overloading in the U.S.A. was deliberate; for the purposes of the defendants' argument that finding is not required. But there is material in the agreed case which would make such a finding not at all improbable. The vessel was not overloaded when she left her loading port on November 2, 1955; she had then three-eighths of an inch to spare. But it seems plain that she was not then sufficiently bunkered to take her across the Atlantic. On November 5 she called at Port Everglades, Florida, for bunkers, and the 600 tons which she then took on caused her loadline to become submerged by about 10 inches. It is hard to believe that that fact was not appreciated at the time. As she went across the Atlantic her load was, of course, lightened by the consumption of bunkers, but, on the other hand, she passed into the winter zone and the net result was that when she arrived in the Mersey her loadline, as I have said, was submerged by more than 11 inches.

It is a misfortune for the defendants that the legal weapon which they are wielding is so much more potent than it need be to achieve their purpose. Believing, rightly or wrongly, that the plaintiffs have deliberately committed a serious infraction of the Act and one which has placed their property in jeopardy, the defendants wish to do no more than to take the profit out of the plaintiffs' dealing. But the principle which they invoke for this purpose cares not at all for the element of deliberation or for the gravity of the infraction, and does not adjust the penalty to the profits unjustifiably earned. The defendants cannot succeed unless they claim the right to retain the whole freight and to keep it whether the offence was accidental or deliberate, serious or trivial. The application of this principle to a case such as this is bound to lead to startling results. Mr. Wilmers does not seek to avert his gaze from the wide consequences. A shipowner who accidentally over-loads by a fraction of an inch will not be able to recover from any of the shippers or consignees a penny of the freight. There are numerous other ille-galities which a ship might commit in the course of the voyage which would have the same effect; Mr. Roskill has referred me by way of example to sec-tion 24 of the Merchant Shipping (Safety Conventions) Act, 1949, which makes it an offence to send a ship to sea laden with grain if all necessary and reasonable precautions have not been taken to prevent the grain from shifting. He has referred me also to the detailed regulations for the carriage of timber — similar in character to regulations under the Factories Acts — which must be complied with if an offence is not to be committed under section 61 of the Act of 1932. If Mr. Wilmers is right, the consequences to shipowners of a breach of the Act of 1932 would be as serious as if owners of factories were unable to recover from their customers the cost of any arti-cles manufactured in a factory which did not in all respects comply with the Acts. Carriers by land are in no better position; again Mr. Wilmers does not shrink from saying that the owner of a lorry could not recover against the consignees the cost of goods transported in it if in the course of the journey it was driven a mile an hour over its permitted speed. If this is really the law, it is very unenterprising of cargo owners and consignees to wait until a criminal conviction has been secured before denying their liabilities. "A ser-vice of trained observers on all our main roads would soon pay for itself." An effective patrol of the high seas would probably prove too expensive, but the maintenance of a "corps of vigilantes" in all principal ports would be well worth while when one considers that the smallest infringement of the statute or a regulation made thereunder would relieve all the cargo own-ers on the ship from all liability for freight.

Of course, as Mr. Wilmers says, one must not be deterred from enunciat-ing the correct principle of law because it may have startling or even cala-mitous results. "But I confess I approach the investigation of a legal proposition which has results of this character with a prejudice in favour of the idea that there may be a flaw in the argument somewhere."

Mr. Wilmers puts his case under three main heads. In the first place he submits that, notwithstanding that the contract of carriage between the par-ties was legal when made, the plaintiffs have performed it in an illegal man-ner by carrying the goods in a ship which was overloaded in violation of the statute. He submits as a general proposition that a person who performs a legal contract in an illegal manner cannot sue upon it, and he relies upon a line of authorities of which *Anderson Ltd. v. Daniel*, [1924] 1 K.B. 138, is probably the best known. He referred particularly to the formulation of the principle by Atkin L.J. in the following passage:

> "The question of illegality in a contract generally arises in connexion with its for-mation, but it may also arise, as it does here, in connexion with its performance. In the former case, where the parties have agreed to something which is prohib-ited by Act of Parliament, it is indisputable that the contract is unenforceable by either party. And I think that it is equally unenforceable by the offending party where the illegality arises from the fact that the mode of performance adopted by the party performing it is in violation of some statute, even though the contract as agreed upon between the parties was capable of being performed in a perfectly legal manner."

As an alternative to this general proposition and as a modification of it,

Mr. Wilmers submits that a plaintiff cannot recover if, in the course of carrying out a legal contract made with a person of a class which it is the policy of a particular statute to protect, he commits a violation of that statute.

Secondly, he relies upon the well-known principle — most recently considered, I think, in *Marles v. Philip Trant & Sons*, [1954] 1 Q.B. 29 — that a plaintiff cannot recover money if in order to establish his claim to it, he has to disclose that he committed an illegal act. These plaintiffs, he submits, cannot obtain their freight unless they prove that they carried the goods safely to their destination, and they cannot prove that without disclosing that they carried them illegally in an overloaded ship.

Thirdly, he relies upon the principle that a person cannot enforce rights which result to him from his own crime. He submits that the criminal offence committed in this case secured to the plaintiffs a larger freight than they would have earned if they had kept within the law. A part of the freight claimed in this case is therefore a benefit resulting from the crime and in such circumstances the plaintiff cannot recover any part of it.

I am satisfied that Mr. Wilmers's chief argument is based on a misconception of the principle applied in *Anderson Ltd. v. Daniel*, which I have already cited. In order to expose that misconception I must state briefly how that principle fits in with other principles relating to illegal contracts. There are two general principles. The first is that a contract which is entered into with the object of committing an illegal act is unenforceable. The application of this principle depends upon proof of the intent, at the time the contract was made, to break the law; if the intent is mutual the contract is not enforceable at all, and, if unilateral, it is unenforceable at the suit of the party who is proved to have it. This principle is not involved here. Whether or not the overloading was deliberate when it was done, there is no proof that it was contemplated when the contract of carriage was made. The second principle is that the court will not enforce a contract which is expressly or impliedly prohibited by statute. If the contract is of this class it does not matter what the intent of the parties is; if the statute prohibits the contract, it is unenforceable whether the parties meant to break the law or not. A significant distinction between the two classes is this. In the former class you have only to look and see what acts the statute prohibits; it does not matter whether or not it prohibits a contract; if a contract is deliberately made to do a prohibited act, that contract will be unenforceable. In the latter class, you have to consider not what acts the statute prohibits, but what contracts it prohibits; but you are not concerned at all with the intent of the parties; if the parties enter into a prohibited contract, that contract is unenforceable.

The principle enunciated by Atkin L.J. and cited above is an offshoot of the second principle that a prohibited contract will not be enforced. If the prohibited contract is an express one, it falls directly within the principle. It must likewise fall within it if the contract is implied. If, for example, an unlicensed broker sues for work and labour, it does not matter that no express contract is alleged and that the claim is based solely on the performance of the contract, that is to say, the work and labour done; it is as much unenforceable as an express contract made to fit the work done. The same reasoning must be applied to a contract which, though legal in form, is performed unlawfully. Jenkins L.J. in his illuminating judgment in *B. and B. Viennese Fashions v. Losane*, [1952] 1 T.L.R. 750, has shown how illogical it would be if the law were otherwise. In that case the regulations required that the seller of utility goods should furnish to the buyer an invoice containing certain particulars. The plaintiff made a contract of sale for non-utility goods, to which the regulations did not apply; but he purported to perform it by delivering to the buyer without objection utility garments to which the regulations did apply; and he did not furnish the invoice. If the court enforced his claim for the price of the garments, it would have, in effect, been enforcing a contract for the supply of utility garments without furnishing an invoice, which, had it originally been made in that form, would have been prohibited. But whether it is the terms of the contract or the performance of it that is called in question, the test is just the same: is the contract, as made or as performed, a contract that is prohibited by the statute?

Mr. Wilmers's proposition ignores this test. On a superficial reading of *Anderson Ltd. v. Daniel* and the cases that followed and preceded it, judges may appear to be saying that it does not matter that the contract is itself legal, if something illegal is done under it. But that is an unconsidered interpretation of the cases. When fully considered, it is plain that they do not proceed upon the basis that in the course of performing a legal contract an illegality was committed; but on the narrower basis that the way in which the contract was performed turned it into the sort of contract that was prohibited by the statute.

All the cases which Mr. Wilmers cited in support of his submission show, I think, that this is the true basis. Some of the earlier cases on which he relied — those in which the principle was first being formulated — show this most clearly; and I take as an example of them *Cope v. Rowlands* (1836), 2 M. & W. 149. In that case the plaintiff brought an action for work and labour done by him as a broker and the plea was that he was not duly licensed to act as a stockbroker pursuant to the statute. The statute imposed a penalty on any unlicensed person acting as a broker. Parke B. (the italics below are those in the report) declared the law to be as follows: "It is perfectly settled, that where the contract which the plaintiff seeks to enforce, be it express or implied, is expressly or by implication forbidden by the common or statute law, no court will lend its assistance to give it effect. It is equally clear that a contract is void if prohibited by a statute, though the statute inflicts a penalty only, because such a penalty implies a prohibition. ... And it may be safely laid down, notwithstanding some dicta apparently to the contrary, that if *the contract* be rendered illegal, it can make no difference, in point of law, whether the statute which makes it so has in view the protection of the revenue, or any other object. The sole question is, whether the statute *means to prohibit the contract?*" After considering the language of the Act Parke B. went on to say that the language "shows clearly that the legislature had in view, as *one* object, the benefit and security of the public in those important transactions which are negotiated by brokers. The clause, therefore, which imposes a penalty, must be taken ... to imply a prohibition of all unadmitted persons to act as brokers, and consequently to prohibit, by necessary inference, all contracts which such persons make for compensation to themselves for so acting; and this is the contract on which this action is ... brought."

Now this language — and the same sort of language is used in all the cases — shows that the question always is whether the statute meant to prohibit the contract which is sued upon. One of the tests commonly used, and frequently mentioned in the later cases, in order to ascertain the true meaning of the statute is to inquire whether or not the object of the statute was to protect the public or a class of persons, that is, to protect the public from claims for services by unqualified persons or to protect licensed persons from competition. Mr. Wilmers (while saying that, if necessary, he would submit that the Act of 1932 was passed, inter alia, to protect those who had property at sea) was unable to explain the relevance of this consideration to his view of the law. If in considering the effect of the statute the only inquiry that you have to make is whether an act is illegal, it cannot matter for whose benefit the statute was passed; the fact that the statute makes the act illegal is of itself enough. But if you are considering whether a contract not expressly prohibited by the Act is impliedly prohibited, such considerations are relevant in order to determine the scope of the statute.

This, then, is the principle which I think is to be derived from the class of cases which Mr. Wilmers cited. Not unnaturally, he cited those cases in which the result at least was consistent with the proposition for which he was contending. Had he cited those cases in which the claim succeeded because the statute was held not to imply a prohibition of any contract, he would, I think, have seen the fallacy in his argument. For that submits the point to the crucial test. The plaintiff does an illegal act, being one prohibited by the statute, but he does it in performance of a legal contract, since the statute is construed as prohibiting the act merely and not prohibiting the contract under which it is done. If in such a case it had been held that it did not matter whether the contract was legal or not since the mode of performing it was illegal, Mr. Wilmers's argument would be well supported. But in fact the contrary has been held. I take as an example of cases of this type, *Wetherell v. Jones* (1832), 3 B. & Ad. 221. The plaintiff sued for the price of spirits sold and delivered. A statute of George IV provided that no spirits should be sent out of stock without a permit. The court held that the permit obtained by the plaintiff was irregular because of his own fault and that he was therefore guilty of a violation of the law, but that the statute did not prohibit the contract. Tenterden C.J. stated the law as follows: "Where a contract which a plaintiff seeks to enforce is expressly, or by implication, forbidden by the statute or common law, no court will lend its assistance to give it effect: and there are numerous cases in the books where an action on the contract has failed, because either the consideration for the promise or the act to be done was illegal, as being against the express provisions of the law, or contrary to justice, morality, and sound policy. But where the consideration and the matter to be performed are both legal, we are not aware that a plaintiff has ever been precluded from recovering by an infringement of the law, not contemplated by the contract, in the performance of something to be done on his part."

The last sentence in this judgment is a clear and decisive statement of the law; it is directly contrary to the contention which Mr. Wilmers advances, which I therefore reject both on principle and on authority.

So Mr. Wilmers's wider proposition fails. Mr. Roskill is right in his submission that the determining factor is the true effect and meaning of the statute, and I turn therefore to consider Mr. Wilmers's alternative proposition that the contract evidenced by the bill of lading is one that is made illegal by the Act of 1932. I have already indicated the basis of this argument, namely, that the statute being one which according to its preamble is passed to give effect to a convention "for promoting the safety of life and property at sea," it is therefore passed for the benefit of cargo owners among others. That this is an important consideration is certainly established by the authorities. But I follow the view of Parke B. in *Cope v. Rowlands*, 2 M. & W. 149, which I have already cited, that it is one only of the tests. The fundamental question is whether the statute means to prohibit the contract. The statute is to be construed in the ordinary way; one must have regard to all relevant considerations and no single consideration, however important, is conclusive.

Two questions are involved. The first — and the one which hitherto has usually settled the matter — is: does the statute mean to prohibit contracts at all? But if this be answered in the affirmative, then one must ask: does this contract belong to the class which the statute intends to prohibit? For example, a person is forbidden by statute from using an unlicensed vehicle on the highway. If one asks oneself whether there is in such an enactment an implied prohibition of all contracts for the use of unlicensed vehicles, the answer may well be that there is, and that contracts of hire would be unenforceable. But if one asks oneself whether there is an implied prohibition of contracts for the carriage of goods by unlicensed vehicles or for the repairing of unlicensed vehicles or for the garaging of unlicensed vehicles, the answer may well be different. The answer might be that collateral contracts of this sort are not within the ambit of the statute.

The relevant section of the Act of 1932, section 44, provides that the ship "shall not be so loaded as to submerge" the appropriate loadline. It may be that a contract for the loading of the ship which necessarily has this effect would be unenforceable. It might be, for example, that the contract for bunkering at Port Everglades which had the effect of submerging the load-line, if governed by English law, would have been unenforceable. But an implied prohibition of contracts of loading does not necessarily extend to contracts for the carriage of goods by improperly loaded vessels. Of course, if the parties knowingly agree to ship goods by an overloaded vessel, such a contract would be illegal; but its illegality does not depend on whether it is impliedly prohibited by the statute, since it falls within the first of the two general heads of illegality I noted above where there is an intent to break the law. The way to test the question whether a particular class of contract is prohibited by the statute is to test it in relation to a contract made in ignorance of its effect.

In my judgment, contracts for the carriage of goods are not within the ambit of this statute at all. A court should not hold that any contract or class of contracts is prohibited by statute unless there is a clear implication, or "necessary inference," as Parke B. put it, that the statute so intended. If a contract has as its whole object the doing of the very act which the statute prohibits, it can be argued that you can hardly make sense of a statute which forbids an act and yet permits to be made a contract to do it; that is a clear implication. But unless you get a clear implication of that sort, I think that a court ought to be very slow to hold that a statute intends to interfere with the rights and remedies given by the ordinary law of contract. Caution in this respect is, I think, especially necessary in these times when so much of commercial life is governed by regulations of one sort or another, which may easily be broken without wicked intent. Persons who deliberately set out to break the law cannot expect to be aided in a court of justice, but it is a different matter when the law is unwittingly broken. To nullify a bargain in such circumstances frequently means that in a case — perhaps of such triviality that no authority would have felt it worth while to prosecute — a seller, because he cannot enforce his civil rights, may forfeit a sum vastly in excess of any penalty that a criminal court would impose; and the sum forfeited will not go into the public purse but into the pockets of someone who is lucky enough to pick up the windfall or astute enough to have contrived to get it. It is questionable how far this contributes to public morality. In *Vita Food Products Inc. v. Unus Shipping Co.*, [1939] A.C. 277, Lord Wright said: "Nor must it be forgotten that the rule by which contracts not expressly forbidden by statute or declared to be void are in proper cases nullified for disobedience to a statute is a rule of public policy only, and public policy understood in a wider sense may at times be better served by refusing to nullify a bargain save on serious and sufficient grounds." It may be questionable also whether public policy is well served by driving from the seat of judgment everyone who has been guilty of a minor transgression. Commercial men who have unwittingly offended against one of a multiplicity of regulations may nevertheless feel that they have not thereby forfeited all right to justice, and may go elsewhere for it if courts of law will not give it to them. In the last resort they will, if necessary, set up their own machinery for dealing with their own disputes in the way that those whom the law puts beyond the pale, such as gamblers, have done. I have said enough, and perhaps more than enough, to show how important it is that the courts should be slow to imply the statutory prohibition of contracts, and should do so only when the implication is quite clear. I have felt justified in saying as much because, to any judge who sits in what is called the Commercial Court, it must be a matter of special concern. This court was instituted more than half a century ago so that it might solve the disputes of commercial men in a way which they understood and appreciated, and it is a particular misfortune for it if it has to deny that service to any except those who are clearly undeserving of it.

I think also that it is proper, in determining the scope of the statute, to have regard to the consequences I have already described and to the inconveniences and injury to maritime business which would follow from upholding the defendants' contention in this case. In the light of all these considerations I should not be prepared to treat this statute as nullifying contracts for the carriage of goods unless I found myself clearly compelled by authority to do so. I can find no such authority in the cases which Mr. Wilmers has cited, nor even any analogous cases in which the law has been stretched as far. Of course, the construction of each Act depends upon its own terms, but I can find no authority in which any Act has been given anything like so wide an effect as Mr. Wilmers wants the Act of 1932 to be given. In the statutes to which the principle has been applied, what was prohibited was a contract which had at its centre — indeed often filling the whole space within its circumference — the prohibited act; contracts for the sale of prohibited goods, contracts for the sale of goods without accompanying documents when the statute specifically said there must be accompanying documents; contracts for work and labour done by persons who were prohibited from doing the whole of the work and labour for which they demanded recompense. It is going a long way further to say that contracts which depend for their performance upon the use of an instrument which has been treated in a forbidden way should also be forbidden. In the only case I have seen where the contention appeared to go as far as that the claim failed. The relevant facts in *Smith v. Mawhood* (1845), 14 M. & W. 452, appear sufficiently from the judgment of Alderson B., where he also dealt with the contention: "But here the legislature has merely said, that where a party carries on the trade or business of a dealer in or seller of tobacco, he shall be liable to a certain penalty, if the house in which he carries on the business shall not have his name, etc., painted on it, in letters publicly visible and legible, and at least an inch long, and so forth. He is liable to the penalty, therefore, by carrying on the trade in a house in which these requisites are not complied with; and there is no addition to his criminality if he makes fifty contracts for the *sale* of tobacco in such a house. It seems to me, therefore, that there is nothing in the Act of Parliament to prohibit every act of sale, but that its only effect is to impose a penalty, for the purpose of the revenue, on the carrying on of the trade without complying with its requisites."

A contract for the sale of tobacco was therefore not to be considered void merely because the premises in which the tobacco was sold did not comply with the law. So it might be said that a contract for carriage of goods is not to be considered void merely because the ship in which they are carried does not comply with the law. But I recognize that each case must be determined by reference to the relevant statute and not by comparison with other cases. I reach my conclusion — in the words of Lord Wright in *Vita Food Products Inc. v. Unus Shipping Co.*, [1939] A.C. 277, 295 — on "the true construction of the statute, having regard to its scope and its purpose and to the inconvenience which would follow from any other conclusion."

In view of the importance of this question, I have thought it right to determine it upon general grounds rather than upon the particular wording of section 44. But I must note that Mr. Roskill also particularly relies upon the wording of subsection (2) of that section. This subsection, to which I have already referred, is the one which says that the fine is to be such "as the court thinks fit to impose having regard to the extent to which the earning capacity of the ship was, or would have been, increased by reason of the submersion." Mr. Roskill submits that this shows that the statute contemplated that, notwithstanding the breach of it, there would be an "earning capacity" and, therefore, that contracts for the payment of freight must be intended to remain alive. I note that a similar point was taken in *Forster v. Taylor* (1834), 5 B. & Ad. 887, 889, but it was not necessary for the court to deal with it.

I turn now to Mr. Wilmers's second point. He submitted that the plaintiffs could not succeed in a claim for freight without disclosing that they had committed an illegality in the course of the voyage; or, put another way, that part of the consideration for the payment of freight was the safe carriage of the goods, and therefore they must show that they carried the goods safely. In the passage I have quoted from the judgment in *Wetherell v. Jones* Tenterden C.J. carefully distinguished between an infringement of the law in the performance of the contract and a case where "the consideration and the matter to be performed" were illegal. There is a distinction there — of the sort I have just been considering — between a contract which has as its object the doing of the very act forbidden by the statute, and a contract whose performance involves an illegality only incidentally. It may be, therefore, that the second point is the first point looked at from another angle. However that may be, there is no doubt that if the plaintiffs cannot succeed in their claim for freight without showing that they carried the goods in an overloaded ship, they must fail.

But, in my judgment, the plaintiffs need show no more in order to recover their freight than that they delivered to the defendants the goods they received in the same good order and condition as that in which they received them. Indeed, they are entitled to recover their freight without deduction (but subject to counterclaim) if the goods they delivered were substantially the same as when loaded: see Scrutton on Charterparties, 16th ed., p. 391, art. 144. It may be true that it is a term of the contract of carriage that the goods should be carried safely. Article III of the Hague Rules provides, for example, in rule 2, "that the carrier shall properly and carefully load, handle, stow, carry, keep, care for and discharge the goods carried." But no one has ever heard of a claim for freight being supported by a string of witnesses describing the loading, handling, stowing, keeping, caring for and discharging the goods. The truth is that if the goods have been delivered safely, it must follow that they have been carried safely. If, therefore, they are proved to have been delivered undamaged, the shipowner need prove no more. The law is that they shall be carried safely — not that they should not be exposed to danger on the voyage. If the plaintiffs had to prove that they were not exposed to danger on the voyage, then no doubt they would also have to prove that the ship complied with all the safety regulations affecting her; but in the claim for freight they need only prove safe delivery. This point fails.

On Mr. Wilmers's third point I take the law from the dictum in *Beresford v. Royal Insurance Co. Ltd.*, [1938] A.C. 586, that was adopted and applied by Lord Atkin: "no system of jurisprudence can with reason include amongst the rights which it enforces rights directly resulting to the person asserting them from the crime of that person." I observe in the first place that in the Court of Appeal in the same case Lord Wright doubted whether this principle applied to all statutory offences. His doubt was referred to by Denning L.J. in *Marles v. Philip Trant & Sons*, [1954] 1 Q.B. 29, 37, which I have already cited. The distinction is much to the point here. The Act of 1932 imposes a penalty which is itself designed to deprive the offender of the benefits of his crime. It would be a curious thing if the operation could be performed twice — once by the criminal law and then again by the civil. It would be curious, too, if in a case in which the magistrates had thought fit to impose only a nominal fine, their decision could, in effect, be overridden in a civil action. But the question whether the rule applies to statutory offences is an important one which I do not wish to decide in the present case. The dicta of Lord Wright and Denning L.J. suggest that there are cases where its application would be morally unjustifiable; but it is not clear that they go as far as saying that the application would not be justified in law. I prefer, therefore, to deal with Mr. Wilmers's submission in another way.

The rights which cannot be enforced must be those "directly resulting" from the crime. That means, I think, that for a right to money or to property to be unenforceable the property or money must be identifiable as something to which, but for the crime, the plaintiff would have had no right or title. That cannot be said in this case. The amount of the profit which the plaintiffs made from the crime, that is to say, the amount of freight which, but for the overloading, they could not have earned on this voyage, was, as I have said, £2,295. The quantity of cargo consigned to the defendants was approximately 35 per cent. of the whole and, therefore, even if it were permissible to treat the benefit as being divisible pro rata over the whole of the cargo, the amount embodied in the claim against the defendants would not be more than 35 per cent. of £2,300. That would not justify the withholding of £2,000. The fact is that the defendants and another cargo owner have between them withheld money, not on a basis that is proportionate to the claim against them, but so as to wipe out the improper profit on the whole of the cargo. I do not, however, think that the defendants' position would be any better if they had deducted no more than the sum attributable to their freight on a pro rata basis. There is no warrant under the principle for a pro rata division; it would be just as reasonable to say that the excess freight should be deemed to attach entirely to the last 427 tons loaded, leaving the freight claim on all the rest unaffected. But in truth there is no warrant for any particular form of division. The fact is that in this type of case no claim or part of a claim for freight can be clearly identified as being the excess illegally earned.

In *Beresford v. Royal Insurance Co. Ltd.* the court dismissed the claim of a personal representative who claimed on policies of life insurance which had matured owing to the assured committing suicide in circumstances that amounted to a crime. Mr. Wilmers submitted that the only benefit which the assured or his estate derived from the claim was the acceleration of the policies and that notwithstanding that some of the policies had been in force for a considerable time and therefore, I suppose, had a surrender value before the suicide was committed, the plaintiff was not allowed to recover anything. So in the present case, he submits, the commission of the crime defeats the whole claim to freight notwithstanding that the earning of the greater part of it was irrespective of the crime.

The comparison does not seem to me to be just. In *Beresford v. Royal Insurance Co. Ltd.*, but for the crime committed by the assured, no part of the policy moneys could have been claimed in that form, that is to say, as money repayable on the happening of the event insured against, or at that time. That does not necessarily mean that, so far as public policy was concerned, the plaintiff could recover nothing. If the plaintiff, for example, had sued for the return of premiums, assuming the contract permitted it, I have not been referred to any observation in the case which would suggest that an action in that form would fail on the grounds of public policy. The claim which the court was considering under the policy depended entirely upon proof of death and the death was a crime. In the present case the right to claim freight from the defendants was not brought into existence by a crime; the crime affected only the total amount of freight earned by the ship.

The result is that there must be judgment for the plaintiffs for £2,000. But the defendants will not have fought the action altogether in vain if it brings to the attention of the competent authorities the fact that section 44 of the Act of 1932 is out of date and ought to be amended. I have already noted that for a similar offence a British master can be imprisoned and it must be very galling for those concerned to see a foreign master do the same thing without the law providing any effective deterrent.

Judgment for plaintiffs.

¹ Merchant Shipping (Safety and Load Line Conventions) Act, 1932, s. 44: "(1) A British load line ship registered in the United Kingdom shall not be so loaded as to submerge in salt water, when the ship has no list, the appropriate load line on each side of the ship, that is to say, the load line indicating or purporting to indicate the maximum depth to which the ship is for the time being entitled under the load line rules to be loaded. (2) If any such ship is loaded in contravention of this section, the owner or master of the ship shall for each offence be liable to a fine not exceeding one hundred pounds and to such additional fine, not exceeding the amount herein-after specified, as the court thinks fit to impose having regard to the extent to which the earning capacity of the ship was, or would have been, increased by reason of the submersion. (3) The said additional fine shall not exceed one hundred pounds for every inch or fraction of an inch by which the appropriate load line on each side of the ship was submerged, or would have been submerged if the ship had been in salt water and had no list." S. 57: "The provisions of section 44 of this Act shall apply to load line ships not registered in the United Kingdom, while they are within any port in the United Kingdom, as they apply to British load line ships registered in the United Kingdom...:"

ARCHBOLDS (FREIGHTAGE) LTD. v. SPANGLETT LTD.

[1961] 1 Q.B. 374 Court of Appeal (England); Sellers, Pearce and Devlin
L.JJ.

APPEAL from Slade J.

The following statement of facts is taken from the judgment of Pearce L.J. Judgment was given for the plaintiffs, Archbolds (Freightage) Ltd., on December 3, 1959, for £3,674 18s. 3d. damages in respect of the loss of a consignment of whisky which was stolen from the defendants. S. Spanglett Ltd., owing to their negligence, while they were transporting it as carriers for the plaintiffs from Leeds to the London docks. Various matters raised in the defence were decided in the plaintiffs' favour, and the issue on this appeal was whether the judge should have held that the plaintiffs could not recover damages because the contract of carriage was illegal.

The following facts were material to this issue: the defendants were fur-niture manufacturers in London and owned five vans for use in their busi-ness. Those vans had "C" licences under the Road and Rail Traffic Act, 1933, which enabled them to carry the defendants' own goods but did not allow them to carry for reward the goods of others. The plaintiffs were car-riers with offices at London and Leeds and also had a clearing house to assist with sub-contracting contracts of carriage. Their vehicles had "A" licences which enabled them to carry the goods of others for reward. When some other carrier was returning home with an empty van having made a delivery, he might ask the plaintiffs if they had a load available for him; and if they had one available, it was an economy for them to sub-contract that load to him instead of sending their own van with the risk of its having to return empty.

At the time of the Suez crisis there was a shortage of petrol and the Min-ister enlarged the scope of "C" licences to permit licensees to carry the goods of others which would normally be carried under [other persons' own] "C" licences. This limited extension was presumably designed to leave the trade of "A" licence-holders unaffected. Although it was not strictly proved, it was assumed that the whisky in question was not whisky that would normally be carried under a "C" licence. Therefore it could not legally be carried for reward on any of the defendants' vans.

The plaintiffs' London office, as a result of a telephone conversation on March 25, 1956, with some unidentified person who spoke from the defendants' office, believed that the defendants' vehicles had "A" licences and were entitled to carry general goods. They therefore employed the defendants to carry for them a part load of goods on the defendants' van which was taking some of the defendants' own furniture from London to the Leeds area.

On March 27, 1956, Randall, the defendants' driver, having delivered those goods, spoke on the telephone to one Field, the traffic manager at the plaintiffs' office in Leeds, in order to see if he could obtain a load for his empty van back from Leeds to London. Randall said who he was, that he was from the defendants and that he had just carried goods from the plaintiffs' London office to Leeds and "if possible would like a return load." He then said: "Have you anything for a covered van?" Field replied that he had 3¾ tons. He left the telephone to make certain that the load was suitable for a covered van, returned to the telephone and told Randall to come to the plaintiffs' Leeds office. Field made no inquiry about Randall's licence because, to use his own words, "I knew he had been loaded by our London Office." Randall came to the office, the van was loaded with 3¾ tons, which was in fact 200 cases of whisky, and set off for the London docks. The whisky was stolen owing to Randall's negligence.

Slade J. held that the plaintiffs did not know that the contract was to be carried out in an illegal manner and that their claim for damages succeeded. The defendants appealed.

Devlin L.J. The effect of illegality upon a contract may be threefold. If at the time of making the contract there is an intent to perform it in an unlawful way, the contract, although it remains alive, is unenforceable at the suit of the party having that intent; if the intent is held in common, it is not enforceable at all. Another effect of illegality is to prevent a plaintiff from recovering under a contract if in order to prove his rights under it he has to rely upon his own illegal act; he may not do that even though he can show that at the time of making the contract he had no intent to break the law and that at the time of performance he did not know that what he was doing was illegal. The third effect of illegality is to avoid the contract ab initio and that arises if the making of the contract is expressly or impliedly prohibited by statute or is otherwise contrary to public policy.

The defendants do not seek to bring this case under either of the first two heads. They cannot themselves enforce the contract because they intended to perform it unlawfully with a van that they knew was not properly licensed for the purpose: but that does not prevent the plaintiffs, who had no such intent and were not privy to it, from enforcing the contract. Nor can it be said that the plaintiffs committed any illegal act. To load a vehicle is not to use it on the road, which is what is forbidden; no doubt loading would be enough to constitute aiding and abetting if the plaintiffs knew of the defendants' purpose (*National Coal Board v. Gamble*), [1959] 1 Q.B. 11, but they did not.

So what the defendants say is that the contract is prohibited by the Road and Rail Traffic Act, 1933, s. 1. In order to see whether the contract falls within the prohibition it is necessary to ascertain the exact terms of the contract and the exact terms of the prohibition. For reasons which I shall explain later, I shall begin by ascertaining the latter. Section 1 of the Act provides that no person shall use a goods vehicle on a road for the carriage of goods for hire or reward except under a licence. Section 2 provides for various classes of licences, "A," "B" and "C." It is agreed that the carriage of the goods which were the subject-matter of this contract required an "A" licence. The fact that the van had a "C" licence does not therefore help one way or the other; and it is admitted that the defendants' use of this van for the carriage of these goods was prohibited. As I have noted, the plaintiffs are not to be treated as using the van because they supplied the load. Section 1 (3) provides that the driver of the vehicle or, if he is an agent or servant, his principal, shall be deemed to be the person by whom the vehicle is being used.

The statute does not expressly prohibit the making of any contract. The question is therefore whether a prohibition arises as a matter of necessary implication. It follows from the decision of this court in *Nash v. Stevenson Transport Ltd.*, [1936] 2 K.B. 128, that a contract for the use of unlicensed vehicles is prohibited. In that case the plaintiff held "A" licences which the defendant wanted to purchase. But the Act of 1933 provides that licences may not be transferred or assigned, and it was therefore agreed that the defendant should run the vehicles in the plaintiff's name so that they might obtain the benefit of his licences. It was held by the court that that was an illegal agreement because the defendant was the person who was using the vehicles and the plaintiff the person who was licensed to use them; thus the user was not the licensee. In the present case there was no contract for the use of the vehicle.

On the other hand, it does not follow that because it is an offence for one party to enter into a contract, the contract itself is void. In *In re Mahmoud and Ispahani*, [1921] 2 K.B. 716, 730, Scrutton L.J. said: "In *Bloxsome v. Williams* (1824), 3 B. & C. 232, the position was that the defendant, a horse dealer, was prohibited from trading on Sunday, but there was nothing illegal in another person making a contract with a horse dealer, except that if he knew that the person with whom he was dealing was a horse dealer and was guilty of breaking the law he might be aiding and abetting him to break the law. But merely to make a contract with a horse dealer, without knowing he was a horse dealer, was not illegal."

The general considerations which arise on this question were examined at length in *St. John Shipping Corporation v. Joseph Rank Ltd.*, [1957] 1 Q.B. 267, 285, and Pearce L.J. has set them out so clearly in his judgment in this case that I need add little to them. Fundamentally they are the same as those that arise on the construction of every statute; one must have regard to the language used and to the scope and purpose of the statute. I think that the purpose of this statute is sufficiently served by the penalties prescribed for the offender; the avoidance of the contract would cause grave inconvenience and injury to innocent members of the public without furthering the object of the statute. Moreover, the value of the relief given to the wrongdoer if he could escape what would otherwise have been his legal obligation might, as it would in this case, greatly outweigh the punishment that could be imposed upon him, and thus undo the penal effect of the statute.

I conclude, therefore, that this contract was not illegal for the reason that the statute does not prohibit the making of a contract for the carriage of goods in unlicensed vehicles and this contract belongs to this class. I am able, therefore, to arrive at my judgment without an examination of the exact terms of the contract. It would have been natural to have begun by looking at the contract; I have not done so because it is doubtful whether the state of the pleadings permits a thorough examination. But as Mr. Karmel's argument before us turned upon its terms, I think that I should deal with them.

The defendants contend that this was a contract of carriage by a specified vehicle, namely, the van SXY902 then being driven by Randall. The plaintiffs agree that it was contemplated that the van SXY902 should be used for the contract but dispute that the contract was so limited. The words used in the contract were "a covered van" and the plaintiffs submit, and the judge has so held, that "it was open to the defendants to carry the goods in any vehicle they liked."

I have reached no final conclusion on this point. Assuming, as for the purposes of this argument I do, that the statute prohibits every contract for the carriage of goods in an unlicensed vehicle, I do not think that the question whether this contract falls within the statute depends on whether it was limited to the use of the vehicle SXY902. According to the defendants' argument, the significance of the point lies in the fact that they have to accept the burden of proving that there was no way in which they could have performed the contract legally. If only the one van could have been used under the contract, they claim to have discharged that burden; otherwise they concede that they cannot prove that they could not, if they had tried, have got hold of some other licensed van. In my judgment, this is not the decisive test.

It is a familiar principle of law that if a contract can be performed in one of two ways, that is, legally or illegally, it is not an illegal contract, though it may be unenforceable at the suit of a party who chooses to perform it illegally. That statement of the law is meaningful if the contract is one which is by its terms open to two modes of performance; otherwise it is meaningless. Almost any contract — certainly any contract for the carriage of goods by road — can be performed illegally; any contract of carriage by road can be performed illegally simply by exceeding the appropriate speed limit. The error in the defendants' argument, I think, is that they are looking at the facts which determine their capacity to perform and not at the terms of the contract. Suppose that the contract were for a vehicle with an "A" licence, or — what is substantially the same thing — for a specified vehicle warranted as holding an "A" licence. That would not be an illegal contract for it would be a contract for the use of a licensed vehicle and not an unlicensed one. If those were the express terms of the contract, it would not be made illegal because all the carrier's vehicles, or the specified vehicle as the case might be, had "C" licences. The most that that could show would be that the carrier might well be unable to perform his contract. Or suppose that the contract were for any "A" vehicle owned by the defendant and the defendant had a fleet of five "A" vehicles and five "C" vehicles. That would be a legal contract and it would not be made illegal because, at the time when it was made, it was physically impossible for the defendant to get any of his "A" vehicles to the loading place in time. If the contract is for a specified vehicle with an "A" licence, loading to begin within a week, it is not illegal because when the contract was made the vehicle had no "A" licence; one might be obtained in time and the court will not decide the question of legality by inquiring whether an "A" licence could or could not have been obtained for it within the week. So in this case it is irrelevant to say that the van SXY902 had in fact not got an "A" licence and could not conceivably have got one in time. The error in the defendants' argument is that they assume that because the parties were contracting about a specified vehicle and because that specified vehicle had in fact (a fact known to one party and not to the other) only a "C" licence, therefore they were contracting about a vehicle with a "C" licence. It is the terms of the contract that matter; the surrounding facts are irrelevant, save in so far as, being known to both parties, they throw light on the meaning and effect of the contract. The question is not whether the vehicle was in fact properly licensed but whether it was expressly or by implication in the contract described or warranted as properly licensed. If it was so described or warranted, then the legal position is, not that the contract could only be performed by a violation of the law, but that unless it could be performed legally, it could not be performed at all. The fact that, as in this case, it may be known to one of the parties at the time of making the contract that he cannot perform it legally and therefore that it will inevitably be broken, does not make the contract itself illegal.

So the correct line of inquiry into the terms of the contract in this case should have been not as to whether it provided for performance by a specified vehicle or by any vehicle that the defendants chose to nominate, but as to whether the defendants warranted or agreed that the vehicle which was to do the work, whether a specified vehicle or any other, was legally fit for the service which it had to undertake, that is, that it had an "A" licence.

I think there is much to be said for the argument that in a case of this sort there is, unless the circumstances exclude it, an implied warranty that the van is properly licensed for the service for which it is required. It would be unreasonable to expect a man when he is getting into a taxicab to ask for an express warranty from the driver that his cab was licensed; the answer, if it took any intelligible form at all, would be to the effect that it would not be on the streets if it were not. The same applies to a person who delivers goods for carriage by a particular vehicle; he cannot be expected to examine the road licence to see if it is in order. But the issue of warranty was not raised in the pleadings or at the trial and so I think it is preferable to decide this case on the broad ground which Pearce L.J. has adopted and with which, for the reasons I have given, I agree.

There are many pitfalls in this branch of the law. If, for example, Mr. Field had observed that the van had a "C" licence and said nothing, he might be said to have accepted a mode of performance different from that contracted for and so varied the contract and turned it into an illegal one: see *St. John Shipping Corporation v. Joseph Rank Ltd.*, [1957] 1 Q.B. 267, 283, 284, where that sort of point was considered. Or, to take another example, if a statute prohibits the sale of goods to an alien, a warranty by the buyer that he is not an alien will not save the contract. That is because the terms of the prohibition expressly forbid a sale to an alien; consequently, the question to be asked in order to see whether the contract comes within the prohibition is whether the buyer is in fact an alien, not whether he represented himself as one. *In re Mahmoud*, [1921] 2 K.B. 716, is that sort of case. The statute forbade the buying and selling of certain goods between unlicensed persons. The buyer falsely represented himself as having a licence. It is not said that he so warranted but, if he had, it could have made no difference. Once the fact was established that he was an unlicensed person the contract was brought within the category of those that were prohibited. *Strongman v. Sincock*, [1955] 2 Q.B. 525, exemplifies another sort of difficulty. It was an action brought by a builder against a building owner to recover the price of building work done. The statute forbade the execution of building operations without a licence. The building owner expressly undertook to obtain the necessary licence and failed to do so; and it was held that the builder could not recover. The builder, I dare say, might have contended that, having regard to the undertaking, the contract he made was for licensed operations and therefore legal. But unfortunately he had himself performed it illegally by building without a licence and he could not recover without relying on his illegal act because he was suing for money for work done. The undertaking might make the contract legal but not the operations. All these cases are distinguishable from the present one, where the contract is not within the prohibition and the plaintiffs themselves committed no illegal act and did not aid or abet the defendants. Apart from the pleading point, it might not matter if the last two cases were not distinguishable, since the plaintiffs could obtain damages for breach of the warranty as in *Strongman v. Sincock*.

Appeal dismissed with costs.

[Sellers L.J. agreed with the others. Pearce L.J. gave judgment to the same effect.]

QUESTION

To what extent would the suggestion made by Devlin L.J. that there may be an implied warranty of legality, solve some of the problems that arose in the cases we have discussed?

ASHMORE v. DAWSON LTD.

[1973] 2 All E.R. 856, Court of Appeal; Lord Denning M.R., Phillimore and Scarman L.JJ.

Lord Denning MR. In February 1967 a big piece of engineering equipment called a tube bank was being carried from Stockton-on-Tees to Hull where it was to be shipped to Poland. It was very heavy. It weighed 25 tons. It was loaded on an articulated lorry. Halfway to Hull that lorry with its load tipped over. Damage was done to the load. It cost £2,225 to repair. The manufacturers claim damages from the hauliers. In answer the hauliers plead that the load was too heavy for the vehicle, and that the contract of carriage, or the performance of it, was illegal.

The relevant regulations are the Motor Vehicles (Construction and Use) Regulations 1966. They were made by virtue of the Road Traffic Act 1960, s 64. Section 64 (2) says:

'... it shall not be lawful to use on a road a motor vehicle or trailer which does not comply with any such regulations as aforesaid...'

In the present case the vehicle was an articulated vehicle with a tractor and trailer. Under reg 73 (2) the maximum weight laden was specified as 30 tons. Now the unladen weight of the vehicle was ten tons. This load (consisting of the tube bank) was 25 tons. So the total weight laden was 35 tons. So it was five tons over the regulation weight. Furthermore, the tube bank was top heavy. It had fittings on the top which made its centre of gravity high. Not only was it in breach of the regulations, but it was a dangerous and unsafe load to be carried on this vehicle along the roads of England. The evidence showed clearly that the only vehicle suitable for this load was a 'low loader', which is underslung so that it can take heavier weights and bigger loads. So the expedition was certainly illegal.

I turn now to consider the contract of carriage. The makers of the tube bank were Ashmore, Benson, Pease & Co Ltd of Stockton-on-Tees, the plaintiffs. Their transport manager was a Mr Bulmer. His assistant was Mr Jones. Two of these tube banks were to be sent from the works at Stockton-on-Tees to the port of Hull. Mr Bulmer told Mr Jones to arrange for the carriage of the two tube banks and to give the work to A V Dawson Ltd, the defendants. That was a small firm in which the principals were Mr Arthur Vernon Dawson, the father, and Mr Maurice Dawson, the son. This firm had ten articulated vehicles. The biggest of them was only a 30 tonner. They had no low loaders. They had worked for Ashmores for several years. Mr Jones knew the whole of their fleet well; and Mr Bulmer had known it for some six months. On getting the instructions, Mr Jones telephoned Dawsons and spoke to Mr Maurice Dawson, the son. He suggested that Maurice Dawson should come up and see the nature of the load. Maurice Dawson did so. The weight of it was shown plainly on the plate and on each tube bank and on the case. It was '25 tons'. It was arranged that Dawsons should take the loads. The price was arranged; it was £55 for the trip for each of the two articulated vehicles. If it had been on low loaders (which Dawsons had not got), the price would have been £85 or more for each; but here it was £55.

Later that day Dawsons sent two of their drivers with the articulated vehicles to get the two loads. The tube banks were loaded on to the trailers. Mr Bulmer was there for a short time. He saw them loaded, and so did Mr Jones. The tube banks were firmly secured by chains.

Early next morning the two drivers came and set off on the journey for Hull. When they were about halfway there, the leading vehicle toppled over. It was driven by Mr Harvey, the best and most experienced driver that Dawsons had. Mr Harvey was asked the cause: 'What do you say caused your lorry to topple over?' He answered: 'The camber in the road to the left plus the weight of the load, plus the height of the load.' The judge found that Mr Harvey made an error of judgment. But that was not the real cause of the toppling over. The real cause was the overweight. The articulated lorry was a most unsuitable vehicle on which to carry it. The whole transaction was illegal, being in breach of the regulations. Assuming, however, that Mr Harvey was negligent, the question is whether the illegality prevents Ashmores from suing for the negligence. This depends on whether the contract itself was unlawful, or its performance was unlawful.

The first question is whether the contract of carriage, when made, was lawful or not. The judge found that it was lawful, because it could have been lawfully performed. He cited *Waugh v Morris* and said:

'I find that this contract was concluded between Jones on behalf of [Ashmores] and Maurice Dawson on behalf of [Dawsons]. I find that Jones was relying on

Maurice Dawson and his company to carry out the contract, a contract which could perfectly easily be carried out lawfully, and that he relied on [Dawsons] to do so. It was not a term of the contract that it should be carried in any particular lorry. The contract was concluded at a time when Mr Jones was asking Mr Maurice Dawson to look at the load and say that he could carry it for the sum offered.'

I am not altogether satisfied with that finding. Mr Jones admitted that he knew a little about motor vehicle construction and the regulations. He was asked by counsel for Dawsons: 'You knew, for example, that there were specific loads for articulated lorries, didn't you?' and he said: 'I would say yes.' I would have thought that Mr Jones, being in the business, would have known that the lorries which Dawsons were going to provide could not lawfully carry these loads.

Although I have these misgivings, I am prepared to accept the judge's finding that the contract was lawful when it was made. But then the question arises: was it lawful in its performance? The judge's attention does not seem to have been drawn to this point. Yet there are authorities which show that illegality in the performance of a contract may disable a person from suing on it, if he participated in the illegality. This was pointed out by Atkin LJ in *Anderson Ltd. v Daniel*, [1924] 1 K.B. 138, in a passage which was quoted by Devlin J in *St John Shipping Corpn v Joseph Rank Ltd:*

> 'The question of illegality in a contract generally arises in connection with its formation, but it may also arise, as it does here, in connection with its performance. In the former case, where the parties have agreed to do something which is prohibited by Act of Parliament, it is indisputable that the contract is unenforceable by either party. And I think that it is equally unenforceable by the offending party where the illegality arises from the fact that the mode of performance adopted by the party performing it is in violation of some statute, even though the contract as agreed upon between the parties was capable of being performed in a perfectly legal manner.'

'That passage was further approved by Jenkins LJ in *B and B Viennese Fashions v Losane*, [1952] 1 All E.R. 909, where he said, 'that illegality in the performance of a contract may avoid it although the contract was not illegal ab initio'.

In this case the parties entered into the performance of the contract when Dawsons' driver took the articulated vehicle (the 30 tonner) up to Ashmores' works to pick up this load. Mr Bulmer, the transport manager, came along and saw it. Mr Jones, his assistant, was there. Both saw this 25 tons tube bank being loaded on to the articulated lorry. Mr Bulmer must have known that this was illegal; and Mr Bulmer's knowledge would affect Ashmores. Mr Jones was asked: 'Mr Bulmer would know the specific loads for articulated lorries, would he not? *A* Like the back of his hand, yes'. Then as to these particular lorries, Mr Jones was asked:

> '*Q* Mr Bulmer would have had all the knowledge in the world and would have known what weight these lorries were permitted to carry but you didn't know? *A* Well, I would say he would have a good idea what they would carry, yes.'

Now Mr Bulmer was not called to give evidence. The reason was because he left the employment of Ashmores some years ago and had gone to Zambia. But he had given a statement in which he had said:

> 'Identical loads to the one in question have been carried on similar vehicles

belonging to G Stiller (Haulage) Ltd, Middleton St George, Darlington, completely without incident.'

On that evidence I think that Mr Bulmer must have known that these articulated lorries of Dawsons were only permitted to carry 20 tons. Nevertheless, realising that 25 tons was too heavy — much too heavy — for them, he was content to let them carry the loads because it had happened before without trouble. He was getting the transport done cheaper too by £30 saved on each trip by each load. Not only did Mr Bulmer know of the illegality; he participated in it by sanctioning the loading of the vehicle with a load in excess of the regulations. That participation in the illegal performance of the contract debars Ashmores from suing Dawsons on it or suing Dawsons for negligence. I know that Dawsons were parties to the illegality. They knew, as well as Mr Bulmer, that the load was overweight in breach of the regulations. But in such a situation as this, the defendants are in a better position. In pari delicto, potior est conditio defendentis.

I would therefore allow the appeal and enter judgment for the Dawsons.

Phillimore LJ. I agree: and indeed I would go further, in that in my judgement this contract was illegal from its inception. The learned judge accepted Mr Jones's evidence — to use his own word — 'completely', although Mr Jones, on the very vital question of whether this type of articulated lorry would have specific loads permissible, contradicted himself. He preferred Mr Jones's evidence to that of either Mr Maurice Dawson or his father; and indeed he went so far as to say that he thought that he was not satisfied that a lengthy conversation which Mr Maurice Dawson had described had ever taken place. Now no doubt there was some material for criticising the evidence both of Mr Maurice Dawson and of his father. That is not altogether surprising since the events in question took place in February 1967 and the case was not brought to trial until the summer of 1972. In the course of Mr Maurice Dawson's evidence he said that after he had seen these cases of machinery which they were to transport, he had a conversation with Mr Bulmer, and he said he told Mr Bulmer that he thought that these articles would be better carried on low loader types of transport; to which the answer that Mr Bulmer gave was that there was not time because they had to be at the docks at Hull on the following morning; and he then proceeded to suggest that in his reluctance to carry these articles on articulated vehicles Mr Maurice Dawson was actuated by fear of a gentleman called Peter Sunter, who apparently ran a low loader transport business and would report to the authorities anyone whom he was able to detect as carrying excessive loads in articulated lorries. He then described how Mr Bulmer had said that a firm called Stillers of Darlington had carried similar weights in their vehicles and had done so without difficulty. It was quite a lengthy conversation which was described, and I find it impossible to hold that this was entirely invented. Moreover, it is exactly in line with a conversation which the father spoke to as having taken place during the course of a telephone conversation which he had with Mr Jones. He said that Mr Jones had told him that these loads were 25 tons each; he had said that they should go by low loader vehicles; and the answer to that was that Mr Jones said he knew that they should, but that Mr Bulmer was trying to economise on transport costs and had given the job to Dawsons for that reason; that he then went on to describe how Stillers had carried similar loads on the articulated lorries without difficulty. It is to be observed that in a statement which Mr Bulmer made in the summer of 1968 he said that 'Identical loads to the one in question have been carried on similar vehicles belonging to G Stiller (Haulage) Ltd, Middleton St George, Darlington, completely without incident.' It seems to me that those conversations to which the father and the son deposed are consistent and consistent only with this contract having been deliberately given to Dawsons in the knowledge that it involved a breach of these regulations and in order to economise on the job.

For those reasons also I would allow this appeal.

Scarman LJ. I also would allow this appeal; but, for myself, I think that this court ought not to disturb the learned judge's finding that the contract was lawful in its inception. The only way in which his finding on that issue can be attacked appears to me to be by placing some reliance on the evidence of one or other or both of the two Dawsons. This court has not had the benefit enjoyed (if that is the correct term) by the judge of having seen those gentlemen in the witness box. Commenting on their evidence generally, he said: 'I found their evidence completely unsatisfactory.' In the face of that sweeping condemnation of their credibility, I am not prepared to speculate as to how much of the Dawsons' evidence has some element of truth and how much has not. If, therefore, one puts on one side, as I think this court must, the evidence of the two Dawsons, one is left with the evidence of Mr Jones. The judge accepted Mr Jones as a reliable witness. When one turns to the evidence of Mr Jones, it is clear that, if his account of the two conversations with Maurice Dawson, which I think constituted the contract, is accurate, then this contract was capable of a lawful performance. Mr Jones describes first a telephone conversation, when he told Mr Maurice Dawson that he had two tube banks weighing 25 tons to go to Hull to be there at 8 a m on Wednesday morning. He then said that he told Mr Dawson that it would be advisable to come up and see the load to see what his vehicles would be carrying. At that moment, assuming that Mr Dawson had shown himself interested in this offer, Mr Jones had plainly suggested to Mr Dawson a job of carrying these two 25 tons loads to Hull, and had invited Mr Dawson to take a look at the loads and to decide what vehicles should carry it. On the Tuesday — I do not think it is clear whether it was Tuesday morning or Tuesday afternoon — Mr Maurice Dawson did come to Ashmores. He went to the site where the tube banks were standing. He saw them and decided to accept the offer. Mr Dawson made no demur as to the feasibility of carrying the loads; and that was the contract. Even if Mr Jones was aware at the time that none of the Dawson-owned articulated lorries could lawfully carry this load, it is not to be implied against him that he had put Dawson on terms that these loads were to be carried in Dawson articulated lorries. It was left to the Dawsons to carry the loads in vehicles that they thought appropriate. The contract was, therefore, capable of being performed lawfully.

The next question is, was this contract lawfully performed? It was not. The loads were carried on two articulated lorries. The all-up weight of each lorry was well over the 30 tons which each was permitted by law to carry. There was therefore a breach of s 64 (2) of the Road Traffic Act 1960. The Dawsons, of course, knew that the performance of the contract was illegal. The question is, did Ashmores, the plaintiffs? The issue of illegal performance, as distinct from illegal formation, was neither discussed nor expressly decided by the judge. It was raised at the trial, though not mentioned in the pleadings. It is raised in this court and it is our duty to consider it. The critical factor is the knowledge of two men, Mr Bulmer and Mr Jones. Mr Bulmer, for the reasons given by Lord Denning MR, was unable to give evidence at the trial; but it is clear that Mr Bulmer did go down to the site where these tube banks were standing and for a time watched them being loaded on to the two Dawson lorries. Mr Jones was there too. Both Mr Bulmer and Mr Jones were very well aware of the nature of the Dawson fleet of lorries. Both of them now knew, if they did not know before, that loads were being placed on articulated lorries. It is said, however, that neither of them knew all the facts constituting the illegality of this performance, because there is no specific evidence that either knew that the unladen weight of these articulated lorries was ten tons each. The court in my view must apply its common sense to the evidence and the materials that it has on this — more especially because in express terms the judge did not deal with it. It is clear from the evidence that Mr Bulmer was well aware of the regulations; Mr Jones said that Mr Bulmer knew them like the back of his hand; further, in my opinion, Mr Bulmer must have known the carrying capacity of the two Dawson lorries he saw being loaded. It would be shutting one's eyes to the obvious were one to say that, as Mr Bulmer watched these loads being placed on these lorries, he was not aware that the lorries were ten tons or thereabouts unladen. He knew the weight of the two loads; he knew the regulations. He must have known that Dawsons were about to commit a breach of the law. My own view is that, had Mr Jones himself addressed his mind to the problem, he also would have been aware of the facts constituting this infringement of the law. But it is enough for the purposes of judgment if Mr Bulmer knew. The question now arises, and it is really a question of law, whether, Mr Bulmer being the transport manager of Ashmores, his knowledge would be sufficient to impose on Ashmores the consequences of being parties to an illegal performance of the contract. Mr Bulmer was their responsible official. But knowledge by itself is not, I think, enough. There must be knowledge plus participation. On this point I would respectfully adopt the language of Lord Denning MR in *J M Allan (Merchandising) Ltd v Cloke*, [1963] 2 Q.B. 340, when he said:

> 'I desire to say that where two people together have the common design to use a subject-matter for an unlawful purpose, so that each participates in the unlawful purpose, then that contract is illegal in its formation: and it is no answer for them to say that they did not know the law on the matter.'

What is applicable to formation is equally applicable to performance. There must be some degree of assent to the illegal performance. In *B and B Viennese Fashions v Losane* Jenkins LJ recognised, I think, the necessity to assent to the illegality; he said:

> 'It is plain from *Anderson, Ltd. v. Daniel* that illegality in the performance of a contract may avoid it although the contract was not illegal ab initio. That being so, one has to consider whether the mode in which the contract was performed, or purported to be performed, in this case sufficed to turn it into an illegal contract.'

A little further on he said:

> 'The plaintiff chose, in purported performance of the contract, to deliver utility garments without an invoice. As a performance of the contract, that was clearly an illegal performance in view of the provisions of art. 10 (1). The defendant firm accepted the goods so delivered and disposed of them.'

In the present case Mr Bulmer could have stopped the loading when he went down to watch it being done. He did not do so, with all his knowledge and experience; and I am driven to the conclusion that he was a participator in the illegality. For these reasons I think this performance was illegal and that Ashmores, through Mr Bulmer, participated in that illegal performance. I would allow the appeal.

I would add one word on a point which was discussed in the course of argument but which does not require to be considered for the purposes of our decision. Counsel for Dawsons at the trial was anxious to call an engineer to explain the circumstances and perhaps the cause of the accident. When he sought to call this witness he was confronted by the learned trial judge with RSC Ord 38, r 6 (1), which says:

> 'In an action arising out of an accident on land due to a collision or apprehended collision, unless at or before the trial the Court otherwise orders, the oral expert evidence of an engineer sought to be called on account of his skill and knowledge as respects motor vehicles shall not be receivable [unless, in effect, a copy of a report from him containing the substance of his evidence has been made available to the other side before the hearing].'

The judge would not permit the engineer to be called, taking the view that the overturning of this lorry when it struck the grass verge of the highway was a collision. Whatever may be the meaning of the word 'collision' (and I accept that there can be a collision between a moving object and a stationary body), the overbalancing of a great lorry because of contact with a grass verge does not seem to me to amount to collision. But, be that as it may, it is unfortunate that the judge shut out the evidence of the expert on a point such as this; for the rule plainly confers on the court a discretion. In my judgment the discretion should have been exercised in favour of the Dawsons. Had the engineering evidence caused any surprise or difficulty to the other side, the surprise could have been adequately dealt with by adjournment.

Appeal allowed.

DAVIDSON AND CO. LTD. v. McLEERY

(1969), 6 D.L.R. (3d) 331. Supreme Court of British Columbia.

ACTION for balance owing on account between stockbroker and client.

Gregory, J.: — This is an action by a firm of stockbrokers against a client for what is, in effect, the balance of a trading account in respect of the sale and purchase of securities over a period long enough that both the *Securities Act*, 1962 (B.C.), c. 55, and the *Securities Act*, 1967 (B.C.), c. 45, apply. However, in the view I take of the case it is unnecessary to consider which transactions came within which Act because the provisions I find it necessary to consider are virtually identical except for the numbering of the sections. Where I refer to a section by number I will use the number in the 1967 Act.

Although a number of defences were raised on the pleadings and relied on in argument, the only one I regard as meritorious enough to consider is that the plaintiff's claim arises through its unlawful act in permitting the defendant's trading to be put through one Frank Head, a "salesman in training" or "sales trainee" employed by the plaintiff brokers who was, to the knowledge of the plaintiff, not licensed under the *Securities Act, 1967* and that the plaintiff's breach of the *Securities Act, 1967* renders its claim unenforceable. This defence, in my judgment, if valid, applies equally to the $9,045 and interest claimed on a promissory note made by the defendant in favour of the plaintiff and to the $2,519.43 claimed in respect of an open account, because the consideration for the note arose by reason of the defendant's trades through Head, the plaintiff's unlicensed sales trainee, no less than did the amount claimed in respect of the open account: See *Skale v. Becker*, [1927] 1 D.L.R. 723, 59 O.L.R. 651.

The only evidence I "heard" was the reading in from examinations for discovery, of the defendant by counsel for the plaintiff and of Douglas Gordon, an officer of plaintiff company, by counsel for the defendant. There was some conflict in the evidence, and I do not have the advantage trial Judges normally have of basing a finding of the reliability of the testimony of a witness in part on his observation of the witness's demeanour in giving his evidence in open Court. Making matters more difficult for me in deciding the facts is that each counsel made the mistake of reading in evidence harmful to his own case and/or helpful to his opponent's.

I direct my attention first to the allegation that the plaintiff's claim arises through its unlawful act in permitting the defendant's trading to be put through by an unlicensed salesman. Section 7 (1) (*c*) provides that:

7(1) No person shall,
(c)   act as a salesman of or on behalf of a person or company in connection with a trade in a security by the person or company unless he is registered as a salesman of the person or company and the person or company is registered as a broker...

Mr. Gordon's evidence was that Head and another unlicensed sales trainee "... were allowed to take orders: they were not allowed to solicit orders". Asked what he meant by "take orders" he replied "If clients came in and were potential clients for the house, for them they were allowed to take the orders." Head was paid on what Gordon called a "bonus arrangement" the main factor considered with respect to the bonus (which was paid once a month) being "... the number of clients that he introduced to the house". He also testified that the number of sales effected by the clients would have "... an indirect bearing on (the bonus)". Asked what he meant by his use of the word "indirect", Gordon testified that "the other factors... we considered in bonusing [were] the length of time that he put in the office, how he was developing as a potential salesman and how he was progressing with his I.D.A. course".

I do not believe that I can accept Gordon's evidence as being entirely truthful. The remuneration paid by the plaintiff to Head varied so greatly that I think the inescapable conclusion is that the remuneration was based chiefly on sales. In July, 1966, Head's total remuneration was $342.50; in August it was $1,388.25; in September $518.75 and in October $1,319.45. It was not until September, 1966, that Head even enrolled in the I.D.A. course and, as far as the evidence indicated, Head began to work for the plaintiff only in June or July so it appears evident to me that if the progress a sales trainee was making with his I.D.A. course and the length of time that he put in in the office had anything at all to do with his remuneration, these were very minor factors indeed in comparison with the amount of business he produced for the plaintiff brokers.

I conclude from Gordon's uncontradicted evidence (that sales trainees were allowed to take orders but not allowed to solicit orders) that Gordon thought that this was neither prohibited by nor an offence under s. 7(1) (c) of the *Securities Act, 1967*: on the other hand I can think of no greater inducement to a sales trainee to disobey the instructions not to solicit orders than to pay the trainee chiefly on the basis of the volume of orders he secured.

There was no evidence led to suggest that Head's handling of orders from the defendant was supervised by any licensed salesman, and on the evidence before me I see no escape from the conclusion that the plaintiff, in breach of the *Securities Act, 1967*, knowingly and willingly allowed an unlicensed employee to trade in securities. (I specifically refrain from expressing any opinion whether or not it would constitute a violation of the *Securities Act, 1967*, for a licensed broker to permit an unlicensed sales trainee to accept orders under the direct supervision of and handled by a licensed salesman, particularly if the trainee were paid a fixed salary.) So much for the "unlawful conduct" on the part of the plaintiff upon which the defence is based and I turn my attention to the defendant.

I have no hesitation in finding on the evidence that the defendant knew that Head was unlicensed. Neither Head nor the plaintiff failed faithfully to carry out the defendant's orders to buy and sell securities, to make proper charges and to render prompt and accurate accounts both of security trades and of the financial position between the plaintiff and defendant as a result of the trades. It is clear therefore that the defendant, whose purchases and sales were made on the basis of his own judgment and accurately carried out, can level no greater criticism at the plaintiff than that the plaintiff was in breach of the *Securities Act, 1967*, by allowing Head to do what the defendant wanted him to do.

This, however, is not the whole story as far as the defendant is concerned because it is clear that he and Head were conspiring with one another to defraud the plaintiff, specifically by allowing the defendant, without the knowledge of any one in the plaintiff's office except Head himself, to trade under the names of four persons, thereby obtaining a line of credit which both Head and the defendant knew the defendant could not get if he were doing all the trading in his own name. If the plaintiff is not entitled to recover because it violated the *Securities Act, 1967*, the defendant will have succeeded in defrauding the plaintiff despite the facts that the plaintiff's violation of the statute was known to and fully concurred in by the defendant and that the defendant suffered no loss or damage whatever thereby.

Counsel for the defendant relied on a number of authorities in support of the defendant's position. One line of cases had to do with the right of a real estate agent to recover commission when the salesman was not licensed according to statute. For example, *Commercial Life Ass'ce Co. v. Drever*, [1948] 2 D.L.R. 241, [1948] S.C.R. 306, a decision of the Supreme Court of Canada and in particular to a paragraph in the judgment of Locke, J., at p. 246:

> It is unfortunate that the services of the respondent [real estate agent], which were an effective cause of the sale, should go unrewarded but, as stated by Lord Mansfield in *Holman v. Johnson* (1775), 1 Cowp. 341 at p. 343, 98 E.R. 1120:
> "The objection, that a contract is immoral or illegal as between plaintiff and defendant, sounds at all times very ill in the mouth of the defendant. It is not for his sake, however, that the objection is ever allowed; but it is founded in general principles of policy, which the defendant has the advantage of, contrary to the

real justice, as between him and the plaintiff, by accident, if I may so say. The principle of public policy is this; ex dolo malo non oritur actio. No Court will lend its aid to a man who founds his cause of action upon an immoral or an illegal act."

While this passage, taken out of context, supports the defendant's position in the case at bar, it must be read in light of the specific statutory provision in the Alberta *Real Estate Agents' Licensing Act* quoted at p. 244:

"No person shall be entitled to recover any compensation for any act done in contravention of the provisions of this Act, or to be reimbursed for any expenditure incurred by him in or in connection with the doing of any such act."

. . .

Quite apart however from the fact that the Real Estate Acts of the several Provinces of Canada seem to contain a specific provision that an unlicensed agent or a licensed agent whose salesman is unlicensed is disentitled to recover a commission, it must be borne in mind that in the case at bar the action is not for the plaintiff's brokerage fees on the defendant's trades but rather for the balance of a trading account owing the plaintiff as a result of securities bought and sold through the plaintiff.

In my judgment the strongest case the defendant's counsel cited in support of his client's position was a decision of the Ontario High Court, *Maschinenfabrik Seydelman K-G v. Presswood Bros. Ltd.*, 47 D.L.R. (2d) 214, [1965] 1 O.R. 177, in which Hughes, J., held that an action by the plaintiff to recover the purchase price of certain electrical machinery sold to the defendant was void and unenforceable because the plaintiff had failed to comply with a regulation under the Ontario *Power Commission Act* requiring the equipment to be approved before sale, ending up with the result that the defendant got the equipment (which incidentally was subsequently approved) without having to pay for it. This case, while not binding upon me, caused me a good deal of concern until I dug a little deeper than counsel had done into the law and found that the decision of Hughes, J., had been reversed by the Ontario Court of Appeal: 53 D.L.R. (2d) 244, [1966] 1 O.R. 316.

Counsel for the defendant also relied on *Montreal Trust Co et al. v. C.N.R. Co.*, [1939] 3 D.L.R. 497, [1939] A.C. 613, 50 C.R.T.C. 1, a decision of the Privy Council. The [D.L.R.] headnote reads as follows:

A lease whereby a railway company director through a nominee leases a residence to the company for its president's use falls within the provision of s. 121 of the Railway Act, R.S.C. 1927, c. 170, prohibiting a director from being interested in any contract with the company, and such a lease is "for his own use and benefit" within the meaning of such provision notwithstanding that the director only acted at the company's request, derived no profit from the transaction, and that the president had an option to purchase the premises for the price paid by the director. The effect of s. 121 was not merely to avoid the director's interest in the prohibited contract but to render it null and void. Hence a claim for rent must be dismissed.

The [D.L.R.] report also contains an editorial note which I think sums up the defendant's position better than I did earlier on in these reasons. The editorial note reads:

It is settled law that a contract prohibited by statute for the protection of the public is illegal and unenforceable. Most of the cases arising under the rule relate to ascertaining whether a contract is impliedly prohibited by statute. Where a penalty is imposed for the doing of an act and it is determined that *one of the* statute's objects is the protection of the public and not merely of the revenue, the act will be deemed prohibited by the statute and illegal.

I do not believe that in any of the cases cited by counsel, not all of which I have referred to, is there any authority for the proposition he asserts on behalf of the defendant which, as I (rather bluntly) put it at p. 335 of these reasons, that because the plaintiff violated the *Securities Act, 1967*, the defendant should succeed in his conspiracy to defraud the plaintiff despite the facts that the plaintiff's breach of the statute was known to and fully concurred in by the defendant and that the defendant suffered no loss or damage whatever thereby.

If this were an action simply to recover brokerage I think, on the authorities, I would have no alternative than to dismiss the action. But as the action is brought for the balance owing the plaintiff on a trading account I believe that I can both follow the authorities binding on me and do justice. If I cannot do both then at least I will try to do justice, and I will not permit the defendant to succeed in his effort to defraud the plaintiff on the mere basis the plaintiff violated a provision of the *Securities Act, 1967*.

There will be judgment for the plaintiff for $12,550.84, interest on $9,045 at 8% per annum from August 6, 1968, to the date judgment is entered and costs.

I direct the District Registrar of the Court to send a copy of my reasons for judgment to the Attorney-General for his consideration of criminal proceedings against the defendant and Head and a copy to the British Columbia Securities Commission for its consideration of the conduct of the plaintiff, not merely because the plaintiff violated the provisions of the *Securities Act, 1967*, but also to give the Commission an opportunity to clarify (or to give the Commission an opportunity to recommend to the Attorney-General that he introduce legislation to clarify) what, if anything, an unlicensed sales trainee should be allowed to do in respect of trading in securities. I request the District Registrar also to return to counsel the copies of the consolidated *Securities Act, 1967* they were good enough to lend me.

Judgment for plaintiff.

[*NOTE*: The decision at trial was affirmed in the Court of Appeal (Robertson, Nemetz and Taggart JJ.A.). The substance of the appellate court's decision is contained in the paragraph reproduced below ((1971), 14 D.L.R. (3d) 756 per Nemetz J.A., for the Court, at p. 759):

... This is not an action by Head against Davidson for the recovery of commission fees on the trades of securities. Rather, it is an action by a broker against a customer for the balance owing to the broker as a result of the broker buying and selling securities for the customer at the customer's request. The action is brought by Davidson against McLeery upon a contract between Davidson and McLeery. Nothing in our *Securities Act, 1962* renders this contract illegal. Since this contract, in my opinion, is neither forbidden by statute nor by common law, the only point which remains to be determined is whether the fact that Davidson's employee, Head, was statutorily prohibited from acting as a salesman so tainted the contract between Davidson and McLeery as to render it unenforceable. No authority was cited to us to support such a proposition. The employee was not a party to this contract. The collateral fact that that employee was not licensed cannot have rendered this contract illegal or unenforceable. Whether Head would be entitled to recover his commission from Davidson is a matter which does not concern us here.

NOTE

The Ontario Court of Appeal was asked by the Ontario Government in *Reference Re Certain Titles to Land in Ontario*, [1973] 2 O.R. 613, to answer certain questions regarding real estate transactions. Confusion about the interpretation of s. 26 (1) of The Planning Act and problems resulting from attempts by conveyancers to avoid its application had created doubts about the validity of the titles to land of many Ontario home purchasers. One question before the Court was as follows:

On January 2, 1969, A, as grantor, executed a deed conveying a parcel of land, Greenacre, to B, as grantee, and the deed was registered on that date. Greenacre was not within an area of subdivision control on that date.

On January 9, 1969, one deed purporting to convey the North half of Greenacre from B to C, and another deed purporting to convey the South half of Greenacre from B to D were executed and registered. Both C and D were trustees or agents for B, or the same beneficial owner.

On January 16, 1969 subdivision control was made to apply to Greenacre.

On January 23, 1969, a deed purporting to convey the North half of Greenacre from C to E was executed and registered.

On January 24, 1969, a deed purporting to convey the South half of Greenacre from D to F was executed and registered.

Both E and F were bona fide purchasers for value.

Question

In Situation 1, did s. 26(4) of The Planning Act prevent the operation of either of the last two deeds?

The relevant section of the Planning Act reads:

26(1) The council of a municipality may by by-law designate any area within the municipality as an area of subdivision control and thereafter no person shall convey land in the area by way of a deed or transfer on any sale, or mortgage or charge land in the area or enter into any agreement that has the effect of granting the use of or right in land in the area directly or by entitlement to renewal for a period of twenty-one years or more unless, ...

(b) The grantor, mortgagor or vendor does not retain the fee or the equity of redemption in any land abutting the land that is being conveyed or otherwise dealt with;

(4) An agreement, conveyance, mortgage or charge made in contravention of this section or a predecessor thereof does not create or convey any interest in land, but this section does not affect an agreement entered into, subject to the express condition contained therein that such agreement is to be effective only if the provisions of this section are complied with.

The court said in this case (p. 627):

The conveyances by B to C of the north half of Greenacre, and by B to D of the south half, resulted in a lawful severance of B's land, since it was made before subdivision control was made applicable thereto. When C conveyed the north half of the property to E, and D conveyed the south half to F, subdivision control was in effect, but neither C nor D "retained the fee or the equity of redemption" in the abutting lands. Thus they were within the exemption provided for by s. 26(1)(b). While C and D were both trustees or agents for B, E and F were bona fide purchasers for value which would entitle us to assume that they were purchasers without notice of the fact that C and D were trustees or agents for B. This excludes the possibility that there was anything on the registered title which disclosed the capacity in which C and D held the lands. In giving them an unqualified conveyance of the respective halves B no doubt retained control over his trustees or agents, but not over the land, and quoad bona fide purchasers for value without notice he had relinquished his dominion or disposing power over the fee. The case is completely unlike the situation in *Forfar* where the grantor explicitly retained a right to appoint to the use of himself or other nominees of his choice. The titles of E and F are valid on another ground, namely that they were completely ignorant of any fact or facts which would constitute the transaction one which was in contravention of the *Planning Act*. It was stated by Pearce, L.J., in *Archbolds (Freightage), Ltd. v. S. Spanglett, Ltd.*, [1961] 1 All E.R. 417 at p. 424:

"The case has been argued with skill and care on both sides, and yet no case has been cited to us establishing the proposition that where a contract is on the face of it legal and is not forbidden by statute, but must in fact produce illegality by reason of a circumstance known to one party only, it should be held illegal so as to debar the innocent party from relief."

Public policy would not, therefore, require that the Court should refuse its aid to E and F.

PROBLEM

Margaret operates a driving school. She gives lessons to Jacky. Jacky does not pay the fee of $200 that Margaret charges. What would happen in each of these cases? (Do not consider the cases cumulatively:)

(a) Margaret had no licence to operate a driving school;

(b) The agreement had not been in the form, nor had it contained all of the terms required by the relevant legislation;

(c) The lessons were given in a park where driving a car was prohibited.

CHAPTER 9

CONTRACTS: POSTSCRIPT AND PRELUDE

Introduction

Throughout this book we have attempted to demonstrate the dynamic nature of contracts and of contract law. Both are being employed to control relationships unheard of only decades ago. The stress has caused much tearing at the seams: long-established doctrine is being challenged successfully; narrow categories are giving way to broader generalizations in terms of the more basic reasons for protecting interests that arise out of contractual relationships and in terms of more general concerns of reasonable and fundamental fairness. The process continues and must be welcomed if the law is to retain its legitimacy in intervening in our affairs.

The materials in the book were designed to assist students in law to cope with these anticipated future developments. The article that follows suggests why and how.

MACNEIL, I.R., "WHITHER CONTRACTS"
(1969), 21 J. of Leg. Ed. 403
Paper for presentation to the panel on contracts. AALS meeting, December 29, 1967.

Two preliminary questions require answering before determination of the optimum content of any law school course of particular name: 1. Is there any such thing? 2. If there is, is it significant enough to future lawyers to justify spending law school time on it?

In a panel on contracts the first question is, therefore: Is there such a thing as contracts? My friends teaching such courses as Contracts 201 (Sales), Contracts 202 (Negotiable Instruments), Contracts 307 (Creditors' Rights), Contracts 312 (Labor Law), Contracts 313 (Corporations) and Contracts 319 (Trade Regulation) delight in telling me that there is no such thing as contracts. There are, they say, sales contracts, negotiable instruments, secured transactions and bankruptcy, collective bargaining agreements, insurance contracts, real estate transactions, Robinson-Patman provisions and a host of other contract-types, but contracts-in-gross there ain't. Having earlier rejected childhood beliefs in the higher abstractions of Samuel Williston's metaphysics, I almost came to believe them. But a personal vested economic interest in the existence of contracts-in-gross caused me to search further. Since you too share that vested interest you will be pleased to know that I have reached the conclusion that contracts exists.

In view of the large number of books on your desks with the unmodified word "contracts" on the spine, some of you will doubtless be inclined to think that the foregoing paragraph is an overt manifestation of the departure of its author from reality. The accuracy of that reflection I am not qualified to debate. I should warn you, however, that I do not propose to maintain that there is such a thing as contracts simply because large numbers of distinguished legal scholars have organized their work as if there is, nor even because the word "contracts" is an important organizing-indexing tool for a large amount of judicial doctrine and to a considerable extent for statutes and administrative law. To do so would raise similar doubts about my mental stability among the many who believe "that there is no such thing as a 'law of contracts' applicable to all consensual transactions, but rather a variety of transaction-types for which the courts and legislatures are developing sets of specialized rules and exceptions as the need arises."

Accepting arguendo that there is no such thing as a "law of contracts" necessitates looking to something besides the law to support a belief that there is such a thing as contracts. The only place to turn is to the human behavior which in common usage is called contractual. Upon doing this one finds that a vast variety of behavior is encompassed, from a child's purchase of a nickel candy bar to an arrangement to build an SST for the government, from a purchase of stock on a stock exchange where neither buyer nor seller ever see each other, to the continuing close relationship found between employer and employee. It is possible to find common elements in that array of behavior, or is the ordinary use of the word "contracts" itself a generalization with no basis in behavior? Happily for our future as first year contracts teachers there are common elements in contractual behavior, in fact at least five of them.

First, every time a relationship seems properly to enjoy the label "contracts" there is, or has been, some cooperation between or among the people connected with it. While this observation distinguishes contracts from behavior like murder, solo fast driving and solitary sunbathing, it does not distinguish it from the building of dams by the Army engineers, the collection of taxes or necking in the moonlight. In short there is a great deal of behavior which would not normally be called contractual. And so, a search for other elements is necessary.

The second common element jumps to the fore, more obviously, indeed, than the first: economic exchange. While borderlines may give us trouble, whenever behavior occurs which we are sure we can call contractual there is always an element of economic exchange in it.

Before examining other elements common to contracts, it is probably desirable to examine briefly the apparent conflict between the presence of economic exchange and the notion that contractual behavior is cooperative behavior. We do, after all, think of economic exchange as being extremely individualistic and selfish, rather than cooperative. Looked at historically or anthropologically, it is readily seen that where tradition and custom dominate production and distributuon of goods and services the society in question is generally less individualistic and more common in structure, operation and attitudes, than are the societies in which exchange dominates. And in our own century a decline in individualism has paralleled a decline in the significance of exchange as the dominant social mechanism, whether one looks at the modern Western welfare state in its many varieties or at frankly socialistic states. (Conversely, the relatively recent innovations in Russia and Eastern Europe which increase the use of market mechanisms have been hailed, in the Western press at least, as evidence of increasing individualism in those countries.) Moreover, our thinking on this score is also influenced by the deification of exchange by Nineteenth (and Twentieth) century laissez faire political economists, and the countervailing consignment of exchange to the works of the devil by Karl Marx and at least some of his successors.

Easy to escape in view of the foregoing is the fact that exchange represents a species of human cooperation. In the first place it is a kind of social behavior — the true lone wolf has no one with whom to exchange goods or services. Nor, of course, can the true lone wolf participate in the specialization of labor which both causes and is caused by exchange. Moreover, exchange involves a *mutual* goal of the parties, namely, the reciprocal transfer of values. And this is true however strongly the "economic man" — the "as-much-as-possible- for-as-little-as-possible-in-return-man" — may dominate the motivations of both parties to an exchange.

The core of cooperation which is involved in the immediate exchange of existing goods tends to expand if the exchange is extended over time. Whether he likes it or not a customer who enters a contract to purchase goods in the future enables the seller to plan his activities with a degree of assurance which he otherwise would probably have lacked. The customer is thereby cooperating in the seller's production or acquisition of the goods in a manner which would not have occurred had the customer simply purchased goods already produced. Requirements and output contracts are prime examples of this. They provide a framework for cooperation in the production of goods in some (but not all) respects not unlike that which would occur if the buyer and seller were to merge their corporate identities. Other contracts which simply expand the time for exchange perform similar cooperative functions.

Continuing exchange relationships also are very likely to involve varying degrees of mutual social contacts. These contracts inevitably lead to cooperative behavior, whether or not it is motivated by heavily economic exchange. Employment relationships are one of the more obvious examples of this kind of contractual behavior. In such contracts the cooperative behavior which in the quick one-shot exchange is obscured by selfish economic motives bursts into view as a panoply of continual cooperative behavior. This cooperation is motivated not only by economic exchange motives, but also by social exchange motives and by whatever altruistic or other internal motives cause men to "get along together."

A third element in contractual behavior is that it involves mutual planning for the future. At the very least each party must decide that he wants what the other proposes to give and is willing to give what the other wants in return. Since in some exchanges this happens very quickly it is easy to overlook the element of mutuality in the planning of the parties for the future. But in the contract which more clearly involves more than an immediate exchange of existing goods, this mutual planning becomes obvious. (Man being a talkative animal such planning is to a considerable extent verbalized in some way.) We have, however, all too often obscured the fact that it is mutual planning of the relationship which is occurring by our focus on assent and its binding (or non-binding) nature in terms of legal sanctions. This focus may make practical sense in quick exchanges, but its value diminishes in the case of continuing relationships. We have further obscured the fact that it is planning we are talking about by our emphasis on such legal concepts as consideration, mutuality, the sanctity of written verbalizations of plans, etc. Nevertheless, it is mutual planning for the future which is so involved in such matters.

The fourth element in contractual behavior is that potential sanctions external to the "contract" itself are incorporated or added to give reinforcement to the relationship. We are perhaps inclined to think of these sanctions as being legal sanctions, but they are, of course, not so limited, and non-legal sanctions, e.g. business ostracism, are not only significant, but often more significant, than legal sanctions.

The fifth element of contractual behavior is that like all social behavior it is subject to social control and social manipulation which may or may not take into account the interest and desire of those engaging in the behavior.

I am tempted to add a sixth common element, but it is not quite as universal among contractual relationships as the others. A great many contracts, however, acquire the characteristics of property, and in particular the characteristic of alienability. This is bound to happen in a market-credit economy, since the contractual relationship very commonly acquires an economic value of its own and tends to be treated like any other economic value owned by someone.

There are thus, it seems to me, five basic elements of contracts: 1. cooperation, 2. economic exchange, 3. planning for the future, 4. potential external sanctions, and, 5. social control and manipulation. There is also a sixth which is equally basic whenever it is present, the property characteristics of contracts. These conclusions, however, answer only the first of the two preliminary questions posed at the beginning of this paper, namely, whether there is any such thing as contracts? The affirmative answer simply brings on the second question: Is contracts a significant enough social phenomenon to justify spending law school time on it?

Given our heavy reliance on a market economy it is not necessary to justify teaching courses relating to important types of exchange relationships, such as distribution of goods and services, collective bargaining, insurance, trade regulation, corporate finance, credit transactions, government contracts, etc. And conceivably a first year law school course could be justified which is no more than a collection of important and representative contract areas, simply to introduce those areas. A strong argument could be made for at least that much of a "contracts" course on the ground that the subsequent curriculum is heavily elective, and that it is desirable for lawyers to be aware of the extent to which economic exchange transactions permeate our economic, social and legal life.

But, can we go farther and justify a course which explores the behavioral elements common to all of contracting? Is it worthwhile to attempt to examine the legal significance of these elements and the varying ways they affect and are affected by the legal system? Since these questions are answered affirmatively in practically every law school curriculum in the United States a great many people may feel that the discussion can stop at this point. But as noted above I agreed not to base my arguments on the position that there is a "law of contracts" in the Willistonian (or perhaps even a Corbinian) sense. Is there, then, any justification for a generalizing first year course in contracts if we abandon, ex hypothesi, a belief in a "law of contracts"?

I am not convinced that the disappearance of a generalized course in contracts from the law school curriculum would be a disaster on the scale of Waterloo. Nor do I think the Western world would collapse if the generalized concept of contracts ceased altogether to be a way of organizing statutes, judicial decisions, administrative action, textbooks, legal digests, etc. I do think, however, that we would lose some of our understanding of the functions and techniques of contracting and of contract law in the various transaction-type areas themselves. In short, recognition that the various transaction-types do have common elements of behavior can lead lawyers, judges, legislators, administrators and even law teachers to a better grasp of and better dealing with each transaction-type itself. To the extent that this is true a generalized contracts course becomes justified, not on the ground that there is a "law of contracts" but on the ground that the common elements in contracts-in-gross present problems and challenges for the legal system which widely cut across transaction-type lines.

All right, you say, prove it. It is, of course, impossible to prove it to a group like this or in a paper like this. All that can be done is to present some of the significant challenges to the legal system and to lawyers which do cut across the transaction-types. They are set out below not in order of significance, but following generally the order in which the common elements have been presented above.

Cooperation. The fact that contracts are fundamentally mechanisms of cooperation, and only mechanisms of conflict when things have gone wrong, presents the legal system with special problems. In the first place, contracts get along very well without the law most of the time, or at least without its active intervention. The law thus has to deal largely with pathological cases. This in itself would not be so very troublesome except for the feedback of precedent: the rule of the pathological case governs the healthy contract too. To the extent that contractual behavior is influenced by the law this feedback can have very significant effect on all contractual behavior. At least two primary problems arise from this. First, the law arising from sick cases is not necessarily the optimum law for healthy cases. Second, the legal system has only limited techniques and abilities to deal with contracts-in-conflict, and must define the contractual relationship quite specifically in order to do so. In contracts-in-cooperation, however, the most important single ingredient often is an unspecific general willingness to cooperate to achieve mutual success in the relationship. The legal system is thus often in the position not unlike that of a scientist who has to dry out a jellyfish before his instruments of examination can be used on it.

Economic exchange. Many of the consequences of the fact that contracts is a mechanism of economic exchange can better be considered subsequently. Three might, however, be noted at this point. First, the overall impact on the legal system of the exchange-credit economy is something of which no lawyer can afford to be unaware of — so too of the impact of the legal system on the exchange-credit economy. Second, exchange-credit is only one of the two major ways in which societies answer basic economic problems, the other being socialist mechanisms which do not depend upon exchange, e.g. public schools, taxation for defense, etc. A lawyer needs to be aware of the similarities and differences between exchange mechanisms and socialist mechanisms and of their legal significance in view of the importance of both in our society. Third, and closely related to the foregoing, a profitable study can be made of the borderlines between exchange and other kinds of relationships. We have been doing this for years in contract courses with respect to family gifts and the doctrine of consideration. But there are borderline areas of far more social significance, e.g. forced exchanges, such as condemnation of property, the duty to bargain in good faith in the NLRA, duties to enter contracts under the various civil rights laws.

Planning for the future. This aspect of contractual behavior is extremely and directly significant to the practicing lawyer irrespective of the nature of the transaction-type with which he is dealing. First, he must be aware of the fact that the primary purpose of the planning of the parties is to achieve a workable operating relationship for the future. Second, as an expert in verbalizing, in questioning, in anticipating problems, etc. the lawyer may be called upon to assist the parties in planning a workable operating relationship. Third, the lawyer as legal technician has two important further planning roles: (a) planning for trouble between the parties, e.g. thinking about and preparing for such things as risks of non-performance, changed circumstances, liquidated damages, arbitration, etc.; (b) planning both to avoid illegality, e.g. Robinson-Patman, and to utilize the law affirmatively, e.g. qualifying the transaction for beneficial tax treatment.

Potential external sanctions. A lawyer needs to know at least the following generalities about this aspect of contracts-in-gross: The most important support for contractual relationships is not a sanction at all, but a continuation of the exchange motivations which led the parties to enter the relationship in the first place. These motivations may continue in effect even after one party has fully performed while the other has not. The motivation causing the debtor in such a case to perform may well be his desire to enter other exchange relationships with the same creditor. Also of great importance are internal command and habit. For example, it simply never dawns on many people not to pay their department store bills on time, or if it does dawn on them the thought is put aside immediately as immoral or otherwise unthinkable. The lawyer needs to know also that informal social and community sanctions are extremely important. So too are non-legal but more formalized community sanctions, as for example, trade association penalties, or mediation or arbitration (even when these are of no legal force). Legal sanctions are but a last resort, however important they may become when in fact resorted to.

Since, when the last resort is reached, the lawyer is practically always involved, it is essential for him to have some understanding of what it is. The kind of development found in the first chapter of Fuller & Braucher, Basic Contract Law (1964) is a proper and very desirable foundation for thinking about contract remedies relating to any transaction-type.

Social control and manipulation. The most obvious example of social control and manipulation of contractual behavior is the one most observed, most noted and the nature of which as a social control is most overlooked. That is the fact that the legal system enforces contracts at all. Its doing so, of course, represents a conscious or unconscious policy of reinforcing market mechanisms by the law, a policy which goes far beyond simply protecting the changes in property interests which may have been effectuated in a completed contract. This policy is what Macaulay has called the market goals of contract law and policy. One of the most important pedagogical aims of a course in contracts should be to bring home to the student the fact that these market goals themselves constitute social control and manipulation, the social value of which in particular instances must be weighed against competing goals.

The competing non-market goals of legal policy in contractual relationships are bifurcated rather than unitary. Since contract, especially when reinforced by legal sanctions reflecting market goal policy, can be a wild and dangerous animal, it is often necessary to control it by limiting its power. Such control can be achieved in numerous ways, some obvious and some not so obvious. For example, certain transaction types or certain contractual provisions may be made illegal in a criminal sense, or may be stripped of legal enforcement. These limitations are obvious enough. Less obvious, however, may be such things as rules of interpretation which may subtly prevent certain types of parties from effectively creating particularly undesirable contractual provisions. Moreover, the limited nature of contract remedies themselves represents an extremely important limitation on the market goal policy — the law does not, for example, consider that goal sufficiently important to make a breach of contract an economic crime punishable criminally.

Limitation on contract power, however, is not the only social alternative to the market goal policy. The contracts of its citizens are far too valuable and important in a market society for the society to refrain from using them affirmatively for its own purposes. There is thus affirmative social manipulation and exploitation of "private" contracts which is an extremely important goal competing not only with market goals, but often with limitation-of-power goals as well. In the heyday of laissez faire this type of manipulation and exploitation was somewhat limited in scope, taxation of certain kinds of contractual relationships and subsidies being the most obvious examples. In the modern mixed economy, however, social manipulation and exploitation of contractual relationships abound. Not only has transaction-type taxation, notably the sales tax and the income tax, increased vastly in importance, but many kinds of social goals are being achieved by other kinds of required (or societally encouraged) appurtenances to contractual relationships. Nowhere is this more evident than in employment relationships with such imposed appurtenances as Social Security, unemployment insurance, workmen's compensation, health and safety requirements, etc. But employment is by no means the only example, it is merely one of the areas where the process started early. A more recent entry into the field is the vast amount of legal manipulation of contractual relationships to try to solve racial and religious discrimination problems. Although the focus thus far in the civil rights area has been on preventing refusal to contract, certainly more and more it will also be on preventing discrimination within established contractual relationships. e.g. preventing price discrimination by supermarkets in the ghetto or racial discrimination in employee promotion.

Thus, throughout contractual relationships three competing social policies are found: market goals, limitation of contract power and affirmative manipulation and social exploitation. The interplay of these policies cuts across transaction-type lines in such a way that study of them in some transaction-types should aid considerably in understanding them in other types of transactions.

Property characteristics of contracts. Just as society in general may exploit contracts made between its citizens, so too may individual third parties seek to take advantage of them. This is, of course, inevitable in any society in which contracts become a significant form of wealth. At least as long as there is a significant market for the subject matter of a contract there may be third party interests of one kind or another. And since markets are available in a great many transaction-types, such legal matters as assignability, third party beneficiaries, etc. are also a proper subject of a generalized contracts course.

To summarize the answer to the second question which started this paper, all five (or six) of the common elements of contractual relations do present to the legal system and to lawyers problems and challenges which cut across transaction-type boundaries. These problems and challenges could be studied in separate transaction-type courses, and it would even be possible to demonstrate in such courses something of their universality. Nevertheless, their great social and practical-lawyer significance call for a unitary contracts course as the most effective way possible to present the elements and their legal ramifications to the students. In the remainder of the paper I propose to set out some thoughts about the content and structure of a course built around these basic elements.

Contents and structure of a unitary contracts course built on the common contract elements. This is not the proper place to develop a thesis that present generalized contract legal doctrine is vastly deficient as a useful organization of the social and legal problems inherent in contractual relationships. And it certainly is not the place to undertake the task of revamping contracts doctrine to present a theoretical model which corresponds to the basic elements in contractual relationships. And even more it is not the place to try to reconcile such a model with the actual outcome of cases, with legislation and administrative law, with business and other social practice, etc. It is, however, an appropriate place to suggest what should be included in a generalized contracts course in order to bring into the open and to develop the common elements of contractual relationships and the common problems and challenges presented to the legal system by them. So too, the basic organization of the teaching materials is a proper subject for consideration.

The reader who has troubled to arrive at this point will already have inferred some of the purposes and goals of a contracts course built on the common contract elements. Nevertheless, it is appropriate to summarize them at this point:

1. To perform its share (or more) of the development goals of all first year courses: learning to read (and write) and developing other communication skills; developing an increased capacity for sustained rational thought; increasing perception of human values and of how to achieve them; developing a workable sense of justice; developing understanding of decision making and engaging in vicarious practice in human problem solving; sharpening abilities to use legal tools such as statutes and precedent.

2. Broadening perceptions of the significance, consequences, roles and limitations of contractual relations in our society.

3. Acquiring some information about and some understanding of specific and important contractual transaction types, e.g., collective bargaining agreements, consumer purchases, franchise agreements, insurance, etc.

4. Developing a general understanding of the interplay of contractual relationships with the legal system, and specific comprehension of contractual legal problems such as dispute settlement, limitations on legal remedies and their effectiveness, those caused by incomplete and flexible planning, by the need of the legal system to reduce cooperative on-going relationships to relatively rigid verbalizations in order to be able to cope

with conflicts, by specific social limitations and exploitations of contractual relationships, etc.

5. Developing an understanding of the role of the lawyer in contractual relationships generally, and specifically with respect to the response of the legal system to contractual relationships.

6. Acquiring elemental skills in the "lawyering" of contracts from negotiation and drafting to advocacy and judging in appellate litigation, to legislating, etc.

Goals such as the foregoing may look very nice in a law school catalog or sound good in a teacher's introductory lecture, but we all know that we are lucky to achieve much of anything we set out to do in the classroom. It would perhaps therefore be better to call them directions, rather than goals. And so the question is, if we set out with these directions in mind, what goes into the contracts course and how does it go in?

First, the areas of human behavior from which materials are selected are as broad as the common elements of contractual behavior. This broad area of selection encompasses not only most of the traditional contract areas, but gives full weight to continuing economic exchange relationships which have tended to drop out of contracts courses, e.g. collective bargaining and other aspects of employment relationships, mediation, arbitration. Perhaps even more important is that it brings into the contracts fold all of the black sheep transaction-types which have tended to slip away as the academic shepherds of contracts have sought to avoid the doctrinal stresses which otherwise would have been caused by legislative, administrative and sometimes judicial regulation. With the return of such transaction-types comes the regulation as an integral part of the contractual relationship. Robinson-Patman, New York Insurance Law, NLRA, Workmen's Compensation, all seem to be as much a proper study of contracts as is the mailbox rule. Indeed, they are considerably more so since they have some current significance — a comment which brings me to the next point.

Second, the subject matter of the materials selected should have some present or future topical significance. This is important to the achievement of almost all the goals enumerated above. Dead problems, however fascinating intellectually, simply do not achieve most of those goals, unless enough history is reincarnated with them so that the student can see them with the full flavor of the social and economic background of their day. This is a pretty tricky thing to pull off with an 1854 English case concerning the well known carriers trading under the name of Pickford & Co. who evidently did not use printed shipping forms. I shall be the first to agree that it is not always easy to tell when a problem is dead and when it is still topically significant — certainly its absence from current reported appellate cases does not conclusively demonstrate its topical demise. Nevertheless, the difficulty does not justify failure to make an attempt. Moreover, I suspect that there would be considerable agreement about what was and what was not topical if a representative group of contracts teachers were to survey current casebooks.

Third, non-legal as well as legal aspects of contractual relationships should be considered. I have in mind in part, but only in part, the sort of formal sociological studies which have been done by Stewart Macaulay and others. In addition to such studies, however, legal materials themselves can often yield a great deal of enlightenment on non-legal aspects of contractual

relations. For example, cases, while the "spawn of trouble" often nevertheless yield much information about the way people "really" conduct themselves in the real world, even when there is no trouble. Moreover, there is
much to be found with respect to "real life" in journals, etc. dealing with
areas of contracts such as collective bargaining agreements, government
contracts, etc. Nor, in spite of my own relative lack of success in digging out
much, am I yet convinced that business school libraries, for example, do not
have something for us. And certainly, such genuinely negotiated form contracts as those of the American Institute of Architects are goldmines of
information about how the parties plan many of the things which have to be
done in connection with the construction of buildings. In short, I do not
think that it is either necessary or desirable to wait until the legal sociolo-
gists have progressed further before making more diligent efforts to work in
considerably more information on contracting in contrast to that on contract law and litigation.

Fourth, since it is impossible to study the elements of contractual behavior with any degree of breadth without going heavily into areas regulated by
statute and administrative law, a considerable volume of statutory law and
administrative regulation and decisions will inevitably be included. This,
plus the fact that even the traditional area of contract doctrine has now
been invaded by the UCC will help the contracts course do its bit towards
remedying the present absurdity of a common law first year curriculum in
an age of legislative and administrative legal dominance. In addition, such
important dispute settling mechanisms as arbitration require treatment with
more care than is now generally devoted to them — perhaps even as much
as we now devote to some of the topically insignificant aspects of the doctrine of consideration. Thus, if the course is broadened as is herein suggested there will inevitably be a marked reduction in reliance on appellate
cases and especially on common law appellate cases, with corresponding
increases in other types of legal materials.

Fifth, it is apparent that a traditional doctrinal organization of the materials, with chapter headings such as consideration, offer and acceptance,
puts nearly insurmountable hurdles in the way of achieving the goals of the
course. For one thing that kind of organization simply does not fit the functional legal problems created by contracts. For another it causes students to
see contracts backwards. They tend to see contractual relations as extrapo-
lations of legal doctrines, rather than see legal doctrines as a response to
contractual relations. Whatever validity this approach may have with
respect to non-market policies in contract law, it is extremely misleading
with respect to market policies, the very area with which traditional doctrines are most at home. The organization should, therefore, be based on
assessments of the most effective way of accomplishing those goals, rather
than doctrinally.

It is not meant to suggest that even the more abstract legal doctrines can
be ignored (except insofar as they have nothing to do with significant modern problems). For example, the doctrine of consideration would be dealt
with as it arises in the legal responses to various problems, e.g. in the mutuality questions arising in output and requirements contracts and franchise
agreements, in the duress problems arising out of adjustments in existing
contracts, in the problems arising from unconscionable contracts, in dealing
with the revocation of offers, etc. On the other hand, whether it would be

dealt with at all in respect to family gifts would depend upon an assessment of the current importance of the revocability of family gift promises. Or such cases might be included for contrasting the utilization of the consideration doctrines with the handling of similar transactions under the Internal Revenue Code (the latter being a significant and lively current problem).

The foregoing paragraphs outline some of the principles which I think should be applied in order to get into the contracts course what is necessary in order to move it in the direction of the goals argued for earlier. Obviously, however, as soon as we take off from the doctrinal organizations now available, the door is open to a host of possible organizations, selections of topic areas, emphases on types of materials, etc. I am doubtless falling down on the job assigned by the esoteric title which we chose for this panel in failing to be more specific as to the measure of the "mix." My justification is that until someone has in fact attempted to make a mix along the foregoing lines there is not much sense in guessing at the proportions with which he would come up.

.   .   .

Re-read the Introduction to this book

INDEX

A

ACCEPTANCE, see Offer and Acceptance

ACCORD AND SATISFACTION,
    effect of economic duress, 2-155
    explanation of, 2-116, 2-149
    parol evidence rule and, 4-15
    part performance and, 2-118

ADHESION CONTRACTS,
    control of contract power and, 6-36
    described, 6-34
    exemption clauses in, 6-106, 6-173
    form or boiler-plate agreement, 6-141
    free enterprise and, 6-26
    in automobile industry, 2-85, 6-35, 6-173, 6-182
    interpretation of, 6-28, 6-143

ADVERTISEMENT,
    "mere puff", 3-24, 6-245
    offer in, 3-23

AGENTS,
    auto dealers as, 6-189
    carriers as, 6-150, 6-195
    consideration and third parties, 2-123, 2-138
    fiduciary duties of, 6-213
    post office as, 3-50, 3-55

ALLOCATION OF RISK,
    determined by commercial context, 1-112
    in automobile industry, 2-89
    in automobile sales, 2-85, 2-94, 6-182
    in contract for personal performance, 4-177
    in determining foreseeability, 1-107, 1-112, 1-122, 1-123
    in exemption clauses, 4-91
    in sale of land, 4-164, 4-185
    insurance as indicator of, 1-121, 6-105
    standard form contracts and, 6-27
    when negotiations broken off, 3-86, 3-88

ASSIGNMENT,
    assignee of contract, rights of, 6-77
    consideration and third parties, 2-123, 2-138
    Consumer Protection Act on, 6-253
    finance companies, car sales, 6-252
    of mortgage, 6-255

ASSUMPSIT, see also Quasi-Contract; Restitution
    consideration and, 2-110
    frustration and, 4-200
    history of, 2-21, 2-110, 7-2
    Moral Obligation and, 2-67

B

BAILMENT,
> in ticket cases, 6-48, 6-54
> negligence, burden of proof, 6-156
> whether licensee or bailee, 6-54

BATTLE OF THE FORMS,
> description of, 3-89
> mutuality in, 2-76
> U.C.C. position on, 3-96
>> assessment of, 3-97
>> considered with respect to disclaimer, 3-93

BENTHAM,
> as a reformer, 8-4
> Benthamite liberal, 2-67
> on Blackstone, 4-42
> on exchange, 1-12
> on property, 1-4

BLANKET ORDER CONTRACTS,
> analysis and description, 2-86
> consideration and, 2-74

BREACH, see Damages; Fraudulent Breach; Repudiation

C

CANCELLATION,
> of franchise agreement, 2-91
> of release in blanket order, 2-88
> repudiation or rescission, 1-150

CAVEAT EMPTOR,
> duty to disclose defects, 4-123
> implied warranty and, 4-71
> in sale of land, 4-163
> outside contracts of sale, 4-127

CHARITABLE SUBSCRIPTIONS, see Gifts

COLLATERAL CONTRACT, see also Misrepresentations; Interpretation
and Implication; Warranties
> hire purchase and, 4-59
> misrepresentation and, 4-26
> warranty and, 4-46, 4-57, 4-84

COMMERCIAL CONTEXT,
> as basis for implication of terms, 2-82
> how determined, 2-78
> intention and, 6-94
> interpretation of contract language and, 2-82, 4-6
> reasons for enforcement in, 2-1

CONDITIONS,
    express conditions, see also Excuses for Defendant's Non-
        Performance; Waiver
        condition for protection of one party, whether waivable, 5-3, 5-4,
            5-5
        generally, 5-1
        interpretation of, 5-13
        oral condition to written agreement, 5-2
        subsequent conduct, admissibility, 4-8
    implied, see Interpretation and Implication; Misrepresentation;
        Warranties
        Consumer Protection Act on, 6-251
        Sale of Goods Act on, 4-62

CONSIDERATION,
    analysis and history of,
        assessment of current situation, 2-191, 6-32
        early development, 2-111
        nineteenth-century developments, 2-56, 2-112
    blanket orders and, 2-74
    case-knife,
        for enforcing gift promises, considered, 2-170
        generally, 2-55
    classic statements, 2-49, 2-54
    detriment as, 3-23
    evidentiary function of, 2-4
    forbearance as,
        classic statement, 2-49
        Restatement on, 2-49
        whether forebearance consideration, 2-50, 2-52
    form and, 2-1, 2-14
    going-transaction adjustments and,
        duress and public policy, 2-98
        economic duress, 2-41
        inadequacy of traditional doctrine, 2-192
        oral variation and rescission, 2-100, 2-105
        third party, 2-120
    gratuitous promises
        gift and, 2-176
        reasons for not enforcing, 2-14
    intention to create legal relations as substitute for, 2-180
    legal duty, performance of as,
        effect of rescission, 2-100
        factors in enforcing, 2-19
        new promise to pay enforced, 2-100, 2-103
        new promise to perform unenforceable, 2-98, 2-99, 2-101, 2-105
        prior contract with third party, 2-120
        public policy, 2-98
    moral obligation as,
        analysis of claim for enforcement, 2-18

CONSIDERATION *continued*
    moral obligation as *continued*
        insufficient even with subsequent promise, 2-63
        insufficient without pre-existing obligation, 2-58
        Lord Mansfield on, 2-67
        where party legally bound to perform, 2-101
    mutual promises and,
        implied mutuality, 2-82
        in exclusive dealing contracts, 2-83
        issues in enforcement of, 2-73
        lack of mutuality, effect of, 2-76
        as a technique for enforcing gifts, considered, 2-171
    nominal consideration,
        enforced, 2-51
        reasons for enforcing, 2-17
    part payment as, see also Accord and Satisfaction
        consideration implied, 2-116
        effect of economic duress, 2-155
        Mercantile Law Amendment Act, quoted, 2-115
        whether prompt part payment is consideration, 2-112, 2-116, 2-155
    past consideration
        analysis, 2-58
        benefit conferred, 2-58
        express promise to pay as, 2-63
        minor's contracts and, 2-72
        no consideration, 2-58, 2-71
        Statute of Limitations and, 2-72
        warranty after sale, 2-71
    seal and, 2-40
    third parties and,
        analysis of concerns, 2-138
        black-letter rule, 2-123
        devices for avoiding black-letter rule, 2-123
        employees as, 2-141
        legal and equitable developments, 2-124
        mortgages and, 2-140
        Restatement on, 2-139
        specific performance, 2-130
        suit on contract made for others, 2-135
        third party performing legal duty, 2-120, 6-197

CONSTRUCTION, see Interpretation and Implication

CONSUMER PROTECTION,
    automobile sales, 6-173
    Consumer Protection Act, 4-65, 6-251, 6-252, 6-253
    fundamental breach, 6-68
    general legislative response, 6-242
    implied warranties and third parties, 4-66, 4-70
    privity and third party concerns, 4-65

CONTRACT, APPROACHES TO,
    basic common elements of, 9-1

CONTRACT, APPROACHES TO *continued*
    doctrinal vs. functional, 2-138
    economic, 1-41, 1-47
    functional, 1-1, 1-37, 2-139
    juristic, 1-42
    Marxist, 6-1, 6-12

CONTROL OF CONTRACT POWER, see also Adhesion Contracts;
    Consumer Protection; Deposits; Exemption Clauses; Legislative Control
    of Contracts; Penalties; Restraint of Trade; Unconscionability
    as a basic element of contracts, 9-4, 9-6
    generally, 6-1

D

DAMAGES, see also Mitigation; Penalties; Quasi-Contract; Remoteness;
    Restitution
    analyses of, 1-37, 1-47, 1-109
    cost of performance or value, 1-19, 1-49, 1-51, 5-28
        Restatement on, 1-22
    difficulty in assessing, effect of, 1-59
    equitable, 1-97
    expectation interest,
        analysis, 1-38
        justification for enforcement, 1-40
    fundamental breach,
        effect of on liability limitation, 6-82, 6-97
    insurance and, 6-102
    lost profit, 1-30, 1-113, 5-46
    mental suffering, 1-130-136
    non-commercial cases
        different concerns in, 1-62
    onus of proving, 1-57
    principles and purposes of,
        general principle of assessment, 1-19
        purpose of, 1-38, 1-46, 1-131, 1-139
    reliance interest,
        as a measure of damages, awarded, 1-60, 1-62
        as a measure of damages, explained, 1-38
    sale of goods, 1-19, 1-27, 1-30
    warranty, breach of, 4-60

DEPOSITS,
    as earnest, 5-42, 5-44
    as part payment, 5-42
    equitable test for refunding, 6-132
    frustration, restitution and, 4-201
    generally, 5-42, 6-117
    nominal, as liquidated damages, 6-137
    whether refundable, 5-41, 5-42, 6-131

DISCLAIMERS, see Exemption Clauses

DURESS, see also Unconscionability
    in on-going transaction, 2-41
    of goods, 6-203
    salvage agreements, 2-36, 6-204
    threatened breach of contract as, 2-41, 2-98
    unfounded allegations, threats, 2-43

E

ENTIRE CONTRACT RULE, 4-198

EQUITY, see also Damages; Estoppel; Rectification; Specific Performance
    defined, 1-75
    equitable fraud, 6-255
    forfeitures,
        equitable test for, 6-133
        supervisory function over, 6-117
    history of, 1-69, 1-74
    misrepresentation and, 4-31
    parol evidence rule and, 4-16
    part performance, development of, 7-5
    protector of reliance, 3-40
    relief for mistake,
        considered, 4-136, 4-157
        introduced, 4-131
    specific performance and, 1-74, 1-80

ESTOPPEL see also Equity
    introduced as technique for protection of reliance, 2-142
    revocation of offer estopped, 2-160
    revocation of waiver estopped, 2-145
    shield, not sword, 2-148
    waiver and, 2-147

EXCUSES FOR DEFENDANT'S NON-PERFORMANCE, see also
    Conditions
    conditions and, classic statements, 5-17
    conditions generally, 5-16
    conditions, terminology, 5-25
    dependant covenants, 5-18
    generally, 5-1
    Sale of Goods Act, on conditions, 5-25
    reasons for refusing non-performance, 5-19, 5-26
    when breach excuse for non-performance, 5-19, 5-26

EXCUSES FOR PLAINTIFF'S NON-PERFORMANCE
    generally, 5-30
    repudiation as, 5-31
    repudiation by defendant, when plaintiff may sue, 5-33, 5-35, 5-40, 5-41
    waiting to sue, danger in, 5-36
    whether innocent party must be ready to perform, 5-31, 5-37

EXEMPTION CLAUSES, see also Fundamental Breach, Penalties
    auto industry, 2-97, 6-173, 6-182
    bailment,
        fundamental breach, 6-154
        whether applicable to, 6-54
    battle of the forms and, 3-93
    binding certification as, 6-114
    fundamental breach,
        bailment, 6-154
        consequences for exemption clause, damages, 6-82, 6-97, 6-111
        hire-purchase, 6-68
        lease, 6-72
    inconsistencies in, 6-67, 6-160
    misrepresentation and, 4-91
    narrow construction of, 6-66, 6-85, 6-152, 6-155
    negotiations and, 6-90
    notice of, discussed, 6-48, 6-62, 6-106, 6-157
    offer and acceptance of, 6-62
    public policy, 6-173
    reasonableness test, 6-153, 6-154, 6-166, 6-172
    statutory origin, effect of, 6-106
    third parties and
        generally, 6-189
        reasonableness, 6-153
        third party not protected, 6-189, 6-198
        third party protected, 6-193, 6-198
    too broad, struck down, 2-78
    uniform disclaimer, auto industry, 2-97, 6-173, 6-182

EXPECTATION INTEREST,
    analysis, 1-38
    justification for enforcement, 1-40, 1-43
    specific performance as protector of, 1-38

F

FIDUCIARY RELATIONSHIP, see Unconscionability

FORESEEABILITY, see Remoteness of Damage

FRAUD, see Misrepresentation

FREEDOM OF CONTRACT,
    adhesion contracts and, 6-23, 6-144, 6-178
    free enterprise and, 6-26

FRUSTRATION,
    analysis, 4-175
    effect of war, 4-176, 4-198, 4-200
    entire contract rule, 4-198
    foundation of contract,
        doctrine introduced, 4-177
        in coronation case, 4-181
        in sale of land, 4-185
    Frustrated Contracts Act, 4-207

FRUSTRATION *continued*
  lease, 4-193
  personal performance, 4-177
  restitution in, 4-200
  sale of goods, 4-193
  sale of land
    foundation of contract, 4-185
    risk, 4-167

FUNDAMENTAL BREACH,
  as a technique, discussed, 6-156
  consequences for other terms of contract, 6-82, 6-97, 6-111
  contracting out of, discussed, 6-82
  interpretation and, 5-15
  negligent performance and, 6-108
  of a bailment, 6-54, 6-156
  of hire purchase, 6-68
  of a lease, 6-72
  test for, 6-101

G

GIFTS, see also Reliance as a Basis for Enforcement
  consideration and enforcement, 2-177
  enforceability, necessity for reliance considered, 2-170
  legislation on, 2-189
  reasons for not enforcing, 2-14
  reliance on, expectation interest protected, 2-168

H

HIRE-PURCHASE,
  collateral contract in, 4-59
  exemption clauses in, 6-93
  explained, 4-231
  fundamental breach of, 6-68

HISTORY,
  of adhesion contracts, 6-26
  of assumpsit, 2-21, 2-110
  of contracts generally, xxx, 2-20
  of consideration, 2-56, 2-110
  of enforcement of executory exchange, 2-15, 2-22

I

ILLEGALITY,
  conspiracy to defraud, 8-74
  contract entered into with illegal act as purpose, 8-55
  criminal, 8-14
  effect of *Lord's Day Act*, 8-21, 8-32
  ex turpi causa, 8-16, 8-30, 8-46
  generally, 8-1

ILLEGALITY *continued*
    illegal in formation, 8-21, 8-33, 8-37
    illegality of performance, 8-50, 8-63, 8-68
    immoral purpose, 8-14
    interpretation, statute not applicable, 8-42
    public policy and, 8-1, 8-19, 8-21, 8-62, 8-80
    purpose of statute, 8-36, 8-38, 8-42, 8-56
    regulatory, 8-19, 8-37, 8-39, 8-63, 8-68
    Restatement on, 8-49

IMPOSSIBILITY, see Frustration

INEQUALITY OF BARGAINING POWER,
    adhesion contracts and, 6-34, 6-54
    analysis of, 1-3
    as test for unconscionability, 6-204, 6-218
    in automobile industry, 2-85, 6-35, 6-173, 6-182

INFANTS, see Minors

INJUNCTION, see Specific Performance

INNOCENT MISREPRESENTATION, see Misrepresentation

INTENTION TO CREATE LEGAL RELATIONS, see Consideration

INTERPRETATION AND IMPLICATION,
    aids to interpretation
        analysis of parol evidence, 4-14
        commercial context, 6-94
        prior negotiations, admissibility of, 4-4, 4-16
        subsequent conduct, admissibility of, 4-8
    generally, 4-1
    implication,
        of bilateral contract, 3-43
        of condition, 4-125, 4-178, 4-194, 6-54
        of contract from parties' conduct, 1-6
        of intent to enter contract, 3-70
        of mutuality, from context, 2-188
        of a reasonable term, 3-66
        of warranty, 4-66, 4-69, 4-71, 4-102, 8-67
        when a court should imply terms, 1-25, 2-57, 3-41, 6-191
    interpretation
        adhesion contracts and, 6-28, 6-34, 6-143
        commercial context and, 6-94
        freedom of contract and, 6-26, 6-37
        modern trends in, 8-13
        oral warranty, effect of, 4-26
        question of law or fact, 4-2
        "reasonable" interpretation of advertisement, 3-25
        statutes and, 8-1
        uncertainty, courts' approach to, 3-78

L

LABOUR,
    collective bargaining, elements of exchange, 1-13, 2-10
    conflict of labour and contract law, 1-90, 1-92
    employees as third parties to contracts, 2-141
    freedom of contract and, 6-41
    injunction to restrain strike, 1-89
    negotiations in good faith, 3-85
    wrongful dismissal, damages for, 1-130

LANGUAGE, see Interpretation and Implication

LEGAL REASONING,
    adjudication, origins of, 1-7
    Benthamite view of, 2-67
    conceptual vs. functional approach, 2-138
    courts as umpires, 2-57
    fact-finding, problems in, xxix, 2-80, 6-199
    functional approach, 6-6
    generally, xxvii
    judge as creative artist, 8-2
    judgments as products of their time, xxvii
    judicial notice, 2-80
    nature of legal argument, 1-110
    precedent, 1-42

LEGISLATIVE CONTROL OF CONTRACTS,
    adhesion contracts and, 6-146
    auto industry, 2-89, 2-91
    generally, 6-242
    history of, 6-40
    impact of legislation, compared, 1-6, 8-2
    Ontario Securities Act, 4-49
    positivist view of, 6-3
    trends in, 6-23

LIMITATION OF LIABILITY, see Exemption Clauses

LIQUIDATED DAMAGES, see Penalties

M

MARXIST APPROACH TO LAW, 6-1, 6-12

MINORS
    capacity to contract, 2-43
    debts contracted during infancy, 2-63
    past consideration, 2-72
    Statute of Frauds and, 7-1

MISREPRESENTATION
    equity and, 4-31
    fraudulent, see also Fraud
        as to identity of party, 4-223
        non est factum, 4-209
        remedies for, 4-79
    innocent,
        no damages for, 4-35, 4-48
        rescission for, 4-30
        warranty and, 4-49
        whether innocent or fraudulent, 4-35
    "mere puff",
        advertising and, 3-24, 6-245
    negligent,
        damages for in contract and tort, 4-85, 4-101, 4-106
        development of remedy for, 4-79
        whether reliance necessary, 4-89
    prior oral representations as, 6-164
    reliance created by, estoppel, 2-142
    unconscionability and, 6-219
    warranty, collateral contract and, 4-44
    whether warranty or, 1-134, 4-44, 4-49, 4-51, 4-57

MISTAKE
    ambiguity and, 3-7
    analysis of, 4-109, 4-142, 4-147
    equitable relief for,
        considered, 4-136
        introduced, 4-131
        sale of land, 4-157
    of identity, see Mistake, Third Parties
    of law, 4-149, 8-33
    third parties and,
        fraud, *non est factum*, 4-209
        mistake of identity of party, 4-223
        third party rights and *non est factum*, 4-217
    time, relevance of, 4-164
    unilateral, analysis, 4-143

MITIGATION,
    classic rule,
        justified, 1-43, 1-48
        stated, 1-140
    generally, 1-139
    reasonableness in mitigating, question of fact, 1-141
    risks taken in mitigating, effect on assessment of damages, 1-151
    when innocent party must mitigate,
        at date of repudiation, 1-142, 1-148, 1-150
        election, 1-142

N

NEGLIGENT MISREPRESENTATION, see Misrepresentation, Tort

NEGOTIATIONS,
    agreement to make an agreement, 3-69
    agreement to negotiate, 3-84
    allocation of risk for reliance, 3-86, 3-88
    as an aid to construction, whether available, 4-4
    duty to bargain in good faith, 3-85
    generally, 3-1
    implication of term to complete negotiations, 3-66
    negotiation complete, then re-opened, 3-70
    U.C.C. on effect of uncertainty, 3-83
    whether clause void for uncertainty, 3-77
    whether negotiations complete, 3-73

NON-COMMERCIAL CONTRACTS, see also Gifts
    damages, 1-62, 1-133
    enforceability, 2-1, 2-14

NON EST FACTUM,
    analysis of, 4-209
    considered, 4-217
    fraudulent misrepresentation and, 4-209
    pleaded, 6-255

O

OFFER AND ACCEPTANCE,
    classic statements on, 3-9, 3-19
        inadequacies of, 2-191
    Civil Code on, 3-32
    consideration and, 2-191
    firm offers, reliance on, 2-191
    "Halfway Up the Flagpole",
        analysis and description, 3-37
        bilateral contract implied, 3-43
        equity as protector of reliance, 3-40
        inadequacy of traditional doctrine, 2-192
        "lowering the flagpole", 3-45
    issues in, 3-2, 3-37
    mail,
        classic statements on, 3-31, 3-49, 3-55
        interpretation of letters, 3-56
        when letter not received, 3-49
        which party to bear risk of mistake, 3-47
    performance as acceptance,
        advertisement, 3-23
        performance of third party, 6-197
        reward, necessity of mutual assent, 3-26, 3-28
        reward, relevance of acceptor's motive, 3-22

OFFER AND ACCEPTANCE *continued*
    revocability,
        approach of foreign legal systems, 3-32
        bilateral contracts and, 3-44
        classic statement, 3-32
        estopped, 2-160
        need for parties to be *ad idem*, 3-32
        Restatement on, 3-37
        revocation immediately before acceptance, 3-37
    silence as acceptance,
        classic statement, 3-62
        exception, 3-62
        legislation, 3-64

P

PAROL EVIDENCE RULE, see also Interpretation and Implication,
    Rectification
    evidentiary or channeling, 2-7
    generally, 4-13
    judicial analysis, 4-20
    oral condition in written agreement, 5-2
    oral variation, whether admissible, 4-16
    oral warranty, effect of, 4-26
    prior negotiations and, 4-4
    role of jury and, 4-3
    stated and analyzed, 4-14

PENALTIES, see also Exemption Clauses
    generally, 6-117
    judicial interference with, principles of,
        dispensing power of court, 6-125
        law does not favour, 1-23
        traditional supervisory function, 6-117
    liquidated damages or penalty, 6-118, 6-120
        reasonability as a test, 6-126
        tests for, 6-119
    lower than actual damages, 6-139
    non-refundable instalments as, 6-131
    pre-estimate of damages,
        as test for liquidated damages, 6-119, 6-125
        nominal deposit as, 6-137

POGO, 4-172

PRIVATE AUTONOMY,
    adhesion contracts, auto industry, 2-94
    as a basis for enforcement, 2-8
    Civil Code on, 1-5
    free enterprise and, 6-34
    proper sphere of, 2-10
    will theory and, 2-9

PRIVITY,
    auto manufacturer and buyer, 2-90, 6-184
    manufacturer, products liability, 4-66, 4-69
    receiver of message, telegraph clerk, 3-5
    stevedores and carriers, no *jus quaesitum tertio*, 6-189

PROMISSORY ESTOPPEL, see Estoppel

PUBLIC POLICY,
    illegal contracts and, 8-1, 8-19, 8-21
    restraint of trade and, 6-121, 6-222, 6-231, 6-234
    unconscionability, U.C.C. and, 6-258

                              Q

QUANTUM MERUIT, see Assumpsit, Quasi-Contract, Restitution

QUASI-CONTRACT, see also Assumpsit, Restitution
    Holmesian theory and, 2-56
    mistake and, 4-147

                              R

RECTIFICATION,
    allowed for mistake, 4-110
    annulment or rectification, choice, 4-113
    prior negotiations, admissibility, 4-4

RELIANCE AS A BASIS FOR ENFORCEMENT,
    economic duress and, 2-155
    family cases,
        consideration doctrine, adequacy of discussed, 2-192
        doctrines for enforcement considered, 2-180
        mutuality, contract implied, 2-188
        reliance on parent's promise, 2-183
    Fuller on, 1-37, 1-109, 2-17, 2-152
    generally, 2-141
    gifts,
        basis for enforcement, considered, 2-170
        reliance protected, 2-168
    issues in, 1-38, 2-1, 2-11, 2-141
    legislation on, 6-249
    misrepresentation and, 4-81, 4-101, 4-106
    mistake and, 4-172
    offer as relied-on promise, 2-160
    private autonomy and, 2-11
    techniques for enforcement,
        bilateral contract implied, 3-43
        equity, 3-40
        estoppel, assessed, 2-147
        estoppel, introduced, 2-142
        estoppel, restrictions on, 2-148

RELIANCE AS A BASIS FOR ENFORCEMENT *continued*
  techniques for enforcement *continued*
    estoppel, shield, not sword, 2-148
    rescission, 4-80
    tort, 2-183
    unilateral contract, 2-165
    waiver, 2-147
  when negotiations broken off, 3-86, 3-88

RELIANCE AS A MEASURE OF DAMAGES, 1-38 (See also Damages)

REMEDIES, see Assumpsit, Cancellation, Damages, Rectification,
  Restitution, Specific Performance

REMOTENESS OF DAMAGE, see also Allocation of Risk
  determined by commercial context, 1-119
  foreseeability, in tort and contract, 1-118, 1-122, 2-57
  generally, 1-106
  notice of special circumstances, 1-107, 1-121, 1-123, 1-124

REPUDIATION,
  damages for, 4-77
  excuse for plaintiff's non-performance, 5-30
  fundamental breach and, 6-82
  Sale of Goods Act on, 5-40
  suit at time of repudiation, 1-142, 1-148, 1-150, 2-34, 5-33
  when innocent party entitled to repudiate, 5-24
  when plaintiff may sue for, 5-33, 5-34, 5-41
  whether innocent party must be ready and willing to perform, 5-31,
    5-37

REPRESENTATION, see Misrepresentation

RECISSION,
  deposits and, 6-131
  entitles claimant to restitution damages, 2-32
  for mistake, 4-149, 4-159
  legislative provisions for, 6-249
  misrepresentation and, 4-31, 4-79
  oral variation and, 2-100, 2-105
  quantum meruit and, 2-34

RESTITUTION, see also Assumpsit, Unjust Enrichment
  as measure of damages, analysis, 1-38
  in event of plaintiff's breach,
    abandonment as bar to, 5-46
    abandonment or substantial performance, 5-48
    contracts for personal service, 5-50, 5-53
    generally, 5-41
    pre-payment not refundable, 5-41
    pre-payment of services, 5-46, 5-51
    pre-payment refundable, 5-42

RESTRAINT OF TRADE,
  damages in, 1-46, 6-120
  duration of agreement, importance of, 6-226, 6-237
  history and analysis, 6-227
  public policy, 6-122, 6-222, 6-231, 6-234
  unconscionability and, 6-221
  when validity determined, 6-224, 6-234

REWARDS, see Offer and Acceptance

RISK, see Allocation of Risk

S

SALE OF GOODS, see Consumer Protection

SALE OF LAND,
  condition in, 8-28
  damages for breach inadequate, 1-74
  damages, measure of, 1-97
  frustration in, 4-167, 4-186
  innocent misrepresentation, rescission, 4-30
  misrepresentation in, 4-35
  mistake in, 4-110, 4-157, 4-159, 4-164
  nominal deposit as liquidated damages, 6-137
  specific performance, 1-74, 1-79, 1-104, 1-105, 3-3, 4-30, 4-110, 5-4
  Statute of Frauds and, 2-30, 7-5, 8-24
  warranty or misrepresentation in, 4-51, 4-102, 4-168

SEALED CONTRACTS
  analysis and history, 2-46
  cautionary function of, 2-4
  channeling function of, 2-5
  claim for rectification of, 4-4
  consideration and, 2-40
  estoppel in, 2-146
  examples of, 2-44
  modified by oral agreement, 2-145
  not adverted to, no effect, 2-38
  restraint of trade and, 6-222

SHIELDS, LONG AND POINTED, 2-160

SIGNING,
  effect of, 6-50, 6-66, 6-159, 6-165
  Statute of Frauds and, 7-8

SPECIFIC PERFORMANCE,
  cost of performance and, 1-26
  delay as bar to,
    generally, 5-42
    laches, 1-100
  distinguished from damages, 4-35

SPECIFIC PERFORMANCE *continued*
    expectation interest and, 1-38
    generally, 1-68, 1-74, 1-79, 2-56
    granted,
        because nominal damages inadequate, 2-130
        for fungibles, 1-80
        for personal employment, 1-92
        for sale of land, 3-3, 4-110, 5-4
        for sale of specific chattel, 1-75
        for supply, 1-77, 1-96
        generally, 1-79
        negative stipulation, personal services, 1-84
        to end illegal strike, 1-88
    history of, 1-69, 1-74
    mutuality, 1-74, 1-80
    refused,
        before breach, 1-82
        discretionarily, 1-84
        innocent misrepresentation, 4-30
        positive covenant for personal services, 1-84
        where refusal would not harm plaintiff, 1-96
        where third party involved, 1-97

STANDARD FORM CONTRACTS, see also Adhesion Contracts, Battle
    of the Forms, Ticket Cases
    form or boiler plate agreements, 6-141

STATUTE OF FRAUDS,
    assumpsit and, 2-27, 2-30
    generally, 7-1
    minor's contracts and, 2-72
    mistake and, 4-112
    negative canalizing effect of, 2-6, 2-7
    oral variation of contract with statute, 2-145

STATUTE OF LIMITATIONS,
    past consideration and, 2-72
    seal, effect of, 2-44
    Statute of Frauds and, 7-7

STATUTES, see also Legislative Control of Contracts
    role in judicial decision making, 8-1

T

THIRD PARTIES, see Consideration, Exemption Clauses,
    Misrepresentation, Mistake, Privity

"TICKET CASES",
    applicability to signed contracts, 6-162
    bailment, fundamental breach of, 6-54
    development of standard form contracts, 6-27
    offer and acceptance in, 6-62
    notice requirement, 6-54, 6-62
    reasonable expectations enforced, 6-48

TORT,
> damages in, compared with contracts, 1-132
> deceit and warranty, 4-80
> foreseeability, tort vs. contract, 1-119, 1-122, 2-57
> misleading advertising and, 4-78
> mixed tort and contract, 2-21
> negligence and fraud, 4-209
> negligent misrepresentation, 4-81, 4-89, 4-101, 4-109
> tortious damage, Statute of Frauds and, 7-3

U

UNCONSCIONABILITY, see also Restraint of Trade
> analysis, 6-202
> Business Practices Act on, 6-249
> equitable principles, 6-44
> fiduciary relationship, 6-207-216
> generally, 6-199
> restraint of trade and, 6-222
> U.C.C. on, 6-146, 6-258
> Unconscionable Transactions Relief Act, 6-253

UNJUST ENRICHMENT
> basis for enforcement, 1-38, 2-12
> duress and, 2-36, 2-41, 2-98
> half-completed exchange as, 2-14
> in assumpsit, 2-23, 2-28, 2-32
> mistake and, 4-147

W

WAIVER,
> analysis of claim for enforcement, 2-17
> condition for protection of one party, whether waivable, 5-3, 5-4, 5-5
> of legal right as consideration, 2-52
> revocation of, effect of reliance, 2-145

WARRANTIES, see also Conditions, Exemption Clauses, Interpretation and Implication
> after sale, whether consideration, 2-71
> automobiles and, 2-95, 4-49, 4-59, 6-173, 6-182
> collateral contract and, 4-46, 4-57
> collateral warranty, 4-84
> Consumer Protection Act on, 6-251
> hire-purchase and, 4-61
> in lease, fundamental breach of, 6-72
> "judicial risk" and, 6-27
> legality, implied warranty of, 8-67
> merchantability, implied, effect of disclaimer, 6-173, 6-184, 6-187
> Sale of Goods Act and, 4-62
> sale of land, 4-168
> whether representation or warranty, 1-134, 4-44, 4-49, 4-51, 4-57